Technology... In a Class By Itself

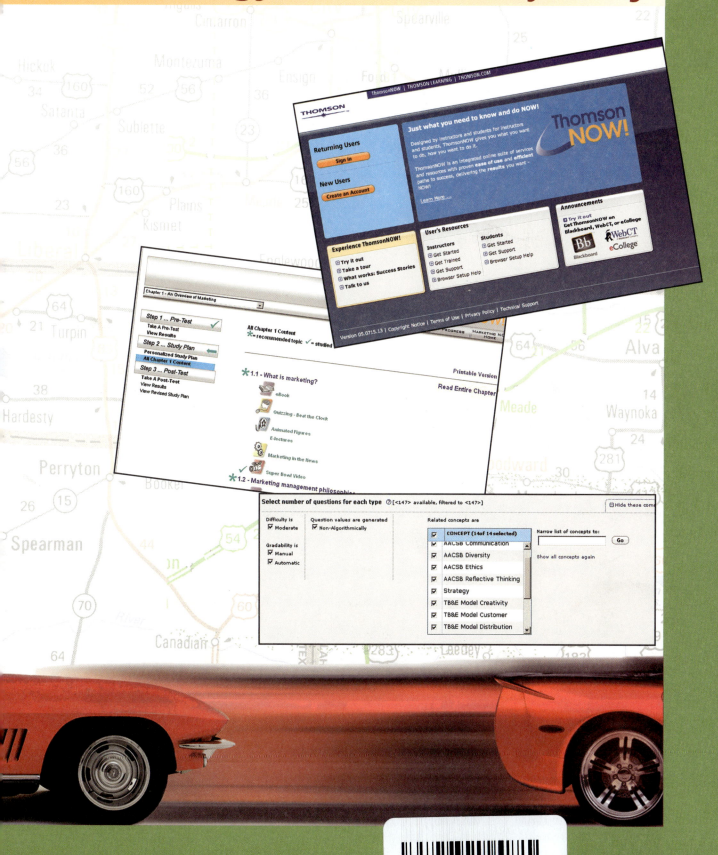

contemporary
MARKETING 13e

contemporary
MARKETING 13e

David L. Kurtz

*Distinguished Professor of Marketing and
R.A. and Vivian Young Chair
of Business Administration*

University of Arkansas

THOMSON

SOUTH-WESTERN

Australia · Brazil · Canada · Mexico · Singapore · Spain · United Kingdom · United States

THOMSON
™
SOUTH-WESTERN

Contemporary Marketing, Thirteenth Edition
David L. Kurtz

VP/Editorial Director:
Jack W. Calhoun

Publisher:
Neil Marquardt

Senior Developmental Editor:
Rebecca von Gillern

Marketing Manager:
Nicole C. Moore

Marketing Communications Manager:
Sarah Greber

Content Project Manager:
Amy Hackett

Manager, Editorial Media:
John Barans

Technology Project Manager:
Kristen Meere

Senior Manufacturing Coordinator:
Diane Gibbons

Production House:
Lachina Publishing Services

Printer:
RR Donnelley
Willard Manufacturing Division

Art Director:
Stacy Jenkins Shirley

Cover and Internal Designer:
Beckmeyer Design

Cover Images:
© Alamy Images

Photography Manager:
Deanna Ettinger

Photo Researcher:
Terri Miller

Library of Congress Control Number:
2006935736

For more information about our products, contact us at:

Thomson Learning Academic
Resource Center

1-800-423-0563

Thomson Higher Education
5191 Natorp Boulevard
Mason, OH 45040
USA

preface

Products often begin their lives as something extraordinary, and as they grow they continue to evolve. The most successful products in the marketplace are those that know their strengths and have branded and marketed those strengths to form a passionate emotional connection with loyal users and relationships with new users every step of the way. Just like the very best brands in the business world, Boone & Kurtz, *Contemporary Marketing*, continues to evolve, both as a product and as a brand. This 13th edition of *Contemporary Marketing* is the first edition written without the collaboration of my longtime co-author, Louis E. (Gene) Boone. As with every good brand, though, the patterns of innovation and excellence established at the beginning remain steadfast. The goals and standards of Boone & Kurtz, *Contemporary Marketing*, remain intact and focused on excellence, as always. I present to you a text and supplement package that will not only show you why we've been the standard-bearer for so long but also prove to YOU and your STUDENTS why Boone & Kurtz remains . . . IN A CLASS BY ITSELF!

Putting Instructors in a Class by Themselves

This new edition's supplement package is designed to propel the instructor into the classroom with all the materials needed to engage students and help them understand text concepts. All the major teaching materials have been combined into one resource—the Instructor's Manual. While this might not sound revolutionary, good brands know that the heart of the product is in its core strengths. In the same way, our new Instructor's Manual combines all of the most important teaching materials in one place. We've included collaborative learning exercises directly in the lecture outline, so you'll know best where to use them. For your convenience, we've also included references to the PowerPoint slides throughout the lecture notes. The Second City Theater, Inc., our brand-new continuing case, is highlighted in all-new part videos, while chapter videos showcase a stellar list of companies, including standard-bearers such as Harley-Davidson and companies doing business with a brand new set of ideals such as American Apparel.

We've heard your appreciation for our PowerPoint Presentations and have gone even one step further: the PowerPoint presentations for this edition are tailored to meet the needs of all instructors, offering three versions: our expanded multimedia collection, the basic collection, and a student version available on our Web site. In addition, our new CERTIFIED TEST BANK, verified multiple times, gives instructors that extra edge needed to drive home key concepts and ignite critical thinking, as well as confidence and assurance when creating and issuing tests. We also listened to your feedback and have incorporated more material on the marketing plan within the ThomsonNOW product. Past users will note that the new edition is less theme driven and designed to emphasize the very best concepts in the marketing world today.

The evolution of a brand or product can be a powerful and compelling undertaking involving every aspect of the marketing process. Understanding this evolution can be a student's best help in understanding how marketing is conducted every day. Every chapter now begins with a new feature called EVOLUTION OF A BRAND. This feature discusses the evolution of the company or product that is the focus of the opening vignette. We've focused our efforts on showing how stellar brands evolve and what this evolution means in the grander scheme of marketing and product management.

Helping Students Stand in a Class by Themselves

With contemporary being the operative word, we've showcased a new, exciting company, The Second City Theater, Inc., a comedy corporation that has produced stars of *Saturday Night Live* and other comedy venues, such as John Belushi and Tina Fey—a company that students can really finding interesting! As always, every chapter is loaded with up-to-the-minute marketing issues and examples to enliven classroom discussion and debate, such as how the Gulf Coast is rebuilding after the devastation of Hurricanes Katrina and Rita as well as a completely new discussion on CAFTA, the Central American Free Trade Agreement, which President Bush signed in 2005. Processes, strategies, and procedures are brought to life through videos highlighting real companies and employees, an inventive business model, and collaborative learning exercises. Brand-new Voice of Experience interviews are placed at the end of each part so that students can see how real-life marketing careers are conducted. And to further enhance the student learning process, we've developed a Principles of Marketing-focused technology product, ThomsonNOW, that integrates personalized learning along with a research database of articles.

HOW BOONE & KURTZ'S *CONTEMPORARY MARKETING* EVOLVED INTO THE LEADING BRAND IN THE MARKET

For more than three decades, *Contemporary Marketing* has provided the latest in content and pedagogy. Our *current* editions have long been the model for our competitors' next editions. Consider Boone & Kurtz's proven record of providing instructors and students with pedagogical firsts:

- *Contemporary Marketing* was the first introductory marketing text written specifically for the student—rather than the instructor—featuring a conversational style that students readily understand and enjoy.

- *Contemporary Marketing* has always been based on marketing research, written the way instructors actually teach the course.

- *Contemporary Marketing* has always employed extensive pedagogy—such as opening vignettes and boxed features—to breathe life into the exciting concepts and issues facing today's marketers.

- *Contemporary Marketing* was the first business text to offer end-of-chapter video cases as well as end-of-part continuing video cases filmed by professional producers, who include text concepts in each video.

- *Contemporary Marketing* was the first to use multimedia technology to integrate all ancillary components: videos, overhead transparencies, and PowerPoint CD-ROMs for both instructors and students—enabling instructors to custom-create lively lecture presentations.

PEDAGOGY

The reason Boone & Kurtz came together to write the first edition of *Contemporary Marketing* was revolutionary. They wanted to write a book about marketing that wasn't an encyclopedia: a text that students would find interesting, a text filled with interesting examples and pedagogy. As with every edition of *Contemporary Marketing*, the 13th edition is packed with new pedagogical features to keep students interested and bring the text topics to life:

- Assessment, Assessment, Assessment: In every marketing department in the country, assessment and assurance of learning among students has become increasingly important. As a result, we've provided you with assessment checks after every main head in every chapter.

- Assurance of Learning Review: Assurance of learning is further enhanced by new end-of-chapter self-quizzes: In addition to ensuring that students are learning throughout the chapter, we've taken assessment one step further by incorporating new end-of-chapter self-quizzes called Assurance of Learning Review. These questions are designed to quickly assess whether students understand the basic concepts covered in the chapter.

- Evolution of a Brand: Products, brands, and people that evolve are the ones that succeed. The evolution of *Contemporary Marketing* is what has put BOONE & KURTZ . . . IN A CLASS BY ITSELF. Every chapter now begins with a new feature called Evolution of a Brand. This feature discusses the evolution of the company or product that is the focus of the opening vignette and what this evolution means in the larger picture of marketing strategy and product management.

- Business Etiquette: Schools realize that it has become increasingly important to understand proper business etiquette when entering the business world, so more and more schools are adding business etiquette to their curriculums. Every chapter of *Contemporary Marketing* contains an Etiquette Tips for Marketing Professionals box, addressing all aspects of proper behavior including communications etiquette, business dinners, and even the most effective way to create customer relationships.

- Voice of Experience: Students often have an amazing ability to grasp chapter concepts and intellectually understand marketing and what a marketing career entails. However, they often do not understand how careers are created and maintained and fail to understand in a real-life sense what a career in marketing may involve on a day-to-day basis. Every part in the text now ends with an interview of an actual marketing professional and includes information about his or her education, career path, and day-to-day responsibilities. These professionals come from all aspects of marketing, from entrepreneurs to vice presidents at some of students' favorite companies. The traits all of them have in common are their hard work, dedication, professionalism, and success. This feature gives students a true understanding of how to launch a real marketing career for themselves through the Voices of Experience.

CONTINUING TO BUILD THE BOONE & KURTZ BRAND

Because the business world moves at an unprecedented pace today, the Principles of Marketing course must race to keep up. Trends, strategies, and practices are constantly changing, though a few things remain the same—the need for excellence and the necessity to evolve and innovate.

You've come to trust *Contemporary Marketing* to cover every aspect of marketing with a critical but fair eye. Let's face it: there are best practices and those we'd never want to repeat. However, both provide learning opportunities and we've always chosen to take a critical look at the way business is being done in the world and help students understand what they need to know in order to have a long and illustrious career in marketing. Keeping this in mind, here are just a few of the important trends and practices we've focused on for this edition:

- Planning a Career in Marketing (section preceding Chapter 1): This popular Boone & Kurtz feature has been revised to include an enhanced discussion of internships as well as a complete update on the current job market. Students in Principles of Marketing courses must keep up with the newest trends and shifts in career fields. The 13th edition of *Contemporary Marketing* helps them answer the question, "Where do I fit in the marketing world?" with an improved discussion of marketing career options.

- Every chapter in the text now includes a section titled Evolution of a Brand that follows the opening vignette and enhances the discussion of whatever brand or product was discussed in that opening scenario. This section also asks students to think critically about what these brands have done and continue to do to remain at the top of their markets.

- Chapter 1 includes the American Marketing Association (AMA) definition of marketing and has an improved section on technology, including coverage of Internet Protocol TV and mobile marketing.

- Chapter 2 now includes examples of the strategic window as well as a completely updated appendix, "Creating an Effective Marketing Plan."

- Two new laws concerning national identity cards and banning the sale of cell phone records have been added to Chapter 3.

- Chapter 4 now focuses more strategically on e-marketing and has an improved discussion of B2B, B2C, and the challenges associated with online marketing and e-business.

- Chapter 5 now includes a discussion on nearshoring along with improved terminology and updated statistics.

- A discussion of CAFTA as well as FTAA information is now included in an updated and improved Chapter 7.

- Blogs and advergames are discussed in Chapter 8, which also now reflects the most current information on marketing research companies and publishers.

- Chapter 9 contains a new expanded section on the cohort effect, and new information and statistics on demographic and psychographic information is included.

- Web services have been added to the discussion on EDI in Chapter 10, and an outdated section on virtual relationships has been deleted.

- Chapter 12's section on category management has been expanded and improved, and information on the Food Allergen Labeling and Consumer Protection Act has been included. RFID information has been added after the discussion of UPCs.

- An improved and more balanced discussion of sponsorships is now included in Chapter 15, and Chapter 16 now includes a discussion of advergames and adware.

- Chapter 17 includes a streamlined and improved discussion of the sales process and also includes a short discussion of cold calling.

- Chapters 18 and 19 have both been updated and include better examples. Chapter 18 also now includes an improved discussion of the modified breakeven concept and yield management.

THE SECOND CITY THEATER INC. CONTINUING VIDEO CASE

You've come to expect only the best from us in choosing our continuing video case company, and we've taken it one step further with our new choice. No other company combines Second City Theater's unique brand of social and political satire with successful and proven business and marketing practices. These unique practices have helped The Second City grow from a small but successful comedy troupe into a large international business. With several theaters in two countries, troupes performing every day all over the world, and performances on international cruise lines, The Second City has found a way to turn comedy into business—and in the process they've had fun! Students and instructors alike know and love many of the famous faces that started performing at Second City—John Belushi, Dan Aykroyd, John Candy, Gilda Radner, Chris Farley, Tina Fey, and the list goes on and on. But how many students realize just how important good business and marketing strategies are in keeping a comedy business that started in 1959 thriving and growing all the way into 2007 and beyond? We've focused on all the aspects of The Second City Theater's marketing strategy so that students can learn—in a way that's interesting and fun. So sit back, get some popcorn, and enjoy the show!

Written case segments at the end of each part of the text contain critical-thinking questions designed to provoke discussion and interaction in the classroom setting. Answers to the questions can be found in the Instructor's Manual, as can a complete video synopsis, a list of text concepts covered in the videos, and even more critical-thinking exercises.

END-OF-CHAPTER VIDEO CASES

In addition to a stellar new continuing video case, we've produced a whole new batch of video cases for each and every chapter, designed to exceed your every expectation. Students need to know the basics about life in the real world of marketing and how businesses succeed and grow—but they don't need a bunch of talking heads putting them to sleep. So although we admit that you will indeed see a few talking heads, they're just there because they really do know what they're talking about, and they have something important for students to hear. But do trust us . . . the videos we've created for this new edition of *Contemporary Marketing* contain so much more!

A complete set of written cases accompanies these chapter videos and can be found in the end-of-book video case appendix. The written segments contain discussion questions. As with the Second City cases, answers to the questions can be found in the Instructor's Manual, as can a complete video synopsis, a list of text concepts covered in the videos, and even more critical-thinking exercises. The video cases are as follows:

Chapter 1: Harley-Davidson Keeps Riders Coming Back

Chapter 2: Timbuk2's Success Is in the Bag

Chapter 3: Organic Valley Farms: Producing Food That's Good for People and the Earth

Chapter 4: Pick Your Bananas Online at Peapod

Chapter 5: Nielsen Media Research Watches the TV Watchers

Chapter 6: High Sierra Sport Company Excels in B2B

Chapter 7: Lonely Planet Brings You the World

Chapter 8: Nielsen Media Research Plays the Rating Game

Chapter 9: Harley-Davidson Rules the Road by Understanding Its Customers

Chapter 10: The Little Guys Home Electronics: Big on Customer Relationships

Chapter 11: Wild Oats Natural Marketplace: Offering Products at their Peak

Chapter 12: Rebranding at JPMorgan Chase

Chapter 13: American Apparel: Supply Fits the Demand

Chapter 14: BP Connects with Drivers

Chapter 15: The Toledo Mud Hens: Family Fun = A Winning Strategy

Chapter 16: BP: Beyond Petroleum

Chapter 17: Harley-Davidson: Selling the Thrill

Chapter 18: Washburn Guitars: How Much Is the Maya Worth?

Chapter 19: Whirlpool: Innovation for Every Price Point

THE *CONTEMPORARY MARKETING* RESOURCE PACKAGE

Since the first edition of this book was published, Boone & Kurtz has exceeded the expectations of instructors, and it quickly became the benchmark for other texts. With its precedent-setting learning materials, *Contemporary Marketing* has continued to improve on its signature package features—equipping students and instructors with the most comprehensive collection of learning tools, teaching materials, and innovative resources available. As expected, the 13th edition continues to serve as the industry benchmark by delivering the most extensive, technologically advanced, user-friendly package on the market.

FOR THE INSTRUCTOR

ThomsonNOW

Designed *by* instructors and students *for* instructors and students, ThomsonNOW gives you what you want to do, how you want to do it. ThomsonNOW is an integrated online suite of services and resources with proven ease of use and efficient paths to success, delivering the results you want—NOW! ThomsonNOW includes self-assessments that generate a personalized study plan, auto-graded homework assignments, a gradebook, an e-book, and more. ThomsonNOW also includes content that is tagged to the core marketing outcomes, as well as to AACSB outcomes. Instructors can track students' progress toward the core outcomes in their class. Figures from the text are used as interactive drag-and-drop exercises, and video clips are included with assignable gradeable questions. Students will find this product fun, and instructors will find it extremely useful. ThomsonNOW also includes seamless integration with WebCT and Blackboard.

Instructor's Manual with Collaborative Learning Exercises and Media Guide (ISBN: 0-324-53657-7)

The 13th edition of *Contemporary Marketing* has a brand-new, extremely easy-to-use Instructor's Manual. This valuable tool completely integrates the various supplements and the text. A detailed lecture outline provides guidance about how to teach the chapter concepts. Collaborative learning exercises are included for each chapter, which give students a completely different way to apply chapter concepts to their own lives. References to the PowerPoint slides are included in the lecture outline. You'll also find answers to all of the end-of-chapter materials and various critical-thinking exercises. Full descriptions of the ThomsonNOW product and BCRC exercises can be found in the Media Guide along with complete video synopses, outlines, and extra questions.

Chapter Video Cases on DVD (ISBN: 0-324-53652-6)

Brand-new end-of-chapter video cases for every chapter of the text focus on successful real companies' processes, strategies, and procedures. Real employees explain real marketing situations with which they have been faced, bringing key concepts from the chapter to life.

The Second City Theater, Inc. Continuing Case Video on DVD (ISBN: 0-324-53652-6)

This brand-new continuing video case combines the entrepreneurial and creative spirit with which Second City was founded with the reality of successful marketing and business strategies. Rarely has a creative enterprise so uniquely brought real business savvy to its success. In these videos we examine the history of the theater company as well as the successful business practices that have allowed for its expansion and growth. The written and video cases are divided into seven sections and are created to be used at the end of each part of the text.

Certified Test Bank (ISBN: 0-324-53656-9)

Containing more than 4,000 questions, this is the most accurate test bank we've had in years. For the first time we've put our test bank through a complete verification process. Every question and answer has been read and reviewed for accuracy by multiple sources. Each chapter of the test bank is organized by chapter objective, and each question categorized by difficulty level, type of question, and text page reference, and has also been tagged for AACSB requirements.

Basic and Expanded PowerPoint Presentations on CD (ISBN: 0-324-53653-4)

After reviewing competitive offerings, we are convinced that our PowerPoint presentations are the best you'll find. We offer two separate collections. The Basic PowerPoint collection contains 10 to 20 slides per chapter. This collection is a basic outline of the chapter, with Web links that bring chapter concepts to life; it also includes figures and tables from the text. The Expanded PowerPoint collection includes 20 to 40 slides per chapter and provides a more complete overview of the chapter. The Expanded collection includes figures and tables from the chapter, Web links, and video links.

JoinIn™ on TurningPoint®

JoinIn on TurningPoint transforms lectures into powerful two-way experiences integrating the interactivity of today's keypad technology right into your Microsoft PowerPoint presentations. Energize your class presentations with JoinIn on TurningPoint, transforming your classroom with seamless integration with Blackboard and WebCT. Visit http://www.thomsonedu.com/joinin for more details. For the 13th edition of *Contemporary Marketing,* we've provided Premium Content TurningPoint slides that are already incorporated into our Expanded PowerPoint collection. These all-new questions cover basic chapter concepts, difficult concepts so you can see student progress, and polling questions for use as opinion-gathering discussion starters.

Instructor's Resource CD (ISBN: 0-324-53654-2)

The IRCD includes electronic versions of all of the instructor supplements: Instructor's Manual, Collaborative Learning Exercises and Media Guide, Test Bank, and Examview testing files and software.

Examview Testing Software on IRCD (ISBN: 0-324-53654-2)

Examview Testing Software is a Windows-based software program that is both easy to use and attractive. We can say with confidence that this is the most accurate test bank we've had in years because it has been through our certification process and every question and answer has been verified multiple times. Each chapter of the test bank is organized by chapter objective, and each question is categorized by difficulty level, type of question, and text page reference, and has also been tagged for AACSB requirements.

Business & Company Resource Center (BCRC)

BCRC puts a complete business library at your students' fingertips. BCRC is a premier online business research tool that allows students to seamlessly search thousands of periodicals, journals, references, financial information sources, market share reports, company histories, and much more. Links to articles and discussion questions for BCRC can be found in ThomsonNOW and on the text Web site at http://www.thomsonedu.com/marketing/boone. View a guided tour of the Business & Company Resource Center at http://www.gale.com/BusinessRC.

Contemporary Marketing, 13th Edition Web Site

Our text Web site (http://www.thomsonedu.com/marketing/boone) is filled with a whole set of useful tools. Instructors will find all the key instructor resources in electronic format: Test Bank, PowerPoint collections, Instructor's Manual with Collaborative Learning Exercises and Media Guide, and BCRC Exercises. Students will also find a host of valuable resources.

Resource Integration Guide (RIG)

The RIG is written to provide the instructor with a clear and concise guide to all of the ancillaries that accompany the text as well as how best to use these items in teaching a Principles of Marketing course. Not only are all of the book's ancillaries organized clearly for you, but we also provide planning suggestions, lecture ideas, and help in creating assignments. This guide will help instructors prepare for teaching the course, execute teaching plans, and evaluate student performance. The RIG can be found on the text Web site (http://www.thomsonedu.com/marketing/boone) in the Instructor's Resource section.

Custom Solutions for *Contemporary Marketing,* 13th Edition

Thomson Custom Solutions develops personalized solutions to meet your business education needs. Match your learning materials to your syllabus and create the perfect learning solution. Consider the following when looking at your customization options for *Contemporary Marketing,* 13th edition:

- Remove chapters you do not cover or rearrange their order, creating a streamlined and efficient text that students will appreciate.

- Add your own material to cover new topics or information, saving you time and providing students with a fully integrated course resource.

Thomson Custom Solutions offers the fastest and easiest way to create unique customized learning materials delivered the way you want. Our custom solutions also include accessing on-demand cases from leading business case providers such as **Harvard Business School Publishing, Ivey, Darden** and **NACRA;** building a tailored text online with http://www.textchoice2.com; and publishing your original materials. For more information about custom publishing options, visit http://www.thomsoncustom .com or contact your local Thomson representative.

FOR THE STUDENT

ThomsonNOW

Designed *by* instructors and students *for* instructors and students, ThomsonNOW gives you what you want to do, how you want to do it. ThomsonNOW is an integrated online suite of services and resources with proven ease of use and efficient paths to success, delivering the results you want— NOW! ThomsonNOW includes self-assessments that generate a personalized study plan, auto-graded homework assignments, a gradebook, an e-book, and more. ThomsonNOW also includes content that is tagged to the core marketing outcomes as well as to AACSB outcomes. Instructors can track students' progress to the core outcomes in their class. Figures from the text are used as interactive drag-and-drop exercises and video clips are included with assignable gradeable questions. Students will find this product fun and instructors will find it extremely useful.

Contemporary Marketing, 13th Edition Web Site

Our text Web site (http://www.thomsonedu.com/marketing/boone) is filled with a whole set of useful tools. Students will find a host of valuable resources including key terms with definitions, quizzes for each chapter, chapter summaries, and recent marketing news tied directly to chapter concepts.

Chapter Audio Reviews

These audio reviews, found in the ThomsonNOW product, contain short summaries of the chapter objectives and major concepts in each chapter and are a good review of reading assignments. Listen to them before you read the chapter as a preview of what's to come—or after you read the chapter as a reinforcement of what you've read. Listen to them on the way to class as a refresher before the lecture—or after you've left class as a review of what the instructor just discussed. However you choose to listen to them, these concise summaries will be helpful in reinforcing all the major concepts for each chapter.

ACKNOWLEDGMENTS

Over the years, *Contemporary Marketing* has benefited from the suggestions of hundreds of marketing instructors. I am most appreciative of their efforts and thoughts. Previous reviewers have included the following people:

Keith Absher
University of North Alabama

Alicia T. Aldridge
Appalachian State University

Amardeep Assar
City University of New York

Tom F. Badgett
Angelo State University

Joe K. Ballenger
Stephen F. Austin State University

Michael Bernacchi
University of Detroit Mercy

David Blanchette
Rhode Island College

Barbara Brown
San Jose State University

Reginald E. Brown
Louisiana Tech University

Marvin Burnett
St. Louis Community College— Florissant

Scott Burton
University of Arkansas

Howard Cox
Fitchberg State University

James Coyle
Baruch College

Elizabeth Creyer
University of Arkansas

Geoff Crosslin
Kalamazoo Valley Community College

William Demkey
Bakersfield College

Michael Drafke
College of DuPage

Joanne Eckstein
Macomb Community College

John Frankel
San Juan College

Robert Georgen
Trident Technical College

Robert Googins
Shasta College

Arlene Green
Indian River Community College

Joel Haynes
State University of West Georgia

Mabre Holder
Roane State Community College

Andrew W. Honeycutt
Clark Atlanta University

Dr. H. Houston
California State University— Los Angeles

John Howe
Santa Ana College

Tom Jensen
University of Arkansas

Marcella Kelly
Santa Monica College

Stephen C. King
Keene State College

Kathleen Krentler
San Diego State University

Laddie Logan
Arkansas State University

Kent Lundin
College of the Sequoias

Patricia Macro
Madison Area Tech College

Frank Markley
Arapahoe Community College

Tom Marshall
Owens Community College

Dennis C. Mathern
The University of Findlay

Lee McGinnis
University of Nebraska

Michael McGinnis
Pennsylvania State University

Norma Mendoza
University of Arkansas

Mohan Menon
University of South Alabama

Anthony Miyazaki
University of Miami

Jerry W. Moorman
Mesa State College

Linda Morable
Richland College

Diane Moretz
Ashland University

Eugene Moynihan
Rockland Community College

Margaret Myers
Northern Kentucky University

Thomas S. O'Connor
University of New Orleans

Nita Paden
Northern Arizona University

George Palz
Erie Community College— North

George Prough
University of Akron

Warren Purdy
University of Southern Maine

Salim Qureshi
Bloomsburg University

Thomas Read
Sierra College

Joel Reedy
University of South Florida

Dominic Rella
Polk Community College

Ken Ridgedell
Southeastern Louisiana University

Fernando Rodriguez
Florida Community College

Lillian Roy
McHenry County College

Arthur Saltzman
California State—San Bernardino

Elise T. Sautter
New Mexico State University

Jonathan E. Schroeder
University of Rhode Island

Farouk Shaaban
Governors State University

John Sondey
South Dakota State University

James Spiers
Arizona State University

David Starr
Shoreline Community College

Bob Stassen
University of Arkansas

Sue Taylor
Belleville Area College

Lars Thording
Arizona State University— West Campus

Rajiv Vaidyanathan
University of Minnesota

Sal Veas
Santa Monica College

Charles Vitaska
Metro State College of Denver

Cortez Walker
Baltimore City Community College

Roger Waller
San Joaquin Delta College

Mary M. Weber
Emporia State University

Vicki L. West
Southwest Texas State University

Elizabeth White
Orange County Community College

David Wiley
Anne Arundel Community College

William Wilkinson
Governors State University

James Williams
Richard Stockton College of New Jersey

Mary Wolfindarger
California State University— Long Beach

Joyce Wood
North Virginia Community College

Earlier contributors include:

Keith Absher	Philip E. Egdorf	Gregory P. Iwaniuk
Kerri L. Acheson	Michael Elliot	Don L. James
Zafar U. Ahmed	Amy Enders	James Jeck
M. Wayne Alexander	Bob Farris	Candida Johnson
Bruce Allen	Lori Feldman	David Johnson
Linda Anglin	Sandra M. Ferriter	Eugene M. Johnson
Allen Appell	Dale Fodness	James C. Johnson
Paul Arsenault	Gary T. Ford	Harold H. Kassarjian
Dub Ashton	Michael Fowler	Bernard Katz
Amardeep Assar	Edward Friese	Stephen K. Keiser
Tom F. Badgett	Sam Fullerton	Michelle Keller
Joe K. Ballenger	Ralph M. Gaedeke	J. Steven Kelly
Wayne Bascom	G. P. Gallo	James H. Kennedy
Richard D. Becherer	Nimish Gandhi	Charles Keuthan
Tom Becker	Sheryl A. Gatto	Maryon King
Richard F. Beltramini	Robert Georgen	Randall S. Kingsbury
Robert Bielski	Don Gibson	Donald L. Knight
Carol C. Bienstock	David W. Glascoff	Linda S. Koffel
Roger D. Blackwell	James Gould	Philip Kotler
Jocelyn C. Bojack	Donald Granbois	Terrence Kroeten
Michele D. Bunn	John Grant	Russell Laczniak
James Camerius	Paul E. Green	Martha Laham
Les Carlson	William Green	L. Keith Larimore
John Carmichael	Blaine Greenfield	Edwin Laube
Jacob Chacko	Matthew Gross	Ken Lawrence
Robert Collins	Robert F. Gwinner	Francis J. Leary, Jr.
Elizabeth Cooper-Martin	Raymond M. Haas	Mary Lou Lockerby
Deborah L. Cowles	John H. Hallaq	James Lollar
Howard B. Cox	Cary Hawthorn	Paul Londrigan
John E. Crawford	E. Paul Hayes	David L. Loudon
Michael R. Czinkota	Hoyt Hayes	Dorothy Maass
Kathy Daruty	Betty Jean Hebel	James C. Makens
Grant Davis	Debbora Heflin-Bullock	Lou Mansfield
Gilberto de los Santos	John (Jack) J. Heinsius	Warren Martin
Carol W. DeMoranville	Sanford B. Helman	James McCormick
Fran DePaul	Nathan Himelstein	Carl McDaniel
Gordon Di Paolo	Robert D. Hisrich	Michael McGinnis
John G. Doering	Ray S. House	James McHugh
Jeffrey T. Doutt	George Housewright	Faye McIntyre
Sid Dudley	Donald Howard	H. Lee Meadow
John W. Earnest	Michael D. Hutt	Mohan Menon

William E. (Gene) Merkle

John D. Milewicz

Robert D. Miller

Laura M. Milner

Banwari Mittal

Harry J. Moak

J. Dale Molander

John F. Monoky

James R. Moore

Thomas M. Moran

Susan Logan Nelson

Colin F. Neuhaus

Robert T. Newcomb

Jacqueline Z. Nicholson

Tom O'Connor

Robert O'Keefe

Sukgoo Pak

Eric Panitz

Dennis D. Pappas

Constantine Petrides

Barbara Piasta

Dennis D. Pitta

Barbara Pletcher

Carolyn E. Predmore

Arthur E. Prell

Bill Quain

Rosemary Ramsey

Thomas C. Reading

Gary Edward Reiman

Glen Riecken

Arnold M. Rieger

C. Richard Roberts

Patrick J. Robinson

William C. Rodgers

William H. Ronald

Bert Rosenbloom

Barbara Rosenthal

Carol Rowery

Ronald S. Rubin

Don Ryktarsyk

Rafael Santos

Duane Schecter

Dennis W. Schneider

Larry J. Schuetz

Bruce Seaton

Howard Seigelman

Jack Seitz

Steven L. Shapiro

F. Kelly Shuptrine

Ricardo Singson

Norman Smothers

Carol S. Soroos

James Spiers

Miriam B. Stamps

William Staples

David Steenstra

Bruce Stern

Robert Stevens

Kermit Swanson

G. Knude Swenson

Cathy Owens Swift

Clint B. Tankersley

Ruth Taylor

Donald L. Temple

Vern Terpstra

Ann Marie Thompson

Howard A. Thompson

John E. Timmerman

Frank Titlow

Rex Toh

Dennis H. Tootelian

Fred Trawick

Richard Lee Utecht

Rajiv Vaidyanathan

Toni Valdez

Peter Vanderhagen

Dinoo T. Vanier

Gayle D. Wasson

Donald Weinrauch

Fred Weinthal

Susan B. Wessels

John J. Whithey

Debbora Whitson

Robert J. Williams

Nicholas C. Williamson

Cecilia Wittmayer

Van R. Wood

Julian Yudelson

Robert J. Zimmer

IN CONCLUSION

I would like to thank Karen Hill of Elm Street Publishing and Ron Jost and Katherine Wilson of Lachina Publishing Services. Their ability to meet tight deadlines is truly appreciated.

Let me conclude by mentioning that the new edition would never have become a reality without the superior efforts of the Thomson South-Western production and marketing teams. My editors Neil Marquardt, Rebecca von Gillern, Amy Hackett, Vicky True, and Kristen Meere provided another *Contemporary Marketing* winner. Special thanks also go to my marketing manager, Nicole Moore.

Dave Kurtz

about the author

During **Dave Kurtz's** high school days, no one in Salisbury, Maryland, would have mistaken him for a scholar. In fact, he was a mediocre student, so bad that his father steered him toward higher education by finding him a succession of backbreaking summer jobs. Thankfully, most of them have been erased from his memory, but a few linger, including picking peaches, loading watermelons on trucks headed for market, and working as a pipefitter's helper. Unfortunately, these jobs had zero impact on his academic standing. Worse yet for Dave's ego, he was no better than average as a high school athlete in football and track.

But four years at Davis & Elkins College in Elkins, West Virginia, turned him around. Excellent instructors helped get Dave on a sound academic footing. His grade point average soared—enough to get him accepted by the graduate business school at the University of Arkansas, where he met Gene Boone. Gene and Dave became longtime co-authors; together they produced more than 50 books. In addition to writing, Dave and Gene were involved in several entrepreneurial ventures.

Today, Dave is back teaching at the University of Arkansas, after tours of duty in Ypsilanti, Michigan; Seattle, Washington; and Melbourne, Australia. He is the proud grandfather of five "perfect" kids and a sportsman with a golf handicap too high to mention. Dave, his wife, Diane, and four demanding canine companions (Daisy, Lucy, Molly, and Sally) live in Rogers, Arkansas. Dave holds a distinguished professorship at the Sam M. Walton College of Business in nearby Fayetteville, home of the Arkansas Razorbacks.

Dear Colleagues,

This edition is dedicated to my longtime co-author, Louis E. "Gene" Boone. Gene passed away after the previous edition was published. Many marketing and business instructors knew Gene over his lengthy and distinguished career. These folks can remember the numerous contributions he made to business education. Gene was truly a pioneer in our discipline. From my perspective, he was my best friend and one of the brightest people I have ever encountered.

At several points in preparing this new edition, I would stop and say to myself, "Gene would or would not have liked this idea." In short, his input is still evident in the 13th edition. And it will remain there in the editions to come.

Gene Boone was arguably the best and most creative business writer of his generation. I intend to ensure that the tradition of excellence he established will be forever part of Boone & Kurtz's *Contemporary Marketing*.

David L. Kurtz
dkurtz@walton.uark.edu

contents in brief

PHOTOS: CORVETTE ADVERTISEMENTS REPRODUCED WITH PERMISSION OF GM CORP. LICENSING GROUP

contents

Opening Vignette
Starbucks: Connecting with Customers   2

Etiquette Tips for Marketing Professionals
Forms of Address: Which One Do You Use, and When?   15

Marketing Success
What's a Google?   18

Solving an Ethical Controversy
FEMA and Katrina: The Hurricane after the Hurricane 25

PHOTO: CORVETTE ADVERTISEMENT REPRODUCED WITH PERMISSION OF GM CORP. LICENSING GROUP

chapter 2
Strategic Planning and the Marketing Process   34

appendix
Creating an Effective Marketing Plan   60

chapter 3
The Marketing Environment, Ethics, and Social Responsibility   74

chapter 4
E-Business in Contemporary Marketing   110

PART 2
UNDERSTANDING BUYERS AND MARKETS 145

chapter 5
Consumer Behavior 146

Opening Vignette
Who Buys Hybrid Cars— and Why? 146

Solving an Ethical Controversy
Kids, Parents, and Violent Video Games 157

Marketing Success
Airlines Make Boarding Easier 162

Etiquette Tips for Marketing Professionals
Handling Angry Customers 168

PART 3
TARGET MARKET SELECTION   245

chapter 8
Marketing Research and Sales Forecasting   246

chapter 9
Market Segmentation, Targeting, and Positioning   278

chapter 10
Relationship Marketing and Customer Relationship Management (CRM)   310

Opening Vignette
Best Buy Bets on Customers 310

Solving an Ethical Controversy
Too Much Data, Not Enough Protection? 322

Etiquette Tips for Marketing Professionals
How to Deal with Rude People 325

Marketing Failure
The Perils of Big Partners 326

PHOTO: CORVETTE ADVERTISEMENT REPRODUCED WITH PERMISSION OF GM CORP. LICENSING GROUP

PART 4
PRODUCT DECISIONS 343

PART 5
DISTRIBUTION DECISIONS   411

chapter 13
Marketing Channels and Supply Chain Management   412

chapter 14
Retailers, Wholesalers, and Direct Marketers   448

PART 6
PROMOTIONAL DECISIONS 485

chapter 15
Integrated Marketing Communications 486

chapter 16
Advertising and Public Relations   524

chapter 19
Pricing Strategies 634

prologue

Planning a Career in Marketing

The Real Deal: A Top Marketer's Job

Al DeGenova is constantly on the move. He serves as director of marketing communications for Grohe America, the U.S. subsidiary for German luxury bath and kitchen fixture manufacturer Grohe Technology AG. DeGenova's job is critical to the success of his company—to create marketing messages that flow from his employer to his customers like water.

To be effective, DeGenova puts in long hours. During an average day, he might respond to e-mails and voice mails about his marketing projects, work with Grohe's public-relations agency on a strategic plan for launching three new product lines, meet with marketing managers who report to him, field calls from sales reps who have questions about customers or products, oversee the creation of sales displays for trade shows, write brochures and press releases, and monitor the advertising and marketing budget. Al DeGenova loves his job. He works hard to balance his career and family life and says he is satisfied with both. "I like the fact that there is a creative element [to my job] because it fits my personality," he comments. He likes going on photo shoots and writing captions for ads, along with thinking up new slogans for brochures. "I like developing advertising because it reaches the widest audience," DeGenova says, "and you have to really think about how you're creating your message." He also likes the autonomy he has—the authority to set his own priorities and those of the managers who report to him. But he quickly notes that he has a boss, too. "I have to get approval for big projects like trade shows, which involve a lot of people."

DeGenova points out that because his firm creates products for consumers in 181 countries, his staff needs to be aware of the product preferences of the different markets. "Every market has its own character," he observes. "In Germany, we sell mostly bath fittings, and we offer flushing systems as well. We don't even include those in our price list [here]. Finishes such as oil-rubbed bronze, polished nickel, polished brass, and satin nickel are big in the United States but not in Europe." He explains that these preferences drive the firm's marketing efforts. "Globally, each country has specific needs versus those of Europe. Marketing to the different countries around the world requires different brochures and different imagery inside those brochures. Europe is fairly homogenous in this regard."

At the end of the day, DeGenova is happy with his choice of marketing as a long-term career, although he sometimes toys with the idea of becoming a novelist or college professor when he retires. And he admits, "the hardest part of [my] job is trying to make everyone happy." That may be the hardest part of any job, in any field. So he shrugs it off and is once again on the move.[1]

briefly *speaking*

"How would like a job where, if you made a mistake, a big red light goes on and 18,000 people boo?"

—Jacques Plante
(1929–1986)
National Hockey League goalie

Overview

Congratulations on your decision to take this course. As a consumer, you already know that marketing is a pervasive element in our lives. In one form or another, it reaches every person. This course will inform you about the different types of marketing messages, show you how they are created, and help you understand the impact they have.

As you begin this course, try to be aware of three important points about marketing: marketing costs are a big component of a product's budget, marketers contribute to society as well as to individual employers, and marketing is the single largest employment category in the U.S. labor force.

MARKETING COSTS ARE A BIG COMPONENT OF A PRODUCT'S TOTAL BUDGET

Approximately 50 percent of the total costs of products you buy are marketing costs. Half of the $199 you pay for an iPod goes to marketing costs—making sure that you are aware of the iPod's existence and its capabilities and persuading you to buy it. Yes, the cost of the high-tech features is an important component, as is the plastic case and earbuds. But marketing expenses also figure into the total cost of the product. The same is true of that Toyota Scion you have your eye on.

But costs alone do not indicate the value of marketing to the success of a product. Marketing sends important messages to consumers and businesses, usually expanding overall sales and spreading production costs over more items sold, reducing the total cost to bring the product to market.

MARKETERS CONTRIBUTE TO SOCIETY AS WELL AS TO INDIVIDUAL EMPLOYERS

Marketing decisions affect everyone's welfare. How much quality should be built into a product? Will people buy a safer product if it costs twice as much as the current version? Should every community adopt recycling programs? Because ethics and social responsibility are critical factors in creating long-term relationships with consumers, business customers, and the community, marketers MUST strive to exceed customer and government expectations of ethical behavior. Be sure to read the "Solving an Ethical Controversy" features included in every chapter. They will get you thinking about ethical issues in marketing and increase your awareness of the importance of maintaining high ethical standards in every dimension of marketing. These features will allow you to examine such current issues as online data protection, the potential effects of violent video games, proper gift-giving policies in the workplace, fair-trade pricing, the blocking of cell phones, food labeling, consumer drug advertising, and many others. The topics also make good springboards for discussion between you and your classmates.

Not only does marketing influence numerous facets of our daily lives, but decisions regarding marketing activities also affect everyone's welfare. Opportunities to advance to more responsible decision-making positions often come sooner in marketing than in most occupations. This combination of challenges and opportunities has made marketing one of the most popular fields of academic study.

Although many paths can lead to the top of the corporate ladder, marketing remains one of the strongest and most popular. The growing global economy depends on proven market leaders in winning the fight to increase a firm's worldwide market shares. Marketing provides a solid background for developing the long-term, loyal relationships with customers that are so necessary for success in the global marketplace.

Top marketers such as Apple Computer, Boeing, Hewlett-Packard, Microsoft, Nike, and Safeco contribute to the overall welfare of society and the environment by offering employee commuters different options. They organize mass transit and van pooling programs, as well as arrange for telecommuting to reduce air pollution.

© ASSOCIATED PRESS, AP

YOU MAY CHOOSE A CAREER IN MARKETING

Even if you aren't sure about a career now, this course may help you decide on a path in marketing. In fact, of the many career paths chosen by business graduates, marketing is the largest employment category in the U.S. labor force, and job growth in the field is expected to accelerate. All firms must somehow get their goods and services into the hands of customers profitably, and doing so is becoming increasingly challenging. So marketing plays a significant role in the survival and growth of all companies—which means that as a field, it will continue to grow.

The U.S. Bureau of Labor Statistics anticipates stiff competition for desirable jobs, with college graduates having "related experience, a high level of creativity, strong communication skills, and computer skills" standing the best chance of landing these jobs. These candidates can expect high earnings along with travel and long work hours, including evenings and weekends.[2]

YOUR QUEST FOR A SUCCESSFUL, REWARDING CAREER

Selecting a career is an important life decision—your career will determine such things as where you live, how much money you make, and for what kind of company you work. That's why *Contemporary Marketing* begins by discussing the best ways to approach career decisions and to prepare for an *entry-level position*—your first permanent employment after leaving school. We then look at a range of marketing careers and discuss employment opportunities in fields related to each major part of the text.

The good news is that the job market is healthy. The average starting salary for marketing graduates is about $35,000.[3] As mentioned earlier, the field of marketing is the largest area of employment in the United States—and employers are continuing to hire. This positive outlook does *not* mean that competition isn't stiff or that you can be casual in your approach to your first job. You are not guaranteed anything. But if you are creative, hardworking, and determined—and if you learn everything you can about business and marketing before you begin your search—you are likely to land a good entry-level position at a company that suits you. During the next few months, you will be introduced to all the key functional areas of marketing. As you learn about marketing concepts, you will also be able to identify areas of employment that you may wish to pursue.

Education will improve your prospects of finding and keeping the right job. Recent college graduates can earn nearly twice what workers with high school diplomas earn.[4] Better educated graduates also find jobs more quickly than others. Applying yourself in class and expanding your experiences through career-directed volunteer efforts, part-time and summer jobs, and high-quality internships—and selecting the right major—will put you well on your way to improving these salary statistics when you launch your career.

In addition to taking classes, try to gain related experience either through a job or by participating in campus organizations. Internships, summer and part-time jobs, and volunteer activities on campus and in your community can also give you valuable hands-on experience while you pursue your education. Work-related experience, whether paid or volunteer, lets a potential employer know you are serious about pursuing your career. It also helps you decide on your own path.

This introduction to planning your career provides you with a brief look at the trends and opportunities available for future marketers in an increasingly diversified, professional field. It describes essential elements of an effective résumé and discusses the latest trends in electronic job searches. Finally, it provides a listing of primary marketing information sources that contain answers to many of the

Companies such as Weyerhaeuser seek to build a diverse, creative workforce. Not only does the company need engineers and information technology specialists, but it also looks for professionals with expertise in sales and marketing.

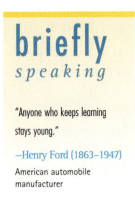
questions typically asked by applicants. This information will provide valuable career-planning assistance in this and other future courses, whether your career plans involve marketing or you decide to major in another field.

Many of the marketing positions you read about throughout this text are described here. Specifically, the job summaries describe the responsibilities and duties that are typically required, as well as the usual career path for each of these marketing-related positions. You might follow a traditional career path, or you might wind up in one of the new types of marketing jobs that are emerging, as Christine Halvorson did. Halvorson, a former freelance writer and Web content editor, responded to an advertisement on Monster.com, which led her to apply for the job of chief blogger at Stonyfield Farm, maker of organic yogurt. Halvorson landed the job and now writes four regular blogs for the company, including the Daily Scoop, a blog about the company itself, and Creating Healthy Kids, which promotes healthful food choices in schools.[5]

Marketing your skills to a prospective employer is much the same as marketing a product to a consumer. Increasingly, job seekers are selling their skills online, bypassing intermediaries such as employment agencies and leveling the playing field between applicant and potential employer. The greatest challenge for online job seekers is learning how to market themselves.

Despite the vast databases and fancy tools of the giant career sites such as Monster.com, HotJobs.com, and CareerBuilder.com, which may receive hundreds of thousands of visits each day, savvy job seekers also zero in on niche boards offering more focused listings. You can find sites that focus specifically on sales, such as SalesJobs.com, and those that emphasize positions for female professionals, such as WomenSportsJobs.com.[6] In all, there are about 40,000 online job boards.[7]

In many instances, students seeking interviews with specific employers or in certain geographic locations go directly to the employer's or region's Web site to learn of available positions. Most employers include an employment site as part of their home page. Some offer virtual tours of what it is like to work for the firm. For example, the Enterprise Rent-a-Car Web site features profiles of young assistant managers as they perform daily work activities. The site points to the skills that employees gain while working there, the friendships formed among workers, opportunities for involvement in the community, the management training program, and available internships.[8]

The key to finding the job you want is letting the market know who you are and what you can do. While few college graduates are hired directly based on their response to an online listing, this approach is often an important first step in zeroing in on specific employers of interest and then soliciting interviews that may lead to job offers. So you should familiarize yourself with the way online job sites work, including those of specific companies.

As you begin your career, you will apply many of the principles and concepts discussed in this text, including how to target a market, capitalize on brand equity, position a product, and use marketing research techniques. Even in jobs that seem remote from the marketing discipline, this knowledge will help you stay focused on the most important aspect of business: the consumer.

STANDING OUT FROM THE CROWD OF JOB SEEKERS

Because high-quality employees provide companies the edge they need in competitive markets, employers need to be choosy in deciding which applicants will make the cut, be interviewed, and possibly be offered a position. And often the applicant's accumulated job and leadership experiences will be key criteria in determining whether he or she is given serious consideration as a potential employee.

Some students continue their studies following graduation and pursue an MBA degree or enter a master's program specially suited to their career goals. But many enter the job market right way, perhaps pursuing an advanced degree later on. Experience is one factor in a prospective employee's favor, and some activities that enhance a candidate's profile are internships and volunteering.

INTERNSHIPS PROVIDE VALUABLE WORK EXPERIENCE

Internships have been described as a critical link in bridging the theory–practice educational gap. They help carry students between the academic present and the professional future. They provide students with an opportunity for learning how classroom theory is applied in real-world business environments.

Internships are gaining popularity for both employers and students or recent grads. The National Association of Colleges and Employers (NACE) reports that employers cite internships as one of the leading qualifications for hiring new employees. During a recent year, more than 53 percent of interns were subsequently hired by their companies as full-time employees, and 62 percent of all new college hires had previous internship experience. Internships give students daily hands-on experience, including specific skills they might not have coming into the job. "Interns don't just pour coffee and do filing," notes Stan Inman, director of career services for NACE. "They get responsibilities and the chance to show their employer that they can succeed at the company."[9]

Start your search for an internship at your college placement office or library. Some college Web sites have catalogs of internships available through organizations, such as the American Association of Advertising Agencies, the Inroads Minority Internship Program, and the Washington Center for Internships and Academic Seminars.[10] Also check with the alumni office, which may have a listing of alumni who are willing to talk with seniors or recent grads about their fields. You can talk with your instructors, visit the Web sites of companies that interest you, and check your local bookstore for career and internship reference guides.

YOUR RÉSUMÉ

Writing a résumé is a vital task, but it doesn't need to be daunting. Your résumé is like a verbal snapshot of you. It tells a potential employer about you, your credentials, and your goals. It provides an all-important first impression of you and may be the only written record available with which an

briefly
speaking

"Ambition is the path to success. Persistence is the vehicle you arrive in."

—Bill Bradley (b. 1943)
Former U.S. Senator, NBA player, and U.S. Olympian

Résumé Blunders

The following is a list of errors that have appeared in résumés, job applications, and cover letters received by Monster.com and CareerBuilder.com:

- "Here are my qualifications for you to overlook."

- "Accomplishments: Completed 11 years of high school."

- "Qualifications: No education or experience."

- "Fired because I fought for lower pay."

- "I am a rabid typist."

- "I am relatively intelligent, obedient, and loyal as a puppy."

- "My objective is simple: I want your job."

- "Please remember dear Sir/Madam, that I have failed in a few subjects in my diploma in computer engineering, and that I have no degree."

- "Reason for leaving: it had to do with the IRS, FBI, and SEC."

- "Reason for leaving: my boss said the end of the world is near."

Sources: "Résumé Faux Pas," Monster.com, **http://content.monster.com**, accessed August 16, 2006; "Résumés from Hell and Their Lessons," CNN.com, March 1, 2006, **http://www.cnn.com**.

figure 1

Functional Résumé

Roberto Chavez
Two Seaside Drive, Apt. 3A
Los Angeles, CA 90026
215-555-7092
RCHAVEZ@hotmail.com

Objective
Joining a growth-oriented company that values highly productive employees. Seeking an opportunity that leads to senior merchandising position.

Professional Experience
Administration
Management responsibilities in a major retail buying office included coordinating vendor relation efforts. Supervised assistant buyers.

Category Management
Experience in buying home improvement and sport, recreation, and fitness categories.

Planning
Leader of a team charged with reviewing the company's annual vendor evaluation program.

Problem Solving
Successfully developed a program to improve margins in the tennis, golf, and fishing product categories.

Work Experience
Senior Buyer
Southern California Department Stores   2006–Present

Merchandiser
Pacific Discount Stores, a division of Southern California
Department Stores   2004–2006

Education
Bachelor of Science degree in business
Double major in marketing and retailing
California State University–San Bernardino   2002–2006

Computer Skills
Proficient with IBM-compatible computers and related software, including spreadsheets, graphics, desktop publishing, and word processing.
Packages: Microsoft Word, Excel, PowerPoint, Adobe PageMaker, CorelDRAW

Familiar with Adobe Photoshop and the Macintosh.

Language Skills
Fluent in speaking and writing Spanish.

---

employer can make a decision about you. Your résumé is a concise summary of your academic, professional, and personal accomplishments; it makes focused statements about you as a student and potential employee.

Three basic formats are used in preparing a résumé. A *chronological résumé* arranges information in reverse chronological order, emphasizing job titles and organizations and describing responsibilities held and duties performed. This format highlights continuity and career growth. A *functional résumé* accents accomplishments and strengths, placing less emphasis on job titles and work history, and often omits job descriptions. A functional résumé prepared by a recent graduate is shown in Figure 1. Some applicants use a *combined résumé* format, which emphasizes skills first, followed by employment history. This format highlights a candidate's potential and suits students who often have little experience directly related to their desired positions.

Regardless of which format you choose, all résumés contain certain information. And they all have the same goal: to interest an employer enough to invite you to apply formally for a job and conduct an interview. A résumé should be concise—no more than a single page. Before writing your résumé, take the time to outline your goals, skills, abilities, education, and work experience and list any relevant volunteer or extracurricular activities. You can pare these down later, but having them in front of you will make it easier to build your final résumé.

Your contact information should appear at the top of the page: full name, address, phone number, and e-mail address. If your e-mail username is "MachoDude" or "SnowboardDoll," replace it with one related to your real name or location to persuade employers to take you seriously. Likewise, avoid using a nickname. Even if all of your friends call you Smitty, cite your name as John A. Smith.

A statement of goals usually follows. Try to be somewhat specific with it. You can say, "My goal is to obtain an entry-level marketing position where I can apply my analytical and organizational skills." Don't state that your goal is to become CEO of the company—that's a long way off, and it doesn't apply to the job at hand.

Your education information generally comes next. State your most recent level of education first. There is no need to list high school unless you attended a specialized school or received particular honors. Include your degree, academic honors, and grade point average if it is above 3.0.

State your work history, including employment, internships, and related volunteer work. Include the name of the organization, the dates you worked there, your job title, and your responsibilities on the job. Provide a statement of your skills, such as leadership, managing others, computer software knowledge, and the like. At the end of your résumé, add a note that you will furnish references on request—do *not* include your references' names and contact information on your résumé.[11]

Whether yours is a traditional résumé on paper or posted on an Internet résumé listing, the important point to remember in creating an effective résumé is to present the most relevant information in a clear, concise manner that emphasizes your best attributes.

briefly
speaking

"A résumé is a balance sheet without any liabilities."

–Robert Half (1918–2001)
American personnel agency executive

COVER LETTER

Your potential employer is typically first introduced to you through a cover letter. Like gift wrapping on a present, a cover letter should attract attention and interest about what is inside. Your letter should be addressed to a specific person—not "to whom it may concern." It should include information about the job for which you are applying, why you are interested in it, a brief summary of your top accomplishments or skills, and a note that you are available for an interview. Close your letter by thanking the person for his or her time and consideration.

Here are a few additional tips:

- Keep your letter to a single page.

- Proofread it several times.

- Be sure to sign your letter.

- Customize the letter to the company or person for whom it is intended, even though you may be writing 10 or 20 such letters.

- Be confident but not arrogant.[12]

LETTERS OF RECOMMENDATION

Letters of recommendation serve as testimonials to your performance in academic and work settings. The best references provide information relevant to the desired industry or marketing specialty as well as opinions of your skills, abilities, and character. You can obtain references from former or current employers, supervisors from volunteer experiences, instructors, and others who can attest to your academic and professional competencies.

An effective letter of recommendation typically contains the following elements:

1. Statement of the length and nature of the relationship between the writer and the job candidate

2. Description of the candidate's academic and career growth potential

3. Review of important achievements

4. Evaluation of personal characteristics (what kind of colleague the candidate will make)

5. Summary of the candidate's outstanding strengths and abilities

Because letters of recommendation take time and effort, it helps to provide a résumé and any other information relevant to the recommendation, along with a stamped, addressed (typed) envelope. When requesting letters of recommendation, allow ample time for your references to compose them—as long as a month is not unusual.

In addition to including a cover letter, résumé, and letters of recommendation, you should include photocopies of transcripts, writing samples, or other examples of work completed. For instance, if you are applying for a position in public relations, advertising, or sports marketing, you may want to include examples of professional writing, graphics, and audiovisual media to support written evidence of your credentials. Research and service projects that resulted in published or unpublished articles may also enhance your portfolio.

USING ELECTRONIC SYSTEMS

Most large firms have moved toward electronic (paperless) résumé processing and applicant-tracking systems. In fact, some human resources experts say outright that the fastest way to get your résumé to the correct person is to use the firm's own online application system. So it's best to prepare a résumé that is compatible with these systems. Figure 2 contains a number of tips for preparing an effective, readable, technology-compatible résumé.

In addition to those tips, keep in mind a few overall rules. First, read the directions for completing and transmitting your résumé or application carefully—and follow them to the letter. If you try to stand out by doing something different, your application will probably be lost or ignored—you will be viewed as someone who might not follow instructions on the job. Second, complete all possible fields, even those that are not required. Third, if the firm offers an optional online assessment test, take it. An employer will appreciate your initiative and can evaluate some of your skills immediately.[13]

Finally, choose effective keywords for your résumé. Employers who review electronic résumés posted on their sites and on big boards save time by using computers to search for keywords in job titles, job descriptions, or résumés to narrow the search. In fact, *manager* is the number one word for which companies search. Regardless of the position you seek, one key to an effective electronic résumé is to use exact words and phrases, emphasizing nouns rather than the action verbs you are likely to use in a print-only résumé. For example, a company looking for a marketing account manager with experience in Microsoft Access, Microsoft Word, and Microsoft Excel programs may conduct computer searches for only résumés that include the job title and the three software programs.

figure 2

Tips for Preparing an Electronic Résumé

Tips for Preparing an Electronic Résumé

- Use a plain font. Use a standard typeface, such as Courier, Times, Arial, Univers, or Futura. Simplicity is key.
- Use 11- to 14-point type sizes.
- Keep your line length to no more than 65 characters (letters, spaces, and punctuation).
- Do not use graphics, bullets, lines, bold, italics, underlines, or shading.
- Use capital letters for your headings.
- Justify your text to the left.
- Use vertical and horizontal lines sparingly. Lines may blur your type.
- Omit parentheses and brackets, even around telephone numbers. These can blur and leave the number unreadable.
- Use white paper and black type.
- Use a laser-quality printer.
- Print on one side of the paper only.
- Don't compress space between letters. Use a second page rather than pack everything into one page and have it scan unclearly.
- Do not staple pages of a résumé together.
- Use industry buzzwords. Keyword searches often look for industry jargon.
- Place your name as the first text on the résumé. Do not put anything else on that line.
- Fax résumés on the *fine mode* setting. It is much easier to read than the *standard mode* setting.
- Do not fold your résumé. A crease makes scanning—and retrieving—difficult.
- If you are sending your résumé in the body of an e-mail transmission, do not distinguish between pages, as the full e-mail will download into the database as one sheet.
- Don't send a résumé as an e-mail attachment unless you are specifically instructed to do so. Many employers discard unsolicited attachments.

Source: Mary Lebeau, "Tips for Electronic Resumes," JobWeb Career Library, **http://www.jobweb.com**, accessed September 8, 2006. Reprinted from JobWeb (www.jobweb.com) with permission of the National Association of Colleges and Employers, copyright holder.

LEARNING MORE ABOUT JOB OPPORTUNITIES

As you continue with your selection and application process, study the various employment opportunities you have identified. Obviously you will like some more than others, but keep an open mind; remember, this is the beginning of a long career. Examine a number of factors when assessing each job possibility:

1. Actual job responsibilities
2. Industry characteristics
3. Nature of the company
4. Geographic location
5. Salary and opportunities for advancement
6. The contribution the job is likely to make to your long-range career opportunities

Many job applicants consider only the most striking features of a job, perhaps its location or the salary offered. However, a comprehensive review of job openings will give you a more balanced perspective of the overall employment opportunity, including both long-run and short-run factors.

JOB INTERVIEWS

Your first goal in your job search is to land an interview with a prospective employer. If the experience is new to you and you feel uncertain or nervous, you can do a lot to turn those feelings into confidence.

briefly *speaking*

"Put it to them briefly so they will read it; picturesquely, so they will remember it—and, above all, accurately, so they will be guided by its light."

—Joseph Pulitzer (1847–1911)
American journalist

Preparing for the Interview

Do your homework. Learn as much as you can about the company, the industry in which it operates, the goods or services it offers, the working environment, and the like. If you are well prepared for the questions you are asked—and prepared to ask educated questions—you are much more likely to have a positive interview experience. You can prepare by researching the following basic information about the firm:

- How long has the firm been in business?

- In what industry does the firm operate? What is its role within the industry?

- Who are the firm's customers? Who are its competitors?

- How is the firm organized? How many people work there? Where are its headquarters? Does it have other offices and production facilities located around the nation or around the world?

- What is the company's mission? Does the company have a written code of ethics?

This information is useful in several ways. Not only will it increase your confidence about the interview, but it may also help you weed out any firms that might not be a good fit for you. You've also shown the interviewer that you are motivated enough to come to the discussion prepared.

You can find this information in many of the same places you looked initially for information about companies at the beginning of your job search. Your school's career center, library, and, most important, the company's own Web site will have much of the information you need. In addition, you can find brief company profiles on business sites such as Hoovers.com, and don't forget to check the various business magazines.

What to Expect in an Interview

You've made the interview appointment, done your research on the company, and chosen the right attire for the occasion according to the "Etiquette Tips for Marketing Professionals" feature on page xlviii. What's next?

Prepare yourself for the questions you will likely be asked. As you gain experience in interviewing, you will recognize variations of similar questions and be able to answer them comfortably. An interviewer needs to get to know you in a short period of time, so he or she will ask questions that deal with your personality, your life and work experience, and decision-making or problem-solving style. Here are a few examples:

- Why did you apply for this job? Why do you want this job?

- What are the requirements of the job as you understand them?

- What are your strengths? What are your weaknesses?

- Are you an organized person? How do you manage your time?

- What were your responsibilities on your last job or internship? How would they apply here?

- What were your biggest successes or failures—in school or work?

- How do you make big decisions? How do you function under pressure?

- Do you work better with other people, or on your own?

- Where do you see yourself in five years?[14]

To prepare effective answers, ask a friend or family member to role-play the interview with you, asking questions so that you have an opportunity to hear yourself respond out loud before the actual interview.

When you arrive for your interview, be sure to confirm the name of the person (or people) who will conduct the interview. If this person is with the human resource department and your interview goes well, he or she will probably recommend you to a manager or supervisor for further interviewing. Some hiring decisions are made by a single supervisor, while others result from joint interviews conducted by both human resources personnel and the immediate supervisor of the prospective employee.

briefly
speaking

"The future belongs to those who believe in the beauty of their dreams."

—Eleanor Roosevelt
(1884–1962)
First lady of the United States
(1933–1945)

Etiquette Tips for Marketing Professionals

How to Dress for Your Job Interview

Landing a job interview is a big step on the road to starting your career. Making the most of the opportunity to create a good impression—and to learn something about the company you might work for—begins with presenting yourself well. You need to be prepared; project confidence, eagerness, and dependability; and look the part. Here are some tips for dressing for the interview. Unless you are applying for a very unusual job, in which case you can actually call ahead and find out what attire is appropriate, these suggestions will serve you well.

1. Dress conservatively. A dark two-piece, single-breasted suit is best for men and women, with a conservative long-sleeved shirt or blouse. Men should choose a conservatively patterned tie. Keep conventional jewelry and makeup to an unnoticeable minimum.

2. Make sure your clothes are clean and well pressed and that there are no runs in stockings or holes in socks.

3. Wear clean, well-polished shoes. Avoid extreme styles or colors; conservative, closed-toe shoes are the best choice.

4. Make sure your nails are clean and short. If you wear polish, use a conservative color or clear.

5. Avoid cologne or perfume—some people are allergic to the scent, particularly in a closed area such as an office.

6. Keep your pockets free of noisy coins and keys or bulging items such as phones or pagers.

7. Leave nose rings, eyebrow rings, and other unusual body ornaments at home. Cover any visible tattoos.

8. Keep your hair neat, groomed, and short (for men) or off your face (for women). Men should be clean shaven.

9. Carry a lightweight portfolio or briefcase (women might carry a leather tote). If you have a cell phone or pager inside it, turn it off.

Looking professional is the first step to conducting a successful interview—and landing a job. So think first what the interviewer would like to see in a job candidate and dress accordingly. Then both you and the interviewer will be more at ease.

Sources: "Dressed for Success," Sam M. Walton College of Business, **http://waltoncollege.uark.edu**, accessed August 17, 2006; Peter Vogt, "Get Polished for Your Interview," Monster.com, **http://interview.monster .com**, accessed August 17, 2006; "Dressing for a Job Interview," CollegeGrad.com, **http://www.collegegrad.com**, accessed August 17, 2006.

The job interview is a time for you to learn about the opportunities a company offers, as well as for the organization to learn about your strengths.

© ERIC AUDRAS/PHOTOALTO/GETTY IMAGES

During a typical interview, the interviewer usually talks little. This approach, referred to as an *open-ended interview*, forces you to talk about yourself and your career goals. This is a major reason why it is important to arrive prepared. If you appear uncertain or disorganized in your thinking, the interviewer may surmise that you have not prepared or aren't serious about the job. Keep the conversation on target; don't ramble on and on. You may also ask questions of the interviewer, so be sure to listen carefully to the responses. Appropriate questions include those about job responsibilities, training, and long-range opportunities for advancement. Don't ask when you will get a raise or promotion or how many vacation days you will receive. In the end, a successful interview represents a mutual exchange of information.

A successful first interview may result in an invitation to return to take a skills test, tour the building, or even meet other managers and co-workers. All of these experiences point toward making the right fit between a company and its potential employees. On the other hand, even after a good interview, you may not be asked back. Do not consider this a personal rejection—the job market is competitive, and companies must make their selections carefully to achieve the best match. It might not have been the right firm or job for you in the long run, and the interviewer realized this. Treat each job application and interview as a chance to build confidence and experience—and eventually, the right job will be yours.

EMPLOYMENT DECISIONS

By now, a firm that is still considering you as a strong candidate knows quite a bit about you. You should also know a lot about the company and whether you want to work there. When the interview process is complete, you may be offered a position with the firm. Your decision to accept the offer should depend on a variety of factors, including the following:

- Do you want to work in this industry?

- Do you want to be a part of the company's mission? Would you be proud to work for this company?

- Could this particular job lead to other opportunities within the company?

- Will you be able to work well with your co-workers and supervisors?

- Can you already see ways that you can learn and contribute your best efforts to the company?

If you are offered the job and decide to accept it, congratulations! Approach your new job with professionalism, creativity, and a willingness to learn. You are on your way to a successful career in marketing.

MARKETING POSITIONS

In order to survive and grow, an organization must market its goods or services. Marketing responsibilities vary among organizations and industries. In a small firm, the owner or president may assume many of the company's marketing responsibilities. A large firm needs experienced sales, marketing, and advertising managers, as well as staff, to coordinate these activities. The "Career Path" features that follow outline major marketing positions, providing job descriptions and projected career paths for each. Each position is also cross-referenced to the chapter in this text that discusses the marketing area in detail.

briefly
speaking

"The best way to get what you want is to help other people get what they want."

–Zig Ziglar (b. 1927)
American motivational speaker

© PHOTOGRAPHER'S CHOICE/GETTY IMAGES

Sales associates learn how to be poised and confident, speak clearly and effectively, and communicate with customers and other staff members—all skills that can translate into future success.

Career Path 1: Marketing, Advertising, Product, and Public Relations Managers

Related Chapters: Chapters 1 and 2 (marketing); Chapters 11 and 12 (product); Chapters 15 and 16 (advertising and public relations)

Marketing management spans a range of positions, including vice president of marketing, marketing manager, sales manager, product manager, advertising manager, promotion manager, and public-relations manager. The vice president directs the firm's overall marketing policy, and all other marketers report through channels to this person. Sales managers direct the efforts of sales professionals by assigning territories, establishing goals, developing training programs, and supervising local sales managers and their personnel. Advertising managers oversee account services, creative services, and media services departments. Promotion managers direct promotional programs that combine advertising with purchase incentives designed to increase the sales of the firm's goods or services. Public-relations managers communicate with the firm's various publics, conduct publicity programs, and supervise the specialists who implement these programs.

Job Description

As with senior management positions in production, finance, and other areas, top marketing management positions often involve long hours and regular travel. Work under pressure is also common to solve problems and meet deadlines. For sales managers, job transfers between headquarters and regional offices may disrupt one's personal life. More than 310,000 marketing, advertising, and public-relations managers are currently employed in the United States. The Bureau of Labor Statistics estimates that the number of these jobs will increase faster than average through the year 2014.[15]

Career Path

A degree in business administration, preferably with a concentration in marketing, is usually preferred for these positions, but for advertising positions, some employers want a bachelor's degree in advertising or journalism. Those looking for jobs in public relations should have a bachelor's degree in public relations or journalism. In highly technical industries, such as computers, chemicals, and electronics, employers may look for bachelor's degrees in science or engineering combined with master's degrees in business administration. Liberal arts students can also find many opportunities, especially if they have business minors. Most managers are promoted from positions such as sales representatives, product or brand specialists, and advertising specialists within their organizations. Skills or traits that are most desirable for these jobs include high motivation levels, maturity, creativity, resistance to stress, flexibility, and the ability to communicate persuasively.[16]

Career Path 2: Sales Representatives and Sales Managers

Related Chapter: Chapter 17

Millions of items are bought and sold every day. The people in the firm who carry out this activity may have a variety of titles—sales representative, account manager, manufacturer's representative, sales engineer, sales agent, retail salesperson, wholesale sales representative, and service sales representative. Sales managers are typically selected from people in the current sales force who have demonstrated that they possess the managerial skills needed to lead teams of sales representatives. In addition, many organizations require that all marketing professionals spend some time in the field to experience the market firsthand and to understand the challenges faced by front-line personnel.

Job Description

Salespeople usually develop prospective client lists, meet with current and prospective customers to discuss the firm's products, and then follow up to answer questions and supply additional information. By knowing the business needs of each customer, the sales representative can identify products that best satisfy these needs. After a customer purchase, they are likely to revisit their customers to ensure that the products are meeting the customers' needs and to explore further business opportunities or referrals provided by satisfied buyers. Some sales of technical products involve lengthy interactions. In these cases, a salesperson may work with several clients simultaneously over a large geographic area. Those responsible for large territories may spend most of their workdays on the phone, receiving and sending e-mail messages, or traveling to provide service to customers. The job outlook for sales managers is positive, with faster-than-average growth through the year 2014. Currently there are more than 337,000 sales managers in the United States.[17]

Work as a sales representative or sales manager can be rewarding for those who enjoy interacting with people, are invigorated by competition, and feel energized by the challenge of expanding sales in their territories. Successful sales professionals—both individual sales reps and sales managers—should be goal oriented, persuasive, self-motivated, and independent. In addition, patience and perseverance are important qualities.

Career Path

The background needed for a position in sales varies according to the product line and market. Most professional sales jobs require a college degree, preferably with a major in business administration or marketing. Many companies run their own formal training programs that can last up to two years for sales representatives in technical industries. This training may take place in a classroom, in the field with a mentor, or most often using a combination of both methods. Sales managers are usually promoted from the field; they are likely to include successful sales representatives who exhibit managerial skills and promise. Sales management positions begin at a local or district level, then advance to positions of increased authority and responsibility such as area, regional, national, and international sales manager.[18]

Career Path 3: Advertising Specialists

Related Chapters: Chapters 15 and 16

Most companies, especially firms serving consumer markets, maintain small groups of advertising specialists who serve as liaisons between the marketer and its outside advertising agencies. The leader of this liaison function is sometimes called a marketing communications manager. Advertising agencies also employ specialists in account services, creative services, and media services. Account services functions are performed by account executives, who work directly with clients. An agency's creative services department develops the themes and presentations of the advertisements. This department is supervised by a creative director, who oversees the copy chief, the art director, and their staff members. The media services department is managed by a media director, who oversees the planning group that selects media outlets for ads. Currently, there are about 4,700 full-service advertising agencies in the United States.[19]

Job Description

Advertising can be one of the most glamorous and creative fields in marketing. Because the field combines the best of both worlds—that is, the tangible and scientific aspects of marketing along with creative artistry—advertising attracts people with a broad array of abilities. As exciting as it may seem, advertising is also stressful. Those in the creative field often have to come up with innovative plans on a tight schedule. Long hours are also common. Advertising professionals must be able to manage their time wisely, be willing to travel, and deal with demanding clients.[20]

Career Path

Most new hires begin as assistants or associates for the position they hope to acquire, such as copywriter, art director, and media buyer. Often a newly hired employee must receive two to four promotions before becoming manager of these functions. A bachelor's degree with broad liberal arts exposure in courses such as graphic arts, communications, psychology, and marketing is usually required for an entry-level position in advertising.[21]

Career Path 4: Public-Relations Specialists

Related Chapters: Chapters 15 and 16

Specialists in public relations strive to build and maintain positive relationships with various publics. They may assist management in drafting speeches, arranging interviews, overseeing company archives, responding to information requests, and handling special events, such as sponsorships and trade shows, that generate promotional benefits for the firm.

Job Description

Public-relations specialists may work hectic schedules to help a firm respond to and manage a crisis or to meet the deadline for a special event. Although public-relations positions tend to be concentrated in large cities near major press services and communications facilities, this is changing as communications technologies allow more freedom of movement. Most public-relations consulting firms are concentrated in New York, Los Angeles, Chicago, and Washington, D.C., and they range in size from hundreds of employees to just a handful.[22]

Essential characteristics for a public-relations specialist include creativity, initiative, good judgment, and the ability to express thoughts clearly and simply—both verbally and in writing. An outgoing personality, self-confidence, and enthusiasm are also recommended traits.

Career Path

A college degree combined with public-relations experience, usually gained through one or more internships, is considered excellent preparation for public relations. Many entry-level public-relations specialists hold degrees with majors in advertising, marketing, public relations, or communications. New employees in larger organizations are likely to participate in formal training programs; those who begin their careers at smaller firms typically work under the guidance of experienced staff members. Entry-level positions carry such titles as research assistant or account assistant. A potential career path includes a promotion to account executive, account supervisor, vice president, and eventually senior vice president.

Career Path 5: Purchasing Agents and Managers

Related Chapter: Chapter 6

In today's competitive business environment, the two key marketing functions of buying and selling are performed by trained specialists. Just as every organization is involved in selling its output to meet the needs of customers, so too must all companies purchase goods and services to operate their businesses and turn out items for sale. Purchasing agents and managers represent a vital component of a company's supply chain.

Job Description

About 350,000 people work as purchasing agents and buyers for firms in the United States. Modern technology has transformed the role of the purchasing agent. The transfer of routine tasks to computers now allows contract specialists, or procurement officers, to focus on products, suppliers, and contract negotiations. The primary function of this position is to purchase the goods, materials, component parts, supplies, and services required by the organization. These buyers ensure that suppliers deliver quality and quantity levels that match the firm's needs; they also secure these inputs at reasonable prices and make them available when needed.

Purchasing agents must develop good working relationships both with colleagues in their own organizations and with suppliers. As the popularity of outsourcing has increased, the selection and management of suppliers have become critical functions of the purchasing department. In the government sector, this role is dominated by strict laws, statutes, and regulations that change frequently.

Most purchasing agents and their managers work in comfortable environments, but they work more than the standard 40-hour week to meet production deadlines or to be ready for special sales, conferences, or other events. Depending on the industry, these specialists may have to work extra hours prior to holidays or certain seasons, such as back-to-school, in order to have enough merchandise to meet demand. Many buyers do at least some travel. Those who work for firms with manufacturing or sources overseas—such as clothing manufacturers—may travel outside the United States.[23]

Career Path

Organizations prefer college-educated candidates for entry-level jobs in purchasing. Strong analytical and communication skills are required for these positions. New hires often begin their careers in extensive company training programs in which they learn procedures and operations. Training may include assignments dealing with production planning. Professional certification is becoming an essential criterion for advancement in both the private and the public sectors. A variety of associations serving the different categories of purchasing confer certifications on agents, including Certified Purchasing Manager, Professional Public Buyer, Certified Public Purchasing Officer, Certified Associate Contract Manager, and Certified Professional Contract Manager.

Career Path 6: Retail and Wholesale Buyers and Merchandise Managers

Related Chapter: Chapter 14

Buyers working for retailers and wholesale businesses purchase goods for resale. Their goal is to find the best possible merchandise at the lowest prices. They also influence the distribution and marketing of this merchandise. Successful buyers must understand what appeals to consumers and what their establishments can sell. Product bar codes and point-of-purchase terminals allow organizations to accurately track goods that are selling and those that are not; buyers frequently analyze this data to improve their understanding of consumer demand. Buyers also check competitors' prices and sales activities and watch general economic conditions to anticipate consumer buying patterns.

Job Description

Approximately 156,000 people are currently employed in the United States as retail and wholesale buyers. These jobs often require substantial travel, as many orders are placed during buying trips to shows and exhibitions. Effective planning and decision-making skills are strong assets in this career. In addition, the job involves anticipating consumer preferences and ensuring that the firm keeps needed goods in stock. Consequently, the people filling these positions must possess such qualities as resourcefulness, good judgment, and self-confidence.[24]

Career Path

Most retail and wholesale buyers begin their careers as assistant buyers or trainees. Larger retailers seek college-educated candidates, and extensive training includes job experience in a variety of positions. Advancement often comes when buyers move to departments or new locations with larger volumes—or become merchandise managers who coordinate or oversee the work of several buyers.

Career Path 7: Marketing Research Analysts

Related Chapter: Chapter 8

These marketing specialists provide information that helps marketers identify and define opportunities. They generate, refine, and evaluate marketing actions and monitor marketing performance. Marketing research analysts devise methods and procedures for obtaining needed decision-oriented data. Once they compile data, analysts evaluate it and then make recommendations to management.

Job Description

Firms that specialize in marketing research and management consulting employ most of the nation's marketing research analysts. These positions are often concentrated in larger cities, such as New York, Los Angeles, and Chicago. Those who pursue careers in marketing research must be able to work accurately with detail, display patience and persistence, work effectively both independently and with others, and operate objectively and systematically. Significant computer and analytical skills are essential for success in this field. Deadlines are typical in this field, but these specialists tend to have fairly regular work hours compared with other marketing professionals. Employment opportunities are expected to grow faster than average through 2014. Marketing and survey researchers occupy about 212,000 jobs in the United States.

Marketing research analysts create methods and procedures for gathering the necessary data to serve their clients. They may design telephone, mail, or Internet surveys to evaluate consumer preferences. They may also conduct in-person interviews or lead focus group discussions. Once they have compiled data, they evaluate information to make recommendations based on their research.[25]

Career Path

A bachelor's degree with an emphasis in marketing provides sufficient qualifications for many entry-level jobs in marketing research. Because of the importance of quantitative skills and the need for competence in using analytical software packages, this professional's education should include courses in mathematics, computer science, and information systems. Students should try to gain experience in conducting interviews or surveys while still in college. A master's degree in business administration or a related discipline is helpful for improving advancement opportunities.[26]

Career Path 8: Logistics: Materials Receiving, Scheduling, Dispatching, and Distributing Occupations

Related Chapter: Chapter 13

Logistics offers a myriad of career positions. Job titles under this broad heading include materials receiving, scheduling, dispatching, materials management executive, distribution operations coordinator, distribution center manager, and transportation manager. The logistics function includes responsibilities for production and inventory planning and control, distribution, and transportation.

Job Description

There are about 53,000 logisticians in the United States in addition to 92,000 transportation, storage, and distribution managers. These positions demand good communication skills and the ability to work effectively under pressure. They involve planning, directing, and coordinating storage or distribution activities according to laws and regulations. A logistician analyzes and coordinates the logistical functions of a firm or organization.[27]

Career Path

Computer skills are highly valued in these jobs. Employers look for candidates with degrees in logistics and transportation. However, graduates in marketing and other business disciplines may succeed in this field.

ADDITIONAL INFORMATION SOURCES

A wealth of helpful career information is continually updated for you at the Boone and Kurtz Web site: www.thomsonedu.com/marketing/boone. You'll find a complete "Marketing Careers" section located under the heading "Marketing Topics" on the left-hand navigation bar. Here you'll learn more about marketing careers and be able to locate currently posted job opportunities. The site provides a vast number of career resources such as links to job sites, career guidance sites, newspaper job ads, and company information. It also provides ways for researching cities of special interest to you.

"The Voice of Experience: Talking about Marketing Careers," a popular feature at the end of each of the seven parts of *Contemporary Marketing*, consists of an interview with a top marketing executive in a major marketing organization. In reading the marketing executive's description of his or her background, the way the position was filled, and the other members of the marketing department, you will be able to compare the similarities—and differences—between this industry and others. Most people interviewed also discuss how to stand out in applying for internships.

The "Personal Development" section of the Web site contains career guidance tips, including interviewing techniques and résumé writing advice. The site is updated regularly.

PART 1

Designing Customer-Oriented Marketing Strategies

CHEVROLET UNLEASHES THE NEW CORVETTE

CORVETTE by Chevrolet

New with 4-wheel disc brakes
'65 CORVETTE

'73 CORVETTE
We gave it radials, a quieter ride, guard beams and a nose job.

Building a better way to see the U.S.A.

CHEVROLET

AN AMERICAN REVOLUTION

STARBUCKS: Connecting with Customers

If you're like a lot of people, you need your cup of coffee in the morning. Maybe it's the aroma, maybe it's the flavor, maybe it's the caffeine—or a combination of all three. You can choose among hundreds of blends. What makes you want one more than another? How do you decide which brand is your favorite? During the last two decades, Starbucks has devoted itself to offering the best cup of coffee a consumer can drink, in enough locations so that everyone can find one.

Starting with a single coffee shop in Seattle, Starbucks now has more than 9,000 stores—with an ultimate goal of 40,000. You can still visit a Starbucks and settle into a cushy armchair with a newspaper and a tall cup of joe. Or you can stop by the Starbucks kiosk in your local Stop & Shop supermarket and pick up a steaming latte to sip while you shop. And while Starbucks has traditionally opened outlets in more upscale urban and suburban neighborhoods—largely because a cup of specialty coffee may cost $3 or more—the company is moving into smaller towns and neighborhoods with more modest standards of living. Currently, the firm is considering a deal with Wal-Mart. "We'd love to be in Wal-Mart parking lots with company-operated stores," says CEO Jim Donald. Starbucks is one of the few restaurants that appeal to consumers of all ages and lifestyles, offering a reprieve from demands of the day. Its coffee shops give teens a place to cluster after school. Moms with strollers routinely gather for a midmorning snack. Office workers congregate for a quick afternoon coffee break.

Chairman Howard Schultz and CEO Jim Donald believe that the secret to Starbucks's success is the company's near-fanatical focus on people. "Our success comes down to the way we connect with our customers, our communities, our farms—with each other," explains Donald. "We just had a four-day leadership conference. The theme was human connection. We didn't once talk about sales and profits. We talked about how we continue to grow and how we connect." So when Starbucks adds new products and new locations, it does so to delight the people it serves. The Starbucks experience is about much more than coffee, although its brews are so distinct that they have their own vocabulary—such as *iced grande* or *skinny latte*. A *barista* makes your drink according to strict standards. All of these features

Marketing: The Art and Science of Satisfying Customers

Chapter Objectives

1 Define *marketing,* explain how it creates utility, and describe its role in the global marketplace.

2 Contrast marketing activities during the four eras in the history of marketing.

3 Explain the importance of avoiding marketing myopia.

4 Describe the characteristics of not-for-profit marketing.

5 Identify and briefly explain each of the five types of nontraditional marketing.

6 Outline the importance of creativity, critical thinking, and the technology revolution in marketing.

7 Explain the shift from transaction-based marketing to relationship marketing.

8 Identify the universal functions of marketing.

9 Demonstrate the relationship between ethical business practices, social responsibility, and marketplace success.

are based on marketing decisions designed to cement a long relationship with the customer—to turn the need for caffeine into a desire for a steaming cup of Starbucks. From the company's development of new beverages such as the popular chilled Frappuccino, to the installation of its Hear Music platform, which allows customers to download songs in Starbucks shops, to sales of CDs and DVDs in its shops, Starbucks pays close attention to discovering and giving consumers what they want.

Starbucks uses the same philosophy of connection to establish its presence around the world. Despite a long tradition of tea drinking in Asia, Starbucks has won converts in China and Japan with specially developed beverages designed to appeal to Chinese and Japanese tastes. Jim Donald sees vast opportunities throughout Europe and Asia and hopes to establish Starbucks in India as well. And of the market back in the United States he observes, "There are 165,000 miles of U.S. roadway that we haven't tapped."

Growth is always tricky for a company that insists on maintaining quality and a close relationship with its customers. "I want to grow big and stay small at the same time," says Donald. "We want to run the company just like we did when we were one store on Pike Place Market in Seattle." Maintaining that cozy feeling with every customer while broadening the firm's customer base may be difficult, but Donald believes it can be

evolution *of a* brand

From Starbucks' modest start with a single store in Pike Place Market in Seattle, the coffee shop has become a national and international sensation that has transformed the industry. The firm concentrates on satisfying its customers, providing much more than a great cup of coffee or other beverage. The company now has more than 9,000 stores but plans to open 30,000 worldwide.

- Starbucks serves a wide variety of beverages to its customers. How has its focus on quality and customer satisfaction helped the company grow? What other features of a visit to Starbucks provide the firm a competitive advantage in the crowded coffee market? Make a list of the goods and services that help the company maintain its edge. What other offerings could help the company continue to serve its customers well?

- Consider Starbucks' growth plans. Is there any limit to its expansion in the U.S. market? What factors does the company need to both watch for and avoid to be successful? Now think about the firm's international growth. If you were a Starbucks executive, what kind of information would you need to know about to enter a foreign market? How could you understand your

done. "Howard [Schultz] has always said that we're not in the coffee business, serving people; we're in the people business, serving coffee." That's a good, strong brew for success.[1]

evolution *of a* **brand** global customers better to ensure success? Make a list of suggestions. Now do some research to see how Starbucks is faring in its expansion. How—and what—has it done in the United States and abroad to achieve its goals?

Chapter Overview

- "I'll only drink Starbucks coffee."
- "I buy all my clothes at Urban Outfitters."
- "The next car I drive will be a Toyota Prius."
- "I go to all the Steelers games at Heinz Field."

These words are music to a marketer's ears. They may echo the click of an online purchase, the *ping* of a cash register, the cheers of fans at a stadium. Customer loyalty is the watchword of 21st-century marketing. Individual consumers and business purchasers have so many goods and services from which to choose—and so many different ways to purchase them—that marketers must continually seek out new and better ways to attract and keep customers. Sometimes they miss the boat, allowing other companies to make the most of opportunities. Amazon.com, which recently cleared $1 billion in quarterly sales, lags far behind Apple in one area of e-business—the digital delivery of music and movies. Completely trounced by Apple's iTunes, Amazon has scurried to come up with a better way to serve music customers. Soon customers who buy a CD at Amazon.com will also receive a digital copy of it, which they can transfer to a portable music player.[2]

The technology revolution continues to change the rules of marketing during this first decade of the 21st century and will continue to do so in years beyond. The combined power of telecommunications and computer technology creates inexpensive global networks that transfer voice messages, text, graphics, and data within seconds. These sophisticated technologies create new types of products, and they also demand new approaches to marketing existing products. Media mogul Rupert Murdoch, chairman of News Corp.—parent company of Fox and MySpace.com—takes a hard line on the news and information industry and the importance of developing new ways to communicate with consumers. "Most newspaper companies still have their heads in the sand, but other media companies are aggressive," he says. "And there are completely new start-up companies. There is a great pace of development, which is very exciting. At News Corp., we have been developing online extensions of traditional media for the last few years."[3]

Communications technology contributes as well to the globalization of today's marketplace, where businesses manufacture, buy, and sell across national borders. You can bid at eBay on a potential bargain or eat a Big Mac or drink Coca-Cola almost anywhere in the world; your DVD or CD player was probably manufactured in China or South Korea. Both Mercedes-Benz and Hyundai SUVs are assembled in Alabama, while some Volkswagens are imported from Mexico. Finished products and components routinely cross international borders, but successful global marketing also requires knowledge to tailor products to regional tastes. A chain restaurant in the South might offer grits instead of hash browns on its breakfast menu.

Rapidly changing business landscapes create new challenges for companies, whether they are giant multinational firms or small bou-

briefly *speaking*

"A sign at Dell headquarters reads 'Think Customer.' A full 90 percent of employees deal directly with customers. What are the universal attributes of the Dell brand? Customer advocacy."

—Mike George
U.S. consumer vice president, Dell

tiques, profit-oriented or not-for-profit. Organizations must react quickly to shifts in consumer tastes, competitive offerings, and other market dynamics. Fortunately, information technologies give organizations fast new ways to interact and develop long-term relationships with their customers and suppliers. In fact, such links have become a core element of marketing today.

Every company must serve customer needs—create customer satisfaction—to succeed. We call customer satisfaction an art because it requires

imagination and creativity and a science because it requires technical knowledge, skill, and experience. Marketing strategies are the tools that marketers use to identify and analyze customers' needs, then show that their company's goods and services can meet those needs. Tomorrow's market leaders will be companies that can make the most of these strategies to create satisfied customers.

This new edition of *Contemporary Marketing* focuses on the strategies that allow companies to succeed in today's interactive marketplace. This

chapter sets the stage for the entire text, examining the importance of creating satisfaction through customer relationships. Initial sections describe the historical development of marketing and its contributions to society. Later sections introduce the technology revolution, the universal functions of marketing, and the relationship between ethical business practices and marketplace success. Throughout the chapter—and the entire book—we discuss customer loyalty and the lifetime value of a customer.

WHAT IS MARKETING?

The production and marketing of goods and services—whether it's a new crop of organically grown vegetables or digital cable service—are the essence of economic life in any society. All organizations perform these two basic functions to satisfy their commitments to society, their customers, and their owners. They create a benefit that economists call **utility**—the want-satisfying power of a good or service. Table 1.1 describes the four basic kinds of utility: form, time, place, and ownership.

Form utility is created when the company converts raw materials and component inputs into finished goods and services. By combining glass, plastic, metals, circuit boards, and other components, Canon makes a digital camera and Pioneer produces a plasma television. With fabric and leather, Prada manufactures its high-fashion line of handbags. With a ship and the ocean, a captain and staff, food and entertainment, Royal Caribbean creates a cruise. Although the marketing function focuses on influencing consumer and audience preferences, the organization's production function creates form utility.

1 Define *marketing,* explain how it creates utility, and describe its role in the global marketplace.

utility Want-satisfying power of a good or service.

table 1.1   Four Types of Utility

TYPE	DESCRIPTION	EXAMPLES	ORGANIZATIONAL FUNCTION RESPONSIBLE
Form	Conversion of raw materials and components into finished goods and services	Dinner at Wendy's; iPod; T-shirt from Urban Outfitters	Production*
Time	Availability of goods and services when consumers want them	Dental appointment; digital photographs; LensCrafters eyeglass guarantee; UPS Next Day Air	Marketing
Place	Availability of goods and services at convenient locations	Soft-drink machines outside gas stations; on-site day care; banks in grocery stores	Marketing
Ownership (possession)	Ability to transfer title to goods or services from marketer to buyer	Retail sales (in exchange for currency or credit card payment)	Marketing

*Marketing provides inputs related to consumer preferences, but creating form utility is the responsibility of the production function.

We don't get you over oceans, mountains and deserts only to be delayed by Chapter 3, Part 319, Regulation 40-2 of CFR Title 7.

WHAT CAN BROWN DO FOR YOU?

When you're trading internationally, your entire investment could be hanging on a single clause. Whether it's a rule overlooked out of hundreds of laws and trade agreements or a misinterpretation by one of dozens of third parties, mistakes like these can cause costly delays.

Fortunately, there's a simple solution. Leave the burden of global compliance to UPS. With over 80 years of experience in international trade, we have the resources and network of people all over

the world to head off problems and facilitate the movement of your goods. And since we deal with the thorniest compliance issues every day, we're up on the very latest, most accurate information.

As your single source for customs brokerage and international trade management solutions, we'll help make sure nothing stands in the way of your global transactions. Including that mountain of paper.

1-800-PICK-UPS

UPS

© 2005 United Parcel Service of America, Inc. UPS, the UPS brandmark, and the color brown are registered trademarks of United Parcel Service of America, Inc. All rights reserved. UPS TradeService, trade consulting and education, and managed services provided by UPS Trade Management Services, Inc.

PHOTO IS PROPERTY OF UPS

UPS creates time utility by delivering packages on time, anywhere in the world.

Marketing creates time, place, and ownership utilities. *Time and place utility* occur when consumers find goods and services available when and where they want to purchase them. Vending machines and convenience stores focus on providing place utility for people buying newspapers, snacks, and soft drinks. Stacey Pecor created time and place utility for women in Vermont who wanted access to trendy, unique fashion without having to travel to Boston or New York. She opened her own boutique called Olive and Bette's. The shop was so successful that she eventually opened boutiques in New York City as well.[4]

The transfer of title to goods or services at the time of purchase creates *ownership utility*. Signing up for the Royal Caribbean cruise or taking home a vintage-inspired T-shirt from Olive and Bette's creates ownership utility.

All organizations must create utility to survive. Designing and marketing want-satisfying goods, services, and ideas are the foundation for the creation of utility. But where does the process start? In the toy industry, manufacturers try to come up with items that children will want to play with—creating utility. But that's not as simple as it sounds. At the Toy Fair held each February in New York, retailers pore through the booths of manufacturers and suppliers, looking for the next Bratz dolls or Lego building blocks—trends that turn into classics and generate millions in revenues over the years.

Companies such as Sirius Satellite Radio and XM Satellite Radio Holdings are creating utility for consumers with satellite radio service. Statistics show that they are succeeding: XM now claims more than 1 million subscribers. As more celebrities sign on as hosts—including Oprah Winfrey and Howard Stern—satellite radio marketers can persuade consumers that they create utility for them. In another area of entertainment, podcasts are creating a buzz. Podcasts—recorded audio files that are distributed through Internet download—create utility through their ability to be stored on computers or digital music devices and played back whenever the consumer wants. Start-up firms such as Odeo.com are scrambling to tap this market as quickly as possible. Odeo.com creates utility by organizing its shows according to topic—users can click on headings such as food and technology. To further help its listeners, Odeo employees scan the site for the best shows and post their "Staff Picks" on the Featured Channels page.[5]

But how does an organization create a customer? Most take a three-step approach: identifying needs in the marketplace, finding out which needs the organization can profitably serve, and developing goods and services to convert potential buyers into customers. Marketing specialists are responsible for most of the activities necessary to create the customers the organization wants. These activities include the following:

- identifying customer needs
- designing products that meet those needs
- communicating information about those goods and services to prospective buyers
- making the items available at times and places that meet customers' needs
- pricing merchandise and services to reflect costs, competition, and customers' ability to buy
- providing the necessary service and follow-up to ensure customer satisfaction after the purchase[6]

A DEFINITION OF MARKETING

The word *marketing* encompasses such a broad scope of activities and ideas that settling on one definition is often difficult. Ask three people to define marketing, and three different definitions are likely to follow. We are exposed to so much advertising and personal selling that most people link marketing only to those activities. But marketing begins long before a product hits the shelf. It involves analyzing customer needs, obtaining the information necessary to design and produce goods or services that match buyer expectations, satisfying customer preferences, and creating and maintaining relationships with customers and suppliers. Marketing activities apply to profit-oriented businesses such as Apple Computer and Zappos.com as well as not-for-profit organizations such as Save the Children and the Red Cross. Even government agencies such as the U.S. Postal Service engage in marketing activities. Today's definition takes all these factors into account. **Marketing** is an organizational function and a set of processes for creating, communicating, and delivering value to customers and for managing customer relationships in ways that benefit the organization and its stakeholders.[7]

The expanded concept of marketing activities permeates all functions in businesses and not-for-profit organizations. It assumes that organizations conduct their marketing efforts ethically and that these efforts serve the best interests of both society and the organization. The concept also identifies the marketing variables—product, price, promotion, and distribution—that combine to provide customer satisfaction. In addition, it assumes that the organization begins by identifying and analyzing who its potential customers are and what they need. At all points, the concept emphasizes creating and maintaining long-term relationships with customers and suppliers.

marketing Organizational function and a set of processes for creating, communicating, and delivering value to customers and for managing customer relationships in ways that benefit the organization and its stakeholders.

TODAY'S GLOBAL MARKETPLACE

Several factors have forced marketers—and entire nations—to extend their economic views to events outside their own national borders. First, international agreements are being negotiated in attempts to expand trade among nations. Second, the growth of electronic business and related computer technologies is allowing previously isolated countries to enter the marketplace for buyers and sellers around the globe. Third, the interdependence of the world's economies is a reality because no nation produces all of the raw materials and finished goods its citizens need or consumes all of its output without exporting some to other countries. Evidence of this interdependence is illustrated by the introduction of the euro as a common currency to facilitate trade among the nations of the European Union and the creation of trade agreements such as the North American Free Trade Agreement (NAFTA) and the World Trade Organization (WTO).

Rising oil prices affect the price that U.S. consumers pay for just about everything—not just gasoline at the pump. Consider the $1 surcharge for a pizza delivery and increased airfares, not to mention heating oil. If the winter is mild, it might not cost so much to heat a house or apartment—but when temperatures drop and more oil and natural gas are used, costs to individual consumers can skyrocket. Threatened or real disruptions in the supply of oil also have dramatic economic impacts. Tribal disputes in Nigeria caused a cutback in oil production there. Hurricane Katrina caused drilling rigs and refineries to shut down temporarily along the U.S. Gulf Coast.[8]

To remain competitive, companies must continually search for the most efficient manufacturing sites and most lucrative markets for their products. U.S. marketers now find tremendous opportunities serving customers not only in traditional industrialized nations but also in Latin America and emerging economies in central and eastern Europe, the Middle East, Asia, and Africa, where rising standards of living create increased customer demand for the latest goods and services. Expanding operations beyond the U.S. market gives domestic companies access to 6.5 billion international customers. In addition, companies based in these emerging economies are beginning to compete as well. Since China's acceptance into the World Trade Organization, its exports have risen tremendously. In one recent year alone, China reported that its exports to the United States rose 30 percent.[9] China has become a manufacturing center for many firms based in other countries. Japan's Fuji Photo Film recently announced that it would shift production of its digital cameras to China.[10]

Service firms also play a major role in today's global marketplace. Although the New York Stock Exchange is based in New York City, investors trade more than $50 billion worldwide every day over the exchange. Softtek, a Mexican software development company with 3,500 employees,

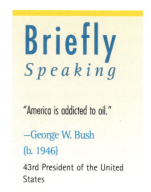

Briefly
Speaking

"America is addicted to oil."

—George W. Bush
(b. 1946)

43rd President of the United States

offers information technology services to many U.S. organizations. By *nearshoring* software design this way, U.S. firms enjoy the efficiency of being in the same time zone—as opposed to hiring firms in India or China.[11]

The United States is also an attractive market for foreign competitors because of its size and the high standard of living that American consumers enjoy. Companies such as Nissan, Sony, and Sun Life of Canada operate production, distribution, service, and retail facilities in the U.S. Foreign ownership of U.S. companies has increased also. Pillsbury and MCA are two well-known firms with foreign parents. Even American-dominated industries such as computer software must contend with foreign competition. Although U.S. firms still hold about 75 percent of the software market, European companies are quickly gaining market share.

Although many global marketing strategies are almost identical to those used in domestic markets, more and more companies are tailoring their marketing efforts to the needs and preferences of consumers in foreign markets. It is often difficult to standardize a brand name on a global basis. The Japanese, for example, like the names of flowers or girls for their automobiles, names like Bluebird, Bluebonnet, Violet, and Gloria. Americans, on the other hand, prefer rugged outdoorsy names like Chevy Tahoe, Jeep Cherokee, and Dodge Challenger.

 assessment check

1. Define *marketing* and explain how it creates utility.
2. What three factors have forced marketers to embrace a global marketplace?

---

2 Contrast marketing activities during the four eras in the history of marketing.

exchange process
Activity in which two or more parties give something of value to each other to satisfy perceived needs.

FOUR ERAS IN THE HISTORY OF MARKETING

The essence of marketing is the **exchange process**, in which two or more parties give something of value to each other to satisfy perceived needs. Often people exchange money for tangible goods such as groceries, clothes, a car, or a house. In other situations, they exchange money for intangible services such as a haircut or a college education. Many exchanges involve a combination of goods and services, such as dinner in a restaurant—where dinner represents the good and the wait staff represents the service. People also make exchanges when they donate money or time to a charitable cause such as Habitat for Humanity.

Although marketing has always been a part of business, its importance has varied greatly. Figure 1.1 identifies four eras in the history of marketing: (1) the production era, (2) the sales era, (3) the marketing era, and (4) the relationship era.

figure 1.1

Four Eras of Marketing History

ERA	Production	Sales	Marketing	Relationship
PREVAILING ATTITUDE	"A good product will sell itself."	"Creative advertising and selling will overcome consumers' resistance and persuade them to buy."	"The consumer rules! Find a need and fill it."	"Long-term relationships with customers and other partners lead to success."
APPROXIMATE TIME PERIOD*	Prior to 1920s	Prior to 1950s	Since 1950s	Since 1990s

THE PRODUCTION ERA

Before 1925, most firms—even those operating in highly developed economies in western Europe and North America—focused narrowly on production. Manufacturers stressed production of quality products and then looked for people to purchase them. The prevailing attitude of this era held that a high-quality product would sell itself. This **production orientation** dominated business philosophy for decades; in fact, business success was often defined solely in terms of production successes.

The production era reached its peak during the early part of the 20th century. Henry Ford's mass-production line exemplifies this orientation. Ford's slogan, "They [customers] can have any color they want, as long as it's black," reflected the prevalent attitude toward marketing. Production shortages and intense consumer demand ruled the day. It is easy to understand how production activities took precedence.

However, building a new product is no guarantee of success, and marketing history is cluttered with the bones of miserable product failures despite major innovations. In fact, more than 80 percent of new products fail. Inventing an outstanding new product is not enough. That product must also fill a perceived marketplace need. Otherwise, even the best-engineered, highest-quality product will fail. Even Henry Ford's horseless carriage took a while to catch on. People were afraid of motor vehicles, which spat out exhaust, stirred up dust on dirt roads, got stuck in mud, and tied up horse traffic. Besides, at the speed of seven miles per hour, they caused all kinds of accidents and disruption. It took savvy marketing by some early salespeople—and eventually a widespread perceived need—to change people's minds about the product. Today, most of us could not imagine life without a car and have refined that need to preferences for certain types of vehicles, including SUVs, convertibles, trucks, and hybrids.

THE SALES ERA

As production techniques in the United States and Europe became more sophisticated, output grew from the 1920s into the early 1950s. As a result, manufacturers began to increase their emphasis on effective sales forces to find customers for their output. In this era, firms attempted to match their output to the potential number of customers who would want it. Companies with a **sales orientation** assume that customers will resist purchasing nonessential goods and services and that the task of personal selling and advertising is to persuade them to buy.

Although marketing departments began to emerge from the shadows of production and engineering during the sales era, they tended to remain in subordinate positions. Many chief marketing executives held the title of sales manager. But selling is only one component of marketing. As marketing scholar Theodore Levitt once pointed out, "Marketing is as different from selling as chemistry is from alchemy, astronomy from astrology, chess from checkers."

THE MARKETING ERA

Personal incomes and consumer demand for goods and services dropped rapidly during the Great Depression of the 1930s, thrusting marketing into a more important role. Organizational survival dictated that managers pay close attention to the markets for their goods and services. This trend ended with the outbreak of World War II, when rationing and shortages of consumer goods became commonplace. The war years, however, created only a pause in an emerging trend in business: a shift in the focus from products and sales to satisfying customer needs.

Emergence of the Marketing Concept

The marketing concept, a crucial change in management philosophy, can be linked to the shift from a **seller's market**—one in which there were more buyers for fewer goods and services—to a **buyer's market**—one in which there were more goods and services than people willing to buy them. When World War II ended, factories stopped manufacturing tanks and ships and started turning out consumer products again, an activity that had, for all practical purposes, stopped in early 1942.

The advent of a strong buyer's market created the need for consumer orientation by businesses. Companies had to market goods and services, not just produce and sell them. This realization has been identified as the emergence of the marketing concept. Marketing would no longer be regarded as a

consumer orientation
Business philosophy incorporating the marketing concept that emphasizes first determining unmet consumer needs and then designing a system for satisfying them.

supplemental activity performed after completing the production process. Instead, the marketer played a leading role in product planning. *Marketing* and *selling* would no longer be synonymous terms.

marketing concept
Company-wide consumer orientation with the objective of achieving long-run success.

Today's fully developed **marketing concept** is a *company-wide consumer orientation* with the objective of achieving long-run success. All facets—and all levels, from top to bottom—of the organization must contribute first to assessing and then to satisfying customer wants and needs. From marketing manager to accountant to product designer, every employee plays a role in reaching potential customers. Even during tough economic times, when companies tend to emphasize cutting costs and boosting revenues, the marketing concept focuses on the objective of achieving long-run success instead of short-term profits. Because the firm's survival and growth are built into the marketing concept, company-wide consumer orientation should lead to greater long-run profits.

Consider Apple Computer. Named first in a list of the top 20 innovative companies worldwide in a poll by Boston Consulting Group, respondents said Apple "delivers great consumer experiences with outstanding design."[12] Apple's popularity has surged with the introduction of its iPod line. Every teen wants one. Every college student wants one. Even baby boomers, who are close to retirement, want one. And where do they download songs? Apple's iTunes Music Store. In a deal with Disney, Apple now offers ABC shows such as *Lost* and *Grey's Anatomy* on its video iPod. And Disney's purchase of Pixar Animation Studios should increase the offerings. Many industry watchers credit Apple's co-founder and CEO Steven Jobs. Jobs, who left the company for twelve years, came back in a big way. Jobs has always been viewed as an innovator, and even his critics concede that he knows how to make what consumers want. And he won't compromise on quality. "I'm as proud of what we don't do as I am of what we do," says Jobs.[13]

relationship marketing
Development and maintenance of long-term, cost-effective relationships with individual customers, suppliers, employees, and other partners for mutual benefit.

A strong market orientation—the extent to which a company adopts the marketing concept—generally improves market success and overall performance. It also has a positive effect on new-product development and the introduction of innovative products. Companies that implement market-driven strategies are better able to understand their customers' experiences, buying habits, and needs. Like Apple, these companies can, therefore, design products with advantages and levels of quality compatible with customer requirements.

You carry the future on your shoulders. Plan for it.

A FINANCIAL GAME PLAN FOR EVERY FAMILY. MetLife knows that just as every family is unique, so are their financial planning goals. Feel secure knowing that our financial advisors offer a diverse range of tools to help your family plan for the future. And the beauty of your plan will be your ability to change it as your goals change over time. Isn't now the right time to start planning for your life with the kind of support that only the nation's #1 insurer can offer? For more information, **call 1-800-MetLife or visit metlife.com**

have you met life today?®

MetLife

MetLife practices relationship marketing by offering long-term programs that help customers plan for the future.

THE RELATIONSHIP ERA

The fourth era in the history of marketing emerged during the final decade of the 20th century and continues to grow in importance. Organizations now build on the marketing era's customer orientation by focusing on establishing and maintaining relationships with both customers and suppliers. **Relationship marketing** involves developing long-term, value-added relationships over time with customers and suppliers. Strategic alliances and partnerships among manufacturers, retailers, and suppliers often benefit everyone. It took a decade and more than $13 billion from four countries to launch the world's largest passenger plane, the Airbus 380. To develop the new aircraft, Airbus merged its partner companies into one large firm. Then it worked with more than 60 airports during the design phase to make sure that they could accommodate the aircraft. By the time Singapore Airlines conducted the first test flight, thirteen other airlines had already placed orders for the Airbus 380.[14] The concept of relationship marketing, which is the current state of customer-driven marketing, is discussed in detail later in this chapter and in Chapter 10.

CONVERTING NEEDS TO WANTS

Every consumer must acquire goods and services on a continuing basis to fill certain needs. Everyone must satisfy the fundamental needs for food, clothing, shelter, and transportation by purchasing items or, in some instances, temporarily using rented property and hired or leased transportation. By focusing on the benefits resulting from these goods and services, effective marketing converts needs to wants. A need for a pair of pants may be converted to a desire for jeans—and further, a desire for jeans from Abercrombie & Fitch or American Eagle Outfitters. The need for food may be converted to a desire for dinner at Pizzeria Uno or groceries from Whole Foods Market. But if the need for transportation isn't converted to a desire for a Dodge Durango or a Honda Odyssey, extra vehicles may sit unsold on a dealer's lot.

Consumers need to communicate. But converting that need to the desire for certain types of communication requires skill. It also requires listening to what consumers want. Consumers' demand for more cell phone and wireless services seems nearly unlimited—providing tremendous opportunities for companies. New products appear continually to feed that demand. The number of Wi-Fi Internet users rose 57 percent in a recent year, laying the groundwork for the next generation of technology— WiMax—which allows even faster Internet access over greater areas. Smaller firms such as NextWeb and Tower-Stream—which has teamed up with telecommunications firm Vonage—are scrambling to grab a piece of the WiMax market, as are big telecom players such as AT&T. All are hoping to offer the services that consumers decide they want.[15]

 assessment check

1. What is the major distinction between the production era and the sales era?
2. What is the marketing concept?
3. Describe the relationship era of marketing.

AVOIDING MARKETING MYOPIA

The emergence of the marketing concept has not been devoid of setbacks. One troublesome problem led marketing scholar Theodore Levitt to coin the term **marketing myopia**. According to Levitt, marketing myopia is management's failure to recognize the scope of its business. Product-oriented rather than customer-oriented management endangers future growth. Levitt cites many service industries—such as dry cleaning and electric utilities—as examples of marketing myopia. But many firms have found innovative ways to reach new markets and develop long-term relationships. Table 1.2 illustrates how firms in a number of industries have overcome myopic thinking by developing broader marketing-oriented business ideas that focus on consumer need satisfaction.

Tim Curtis took a second look at his business—waste management—and found a way to turn it into something much more. The search for alternative energy sources is a growing field, filled with people who use their imaginations not just to create products but to find imaginative ways to reach new

 3 Explain the importance of avoiding marketing myopia.

marketing myopia
Management's failure to recognize the scope of its business.

---

table 1.2   Avoiding Marketing Myopia

COMPANY	MYOPIC DESCRIPTION	COMPANY MOTTO—AVOIDING MYOPIA
General Electric	An appliance company	Imagination at Work
AT&T	A phone company	Your World Delivered
Visa	A credit card company	Life Takes Visa
Michelin	A tire manufacturer	A Better Way Forward
Nokia	A cell phone manufacturer	Connecting People
Southwest Airlines	An airline	A Symbol of Freedom

customers. Instead of just removing unwanted materials from warehouses, tanks, and dumpsters, Curtis's firm, called Liquid Resources, now takes cast-off liquid products from manufacturers—such as beer, soda, and juice drinks—smashes the containers, ferments and distills the liquid contents, then converts the liquid to fuel-grade ethanol. Another firm, called Renewable Environmental Solutions, converts remains from a Butterball turkey processing plant into barrels of crude oil. Experts anticipate a huge of wave of innovative products and marketing in the energy industry over the next few years.[16]

✓ *assessment check*

1. What is marketing myopia?
2. Give an example of how a firm can avoid marketing myopia.

EXTENDING THE TRADITIONAL BOUNDARIES OF MARKETING

Today's organizations—both profit-oriented and not-for-profit—recognize universal needs for marketing and its importance to their success. During a television commercial break, viewers might be exposed to an advertisement for a Nissan Altima, an appeal to help feed children in foreign countries, a message by a political candidate, and a commercial for McDonald's—all in the space of about two minutes. Two of these ads are paid for by firms attempting to achieve profitability and other objectives. The appeal for funds to feed children and the political ad are examples of communications by not-for-profit organizations and individuals.

MARKETING IN NOT-FOR-PROFIT ORGANIZATIONS

Nearly 10 percent of the U.S. workforce works or volunteers in one or more of the 1.6 million not-for-profit organizations across the country. In total, these organizations generate hundreds of billions of dollars of revenues each year through contributions and from fund-raising activities. That makes not-for-profit organizations big business.

Not-for-profit organizations operate in both public and private sectors. Federal, state, and local firms pursue service objectives that are not keyed to profitability targets. The Federal Trade Commission oversees business activities; a state's department of motor vehicles issues car registrations and driver's licenses; a local school council is responsible for maintaining educational standards for its district. The private sector has an even greater array of not-for-profit organizations, including hospitals, libraries, the American Kennel Club, and the American Heart Association. Regardless of their size or location, all of these organizations need funds to operate. Adopting the marketing concept can make a great difference in their ability to meet their service objectives.

Colonial Williamsburg wants to attract more children to its re-created village in Virginia. So the museum recently developed Revolutionary City, a series of interactive vignettes designed to get all visitors to participate. Actors posing as soldiers, slaves, tavern workers, and other citizens stroll through the village seeking advice and help from unsuspecting visi-

© ASSOCIATED PRESS, AP

Colonial Williamsburg is a not-for-profit organization that teaches history through its realistic re-creations. It hopes to connect with younger people through a variety of special programs and events.

tors. A slave may beg for assistance in fleeing; a soldier may try to enlist more troops. "The idea is to bring life to that period," explains Rex Ellis of the Colonial Williamsburg Foundation.[17] And if kids think the experience is interesting, they'll tell other kids.

Some not-for-profits form partnerships with business firms that promote the organization's cause or message. Target Stores funded a facility called Target House, which provides long-term housing for families with children who are being treated at St. Jude Children's Research Hospital. The house has apartments and common areas where families can gather and children can play. Celebrities have also contributed to the house. Golf pro Tiger Woods sponsored a library, singer Amy Grant furnished a music room, and Olympic gold-medalist Scott Hamilton donated a fitness center and art room.[18]

Generally, the alliances formed between not-for-profit organizations and commercial firms benefit both. The reality of operating with multimillion-dollar budgets requires not-for-profit organizations to maintain a focused business approach. Consider some current examples:

- America's Second Harvest receives assistance from food manufacturers and grocery stores in distributing 2 billion pounds of food and grocery products to needy Americans. Participating businesses include Campbell Soup Company, The Coca-Cola Company, General Mills, Safeway, and Wal-Mart.[19]

- Corporate Angel Network works with the National Business Aviation Association to provide free transportation for cancer patients traveling to and from their treatments using empty seats on corporate jets.

- U2 band founder Bono recently launched a line of clothing called Red, in an effort to raise money for the Global Fund to Fight AIDS, Tuberculosis, and Malaria. American Express, Converse, Giorgio Armani, and The Gap have pledged to sell the Red-themed products and donate some of the proceeds to the fund. American Express offers a red credit card, and Armani sells a stylish pair of red sunglasses.[20]

The diversity of not-for-profit organizations suggests the presence of numerous organizational objectives other than profitability. In addition to their organizational goals, not-for-profit organizations differ from profit-seeking firms in several other ways.

CHARACTERISTICS OF NOT–FOR–PROFIT MARKETING

4 Describe the characteristics of not-for-profit marketing.

The most obvious distinction between not-for-profit organizations and for-profit—commercial—firms is the financial **bottom line**, business jargon that refers to the overall profitability of an organization. For-profit organizations measure profitability in terms of sales and revenues, and their goal is to generate revenues above and beyond their costs to make money for all stakeholders involved, including employees, shareholders, and the organization itself. Not-for-profit organizations hope to generate as much revenue as possible to support their causes, whether it is feeding children, preserving wilderness, or helping single mothers find work. Historically, not-for-profits have had less exact goals and marketing objectives than for-profit firms, but in recent years many of these groups have recognized that to succeed, they must develop more cost-effective ways to provide services, and they must compete with other organizations for donors' dollars. Marketing can help them accomplish these tasks.

Other distinctions exist between the two types of organizations as well, each of which influences marketing activities. Like profit-seeking firms, not-for-profit organizations may market tangible goods and/or intangible services. The Public Broadcasting Service (PBS) offers videotapes and DVDs of its shows and related items in its catalog (tangible items) as well as broadcasting a variety of noncommercial programs (intangible services). But profit-seeking businesses tend to focus their marketing on just one public—their customers. Not-for-profit organizations, however, must often market to multiple publics, which complicates decision making about the correct markets to target. Many deal with at least two major publics—their clients and their sponsors—and often many other publics as well. A college or university targets prospective students as clients of its marketing program, but it also markets to current students, parents of students, major donors, alumni, faculty, staff, local businesses, and local government agencies.

A customer or service user of a not-for-profit organization may have less control over the organization's destiny than do customers of a profit-seeking firm. Not-for-profit organizations also often possess some degree of monopoly power in a given geographic area. An individual contributor might object to United Way's inclusion of a particular local agency, but that agency will receive a portion of that donor's contribution.

In another potential problem, a resource contributor—whether a cash donor, a volunteer, or someone who provides office space—may try to interfere with the marketing program to promote the message that he or she feels is relevant.

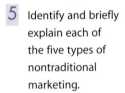

assessment check

1. What is the most obvious distinction between a not-for-profit organization and a commercial organization?
2. Why do for-profit and not-for-profit organizations sometimes form alliances?

5 Identify and briefly explain each of the five types of nontraditional marketing.

NONTRADITIONAL MARKETING

As marketing evolved into an organization-wide activity, its application has broadened far beyond its traditional boundaries of for-profit organizations that create and distribute tangible goods and intangible services. In many cases, broader appeals focus on causes, events, individuals, organizations, and places in the not-for-profit sector. In other instances, they encompass diverse groups of profit-seeking individuals, activities, and organizations. Table 1.3 lists and describes five major categories of nontraditional marketing: person marketing, place marketing, cause marketing, event marketing, and organization marketing. These categories can overlap—promotion for an organization may also encompass a cause; a promotional campaign may focus on both an event and a place.

PERSON MARKETING

person marketing
Marketing efforts designed to cultivate the attention, interest, and preferences of a target market toward a person (perhaps a political candidate or celebrity).

Person marketing involves efforts designed to cultivate the attention, interest, and preferences of a target market toward a celebrity or authority figure. Celebrities can be real people or fictional characters. To help gain additional viewers, CBS News promotes its new anchor, Katie Couric, who gained popularity during her fifteen-year stint as co-host of NBC's *Today* show. The network hopes viewers will tune in because they like to watch her. Political candidates engage in person marketing as well, as they promote their candidacy for office. Authors such as Suze Orman of *The Road to Wealth* use person marketing to promote their books. Oprah Winfrey uses person marketing to promote her *O* magazine, where she appears on every cover. The "Etiquette Tips for Marketing Professionals" feature provides guidelines for putting your best foot forward in business situations.

table 1.3   Categories of Nontraditional Marketing

TYPE	BRIEF DESCRIPTION	EXAMPLES
Person marketing	Marketing efforts designed to cultivate the attention and preference of a target market toward a person.	Celebrity Toby Keith, country singer Athlete Peyton Manning, Indianapolis Colts' quarterback Political candidate John McCain, U.S. Senator, Arizona
Place marketing	Marketing efforts designed to attract visitors to a particular area; improve consumer images of a city, state, or nation; and/or attract new business	Las Vegas: What happens here, stays here. Texas: It's like a whole other country. Toronto, Ontario: The world within a city.
Cause marketing	Identification and marketing of a social issue, cause, or idea to selected target markets	"21 means 21" "Live strong"
Event marketing	Marketing of sporting, cultural, and charitable activities to selected target markets	2008 Beijing Summer Olympics Susan G. Komen Race for the Cure
Organization marketing	Marketing efforts of mutual-benefit organizations, service organizations, and government organizations that seek to influence others to accept their goals, receive their services, or contribute to them in some way	United Way brings out the best in all of us. American Red Cross: Together, we can save a life. The Nature Conservancy: Saving the last great places on Earth.

Etiquette Tips for Marketing Professionals

Forms of Address: Which One Do You Use, and When?

When you meet someone new in a professional situation, do you say "Mr.," "Dr.," or "Ms.," and hope you've got it right? Most people have experienced this confusion at one time or another. Whether you're interviewing for a job or making a sales call, you are marketing yourself to the other person—and you want to make sure you address that person with the correct title. Here are a few guidelines to help you navigate the maze successfully:

1. Always use a title and last name until you are asked to use a person's first name. Even if you are introduced to someone by first name—such as Patricia Graham—continue to address her as "Ms. Graham" until she specifically invites you to do otherwise. In many cultures, first names are never used in business situations.
2. Listen. If someone else makes an introduction for you, pay attention to the way the introduc-

tion is made. Make a mental note of which form of address is used.
3. Introduce a lower-ranking person to a higher-ranking person. For example, you might introduce your new assistant to a department manager by saying, "Ms. Lopez, this is my new assistant, Jeremy Morgan."
4. If you aren't certain which title to use, at least make an attempt by saying "Mr." or "Ms." Through conversation—or the help of someone else who is present—you will be able to refine the title to "Dr.," "Senator," or "Mrs.," if appropriate.

Sources: Susan Bryant, "Business Etiquette You Should Know," Monster.com, **http://wlb.monster.com**, accessed February 2, 2006; Hilka Klinkenberg, "Manners Mom Never Taught You," Novatrain, **http://www.novatrain.com**, accessed February 2, 2006; Lydia Ramsay, "Minding Your Global Manners," Business Know-How, **http://www.businessknowhow.com**, accessed February 2, 2006.

An extension of person marketing involves *celebrity endorsements,* in which well-known athletes, entertainers, and experts or authority figures promote products for companies or social causes for not-for-profit organizations. Golfer Tiger Woods, tennis player Maria Sharapova, NASCAR racer Jeff Gordon, and actress Uma Thurman can all be seen in ads for Tag Heuer watches. Singer Clint Black does commercials for Wal-Mart, which distributes his CDs. Actor William Shatner can be seen in ads for Priceline.com, while his former *Star Trek* co-star Leonard Nimoy promotes the pain reliever Aleve. Actress Kirstie Alley encourages women to join the Jenny Craig program to lose weight. Athletes are the big winners in the celebrity endorsement arena—NBA Cleveland Cavaliers star LeBron James has multimillion-dollar endorsement deals with Nike, Upper Deck, and Coca-Cola. Pittsburgh Steelers quarterback Ben Roethlisberger raked in a reported $4.5 million in endorsements within weeks of a Super Bowl win.[21] And Nike has a ten-year endorsement deal with baseball player Alex Rodriguez—A-Rod—above and beyond his $252 million salary from the New York Yankees.

Briefly Speaking

"How bad a day can it be if you're looking at the right side of the grass?"

—Michael Bloomberg (b. 1942)
Mayor of New York City

PLACE MARKETING

Another category of nontraditional marketing is **place marketing**, which attempts to attract customers to particular areas. Cities, states, regions, and countries publicize their tourist attractions to lure vacation travelers. They also promote themselves as good locations for businesses. Place marketing has become more important in the world economy—not only for tourism but also to recruit business and workers. As they rebuild, cities or regions that have suffered war or natural disasters may advertise reopening attractions to tourists alongside opportunities to businesses. The reopening of a zoo in postwar Afghanistan received worldwide attention, as did the first Mardi Gras celebration in New Orleans after Hurricane Katrina. Vietnam has been a country of growing interest to Vietnam veterans and their children or grandchildren.

place marketing
Marketing efforts to attract people and organizations to a particular geographic area.

IMAGE COURTESY OF THE ADVERTISING ARCHIVES

100% PURE NEW ZEALAND

Flowering in late Spring the Mount Cook Lily is one of 415 mountain plants that are unique to the South Island's magnificent Mount Cook region. Whether you're there to take in the snow-clad peaks or heli-ski down them, the alpine air and piercing light will refresh you like nothing else on earth.   www.newzealand.com

New Zealand uses place marketing to attract tourists. Here it promotes the breathtaking scenery of its Mount Cook region.

Place marketing can be a showcase for ingenuity. Sheboygan, Wisconsin, is popularly known as the "Bratwurst Capital of the World." But it wants to become the first private spaceport in the Midwest. The area, which for years has been launching small rockets 35 miles in the air as part of its Rockets for Schools program, sits right next to a huge chunk of restricted airspace. This restriction would allow rockets to be sent into the upper atmosphere without colliding with other flight traffic. The Federal Aviation Administration (FAA) has already authorized Sheboygan to launch suborbital flights, and both state and federal officials are convinced the plan would work. Businesspeople are in agreement as well. The idea of Sheboygan as a place where people can catch the next rocket into space may very well take flight.[22]

In another area of the country, you wouldn't necessarily think of West Virginia as a hub for skiers. But the town of Davis is home to Timberline Four Seasons Ski Resort, which boasts up to 160 inches of snow per year on its Herz Mountain. Although it is often overlooked by skiers who routinely travel north and west, locals are convinced that their mountain is about to be discovered. In addition to skiing, the area promotes mountain bike races and hiking in the summer.[23]

CAUSE MARKETING

A third category of nontraditional marketing, **cause marketing**, refers to the identification and marketing of a social issue, cause, or idea to selected target markets. Cause marketing covers a wide range of issues, including literacy, physical fitness, family planning, control of overeating, environmental protection, elimination of birth defects, child-abuse prevention, and punishment of convicted drunk drivers.

cause marketing Identification and marketing of a social issue, cause, or idea to selected target markets.

event marketing Marketing of sporting, cultural, and charitable activities to selected target markets

As mentioned earlier, an increasingly common marketing practice is for profit-seeking firms to link their products to social causes—it's a win-win situation for everyone. Another common practice is for several not-for-profit organizations to band together for a single cause. After Hurricane Katrina devastated the Gulf Coast, organizations such as the American Society for the Prevention of Cruelty to Animals (ASPCA), the Humane Society of the United States, Adopt-a-Pet, and others came together to rescue, treat, and care for animal victims of the storm. In one effort, these groups donated $150,000 worth of heartworm treatments for the animals, because of the increased number of disease-carrying mosquitoes after the hurricane.[24]

Surveys show strong support for cause-related marketing by both consumers and company employees. In a recent survey, 92 percent of consumers had a more positive image of companies that support important social causes, and four of five respondents said that they would change brands to support a cause if the price and quality of the two brands remained equal. Cause marketing can help build relationships with customers.

EVENT MARKETING

Event marketing refers to the marketing of sporting, cultural, and charitable activities to selected target markets. It also includes the sponsorship of such events by firms seeking to increase public awareness and bolster their images by linking themselves and their products to the events. Sports sponsorships have gained effectiveness in increasing brand recognition, enhancing image, boosting purchase volume, and increasing popularity with sports fans in demographic segments corresponding to sponsor business goals.

Some people might say that the premier sporting event is baseball's World Series. Others claim it's the Olympics. Still others might argue that it's the Super Bowl, which some consumers claim they watch only to see the debut of commercials. Those commercials are expensive—they can cost as much as $2.5 million for 30 seconds of airtime, or $83,333 a second. But they reach an estimated 90 million viewers. Companies now also feed their commercials to Web sites and make them available for downloading to personal computers and video iPods. Experienced marketers caution that firms planning such a big expenditure should make it part of a larger marketing plan, not just a single shot at fame.[25]

For those who prefer the international pageantry of the Olympics, marketers have plenty of plans. The promotion of upcoming Olympics—both summer and winter—begins years in advance. Before the end of each Olympics, hosts of the next games unveil their logo and the marketing takes off from there. Corporate sponsors such as Adidas and Nike try to target the next Olympic gold medal winners, draping them in clothing and gear with company logos. The 2008 Olympics in Beijing, China, are particularly important because of the huge consumer market there. Sales of premium sportswear already tops $350 million for Nike and $300 million for Adidas, and both firms are seeking an even bigger piece of the pie. Adidas paid between $80 million and $100 million in cash and uniforms to be an official sponsor of the Beijing Olympics, but the company believes the investment will pay off in sales and long-term relationships with Chinese consumers.[26]

Event marketers continued to find ways to help the victims of Hurricane Katrina months after the storm. Six months after the hurricane hit, American Express, Shell, and health insurance provider Tenet Choices were among the firms to sponsor Jazzfest, a benefit jazz festival held to raise money for hurricane victims. A group of 140 women from the New Orleans area called Women of the Storm went to Capitol Hill in Washington, D.C., to pressure lawmakers for more relief funding.[27]

ORGANIZATION MARKETING

Organization marketing attempts to influence people to accept the goals of, receive the services of, or contribute in some way to an organization. Organization marketing includes mutual-benefit organizations (Service Employees International Union and the Republican and Democratic political parties), service and cultural organizations (Baylor College of Medicine, DePaul University, St. Louis Barnes-Jewish Hospital, and the National Air and Space Museum), and government organizations (the U.S. Coast Guard, the Newark Police Department, the Sacramento Fire Department, and the U.S. Postal Service). Colleges and universities use organizational marketing to help raise funds. The University of North Carolina now leads all colleges and universities in the sale of licensed merchandise—the school receives around $3.5 million a year from these sales.[28]

Marketers for the U.S. Department of Defense (DOD) recently took an unconventional approach to marketing by appealing to the parents of potential soldiers. The DOD launched several commercials focusing on the value of a military career from the point of view of parents. "When young adults are making the decision to join the Army, there is no one they seek approval from more than their parents," explains Col. Thomas Nickerson, director of strategic outreach for the U.S. Army Accessions Command. "Because of this, it is important we engage in a dialogue with parents to further educate them about the tangible and intangible benefits of a career in the U.S. Army."[29]

organization marketing
Marketing by mutual-benefit organizations, service organizations, and government organizations intended to influence others to accept their goals, receive their services, or contribute to them in some way.

 assessment check

1. Identify the five major categories of nontraditional marketing.

2. Give an example of a way in which two or more of these categories might overlap.

CREATIVITY AND CRITICAL THINKING

 6 Outline the importance of creativity, critical thinking, and the technology revolution in marketing.

The challenges presented by today's complex and technologically sophisticated marketing environment require creativity and critical-thinking skills from marketing professionals. **Creativity** is a human activity that produces original ideas or knowledge, frequently by testing combinations of ideas or data to produce unique results. It is an extremely valuable skill for marketers. Creativity helps them develop novel solutions to perceived marketing problems. It has been a part of the human endeavor since the beginning of time. Leonardo da Vinci conceived his idea for a helicopter after watching leaves twirl in the wind. Swiss engineer George de Mestral, noticing that burrs stuck to his wool socks because of their tiny hooks, invented Velcro. Companies rely on creativity at all levels. After spending years in the shadow of Coca-Cola, Pepsi has emerged in its own spotlight. The firm still sells less cola than Coke, but creative marketing has placed it squarely in the forefront of a broadened soft drink and snack-food industry. Instead of focusing on one type of drink, Pepsi began to develop sports drinks and flavored water, which more and more consumers wanted. Pepsi's Aquafina is now the number one water brand, and the firm's Gatorade boasts 80 percent of the sports drink market.[30]

Critical thinking refers to the process of determining the authenticity, accuracy, and worth of information, knowledge, claims, and arguments. Critical thinkers do not take information at face value and simply assume that it is accurate; they analyze the data themselves and develop their own opinions and conclusions. Critical thinking requires discipline and sometimes a cooling-off period after the creative fire of a new idea. In many instances, it requires analyzing what went wrong with an idea or a process and figuring out how to make it right. PepsiCo, just mentioned, certainly relied on critical thinking to support its new product strategy. Microsoft has joined its MSN Internet product group and its research unit to form an Internet research lab to develop and evaluate new products. "Its goal is to hit the sweet spot in the middle between science and engineering, where each is . . . better together," explains Microsoft's Gary William Flake, who heads up the new project.[31]

THE TECHNOLOGY REVOLUTION IN MARKETING

As we move through the first decade of the 21st century, we also enter a new era in communication, considered by some as unique as the 15th-century invention of the printing press or the first radio and television broadcasts early in the 20th century. **Technology** is the business application of knowledge based on scientific discoveries, inventions, and innovations. Interactive multimedia technologies including computer networks, Internet services, and wireless devices have revolutionized the way people store, distribute, retrieve, and present information. These technologies link employees, suppliers, and customers throughout the world. Technological advances continuously revolutionize marketing. Now that more than half of all U.S. homes and apartments contain at least one personal computer, online services and the Internet offer a new medium over which companies can market products and offer customer service. Because online sales in the United States reached more than $143 billion in a recent year, marketers are doing their best to make the most of this medium. The "Marketing Success" feature discusses one company that helped revolutionize online marketing.

Marketers can develop targeted marketing campaigns and zoned advertising programs for consumers located within a certain distance from a store and even within specific city blocks. Cairo.com collects local advertising flyers and posts them online so shoppers will know which local stores offer the best deals. ShopLocal LLC offers a similar service but also compares prices of online merchants with those of local stores.[32]

 ## marketing success   What's a Google?

Background. When Sergey Brin and Larry Page founded Internet search engine Google roughly a decade ago, most people had never heard the mathematical term *googol*, which refers to the number 1 followed by 100 zeros. But the name fit the new software company, whose "mission is to organize the world's information and make it universally accessible and useful."

The Challenge. Brin and Page had created a service that would change the way people communicate and conduct business—but to be successful, they had to make the product easy for people to find and use.

The Strategy. The Google Web site has a clean, clear design with simple prompts that are easy for anyone to follow. The Google search engine returns its results in less than half a second. More important, it delivers accurately the type of information a user is looking for. Google provides features such as a spell checker, translation of foreign language Web pages, and a calculator. All of these features are free to the user. As a business, Google generates much of its revenue through advertising that is clearly separated from search results, so users do not become confused or frustrated by unwanted advertising images.

Technology can also open up entirely new markets. Cell phones have helped bring the entire continent of Africa into the world marketplace. With a cell phone in hand, farmers no longer have to trek miles to a pay phone to negotiate prices for their goods. Wildlife researchers use cell phone signals to track endangered animals, and fishermen can call ahead to the mainland to find out where to take their catch.[33]

INTERACTIVE AND INTERNET MARKETING

Interactive media technologies combine computers and telecommunications resources to create software that users can control. They allow people to digitize reports and drawings and transmit them, quickly and inexpensively, over phone lines, coaxial cables, or fiber-optic cables. People can subscribe to personalized news services that deliver article summaries on specified topics directly to their fax machines or computers. They can communicate via e-mail, voice mail, fax, videoconferencing, and computer networks; pay bills using online banking services; and use online resources to get information about everything from theater events to a local Toyota dealer's special sale. People can make phone calls via the Internet using voice over Internet protocol (VoIP). Many calls are now transmitted via VoIP because it is cheaper than conventional phone lines—presenting a potentially important interactive medium for marketers.

The World Wide Web provides marketers with tremendous interactive technologies. Compared with traditional media, the hypermedia resources of the Web offer a number of advantages. Data move in seconds, and interactive control gives users quick access to other information resources through related pages, at either the same or other sites, and easy navigation through documents. Because the medium is dynamic, Web site sponsors can easily keep information current. Multimedia capacities increase the attractiveness of documents and sites.

Interactive marketing refers to buyer–seller communications in which the customer controls the amount and type of information received from a marketer. This technique provides immediate access to key product information when the consumer wants it. Interactive marketing allows marketers and consumers to customize their communication. Customers may come to companies for information, creating opportunities for one-to-one marketing. Kimberly-Clark, maker of Kleenex, launched three Web sites as part of its sponsorship of the Winter Olympics in Turin, Italy. One site featured photos and stories of athletes' mothers—with an e-mail address at which viewers could contact the Olympic moms and ask them questions. The other two sites promoted sweepstakes for Kimberly-Clark products and other prizes.[34]

Interactive marketing can also allow larger exchanges, in which consumers can communicate with one another using e-mail or electronic bulletin boards. These electronic conversations establish innovative relationships between users and the technology, providing customized information based on users' interests and levels of understanding. Marketers can also use Web logs (blogs) and wireless phones to foster these communications. Yahoo! has been testing Shoposphere, a networking site

The Outcome. Google continues to grow and move into new markets such as China, new relationships such as a partnership with Sun Microsystems to develop new software to protect computers against harmful programs such as spyware, and new products such as geographical search and view feature Google Earth. The firm has also started selling video content such as CBS TV programs and professional basketball games. Still, Google's marketers and executives remain focused on delivering information and services in ways that improve people's lives. "We believe strongly that in the long term, we will be better served . . . by a company that does good things for the world even if we forgo some short-term gains," wrote Brin and Page in a founders' letter that accompanied the firm's initial public offering of stock. "We aspire to make Google an institution that makes the world a better place."

Sources: Adi Ignatius, "In Search of the Real Google," *Time*, February 20, 2006, pp. 36–49; Steven Levy, "Google and the China Syndrome," *Newsweek*, February 13, 2006, p. 14; Mike Langberg, "In China, Google Founders Wake up to the Real World," *Seattle Times*, January 30, 2006, **http://seattletimes.nwsource.com**; Google Web site, **http://www.google.com**, accessed January 27, 2006; "Google, Sun & Harvard vs. Spyware and AdWare," *Search Engine Journal*, January 25, 2006, **http://www.searchenginejournal.com**; Nicholas Hoover, "Google Secrets," *Optimize*, January 2006, **http://www.optimizemagazine.com**.

within its own shopping site that lists reviews, blogs, and shopping lists posted by members. For example, a card game enthusiast can post a "Poker Night" shopping list telling new players where to find the essentials—including table, strategy books, and accessories.[35]

Internet protocol television (IPTV) is another interactive technology for marketers and consumers alike to embrace. IPTV allows a two-way digital broadcast signal to be sent through a telephone or cable network by way of a broadband connection. AT&T and Verizon Communications both plan to offer a full range of IPTV services soon. Services in the works include Caller ID, e-mail, and voice mail on television; the ability to program a digital video recorder from a cell phone; the capability to pull up sports statistics during a game; and the possibility of viewing events from multiple camera angles.[36]

Interactive promotions put the customer in control. Consumers can easily get tips on product usage and answers to customer service questions. They can also tell the company what they like or dislike about a product, and they can just as easily click the exit button and move on to another area. As interactive promotions grow in number and popularity, the challenge will be attracting and holding consumer attention.

BROADBAND

Broadband technology—an always-on Internet connection that runs at 200 kilobytes per second or higher—can deliver large amounts of data at once, making online marketing even faster and easier than it was a few years ago. Consumers can access Web pages and sites can process credit card purchases much more quickly via broadband. The number of households with broadband connections is increasing rapidly because of this speed advantage. More than 50 percent of all online U.S. households use a broadband Internet connection, even though subscription costs are higher than other connections. The United States is certainly not the only market that has embraced broadband. For example, South Korea has discovered its benefits. About 11 million South Korean households—70 percent of the nation's citizens—have a broadband connection. Broadband is growing in the United Kingdom, Europe, and China as well.

Wireless technology is an important tool in 21st-century marketing.

WIRELESS

More and more consumers now have Internet connections via **wireless technology** for their laptop and handheld computers, which is both a challenge and an opportunity for marketers. About 41 percent of Internet users in the United States are "wireless ready," which means they use wireless devices such as cell phones or notebook computers to access the Web and check their e-mail. As this percentage increases, the stage is set for **mobile marketing**—marketing messages transmitted via wireless technology.

Wireless ads offer tremendous potential to target certain audiences. And because these ads appear by themselves on a handheld user's screen, they command more attention than a traditional banner ad on a computer screen would. Although 70 percent of consumers say they would prefer to download ad-free content to their handheld devices, 20 percent say they would still download ad-supported content.[37] And many consumers are interested in watching live television programs on the go—another opportunity for mobile marketing. Through MobiTV and SmartVideo, consumers can order live programming from providers such as ABC News. Companies such as Motorola, Intel, Nokia, and Texas Instruments are joining together to enable live broadcasts. And the Mobile Marketing Association (MMA), along with major firms Verizon Wireless, MobiTV, AOL, and Zingy, are discussing the best ways to engage in mobile video advertising. "We all believe that it is going to be a significantly large opportunity," predicts Laura Marriott of the MMA.[38] One research firm predicts that the global mobile commerce market—mobile entertainment downloads, ticket purchases, and other transactions—will soon reach $88 billion.[39]

 assessment check

1. Define *creativity* and *critical thinking*.
2. Why are both of these attributes important for marketers?
3. Why is interactive marketing an important tool for marketers?

FROM TRANSACTION-BASED MARKETING TO RELATIONSHIP MARKETING

7 Explain the shift from transaction-based marketing to relationship marketing.

As marketing progresses through the 21st century, a significant change is taking place in the way companies interact with customers. The traditional view of marketing as a simple exchange process, or **transaction-based marketing,** is being replaced by a different, longer-term approach that emphasizes building relationships with one customer at a time. Traditional marketing strategies focused on attracting customers and closing deals. Today's marketers realize that, although it's important to attract new customers, it's even more important to establish and maintain a relationship with them so they become loyal repeat customers. These efforts must expand to include suppliers and employees as well. Over the long term, this relationship may be translated to the **lifetime value of a customer**—the revenues and intangible benefits that a customer brings to an organization over an average lifetime, minus the investment the firm has made to attract and keep the customer.

Marketers realize that consumers are getting more and more sophisticated. They quickly recognize marketing messages and may turn away from them if the messages don't contain information that consumers want and need. So marketers need to develop new techniques to establish and build trusting relationships between companies and their customers.[40] As defined earlier in this chapter, relationship marketing refers to the development, growth, and maintenance of long-term, cost-effective exchange relationships with individual customers, suppliers, employees, and other partners for mutual benefit. It broadens the scope of external marketing relationships to include suppliers, customers, and referral sources. In relationship marketing, the term *customer* takes on a new meaning. Employees serve customers within an organization as well as outside it; individual employees and their departments are customers of and suppliers to one another. They must apply the same high standards of customer satisfaction to intradepartmental relationships as they do to external customer relationships. Relationship marketing recognizes the critical importance of internal marketing to the success of external marketing plans. Programs that improve customer service inside a company also raise productivity and staff morale, resulting in better customer relationships outside the firm.

Relationship marketing gives a company new opportunities to gain a competitive edge by moving customers up a loyalty ladder—from new customers to regular purchasers, then to loyal supporters of the firm and its goods and services, and finally to advocates who not only buy its products but recommend them to others, as shown in Figure 1.2.

Relationship building begins early in marketing. It starts with determining what customers need and want, then developing high-quality products to meet those needs. It continues with excellent customer service during and after purchase. It also includes programs that encourage repeat

figure 1.2

Converting New Customers to Advocates

(Advocate / Loyal Supporter / Regular Purchaser / New Customer)

purchases and foster customer loyalty. Marketers may try to rebuild damaged relationships or rejuvenate unprofitable customers with these practices as well. Sometimes modifying a product or tailoring customer service to meet the needs of these customers can go a long way toward rebuilding a relationship.

By converting indifferent customers into loyal ones, companies generate repeat sales. The cost of maintaining existing customers is far below the cost of finding new ones, and these loyal customers are profitable. Some of the best repeat customers are those who are also willing to spread the word—create a buzz—about a product. **Buzz marketing** can be very effective in attracting new customers by bridging the gap between a company and its products. Companies as diverse as Microsoft and Build-a-Bear Workshop have tapped customers to create buzz about their products. Firms that make the most efficient use of buzz marketing warn that it is not a "one-way" approach to building customer relationships. "It's not about creating a better megaphone," explains Bill Hamilton, CEO of screen-capture software developer TechSmith. "To be successful, companies need better conversations with their customers." At TechSmith, one marketer estimates that she chats with as many as 400 "customer evangelists" a month via e-mail, instant messaging, phone, and private forums.[41] Motor scooter firm Vespa recently asked two enthusiastic Vespa fans to participate as bloggers on the firm's Web site. "Vespa has incredible fans, and we thought the best approach was to let customers tell their stories online," says Steve Rubel of CooperKatz, which Vespa hired to do its online marketing. Although the Vespa bloggers aren't paid in cash, they receive some free accessories and get to be the first to try out new models.[42]

Effective relationship marketing often relies heavily on information technologies such as computer databases that record customers' tastes, price preferences, and lifestyles. This technology helps companies become one-to-one marketers that gather customer-specific information and provide individually customized goods and services. The firms target their marketing programs to appropriate groups rather than relying on mass-marketing campaigns. Companies that study customer preferences and react accordingly gain distinct competitive advantages.

DEVELOPING PARTNERSHIPS AND STRATEGIC ALLIANCES

Relationship marketing does not apply just to individual consumers and employees. It also affects a wide range of other markets, including business-to-business relationships with the firm's suppliers and distributors as well as other types of corporate partnerships. In the past, companies have often viewed their suppliers as adversaries against whom they must fiercely negotiate prices, playing one off against the other. But this attitude has changed radically as both marketers and their suppliers discover the benefits of collaborative relationships.

strategic alliance Partnerships in which two or more companies combine resources and capital to create competitive advantages in a new market.

The formation of *strategic alliances*—partnerships that create competitive advantages—is also on the rise. Alliances take many forms, including product development partnerships that involve shared costs for research and development and marketing, and vertical alliances in which one company provides a product or component to another firm, which then distributes or sells it under its own brand. Yahoo! and TiVo joined forces to blend some of their services. The two companies collaborated to offer Yahoo's Internet-based content through TiVo's digital recording devices. People who go to Yahoo's TV page can now click on a record-to-TiVo button directly from a TV program listing to schedule recordings remotely. The firms also offer more Yahoo! content via TiVo.[43]

Not-for-profit organizations often use strategic alliances to raise awareness and funds for their causes. Samsung partnered with the Turin Winter Olympics to create the Wireless Olympic Works to provide the wireless interface for people to receive real-time information and results from various events. *National Geographic* teamed up with Oriental Weavers to create a line of rugs inspired by world cultures. The National Geographic Society's proceeds from this collection go to its World Cultures Fund, which supports the study and a preservation of world cultures.

 assessment check

1. How does relationship marketing give companies a competitive edge?
2. What is a strategic alliance?

COSTS AND FUNCTIONS OF MARKETING

8   Identify the universal functions of marketing.

Firms must spend money to create time, place, and ownership utilities. Numerous attempts have been made to measure marketing costs in relation to overall product costs, and most estimates have ranged between 40 and 60 percent of total costs. On average, half of the costs involved in a product, such as a Subway sandwich, a Subaru Imprezia, or a trip to the Bahamas, can be traced directly to marketing. These costs are not associated with wheat, metal, or other raw materials. Nor are they associated with baking, welding, or any of the other production functions necessary for creating form utility. What functions does marketing perform, and why are they important in creating customer satisfaction?

As Figure 1.3 reveals, marketing is responsible for the performance of eight universal functions: buying, selling, transporting, storing, standardizing and grading, financing, risk taking, and securing marketing information. Some functions are performed by manufacturers, others by retailers, and still others by marketing intermediaries called **wholesalers.**

Buying and selling, the first two functions shown in Figure 1.3, represent **exchange functions.** Buying is important to marketing on several levels. Marketers must determine how and why consumers buy certain goods and services. To be successful, they must try to understand consumer behavior. In addition, retailers and other intermediaries must seek out products that will appeal to their customers. Because they generate time, place, and ownership utilities through these purchases, marketers must anticipate consumer preferences for purchases to be made several months later. Selling is the second half of the exchange process. It involves advertising, personal selling, and sales promotion in an attempt to match the firm's goods and services to consumer needs.

Transporting and storing are **physical distribution functions.** Transporting involves physically moving goods from the seller to the purchaser. Storing involves warehousing goods until they are needed for sale. Manufacturers, wholesalers, and retailers all typically perform these functions.

The final four marketing functions—standardizing and grading, financing, risk taking, and securing marketing information—are often called **facilitating functions** because they help the marketer perform the exchange and physical distribution functions. Quality and quantity control standards and grades, frequently set by federal or state governments, reduce the need for purchasers to inspect each item. For example, if you request a certain size tire for your automobile, you expect to get it.

Financing is another marketing function because buyers often need access to funds to finance inventories prior to sales. Manufacturers often provide financing for their wholesale and retail customers. Some types of wholesalers perform similar functions for their markets. Finally, retailers frequently allow their customers to buy on credit, with either store charge cards or major credit cards.

figure 1.3

Eight Universal Marketing Functions

The seventh function, risk taking, is part of most ventures. Manufacturers create goods and services based on research and their belief that consumers need them. Wholesalers and retailers acquire inventory based on similar expectations of future consumer demand. Entrepreneurial risk takers accommodate these uncertainties about future consumer behavior when they market goods and services.

The final marketing function involves securing marketing information. Marketers gather information about potential customers—who they are, what they buy, where they buy, and how they buy. By collecting and analyzing marketing information, marketers can understand why consumers purchase some goods while passing others by. This information also helps determine what consumers want and need—and how to offer goods and services to satisfy them. So marketing is the direct connection between a firm and its customers, the link that helps build and maintain lasting relationships.

 assessment check

1. **Which two marketing functions represent exchange functions?**
2. **Which two functions represent physical distribution functions?**
3. **Which four functions are facilitating functions?**

 9 Demonstrate the relationship between ethical business practices, social responsibility, and marketplace success.

ETHICS AND SOCIAL RESPONSIBILITY: DOING WELL BY DOING GOOD

Ethics are moral standards of behavior expected by a society. Most companies do their best to abide by an ethical code of conduct, but sometimes organizations and their leaders fall short. Several years ago, the Texas-based energy giant Enron collapsed, taking with it the retirement savings of its employees and investors. In another scandal, executives from Tyco were convicted of using millions of company dollars for their personal benefit. And chemical manufacturer Monsanto was convicted not only of polluting water sources and soil in a rural Alabama area for decades but of ignoring evidence its own scientists had gathered indicating the extent and severity of the pollution.

Despite these and other alleged breaches of ethical standards, most businesspeople follow ethical practices. More than half of all major corporations now offer ethics training to employees, and most corporate mission statements include pledges to protect the environment, contribute to communities, and improve workers' lives. This book encourages you to follow the highest ethical standards throughout your business and marketing career. Because ethics and social responsibility are so important to marketers, each chapter in this book contains a critical-thinking feature titled "Solving an Ethical Controversy." This chapter's feature explores the problems of responding to large-scale natural disaster.

Social responsibility involves marketing philosophies, policies, procedures, and actions whose primary objective is to enhance society. Social responsibility often takes the form of philanthropy, which involves making gifts of money or time to humanitarian causes. Many firms—both large and small—include social responsibility programs as part of their overall mission. These programs often produce such benefits as improved customer relationships, increased employee loyalty, marketplace success, and improved financial performance. Timberland, a manufacturer of boots, outdoor clothing, and accessories, is well known for its high ethical standards and socially responsible programs. The company donates large sums of money to charities each year, and its employees are given paid time off to volunteer for their favorite organizations—from the animal shelter to the local preschool. The company also welcomes ideas for socially responsible programs from its employees.[44] As part of a recent project to benefit St. Helena's Residence, a foster-care home for girls in New York City, many businesses—including Lowe's, Drexel Heritage, and Taylor-Made Contractors—donated goods and services to renovate the house, under the direction of *O at Home,* a magazine founded by Oprah Winfrey.[45]

Recent recipients of the prestigious annual awards given by the Committee to Encourage Corporate Philanthropy (CECP) include Cisco Systems, Grand Circle, and KaBOOM! Cisco

Solving an Ethical Controversy

FEMA and Katrina: The Hurricane after the Hurricane

Even before the winds died down and the skies over Alabama, Louisiana, and Mississippi began to clear, it was clear that the Federal Emergency Management Agency (FEMA) had failed to respond efficiently or effectively to the region devastated by Hurricane Katrina. In addition, local police and firefighters were criticized for not evacuating the elderly and disadvantaged or protecting citizens who had remained behind. Fingers were pointed, FEMA chief Michael Brown left, and a flurry of arguments followed. Meanwhile, survivors waited on rooftops to be rescued, evacuees huddled in substandard shelters, and separated family members desperately searched for each other.

Amid the confusion, corporations such as Wal-Mart, Home Depot, and Lowe's stepped in to help. Home Depot set up several temporary sites along the Gulf Coast, which they stocked with lumber and building supplies. Lowe's stocked its stores with similar supplies. "We need to build the best level of service possible," said a Lowe's spokeswoman. Wal-Mart established an Emergency Contact Service that helped people search for missing loved ones, and set up a gift registry for storm victims.

Should private corporations, which have other challenges to deal with, be asked to assist governments during emergencies?

PRO

1. Disasters of such magnitude as Hurricane Katrina create massive destruction. The more organizations that can prepare for and respond to disasters, the better. The federal and local governments should concentrate on coordinating all parties into an effective response.
2. Some private organizations have the needed supplies such as food, water, and clothing to help people in need immediately. They also know their customers well because they serve them day to day. Wal-Mart used its familiar stores and staff to distribute 2,500 trailer loads of water and emergency

supplies immediately after the storm. The firm also donated 150 computers to Red Cross shelters to help evacuees locate loved ones. Home Depot had supply trucks ready for deployment even before the hurricane hit. "In this kind of atmosphere, speed is incredibly important," said Carl Liebert, executive vice president at Lowe's.

CON

1. Despite their valiant efforts, private companies can't possibly fulfill such great needs. They have their own stockholders, employees, and operations to worry about. Governments should be responsible for ensuring the safety and well-being of citizens during disasters.
2. Although the response to Katrina was not adequate, governments have professionals who are the best equipped in both training and supplies to handle emergencies. Those first responders just need to do a better job of carrying out their plans and coordinating efforts.

Summary

While it could be said that Katrina delivered a black eye to the federal, state, and local governments, the disaster gave private companies a chance to shine. In fact, the public confidence and trust in private firms such as Wal-Mart and Home Depot was boosted to a new high. The efforts of these and other firms will not only go a long way toward rebuilding a region but also generate strong loyalty from customers in the future.

Sources: Jeanne Meserve, "FEMA Failed to Accept Katrina Help, Documents Say," CNN Washington Bureau, January 30, 2006, http://www.cnn.com; Anne D'innocenzio, "Home Depot and Lowe's Plan Big Role in Rebuilding of Gulf Coast," *San Diego Union-Tribune*, October 17, 2005, http://www.signonsandiego.com; "The Home Depot Launches 'Rebuilding Hope & Homes' to Assist in Long-Term Hurricane Katrina Recovery," PR Newswire, September 20, 2005, http://sev.prnewswire.com; "Wal-Mart Opens Gift Registry for Hurricane Katrina Victims," PR Newswire, September 12, 2005, http://sev.prnewswire.com; Michael Barbara and Justin Gillis, "Wal-Mart at Forefront of Hurricane Relief," *Washington Post*, September 6, 2005, http://www.washingtonpost.com; Julie Schmit, "Home Supply Stores Started Prep Work Early," *USA Today*, September 1, 2005, http://www.usatoday.com.

Our cleaner coal technology will create energy with less emissions than traditional coal plants. When we use our ecomagination, we like to keep it clean. To learn more, visit ge.com/ecomagination.

GE imagination at work

© 2005 GENERAL ELECTRIC COMPANY

GE engages in ethical and socially responsible business practices through its "economagination" program. Here GE showcases its cleaner coal technology, which reduces emissions into the environment.

made a $40 million commitment to an education initiative to aid victims of Hurricane Katrina, and offers a global Leadership Fellows Program to employees who want to work full time for not-for-profit organizations for up to one year—at no cost to the not-for-profit organizations. Grand Circle, a leader in international travel, has a variety of programs through which it supports the communities that its customers visit. The Grand Circle Foundation currently funds 87 schools and youth programs around the world. KaBOOM! and Home Depot work together to revitalize communities by creating play spaces for children. One recent project created or renovated 1,000 play spaces in 1,000 days.[46]

✔ assessment check

1. Define *ethics.*
2. What is *social responsibility?*

Strategic Implications of Marketing in the 21st Century

Unprecedented opportunities have emerged out of electronic commerce and computer technologies in business today. These advances and innovations have allowed organizations to reach new markets, reduce selling and marketing costs, and enhance their relationships with customers and suppliers. Thanks to the Internet, commerce has grown into a global market.

As a new universe for consumers and organizations is created, marketers must learn to be creative and think critically about their environment. Profit-seeking and not-for-profit organizations must broaden the scope of their activities to prevent myopic results in their enterprises.

Marketers must constantly look for ways to create loyal customers and build long-term relationships with those customers, often on a one-to-one basis. They must be able to anticipate customer needs and satisfy them with innovative goods and services. They must be able to do this faster and better than the competition. And they must conduct their business according to the highest ethical standards.

REVIEW OF CHAPTER OBJECTIVES

1   Define *marketing,* explain how it creates utility, and describe its role in the global marketplace.

Marketing is an organizational function and a set of processes for creating, communicating, and delivering value to customers and for managing customer relationships in ways that benefit the organization and its stakeholders. Utility is the want-satisfying power of a good or service. Four basic kinds of utility exist: form, time, place, and ownership. Marketing creates time, place, and ownership utilities. Three factors have forced marketers to embrace a global marketplace: expanded international trade agreements; new technologies that have brought previously isolated nations to the marketplace; and greater interdependence of the world's economies.

2   Contrast marketing activities during the four eras in the history of marketing.

During the production era, businesspeople believed that quality products would sell themselves. The sales era emphasized convincing people to buy. The marketing concept emerged during the marketing era, in which there was a company-wide focus on consumer orientation with the objective of achieving long-term success. The relationship era focuses on establishing and maintaining relationships between customers and suppliers. Relationship marketing involves long-term, value-added relationships.

3   Explain the importance of avoiding marketing myopia.

Marketing myopia is management's failure to recognize a company's scope of business. It focuses marketers too narrowly on products and thus misses potential opportunities to satisfy customers. To avoid it, companies must broadly define their goals so they focus on fulfilling consumer needs.

4   Describe the characteristics of not-for-profit marketing.

Not-for-profit organizations operate in both public and private sectors. The biggest distinction between not-for-profits and commercial firms is the bottom line—whether the firm is judged by its profitability levels. Not-for-profit organizations may market to multiple publics. A customer or service user of a not-for-profit organization may have less control over the organization's destiny than do customers of a profit-seeking firm. In addition, resource contributors to not-for-profits may try to influence the organization's activities. Not-for-profits and for-profits may form alliances that effectively promote each other's causes and services.

5   Identify and briefly explain each of the five types of nontraditional marketing.

Person marketing focuses on efforts to cultivate the attention, interest, and preferences of a target market toward a celebrity or noted figure. Place marketing attempts to attract visitors and businesses to a particular destination. Cause marketing identifies and markets a social issue, cause, or idea. Event marketing promotes sporting, cultural, charitable, or political activities. Organization marketing attempts to influence others to accept the organization's goals or services and contribute to it in some way.

6   Outline the importance of creativity, critical thinking, and the technology revolution in marketing.

Creativity produces original ideas, while critical thinking determines the authenticity, accuracy, and worth of any information, knowledge, claims, or arguments. These two processes combine to develop innovation and analyze the best course of action for a firm. Technology is the business application of knowledge based on scientific discoveries, inventions, and innovations. Interactive technologies allow marketers direct communication with customers, permit more meaningful exchanges, and put the customer in control.

7 Explain the shift from transaction-based marketing to relationship marketing.

Relationship marketing represents a dramatic change in the way companies interact with customers. The focus on relationships gives a firm new opportunities to gain a competitive edge by moving customers up a loyalty ladder from new customers to regular purchasers and then to loyal supporters and advocates. Over the long term, this relationship may be translated to the lifetime value of a customer. Organizations may form partnerships—called *strategic alliances*—to create a competitive advantage. These alliances may involve product development, raising awareness, and other activities.

8 Identify the universal functions of marketing.

Marketing is responsible for eight universal functions, divided into three categories: (1) exchange functions (buying and selling); (2) physical distribution (transporting and storing); and (3) facilitating functions (standardization and grading, financing, risk taking, and securing market information).

9 Demonstrate the relationship between ethical business practices, social responsibility, and marketplace success.

Ethics are moral standards of behavior expected by a society. Companies that promote ethical behavior and social responsibility usually produce increased employee loyalty and a better public image. This image often pays off in customer growth, since many buyers want to associate themselves with—and be customers of—such firms. Social responsibility involves marketing philosophies, policies, procedures, and actions whose primary objective is the enhancement of society. These actions also generally promote a firm's public image.

✓ *assessment check* **answers**

1.1 Define *marketing* and explain how it creates utility.

Marketing is an organizational function and a set of processes for creating, communicating and delivering value to customers and for managing customer relationships in ways that benefit the organization and its stakeholders. It creates time, place, and ownership utilities.

1.2 What three factors have forced marketers to embrace a global marketplace?

International agreements are being negotiated in attempts to expand trade among nations. The growth of technology is bringing previously isolated countries into the marketplace. The interdependence of the world's economies is now a reality.

2.1 What is the major distinction between the production era and the sales era?

During the production era, businesspeople believed that quality products would sell themselves. But during the sales era, emphasis was placed on selling—persuading people to buy.

2.2 What is the marketing concept?

The marketing concept is a company-wide consumer orientation with the objective of achieving long-term success.

2.3 Describe the relationship era of marketing.

The relationship era focuses on building long-term, value-added relationships over time with customers and suppliers.

3.1 What is marketing myopia?

Marketing myopia is management's failure to recognize the scope of a company's business.

✓ *assessment check* **answers**

3.2   Give an example of how a firm can avoid marketing myopia.

A firm can find innovative ways to reach new markets with existing goods and services.

4.1   What is the most obvious distinction between a not-for-profit organization and a commercial organization?

The biggest distinction between for-profit and not-for-profit organizations is the bottom line—whether an organization is judged by its profitability.

4.2   Why do for-profit and not-for-profit organizations sometimes form alliances?

For-profits and not-for-profits may form alliances to promote each other's causes and services. For-profits may do so as part of their social responsibility programs.

5.1   Identify the five major categories of nontraditional marketing.

The five categories of nontraditional marketing are person, place, cause, event, and organization marketing.

5.2   Give an example of a way in which two or more of these categories might overlap.

Overlap can occur in many ways. An organization might use a person to promote its cause or event. Two organizations might use one marketing effort to promote an event and a place—for example, NBC Sports and the National Thoroughbred Racing Association combining to promote the Kentucky Derby at Churchill Downs.

6.1   Define *creativity* and *critical thinking*.

Creativity produces original ideas or knowledge. Critical thinking is the process of determining the authenticity, accuracy, and worth of information, knowledge, claims, or arguments.

6.2   Why are both of these attributes important for marketers?

Creativity and critical thinking are important for marketers because they generate new ideas and then use discipline to analyze the best course of action.

6.3   Why is interactive marketing an important tool for marketers?

Interactive marketing technologies create direct communication with customers, allow larger exchanges, and put the customer in control.

7.1   How does relationship marketing give companies a competitive edge?

Relationship marketing can move customers up a loyalty ladder, generating repeat sales and long-term relationships.

7.2   What is a strategic alliance?

A strategic alliance is a partnership formed between two organizations to create a competitive advantage.

8.1   Which two marketing functions represent exchange functions?

Buying and selling are exchange functions.

8.2   Which two functions represent physical distribution functions?

Transporting and storing are physical distribution functions.

assessment check **answers**

8.3 Which four functions are facilitating functions?

The facilitating functions are standardization and grading, financing, risk taking, and securing market information.

9.1 Define *ethics*.

Ethics are moral standards of behavior expected by a society.

9.2 What is *social responsibility*?

Social responsibility involves marketing philosophies, policies, procedures, and actions whose primary objective is the enhancement of society.

MARKETING TERMS YOU NEED TO KNOW

utility 5

marketing 7

exchange process 8

consumer orientation 9

marketing concept 10

relationship marketing 10

marketing myopia 11

person marketing 14

place marketing 15

cause marketing 16

event marketing 16

organization marketing 17

strategic alliance 22

OTHER IMPORTANT MARKETING TERMS

production orientation 9

sales orientation 9

seller's market 9

buyer's market 9

bottom line 13

creativity 17

critical thinking 18

technology 18

interactive marketing 19

Internet protocol television (IPTV) 20

broadband technology 20

wireless technology 20

mobile marketing 20

transaction-based marketing 21

lifetime value of a customer 21

buzz marketing 22

wholesalers 23

exchange functions 23

physical distribution functions 23

facilitating functions 23

ethics 24

social responsibility 24

ASSURANCE OF LEARNING REVIEW

1. Identify the four types of utility, and give an example of each.
2. What condition in the marketplace gave rise to the need for a consumer orientation by businesses after World War II?
3. Define *relationship marketing* and describe how it fits into the marketing concept.
4. Why do not-for-profit organizations need to engage in marketing efforts?
5. Give an example of how Big Apple Bagels could use one or more of the nontraditional marketing techniques to promote the opening of a new franchise.
6. What might be some of the benefits of mobile marketing for firms that use it to reach out to consumers?
7. Describe the significance of the shift from transaction-based marketing to relationship marketing. When does relationship building begin?
8. Identify the two exchange functions of marketing and explain why they are important to the overall marketing program.
9. How does the physical distribution function create utility?
10. How do ethics and social responsibility help a firm achieve marketplace success?

PROJECTS AND TEAMWORK EXERCISES

1. Consider each of the following firms and describe how the firm's goods and/or services can create different types of utility. If necessary, go online to the company's Web site to learn more about it. You can do this alone or in a team.
   a. Olive Garden, Red Robin, Chili's, or another restaurant chain
   b. Snapfish or other online digital photo service
   c. Busch Gardens
   d. eBay
   e. Supervalu supermarkets

2. With a classmate, choose a U.S.-based company whose products you think will do well in certain markets overseas. Suggestions include Pizza Hut, Cuts Fitness (for Men) or Curves (for Women), iSold It, Burton Snowboards, or American Eagle Outfitters. The company can be anything from a music group to a clothing retailer—anything that interests you. Then write a plan for how you would target and communicate with overseas markets.

3. Choose a company that interests you from the following list, or select one of your own. Research the company online, through business magazines, or through other sources to learn what seems to be the scope of its business. Write a brief description of the company's scope of business as it is now. Then describe strategies for avoiding marketing myopia, expanding the company's scope of business over

the next ten years. Use your creativity and critical-thinking skills to come up with ideas.
   a. DHL (delivery service)
   b. Carnival Cruise Lines
   c. Olympus
   d. E*Trade
   e. Apple Computer

4. With a classmate, choose one of the following not-for-profit organizations. Then come up with a for-profit firm with which you think your organization could form a strategic alliance. Create a presentation—an ad, a poster, or the like—illustrating and promoting the partnership.
   a. U.S. Postal Service
   b. Make-a-Wish Foundation
   c. Habitat for Humanity
   d. American Cancer Society
   e. American Kennel Club

5. With a classmate, choose one of the following for-profit organizations. Then create a presentation using person, place, cause, event, or organization marketing to promote its products.
   a. MasterCard
   b. L'Oréal Paris
   c. Trek bicycles
   d. T-Mobile
   e. Subway

CRITICAL-THINKING EXERCISES

1. How does an organization create a customer?
2. How can marketers use interactive marketing to convert needs to wants and ultimately build long-term relationships with customers?
3. Why is utility such an important feature of marketing?
4. What benefits—monetary and nonmonetary—do social responsibility programs bring to a business?

5. Why is determining the lifetime value of a customer an important analysis for a company to make?
6. Why is it important for a firm to establish high ethical standards for its business practices? What role do you think marketers play in implementing these high standards?

ETHICS EXERCISE

While you are being interviewed for a job as a marketer for a large company that manufactures boxed, prepared meals—such as macaroni and cheese or chicken with biscuits—the interviewer steps outside the office. From where you are sitting, you can see a stack of papers on the interviewer's desk that contains advertisements by a competitor who makes similar products. You have an interview scheduled with the competitor for the following week.

1. Would you take a quick look at the ads—and any accompanying marketing notes—while the interviewer is out of the office? Why or why not?
2. In your next interview, would you tell the competitor that you saw the ads? Why or why not?
3. When the interviewer returns, would you mention the ads and offer your own commentary on them? Why or why not?

INTERNET EXERCISES

1. **Exploring the AMA's Web site.** The American Marketing Association's Web site contains lots of useful and interesting information for students. One section is devoted to careers. Visit the AMA's Web site (http://www.marketingpower.com), click on *Marketing Jobs and Career Services*, and then click on Career Strategies and Tips. Answer the following questions:

   a. According to a recent survey of hiring managers, what is the best way for a job seeker to follow up after he or she submits a résumé?

   b. What is the primary means of communication used by managers today?

   c. What are three dos and don'ts for attending a business luncheon?

2. **Job outlook for marketing professionals.** The U.S. Bureau of Labor Statistics compiles data about occupations and makes forecasts concerning future employment growth. Visit the BLS Web site (http://www.bls.gov) and click on *Occupational Outlook Handbook*. Click on *Management* and then *Advertising, Marketing, Promotions, Public Relations, and Sales Managers*. Review the material and answer the following questions:

   a. What are the three significant points about the outlook for those considering a career in marketing?

   b. Of the total employed as managers in the various marketing-related occupations, how many are employed as sales managers? Which industry (or industries) employs the largest number of sales managers?

   c. What is the outlook for growth in the various marketing-related occupations over the next few years?

Note: Internet Web addresses change frequently. If you don't find the exact site listed, you may need to access the organization's home page and search from there or use a search engine such as Google.

CASE 1.1   Golfers Are Joining the Hybrid Club

If you're a golfer, you know the difference between a wood and an iron. They're both clubs, but a fairway wood is the club you normally use to hit the ball long distances. An iron is used for greater accuracy. Golfers have their favorite clubs—those they feel confident will blast them out of sand traps or pitch them onto the green or just know they can hit straight when the pressure is on. Over the years, they may exchange a putter or replace a worn driver, but they remain loyal to clubs that fit their swing and particular brand of game. The only way they'll change is if they know with certainty that a new club will significantly improve their game.

Recently, some golf club manufacturers have begun to stir this devotion up. Companies such as Calloway, Taylor-Made, Ping, and Nike Golf have introduced hybrid clubs—clubs designed to capture the best features of both fairway wood and iron. Manufacturers have shifted the center of gravity in the hybrid to the back and bottom of the club. This helps launch the ball high into the air. The flat face gives the ball a spin, allowing it to stop faster and with greater accuracy. But figuring out the technology was just the first challenge for these firms. Getting golfers to switch is another game altogether. Marketers have found ways to use different types of marketing to get their message across to golfers.

Celebrities can do a lot to spark the popularity of a new golf product. So manufacturers have tapped celebrity golfers from around the world to promote the hybrid clubs.

Eight-time LPGA champion Rachel Hetherington of Australia touts the benefits of her Hogan Edge CFT hybrid club in an interview for *Golf for Women* magazine. "My hybrid has transformed the long-iron shots I used to hate," she says. Events that feature charitable causes and golf stars have been a hit as well. At a recent benefit golf tournament sponsored by the Children's Aid Foundation—which raised nearly a quarter of a million dollars—ladies had the opportunity to try out some of the hybrid clubs under the eye of LPGA golf star Sandra Post. A Canadian firm held nearly six months' worth of weekly sweepstakes in which it gave away hybrid clubs. Magazines such as *Golf Digest* and Web sites such as PGATOUR.com give constant reviews and updates on the new equipment as well.

As hybrids move on to their next generation, manufacturers are always listening to what their customers want. In developing its Slingshot Tour Hybrid, the Nike Golf design team incorporated suggestions from the players themselves. "The mandate from the players was that it would need to have clean lines, compact shape, and minimal offset," stated Nike Golf. The firm listened—and then staff members went out on the links with the new clubs and played the PGA Tour season.

Marketers are hoping that amateurs will follow the pros' lead and try the hybrids. "Hybrid clubs have helped make the game more enjoyable and playable, for many more golfers," says Dan Murphy, director of marketing for precept Golf. "And that goes both for average players and better players." More enjoyment may mean more players and more games played, and ultimately more hybrid clubs sold.

Questions for Critical Thinking

1. Describe the role of relationship marketing in the making the hybrid clubs successful in the marketplace.
2. What type of strategic alliances could golf equipment manufacturers use to promote their hybrids?

Sources: "Golf Equipment," Golf Equipment Source, **http://www. golfequipmentsource.com**, accessed February 2, 2006; "Adams IDEA Hybrid Irons Sweepstakes," The Golf Channel, **http://www.thegolfchannel. com**, accessed February 2, 2006; "Women's Golf Classic Scores a Great Day for a Great Cause," Children's Aid Foundation, **http://www.cafdn.org**, accessed February 2, 2006; Chuck Stogel, "Companies Expanding Lineups to Suit Hybrid Club Buzz," PGATOUR.com, **http://www.pgatour.com**, accessed February 2, 2006; "Nike Golf's Slingshot Franchise," Golf Business Wire, January 11, 2006, **http://www.golfbusinesswire.com**; E. Michael Johnson, "Help Is on the Way," *Golf Digest,* March/April 2005, **http://www.golfdigest.com**; Rachel Hetherington with Stina Sternberg, "5 Ways to Use Your Hybrid Club," *Golf Digest,* March/April 2005, **http://www.golfdigest.com**.

VIDEO CASE 1.2 Harley–Davidson Keeps Riders Coming Back

The written video case on Harley-Davidson appears on page VC-2. The recently filmed Harley-Davidson video is designed to expand and highlight the concepts in this chapter and the concepts and questions covered in the written video case.

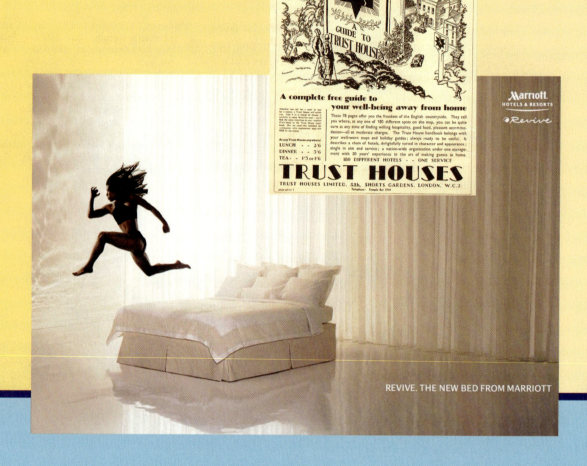

REVIVE. THE NEW BED FROM MARRIOTT

Westin Starts the Bed Wars

What's the first thing most people do when they check into a hotel room? They test the bed, of course. And hotels are finally realizing why that initial impression is so important to establishing a good relationship with guests. Whether they're traveling for business or pleasure, what people really want is a good night's sleep, and they're willing to pay for it.

Recently, after reviewing mattresses and pillows for over a year and recruiting staff and guests to test 50 different beds in one of its ballrooms, Westin Hotels & Resorts decided to offer the Heavenly Bed, featuring a Simmons mattress with a pillow top and 900 individual coils. Luxurious linens, pillows, and duvets completed the sleep set. The result? The first guest to sleep in a Heavenly Bed begged to be allowed to buy it the following morning, and that request was followed by dozens more within the week.

Soon Westin decided to give guests what they wanted, and the company began offering the Heavenly Bed for retail sale, complete with almost a dozen high-quality accessories such as a down blanket, sheets, pillows, bed skirt, and duvet. The response was eye opening. About 3,000 beds were purchased through catalog and online sales at $3,115 for a queen-size bed and $3,615 for a king. This success prompted Westin to partner with Nordstrom's to sell the bed in 48 of its stores nationwide and by special order in others. One industry expert calls the Heavenly Bed "one of the great marketing ideas in lodging in the last decade." Westin expects sales of the beds and separate purchases of sheet-and-pillow sets to top $8 million a year.

"We're the first hotel company to do something like this," says Westin's senior vice president. "Being first into the market is a huge advantage. We feel good that, although people are trying to duplicate what we've done, nobody has reached the level that we're at after five years."

That's not for lack of trying, however. Every major hotel chain has jumped to upgrade its beds and linens in properties around the world, investing millions of dollars in playing catch-up. Radisson has new custom-designed Sleep Number beds and new bedding. Hyatt has adopted pillow-top mattresses. Marriott spent nearly $190 million on upgraded beds

Strategic Planning and the Marketing Process

Chapter Objectives

1 Distinguish between strategic planning and tactical planning.

2 Explain how marketing plans differ at various levels in an organization.

3 Identify the steps in the marketing planning process.

4 Describe successful planning tools and techniques, including Porter's Five Forces model, first and second mover strategies, SWOT analysis, and the strategic window.

5 Identify the basic elements of a marketing strategy.

6 Describe the environmental characteristics that influence strategic decisions.

7 Describe the methods for marketing planning, including business portfolio analysis and the BCG matrix.

and linens alone and dubbed their new product the "Revive" bed. The Windsor Hotel in Melbourne, Australia, offers guests a choice of ten different types of pillows, including an aromatherapy model. Hyatt has introduced the Grand Bed, with a 13½-inch pillow-top mattress, and luxury-quality linens. Crowne Plaza sells its Serta beds online, while Hilton and Marriott are offering sets of linens for sale at their Web sites.

But, fearing being caught napping again, the competition has introduced even more sleep-inducing extras to offer weary guests. Crowne Plaza has separate floors called "quiet zones," where no housekeeping services are conducted before 10 A.M. and no children are lodged. The company also hired a sleep doctor to advise it on guests' relaxation needs, and it now offers a sleep kit including eye mask, earplugs, night light, lavender aromatherapy spray, and a sleep CD. Hilton's rooms have connection cables for MP3 players such as the iPod, and even moderate

and budget chains such as Red Roof Inn and Best Western are offering hypoallergenic pillows and triple sheeting on their beds. The bed wars have even spread to the cruise industry, in which Carnival, Holland America, Royal Caribbean, Windstar, and Radisson Seven Seas are battling it out with upgraded mattresses, luxury linens, free robes and iPods, and upscale toiletries.

evolution *of a* brand

Westin Hotels & Resorts made a bold strategic move to differentiate itself from the competition when it introduced the Heavenly Bed. The company spent more than a year researching 50 different beds to come up with the perfect combination of mattress, linens, pillows, and duvets for its guests. The change was an instant hit with guests, some of whom wanted to buy one for their homes. Other hotel chains soon followed Westin's lead, introducing their own upgraded beds and other products to pamper guests with a terrific night's sleep.

- The Heavenly Bed's introduction changed customers' perceptions of the hotel industry. Being the first to market a product can be risky, but other chains noticed Westin's success and quickly entered the luxury bed race with their own offerings. Do some research on Westin Hotels & Resorts and the Heavenly Bed. Is the Heavenly Bed still first in the market? How is Westin competing in the hospitality industry overall? Have the Heavenly Bed's retail sales continued to be strong? Has the company modified the product since it was introduced?

Meanwhile, hotels are tossing out their stain-hiding bedspreads and revving up their laundries in recognition of what guests have always known—that only white linens and comforters can really be as clean as home. [1]

Chapter Overview

- More and more women are buying trucks. Should we add features to our trucks that are designed specifically for our female customers?

- We have fewer customers eating at our restaurant on weekends. Should we revamp our menu? Lower our prices? Use special promotions? Update the dining room décor?

- Recent marketing research shows that we are not reaching our customer target—consumers in their early to mid-20s. Should we consider another advertising agency?

Marketers face strategic questions every day—planning strategy is a critical part of their job. The marketplace changes continually in response to changes in consumer tastes and expectations, technological developments, competitors' actions, economic trends, and political and legal events, as well as product innovations and pressures from suppliers and distributors. Although the causes of these changes often lie outside a marketer's control, effective planning can anticipate many of the changes. Westin Hotels saw a market need for comfortable, luxurious sleep, and the hotel chain devised a plan to offer it. When the concept took off, Westin found a way to let customers take the benefits home.

This chapter provides an important foundation for analyzing all aspects of marketing by demonstrating the importance of gathering reliable information to create an effective plan. These activities provide a structure for a firm to use its unique strengths. Marketing planning identifies the markets a company can best serve as well as the most appropriate mix of approaches to satisfy the customers in those markets. While this chapter focuses on planning, we will examine in greater detail the task of marketing research and decision making in Chapter 8.

MARKETING PLANNING: THE BASIS FOR STRATEGY AND TACTICS

Everyone plans. We plan which courses we want to take, which movie we want to see, and which outfit to wear to a party. We plan where we want to live and what career we want to pursue. Marketers plan as well. **Planning** is the process of anticipating future events and conditions and of determining the best way to achieve organizational objectives. Of course, before marketing planning can even begin, an organization must define its objectives. Planning is a continuous process that includes identifying objectives and then determining the actions through which a firm can attain those objectives. The planning process creates a blueprint for marketers, executives, production staff, and everyone else in the organization to follow for achieving organizational objectives. It also defines checkpoints so that people within the organization can compare actual performance with expectations to indicate whether current activities are moving the organization toward its objectives.

Planning is important for both large and small companies. Microsoft CEO Steve Ballmer recently announced the company's biggest reorganization in several years, planned to help the company respond faster to the never-ending changes in the technology marketplace. Its seven divisions have been forged into three new groups—Platform Products & Services, which includes Windows; the Business Group, which includes Office and Microsoft Business Solutions; and the Entertainment & Devices division, which includes Xbox. "Our goal in making these changes," Ballmer told employees, "is to enable Microsoft to achieve greater agility in managing the incredible growth ahead and executing our software-based services strategy."[2]

At the other end of the size spectrum, newlyweds Jennifer Melton and Brennan Johnson started their business, called Cloud Star, with a simple plan. Jennifer began making their German shepherd's food at home when she realized that the pet, adopted from a shelter, had severe allergies to commercial dog foods. After getting an overwhelmingly positive response to their home-baked treats at animal shelter bake sales, Melton and Johnson began to market their own line of bake-at-home dog treats, called Buddy Biscuits, that were free of many of the ingredients often found in commercial foods. Within a few years, they added dog shampoos and conditioners to their product line. They base much of their planning on feedback from customers. "Most of our growth and our decisions for which area we wanted to go into have been from listening to our customers and what they want from us," explains Melton.[3]

Marketing planning—implementing planning activities devoted to achieving marketing objectives—establishes the basis for any marketing strategy. Product lines, pricing decisions, selection of appropriate distribution channels, and decisions relating to promotional campaigns all depend on plans formulated within the marketing organization.

An important trend in marketing planning centers on relationship marketing, which is a firm's

planning Process of anticipating future events and conditions and of determining the best way to achieve organizational objectives.

marketing planning Implementing planning activities devoted to achieving marketing objectives.

DES JENSON/BLOOMBERG NEWS/LANDOV

Apple Computer's long-range plans for its music service included broadening its market to provide software for non-Apple PCs. So Hewlett-Packard PCs now come already loaded with Apple's iTunes software.

effort to develop long-term, cost-effective links with individual customers and suppliers for mutual benefit. Good relationships with customers can arm a firm with vital strategic weapons, as home improvement retailers such as Home Depot and Lowe's have become aware. The "Marketing Success" feature describes their battle to forge new relationships with the rising number of women do-it-yourselfers.

Many companies now include relationship-building goals and strategies in their plans. Relationship marketers frequently maintain databases to track customer preferences. These marketers may also manipulate product spreadsheets to answer what-if questions related to prices and marketing performance. In the business-to-business marketplace, software giant Oracle hopes to save its customers tens of millions of dollars every year on expensive consulting services. By acquiring Siebel Systems, a maker of customer-relationship-management software, Oracle closed a gap in its product line and hopes to become the top one-stop supplier of business software applications in accounting, sales, and human resources departments. With Siebel's software and Oracle's databases and applications servers, "existing Oracle customers are going to get much better CRM software out of this," says one industry expert. [4]

 Distinguish between strategic planning and tactical planning.

strategic planning
Process of determining an organization's primary objectives and adopting courses of action that will achieve these objectives.

tactical planning
Planning that guides the implementation of activities specified in the strategic plan.

STRATEGIC PLANNING VERSUS TACTICAL PLANNING

Planning is often classified on the basis of its scope or breadth. Some extremely broad plans focus on long-range organizational objectives that will significantly affect the firm for five or more years. Other more targeted plans cover the objectives of individual business units over shorter periods.

Strategic planning can be defined as the process of determining an organization's primary objectives and adopting courses of action that will achieve these objectives. This process includes, of course, allocation of necessary resources. The word *strategy* dates back to a Greek term meaning "the general's art." Strategic planning has a critical impact on a firm's destiny because it provides long-term direction for its decision makers.

Strategic planning is complemented by **tactical planning,** which guides the implementation of activities specified in the strategic plan. Unlike strategic plans, tactical plans typically address shorter-term actions that focus on current and near-future activities that a firm must complete to implement its larger strategies. As Eastman Kodak's traditional camera and film business continues its sharp decline, CEO Antonio Perez faces the challenge of getting through a few difficult years of plummeting sales, cutbacks, and layoffs while implementing a new strategy, focusing on the company's core strength in digital imaging. "Digital imaging . . . is the DNA of the company and what we really do well—better than anyone else in the world," says Perez. "We eliminated any other business where we didn't think we could be No. 1 or 2." Tactics that support the new strategy

✓ assessment check

1. Define *planning*.
2. Give an example of strategic planning and tactical planning.

 marketing success   Home Depot versus Lowe's

Background. Home Depot and Lowe's—the nation's two biggest hardware and appliance retailers—are long-time rivals, particularly in the do-it-yourself market, where men have traditionally been the biggest customers. Female customers in both stores tended to buy their husbands tools so they could use them around the house. But changes in society brought changes in customer needs.

The Challenge. With recent shifts in gender roles and the rise in female-headed households, marketers wanted to reassess the home improvement market. A survey conducted by Sears confirmed that more than 80 percent of female homeowners polled not only admire women who are skilled in home

repair but also feel independent themselves when they work with tools. Other marketers became aware of the trend, too. "We took a step back and listened to our female customers," says a Lowe's spokesperson. Wider aisles, brighter lighting, and clear displays helped attract women to Lowe's stores, as did free once-a-month how-to seminars and "recipe cards" with instructions for weekend projects. But Home Depot wasn't as quick to respond and lagged behind.

The Strategy. Beginning with a huge face-lift at all its stores, including better lighting, brighter signs, and a bigger selection of appliances, Home Depot has followed Lowe's lead by also attracting women to its stores. "I see

include developing the first Wi-Fi camera and the first dual-lens digital camera, and partnering with Motorola to build better camera phones. As for traditional photography, says Perez, "We will always sell film as long as there are customers to buy it."[5]

PLANNING AT DIFFERENT ORGANIZATIONAL LEVELS

2 Explain how marketing plans differ at various levels in an organization.

Planning is a major responsibility for every manager, so managers at all organizational levels devote portions of their workdays to planning. However, the amount of time spent on planning activities and the types of planning typically vary. Interruptions, such as all managers face every day, are one of the great impediments to planning. Check the "Etiquette Tips for Marketing Professionals" feature for some tactful ways to minimize interruptions in your workday.

Top management—the board of directors, chief executive officers (CEOs), chief operating officers (COOs), and functional vice presidents, such as chief marketing officers—spend greater proportions of their time planning than do middle-level and supervisory-level managers. Also, top managers usually focus their planning on long-range strategic issues. In contrast, middle-level managers—such as advertising executives, regional sales managers, and marketing research directors—tend to focus on operational planning, which includes creating and implementing tactical plans for their own units. Supervisors often develop specific programs to

COURTESY OF HOME DEPOT

To help cement strong relationships with homeowners who *don't* want to do it themselves, Home Depot offers not only lumber, tiles, cabinets, and appliances but also installation through its network of licensed and insured tradespeople.

a power drill in my future," said one woman attending her third Home Depot class, this time on power tools. Some 200,000 women have attended Home Depot Do It Herselfer workshops, and many types of training sessions and seminars have been well-attended weekly or monthly offerings at the stores.

The Outcome. Drawing more women into its stores has helped Home Depot in several ways. Its share of the home appliance market has tripled to 9 percent, for instance, and it continues to work at changing customers' perceptions of the chain from a warehouse to a retail outlet. Other big retailers such as Sears are getting into the act. Although these stores are all very careful not to pander to women or squeeze out male shoppers, at least one firm, Barbara K Enterprises, has benefited from the change in the industry—it is marketing a new line of tools designed especially for women.

Sources: Lowe's Web site, **http://www.lowes.com**, accessed February 24, 2006; Miriam Gottfried, "Repair Job," *Forbes*, December 26, 2005, p. 132; Michelle Kearns, "Lowe's Takes on Home Depot for Home-Improvement Dollar," *Buffalo News*, October 9, 2005, **http://www.buffalo.com**; Amy Tsao, "Retooling Home Improvement," *BusinessWeek*, February 14, 2005, **http://www.businessweek.com**.

Etiquette Tips for Marketing Professionals

How to Handle Interruptions

Managers at all levels of an organization are interrupted every few minutes, every day. Interruptions are part of a manager's day that can't be avoided. Because they're estimated to use up more than one-fourth of every employee's workday, however, interruptions can make planning very difficult. Here are some suggestions for dealing with them tactfully.

1. If someone stops by just to chat, say something friendly but unmistakable such as, "I'm sorry I don't have time to talk right now. Can we catch up later?"

2. If your office is located near the copier or water cooler where people gather, try turning your desk away from the doorway or getting a partition, a file cabinet, or even a large plant to shield you from view.

3. Remove extra chairs from your office or cubicle to make it a less inviting place for others to kill time.

4. Discourage visitors who linger too long by getting up and moving away from your desk, by picking up some work or positioning yourself in front of your computer, or even by excusing yourself to go to the restroom.

5. If someone who reports to you asks to see you and you must make time, but you can't do it immediately, acknowledge the person's request and its importance to both of you. Then suggest a time that works for you. For instance, "Seth, I agree it's important for us to discuss this. I really have to finish this e-mail before noon. Let's meet in your office at one o'clock."

6. If your boss asks to see you and you're in the middle of something, use a similar strategy but let him or her choose the time. "Clare, I know that's a critical discussion we need to have. I'm trying to finish the e-mail you asked me to send to the sales staff by the noon deadline. Would you like me to finish that up, or should I put it off so we can meet now?"

7. If you really need a block of time without interruptions, ask your staff and co-workers to respect that time, forward phone calls, turn off your cell phone and pager, and if you have a door, close it.

8. If you must answer the phone, do it promptly, thank the person for calling, and get a callback number. Say, "I'm meeting with someone now, but I'll get back you right after the meeting," and be sure to do so.

9. Avoid creating interruptions for others by asking yourself before phoning them whether they really need to hear from you right now. If not, call later.

Sources: "Controlling Office Interruptions," Life Organizers.com, **http://www.lifeorganizers.com**, accessed February 9, 2006; "10 Easy-to-Learn Tips on Handling Interruptions," Performance.com, **http://www.superperformance.com**, accessed February 9, 2006; "Business Etiquette," Newspaper Association of America, **http://www.naa.org**, accessed October 7, 2005; Bob Lang, "Proper Business Etiquette for Using Electronic Communicating Devices," **http://www.baltimoremd.com**, accessed October 7, 2005; "Interruptions Cost $588B," *Red Herring*, September 8, 2005, **http://www.redherring.com**; "Peter Post," *Boston Globe*, July 31, 2005, **http://www.boston.com**.

meet goals in their areas of responsibility. Table 2.1 summarizes the types of planning undertaken at various organizational levels.

When it is most effective, the planning process includes input from a wide range of sources: employees, suppliers, and customers. Some marketing experts advocate developing a network of "influencers"—people who have influence over other people's opinions through authority, visibility, or expertise—to provide input and spread the word about company plans and products. Valuable input can come from almost anywhere. When De Beers, the diamond company, opened its first retail store in Manhattan recently, it held a huge opening party with nearly 1,000 celebrity guests. But before the party, a gathering of less than 150 very special and influential guests was held. "Some of the richest people in the world are in these rooms," said a De Beers jewelry expert who attended the party. "There are women here who would buy a $10,000 ring and forget about it in a week."[6]

 assessment check

1. How do marketing plans differ at different levels of the organization?

2. Why is it important to get input from others when planning?

table 2.1   Planning at Different Managerial Levels

MANAGEMENT LEVEL	TYPES OF PLANNING EMPHASIZED AT THIS LEVEL	EXAMPLES
Top Management		
Board of directors	Strategic planning	Organization-wide objectives; fundamental strategies; long-term plans; total budget
Chief executive officer (CEO)		
Chief operating officer (COO)		
Divisional vice presidents		
Middle Management		
General sales manager	Tactical planning	Quarterly and semiannual plans; divisional budgets; divisional policies and procedures
Business unit manager		
Director of marketing research		
Supervisory Management		
Regional sales manager	Operational planning	Daily and weekly plans; unit budgets; departmental rules and procedures
Supervisor—telemarketing office		

STEPS IN THE MARKETING PLANNING PROCESS

3 Identify the steps in the marketing planning process.

The marketing planning process begins at the corporate level with the definition of a firm's mission. It then determines its objectives, assesses its resources, and evaluates environmental risks and opportunities. Guided by this information, marketers within each business unit then formulate a marketing strategy, implement the strategy through operating plans, and gather feedback to monitor and adapt strategies when necessary. Figure 2.1 shows the basic steps in the process.

DEFINING THE ORGANIZATION'S MISSION AND OBJECTIVES

The planning process begins with defining the firm's **mission,** the essential purpose that differentiates the company from others. The mission statement specifies the organization's overall goals and operational scope and provides general guidelines for future management actions. Adjustments in this statement reflect changing business environments and management philosophies.

mission Essential purpose that differentiates one company from others.

figure 2.1

The Marketing Planning Process

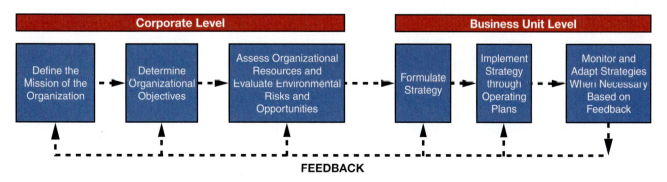

FEEDBACK

Although business writer Peter Drucker cautioned that an effective mission statement should be brief enough "to fit on a T-shirt," organizations typically define themselves with slightly longer statements. A statement may be lengthy and formal or brief and informal. Here are several examples:

- 3M: "To solve unsolved problems innovatively."

- Mary Kay Cosmetics: "To give unlimited opportunity to women."

- Merck: "To preserve and improve human life."

- Wal-Mart: "Always low prices."

- Intel: "To delight our customers, employees, and shareholders by relentlessly delivering the platform and technology advancements that become essential to the way we work and live."

- MD Anderson Cancer Center: "Making cancer history."

- Google: "To organize the world's information and make it universally accessible and useful."

An organization lays out its basic **objectives,** or goals, in its complete mission statement. These objectives guide development of supporting marketing objectives and plans. Soundly conceived objectives should state specific intentions such as the following:

- Generate a 10 percent profit over the next twelve months

- Attain a 20 percent share of the market by 2010

- Add 50 new stores within the next year

- Develop twelve new products in 24 months

- Expand operations to China by 2012

- Cut operating costs by 5 percent

ASSESSING ORGANIZATIONAL RESOURCES AND EVALUATING ENVIRONMENTAL RISKS AND OPPORTUNITIES

The third step of the marketing planning process is to assess an organization's strengths, weaknesses, and available opportunities. Organizational resources include the capabilities of the firm's production, marketing, finance, technology, and employees. An organization's planners pinpoint its strengths and weaknesses. Strengths help them set objectives, develop plans for meeting those objectives, and take advantage of marketing opportunities.

Chapter 3 will discuss environmental factors that affect marketing opportunities. Environmental effects can emerge both from within the organization and from the external environment. For example, the technological advances provided by the Internet have transformed how people communicate and do business around the world. In fact, the Internet itself has created entirely new categories of business.

FORMULATING, IMPLEMENTING, AND MONITORING A MARKETING STRATEGY

Once a firm's marketers figure out their company's best opportunities, they can develop a marketing plan designed to meet the overall objectives. A good marketing plan revolves around an efficient, flexible, and adaptable marketing strategy.

A **marketing strategy** is an overall, company-wide program for selecting a particular target market and then satisfying consumers in that market through a careful blending of the elements of the marketing mix—product, distribution, promotion, and price—each of which is a subset of the overall marketing strategy.

In the two final steps of the planning process, marketers put the marketing strategy into action; then they monitor performance to ensure that objectives are being achieved. Sometimes strategies need to be modified if the product's or company's actual performance is not in line with expected results. U.S. fast-food chains are discovering that although consumers say they want more nutritious meals when they eat out, they don't often follow through and order them. So Ruby Tuesday, the first chain to list nutrition information for every item on its menu, has eliminated a number of healthful new dishes from its heavily advertised Smart Eating program in the wake of lackluster sales. It moved calorie and fat information to the back of the menu, restored the large portions of fries and pasta it used to serve, and went back to promoting its big burgers. Other chains have scaled back as well. Says the chief concept officer for Burger King, "The gap between what [diners] say and what they do is just huge. Therein lies the challenge for business, because there is simply not enough behavior shift to build a business around."[7]

THE HERSHEY COMPANY

To meet consumers' often conflicting needs—for a sweet snack and healthful ingredients—Hershey Foods created its SnackBarz line. The Reese's, Hershey's, and S'mores bars combine the taste of the company's well-known snacks with ingredients containing calcium, iron, and vitamins.

 assessment check

1. Distinguish between an organization's mission and its objectives.
2. What is the importance of the final step in the marketing planning process?

SUCCESSFUL STRATEGIES: TOOLS AND TECHNIQUES

4 Describe successful planning tools and techniques, including Porter's Five Forces model, first and second mover strategies, SWOT analysis, and the strategic window.

We can identify a number of successful marketing planning tools and techniques. This section discusses four of them: Porter's Five Forces model, first and second mover strategies, SWOT analysis, and the strategic window. All planning strategies have the goal of creating a **sustainable competitive advantage** for a firm, in which other companies simply cannot provide the same value to their customers that the firm does—no matter how hard they try.

PORTER'S FIVE FORCES MODEL

A number of years ago, the renowned business strategist and one of the world's best-known business academics Michael E. Porter identified five competitive forces that influence planning strategies in a model called **Porter's Five Forces.** Porter later updated his model to include the impact of the Internet on the strategies that businesses use. As illustrated by Figure 2.2, the five forces are potential new entrants; bargaining power of buyers; bargaining power of suppliers; threat of substitute products; and rivalry among competitors.

Porter's Five Forces Model developed by strategy expert Michael Porter that identifies five competitive forces that influence planning strategies: the threat of new entrants, the bargaining power of buyers, the bargaining power of suppliers, the threat of substitute products, and rivalry among competitors.

figure 2.2

Porter's Five
Forces Model

Source: Adapted with
permission of The Free
Press, a division of Simon
& Schuster Adult Publishing
Group. From *Competitive
Strategy: Techniques for
Analyzing Industries and
Competitors* by Michael
E. Porter. Copyright ©
1980, 1998 by The Free
Press. All rights reserved.

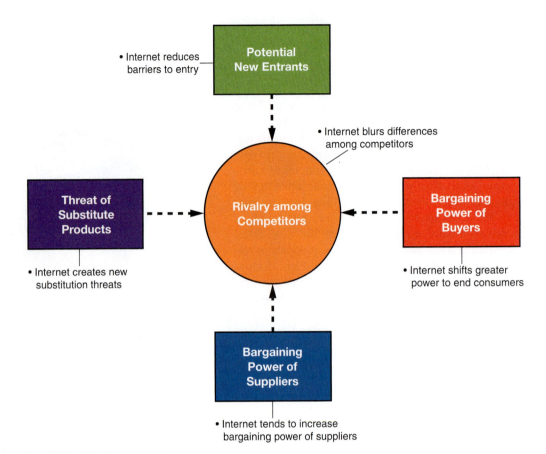

- Internet reduces barriers to entry

Potential New Entrants

- Internet blurs differences among competitors

Threat of Substitute Products

Rivalry among Competitors

Bargaining Power of Buyers

- Internet creates new substitution threats

- Internet shifts greater power to end consumers

Bargaining Power of Suppliers

- Internet tends to increase bargaining power of suppliers

The Internet has increased competition in many industries. Travel agents once had a stranglehold on the travel industry, but now consumers can set up their vacations directly through online services such as Expedia.

Potential new entrants are sometimes blocked by the cost or difficulty of entering a market. It is a lot more costly and complicated to begin building aircraft than it is to start up an Internet résumé service. In fact, the Internet has reduced the barriers to market entry in many industries.

If customers have considerable bargaining power, they can greatly influence a firm's strategy. The Internet can increase a customer's buying power by providing information that might not otherwise be easily accessible such as alternate suppliers and price comparisons. Before going to the showroom, for instance, car buyers can check out the true value of a trade-in at Web sites such as CarMax.com and research new-car costs at Edmunds.com.[8]

The number of suppliers available to a manufacturer or retailer affects their bargaining power. If a seafood restaurant in the Midwest has only one supplier of Maine lobsters, that supplier has significant bargaining power. But seafood restaurants along the coast of Maine have many lobster suppliers available, which gives their suppliers less bargaining power.

If customers have the opportunity to replace a company's products with goods or services from a competing firm or industry, the company's marketers may have to find a new market, change prices, or compete in other ways to maintain an advantage. Sometimes substitute products drive companies out of business altogether. That was the case for NYCD, a small record shop that was one of New York City's last independent stores selling new and used records and CDs. An instant hit when it opened in 1993, the store fell victim to several trends, the most influential of which was the increasing ease of music downloading. The store's owners knew the end had come when a Yellow Book saleswoman entered the store to try to sell them ad space. Her assistant picked up a CD from a display, and the saleswoman blurted out, "Oh, don't buy that. I'll burn you a copy at home."[9]

The four previous forces influence the rivalry among competitors. In addition, issues such as cost and differentiation or lack of differentiation of products—along with the Internet—influence the strategies that companies use to stand out from their competitors. With increased availability of information, which tends to level the playing field, rivalry heats up among competitors, who try to differentiate themselves from the crowd.

FIRST MOVER AND SECOND MOVER STRATEGIES

Some firms like to adopt a **first mover strategy**—attempting to capture the greatest market share and develop long-term relationships by being the first to enter the market with a product or service, as Westin Hotels did in the chapter-opening story about the Heavenly Bed. Being first may also refer to entering new markets with existing products or creating significant innovations that effectively turn an old product into a new one. Naturally, this strategy has its risks—companies that follow can learn from mistakes by first movers.[10] Apple has held firmly to the lead it established with its iTunes online music store, recently passing the 1 billion mark in downloads purchased. That success grew directly from Apple's leading the way in the market for digital music players, in which the iPod still dominates, with about 78 percent of the U.S. market and about half the market worldwide. "With each passing year since [iTunes] was introduced," says an industry authority, "Apple has continued to expand its lead both on the hardware side and the service side. It's certainly become more difficult for its competitors."[11]

On the other hand, Apple failed terribly with another first mover introduction, its Newton handheld computer, while other firms overtook the lead in the market. Businesses often thrive on a **second mover strategy,** observing closely the innovations of first movers and then improving on them to gain advantage in the marketplace. Target has benefited greatly from being next in line to industry leader Wal-Mart, for instance. Wal-Mart's every move—new store openings, employee benefits packages, and squeezing suppliers—is scrutinized in the press. But Target, whose benefits are not much different from Wal-Mart's and which also wrings tough concessions from suppliers, has a much lower profile in the public's mind and generates less controversy.[12]

SWOT ANALYSIS

An important strategic planning tool, **SWOT analysis,** helps planners compare internal organizational strengths and weaknesses with external opportunities and threats. (SWOT is an acronym for *strengths, weaknesses, opportunities,* and *threats.*) This form of analysis provides managers with a critical view of the organization's internal and external environments and helps them evaluate the firm's fulfillment of its basic mission.

DRINK MORE WATER

AQUAFINA
Pure Water · Perfect Taste

COURTESY OF PEPSI-COLA NORTH AMERICA

AQUAFINA is a registered trademark of PepsiCo, Inc.

AQUAFINA
Pure Water · Perfect Taste
www.aquafina.com

PepsiCo marketers have focused the company's strategy on its entire product lineup, including alternative beverage brands, such as Aquafina, and snack products.

first mover strategy
Theory advocating that the company that is first to offer a product in a marketplace will be the long-term market winner.

second mover strategy
Theory that advocates observing closely the innovations of first movers and then improving on them to gain advantage in the marketplace.

SWOT analysis Analysis that helps planners compare internal organizational strengths and weaknesses with external opportunities and threats.

Briefly
Speaking

"Innovation is the central issue in economic prosperity."

—Michael Porter (b. 1947)
American management theorist and writer

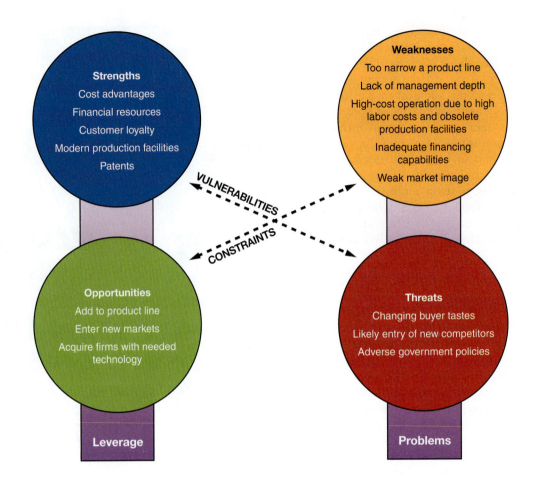

A company's strengths reflect its **core competencies**—what it does well. Core competencies are capabilities that customers value and competitors find difficult to duplicate. As Figure 2.3 shows, matching an internal strength with an external opportunity produces a situation known as *leverage*. Marketers face a problem when environmental threats attack their organization's weaknesses. Planners anticipate constraints when internal weaknesses or limitations prevent their organization from taking advantage of opportunities. These internal weaknesses can create vulnerabilities for a company—environmental threats to its organizational strength.

SBC Telecommunications hoped to overcome the weakness of slow revenue growth by purchasing competitor AT&T. One strength the combined company will leverage is its new name, AT&T, whose history in telecommunications stretches back more than 120 years. AT&T was recently named the most admired U.S. telecommunications company by *Fortune* magazine. The new AT&T, which replaces Verizon as the largest U.S. phone company by sales, will exploit a huge opportunity and expand its global network to Europe, the Middle East, Africa, and Latin America. AT&T is offering wireless services in more than 125 countries and has earmarked more than $8 billion to invest in the expansion. At the same time, AT&T is partnering with Yahoo! to capitalize on another opportunity closer to home. The two companies will let users of Cingular wireless phones access the photos, e-mail, instant messages, and address books stored in their Yahoo! accounts. In this venture AT&T faces the threat of competition from a joint venture by Google and EarthLink to offer free wireless Internet access in San Francisco. AT&T is still not finished with its merger plans; the company is acquiring another former Baby Bell company, BellSouth.[13]

strategic window Limited periods during which the key requirements of a market and the particular competencies of a firm best fit together.

THE STRATEGIC WINDOW

The success of products is also influenced by conditions in the market. Professor Derek Abell has suggested the term **strategic window** to define the limited periods during which the key requirements of a market and the particular competencies of a firm best fit together.[14] The view through a strategic window shows planners a way to relate potential opportunities to company capabilities. Such a view requires a thorough analysis of (1) current and projected external environmental conditions, (2) current and projected internal company capabilities, and (3) how, whether, and when the firm can feasibly reconcile environmental conditions and company capabilities by implementing one or more marketing strategies.

"China has begun to enter the age of mass car consumption. This is a great and historic advance," says China's state-run news agency, Xinhua. In just a few years, demand for cars has soared in China, and the government has funneled the equivalent of billions of dollars into building highways; only the United States has more miles of motorways. Carmakers at home and abroad are watching this strategic window carefully. "China is going to become the second-largest market in the world sometime over the next two or three years," says the head of China distribution for Ford. After that, he believes, it could be the world's biggest market.[15]

 assessment check

1. Briefly explain each of Porter's Five Forces.
2. What are the benefits and drawbacks of a first mover strategy?
3. What are the four components of the SWOT analysis? What is a strategic window?

ELEMENTS OF A MARKETING STRATEGY

5 Identify the basic elements of a marketing strategy.

Success for a product in the marketplace—whether it is a tangible good, a service, a cause, a person, a place, or an organization—depends on an effective marketing strategy. It's one thing to develop a great product, but if customers don't get the message about it, the product will die. An effective marketing strategy reaches the right buyers at the right time, persuades them to try the product, and develops a strong relationship with them over time. The basic elements of a marketing strategy consist of (1) the target market and (2) the marketing mix variables of product, distribution, promotion, and price that combine to satisfy the needs of the target market. The outer circle in Figure 2.4 lists environmental characteristics that provide the framework within which marketing strategies are planned.

THE TARGET MARKET

A customer-driven organization begins its overall strategy with a detailed description of its **target market:** the group of people toward whom the firm decides to direct its marketing efforts and ultimately its merchandise. Kohl's department stores serve a target market of consumers purchasing for themselves and their families. Other companies, such as Boeing, market most of their products to business buyers such as American Airlines and government purchasers. Still other firms provide goods and services to retail and wholesale buyers. In every instance, however, marketers pinpoint their target markets as accurately as possible. Although the concept of dividing markets into specific segments is discussed in more detail in Chapter 9, it's important to understand the idea of targeting a market from the outset. That's what Toyota did when it made its third attempt to crack the market for big pickup trucks in the United States with its Tundra. After building trucks that were too small and too light for customers who were happy buying from Detroit's Big Three automakers, this time Toyota's designers and engineers learned the culture of the Sun Belt states, going to NASCAR events, camping at ranches in South Texas and Oklahoma, and tagging along to RV camps with families in their target market. "Toyota realized it needs to be the best in class," says a San Antonio dealer who advised Toyota on the new Tundra. "When other truck owners park next to this Tundra," he predicts, "they'll feel like they're in a solar eclipse."[16]

Diversity plays an ever-increasing role in targeting markets. According to the U.S. Census Bureau, the rapidly growing Hispanic population in the

figure 2.4

Elements of a Marketing Strategy and Its Environmental Framework

United States has now surpassed African Americans as the largest minority group. The census reports more than 41 million Hispanics in America, or one of every seven people in the United States.[17] With this phenomenal growth, marketers would be wise to pay attention to these and other markets—including women, seniors, and children of baby boomers—as they develop goods and services to offer consumers. The hotel industry, for instance, is increasingly courting female business travelers with women-only floors. Frills such as silky bathrobes, scents in the bathroom, specially selected books and magazines by the bedside, and better-branded toiletries are just a few of the amenities. Also high on the list of advantages appreciated by female travelers is the extra security many hotels offer, including escort service, rooms near the elevators, programmed key cards for floor and room access, and discretion in telling the guest her room number so no one overhears.[18]

MARKETING MIX VARIABLES

After marketers select a target market, they direct their company's activities toward profitably satisfying that segment. Although they must manipulate thousands of variables to reach this goal, marketing decision making can be divided into four strategies: product, distribution, promotion, and pricing strategies. The total package forms the **marketing mix**—the blending of the four strategic elements to fit the needs and preferences of a specific target market. While the fourfold classification is useful to study and analyze, remember that the marketing mix can—and should—be an ever-changing combination of variables to achieve success.

marketing mix Blending of the four strategy elements—product, distribution, promotion, and pricing—to fit the needs and preferences of a specific target market.

Figure 2.4 illustrates the focus of the marketing mix variables on the central choice of the target market. In addition, decisions about product, distribution, promotion, and price are affected by the environmental factors in the outer circle of the figure. The environmental variables may play a major role in the success of a marketing program, and marketers must consider their probable effects.

Product Strategy

In marketing, the word *product* means more than a good, service, or idea. Product is a broad concept that also encompasses the satisfaction of all consumer needs in relation to a good, service, or idea. So **product strategy** involves more than just deciding what goods or services the firm should offer to a group of consumers. It also includes decisions about customer service, package design, brand names, trademarks, patents, warranties, the life cycle of a product, positioning the product in the marketplace, and new-product development. Hewlett-Packard (HP), already a leader in the market for computer printers and digital photo printers, is moving into retail photo printing with the introduction of its Photosmart Express self-service photo kiosk. The kiosk printer is the first to use ink-jet technology in this market. It includes an easy-to-use touch screen to guide customers through the process of producing 4-by-6-inch prints in as little as five seconds. HP faces stiff competition from Fuji and Kodak, but the kiosk printer is "basically closing a loop," says an analyst in the digital imaging market. "They can generate revenue from home printing, online printing, and now, retail printing."[19]

Distribution Strategy

Marketers develop **distribution strategies** to ensure that consumers find their products in the proper quantities at the right times and places. Distribution decisions involve modes of transportation, warehousing, inventory control, order processing, and selection of marketing channels. Marketing channels are made up of institutions such as retailers and wholesalers—intermediaries that may be involved in a product's movement from producer to final consumer.

Technology is opening new channels of distribution in many industries. Computer software, a product made of digital data files, is ideally suited to electronic distribution. But all kinds of other products are now bought and sold over the Internet as well. By affecting everything from warehousing to order processing, technology has made the success of Amazon.com and eBay possible. Although these firms operate differently, both rely on technology for various distribution tasks.

Distribution is the perfect place for many companies to form alliances. Sony's music division signed an agreement with Universal Music Group to form Duet, an online music service that will make thousands of songs available to consumers legally over the Internet. Distribution considerations can also lead to strategic organizational decisions. Dow Jones has reorganized its business units, which include the *Wall Street Journal,* around its customers. Instead of print and electronic divisions, it will now deliver content based on the market: the consumer or the business customer.[20]

Promotion Strategy

Promotion is the communications link between sellers and buyers. Organizations use varied ways to send messages about their goods, services, and ideas. They may communicate messages directly through salespeople or indirectly through advertisements and promotions. When it unveiled the new Eclipse Spyder, Mitsubishi acted on marketing research indicating that Americans are intrigued by Japanese culture, including its art, fashion, and food. So the carmaker celebrated its new-product introduction to the strains of pounding Japanese rock and a performance by Japanese drummers in native dress.[21]

In developing a promotional strategy, marketers blend the various elements of promotion to communicate most effectively with their target market. Many companies use an approach called **integrated marketing communications (IMC)** to coordinate all promotional activities so that the consumer receives a unified and consistent message. Consumers might receive newsletters, e-mail updates, discount coupons, catalogs, invitations to company-sponsored events, and any number of other types of marketing communications about a product. Toyota dealers mail maintenance and service reminders to their customers. New England–based Shaw's Supermarkets places discount coupons in local newspapers. A political candidate may send volunteer workers through a neighborhood to invite voters to a special reception.

KRAFT FOODS, INC. CALIFORNIA PIZZA KITCHEN, INC.

California Pizza Kitchen has broadened the distribution strategy for its gourmet pizzas. In addition to eating at its trendy restaurants, consumers can now pick up such selections as the margherita pizza from their local grocer's freezer.

Pricing Strategy

Pricing strategy deals with the methods of setting profitable and justifiable prices. It is closely regulated and subject to considerable public scrutiny. One of the many factors that influence a marketer's pricing strategy is competition. The computer industry has become all too familiar with price cuts by both current competitors and new market entrants. After years of steady growth, the market has become saturated with low-cost computers, driving down profit margins even farther. There's plenty of competition in the air travel and automobile manufacturing industries as well. Two new air carriers, Eos Airlines and MAXjet Airways, are courting business and first-class passengers between New York and London with strikingly different pricing strategies. Eos offers its 48 flatbed seats for $6,500 round trip, about half as much as first-class fares on established carriers, while MAXjet has only business class available in its 102-seat cabins, priced at $1,560 round-trip. "We want to bring affordable business travel to a wider segment of the market," says MAXjet's CEO. Commenting on their different pricing strategies, one observer says, "For every seat that Eos sells, MAXjet will need to sell 10."[22] A good pricing strategy should create value for customers, building and strengthening their relationship with a firm and its products.

 assessment check

1. What are the two components of every marketing strategy?

2. Identify the four strategic elements of the marketing mix.

6   Describe the environmental characteristics that influence strategic decisions.

THE MARKETING ENVIRONMENT

Marketers do not make decisions about target markets and marketing mix variables in a vacuum. They must take into account the dynamic nature of the five dimensions of the marketing environment shown back in Figure 2.4: competitive, political-legal, economic, technological, and social-cultural factors.

Concerns about the natural environment have led to new regulations concerning air and water pollution. Automobile engineers, for instance, have turned public concerns and legal issues into opportunities by developing hybrid cars. These new models are fueled by dual energy: a gasoline engine and an electric motor. Toyota was the first to enter the market with its Prius, which depends on both an electric motor and a backup gasoline engine. Note that the marketing environment is fertile ground for innovators and entrepreneurs.

Businesses are increasingly looking to foreign shores for new growth markets. China-based Lenovo Group, the third-largest computer maker in the world, is taking its first steps in the United States and other foreign markets with low-priced desktops and notebooks designed for consumers and small businesses. The company recently purchased IBM's stagnant personal computer business. "Lenovo will offer the new PCs as the smart choice for today's most savvy entrepreneurs, priced to fit the budgets and computer needs of even the smallest firms," says its chief marketing officer.[23]

Technology has changed the marketing environment as well, partly with the advent of the Internet. Throughout this text, you will encounter examples of the ways the Internet and other technological developments are continuously altering how firms do business. And as technology forces these changes, other aspects of the environment must respond. Sometimes legal disputes arise over who owns which innovations. A long-running patent infringement suit brought against Research In Motion (RIM), the maker of the BlackBerry handheld device, was recently settled for a onetime payment of $612.5 million days before an injunction was expected to shut down the popular wireless e-mail service. In return for the settlement, NTP, which brought the suit, issued Research In Motion a license to use its patented technology in the future. The end of the case followed several setbacks for both sides and was a particular relief to corporate BlackBerry customers. "It was going to be a nightmare because we have 3,000 BlackBerry users," said a UPS spokesperson.[24] Amazon.com founder and chief executive Jeff Bezos has suggested that software and Internet patents should have a shorter life span than other patents—perhaps because of the rapid changes in technology—and that they should be open to public comment before being issued.

Competition is never far from the marketer's mind. Among the companies finding themselves increasingly vulnerable to competition from the Internet, for instance, are media giants such as the *New York Times,* Walt Disney, the major TV networks, and magazine and book publishers. Digital and online business entrepreneurs are looking for versatile ways to offer competing content and services to users everywhere, faster and more cheaply than ever before. Google, Yahoo!, and Comcast are posting record earnings. Microsoft is shifting more and more resources to the Internet, while the number two newspaper chain in the United States, Knight Ridder, is being broken up and sold because of declining ad revenue.[25]

Some experts have coined the phrase **rule of three,** meaning that in any industry, the three strongest, most efficient companies dominate between 70 and 90 percent of the market. Here are a few examples—all of which are household names:

- *Fast-food restaurants:* McDonald's, Burger King, Wendy's

- *Cereal manufacturers:* General Mills, Kellogg's, Post

- *Running shoes:* Nike, Fila USA, Reebok

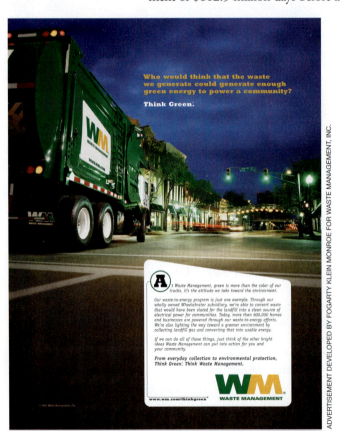

Who would think that the waste we generate could generate enough green energy to power a community?

Think Green.

A t Waste Management, green is more than the color of our trucks, it's the attitude we take toward the environment.

Our waste-to-energy program is just one example. Through our wholly owned Wheelabrator subsidiary, we're able to convert waste that would have been slated for the landfill into a clean source of electrical power for communities. Today, more than 600,000 homes and businesses are powered through our waste-to-energy efforts. We're also lighting the way toward a greener environment by collecting landfill gas and converting that into usable energy.

If we can do all of those things, just think of the other bright ideas Waste Management can put into action for you and your community.

From everyday collection to environmental protection, *Think Green. Think Waste Management.*

WM WASTE MANAGEMENT
www.wm.com/thinkgreen

Increasing concern for the environment and dependence on foreign oil have led some companies to provide creative solutions to both problems. Waste Management has developed programs to create energy from waste that once would have gone into a landfill. The trash hauler has worked to create power from naturally occurring landfill gas.

Solving an Ethical Controversy

Should Retailers Ban the Salvation Army from Their Sidewalks?

During a recent Christmas season, Target banned the Salvation Army's traditional bell ringers and red collection kettles from its stores, angering shoppers nationwide. The company said it was simply enforcing its existing rules against solicitation on store premises, but the venerable Christian charity claimed that the snub could cost it $9 million in donations, with repercussions not only at Christmas but throughout the year. The move hurt Target, too. "I don't plan to buy another thing at Target until they change their policy toward the Salvation Army," said one clergy member who, like many others, urged churchgoers to boycott the store. Meanwhile, at 3,800 Wal-Mart and Sam's Club locations around the country, the Salvation Army's traditional red kettle and bell-ringing season was extended to allow the charity to raise extra money for hurricane relief after Katrina devastated New Orleans.

Is it ethical for retailers to ban charitable groups from their stores?

PRO

1. Many other big retailers such Best Buy, Home Depot, and Barnes and Noble also prohibit solicitations. It is not an unusual policy and is not aimed directly at any one charity.
2. Target already donates more than $100 million a year to charities, including the Salvation Army. The

firm just doesn't want charities to pressure customers on their sidewalks.

CON

1. With so many disasters in recent years, the Salvation Army deserves as many opportunities as it can get to help people by collecting donations.
2. With sidewalk donations, customers are afforded an easy way to contribute to the charity's many efforts for those in need, increasing goodwill to the store.

Summary

Target stood its ground in prohibiting the Salvation Army from soliciting at its stores. However, the two organizations created a partnership to operate an online regional project called Target/Salvation Army Wish List, intended to help individuals and families in need along the Gulf Coast and around the country. Donors could visit the Web site; choose a gift such as warm bedding, socks, or battery-powered lanterns; and purchase it from Target to be donated for hurricane relief.

Sources: Target Web site, **http://www.target.com/**, accessed January 25, 2006; "Churches and Wal-Mart Help Rescue Salvation Army from Target's Snub," NewsMax.com, December 16, 2004, **http://www.newsmax.com**, accessed January 25, 2006; Don Teague, "Target Bans Salvation Army Solicitations," MSNBC, December 13, 2004, **http://www.msnbc.com**, accessed January 25, 2006.

- *Supermarkets:* Wal-Mart, Kroger, Supervalu
- *Pharmaceuticals:* Merck, Pfizer, Bristol-Myers Squibb[26]

While it may seem like an uphill battle for the remaining companies in any given industry, they can find a strategy for gaining competitive ground.

In the highly competitive airline industry, discounters such as JetBlue and Southwest have managed to thrive when some of the larger airlines such as USAirways have been pushed into bankruptcy. JetBlue appeals to value-oriented consumers—and delivers by offering services that the larger airlines have reduced or cut out altogether. JetBlue promises a friendly crew, large overhead bins for carry-on luggage, leather seating, a new terminal in the landmark TWA building at JFK International Airport in New York City, and live satellite TV at every seat. Recently JetBlue was rated by one survey as the number one airline in the United States. It's about "bringing humanity back to air travel," says CEO David G. Neeleman.[27]

The social-cultural environment includes a variety of factors, including prevailing cultural norms. Sometimes a company policy can have unintended consequences when store customers feel that it betrays their cultural norms, as Target found out when it banned charity solicitations on its premises (see the "Solving an Ethical Controversy" feature).

assessment check

1. What are the five dimensions of the marketing environment?
2. How does technology influence the marketing environment?

The marketing environment provides a framework for all marketing activity. Marketers consider environmental dimensions when they develop strategies for segmenting and targeting markets and when they study consumer and organizational buying behavior.

7 Describe the methods for marketing planning, including business portfolio analysis and the BCG matrix.

METHODS FOR MARKETING PLANNING

As growing numbers of companies have discovered the benefits of effective marketing planning, they have developed planning methods to assist in this important function. This section discusses two useful methods: the strategic business unit concept and the market share/market growth matrix.

BUSINESS PORTFOLIO ANALYSIS

strategic business units (SBUs) Key business units within diversified firms.

Although a small company may offer only a few items to its customers, a larger organization frequently offers and markets many products to widely diverse markets. Bank of America offers a wide range of financial products to businesses and consumers; Kraft Foods stocks supermarket shelves with everything from macaroni and cheese to mayonnaise. Top managers at these larger firms need a method for spotting product lines that deserve more investment as well as lines that aren't living up to expectations. So they conduct a **portfolio analysis,** in which they evaluate their company's products and divisions to determine which are strongest and which are weakest. Much as securities analysts review their portfolios of stocks and bonds, deciding which to retain and which to discard, marketing planners must assess their products, the regions in which they operate, and other marketing mix variables. This is where the concept of an SBU comes in.

Strategic business units (SBUs) are key business units within diversified firms. Each SBU has its own managers, resources, objectives, and competitors. A division, product line, or single product may define the boundaries of an SBU. Each SBU pursues its own distinct mission and often develops its own plans independently of other units in the organization.

Strategic business units, also called **categories,** focus the attention of company managers so that they can respond effectively to changing consumer demand within limited markets. Companies may have to redefine their SBUs as market conditions dictate. Hewlett-Packard recently created a separate new company unit for its iPaq handheld computer, splitting handhelds from its operations for laptops, desktops, and workstations.[28]

THE BCG MATRIX

To evaluate each of their organization's strategic business units, marketers need some type of portfolio performance framework. A widely used framework was developed by the Boston Consulting Group. This **market share/market growth matrix** places SBUs in a four-quadrant chart that plots market share—the percentage of a market that a firm controls—against market growth potential. The position of an SBU along the horizontal axis indicates its market share relative to those of competitors in the industry. Its position along the vertical axis indicates the annual growth rate of the market. After plotting all of a firm's business units, planners divide them according to the matrix's four quadrants. Figure 2.5 illustrates this

One holiday tradition worth keeping.

This holiday season, Wal-Mart will match, dollar for dollar, funds donated to The Salvation Army bell ringers at any Wal-Mart or SAM'S CLUB location, up to one million dollars. So please, give generously. And help Wal-Mart support The Salvation Army, a tradition that brings help, and hope, to our friends and neighbors in need. Together, we can make the season a little brighter for those who need it most.

WAL★MART
Walmart.com

With the onslaught of natural disasters, Wal-Mart made a strategic decision to continue its tradition of allowing Salvation Army bell ringers to gather contributions in front of its stores. In addition, the company matched, dollar for dollar, donations up to $1 million at any Wal-Mart or Sam's Club location.

matrix by labeling the four quadrants stars, cash cows, question marks, and dogs. Firms in each quadrant require a unique marketing strategy.

Stars represent units with high market shares in high-growth markets. These products or businesses are high-growth market leaders. Although they generate considerable income, they need inflows of even more cash to finance further growth. Apple's popular iPod is the number one selling portable digital music player in the world, but because of rapidly changing technology, Apple will have to continue to invest in ways to update and upgrade the player. The introduction of new models that can store and play video content such as music videos and television reruns is one example of Apple's market growth strategy.[29]

Cash cows command high market shares in low-growth markets. Marketers for such an SBU want to maintain this status for as long as possible. The business produces strong cash flows, but instead of investing heavily in the unit's own promotions and production capacity, the firm can use this cash to finance the growth of other SBUs with higher growth potentials. For instance, Microsoft might use the profits from sales of its Windows operating system to finance research and development for new Internet-based technologies.

Question marks achieve low market shares in high-growth markets. Marketers must decide whether to continue supporting these products or businesses, because question marks typically require considerably more cash than they generate. If a question mark cannot become a star, the firm should pull out of the market and target other markets with greater potential. With a new CEO, Six Flags is looking for ways to bring new customers to its 29 theme parks around the country. The shareholders have been promised change, and everything is up for grabs, including the ad campaign, the rides, and the parks themselves. "This industry relies too much on big rides," says CEO Mark Shapiro. "We have to diversify. We have to focus on more concerts and more themed attractions." Industry experts agree, saying that renewed ties with Hollywood—film producer Harvey Weinstein has recently joined the Six Flags board—could help make the parks a family destination again.[30]

Dogs manage only low market shares in low-growth markets. SBUs in this category promise poor future prospects, and marketers should withdraw from these businesses or product lines as quickly as possible. In some cases, these products can be sold to other firms, where they are a better fit. As mentioned previously, IBM sold its PC business to Lenovo so that it could concentrate on its business services.

figure 2.5

BCG Market Share/Market Growth Matrix

assessment check

1. What are SBUs?
2. Identify the four quadrants in the BCG matrix.

Strategic Implications of Marketing in the 21st Century

Never before has planning been as important to marketers as the 21st century speeds ahead with technological advances. Marketers need to plan carefully, accurately, and quickly if their companies are to gain a competitive advantage in today's global marketplace. They need to define their organization's mission and understand the different methods for formulating a successful marketing strategy. They must consider a changing, diverse population and the boundaryless business environment created by the Internet. They must be able to evaluate when it's best to be first to get into a market and when it's best to wait. They need to recognize when they've got a star and when they've got a dog—when to hang on and when to let go. As daunting as this seems, planning can reduce the risk and worry of bringing new goods and services to the marketplace.

REVIEW OF CHAPTER OBJECTIVES

1   Distinguish between strategic planning and tactical planning.

Strategic planning is the process of identifying an organization's primary objectives and adopting courses of action toward these objectives. In other words, strategic planning focuses on the big picture of which industries are central to a firm's business. Tactical planning guides the implementation of the activities specified in the strategic plan. Once a strategy is set, operational managers devise methods (tactics) to achieve the larger goals.

2   Explain how marketing plans differ at various levels in an organization.

Top management spends more time engaged in strategic planning than do middle- and supervisory-level managers, who tend to focus on narrower, tactical plans for their units. Supervisory managers are more likely to develop specific plans designed to meet the goals assigned to them—for example, streamlining production processes so that they operate more efficiently.

3   Identify the steps in the marketing planning process.

The basic steps in the marketing planning process are defining the organization's mission and objectives; assessing organizational resources and evaluating environmental risks and opportunities; and formulating, implementing, and monitoring the marketing strategy.

4   Describe successful planning tools and techniques, including Porter's Five Forces model, first and second mover strategies, SWOT analysis, and the strategic window.

Porter's Five Forces are identified as the five competitive factors that influence planning strategies: potential new entrants, bargaining power of buyers, bargaining power of suppliers, threat of substitute products, and rivalry among competitors. With a first mover strategy, a firm attempts to capture the greatest market share by being first to enter the market; with a second mover strategy, a firm observes the innovations of first movers and then attempts to improve on them to gain advantage. SWOT analysis (strengths, weaknesses, opportunities, and threats) helps planners compare internal organizational strengths and weaknesses with external opportunities and threats. The strategic window identifies the limited periods during which the key requirements of a market and the competencies of a firm best fit together.

5   Identify the basic elements of a marketing strategy.

Development of a marketing strategy is a two-step process: (1) selecting a target market and (2) designing an effective marketing mix to satisfy the chosen target. The target market is the group of people toward whom a company decides to direct its marketing efforts. The marketing mix blends four strategy elements to fit the needs and preferences of a specific target market. These elements are product strategy, distribution strategy, promotion strategy, and pricing strategy.

6   Describe the environmental characteristics that influence strategic decisions.

The five dimensions of the marketing environment are competitive, political-legal, economic, technological, and social-cultural. Marketers must be aware of growing cultural diversity in the global marketplace.

7   Describe the methods for marketing planning, including business portfolio analysis and the BCG matrix.

The business portfolio analysis evaluates a company's products and divisions, including strategic business units (SBUs). The SBU focuses the attention of company managers so that they can respond effectively to changing consumer demand within certain markets. The BCG matrix places SBUs in a four-quadrant chart that plots market share against market growth potential. The four quadrants are stars, cash cows, dogs, and question marks.

assessment check **answers**

1.1 Define *planning*.

Planning is the process of anticipating future events and conditions and of determining the best way to achieve organizational objectives.

1.2 Give an example of strategic planning and tactical planning.

Eastman Kodak's strategic plans include focusing on the company's core strength in digital imaging. The company's tactical plans include developing the first Wi-Fi camera and the first dual-lens digital camera, and partnering with Motorola to build better camera phones.

2.1 How do marketing plans differ at different levels of the organization?

Top managers usually focus their planning activities on long-range strategic issues. In contrast, middle-level managers focus on operational planning, which includes creating and implementing tactical plans for their own units. Supervisors develop specific programs to meet the goals in their areas of responsibility.

2.2 Why is it important to get input from others when planning?

Input from a variety of sources—other employees, suppliers, or customers—helps ensure that many ideas are considered. Involving those people in planning can also turn them into advocates for the plan.

3.1 Distinguish between an organization's mission and its objectives.

The firm's mission is the essential purpose that differentiates the company from others. Its objectives guide development of supporting marketing objectives and plans.

3.2 What is the importance of the final step in the marketing planning process?

In the final step of the marketing planning process, managers monitor performance to ensure that objectives are being achieved.

4.1 Briefly explain each of Porter's Five Forces.

Porter's Five Forces are the threats of potential new entrants, which increases competition in a market; bargaining power of buyers, which can depress prices; bargaining power of suppliers, which can increase cost or reduce selection; threat of substitute products, which can lure customers to other products; and rivalry among competitors, which can bring about price wars or divert companies from their main goals.

4.2 What are the benefits and drawbacks of a first mover strategy?

The benefits of a first mover strategy include being able to capture the greatest market share and develop long-term relationships with customers. Disadvantages include the possibility that companies that follow can learn from mistakes by first movers.

4.3 What are the four components of the SWOT analysis? What is a strategic window?

SWOT analysis helps planners compare internal organizational strengths and weaknesses with external opportunities and threats. SWOT is an acronym for *strengths, weaknesses, opportunities,* and *threats*. A strategic window defines the limited periods during which the key requirements of a market and the particular competencies of a firm best fit together.

5.1 What are the two components of every marketing strategy?

The basic elements of a marketing strategy are (1) the target market and (2) the marketing mix variables.

5.2 Identify the four strategic elements of the marketing mix.

The marketing mix consists of product, distribution, promotion, and price strategies.

assessment check **answers**

6.1   What are the five dimensions of the marketing environment?

The five dimensions of the marketing environment are competitive, political-legal, economic, technological, and social-cultural factors.

6.2   How does technology influence the marketing environment?

The Internet and other technological developments continuously alter how firms do business. And as technology forces these changes, other aspects of the environment must respond.

7.1   What are SBUs?

Strategic business units (SBUs) are key business units within diversified firms. Each SBU has its own managers, resources, objectives, and competitors.

7.2   Identify the four quadrants in the BCG matrix.

The BCG matrix labels SBUs stars, cash cows, question marks, and dogs.

MARKETING TERMS YOU NEED TO KNOW

planning 37
marketing planning 37
strategic planning 38
tactical planning 38

mission 41
Porter's Five Forces 43
first mover strategy 45
second mover strategy 45

SWOT analysis 45
strategic window 46
marketing mix 48
strategic business units (SBUs) 52

OTHER IMPORTANT MARKETING TERMS

objectives 42
marketing strategy 42
sustainable competitive advantage 43
core competencies 46
target market 47

product strategy 48
distribution strategy 48
promotion 49
integrated marketing communications
   (IMC) 49

pricing strategy 49
rule of three 50
portfolio analysis 52
category 52
market share/market growth matrix 52

ASSURANCE OF LEARNING REVIEW

1. State whether each of the following illustrates strategic or tactical planning:
   a. Wal-Mart decides to enter the Japanese market.
   b. A local bakery decides to add coffee to its list of offerings.
2. Summarize in one or two sentences a strategic plan that a top manager in a business unit might be involved with. Now state in a sentence or two a tactical plan that a middle-level manager might focus on.
3. What is the difference between a firm's mission and its objectives?
4. Define *marketing strategy*.
5. Over which of Porter's Five Forces do consumers have the greatest influence?

6. Cite examples of firms that have succeeded with first and second mover strategies.
7. When using the strategic window, what three factors must marketers analyze?
8. Why is identifying a target market so important to a company?
9. Give an example of each of the four strategies in the marketing mix.
10. Identify a major way in which technology has changed the marketing environment in the last five years.
11. What is another name for SBUs?
12. Describe the characteristics of each of the four quadrants in the BCG matrix.

PROJECTS AND TEAMWORK EXERCISES

1. Choose a company whose goods and services are familiar to you. With at least one other classmate, formulate a mission statement for that company.

2. Once you have formulated the mission statement for your firm, identify at least five objectives.

3. Create a SWOT analysis for yourself, listing your own personal strengths, weaknesses, opportunities, and threats.

4. ABC has made some of its TV shows (such as *Lost* and *Desperate Housewives*) available for download to iPods and to PCs. Discuss how this strategy demonstrates a strategic window for the company.

5. Use your library or an Internet search engine to collect information on one of the following companies (or select one of your own). Identify the firm's target market(s). Note that a large company might have more than one target market. Write a brief proposal for a marketing strategy to reach that market.
   a. MasterCard
   b. Costco
   c. Volkswagen
   d. Old Navy

6. With a classmate, choose a company whose products you have purchased in the past. Create two ads for one of the company's products (or product lines). One ad should focus on the product itself—its features, packaging, or brand name. The second ad should focus on pricing. Present your ads to the class for discussion. Which ad is more effective for the product and why?

7. On your own or with a classmate, research a firm that has been around for a long time, such as Ford, General Electric, or DuPont. Use your research to determine the ways that technology has changed the marketing environment for your firm. Present your findings in class.

8. Suppose you are a marketer for a large U.S. toy manufacturer. Top executives at the company have determined that growth overseas is an essential objective, and they want you to look at the Indian market's potential in the next five years. Write a memo to your manager explaining how you think the social-cultural environment may affect your firm's marketing strategy overseas.

9. Team up with one or more classmates to research companies on the Web, looking for firms that have created successful SBUs such as L. L. Bean's outdoor and fitness department that is aimed at women. Then create an advertisement for one of those SBUs.

10. Go back to the firm you selected in question 5 (or choose a different firm). Further research the company's products so you can create a hypothetical BCG matrix for some of the company's products. Which products are the stars? Which are the cash cows and question marks? Are there any dogs?

CRITICAL-THINKING EXERCISES

1. Why is it important from a marketing standpoint for an organization to define its goals and objectives?

2. What are the potential benefits and drawbacks if a firm strays from its core competencies?

3. Describe a consumer product that you think is particularly vulnerable to substitution. If you were a marketer for that product, what steps might you take to defend your product's position?

4. Suppose you were a marketer for a luxury skin-care line. What factors in the marketing environment might affect your marketing strategy and why?

5. Suppose you were a marketer for a small firm trying to enter one of the dominant industries illustrating the rule of three. Which marketing strategy might you select and why?

ETHICS EXERCISE

Suppose you work for a company that makes surfboards. As part of the marketing team, you have helped create a SWOT analysis for the company and have discovered some good and not-so-good things about your employer. Strengths include customer loyalty, a patented design, and competitive prices. The company has been based on the West Coast, but the owner sees an opportunity to enter the market on the East Coast. But you are concerned about the firm's weaknesses—the product line is narrow, you suspect the company doesn't have the financial resources to expand right now, and the owner keeps a tight rein on everything.

1. Should you speak to your manager about your concerns or keep quiet? Why?

2. Would you look for a job at another firm or remain loyal to the one you work for? Why?

INTERNET EXERCISES

1. **Strategic versus tactical planning.** Review the chapter material on the differences between strategic and tactical planning. Visit the company Web sites listed here and, by searching news and announcements, determine whether the decisions listed were the result of strategic planning, tactical planning, or a combination of the two. Be prepared to defend your conclusions.
   a. The decision by Airbus (http://www.airbus.com) to proceed with the launch of the A380, the world's largest commercial airliner
   b. Wal-Mart Stores' (http://www.walmartstores.com) international expansion plans
   c. The recent decision by Eastman Kodak (http://www.kodak.com) to discontinue the manufacture and distribution of most film cameras

2. **Marketing planning methods.** Two marketing planning methods described in Chapter 2 were business portfolio analysis and the BCG matrix. Review the material and then perform the following exercises:

   a. Go to the Web site of 3M (http://www.mmm.com). Based on the information you find, divide 3M into its main strategic business units.
   b. Philips is a large Dutch-based diversified company specializing in consumer electronics and products. Go to the firm's U.S. Web site (http://www.philipsusa.com). Select five product lines, such as televisions and electric shavers. Classify each product in the BCG matrix. Justify your classifications.
   c. It is not uncommon for companies to sell individual products, or even complete product lines, to other companies. Using Google or another Internet search engine, identify a recent product sale. Using business portfolio analysis or the BCG matrix, prepare a brief report discussing why the seller sold the product and why the buyer purchased it.

Note: Internet Web addresses change frequently. If you don't find the exact site listed, you may need to access the organization's home page and search from there or use a search engine such as Google.

 CASE 2.1   A Farewell to Regional Jets?

Not too long ago, small regional jets, which carry 50 passengers in a single class, were the craft of choice among airlines, who ordered the $24 million planes by the dozen. With business travel booming, regional jets seemed to be an ideal solution for service to midsize cities. The two biggest manufacturers of the planes, Montreal-based Bombardier and Embraer of Brazil, considered them the stars of their product lineup and couldn't make them fast enough. Soon there were about 1,600 regional jets in the air, carrying about 20 percent of all domestic passengers.

Then the marketing environment changed as low-priced competitors moved into the business travel market, and business slumped generally following the September 11, 2001, terrorist attacks. To bring back passengers, many carriers flying regional jets reconsidered their pricing strategies and lowered fares, making the jets, which aren't very fuel-efficient, even more costly to fly. Delta Air Lines and Northwest, which both used regional jets on many flights, filed for bankruptcy. Delta returned 30 of its leased jets, and Northwest put an order for 13 on hold. Independence Air sold or returned 29 jets and took 28 more out of service, then ceased all flights. Industry experts predict that as many as 200 regional jets will soon end up in storage.

"The day of the regional jet is over, in terms of demand," said one airline industry consultant. "They can't make money." In a few short years, the market for regional jets had dried up.

Bombardier and Embraer were ready, however, with revised strategic plans. Soon they began rolling out a new breed of regional jet. Carrying between 70 and 100 passengers, the new craft are economical and roomy enough to have separate first-class sections, an amenity that business travelers crave. While most observers believe that the smaller jets won't disappear altogether, there's little doubt that they have seen their day. Because they were cramped and uncomfortable, frequent travelers probably won't miss them. But Bombardier, which guaranteed its airline customers that regional jets would have resale value, might face a $2.6 billion bill when the 50-seaters hit the used-airplane market.

Questions for Critical Thinking

1. What are some of the strengths, weaknesses, opportunities, and threats that face the aircraft manufacturing industry, as represented by Bombardier and Embraer?

2. Which elements of the marketing mix have airlines emphasized in their battle to retain their business passengers? Do you think they have chosen the most effective strategies? Why or why not?

Sources: "United One-Ups Small Regional Jets," *USA Today,* February 6, 2006, **http://www.usatoday.com**; Joe Sharkey, "No Room for the Passengers, Never Mind the Carry-Ons," *New York Times,* January 31, 2006, **http://www.nytimes.com**; Marilyn Adams, "Regional Jets Appear on Endangered Species List," *USA Today,* November 2, 2005, p. 1B; "The Rise and Fall of Regional Jets," Marginal Revolution, November 2005, **http://www.marginalrevolution.com**.

 VIDEO CASE 2.2   Timbuk2's Success Is in the Bag

The written video case on Timbuk2 appears on page VC-3. The recently filmed Timbuk2 video is designed to expand and highlight the concepts in this chapter and the concepts and questions covered in the written video case.

appendix

Creating an Effective Marketing Plan

Overview

- "What are our mission and goals?"

- "Who are our customers?"

- "What types of products do we offer?"

- "How can we provide superior customer service?"

These are some of the questions addressed by a **marketing plan**—a detailed description of the resources and actions needed to achieve stated marketing objectives.

Chapter 2 discussed **strategic planning**—the process of anticipating events and market conditions and deciding how a firm can best achieve its organizational objectives. Marketing planning encompasses all the activities devoted to achieving marketing objectives, establishing a basis for designing a marketing strategy. This appendix

deals in depth with the formal marketing plan, which is part of an organization's overall business plan. At the end of this appendix, you'll see what an actual marketing plan looks like. Each plan component for a hypothetical firm called Blue Sky Clothing is presented.

marketing plan Detailed description of the resources and actions needed to achieve stated marketing objectives.

strategic planning Process of anticipating events and market conditions and deciding how a firm can best achieve its organizational objectives.

business plan Formal document that outlines a company's objectives, how they will be met, how the business will obtain financing, and how much money the company expects to earn.

COMPONENTS OF A BUSINESS PLAN

A company's **business plan** is one of its most important documents. The business plan puts in writing all of the company's objectives, how they will be met, how the business will obtain financing, and how much money the company expects to earn over a specified time period. Although business plans vary in length and format, most contain at least some form of the following components:

- An *executive summary* briefly answers the *who, what, when, where, how,* and *why* questions for the plan. Although the summary appears early in the plan, it is typically written last, after the firm's executives have worked out the details of all the other sections.

- A *competitive analysis* section focuses on the environment in which the marketing plan is to be implemented. Although this section is more closely associated with the comprehensive business plan, factors specifically influencing marketing are likely to be included here.

- The *mission statement* summarizes the organization's purpose, vision, and overall goals. This statement provides the foundation on which further planning is based.

- The overall business plan includes a series of *component* plans that present goals and strategies for each functional area of the enterprise. They typically include the following:

- The *marketing plan,* which describes strategies for informing potential customers about the goods and services offered by the firm as well as strategies for developing long-term relationships. At the end of this appendix, a sample marketing plan for Blue Sky Clothing is presented.

- The *financing plan,* which presents a realistic approach for securing needed funds and managing debt and cash flows.

- The *production plan,* which describes how the organization will develop its products in the most efficient, cost-effective manner possible.

- The *facilities plan,* which describes the physical environment and equipment required to implement the production plan.

- The *human resources plan,* which estimates the firm's employment needs and the skills necessary to achieve organizational goals, including a comparison of current employees with the needs of the firm, and which establishes processes for securing adequately trained personnel if a gap exists between current employee skills and future needs.

This basic format encompasses the planning process used by nearly every successful organization. Whether a company operates in the manufacturing, wholesaling, retailing, or service sector (or a combination), the components described here are likely to appear in its overall business plan. Regardless of the size or longevity of a company, a business plan is an essential tool for a firm's owners because it helps them focus on the key elements of their business. Even small firms that are just starting out need a business plan to obtain financing. Figure 1 shows the outline of a business plan for Blue Sky Clothing.

CREATING A MARKETING PLAN

Keep in mind that a marketing plan should be created in conjunction with the other elements of a firm's business plan. In addition, a marketing plan often draws from the business plan, restating the executive summary, competitive analysis, and mission statement to give its readers an overall view of the firm. The marketing plan is needed for a variety of reasons:

- to obtain financing, because banks and most private investors require a detailed business plan—including a marketing plan component—before they will even consider a loan application or a venture capital investment

- to provide direction for the firm's overall business and marketing strategies

- to support the development of long-term and short-term organizational objectives

- to guide employees in achieving these objectives

- to serve as a standard against which the firm's progress can be measured and evaluated

In addition, the marketing plan is where a firm puts into writing its commitment to its customers and to building long-lasting relationships. After creating and implementing the plan, marketers must reevaluate it periodically to gauge its success in moving the organization toward its goals. If changes are needed, they should be made as soon as possible.

FORMULATING AN OVERALL MARKETING STRATEGY

Before writing a marketing plan, a firm's marketers formulate an overall marketing strategy. A firm may use a number of tools in marketing planning, including business portfolio analysis and the BCG matrix. Its executives may conduct a SWOT analysis, take advantage of a strategic window, study Porter's Five Forces model as it relates to their business, or consider adopting a first or second mover strategy, all of which are described in Chapter 2.

figure 1

Outline of a Business Plan

The Blue Sky Clothing Business Plan

I. Executive Summary
- Who, What, When, Where, How, and Why

II. Table of Contents

III. Introduction
- Mission Statement
- Concept and Company
- Management Team
- Product

IV. Marketing Strategy
- Demographics
- Trends
- Market Penetration
- Potential Sales Revenue

V. Financing the Business
- Cash Flow Analysis
- Pro Forma Balance Sheet
- Income Statement

VI. Facilities Plan
- Physical Environment
- Equipment

VII. Human Resources Plan
- Employment Needs and Skills
- Current Employees

VIII. Résumés of Principals

spreadsheet analysis
Grid that organizes numerical information in a standardized, easily understood format.

In addition to the planning strategies discussed in Chapter 2, marketers are likely to use **spreadsheet analysis,** which lays out a grid of columns and rows that organize numerical information in a standardized, easily understood format. Spreadsheet analysis helps planners answer various "what if" questions related to the firm's financing and operations. The most popular spreadsheet software is Microsoft Excel. A spreadsheet analysis helps planners anticipate marketing performance given specified sets of circumstances. For example, a spreadsheet might project the outcomes of different pricing decisions for a new product, as shown in Figure 2.

Once general planning strategies are determined, marketers begin to flesh out the details of the marketing strategy. The elements of a marketing strategy include identifying the target market, studying the marketing environment, and creating a marketing mix.

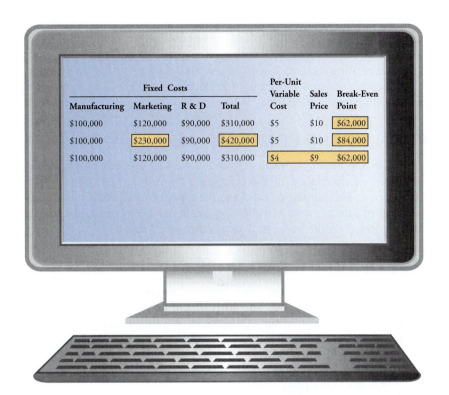

Fixed Costs				Per-Unit Variable Cost	Sales Price	Break-Even Point
Manufacturing	Marketing	R & D	Total			
$100,000	$120,000	$90,000	$310,000	$5	$10	$62,000
$100,000	$230,000	$90,000	$420,000	$5	$10	$84,000
$100,000	$120,000	$90,000	$310,000	$4	$9	$62,000

When marketers have identified the target market, they can develop the optimal marketing mix to reach their potential customers:

- *Product strategy.* Which goods and services should the company offer to meet its customers' needs?

- *Distribution strategy.* Through which channel(s) and physical facilities will the firm distribute its products?

- *Promotional strategy.* What mix of advertising, sales promotion, and personal selling activities will the firm use to reach its customers initially and then develop long-term relationships?

- *Pricing strategy.* At what level should the company set its prices?

THE EXECUTIVE SUMMARY, COMPETITIVE ANALYSIS, AND MISSION STATEMENT

Because these three elements of the business plan often reappear in the marketing plan, it is useful to describe them here. Recall that the executive summary answers the *who, what, when, where, how,* and *why* questions for the business. The executive summary for Google would include references to its current strategic planning process for its search services, which relies on developing new "ways in which technology can improve upon existing ways of doing business."[1] It would go on to answer questions such as who is involved (key people and organizations), what length of time the plan represents, and how the goals will be met.

The competitive analysis focuses on the environment in which the marketing plan is to be implemented. For Cabrera Capital Markets, a small minority-owned investment bank and brokerage firm, staying competitive is all about harnessing technology. Martin Cabrera invested in the NYFIX trading system and saw his annual revenues jump $500,000 the following year. "We have the same bells and whistles that Goldman Sachs and Lehman [Brothers] has," says Cabrera. "So it allows us to compete with all the institutions in the business."[2]

The mission statement puts into words an organization's overall purpose and reason for being. Starbucks' mission statement is to "establish Starbucks as the premier purveyor of the finest coffee in the world while maintaining our uncompromising principles while we grow." The guiding principles for employees include treating each other with respect and dignity, embracing diversity, applying the highest standards of excellence to the creation of Starbucks' many products, and developing "enthusiastically satisfied customers all of the time."[3]

DESCRIPTION OF THE COMPANY

Near the beginning of the marketing plan—typically following the executive summary and before the mission statement—a description of the company is included. The company description may include a brief history or background of the firm, the types of products it offers or plans to introduce, recent successes or achievements—in short, it consists of a few paragraphs containing the kind of information often found on the home page of a company's Web site.

STATEMENT OF GOALS AND CORE COMPETENCIES

The plan then includes a statement of the firm's goals and its core competencies—the things it does extremely well or better than anyone else. The goals should be specific and measurable and may be divided into financial and nonfinancial aims. A financial goal might be to add 75 new franchises in the next twelve months or to reach $10 million in revenues. A nonfinancial goal might be to enter the European market or to add a new product line every other year. A stated goal for U.S. automakers is their plan to double production of flexible-fuel vehicles that can run on gasoline and ethanol blends by 2010, to 2 million cars a year.[4]

Core competencies make a firm stand out from everyone else in the marketplace. Costco's core competency is offering a wide variety of goods at low prices, including unexpected bargains such as luxury-brand watches and Dom Perignon champagne. Jim Sinegal, co-founder and CEO, is known for keeping costs low, but not wages and benefits. He believes strongly in the value of his company's nearly 119,000 employees and rewards them well. "Our attitude," he says, "is that if you hire good people and pay them a fair wage, then good things will happen for the company."[5]

Small businesses often begin with a single core competency and build their business and reputation on it. It is important for a new firm to identify its core competency in the marketing plan so that investors or banks understand why they should lend the firm money to get started or to grow to the next stage. Leslie Blesius successfully fended off competitors such as Pottery Barn and Restoration Hardware when she was establishing her upscale home furnishings shop in Highland Park, Illinois. She focused on what she did better than the chains, offering personalized services such as in-home consultations and installations, more selection, and more custom options. "It's all about how much we can help," Blesius says. Her strategy was so successful that she was able to survive and even expand, offering new furniture lines and opening a bed-and-bath section.[6]

OUTLINE OF THE MARKETING ENVIRONMENT (SITUATION ANALYSIS)

Every successful marketing plan considers the marketing environment—the competitive, economic, political-legal, technological, and social-cultural factors that affect the way a firm formulates and implements its marketing strategy. Marketing plans may address these issues in different ways, but the goal is to present information that describes the company's position or situation within the marketing environment. J. Crew, for instance, has a well-known brand name and a CEO with an impressive track record, Mickey Drexler, who previously headed The Gap. Says one industry watcher, "It's very much a merchant-driven company, dealing with an upper-income demographic that is spot-on to the current environment." So a marketing plan for J. Crew would include an evaluation of competing stores such as The Gap and Urban Outfitters; any technological advances that would affect such factors as merchandise distribution or inventory; social-cultural issues such as fashion preferences and spending habits of customers; and economic issues affecting a pricing strategy.

One such method for outlining the marketing environment in the marketing plan is to include a SWOT analysis, described in Chapter 2. SWOT analysis identifies the firm's strengths, weaknesses, opportunities, and threats within the marketing environment. A SWOT analysis for J. Crew might include strengths such as its corporate leadership, brand name, and upscale target market. Weaknesses might include the risks inherent in the business of correctly spotting fashion trends. A major opportunity lies in the fact that J. Crew can expand almost anywhere—in fact, it plans to add between 25 and 35 new stores every year—and it will also expand its offerings to include a line of children's wear, a lower-priced casual line, and wedding attire. Threats include competition from other trendy stores, sudden changes in customer preferences, and economic dips that affect spending.[7] A SWOT analysis can be presented in chart format so that it is easy to read as part of the marketing plan. The sample marketing plan in this appendix includes a SWOT analysis for Blue Sky Clothing.

THE TARGET MARKET AND MARKETING MIX

The marketing plan identifies the target market for the firm's products. The target market for Whirlpool's pedestal-mounted washing machine and Moen's sleek shower grab bar is baby boomers, the oldest of whom are entering their 60s.[8] For another target market, Toyota's planned spin-off series of the hit TV drama *Prison Break* consists of two-minute episodes for mobile phones. The target market is young consumers.[9] And marketers promoting bands such as Girl Authority, a squeaky-clean nine-girl band with a new album, are aiming at both preteen girls and parents looking for wholesome entertainment for their kids.[10]

The marketing plan also discusses the marketing mix that the firm has selected for its products. When Nokia launched its N-Gage, a handset that plays games, the company used a marketing mix that included product, distribution, promotion, and pricing strategies. By expanding its well-known communications product line to include a handheld game device, Nokia set its new product in direct competition with game machines made by Nintendo and Sony but expanded the social aspect of its system by offering simplified game development based on the Internet's Java technology. This feature allows players to communicate with friends while in the game. The company negotiated deals with major wireless service providers such as Cingular to distribute N-Gage. And the product's distribution expanded when the company began offering trials, purchase, and downloads of popular games from its Web site, **http://www.n-gage.com**. Nokia spent an estimated $100 million promoting the initial handset. Drawing on the success of a well-known software marketer, Nokia announced a new partnership with leading international video game developer Gameloft. N-Gage had an initial retail price of $200, but Nokia dropped its base price to $99 for customers who prepay for wireless service. Also, wireless carriers offer special discounted prices for N-Gage, depending on the service contract customers select.[11]

BUDGET, SCHEDULE, AND MONITORING

Every marketing plan requires a budget, a time schedule for implementation, and a system for monitoring the plan's success or failure. Entrepreneur Jeff Riggs started planning years in advance to qualify for the more than $1 million in loans he needed to realize his dream—to buy a plot of land in his native Montana and build and operate the first Wheat Montana franchise restaurant. Because he earned a basketball scholarship, Riggs was able to apply the money his parents would have spent on college tuition to buying residential property. With the financial base that his rental incomes afforded, he was able to obtain three loans and open his restaurant. The expenses he forecasted in his business plan were on target, and his revenues exceeded his initial estimates. So Riggs, only 27, opened another franchise. His goal is to operate four stores when he is 30.[12] Typically, a budget includes a breakdown of the costs incurred as the marketing program is implemented, offset by projected sales, profits, and losses over the time period of the program.

Most long-range marketing plans encompass a two- to five-year period, although companies that do business in industries such as auto manufacturing, pharmaceuticals, or lumber may extend their marketing plans further into the future because it typically takes longer to develop these products. However, marketers in most industries will have difficulty making estimates and predictions beyond five years because of the many uncertainties in the marketplace. Firms also may opt to develop short-term plans to cover marketing activities for a single year.

The marketing plan, whether it is long term or short term, predicts how long it will take to achieve the goals set out by the plan. A goal may be opening a certain number of new stores, increasing market share, or achieving an expansion of the product line. Finally, the marketing program is monitored and evaluated for its performance. Monthly, quarterly, and annual sales targets are usually tracked; the efficiency with which certain tasks are completed is determined; customer satisfaction is measured, and so forth. All of these factors contribute to the overall review of the program.

At some point, a firm may implement an *exit strategy,* a plan for the firm to leave the market. A common way for a large company to do this is to sell off a business unit. A number of these strategies have been implemented recently. Cendant sold its travel services division, Travelport, for more than $4 billion in cash, after first considering a plan to spin the division off as a separate business. Travelport owns the popular Orbitz and CheapTickets Web sites and was purchased by an affiliate of equity firm The Blackstone Group.[13]

Another example of an exit strategy is Wal-Mart's decision to leave South Korea, selling its stores there after failing to make a success of its sixteen South Korean outlets. The stores were sold to Shinsegae, a local retailer, for nearly $900 million. Wal-Mart was following in the backtracking footsteps of several other multinationals, including Nokia, Nestlé, Carrefour, and Google, all of which have exited the demanding South Korean market.[14]

SAMPLE MARKETING PLAN

The following pages contain an annotated sample marketing plan for Blue Sky Clothing. At some point in your career, you will likely be involved in writing—or at least contributing to—a marketing plan. And you'll certainly read many marketing plans throughout your business career. Keep in mind that the plan for Blue Sky is a single example; no one format is used by all companies. Also, the Blue Sky plan has been somewhat condensed to make it easier to annotate and illustrate the most vital features. The important point to remember is that the marketing plan is a document designed to present concise, cohesive information about a company's marketing objectives to managers, lending institutions, and others who are involved in creating and carrying out the firm's overall business strategy.

FIVE-YEAR MARKETING PLAN
BLUE SKY CLOTHING, INC.

TABLE OF CONTENTS

EXECUTIVE SUMMARY

This five-year marketing plan for Blue Sky Clothing has been created by its two founders to secure additional funding for growth and to inform employees of the company's current status and direction. Although Blue Sky was launched only three years ago, the firm has experienced greater-than-anticipated demand for its products, and research has shown that the target market of sports-minded consumers and sports retailers would like to buy more casual clothing than Blue Sky currently offers. As a result, Blue Sky wants to extend its current product line as well as add new product lines. In addition, the firm plans to explore opportunities for online sales. The marketing environment has been very receptive to the firm's high-quality goods—casual clothing in trendy colors with logos and slogans that reflect the interests of outdoor enthusiasts around the country. Over the next five years, Blue Sky can increase its distribution, offer new products, and win new customers.

The executive summary outlines the *who, what, where, when, how,* and *why* of the marketing plan. Blue Sky is only three years old and is successful enough that it now needs a formal marketing plan to obtain additional financing from a bank or private investors for expansion and the launch of new products.

COMPANY DESCRIPTION

Blue Sky Clothing was founded three years ago by entrepreneurs Lucy Neuman and Nick Russell. Neuman has an undergraduate degree in marketing and worked for several years in the retail clothing industry. Russell operated an adventure business called Go West!, which arranges group trips to locations in Wyoming, Montana, and Idaho, before selling the enterprise to a partner. Neuman and Russell, who have been friends since college, decided to develop and market a line of clothing with a unique—yet universal—appeal to outdoor enthusiasts.

Blue Sky Clothing reflects Neuman's and Russell's passion for the outdoors. The company's original cotton T-shirts, baseball caps, and fleece jackets and vests bear logos of different sports—such as kayaking, mountain climbing, bicycling, skating, surfing, and horseback riding. But every item shows off the company's slogan: "Go Play Outside." Blue Sky sells clothing for both men and women, in the hottest colors with the coolest names—such as sunrise pink, sunset red, twilight purple, desert rose, cactus green, ocean blue, mountaintop white, and river rock gray.

Blue Sky attire is currently carried by small retail stores that specialize in outdoor clothing and gear. Most of these stores are concentrated in northern New England, California, the Northwest, and a few states in the South. The high quality, trendy colors, and unique message of the clothing have gained Blue Sky a following among consumers between ages 25 and 45. Sales have tripled in the last year alone, and Blue Sky is currently working to expand its manufacturing capabilities.

Blue Sky is also committed to giving back to the community by contributing to local conservation programs. Ultimately, the company would like to develop and fund its own environmental programs. This plan will outline how Blue Sky intends to introduce new products, expand its distribution, enter new markets, and give back to the community.

The company description summarizes the history of Blue Sky—how it was founded and by whom, what its products are, and why they are unique. It begins to "sell" the reader on the growth possibilities for Blue Sky.

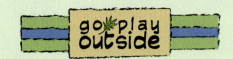

BLUE SKY'S MISSION AND GOALS

Blue Sky's mission is to be a leading producer and marketer of personalized, casual clothing for consumers who love the outdoors. Blue Sky wants to inspire people to get outdoors more often and enjoy family and friends while doing so. In addition, Blue Sky strives to design programs for preserving the natural environment.

During the next five years, Blue Sky seeks to achieve the following financial and nonfinancial goals:

- *Financial goals*

  1. Obtain financing to expand manufacturing capabilities, increase distribution, and introduce two new product lines.

  2. Increase revenues by at least 50 percent each year.

  3. Donate at least $25,000 a year to conservation organizations.

- *Nonfinancial goals*

  4. Introduce two new product lines—customized logo clothing and lightweight luggage.

  5. Enter new geographic markets, including southwestern and mid-Atlantic states.

  6. Develop a successful Internet site, while maintaining strong relationships with retailers.

  7. Develop its own conservation program aimed at helping communities raise money to purchase open space.

CORE COMPETENCIES

Blue Sky seeks to use its core competencies to achieve a sustainable competitive advantage, in which competitors cannot provide the same value to consumers that Blue Sky does. Already Blue Sky has developed core competencies in (1) offering a high-quality, branded product whose image is recognizable among consumers; (2) creating a sense of community among consumers who purchase the products; and (3) developing a reputation among retailers as a reliable manufacturer, delivering the requested number of products on schedule. The firm intends to build on these competencies through marketing efforts that increase the number of products offered as well as distribution outlets.

By forming strong relationships with consumers, retailers, and suppliers of fabric and other goods and services, Blue Sky believes it can create a sustainable competitive advantage over its rivals. No other clothing company can say to its customers with as much conviction, "Go Play Outside"!

SITUATION ANALYSIS

The marketing environment for Blue Sky represents overwhelming opportunities. It also contains some challenges that the firm believes it can meet successfully. Table A illustrates a SWOT analysis of the company conducted by marketers to highlight Blue Sky's strengths, weaknesses, opportunities, and threats.

The SWOT analysis presents a thumbnail sketch of the company's position in the marketplace. In just three years, Blue Sky has built some impressive strengths while looking forward to new opportunities. Its dedicated founders, the growing number of brand-loyal customers, and sound financial management place the company in a good position to grow.

It is important to state a firm's mission and goals, including financial and nonfinancial goals. Blue Sky's goals include growth and profits for the company as well as the ability to contribute to society through conservation programs.

This section reminds employees as well as those outside the company (such as potential lenders) exactly what Blue Sky does so well and how it plans to achieve a sustainable competitive advantage over rivals. Note that here and throughout the plan, Blue Sky focuses on relationships.

The situation analysis provides an outline of the marketing environment. A SWOT analysis helps marketers and others identify clearly a firm's strengths, weaknesses, opportunities, and threats. Again, relationships are a focus. Blue Sky has also conducted research on the outdoor clothing market, competitors, and consumers to determine how best to attract and keep customers.

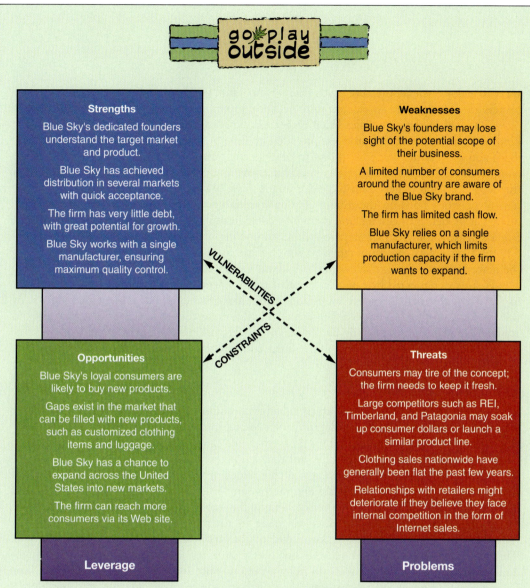

go play outside

Strengths

Blue Sky's dedicated founders understand the target market and product.

Blue Sky has achieved distribution in several markets with quick acceptance.

The firm has very little debt, with great potential for growth.

Blue Sky works with a single manufacturer, ensuring maximum quality control.

Weaknesses

Blue Sky's founders may lose sight of the potential scope of their business.

A limited number of consumers around the country are aware of the Blue Sky brand.

The firm has limited cash flow.

Blue Sky relies on a single manufacturer, which limits production capacity if the firm wants to expand.

Opportunities

Blue Sky's loyal consumers are likely to buy new products.

Gaps exist in the market that can be filled with new products, such as customized clothing items and luggage.

Blue Sky has a chance to expand across the United States into new markets.

The firm can reach more consumers via its Web site.

Threats

Consumers may tire of the concept; the firm needs to keep it fresh.

Large competitors such as REI, Timberland, and Patagonia may soak up consumer dollars or launch a similar product line.

Clothing sales nationwide have generally been flat the past few years.

Relationships with retailers might deteriorate if they believe they face internal competition in the form of Internet sales.

VULNERABILITIES

CONSTRAINTS

Leverage

Problems

However, as Blue Sky considers expansion of its product line and entry into new markets, the firm will have to guard against marketing myopia (the failure to recognize the scope of its business) and quality slippages. As the company finalizes plans for new products and expanded Internet sales, its management will also have to guard against competitors who attempt to duplicate the products. However, building strong relationships with consumers, retailers, and suppliers should help thwart competitors.

COMPETITORS IN THE OUTDOOR CLOTHING MARKET

The outdoor retail sales industry sells about $5 billion worth of goods annually, ranging from clothing to equipment. The outdoor apparel market has many entries. L. L. Bean, REI, Timberland, Bass Pro Shops, Cabela's, The North Face, and Patagonia are among the most recognizable companies that offer these products. Smaller competitors such as Title IX, which offers athletic clothing for women, and Ragged Mountain, which sells fleece clothing for skiers and hikers, also capture some of the market. The outlook for the industry in general—and Blue Sky in particular—is positive for several reasons. First, consumers are participating in and investing in recreational activities that are near their homes. Second, consumers are looking for

ways to enjoy their leisure time with friends and family without overspending. Third, consumers are gaining more confidence in the economy and are willing and able to spend more.

While all of the companies listed earlier can be considered competitors, none offers the kind of trendy, yet practical products provided by Blue Sky—and none carries the customized logos and slogans that Blue Sky plans to offer in the near future. In addition, most of these competitors sell performance apparel in high-tech manufactured fabrics. With the exception of the fleece vests and jackets, Blue Sky's clothing is made of strictly the highest-quality cotton, so it may be worn both on the hiking trail and around town. Finally, Blue Sky products are offered at moderate prices, making them affordable in multiple quantities. For instance, a Blue Sky T-shirt sells for $15.99, compared with a competing high-performance T-shirt that sells for $29.99. Consumers can easily replace a set of shirts from one season to the next, picking up the newest colors, without having to think about the purchase.

A survey conducted by Blue Sky revealed that 67 percent of responding consumers prefer to replace their casual and active wear more often than other clothing, so they are attracted by the moderate pricing of Blue Sky products. In addition, as the trend toward health-conscious activities and concerns about the natural environment continue, consumers increasingly relate to the Blue Sky philosophy as well as the firm's contributions to socially responsible programs.

THE TARGET MARKET

> Blue Sky has identified its customers as active people between ages 25 and 45. However, that doesn't mean someone who is older or prefers to read about the outdoors isn't a potential customer as well. By pinpointing where existing customers live, Blue Sky can plan for growth into new outlets.

The target market for Blue Sky products is active consumers between ages 25 and 45—people who like to hike, rock climb, bicycle, surf, figure skate, in-line skate, ride horses, snowboard or ski, kayak, and other such activities. In short, they like to "Go Play Outside." They might not be experts at the sports they engage in, but they enjoy themselves outdoors.

These active consumers represent a demographic group of well-educated and successful individuals; they are single or married and raising families. Household incomes generally range between $60,000 and $120,000 annually. Despite their comfortable incomes, these consumers are price conscious and consistently seek value in their purchases. Regardless of their age (whether they fall at the upper or lower end of the target range), they lead active lifestyles. They are somewhat status oriented but not overly so. They like to be associated with high-quality products but are not willing to pay a premium price for a certain brand. Current Blue Sky customers tend to live in northern New England, the South, California, and the Northwest. However, one future goal is to target consumers in the Mid-Atlantic states and Southwest as well.

THE MARKETING MIX

> The strongest part of the marketing mix for Blue Sky involves sales promotions, public relations, and nontraditional marketing strategies such as attending outdoor events and organizing activities such as day hikes and bike rides.

The following discussion outlines some of the details of the proposed marketing mix for Blue Sky products.

PRODUCT STRATEGY. Blue Sky currently offers a line of high-quality outdoor apparel items including cotton T-shirts, baseball caps, and fleece vests and jackets. All bear the company logo and slogan, "Go Play Outside." The firm has researched the most popular colors for its items and given them names that consumers enjoy—sunset red, sunrise pink, cactus green, desert rose, and river rock gray, among others. Over the next five years, Blue Sky plans to expand the product line to include customized clothing items. Customers may select a logo that represents their sport—say, rock climbing. Then they can add a slogan to match the logo, such as "Get Over It." A baseball cap with a bicyclist might bear the slogan, "Take a Spin." At the beginning, there would be ten new logos and five new slogans; more would be added later.

Eventually, some slogans and logos would be retired, and new ones introduced. This strategy will keep the concept fresh and prevent it from becoming diluted with too many variations.

The second way in which Blue Sky plans to expand its product line is to offer items of lightweight luggage—two sizes of duffel bags, two sizes of tote bags, and a daypack. These items would also come in trendy and basic colors, with a choice of logos and slogans. In addition, every product would bear the Blue Sky logo.

DISTRIBUTION STRATEGY. Currently, Blue Sky is marketed through regional and local specialty shops scattered along the California coast, into the Northwest, across the South, and in northern New England. So far, Blue Sky has not been distributed through national sporting goods and apparel chains. Climate and season tend to dictate the sales at specialty shops, which sell more T-shirts and baseball caps during warm weather and more fleece vests and jackets during colder months. Blue Sky obtains much of its information about overall industry trends in different geographic areas and at different types of retail outlets from its trade organization, Outdoor Industry Association.

Over the next three years, Blue Sky seeks to expand distribution to retail specialty shops throughout the nation, focusing next on the southwest and mid-Atlantic regions. The firm has not yet determined whether it would be beneficial to sell through a major national chain such as REI or Bass Pro Shops, as these outlets could be considered competitors.

In addition, Blue Sky plans to expand online sales by offering the customized product line via Internet only, thus distinguishing between Internet offerings and specialty shop offerings. Eventually, we may be able to place Internet kiosks at some of the more profitable store outlets so that consumers could order customized products from the stores. Regardless of its expansion plans, Blue Sky fully intends to monitor and maintain strong relationships with distribution channel members.

PROMOTION STRATEGY. Blue Sky communicates with consumers and retailers about its products in a variety of ways. Information about Blue Sky—the company as well as its products—is available via the Internet, through direct mailings, and in person. The firm's promotional efforts also seek to differentiate its products from those of its competitors.

The company relies on personal contact with retailers to establish the products in their stores. This contact, whether in person or by phone, helps convey the Blue Sky message, demonstrate the products' unique qualities, and build relationships. Blue Sky sales representatives visit each store two or three times a year and offer in-store training on the features of the products for new retailers or for those who want a refresher. As distribution expands, Blue Sky will adjust to meet greater demand by increasing sales staff to make sure its stores are visited more frequently.

Sales promotions and public relations currently make up the bulk of Blue Sky's promotional strategy. Blue Sky staff works with retailers to offer short-term sales promotions tied to events and contests. In addition, Nick Russell is currently working with several trip outfitters to offer Blue Sky items on a promotional basis. Because Blue Sky also engages in cause marketing through its contribution to environmental programs, good public relations have followed.

Nontraditional marketing methods that require little cash and a lot of creativity also lend themselves perfectly to Blue Sky. Because Blue Sky is a small, flexible organization, the firm can easily implement ideas such as distributing free water, stickers, and discount coupons at outdoor sporting events. During the next year, the company plans to engage in the following marketing efforts:

- Create a Blue Sky Tour, in which several employees take turns driving around the country to campgrounds to distribute promotional items such as Blue Sky stickers and discount coupons.

- Attend canoe and kayak races, bicycling events, and rock climbing competitions with our Blue Sky truck to distribute free water, stickers, and discount coupons for Blue Sky shirts or hats.

- Organize Blue Sky hikes departing from participating retailers.

- Hold a Blue Sky design contest, selecting a winning slogan and logo to be added to the customized line.

PRICING STRATEGY. As discussed earlier in this plan, Blue Sky products are priced with the competition in mind. The firm is not concerned with setting high prices to signal luxury or prestige, nor is it attempting to achieve the goals of offsetting low prices by selling large quantities of products. Instead, value pricing is practiced so that customers feel comfortable purchasing new clothing to replace the old, even if it is just because they like the new colors. The pricing strategy also makes Blue Sky products good gifts—for birthdays, graduations, or "just because." The customized clothing will sell for $2 to $4 more than the regular Blue Sky logo clothing. The luggage will be priced competitively, offering a good value against its competition.

BUDGET, SCHEDULE, AND MONITORING

Though its history is short, Blue Sky has enjoyed a steady increase in sales since its introduction three years ago. Figure A shows these three years, plus projected sales for the next three years, including the introduction of the two new product lines. Additional financial data are included in the overall business plan for the company.

An actual plan will include more specific financial details, which will be folded into the overall business plan. For more information, see the "Financial Analysis in Marketing" appendix at the end of this book. In addition, Blue Sky states that at this stage, it does not have plans to exit the market by merging with another firm or making a public stock offering.

figure A

Annual Sales for Blue Sky Clothing: 2007–2012

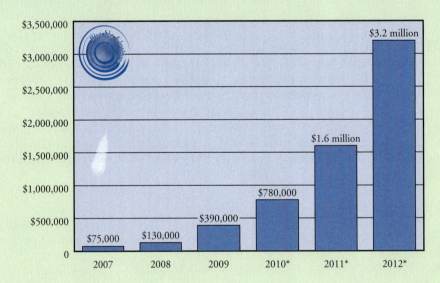

*Projected sales

The timeline for expansion of outlets and introduction of the two new product lines is shown in Figure B. The implementation of each of these tasks will be monitored closely and evaluated for its performance.

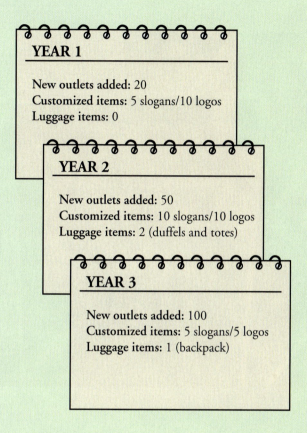

YEAR 1

New outlets added: 20
Customized items: 5 slogans/10 logos
Luggage items: 0

YEAR 2

New outlets added: 50
Customized items: 10 slogans/10 logos
Luggage items: 2 (duffels and totes)

YEAR 3

New outlets added: 100
Customized items: 5 slogans/5 logos
Luggage items: 1 (backpack)

figure B

Timeline for First Three
Years of Marketing Plan

Blue Sky anticipates continuing operations into the foreseeable future, with no plans to exit this market. Instead, as discussed throughout this plan, the firm plans to increase its presence in the market. At present, there are no plans to merge with another company or to make a public stock offering.

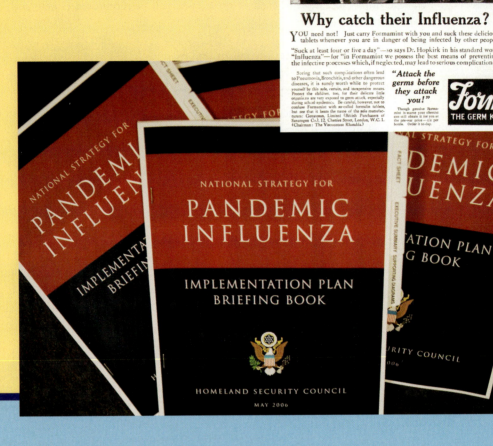

CHAPTER 3

Risky Business: Avian Flu and the Marketplace

More and more people travel today. As they visit places around the globe, they are exposed to all kinds of serious—and sometimes contagious—diseases. Some can prevented by vaccinations; others have no known cures. Stories about the respiratory illness SARS and now avian flu—both of which originated in Asia—have filled the news for several years. While some people shrug and point out that the avian flu virus has yet to be spread from human to human, health officials worry about the potential of an avian flu pandemic, capable of killing millions of people in a single sweep. The threat of avian flu affects businesspeople who travel and the travel industry itself. But it also has the capacity to stretch the limits of the political, technological, and legal systems in affected countries.

Because Hawaii is the U.S. state nearest to Asia, officials there worry that not only travelers but also migrating birds could bring the flu home to roost in their state. Hawaii depends on tourism for much of its income, and food and supplies are routinely shipped into the state. So Hawaiians have gone to great lengths to prepare for a possible invasion of avian flu. Scientists now routinely test birds, and labs are open to test samples from humans, too. Businesses and hospitals are also making preparations, stockpiling supplies in case shipping is cut off due to quarantines. The Centers for Disease Control requires airlines to notify them of any arriving passengers with avian flu symptoms so that they can be tested by state health officials. "Avian flu is a little like watching for that hurricane, and people

here take it seriously," explains Chris Chelsea, who maps the spread of the virus for the Pacific Disaster Center on Maui.

While Hawaii remains on the front lines of surveillance for the virus, the Congressional Budget Office warns that if avian flu does become a human flu and spread rapidly across the United States, roughly a third of the population—90 million people—could become ill. This possible disaster could mean a $167 billion loss to the economy, in addition to the health and lives of people. Sales of many goods and services such as restaurant meals and vacations would likely plummet, although online purchases and telephone orders might increase. While no one wants this grave scenario to happen, one expert warns that "pandemics aren't

The Marketing Environment, Ethics, and Social Responsibility

Chapter Objectives

1. Identify the five components of the marketing environment.

2. Explain the types of competition marketers face and the steps necessary for developing a competitive strategy.

3. Describe how marketing activities are regulated and how marketers can influence the political-legal environment.

4. Outline the economic factors that affect marketing decisions and consumer buying power.

5. Discuss the impact of the technological environment on a firm's marketing activities.

6. Explain how the social-cultural environment influences marketing.

7. Describe the ethical issues in marketing.

8. Identify the four levels of the social responsibility pyramid.

optional—they occur. The only question is whether this one will be the next one."

Looking at the brighter side, a vaccine for avian and other strains of influenza does exist. But the vaccine must be manufactured under strict quality and legal controls, by certain firms, in specified quantities. The medicine must also arrive in time to be administered before the virus hits the general population. In the United States, the Food and Drug Administration (FDA) is in charge of approving and regulating vaccines. Currently, firms outside the United States make most of the vaccines, including a European subsidiary of GlaxoSmithKline and Sanofi-Pasteur. Another major supplier, Chiron, was shut down when its vaccine supply was discovered to be contaminated. Recently the FDA issued new, streamlined guidelines for vaccine manufacturers to bring their products to the marketplace. However, in exchange for speeding the process of approval, firms must agree to conduct follow-up studies on their vaccines once they are being used. "Having more manufacturers of influenza vaccine licensed in

the U.S., and having more vaccine dosages, is critical to public health," says Mike Leavitt, secretary of the Department of Health and Human Services.

evolution
of a brand

A nervous world is watching the progress of avian flu. So far, the spread has still been limited to people with very close contact with poultry—mostly in Asia. If widespread human-to-human transmission of avian flu does become a reality, a vaccine targeted directly to that strain of the virus could be manufactured within about six months of its discovery. But mass production to prevent the spread of the disease would take more time. In the meantime, health officials would look to medications, such as Tamiflu, that can be taken orally within 48 hours to lessen the effects of flu in a patient.

Tamiflu, manufactured by Swiss-based firm Roche Pharmaceuticals, was approved for use to treat many strains of influenza in the United States in 1999. It is available by prescription and helps lessen the symptoms of flu in patients who already have the disease. Tamiflu does not prevent influenza; instead, it attacks the virus already in the patient to lessen the severity and duration of symptoms. Currently, most doctors are refraining from writing prescriptions for individual patients to stockpile—just in case they need it. Doing this allows the manufacturer to provide its doses to governments, which can then distribute the medication to targeted areas to help control the spread of flu outbreaks.[1]

- The U.S. secretary of Health and Human Services, Mike Leavitt, has set a goal for the nation to stockpile enough Tamiflu to treat one-fourth

A public health issue can very quickly become an economic issue, affecting most segments of the marketing environment. In Europe, Asia, and other areas of the world, avian flu is already damaging certain businesses. The European Union, a large exporter of poultry, has seen a significant downturn in demand. "What happens . . . depends a lot on how consumers view imported versus domestically produced product," explains one industry expert. "The European Union is a very large exporter of poultry. They usually export about a million tons a year. And so, that's basically trade bans on European products."[2]

Chapter Overview

Change is a fact of life for all people, including marketers. Adapting to change in an environment as complex and unpredictable as the one dealing with avian flu is perhaps the supreme challenge.

Although some change may be the result of sudden crises, more often it is the result of a gradual trend in lifestyle, income, population, and other factors. General Motors is clinging to its spot as the world's largest automaker. Changes in the economy, increased competition, rising production and fuel costs, and consumer preferences recently caused the firm to cut 30,000 jobs and close nine North American plants. Toyota is waiting in the wings.[3] Technology can trigger a sudden change in the marketplace: in one fell swoop, it appeared that Internet music downloads had replaced traditional CDs. And within

mere months of offering its first iPod, Apple introduced the video iPod.

Marketers must anticipate and plan for change. They must set goals to meet the concerns of customers, employees, shareholders, and members of the general public. Industry competition, legal constraints, the impact of technology on product designs, and social concerns are some of the many important factors that shape the business environment. All potentially have impact on a firm's goods and services. Although external forces frequently are outside the marketing manager's control, decision makers must still consider those influences together with the variables of the marketing mix in developing—and occasionally modifying—marketing plans and strategies that take these environmental factors into consideration.

This chapter begins by describing five forces in marketing's external environment—competitive, political-legal, economic, technological, and social-cultural. Figure 3.1 identifies them as the foundation for making decisions that involve the four marketing mix elements and the target market. These forces provide the frame of reference within which all marketing decisions are made. The second focus of this chapter is marketing ethics and social responsibility. That section describes the nature of marketers' responsibilities both to business and to society at large.

1   Identify the five components of the marketing environment.

environmental scanning Process of collecting information about the external marketing environment to identify and interpret potential trends.

ENVIRONMENTAL SCANNING AND ENVIRONMENTAL MANAGEMENT

Marketers constantly monitor crucial trends and developments in the business environment. **Environmental scanning** is the process of collecting information about the external marketing environment to identify and interpret potential trends. The goal of this process is to analyze the information and decide whether these trends represent significant opportunities or pose major threats to the company. The firm can then determine the best response to a particular environmental change.

After the first case of mad cow disease in the United States was confirmed, some consumers were afraid to eat beef. Producers of so-called natural or organic beef recognized an opportunity in the marketplace—increased demand for their products. So they swung into action, shifting to more aggressive marketing tactics to demonstrate that their meat was safe for consumers. They pointed out that their beef, produced without artificial growth hormones or most antibiotics, was obtained from cows fed vegetarian diets and was monitored throughout the production process. Even though their beef costs more, these marketers made inroads. Organic farming currently ranks as one of the fastest-growing segments of U.S. agriculture.

But the fear of contaminated beef didn't stop at the U.S. borders. South Korea, the third-largest market for U.S. beef, banned imports of the beef. Japan closed its doors on U.S. beef when the country received a faulty veal shipment. Several years later, South Korea—along with 68 other countries—agreed to begin receiving U.S. beef again, under strict regulations. Japan continued its negotiations and discovered its own case of mad cow disease.[4]

Environmental scanning is a vital component of effective **environmental management.** Environmental management involves marketers' efforts to achieve organizational objectives by predicting and influencing the competitive, political-legal, economic, technological, and social-cultural environments. In the political-legal environment, managers who seek modifications of regulations, laws, or tariff restrictions may lobby legislators or contribute to the campaigns of sympathetic politicians. In response to criticism, Pharmaceutical Research and Manufacturers of America, a group that represents the pharmaceuticals industry, created its own voluntary code of

environmental management Attainment of organizational objectives by predicting and influencing the competitive, political-legal, economic, technological, and social-cultural environments.

figure 3.1

Elements of the Marketing Mix within an Environmental Framework

...Duane Dorenkamp, the Willises, the Ostermans, the Blackfords and the dozens of other family farmers across the Midwest who raise pork the old-fashioned way. Naturally.

These are the farmers of Niman Ranch, the fine folks who provide much of the pork we use in our carnitas. We've visited their farms, walked their fields, even met their families.

What sets these farmers apart is their commitment to sustainable agriculture. That means their pigs are raised with plenty of room to roam and socialize. They eat only corn, soy and other natural grains and grasses. And since Niman Ranch pigs are free from the unhealthy, cramped conditions of mass-produced corporate hog operations, they don't need or receive antibiotics.

So that's why our carnitas are made from all the Niman Ranch pork we can buy. We think it's the best-tasting pork available.

Duane's betting the farm you'll agree.

Chipotle.

TRY A LITTLE TENDERNESS
FIND YOURS @ CHIPOTLE.COM

Capitalizing on the trend for organic foods, Chipotle fast-food restaurants offer customers fresh ingredients such as chicken, pork, and beef that are raised without growth hormones or antibiotics.

✓ **assessment check**

1. Define *environmental scanning*.

2. How does environmental scanning contribute to environmental management?

competitive environment
Interactive process that occurs in the marketplace among marketers of directly competitive products, marketers of products that can be substituted for one another, and marketers competing for the consumer's purchasing power.

conduct for advertising prescription drugs on TV and in print. The code includes guidelines for creating serious, informative ads that point to a drug's risks as well as benefits. "We don't make ice cream or handbags or automobiles," observed Bill Tauzin, president of the organization. "We make products that save lives."[5]

For many domestic and international firms, competing with established industry leaders frequently involves **strategic alliances**—partnerships with other firms in which the partners combine resources and capital to create competitive advantages in a new market. Strategic alliances are especially common in international marketing, in which partnerships with local firms provide regional expertise for a company expanding its operations abroad. According to one study, about 35 percent of all corporate revenues worldwide are the result of some kind of strategic alliance.[6] Members of such alliances share risks and profits. Alliances are considered essential in a country such as China, where laws require foreign firms doing business there to work with local companies.

Through successful research and development efforts, firms may influence changes in their own technological environments. A research breakthrough may lead to reduced production costs or a technologically superior new product. While changes in the marketing environment may be beyond the control of individual marketers, managers continually seek to predict their impact on marketing decisions and to modify operations to meet changing market needs. Even modest environmental shifts can alter the results of those decisions.

THE COMPETITIVE ENVIRONMENT

As organizations vie to satisfy customers, the interactive exchange creates the **competitive environment.** Marketing decisions by individual firms influence consumer responses in the marketplace. They also affect the marketing strategies of competitors. As a consequence, marketers must continually monitor their competitors' marketing activities—their products, distribution channels, prices, and promotional efforts.

Few organizations have **monopoly** positions as the sole supplier of a good or service in the marketplace. Utilities, such as natural gas, electricity, water, and cable TV service, have traditionally accepted considerable regulation from local authorities who controlled such marketing-related factors as rates, service levels, and geographic coverage. In exchange, the utilities gained exclusive rights to serve a particular group of consumers. But the **deregulation movement** of the past three decades has ended total monopoly protection for most utilities. Many shoppers can choose from alternative cable TV and Internet providers, cell phone and traditional telephone carriers, and even gas and electric utilities. Some firms, such as pharmaceuticals giants Merck and Pfizer, have *temporary* monopolies provided by patents on new drugs. When the FDA approves a new drug for lowering cholesterol or improving sleep, its manufacturer is typically granted exclusive rights to produce and market the product during the life of the patent. Theoretically, this gives the manufacturer a chance to recoup the millions spent on developing and launching the drug. Once the patent expires, all bets are off—and competitors can flood the market with generic versions of the drug.

Through industry megamergers, some companies try to dominate markets without creating illegal monopolies. As a result of mergers, the telecommunications industry is now dominated by a few giants. Twenty years ago, AT&T—often called "Ma Bell"—was forced to split into local "Baby Bells" as the result of an **antitrust** case that determined the firm had become a monopoly. But a few years ago, SBC Communications bought the smaller, reorganized AT&T for $16 billion, re-creating the largest telecommunications firm in the United States—called AT&T. A year later, the new AT&T acquired BellSouth, giving the firm 49 million access lines. Cingular Wireless, which has a joint venture with BellSouth, is now the nation's largest U.S. wireless carrier, with 54 million subscribers.[7]

Rather than seeking sole dominance of a market, corporations increasingly prefer to share the pie with just a few rivals. Referred to by economists as an **oligopoly,** this structure of a limited number of sellers in an industry in which high start-up costs form barriers to keep out new competitors deters newcomers from breaking into markets, while ensuring that corporations remain innovative. In one of the numerous ongoing antitrust actions being pursued against Microsoft, the European Committee for Interoperable Systems (ECIS)—which includes firms such as IBM, Oracle, Nokia, RealNetworks, and Sun Microsystems—has filed a complaint alleging that Microsoft does not make its Office program compatible with competing programs, and continues to engage in unethical bundling of certain products.[8]

TYPES OF COMPETITION

Marketers face three types of competition. The most *direct* form occurs among marketers of similar products, as when an ExxonMobil station opens across the street from a Shell retail outlet. The cell phone market provides consumers with such alternative suppliers as Verizon, Cingular, and T-Mobile.

Costco—which sells everything from home generators to birthday cakes—also takes direct aim at luxury retailers. Costco offers diamond jewelry, cashmere sweaters, and Coach and Kate Spade handbags. And in a new venture with Synergy Brands, the retailer will sell Synergy's line of designer luxury goods, including handbags, wallets, briefcases, and other goods. "The new line fits with Costco's history of success with luxury products, which contribute to the treasure hunt atmosphere the company tries to deliver to its clubs," writes one industry watcher.[9]

A second type of competition is *indirect,* involving products that are easily substituted. In the fast-food industry, pizza competes with chicken, hamburgers, and tacos. In entertainment, a movie could be substituted for a concert or a night at the bowling alley. Six Flags and Universal Studios amusement parks—traditional hot spots for family vacations—now compete with outdoor adventure trips. One of every two U.S. adults will decide not to make this year's vacation a tranquil week at the beach or a trip to Disney World. Instead, they'll choose to do something more adventurous—thrill-filled experiences such as skydiving, whitewater rafting, or climbing Mount Rainier. So marketers have to find ways to attract consumers to their specific brand as well as to their type of product.

A change such as a price increase or an improvement in a product's attributes can also affect demand for substitute products. As the prices for one type of energy soar, consumers look for cheaper—and more environmentally friendly—alternatives. State regulators in California recently approved $3 billion in customer rebates in an effort to encourage residents to install solar panels in the roofs of their houses. U.S. mining companies are now taking another look at uranium to fuel more nuclear power plants. And Japanese scientists have announced that they can extract gasoline from cattle dung. "The new technology will be a boon for livestock breeders," who have to struggle to find ways to dispose of nearly half a million tons of waste per year, notes a Japanese agricultural engineering professor.[10]

One substitute, the Internet access known as wireless fidelity, or *Wi-Fi,* has experienced a rocky start-up. While industry observers project that every laptop and handheld computer will soon be able to receive Wi-Fi, it's difficult to predict how many people will use it. A wireless network allows computers, printers, and other devices to be

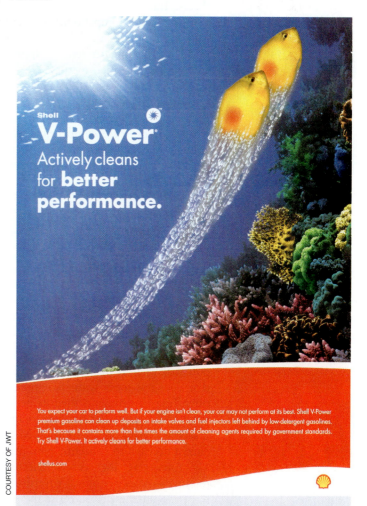

COURTESY OF JWT

Shell promotes the benefits of its V-Power gasoline, which is formulated to clean up engine deposits left by low-detergent gasolines. The company says this gasoline contains more than five times the amount of cleaning agents required by federal government standards.

connected without the inconvenience of stringing cables in traditional office or home settings. Wi-Fi is a wireless network that connects various devices and allows them to communicate with one another through radio waves. Any PC with a Wi-Fi receptor can connect with the Internet at so-called *hot spots*—locations with a wireless router and a high-speed Internet modem. By one estimate, the number of registered hot spots worldwide now exceeds 70,000.[11] They are found in a variety of places, including airports, libraries, and coffee shops. For instance, most Starbucks shops are Wi-Fi hot spots. Some hot spots provide free Internet access, while others are fee based. More and more coffee shops, bookstores, and even cities are offering free Wi-Fi hot spots for at least a few hours at a time. Many hotels, though, still charge their guests a daily fee for wireless access.

Many believe that the successor to Wi-Fi will be *WiMAX*, a new wireless standard. WiMAX recently got a huge boost when Intel announced that it would begin producing computer chips incorporating this new wireless standard.[12] Unlike Wi-Fi's relatively limited geographic coverage area—generally around 300 feet—a single WiMAX access point can provide coverage over many miles. Hundreds of cities, including San Francisco and Philadelphia, have announced plans to build WiMAX networks that will, in essence, turn these cities into giant hot spots. WiMAX also has the potential to bring high-speed Internet access to rural areas where traditional forms of broadband are too expensive or impractical. For instance, Morrow County, Oregon, has only 11,000 people but covers more than 2,000 square miles. WiMAX is the only practical and cost-effective way to provide broadband access to this sparsely populated region. So Morrow County became one of the first rural areas in the country to be blanketed by a WiMAX network.[13]

The final type of competition occurs among all organizations that compete for consumers' purchases. Traditional economic analysis views competition as a battle among companies in the same industry (direct competition) or among substitutable goods and services (indirect competition). But marketers know that *all* firms compete for a limited number of dollars that consumers can or will spend. In this broader sense, competition means that purchase of a Honda Accord might compete with a Holland America cruise.

Because the competitive environment often determines the success or failure of a product, marketers must continually assess competitors' marketing strategies. New products, updated features or technology, increased service, and lower prices are all variations that marketers look for. When changes occur in the competition, marketers must decide how to respond.

DEVELOPING A COMPETITIVE STRATEGY

Marketers at every successful firm must develop an effective strategy for dealing with the competitive environment. One company may compete in a broad range of markets in many areas of the world. Another may specialize in particular market segments, such as those determined by customers' geographic location, age, or income characteristics. Determining a **competitive strategy** involves answering the following three questions:

1. Should we compete?

2. If so, in what markets should we compete?

3. How should we compete?

The answer to the first question depends on the firm's resources, objectives, and expected profit potential. A firm may decide not to pursue or continue operating a potentially successful venture that does not mesh with its resources, objectives, or profit expectations. Semiconductor manufacturer Texas Instruments shed its defense electronics business unit, which makes missile sensors and radar and night-vision systems, to an aircraft company where this unit was a better fit. When pharmaceutical giant Merck spun off Medco, its profitable pharmacy-benefits-management subsidiary, it cited a decision to concentrate on its core business—developing breakthrough medicines.

Answering the second question requires marketers to acknowledge their firm's limited resources—sales personnel, advertising budgets, product development capability, and the like. They must allocate these resources to the areas of greatest opportunity. Some companies gain access to new markets or new technologies through acquisitions or mergers. By acquiring MCI, Verizon Communications gained access to a huge, international long-distance telecommunications and data network, along with hundreds of thousands of existing MCI residential and business customers.

Answering the third question on the list requires marketers to make product, distribution, promotion, and pricing decisions that give the firm a competitive advantage in the marketplace. Firms can compete on a variety of bases, including product quality, price, and customer service. Starbucks, Dunkin' Donuts, and McDonald's all sell coffee. But after looking at the competition, McDonald's brought a premium coffee supplier on board. It is now selling richer, more flavorful coffee—for about 20 cents more per cup. But the price is still less than that of competing coffee brands Starbucks and Dunkin' Donuts. Starbucks, however, continues with its competitive strategy of offering premium coffee in a setting where customers like to relax and linger. Dunkin' Donuts, whose focus has traditionally been in New England, is expanding across the country with the goal of competing directly with Starbucks.[14]

TIME-BASED COMPETITION

With increased international competition and rapid changes in technology, a steadily growing number of firms are using time as a strategic competitive weapon. **Time-based competition** is the strategy of developing and distributing goods and services more quickly than competitors. Although a video option on cell phones came late to the U.S. market, the new feature was a big hit, attracting new customers to cell phone providers. The flexibility and responsiveness of time-based competitors enable them to improve product quality, reduce costs, and expand product offerings to satisfy new market segments and enhance customer satisfaction.

In rapidly changing markets—particularly those that involve technology—time-based competition is critical to a firm's success. Google and CBS both offer their own news to mobile phone users. In addition, several other firms—T-Mobile, Sony Ericsson, and Motorola—have announced partnerships with Google that position a Google search bar on mobile phones. In the race for digital entertainment customers, Apple launched a new minicomputer designed as a "hub" for consumers' digital entertainment, as well as a home stereo system linked to the iPod.[15]

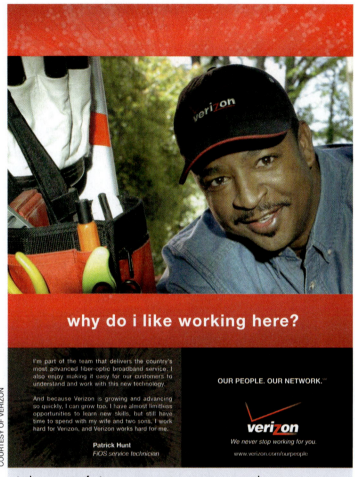

COURTESY OF VERIZON

As the competition for Internet access continues to grow among telecommunications companies, so does Verizon's fiber-optic network. The network can deliver fast broadband connections to customers' homes.

 assessment check

1. Distinguish between direct and indirect competition and give an example of each.
2. What is time-based competition?

THE POLITICAL-LEGAL ENVIRONMENT

Before you play the game, learn the rules! You may find it hard to win a new game without first understanding the rules. Yet some businesspeople exhibit a lack of knowledge about marketing's **political-legal environment**—the laws and their interpretations that require firms to operate under competitive conditions and to protect consumer rights. Ignorance of laws, ordinances, and regulations or noncompliance with them can result in fines, negative publicity, and expensive civil damage suits.

The existing U.S. legal framework was constructed piecemeal, often in response to issues that were important when individual laws were enacted. Businesspeople must be diligent to understand the legal system's relationship to their marketing decisions. Numerous laws and regulations affect those decisions, many of them vaguely stated and inconsistently enforced by a multitude of different authorities.

political-legal environment Component of the marketing environment consisting of laws and their interpretations that require firms to operate under competitive conditions and to protect consumer rights.

Federal, state, and local regulations affect marketing practices, as do the actions of independent regulatory agencies. These requirements and prohibitions touch on all aspects of marketing decision making: designing, labeling, packaging, distributing, advertising, and promoting goods and services. To cope with the vast, complex, and changing political-legal environment, many large firms maintain in-house legal departments; small firms often seek professional advice from outside attorneys. All marketers, however, should be aware of the major regulations that affect their activities.

GOVERNMENT REGULATION

3 Describe how marketing activities are regulated and how marketers can influence the political-legal environment.

The history of U.S. government regulation can be divided into four phases. The first phase was the *antimonopoly period* of the late 19th and early 20th centuries. During this era, major laws such as the Sherman Antitrust Act, Clayton Act, and Federal Trade Commission Act were passed to maintain a competitive environment by reducing the trend toward increasing concentration of industry power in the hands of a small number of competitors. Laws enacted more than 100 years ago still affect business in the 21st century.

The Microsoft case is a good example of antitrust legislation at work. The U.S. Department of Justice found the software powerhouse guilty of predatory practices designed to crush competition. By bundling its own Internet Explorer browser with its Windows operating system—which runs 90 percent of the world's personal computers—Microsoft grabbed the majority of the market from rival Netscape. It also bullied firms as large as America Online to drop Netscape Navigator in favor of its browser. Microsoft's supporters countered that consumers have clearly benefited from the integrated features in Windows and that its bundling decisions were simply efforts to offer customer satisfaction through added value.

The second phase, aimed at *protecting competitors,* emerged during the Great Depression era of the 1930s, when independent merchants felt the need for legal protection against competition from larger chain stores. Among the federal legislation enacted was the Robinson-Patman Act. The third regulatory phase focused on *consumer protection.* The objective of consumer protection underlies most laws—with good examples including the Sherman Act, FTC Act, and Federal Food and Drug Act. Additional laws have been enacted over the past 40 years. The fourth phase, *industry deregulation,* began in the late 1970s and continues to the present. During this phase, government has sought to increase competition in such industries as telecommunications, utilities, transportation, and financial services by discontinuing many regulations and permitting firms to expand their service offerings to new markets.

The newest regulatory frontier is *cyberspace.* Federal and state regulators are investigating ways to police the Internet and online services. The FTC, along with private organizations and other government agencies, has created a site, **http://www.onguardonline.gov**, where consumers can take quizzes designed to educate them about ID theft, spam (junk e-mail), phishing (luring consumers to provide personal information), and online shopping scams. But cybercrime is spreading quickly. Attacks by malicious software that contain codes capable of stealing account logons, passwords, and other confidential data are on the rise. Nearly 10 million households that engage in online banking have had their computers infected by keystroke loggers, programs that give cybercrooks access to deposits. In addition, cybercrooks can create new accounts and obtain credit cards with stolen identities.[16]

Privacy and child protection issues are another important—but difficult—enforcement challenge. With the passage of the Children's Online Privacy Protection Act, Congress took the first step in regulating what children are exposed to on the Internet. The primary focus is a set of rules regarding how and when marketers need to get parental permission before obtaining marketing research information from children over the Web. Finally, the government's Do Not Call Registry, a list to which consumers can add their phone numbers—including cell phones—to avoid telemarketing calls, provides protection for consumers who do not want to be contacted by telemarketers. A violation can result in a $10,000 fine for the offending firm. However, telemarketers for not-for-profit organizations, companies with which the consumer has an existing relationship, and political candidates are exempt from the law.[17]

Table 3.1 lists and briefly describes the major federal laws affecting marketing. Legislation covering specific marketing practices, such as product development, packaging, labeling, product warranties, and franchise agreements, is discussed in later chapters.

Briefly
Speaking

"Consumers want more control over their telephones. Today we give it to them."

—Michael K. Powell (b. 1963)

Former chairman, Federal Communications Commission (announcing the implementation of the National Do Not Call Registry)

table 3.1 Major Federal Laws Affecting Marketing

DATE	LAW	DESCRIPTION
A. LAWS MAINTAINING A COMPETITIVE ENVIRONMENT		
1890	Sherman Antitrust Act	Prohibits restraint of trade and monopolization; identifies a competitive marketing system as national policy goal.
1914	Clayton Act	Strengthens the Sherman Act by restricting such practices as price discrimination, exclusive dealing, tying contracts, and interlocking boards of directors where the effect "may be to substantially lessen competition or tend to create a monopoly"; amended by the Celler-Kefauver Antimerger Act to prohibit major asset purchases that would decrease competition in an industry.
1914	Federal Trade Commission Act (FTC)	Prohibits unfair methods of competition; establishes the Federal Trade Commission, an administrative agency that investigates business practices and enforces the FTC Act.
1938	Wheeler-Lea Act	Amends the FTC Act to outlaw additional unfair practices; gives the FTC jurisdiction over false and misleading advertising.
1998	Digital Millennium Copyright Act	Protects intellectual property rights by prohibiting copying or downloading of digital files
B. LAWS REGULATING COMPETITION		
1936	Robinson-Patman Act	Prohibits price discrimination in sales to wholesalers, retailers, or other producers; prohibits selling at unreasonably low prices to eliminate competition.
1993	North American Free Trade Agreement (NAFTA)	International trade agreement between Canada, Mexico, and the United States designed to facilitate trade by removing tariffs and other trade barriers among the three nations.
C. LAWS PROTECTING CONSUMERS		
1906	Federal Food and Drug Act	Prohibits adulteration and misbranding of food and drugs involved in interstate commerce; strengthened by the Food, Drug, and Cosmetic Act (1938) and the Kefauver-Harris Drug Amendment (1962).
1970	National Environmental Policy Act	Establishes the Environmental Protection Agency to deal with various types of pollution and organizations that create pollution.
1971	Public Health Cigarette Smoking Act	Prohibits tobacco advertising on radio and television.
1972	Consumer Product Safety Act	Created the Consumer Product Safety Commission, which has authority to specify safety standards for most products.
1998	Children's Online Privacy Protection Act	Empowers FTC to set rules regarding how and when marketers must obtain parental permission before asking children marketing research questions.
1999	Anticybersquatting Consumer Protection Act	Bans the bad-faith purchase of domain names that are identical or confusingly similar to existing registered trademarks.
2001	Electronic Signature Act	Gives electronic signatures the same legal weight as handwritten signatures.
2005	Real ID Act	Signed into law by President George W. Bush in May 2005. Going into effect in 2008; it establishes and implements regulations for state driver's license and identification document security standards.
2006	Consumer Telephone Records Act	Prohibits the sale of cell phone records.
D. LAWS DEREGULATING SPECIFIC INDUSTRIES		
1978	Airline Deregulation Act	Grants considerable freedom to commercial airlines in setting fares and choosing new routes.
1980	Motor Carrier Act and Staggers Rail Act	Significantly deregulates trucking and railroad industries by permitting them to negotiate rates and services.
1996	Telecommunications Act	Significantly deregulates the telecommunications industry by removing barriers to competition in local and long-distance phone and cable and television markets.
2003	Amendments to the Telemarketing Sales Rule	Created a national Do Not Call Registry, which prohibits telemarketing calls to registered telephone numbers; restricted the number and duration of telemarketing calls generating dead air space with use of automatic dialers; cracked down on unauthorized billing; and required telemarketers to transmit their caller ID information. Telemarketers must check the Do Not Call list quarterly, and violators could be fined as much as $11,000 per occurrence. Excluded from the registry's restrictions are charities, opinion pollsters, and political candidates.

Marketers must also monitor state and local laws that affect their industries. Many states, for instance, allow hard liquor to be sold only in liquor stores, while others prohibit the sale of alcoholic beverages on Sunday. California's stringent regulations for automobile emissions require special pollution control equipment on cars sold in the state.

GOVERNMENT REGULATORY AGENCIES

Federal, state, and local governments have established regulatory agencies to enforce laws. At the federal level, the Federal Trade Commission (FTC) wields the broadest powers of any agency to influence marketing activities. The FTC enforces laws regulating unfair business practices and stops false and deceptive advertising. It regulates communication by wire, radio, and television. Other federal regulatory agencies include the Consumer Product Safety Commission, the Federal Power Commission, the Environmental Protection Agency (EPA), and the Food and Drug Administration (FDA). An advisory panel recently asked the FDA to ban nonprescription inhalers such as Primatene Mist for asthma symptoms because of the propellant they contain. However, Primatene's manufacturer, Wyeth, argued that the product meets all the criteria necessary to be considered an essential medication for consumers.[18]

The FTC uses several procedures to enforce laws. It may issue a consent order through which a business accused of violations can agree to voluntary compliance without admitting guilt. If a business refuses to comply with an FTC request, the agency can issue a cease-and-desist order, which gives a final demand to stop an illegal practice. Firms often challenge cease-and-desist orders in court. The FTC can require advertisers to provide additional information about products in their advertisements, and it can force firms using deceptive advertising to correct earlier claims with new promotional messages. In some cases, the FTC can require a firm to give refunds to consumers misled by deceptive advertising.

The FTC and U.S. Department of Justice can stop mergers if they believe the proposed acquisition will reduce competition by making it harder for new companies to enter the field. In recent years, these agencies have taken a harder line on proposed mergers, especially in the computer, telecommunications, financial services, and healthcare sectors.

Removing regulations also changes the competitive picture considerably. Following deregulation of the telecommunications and utilities industries, suppliers no longer have exclusive rights to operate within a territory. Natural gas utilities traditionally competed with electric companies to supply homeowners and businesses with energy needs. Because of deregulation, they now also compete with other gas companies. The restructuring of the electricity industry by state took hold immediately in the Northeast, ranging from Maine to Virginia and reaching through the Midwest in Ohio, Michigan, and Illinois. (Indiana and Vermont abstained.) Texas, Arizona, and Oregon also jumped on the bandwagon. But several states delayed deregulation activities, and California actually suspended them altogether. Restructuring caused major headaches for some utilities, leading to shortages and blackouts in the East and an inability to coordinate service with needs, nonmaintenance of power lines, and lack of funds for operating or decommissioning nuclear power plants.[19] Thus, while deregulation may be designed to promote competition and provide better service and prices for consumers, it doesn't always work as planned.

The latest round of deregulation brought the passage of the Telecommunications Act of 1996 and its 2003 amendment, the Do Not Call law mentioned earlier. The Telecommunications Act removed barriers between local and long-distance phone companies and cable companies. It allowed the so-called Baby Bells—the seven regional Bell operating companies—to offer long-distance service; at the same time, long-distance companies were able to offer local service. Satellite television providers such as Dish Network and DirecTV and cable companies such as Comcast can offer phone service, while phone companies can get into the cable business. The change promises huge rewards for competitive winners. Consumers can shop around for the best deals and packages as more companies compete for their business by packaging services at reduced prices.

OTHER REGULATORY FORCES

Public and private consumer interest groups and self-regulatory organizations are also part of the legal environment. Consumer interest organizations have mushroomed in the past 25 years, and today hundreds of groups operate at national, state, and local levels. These organizations seek to protect consumers in as many areas as possible. Citing the need for a standardized credit scoring system, three major credit-reporting agencies—Equifax, Experian, and TransUnion—created a new collaborative system called VantageScore. But Consumer Federation of America, a not-for-profit consumer group, criticized the new system for not examining the accuracy of the credit reports themselves—on which the scores are based.[20] The Coalition for Fire-Safe Cigarettes is working to pressure tobacco companies to produce cigarettes that will not smolder and start fires if left unattended. Bills mandating fire-safe cigarettes have been passed in California, New York, Vermont, and all of Canada and are being considered in eleven other U.S. states. "We should not have a patchwork of cigarette fire safety in this country," notes Jim Burns, president of the National Association of State Fire Marshals. "The tobacco companies can put an early end to this process by agreeing to manufacture only fire-safe cigarettes."[21]

Other groups attempt to advance the rights of minorities, senior citizens, and other special-interest causes. The power of these groups has also grown. AARP (formerly known as the American Association of Retired Persons), wields political and economic power, particularly as more and more people reach retirement age. Animal rights groups are also a powerful influence on business. The American Humane Association (AHA) grants the disclaimer "No Animals Were Harmed" to moviemakers who use animals in their films. It is the only organization authorized by movie studios to monitor the use and care of animals on the set. However, the group recently found itself at odds with other animal rights groups when it refused to sign on to a campaign to prohibit all use of primates in movies. "Rather than sign on that [apes] can't be used in entertainment, we can protect their safety," argued Marie Belew Wheatley, president of AHA.[22]

Self-regulatory groups represent industries' attempts to set guidelines for responsible business conduct. The Council of Better Business Bureaus is a national organization devoted to consumer service and business self-regulation. The council's National Advertising Division (NAD) promotes truth and accuracy in advertising. It reviews and advocates voluntary resolution of advertising-related complaints between consumers and businesses. If NAD fails to resolve a complaint, an appeal can be made to the National Advertising Review Board, which is composed of advertisers, ad agency representatives, and public members. In addition, many individual trade associations set business guidelines and codes of conduct and encourage members' voluntary compliance.

In an effort to protect consumer privacy and curb unwanted mail or phone solicitations, the Direct Marketing Association (DMA) recently approved new rules requiring customers to be notified if information about them—including their name and address—was being shared with other marketers. Companies must also tell consumers that they have the option not to have their information shared. These rules apply to thousands of member companies, including Internet firms, banks, publishers, and retailers.[23]

As mentioned earlier, regulating the online world poses a challenge. Favoring self-regulation as the best starting point, the FTC sponsored a privacy initiative for consumers, advertisers, online companies, and others as a way to develop voluntary industry privacy guidelines. The Interactive Services Association is also working on its own privacy standards.

CONTROLLING THE POLITICAL–LEGAL ENVIRONMENT

Most marketers comply with laws and regulations. Doing so not only serves their customers but also avoids legal problems that could ultimately damage a firm's image and hurt profits. Yet marketers fight regulations they consider unjust. Most marketers agree that workers deserve health care, though many disagree on who should pay for it. With rising costs to provide care for uninsured workers, laws in more than 20 states now dictate how much healthcare service employees should receive, as described in the "Marketing Failure" feature. Some marketers are upset about the new laws, saying they may actually do more harm than good.

Consumer groups and political action committees within industries may try to influence the outcome of proposed legislation or change existing laws by engaging in political lobbying or boycotts. Lobbying groups frequently enlist the support of customers, employees, and suppliers to assist their efforts. The Universal Service Fund (USF)

assessment check

1. Identify the four phases of U.S. government regulation of business. What is the newest frontier?

2. Which federal agency wields the broadest regulatory powers for influencing marketing activities?

seeks to subsidize telecommunications to rural and disadvantaged areas by essentially taxing the Internet. However, critics charge that current USF money doesn't end up where it is supposed to and that taxation will "discourage investment, slow connection speeds, and cost consumers extra money."[24]

 4 Outline the economic factors that affect marketing decisions and consumer buying power.

THE ECONOMIC ENVIRONMENT

The overall health of the economy influences how much consumers spend and what they buy. This relationship also works the other way. Consumer buying plays an important role in the economy's health; in fact, consumer spending accounts for nearly 70 percent of the nation's total **gross domestic product (GDP),** which is the sum of all goods and services produced by a nation in a year.[25] Because marketing activities are directed toward satisfying consumer wants and needs, marketers must first understand how economic conditions influence the purchasing decisions that consumers make.

economic environment
Factors that influence consumer buying power and marketing strategies, including stage of the business cycle, inflation and deflation, unemployment, income, and resource availability.

Marketing's **economic environment** consists of factors that influence consumer buying power and marketing strategies. They include the stage of the business cycle, inflation and deflation, unemployment, income, and resource availability.

STAGES IN THE BUSINESS CYCLE

Historically, the economy has tended to follow a cyclical pattern consisting of four stages: prosperity, recession, depression, and recovery. Consumer buying differs in each stage of the **business cycle,** and marketers must adjust their strategies accordingly. In times of prosperity, consumer spending maintains a brisk pace, and buyers are willing to spend more for premium versions of well-known brands. Growth in services such as banking and restaurants usually indicates a strong economy. When economists predict such conditions as low inflation and low unemployment, marketers respond by offering new products, increasing their promotional efforts, and expanding distribution. They might even raise prices to widen profit margins. But high prices for some items—such as energy—can affect businesses and consumers alike. Hakan Swahn, owner of a restaurant group in New York, pays more for light and heat than he did in past years. But another factor worries him as well—the rising price of seafood. "Fish has had an impact on us," he notes. "I feel that has gone up pretty substantially. I feel more uneasy about the price of seafood than anything else."[26] As a marketer, Swahn must figure out how to attract and serve his customers despite rising costs.

During the most recent economic slowdown, consumers focused on more basic, functional products that carried lower price tags. They limited travel, restaurant meals, and entertainment. They skipped expensive vacations and cooked their own meals. But they did one surprising thing—they invested in improving their homes. Instead of buying larger homes or vacation properties, they spruced up what they had—which kept the home improvement industry going. During a recession, marketers consider lowering prices and increasing promotions that include special offers to stimulate demand. They may also launch special value-priced products likely to appeal to cost-conscious buyers.

 marketing failure Healthcare Legislation: Do Wal-Mart Workers Win or Lose?

Background. In the United States, healthcare insurance is most often provided by employers. And employees naturally want the best healthcare that is available. But often debate rages about how much—or what type—of benefits should be an employer's responsibility. That's the problem faced by many firms, including retail giant Wal-Mart.

The Challenge. More than 20 states have set minimum insurance standards for employees. This requirement has huge implications for an employer like Wal-Mart, which operates 3,800 stores in all 50 states, employing

1.3 million workers. Citing the cost of implementing the state-mandated plan in Maryland, Wal-Mart says that in addition to complying with the new law, it would like to offer its cost-cutting expertise to gain efficiencies in the U.S. healthcare system.

The Outcome. Wal-Mart offers eighteen different health plans. Some plans start for as little as $11 per month for the employee and $9 per month for a child, and deductibles range from $350 to $2,000. The firm also began covering part-time workers under its group plan, lowered the waiting period

ICON: © GETTY IMAGES

Consumer spending sinks to its lowest level during a depression. The last true depression in the United States occurred during the 1930s. Although a severe depression could occur again, most experts see it as a slim possibility. Through its monetary and fiscal policies, the federal government attempts to control extreme fluctuations in the business cycle that lead to depression.

In the recovery stage, the economy emerges from recession and consumer purchasing power increases. But while consumers have money to spend, caution often restrains their willingness to buy. A family might buy a new car if no-interest financing is available. A couple might decide to book a trip through a discount travel firm such as Expedia.com or Travelocity. Companies like these can make the most of an opportunity and develop loyal customers by offering superior service at lower prices. Recovery still remains a difficult stage for businesses just climbing out of a recession because they must earn profits while trying to gauge uncertain consumer demand. Many cope by holding down costs. Some trim payrolls and close branch offices. Others cut back on business travel budgets, substituting teleconferencing and videoconferencing.

Business cycles, like other aspects of the economy, are complex phenomena that, despite the efforts of government, businesspeople, and others to control them, sometimes have a life of their own. Unforeseen natural disasters such as Hurricane Katrina, major tragedies such as the attacks of September 11, 2001, and the effects of war or peace all have an impact on business and the economy as a whole. The most effective marketers know how to recognize ways to serve their customers during the best of times—and the worst of times.

Waking to the music of tropical birds greeting the sunrise
An afternoon stroll on the golden beaches
Dinner at one of the best restaurants in the world

It doesn't get better than Barbados

BARBADOS
www.visitbarbados.co.uk

IMAGE COURTESY OF THE ADVERTISING ARCHIVES

During an economic recovery, consumers feel more comfortable spending money on luxuries, such as foreign vacations.

INFLATION AND DEFLATION

A major constraint on consumer spending, which can occur during any stage of the business cycle, is **inflation**—rising prices caused by some combination of excess demand and increases in the costs of raw materials, component parts, human resources, or other factors of production. Inflation devalues money by reducing the products it can buy through persistent price increases. These rising prices

Who is helping two-thirds of new US ethanol plants meet the nation's future energy needs? We are.

automation & control • building technologies • energy & power • financial services • hearing solutions • home appliances • information & communication
lighting • material handling • medical solutions • transportation • water technologies   usa.siemens.com

Innovations from Siemens can be found everywhere. One of our specialties is providing automation equipment that processes 70% of growing US ethanol production. We recognize the need for more alternative fuels in the US, and greater production quantities lead to better prices and availability, resulting in overall fuel efficiency. We're also developing technologies, like a natural gas control unit, that enable traditional vehicles to take advantage of compressed natural gas (CNG) and other more environmentally friendly fuel options. At Siemens, our innovations help turn dreams into reality.

SIEMENS
Global network of innovation

PHOTO COURTESY OF GETTY IMAGES

Because of price volatility, the cost of gasoline is not counted in the inflation rate. But smart marketers such as German-based Siemens are working to provide U.S. consumers alternative fuels such as ethanol to reduce dependence on foreign oil.

increase marketers' costs, such as expenditures for wages and raw materials, and the resulting higher prices may therefore negatively affect sales. U.S. inflation hit a heart-stopping high in 1979 of 13.3 percent. Currently, inflation hovers around 2.2 percent.[27]

If inflation is so bad, is its opposite, *deflation,* better? At first, it might seem so. Falling prices mean that products are more affordable. But deflation can be a long and damaging downward spiral, causing a freefall in business profits, lower returns on most investments, and widespread job layoffs. The last time the United States experienced significant deflation was in the Great Depression of the 1930s. During a recent recession, economists worried about deflation, as interest rates declined and some product prices declined. But rates and prices stabilized.

Unemployment

Unemployment is defined as the proportion of people in the economy who are actively seeking work but do not have jobs. Unemployment rises during recessions and declines in the recovery and prosperity stages of the business cycle. Like inflation, unemployment affects the way consumers behave. Unless unemployment insurance, personal savings, and union benefits effectively offset lost earnings, unemployed people have relatively little money to spend—they buy food, pay the rent or mortgage, and try to keep up with utility bills.

Currently unemployment hovers under 5 percent nationally, which indicates that the economy is growing. "Economic growth remains solid and the economy could create over 2 million jobs this year," predicts one senior financial economist.[28] Not surprisingly, the creation of more jobs helps strengthen consumer spending.

Income

Income is another important determinant of marketing's economic environment because it influences consumer buying power. By studying income statistics and trends, marketers can estimate market potential and plan to target specific market segments. U.S. household incomes have grown in recent years. Coupled with a low rate of inflation, this increase has boosted purchasing power for millions of consumers. A rise in income represents a potential for increasing overall sales. However, many marketers are particularly interested in **discretionary income,** the amount of money people have to spend after buying necessities such as food, clothing, and housing. Those whose industry involves the necessities seek to turn those needs into preferences for their goods and services.

Changes in average earnings powerfully affect discretionary income. Historically, periods of major innovation have been accompanied by dramatic increases in living standards and rising incomes. Automobiles, televisions, telephones, and computers are just a few of the innovations that have changed consumers' lives—and standards of living. The Bureau of Economic Analysis, a division of the U.S. Department of Commerce, tracks personal income and discretionary income in the United States, then determines how much of that income is spent on personal consumption.[29] Marketers can use these figures to plan their approaches to everything from product development to the promotion of their goods and services.

Income also affects how much money individuals can and will donate to not-for-profit organizations. The "Etiquette Tips for Marketing Professionals" feature can steer you through the maze of decisions involved in making such donations at work.

Etiquette Tips for Marketing Professionals

To Give or Not to Give—at the Office

Just about everyone wants to support a good cause. Most of us have our favorites, depending on where we live and which issues strike us close to the heart. At the workplace, on occasion you might be asked to donate to a certain charity or nonprofit organization. Here are a few tips for sorting through these requests and deciding whether to participate:

1. If you are unfamiliar with the organization, ask for information about whom it serves, where, and in what ways. Ask how donations are used.
2. Consider whether the organization is consistent with your own views. Would you support it outside the workplace?
3. If you decide to contribute, do so within your own means. Don't feel obligated to make a donation that you cannot afford. Be sure that donations are collected anonymously, and ask for a receipt for your tax records.
4. If you prefer to decline, do so politely. You might have several reasons for deciding not to contribute—your own expenses, other charita-

ble obligations, or a different point of view from that of the organization. You do not have to give an elaborate explanation. Simply say, "I'm sorry, but I'm not able to contribute at this time."
5. If you feel pressure after declining, recognize that charitable donations—even if they are supported by your manager or the company as a whole—are not required of you. You cannot be fired for declining to contribute.
6. If you want to support the mission of the organization but cannot make a financial donation at the moment, offer to volunteer in some way. You may be asked to help in the fundraising effort.
7. Try to keep your decision private instead of discussing it with others.

Sources: "Letting Shareholders Choose Their Own Charities," *Warren Buffett Secrets,* **http://www.buffettsecrets.com**, accessed March 2, 2006; United Way Web site, **http://www.unitedway.org**, accessed March 2, 2006; Caren Chesler, "Buttonholed!" *Investment Dealers' Digest,* February 27, 2006.

Resource Availability

Resources are not unlimited. Shortages—temporary or permanent—can result from several conditions, including lack of raw materials, component parts, energy, or labor. U.S. business executives and government officials continue to be concerned about the nation's dependence on imported oil and the effect shortages can have on the economy. As talks between the European Union and leaders in Iran about Iran's nuclear capabilities broke down, economists worried that Iran—the second-largest oil producer in the Organization of the Petroleum Exporting Countries (OPEC)—could withhold its supply. Also, attacks by Nigerian militants on oil production facilities have slowed production there. Nigeria is the largest oil producer in Africa, and the eleventh-largest in the world. In addition, terrorist threats to Saudi Arabia's oil industry infrastructure—including an attempted attack on one of its major oil-exporting terminals—have caused worldwide concern.[30]

One reaction to a shortage is **demarketing,** the process of reducing consumer demand for a product to a level that the firm can reasonably supply. Oil companies publicize tips for consumers on how to cut gasoline consumption, and utility companies encourage homeowners to install more insulation to reduce heating costs. Many cities promote mass transit and carpooling for consumers. A shortage presents marketers with a unique set of challenges. They may have to allocate limited supplies, a sharply different activity from marketing's traditional objective of expanding sales volume. Shortages may require marketers to decide whether to spread limited supplies over all customers or limit purchases by some customers so that the firm can completely satisfy others.

Marketers have also devised ways to deal with increased demand for fixed amounts of resources. Reynolds Metal addresses the dwindling supply of aluminum through its recycling programs, including cash-paying vending machines. The city of Honolulu has three such "reverse" vending machines outside

demarketing Process of reducing consumer demand for a good or service to a level that the firm can supply.

figure 3.2

Goods Still Manufactured Primarily in the United States

Source: Data from the U.S. Census Bureau, as cited in Mark Trumbull, "Trade Gap Aside, a Lot Still 'Made in the USA,'" *Christian Science Monitor*, February 13, 2006, http://www.csmonitor.com.

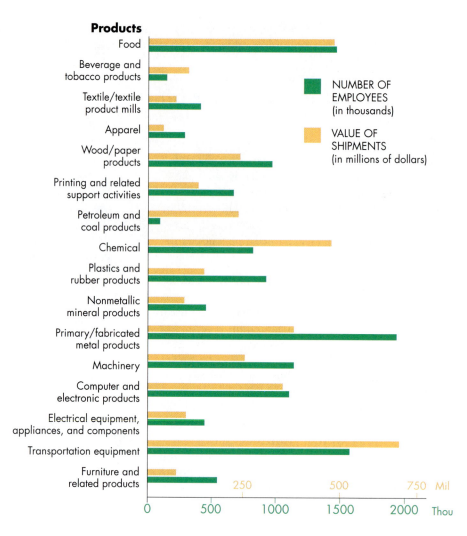

its municipal building. Consumers deposit their empty beverage cans or bottles into a machine, which spits out a receipt. Then they insert the receipt into an adjacent InstaDeem machine, which automatically redeems the receipt for cash. The reverse vending system not only addresses the issue of shortages but also deals with potential waste in a socially responsible way. And it creates time and place utility for consumers who want to recycle their cans and bottles. "This kind of automation allows us to bring more convenience to all the residents on the island for redeeming their deposits," notes Suzanne Jones, the city's recycling coordinator. "The more convenient, the higher the recycle rates are going to be."[31]

THE INTERNATIONAL ECONOMIC ENVIRONMENT

In today's global economy, marketers must also monitor the economic environment of other nations. Just as in the United States, a recession in Europe or Japan changes consumer and business buying habits. Changes in foreign currency rates compared with the U.S. dollar also affect marketing decisions. Labor costs and other factors affect firms' decisions to shift manufacturing operations overseas, decisions that may result in cutbacks in U.S. jobs and boosts to other nations' workforces. Although U.S. workers worry about the number of jobs sent overseas, some manufacturing remains strong in the United States. While workers in Asia assemble computers, production of computer chips often remains in the United States. Figure 3.2 tallies the manufacturing industries that remain strong in the United States.

As China exports more and more goods to the world and to the United States in particular, some people voice concern over the widening trade gap. Only recently have broad economic reforms allowed China to play in the global marketplace. Today the currency reserves in China's central bank surpass those of Japan. The world's largest shopping mall is located in Beijing, and two-thirds of all DVD players and other electronic equipment are produced in China. Some economists believe that it is only a matter of time before China's economy overtakes that of the United States.[32]

Politics in other countries affect the international economic environment, as well. Elections in countries such as Brazil and Mexico could result in a shift away from free-market policies. Turmoil in Venezuela could affect the oil industry.

But some valuable lessons have been learned. Whereas developing nations often relied on private funds from industries and organizations to jump-start their economies a decade ago, they now look to establish and build strong export industries. Global demand for certain commodities has helped these nations—such as Argentina, which exports soybeans—strengthen their economies.[33]

✓ assessment check

1. Identify and describe briefly the four stages of the business cycle.

2. Explain how inflation and income affect consumer buying decisions.

THE TECHNOLOGICAL ENVIRONMENT

The **technological environment** represents the application to marketing of knowledge based on discoveries in science, inventions, and innovations. Technology leads to new goods and services for consumers; it also improves existing products, offers better customer service, and often reduces prices through new, cost-efficient production and distribution methods. Technology can quickly make products obsolete—e-mail, for example, quickly eroded both letter writing and the market for fax machines—but it can just as quickly open new marketing opportunities, in entirely new industries.

Pets have been wearing RFID—radio-frequency identification—transmitters for years, in case they got lost. Now RFID tags are used in many industries to locate everything from library books to laundry detergent. An RFID tag contains a computer chip with an antenna. A reader scans the tag and transmits the data from the tag to a computer. This innovation means that retailers, manufacturers, and others can locate and track inventory without opening packages. One medical center is even considering using RFID microchips to help locate wandering Alzheimer's patients. And the U.S. military uses RFID to locate ammunition and supplies. Critics warn that improper use of RFID technology could lead to loss of privacy because products or people could be tracked without their knowledge.[34]

Technology can address social concerns. In response to pressure from the World Trade Organization and the U.S. government, Japanese automakers were first to use technology to develop more fuel-efficient vehicles and reduce dangerous emissions with offerings such as the Toyota Prius and a hybrid version of the Honda Civic. Both vehicles run on a combination of gasoline and electricity. Two biotech firms in California have been researching ways to reduce the cost of making ethanol fuel out of cellulose materials—crop waste, weeds, forest underbrush, garbage, anything organic. Bill Gates, founder of Microsoft, has invested $84 million in another ethanol firm. The National Resources Defense Council predicts that cellulose biomass energy made from waste, grass, and other materials could account for about half of current transportation petroleum in as little as 40 years.[35]

Industry, government, colleges and universities, and other not-for-profit institutions all play roles in the development of new technology—but improvements often come at a price. Research and development efforts by private industry represent a major source of technological innovation, as in the pharmaceutical industry. The cost of bringing a new drug to market can run as high as $1.7 billion, according to a report by the FDA. "The development cost is so high that pharmaceutical companies can only afford to market blockbusters," concedes the dean of the Graduate College at Illinois Institute of Technology. As a result, eleven universities have joined with the FDA in a partnership called the National Institute of Pharmaceutical Technology and Education to find ways to solve this problem.[36]

Another major source of technology is the federal government, including the military. Air bags originated from Air Force ejection seats, digital computers were first designed to calculate artillery trajectories, and the microwave oven is a derivative of military radar systems. Even the Internet was first developed by the U.S. Department of Defense as a secure military communications system. Although the United States has long been the world leader in research, competition from rivals in Europe, Japan, and other Asian countries is intense. Despite the dominance of U.S. auto brands in the past, Japanese cars have surged ahead in popularity. But the real surprise is that China is motoring right along as well. If you've never heard of Tianjin FAW Xiali Automobile Co., Ltd., you probably will in the next few years. While this automaker and three others now account for nearly 25 percent of the Chinese market, they have bigger plans: look for their cars in the United States soon.[37]

5 Discuss the impact of the technological environment on a firm's marketing activities.

technological environment Application to marketing of knowledge based on discoveries in science, inventions, and innovations.

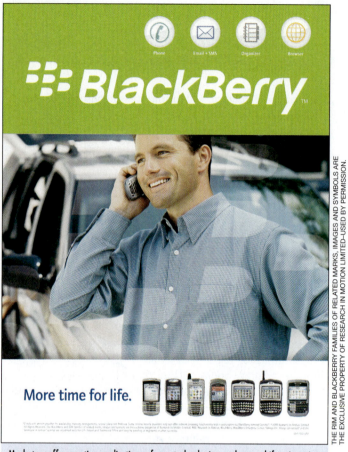

More time for life.

THE RIM AND BLACKBERRY FAMILIES OF RELATED MARKS, IMAGES AND SYMBOLS ARE THE EXCLUSIVE PROPERTY OF RESEARCH IN MOTION LIMITED–USED BY PERMISSION.

Marketers offer creative applications of new technologies, such as multifunction wireless devices offering phone service, Internet connection, and e-mail.

 **assessment check**

1. What are some of the consumer benefits of technology?
2. Why must marketers monitor the technological environment?

APPLYING TECHNOLOGY

Marketers monitor the technological environment for a number of reasons. Creative applications of new technologies not only give a firm a definite competitive edge but can also benefit society. Marketers who monitor new technology and successfully apply it may also enhance customer service. Boeing is equipping its aircraft with Wi-Fi access so that passengers with laptops can log on to the Internet while in flight. This service is particularly helpful to business travelers who want to make the most of their workday in flight. Boeing predicts that the move will pay off. "Wi-Fi is on an explosive growth path," says Boeing's president, Scott E. Carson.[38]

VoIP—which stands for *voice over Internet protocol*—is an alternative to traditional telecommunications services provided by companies such as Qwest. The telephone is not connected to a traditional phone jack but instead is connected to a personal computer with any type of broadband Internet connection. Special software transmits phone conversations over the Internet, rather than through telephone lines. A VoIP user dials the phone as usual. Recipients can receive calls made using VoIP through regular telephone connections—land or wireless. Moreover, you can call another person who has VoIP using a regular landline or cell phone. A growing number of consumers and businesses have embraced VoIP, mainly because of the cost savings and the extra features offered by VoIP. One of the largest VoIP providers, with more than 1 million business and residential customers, is New Jersey–based Vonage. The company offers business and residential customers calling plans that are priced well below those offered by traditional telecommunications companies and include services such as call waiting and three-way calling at no extra charge.[39]

As convenient as the Internet, cell phones, and Wi-Fi are for businesspeople and consumers, the networks that facilitate these connections aren't yet compatible with each other. So engineers are working on a new standard that would enable these networks to connect with each other—paving the way for melded services such as video exchanges between a cell phone and a computer. Called the Internet Protocol Multimedia Subsystem (IPMS), the new standard will attempt to create a common interface so that data can be carried across networks between different devices.[40] The implications for various communications providers are enormous—not only will they find new ways to cooperate but they will also find new ways to compete. Subsequent chapters discuss in more detail how companies apply technologies—such as databases, blogs, and interactive promotional techniques—to create a competitive advantage.

6 Explain how the social-cultural environment influences marketing.

social-cultural environment Component of the marketing environment consisting of the relationship between the marketer, society, and culture.

THE SOCIAL-CULTURAL ENVIRONMENT

As a nation, the United States is becoming older, more affluent, and more culturally diverse. The birthrate is falling, and subculture populations are rising. People express concerns about the natural environment, buying ecologically friendly products that reduce pollution. They value their time with family and friends, cooking meals at home and exchanging vacation photos over the Internet. Marketers need to track these trends to be sure they are in tune with consumers' needs and desires. These aspects of consumer lifestyles help shape marketing's **social-cultural environment**—the relationship between marketing, society, and culture.

To remain competitive, marketers must be sensitive to society's demographic shifts and changing values. These variables affect consumers' reactions to different products and marketing practices. As the baby boom generation—those born between 1946 and 1965—reaches middle age and retirement, marketers are scrambling to identify this generation's needs and wants. Fueled by hopes of a long life with plenty of time and money to spend, the baby boom generation views retirement much differently than their predecessors did. Marketers already know that boomers want to travel and enjoy their leisure time. But they aren't playing shuffleboard—they are taking up fly fishing, yoga, and boating. They are also spending money on vacation homes and in craft stores. Some are even starting a second career, establishing their own small businesses. Aging boomers also need healthcare goods and services—as they live longer, they may need everything from physical therapy for a repaired knee to a motorized scooter to get around.[41]

Another social-cultural consideration is the increasing importance of cultural diversity. The United States is a mixed society composed of various submarkets, each with its unique values, cultural characteristics, consumer preferences, and purchasing behaviors. Satellite and cable TV companies now offer more Spanish-language programming in an effort to attract the millions of Hispanic viewers in the United States. The market that was once dominated by Spanish-language networks Univision and Telemundo is facing new competition from Comcast, Cablevision, Time Warner Cable, Dish Network, and DirecTV. Traditionally, TV shows targeted for Hispanics were mostly imported from Mexico. However, 15 million viewers from other regions of Latin America didn't get any programming from their own countries. Now, the choices are broader—most Latin American countries are represented by at least one channel.[42]

Marketers also need to learn about cultural and societal differences among countries abroad, particularly as business becomes more and more global. Marketing strategies that work in the United States often fail when directly applied in other countries, and vice versa. In many cases, marketers must redesign packages and modify products and advertising messages to suit the tastes and preferences of different cultures. Chapter 7 explores the social-cultural aspects of global marketing.

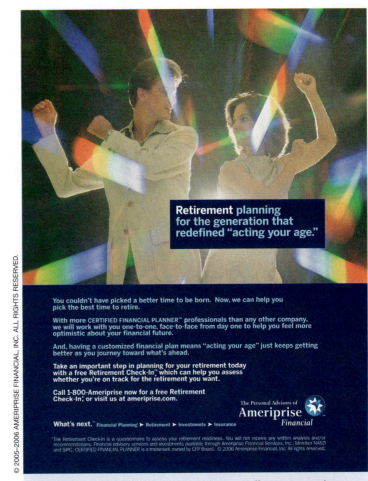

As the baby boomer generation ages, many marketers are offering services such as financial planning to make their retirement or second careers more comfortable.

CONSUMERISM

Changing societal values have led to **consumerism,** defined as a social force within the environment that aids and protects the consumer by exerting legal, moral, and economic pressures on business and government. Today everyone—marketers, industry, government, and the public—is acutely aware of the impact of consumerism on the nation's economy and general well-being.

In recent years, marketers have witnessed increasing consumer activism. Based on complaints from an animal welfare group, the FTC recently approved a labeling change for egg cartons. The old label, "Animal Care Certified," was replaced by a new label, "United Egg Producers Certified." According to the animal welfare group, the previous label led consumers to believe that all hens were uniformly treated the same, humane way. The new label "allows consumers to make more informed buying choices," noted the executive director of the group.[43]

But firms cannot always adjust to meet the demands of consumer groups. The choice between pleasing all consumers and remaining profitable—thus surviving—defines one of the most difficult dilemmas facing business. Given these constraints, what do consumers have the right to expect from

consumerism Social force within the environment that aids and protects the consumer by exerting legal, moral, and economic pressures on business and government.

the companies from which they buy goods and services? The most frequently quoted answer to this question comes from a speech made by President John F. Kennedy more than four decades ago. Although this list does not amount to a definitive statement, it offers good rules of thumb that explain basic **consumer rights:**

consumer rights List of legitimate consumer expectations suggested by President Kennedy.

1. *The right to choose freely.* Consumers should be able to choose from among a range of goods and services.

2. *The right to be informed.* Consumers should be provided with enough education and product information to enable them to be responsible buyers.

3. *The right to be heard.* Consumers should be able to express their legitimate displeasure to appropriate parties—that is, sellers, consumer assistance groups, and city or state consumer affairs offices.

4. *The right to be safe.* Consumers should be assured that the goods and services they purchase are not injurious with normal use. Goods and services should be designed so that the average consumer can use them safely.

These rights have formed the conceptual framework of much of the legislation enacted during the first 40 years of the consumer rights movement. However, the question of how best to guarantee them remains unanswered. Sometimes state or federal authorities step in. California's "lemon law" gives car dealers only three chances to repair a defective auto. Food-labeling regulations force disclosure of such details as expiration date, ingredients, and nutritional values on packaged foods. In response to a lawsuit filed by an individual consumer and the Center for Science in the Public Interest, PepsiCo agreed to change the label on its Tropicana Peach Papaya and Strawberry Melon drinks. Although the firm claimed that the old label actually met FDA guidelines, PepsiCo said it would change the label because "we just want to take every opportunity to provide nutrition information about our products and clearly communicate what's inside each package."[44]

Consumers' right to safety encompasses a vast range of products, from automobiles to children's toys. Sometimes it seems as though safety recalls are reported in the media too regularly. You might even receive a letter in the mail from a manufacturer informing you of a recall for a part on your refrigerator or car. One recent winter, the U.S. Consumer Product Safety Commission and Decathlon USA jointly announced a recall of one of Decathlon's models of snowboard bindings. It was discovered that the binding's plastic base could break during use, which could cause an accident or injury. Consumers were instructed to return the bindings immediately to any Decathlon store for a gift certificate and reimbursement—along with a free pair of self-heating snow gloves.[45]

Consumerism, along with the rest of the social-cultural environment for marketing decisions at home and abroad, is expanding in scope and importance. Today, no marketer can initiate a strategic decision without considering the society's norms, values, culture, and demographics. Understanding how these variables affect decisions is so important that some firms have created a new position—typically, manager of public policy research—to study the changing societal environment's future impact on their organizations.

 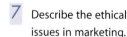 **assessment check**

1. Define *consumerism*.
2. Identify the four consumer rights.

7 Describe the ethical issues in marketing.

ETHICAL ISSUES IN MARKETING

The five environments described so far in this chapter do not completely capture the role that marketing plays in society and the consequent effects and responsibilities of marketing activities. Because marketing is closely connected with various public issues, it invites constant scrutiny. Moreover, since marketing acts as an interface between an organization and the society in which it operates, marketers often carry much of the responsibility for dealing with social issues that affect their firms.

Marketing operates outside the firm. It responds to that outside environment, and in turn is acted on by environmental influences. Relationships with employees, suppliers, the government,

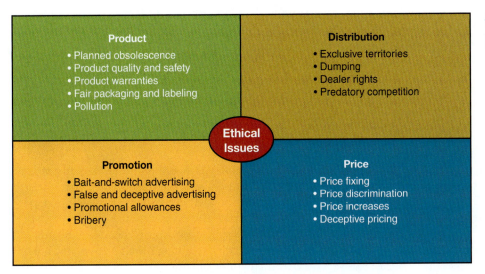

figure 3.3
Ethical Questions in Marketing

consumers, and society as a whole frame the social issues that marketers must address. The way that marketers deal with these social issues has a significant effect on their firm's eventual success. The diverse social issues that marketers face can be divided into two major categories: marketing ethics and social responsibility. While these two categories certainly overlap, this simple classification system provides a method for studying these issues.

The wave of corporate fraud and conflicts of interest on Wall Street and in big business during the past decade is still being addressed in the form of court trials and guilty pleas by wrongdoers. Cases against senior executives at Enron and Tyco International brought jail sentences for those who were convicted. Other companies have responded proactively, by tightening their own ethical codes and even hiring managers whose role is specifically to enforce them. More than 600 U.S. companies now have such managers, including Dun & Bradstreet, Dow Corning, Texas Instruments, Wal-Mart, and even the Internal Revenue Service.[46]

Environmental influences have directed increased attention toward **marketing ethics,** defined as marketers' standards of conduct and moral values. Ethics concern matters of right and wrong: the responsibility of individuals and firms to do what is morally right. As Figure 3.3 shows, each element of the marketing mix raises its own set of ethical questions. Before any improvements to a firm's marketing program can be made, each element must be evaluated.

Creating an ethics program may be complicated and time consuming, but it is worthwhile. Some firms take their cue from the U.S. Federal Sentencing Guidelines for Organizations, which provides a framework for evaluating misconduct in business activities, such as fraud or price fixing. After discovering that similar cases had been resolved differently by courts, the U.S. Sentencing Commission enacted guidelines in 1991 that rely on what legislators call the stick-and-carrot approach to corporate ethics: The financial penalties that the courts can impose for wrongdoing are the stick, while the existence of an effective ethics program can reduce the fines the courts can set, which serves as the carrot. The sentencing guidelines act as an incentive for corporations to implement effective ethics compliance programs—if they are hauled into court, the existence of such a program can help reduce fines or sentences. Figure 3.4 presents a step-by-step framework for building an effective program. Because training employees—and students—to behave in an ethical manner is so important, some firms and universities have taken

marketing ethics Marketers' standards of conduct and moral values.

figure 3.4
Ten Steps for Corporations to Improve Standards of Business Ethics

1. Appoint a senior-level ethics compliance officer.
2. Set up an ethics code capable of detecting and preventing misconduct.
3. Distribute a written code of ethics to employees, subsidiaries, and associated companies and require all business partners to abide by it.
4. Conduct regular ethics training programs to communicate standards and procedures.
5. Establish systems to monitor misconduct and report grievances.
6. Establish consistent punishment guidelines to enforce standards and codes.
7. Encourage an open-door policy, allowing employees to report cases of misconduct without fear of retaliation.
8. Prohibit employees with a track record of misconduct from holding positions with substantial discretionary authority.
9. Promote ethically aware and responsible managers.
10. Continually monitor effectiveness of all ethics-related programs.

Source: Adapted from O. C. Ferrell, John Fraedrich, and Linda Ferrell, *Business Ethics: Ethical Decision Making and Cases,* Sixth Edition, pp. 61–62 and 172–173. Copyright © 2005 by Houghton Mifflin Company. Reprinted with permission.

Solving an Ethical Controversy

Corporate Criminals in the Classroom

The scene plays out in colleges and universities across the country: convicted corporate criminals as guest speakers in business classes, talking about business ethics. One such speaker is Walter Pavlo, who pleaded guilty to stealing $6 million in a fraud scheme at MCI. Pavlo presents his story in a personable style, claiming that he was actually scared as he took part in the crime. While the idea of recruiting former criminals to teach business ethics appeals to some, others argue that it may actually glamorize corporate crime.

Should corporate criminals teach business ethics in the classroom?

PRO

1. No one knows better what goes on in the mind of someone who commits corporate crime than the person who actually committed it. This person also knows firsthand the consequences—jail time, difficulty finding work afterward, and a lifelong stigma.
2. The need for ethics training in the classroom is great, and personal experience can bring the subject alive, says Mark Morze, another executive who spent five years in jail for a major fraud crime. "We are living in a society that has an extreme lack of ethics. We are not teaching ethics at home or in school. That's just amazing to me."

CON

1. Convicted criminals should not be allowed to profit from activities related to their crimes, yet these speakers are now part of a major new business ethics industry.
2. The speaker's subsequent success may seem to overshadow the crime. Although Walter Pavlo encountered many difficulties as a result of his conviction, he discovered that companies wanted to hire him to teach their employees about business ethics—and he began a whole new career.

Summary

The growing industry of business ethics indicates that companies and schools take the situation seriously. The aim is to help students who become employees—and who might never think of themselves as capable of committing a crime—make the right decisions. "Most people are good, and then they enter an arena with incredibly high pressure," explains Terry Halbert, the professor at Temple University who invited Walter Pavlo to speak. "Many people aren't prepared for what follows. I want to bring it to life."

Sources: American Psychological Association book review of Shadd Maruna, *Making Good: How Ex-Convicts Reform and Rebuild Their Lives,* http://www.apa.org, accessed March 2, 2006; Greg Farrell and Jayne O'Donnell, "Ethics Training as Taught by Ex-Cons: Crime Doesn't Pay," *USA Today,* November 16, 2005, pp. B1–B2; Jayne O'Donnell, "Former Duo of Deceit Now Lecture Students about Ethics," *USA Today,* April 18, 2005, http://www.usatoday.com.

an unusual step: they are inviting convicted corporate criminals to speak to employees and students about their mistakes and the consequences of their actions. As the "Solving an Ethical Controversy" feature points out, not everyone agrees with this approach.

Ensuring ethical practices means promising customers and business partners not to sacrifice quality and fairness for profit. In exchange, organizations hope for increased customer loyalty toward their brands. Yet issues involving marketing ethics are not always clear-cut. The issue of cigarette advertising, for example, has divided the ranks of advertising executives. Is it right for advertisers to promote a product that, while legal, has known health hazards?

For years, charges of unethical conduct have plagued the tobacco industry. In the largest civil settlement in U.S. history, tobacco manufacturers agreed to pay $206 billion to 46 states. Four other states—Florida, Minnesota, Mississippi, and Texas—had separate settlements totaling another $40 billion. The settlement frees tobacco companies from state claims for the cost of treating sick smokers. For their part, cigarette makers can no longer advertise on billboards or use cartoon characters in ads, nor can they sell nontobacco merchandise containing tobacco brands or logos. However, several years later, the penalties were softened, particularly those that involved funding smoking-cessation programs—fines dropped from $130 billion to $10 billion.[47]

People develop standards of ethical behavior based on their own systems of values, which help them deal with ethical questions in their personal lives. However, the workplace may generate serious conflicts when individuals discover that their ethical beliefs are not necessarily in line with those of their employer. For example, employees may think that shopping online during a lunch break using a work computer is fine, but the company may decide otherwise. The questionnaire in Figure 3.5 highlights other everyday ethical dilemmas.

How can these conflicts be resolved? In addition to individual and organizational ethics, individuals may be influenced by a third basis of ethical authority—a professional code of ethics that transcends both organizational and individual value systems. A professional peer association can exercise collective oversight to limit a marketer's individual behavior. Any code of ethics must anticipate the variety of problems that marketers are likely to encounter. Promotional matters tend to receive the greatest attention, but ethical considerations also influence marketing research, product strategy, distribution strategy, and pricing.

ETHICS IN MARKETING RESEARCH

Invasion of personal privacy has become a critical issue in marketing research. The proliferation of databases, the selling of address lists, and the ease with which consumer information can be gathered through Internet technology have all increased public concern. The issue of privacy will be explored in greater detail in Chapter 4. One marketing research tool that is particularly problematic is the promise of cash or gifts in return for marketing information that can then be sold to direct marketers. Consumers commonly disclose their personal information in return for an e-mail newsletter or a favorite magazine.

Privacy issues have mushroomed with the growth of the Internet, with huge consequences to both consumers and marketers. CardSystems, a credit card processor, mistakenly released financial data on 40 million consumers to a hacker. CitiGroup lost data on 3.9 million customers when unencrypted backup tapes it had shipped disappeared.[48] When consumer data broker ChoicePoint admitted that records containing personal financial information on 163,000 consumers had been exposed, the FTC charged that ChoicePoint's security procedures were inadequate and violated consumers' privacy rights along with federal laws. ChoicePoint was ordered to pay $10 million in civil penalties and $5 million in consumer fines.[49] "The thing about a breach like ChoicePoint's is, it's so much more serious—because if organized crime buys the data, you can be pretty sure they're

Briefly Speaking

"At this moment, America's greatest economic need is higher ethical standards—standards enforced by strict laws and upheld by responsible business leaders. There is no capitalism without conscience; there is no wealth without character."

—George W. Bush (b. 1946)
43rd president of the United States

figure 3.5

Test Your Workplace Ethics

Source: Ethics Officer Association, Belmont, Massachusetts; Leadership Group, Wilmette, Illinois; surveys sampled a cross-section of workers at large companies and nationwide; used with permission from Ethics Officer Association.

Office Technology

1. Is it wrong to use company e-mail for personal reasons?
   ❑Yes   ❑No

2. Is it wrong to use office equipment to help your children or spouse do schoolwork?
   ❑Yes   ❑No

3. Is it wrong to play computer games on office equipment during the workday?
   ❑Yes   ❑No

4. Is it wrong to use office equipment to do Internet shopping?
   ❑Yes   ❑No

5. Is it unethical to blame an error you made on a technological glitch?
   ❑Yes   ❑No

6. Is it unethical to visit pornographic Web sites using office equipment?
   ❑Yes   ❑No

Gifts and Entertainment

7. What's the value at which a gift from a supplier or client becomes troubling?
   ❑$25   ❑$50   ❑$100

8. Is a $50 gift to a boss unacceptable?
   ❑Yes   ❑No

9. Is a $50 gift from the boss unacceptable?
   ❑Yes   ❑No

10. Of gifts from suppliers: Is it OK to take a $200 pair of football tickets?
    ❑Yes   ❑No

11. Is it OK to take a $120 pair of theater tickets?
    ❑Yes   ❑No

12. Is it OK to take a $100 holiday food basket?
    ❑Yes   ❑No

13. Is it OK to take a $25 gift certificate?
    ❑Yes   ❑No

14. Can you accept a $75 prize won at a raffle at a supplier's conference?
    ❑Yes   ❑No

Truth and Lies

15. Due to on-the-job pressure, have you ever abused or lied about sick days?
    ❑Yes   ❑No

16. Due to on-the-job pressure, have you ever taken credit for someone else's work or idea?
    ❑Yes   ❑No

Credit card companies are facing increased scrutiny about customer privacy issues. Invasion of privacy and personal identity theft have increased with the use of the Internet.

going to use it," warns Garnet Steen, president of RelyData, which offers identity theft recovery services. "That's a little different from saying that a state university's database got hacked, when it could have been just some computer-science students flexing their muscles."[50]

Several agencies, including the FTC, offer assistance to Internet consumers. Consumers can go to **http:// www.ftc.gov/privacy** for information. The Direct Marketing Association also provides services, such as the Mail, Telephone, and E-Mail Preference Services, to help consumers get their names removed from marketers' targeted lists. Registration for the U.S. government's Do Not Call Registry is available at (888) 382-1222 and **http:// www.donotcall.gov**. Unlistme.com and Junkbusters are free Web services that also help consumers remove their names from direct mail and telemarketing lists.

ETHICS IN PRODUCT STRATEGY

Product quality, planned obsolescence, brand similarity, and packaging all raise ethical issues. Feeling the competition, some marketers have tried packaging practices that might be considered misleading, deceptive, or unethical. Larger packages take up more shelf space, and consumers notice them. An odd-sized package makes price comparisons difficult. Bottles with concave bottoms give the impression that they contain more liquid than they actually do. Are these packaging practices justified in the name of competition, or are they deceptive? Growing regulatory mandates appear to be narrowing the range of discretion in this area.

How do you evaluate the quality of a product like a soft drink? By flavor or by ingredients? Citing several studies, some consumer advocates say that the ingredients in soda—mainly the high sugar content—can be linked to obesity in consumers, particularly children. Not surprisingly, the beverage industry disagrees, arguing that lack of exercise and a poor diet in general are greater contributors to weight gain than regular consumption of soda. But one of the nation's leading epidemiologists, the American Cancer Society's Dr. Michael Thun, wants to see new labels on soda cans. "I think it would be a good candidate for a warning," he observes.[51]

ETHICS IN DISTRIBUTION

Two ethical issues influence a firm's decisions regarding distribution strategy:

1. What is the appropriate degree of control over the distribution channel?

2. Should a company distribute its products in marginally profitable outlets that have no alternative source of supply?

The question of channel control typically arises in relationships between manufacturers and franchise dealers. For example, should an automobile dealership, a gas station, or a fast-food outlet be forced to purchase parts, materials, and supplementary services from the parent organization?

The second question concerns marketers' responsibility to serve unsatisfied market segments even if the profit potential is slight. Should marketers serve retail stores in low-income areas, serve users of limited amounts of the firm's product, or serve a declining rural market? These problems are difficult to resolve because they often involve individuals rather than broad segments of the general public. An important first step is to ensure that the firm consistently enforces its channel policies.

ETHICS IN PROMOTION

Promotion raises many ethical questions, because it is the most direct link between a firm and its customers. Personal selling has always been a target of criticism—and jokes about untrustworthiness. Used-car dealers, horse traders, and purveyors of quick remedies have been the targets of such barbs. But promotion covers many areas, ranging from advertising to direct marketing—and it is vital for marketers to monitor their ethics in all marketing communications. Truth in advertising—representing accurately a product's benefits and drawbacks, warranties, price, and availability—is the bedrock of ethics in promotion.

Marketing to children has been under close scrutiny for many years because children have not yet developed the skills to receive marketing messages critically. They simply believe everything they see and hear. For example, snack foods, candy, soda, and other junk foods are for sale in abundant quantities in many schools throughout the country, where children are a captive audience. Organizations now pay to advertise on school buses in some communities, including Denver and Miami. While participating schools argue that the advertising revenues actually help students through funded programs, critics disagree. "It teaches children that . . . they're for sale," warns Gary Ruskin, executive director of the consumer group Commercial Alert.[52]

Some companies are taking a stance against promoting certain products to children. Kraft Foods recently announced plans to cut back on advertising fatty and sugary foods to children, adding new logos to its food and drinks that highlight its more nutritional offerings. Competitors such as Quaker Oats and General Mills soon followed suit. "This is a great step by Kraft," said Margo Wootan, nutrition policy director for the Center for Science in the Public Interest. "This will help support parents' efforts to get their kids to eat better. I think we are going to see more of these changes."[53]

Promoting certain products to college students can raise ethical questions as well. College students are a prime market for firms that sell everything from electronics to beer. And it's the beer that has people worried, particularly because laws prohibit the sale of alcohol to anyone under age 21. Even if they don't drink illegally, students can collect and wear promotional hats, shirts, duffle bags, and other items that display popular alcohol names and logos. According to researcher Dr. James D. Sargent, "promotional items are related to early onset drinking, and I think the responsible thing to do would be for these industries to quit distributing them."[54]

ETHICS IN PRICING

Pricing is probably the most regulated aspect of a firm's marketing strategy. As a result, most unethical price behavior is also illegal. Some aspects of pricing, however, are still open to ethics abuses. For example, should some customers pay more for merchandise if distribution costs are higher in their areas? Do marketers have an obligation to warn vendors and customers of impending price, discount, or return policy changes?

After Hurricane Katrina hit the Gulf Coast, gasoline prices skyrocketed—not just in the affected region, but all over the United States. Upon investigation, more than 400 gas stations in New Jersey were found to have raised their prices more than once every 24 hours, charged more than their posted prices, and failed to maintain proper records. The state sued Sunoco, Amerada Hess, Motiva Shell, and several independent operators for their price violations.[55]

Credit card companies often walk a fine line between ethical and unethical pricing practices. While consumers are almost always informed of credit card terms on their agreements, the print is usually tiny and the language hard to understand. For instance, a credit card issuer might advertise the benefits of its premium card. But the fine print explains that the firm is allowed to substitute a different plan—with a higher interest rate—if the applicant doesn't qualify for the premium card. In addition, certain laws allow companies to levy charges that consumers might not be aware of. For

assessment check

1. Define *marketing ethics.*
2. Identify the five areas in which ethics can be a problem.

example, under a provision called *universal default,* a company may legally raise its interest rate on a card if the customer is late paying other bills—even if that credit card is paid on time.[56]

All these concerns must be dealt with in developing a professional ethic for pricing products. The ethical issues involved in pricing for today's highly competitive and increasingly computerized markets are discussed in greater detail in Chapters 18 and 19.

8 Identify the four levels of the social responsibility pyramid.

social responsibility
Marketing philosophies, policies, procedures, and actions that have the enhancement of society's welfare as a primary objective.

SOCIAL RESPONSIBILITY IN MARKETING

Companies can do business in such a way that everyone benefits—customers, the companies themselves, and society as a whole. While ethical business practices are vital to a firm's long-term survival and growth, **social responsibility** raises the bar even higher. In marketing, social responsibility involves accepting an obligation to give equal weight to profits, consumer satisfaction, and social well-being in evaluating a firm's performance. In addition to measuring sales, revenues, and profits, a firm must also consider ways in which it has contributed to the overall well-being of its customers and society.

Social responsibility allows a wide range of opportunities for companies to shine. If they are reluctant at first, government legislation can mandate socially responsible actions. Government may require firms to take socially responsible actions in matters of environmental policy, deceptive product claims, and other areas. Also, consumers, through their power to repeat or withhold purchases, may force marketers to provide honest and relevant information and fair prices. The four dimensions of social responsibility—economic, legal, ethical, and philanthropic—are shown in Figure 3.6. The first two dimensions have long been recognized, but ethical obligations and the need for marketers to be good corporate citizens have increased in importance in recent years.

The locus for socially responsible decisions in organizations has always been an important issue. But who should accept specific accountability for the social effects of marketing decisions? Responses include the district sales manager, the marketing vice president, the firm's CEO, and even the board of directors. Probably the most valid assessment holds that all marketers, regardless of their stations in the organization, remain accountable for the social aspects of their decisions.

figure 3.6

The Four Step Pyramid of Social Responsibility

Source: The Four Step Pyramid of Corporate Social Responsibility from *Business Horizons,* Vol 34, 1991, page 92, Freeman & Liedtka, "Corp. Social Responsibility." Reprinted from *Business Horizons* © 1991 with permission from Elsevier.

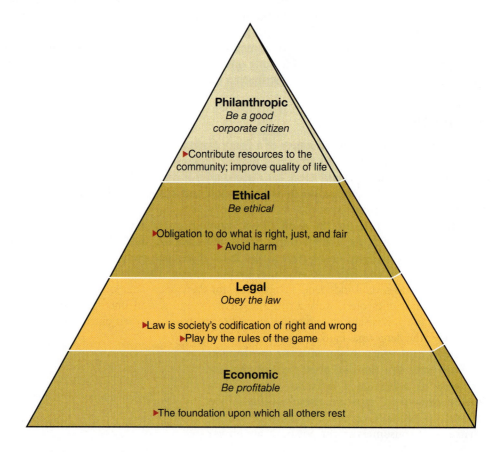

Philanthropic
Be a good corporate citizen
▶Contribute resources to the community; improve quality of life

Ethical
Be ethical
▶Obligation to do what is right, just, and fair
▶ Avoid harm

Legal
Obey the law
▶Law is society's codification of right and wrong
▶Play by the rules of the game

Economic
Be profitable
▶The foundation upon which all others rest

MARKETING'S RESPONSIBILITIES

The concept of business's social responsibility traditionally has concerned managers' relationships with customers, employees, and stockholders. In general, managers traditionally have felt responsible for providing quality products at reasonable prices for customers, adequate wages and decent working environments for employees, and acceptable profits for stockholders. Only occasionally did the concept extend to relations with the government and rarely with the general public.

Today, corporate responsibility has expanded to cover the entire framework of society. A decision to temporarily delay the installation of a pollution-control device may satisfy the traditional sense of responsibility. Customers would continue to receive an uninterrupted supply of the plant's products, employees would not face layoffs, and stockholders would still receive reasonable returns on their investments. Contemporary business ethics, however, would not accept this choice as socially responsible.

Contemporary marketing decisions must consider their global effect. Some clothing manufacturers and retailers have come under fire for buying from foreign suppliers who force employees to work in dangerous conditions or pay less than a living wage. Giant pharmaceuticals companies, for example, that refuse to allow the development of low-cost versions of their patented drugs to combat epidemics in Africa of diseases such as AIDS, malaria, or tuberculosis have been accused of ignoring the global reach of corporate responsibility. Marketers must also consider the long-term effects of their decisions and the well-being of future generations. Manufacturing processes that damage the environment or that use up natural energy resources are easy targets for criticism.

Marketers can use several methods to help their companies behave in socially responsible ways. Chapter 1 discussed cause marketing as one channel through which firms can promote social causes—and at the same time benefit by linking their people and products to worthy undertakings. Socially responsible marketing involves campaigns that encourage people to adopt socially beneficial behaviors, whether they be safe driving, eating more nutritious food, or improving the working conditions of people half a world away. And organizations that sponsor socially responsible programs not only help society but also develop goodwill for an organization, which could help the bottom line in the long run.

One way entire communities can benefit is through socially responsible investing. Many local banks and credit unions are committed to investing in their own communities. When consumers purchase CDs or open money market accounts or savings accounts, the bank or credit union can use the money to finance loans for affordable housing or for small businesses. Consumers still get the interest on their accounts, and the money is being used to improve the community. The U.S. Treasury Department has certified about 750 community development financial institutions (CDFIs) that serve neighborhoods that might otherwise be overlooked and educating low-income borrowers.[57]

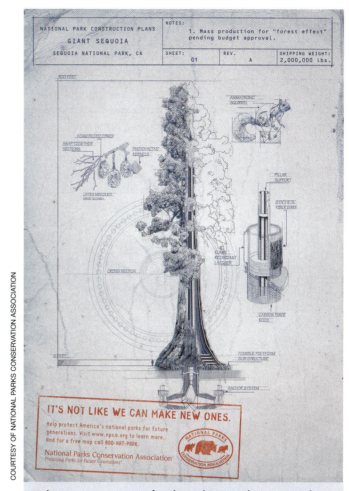

Marketers can raise awareness of worthy social causes, such as preserving the nation's parks, as this promotion for the National Parks Conservation Association does.

COURTESY OF NATIONAL PARKS CONSERVATION ASSOCIATION

Briefly Speaking

"There's no incompatibility between doing the right thing and making money."

—William Clay Ford, Jr. (b. 1957)

CEO, Ford Motor Company

MARKETING AND ECOLOGY

Ecology—the relationship between organisms and their natural environments—has become a driving force in influencing how businesses operate. Many industry and government leaders rank the protection of the environment as the biggest challenge facing today's corporations. Environmental issues such as water pollution, waste disposal, acid rain, depletion of the ozone layer, and global

green marketing
Production, promotion, and reclamation of environmentally sensitive products.

warming affect everyone. They influence all areas of marketing decision making, including product planning and public relations, spanning such topics as planned obsolescence, pollution control, recycling waste materials, and resource conservation.

In creating new-product offerings that respond to consumer demands for convenience by offering extremely short-lived products, such as disposable diapers, ballpoint pens, razors, and cameras, marketers occasionally find themselves accused of intentionally offering products with limited durability—in other words, of practicing **planned obsolescence.** In addition to convenience-oriented items, other products become obsolete when rapid changes in technology create superior alternatives. In the computer industry, changes take place so quickly that lawmakers in several states have proposed legislation to force manufacturers to take back "e-waste"—used PCs and other technology products that contain toxic chemicals. For example, HP now supplies its printers with two cartridges—one for color and one for black. The replacement packs for each cartridge come with a self-addressed, postage-paid pouch to mail empty cartridges back to the company for reuse. Retailer Staples provides customers with plastic bags in which they can put empty cartridges. Any customer who returns the bag with empty cartridges to a Staples store receives a $3 coupon for each empty cartridge.

Public concern about pollution of such natural resources as water and air affects some industries, such as pharmaceuticals or heavy-goods manufacturing, more than others. Still, the marketing system annually generates billions of tons of packaging materials such as glass, metal, paper, and plastics that add to the world's growing piles of trash and waste. Recycling such materials, as HP and Staples do, is another important aspect of ecology. Recycling can benefit society by saving natural resources and energy as well as by alleviating a major factor in environmental pollution—waste disposal.

Alliances can be effective in dealing with the problem of waste disposal. Not-for-profit Goodwill Industries and Dell recently launched the San Francisco Bay Area Computer Recycling Project, which offers drop-off recycling and reuse opportunities for unwanted computers to area residents—for free. Whereas many recycling posts charge fees of as much as $20 to deposit old computers and other electronics, this program charges consumers nothing. According to the two organizations, the goal of the initiative is to "divert at least 1 million pounds of used computers and computer equipment from landfills over one year and to provide education on the importance of proper computer disposal."[58]

Many companies respond to consumers' growing concern about ecological issues through **green marketing**—production, promotion, and reclamation of environmentally sensitive products. In the green marketing revolution of the early 1990s, marketers were quick to tie their companies and products to ecological themes. Consumers have responded by purchasing more and more of these goods, providing profits and opportunities for growth to the companies that make and sell them. Auto manufacturers such as Toyota and Honda are already making second-generation hybrid autos. Starbucks offers its own Ethos bottled water, along with a pledge to donate 5 cents from every bottle toward a $10 million program that will help improve drinking-water conditions around the world. Wal-Mart has built a 206,000-square-foot store in Texas that is designed to be sustainable. General Electric has announced a corporate initiative called Ecomagination, backed by a $1.5 billion yearly investment in research on cleaner technologies. GE has also launched an ad campaign that highlights the environmental benefits of specific products and services.[59]

Used batteries and electronics can create environmental problems when they decompose. For more than a decade, not-for-profit organization Rechargeable Battery Recycling Corporation has collected and recycled millions of batteries and cell phones. The organization assists communities and companies with their recycling efforts.

One area of green marketing that is booming is the organic food industry. Of the 106 million households in the United States, 13 million now say they buy organic products consistently. But marketers and consumers alike have struggled to understand exactly what *organic* means. Marketers must use the term accurately in labeling, and consumers want to know what they are buying. According to the U.S. Department of Agriculture, "Organic food is produced by farmers who emphasize the use of renewable resources and the conservation of soil and water to enhance environmental quality for future generations." The USDA also specifies that certified organic meat, poultry, eggs, and dairy products must be produced by animals raised without antibiotics or growth hormones. A product that has a "USDA organic" seal certifies that it is at least 95 percent organic. Because it takes an average of three years for a farmer to receive USDA certification—an expensive process—prices for organic products are usually higher.[60]

 assessment check

1. **Identify the four levels of the social responsibility pyramid.**
2. **What are the benefits of green marketing?**

Strategic Implications of Marketing in the 21st Century

Marketing decisions that businesses make are influenced by changes in the competitive, political-legal, economic, technological, and social-cultural environments. Marketing ethics and social responsibility will continue to play important roles in business transactions in your hometown and around the globe.

As the Internet and the rapid changes in technology that it represents are fully absorbed into the competitive environment, competition will become even more intense than it is today. Much of the competition will result from innovations in technology and scientific discoveries. Business in the 21st century will be propelled by information technologies, but sustained by creative thinking and the willingness of marketers to meet challenges. Marketers will face new regulations as the political and legal environment responds to changes in the United States and abroad. As the population ages and the social-cultural environment evolves, marketers will seek to meet the demands for new goods and services for consumers, such as increased health care. As always, they will try to anticipate and make the most of every opportunity afforded by the business cycle.

Ethics and social responsibility must underlie everything that marketers do in the 21st century—those who find ways to "do well by doing good" will succeed.

REVIEW OF CHAPTER OBJECTIVES

1 Identify the five components of the marketing environment.

The five components of the marketing environment are (1) the *competitive environment*—the interactive process that occurs in the marketplace as competing organizations seek to satisfy markets; (2) the *political-legal environment*—the laws and interpretations of laws that require firms to operate under competitive conditions and to protect consumer rights; (3) the *economic environment*—environmental factors resulting from business fluctuations and resulting variations in inflation rates and employment levels; (4) the *technological environment*—application to marketing of knowledge based on discoveries in science, inventions, and innovations; and (5) the *social-cultural environment*—the component of the marketing environment consisting of the relationship between the marketer and society and its culture.

2   Explain the types of competition marketers face and the steps necessary for developing a competitive strategy.

Three types of competition exist: (1) direct competition among marketers of similar products; (2) competition among goods or services that can be substituted for one another; and (3) competition among all organizations that vie for the consumer's purchasing power. To develop a competitive strategy, marketers must answer the following questions: (1) Should we compete? The answer depends on the firm's available resources and objectives as well as its expected profit potential. (2) If so, in what markets should we compete? This question requires marketers to make product, pricing, distribution, and promotional decisions that give their firm a competitive advantage. (3) How should we compete? This question requires marketers to make the technical decisions involved in setting a comprehensive marketing strategy.

3   Describe how marketing activities are regulated and how marketers can influence the political-legal environment.

Marketing activities are influenced by federal, state, and local laws that require firms to operate under competitive conditions and to protect consumer rights. Government regulatory agencies such as the Federal Trade Commission enforce these laws and identify and correct unfair marketing practices. Public and private consumer interest groups and industry self-regulatory groups also affect marketing activities. Marketers may seek to influence public opinion and legislative actions through advertising, political action committees, and political lobbying.

4   Outline the economic factors that affect marketing decisions and consumer buying power.

The primary economic factors are (1) the stage in the business cycle, (2) inflation and deflation, (3) unemployment, (4) income, and (5) resource availability. All are vitally important to marketers because of their effects on consumers' willingness to buy and consumers' perceptions regarding changes in the marketing mix variables.

5   Discuss the impact of the technological environment on a firm's marketing activities.

The technological environment consists of application to marketing of knowledge based on discoveries in science, inventions, and innovations. This knowledge can provide marketing opportunities: it results in new products and improves existing ones, and it is a frequent source of price reductions through new production methods or materials. Technological applications also pose a threat because they can make existing products obsolete overnight. The technological environment demands that marketers continually adapt to change, because its scope of influence reaches into consumers' lifestyles, competitors' products, and industrial users' demands.

6   Explain how the social-cultural environment influences marketing.

The social-cultural environment is the relationship between marketing, society, and culture. To remain competitive, marketers must be sensitive to society's demographic shifts and changing values, which affect consumers' reactions to different products and marketing practices. Marketers must consider the increasing importance of cultural diversity, both in the United States and abroad. Changing societal values have led to consumerism. Consumerism is the social force within the environment designed to aid and protect the consumer by exerting legal, moral, and economic pressures on business. Consumer rights include the following: (1) the right to choose freely, (2) the right to be informed, (3) the right to be heard, and (4) the right to be safe.

7   Describe the ethical issues in marketing.

Marketing ethics encompass the marketer's standards of conduct and moral values. Each element of the marketing mix raises its own set of ethical questions. Ethics in product strategy may involve quality and safety, packaging and labeling, and pollution. Ethics in distribution may involve territorial decisions. In promotion, ethical issues include honesty in advertising and promotion to children. Pricing may raise questions about price fixing and discrimination, increases, and deceptive pricing.

8   **Identify the four levels of the social responsibility pyramid.**

The four levels of social responsibility are (1) *economic*—to be profitable, the foundation upon which the other three levels of the pyramid rest; (2) *legal*—to obey the law, society's codification of right and wrong; (3) *ethical*—to do what is right, just, and fair and to avoid wrongdoing; and (4) *philanthropic*—to be a good corporate citizen, contributing to the community and improving quality of life.

 assessment check **answers**

1.1   Define *environmental scanning.*

Environmental scanning is the process of collecting information about the external marketing environment to identify and interpret potential trends.

1.2   How does environmental scanning contribute to environmental management?

Environmental scanning contributes to environmental management by providing current information about the five different environments so marketers can predict and influence changes.

2.1   Distinguish between direct and indirect competition and give an example of each.

Direct competition occurs among marketers of similar products, such as auto manufacturers or gas stations. Indirect competition involves products that are easily substituted. Pizza could compete with fried chicken or tacos. Busch Gardens could compete with a trip to a baseball game.

2.2   What is time-based competition?

Time-based competition is the strategy of developing and distributing goods and services more quickly than competitors.

3.1   Identify the four phases of U.S. government regulation of business. What is the newest frontier?

The four phases of government regulation of business are the antimonopoly period, protection of competitors, consumer protection, and industry regulation. The newest frontier is cyberspace.

3.2   Which federal agency wields the broadest regulatory powers for influencing marketing activities?

The Federal Trade Commission (FTC) has the broadest regulatory authority.

4.1   Identify and describe briefly the four stages of the business cycle.

The four stages of the business cycle are prosperity, recession, depression, and recovery.

4.2   Explain how inflation and income affect consumer buying decisions.

Inflation devalues money and therefore may restrict some purchasing, particularly goods and services that are not considered necessary. Income also influences consumer buying power—the more discretionary income a household has, the more goods and services can be purchased.

5.1   What are some of the consumer benefits of technology?

Technology can lead to new or improved goods and services, offer better customer service, and reduce prices. It can also address social concerns.

5.2   Why must marketers monitor the technological environment?

Marketers need to monitor the technological environment in order to stay current with—and possibly ahead of—competitors. If they don't, they may wind up with obsolete offerings.

6.1   Define *consumerism.*

Consumerism is a social force within the environment that aids and protects the buyer by exerting legal, moral, and economic pressures on business.

✓ *assessment check* answers

6.2 Identify the four consumer rights.

The four consumer rights are as follows: the right to choose freely, the right to be informed, the right to be heard, and the right to be safe.

7.1 Define *marketing ethics*.

Marketing ethics refers to the marketer's standards of conduct and moral values.

7.2 Identify the five areas in which ethics can be a problem.

The five areas of ethical concern for marketers are marketing research, product strategy, distribution, promotion, and pricing.

8.1 Identify the four levels of the social responsibility pyramid.

The four levels of social responsibility are economic, legal, ethical, and philanthropic.

8.2 What are the benefits of green marketing?

Green marketing, which responds to consumers' growing concerns about ecological issues, offers consumers high-quality products without health risks or damage to the environment. Marketers who engage in green marketing may find themselves in a booming industry such as organic foods.

MARKETING TERMS YOU NEED TO KNOW

environmental scanning 77

environmental management 77

competitive environment 78

political-legal environment 81

economic environment 86

demarketing 89

technological environment 91

social-cultural environment 92

consumerism 93

consumer rights 94

marketing ethics 95

social responsibility 100

green marketing 102

OTHER IMPORTANT MARKETING TERMS

strategic alliance 78

monopoly 78

deregulation movement 78

antitrust 78

oligopoly 79

competitive strategy 80

time-based competition 81

gross domestic product (GDP) 86

business cycle 86

inflation 87

unemployment 88

discretionary income 88

VoIP 92

ecology 101

planned obsolescence 102

ASSURANCE OF LEARNING REVIEW

1. Why is environmental scanning an important activity for marketers?
2. What are the three different types of competition? Give an example of each.
3. What are the three questions marketers must ask before deciding on a competitive strategy?
4. What is the function of the Federal Trade Commission? The Food and Drug Administration?
5. Describe an industry or firm that you think might be able to weather an economic downturn and explain why.
6. Why do marketers monitor the technological environment?
7. How might marketers make the most of shifts in the social-cultural environment?
8. Describe the importance of consumer rights in today's marketing activities.
9. Why is it worthwhile for a firm to create an ethics program?
10. How can social responsibility benefit a firm as well as the society in which it operates?

PROJECTS AND TEAMWORK EXERCISES

1. With a classmate, choose two firms that compete directly with each other. Select two of the following or choose your own. Then develop a competitive strategy for your firm while your partner develops a strategy for his or hers. Present the two strategies to the class. How are they similar? How are they different?
   a. Home Depot and Lowe's
   b. Apple and Dell
   c. Busch Gardens and Six Flags
   d. Visa and MasterCard
   e. Honda and Ford
   f. Sara Lee and Kraft Foods

2. Track your own consumer purchasing decisions as they relate to your income. Compare your decisions during the college year and the summer. Do you have a summer job that increases your income? How does that affect your decisions?

3. The U.S. Postal service essentially enjoys a monopoly on the delivery of most mail. With a classmate, develop a strategy for a business that would compete with the USPS in areas that firms such as UPS, FedEx, and DHL do not already address.

4. Choose one of the following products. Working in pairs or small groups, present arguments for and against having the United States impose certain regulations on the advertising of your product. (Note that some products already do have regulations—you can argue for or against them.)
   a. alcoholic beverages
   b. tobacco
   c. casinos
   d. prescription medications

5. With a classmate, research one of the recent large cases involving unethical and illegal activities by executives for companies such as Enron, Tyco, MCI, and Martha Stewart Living Omnimedia. Describe the charges made against these executives and the outcome. Do you think they were fairly charged and punished? Why or why not?

CRITICAL-THINKING EXERCISES

1. Suppose you and a friend want to start a company that markets frozen fish dinners. What are some of the questions about the competitive environment that you would like to have answered before you begin production? How will you determine whom your customers are likely to be? How will you reach them?

2. Emissions standards for motorcycles took effect in 2006 under rules adopted by the Environmental Protection Agency. There were no previous emissions controls for motorcycles at all, but even under the new laws, "dirt" bikes for off-road use will be exempt, and manufacturers producing fewer than 3,000 vehicles a year were allowed an extra two years to comply. The new standards add about $75 to the average cost of a motorcycle according to the EPA, but $250 according to the Motorcycle Industry Council. Why do you think motorcycle makers have not adopted voluntary emissions standards? Should they have done so? Why or why not?

3. The social-cultural environment can have a strong influence on the decisions marketers must make. In recent years, animal rights groups have targeted the manufacture and sale of *foie gras,* a European food delicacy made from goose and duck liver. Activists cite the cruel treatment of these birds, while chefs and restaurant owners claim otherwise. Animal rights groups are pressuring restaurants to stop serving foie gras. Others argue that consumers should be allowed a choice. What aspects of the social-cultural environment are affecting the marketing of foie gras? Which of the other components of the marketing environment may come into play, and how?

4. Nearly 400 million rebates—worth about $6 billion—are offered to U.S. consumers by marketers every year. But do consumers like them? Often rebates require more effort than a consumer is willing to make to receive the cash back. Critics of the promotional effort say that marketers know this—and are banking on consumers' not redeeming them. One expert estimates that this translates to about $2 billion of extra income in the pockets of retailers and manufacturers.[61] Do you think rebate programs are ethical? Why or why not?

5. The disposal of nuclear waste has been an ongoing public safety issue, one with which marketers who work for nuclear power companies must deal. This material is currently stored at 126 sites around the nation. The U.S. Department of Energy (DOE) is obtaining a license to proceed with the construction of a single nuclear repository at Yucca Mountain in Nevada.[62] Supporters of the site argue that Yucca Mountain is critical to building America's nuclear power capacity, while critics are skeptical of its safety and usefulness. As a marketer, how would you approach this issue?

ETHICS EXERCISE

Some retail firms protect their inventory against theft by locking their premises after hours even though maintenance and other workers are inside the stores working all night. Employees have charged that they are forbidden to leave the premises during work hours and that during an emergency, such as illness or injury, precious time is lost waiting for a manager to arrive who is authorized to unlock the doors. Although workers could open an emergency exit, in some cases they claim that they will be fired for doing so. Employers assert that managers with keys are on the premises (or minutes away) and that locking employees in ensures their own safety as well as cutting down on costly "shrinkage."

1. Under what circumstances, if any, do you think locking employees in at night is appropriate?
2. If you feel this practice is appropriate, what safeguards do you think should be put into effect? What responsibilities do employers and employees have in such circumstances?

INTERNET EXERCISES

1. **Developing a competitive strategy.** Review the material in the chapter on how companies develop a competitive strategy, including the key questions that must be answered.
   a. Visit the Web site of a company such as Procter & Gamble (http://www.pg.com) or Colgate (http://www.colgate.com). Pick one of the company's products and analyze how the firm answered each of the key questions when it developed a competitive strategy for the product you selected.
   b. Gatorade (http://www.gatorade.com) and PowerAde (http://www.powerade.com) are the two leading brands in the growing market for sports drinks. Gatorade is a Pepsi brand and PowerAde is a Coke brand. Visit each product's Web site and compare and contrast the competitive strategies used by both companies to build their respective brands.
   c. Companies discontinue products from time to time. Using Google or another search engine, identify a product that has recently been discontinued. Research the product and the company that produced it, and write a brief report summarizing the reasons behind the decision.

2. **Ethics and social responsibility.** Many companies use the Web to highlight their ethical standards and social responsibility. Visit each of the following Web sites and prepare a brief summary of what you found.
   a. Green marketing and environmentalism: Ford Motor Company (http://www.ford.com/en/goodworks/environment/default.htm)
   b. Coffee producers and fair trade: Starbucks (http://www.starbucks.com/aboutus/default.asp)
   c. Ethical standards and credo: Johnson & Johnson (http://www.jnj.com/our_company/our_credo/index.htm)

Note: Internet Web addresses change frequently. If you don't find the exact site listed, you may need to access the organization's home page and search from there or use a search engine such as Google.

ETHICS QUESTIONNAIRE ANSWERS

Questionnaire is on page 97

1. 34% said personal e-mail on company computers is wrong
2. 37% said using office equipment for schoolwork is wrong
3. 49% said playing computer games at work is wrong
4. 54% said Internet shopping at work is wrong
5. 61% said its unethical to blame your error on technology
6. 87% said it's unethical to visit pornographic sites at work
7. 33% said $25 is the amount at which a gift from a supplier or client becomes troubling, while 33% said $50, and 33% said $100
8. 35% said a $50 gift to the boss is unacceptable
9. 12% said a $50 gift from the boss is unacceptable
10. 70% said it's unacceptable to take the $200 football tickets
11. 70% said it's unacceptable to take the $120 theater tickets
12. 35% said it's unacceptable to take the $100 food basket
13. 45% said it's unacceptable to take the $25 gift certificate
14. 40% said it's unacceptable to take the $75 raffle prize
15. 11% reported they lied about sick days
16. 4% reported they have taken credit for the work or ideas of others

CASE 3.1   The Selling of Cell Phone Logs

Someone's listening to you. Specifically, someone may have access to your cell phone records. In recent years, online Web sites called "information brokers" have conducted business by gathering a wide range of personal information about consumers and selling it to anyone willing to pay for it. Despite the Telecommunications Act of 1996, this information includes consumers' call records, which may be sold by the phone companies to their affiliates, agents, and partners involved in joint ventures. The information could potentially be used for all kinds of purposes, from unethical marketing to identity theft. One Web site, Locatecell.com, openly promised to provide records of up to 100 outbound calls placed from any phone for $110 to $125. For $95, the site would supply any working cell phone number.

Recently, however, consumer advocacy groups have linked arms with two of the nation's top regulatory agencies—the Federal Communications Commission (FCC) and the Federal Trade Commission (FTC) to crack down on the sale of cell phone logs, which affects millions of consumers. "I've got a cell phone," said Senator Daniel K. Inouye of Hawaii. "All of us have got cell phones. Just the thought of someone passing [my call log] information to others—it horrifies me." While the Telecommunications Act prohibits obtaining a person's financial information under false pretexts, it does not address the issue of telephone records. In addition to financial data, the loss of personal information could leave someone vulnerable to personal crime—stalking, harassment, or worse. "These records can include some of the most private personal information about an individual," warned Jonathan Adelstein of the FCC.

As the Consumer Telephone Records Act of 2006 was being introduced to block the sale of cell phone records, FCC chairman Kevin Martin noted, "I believe Congress could specifically make illegal the commercial availability of consumers' phone records. If any entity is found to be selling this information for a fee, regardless of how it obtained such information, it would face liability." The stricter law works on both sides, making it a federal offense for information brokers to obtain unauthorized records as well as for phone companies to sell them.

Recognizing their own risk—and ethical responsibility—some cell phone companies have taken independent steps to block the sale of phone records. Cingular Wireless obtained a restraining order against Locatecell.com and similar companies, claiming that employees of these services pose as cell phone customers to wrangle personal information from Cingular representatives. The information is then sold. "This is something we take very seriously," said Mark Seigel of Cingular Wireless. "Nothing is more important to us than the privacy of our customers' records." Verizon Wireless filed a lawsuit against information brokers in Tennessee and Florida. The carriers support the stricter legislation, saying it helps them do their job. "We need the assistance of the law enforcement community here," says Joe Farren, a spokesman for CTIA, which represents the wireless phone industry. In the long run, protecting customers isn't just ethical business—it's good business.

Questions for Critical Thinking

1. In what ways is the political-legal environment important to marketers who work for cell phone companies? Do you agree with the implementation of stricter legislation against the sale of cell phone records? Why or why not?
2. Describe some additional ethical steps that cell phone companies might take to protect the privacy of their customers.

Sources: Peter Hardin, "Theft of Call Logs on Radar; Congress Could Act Soon on Cell-Phone Records Being Stolen," *RedOrbit*, February 9, 2006, **http://www.redorbit.com**; Roy Mark, "Feds Say: Ban All Sales of Phone Records," Internet.com, February 2, 2006, **http://www.internetnews.com**; Grant Gross, "Update—Legislation Would Prohibit Sale of Phone Call Logs," InfoWorld, January 18, 2006, **http://www.infoworld.com**; "Schumer Unveils Bipartisan Bill to Stop Sale of Cell Phone Call Logs," U.S. Senate press release, January 18, 2006, **http://www.senate.gov**; Peter Svensson, "Calling Records Sales Face New Scrutiny," Associated Press, January 18, 2006, **http://news.yahoo.com**; "Feds Probe Sale of Personal Phone Records," Associated Press, January 17, 2006, **http://news.yahoo.com**; Leslie Cayley, "Cingular Goes after Firms Selling Call Records," *USA Today*, January 16, 2006, **http://www.usatoday.com**.

VIDEO CASE 3.2   Organic Valley Farms: Producing Food That's Good for People and the Earth

The written video case on Organic Valley Farms appears on page VC-4. The recently filmed Organic Valley Farms video is designed to expand and highlight the concepts in this chapter and the concepts and questions covered in the written video case.

CHAPTER 4

Southwest Airlines Spreads Its Wings

Southwest Airlines has a long history of innovation, including offering employees the first profit-sharing plan in the U.S. airline industry. The company is widely recognized as a great place to work, has an enviable on-time and baggage-handling record, and is one of the country's most admired and most financially successful corporations. Southwest's 31,000 employees make sure 3,000 low-cost, low-fare flights reach 62 U.S. cities each day.

But Southwest's distinctive brand of success doesn't stop at the airport terminal. Its Web site, http://www.southwest.com, was the first airline home page on the Internet. A team of five employees labored nine months to create the site, and now it is the largest—and most profitable—airline site on the Web.

More than half of the tickets booked on Southwest flights are sold online, and the percentage of passenger revenue being generated by online bookings has been rising steadily, recently reaching about 70 percent. More than half the airline's customers check in online or at an airport kiosk, and passengers can now reach the Southwest site through Web-enabled handheld devices as well.

"With the growing popularity of Web-enabled mobile devices, we wanted to offer our customers the convenience of checking in for their flight wherever they may be," said the company's vice president of marketing. "This is just one more example of how we are striving to make the travel experience even easier for our customers."

Southwest has expanded its online presence in a number of other creative ways. It offers a weekly e-mail service called Click 'n Save that promotes air, hotel, car rental, vacation, cruise, and other specials and packages. This free service has enrolled more than 5 million people. Tabs on the company's home page take visitors to vacation and cruise deals and special packages with one click. There they can search by destination or by departure city, price various trips, compare special deals, and book any combination of air, car, and hotel they want. They can even access 24-hour traveler assistance at the site. For its Hispanic customers, the carrier has also developed a booking site, http://www.southwest.com/vamonos, for making reservations and getting airport information and route maps

TOP PHOTO: IMAGE COURTESY OF THE ADVERTISING ARCHIVES
BOTTOM PHOTO: ASSOCIATED PRESS, AP

E-Business in Contemporary Marketing

Chapter Objectives

1   Define *e-business* and discuss how marketers use the Internet to achieve business success.

2   Distinguish between a corporate Web site and a marketing Web site.

3   List the major forms of B2B e-marketing.

4   Explain business-to-consumer (B2C) e-marketing.

5   Identify online buyers and sellers.

6   Describe some of the challenges associated with online marketing and e-business.

7   Discuss how marketers use the communication function of the Web as part of their online marketing strategies.

8   Outline the steps involved in developing successful e-business Web sites and identify methods for measuring Web site effectiveness.

all in Spanish. Company policies, travel tips, and other helpful information are also provided.

Southwest brings business travelers their own free online booking and travel management tool, SWABIZ, accessed from the home page. That site offers travel discounts and a frequent-traveler reward program, and it also helps corporate travel managers track, manage, and report business travel for their firms. Enrollments have increased 44 percent in the last year.

In yet another innovation, DING!, a free downloadable computer application, brings exclusive Southwest offers directly to customers' desktops in the form of live updates. DING! also provides quick access to online check-in tools and lets customers check flight status online.

Need a special gift in a hurry? You can buy a Southwest gift card online, and within an hour the company will send a free e-mail announcement to the recipient for you. The gift card never expires and can be redeemed through one of the company's six reservations centers, at a Southwest airport ticket counter, or, of course, online. About the only thing the Southwest Airlines Web site can't do yet is fly.[1]

evolution *of a* brand

Southwest Airlines began in 1971 with three jets serving Dallas, Houston, and San Antonio, after co-founders Rollin King and Herb Kelleher decided that success lay in taking passengers where they wanted to go, when they wanted to fly, on time at the lowest possible fares. Now one of the largest airlines in the country, Southwest flies more than 70 million passengers a year on 436 jets.

The firm grew rapidly, promoting itself as a fun way to fly and offering innovative conveniences such as self-ticketing machines and open seating. Low fares were a consistent theme and, along with a sterling record of on-time arrivals, helped the company achieve numerous awards for customer satisfaction. By the mid-1990s the company had introduced ticketless travel, expanded it to an online service, and racked up four consecutive industry "triple crowns"—for best on-time record, best baggage handling, and fewest customer complaints. To reduce waiting time for customers and improve the airport experience after 9/11, Southwest installed nearly 250 check-in kiosks in airports around the country.

The airline has been consistently profitable for more than 30 years and continues to add routes and destinations to its offerings.

Chapter Overview

During the past decade, marketing has become the cutting-edge tool for success on the Internet. Profit-seeking organizations are not the only benefactors of the Internet; organizations of all kinds are beginning to emphasize marketing's role in achieving set goals. Colleges and universities, charities, museums, symphony orchestras, and hospitals now employ the marketing concept discussed in Chapter 1: providing customers the goods and services they want to buy when they want to buy them. Contemporary marketing continues to perform its function of bringing buyers and sellers together; it just does it faster and more efficiently than ever before. With just a few ticks of the clock and a few clicks of a mouse, the Internet revolutionizes

e-business Firm that targets customers by collecting and analyzing business information, conducting customer transactions, and maintaining online relationships with customers.

every aspect of life. New words have emerged, such as *shopping blog, RSS, VoIP,* and *XML;* and old words have new meanings never imagined a few years ago: *Web, Net, surfer* and *server, banner* and *browsers, online* and *offline.*

Electronic Business (or **e-business**) refers to conducting business via the Internet and has turned virtual reality into reality. With a computer and Internet access, a virtual marketplace is open 24 hours a day, 7 days a week, to provide almost anything anywhere to anyone, including clothes, food, entertainment, medicine, and information. You can pay your cell phone bill, make travel reservations, do research for a term paper, post a résumé at an employment bulletin board, or buy a used car—

Briefly Speaking

"The Internet has been the most fundamental change during my lifetime and for hundreds of years. Someone the other day said, 'It's the biggest thing since [the printing of the Gutenberg Bible],' and then someone else said, 'No, it's the biggest thing since the invention of writing.'"

—Rupert Murdoch
(b. 1931)
U.S. publisher and businessman

perhaps at a lower price than you could in person.

Internet marketers can reach individual consumers or target organizations worldwide through a vast array of computer and communications technologies. In just a few short years, hundreds of thousands of companies large and small have been connected to electronic marketing channels. The size and scope of e-business is difficult to understate. For instance, according to the U.S. Census Bureau, online retail sales in the United States totaled almost $86 billion in a recent year. During that year, online retail sales grew by more than 23 percent, or more than three times the overall growth rate in retail sales.[2]

E-business involves much more than just buying and selling goods and services. Some surveys suggest that the Web is the number one medium for new-product information, eclipsing catalogs, print ads, and trade shows. The Internet allows retailers and vendors to exchange vital information, improving the overall functioning of supply and distribution, lowering costs, and increasing profits. Moreover, an increasing number of Americans now get some of their news and information from *blogs* (online journals) rather than from traditional media such as television and newspapers. Consequently, a growing number of businesses are using blogs to put human faces on their organizations and communicate directly with customers.

In the past decade, the number of Internet users in the United States and worldwide has grown dramatically. Today an estimated 203 million Americans—more than two-thirds of the population—access the Internet at home, at school, at work, or at public access sites. Worldwide, the number of Internet users is around 1 billion.[3] Figure 4.1 shows the top ten nations in terms of Internet users and Internet penetration (the percentage of a nation's population who use the Internet). As the figure shows, although the United States leads the world in number of Internet users, it ranks only seventh in Internet penetration.

While some of the novelty has worn off, the Internet has become a significant presence in the daily lives of people throughout the world. For example, according to recent surveys, around 50 million Americans get most of their news from the Web and more than 25 million have sold something online.[4] Another report estimates that both the average Briton and the average American spend more time online than watching television today.[5]

In spite of the past success and future potential of the Internet, issues and concerns relating to e-business remain. Some highly touted e-business applications have proven less than successful, cost savings and profits have occasionally been elusive, and many privacy and security issues still linger. Nevertheless, the benefits and potential of e-business outweigh the concerns and problems.

This chapter examines the current status and potential of e-business and e-marketing. We begin by describing the scope of e-business and outline how marketers use the Internet to succeed. Next, we distinguish between a corporate (or organizational) Web site and a marketing Web site.

figure 4.1

Number of Internet Users and Internet Penetration Rate (by country)

Source: World Internet Statistics, **http://www.internetworldstats. com**, accessed May 10, 2006.

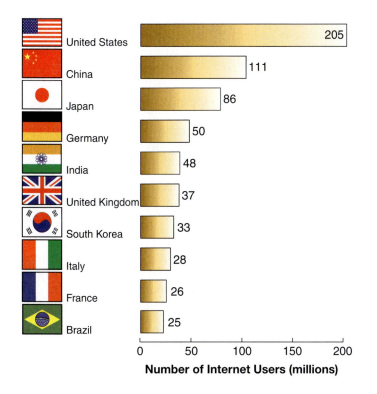

Number of Internet Users (millions)	
United States	205
China	111
Japan	86
Germany	50
India	48
United Kingdom	37
South Korea	33
Italy	28
France	26
Brazil	25

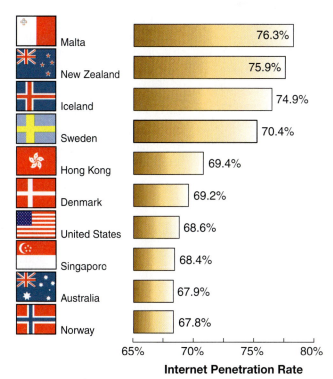

Internet Penetration Rate	
Malta	76.3%
New Zealand	75.9%
Iceland	74.9%
Sweden	70.4%
Hong Kong	69.4%
Denmark	69.2%
United States	68.6%
Singapore	68.4%
Australia	67.9%
Norway	67.8%

This discussion is followed by a review of the major types of B2B e-marketing. We then explore the types of goods and services most often marketed via the Internet, along with a profile of online buyers and sellers. Next, we describe some of the challenges associated with e-business and e-marketing. How marketers use the communication function of the Internet is discussed next. We conclude the chapter by examining how to access the effectiveness of e-marketing.

WHAT IS E-BUSINESS?

Today *e-business* is used to describe the wide range of business activities that take place via Internet applications, such as e-mail and virtual shopping carts. E-business can be divided into the following five broad categories: (1) *e-tailing* or virtual storefronts on Web sites; (2) business-to-business transactions; (3) electronic data interchanges (EDI), the business-to-business exchange of data; (4) e-mail, instant messaging, blogs, podcasts, and other Web-enabled communication tools and their use as media for reaching prospective and existing customers; and (5) the gathering and use of demographic, product, and other information through Web contacts.

e-marketing Strategic process of creating, distributing, promoting, and pricing goods and services to a target market over the Internet or through digital tools.

The component of e-business of particular interest to marketers is *electronic marketing* (**e-marketing**), the strategic process of creating, distributing, promoting, and pricing goods and services to a target market over the Internet or through such digital tools as smart phones. E-marketing is the means by which e-business is achieved. It encompasses such activities as the following:

- legally downloading music and videos from Apple Computer's iTunes Web site (http://www.itunes.com)

- booking a flight to Chicago on Orbitz.com to attend a job fair

- researching computer printers on CNet.com and then placing an order at Newegg.com

- accessing research site LexisNexis through your college's wireless network, allowing you to work on a paper at home and then ordering a pizza for later delivery from PapaJohns.com

The application of these electronic tools to contemporary marketing has the potential to greatly reduce costs and increase customer satisfaction by increasing the speed and efficiency of marketing interactions. Just as e-business is a major function of the Internet, e-marketing is an integral component of e-business.

A closely related but somewhat narrower term than *e-marketing* is *online marketing*. While electronic marketing can encompass digital technologies ranging from DVDs to interactive store kiosks that do not involve computers, online marketing refers to marketing activities that connect buyers and sellers electronically through interactive computer systems.

CAPABILITIES AND BENEFITS OF E-MARKETING

E-business offers countless opportunities for marketers to reach consumers. This radical departure from traditional brick-and-mortar operations provides the following benefits to contemporary marketers, as shown in Table 4.1.

- *Global reach.* The Net eliminates the geographic protections of local business. For instance, Artezen is a home-design retailer based in Bloomington, Illinois. Its customers, however, are located all over the country—California is one of its largest markets. "Online is the great equalizer," according to store owner Melanie Shellito.[6]

interactive marketing Buyer–seller communications in which the customer controls the amount and type of information received from a marketer through such channels as the Internet and virtual reality kiosks.

- *Personalization.* Only a handful of Gateway computers are waiting for customers to purchase at any one time. The production process begins when an order is received and ends a day or two later when the PC is shipped to the customer. Not only does this approach better satisfy customer needs, but it also sharply reduces the amount of inventory Gateway has to carry.

- *Interactive marketing.* One of the largest online retailers is Amazon.com. It uses a concept called **interactive marketing.** This approach, which consists of buyer–seller communications in which the customer controls the amount and type of information received from a marketer, has been

table 4.1	E-Commerce Capabilities	
CAPABILITY	**DESCRIPTION**	**EXAMPLE**
Global reach	The ability to reach anyone connected to a PC anywhere in the world.	EBay—the online auction site—links buyers and sellers throughout the world.
Personalization	Creating products to meet customer specifications.	Lands' End offers online shoppers custom-made shirts, slacks, and jeans.
Interactive marketing	Buyer–seller communications through such channels as the Internet and interactive kiosks.	Best Buy stores have a "Computer Creation Station" that lets customers design and order custom-made personal computers.
Right-time marketing	The ability to provide a product at the exact time needed.	UPS customers can place service orders online and track shipments 24/7.
Integrated marketing	Coordination of all promotional activities to produce a unified, customer-focused promotional message.	Southwest Airlines use the slogans "A Symbol of Freedom" and "You're Now Free to Move around the Country" in both online and offline promotions.

used by marketers for over a decade. Point-of-sale brochures and coupon dispensers located in supermarkets are simple forms of interactive marketing. However, when digital tools such as the Internet are included in interactive marketing efforts, the results are infinitely improved for the seller and buyer alike.

- *Right-time marketing.* Online retailers, such as BN.com and REI.com, can provide products when and where customers want them.

- *Integrated marketing.* The Internet enables the coordination of all promotional activities and communication to create a unified, customer-oriented promotional message.

In addition to the benefits listed here, an effective online presence can improve the performance of traditional marketing operations. For instance, a study by e-business research firm Jupiter Media Metrix found that half of customers use a retailer's Web site primarily for research before buying a product in the retailer's physical store.[7] As noted earlier, some surveys suggest that the Web has become the primary source of product information. A study by marketing and business research firm The Dieringer Group found that a significant segment of American consumers—perhaps as many as 83 million—rely on the Internet nearly twice as much for local purchasing information compared with traditional media such as newspaper, local TV, or radio ads. For each dollar these consumers spent online, the study found, they spent $1.60 offline at local stores.[8]

 assessment check

1. Define *e-business.*
2. Explain the difference between e-business and e-marketing.
3. What are the major benefits of e-marketing?

2 Distinguish between a corporate Web site and a marketing Web site.

corporate Web site Site designed to increase a firm's visibility, promote its offerings, and provide information to interested parties.

TYPES OF BUSINESS WEB SITES

Virtually all businesses today have Web sites. They may offer general information, electronic shopping, and promotions such as games, contests, and online coupons. Type in the firm's Internet address, and the Web site's home page appears on your computer screen.

Two types of company Web sites exist. Many firms have established **corporate Web sites** to increase their visibility, promote their offerings, and provide information to interested parties. Rather than selling goods and services directly, these sites attempt to build customer goodwill and assist channel members in their marketing efforts. For example, the Web site for Levi's jeans offers detailed

marketing Web site
Site whose main purpose is to increase purchases by visitors.

product information and a chance to view recent commercials. Consumers who want to buy jeans, however, can link to the Web sites of retailers such as Kohl's and JCPenney. In addition to using the Web to communicate product information and build relationships with customers, many companies also use their corporate Web sites for a variety of other purposes, including disseminating financial information to investors, giving prospective employees the opportunity to apply online for jobs, and providing a communication channel for customers and other interested parties via e-mail, blogs, and online forums.

Although **marketing Web sites** often include information about company history, products, locations, employment opportunities, and financial information, their goal is to increase purchases by visitors. For instance, Starbucks' Web site contains all of the information traditionally found on a corporate Web site, but it also includes an online store selling everything from coffee to espresso machines. Many marketing Web sites try to engage consumers in interactions that will move them closer to a demonstration, trial visit, purchase, or other marketing outcome. Some marketing Web sites, such as Sony.com, are quite complex. Visitors can link to pages for Sony Pictures Entertainment (with movie trailers and sweepstakes), Sony Music (audio and video clips plus news about recordings), and Sony Online Entertainment (online games plus information about games and gaming systems), among other possibilities.

✓ *assessment check*

1. Explain the difference between a corporate Web site and a marketing Web site.

2. Visit the Web site for Urban Outfitters (http://www.urbanoutfitters.com). Is it a corporate Web site or a marketing Web site?

Corporate Web sites such as this one from Ford Motor Company provide consumers general information about the company, its history and operations, current events, and products. Marketing Web sites such as The Gap's are intended primarily to provide convenient shopping for customers.

 List the major forms of B2B e-marketing.

B2B E-MARKETING

FedEx's Web site is not designed to be flashy. It doesn't contain fancy graphics or streaming video clips. Instead, it provides lots of practical information to help the firm's customers. The site enables customers to check rates, compare services, schedule package pickups and deliveries, track shipments, and order shipping supplies. This information is vital to FedEx's customers, most of whom are businesses. Customers access the site thousands of times a day.

Business-to-business, known as **B2B, e-marketing** is the use of the Internet for business transactions between organizations. Although most people are familiar with such online firms as Amazon.com and eBay, consumer transactions are dwarfed by their B2B counterparts. According to the U.S. Census Bureau, more than 90 percent of e-business activity consists of B2B transactions. Moreover, the Census Bureau reports, B2B e-business transactions make up more than 10 percent of all B2B transactions.[9]

business-to-business (B2B) e-marketing Use of the Internet for business transactions between organizations.

In addition to generating sales revenue, B2B e-marketing also provides detailed product descriptions whenever they are needed. Payments and other information are exchanged on the Web. Moreover, B2B e-marketing can slash order-processing expenses. Business-to-business transactions, which typically involve more steps than consumer purchases, can be much more efficient on the Internet. Orders placed over the Internet typically contain fewer errors than handwritten ones, and when mistakes occur, the technology can quickly locate them. So the Internet is an attractive option for business buying and selling. In some industries, relying on the Internet to make purchases can reduce costs by almost 25 percent.

B2B e-marketing activity has become more varied in recent years. In addition to using the Web to conduct individual sales transactions and provide product information, companies are using such tools as EDI, extranets, private exchanges, Web services, electronic exchanges, and e-procurement, discussed next.

IMAGE COURTESY OF THE ADVERTISING ARCHIVES

Software from vendors such as Microsoft allows employees of a business to link directly with their partners and suppliers, streamlining distribution and production functions.

ELECTRONIC DATA INTERCHANGE, WEB SERVICES, EXTRANETS, AND PRIVATE EXCHANGES

One of the oldest applications of technology to business transactions is *electronic data interchange (EDI),* computer-to-computer exchanges of price quotations, purchase orders, invoices, and other sales information between buyers and sellers. EDI requires compatible hardware and software systems to exchange data over a network. Use of EDI cuts paper flow, speeds the order cycle, and reduces errors. In addition, by receiving daily inventory status reports from vendors, companies can set production schedules to match demand.

Early EDI systems were limited due to the requirement that all parties had to use the same computer operating system. So a company using UNIX couldn't easily link with a company using Windows NT. That changed with the introduction of *Web services*—Internet-based systems that allow parties to communicate electronically with one another regardless of the computer operating system they use. Web services rely on open source XML (Extensible Markup Language, a formatting language) standards. EDI and Web services are discussed in more detail in Chapter 10.

The Internet also offers an efficient way for businesses to collaborate with vendors, partners, and customers through *extranets,* secure networks used for e-marketing and accessible through the firm's Web site by external customers, suppliers, or other authorized users. Extranets go beyond ordering and fulfillment processes by giving selected outsiders access to internal information. As with other forms of e-marketing, extranets provide additional benefits such as enhanced relationships with business partners. Ford Motor Credit recently established an extranet to facilitate the processing of credit applications from Ford dealers. It now processes around half of all the applications that come from Ford dealers, or more than 150,000 per day.[10]

Security and access authorization remain critical issues, and most companies create virtual private networks that protect information traveling over public communications media. These networks control who uses a company's resources and what users can access. Also, they cost considerably less than leasing dedicated lines.

The next generation of extranets is the *private exchange,* a secure Web site at which a company and its suppliers share all types of data related to e-marketing, from product design through delivery of orders. A private exchange is more collaborative than a typical extranet, so this type of arrangement has sometimes been called *c-business.* The participants can use it to collaborate on product ideas, production scheduling, distribution, order tracking, and any other functions a business wants to include. For example, Wal-Mart Stores has a private exchange it calls *retail link.* The system permits Wal-Mart employees to access detailed sales and inventory information. Suppliers such as Procter & Gamble and Nestlé, in turn, can look up Wal-Mart sales data and forecasts to manage their own inventory and logistics, helping them better meet the needs of the world's largest retailer and its millions of customers worldwide.

ELECTRONIC EXCHANGES AND E-PROCUREMENT

The earliest types of B2B e-business usually consisted of a company setting up a Web site and offering information and products to any buyer willing to make online purchases. Then entrepreneurs created **electronic exchanges,** online marketplaces that bring buyers and sellers together in one electronic marketplace and cater to a specific industry's needs. One of the earliest electronic exchanges, FreeMarkets, allowed suppliers to compete for the business of organizational buyers who might be purchasing anything from gears to printed circuit boards. The idea was to improve the efficiency of the purchase process for hundreds of industrial products.

Initially, many believed that electronic exchanges would become one of the most popular uses of the Internet. It didn't quite work out that way. Approximately 15,000 electronic exchanges were launched within a few years. Today, however, less than 20 percent remain. The others either merged or simply disappeared. Even FreeMarkets was acquired by e-business software firm Ariba. Only electronic exchanges specializing in electronic components and transportation services have proven consistently successful.[11]

Why was the performance of many electronic exchanges so disappointing? Experts believe that many suppliers weren't happy with the pressure to come in with the lowest bid each time a satisfied long-term buyer decided to make a new purchase. Moreover, many buyers decided that they preferred to cultivate long-term relationships with their suppliers, even if those suppliers charged slightly higher prices occasionally. Purchasing agents simply didn't see enough benefits from electronic exchanges to abandon suppliers they knew.[12]

Evolving from electronic exchanges has been **e-procurement,** Web-based systems that enable all types of organizations to improve the efficiency of their bidding and purchasing processes. Ariba, the company that acquired FreeMarkets, offers a variety of e-procurement software products. Many large corporations, such as Saks and Unilever, use Ariba products such as Buyer for purchasing goods and services. Unilever reports that Buyer and other Ariba e-procurement software have saved the company tens of millions of dollars. Saks believes that Buyer has cut purchase negotiation times from four months to six weeks and saved the company 10 to 20 percent off regular, published prices.[13]

E-procurement also benefits the public sector. For instance, the state of North Carolina has instituted a program called NC E-Procurement. The program combines the use of Internet technology with traditional procurement practices to streamline the purchasing process and reduce

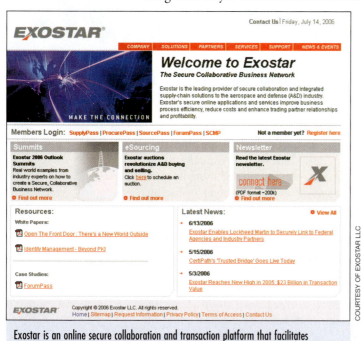

Exostar is an online secure collaboration and transaction platform that facilitates e-procurement for companies in the global aerospace and defense industry.

costs. State and local governmental agencies, public schools, and state-supported colleges can use the system to purchase a variety of products from approved vendors. According to officials, "E-Procurement has reduced prices for goods and services through volume discounts and also enables administrative and operational cost savings by streamlining processing and interactions with vendors/suppliers." One North Carolina county reported saving more than 30 percent on printer supplies by using E-Procurement.[14]

assessment check

1. What is B2B e-marketing? How large is it relative to consumer e-marketing?
2. Define *EDI* and *Web services*.
3. Briefly explain how e-procurement works.

ONLINE SHOPPING AND B2C E-MARKETING

One area of e-business that has consistently grabbed news headlines is Internet shopping. Known as **business-to-consumer,** or **B2C, e-marketing,** it involves selling directly to consumers over the Internet. Driven by convenience and improved security for transmitting credit card numbers and other financial information, online retail sales, sometimes called *e-tailing,* have grown rapidly in recent years. According to the U.S. Census Bureau, online retail sales now amount to roughly 3 percent of all retail sales; less than five years ago, online retail sales made up around .05 percent of retail sales.[15] Currently, an estimated 30 percent of the U.S. population shops online. Within the next couple of years, around half of American consumers will make purchases online.[16]

Most people think of the Web as a giant cybermall of retail stores selling millions of goods online. However, service providers are also important participants in e-marketing, including providers of financial services. Brick-and-mortar banks such as Wachovia and brokerage firms such as Charles Schwab have greatly expanded their online services. In addition, many new online service providers are rapidly attracting customers who want to do more of their own banking and investment trading at whatever time and day suits them. Bank of America—the nation's largest bank—is also the leader in online banking. Its success is profiled in the "Marketing Success" feature.

Another point to remember is that there are basically two types of B2C Web sites: shopping sites and informational sites. The Gap has a shopping site (http://www.gap.com). Customers can view product information and place orders online. By contrast, Toyota's Web site (http://www.toyota.com) is informational only. Consumers can view detailed product information, compare financing alternatives, even request a price quote from a local dealer. They *cannot,* however, buy a new car online.

ELECTRONIC STOREFRONTS

Virtually all major retailers have staked their claims in cyberspace by setting up **electronic storefronts,** Web sites where they offer items for sale to consumers. Wal-Mart's electronic storefront, Walmart.com, has expanded its online offerings substantially over the past few years. It also began offering more upscale merchandise recently on WalmMart.com, including cashmere scarves, eighteen-carat white gold rings, and 60-inch plasma televisions. This online strategy is part of the retailer's overall effort to lure more affluent shoppers and better compete with firms such as Target. Walmart.com is also a testing ground for merchandise the company might decide to carry in its regular stores.[17]

Clothing retailer Lands' End used to generate virtually all of its orders by telephone. A few years ago, the company decided to turn to B2C e-marketing to boost sales and reduce costs. Lands' End offers a full array of online services, such as its virtual model that allows consumers to "try on" clothes before they buy. Online customers can communicate with customer service representatives in real time, and two customers can even shop on the site simultaneously—just as if they were shopping together in a traditional store.

Generally, online retailers—such as LLBean.com and BestBuy.com—provide an online catalog where visitors click on items they want to buy. These items are placed in a file called an **electronic shopping cart.** When the shopper indicates that he or she wants to complete the transaction, the items in the electronic shopping cart are listed on the screen, along with the total amount due, so that the customer can review the whole order and make changes before paying.

4 Explain business-to-consumer (B2C) e-marketing.

business-to-consumer (B2C) e-marketing Selling directly to consumers over the Internet.

electronic storefront Company Web site that sells products to customers.

One factor that experts think will have a significant influence on the growth in online shopping is the increased availability of broadband Internet connections. According to data from the Pew Internet and American Life Project, close to 60 percent of American Internet users now have broadband connections, and the percentage is rising.[18] This trend is significant for e-tailers because on average, broadband users are online more often, for longer periods of time, and, most important, spend more online than narrowband users. Typically, today around 70 percent of all online retail purchases are conducted over broadband connections. Broadband shoppers also spend approximately 34 percent more online than narrowband shoppers.[19]

BENEFITS OF B2C E-MARKETING

Many consumers prefer shopping online to the time needed to drive to a store and select purchases. One recent survey revealed that more than half of all consumers responded that they enjoy shopping online more than in stores. Moreover, 75 percent of women in the 31-to-40 age group said that the Internet was their preferred purchasing method.[20] Why do consumers shop online? Three main reasons are most often cited in consumer surveys: price, convenience, and personalization.

Lower Prices

Many of the best deals on products, such as airfares and hotels, can be found at sites on the Internet. If you call Delta Airlines' toll-free number, before you can speak to an agent a recorded voice invites you to "visit Delta.com, where lower fares may be available." Visitors to BN.com—the online store of bookseller Barnes and Noble—find that many best sellers are discounted by up to 40 percent. At retail Barnes and Noble stores, best sellers are marked down by only 30 percent. Anyone who has ever searched both the Web and traditional stores for the best price for software or a newly issued CD can find it online. In fact, almost 60 percent of Web shoppers cited lower prices as a motivation for shopping online.[21]

The Web is an ideal method for savvy shoppers to compare prices from dozens—even hundreds—of sellers. Online shoppers can compare features and prices at their leisure, without being pressured by a salesperson or having to conform to the company's hours of operation. Say, for instance, you're in the market for a new computer monitor. **Bots,** one of the newer e-business tools, aid consumers in comparison shopping. Bots—short for *robots*—are search programs that check hundreds of sites, gather and assemble information, and bring it back to the sender. For instance, at Shopping.com, you can specify the type and size of monitor you're looking for and the Web site displays a list of the highest-ranked monitors, along with the e-tailer offering the best price on each item and estimated shipping expenses. The Web site even ranks the e-tailers by customer experience and tells you whether a particular model is in stock.

marketing success   Bank of America Clicks with Online Customers

Background. Bank of America is one of the largest financial institutions in the world, with customers including individual consumers, small businesses, and large corporations. Its 5,800 retail offices, thousands of ATMs, and popular online banking Web site bring customers a full line of banking, investing, and asset- and risk-management services.

The Challenge. Online banking is growing rapidly, according to a recent survey of consumer behavior in the banking industry. The number of customers banking and paying bills online recently reached 53 million and now includes one in every four adults. Bank of America, which serves about one-fourth of U.S. households with its traditional retail banking services, faced stiff competition in the online banking business from big competitors such as Citibank, Wachovia, and Chase/Bank One.

The Strategy. With customers becoming more used to the ease and convenience of online banking, Bank of America needed not just to convert customers to the idea of Internet banking but also to draw them specifically to its own site. To generate interest and reassure customers, Bank of America decided to focus on safety. The bank's e-commerce executive described its two-pronged approach this way: "We've made security and simplicity our top

Convenience

A second important factor in prompting online purchases is shopper convenience. Cybershoppers can order goods and services from around the world at any hour of the day or night. Most e-tailers allow customers to register their credit card and shipping information for quick use in making future purchases. Customers are required to select a user name and password for security. Later, when they place another order, registered customers are asked to type in their password. E-tailers typically send an e-mail message confirming an order and the amount charged to the buyer's credit card. Another e-mail is sent once the product is shipped, along with a tracking number, which the customer can use to follow the order through the delivery process.

Personalization

While online shopping transactions often operate with little or no human interac-

COURTESY OF SHOPZILLA

Shopzilla is the largest shopping search site that allows consumers to find, compare, and buy any product from any store on the Web. It features more than 30 million products from 75,000 stores.

tion, successful B2C e-marketing companies know how important personalization is to the quality of the shopping experience. Customer satisfaction is greatly affected by the marketer's ability to offer service tailored to many customers. But each person expects a certain level of customer service. Consequently, most leading online retailers offer customized features on their Web sites.

The early years of e-business saw Web marketers casting their nets broadly in an effort to land as many buyers as possible. Today, the emphasis has turned toward creating loyal customers who are likely to make repeat purchases. How does personalized marketing work online? Say you buy a book at Amazon.com and register with the site. The site welcomes you back for your next purchase by name. Using special software that analyzes your previous purchases, it also suggests several other books you might like. You even have the option of receiving periodic e-mails from Amazon.com informing you of new products. Many other leading e-tailers have adopted similar types of personalized marketing.

priorities." A two-way authentication system to help users distinguish the real banking Web site from fraudulent sites, free online and cell phone alerts about account information and passwords, stronger identification and passcode features, paperless statements, and a live-chat help line are some of the security features the bank continues to roll out and improve.

The Outcome. Bank of America has twice ranked at the top of an industry online-banking safety scorecard. More than half of U.S. consumers who pay bills online do so through Bank of America, and more than one in three who bank online use the company's Web site and online services.

Sources: Binyamin Appelbaum, "BofA Dominates Online Banking," Knight Ridder Tribune Business News, April 11, 2006, p. 1; "Bank of America Reaches 15 Million Online Banking Customers," PR Newswire, April 11, 2006, **http://www.prnewswire.com**; "ComScore Study Reveals the Number of Online Banking Customers Has Grown," PR Newswire, April 10, 2006, **http://www.prnewswire.com**; Taylor Moore, "Online Banking Comes of Age," Lane Report, March 1, 2005, p. 26.

assessment check

1. **What is B2C e-marketing?**
2. **Explain the difference between a shopping Web site and an informational Web site.**
3. **Discuss the benefits of B2C e-marketing.**

Some Web sites offer customized products to match individual consumer requirements. For instance, Nike offers online shoppers the opportunity to customize a running shoe, personalizing such features as the outsole, the amount of cushioning, and the width. The personalized shoe costs about $10 more than buying a product off the store shelves.

5   Identify online buyers and sellers.

ONLINE BUYERS AND SELLERS

The Pew Internet and American Life Project regularly collects and analyzes data about Americans' Internet usage, including online buying behavior. A recent survey paints a comprehensive picture of the characteristics of online users and buyers. Some of the key findings of the report are summarized in Figure 4.2. While the typical Internet user, according to the study, is still relatively young, highly educated, urban or suburban, and affluent, the characteristics of online buyers are changing. For instance, since 2000, use of the Internet among older Americans has increased faster than it has among younger Americans. Moreover, today a broader range of Internet users now purchase products online compared with a few years ago. In 2000, men made up the majority of online shoppers.[22] Today, women outshop men online.[23]

figure 4.2

Characteristics of U.S. Internet Users

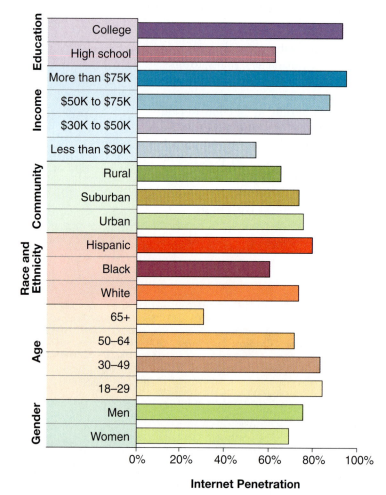

Internet Penetration

Source: Pew Internet and American Life Project, "Demographics of Internet Users," **http://www. pewinternet.org**, accessed April 24, 2006.

Realizing that customers would have little or no opportunity to rely on many of the sense modes—smelling the freshness of direct-from-the-oven bread, touching the soft fabric of a new cashmere sweater, or squeezing fruit to assess its ripeness—early online sellers focused on offering products that consumers were familiar with and tended to buy frequently, such as books and music. Other popular early online offerings included computer hardware and software, and airline tickets.

Figure 4.3 shows the five fastest-growing products sold online during a recent holiday shopping period. While overall online retail sales rose by around 25 percent, online sales of apparel increased by more than 35 percent. Other fast-growing categories included computer software, home and garden products, toys, and jewelry.[24] A few years ago, apparel, home and garden products, toys, and jewelry were rarely sold online.

Experts believe that in the coming years online sales of apparel, prescription drugs, and home products will grow more rapidly than other products as the characteristics of Internet users continue to change. Because women—who spend more money on apparel than men do—will continue to become a larger and larger share of Internet users and shoppers, online apparel sales are likely to stay hot. Similarly, as the population of online users over age 55 grows, so will online sales of prescription drugs.

assessment check

1. **Who shops online? Are the characteristics of online shoppers changing?**
2. **List the fastest-growing products sold online.**

Kitchen products, small appliances, and large appliances—which typically are bought more frequently by women and older consumers—are also expected to experience strong growth in the near future. [25]

E-BUSINESS AND E-MARKETING CHALLENGES

For all their advantages, e-business and e-marketing face some problems and challenges. Some of the most significant include developing safe online payment systems, protecting consumer privacy, preventing fraud, improving site design and customer service, and eliminating potential channel conflicts.

6 Describe some of the challenges associated with online marketing and e-business.

ONLINE PAYMENT SYSTEMS

In response to consumer concerns about the safety of sending credit card numbers over the Internet, companies have developed secure payment systems. Internet browsers, such as Microsoft Internet Explorer, contain sophisticated encryption systems to protect sensitive information. **Encryption** is the process of encoding data for security purposes. When such a system is active, users see a special icon that indicates that they are at a protected Web site.

To further increase consumer security, most companies involved in e-business, including all major credit card companies, use **Secure Sockets Layer (SSL)** technology to encrypt information and provide authentication. SSL consists of a public key and a private key. The public key is used to encrypt information and the private key is used to decipher it. When a browser points to a domain with an SSL certificate, the technology authenticates the server and the visitor and establishes an encryption method and a unique session key. Both parties can then begin a secure session that guarantees message privacy and integrity. VeriSign is one of the leading providers of SSL technology used by more than 90 percent of *Fortune* 500 companies and the nation's ten largest banks.[26]

Some online retailers offer shoppers the option of setting up electronic wallets. An **electronic wallet** is a computer data file at an e-business site's checkout counter that contains credit card information and owner identification. With electronic wallets, customers do not have to retype personal information each time they make a purchase at that site. Consumers simply click on the electronic wallet after selecting items, and their credit card payment information, name and address, and preferred mailing method are transmitted instantly.

PRIVACY ISSUES

Consumers worry that information about them will become available to others without their permission. In fact, marketing

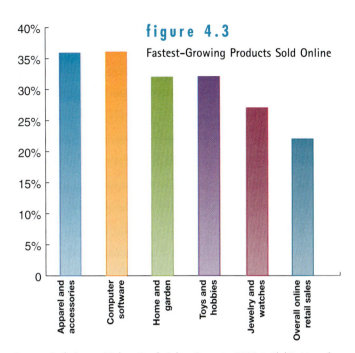

figure 4.3
Fastest-Growing Products Sold Online

Source: Enid Burns, "Online Retail Sales Grew in 2005," ClickZ Network, **http://www.clickz.com**, accessed May 10, 2006.

Visa promotes the advantages of online bill payment over sending checks through regular mail, which could get lost, stolen, or even eaten by a pet. The firm allows consumers to set up automatic payment of monthly bills and avoid the time and hassle of writing checks and finding stamps.

research indicates that privacy is one of the top concerns of Internet users and may impede the growth of e-business. For instance, during a recent holiday shopping period, 78 percent of regular Internet users surveyed expressed concerns about the security at online retailers. More than one-third said that security concerns would affect their online shopping a great deal. Consumers' top security concern, the survey reports, is protection of personal information.[27]

As the earlier discussion of Internet payments explained, concern about the privacy of credit card numbers has led to the use of secure payment systems. To add to those security systems, e-marketing sites involving personal information require passwords as a form of authentication—that is, to determine that the person using the site is actually the one authorized to have access to the account. More recently, **electronic signatures** have become a way to enter into legal contracts such as home mortgages and insurance policies online. With an e-signature, an individual obtains a form of electronic identification and installs it in his or her Web browser. Signing the contract involves looking up and verifying the buyer's identity with this software.

Thanks to *cookies* and *spyware*—software used to automatically collect data from Internet browsers, online companies can track their customers' shopping and viewing habits. The way that companies use these technologies has the potential both to make visits to the Web site more convenient and to invade computer users' privacy. Amazon.com, for instance, has long employed sophisticated data collection systems to track customer habits. The "Solving an Ethical Controversy" feature describes Amazon's latest technologies and debates the privacy and security concerns these technologies raise.

Most consumers want assurances that any information they provide won't be sold to others without their permission. In response to these concerns, online merchants take steps to protect consumer information. For example, many Internet companies have signed on with Internet privacy organizations such as TRUSTe. By displaying the TRUSTe logo on their Web sites, they indicate that they have promised to disclose how they collect personal data and what they do with the information. Prominently displaying a privacy policy is an effective way to build customers' trust.

Such privacy features may become a necessary feature of Web sites if consumer concerns continue to grow. They also may become legally necessary. Already in the United States, the *Children's Online Privacy Protection Act* (*COPPA*) requires that Web sites targeting children younger than age 13 obtain "verifiable parental consent" before collecting any data that could be used to identify or contact individual users, including names and e-mail addresses.

Organizations, too, are concerned about the privacy of their data, and with good reason. For instance, personal data of almost 60,000 people affiliated with California State University, Chico, were recently stolen by computer hackers. This incident closely followed a similar case of identity theft in which personal data for more than 145,000 people were exposed by a security breach at ChoicePoint, a firm that collects and stores consumer financial data.[28]

To prevent such intrusions, companies install combinations of hardware and software called *firewalls* to keep unauthorized Net users from tapping into private corporate data. A **firewall** is an electronic barrier between a company's internal network and the Internet that limits access into and out of the network. However, an impenetrable firewall is difficult to find. A determined and skilled hacker can often gain access. So it is important for firms to test their Web sites and networks for vulnerabilities and back up critical data in case an intruder breaches security measures.

INTERNET FRAUD

Fraud is another impediment to the growth of e-business and e-marketing. The Internet Crime Complaint Center (http://www.ic3.gov), run by the FBI, compiles complaints concerning Internet fraud. According to recent statistics, the IC3 logged more than 231,000 complaints during a recent year, an increase of almost 12 percent from the prior year. Online auctions were the number one source of fraud complaints. Approximately 65 percent of the total Internet-related fraud complaints referred to law enforcement agencies dealt with online auctions. Auction fraud includes merchandise that does not match the description the bidder was given, such as fraudulent paintings, and products that were purchased but never delivered. Nondelivery of merchandise, credit/debit card fraud, invest-

Solving an Ethical Controversy

Amazon.com: Helpful or Intrusive?

Amazon.com is one of the premier Internet retailers. The company earns nearly $7 billion in sales and ships items including books, music, DVDs, electronics, and thousands of other products stocked by partners such as Target, Macy's, and Toys "R" Us. Amazon even competes against eBay, with nearly a million third-party sellers accounting for a quarter of its sales. The site has "developed an extremely loyal customer base, and they've cultivated that by continually lowering prices and adding features to their Web site," said an industry expert.

Many of those features are designed to make shopping a personalized experience. Software tools help Amazon suggest new products when customers log on, narrow their site searches, track favorite authors and topics, read recommended blogs, and even avoid buying stuff they have already purchased. Privacy advocates, however, fear that by storing the vast amounts of personal information about buying habits that allow this kind of "relationship building," Amazon might be getting a little too personal, particularly if the data becomes vulnerable to theft or misuse. One objection is that the company doesn't request customer permission to collect the data or offer a way to erase it.

Should online retailers such as Amazon.com continue to collect personal information about customers without permission?

PRO

1. The benefits of personalized Internet shopping outweigh the possible risks for those who choose to use it.
2. Online retailers collect little more information than consumers already make available when they bank online or use a credit card in a store.

CON

1. Customers should be offered a chance to opt out of the data collection process if they choose.
2. Retailers cannot guarantee the security of the information.

Summary

As Amazon grows, it must compete with the leading Internet search engines as well as rival retailers including Netflix and iTunes. Its new search engine, called A9.com, ranks well behind Yahoo! and Google in popularity, but it includes a powerful "people" search feature for business users, who can monitor and manage their own information. The company continues to promise that it will not violate any privacy laws.

Sources: Elinor Mills, "A9 Searches for Purpose," C/Net News, February 10, 2006, **http://insight.zdnet.co.uk**; Antone Gonsalves, "Amazon.com A9 Search Engine Adds Zoom People Search," Tech Web, January 17, 2006, **http://www.techweb.com**; Elizabeth M. Gillespie, "Amazon.com Sitting Pretty 10 Years Later," Associated Press, July 5, 2005, **http://news.yahoo.com**.

ment fraud, and identify theft also made up major categories of Internet-related complaints referred to law enforcement agencies.[29]

One growing type of Internet fraud is called **phishing.** It is a high-tech scam that uses e-mail or pop-up messages that claim to be from familiar businesses or organizations such as banks, Internet service providers, or even government agencies. The message usually asks the reader to "update" or "validate" account information, often stating that some dire consequence will occur if the reader doesn't respond. The purpose of phishing is to get unsuspecting victims to disclose personal information such as credit card numbers, bank account numbers, Social Security numbers, or computer passwords. Phishing is also commonly used to distribute viruses and malicious spyware programs to computer users. As the Federal Trade Commission advises, if you receive an e-mail or pop-up message that asks for personal information, don't reply or click on the link in the message no matter how authentic the message or pop-up appears. Legitimate companies don't ask for personal or financial information via e-mail or pop-ups.[30]

phishing High-tech scam that uses authentic-looking e-mail or pop-up messages to get unsuspecting victims to reveal personal information.

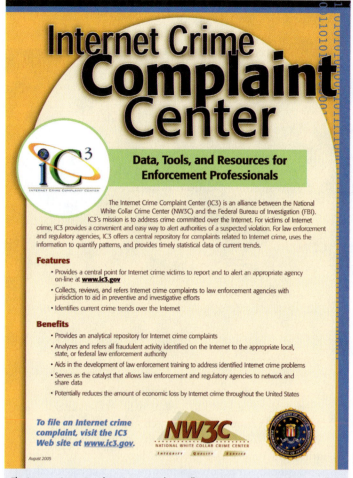

The Internet Crime Complaint Center's Web site allows victims to report suspicious or illegal activities and alert law enforcement agencies so that they can track, analyze, and investigate Internet crimes.

Payment fraud is another growing problem for many e-tailers. Orders are placed online and paid for using a credit card, and the retailer ships the merchandise. Then the cardholder asks the credit card issuer for a chargeback to the e-tailer, claiming that he or she never made the purchase or never received the merchandise. Some claims are legitimate, but many involve fraud. Because an online purchase doesn't require a customer's signature or credit card imprint, the merchant, not the card issuer, bears the liability in most fraud cases. Some estimates of payment fraud are as high as 24 cents per $100 of online sales, three to four times the overall rate of credit card fraud.[31] E-tailers are trying to reduce payment fraud by employing software that spots fraud before it happens, using payment verification services offered by credit card companies, such as Visa, and even hiring companies that specialize in fighting credit card chargebacks.

WEB SITE DESIGN AND SERVICE

For firms to attract customers—and keep them—e-marketers must meet buyers' expectations. For instance, customers want to find products easily and have questions answered quickly. However, Web sites are not always well designed and easy to use. In fact, the percentage of online customers who abandon their shopping carts prior to completing purchases is estimated to be as high as 70 percent. Poor site design or a lack of customer service are two commonly cited reasons for shopping cart abandonment.[32]

Moreover, surveys suggest that negative online experiences pose risks to retailers' brands. For example, 82 percent of consumers polled said they'd be less likely to return to a Web site where they had a frustrating experience, and one-third said that a negative online experience would make them less likely to purchase products at the retailer's physical stores. Some of the most frequently cited negative online experiences were poor site navigation, problems with checkout (such as the process taking too long), and inadequate product information.[33]

Another challenge to successful e-business is merchandise delivery and returns. Retailers sometimes have trouble making deliveries to on-the-go consumers. And consumers don't want to wait for packages to be delivered. Also, if customers aren't satisfied with products, then they have to arrange for pickup or send packages back themselves.

Retailers have begun to address these issues. Most have systems on their Web sites that allow customers to track orders from placement to delivery. E-tailers have also worked hard on a process known as *reverse logistics*. Detailed directions on how to return merchandise, including preprinted shipping labels, are included in orders. A few, such as Nordstrom's and Chef's Catalog, even pay the shipping cost for returns.

Many of the so-called "pure play" dot-com retailers—those without traditional stores or catalogs—didn't survive for very long. They had no history of selling and satisfying customers. Because of expertise in all parts of retailing, companies that combine their store and catalog operations with e-business—such as Eddie Bauer and REI—have generally been more successful than those with little or no retail experience. For instance, according to one recent survey, QVC and L. L. Bean received the highest overall online customer satisfaction ratings. Both companies are experienced traditional retailers.[34]

The same lesson also applies to other service industries. To be successful at e-business, a firm must establish and maintain competitive standards for customer service. When it began offering customers the opportunity to check flight schedules and purchase tickets online, Southwest Airlines worked hard to make sure its Web site had the same high service standards the airline is known for. As noted in the chapter's opening example, Southwest.com has proved both very popular and profitable.

CHANNEL CONFLICTS

Companies spend time and money to nurture relationships with their partners. But when a manufacturer uses the Internet to sell directly to customers, it can compete with its usual partners. Retailers often have their own Web sites, so they don't want their suppliers competing with them for sales. As e-business broadens its reach, producers must decide whether these relationships are more important than the potential of selling directly on the Web. Conflicts between producers, wholesalers, and retailers are called **channel conflicts.**

Mattel, well known for producing toys such as Barbie, Cabbage Patch dolls, and Matchbox cars, sells most of its products in toy stores and toy departments of other retailers, such as Target and Wal-Mart. The company wants an Internet presence, but it would cut the retailers out of this important source of revenue if it sold toys online to consumers. Mattel cannot afford to lose the goodwill and purchasing power of major retailers such as Toys "R" Us. So the company sells only specialty products online, including pricey American Girl dolls.

Pricing is another potential area of conflict. In their eagerness to establish themselves as Internet leaders, some companies have sold merchandise at discount prices. American Leather sells custom leather furniture through upscale retailers, and each dealer serving a geographic area has an exclusive contract for the collections it offers in its area. But at least one dealer began offering American Leather furniture at a discount to customers outside its market area. Other dealers complained, so American Leather established a policy that dealers were not to advertise the company's products on the Internet. Instead, American Leather offered links to local dealers on its own Web site and made plans to allow buyers to order online, with the sale to be directed to the dealer serving the consumer's geographic area.

 assessment check

1. What are the major challenges to growth in e-business and e-marketing?
2. Describe phishing.
3. Explain how e-marketing can create channel conflicts.

USING THE WEB'S COMMUNICATION FUNCTION

7 Discuss how marketers use the communication function of the Web as part of their online marketing strategies.

There are four main functions of the Internet: e-business, entertainment, information, and communication. Even though e-business is a significant activity, and is growing rapidly, communication still remains the most popular Web function. For instance, it is estimated that the volume of e-mail today exceeds regular mail (sometimes jokingly called *snail mail*) by something like ten to one. It's not surprising, therefore, that contemporary marketers use the communication function of the Internet to advance their organizational objectives.

Companies have long used e-mail to communicate with customers, suppliers, and other partners. Most companies have links on their Web sites that allow visitors to send e-mail directly to the most appropriate person or division within the company. For instance, if you have a question concerning an online order from Chef's Catalog, you can click on a link on the retailer's Web site and send an e-mail to a customer service representative. Many online retailers have gone even further by offering their customers live help. Using a form of instant messaging, live help provides a real-time communication channel between customers and customer service representatives.

Firms also use e-mail to inform customers about events such as new products and special promotions. While using e-mail in this manner can be quite cost effective, companies have to be careful. A growing number of customers consider such e-mails to be **spam**, the popular name for junk e-mail. In fact, in a recent survey, one of the leading reasons consumers gave for reducing online shopping was "receiving unsolicited e-mail or spam" after an online purchase.[35] Moreover, many Internet users employ so-called *spam filters* that automatically eliminate junk e-mail from their inboxes.

spam Popular name for junk e-mail.

E-mail software such as QuickMail
contains spam filters to help control
and reduce unwanted messages.

blog Short for *Web log*—
an online journal for an
individual or organiza-
tion.

ONLINE COMMUNITIES

In addition to e-mail, many firms use Internet forums, newsgroups, electronic bulletin boards, and Web communities that appeal to people who share common interests. All of these sites take advantage of the communication power of the Internet which, as noted earlier in the chapter, is still a main reason why people go online. Members congregate online and exchange views and information on topics of interest. These communities may be organized for commercial or noncommercial purposes.

Online communities can take several forms, but all offer specific advantages to users and organizations alike. Online forums, for instance, are Internet discussion groups. Users log in and participate by sending comments and questions or receiving information from other forum members. Forums may operate as electronic bulletin boards, as libraries for storing information, or even as a type of classified ad directory. Firms often use forums to ask questions and exchange information with customers. Adobe, which designs such software as Acrobat and Photoshop, operates a "user-to-user" forum on its Web site as a support community for its customers. Customers who share common personal and professional interests can congregate, exchange industry news and practical product tips, share ideas, and—equally important—create publicity for Adobe products.

Newsgroups are noncommercial Internet versions of forums. Here people post and read messages on specific topics. Tens of thousands of newsgroups are on the Internet, and the number continues to rise. **Electronic bulletin boards** are specialized online services that center on a specific topic or area of interest. For instance, mountain bikers might check online bulletin boards to find out about the latest equipment, new places to ride, or current weather conditions in popular biking locations. While newsgroups resemble two-way conversations, electronic bulletin boards are more like announcements.

Online communities are not limited to consumers. They also facilitate business-to-business marketing. Using the Internet to build communities helps companies find other organizations, including suppliers, distributors, and competitors that may be interested in forming an alliance. Marketers who want to expand internationally frequently seek advice from other members of their online community.

BLOGS

Another type of online communication method that is gaining popularity is the **blog.** Short for *Web log,* a blog is a Web page that serves as a publicly accessible journal for an individual or organization. Typically updated daily, or even more frequently, these hybrid diary-guide sites are read regularly by almost 30 percent of American Internet users. Using *RSS (Really Simple Syndication)* software, readers are continually kept up-to-date on new material posted on their favorite blogs whenever they are online. Unlike e-mail and instant messaging, blogs let readers post comments and ask questions aimed at the author (called a *blogger*). Some blogs today also incorporate **wikis.** A wiki is a Web page that anyone can edit so that a reader can, in addition to asking questions or posting comments, actually make changes to the Web page. **Podcasts** are another emerging technology. Anyone from bloggers to traditional media sources can prepare an audio or video recording and then post it to a Web site from which it can be downloaded to any digital device that can play the file. According to the Web site iPodder.org, more than 3,000 podcasts operate worldwide.[36]

Given the growing interest in blogs and podcasts, it hasn't taken long for marketers to incorporate them into their e-business strategies. GreenCine—a small online DVD rental company—partially credits its blog for a sharp increase in revenues. Films critiqued by the blog's two writers are often snapped up immediately by renters.[37] Moreover, many believe that corporate blogs, if done properly, can also help build brand trust. An example is iLounge.com, a blog hosted by Apple that lets users discuss their ideas for the next-generation iPod. David Eastman, managing director of Agency.com, believes that iLounge.com benefits Apple in two ways. First, it helps build the iPod brand; second, it gives Apple marketers ideas to improve the design of its most successful product. On the other hand, Eastman believes that some blogs can end up hurting their brands. An example—in Eastman's opinion—is the blog hosted by Cadbury Schweppes for its Raging Cow milk drink. According to Eastman, it came across poorly because all it featured were product-endorsing comments from children. [38]

Some observers were skeptical when GM started a corporate blog written by the company's vice chairman, Robert Lutz, thinking most Internet users would dismiss it as nothing more than corporate public relations. Now many of these same observers give *FastLane* (the official name of GM's blog) high marks and consider it a marketing success. The site discusses topics such as GM design, new product launches, and the company's overall business strategy. Podcasts are also available, including a recent clip coinciding with the launch of the new Corvette. FastLane averages 4,000 to 5,000 hits per day, and each posting by Lutz typically receives between 60 and 100 comments, both positive and negative. According to experts, one reason why FastLane works is that GM is willing to accept and post criticism, and as a result, the blog comes across as being inclusive and genuine. [39]

Many companies allow, and even encourage, employees to start their own blogs, believing that employee blogs can serve useful functions. For example, Kevin Dugan works as a public-relations consultant and is a blogger. Displayed on Dugan's blog is a disclaimer stating that the opinions expressed are his and are not necessarily those of his employer or its clients. However, both Dugan and his firm believe that his blog is more than just a soapbox—it indirectly markets the firm's work and philosophies. [40]

Some companies, however, have strict policies about the content of employee blogs, and some employees have even been disciplined over what their employers thought was improper blogging. However, most companies today still have no official policies regarding employee blogs. The "Etiquette Tips for Marketing Professionals" feature offers some commonsense tips for would-be employee bloggers.

WEB-BASED PROMOTIONS

Rather than relying completely on their Web sites to attract buyers, companies frequently expand their reach in the marketplace by placing ads on sites their prospective customers are likely to visit. **Banner ads,** the most common form of Internet advertising, are typically small, strip messages placed in high-visibility areas of frequently visited Web sites. **Pop-up ads** are separate windows that pop up with an advertising message. The effectiveness of pop-up ads, however, is questionable. First, scam artists use pop-ups. Second, many Internet users simply hate pop-up ads—even those from legitimate companies. Consequently, most ISPs now offer software that blocks pop-up ads. Google and Microsoft also offer free pop-up ad-blocking software.

Another type of online advertising gaining popularity is so-called **search marketing.** Most firms make sure that they are listed with the major search engines such as Google. But that is not enough to ensure visibility with consumers. A single search for an item—say, plastic fasteners—may yield thousands of sites, many of which may not even be relevant. To overcome this problem, companies pay search engines fees to have their Web sites or ads pop up after a user enters certain words into the search engine, or to make sure that their firm's listing appears toward the top of the search results. Google and other search engines now include "Sponsored Links" on the right side of the search results page. A user who clicks on one of the sites listed under Sponsored Links is taken to that site, and the company pays the search engine a small fee. Many experts consider search marketing the most cost-effective form of Web-based advertising. As a result, it is growing rapidly. According to research firm eMarketer, search marketing expenditures could soon reach $10 billion. [41]

COURTESY OF WWW.FASTLANE.GMBLOGS.COM

FastLane is GM executive Robert Lutz's corporate blog, where he posts messages to update interested consumers on the latest news and video podcasts from the company.

search marketing Paying search engines, such as Google, a fee to make sure that the company's listing appears toward the top of the search results.

Etiquette Tips for Marketing Professionals

Blogging Basics

All companies have Web sites, and a growing number also operate corporate blogs. Usually written by trusted employees to present a human face to customers, company blogs can serve as useful forums for touting new products, squashing rumors, and fielding customer complaints.

But bloggers who write about their companies unofficially, in personal blogs, should be careful about what they say. Indiscretion has cost more than one outspoken employee a job. Here are some guidelines for bloggers, especially those who want to write about their workplace, boss, or colleagues.

1. Think before you write, and don't post anything you wouldn't want to see in the newspaper.
2. Check your facts before you post.
3. Make sure you don't confuse free speech with irresponsible speech.
4. Ask yourself whether your readers really need to know the content of your post.

5. Don't post when you're angry. You'll say things you may regret.
6. Don't respond to reader comments when you're angry, and never say something you wouldn't say in person.
7. Never name names. Even if you use pseudonyms, supporting detail can identify the people you write about, as it did in the case of at least one fired blogger.
8. Avoid pranks and hoaxes; they will misfire.
9. Don't make the mistake of thinking a negative blog about your firm or industry will help your career. It won't.
10. Accept that if what you write is negative or controversial, you won't remain anonymous for long.

Sources: Enid Burns, "Executive Slow to See Value of Corporate Blogging," ClickZ Network, May 9, 2006, **http://www.clickz.com**; Sarah Todd, "Blogging Etiquette," Information & Communication Technology in Education, April 19, 2006, **http://www.ictineducation.org**; Steve Johnson, "Blogs Can Bite," *Chicago Tribune*, August 15, 2005, pp. 1, 10.

Another way in which companies use the Web to promote their products is through online coupons. For instance, customers can visit a company's Web site—such as Procter & Gamble's (http://www.pg.com)—to learn about a new product and then print a discount coupon redeemable at participating retailers. Consumers can also find virtual coupons on their PCs by such criteria as business name, location, and keyword and then download and print them. ValPak Marketing Systems, a longtime leader in the paper coupon industry, now offers the online equivalent at its Web site (http://www.valpak.com).

 assessment check

1. What are online communities? Explain how online communities can help companies market their products and improve customer service.
2. What are blogs, wikis, and podcasts?
3. Explain the difference between a banner ad, a pop-up ad, and search marketing.

MANAGING A WEB SITE

An e-business Web site can serve many purposes. It can broaden customer bases, provide immediate access to current catalogs, accept and process orders, and offer personalized customer service. As technology becomes increasingly easy to use, anyone with a computer and Internet access can open an Internet account and place a simple Web site on the Internet. How people or organizations use their sites to achieve their goals determines whether their sites will succeed. Figure 4.4 lists some key questions to consider in developing a Web site.

DEVELOPING SUCCESSFUL WEB SITES

Most Web experts agree: "It is easier to build a bad Web site than a good one." When judging Web sites, success means different things to different businesses. One firm might feel satisfied by maintaining a popular site that conveys company information or reinforces name recognition—just as a billboard or magazine ad does—without requiring any immediate sales activity. Web sites like those of the *Los Angeles Times* and *USA Today* draw many visitors who want the latest news, and Yahoo!, Google, and ESPN.com are successful because they attract heavy traffic. As well as enhancing their brands, popular Web sites such as these add to their success by selling advertising space to other businesses.

Internet merchants need to attract customers who conduct business on the spot. Some companies find success by hosting Web sites that offer some value-added service to create goodwill for potential customers. Organizations such as the Mayo Clinic and accounting giant Ernst & Young provide useful information or links to related sites that people frequently visit. But to get people to stay at the site and complete a transaction, the site must also be secure, reliable, and easy to use.

Planning and Preparation

What is the company's goal for its Web site? Answering this question is the first and most important step in the Web site development process. For broadband telephone service provider Vonage, the primary objective is to sign up new customers. So the Web site designers put a link called "Sign Up Now" prominently in the upper portion of the home page.

8 Outline the steps involved in developing successful business Web sites and identify methods for measuring Web site effectivenss.

Yahoo! helps businesses increase their visibility to consumers online.

figure 4.4

Questions to Consider in Developing a Web Site

- What is the purpose of the Web site?
  - How can we attract repeat visitors?

- What external links should be established to draw visitors to the site?
- What internal links to databases and other corporate resources are needed?

- What should the domain name be?
- How should it work?
- What should the site contain?

- Who should put the site on the Net—company or Web host?

- How much money should be spent to set up and maintain the site?
- How current does information on the site need to be?

Telephone service provider Vonage maintains a Web site to provide a convenient method for customers to learn about products, services, and account information.

Objectives for the Web site also determine the scope of the project. If the company's goal is to sell merchandise online, the site must incorporate a way for customers to place orders and ask questions about products, as well as links to the company's databases to track inventory and deliveries. The plan should include not only the appearance of the Web site but also the company's behind-the-scenes resources for making the Web site deliver on its promises.

Other key decisions include whether to create and maintain a site in-house or to contract with outside designers. Some companies prefer to retain control over content and design by producing their own sites. However, because acquiring the expertise to develop Web sites can be very time-consuming, hiring specialists may be more cost effective. Often companies such as Macromedia provide both software and consulting services to clients for their Web sites.

Naming the Web site is another important early step in the planning process. A domain name should reflect the company and its products and be easy to remember. However, with millions of domain names already registered, the search for a unique, memorable, and easily spelled name can be difficult.

Content and Connections

Content is one of the most important factors in determining whether visitors return to a site. People obviously are more inclined to visit a site that provides material that interests them. Many e-business Web sites try to distinguish themselves by offering additional features. For example, Williams-Sonoma's Web site lures traffic to the site with weekly menu planners; printer-ready recipes; and features that convert menus between metric and U.S. measurement systems, adjust measurements for different numbers of servings, and create shopping lists for menus. Many sites offer links to other sites that may interest visitors.

Standards for good content vary for every site, but available resources should be relevant to viewers, easy to access and understand, updated regularly, and written or displayed in a compelling, entertaining way. When the World Wide Web was a novelty, a page with a picture and a couple of paragraphs of text seemed entertaining. But such "brochureware" falls far short of meeting today's standards for interactivity, including the ability to accept customer data and orders, keep up-to-the-minute inventory records, and respond quickly to customer questions and complaints. Also, today's Internet users are less patient about figuring out how to make a site do what it promises. They won't wait ten minutes for a video clip to download or click through five different pages to complete a purchase.

After making content decisions and designing the site, the next step is connect to the Internet by placing the required computer files on a server. Companies can have their own dedicated Web servers or contract to place their Web sites on servers at ISPs or other host companies. Most small businesses lack the necessary expertise to set up and run their own servers; they are better off outsourcing to meet their hosting and maintenance needs. They also need to draw business to their site. This usually requires a listing with the major search engines, such as Google, Ask.com, and Yahoo!.

Costs and Maintenance

As with any technological investment, Web site costs are an important consideration. The highly variable cost of a Web site includes not only development expenses but also the cost of placing the site on a Web server, maintaining and updating it, and promoting it. A reasonably tech-savvy employee with off-the-shelf software can create a simple piece of brochureware for a few hundred dollars. A Web site that can handle e-business will cost at least $10,000. Creating it requires understanding how to link the Web site to the company's other information systems.

Although developing a commercial Web site with interactive features can cost tens of thousands of dollars, putting it online can cost as little as $11.95 a month for a spot on the server of a Web host such as Yahoo! And Web hosts deliver a huge audience. In a typical week, more than 30 million people visit Yahoo!

It's also important for a Web site to stay current. Visitors don't return to a site if they know that the information never changes or that claims about inventory or product selection are not current. Consequently, updating design and content is another major expense. In addition, site maintenance should include running occasional searches to test that links to the company's Web site are still active.

MEASURING WEB SITE EFFECTIVENESS

How does a company gauge the return from investing in a Web site? Measuring the effectiveness of a Web site is tricky, and the appropriate process often depends on the purpose of the Web site. Figure 4.5 lists some measures of effectiveness. Profitability is relatively easy to measure in companies that generate revenues directly from online product orders, advertising, or subscription sales. As noted at the beginning of the chapter, Southwest Airlines generates more than $3 billion annually in revenue from Southwest.com. However, what's not clear is how many of those tickets Southwest would have sold through other channels if Southwest.com did not exist. Also, there is evidence that so-called **Web-to-store shoppers**—a group that favors the Internet primarily as a research tool and time-saving device for retail purchases made in stores—are a significant consumer niche.[42]

For many companies, revenue is not a major Web site objective. Most company Web sites are classified as corporate Web sites, not shopping sites, meaning that firms use their sites to showcase their products and to offer information about their organizations. For such companies, online success is measured by increased brand awareness and brand loyalty, which presumably translates into greater profitability through offline transactions.

Some standards guide efforts to collect and analyze traditional consumer purchase data, such as how many Illinois residents purchased new Toyotas the previous year, watched *24* on Fox, or tried Wendy's new Frescata sandwiches. Still, the Internet presents several challenges for marketers. Although information sources are getting better, it is difficult to be sure how many people use the Internet, how often, and what they actually do online. Some Web pages display counters that measure the number of visits. However, the counters can't tell whether someone has spent time on the page or skipped over it on the way to another site, or whether that person is a first-time or repeat viewer.

Advertisers typically measure the success of their ads in terms of **click-through rates,** meaning the percentage of people presented with a banner ad who click on it, thereby linking to a Web site or a pop-up page of information related to the ad. Recently, the average click-through rate has been declining to about 0.5 percent of those viewing an ad. This rate is much lower than the 1.0 to 1.5 percent response rate for direct-mail advertisements. Low click-through rates have made Web advertising less attractive than it was when it was new and people were clicking on just about anything online. Selling advertising has therefore become a less reliable source of e-business revenues.

As e-business gains popularity, new models for measuring its effectiveness are being developed. A basic measurement is the **conversion rate,** the percentage of visitors to a Web site who make purchases. A conversion rate of 3 to 5 percent is average by today's standards. A company can use its advertising cost, site traffic, and conversion rate data to find out the cost to win each

click-through rate Percentage of people presented with a banner ad who click on it.

conversion rate Percentage of visitors to a Web site who make a purchase.

figure 4.5

Measures of Web Site Effectiveness

customer. E-business companies are trying to boost their conversion rates by ensuring that their sites download quickly, are easy to use, and deliver on their promises. Many are turning to one of several firms that help companies improve the performance of their Web sites. For example, CompUSA—a computer and electronics retailer—turned to Web consultant Coremetrics to help it improve the overall performance of its Web site. Using Coremetrics Online Analytics, CompUSA identified the specific online shopping tools that played a role in creating loyal, high-volume customers. By improving these tools and making them more accessible on its Web site, CompUSA increased its revenues by more than $2 million.[43]

Besides measuring click-through and conversion rates, companies can study samples of consumers. Research firms such as Media Metrix and RelevantKnowledge recruit panels of computer users to track Internet site performance and evaluate Web activity; this service works in much the same way that television rating firm ACNielsen monitors television audiences. The WebTrends service provides information on Web site visitors, including where they come from, what they see, and the number of "hits," or visits to the site, during different times of the day. Other surveys of Web users investigate their brand awareness and their attitudes toward Web sites and brands.

 assessment check

1. What are the basic questions a company should ask itself when planning a Web site?

2. How does the type of Web site affect measures of effectiveness?

3. Explain the difference between click-through rate and conversion rate.

Strategic Implications of Marketing in the 21st Century

The future is bright for marketers who continue to take advantage of the tremendous potential of e-business and e-marketing. Online channels, such as podcasts, that seem cutting edge today will be eclipsed within the next decade by newer technologies, some of which haven't even been invented yet. First and foremost, e-business empowers consumers. For instance, already a significant percentage of car buyers show up at a dealership armed with information on dealer costs and option packages—information they obtained online. And the percentage of informed car buyers is only going to increase. This

trend isn't about being market led or customer focused; it is about consumer control. Some argue that the Internet represents the ultimate triumph of consumerism.

Since the end of World War II, there has been a fundamental shift in the retailing paradigm from Main Street to malls to superstores. Each time the framework shifted, a new group of leaders emerged. The old leaders often missed the early warning signs because they were easy to ignore. When the first Wal-Mart and Home Depot stores appeared, how many really understood what the impact of these large retailers would

be on the marketing environment? Similarly, marketers must understand the potential impact of the Web. Initially some experts predicted the death of traditional retailing. This hasn't happened and probably will never happen. Rather, what has occurred has been a marketing evolution for organizations that embrace Internet technologies as essential parts of their marketing strategies. E-business is fueled by information; marketers who effectively use the wealth of data available will not only survive but thrive in cyberspace.

REVIEW OF CHAPTER OBJECTIVES

1 Define *e-business* and discuss how marketers use the Internet to achieve business success.

E-business involves targeting customers by collecting and analyzing business information, conducting customer transactions, and maintaining online relationships with customers by means of computer networks such as the Internet. E-marketing is the strategic process of creating, distributing, promoting, and pricing goods and services to a target market over the Internet. The capabilities and benefits of e-business and e-marketing include the elimination of geographical boundaries, personalized marketing, interactive marketing, right-time marketing, and integrated marketing.

2 Distinguish between a corporate Web site and a marketing Web site.

Virtually all businesses have Web sites. Generally, these sites can be classified as either corporate Web sites or marketing Web sites. Corporate Web sites are designed to increase the firms' visibility, promote their offerings, and provide information to interested parties. Marketing Web sites are also designed to communicate information and build customer relationships, but the main purpose of marketing Web sites is to increase purchases by site visitors.

3 List the major forms of B2B e-marketing.

B2B e-marketing is the process of selling goods and services through Internet-based exchanges of data. Electronic data interchange was an early use of technology to conduct business transactions. B2B e-marketing includes product information; ordering, invoicing, and payment processes; and customer service. In a B2B context, e-business uses Internet technology to conduct transactions between two organizations via Web services, extranets, private exchanges, electronic exchanges, and e-procurement.

4 Explain business-to-consumer (B2C) e-marketing.

Business-to-consumer (B2C) e-marketing is maturing. B2C uses the Internet to connect companies directly with consumers. E-tailing and electronic storefronts are the major forms of B2C online sales channels. B2C Web sites are either shopping sites or informational sites. Products can be purchased on shopping sites, while informational sites provide product information along with links to sellers. Benefits of B2C e-marketing include lower prices, increased convenience, and product personalization.

5 Identify online buyers and sellers.

Traditionally, online users tended to live in urban areas, earn more than $75,000 per year, and have college degrees. However, in recent years the typical Internet user has gotten older and less affluent. Also, most online shoppers today are women. All of these trends mean that the typical online shopper is looking more and more like the average consumer. As the characteristics of online shoppers change, so too will the mix of items sold online. For instance, as the average age of Internet users rises, online sales of prescription drugs should increase.

6 Describe some of the challenges associated with online marketing and e-business.

One of the challenges to e-business is developing safe online payment methods. Most firms involved in e-business use Secure Sockets Layer technology to encrypt information and provide authentication. Electronic wallets are secure data files at Web sites that contain customer information so that customers don't have to retype personal information each time they make a purchase. The growth of e-business has also been hampered by consumer security and privacy concerns and fraud. In addition, poor Web site design and service, unreliability of delivery and returns, and lack of retail expertise has limited e-business success. The Internet can also generate conflict among manufacturers, wholesalers, and retailers.

7 **Discuss how marketers use the communication function of the Web as part of their online marketing strategies.**

Communication remains the most popular function of the Internet. Companies have long used e-mail to communicate with customers, suppliers, and other partners. Online communities are groups of people who share common interests. Companies use online communities such as forums and electronic bulletin boards to communicate with and obtain feedback from customers and other partners. Blogs are online journals that have gained popularity in recent years. Wikis are Web pages that anyone can edit, and podcasts are audio and video files that can be downloaded from the Web to any digital device. Companies have just begun to explore the potential of blogs, wikis, and podcasts. Web-based promotions include advertising on other Web sites using banner ads and pop-up ads, search marketing, and online coupons. Banner ads are strip messages placed in high-visibility areas of frequently visited Web sites. A pop-up ad is a separate window that pops up with an advertising message. Search marketing is an arrangement by which a firm pays a search engine such as Google a fee to make sure that the firm's listing appears toward the top of the search results.

8 **Outline the steps involved in developing successful e-business Web sites and identify methods for measuring Web site effectiveness.**

Businesses establish Web sites to expand their customer bases, increase buyer awareness of their products, improve consumer communications, and provide better service. Before designing a Web site, a company's decision makers must first determine what they want to achieve with the site. Other important decisions include who should create, host, and manage the site; how to promote it; and how much funding to allocate. Successful Web sites contain informative, up-to-date, and visually appealing content. Sites should also download quickly and be easy to use. Finally, management must develop ways of measuring how well a site accomplishes its objectives. Common methods of measuring the effectiveness of Web sites include profitability, click-through rates, and conversion rates.

 assessment check **answers**

1.1   Define *e-business*.

E-business involves targeting customers by collecting and analyzing business information, conducting customer transactions, and maintaining online relationships with customers by means of the Internet or private computer networks.

1.2   Explain the difference between e-business and e-marketing.

E-marketing is the strategic process of creating, distributing, promoting, and pricing goods and services to a target market over the Internet.

1.3   What are the major benefits of e-marketing?

The major benefits of e-business include the elimination of geographical boundaries, personalized marketing, interactive marketing, right-time marketing, and integrated marketing.

2.1   Explain the difference between a corporate Web site and a marketing Web site.

A corporate Web site is designed to increase a firm's visibility, promote its offerings, and provide information for interested parties. A marketing Web site generally includes the same information found on a corporate Web site but is also designed to increase sales by site visitors.

2.2   Visit the Web site for Urban Outfitters (http://www.urbanoutfitters.com). Is it a corporate Web site or a marketing Web site?

Urban Outfitters is a marketing Web site. It offers, for instance, an online store.

assessment check **answers**

3.1 What is B2B e-marketing? How large is it relative to consumer e-marketing?

B2B e-marketing is the use of the Internet for business transactions between organizations. By some estimates, 80 percent or more of all e-marketing activity consists of B2B transactions.

3.2 Define *EDI* and *Web services.*

An EDI is a computer-to-computer exchange of invoices, purchase orders, price quotations, and other sales information between buyers and sellers. All parties must use the same computer operating system. Web services consist of Internet-based systems that allow parties to communicate and exchange data regardless of the computer operating system they used.

3.3 Briefly explain how e-procurement works.

E-procurement systems are Web-based systems that enable all types of organizations to improve the efficiency of their bidding and purchasing processes.

4.1 What is B2C e-marketing?

B2C e-marketing uses the Internet to connect companies directly with consumers through either shopping sites or informational sites.

4.2 Explain the difference between a shopping Web site and an informational Web site.

Consumers can purchase products on shopping sites, while informational sites provide product information along with links to sellers. However, consumers cannot actually purchase products on informational sites.

4.3 Discuss the benefits of B2C e-marketing.

Benefits of B2C e-marketing include lower prices, increased convenience, and personalization.

5.1 Who shops online? Are the characteristics of online shoppers changing?

The typical online shopper is still more affluent and more educated than the average consumer. In addition, online shoppers tend to live in urban and suburban areas. However, the characteristics of the typical online shopper are changing. While men used to shop more frequently online than women did, today more women shop online than do men.

5.2 List the fastest-growing products sold online.

The fastest-growing products sold online include apparel, computer software, home and garden products, toys, and jewelry.

6.1 What are the major challenges to growth in e-business and e-marketing?

The major challenges include developing safe online payment systems, security and privacy concerns, and fraud. In addition, poor Web site design and service, unreliability of delivery and returns, and lack of retail expertise have limited e-business success.

6.2 Describe phishing.

Phishing is a scam that uses e-mail or pop-up messages that claim to be from familiar banks, Internet service providers, or other organizations asking for personal information. The purpose of phishing is to get unsuspecting victims to disclose personal information such as credit card numbers.

6.3 Explain how e-marketing can create channel conflicts.

The Internet can generate conflict among manufacturers, wholesalers, and retailers—so-called channel conflicts. For instance, a channel conflict could be created when a manufacturer sells its products online for less than its partners—local retailers—charge.

assessment check **answers**

7.1   What are online communities? Explain how online communities can help companies market their products and improve customer service.

Online communities can take several forms and include Internet discussion groups and electronic bulletin boards. Users log in and participate by sending comments and questions, or receiving information from other forum members. Companies use online communities to ask questions and exchange information with customers.

7.2   What are blogs, wikis, and podcasts?

A blog, short for *Web log*, is a Web page that serves as a publicly accessible journal for an individual or organization. A wiki is a Web page that anyone can edit. A podcast is an audio or video file that can be downloaded from a Web site to a digital device. Companies are starting to use blogs, wikis, and podcasts as tools to build and maintain customer relationships.

7.3   Explain the difference between a banner ad, a pop-up ad, and search marketing.

Banner ads are strip messages placed in high-visibility areas of frequently visited Web sites. A pop-up ad is a separate window that pops up with an advertising message. Search marketing is an arrangement by which a firm pays a search engine—such as Google—a fee to make sure that the firm's listing appears toward the top of the search results.

8.1   What are the basic questions a company should ask itself when planning a Web site?

The first question deals with the purpose of the Web site. The second deals with whether the firm should develop the site itself or outsource it to a specialized firm. The third question is determining the name of the site.

8.2   How does the type of Web site affect measures of effectiveness?

For a shopping site, profitability is an important measure of effectiveness, though profitability can be difficult to measure given the presence of Web-to-store shoppers. For company Web sites, online success is measured by increased brand awareness and loyalty, which presumably translate into greater profitability through offline transactions.

8.3   Explain the difference between click-through rate and conversion rate.

The click-through rate is the percentage of viewers who, when presented with a banner ad, click on it. The conversion rate is the percentage of visitors to a Web site who actually make purchases.

MARKETING TERMS YOU NEED TO KNOW

e-business 112
e-marketing 114
interactive marketing 114
corporate Web site 115
marketing Web site 116

business-to-business (B2B) e-marketing 117
business-to-consumer (B2C) e-marketing 119
electronic storefronts 119
phishing 125
spam 127

blog 128
search marketing 129
click-through rate 133
conversion rate 133

OTHER IMPORTANT MARKETING TERMS

electronic exchange 118
e-procurement 118
electronic shopping cart 119
bot 120
encryption 123
Secure Sockets Layer (SSL) 123

electronic wallet 123
electronic signatures 124
firewall 124
channel conflict 127
electronic bulletin board 128
wiki 128

podcast 128
banner ad 129
pop-up ad 129
Web-to-store shoppers 133

ASSURANCE OF LEARNING REVIEW

1. List the five e-business categories.
2. Explain how a Web presence can improve the performance of traditional brick-and-mortar operations.
3. Describe the type and purpose of information found on a corporate Web site.
4. Which is larger, B2B or B2C e-marketing?
5. What is an electronic exchange? Why have they proven less successful than many people originally projected?
6. List the reasons consumers give for why they shop online.
7. Describe some of the privacy concerns of online shoppers.
8. What is purchase fraud?
9. Discuss how companies can use blogs.
10. Describe the issues that go into planning and preparing a Web site. How does the purpose of the Web site affect its planning and preparation?

PROJECTS AND TEAMWORK EXERCISES

1. In small teams, research the benefits of purchasing the following products online:
   a. notebook computers
   b. hotel rooms in Orlando
   c. women's business wear
   d. auto insurance
2. Assume that your team is assigned to develop the Web site for a large online clothing retailer that also has traditional retail stores. Research the characteristics of Web users and online shoppers. What features would you want to incorporate into your Web site?
3. How can marketers use the concept of community to add value to their products? Give a real-world example of each of the types of communities discussed in the chapter.
4. Working with a small group, assume that your group designs e-business Web sites. Identify a local company that operates with little or no online presence. Outline a proposal that explains the benefits to the firm of either going online or sig-

nificantly expanding its online presence. Sketch out what the firm's Web site should look like and the functions it should perform.
5. Working with a partner, identify and visit ten different e-business Web sites. These can be either B2C or B2B sites. Which of these sites, in your opinion, have the highest and lowest conversion rates? Explain your choices and suggest some ways in which the conversion rates of all ten sites could be improved.
6. Identify a local company that has an extensive online presence. Arrange to interview the person in charge of the company's Web site. Ask him or her the following questions:
   a. How was the Web site developed?
   b. Did the company develop the site in-house or did it outsource the task?
   c. How often does the company make changes to the site?
   d. In the opinion of the company, what are the advantages and disadvantages of going online?

CRITICAL THINKING EXERCISES

1. How are the profiles of online buyers and sellers changing? What are some of the strategic implications of these shifts to online marketers?
2. Some marketers argue that search marketing is a more effective means of using the Web to advertise than traditional pop-up or banner ads. Research the concept of search marketing. What are some of the benefits of using search marketing?
3. Assume that you work for a U.S. company that markets its products throughout the world. Its current online presence outside the United States is limited. Outline some steps the company should take to expand its online presence internationally.
4. Visa offers a service called Verified by Visa. The purpose is to reduce Internet-related fraud (MasterCard and American Express have similar services). Research "Verified by Visa" and prepare a report summarizing the program and how it protects both buyers and sellers.
5. One factor that appears to be impeding the growth in online sales is consumers' fear of receiving unsolicited e-mail after a purchase is made. Given that fear, should companies continue to use e-mail to communicate with customers? If so, how?

ETHICS EXERCISE

One of the lingering impediments to e-business revolves around privacy concerns. Virtually all Web sites collect user data. Internet service providers, for example, can track where users go on the Web and store that information. Search engines keep detailed data on Internet searches by users. Those arguing that additional privacy laws and regulations are needed claim that users never know exactly what information is being collected, nor when it is being collected. Moreover, there is no means for determining whether Web sites follow their own privacy policies.

On the other hand, some say that current laws and regulations are adequate because they make it illegal for firms to misrepresent their privacy policies or fail to disclose material information. Furthermore, there is no evidence that Internet companies are qui-

etly passing on material customer information to outside parties. Aside from the strictly legal issues, Web privacy raises a number of ethical issues as well.

Assume that your company collects and stores personal information about its online customers. The company's privacy policy allows the company to give limited amounts of that information to "selected" third parties.

1. Is this policy, in your opinion, appropriate and adequate? What ethical issues does your company's policy raise?
2. How would you change the privacy policy to reflect your ethical concerns?
3. From strictly an economic perspective, is the company's existing policy adequate and appropriate?

INTERNET EXERCISES

1. **Trends in Web usage worldwide.** One source of statistics on the Web is ClickZ Network (http://www.clickz.com). Go to the statistics section of the ClickZ Web site and read the most recent report on international Web traffic.
   a. Which countries have experienced the fastest growth in regular Internet users over the past year?
   b. Which countries have the highest percentage of broadband users? What other trends in broadband adoption and usage are evident?
   c. How much country-by-country variation is there in online activities? In other words, are citizens in some countries more or less likely to shop online?
2. **Online shopping.** Assume that you're in the market for a digital camera. Complete the following exercises.
   a. Go to CNet.com (http://www.cnet.com) and research digital cameras. Decide what features you would like

and generally how much you'd like to spend. Narrow your list to three or four specific makes and models.
   b. Visit at least three retailers that sell the makes and models you identified, including at least one that doesn't have retail stores. Which site did you like the best? Which site did you like the least? Did you identify any advantages to shopping at an online retailer that also has traditional stores?
   c. Shop for the makes and models of cameras you identified using one of the major shopping bots. Comment on your experience.

Note: Internet Web addresses change frequently. If you don't find the exact site listed, you may need to access the organization's home page and search from there or use a search engine such as Google.

CASE 4.1   iTunes and the Future of Music

By any measure, Apple dominates the world of legal music downloads. Its iTunes Music Store, pumped by the company's sale of more than 42 million iPod players, has grown in just a few years to account for 83 percent of the downloadable music sold on the Internet. Selling songs for 99 cents at a rate of 3 million a day—or

1 billion a year—the iTunes operation just breaks even financially, after royalties and operating costs are taken out. But iTunes and the iPod go hand in hand, and the highly profitable little iPod now accounts for half of Apple's revenues. As one industry observer said of iTunes, the iPod, and Apple's proprietary music software, "It's really very dif-

ficult to separate any of those elements" in accounting for their market power.

But there's room for competition in the $13 billion worldwide retail music business, and competitors won't be the only problem iTunes faces in the near future. Music piracy is still a threat, and Apple has used the availability of free (though illegal) downloads to argue against variable pricing in its recent contract renewal negotiations with the four biggest recording companies—Sony BMG, Universal, Warner Music, and EMI. "Music labels would much rather have variable prices, so they can charge more for hits and perhaps less for older tracks," said an industry expert. "Apple likes the $0.99 price because it is simple, uniform, not too high to discourage buyers, and very easy to administer and merchandise." In addition, as CEO Steve Jobs told a press conference, the price for legal downloading must compete with the free cost of illegal networks. Apple won its point and will continue to sell songs for 99 cents.

So will Microsoft. Microsoft is offering an online music service, in partnership with MTV, to compete directly against iTunes with 2 million songs, compared with iTunes's 3 million. For a subscription fee of about $10 a month, it also offers access to 130 radio stations of all genres and 500 different playlists. Called URGE, the new service uses Microsoft's Media Player software and comes with a fourteen-day free trial.

Another challenge to iTunes's dominance may come from Samsung's new Helix, a tiny radio and music player that can pick up XM Satellite Radio's 70 commercial-free stations and play back up to 750 downloaded songs. Users can store songs they hear on the radio by simply pressing Record to capture the track from the beginning for instant music portability—no computer required.

And legal challenges looming from France may spread internationally. Legislation is working its way through the French National Assembly to compel iTunes and other online music stores with proprietary music management software to open their code to others. If passed, the law will support a push to standardize formats across the industry so that songs from any vendor could be played on any digital player. An iTunes download, say, could then be used on the Linux operating system, just as any music CD can play on any CD device. Savvy users of music downloads can already work around the compatibility problem, and with Apple's market domination, it hasn't hampered many music fans. But some observers think that whatever the outcome in France, other countries will follow France's example. Still, they'll have to get there before the hackers do.

Questions for Critical Thinking

1. Apple has said that if the French legislation passes, it will consider giving up the French share of its business by pulling iTunes from the French market. Could such a strategy succeed? Do you think it would be wise from a marketing standpoint? Why or why not?

2. iTunes now carries music videos and short films for downloading, as well as hit TV shows including *24*, *Prison Break*, and *SpongeBob SquarePants.* What type of marketing strategy is behind these additions to the iTunes library? How successful do you think it will be?

Sources: David Pogue, "XM Radio Fans Can Record It if They Hear It," *New York Times,* May 25, 2006, **http://www.nytimes.com**; Matthieu Demeestere, "Microsoft, MTV Challenge Apple iTunes," Agence-France Presse, May 17, 2006, **http://www.afp.com**; Brian Holmes, "Fox Shows to Debut on iTunes," *Earth Times,* May 10, 2006, **http://www.earthtimes.org**; Walaika K. Haskins, "Apple Wins iTunes Price Battle," Newsfactor Network, May 2, 2006, **http://www.newsfactor.com**; Rob Pegoraro, "France Takes a Shot at iTunes," *Washington Post,* March 26, 2006, **http://www.washingtonpost.com**; Doreen Carvajal, "Paris Acts to Open up Online Sales of Music," *International Herald Tribune,* March 22, 2006, **http://www.iht.com**; Matthew Yi, "One Billion Songs Sold on iTunes in 3 Years," *San Francisco Chronicle,* February 24, 2006, **http://www.sfgate.com**; Mike Musgrove, "Bit Hit of the Holidays: 14 Million iPods Sold," *Washington Post,* January 11, 2006, **http://www.washingtonpost.com.**

VIDEO CASE 4.2   Pick Your Bananas Online at Peapod

The written video case on Peapod appears on page VC-5. The recently filmed Peapod video is designed to expand and highlight the concepts in this chapter and the concepts and questions covered in the written video case.

Talking about Marketing Careers with. . .

MICHAEL L. HUTZEL, JR.
DIRECTOR OF STRATEGIC INITIATIVES
RDI MARKETING SERVICES, INC.

Knowledge is power, especially in today's competitive business environment. Organizations and their marketers continually look for ways to understand their customers and the products they purchase—or would like to purchase. The day-to-day contact firms have with those customers can provide key insights. Ohio-based RDI Marketing Services, Inc., helps contemporary marketers with their customer contact and research needs by providing inbound and outbound telemarketing services. Its staff offer customized, personal service for such major business initiatives as marketing research for new-product development, understanding customer perceptions of current practices or special promotions, sales, and industry-wide product recalls.

RDI is a strategic partner to its clients, tailoring its services to fit the project. Its employees consult with an organization's staff and offer expertise in developing marketing plans, drafting questionnaires and scripts, and using technology effectively to reach different markets. Here to discuss RDI's current activities and future plans is Michael L. Hutzel, Jr., the company's direc-

tor of strategic initiatives. He agreed to a brief Q&A session to give us some background on building and maintaining a successful operation.

Q: Providing service and expertise to help *Fortune* 500 companies in their marketing efforts is a high-profile position. What is your educational background, and what experiences helped you work your way up the career ladder?

A: Ironically, most of my education in the marketing field is hands-on. I do have, however, a bachelor's degree in English as well as a master's in English education, both from The Ohio State University. This educational background has been extremely helpful in the writing of client scripts and proposals and in the bidding process. It has also been helpful with client meetings. My five years of experience in the classroom prepared me very well for the types of individual and group interactions that I now experience on a daily basis.

As for marketing experiences, nothing has proven more valuable to me. I remained tied to the marketing industry, one way or another, throughout my college career, mostly with part-time work. Initially, it was the type of job that allowed flexibility around constantly changing college courses, and it turned into a career. Learning to be flexible, understanding client needs, and embracing the changes of technology are key to developing a career in this field. And, of course, there is no substitute for hard work. Projects in this industry, much like the creation of a Web site, tend to be very "front-end" loaded. A lot of thankless hours go into the beginning of a project or new client relationship, but normally it is worth the haul.

Q: You are the Director of Strategic Initiatives at RDI. Tell us a bit about what your job involves. What is a typical day like for you?

A: First, there is no such thing as "typical." Honestly, though, that is part of the

appeal. We have dozens of clients with very distinct needs that are ever changing. The reality of what we do is to service those clients in the best ways possible, which often means change, sometimes as frequently as by the hour.

My job entails two major aspects: operations and client relations. I serve as a client liaison to see that new projects get up and running as efficiently and effectively as possible. This means that I am involved in client meetings, normally to discuss upcoming needs and to evaluate the best plan of attack that is cost-effective for all involved. I have to stay intricately involved with operations so that I see the project though from inception to implementation. Because of this function, I need to have a thorough understanding of how the call center works—the human and technological resources—and be able to appropriately identify what is the best plan of action. After a project is under way, I facilitate necessary changes and maintain an ongoing relationship with the client.

Q: Your firm depends on solid relationships with such major clients as General Electric, Integrity Pharmaceuticals, and Sara Lee Corp. How do you develop and help strengthen those relationships?

A: Client relationships are the nucleus around which we all function. Quite simply, without them we would not be in existence. The initial development of these relationships comes from a wide variety of places. We are fortunate to have solid history, which allows us to work a great deal from client referrals. However, we never rest on our laurels and have an executive team, of which I am part, that focuses on exploring opportunities with clients in industries with which we are familiar, since we have a good understanding of what some of their needs might be. We also are constantly looking into other industries as well, to see if there is another niche we can explore. The premise from which we work is simple: to seek out and foster relationships in any industry in which the relationship can be mutually beneficial.

As for strengthening current relationships, this too has a high priority. Regular and positive contact seems to be the most effective for us. Each client is given several points of contact, typically executives, who can be available to address ongoing needs and concerns.

Q: We hear a lot about the importance of quality in providing services these days. How does RDI set quality standards, train employees, monitor their performance, and motivate them to perform their best for your clients?

A: RDI has worked very diligently to develop some of the highest standards in the business. Quality control is taken very seriously. So much so, that an entire department is dedicated just to that. Most of the quality control begins in the human resources department and is followed through with our Quality Assurance department. We have folks working literally around the clock to assure that the standards of our clients are met.

We are also very proud that we adopt a "promote from within" policy. This serves as incredible motivation for those who are beginning a career here. I have seen folks in my tenure here begin as hourly CSRs (client service representatives), spending their entire day on the phone in a cubicle, rise to team leads, supervisors, and even full-blown managers. It does wonders for maintaining team rapport and motivates those who want to grow within the company.

Q: We noticed that your firm provides multilingual call center services for clients at its center in Nogales, Arizona. How important is that service to your firm? Is this a growing part of your business?

A: To be competitive, offering such services is absolutely crucial. Our clients appeal to a wide range of consumers, and we have to adjust to fit their needs. The world is no longer a place of "us and them." Almost every major successful industry embraces diversity and utilizes the skills multiple cultures possess. The consumer base is the quintessential melting pot, and consumers are becoming increasingly informed. It used to be that offering such services was consid-

ered cutting edge; now I would argue it is essential as a fundamental service. Ultimately, it is the consumer who drives the market, and their needs must be met, by both our firm and our clients.

Q: We read nearly every week about the importance of outsourcing to today's marketers. As a company providing such services, how does your firm help clients formulate their strategic marketing plans?

A: We become as involved as our clients need us to be. Unfortunately, this too has no "typical" parameters. We do attempt to initiate our service in a standard approach, but normally it is very quickly tailored to what the client's ongoing needs may be. Often, we start with successful strategies that are time tested, particularly if a new client is in an industry with which we are familiar. If both the client and the industry are new to us, we try to draw from past success with clients who are most like the new client, or spend a great deal of effort to research the particular industry our new client is in. Understanding a client's industry, and more specifically their customer base, can go a long way in helping to determine a client's potential needs.

Q: Critical to developing and keeping customers' trust is operating in an ethical manner. In your field, confidentiality is an issue that must surface often. How important are confidentiality and security to RDI? How do you ensure the safety of client information?

A: Technology being what it is, this is probably a question better suited for our I.T. department. I can tell you, though, that we go to extreme measures in this age of constant security risks to protect our clients' data. We have security clearance in our buildings, electronic badges with varying levels of clearance, and similar clearance levels for logging in and out of computers, the server, and any of our storage databases. We expend a great deal of financial and human resources to ensure this.

Q: Marketers have been quick to adopt new technologies to help them achieve their goals. What new technologies, such as the Internet and telecommunications, do you use in your daily work? How have they helped your firm compete in the marketplace?

A: Depending on the project and its needs, different sources of technology are used. Telephony, point-to-point communication, I3 for remote access, INT5 dedicated servers, virtual private networks (VPNs), Internet, interactive voice response (IVR) are all just a few of the systems we use. The bottom line is that technology is one of the pillars in what we do on a daily basis. The trick to staying competitive is not always having the latest, greatest equipment. I would argue it is more about understanding what the available technologies have to offer, exploiting those technologies to their utmost capacities, and making sure that any new technologies will communicate efficiently with the current ones already in place.

Q: Students are always interested to hear advice on how to get started in their marketing careers. They read about the importance of gaining experience through volunteer activities and internships. What practical insights can you give to our readers to give them a head start?

A: I would say that getting as much exposure to as many firms as possible would be a good start. Do homework on each firm before volunteering or interning so there is a good base from which to make a decision. I would also say that it would be smart to get some idea of what interests them the most. Is it marketing or operations, sales or client development? There are several distinct courses that a professional can run in this industry, and although they may intertwine, they require very different skill sets. Look, listen, and be willing to learn from those who are successful; they have gems of wisdom to share, said or unsaid. Most important, never forget that at the end of the day all successful firms are fueled by the consumer. Consumers are what make us possible.

Laughter's Part of the Plan

The Second City (SC) cultivates a unique relationship with its customer when its actors step on stage and confidently ask the audience for "a suggestion of anything at all." This bold request that launches the actors into a series of hilarious improvisations has been with the company since its beginning. On December 16, 1959, a group of University of Chicago students began performing sketch and improvisational comedy in a local coffee shop. Soon playing to sold-out crowds, The Second City found its name, identity, and first marketing move all in one place. Journalist A. J. Leibling had lambasted Chicago in a series of articles dubbing the town "The Second City" as he saw it subpar to cities such as New York and Paris. The cast of Second City proceeded to use headlines and cutting-edge comedy to reclaim the put-down and produce a nonstop series of compelling comedy revues. Training some of the greatest names in comedy, SC has developed a theater company that has captured the hearts of the entertainment industry for decades.

The Second City has expanded from its theatrical roots in the "Windy City" to become a brand recognized throughout the world. On the television screen; on stages in Toronto, Detroit, Las Vegas, and Denver; at college assemblies, in corporate events; across the internet; and even on the high seas with performances for Norwegian Cruise Lines, Second City operates a marketing plan as bold and captivating as its comedy.

Its long lists of famous alumni are a cherished legacy for the company. As actors such as John Candy, Mike Myers, and Tina Fey have ascended to stardom, they have become the faces of The Second City, leading the customer right to the very stage whence these stars first shined. The Second City has formulated its marketing concept around the talent and exposure of its comedic success stories throughout the last 50 years.

Kelly Leonard, Second City's vice president, recognizes how SC's continued growth has fostered its target market. "We keep a presence in promoting ourselves to concierges, convention bureaus and other visitor/tourist related groups. We are a strong tourist destination, so we like to keep our face in front of that market." Their product, their talent, has been seen around the world. So when tourists visit Chicago, a stop at The Second City makes for a fun night of entertainment. This is the most significant relationship for the company. It treats the audience to a night of sketch comedy based on current headlines and cultural issues, followed by a free set of improvisational comedy, the company's signature art form. The audience sits just feet away from Second City's product, its actors, who could jump into the lights of Hollywood in the blink of an eye.

The Second City performs new comedy revues around the globe to turn its recognizable brand into an accessible product. Its first international move was in 1973 when founder Bernie Sahlins and Andrew Alexander, the company's chief executive officer, launched a new SC theater in Toronto. The stage has cultivated the talents of actors such as Martin Short, Rick Moranis, and Dan Aykroyd. It also provided Alexander with the cast of SC's first move onto the television medium, *Second City Television*. SCTV became the biggest promotional agent for the company to-date, and developed a relationship with SC's audience across international lines.

Today, The Second City keeps focused on its core initiative: to find, cultivate, and produce great comedic talent. For the consumer, this means ground-breaking talent from the early generations of Alan Arkin and Barbara Harris to more recent graduates such as Horatio Sanz and Steven Colbert.

The Second City has theaters in Chicago, Toronto, Detroit, Las Vegas, and Denver. Each of these operates with SC's concentration on current events and improvisation to orient shows around the creative tradition of the company. It also provides a convenient frame of reference for its consumer. To reach their respective audiences, the theaters employ distinctive marketing strategies. In Detroit, shows are tailored to the local audience. In Las Vegas, The Second City stands out as a comparatively less-glamorized venue, in an overglamorized city; in Detroit and Denver, the two newer establishments, shows and promotion are building a core audience in the community; and in Chicago, the theater supplements its flagship Mainstage with additional, more eclectic shows to reattract the local crowd.

Understanding its tourist appeal and the tourist industry helped Second City's top management find a new market. VP Kelly Leonard noticed an opportunity with Norwegian Cruise Lines to produce Second City revues for vacationing travelers, which resulted in an exclusive deal with the company. Aboard ship, SC performs for a demographic similar to its tourist market. Consequently Second City Theatricals distributes SC comedy around the globe and has an exciting strategic alliance with the cruise line.

Marketers at The Second City appreciate the fact that awareness of their company is spread primarily by word of mouth. The Second City works to enrich this initial relationship by expanding the mix of services offered by the company. Kelly Leonard attributes Second City's success in forming long-term relationships with consumers through "our expanded services. . . . We offer workshops and shows in the high schools; we play the colleges; we provide corporate entertainment—basically, we're creating a series of in's that cross over a variety of ages and experiences. The more stuff that we can create that is pure to what we do, the better we are positioning ourselves for the future."

The Second City has always been an intensely creative business environment. Since it first began as a daring startup theater company, it has attracted innovators both on and off its stage. It has also attracted an audience wanting to think, interact, and most of all, laugh about whatever it is that they've been thinking about, that suddenly became their "suggestion" for the night.

Questions

1. What is Second City's target market? What decisions has it made based on this knowledge?
2. How do you think the Second City chooses where to put its theaters?
3. Explain the short and long-term aspects of Second City's relationship with its customer.
4. How does The Second City vary its product to account for varying locations?

PART 2

Understanding Buyers and Markets

CHEVROLET UNLEASHES THE NEW CORVETTE

CORVETTE
by Chevrolet

New with 4-wheel disc brakes
'65 CORVETTE

'73 CORVETTE
We gave it radials, a quieter ride, guard beams and a nose job.

Building a better way to see the U.S.A.

CHEVROLET

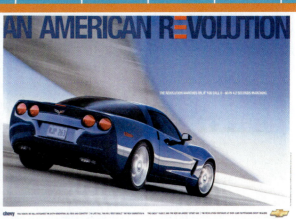

AN AMERICAN REVOLUTION

chevy

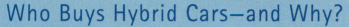

CHAPTER 5

Who Buys Hybrid Cars—and Why?

If you could buy a new car today, what would it be? Maybe you'd choose a pickup truck for power and durability. Or what about that sleek sports car? Or you might be practical—as long as you turn the ignition key and the car starts, you're happy. Have you ever thought about a hybrid? Many people today are.

Gas/electric hybrid vehicles are fueled by a combination of gasoline and battery-powered electricity. As a result, they are more fuel efficient than gas-only vehicles, and they produce fewer emissions. But although a few years ago hybrids were considered the domain of quirky auto engineers and consumers whose primary concern was saving the planet, they are now increasingly cruising the main streets and highways across the nation. Consumers have stopped just looking and are driving them off the dealers' lots. And more and more auto manufacturers are paying attention.

Toyota and Honda were two of the first major auto manufacturers to put a hybrid model on the market. The Toyota Prius and Honda Civic hybrid have now been through several model years. Both companies are also producing hybrid versions of their most popular cars. Toyota offers a hybrid Highlander SUV and Camry, along with the luxury Lexus RX400h. Honda offers a hybrid Accord in addition to its Civic. As more consumers are taking the hybrids for a test-drive, American and European manufacturers have begun rolling out their own versions. Chevrolet has introduced a hybrid Malibu, and Ford a hybrid Fusion and Five Hundred.

But what about consumers who can't let go of the wheel of their SUV or pickup? Americans are known for their love affair with trucks and SUVs; many wouldn't consider downsizing to a sedan, no matter how much gas they might save. No need to worry—automakers haven't forgotten those consumers. Soon hybrid versions of the Chevy Silverado and Tahoe, the Saturn Vue, the GMC Sierra, and others will be rolling off the assembly line. Sweden's AB Volvo—one of the world's biggest truck manufacturers—has unveiled its own new technology for cutting fuel consumption in heavy vehicles. The company plans to launch hybrid vehicles powered by diesel engines backed by electric batteries charged with the energy released from the brakes. Volvo knows what it's doing—the firm also makes buses and Mack

Consumer Behavior

Chapter Objectives

1 Define *consumer behavior* and describe the role it plays in marketing decisions.

2 Describe the interpersonal determinants of consumer behavior: cultural, social, and family influences.

3 Explain each of the personal determinants of consumer behavior: needs and motives, perceptions, attitudes, learning, and self-concept theory.

4 Distinguish between high-involvement and low-involvement purchase decisions.

5 Outline the steps in the consumer decision process.

6 Differentiate among routinized response behavior, limited problem solving, and extended problem solving by consumers.

trucks. "There is a growing interest in the market to reduce fuel consumption," explains Volvo's CEO Leif Johansson. "We now have a technology that is interesting from a commercial viewpoint . . . for a hybrid market for heavy vehicles."

Why are consumers gravitating toward hybrids? Reducing fuel consumption is one issue. Each gallon of gasoline *not* burned by a vehicle prevents the release of emissions that combine to create nineteen pounds of carbon dioxide in the atmosphere. But preventing pollution is not the whole story. With fluctuating—sometimes soaring—gas prices, cars and trucks that use less gas simply make sense. Critics argue that the high purchase price of many hybrid vehicles, which can run several thousand dollars above their gas-only counterparts, offset gasoline savings. But *Consumer Reports* recently reported that the Toyota Prius and Honda Civic Hybrid recovered their initial costs in the first five years or 75,000 miles of ownership, actually saving owners $300 to $400. Other models still lag in savings.

Another issue is government incentives. Tax breaks have contributed to hybrid owners' overall savings. Under a new federal energy bill, drivers who purchase a hybrid qualify for a tax credit ranging

from $250 to $3,150, depending on the size and weight of the vehicle. Some cities now allow drivers of hybrids to use carpool lanes, a potential benefit to harried commuters.

evolution *of a* brand

Hybrid vehicles were introduced in the U.S. market around the turn of the 21st century. Since that time, sales of hybrid cars and trucks have been roughly doubling every year. Still, hybrids currently make up a small fraction of total car sales annually. But industry experts think the percentage of hybrid vehicles sold will grow rapidly in coming years.

- The Toyota Prius and Honda Civic Hybrid were two of the first hybrid vehicles to hit American roadways. At the time of this writing, they are the two most popular brands of

hybrids on the market. Do some research into the sales of the Prius and Civic Hybrid to see why consumers are buying the cars. What factors seem to be influencing consumers in their purchases? Are the Prius and Civic Hybrid still the top-selling models? Why or why not? What factors have influenced their increase or decrease in sales?

- Investigate whether sales of hybrid vehicles are linked to any specific geographic areas. If they are more popular in certain places, list the factors that lead those consumers to buy hybrids. Do social or cultural issues enter into

Finally, customer satisfaction is high for hybrids. Current owners typically score them well on surveys of reliability and performance. "These benefits add up to an inviting package for many car buyers who are willing to pay a premium for a hybrid," concludes *Consumer Reports*.[1]

evolution *of a* **brand** consumers' decisions in certain cities or states? If so, list the characteristics you found for those hybrid buyers. How do they differ from the average car buyer?

Chapter Overview

Why do you head for Pizza Hut whenever you have a craving for extra cheese and pepperoni? Why does your roommate stock Odwalla juices in the fridge? Why does your best friend drive five miles out of the way for Starbucks—when the local coffee shop is much closer? The answers to these questions aren't obvious, and they directly affect every aspect of marketing strategy, including the development of a product, the level at which it is priced, and the way it is promoted. Developing a marketing strategy requires an understanding of the process by which individual consumers buy goods and services for their own use and organizational buyers purchase business products for their organizations.

A variety of influences affect both individuals buying items for themselves and personnel purchasing products for their firms. This chapter focuses on individual purchasing behavior, which applies to all of us as consumers. **Consumer behavior** is the process through which the ultimate buyer makes purchase decisions

consumer behavior Process through which buyers make purchase decisions.

from toothbrushes to autos to vacations. Chapter 6 will shift the focus to business buying decisions.

The study of consumer behavior builds on an understanding of human behavior in general. In their efforts to understand why and how consumers make buying decisions, marketers borrow extensively from the sciences of psychology and sociology. The work of psychologist Kurt Lewin, for example, provides a useful classification scheme for influences on buying behavior. Lewin's proposition is

$$B = f(P, E)$$

This statement means that behavior (*B*) is a function (*f*) of the interactions of personal influences (*P*) and pressures exerted by outside environmental forces (*E*).

1 Define *consumer behavior* and describe the role it plays in marketing decisions.

Briefly Speaking

"A [fan] is a person who sits forty rows up in the stands and wonders why a seventeen-year-old kid can't hit another seventeen-year-old kid with a ball from forty yards away . . . and then he goes out to the parking lot and can't find his car."

—Chuck Mills (b. 1928)
American college football coach

The statement is usually rewritten to apply to consumer behavior as follows:

$$B = f(I, P)$$

Consumer behavior (*B*) is a function (*f*) of the interactions of interpersonal influences (*I*)—such as culture, friends, classmates, co-workers, and relatives—and personal factors (*P*) such as attitudes, learning, and perception. In other words, inputs from others and an individual's psychological makeup affect his or her purchasing behavior. Before looking at how consumers make purchase decisions, we first consider how both interpersonal and personal factors affect consumers.

✓ assessment check

1. **Why is the study of consumer behavior important to marketers?**
2. **Describe Kurt Lewin's proposition.**

INTERPERSONAL DETERMINANTS OF CONSUMER BEHAVIOR

2 Describe the interpersonal determinants of consumer behavior: cultural, social, and family influences.

You don't live in a bubble—and you don't make purchase decisions there. You might not be aware of it, but every buying decision you make is influenced by a variety of external and internal factors. Consumers often decide to buy goods and services based on what they believe others expect of them. They may want to project positive images to peers or to satisfy the expectations of family members. They may buy a certain book because someone they respect recommended it. Or they may make reservations at a particular restaurant based on a good review in the newspaper. They may even buy a home in a neighborhood that they think will impress their family and friends. Marketers recognize three broad categories of interpersonal influences on consumer behavior: cultural, social, and family influences.

CULTURAL INFLUENCES

Culture can be defined as the values, beliefs, preferences, and tastes handed down from one generation to the next. Culture is the broadest environmental determinant of consumer behavior. Marketers need to understand its role in consumer decision making, both in the United States and abroad. They must also monitor trends in cultural values as well as recognize changes in these values.

culture Values, beliefs, preferences, and tastes handed down from one generation to the next.

Marketing strategies and business practices that work in one country may be offensive or ineffective in another. Strategies may even have to be varied from one area of a country to another. Nowhere is that more true than the United States, where the population continues to diversify at a rapid rate. In Nashville, the Music City Motorplex has taken down its old signs and put up new ones—in Spanish and English. The racetrack, which is located near a large Hispanic community, has also hired bilingual personnel and announcers.[2] In Chicago, Kraft Foods introduced its *De tu Cocina a tu Tierra* program, which invites Hispanic moms to enter their favorite traditional dishes in a Kraft Kitchens contest to win a trip to a destination of their choosing.[3] In Texas, Wal-Mart offers a variety of goods and services tailored to Hispanic consumers, ranging from a line of Mexican-inspired bathroom and dining accessories designed by Zarela Martinez to its own Spanish-language magazine, *Viviendo.*[4]

Core Values in U.S. Culture

Some cultural values change over time, but basic core values do not. The work ethic and the desire to accumulate wealth are two core values in American society. Even though the typical family structure and family members' roles have shifted in recent years, American culture still emphasizes the importance of family and home life. This value is strengthened during times of upheaval such as after the events of September 11, 2001, or Hurricane Katrina several years later. Other core values include education, individualism, freedom, youth, health, physical activity, humanitarianism, and efficiency. You can probably recognize yourself in some of these core values. Each of these values influences consumer behavior, including your own.

Values that change over time also have their effects. As technology rapidly changes the way people exchange information, consumers adopt values that include communicating with anyone, anytime, anywhere in the

GO RVING AND THE RICHARDS GROUP

The importance of family is a core value in U.S. culture. This ad promotes a family vacation in an RV.

world. The generation that includes older teens and young twenties is the most skilled at using new communications technologies. They keep in touch with friends, classmates, and co-workers via PC, cell phone, BlackBerry, and other devices. They create personal Web pages and blogs and send photos to each other via Shutterfly.com. Nearly 80 percent of online teens and adults under age 28 surveyed report that they regularly visit or create blogs. Sixty percent say they send text messages via cell phone.[5] These changes in consumer behavior signal a change in values.

International Perspective on Cultural Influences

Cultural differences are particularly important for international marketers. Marketing strategies that prove successful in one country often cannot extend to other international markets because of cultural variations. Europe is a good example, with many different languages and a wide range of lifestyles and product preferences. Even though the continent is becoming a single economic unit as a result of the expansion of the European Union and the widespread use of the euro as currency, cultural divisions continue to define multiple markets.

Packaging is one area where marketers must be careful. A few years ago, McDonald's announced that all 30,000 of its restaurants in 100 countries would feature the same packaging for its food and beverages. Wrappers would feature photos of real consumers enjoying themselves by playing sports, listening to music, or reading to children. Two years later, the firm dropped the idea, adopting instead localized packaging including nutritional labels. Why did McDonald's do such a turnabout? People in different countries value different activities. They also want different information on package labels.

China, which is an emerging market with enormous potential, is also filled with marketing pitfalls. When Nestlé introduced coffee to Chinese consumers, the firm learned through trial and error that it had to offer a mixture of coffee, cream, and sugar that tasted just right to the Chinese palate. After its adjustments, the firm dominated the coffee category in China. Starbucks noticed and has now entered the Chinese market.[6]

Subcultures

Cultures are not homogeneous groups with universal values, even though core values tend to dominate. Each culture includes numerous **subcultures**—groups with their own distinct modes of behavior. Understanding the differences among subcultures can help marketers develop more effective marketing strategies.

The United States, like many nations, is composed of significant subcultures that differ by ethnicity, nationality, age, rural versus urban location, religion, and geographic distribution. The southwestern lifestyle emphasizes casual dress, outdoor entertaining, and active recreation. Mormons refrain from buying or using tobacco and liquor. Orthodox Jews purchase and consume only kosher foods. Understanding these and other differences among subcultures contributes to successful marketing of goods and services.

America's population mix is changing. By 2050, the nation's racial and ethnic minority groups will represent nearly half the total U.S. population. The number of African Americans is expected to increase from just under 36 million to more than 61 million during this time, representing 14.6 percent of the population. Hispanic and Asian populations will grow also—Hispanics will account for nearly 25 percent

KEN PICKETT/WPN

Just one of the benefits of the United States' many subcultures is the nation's cuisine. Asian, Italian, Hispanic, Caribbean: each group adds its own unique twist to America's palate. Shown here are Hmong immigrants selling traditional Southeast Asian vegetables at a farmers' market in Minnesota.

and Asians 8 percent of the population. In addition, women will continue to outnumber men in the United States.[7] Marketers need to be sensitive to these changes and to the differences in shopping patterns and buying habits among ethnic segments of the population. Businesses can no longer succeed by selling one-size-fits-all products; they must consider consumer needs, interests, and concerns when developing their marketing strategies.

Marketing concepts may not always cross cultural boundaries without changes. For example, new immigrants may not be familiar with cents-off coupons and contests. Marketers may need to provide specific instructions when targeting such promotions to these groups.

According to the U.S. Census Bureau, the three largest and fastest-growing U.S. ethnic subcultures are Hispanics, African Americans, and Asians. Figure 5.1 shows the proportion of the U.S. population made up of minority groups. Although no ethnic or racial subculture is entirely homogeneous, researchers have found that each of these three ethnic segments has identifiable consumer behavior profiles.

Hispanic-American Consumers

Marketers face several challenges in appealing to Hispanic consumers. The 41 million Hispanics in the United States are not a homogeneous group. They come from a wide range of countries, each with its own culture. Two-thirds come from Mexico, one in seven is Central and South American, one in twelve is Puerto Rican, and nearly 4 percent are Cuban. The common trait they share is a connection to Latin America—through either immigration or ancestry. As the Hispanic population shifts to include second- and third-generation immigrants, changes in attitudes and values may occur as well. Even the word *Hispanic* is not universal; Puerto Ricans and Dominicans in New York and Cubans in southern Florida refer to themselves as Hispanic, but many Mexican and Central Americans in the southwestern United States prefer to be called Latinos. Not surprisingly, the cultural differences among these different segments often affect consumer preferences.

More important than differences in national origin are differences in **acculturation**, or the degree to which newcomers have adapted to U.S. culture. Acculturation plays a vital role in consumer behavior. For instance, marketers should not assume that all Hispanics understand Spanish. By the third generation after immigration, most Hispanic Americans speak only English.

Hispanics can be divided into three major acculturation groups:

- *Largely unacculturated Hispanics* (about 28 percent of the United States Hispanic population) were typically born outside the United States and have lived in the country for less than ten years. Seventy-two percent speak only Spanish, and most identify themselves by their country of origin rather than as Hispanic or Latino.

- *Partially acculturated Hispanics* (approximately 59 percent) were born in the United States or have lived here for more than ten years. Half are bilingual, speaking English at work and Spanish at home—meaning that marketers can reach them in either language. The other half speak English exclusively.

- *Highly acculturated Hispanics* (13 percent) were usually born and raised in the United States. Only 22 percent are bilingual, while 78 percent consider English their dominant language. More than half refer to themselves as American, while about 20 percent each refer to themselves as Hispanic or by country of origin.[8]

figure 5.1

Ethnic and Racial Minorities as a Percentage of the Total U.S. Population

Source: Data from the U.S. Census Bureau, "USA Statistics in Brief—Race and Hispanic Origin," December 29, 2005, **www.census.gov**, accessed March 15, 2006.

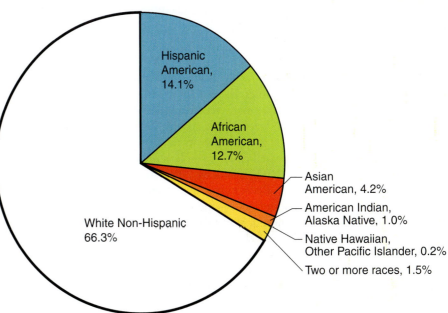

Hispanic American, 14.1%

African American, 12.7%

Asian American, 4.2%

American Indian, Alaska Native, 1.0%

Native Hawaiian, Other Pacific Islander, 0.2%

Two or more races, 1.5%

White Non-Hispanic 66.3%

Research reveals several other important points:

- The Hispanic market is large and fast growing. Already the United States is home to the fifth-largest Hispanic population in the world; only the populations of Argentina, Colombia, Mexico, and Spain are bigger.

- Hispanics tend to be young, with a median age of 25 compared with a median age of 36 for the general U.S. population.

- Although Hispanics are concentrated geographically in California, Florida, New Mexico, New York, and Texas, they are settling in other states as well. Georgia, Nebraska, and Washington are experiencing rapid rates of growth. Half of all U.S. Hispanics now live in Hispanic-minority neighborhoods, making them less concentrated than the African American population.[9]

Hispanics tend to have larger households than non-Hispanics, making them good customers for products sold in bulk. They spend more on their children than do parents in other subcultures, especially on clothing. Hispanics also place great importance on keeping in touch with relatives in other countries, making them excellent customers for phone cards, air travel, and wire transfers of money. In addition, Hispanics make more visits to pizza and chicken chain restaurants than do general-market consumers and bring along with them a larger group of family members and friends. These are all trends that marketers who want to reach this group of consumers should consider.

African American Consumers

The continuously growing African American market offers a tremendous opportunity for marketers who understand its buying patterns. The African American population stands at nearly 38 million people. But that segment is expected to grow to more than 61 million by 2050.[10] The buying power of these consumers is projected to hit $1 trillion by 2010. Smart marketers recognize the opportunities in this segment. Don Montuori, publisher of *Packaged Facts,* points out that purchasing in some African American markets outpaces that of Hispanics, including those with incomes greater than $50,000, owner-occupied households, married-couple families, and African American women.[11]

Recognizing these opportunities, Renaissance Urban Media Group launched *Mecca Magazine,* an upscale glossy magazine aimed at African Americans who live and work in the Atlanta area. Mark Pettit, president and CEO of marketing firm Creaxion, says, "Atlanta's African-American community is one of the largest, most affluent and successful in the nation."[12]

As with any other subculture, marketers must avoid approaching all African American consumers in the same way; demographic factors such as income, age, language, and educational level must be considered. Most African Americans are descended from families who have lived in the United States. for generations, but some are recent immigrants. And they are members of every economic group.

Asian American Consumers

Marketing to Asian Americans presents many of the same challenges as reaching Hispanics. Like Hispanics, the country's more than 12 million Asian Americans are spread among culturally diverse groups, many retaining their own languages. The Asian American subculture consists of more than two dozen ethnic groups, including Chinese, Filipinos, Indians, Japanese, Koreans, and Vietnamese. Each group brings its own language, religion, and value system to purchasing decisions. Asian Americans taken as a whole represent $579 billion in buying power and are expected to number more than 33 million by 2050, so marketers need to search for efficient ways to reach them.[13]

Recognizing that Asian American women are often more petite than women of other racial backgrounds—and often have difficulty finding clothes that fit—Sears has launched the idea of multicultural stores that will offer Asian American women and other minorities the styles, fabrics, and sizes of clothing that they want. Sears designers have come up with new colors and specially sized styles cut to fit Asian Americans. The new clothing was launched in 97 of the firm's 870 stores nationwide, concentrated where Asian Americans live.[14]

Marketers in other industries are trying much harder than they did in the past to learn what Asian American consumers really want and need. One research firm for the grocery industry is conducting an extensive survey. "We will be going into people's homes to see what brands they have in their refrigerators and how they use those brands, as well as [into] supermarkets and other venues," says Tanya Raukko, director of strategic planning at InterTrend. "This is the kind of research that is needed to demystify for marketers how Asians connect with their brands." When Kraft began testing some new products it had developed through a partnership with 99 Ranch, the largest Asian grocery chain in the United States, the firm's marketers discovered that consumers didn't necessarily want more Asian-style products. Instead, they wanted to learn more about how to use American products. Still, the firm is committed to offering plenty of choices in both categories.[15]

SOCIAL INFLUENCES

As a consumer, you belong to a number of social groups. Your earliest group experience came from membership in a family. As you began to grow, you might have joined a group of friends in day care or in the neighborhood. Later, you might have played on a soccer team, joined the drama club at school, or worked as part of a volunteer group in the community. By the time you became an adult, you had already been a member of many social groups—as you are now.

Group membership influences an individual consumer's purchase decisions and behavior in both overt and subtle ways. Every group establishes certain norms of behavior. **Norms** are the values, attitudes, and behaviors that a group deems appropriate for its members. Group members are expected to comply with these norms. Members of such diverse groups as the Harley Owners Group (H.O.G.), Friends of the Earth, and the local country club tend to adopt their organization's norms of behavior. Norms can even affect nonmembers. Individuals who aspire to membership in a group may adopt its standards of behavior and values.

Differences in group status and roles can also affect buying behavior. **Status** is the relative position of any individual member in a group; **roles** define behavior that members of a group expect of individuals who hold specific positions within that group. Some groups (such as the American Medical Association) define formal roles, and others (such as a book club among friends) impose informal expectations. Both types of groups supply each member with both status and roles; in doing so, they influence that person's activities—including his or her purchase behavior.

People often make purchases designed to reflect their status within a particular group. This is particularly true when the purchase is considered expensive by society. In the past few years, consumers considered affluent spent money on home redecorating and remodeling, as well as new cars. But the new norm for membership in the affluent group is the purchase of an experience, like a luxury cruise on the Mediterranean. "As you accumulate wealth, you don't need to buy another BMW," explains Scott Schroeder, president and CEO of marketing firm Cohorts. "Those needs are met, but the need for experience is deeper, and the market is reinventing itself and is responding to that."[16]

In a countertrend, some Americans have decided to simplify their lives by reducing their consumption drastically. A group of friends in San Francisco started the Compact, named after the Mayflower Compact, the agreement the Pilgrims made in 1620 to live by higher principles. Members of the modern Compact swear to buy nothing new but food, medicine, and toiletries. They shop at thrift stores, plant gardens, lend each other camping gear or other occasional-use items, and recycle and reuse whatever they can. The group now has a Web site on Yahoo! where members can sign up.[17]

One of the influences on consumer behavior is membership in a social group. Verizon promotes its unlimited "in" calling to other members of its service plan.

The Asch Phenomenon

Groups influence people's purchase decisions more than they realize. Most people adhere in varying degrees to the general expectations of any group that they consider important, often without conscious awareness. The surprising impact of groups and group norms on individual behavior has been called the **Asch phenomenon,** named after social psychologist S. E. Asch, who through his research first documented characteristics of individual behavior.

Asch found that individuals conformed to majority rule, even if that majority rule went against their beliefs. The Asch phenomenon can be a big factor in many purchase decisions, from major choices such as buying a car to deciding whether to buy a pair of shoes on sale.

Reference Groups

reference groups People or institutions whose opinions are valued and to whom a person looks for guidance in his or her own behavior, values, and conduct, such as family, friends, or celebrities.

Discussion of the Asch phenomenon raises the subject of **reference groups**—groups whose value structures and standards influence a person's behavior. Consumers usually try to coordinate their purchase behavior with their perceptions of the values of their reference groups. The extent of reference group influence varies widely among individuals. Strong influence by a group on a member's purchase requires two conditions:

1. The purchased product must be one that others can see and identify.

2. The purchased item must be conspicuous; it must stand out as something unusual, a brand or product that not everyone owns.

Reference group influence would significantly affect the decision to buy a luxury home in an upscale neighborhood, but probably wouldn't have an impact on the decision to buy a loaf of bread—unless that loaf of bread was purchased at a gourmet bakery. Reference group influence can affect the decision to buy a certain brand of athletic clothing or sports equipment, but probably not athletic socks. When millionaire Denis Tito paid the Russian Space agency $20 million in a highly publicized move, he created his own reference group—the first tourist in outer space. He spent a week at the International Space Station with the cosmonauts working there. "There's really nothing like it," Tito recalls. "I've had my dream." Closer to home, more than 300 wealthy individuals fork over $65,000 each year for the chance to climb the world's highest peak, Mt. Everest.[18]

Children are especially vulnerable to the influence of reference groups. They often base their buying decisions on outside forces such as what they see on television, opinions of friends, and fashionable products among adults. Advertising, especially endorsements by celebrities, can have even greater impacts on children than on adults, in part because children want so badly to belong to aspirational groups.[19]

Social Classes

W. Lloyd Warner's research identified six classes within the social structures of both small and large U.S. cities: the upper-upper, lower-upper, upper-middle, and lower-middle classes, followed by the working class and lower class. Class rankings are determined by occupation, income, education, family background, and residence location. Note that income is not always a primary factor; pipe fitters paid at union scale earn more than many college professors, but their purchase behavior may be quite different. Still, the ability to make certain purchases—such as a private jet or an ocean-view home—is an important factor in determining class.

Family characteristics, such as the occupations and incomes of one or both parents, have been the primary influences on social class. As women's careers and earning power have increased over the past few decades, marketers have begun to pay more attention to their position as influential buyers.

People in one social class may aspire to a higher class and therefore exhibit buying behavior common to that class rather than to their own. Middle-class consumers often buy items they associate with the upper classes. Marketers of certain luxury goods appeal to these consumers. Coach, Tiffany, and Bloomingdale's—all traditionally associated with high-end luxury goods—now offer their items in price ranges and locations accessible to middle-class consumers. Although the upper-income classes themselves account for a very small percentage of the population, many more consumers now treat themselves to prestigious products, such as antique carpets or luxury cars.

Marketers for exclusive credit cards now try to attract consumers in higher social classes by offering special services. They know that these consumers can buy whatever they want, so they try to differentiate themselves by offering unique benefits. Master-Card and Visa issue prestige cards that can get holders tickets to the Super Bowl or reserve tickets to the hottest shows on Broadway. The annual fees aren't staggering—only about $85—but applicants must earn at least $125,000 to receive the cards. The Centurion card from American Express is issued by invitation only and is so exclusive that details about it aren't available on the firm's Web site. Terms include an annual fee of $2,500 and required spending of $5,000 per month. American Express won't reveal the names of its cardhold-

IMAGE COURTESY OF THE ADVERTISING ARCHIVES

Luxury goods appeal to those aspiring to a higher social class.

ers, but a certain mystique surrounds the Centurion card, its members, and its privileges, which include complimentary companion airline tickets on transatlantic flights and personal shoppers at upscale stores such as Escada and Saks. And American Express isn't talking. "Our customers want to remain private and we want to maintain that this card is exclusive," says a spokesperson for American Express.[20]

opinion leaders Trendsetters who purchase new products before others in a group and then influence others in their purchases.

Opinion Leaders

In nearly every reference group, a few members act as **opinion leaders.** These trendsetters are likely to purchase new products before others in the group and then share their experiences and opinions via word of mouth. As others in the group decide whether to try the same products, they are influenced by the reports of opinion leaders.

Generalized opinion leaders are rare; instead, individuals tend to act as opinion leaders for specific goods or services based on their knowledge of and interest in those products. Their interest motivates them to seek out information from mass media, manufacturers, and other sources and, in turn, transmit this information to associates through interpersonal communications. Opinion leaders are found within all segments of the population.

Information about goods and services sometimes flows from the Internet, radio, television, and other mass media to opinion leaders and then from opinion leaders to others. In other instances, information flows directly from media sources to all consumers. In still other instances, a multistep flow carries information from mass media to opinion leaders and then on to other opinion leaders before dissemination to the general public. Figure 5.2 illustrates these three types of communication flow.

Some opinion leaders influence purchases by others merely through their own actions. Tour de France winner Lance Armstrong has influenced different types of purchases, ranging from bicycles to the yellow stretch bracelets sold to raise money for the Lance Armstrong Foundation, which supports cancer research. Consumers who purchase new bikes are opting for road bikes instead of the previously popular mountain bikes—often because of Armstrong's influence. But they aren't necessarily training to race like Armstrong did. Instead, they are riding for recreation.[21]

figure 5.2

Alternative Channels for Communications Flow

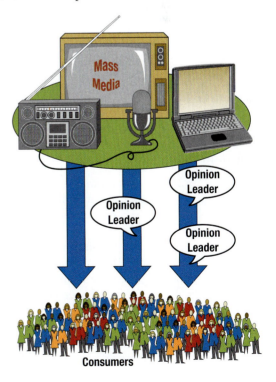

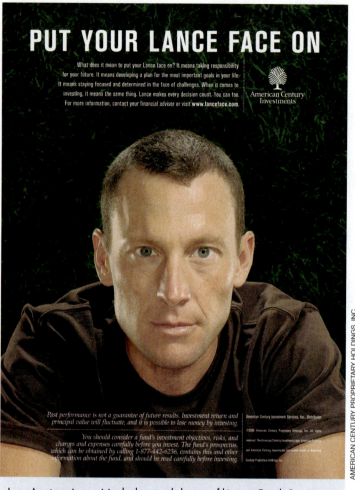

PUT YOUR LANCE FACE ON

What does it mean to put your Lance face on? It means taking responsibility for your future. It means developing a plan for the most important goals in your life. It means staying focused and determined in the face of challenges. When it comes to investing, it means the same thing. Lance makes every decision count. You can too. For more information, contact your financial advisor or visit www.lanceface.com.

American Century
Investments

Past performance is not a guarantee of future results. Investment return and principal value will fluctuate, and it is possible to lose money by investing.

American Century Investment Services, Inc., Distributor.

©2006 American Century Proprietary Holdings, Inc. All rights reserved. The American Century Investments logo, American Century and American Century Investments are service marks of American Century Proprietary Holdings, Inc.

You should consider a fund's investment objectives, risks, and charges and expenses carefully before you invest. The fund's prospectus, which can be obtained by calling 1-877-442-6236, contains this and other information about the fund, and should be read carefully before investing.

AMERICAN CENTURY PROPRIETARY HOLDINGS, INC.

Lance Armstrong is an opinion leader not only because of his seven Tour de France wins but also because he is a cancer survivor. Here American Century Investments encourages investors to take responsibility for their financial future by "putting their Lance face on."

FAMILY INFLUENCES

Most people are members of at least two families during their lifetimes—the ones they are born into and those they eventually form later in life. The family group is perhaps the most important determinant of consumer behavior because of the close, continuing interactions among family members. Like other groups, each family typically has norms of expected behavior and different roles and status relationships for its members. These influences may mean that what is considered appropriate in one family may be inappropriate in another, as in the case of violent video games described in the "Solving an Ethical Controversy" feature.

According to the U.S. Census Bureau, the structure of families has been steadily changing over the last century. In 1900, 80 percent of households were headed by married couples; today, only 53 percent are. A century ago, half of all households consisted of extended families, with six or more people living under one roof; today, only 10 percent of such households exist. Today, three of every five married women and 69 percent of single women work outside the home, as compared with 6 percent of married women and 44 percent of single women in the year 1900. In addition, the combined workweek of a husband and wife with children has increased from 59 hours in 1979 to 68 hours currently.[22] These statistics have important implications for marketers because they indicate a change in who makes buying decisions. Still, marketers describe the role of each spouse in terms of these four categories:

1. *Autonomic role* is seen when the partners independently make equal numbers of decisions. Personal-care items would fall into the category of purchase decisions each would make for himself or herself.

2. *Husband-dominant role* occurs when the husband usually makes certain purchase decisions. Buying a life insurance policy is a typical example.

3. *Wife-dominant role* has the wife making most of certain buying decisions. Children's clothing is a typical wife-dominant purchase.

4. *Syncratic role* refers to joint decisions. The purchase of a house follows a syncratic pattern.

The increasing occurrence of the two-income family means that women have a greater role in making family purchase decisions. Today, women have more say in large-ticket family purchases such as automobiles and computers. And studies show that women take the lead in choosing entertainment such as movies and restaurants.[23] Studies of family decision making have also shown that households with two wage earners are more likely than others to make joint purchasing decisions. Members of two-income households often do their shopping in the evening and on weekends because of the number of hours spent at the workplace, as mentioned earlier. Shifting family roles have created new markets for a variety of products. Goods and services that save time, promote family togetherness, emphasize safety, or encourage health and fitness appeal to the family values and influences of today.

Children and Teenagers in Family Purchases

Children and teenagers represent a huge market—more than 50 million strong—and they influence what their parents buy, from cereal to automobiles. These consumers are exposed to many marketing messages, and they are far more sophisticated than their parents or grandparents were at

Solving an Ethical Controversy

Kids, Parents, and Violent Video Games

Who buys and plays video games? Teenage boys are probably the biggest group of video game consumers. But adults—including the parents of children and teenagers—account for 35 percent of video game players. Eighty percent of these parents view video gaming as family entertainment instead of watching a movie or playing a round of Monopoly. But there is a darker side to video gaming. While many games are harmless, others contain violence and sexually explicit material. Some psychologists worry that prolonged exposure to images in these games can result in more violent, aggressive behavior by children and teens. Although there is a rating system, some game manufacturers allegedly circumvent it by embedding hidden images in their games. And children or teens have easy access to games that are intended for an adult audience.

Should there be stricter laws limiting the sale of video games?

PRO

1. Children are a vulnerable audience. "Generally, the research shows that violence in video games increases children's aggressive behavior and decreases their helpful behavior," notes psychologist Elizabeth Carli.
2. Playing a violent video game is more harmful than watching a violent television show. "If you are actively involved in learning, you remember things better," says Carli. "So in a game you do things over and over again, whereas in the movies or on television you watch it once. And in the game there is reinforcement for it. So if it is killing people that you're doing, you get a reward for that."

CON

1. Critics of the studies linking video games to aggressive behavior cite numerous flaws in the research. They claim that violence is part of mainstream entertainment in the United States, and other media should be examined just as closely.
2. Two-thirds of parents in one survey said that it is not the role of government to shield children from violent games—parents should take that responsibility.

Summary

Deciding not to wait for new federal laws, the City of Los Angeles recently sued the makers of the game Grand Theft Auto—San Andreas, which features characters who commit murder and make drug deals. The city alleges that Rockstar Games deliberately embedded a "minigame" within the larger game that allows characters to engage in explicit sexual acts. "Businesses have an obligation to truthfully disclose the content of their products—whether in the food we eat or the entertainment we consume," argues city attorney Rocky Delgadillo. Meanwhile, the American Psychological Association encourages parents to help educate their children to become more "media literate" so that they understand what they are seeing, playing, and doing.

Sources: "Attorney Sues 'Grand Theft Auto' Makers," Associated Press, January 27, 2006, http://news.yahoo.com; May Wong, "Survey: More Parents Playing Video Games," Associated Press, January 26, 2006, http://news.yahoo.com; Benjamin Radford, "Reality Check on Video Game Violence," Live Science, December 2005, http://www.livescience.com; Daniel DeNoon, "Psychologists Attack Violent Video Games," WebMD, August 19, 2005, http://www.webmd.com.

the same age. They also have greater influence over the goods and services their families purchase—in addition to the spending power they bring to their own purchases. Preteens and teens wield a whopping $192 billion in purchasing power each year, and marketers are taking notice. Individualism is a key trait among this consumer group. Apple appeals to teens' desire for individuality with the iPod—kids can load and play whatever music they want, whenever they want, by themselves. Threadless.com is a Web site where teens can create individualized T-shirts—instead of buying the same ones their friends have. PepsiCo created a line of drinks called Pepsi Blue, which it promotes by sponsoring events at places where teens like to gather, instead of promoting the line with television commercials.[24]

Even after they grow up, children continue to play roles in family consumer behavior. Studies show that 73 percent of people communicate with at least one family member every day—by phone, by e-mail, or in person. Sixty-five percent of adult children who have a living parent reside within an hour's drive of the parent. More than six in ten report that their most frequent contact is with their mother.[25] With this much communication taking place, conversation about goods or services such as cars, clothes, healthcare, lawn service, and vacations is likely to occur. Marketers can use these statistics to determine how to reach the most influential consumers in a family.

assessment check

1. List the interpersonal determinants of consumer behavior.
2. What is a subculture?
3. Describe the Asch phenomenon.

---

3 Explain each of the personal determinants of consumer behavior: needs and motives, perceptions, attitudes, learning, and self-concept theory.

PERSONAL DETERMINANTS OF CONSUMER BEHAVIOR

Consumer behavior is affected by a number of internal, personal factors in addition to interpersonal ones. Each individual brings unique needs, motives, perceptions, attitudes, learned responses, and self-concepts to buying decisions. This section looks at how these factors influence consumer behavior.

NEEDS AND MOTIVES

need Imbalance between a consumer's actual and desired states.

Individual purchase behavior is driven by the motivation to fill a perceived need. A **need** is an imbalance between the consumer's actual and desired states. A person who recognizes or feels a significant or urgent need then seeks to correct the imbalance. Marketers attempt to arouse this sense of urgency by making a need "felt" and then influencing consumers' motivation to satisfy their needs by purchasing specific products.

motive Inner state that directs a person toward the goal of satisfying a need.

Motives are inner states that direct a person toward the goal of satisfying a need. The individual takes action to reduce the state of tension and return to a condition of equilibrium.

Maslow's Hierarchy of Needs

Psychologist Abraham H. Maslow developed a theory that characterized needs and arranged them into a hierarchy. Maslow identified five levels of needs, beginning with physiological needs and progressing to the need for self-actualization. A person must at least partially satisfy lower-level needs, according to Maslow, before higher needs can affect behavior. In developed countries, where relatively large per-capita incomes allow most people to satisfy the basic needs on the hierarchy, higher-order needs may be more important to consumer behavior. Table 5.1 illustrates products and marketing themes designed to satisfy needs at each level.

Physiological Needs

Needs at the most basic level concern essential requirements for survival, such as food, water, shelter, and clothing. Pur promotes its water filtration system with the slogan, "Your water should be Pur." Its ads emphasize the need for clean water: "When you realize how often water touches your family's life, you discover just how important healthy, great-tasting water is."

Safety Needs

Second-level needs include security, protection from physical harm, and avoidance of the unexpected. To gratify these needs, consumers may buy disability insurance or security devices. Aetna, which provides a wide range of insurance products, uses the slogan "We want you to know." Its ads focus on the power of information in making educated insurance purchases.

Social/Belongingness Needs

Satisfaction of physiological and safety needs leads a person to attend to third-level needs—the desire to be accepted by people and groups important to that individual. To satisfy this need, people may join organizations and buy goods or services that make them feel part of a group. American Express

table 5.1		Marketing Strategies Based on Maslow's Hierarchy of Needs
PHYSIOLOGICAL NEEDS	*Products*	Vitamins, medicines, food, bottled water, exercise equipment
	Marketing themes	Bayer—"Science for a better life"; Puffs facial tissues—"A nose in need deserves Puffs indeed"; Ocean Spray cranberry juice—"Crave the wave"
SAFETY NEEDS	*Products*	Auto air bags, burglar alarm systems, retirement investments, insurance, computer antivirus software, smoke and carbon monoxide detectors
	Marketing themes	Fireman's Fund Insurance—"License to get on with it"; Internet Security Systems—"Ahead of the threat"; Volvo—"Protect the body. Ignite the soul."
BELONGINGNESS	*Products*	Beauty aids, entertainment, clothing, cars, clubs
	Marketing themes	Old Navy clothing—"Spring break from coast to coast"; Washington Mutual banks—"More human interest"; Marriott rewards—"Be here faster"
ESTEEM NEEDS	*Products*	Clothing, cars, jewelry, hobbies, beauty spa services
	Marketing Themes	Lexus automobiles—"The relentless pursuit of perfection"; Van Cleef & Arpels—"The pleasure of perfection"; Jenn-Air kitchen appliances—"The sign of a great cook"; Tag Heuer watches—"What are you made of?"
SELF-ACTUALIZATION	*Products*	Education, cultural events, sports, hobbies, luxury goods, technology, travel
	Marketing themes	Gatorade—"Is it in you?"; DePaul University—"Turning goals into accomplishments"; Dodge cars and trucks—"Grab life by the horns"; Southwest Airlines—"You are now free to move about the country"

advertises its Membership Rewards program, which features the ability to use its frequent-flyer points on almost any airline, as if it is an exclusive club.

Esteem Needs

People have a universal desire for a sense of accomplishment and achievement. They also wish to gain the respect of others and even to exceed others' performance once lower-order needs are satisfied. Las Vegas's luxury hotel Bellagio advertises with the slogan, "Look behind you. That's the pecking order."

Self-Actualization Needs

At the top rung of Maslow's ladder of human needs is people's desire to realize their full potential and to find fulfillment by expressing their unique talents and capabilities. Companies specializing in exotic adventure or educational trips aim to satisfy consumers' needs for self-actualization. Not-for-profit organizations that invite paying volunteers to assist in such projects as archaeological digs or building homes for the needy appeal to these needs as well. MasterCard's well-known "priceless" ads often feature the satisfaction of self-actualization needs.

Maslow noted that a satisfied need no longer has to be met. Once the physiological needs are met, the individual moves on to pursue satisfaction of higher-order needs. Consumers are periodically motivated by the need to relieve thirst and hunger, but their interests soon return to focus on satisfaction of safety, social, and other needs in the hierarchy. But people may not always progress through the hierarchy; they may fixate on a certain level. For example, consumers who live through an economic downturn may always be motivated to save money. Marketers can use this as an opportunity by offering money-saving goods and services.

Critics have pointed out a variety of flaws in Maslow's reasoning. For example, some needs can be related to more than one level, and not every individual progresses through the needs hierarchy in the same order; some bypass social and esteem needs and are motivated by self-actualization needs. But the hierarchy of needs can offer an effective guideline for marketers who want to study consumer behavior.

PERCEPTIONS

perception Meaning that a person attributes to incoming stimuli gathered through the five senses.

Perception is the meaning that a person attributes to incoming stimuli gathered through the five senses—sight, hearing, touch, taste, and smell. Certainly a buyer's behavior is influenced by his or her perceptions of a good or service. Researchers now recognize that people's perceptions depend as much on what they *want* to perceive as on the actual stimuli. For this reason, Nordstrom and Target are perceived differently, as are Godiva chocolates and Hershey bars. A person's perception of an object or event results from the interaction of two types of factors:

1. *Stimulus factors*—characteristics of the physical object such as size, color, weight, and shape

2. *Individual factors*—unique characteristics of the individual, including not only sensory processes but also experiences with similar inputs and basic motivations and expectations

Perceptual Screens

The average American consumer is constantly bombarded by marketing messages. According to the Food Marketing Institute, a typical supermarket now carries 30,000 different packages, each serving as a miniature billboard vying to attract consumers' attention. More than 6,000 commercials are aired on network TV each week. Prime-time TV shows on both network and cable stations carry more than fifteen minutes of advertising every hour.[26] Thousands of businesses have set up Web sites to tout their offerings, and supermarkets now display flat-panel screens with videos giving menu advice and preparation instructions in various departments and at the checkout. Marketers also stamp their messages on everything from popcorn bags in movie theaters to airsickness bags on planes.

This marketing clutter has caused consumers to ignore many promotional messages. People respond selectively to messages that manage to break through their **perceptual screens**—the mental filtering processes through which all inputs must pass. The proliferation of TV commercials has advertising researchers worried. "It may never be that commercials drive people away from the set, but it makes them pay less attention to avoid the irrelevant interruptions," says Tim Brooks, TV historian and research chief at the cable station Lifetime.[27]

All marketers struggle to determine which stimuli evoke positive responses from consumers. They must learn how to grab a consumer's attention long enough to watch a commercial, read an advertisement, listen to a sales pitch, or react to a point-of-purchase display. Marketers want their messages to stand out in the crowd.

One way to break through clutter is to run large ads. Doubling the size of an ad in printed media increases its attention value by about 50 percent. Other methods for enhancing contrast include arranging a large amount of white space around a printed area or placing white type on a dark background. Vivid illustrations and photos can also help to break through clutter in print ads. Using color creatively can help break through clutter. Color is so suggestive that its use on product packaging and logos is often the result of a long and careful process of selection. Red grabs the attention, and orange has been shown to stimulate appetite. Blue is associated with water—you'll find blue on cleaning products. Green connotes low-fat or healthful food products.

The psychological concept of closure also helps marketers create a

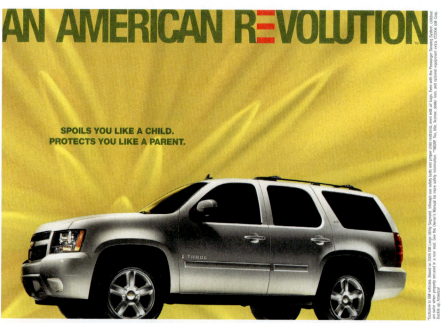

Chevy uses closure in its "An American Revolution" tag line. The bright ad also helps break through consumers' perceptual screens.

message that stands out. *Closure* is the human tendency to perceive a complete picture from an incomplete stimulus. Advertisements that allow consumers to do this often succeed in breaking through perceptual screens. In an ad campaign for its cars and trucks that includes the tag line, "AN AMERICAN REVOLUTION," Chevrolet marketers replaced the *E* in *REVOLUTION* with three red bars so that it appears to be an American flag. The word is still legible, as readers mentally change the bars into the letter. The effect is subtle, but it helps reinforce the "made in America" concept.

Word-of-mouth marketing can be another effective way to break through consumers' perceptual screens. Several brewing companies have recently revived older brands of beer that were once popular, such as Rheingold, Pabst Blue Ribbon (PBR), and Utica Club. Dubbed "retro beers," these brands are enjoying new life in the frosted mugs of the twentysomething generation. Marketers have decided that the best way to promote these beers is through word of mouth instead of a big ad campaign, which they fear would actually kill the buzz created by consumers themselves. "More than anything, we're just letting it go by word of mouth," says Fred Matt, vice president of Matt Brewing, which makes Utica Club in upstate New York.[28]

A new tool that marketers are exploring is the use of virtual reality. Some companies have created presentations based on virtual reality that display marketing messages and information in a three-dimensional format. Eventually, experts predict, consumers will be able to tour resort areas via virtual reality before booking their trips or to walk through the interiors of homes they are considering buying via virtual reality. Virtual reality technology may allow marketers to penetrate consumer perceptual filters in a way not currently possible with other forms of media.

With selective perception at work screening competing messages, it is easy to see the importance of marketers' efforts in developing brand loyalty. Satisfied customers are less likely to seek information about competing products. Even when competitive advertising is forced on them, they are less apt than others to look beyond their perceptual filters at those appeals. Loyal customers simply tune out information that does not agree with their existing beliefs and expectations.

Subliminal Perception

Almost 50 years ago, a New Jersey movie theater tried to boost concession sales by flashing the words *Eat Popcorn* and *Drink Coca-Cola* between frames of actress Kim Novak's image in the movie *Picnic*. The messages flashed on the screen every five seconds for a duration of one three-hundredth of a second each time. Researchers reported that these messages, though too short to be recognizable at the conscious level, resulted in a 58 percent increase in popcorn sales and an 18 percent increase in Coke sales. After the findings were published, advertising agencies and consumer protection groups became intensely interested in **subliminal perception**—the subconscious receipt of incoming information.

Subliminal advertising is aimed at the subconscious level of awareness to circumvent the audience's perceptual screens. The goal of the original research was to induce consumer purchases while keeping consumers unaware of the source of the motivation to buy. All later attempts to duplicate the test findings were unsuccessful. Although subliminal advertising is considered manipulative, it is exceedingly unlikely to induce purchasing except by people already inclined to buy. There are three reasons for this:

1. Strong stimulus factors are required just to get a prospective customer's attention.

2. Only a very short message can be transmitted.

3. Individuals vary greatly in their thresholds of consciousness. Messages transmitted at the threshold of consciousness for one person will not be perceived at all by some people and will be all too apparent to others. The subliminally exposed message "Drink Coca-Cola" may go unseen by some viewers, while others may read it as "Drink Pepsi-Cola," "Drink Cocoa," or even "Drive Slowly."

Despite the findings about subliminal advertising, however, neuroscientists do know that emotions—including those that a person may not be consciously aware of—play a vital role in decision making, and marketers are looking to find ways to elicit emotions that motivate people toward a purchase. *Neuromarketing* has already taken some concrete forms. Retailers such as Supervalu and Walgreens have adopted hypersonic sound technology, which beams commercials to individual customers in stores—say, when they are standing in the checkout line or in the cereal aisle. Magazine publisher Condé Nast used a patented metaphor elicitation technique from the firm Olson Zaltman—which uncovers unconscious associations in people's minds—to create its Point of Passion campaign for trade publications, billboards, and Internet messages.[29]

ATTITUDES

Perception of incoming stimuli is greatly affected by attitudes. In fact, a consumer's decision to purchase an item is strongly based on his or her attitudes about the product, store, or salesperson.

attitudes Person's enduring favorable or unfavorable evaluations, emotions, or action tendencies toward some object or idea.

Attitudes are a person's enduring favorable or unfavorable evaluations, emotions, or action tendencies toward some object or idea. As they form over time through individual experiences and group contacts, attitudes become highly resistant to change. New fees, a change in service hours, or other policy changes can be difficult for customers to accept. Because favorable attitudes likely affect brand preferences, marketers are interested in determining consumer attitudes toward their offerings. Numerous attitude-scaling devices have been developed for this purpose.

Attitude Components

An attitude has cognitive, affective, and behavioral components. The *cognitive* component refers to the individual's information and knowledge about an object or concept. The *affective* component deals with feelings or emotional reactions. The *behavioral* component involves tendencies to act in a certain manner. For example, in deciding whether to shop at a floor covering store, a consumer might obtain information about what the store offers from advertising, personal visits, and input from family, friends, and associates—the cognitive component. The consumer might also receive affective input by listening to others about their shopping experiences at this store. Other affective information might lead the person to make a judgment about the type of people who seem to shop there—whether they represent a group with which he or she would like to be associated. Then, the consumer may ultimately decide to have the store install carpet in the living room—the behavioral component. All three components maintain a relatively stable and balanced relationship to one another. Together, they form an overall attitude about an object or idea.

These influences on attitude confirm what one research firm found when it surveyed consumers about their choice of floor covering stores. The survey gave consumers five factors that might steer them toward one store or another. Nearly one-third said the greatest influence was having shopped at the store before, followed by word-of-mouth influence from family and friends at 26 percent. Having an accessible store location came in third at 12 percent, while advertising and liking the image created in the shop window each brought in 6 percent of the vote.[30]

Changing Consumer Attitudes

As a favorable consumer attitude provides a vital condition for marketing success, how can a firm lead prospective buyers to adopt such an attitude toward its products? Marketers have two choices:

Briefly
Speaking

"Treat your customers like they own you, because they do."

—Mark Cuban (b. 1958)
Co-founder, HDNet, and owner of the Dallas Mavericks NBA team

---

marketing success   Airlines Make Boarding Easier

Background. Everyone who has ever boarded a plane has been caught by that traffic jam in the aisle. As your seating row is called, you jostle with other passengers who "fight for control of overhead bins, pushing, shoving, hoisting and heaving huge, overstuffed bags into too little space," says the Association of Flight Attendants. There must be a better way, you think. United, Delta, America West, AirTran, and other airlines agree. And they're finally doing something about it.

The Challenge. Traditionally, most airlines—except Southwest, which does not assign seats—boarded passengers from back to front, according to their seat assignments. How could they find a better way to herd several dozen—or several hundred—people into a tight space quickly, smoothly, and efficiently?

The Strategy. United and America West now load passengers according to their seat letter—window passengers board first, then middle-seat fliers, then aisle-seat travelers. Passengers who are traveling together may board together. Delta and AirTran each uses a variation on the system. Southwest continues with its random seating and boarding plan.

(1) attempt to produce consumer attitudes that will motivate purchase of a particular product or (2) evaluate existing consumer attitudes and then make the product features appeal to them.

If consumers view an existing good or service unfavorably, the seller may redesign it or offer new options. Several airlines have decided to change the way they board passengers on flights, in an effort to change negative attitudes into positive ones, as described in the "Marketing Success" feature.

Or an attitude may not be unfavorable—just one that does not motivate the consumer toward a purchase. Wal-Mart marketers discovered that upscale consumers view the deals they get on peanut butter, paper towels, and laundry detergent at Wal-Mart as good, but they go elsewhere to purchase fine wine, jewelry, and high-end electronics. So in an effort to change these consumers' attitudes, Wal-Mart recently built a new store in Texas that caters specifically to them. This chic Wal-Mart Supercenter offers premium foods, clothing, electronics, housewares, and fitness products—along with a café wired for Wi-Fi Internet access, wider aisles, and restrooms decorated in faux marble. If the store succeeds, Wal-Mart will begin to add those items in existing stores in more affluent neighborhoods, and may even build more stores for its wealthy customers.[31]

Modifying the Components of Attitude

Attitudes frequently change in response to inconsistencies among the three components. The most common inconsistencies result when new information changes the cognitive or affective components of an attitude. Marketers can modify attitudes by providing evidence of product benefits and by correcting misconceptions. Marketers may also change attitudes by engaging buyers in new behavior. Free samples, for instance, can change attitudes by getting consumers to try a product.

Sometimes new technologies can encourage consumers to change their attitudes. Some people are reluctant to purchase clothing online because they are afraid it will not fit properly. To address these concerns, e-retailer Lands' End (now part of Sears) introduced a "virtual model" feature on its Web site. People who visit the site answer a series of questions about height, body proportions, and hair color, and the software creates a three-dimensional figure reflecting their responses. Consumers can then adorn the electronic model with Lands' End garments to get an idea of how various outfits might look on them. Of course, for the electronic model to be correct, shoppers must enter information about their bodies accurately instead of simply relying on their perception of themselves.

LEARNING

Marketing is concerned as seriously with the process by which consumer decisions change over time as with the current status of those decisions. **Learning,** in a marketing context, refers to immediate or expected changes in consumer behavior as a result of experience. The learning process includes the component of **drive,** which is any strong stimulus that impels action. Fear, pride, desire for money, thirst, pain avoidance, and rivalry are examples of drives. Learning also relies on a **cue**—that is, any

learning Knowledge or skill that is acquired as a result of experience, which changes consumer behavior.

The Outcome. United reports that boarding is now completed four or five minutes sooner than it was before the airline changed its procedure, which translates to $1 million in savings per year by reducing idle time for expensive aircraft. America West, which is now part of US Airways, says that the new process shaves about two minutes off the boarding time. The same holds true for the deboarding process. "From a customer's perspective, you obviously gain a tremendous benefit," says Sean Donohue, vice president of Ted, a subsidiary of United. "You can get off the airplane faster, and you can get on the airplane faster."

Sources: Jane Engle, "Much Carrying On about the Carry-Ons," *Chicago Tribune*, March 12, 2006, **http://www.chicagotribune.com**; Chris Walsh, "United to Halve Boarding Time," *Rocky Mountain News*, January 12, 2006, **http://www.rockymountainnews.com**; Roger Yu, "Airlines Change How They Herd Us Aboard," *USA Today*, January 10, 2006, p. B1.

object in the environment that determines the nature of the consumer's response to a drive. Examples of cues are a newspaper advertisement for a new Thai restaurant (a cue for a hungry person) and a Shell sign near an interstate highway (a cue for a motorist who needs gasoline).

A **response** is an individual's reaction to a set of cues and drives. Responses might include reactions such as purchasing Frontline flea and tick prevention for pets, dining at Quizno's, or deciding to enroll at a particular community college or university.

Reinforcement is the reduction in drive that results from a proper response. As a response becomes more rewarding, it creates a stronger bond between the drive and the purchase of the product, likely increasing future purchases by the consumer. Reinforcement is the rationale that underlies frequent-buyer programs, which reward repeat purchasers for their loyalty. These programs may offer points for premiums, frequent-flyer miles, and the like. However, so many companies now offer these programs that marketers must find ways to differentiate them. Zeroing in on a common complaint of consumers who try to redeem rewards points—that it takes too long to earn enough points for rewards of any real value—Citi introduced its "Thank You" program, which lowers the number of points required. Citi card holders may now receive electronics, travel, and gift certificates without having to earn so many points. In addition, Citi's Simplicity cards have no annual fee—unlike those of American Express and some Visa Extra cards.[32]

Applying Learning Theory to Marketing Decisions

Learning theory has some important implications for marketing strategists, particularly those involved with consumer packaged goods. Marketers must find a way to develop a desired outcome such as repeat purchase behavior gradually over time. **Shaping** is the process of applying a series of rewards and reinforcements to permit more complex behavior to evolve.

Both promotional strategy and the product itself play a role in the shaping process. Marketers want to motivate consumers to become regular buyers of certain merchandise. Their first step in getting consumers to try the product might be to offer a free-sample package that includes a substantial discount coupon for the next purchase. This example uses a cue as a shaping procedure. If the item performs well, the purchase response is reinforced and followed by another inducement—the coupon. The reason that a sample works so well is that it allows the consumer to try the product at no risk. "Trial reduces risk, the less risk the greater the certainty, the better satisfaction [a consumer] has with a product," explains Paul Hunt of the research and consulting firm Advantage Group. "The sample product provides a guarantee for the consumer."[33]

The second step is to entice the consumer to buy the item with little financial risk. The discount coupon enclosed with the free sample prompts this action. Suppose the package that the consumer purchases has still another, smaller discount coupon enclosed. Again, satisfactory product performance and the second coupon provide reinforcement.

The third step is to motivate the person to buy the item again at a moderate cost. A discount coupon accomplishes this objective, but this time the purchased package includes no additional coupon. The only reinforcement comes from satisfactory product performance.

The final test comes when the consumer decides whether to buy the item at its true price without a discount coupon. Satisfaction with product performance provides the only continuing reinforcement. Repeat purchase behavior is literally shaped by effective application of learning theory within a marketing strategy context.

Samples can help guide a consumer toward a purchase. Benjamin Moore provides two-ounce color samples of 260 of its colors to help consumers choose the perfect paint.

SELF-CONCEPT THEORY

The consumer's **self-concept**—a person's multifaceted picture of himself or herself—plays an important role in consumer behavior. Say a young woman views herself as bright, ambitious, and headed for a successful marketing career. She'll want to buy attractive clothes and jewelry to reflect that image of herself. Say an older man views himself as young for his age; he may purchase a sports car and stylish clothes to reflect his self-concept.

The concept of self emerges from an interaction of many of the influences—both personal and interpersonal—that affect buying behavior. A person's needs, motives, perceptions, attitudes, and learning lie at the core of his or her conception of self. In addition, family, social, and cultural influences affect self-concept.

A person's self-concept has four components: real self, self-image, looking-glass self, and ideal self. The *real self* is an objective view of the total person. The *self-image*—the way an individual views himself or herself—may distort the objective view. The *looking-glass self*—the way an individual thinks others see him or her—may also differ substantially from self-image because people often choose to project different images to others than their perceptions of their real selves. The *ideal self* serves as a personal set of objectives, because it is the image to which the individual aspires. When making purchasing decisions, consumers are likely to choose products that move them closer to their ideal self-images.

self-concept Person's multifaceted picture of himself or herself.

✓ *assessment check*

1. Identify the personal determinants of consumer behavior.
2. What are the human needs categorized by Abraham Maslow?
3. How do perception and learning differ?

THE CONSUMER DECISION PROCESS

4 Distinguish between high-involvement and low-involvement purchase decisions.

Although they might not be aware of it, consumers complete a step-by-step process in making purchasing decisions. The time and effort devoted to a particular purchasing decision depend on how important it is.

Purchases with high levels of potential social or economic consequences are said to be **high-involvement purchase decisions.** Buying a car, purchasing a condominium, or deciding where to go to college are examples of high-involvement decisions. Routine purchases that pose little risk to the consumer are **low-involvement purchase decisions.** Purchasing a candy bar from a vending machine is a good example.

Consumers generally invest more time and effort in buying decisions for high-involvement products than in those for low-involvement products. A home buyer will visit a number of listings, compare asking prices, apply for a mortgage, have the selected house inspected, and even have friends or family members visit the home before signing the final papers. Few buyers invest that much effort in choosing a brand of orange juice at the supermarket. Believe it or not, though, they will still go through the steps of the consumer decision process—but on a more compressed scale.

Figure 5.3 shows the six steps in the consumer decision process. First, the consumer recognizes a problem or unmet need, searches for appropriate goods or services, and evaluates the alternatives before making a purchase decision. The next step is the actual purchase.

PRNEWSFOTO/WM. WRIGLEY JR. COMPANY

Chewing gum is an example of a low-involvement purchase.

assessment check

1. Differentiate between high-involvement decisions and low-involvement decisions.

2. Categorize each of the following as a high- or low-involvement product: shampoo, computer, popcorn, apartment, cell phone service.

After buying the item, the consumer evaluates whether he or she made the right choice. Much of marketing involves steering consumers through the decision process in the direction of a specific product.

Consumers apply the decision process in solving problems and taking advantage of opportunities. Such decisions permit them to correct differences between their actual and desired states. Feedback from each decision serves as additional experience in helping guide subsequent decisions.

PROBLEM OR OPPORTUNITY RECOGNITION

5 Outline the steps in the consumer decision process.

During the first stage in the decision process, the consumer becomes aware of a significant discrepancy between the existing situation and a desired situation. You have experienced this yourself. Perhaps you open the refrigerator door and find little food there. By identifying the problem—not enough food in the refrigerator—you can resolve it with a trip to the grocery store. Sometimes the problem is more specific. You might have a full refrigerator, but no mustard or mayonnaise for sandwiches. This problem requires a solution as well.

Suppose you are unhappy with a particular purchase—say, a brand of cereal. The cereal might be too sweet or too crunchy. Or maybe you just want a change from the same old cereal every morning. This is the recognition of another type of problem or opportunity—the desire for change.

What if you just got a raise at work? You might decide to splurge on dinner at a restaurant. Or you might want to try a gourmet prepared take-home dinner from the supermarket. Both dinners are more expensive than the groceries you have always bought, but now they are within financial reach. The marketer's main task during this phase of the decision-making process is to help prospective buyers identify and recognize potential problems or needs. This task may take the form of advertising, promotions, or personal sales assistance. A supermarket employee might suggest appetizers or desserts to accompany the gourmet take-home dinner.

SEARCH

figure 5.3

Integrated Model of the Consumer Decision Process

Source: Roger Blackwell, Paul W. Miniard, and James F. Engel, *Consumer Behavior*, 10th ed. (Mason, OH: South-Western, 2006).

During the second step in the decision process, a consumer gathers information about the attainment of a desired state of affairs. This search identifies different ways to solve the problem. A high-involvement purchase might mean conducting an extensive search for information, whereas a low-involvement purchase might require much less research.

The search may cover internal or external sources of information. An internal search is simply a mental review: Is there past experience with the product? Was it good or bad? An external search involves gathering information from all kinds of outside sources—for instance, family, friends, co-workers or classmates, advertisements or salespeople, online reviews, and consumer

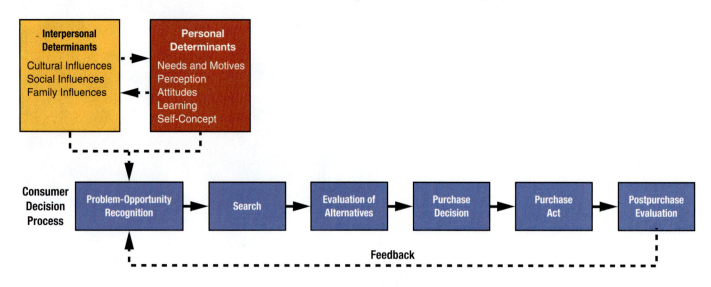

magazines. Because conducting an external search requires time and effort, it is usually done for high-involvement purchases.

The search identifies alternative brands or models for consideration and possible purchase. The number of alternatives that a consumer actually considers in making a purchase decision is known in marketing as the **evoked set.** In some searches, consumers already know of the brands that merit further consideration; in others, their external searches develop such information. The number of brands included in the evoked set vary depending on both the situation and the person. An immediate need—such as filling a nearly empty gas tank during a road trip—might limit the evoked set. But a driver with half a tank of gas, with more time to make a decision, might expand the evoked set to choose from a broader range of options.

Consumers now choose among more alternative products than ever before. This variety can confuse and complicate the analysis that narrows the range of choices. Instead of comparing one or two brands, a consumer often faces a dizzying array of brands and subbrands. Products that once included only regular and decaffeinated coffee are now available in many different forms—cappuccino, latte, skinny latte, flavored coffee, espresso, and iced coffee, just to name a few possibilities. Recognizing this—and wanting to help consumers find their way through the maze of choices—some firms have set up online shopping sites where consumers can compare products. Yahoo! has a site with free pricing guides and other points of comparison for products in many categories. Consumers love it because they can visit one site and make side-by-side comparisons anytime, anywhere. "We are entering a new era [in comparison shopping]," says the general manager of Yahoo's shopping site. "Now, we are all trying to figure out ways to differentiate ourselves."[34]

evoked set Number of alternatives that a consumer actually considers in making a purchase decision.

EVALUATION OF ALTERNATIVES

The third step in the consumer decision process is to evaluate the evoked set of options. Actually, it is difficult to completely separate the second and third steps because some evaluation takes place as the search progresses; consumers accept, distort, or reject information as they receive it. For example, knowing that you are looking for a new jacket, your roommate might tell you about this great new apparel store she visited recently. But you don't particularly like her taste in clothes, so you reject the information, even though the store might have some nice things.

The outcome of the evaluation stage is the choice of a brand or product in the evoked set, or possibly a decision to keep looking for alternatives. To complete this analysis, the consumer must develop a set of evaluative criteria to guide the selection. **Evaluative criteria** are the features that a consumer considers in choosing among alternatives. These criteria can either be objective facts (government tests of an automobile's miles-per-gallon rating) or subjective impressions (a favorable view of American Eagle clothing). Common criteria include price, brand name, and country of origin. Evaluative criteria can vary with the consumer's age, income level, social class, and culture; what's important to a senior citizen might not matter at all to a college student. If you were in the market for a flat panel TV, your criteria might include price and brand name. A Samsung 50-inch HDTV sells for as much as $2,500 retail. But a Vizio TV sells for much less. You must decide which is most important to you—the known brand name of Samsung or the lower price offered by Vizio's maker.[35]

evaluative criteria Features that a consumer considers in choosing among alternatives.

Marketers attempt to influence the outcome of this stage in three ways. First, they try to educate consumers about attributes that they view as important in evaluating a particular class of goods. They also identify which evaluative criteria are important to an individual and attempt to show why a specific brand fulfills those criteria. Finally, they try to induce a customer to expand the evoked set to include the product being marketed.

PURCHASE DECISION AND PURCHASE ACT

The search and alternative evaluation stages of the decision process result in the purchase decision and the actual purchase. At this stage, the consumer has evaluated each alternative in the evoked set based on his or her personal set of evaluative criteria, and narrowed the alternatives down to one.

The consumer then decides where—or from whom—to make the purchase. Sometimes this decision is part of the evaluation; perhaps one seller is offering a better price or better warranty than another. The purchase may be made online or in person at a retail store. The delivery options might also influence the decision of where to purchase an item. For example, a local electronics store might deliver your flat panel TV for free, whereas an online retailer might charge $50 for delivery.

Etiquette Tips for Marketing Professionals

Handling Angry Customers

Part of building healthy, long-lasting relationships with customers is learning how to deal with them when they are dissatisfied or downright irate about the quality of goods and services they have received. Regardless of what kind of business you are in, at some point you will probably encounter someone who is upset. If you take a deep breath and follow these tips, you may find that you can handle the situation better than you thought you could. If all goes well, you may even strengthen your firm's relationship with that particular customer.

1. *Remain calm.* This is the most important rule for handling just about any interaction. Keep in mind that the customer isn't upset at you, personally—just frustrated with a product. If you respond to someone's anger by getting angry yourself, the situation will only get worse. So keep cool, and the other person may cool down more quickly as well.

2. *Be respectful.* Be polite and respectful of the other person's feelings and state of mind. If you remain calm and considerate, you can help the customer focus specifically on the problem at hand.

3. *Listen carefully.* Everyone wants to be heard. Ask the customer to describe the problem to you. Listen carefully, and take notes if possible. As the person talks, he or she may begin to calm down.

4. *Confirm the problem.* When you think the customer has finished describing the complaint, repeat it back so you are sure you understand completely. Simply say, "Let me make sure I have understood you correctly," and restate the problem.

5. *Take responsibility for the next step.* If you have the authority to solve the problem, tell the customer exactly what you are going to do and when. If you do not have the authority, say so—and then explain what the next step will be. If at all possible, promise to follow the problem through to its solution, even if you are not able to make the correction yourself. A follow-up call to make sure the problem is resolved—and the customer is satisfied—is one more step toward building a lifelong relationship.

Sources: "Telephone Etiquette Guide," California State University–Fullerton, **http://www.fullerton.edu**, accessed March 14, 2006; Gene Mage, "How to Deal with an Enraged Customer," *Making It Work*, **http://www.makingitwork.com**, accessed March 14, 2006; Nancy Friedman, "Strategies for Handling Irate Callers," *Networking Today*, **http://www.networkingtoday.ca**, accessed March 14, 2006.

POSTPURCHASE EVALUATION

The purchase act produces one of two results. The buyer feels either satisfaction at the removal of the discrepancy between the existing and desired states or dissatisfaction with the purchase. Consumers are generally satisfied if purchases meet—or exceed—their expectations.

cognitive dissonance
Imbalance among knowledge, beliefs, and attitudes that occurs after an action or decision, such as a purchase.

Sometimes, however, consumers experience some postpurchase anxieties called **cognitive dissonance.** This anxiety results from an imbalance among a person's knowledge, beliefs, and attitudes. You might experience some dissonance once your flat panel TV is delivered if you can't figure out how to use it, if you are worried about spending too much money, or if you discover that the one you chose doesn't have all the features you thought it had. You might decide to complain to the seller if you are dissatisfied with your purchase, as discussed in the "Etiquette Tips for Marketing Professionals" feature.

Dissonance is likely to increase (1) as the dollar value of a purchase increases, (2) when the rejected alternatives have desirable features that the chosen alternatives do not provide, and (3) when the purchase decision has a major effect on the buyer. In other words, dissonance is more likely with high-involvement purchases than with those that require low involvement. If you buy a diet soda and don't like the flavor, you can toss it and buy a different one. But if you have spent more than

$1,000 on a flat panel TV and you aren't satisfied with it, you will most likely experience dissonance. You might try to reduce the dissonance by focusing on good reviews about your choice or show a friend all the neat features on your TV—without pointing out anything you find dissatisfactory. Or you might read ads for your selected brand while ignoring advertisements for the one you didn't choose.

Marketers can help buyers reduce cognitive dissonance by providing information that supports the chosen item. Automobile dealers recognize the possibility of "buyer's remorse" and often follow up purchases with letters or telephone calls from dealership personnel offering personal attention to any customer problems. Advertisements that stress customer satisfaction also help reduce cognitive dissonance.

A final method of dealing with cognitive dissonance is to change products. The consumer may ultimately decide that one of the rejected alternatives would have been the best choice and vows to purchase that item in the future. Marketers may capitalize on this with advertising campaigns that focus on the benefits of their products or with tag lines that say something like, "If you're unhappy with them, try us." But making a different choice isn't always an option, particularly if the item requires a large investment in time and money. Homebuyers who decide they are not satisfied with their purchase once they move in usually can't change options quickly or easily, so they must find another way to reduce dissonance.

Sunglass Hut, owned by Luxotica Group, helps reduce cognitive dissonance after purchase by offering its unconditional guarantee to exchange both nonprescription and prescription sunglasses for 30 days until customers are satisfied—or they can get their money back.

CLASSIFYING CONSUMER PROBLEM-SOLVING PROCESSES

As mentioned earlier, the consumer decision processes for different products require varying amounts of problem-solving efforts. Marketers recognize three categories of problem-solving behavior: routinized response, limited problem solving, and extended problem solving. The classification of a particular purchase within this framework clearly influences the consumer decision process.

 assessment check

1. List the steps in the consumer decision process.
2. What is meant by the term *evoked set*?
3. What are evaluative criteria?

Routinized Response Behavior

Consumers make many purchases routinely by choosing a preferred brand or one of a limited group of acceptable brands. This type of rapid consumer problem solving is referred to as **routinized response behavior.** A routine purchase of the same brand of dog food or the renewal of a magazine subscription are examples. The consumer has already set evaluative criteria and identified available options. External search is limited in such cases, which characterize extremely low-involvement products.

Limited Problem Solving

Consider the situation in which the consumer has previously set evaluative criteria for a particular kind of purchase but then encounters a new, unknown brand. The introduction of a new shampoo is an example of a **limited problem-solving** situation. The consumer knows the evaluative criteria for the product, but has not applied these criteria to assess the new brand. Such situations demand

6 Differentiate among routinized response behavior, limited problem solving, and extended problem solving by consumers.

moderate amounts of time and effort for external searches. Limited problem solving is affected by the number of evaluative criteria and brands, the extent of external search, and the process for determining preferences. Consumers making purchase decisions in this product category are likely to feel involvement in the middle of the range.

 assessment check

1. What is routinized response behavior?
2. What does limited problem solving require?
3. Give an example of an extended problem-solving situation.

Extended Problem Solving

Extended problem solving results when brands are difficult to categorize or evaluate. The first step is to compare one item with similar ones. The consumer needs to understand the product features before evaluating alternatives. Most extended problem-solving efforts involve lengthy external searches. High-involvement purchase decisions—cars, homes, and colleges—usually require extended problem solving.

Strategic Implications of Marketing in the 21st Century

Marketers who plan to succeed with today's consumers need to understand how their potential market behaves. Cultural influences play a big role in marketers' relationships with consumers, particularly as firms conduct business on a global scale but also as they try to reach diverse populations in the United States. In addition, family characteristics are changing—more women are in the workforce—which forecasts a change in the way families make purchasing decisions. Perhaps the most surprising shift in family spending is the amount of power—and money—children and teenagers now wield in the marketplace. These young consumers are becoming more and more involved, and in some cases know more about certain products, such as electronics, than their parents do, and very often influence purchase decisions. This holds true even with high-involvement purchases such as SUVs.

Marketers constantly work toward changing or modifying components of consumers' attitudes about their products to gain a favorable attitude and purchase decision. Finally, they refine their understanding of the consumer decision process and use their knowledge to design effective marketing strategies.

REVIEW OF CHAPTER OBJECTIVES

1 Define *consumer behavior* and describe the role it plays in marketing decisions.

Consumer behavior refers to the buyer behavior of individual consumers. Consumer behavior plays a huge role in marketing decisions, including what goods and services to offer, to whom, and where. If marketers can understand the factors that influence consumers, they can develop and offer the right products to those consumers.

2 Describe the interpersonal determinants of consumer behavior: cultural, social, and family influences.

Cultural influences, such as the general work ethic or the desire to accumulate wealth, come from society. Core values may vary from culture to culture. Group or social influences include social class, opinion leaders, and reference groups with which consumers may want to be affiliated. Family influences may come from parents, grandparents, or children.

3   Explain each of the personal determinants of consumer behavior: needs and motives, perceptions, attitudes, learning, and self-concept theory.

A need is an imbalance between a consumer's actual and desired states. A motive is the inner state that directs a person toward the goal of satisfying a need. Perception is the meaning that a person attributes to incoming stimuli gathered through the five senses. Attitudes are a person's enduring favorable or unfavorable evaluations, emotions, or action tendencies toward something. In self-concept theory, a person's view of himself or herself plays a role in purchasing behavior. In purchasing goods and services, people are likely to choose products that move them closer to their ideal self-images.

4   Distinguish between high-involvement and low-involvement purchase decisions.

Purchases with high levels of potential social or economic consequences are called high-involvement purchase decisions. Examples include buying a new car or home. Routine purchases that pose little risk to the consumer are called low-involvement purchase decisions. Choosing a candy bar or a newspaper are examples.

5   Outline the steps in the consumer decision process.

The consumer decision process consists of six steps: problem or opportunity recognition, search, alternative evaluation, purchase decision, purchase act, and postpurchase evaluation. The time involved in each stage of the decision process is determined by the nature of the individual purchases.

6   Differentiate among routinized response behavior, limited problem solving, and extended problem solving by consumers.

Routinized response behavior refers to repeat purchases made of the same brand or limited group of items. Limited problem solving occurs when a consumer has previously set criteria for a purchase but then encounters a new brand or model. Extended problem solving results when brands are difficult to categorize or evaluate. High-involvement purchase decisions usually require extended problem solving.

✓ *assessment check* **answers**

1.1   Why is the study of consumer behavior important to marketers?

If marketers can understand the behavior of consumers, they can offer the right products to consumers who want them.

1.2   Describe Kurt Lewin's proposition.

Kurt Lewin proposed that behavior (*B*) is the function (*f*) of the interactions of personal influences (*P*) and pressures exerted by outside environmental forces (*E*). This research sheds light on how consumers make purchase decisions.

2.1   List the interpersonal determinants of consumer behavior.

The interpersonal determinants of consumer behavior are cultural, social, and family influences.

2.2   What is a subculture?

A subculture is a group within a culture that has its own distinct mode of behavior.

2.3   Describe the Asch phenomenon.

The Asch phenomenon is the impact of groups and group norms on individual behavior.

assessment check **answers**

3.1   Identify the personal determinants of consumer behavior.

The personal determinants of consumer behavior are needs and motives, perceptions, attitudes, learning, and self-concept theory.

3.2   What are the human needs categorized by Abraham Maslow?

The human needs categorized by Abraham Maslow are physiological, safety, social/belongingness, esteem, and self-actualization.

3.3   How do perception and learning differ?

Perception is the meaning that a person attributes to incoming stimuli. Learning refers to immediate or expected changes in behavior as a result of experience.

4.1   Differentiate between high-involvement decisions and low-involvement decisions.

High-involvement decisions have high levels of potential social or economic consequences, such as selecting an Internet service provider. Low-involvement decisions pose little financial, social, or emotional risk to the buyer, such as a newspaper or gallon of milk.

4.2   Categorize each of the following as a high- or low-involvement product: shampoo, computer, popcorn, apartment, cell phone service.

High-involvement products are the computer, apartment, and cell phone service. Low-involvement products are the shampoo and popcorn.

5.1   List the steps in the consumer decision process.

The steps in the consumer decision process are problem or opportunity recognition, search, alternative evaluation, purchase decision, purchase act, and postpurchase evaluation.

5.2   What is meant by the term *evoked set*?

The evoked set is the number of alternatives that a consumer actually considers in making a purchase decision.

5.3   What are evaluative criteria?

Evaluative criteria are the features that a consumer considers in choosing among alternatives.

6.1   What is routinized response behavior?

Routinized response behavior is the repeated purchase of the same brand or limited group of products.

6.2   What does limited problem solving require?

Limited problem solving requires a moderate amount of a consumer's time and effort.

6.3   Give an example of an extended problem solving situation.

An extended problem solving situation might involve the purchase of a car or a college education.

MARKETING TERMS YOU NEED TO KNOW

consumer behavior 148
culture 149
reference groups 154
opinion leaders 155
need 158

motive 158
perception 160
attitudes 162
learning 163
self-concept 165

evoked set 167
evaluative criteria 167
cognitive dissonance 168

OTHER IMPORTANT MARKETING TERMS

subcultures 150	perceptual screen 160	shaping 164
acculturation 151	subliminal perception 161	high-involvement purchase decision 165
norms 153	drive 163	low-involvement purchase decision 165
status 153	cue 163	routinized response behavior 169
roles 153	response 164	limited problem solving 169
Asch phenomenon 154	reinforcement 164	extended problem solving 170

ASSURANCE OF LEARNING REVIEW

1. Why is it important for marketers to understand cultural influences in the countries where they plan to market their goods and services?
2. Describe a subculture with which you are familiar.
3. Choose a group that you identify with or are a member of. Identify the norms of that group. What is your status in the group? What is your role?
4. Identify and describe the four categories of roles that spouses can play in making purchase decisions.
5. Describe the two factors that interact to create a person's perception of an object. How is this important for marketers?
6. What is subliminal perception? Is it an effective marketing tool? Why or why not?
7. What is shaping? How would you use shaping to motivate consumers toward a new type of skin care made with vitamins and minerals?
8. Describe the problem or opportunity recognition stage of a recent purchase you made. How did it lead you to the next step?
9. Suppose you were going to look for a new place to live next year. What would be your evaluative criteria?
10. Why is it important for marketers to recognize into which category of problem solving their goods and services fall?

PROJECTS AND TEAMWORK EXERCISES

1. Choose a partner. Each of you should think about your participation in family purchases. How much influence do you have on your family's decisions? Has this influence changed over time? Why or why not? Compare your answers with those of your partner.
2. With a classmate, watch a half hour of television or go to a place on the Internet where you may find advertisements. Of all the advertisements you see in that time period, note which one made the greatest impression on you, and describe why it did. (Did you remember the product? The slogan? The background music? The spokesperson?) Compare your response with your classmate's.
3. With a classmate, select a good or service that may have suffered from a poor image recently—it may have performed poorly in the public eye or simply gone out of style. Think about how you would go about changing consumers' attitudes toward the product, and present your plan to the class.
4. On your own or with a classmate, select a print advertisement and identify its cognitive, affective, and behavioral components as well as your attitude toward the advertisement. Discuss the advertisement with your class.
5. Choose a partner and select a low-involvement, routinized consumer product such as toothpaste or detergent. Create an ad that you think could stimulate consumers to change their preferred brand to yours.

CRITICAL-THINKING EXERCISES

1. Describe what you think the core values of U.S. culture are. Do you share all of those values? Why or why not?
2. Describe a good or service toward which you have changed your attitude. What influences caused you to make the change? If you haven't experienced a change, describe a good or service toward which you have a strong attitude—and how marketers might be able to change your attitude.
3. Describe a recent high-involvement purchase that you made. What and who influenced the purchase? On Maslow's hierarchy, what needs did you think the purchase would satisfy? Were those needs actually satisfied? Why or why not?
4. Outline three of the four components of your self-concept: self-image, looking-glass self, and ideal self. How close do you think these are to your real self?
5. Think about a purchase that created cognitive dissonance within you after the purchase was made. How did you resolve the anxiety created by the purchase?

ETHICS EXERCISE

Marketing directly to children has become a controversial strategy because there are so many different ways to influence children—through their families and their friends, at school, and through media ranging from TV to the Internet. But children and teens wield a great deal of spending power—almost $200 billion each year—so marketers are naturally tempted to aim many messages at them. Using what you know about consumer behavior, evaluate an advertisement or commercial that is clearly aimed at this young group of consumers.

1. Who would be the reference group that children might aspire to in their purchase of the product in the ad? In Maslow's hierarchy, what needs might the product satisfy?
2. Might the ad mislead children in any way? If so, how?
3. How would you evaluate this advertisement from an ethical standpoint?

INTERNET EXERCISES

1. **Targeting Hispanic consumers**. As noted in the chapter, Hispanics make up a growing percentage of American consumers. Review the material on Hispanic consumers in Chapter 5 and then complete the following exercises.
   a. The U.S. Census Bureau is a major source of demographic data. Visit the Bureau's Web site (http://www.census.gov). Click on *People & Households* and then *Hispanic Origin*. Review the data tables from the most recent surveys. Prepare a summary comparing the age distribution, population growth rate, and income of Hispanics with non-Hispanics.
   b. Select a major consumer products or food company, such as General Mills (http://www.generalmills.com), Tyson Foods (http://www.tyson.com), or Unilever (http://www.unilever.com). Write a report summarizing the company's efforts to target this important consumer segment.
   c. HispanoClick.com is one of many marketing research and consulting firms that helps other companies market to His-

   panics. Visit the Web site (http://www.hispanoclick.com) and review the services offered by HispanoClick.com. How does the firm help clients market to each of the three major acculturation groups of Hispanics?

2. **Consumer decision process**. Assume you're in the market for each of the following products. Follow the first three steps in the consumer decision process model shown in the text (problem-opportunity recognition, search, and evaluation of alternatives). Use the Web to aid in your decision process. For which of the three products did you find the Web the most helpful? The least helpful?
   a. A new or used vehicle.
   b. A notebook computer.
   c. A vacation in Maui.

Note: Internet Web addresses change frequently. If you don't find the exact site listed, you may need to access the organization's home page and search from there or use a search engine such as Google.

CASE 5.1   Burger King's Whopper-Sized Portions

Burger King is bucking a trend. While other chain restaurants are catering to health- and fitness-conscious diners, Burger King is serving up meals to those who want their food filled with the flavors that only fat and salt can provide. Under pressure from the media and consumer advocacy groups as the biggest fast-food restaurant, McDonald's is trying to appease critics with more healthful menu offerings. Applebee's—which offers both eat-in and take-out meals—has joined forces with Weight Watchers to offer meals for consumers who want to trim their waistlines. But Burger King feels no such pressure. Instead, the company has

figured out who eats at Burger King and what they want. And it intends to serve it to them.

Choosing where and what to eat may not seem like a huge decision, but it involves a number of factors. Consumers may be influenced by cost, by their friends and family, by the location of the restaurant and how much time the meal will take, and by their perception of or attitude toward the restaurant and its food. Thinking that its customers wanted a low-fat menu, Burger King struggled to sell several such items before changing course altogether. A marketing survey revealed that although only 18 percent of the population called themselves regular fast-food eaters, these customers accounted for 49 percent of Burger King's business. Company executives call them Super Fans—men age 18 to 34 who are avid football fans and whose "gray collar" jobs aren't the most important aspect of their lives. These guys like spicy chicken sandwiches smothered in pepperjack cheese and jalapeños. They want a hot jolt of joe in the morning, so Burger King has introduced a new brand of coffee with 40 percent caffeine. And they are downing the 760-calorie Enormous Omelet Sandwich—no less than two omelets and cheese slices, three strips of bacon, and a sausage patty in a bun—in record numbers. "It's designed for people who like to start the day with a hearty breakfast," remarks Denny Post, chief product officer for Burger King. Priced at $2.99, it seems like a bargain. The new omelet sandwich has helped increase breakfast sales 20 percent.

Burger King hasn't stopped there. In conjunction with the launch of Universal Pictures' *King Kong* film, Burger King offered up a new Triple Whopper. With three beef patties, American cheese, lettuce, tomato, ketchup, mayonnaise, pickles, and onions on a bun, the new sandwich weighs in at a monstrous 1,230 calories and 82 grams of fat. Long after the movie went to DVD, burger fans are still loving the Triple Whopper. The sandwich sells for around $3.99, but that's still much less than a burger would cost at the average eat-in restaurant. Why do people love these high-calorie, high-fat foods? They taste good.

Another reason that Burger King is so hot these days is that people's busy schedules have only gotten busier. A mom who picks up her kids at soccer practice at 6:30 P.M. doesn't have time to cook dinner. A young professional who usually works through lunch doesn't have time to go to a restaurant. A carpenter whose job starts at 7:00 A.M. doesn't have time for a home-cooked breakfast. "People used to eat three squares," explains Dennis Lombardi, a food consultant. "But traditional eating patterns no longer exist." So Burger King is reaching for consumers who need to eat on the run. That means meals as well as snacks—which may also turn into meals. One survey discovered that 20 years ago, 45 percent of consumers said they did not eat snacks. Today, only 26 percent fall into this category. To meet this demand, Burger King introduced chicken fries—spicy, four-inch-long fried sticks made of white-meat chicken. Served in a cardboard box, they look like a combination of chicken fingers and french fries.

The fast-food industry reaps roughly $135 billion a year feeding U.S. consumers, which means that despite nutrition-centered criticism from some groups, consumers like what they are being served. Burger King has figured out who its customers are and what they like to eat, and customers drive the business.

Questions for Critical Thinking

1. What factors are involved in your own decisions about where and what to eat? Is this usually a high-involvement or low-involvement decision? Where do you eat most often? Why?

2. Do you think Burger King is making a good marketing decision to focus essentially on one group of consumers—the Super Fans? Why or why not?

Sources: Bruce Horovitz, "Burger King Gets New CEO as IPO Nears," *USA Today*, April 10, 2006, p. 7B; Michael S. Rosenwald, "Why America Has to Be Fat," *Washington Post*, January 22, 2006, **http://www.washingtonpost.com**; "Burger King Launches King-Size Meal," AllBusiness, January 3, 2006, **http://www.allbusiness.com**; "Triple Whopper: Portion Fit for King Kong," Diet-Blog, December 30, 2005, **http://www.diet-blog.com**; Amy Johannes, "Burger King Launches Gorilla-Sized Burger for *King-Kong* Tie-In," *Promo*, December 15, 2005, **http://promomagazine.com**; Bruce Horovitz, "Marketers Cash in as Nation Bellies Up to Snack Bar," *USA Today*, June 8, 2005, **http://www.usatoday.com**; Bret Beun, "A Really Big Idea," *Newsweek*, May 23, 2005, p. 48; "A BIG Breakfast at Burger King," CNN Money.com, March 29, 2005, **http://money.cnn.com**.

VIDEO CASE 5.2   Nielsen Media Research Watches the TV Watchers

The written video case on Nielsen Media Research appears on page VC-6. The recently filmed Nielsen Media Research video is designed to expand and highlight the concepts in this chapter and the concepts and questions covered in the written video case.

CHAPTER 6

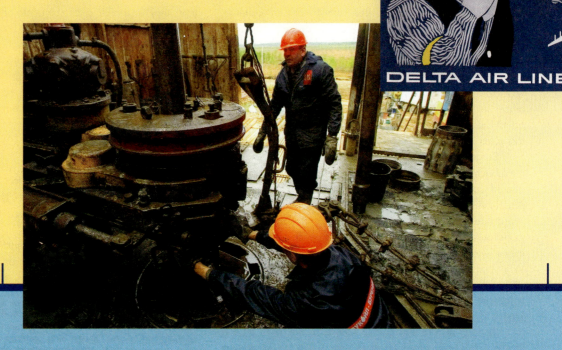

The Biggest Rebuilding Effort Ever

The combined fury of Hurricanes Katrina and Rita wrought havoc on New Orleans and the rest of the Gulf Coast. In addition to the hundreds of lives that were lost, thousands of homes and other buildings were flooded or destroyed, roads and bridges were damaged, water supplies were contaminated, and offshore equipment such as oil-drilling rigs and platforms was battered.

In what will probably be the biggest and most expensive government rebuilding effort in U.S. history, the federal government and the Federal Emergency Management Agency (FEMA) launched a massive process of hiring companies that could provide tools, materials, and expertise for restoring power, communication, and transportation in the area and, most important, for rebuilding homes and getting offshore oil pro-

duction up and running again. Congress approved billions of dollars to be spent in relief efforts, and contracts to work in the relief and rebuilding effort quickly went out to firms including Halliburton, Shaw Group, Bechtel National, Fluor, CH2M Hill, and Dewberry Technologies. Many of these firms already counted the U.S. government as a customer, because they have contracts for rebuilding work in Iraq.

In Louisiana, among the specific tasks the government needed to do were draining flooded areas of New Orleans, cleaning up debris, repairing levees and buildings that could be saved, and restoring utilities. Firms were also hired to identify areas in the state to serve as sites for temporary housing, to bring trailers and prefabricated houses there, and to connect the temporary

dwellings to electricity, water, and sanitary systems. Also needed were software planning and reporting tools to help oversee the process. Contractors went right to work, some in advance of signed deals with the government, and some were steadily hiring workers and subcontractors as the rebuilding process proceeded.

In the Gulf of Mexico, repair of the damaged rigs and platforms, which had withstood waves taller than an eight-story building and winds of more than 175 miles per hour, were quickly under way. Many miles of pipelines were also badly damaged, as were the electronic systems that operate and monitor gas and oil production and transport. About one-fourth of the oil-producing capacity was shut down in the nation's biggest energy hub, and natural gas production

Business-to-Business (B2B) Marketing

Chapter Objectives

1. Explain each of the components of the business-to-business (B2B) market.

2. Describe the major approaches to segmenting business-to-business (B2B) markets.

3. Identify the major characteristics of the business market and its demand.

4. Discuss the decision to make, buy, or lease.

5. Describe the major influences on business buying behavior.

6. Outline the steps in the organizational buying process.

7. Classify organizational buying situations.

8. Explain the buying center concept.

9. Discuss the challenges of and strategies for marketing to government, institutional, and international buyers.

---

dropped by 15 percent after the storm. Underwater robots dug through damaged equipment, and crews worked to retrieve rigs that had snapped and drifted as much as 60 miles from their moorings. A spokesperson for Chevron said, "All the components of the production system have to be in place" for output to return to normal levels.

Among those "components of the system" were oil company employees, many of whom had lost their homes, and local contractors who had lost their equipment to the storm. With ships, crews, marine technicians, and other experts in short supply, available workers were helped and supported by teams of divers and technicians from Canada. The massive effort is under way, but it will take years of hard work, hope, and some luck to bring back the Gulf Coast region.[1]

evolution *of a* brand

New Orleans has always been a city with pluck and determination. Its citizens have knowingly lived within the shadows of the levees that kept the raging waters of the Mississippi out. They have celebrated life in all its quirky forms during annual Mardi Gras festivals, danced and played in bands during funeral processions, and built a city with charm and a zest for life. But even New Orleans met its match when Hurricane Katrina roared ashore, punching holes in levees, snapping trees and power lines, and flooding vast stretches of the city. With rebuilding efforts under way, people continue to question whether the city can return to its former glory—or if not, what sort of city the new Big Easy will be.[2]

- A question mark in New Orleans's rebuilding efforts has been how much—and for how long—the federal government will pay to restore the city. Research the current government funding levels for reconstruction. How much has been paid and pledged to construction firms and other businesses to rebuild the city? What are the sources of the funds—are any private monies available in addition to those provided by the government? What types of businesses has the government contracted to do the reconstruction? What progress has been made and where has it occurred?

- Businesses are the lifeblood of a city, providing needed goods and services to consumers and providing jobs for local residents. Research the current state of New Orleans's businesses. How have they fared in the recovery effort? What sort of assistance is being provided to help them get reestablished? Where is it coming from? What types of businesses have thrived and which have failed? In your opinion, will New Orleans be able to return to its former status? Present the reasons for your viewpoint.

Chapter Overview

We are all aware of the consumer marketplace. As consumers, we're involved in purchasing needed items almost every day of our lives. In addition, we can't help noticing the barrage of marketing messages aimed at us through a variety of media. But the business-to-business marketplace is, in fact, significantly larger. U.S. companies pay more than $300 billion each year just for office and maintenance supplies. Government agencies contribute to the business-to-business market even further; for example, the Department of Defense budget for one recent year was nearly $500 billion.[3] Worldwide business-to-business commerce conducted over the Internet now totals nearly $2

business-to-business (B2B) marketing
Organizational sales and purchases of goods and services to support production of other products, to facilitate daily company operations, or for resale.

trillion.[4] Whether conducted through face-to-face transactions, via telephone, or over the Internet, business marketers each day deal with complex purchasing decisions involving multiple decision makers. They range from simple reorders of previously purchased items to complex buys for which materials are sourced from all over the world. As illustrated by the opening vignette, they often involve the steady building of relationships between sellers and customers as well as the ability to respond quickly to unique and changing circumstances. Customer satisfaction and customer loyalty are major factors in the development of these long-term relationships.

This chapter discusses buying behavior in the business or organizational market. **Business-to-business, or B2B, marketing** deals with organizational sales and purchases of goods and services to support production of

other products, to facilitate daily company operations, or for resale. But you ask, "How do I go about distinguishing between consumer purchases and B2B transactions?" Actually, it's pretty simple. Just ask yourself two questions:

1. Who is buying the good or service?

2. Why is the purchase being made?

Consumer buying involves purchases made by individual people. We purchase items for our own use and enjoyment—and not for resale. By contrast, B2B purchases are made by businesses, government, and marketing intermediaries to be resold, combined with other items to create a finished product for resale, or used up in the day-to-day operations of the organization. So answer the two questions—"Who is buying?" and "Why?"—and you have the answer.

NATURE OF THE BUSINESS MARKET

Firms usually sell fewer standardized products to organizational buyers than to ultimate consumers. Although you might purchase a cell phone for your personal use, a company generally has to purchase an entire communications system from a supplier such as Nortel, whose Meridian Communications Portfolio offers digital voice and Internet technology in a single network.[5] Purchases such as this require greater customization, more decision making, and usually more decision makers. So the buying and selling process becomes more complex, often involving teams of decision makers and taking an average of 6 to 36 months to complete.[6] Because of the complexity of the purchases, customer service is extremely important to B2B buyers. Advertising plays a much smaller role in the business market than in the consumer market, although advertisements placed in business magazines or trade publications are common. Business marketers advertise primarily to announce new products, to enhance their company image and presence, and to attract potential customers who would then deal directly with a salesperson. Personal selling plays a much bigger role in business markets than in consumer markets, distribution channels are shorter, customer relationships tend to last longer, and purchase decisions can involve multiple decision makers. Table 6.1 compares the marketing practices commonly used in both B2B and consumer marketing.

Like final consumers, an organization purchases products to fill needs. However, its primary need—meeting the demands of its own customers—is similar from firm to firm. A manufacturer buys raw materials such as wood pulp, fabric, or grain to create the company's product. A wholesaler or retailer buys the manufactured products—paper, clothing, or cereal—to resell. Mattel buys everything from plastic to paints to produce its toys; Toys "R" Us buys finished toys to sell to the public, and passenger airlines buy and lease aircraft from manufacturers such as Boeing and Airbus. The "Marketing Success" feature discusses how these two companies compete for orders. Institutional purchasers such as government agencies and nonprofit organizations also buy products to meet the needs of their constituents, whether it is global positioning system (GPS) mapping devices or meals ready to eat (MRE) for troops in the field.

Companies also buy services from other businesses. A firm may purchase law and accounting services, an office-cleaning service, a call center service, or a recruiting service. Jan-Pro is a commercial cleaning service company that has been in business since 1991. The chain has more than 75 master franchise offices throughout the United States and Canada and more than 4,300 individual franchise operations in the United States alone.[7]

Environmental, organizational, and interpersonal factors are among the many influences in B2B markets. Budget, cost, and profit considerations all play parts in business buying decisions. In addition, the business buying process typically involves complex interactions among many people. An organization's goals must also be considered in the B2B buying process. Later sections of the chapter will explore these topics in greater detail.

a mountain of copy paper: $98
(knowing it gets you that much closer to a mountain bike: priceless)

With the MasterCard BusinessCard; the rewards really mount up. From cash back to great gifts to free travel and more, you'll find your everyday business purchases have never been more rewarding. Visit mastercardbusiness.com or call 1-866-MC WORKING there are some things money can't buy. for everything else there's MasterCard.

The B2B market includes customers as large as the federal government and as small as individual entrepreneurs. MasterCard promotes the convenience of its Business Card with its rewards program for frequent purchasers.

table 6.1	Comparing Business-to-Business Marketing and Consumer Marketing	
	BUSINESS-TO-BUSINESS MARKETING	**CONSUMER MARKETING**
Product	Relatively technical in nature, exact form often variable, accompanying services very important	Standardized form, service important but less than for business products
Promotion	Emphasis on personal selling	Emphasis on advertising
Distribution	Relatively short, direct channels to market	Product passes through a number of intermediate links en route to consumer
Customer Relations	Relatively enduring and complex	Comparatively infrequent contact, relationship of relatively short duration
Decision-making Process	Diverse group of organization members makes decision	Individual or household unit makes decision
Price	Competitive bidding for unique items, list prices for standard items	List prices

Some firms focus entirely on business markets. For instance, DuPont sells materials such as polymers, coatings, and color technologies to manufacturers that use them in a variety of products. Caterpillar makes construction and mining equipment, diesel and natural gas engines, and industrial gas turbines. SAP America provides collaborative business software that lets companies work with customers and business partners using databases and other applications from every major software vendor. Other firms sell to both consumer and business markets. Herman Miller makes award-winning office furniture as well as stylish furniture for the home, and Intel's digital and wireless computer technology is found in business computing systems and personal computers. Note also that marketing strategies developed in consumer marketing are often appropriate for the business sector, too. Final consumers are often the end users of products sold into the business market and, as explained later in the chapter, can influence the buying decision.

The B2B market is diverse. Transactions can range from orders as small as a box of paper clips or copy machine toner for a home-based business to transactions as large as thousands of parts for an automobile manufacturer or massive turbine generators for an electric power plant. As mentioned earlier, businesses are also big purchasers of services, such as telecommunications, computer consulting, and transportation services. Four major categories define the business market: (1) the commercial market, (2) trade industries, (3) government organizations, and (4) institutions.

COMPONENTS OF THE BUSINESS MARKET

> **1** Explain each of the components of the business-to-business (B2B) market.

commercial market
Individuals and firms that acquire products to support, directly or indirectly, production of other goods and services.

trade industries Retailers or wholesalers that purchase products for resale to others.

reseller Marketing intermediaries that operate in the trade sector.

The **commercial market** is the largest segment of the business market. It includes all individuals and firms that acquire products to support, directly or indirectly, production of other goods and services. When Hewlett-Packard buys computer chips from Intel, when Sara Lee purchases wheat to mill into flour for an ingredient in its breads, and when a plant supervisor orders lightbulbs and cleaning supplies for a factory in Tennessee, these transactions all take place in the commercial market. Some products aid in the production of other items (the computer chips). Others are physically used up in the production of a good or service (the wheat). Still others contribute to the firm's day-to-day operations (the maintenance supplies). The commercial market includes manufacturers, farmers, and other members of resource-producing industries, construction contractors, and providers of such services as transportation, public utilities, financing, insurance, and real-estate brokerage.

The second segment of the organizational market, **trade industries,** includes retailers and wholesalers, known as **resellers,** who operate in this sector. Most resale products, such as clothing, appliances, sports equipment, and automobile parts, are finished goods that the buyers sell to final consumers. In other cases, the buyers may complete some processing or repackaging before reselling the products. A retail meat market may purchase a side of beef and then cut individual pieces for its customers. Lumber dealers and carpet retailers may purchase in bulk and then provide quantities and sizes to meet customers' specifications. In addition to resale products, trade industries buy computers, display shelves, and other products needed to operate their businesses. These goods, as well as

 marketing success   Boeing Soars to New Heights

Background. After years of head-to-head competition in the market for commercial and military aircraft, it seemed as though Boeing would finally take a back seat to its longtime rival Airbus. Boeing's profits were slowing, orders were down, its stock price had dropped, and it hadn't launched a new model in more than dozen years.

The Challenge. Boeing needed to figure out what its customers—major air carriers and the various governments—would want to buy in the coming years. Airbus was counting on passengers wanting cheaper flights to hub cities, which airlines would provide via Airbus's own big planes. Travelers then would transfer to connecting flights on smaller planes.

maintenance items, and specialized services such as scanner installation, newspaper inserts, and radio advertising all represent organizational purchases. Wendy Almquist founded Beans Wax Candle Co., a wholesale soy candle business based in Maple Grove, Minnesota. The company supplies candles for customers such as Carlson Marketing Group, Almquist's former employer, which offers the candles as incentive gifts, and the garden retailer Smith & Hawken, which sells the candles under its private label.[8]

The government category of the business market includes domestic units of government—federal, state, and local—as well as foreign governments. This important market segment makes a wide variety of purchases, ranging from highways to social services. The primary motivation of government purchasing is to provide some form of public benefit, such as national defense or pollution control. But government agencies have also become creative when it comes to selling—local police departments and state and federal agencies are selling unclaimed shipments, confiscated goods, and unclaimed items found in safe-deposit boxes on eBay. Lucky bidders might be able to buy a custom yacht for their business, a sausage grinder for their restaurant, or an auto transmission for their delivery truck through an Internet auction.[9]

Institutions, both public and private, are the fourth component of the business market. This category includes a wide range of organizations, such as hospitals, churches, skilled care and rehabilitation centers, colleges and universities, museums, and not-for-profit agencies. Some institutions—such as in higher education—must rigidly follow standardized purchasing procedures, but others have less formal buying practices. Business-to-business marketers often benefit by setting up separate divisions to sell to institutional buyers.

Commercial markets include computer chips, such as Intel's Centrino mobile technology, which is used in Toshiba's wireless notebook PCs.

© JUSTIN SULLIVAN/GETTY IMAGES

B2B MARKETS: THE INTERNET CONNECTION

While consumers' use of Internet markets receives the bulk of public attention, more than 94 percent of all Internet sales are B2B transactions.[10] Many business-to-business marketers have set up private portals that allow their customers to buy needed items. Service and customized pages are

---

The Strategy. Boeing bet on passengers wanting to fly directly to their destinations, bypassing hubs and connecting flights for the convenience of one takeoff and landing. Its fuel-efficient, midsized 777 wide-body recently shattered the distance record for commercial flight, covering nearly 13,500 miles in a single flight. And the company is introducing its new 787 jet, with high-tech features to save even more fuel, a significant operating cost.

The Outcome. Boeing was right. The aircraft maker's order book is full, and its stock price has tripled in the last couple of years. Although

industry analysts say both companies are so good at what they do that neither eclipses the other for long, at the moment, Boeing has come out on top.

Sources: "Boeing Poised for Supremacy over Airbus: Barron's," Reuters, March 12, 2006, http://news.yahoo.com; Steve Gelsi, "Boeing Gaining Altitude, Barron's Says," MarketWatch, March 11, 2006, http://www.marketwatch.com; Andrew Romano, "Boeing's New Tailwind," Newsweek, December 5, 2005, p. 45.

accessed through passwords provided by B2B marketers. Online auctions and virtual marketplaces offer other ways for buyers and vendors to connect with each other over the Internet.

During the early Internet boom, start-up companies rushed to connect buyers and sellers without considering basic marketing principles such as targeting their market and making sure to fulfill customers' needs. As a result, many of these companies failed. But the companies that survived—and new firms that have learned lessons from the mistakes of the old—have established a much stronger marketing presence. For instance, they recognize that their business customers have a lot at stake and expect greater value and utility from the goods and services they purchase.[11]

The Internet also opens up foreign markets to sellers. One such firm, a cotton exchange called The Seam, survived the Internet boom and bust and now connects U.S. cotton traders instantaneously with textile mills from countries including Turkey, Brazil, and China. The Seam is expanding its services into the wholesale peanut market worldwide.[12]

DIFFERENCES IN FOREIGN BUSINESS MARKETS

When The Seam first moved into other countries, its marketers had to consider the fact that foreign business markets may differ due to variations in government regulations and cultural practices. Some business products need modifications to succeed in foreign markets. In Australia, Japan, and Great Britain, for instance, motorists drive on the left side of the road. Automobiles must be modified to accommodate such differences.

Business marketers must be willing to adapt to local customs and business practices when operating abroad. They should also research cultural preferences. Factors as deceptively simple as the time of a meeting and methods of address for associates can make a difference. A company even needs to consider what ink colors to use for documents because colors can have different meanings in different countries.

assessment check

1. Define *B2B marketing*.
2. What is the commercial market?

2 Describe the major approaches to segmenting business-to-business (B2B) markets.

SEGMENTING B2B MARKETS

Business-to-business markets include wide varieties of customers, so marketers must identify the different market segments they serve. By applying market segmentation concepts to groups of business customers, a firm's marketers can develop a strategy that best suits a particular segment's needs. The overall process of segmenting business markets divides markets based on different criteria, usually organizational characteristics and product applications. Among the major ways to segment business markets are demographics (size), customer type, end-use application, and purchasing situation.

SEGMENTATION BY DEMOGRAPHIC CHARACTERISTICS

As with consumer markets, demographic characteristics define useful segmentation criteria for business markets. For example, firms can be grouped by size, based on sales revenues or number of employees. Marketers may develop one strategy to reach *Fortune 500* corporations with complex purchasing procedures and another strategy for small firms in which decisions are made by one or two people. To attract more small-business customers, Bank of America is expanding its already large lead in the small-business loan market to an online banking service targeted exclusively at small businesses in California. The bank has already beefed up its offerings to the smallest small businesses, with short-term loans backed by the business owner's credit or home equity.[13]

SEGMENTATION BY CUSTOMER TYPE

Another useful segmentation approach groups prospects according to type of customer. Marketers can apply this concept in several ways. They can group customers by broad categories—

manufacturer, service provider, government agency, not-for-profit organization, wholesaler, or retailer—and also by industry. These groups may be further divided using other segmentation approaches discussed in this section.

Customer-based segmentation is a related approach often used in the business-to-business marketplace. Organizational buyers tend to have much more precise—and complex—requirements for goods and services than ultimate consumers do. As a result, business products often fit narrower market segments than consumer products do. This fact leads some firms to design business goods and services to meet detailed buyer specifications. Pasadena-based Tetra Tech FW provides a variety of environmental services, including technology development, design, engineering, and pollution remediation for organizations around the world. Because the company's customers include government agencies as well as private firms—and because customers' needs are different—Tetra Tech FW offers a range of programs to suit each type of customer. For instance, the firm provides consulting services for utilities, helps communities clean up polluted water sources, and even conducts missions to clear public and private sites of unexploded ordnance.[14]

North American Industry Classification System (NAICS)

In the 1930s, the U.S. government set up a uniform system for subdividing the business marketplace into detailed segments. The Standard Industrial Classification (SIC) system standardized efforts to collect and report information on U.S. industrial activity.

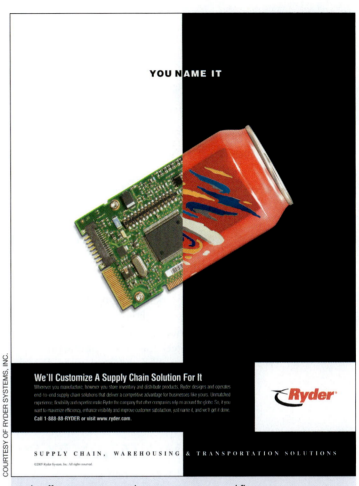

Ryder offers its customers warehousing, transportation, and fleet management services "wherever you manufacture, however you store inventory and distribute products." By serving the needs of different types of firms, Ryder segments its customers by type.

SIC codes divided firms into broad industry categories: agriculture, forestry, and fishing; mining and construction; manufacturing; transportation, communication, electric, gas, and sanitary services; wholesale trade; retail trade; finance, insurance, and real-estate services; public administration; and nonclassifiable establishments. The system assigned each major category within these classifications its own two-digit number. Three-digit and four-digit numbers further subdivided each industry into smaller segments.

For roughly 70 years, B2B marketers used SIC codes as a tool for segmenting markets and identifying new customers. The system, however, became outdated with implementation of the North American Free Trade Agreement (NAFTA). Each NAFTA member—the United States, Canada, and Mexico—had its own system for measuring business activity. NAFTA required a joint classification system that would allow marketers to compare business sectors among the member nations. In effect, marketers required a segmentation tool they could use across borders. The **North American Industry Classification System (NAICS)** replaced the SIC and provides more detail than was previously available. NAICS created new service sectors to better reflect the economy of the 21st century. They include information; health care and social assistance; and professional, scientific, and technical services.

Table 6.2 demonstrates the NAICS system for wholesale stationery and office supplies. NAICS uses six digits, compared with the four digits used in the SIC. The first five digits are fixed among the members of NAFTA. The sixth digit can vary among U.S., Canadian, and Mexican data. In short, the sixth digit accounts for specific data needs of each nation.[15]

customer-based segmentation Dividing a business-to-business market into homogeneous groups based on buyers' product specifications.

North American Industry Classification System (NAICS) Classification used by NAFTA countries to categorize the business marketplace into detailed market segments.

table 6.2	NAICS Classification for Stationery and Office Supplies Merchant Wholesalers
42	Merchant wholesalers
424	Merchant wholesalers, nondurable goods
4241	Paper and paper product merchant wholesalers
42412	Stationery and office supplies merchant wholesalers
424120	Stationery and office supplies merchant wholesalers in the U.S. industry

Source: NAICS, U.S. Census Bureau, **http://www.census.gov**, accessed March 24, 2006.

SEGMENTATION BY END-USE APPLICATION

end-use application segmentation Segmenting a business-to-business market based on how industrial purchasers will use the product.

A third basis for segmentation, **end-use application segmentation,** focuses on the precise way in which a business purchaser will use a product. For example, a printing equipment manufacturer may serve markets ranging from a local utility to a bicycle manufacturer to the U.S. Department of Defense. Each end use of the equipment may dictate unique specifications for performance, design, and price. Praxair, a supplier of industrial gases, for example, might segment its markets according to user. Steel and glass manufacturers might buy hydrogen and oxygen, while food and beverage manufacturers need carbon dioxide. Praxair also sells krypton, a rare gas, to companies that produce lasers, lighting, and thermal windows. Many small and medium-sized companies also segment markets according to end-use application. Instead of competing in markets dominated by large firms, they concentrate on specific end-use market segments.

SEGMENTATION BY PURCHASE CATEGORIES

Firms have different structures for their purchasing functions, and B2B marketers must adapt their strategies according to those organizational buyer characteristics. Some companies designate centralized purchasing departments to serve the entire firm, and others allow each unit to handle its own buying. A supplier may deal with one purchasing agent or several decision makers at various levels. Each of these structures results in different buying behavior.

When the buying situation is important to marketers, they typically consider whether the customer has made previous purchases or if this is the customer's first order. Directron.com, for instance, is a discount computer superstore that offers discounts for repeat customers and volume buyers.[16]

Increasingly, businesses that have developed **customer relationship management (CRM)** systems—strategies and tools that reorient an entire organization to focus on satisfying customers—can segment customers in terms of the stage of the relationship between the business and the customer. A B2B company, for example, might develop different strategies for newly acquired customers than it would for existing customers to which it hopes to sell new products. Similarly, building loyalty among satisfied customers requires a different approach than developing programs to "save" at-risk customer relationships. CRM will be covered in more depth in Chapter 10.

 assessment check

1. **What are the four major ways marketers segment business markets?**

2. **What is the NAICS?**

3 Identify the major characteristics of the business market and its demand.

CHARACTERISTICS OF THE B2B MARKET

Businesses that serve both B2B and consumer markets must understand the needs of their customers. However, several characteristics distinguish the business market from the consumer market:

(1) geographic market concentration, (2) the sizes and numbers of buyers, (3) the purchase decision process, and (4) buyer–seller relationships. The next sections consider how these traits influence business-to-business marketing.

GEOGRAPHIC MARKET CONCENTRATION

The U.S. business market is more geographically concentrated than the consumer market. Manufacturers converge in certain regions of the country, making these areas prime targets for business marketers. For example, the Midwestern states that make up the East North Central region—Ohio, Indiana, Michigan, Illinois, and Wisconsin—lead the nation in manufacturing concentration, followed by the Middle Atlantic and South Atlantic regions.[17]

Certain industries locate in particular areas to be close to customers. Firms may locate sales offices and distribution centers in these areas to provide more attentive service. It makes sense that the Washington, D.C., area is favored by companies that sell to the federal government.

In the automobile industry, suppliers of components and assemblies frequently build plants close to their customers. Ford recently established a first-of-its-kind campus for suppliers near its Chicago assembly plant. The campus allows suppliers to produce or assemble products close to the plant, reducing costs, controlling parts inventory, and increasing flexibility.[18] As Internet-based technology continues to improve, allowing companies to transact business even with distant suppliers, business markets may become less geographically concentrated. Much of government spending, for example, is now directed through the Internet.

SIZES AND NUMBERS OF BUYERS

In addition to geographic concentration, the business market features a limited number of buyers. Marketers can draw on a wealth of statistical information to estimate the sizes and characteristics of business markets. The federal government is the largest single source of such statistics. Every five years, it conducts both a Census of Manufacturers and a Census of Retailing and Wholesaling, which provide detailed information on business establishments, output, and employment. Many government units and trade organizations also operate Web sites that contain helpful information.

Many buyers in limited-buyer markets are large organizations. The international market for jet engines is dominated by three manufacturers: United Technology's Pratt & Whitney unit, General Electric, and Rolls-Royce. These firms sell engines to Boeing and the European consortium, Airbus Industrie. These aircraft manufacturers compete for business from passenger carriers such as Northwest Airlines, British Airways, KLM, and Singapore Airlines, along with cargo carriers such as DHL, Federal Express, and United Parcel Service.

Trade associations and business publications provide additional information on the business market. Private firms such as Dun & Bradstreet publish detailed reports on individual companies. These data serve as a useful starting point for analyzing a business market. Finding data in such a source requires an understanding of the NAICS, which identifies much of the available statistical information.

THE PURCHASE DECISION PROCESS

To market effectively to other organizations, businesses must understand the dynamics of the organizational purchase process. Suppliers who serve business-to-business markets must work with multiple buyers, especially when selling to larger customers. Decision makers at several levels may influence final orders, and the overall process is more formal and professional than the consumer purchasing process. Purchasers typically require a longer time frame because B2B involves more complex decisions. Suppliers must evaluate customer needs and develop proposals that meet technical requirements and specifications. Also, buyers need time to analyze competing proposals. Often decisions require more than one round of bidding and negotiation, especially for complicated purchases.

Briefly
Speaking

"I would rather have a million friends than a million dollars."

—Edward V. Rickenbacker (1890–1973)
American aviator

Solving an Ethical Controversy

How Should Buying Firms Deal with Vendors?

I t's not unusual for vendors to give their valued customers gifts of various types, but many companies have strict rules about what buyers can accept. At ADP, for instance, "other than for modest gifts given or received in the normal course of business (including travel or entertainment), neither you nor your relatives may give gifts to, or receive gifts from, ADP's clients and vendors. Other gifts may be given or accepted only with prior approval of your senior management." Sybase cautions its purchasing staff, "Never offer or give gifts or favors to anyone in connection with any government contracting activity, including 'kickbacks' to any customer who is a prime contractor with a government entity." The University of Nebraska, Omaha, says simply, "Decline personal gifts or gratuities."

Is it acceptable for buyers to receive gifts or gratuities from vendors?

PRO

1. Most buyers can be trusted to make the right decision about vendors based on criteria such as price and quality rather than gifts.
2. Gifts of nominal value are simply a way of thanking important customers and do not influence sales.

CON

1. It's too difficult to make impartial decisions about which vendors to use if you accept anything of material value from them.
2. Such gifts merely drive up the cost of doing business, which hurts customers and shareholders in the long run.

Summary

Even if a buyer's company holds a fairly lenient attitude toward accepting gifts from vendors, good judgment backed by strong personal ethics should govern all B2B purchasing decisions. In most situations there is no lack of real criteria—such as price, quality, speed of delivery, and level of service—on which to base a buying decision. Gifts and gratuities should never cloud the decision process.

Sources: "Code of Business Conduct and Ethics," Automatic Data Processing, **http://www.adp.com**, accessed March 7, 2006; "Statement of Values and Business Ethics," Sybase, **http://www.sybase.com**, accessed March 7, 2006; "Code of Ethics," University of Nebraska, Omaha, **http://www.unomaha.edu**, accessed March 7, 2006.

BUYER–SELLER RELATIONSHIPS

An especially important characteristic of B2B marketing is the relationship between buyers and sellers. These relationships are often more complex than consumer relationships, and they require superior communication among the organizations' personnel. Satisfying one major customer may mean the difference of millions of dollars to a firm. The "Solving an Ethical Controversy" feature discusses an important question many buyers and sellers face.

Relationship marketing involves developing long-term, value-added customer relationships. A primary goal of business-to-business relationships is to provide advantages that no other vendor can provide—for instance, lower price, quicker delivery, better quality and reliability, customized product features, or more favorable financing terms. For the business marketer, providing these advantages means expanding the company's external relationships to include suppliers, distributors, and other organizational partners. It also includes managing internal relationships between departments. Sun Microsystems helped the Taxi and Logistics Division of the Seoul (South Korea) City Hall update its information technology infrastructure, installing new computer servers so that registration of automobiles and two-wheeled vehicles could continue to run smoothly as demand for its services climbed. Each of the two new servers includes one domain for car registration and another for two-wheeled vehicles, plus two more domains designated as standbys.[19]

Close cooperation, whether through informal contacts or under terms specified in contractual partnerships and strategic alliances, enables companies to meet buyers' needs for quality products and customer service. This holds true both during and after the purchase process. Tetra Tech FW, mentioned earlier, has formal Client Service Quality and Shared Vision programs, which are designed to engage customers in continuous communication leading to customer satisfaction.

Relationships between for-profit and not-for-profit organizations are just as important as those between two commercial organizations. Wal-Mart is a longtime corporate sponsor of Children's Miracle Network, an international organization that helps improve children's health and welfare by raising funds for state-of-the-art care, cutting-edge research, and education. Wal-Mart has raised and donated more than $300 million to 170 children's hospitals in the network.[20]

© ASSOCIATED PRESS, AP

Nike and Apple worked together to create the Nike Air Zoom Moire shoe, the first footwear designed to work with Apple's iPod. Developing new products and services required close cooperation and superior communication between partnering firms.

EVALUATING INTERNATIONAL BUSINESS MARKETS

Business purchasing patterns differ from one country to the next. Researching these markets poses a particular problem for B2B marketers. Of course, as explained earlier, NAICS has corrected this problem in the NAFTA countries.

In addition to assessing quantitative data such as the size of the potential market, companies must also carefully weigh its qualitative features. This process involves considering cultural values, work styles, and the best ways to enter overseas markets in general. LG Electronics, a $38 billion global appliance and electronics maker based in South Korea, focuses on understanding the particulars of important local markets in all its new-product introductions. LG conducts in-country research and opens local manufacturing and marketing facilities. The company's Middle East marketing director says, "Gone are the days where you could just roll out one product for the global market. We speak to consumers individually." Some of the company's products include a programmable Russian karaoke phone, a kimchi fridge to isolate the strong odor of South Korea's national dish and keep it away from other foods, a microwave with a skewer rack and special heat setting for kebabs that is marketed in Iran, and a fridge for Saudi Arabia that includes a special bin to hold dates at their ideal temperature.[21]

global sourcing Purchasing goods and services from suppliers worldwide.

In today's international marketplace, companies often practice **global sourcing,** which involves purchasing goods and services from suppliers worldwide. This practice can result in substantial cost savings. Office Depot plans to expand its wood-fiber purchases to northern Canada, Russia, and the Far East.[22] Clothing maker Coldwater Creek uses suppliers in Hong Kong and New Delhi.[23] And U.S. financial institutions are looking at outsourcing check and payment processing in eastern Europe and parts of Asia.[24]

Global sourcing requires companies to adopt a new mindset; some must even reorganize their operations.

✓ **assessment check**

1. Why is geographic segmentation important in the B2B market?

2. In what ways is the buyer–seller relationship important in B2B marketing?

3. What is global sourcing?

Among other considerations, businesses sourcing from multiple multinational locations should streamline the purchase process and minimize price differences due to labor costs, tariffs, taxes, and currency fluctuations.

BUSINESS MARKET DEMAND

The previous section's discussion of business market characteristics demonstrated considerable differences between marketing techniques for consumer and business products. Demand characteristics also differ in these markets. In business markets, the major categories of demand include derived demand, volatile demand, joint demand, inelastic demand, and inventory adjustments. Figure 6.1 summarizes these different categories of business market demand.

DERIVED DEMAND

The term **derived demand** refers to the linkage between demand for a company's output and its purchases of resources such as machinery, components, supplies, and raw materials. The demand for computer microprocessor chips is *derived* from the demand for personal computers. If more businesses and individuals buy new computers, the demand for chips increases; if fewer computers are sold, the demand for chips decreases. In recent years, worldwide slowdowns in sales of personal computers reduced demand for chips. But STATS ChipPAC, Southeast Asia's biggest packager of semiconductors, expects to make its first profit in several years. The company runs tests of specialized chips used in products such as the iPod and LCD televisions, and these electronic products are enjoying a big resurgence in demand.[25]

Organizational buyers purchase two general categories of business products: capital items and expense items. Derived demand ultimately affects both. Capital items are long-lived business assets that must be depreciated over time. *Depreciation* is an accounting term that refers to charging a portion of a capital item's cost as a deduction against the company's annual revenue for purposes of determining its net income. Examples of capital items include major installations such as new manufacturing plants, office buildings, and computer systems.

Expense items, in contrast, are items consumed within short time periods. Accountants charge the cost of such products against income in the year of purchase. Examples of expense items include the supplies necessary to operate the business, ranging from copy paper to machine lubricants.

figure 6.1

Categories of Business Market Demand

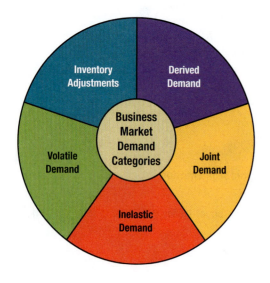

VOLATILE DEMAND

Derived demand creates volatility in business market demand. Assume that the sales volume for a gasoline retailer is increasing at an annual rate of 5 percent. Now suppose that the demand for this gasoline brand slows to a 3 percent annual increase. This slowdown might persuade the firm to keep its current gasoline pumps and replace them only when market conditions improve. In this way, even modest shifts in consumer demand for a gasoline brand would greatly affect the pump manufacturer.

JOINT DEMAND

Another important influence on business market demand is **joint demand,** which results when the demand for one business product is related to the demand for another business product used in combination with the first item. Both lumber and concrete are required to build most homes. If the lumber supply falls, the drop in housing construction will most likely affect the demand for concrete. Another example is the joint demand for electrical power and large turbine engines. If consumers decide to conserve power, demand for new power plants drops, as does the demand for components and replacement parts for turbines.

INELASTIC DEMAND

Inelastic demand means that demand throughout an industry will not change significantly due to a price change. If the price of lumber drops, a construction firm will not necessarily buy more lumber from its suppliers unless another factor—such as lowered mortgage interest rates—causes more consumers to purchase new homes.

INVENTORY ADJUSTMENTS

Adjustments in inventory and inventory policies can also affect business demand. Assume that manufacturers in a particular industry consider a 60-day supply of raw materials the optimal inventory level. Now suppose that economic conditions or other factors induce these firms to increase their inventories to a 90-day supply. The change will bombard the raw-materials supplier with new orders.

Furthermore, **just-in-time (JIT)** inventory policies seek to boost efficiency by cutting inventories to absolute minimum levels and by requiring vendors to deliver inputs as the production process needs them. JIT allows companies to better predict which supplies they will require and the timing for when they will need them, markedly reducing their costs for production and storage. Widespread implementation of JIT has had a substantial impact on organizations' purchasing behavior. Firms that practice JIT tend to order from relatively few suppliers. In some cases, JIT may lead to **sole sourcing** for some items—in other words, buying a firm's entire stock of a product from just one supplier. Electronic data interchange (EDI) and quick-response inventory policies have produced similar results in the trade industries. The latest inventory trend, **JIT II,** leads suppliers to place representatives at the customer's facility to work as part of an integrated, on-site customer–supplier team. Suppliers plan and order in consultation with the customer. This streamlining of the inventory process improves control of the flow of goods.

Although inventory adjustments are critical in manufacturing processes, they are equally vital to wholesalers and retailers. Perhaps nowhere is inventory management more complex than at Wal-Mart, the largest retailer in the world, with more than $320 billion in sales per year. With no signs of slowing down, suppliers such as Procter & Gamble and Unilever—giants themselves—work closely with Wal-Mart to monitor and adjust inventory as necessary. Other suppliers, such as Remington, Revlon, and Hershey Foods, generate at least 20 percent of their total income from Wal-Mart, so inventory management is critical for those companies as well.[26]

 assessment check

1. How does derived demand create volatile demand?
2. Give an example of joint demand.
3. How might JIT II strengthen marketing relationships?

THE MAKE, BUY, OR LEASE DECISION

 4 Discuss the decision to make, buy, or lease.

Before a company can decide what to buy, it should decide whether to buy at all. Organizational buyers must figure out the best way to acquire needed products. In fact, a firm considering the acquisition of a finished good, component part, or service has three basic options:

1. Make the good or provide the service in-house.
2. Purchase it from another organization.
3. Lease it from another organization.

Manufacturing the product itself, if the company has the capability to do so, may be the best route. It may save a great deal of money if its own manufacturing division does not incur costs for overhead that an outside vendor would otherwise charge.

On the other hand, most firms cannot make all the business goods they need. Often it would be too costly to maintain the necessary equipment, staff, and supplies. As a result, purchasing from an outside vendor is the most common choice. Xerox manufactures more than eighteen different types of color printers to meet nearly any business need—from affordable color laser printers to high-performance ink-jet printers. Its wide array of products, coupled with its track record of a century of supplying businesses, has made it a leader in the B2B printer market.[27] Companies can also look outside their own plants for goods and services that they formerly produced in-house, a practice called *outsourcing* that the next section will describe in more detail.

In some cases, however, a company may choose to lease inputs. This option spreads out costs compared with lump-sum costs for up-front purchases. The company pays for the use of equipment for a certain time period. A small business may lease a copier for a few years and make monthly payments. At the end of the lease term, the firm can buy the machine at a prearranged price or replace it with a different model under a new lease. This option can provide useful flexibility for a growing business, allowing it to easily upgrade as its needs change.

Companies can also lease sophisticated computer systems and heavy equipment. For example, some airlines prefer to lease airplanes rather than buy them outright because short-term leases allow them to adapt quickly to changes in passenger demand.

THE RISE OF OFFSHORING AND OUTSOURCING

offshoring Movement of high-wage jobs from one country to lower-cost overseas locations.

Chances are, if you dial a call center for a firm such as America Online, Dell, GE, American Express, or Nestlé, your call may be answered by someone in India.[28] Microsoft recently nearly doubled its workforce in India to 7,000, and IBM employs nearly 50,000 Indians.[29] In recent years, a political firestorm has been ignited by the movement of U.S. jobs to lower-cost overseas locations, a business practice referred to as **offshoring.** This relocation of business processes to a lower-cost location can involve production offshoring or services offshoring. China has emerged as the preferred destination for production offshoring, while India has emerged as the dominant player in services offshoring.

nearshoring Moving jobs to vendors in countries close to the business's home country.

China still leads the way in offshore manufacturing, making two-thirds of the world's copiers, microwaves, DVD players, and shoes, and virtually all of the world's toys. It is expected to become a source of service outsourcing for many, although most of its 8,000-plus software services providers are tiny firms with fewer than 2,000 employees each. Such small firms are seen as risky business partners, with less ability to hang on to their key players and fewer financial resources to survive long term. Fragmented Chinese firms hoping to do business with firms that need such services face another obstacle—the possibility that Indian companies may buy them up and consolidate them to expand their own operations.[30]

outsourcing Using outside vendors to provide goods and services formerly produced in-house.

Some U.S.-based firms want to remain closer to home but take advantage of the benefits of locating some of their operations overseas. Mexico and Canada are attractive locations for these **nearshoring** operations. In today's highly competitive marketplace, firms look outside the United States to improve efficiency and cut costs on just about everything including customer service, human resources, accounting, information technology, manufacturing, and distribution. **Outsourcing,** using outside vendors to produce goods and services formerly produced in-house or in-country, is a trend that continues to rise. Businesses outsource for several reasons: (1) they need to reduce costs to remain competitive; (2) they need to improve the quality and speed of software maintenance and development; and (3) outsourcing has begun to offer greater value than ever before.

Outsourcing allows firms to concentrate their resources on their

REUTERS/JAGADEESH NV/LANDOV

India has an educated workforce, relatively low wage rates, and high-tech telecommunications systems. So, many U.S. companies decide to outsource their service calls to centers such as this one in Bangalore.

core business. It also allows access to specialized talent or expertise that does not exist within the firm. The most frequently outsourced business functions include information technology (IT) and human resources, with other white-collar service jobs such as accounting, drug research, technical R&D, and film animation increasingly being outsourced as well.[31] Although most outsourcing is done by North American–based companies, the practice is rapidly becoming commonplace in Asia, Europe, and Central America. Software is now a $200 billion-a-year industry in the United States. But many firms are now outsourcing their business to other countries, particularly India. One reason is the cost of labor—a starting call center operator or a programmer with a college degree earns around $10,000 a year. Another reason is the large pool of highly educated, English-speaking workers. In a new twist on outsourcing, some Indian firms may soon be hiring increasing numbers of Americans, as they aim higher and look to form full-fledged business partners with their U.S. customers. The numbers are still small, but because higher-level consulting services are based on close customer relationships, it makes sense to hire more Americans.[32]

Eastern Europe is becoming an increasingly popular outsourcing location thanks to its multilingual population. Giants such as Boeing, BMW, General Motors, Siemens, and Nortel contract with small programming firms in Bulgaria, while IBM, Hewlett-Packard, Oracle, and French telecom firm Alcatel have support centers or software labs in Romania. German software powerhouse SAP AG has a Bulgarian research lab with 180 engineers who write Java software for SAP's innovative products around the world. "There is an exceptionally high level of talent in Eastern Europe," says Kasper Rorsted, managing director for Europe, Middle East, and Africa at Hewlett-Packard.[33]

Outsourcing can be a smart strategy if a company chooses a vendor that can provide high-quality products and perhaps at a lower cost than could be achieved on the company's own. This priority allows the outsourcer to focus on its core competencies. Successful outsourcing requires companies to carefully oversee contracts and manage relationships. Some vendors now provide performance guarantees to assure their customers that they will receive high-quality services that meet their needs.

PROBLEMS WITH OFFSHORING AND OUTSOURCING

Offshoring and outsourcing are not without their downsides. Many companies discover that their cost savings are less than vendors sometimes promise. Also, companies that sign multiyear contracts may find that their savings drop after a year or two. When proprietary technology is an issue, outsourcing raises security concerns. Similarly, companies that are protective of customer data and relationships may think twice about entrusting functions such as customer service to outside sources.

In some cases, outsourcing and offshoring can reduce a company's ability to respond quickly to the marketplace, or they can slow efforts in bringing new products to market. Suppliers that fail to deliver goods promptly or provide required services can adversely affect a company's reputation with its customers.

Outsourcing and offshoring are controversial topics with unions, especially in the auto industry, as the percentage of component parts made in-house has steadily dropped. These practices can create conflicts between nonunion outside workers and in-house union employees, who fear job loss. Management initiatives to outsource jobs can lead to strikes and plant shutdowns. Even if they do not lead to disruption in the workplace, outsourcing and offshoring can have a negative impact on employee morale and loyalty.

assessment check

1. Identify two potential benefits of outsourcing.
2. Identify two potential problems with outsourcing.

THE BUSINESS BUYING PROCESS

 Describe the major influences on business buying behavior.

Suppose that CableBox, Inc., a hypothetical manufacturer of television decoder boxes for cable TV service providers, decides to upgrade its manufacturing facility with $1 million in new automated assembly equipment. Before approaching equipment suppliers, the company must analyze its needs, determine goals that the project should accomplish, develop technical specifications for the equipment, and set a budget. Once it receives vendors' proposals, it must evaluate them and select the best one. But what does *best* mean in this context? The lowest price or the best warranty and service contract? Who in the company is responsible for such decisions?

The business buying process is more complex than the consumer decision process. Business buying takes place within a formal organization's budget, cost, and profit considerations. Furthermore, B2B and institutional buying decisions usually involve many people with complex interactions among individuals and organizational goals. For instance, purchasing agents for Healthcare Materials Management Services, the procurement arm of St. Joseph's Health Care London (SJHC) in Canada, must verify the signature on each procurement request before processing it, to be sure it is that of an authorized SJHC representative.[34] To understand organizational buying behavior, business marketers require knowledge of influences on the purchase decision process, the stages in the organizational buying model, types of business buying situations, and techniques for purchase decision analysis.

INFLUENCES ON PURCHASE DECISIONS

B2B buying decisions react to various influences, some external to the firm and others related to internal structure and personnel. In addition to product-specific factors such as purchase price, installation, operating and maintenance costs, and vendor service, companies must consider broader environmental, organizational, and interpersonal influences.

Environmental Factors

Environmental conditions such as economic, political, regulatory, competitive, and technological considerations influence business buying decisions. CableBox may wish to defer purchases of the new equipment in times of slowing economic activity. During a recession, sales to cable companies might drop because households hesitate to spend money on cable service. The company would look at the derived demand for its products, possible changes in its sources of materials, employment trends, and similar factors before committing to such a large capital expenditure.

Environmental factors can also include natural disasters such as Hurricane Katrina. Viking Energy Management serves as a purchasing agent for companies needing fuels such as natural gas, electricity, and gasoline. After the hurricane, when local fuel oil prices were rising so fast they doubled within 30 days, Viking's owners Bryant and Kim Austin Lee decided to help their customers by locking in fuel prices ahead of time. Bryant explains, "What we saw was that the business had to change from being focused on procurement to being focused on quantifying risk and helping clients manage the cost and getting the energy they need."[35]

Political, regulatory, and competitive factors also come into play in influencing purchase decisions. Passage of a law freezing cable rates would affect demand, as would an introduction of a less expensive decoder box by a competitor. Finally, technology plays a role in purchase decisions. A few years ago, cable-ready televisions decreased demand for set-top boxes, and smaller, more powerful satellite dishes have cut into the market for cable TV, reducing derived demand. But customers still need the boxes to access premium channels and movies, even with digital service. CableBox can benefit from technological advances, too. As more homes want fast Internet connections, adding cable modems to its product line may present a growth opportunity.

Organizational Factors

Successful business-to-business marketers understand their customers' organizational structures, policies, and purchasing systems. A company with a centralized procurement function operates differently from one that delegates purchasing decisions to divisional or geographic units. Trying to sell to the local store when head office merchandisers make all the decisions would clearly waste salespeople's time. Buying behavior also differs among firms. For example, centralized buying tends to emphasize long-term relationships, whereas decentralized buying focuses more on short-term results. Personal selling skills and user preferences carry more weight in decentralized purchasing situations than in centralized buying.

How many suppliers should a company patronize? Because purchasing operations spend more than half of each dollar their companies earn, consolidating vendor relationships can lead to large cost savings. However, a fine line separates maximizing buying power from relying too heavily on a few suppliers. Many companies engage in **multiple sourcing**—purchasing from several vendors.

Etiquette Tips for Marketing Professionals

Keeping Customers out of Voice Response Hell

You've probably been on the receiving end of a company's customer service operation that consists entirely of recorded menus and messages. Though they can save nearly 80 percent of the cost of having a human operator take a service call, fourteen of fifteen automated response systems failed in a recent survey of customers. Here are some ways to help your own customers avoid the frustrations that many feel during such phone calls.

1. Tailor your menus to suit different kinds of customers. New voice response systems can provide you with information about incoming callers based only on the originating phone number, so you can offer each caller the right menu from the start.

2. Because you can identify incoming callers, route important ones immediately to live operators in relevant departments such as collections, account management, or marketing, instead of putting them on hold.

3. Make sure your system can route calls to employees who are working at home or on the road. If they're the right people for your customers to talk to, keep them accessible to your callers.

4. Don't set the system up to automatically cross-sell products to customers who must wait on hold. Cross-selling is a major complaint among half of customers surveyed about voice response systems.

5. Ensure that your system answers calls promptly, minimizes the time on hold, and doesn't force callers to repeat information or continually identify themselves.

6. Make it easy to reach a human voice. Remember that most of your competitors will let most of their customers get trapped in voice-response systems. Be the one who doesn't.

Sources: "When to Take the Call and When to Use Voicemail," Earnware Corporation, **http://www.earnware.com**, accessed March 7, 2006; David H. Freedman, "Service with a Smile. Really," *Inc.*, October 2005, pp. 75–76; Alexandra DeFelice, "A Business Imperative: Improve Service Now," Destination CRM.com, July 26, 2005, **http://www.destinationcrm.com**.

Spreading orders ensures against shortages if one vendor cannot deliver on schedule. However, dealing with many sellers can be counterproductive and take too much time. Each company must set its own criteria for this decision.

Interpersonal Influences

Many people may influence B2B purchases, and considerable time may be spent obtaining the input and approval of various organization members. Both group and individual forces are at work here. When committees handle buying, they must spend time to gain majority or unanimous approval. Also, each individual buyer brings to the decision process individual preferences, experiences, and biases.

Business marketers should know who will influence buying decisions in an organization for their products and should know each of their priorities. To choose a supplier for an industrial press, for example, a purchasing manager and representatives of the company's production, engineering, and quality-control departments may jointly decide on a supplier. Each of these principals may have a different point of view that the vendor's marketers must understand.

To effectively address the concerns of all people involved in the buying decision, sales personnel must be well versed in the technical features of their products. They must also interact well with employees of the various departments involved in the purchase decision. Sales representatives for medical products—traditionally called "detailers"—frequently visit hospitals and doctors' offices to discuss the advantages of their new products and leave samples with clinical staff. Representatives for IBM would most likely try to talk with staff who would potentially use its Linux application. See the "Etiquette Tips for Marketing Professionals" feature for some ideas about how to manage telephone communications if your company has an automated voice-response system to answer calls from customers.

Briefly *Speaking*

"Tell me who's your friend and I'll tell you who you are."

—Russian proverb

The Role of the Professional Buyer

Many large organizations attempt to make their purchases through systematic procedures employing professional buyers. In the trade industries, these buyers, often referred to as **merchandisers,** secure needed products at the best possible prices. Nordstrom has buyers for shoes and clothing that will ultimately be sold to consumers. Ford has buyers for components that will be incorporated into its cars and trucks. A firm's purchasing or merchandising unit devotes all of its time and effort in determining needs, locating and evaluating alternative suppliers, and making purchase decisions.

Purchase decisions for capital items vary significantly from those for expense items. Firms often buy expense items routinely with little delay. Capital items, however, involve major fund commitments and usually undergo considerable review.

One way in which a firm may attempt to streamline the buying process is through **systems integration,** or centralization of the procurement function. One company may designate a lead division to handle all purchasing. Another firm may choose to designate a major supplier as the systems integrator. This vendor then assumes responsibility for dealing with all of the suppliers for a project and for presenting the entire package to the buyer. In trade industries, this vendor is sometimes called a **category advisor** or **category captain.**

A business marketer may set up a sales organization to serve national accounts that deals solely with buyers at geographically concentrated corporate headquarters. A separate field sales organization may serve buyers at regional production facilities.

Corporate buyers often use the Internet to identify sources of supplies. They view online catalogs and Web sites to compare vendors' offerings and to obtain product information. Some use Internet exchanges to extend their supplier networks.

assessment check

1. Identify the three major factors that influence purchase decisions.

2. What are the advantages and disadvantages of multiple sourcing?

6 Outline the steps in the organizational buying process.

MODEL OF THE ORGANIZATIONAL BUYING PROCESS

An organizational buying situation takes place through a sequence of activities. Figure 6.2 illustrates an eight-stage model of an organizational buying process. The additional steps arise because business purchasing introduces new complexities that do not affect consumers. Although not every buying situation requires all these steps, this figure provides a good overview of the whole process.

Stage 1: Anticipate or Recognize a Problem/Need/Opportunity and a General Solution

Both consumer and business purchase decisions begin when the recognition of problems, needs, or opportunities triggers the buying process. Perhaps a firm's computer system has become outdated or an account representative demonstrates a new service that could improve the company's performance. Companies may decide to hire an outside marketing specialist when their sales stagnate.

figure 6.2

Stages in the B2B Buying Process

Source: Based on Michael D. Hutt and Thomas W. Speh, *Business Marketing Management: B2B*, 9th ed. (Mason, OH: South-Western, 2007).

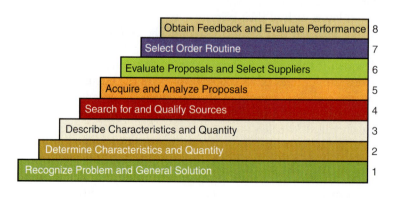

Stage
8 Obtain Feedback and Evaluate Performance
7 Select Order Routine
6 Evaluate Proposals and Select Suppliers
5 Acquire and Analyze Proposals
4 Search for and Qualify Sources
3 Describe Characteristics and Quantity
2 Determine Characteristics and Quantity
1 Recognize Problem and General Solution

The problem may be as simple as needing to provide a good cup of coffee to a firm's employees. "These people needed to be caffeinated, and when they left the office to get coffee, it was lost billable hours," says Nick Lazaris, CEO of Wakefield, Massachusetts–based Keurig, a firm that sells a patented coffee machine to corporations.[36]

Stage 2: Determine the Characteristics and Quantity of a Needed Good or Service

The coffee problem described in Stage 1 translated into a service opportunity for Keurig. The small firm was able to offer a coffee system that would brew one perfect cup of coffee at a time, according to the preferences of each employee. PricewaterhouseCoopers became one of Keurig's first customers, followed by other accounting firms, law practices, and medical offices.[37]

Stage 3: Describe Characteristics and the Quantity of a Needed Good or Service

After determining the characteristics and quantity of needed products, B2B buyers must translate these ideas into detailed specifications. PricewaterhouseCoopers and subsequent customers told Keurig that they wanted a foolproof, individual coffee maker. The Keurig system supplies a plastic K-cup containing ground coffee that the individual simply places in the coffee maker—no measuring of water or coffee is required. Out comes the perfect cup of coffee.[38] Firms could easily base the quantity requirements of the Keurig system on the number of coffee-drinking employees they have or the amount of space they occupy.

Stage 4: Search for and Qualify Potential Sources

Both consumers and businesses search for good suppliers of desired products. The choice of a supplier may be relatively straightforward—because there was no other machine like it, PricewaterhouseCoopers had no trouble selecting the Keurig coffee system. Other searches may involve more complex decision making. A company that wants to buy a group life and health insurance policy, for example, must weigh the varying provisions and programs of many different vendors.

Stage 5: Acquire and Analyze Proposals

The next step is to acquire and analyze suppliers' proposals, which are often submitted in writing. If the buyer is a government or public agency, this stage of the purchase process may involve competitive bidding. During this process, each marketer must develop its bid, including a price, that will satisfy the criteria determined by the customer's problem, need, or opportunity. While competitive bidding is less common in the business sector, a company may follow the practice to purchase nonstandard materials, complex products, or products that are made to its own specifications.

Stage 6: Evaluate Proposals and Select Suppliers

Next in the buying process, buyers must compare vendors' proposals and choose the one that seems best suited to their needs. Proposals for sophisticated equipment, such as a large computer networking system, can include considerable differences among product offerings, and the final choice may involve trade-offs.

Price is not the only criterion for the selection of a vendor. Relationship factors such as communication and trust may also be important to the buyer. Other issues include reliability, delivery record, time from order to delivery, quality, and order accuracy. For DHL, the ability to track valuable items such as high-definition TVs in transit to repair shops was an important consideration in choosing companies to help expand its radio frequency identification (RFID) projects. The company has partnered with IBM, Intel, Royal Philips Electronics N.C., and SAP AG for this service.[39]

Stage 7: Select an Order Routine

Once a supplier has been chosen, buyer and vendor must work out the best way to process future purchases. Ordering routines can vary considerably. Most orders will, however, include product descriptions, quantities, prices, delivery terms, and payment terms. Today, companies have a variety of options for submitting orders: written documents, phone calls, faxes, or electronic data interchange.

Stage 8: Obtain Feedback and Evaluate Performance

At the final stage, buyers measure vendors' performances. Sometimes this judgment may involve a formal evaluation of each supplier's product quality, delivery performance, prices, technical knowledge, and overall responsiveness to customer needs. At other times, vendors may be measured according to whether they have lowered the customer's costs or reduced its employees' workloads. In general, bigger firms are more likely to use formal evaluation procedures, while smaller companies lean toward informal evaluations. Regardless of the method used, buyers should tell vendors how they will be evaluated. DHL, for instance, wants its RFID project to result in "dramatically" improved shipment visibility, to save transport time, and to reduce needed scanning processes by 90 percent.[40]

Sometimes firms rely on independent organizations to gather quality feedback and summarize results. J. D. Power and Associates conducts research and provides information to a variety of firms so that they can improve the quality of their goods and services.

 assessment check

1. Why does the organizational buying process contain more steps than the consumer buying process?
2. List the steps in the organizational buying process.

7 Classify organizational buying situations.

CLASSIFYING BUSINESS BUYING SITUATIONS

As discussed earlier, business buying behavior responds to many purchasing influences such as environmental, organizational, and interpersonal factors. This buying behavior also involves the degree of effort that the purchase decision demands and the levels within the organization where it is made. Like consumer behavior, marketers can classify B2B buying situations into three general categories, ranging from least to most complex: (1) straight rebuying, (2) modified rebuying, and (3) new-task buying. Business buying situations may also involve reciprocity. The following sections look at each type of purchase.

Straight Rebuying

The simplest buying situation is a **straight rebuy,** a recurring purchase decision in which a customer reorders a product that has satisfied needs in the past. The buyer already likes the product and terms of sale, so the purchase requires no new information. The buyer sees little reason to assess competing options and so follows a routine repurchase format. A straight rebuy is the business market equivalent of routinized response behavior in the consumer market. Purchases of low-cost items such as paper clips and pencils for an office are typical examples of straight rebuys. Reorders of coffee from Keurig would also be straight rebuys. Marketers who maintain good relationships with customers by providing high-quality products, superior service, and prompt delivery can go a long way toward ensuring straight rebuys.

Modified Rebuying

In a **modified rebuy,** a purchaser is willing to reevaluate available options. Buyers may see some advantage in looking at alternative offerings within their established purchasing guidelines. They might take this step if their current supplier has let a rebuy situation deteriorate because of poor service or delivery performance. Price, quality, and innovation differences can also provoke modified rebuys. Modified rebuys resemble limited problem solving in consumer markets.

B2B marketers want to induce current customers to make straight rebuys by responding to all of their needs. Competitors, on the other hand, try to lure those buyers away by raising issues that will persuade them to reconsider their decisions.

New-Task Buying

The most complex category of business buying is **new-task buying**—first-time or unique purchase situations that require considerable effort by the decision makers. The consumer market equivalent of new-task buying is extended problem solving. Pittsburgh-based PPG Industries operated a range of legacy and new software programs and packages in its sixteen business units. When it was ready to construct a network to allow it to integrate information with its customers, suppliers, and other partners, PPG knew that both the benefits and the investment in the network would be high, making the choice of platform of the highest importance. "In selecting a platform," says the company's vice president of information technology, "we had to be able to communicate and establish relationships with a single individual all the way up to the largest companies in the world." In the end, the company chose Microsoft's .NET platform.[41]

A new-task buy often requires a purchaser to carefully consider alternative offerings and vendors. A company entering a new field must seek suppliers of component parts that it has never before purchased. This new-task buying would require several stages, each yielding a decision of some sort. These decisions would include developing product requirements, searching out potential suppliers, and evaluating proposals. Information requirements and decision makers can complete the entire buying process, or they may change from stage to stage.

Reciprocity

Reciprocity—a practice of buying from suppliers that are also customers—is a controversial practice in a number of procurement situations. An office equipment manufacturer may favor a particular supplier of component parts if the supplier has recently made a major purchase of the manufacturer's products. Reciprocal arrangements traditionally have been common in industries featuring homogeneous products with similar prices, such as the chemical, paint, petroleum, rubber, and steel industries.

Reciprocity suggests close links among participants in the organizational marketplace. It can add to the complexity of B2B buying behavior for new suppliers who are trying to compete with preferred vendors. Although buyers and sellers enter into reciprocal agreements in the United States, both the Department of Justice and the Federal Trade Commission view them as attempts to reduce competition. Outside the United States, however, governments may take more favorable views of reciprocity. Business-to-business buyers in Canada, for instance, see it as a positive, widespread practice. In Japan, close ties between suppliers and customers are common.

COURTESY OF BT

Voice is just data for your ears.

It's the 21st century. Why are you still running separate networks for voice and data?

BT can guide you to a converged future where simplicity and agility cost less. Where efficiency, service quality and customer delight are easier to achieve.

With over two decades of experience serving the needs of global customers, BT can show you the right roadmap for your journey to convergence.

Talk to us.
www.bt.com/networked

BT brings it all together:
- Network Convergence
- Security Services
- Mobility Solutions
- IP Contact Centres
- Service-Oriented Infrastructures

On a global scale.

BT Bringing it all together

The purchase of a communications network to integrate a company's voice and data applications into one system, such as BT supplies, is usually a new-task purchase.

ANALYSIS TOOLS

Two tools that help professional buyers improve purchase decisions are value analysis and vendor analysis. **Value analysis** examines each component of a purchase in an attempt to either delete the item or replace it with a more cost-effective substitute. Airplane designers have long recognized the need to make planes as light as possible. Value analysis supports using DuPont's synthetic material Kevlar in airplane construction because it weighs less than the metals it replaces. The resulting fuel savings are significant for the buyers in this marketplace.

Vendor analysis carries out an ongoing evaluation of a supplier's performance in categories such as price, EDI capability, back orders, delivery times, liability insurance, and attention to special requests. In some cases, vendor analysis is a formal process. Some buyers use a checklist to assess a vendor's performance. A checklist quickly highlights vendors and potential vendors that do not satisfy the purchaser's buying requirements.

8 Explain the buying center concept.

buying center Participants in an organizational buying action.

THE BUYING CENTER CONCEPT

The buying center concept provides a vital model for understanding B2B buying behavior. A company's **buying center** encompasses everyone who is involved in any aspect of its buying activity. A buying center may include the architect who designs a new research laboratory, the scientist who works in the facility, the purchasing manager who screens contractor proposals, the chief executive officer who makes the final decision, and the vice president of research who signs the formal contracts for the project. Buying center participants in any purchase seek to satisfy personal needs, such as participation or status, as well as organizational needs. A buying center is not part of a firm's formal organizational structure. It is an informal group whose composition and size vary among purchase situations and firms.

BUYING CENTER ROLES

Buying center participants play different roles in the purchasing decision process, which are summarized in Figure 6.3. **Users** are the people who will actually use the good or service. Their influence on the purchase decision may range from negligible to extremely important. Users sometimes initiate purchase actions by requesting products, and they may also help develop product specifications. Users often influence the purchase of office equipment. Office Depot knows this. Recently the company redesigned its office supply stores to make them more attractive to shoppers. The new layout includes a fresh color scheme and graphics, and a "pod" structure that displays related or complementary items, such as binding and filing products, in horseshoe-shaped pods along the walls where customers can find them easily. The modular fixtures can be adapted to Office Depot stores of any size and shape, and they are lower in height to allow salespeople to more easily find customers and offer assistance.[42]

Gatekeepers control the information that all buying center members will review. They may exert this control by distributing printed product data or advertisements or by deciding which salespeople will speak to which individuals in the buying center. A purchasing agent might allow some salespeople to see the engineers responsible for developing specifications but deny others the same privilege. The office manager for a medical group may decide whether to accept and pass along sales literature from a pharmaceutical detailer or sales representative.

Influencers affect the buying decision by supplying information to guide evaluation of alternatives or by setting buying specifications. Influencers are typically technical staff such as engineers or quality-control specialists. Sometimes a buying organization hires outside consultants, such as architects, who influence its buying decisions.

The **decider** chooses a good or service, although another person may have the formal authority to do so. The identity of the decider is the most difficult role for salespeople to pinpoint. A firm's buyer may have the formal authority

figure 6.3

Buying Center Participants and Their Roles

Buyer
Person who has formal authority to purchase

Users
Those who use the product

Gatekeeper
Person who controls information flow

Buying Center

Decider
Person who chooses the product

Influencer
Those who supply technical information or specifications

to buy, but the firm's chief executive officer may actually make the buying decision. Alternatively, a decider might be a design engineer who develops specifications that only one vendor can meet.

The **buyer** has the formal authority to select a supplier and to implement the procedures for securing the good or service. The buyer often surrenders this power to more influential members of the organization, though. The purchasing manager often fills the buyer's role and executes the details associated with a purchase order.

B2B marketers face the task of determining the specific role and the relative decision-making influence of each buying center participant. Salespeople can then tailor their presentations and information to the precise role that an individual plays at each step of the purchase process. Business marketers have found that their initial—and in many cases, most extensive—contacts with a firm's purchasing department often fail to reach the buying center participants who have the greatest influence, because these people may not work in that department at all.

Consider the selection of meeting and convention sites for trade or professional associations. The primary decision maker could be an association board or an executive committee, usually with input from the executive director or a meeting planner; the meeting planner or association executive might choose meeting locations, sometimes with input from members; finally, the association's annual-meeting committee or program committee might make the meeting location selection. Because officers change periodically, centers of control may change frequently. As a result, destination marketers and hotel operators constantly assess how an association makes its decisions on conference locations.

INTERNATIONAL BUYING CENTERS

Two distinct characteristics differentiate international buying centers from domestic ones. First, marketers may have trouble identifying members of foreign buying centers. In addition to cultural differences in decision-making methods, some foreign companies lack staff personnel. In less developed countries, line managers may make most purchase decisions.

Second, a buying center in a foreign company often includes more participants than U.S. companies involve. International buying centers employ from 1 to 50 people, with 15 to 20 participants being commonplace. Global B2B marketers must recognize and accommodate this greater diversity of decision makers.

International buying centers can change in response to political and economic trends. Many European firms once maintained separate facilities in each European nation to avoid tariffs and customs delays. When the European Union lowered trade barriers between member nations, however, many companies closed distant branches and consolidated their buying centers. The Netherlands has been one of the beneficiaries of this trend.

Still, marketers who are flexible and quick to respond to change can get a jump on the competition in foreign markets if they can readily identify the decision maker in the process. When China's computer maker, Lenovo Group, purchased IBM's personal computer business, it decided to sidestep some of the cultural hurdles of doing business abroad when language, customer needs, and management styles all differ from those of the home country. Lenovo retained many of IBM's key executives from the PC division when it finalized the purchase of the company.[43]

TEAM SELLING

To sell effectively to all members of a firm's buying center, many vendors use **team selling,** combining several sales associates or other staff to help the lead account representative reach all those who influence the purchase decision. Team selling may be extended to include members of the seller firm's own supply network into the sales situation. Consider the case of small resellers of specialized computer applications whose clients require high levels of product knowledge and access to training. By working with its supply network—for example, by forming alliances with suppliers to provide training or ongoing service to end clients—resellers are able to offer a higher degree of support.

 assessment check

1. Identify the five roles of people in a buying center decision.

2. What are some of the problems that U.S. marketers face in dealing with international buying centers?

9 Discuss the challenges of and strategies for marketing to government, institutional, and international buyers.

DEVELOPING EFFECTIVE BUSINESS-TO-BUSINESS MARKETING STRATEGIES

A business marketer must develop a marketing strategy based on a particular organization's buying behavior and on the buying situation. Clearly, many variables affect organizational purchasing decisions. This section examines three market segments whose decisions present unique challenges to B2B marketers: units of government, institutions, and international markets. Finally, it summarizes key differences between consumer and business marketing strategies.

CHALLENGES OF GOVERNMENT MARKETS

Government agencies—federal, state, and local—together make up the largest customer group in the United States. More than 85,000 government units buy a wide variety of products, including office supplies, furniture, concrete, vehicles, grease, military aircraft, fuel, and lumber, to name just a few.

To compete effectively, business marketers must understand the unique challenges of selling to government units. One challenge results because government purchases typically involve dozens of interested parties who specify, evaluate, or use the purchased goods and services. These parties may or may not work within the government agency that officially handles a purchase.

Government purchases are also influenced by social goals, such as minority subcontracting programs. Government entities such as the U.S. Postal Service strive to maintain diversity in their suppliers by making a special effort to purchase goods and services from small firms and companies owned by minorities and women.[44] The government also relies on its prime suppliers to subcontract to minority businesses.

Contractual guidelines create another important influence in selling to government markets. The government buys products under two basic types of contracts: fixed-price contracts, in which seller and buyer agree to a set price before finalizing the contract, and cost-reimbursement contracts, in which the government pays the vendor for allowable costs, including profits, incurred during performance of the contract. Each type of contract has advantages and disadvantages for B2B marketers. Although the fixed-price contract offers more profit potential than the alternative, it also carries greater risks from unforeseen expenses, price hikes, and changing political and economic conditions.

Government Purchasing Procedures

Many U.S. government purchases go through the General Services Administration (GSA), a central management agency involved in areas such as procurement, property management, and information resources management. The GSA buys goods and services for its own use and for use by other government agencies. In its role as, essentially, the federal government's business manager, it purchases billions of dollars' worth of products. The Defense Logistics Agency (DLA) serves the same function for the Department of Defense.

By law, most federal purchases must be awarded on the basis of bids, or written sales proposals, from vendors. As part of this process, government buyers develop specifications—detailed descriptions of needed items—for prospective bidders. U.S. government purchases must comply with the Federal Acquisition Regulation (FAR), a 30,000-page set of standards originally designed to cut red tape in government purchasing. FAR standards have been further complicated by numerous exceptions issued by various government agencies. Because they provide services to various federal government agencies such as the Department of Energy, Environmental Protection Agency, and Department of Defense, large environmental engineering firms such as MACTEC, Tetra Tech FW, and Weston Solutions typically have procurement and contract specialists on staff. These specialists stay current with FAR standards and conduct internal quality-assurance and quality-control programs to make sure these standards are followed by their companies.

Recent reforms have attempted to speed purchasing and increase flexibility. They include an increased reliance on fast, easy-to-use, prenegotiated contracts with multiple vendors; elimination of detailed specifications for readily available commercial products; paperwork reduction; and the use of government-issued credit cards to make small buys.[45]

State and local government purchasing procedures resemble federal procedures. Most states and many large cities have created buying offices similar to the GSA. Detailed specifications and open bidding are common at this level as well. Many state purchasing regulations give preference to in-state bidders.

Government spending patterns may differ from those in private industry. Because the federal government's fiscal year runs from October 1 through September 30, many agencies spend much of their procurement budgets in the fourth quarter, from July 1 to September 30. They hoard their funds to cover unexpected expenditures, and if they encounter no such problems, they find themselves with money to spend in late summer. Companies understand this system and keep their eyes on government bulletins, so they can bid on the listed agency purchases, which often involve large amounts of money.

Online with the Federal Government

Like their colleagues in the private sector, government procurement professionals are streamlining purchasing procedures with new technology. Rather than paging through piles of paper catalogs and submitting handwritten purchase orders, government buyers now prefer online catalogs that help them compare competing product offerings. In fact, vendors find business with the government almost impossible unless they embrace electronic commerce.

Vendors can sell products to the federal government through three electronic options. Web sites provide a convenient method of exchanging information for both parties. Government buyers locate and order products, paying with a federally issued credit card, and the vendors deliver the items within about a week. Another route is through government-sponsored electronic ordering systems, which help standardize the buying process. GSA Advantage allows federal employees to order products directly over the Internet at the preferred government price.[46] The Electronic Posting System sends automatic notices of opportunities to sell to the government to more than 29,000 registered vendors. The Phoenix Opportunity System, set up by the Department of Commerce, provides a similar service for minority-owned companies. A pilot program at the Treasury is testing an electronic check-payment system to speed up the settling of vendor invoices.

Despite these advances, many government agencies remain less sophisticated than private-sector businesses. The Pentagon, for instance, is still coping with procurement procedures that were developed over the last 50 years. However, it is introducing a streamlined approach to defense contracting that reduces the time necessary to develop specifications and select suppliers.

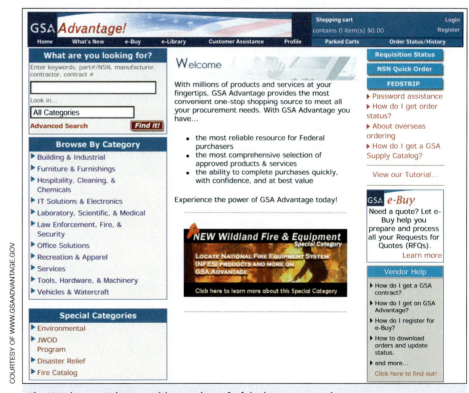

COURTESY OF WWW.GSAADVANTAGE.GOV

The GSA Advantage Web site consolidates purchasing for federal government employees.

CHALLENGES OF INSTITUTIONAL MARKETS

Institutions constitute another important market. Institutional buyers include a wide variety of organizations, such as schools, hospitals, libraries, foundations, clinics, churches, and not-for-profit agencies.

Institutional markets are characterized by widely diverse buying practices. Some institutional purchasers behave like government purchasers because laws and political considerations determine their buying procedures. Many of these institutions, such as schools and prisons, may even be managed by government units.

Buying practices can differ between institutions of the same type. In a small hospital, the chief dietitian may approve all food purchases, while in a larger medical facility, food purchases may go through a committee consisting of the dietitian and a business manager, purchasing agent, and cook. Other hospitals may belong to buying groups, perhaps health maintenance organizations or local hospital cooperatives. Still others may contract with outside firms to prepare and serve all meals.

Within a single institution, multiple buying influences may affect decisions. Many institutions, staffed by professionals such as physicians, nurses, researchers, and instructors, may also employ purchasing managers or even entire purchasing departments. Conflicts may arise among these decision makers. Professional employees may prefer to make their own purchase decisions and resent giving up control to the purchasing staff. This conflict can force a business marketer to cultivate both professionals and purchasers. A detailer for a pharmaceuticals firm must convince physicians of the value to patients of a certain drug while simultaneously convincing the hospital's purchasing department that the firm offers competitive prices, good delivery schedules, and prompt service. The pharmaceuticals industry spends between $8,000 and $15,000 per physician on marketing every year.[47] Some observers see a new trend among some doctors to reject free gifts and samples often offered by drug company representatives, which might create additional conflicts in the purchasing process.[48]

Group purchasing is an important factor in institutional markets because many organizations join cooperative associations to pool purchases for quantity discounts. Universities may join the Education and Institutional Purchasing Cooperative; hospitals may belong to regional associations; and chains of profit-oriented hospitals such as HCA Healthcare can also negotiate quantity discounts. Central headquarters staff usually handles purchasing for all members of such a chain.

Diverse practices in institutional markets pose special challenges for B2B marketers. They must maintain flexibility in developing strategies for dealing with a range of customers, from large cooperative associations and chains to midsize purchasing departments and institutions to individuals. Buying centers can work with varying members, priorities, and levels of expertise. Discounts and effective distribution functions play important roles in obtaining—and keeping—institutions as customers.

CHALLENGES OF INTERNATIONAL MARKETS

To sell successfully in international markets, business marketers must consider buyers' attitudes and cultural patterns within areas where they operate. In Asian markets, a firm must maintain a local presence to sell products. Personal relationships are also important to business deals in Asia. Companies that want to expand globally often need to establish joint ventures with local partners. International marketers must also be poised to respond to shifts in cultural values.

Local industries, economic conditions, geographic characteristics, and legal restrictions must also be considered in international marketing. Many local industries in Spain specialize in food and wine; therefore, a maker of forklift trucks might market smaller vehicles to Spanish companies than to German firms, which require bigger, heavier trucks to serve the needs of that nation's large automobile industry.

Remanufacturing—efforts to restore worn-out products to like-new condition—can be an important marketing strategy in a nation that cannot afford to buy new products. Developing countries often purchase remanufactured factory machinery, which costs 35 to 60 percent less than new equipment.

Foreign governments represent another important business market. In many countries, government or state-owned companies dominate certain industries, such as construction and other infrastructure sales. Additional examples include airport and highway construction, telephone system equipment, and computer networking equipment. Sales to a foreign government can involve an array of regulations. Many governments, like that of the

 assessment check

1. What are some influences on government purchases?

2. Why is group purchasing important in institutional purchases?

3. What special factors influence international buying decisions?

United States, limit foreign participation in their defense programs. Joint ventures and countertrade are common, as are local content laws, which mandate domestic production of a certain percentage of a business product's components.

Strategic Implications of Marketing in the 21st Century

To develop marketing strategies for the B2B sector, marketers must first understand the buying practices that govern the segment they are targeting, whether it is the commercial market, trade industries, government, or institutions. Similarly, when selling to a specific organization, strategies must take into account the many factors that influence purchasing. B2B marketers must identify people who play the various roles in the buying decision. They must also understand how these members interact with one another, other members of their own organization, and outside vendors. Marketers must be careful to direct their marketing efforts to their organization, to broader environmental influences, and to individuals, who operate within the constraints of the firm's buying center.

REVIEW OF CHAPTER OBJECTIVES

1 Explain each of the components of the business-to-business (B2B) market.

The B2B market is divided into four segments: the commercial market, trade industries, governments, and institutions. The commercial market consists of individuals and firms that acquire products to be used, directly or indirectly, to produce other goods and services. Trade industries are organizations, such as retailers and wholesalers, that purchase for resale to others. The primary purpose of government purchasing, at federal, state, and local levels, is to provide some form of public benefit. The fourth segment, institutions, includes a diverse array of organizations, such as hospitals, schools, museums, and not-for-profit agencies.

2 Describe the major approaches to segmenting business-to-business (B2B) markets.

Business markets can be segmented by (1) demographics, (2) customer type, (3) end-use application, and (4) purchasing situation. The North American Industry Classification System (NAICS), instituted after the passage of NAFTA, helps further classify types of customers by the use of six digits.

3 Identify the major characteristics of the business market and its demand.

The major characteristics of the business market are geographic concentration, size and number of buyers, purchase decision procedures, and buyer–seller relationships. The major categories of demand are derived demand, volatile demand, joint demand, inelastic demand, and inventory adjustments.

4 Discuss the decision to make, buy, or lease.

Before a company can decide what to buy, it must decide whether to buy at all. A firm has three options: (1) make the good or service in-house; (2) purchase it from another organization; or (3) lease it from another organization. Companies may outsource goods or services formerly produced in-house to other companies either within their own home country or to firms in other countries. The shift of high-wage jobs from the home country to lower-wage locations is known as offshoring. If a company moves production to a country close to its own borders, it uses a nearshoring strategy. Each option has its benefits and drawbacks, including cost and quality control.

5   Describe the major influences on business buying behavior.

B2B buying behavior tends to be more complex than individual consumer behavior. More people and time are involved, and buyers often seek several alternative supply sources. The systematic nature of organizational buying is reflected in the use of purchasing managers to direct such efforts. Major organizational purchases may require elaborate and lengthy decision-making processes involving many people. Purchase decisions typically depend on combinations of such factors as price, service, certainty of supply, and product efficiency.

6   Outline the steps in the organizational buying process.

The organizational buying process consists of eight general stages: (1) anticipate or recognize a problem/need/opportunity and a general solution; (2) determine characteristics and quantity of needed good or service; (3) describe characteristics and quantity of needed good or service; (4) search for and qualify potential sources; (5) acquire and analyze proposals; (6) evaluate proposals and select supplier(s); (7) select an order routine; and (8) obtain feedback and evaluate performance.

7   Classify organizational buying situations.

Organizational buying situations differ. A straight rebuy is a recurring purchase decision in which a customer stays with an item that has performed satisfactorily. In a modified rebuy, a purchaser is willing to reevaluate available options. New-task buying refers to first-time or unique purchase situations that require considerable effort on the part of the decision makers. Reciprocity involves buying from suppliers that are also customers.

8   Explain the buying center concept.

The buying center includes everyone who is involved in some fashion in an organizational buying action. There are five buying center roles: users, gatekeepers, influencers, deciders, and buyers.

9   Discuss the challenges of and strategies for marketing to government, institutional, and international buyers.

A government purchase typically involves dozens of interested parties. Social goals and programs influence government purchases. Many U.S. government purchases involve complex contractual guidelines and often require detailed specifications and a bidding process. Institutional markets are challenging because of their diverse buying influences and practices. Group purchasing is an important factor, because many institutions join cooperative associations to get quantity discounts. An institutional marketer must be flexible enough to develop strategies for dealing with a range of customers. Discounts and effective distribution play an important role. An effective international business marketer must be aware of foreign attitudes and cultural patterns. Other important factors include economic conditions, geographic characteristics, legal restrictions, and local industries.

✓ *assessment check* **answers**

1.1 Define *B2B marketing*.
Business-to-business, or B2B, marketing deals with organizational purchases of goods and services to support production of other products, to facilitate daily company operations, or for resale.

1.2 What is the commercial market?
The commercial market consists of individuals and firms that acquire products to be used, directly or indirectly, to produce other goods and services.

2.1 What are the four major ways marketers segment business markets?
Business markets can be segmented by (1) demographics, (2) customer type, (3) end-use application, and (4) purchasing situation.

assessment check **answers**

2.2 What is the NAICS?

The North American Industry Classification System (NAICS) is a unified system for Mexico, Canada, and the United States to classify customers and ease trade.

3.1 Why is geographic segmentation important in the B2B market?

Certain industries locate in particular areas to be close to customers. Firms may choose to locate sales offices and distribution centers in these areas to provide more attentive service. For example, the Washington, D.C., area is favored by companies that sell to the federal government.

3.2 In what ways is the buyer–seller relationship important in B2B marketing?

Buyer–seller relationships are often more complex than consumer relationships, and they require superior communication among the organizations' personnel. Satisfying one major customer may mean the difference of millions of dollars to a firm.

3.3 What is global sourcing?

Global sourcing involves contracting to purchase goods and services from suppliers worldwide.

3.4 How does derived demand create volatile demand?

Assume that the sales volume for a gasoline retailer is increasing at an annual rate of 5 percent. Now suppose that the demand for this gasoline brand slows to a 3 percent annual increase. This slowdown might persuade the firm to keep its current gasoline pumps and replace them only when market conditions improve. In this way, even modest shifts in consumer demand for a gasoline brand would greatly affect the pump manufacturer.

3.5 Give an example of joint demand.

Both lumber and concrete are required to build most homes. If the lumber supply falls, the drop in housing construction will most likely affect the demand for concrete.

3.6 How might JIT II strengthen marketing relationships?

JIT II leads suppliers to place representatives at the customer's facility to work as part of an integrated, on-site customer–supplier team. Suppliers plan and order in consultation with the customer. This streamlining of the inventory process improves control of the flow of goods.

4.1 Identify two potential benefits of outsourcing.

Outsourcing allows firms to concentrate their resources on their core business. It also allows access to specialized talent or expertise that does not exist within the firm.

4.2 Identify two potential problems with outsourcing.

Many companies discover that their cost savings are less than vendors sometimes promise. Also, companies that sign multiyear contracts may find that their savings drop after a year or two.

5.1 Identify the three major factors that influence purchase decisions.

In addition to product-specific factors such as purchase price, installation, operating and maintenance costs, and vendor service, companies must consider broader environmental, organizational, and interpersonal influences.

5.2 What are the advantages and disadvantages of multiple sourcing?

Spreading orders ensures against shortages if one vendor cannot deliver on schedule. However, dealing with many sellers can be counterproductive and take too much time.

6.1 Why does the organizational buying process contain more steps than the consumer buying process?

The additional steps arise because business purchasing introduces new complexities that do not affect consumers.

6.2 List the steps in the organizational buying process.

The steps in organizational buying are (1) anticipate or recognize a problem/need/opportunity and a general solution; (2) determine characteristics and quantity of needed good or service; (3) describe characteristics and quantity of needed good or service; (4) search for and qualify potential sources; (5) acquire and analyze proposals; (6) evaluate proposals and select supplier(s); (7) select an order routine; and (8) obtain feedback and evaluate performance.

assessment check **answers**

7.1   What are the four classifications of business buying situations?

The four classifications of business buying are (1) straight rebuying, (2) modified rebuying, (3) new-task buying, and (4) reciprocity.

7.2   Differentiate between value analysis and vendor analysis.

Value analysis examines each component of a purchase in an attempt to either delete the item or replace it with a more cost-effective substitute. Vendor analysis carries out an ongoing evaluation of a supplier's performance in categories such as price, EDI capability, back orders, delivery times, liability insurance, and attention to special requests.

8.1   Identify the five roles of people in a buying center decision.

There are five buying center roles: users (those who use the product), gatekeepers (those who control the flow of information), influencers (those who provide technical information or specifications), deciders (those who actually choose the product), and buyers (those who have the formal authority to purchase).

8.2   What are some of the problems that U.S. marketers face in dealing with international buying centers?

International buying centers pose several problems. In addition to cultural differences in decision-making methods, some foreign companies lack staff personnel, so in less developed countries, line managers may make most purchase decisions. A buying center in a foreign company often includes more participants than U.S. companies involve. Also, international buying centers can change in response to political and economic trends.

9.1   What are some influences on government purchases?

Social goals and programs often influence government purchases.

9.2   Why is group purchasing important in institutional purchases?

Group purchasing is an important factor because many institutions join cooperative associations to get quantity discounts.

9.3   What special factors influence international buying decisions?

An effective international business marketer must be aware of foreign attitudes and cultural patterns. Other important factors include economic conditions, geographic characteristics, legal restrictions, and local industries.

MARKETING TERMS YOU NEED TO KNOW

business-to-business (B2B) marketing 178
commercial market 180
trade industries 180
reseller 180
customer-based segmentation 183

North American Industry Classification System (NAICS) 183
end-use application segmentation 184
global sourcing 187
offshoring 190

nearshoring 190
outsourcing 190
buying center 198

OTHER IMPORTANT MARKETING TERMS

customer relationship management (CRM) 184
derived demand 188
joint demand 188
inelastic demand 189
just-in-time (JIT)/just-in-time II (JIT II) 189
sole sourcing 189
multiple sourcing 193

merchandisers 194
systems integration 194
category advisor (category captain) 194
straight rebuy 196
modified rebuy 196
new-task buying 197
reciprocity 197
value analysis 197

vendor analysis 198
user 198
gatekeeper 198
influencer 198
decider 198
buyer 199
team selling 199
remanufacturing 202

ASSURANCE OF LEARNING REVIEW

1. Which is the largest segment of the business market? What role does the Internet play in the B2B market? What role do resellers play in the B2B market?

2. How is customer-based segmentation beneficial to B2B marketers? Describe segmentation by purchasing situation.

3. How do the sizes and numbers of buyers affect B2B marketers? Why are buyer–seller relationships so important in B2B marketing?

4. Give an example of each type of demand.

5. For what reasons might a firm choose an option other than making a good or service in-house? Why is outsourcing on the rise? How is offshoring different from outsourcing?

6. What are some of the environmental factors that may influence buying decisions? Identify organizational factors that

may influence buying decisions. Describe the role of the professional buyer.

7. Why are there more steps in the organizational buying process than in the consumer buying process? Explain why feedback between buyers and sellers is important to the marketing relationship.

8. Give an example of a straight rebuy and a modified rebuy. Why is new-task buying more complex than the first two buying situations?

9. In the buying center, who is a marketer likely to encounter first? In the buying center, who has the formal authority to make a purchase? What is the purpose of team selling?

10. Describe some of the factors that direct U.S. government purchases. Why are institutional markets particularly challenging?

PROJECTS AND TEAMWORK EXERCISES

1. In small teams, research the buying process through which your school purchases the following products:
   a. lab equipment for one of the science labs
   b. the school's telecommunications system
   c. food for the cafeteria
   d. classroom furniture
   Does the buying process differ for any of these products? If so, how?

2. As a team or individually, choose a commercial product, such as computer chips, flour for baking, paint, or equipment, and research and analyze its foreign market potential. Report your findings to the class.

3. In pairs or individually, select a firm in your area and ask to interview the person who is in charge of purchasing. In particular, ask the person about the importance of buyer–seller relationships in his or her industry. Report your findings to the class.

4. In pairs, select a business product in one of two categories—capital or expense—and determine how derived demand will affect the sales of the product. Create a chart showing your findings.

5. As a team, research a firm such as Microsoft or Boeing to learn how it is using outsourcing or offshoring. Then report on what you think the benefits and drawbacks to the firm might be.

6. Imagine that you and your teammates are buyers for a firm such as Starbucks, Dick's Sporting Goods, Marriott, or another firm you like. Map out a logical buying process for a new-task purchase for your organization.

7. Form a team to conduct a hypothetical team selling effort for the packaging of products manufactured by a food company such as Kraft or General Mills. Have each team member cover a certain concern, such as package design, delivery, and payment schedules. Present your marketing effort to the class.

8. Conduct research into the U.S. government's purchasing process. Select a federal agency or department, such as the Environmental Protection Agency, National Aeronautics and Space Administration (NASA), or the Department of Health and Human Services. What types of purchases does it make? What is the range of contract amounts? Who are the typical suppliers? What type of process is involved in buying?

9. Find an advertisement with marketing messages targeted for an institutional market. Analyze the ad to determine how the marketer has segmented the market, who in the buying center might be the target of the ad, and what other marketing strategies may be apparent.

10. In teams, research the practice of remanufacturing of business products such as factory machinery for foreign markets. What challenges do marketers of such products face?

CRITICAL-THINKING EXERCISES

1. Imagine that you are a wholesaler for dairy products such as yogurt and cheese, which are produced by a cooperative of small farmers. Describe what steps you would take to build relationships with both the producers—farmers—and retailers such as supermarkets.

2. Describe an industry that might be segmented by geographic concentration. Then identify some of the types of firms that might be involved in that industry. Keep in mind that these companies might be involved in other industries as well.

3. Imagine that you are in charge of making the decision to lease or buy a fleet of automobiles for the limousine service for which you work. What factors would influence your decision and why?

4. Do you think online selling to the federal government benefits marketers? What might be some of the drawbacks to this type of selling?

ETHICS EXERCISE

Suppose you work for a well-known local restaurant, and a friend of yours is an account representative for a supplier of restaurant equipment. You know that the restaurant owner is considering upgrading some of the kitchen equipment. Although you have no purchasing authority, your friend has asked you to arrange a meeting with the restaurant owner. You have heard unflattering rumors about this supplier's customer service.

1. Would you arrange the meeting between your friend and your boss?

2. Would you mention the customer-service rumors either to your friend or your boss?

3. Would you try to influence the purchase decision in either direction?

INTERNET EXERCISES

1. **Small-business assistance.** A variety of state and federal governmental agencies, along with financial services firms, offer several types of assistance to small business. Visit each of the Web sites listed and prepare a brief summary of what each offers small-business marketers.
   a. Small Business Administration: http://www.sba.gov
   b. State of Illinois: http://business.illinois.gov/sbr.cfm
   c. American Express: http://www.americanexpress.com (click on Small Business)

2. **Selling to national retailers.** A high percentage of B2B marketing consists of manufacturers selling products to national retailers. Each retailer establishes standards for vendors. Visit each of the following Web sites to learn more about what it takes to sell products to that retailer. Prepare a report on your findings.
   a. Home Depot: http://corporate.homedepot.com/wps/portal (click on For Suppliers)
   b. JCPenney: http://www.jcpenney.net/company/supplier/index.htm
   c. Wal-Mart Stores: http://www.walmartstores.com (click on Suppliers)

Note: Internet Web addresses change frequently. If you don't find the exact site listed, you may need to access the organization's home page and search from there or use a search engine such as Google.

CASE 6.1   Chip Wars: Intel vs. AMD in the B2B Market

Do you know what kind of microprocessor chip powers your computer or laptop? Do you care? Not long ago, consumers were happy to buy computers with Intel chips inside, and Intel was happy to count on orders from Dell and other manufacturers who were eager to give consumers what they wanted. But in the last few years, that situation has changed.

Fewer consumers are paying attention to what's inside their computers today, partly because microchip technology is becoming more complex and more confusing to the average computer user. But an even more threatening development to Intel is the rise of a small but feisty competitor called Advanced Micro Devices (AMD), which is battling Intel on several levels.

Not only is AMD producing a chip that some observers say is a better product than Intel markets, but the company is also mounting a legal challenge. Intel holds an 80 percent market share (by unit volume), which AMD calls an unlawful monopoly. AMD claims that Intel has also forced computer makers and retailers to use or carry its products. AMD filed charges that Intel used these illegal sales tactics on three continents. None of the legal dust has settled yet, but in the meantime AMD finally overtook Intel in the U.S. retail market for personal computers.

Intel is fighting back, and AMD's hard-won lead may not last for long. Both companies are hard at work trying to produce faster, more powerful chips at lower cost. Intel's CEO Paul Otellini says its most important competitive asset is the firm's sheer scale of manufacturing capacity and its newer, faster chips to replace its Pentium 4 processor. The company already has four factories making the new chips and is shifting other factories over. In addition to faster processing, the new chips require less power. Intel also inked a deal to put its chips in Apple computers for the first time, starting with a laptop bearing the new Napa chip. And Dell, one of Intel's largest customers, is showing no signs of disloyalty.

Intel's senior vice president for digital enterprise sums up its strategy: "We're going to ramp it like crazy and deliver it in volume. . . . It's a better product, and people buy better products."

Questions for Critical Thinking

1. In what ways do Intel and AMD create value for their business customers?
2. How important is it for a chip manufacturer to market its B2B products (microprocessor chips) to end users in the personal computer market who aren't particularly tech-savvy? What advantages or disadvantages does such a strategy offer?

Sources: Michael Kanellos, "Intel CEO Throws Down Gauntlet to AMD," CNet News.com, March 10, 2006, **http://news.com.com**; Frank Mitchell Russell, "Chip Giant Intel Ramps Up Microprocessor War with AMD," *San Jose Mercury News*, March 7, 2006, **http://www.mercurynews.com**; Mark LaPedus, "Intel vs. AMD Becomes an Epic," *InformationWeek*, December 16, 2005, **http://www.informationweek.com**; Megan Barnett, "A Chip on His Shoulder," *U.S. News & World Report*, October 17, 2005, pp. EE12–EE16.

VIDEO CASE 6.2   High Sierra Sport Company Excels in B2B

The written case on High Sierra appears on page VC-8. The recently filmed High Sierra video is designed to expand and highlight the concepts in this chapter and the concepts and questions covered in the written video case.

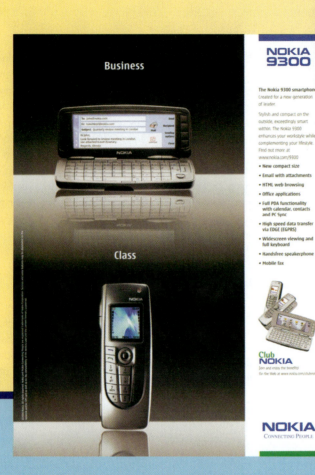

Finland and Nokia: Hot Competitors in a Cold Climate

Winters are cold and dark in Finland. They linger for months across all the Scandinavian countries. But Finland is a hot competitor in the global economy. According to the World Economic Forum, Nordic countries in general are more competitive than many other regions in the world, including Europe and Japan. And Finland tops all the charts, while the United States—the world's largest economy—ranks second. What makes Finland so important in the world marketplace? Economic experts say that Finland has a well-educated workforce, a population that knows how to use technology, and a well-managed economy. The country welcomes and nurtures new businesses, even though tax rates are high. The World Economic Forum calls Finland "one of the most innovative business environments in the world."

Nokia, the world's leading cell phone maker, is one of Finland's best-known companies. With $35 billion in annual sales, Nokia is a major contributor to Finland's economy. Famous for its phone design, Nokia introduced the first digital hand portable GSM phone, the first handset with changeable colors, and the first wireless application protocol (WAP) phone. But Nokia is really known for the aesthetics of its phones—designs that have turned phones into fashion accessories, or even jewelry. Design chief Frank Nuovo likens his company's phones to a person's watch. "If you buy a watch you wear it all the time," he explains. "It's on your person, and so it has a higher emotional purchase level—it has to fit your body, and yourself, as you are projecting yourself. Of all the technological products

that have been developed, the mobile phone has the potential to be on the same level as the watch or the purse." With fashion in mind, Nokia began offering consumers phones in different colors, with changeable covers, and with slight shape variations that differentiated its phones from those of its competitors. Then the firm went a step farther by hiring photographer and director David LaChapelle, who helped produce a marketing campaign called "Distinctly Bold." Consumers who visit the company Web site today can find all kinds of tips for coordinating a fashionable wardrobe—with a cell phone, of course.

But competitors such as Samsung and Motorola were closing in on Nokia. Nuovo likes to say that these firms were merely imitating Nokia's successes, but the

Global Marketing

fact was that they were gaining ground rapidly. "What happened is everybody had targeted the number one player and all of our successes," he argues. "They copied so many of our successes, they took our successes and innovated on top, and it's a natural evolution of the market for the gap to close." But instead of allowing the competition to roll over them, Nokia designers surged ahead once again with new designs that integrated beauty and function. A recent ad for its new 8800 model calls the phone "a perfect moment when aesthetics and functionality meet in perfect harmony."

Industry experts agree that one reason Nokia is so successful is that it creates universal designs—they are useful and appealing to consumers from many cultures. Frank Nuovo calls it Nokia DNA. "It is a physical characteristic and a usability style," he tries to explain. His designers draw from every aspect of life. They study men and women to learn what each wants in a product. And perhaps most important, the design team is made up of employees from 30 different countries. But there is no question that Nokia's philosophy is rooted in Finland and the Finnish values of performance, utility, and simplicity—not to mention the country's focus on technology. Economists suggest that other nations, particularly those in Europe, might benefit from examining this small nation's way of life. Finland markets itself the same way Nokia does—with optimism, innovation, and practicality, with an enthusiastic approach to getting the job done.[1]

evolution
of a brand

Nokia is one of the most successful mobile communications companies in the world. Since the beginning of the 1990s, the firm has concentrated on its core business of telecommunications, when it sold its information technology and basic telecommunications operations. For more than a decade, the company ruled the cell phone industry. But the company missed a significant shift in the market when competitors introduced the "clamshell" folding handset. As a result, Nokia lost some market share to competitors Motorola, Sony Ericsson, Samsung, and LG Electronics. In response, the firm refocused its design efforts by forming a design team made up of men and women from 30 nationalities to reap the creative benefits of diversity in gender and cultural backgrounds.

- Finland, Nokia's home country, puts 3.5 percent of its gross domestic product into research and development. In comparison, the United States invests about 2.6 percent, and the European Union as a whole less than 2 percent. But as in other developed countries, Finland has an aging population, with fewer young people and a growing senior sector. What opportunities and challenges do these facts present the company? How can it exploit its strengths and reduce its weaknesses?

Chapter Overview

Global trade now accounts for at least 27 percent of the U.S. gross domestic product (GDP), compared with 10 percent 30 years ago. Figure 7.1 shows the top ten nations with which the United States trades. Those ten countries account for nearly 70 percent of U.S. imports and two-thirds of U.S. exports.[2]

Global trade can be divided into two categories: **exporting**, marketing domestically produced goods and services abroad, and **importing**, purchasing foreign goods and services. Global trade is vital to a nation and its marketers for several reasons. It expands markets, makes production and distribution economies possible, allows companies to explore growth opportunities in other nations, and makes them less dependent on economic conditions in their home nations. Many also find that global marketing and trade can help them meet customer demand, reduce costs, and

exporting Marketing domestically produced goods and services in foreign countries.

importing Purchasing foreign goods and services.

figure 7.1

Top U.S. Trading Partners—Total Trade Including Exports and Imports

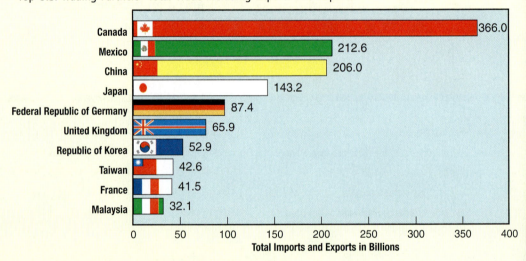

Country	Total Imports and Exports in Billions
Canada	366.0
Mexico	212.6
China	206.0
Japan	143.2
Federal Republic of Germany	87.4
United Kingdom	65.9
Republic of Korea	52.9
Taiwan	42.6
France	41.5
Malaysia	32.1

Source: Data from U.S. Census Bureau, "Top Trading Partners—Total Trade, Exports, Imports," Foreign Trade Division, **http://www.census.gov/foreign-trade/statistics**, accessed March 27, 2006.

provide valuable information on potential markets around the world.

For North American marketers, trade with foreign markets is especially important because the U.S. and Canadian economies represent a mature market for many products. Outside North America, however, it is a different story. Economies in many parts of sub-Saharan Africa, Asia, Latin America, Europe, and the Middle East are growing rapidly. This opens up new markets for U.S. products as consumers

in these areas have more money to spend and as the need for American goods and services by foreign companies expands. Exports of high-tech capital goods account for more than one-third of U.S total exports worldwide.[3] Global trade also builds employment. The United Nations estimates that 65,000 transnational corporations are operating today, employing more than 54 million workers directly and through subsidiaries. Many of these companies and their subsidiaries represent **related party trade,** which includes trade by U.S. companies with their subsidiaries overseas as well as trade by U.S. subsidiaries of foreign-owned firms with their parent companies. According to the U.S. Department of Commerce, related party trade accounts for $950 billion each year.[4] Because importing and exporting of so many goods and services play such an important role in the U.S. economy, your future job might very well involve global marketing, either here in the United States or overseas.

Global marketers carefully evaluate the marketing concepts described in other chapters. However, transactions that cross national borders involve additional considerations. For example, different laws, varying levels of technological capability, economic conditions, cultural and business norms, and consumer preferences often require new strategies. Companies that want to market their products worldwide must reconsider each of the marketing variables—product, distribution, promotion, and price—in terms of the global marketplace. To succeed in global marketing, today's marketers answer questions such as these:

- How do our products fit into a foreign market?

- How can we turn potential threats into opportunities?

- Which strategic alternatives will work in global markets?

Many of the answers to these questions can be found by studying techniques used by successful global marketers. This chapter first considers the importance and characteristics of foreign markets. It then examines the international marketing environment, the trend toward multinational economic integration, and the steps that most firms take to enter the global marketplace. Next, the importance of developing a global marketing mix is discussed. The chapter closes with a look at the United States as a target market for foreign marketers.

THE IMPORTANCE OF GLOBAL MARKETING

1 Describe the importance of global marketing from the perspectives of the individual firm and the nation.

As the list of the world's ten largest corporations shown in Table 7.1 reveals, more than half of these companies are headquartered in the United States. For most U.S. companies—both large and small—global marketing is rapidly becoming a necessity. The demand for foreign products in the fast-growing

table 7.1 World's Ten Largest Marketers (Ranked by Annual Sales)

RANK	COMPANY	COUNTRY	INDUSTRY	SALES (IN BILLIONS OF DOLLARS)
1	ExxonMobil	United States	Oil and gas	$328
2	Wal-Mart Stores	United States	Retailing	312
3	Royal Dutch/Shell Group	Netherlands	Oil and gas	307
4	BP	United Kingdom	Oil and gas	249
5	General Motors	United States	Consumer durable goods	193
6	Chevron	United States	Oil and gas	185
7	Ford Motor	United States	Consumer durable goods	178
8	DaimlerChrysler	Germany	Consumer durable goods	177
9	Toyota Motor	Japan	Consumer durable goods	173
10	ConocoPhillips	United States	Oil and gas	162

Source: Data from Scott DeCarlo, "The Forbes Global 2000: Ranked by Annual Sales," *Forbes*, March 30, 2006, **http://www.forbes.com**.

economies of Pacific Rim and other Asian nations offers one example of the benefits of thinking globally. In a recent year, U.S. exports to China alone rose 19 percent, to almost $42 billion.[5] This surge is partly because Asian consumers believe American goods are higher quality and a better value than those made in their own countries, as described in the "Marketing Success" feature. International marketers recognize how the slogan "Made in the USA" yields tremendous selling power throughout the world. As a result, overseas sales are important revenue sources for many U.S. firms.

Over the last decade, U.S. goods exports have increased 78 percent. Manufacturing exports rose 81 percent, high technology exports went up 77 percent, and agriculture exports increased 42 percent.[6] Among the leading U.S. firms in terms of the portion of their revenues generated from exports are Boeing, Intel, Motorola, Caterpillar, and Sun Microsystems.

Wal-Mart currently ranks as the world's largest private employer, with 1.5 million people, and the largest retailer; its annual sales are 50 percent greater than those of Target, Sears, Costco, and Kmart combined. The retail giant is currently devoting billions of dollars in expansion efforts abroad in Great Britain, the European mainland, Japan, South America, and Central America. Citigroup is also striving for global dominance through foreign markets. Now operating in 54 countries outside the United States, Citigroup is beating the bushes looking for customers overseas. No customer is too small to serve, including a Brazilian worker who needs a $450 loan to cover his daughter's medical bills.[7]

The rapid globalization of business and the boundless nature of the Internet have made it possible for every marketer to become an international marketer. However, becoming an Internet global marketer is not necessarily easy. While larger firms have the advantage of more resources and wider distribution systems, smaller companies can build Web sites for as little as a few hundred dollars and can bring products to market quickly. PayPal, the online payment service owned by eBay, helps such firms complete transactions with their customers. Blue Jeans Cable, a small online provider of custom audio and video cable, turned to PayPal to collect customer payments from anywhere in the world. "We are basically a cash-financed business, so getting paid up front for products is critical," explains Blue Jeans Cable's Kurt Denke.[8]

Just as some firms depend on foreign and Internet sales, others rely on purchasing raw materials abroad as input for their domestic manufacturing operations. A North Carolina furniture manufacturer may depend on purchases of South American mahogany, while 21st-century furniture retailers are taking advantage of increased Chinese-made styling and quality and their traditionally low prices. The top five U.S. imports are computers and office equipment, crude oil, clothing, telecommunications equipment, and agricultural products.

SERVICE AND RETAIL EXPORTS

Manufacturing no longer accounts for the lion's share of annual production output in the United States. Today, three of every five dollars included in the nation's gross domestic product (GDP)

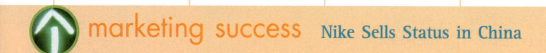

marketing success   Nike Sells Status in China

Background. Nike is an American company with a strong brand, and its logo—the swoosh—is recognized almost anywhere. Founded in the mid-1960s by Phil Knight, the company established itself in the minds of consumers with ads for its running shoes featuring Michael Jordan and other athletes. Today, Nike includes brands such as Converse, Starter, Cole Haan, and Bauer. To continue its success, the firm needs to grow globally.

The Challenge. How does an American firm crack the enormous potential market in China? Nike is determined to outfit millions of Chinese consumers with shoes bearing the swoosh—and is well on the road to doing so.

The Strategy. As soon as the Chinese government began to allow foreign products to be marketed to its citizens, Nike was there. Many of its shoes were already manufactured in Asia, so the leap seemed to be a natural one. Nike launched a TV commercial in China featuring track and field star Liu Xiang becoming his nation's first Olympic gold medalist in hurdling at the Athens Olympics. Instead of focusing on running shoes, however, the ad focused on Chinese pride. The commercial was a hit. Positioning itself for the 2008 Beijing Olympics, Nike is driving hard in China, opening an average of 1.5 new stores each day, using marketing messages that emphasize status and pride rather than the benefits of its products.

comes from services—banking, entertainment, business and technical services, retailing, and communications. Although manufacturing exports are healthier than they were a decade ago, these figures represent a profound shift from a largely manufacturing to a largely service economy. Still, manufacturers as diverse as General Motors and Procter & Gamble strive to serve growing markets such as China. GM offers a wide range of car models to Chinese consumers, while P&G offers some of its most popular brands such as Tide and Crest.[9]

In addition to agricultural products and manufactured goods, the United States is the world's largest exporter of services and retailing. Of the approximately $290 billion in annual U.S. service exports, more than half comes from travel and tourism—money spent by foreign nationals visiting the United States.

American furniture retailers Stickley, Drexel Heritage, Henredon, and Thomasville all use imported mahogany from South America and the Philippines in their furniture lines.

But China is expected to become the number one tourist destination in the world before 2020. The World Trade Organization predicts that China will host 137 million overnight tourists annually by then. In turn, nearly 29 million Chinese citizens are now traveling abroad each year, making China the largest source of international tourists in Asia. Experts predict that number could reach 50 million by the end of the decade.[10]

The most profitable U.S. service exports are business and technical services, such as engineering, financial, computing, legal services, insurance, and entertainment. The financial services industry, already a major presence outside North America, is expanding globally via the Internet. Nearly half the world's active Web population visits a finance Web site at least once a month, with online stock trading and banking leading the way. And more than one of every four Europeans with Internet access currently banks online. A glance at the increasing number of foreign companies listed on the New York Stock Exchange illustrates the importance of global financial services. A number of global service exporters are household names in the United States: American Express, AT&T, Citigroup, Disney, and Allstate Insurance. Many earn a substantial percentage of their revenues from

The Outcome. According to one survey, Chinese consumers now view Nike as the "coolest brand." Sales increased 66 percent in one year, to $300 million, an indication that Chinese consumers continue to be hungry for Western goods. The new Chinese middle class "seeks Western culture," says social scientist Zhang Wanli. "Nike was smart because it didn't enter China selling usefulness, but selling status."

Sources: Matthew Forney, "How Nike Figured Out China," *Time,* http://www.time.com, accessed March 24, 2006; Jon Birger and David Stires, "CEO on the Hot Seat," CNN Money.com, February 6, 2006, http://money.cnn.com; Andrew Patterson, "Phil Knight's Not Diversified," Motley Fool, February 3, 2006, http://www.fool.com.

international sales. Others are smaller firms, such as the many software firms that have found overseas markets receptive to their products. Still others are nonprofit organizations such as the U.S. Postal Service, which is attempting to increase overall revenues by operating a worldwide delivery service. The service competes with for-profit firms such as DHL, UPS, and Federal Express.

The entertainment industry is another major service exporter. Movies, TV shows, and music groups often travel to the ends of the earth to entertain their audiences. Almost a century of exposure to U.S.-made films, television programs, and, more recently, music video clips has made international viewers more familiar with American culture and geography than that of any other nation on earth. However, some markets are more receptive to American entertainment than others, depending on their own culture and language barriers. A Los Angeles–based film production company, Nu Image, is trying to purchase Boyana Film Studios in Sofia, Bulgaria. Nu Image has already made nearly 50 movies in Bulgaria in less than a decade and wants to establish a physical presence in eastern Europe. Why? A U.S. film producer can cut more than 50 percent of the cost of producing a movie by setting up shop in Bulgaria. So far, Nu Image has created 600 new jobs in Sofia, but Boyana's owners aren't eager to sell. They worry that the U.S. firm will not create movies that reflect Bulgarian culture and preferences.[11]

U.S. retailers, ranging from Foot Locker and The Gap to Office Depot and Costco, are opening stores around the world at rapid paces. Recently, Russian consumers have increased their purchases—in fact, the new Mega-1 mall in southern Moscow is often jammed with shoppers. They browse through Swedish home furnishings retailer IKEA and visit a host of other boutiques filled with U.S. merchandise. One survey reports that Mega-1 is the busiest shopping center in the world, with 52 million visitors a year. Although Russian workers generally earn less than those in the United States, they have fewer expenses. In fact, 70 percent of Russian income is disposable—available for spending—compared with 40 percent in Western countries such as the United States.[12]

BENEFITS OF GOING GLOBAL

Besides generating additional revenue, firms expand their operations outside their home country to gain other benefits, including new insights into consumer behavior, alternative distribution strategies, and advance notice of new products. By setting up foreign offices and production facilities, marketers may encounter new products, new approaches to distribution, or clever new promotions that they may be able to apply successfully in their domestic market or in other international markets.

Global marketers are typically well positioned to compete effectively with foreign competitors. A major key to achieving success in foreign markets is a firm's ability to adapt its products to local preferences and culture. To satisfy China's large and diverse population, Samsung offers a variety of models and price ranges on its appliances and electronics. Samsung marketers know that people who live in the hot and muggy climate of Guangdong province need larger refrigerators than those who live in the north. And Procter & Gamble knows that rural Chinese consumers need a lower-priced Tide than those who live in the city. So P&G sells Tide Clean White throughout the countryside while city dwellers can pick up Tide Triple Action.[13]

A product as seemingly universal as pizza must be localized as well. Papa John's pizza now has more than 400 pizza shops in eighteen countries, with plans for another 400 over the next few years. CEO Nigel Travis points out that ethnic preferences, income levels, and even religious prohibitions against certain ingredients have an effect on the types of pizza each shop makes and serves. Consumers in some countries would rather eat their pizza in a restaurant, while others prefer home delivery. So Papa John's relies heavily on marketers and other employees who know each market thoroughly. "We now have a lot of people with international experience," says Travis. "When you go into other markets, you have to be aware of local tastes."[14]

Because companies must perform the marketing functions of buying, selling, transporting, storing, standardizing and grading, financing, risk taking, and obtaining market information in both domestic and global

 assessment check

1. Define *importing* and *exporting*.
2. What is the largest category of exports from the United States?
3. What must global marketers be able to do effectively to reach foreign markets?

markets, some may question the wisdom of treating global marketing as a distinct subject. But as this chapter will explain, there are similarities and differences that influence strategies for both domestic and global marketing.

THE INTERNATIONAL MARKETING ENVIRONMENT

2 Identify the major components of the environment for global marketing.

As in domestic markets, the environmental factors discussed in Chapter 3 have a powerful influence on the development of a firm's global marketing strategy. Marketers must pay close attention to changing demand patterns as well as competitive, economic, social-cultural, political-legal, and technological influences when they venture abroad.

INTERNATIONAL ECONOMIC ENVIRONMENT

A nation's size, per-capita income, and stage of economic development determine its prospects as a host for international business expansion. Nations with low per-capita incomes may be poor markets for expensive industrial machinery but good ones for agricultural hand tools. These nations cannot afford the technical equipment that powers an industrialized society. Wealthier countries may offer prime markets for many U.S. industries, particularly those producing consumer goods and services and advanced industrial products.

But some less industrialized countries are growing fast. India and China, for example, may rival the United States in world economic importance in a generation or two. Although the U.S. per-capita income of $41,800 ranks way above China's $6,200 and India's $3,400, these nations have far larger populations and thus more potential human capital to develop in the future.[15] Their ability to import technology and foreign capital, as well as to train scientists and engineers and invest in research and development, ensures that their growth will be rapid and their income gaps with the United States will close quickly. Together, India and China have contributed one-third of the global GDP in the past few years.[16]

Infrastructure, the underlying foundation for modern life and efficient marketing that includes transportation, communications, banking, utilities, and public services, is another important economic factor to consider when planning to enter a foreign market. An inadequate infrastructure may constrain marketers' plans to manufacture, promote, and distribute goods and services in a particular country. People living in countries blessed by navigable waters often rely on them as inexpensive, relatively efficient alternatives to highways, rail lines, and air transportation. Thai farmers use their nation's myriad rivers to transport their crops. Their boats even become retail outlets in so-called floating markets like the one located outside the capital city of Bangkok. Often the population in rural areas begins to shift to where the infrastructure is more developed. This change is happening in both China and India, where people are moving to cities and coastal areas.[17] Marketers expect developing economies to have substandard utility and communications networks. China encountered numerous problems in establishing a 21st-century communications industry infrastructure. The Chinese government's answer was to bypass the need for landline telephone connections by leapfrogging technologies and moving directly to cell phones.

© KYODO/LANDOV

As part of its infrastructure, Japan has an extensive and modern railway system.

exchange rate Price of one nation's currency in terms of another country's currency.

Changes in exchange rates can also complicate international marketing. An **exchange rate** is the price of one nation's currency in terms of another country's currency. Fluctuations in exchange rates can make a nation's currency more or less valuable compared with those of other nations. In today's global economy, imbalances in trade, dependence on fossil fuels, and other conditions affect the currencies of many countries, not just one or two.[18]

At the beginning of the 21st century, most members of the European Union switched to the euro as the replacement to their traditional francs and liras. The long-range idea behind the new currency is that switching to a single currency will strengthen Europe's competitiveness in the global marketplace. Russian and many eastern European currencies are considered *soft currencies* that cannot be readily converted into such hard currencies as the dollar, euro, or Japanese yen.

INTERNATIONAL SOCIAL-CULTURAL ENVIRONMENT

Before entering a foreign country, marketers should study all aspects of that nation's culture, including language, education, religious attitudes, and social values. The French love to debate and are comfortable with frequent eye contact. In China, humility is a prized virtue, colors have special significance, and it is insulting to be late. Swedes value consensus and do not use humor in negotiations. The "Etiquette Tips for Marketing Professionals" feature offers some examples that will help you deal with cultural differences that arise in business dealings with foreign guests.

Language plays an important role in global marketing. Table 7.2 lists the world's ten most frequently spoken languages. Marketers must make sure not only to use the appropriate language or languages for a country but also to ensure that the message is correctly translated and conveys the intended meaning.

Firms that rely on call centers located in India and staffed by Indian nationals have discovered an occasional language gap. But these employees do speak English, which is the second most spoken language in the world. Despite some glitches, the call centers, along with other outsourced operations, are booming—creating jobs and a new middle class in India. Workers now have money to spend, and have begun to value goods and services that only a few years ago would not have been considered desirable or even appropriate. About 9 percent of the urban Indian household spending now goes toward personal-care goods and services. "A generation ago, there's no way that the Indian male would have been spending this sort of money on his looks," says Hemant Mehta, an Indian marketing researcher.[19]

Briefly
Speaking

"There have been many definitions of hell, but for the English the best definition is that it is a place where the Germans are the police, the Swedish are the comedians, the Italians are the defence force, Frenchmen dig the roads, the Belgians are the pop singers, the Spanish run the railways, the Turks cook the food, the Irish are the waiters, the Greeks run the government, and the common language is Dutch."

—David Frost (b. 1939)
English author and TV show host

table 7.2	The World's Most Frequently Spoken Languages	
RANK	**LANGUAGE**	**NUMBER OF SPEAKERS**
1	Mandarin (Chinese)	1 billion +
2	English	514 million
3	Hindustani	496 million
4	Spanish	425 million
5	Russian	275 million
6	Arabic	256 million
7	Bengali	215 million
8	Portuguese	194 million
9	Malay-Indonesian	176 million
10	French	129 million

Source: Data from "Most Widely Spoken Languages in the World," **http://www.infoplease.com,** accessed March 27, 2006.

Etiquette Tips for Marketing Professionals

Entertaining Foreign Guests

In today's global marketplace, you have a good chance of attending—or even hosting—a function at which foreign customers or colleagues are your firm's guests. Although you may feel nervous about the event, knowing how to act correctly will help you and your guests relax and feel comfortable. The best thing you can do is plan ahead and learn what you can about the culture that your guests represent. Keep in mind that different cultures have different norms of behavior—being on time is very important to Europeans, whereas being late is acceptable to Latin Americans. Here are some hints that should help make the gathering a success.

1. Many business discussions—and deals—take place over a meal. So brush up on your table manners. Even if your guests have slightly different customs, they will recognize your good etiquette. "What turns foreigners off the most is the lack of protocol and table manners that American businesspeople have. I constantly hear complaints about it," warns Samantha von Sperling of Polished Social Image Consultants.

2. Treat your guests with more formality than you might think is necessary. Foreign businesspeople expect more formality than Americans do. For example, men should stand to greet women.

3. If you are at a restaurant, assist your guests if they appear to need help with the menu. If they are uncertain, recommend something that is easy to eat—pass by the lobster or ribs. Try to ascertain ahead of time whether they will expect multiple courses, and help them order accordingly.

4. Take the time to establish a relationship, particularly with Chinese or South American guests. Don't jump into business discussions over appetizers. Instead, chat about nonbusiness issues, but don't ask overly personal questions or talk too much about yourself. If English is a second language for your guests, be sure to speak clearly and try to avoid slang or other expressions that are difficult to interpret.

5. Above all, treat your guests with respect, and remember that the ultimate goal of good manners is to make everyone at the gathering feel comfortable—regardless of the business outcome. "Treating people with respect, consideration and honesty . . . that's really the key," says Peter Post of the Emily Post Institute. "And sincerity is an important part of it, that the things you are doing are coming from the heart."

Sources: Business English Training, **http://www.business-english-training. com/chinawork.htm**, accessed March 24, 2006; "Hosting Foreign Visitors," U.S. Department of Energy Chicago Operations Office, **http://www.ch.doe.gov**, accessed March 14, 2006; Mary K. Pratt, "Sensitivity, Planning Key to Hosting Foreign Clients," *Boston Business Journal*, August 15, 2005, **http://boston.bizjournals.com**.

INTERNATIONAL TECHNOLOGICAL ENVIRONMENT

More than any innovation since the telephone, Internet technology has made it possible for both large and small firms to be connected to the entire world. The Internet transcends political, economic, and cultural barriers, reaching to every corner of the globe. It has made it possible for traditional brick-and-mortar retailers to add new business channels. It also helps developing nations become competitive with industrialized nations. However, a huge gap still exists between the regions with the greatest Internet usage and those with the least. Asia, Europe, and North America together account for nearly 87 percent of the world's total Internet usage, Latin America and the Caribbean follow with almost 8 percent, while Africa accounts for less than 3 percent, Oceania/Australia just below 2 percent, and the Middle East also below 2 percent. Despite those numbers, Africa's usage grew 430 percent in just one year, and the Middle East jumped nearly 400 percent.[20]

Technology presents challenges for global marketers that extend beyond the Internet and other telecommunications innovations. A major issue involving food marketers competing in Europe is

60% of Japanese computer games
are designed in North England.

Game on.

It's not easy to impress the Japanese. Their exacting standards mean only a limited number of companies actually make the grade. So it's quite an accolade for North England to achieve such a high percentage, particularly as most of these games are worldwide best sellers. Expertise in technology and electronics isn't limited simply to computer games. From online gambling software to intelligent applications for mobile phones and Wi Fi telecoms, U.S. companies are extensively utilizing the region's specialist skills, so it's no coincidence that the top global electronics companies have their headquarters in North England. To date, over 1200 American companies here, have moved up to the next level. Ready to play? Visit www.northengland.com

THE NORTH of ENGLAND
INWARD INVESTMENT AGENCY

SUCCESS FOLLOWS SUCCESS.

Asia, Europe, and the United States combined use the greatest amount of Internet and electronic technologies in the world. Shown here is the Worms video game, which was created in England for the Japanese market.

genetic reengineering. Although U.S. grocery shelves are filled with foods grown with genetically modified organisms (GMOs), most Americans are unaware they are eating GMO foods because no labeling disclosures are required. However, in Europe, several organizations have moved to ban these foods. Local and regional authorities have declared themselves "GMO-free," but the European Court of Justice has yet to issue a ruling that would ban GMOs throughout the European Union.[21] This complex issue affects almost every marketer in the global food industry.

INTERNATIONAL POLITICAL-LEGAL ENVIRONMENT

Global marketers must continually stay abreast of laws and trade regulations in each country in which they compete. Political conditions often influence international marketing as well. Political unrest in places such as the Middle East, Africa, eastern Europe, Spain, and South America sometimes results in acts of violence, such as destruction of a firm's property or even deaths from bombings or other terrorist acts. As a result, many Western firms have set up internal **political risk assessment (PRA)** units or turned to outside consulting services to evaluate the political risks of the marketplaces in which they operate.

The political environment also involves labor conditions in different countries. In Europe, dockworkers went on strike and demonstrators fought police and smashed windows in the European Parliament building to protest legislation that would liberalize cargo handling at ports. Unions worried that the bill would eliminate jobs and reduce wages, while cargo-handling firms worried that they would lose contracts to competitors.[22]

The legal environment for U.S. firms operating abroad results from three forces: (1) international law, (2) U.S. law, and (3) legal requirements of host nations. International law emerges from treaties, conventions, and agreements among nations. The United States has many **friendship, commerce, and navigation (FCN) treaties** with other governments. These agreements set terms for various aspects of commercial relations with other countries, such as the right to conduct business in the treaty partner's domestic market. Other international business agreements concern worldwide standards for various products, patents, trademarks, reciprocal tax treaties, export control, international air travel, and international communications.

Since the 1990s, Europe has pushed for mandatory **ISO (International Organization for Standardization) certification**—internationally recognized standards that ensure that a company's goods, services, and operations meet established quality levels. The organization has two sets of standards: The ISO 9000 series of standards sets requirements for quality in goods and services; the ISO 14000 series sets standards for operations that minimize harm to the environment. Today, many U.S. companies follow these certification standards as well. Currently, about 760,900 organizations in 154 countries participate in both series.[23] The International Monetary Fund, another major player in the international legal environment, lends foreign exchange to nations that require it to conduct international trade. These agreements facilitate the entire process of world marketing. However, there are no international laws for corporations—only for governments. So marketers include special provisions in contracts, such as which country's courts have jurisdiction.

The second dimension of the international legal environment, U.S. law, includes various trade regulations, tax laws, and import/export requirements that affect international marketing. One important law, the Export Trading Company Act of 1982, exempts companies from antitrust regulations so that they can form export groups that offer a variety of products to foreign buyers. The law seeks to make it easier for foreign buyers to connect with U.S. exporters. The controversial Helms-Burton Act of 1996 strengthened international trade sanctions against the Cuban government. A decade later, argument still raged over whether the law should remain on the books or be repealed.[24] The Foreign Corrupt Practices Act, which makes it illegal to bribe a foreign official in an attempt to solicit new or repeat sales abroad, has had a major impact on international marketing. The act also mandates that adequate accounting controls be installed to monitor internal compliance. Violations can result in a $1 million fine for

© ASSOCIATED PRESS, AP

U.S. laws regulate the flow of certain goods, such as prescription drugs, to and from the United States.

the firm and a $10,000 fine and five-year imprisonment for the individuals involved. This law has been controversial, mainly because it fails to clearly define what constitutes bribery. The 1988 Trade Act amended the law to include more specific statements of prohibited practices.

Finally, legal requirements of host nations affect foreign marketers. Both Google and Yahoo! have faced such challenges in China. The Chinese government limits Internet access of its citizens, including Web sites considered objectionable and e-mail messaging or blogging. Congress is investigating whether these two firms collaborated too closely with the Chinese government to restrict such access, while the companies argue that it is their responsibility to follow local laws.[25]

TRADE BARRIERS

Assorted trade barriers also affect global marketing. These barriers fall into two major categories: **tariffs**—taxes levied on imported products—and administrative, or nontariff, barriers. Some tariffs impose set taxes per pound, gallon, or unit; others are calculated according to the value of the imported item. Administrative barriers are more subtle than tariffs and take a variety of forms such as customs barriers, quotas on imports, unnecessarily restrictive standards for imports, and export subsidies. Because the GATT and WTO agreements (discussed later in the chapter) eliminated tariffs on many products, countries frequently use nontariff barriers to boost exports and control the flows of imported products.

tariff Tax levied against imported goods.

The United States and other nations continually negotiate tariffs and other trade agreements. One such recent agreement, the U.S.–Central American Free Trade Agreement and Dominican Republic (CAFTA-DR), seeks to streamline and reduce the costs involved in exporting goods among the six countries covered by the agreement—Costa Rica, El Salvador, Guatemala, Honduras, Nicaragua, and the Dominican Republic. While the United States already considers these nations trading partners, the agreement should pave the way for smoother exchanges over time. Better infrastructures as well as increasing incomes make these promising markets for global firms.[26]

Tariffs

The United States has long been the champion of free trade throughout the world, but recently, with shrinking economies of industrialized foreign nations and a growing number of developing countries that are struggling to stabilize their economies, U.S. legislators have been pressured to protect domestic industries from troubles abroad. But moves designed to protect business at home are often a double-edged sword. They also frequently end up penalizing domestic consumers because prices typically rise under protectionist regulations. In a program that many call outdated, the U.S. government sets high tariffs on imported sugar to support U.S. sugar production. So U.S. consumers generally wind up paying higher prices for sugar, which are about double the worldwide prices.[27]

Tariffs can be classified as either revenue or protective tariffs. **Revenue tariffs** are designed to raise funds for the importing government. For years, most U.S. government revenue came from this source. **Protective tariffs,** which are usually higher than revenue tariffs, are designed to raise the retail price of an imported product to match or exceed that of a similar domestic product. Some countries use tariffs in a selective manner to discourage certain consumption practices and thereby reduce access to their local markets. For example, the United States has tariffs on luxury items such as Rolex watches and Russian caviar. In 1988, the United States passed the Omnibus Trade and Competitiveness Act to remedy what it perceived as unfair international trade conditions. Under the so-called Super 301 provisions of the law, the United States can now single out countries that unfairly impede trade with U.S. domestic businesses. If these countries do not open their markets within eighteen months, the law requires retaliation in the form of U.S. tariffs or quotas on the offenders' imports into this country.

Tariffs can also be used to gain bargaining clout with other countries, but they risk adversely affecting the fortunes of domestic companies. One industry that causes great debate between countries is agriculture. Currently, the United States and the European Union (EU) are locked in disagreement over the high tariffs imposed by the EU on agricultural products from developing nations.[28]

Other Trade Barriers

In addition to direct taxes on imported products, governments may erect a number of other barriers, ranging from special permits and detailed inspection requirements to quotas on foreign-made items in an effort to stem the flow of imported goods—or halt them altogether. European shoppers pay about twice the price for bananas that North Americans pay. The reason for these high prices? Through a series of import license controls, Europe allows fewer bananas to be imported than people want to buy. Even worse, the European countries set up a system of quotas designed to support banana growing in former colonies in Africa and Asia, which restricts imports from Latin America and Caribbean countries. Although the EU tried to modify the system, the World Trade Organization (WTO) rejected the new proposal, saying it did not do enough to provide market access for these countries.[29]

import quotas Trade restrictions that limit the number of units of certain goods that can enter a country for resale.

Other forms of trade restrictions include import quotas and embargoes. **Import quotas** limit the number of units of products in certain categories that can cross a country's border for resale. The quota is supposed to protect domestic industry and employment and to preserve foreign exchange, but it doesn't always work that way. Since the late 1950s, the United States has had quotas affecting the apparel industry—whether they involve certain textiles or the manufacturing of the clothes themselves. However, foreign companies often find loopholes in the quota systems and wind up not only with huge profits but also plenty of jobs for their own workers. China and the United States have been locked in a battle over quotas on textiles and apparel. Recently, the U.S. government imposed a new limit of a 7.5 percent increase on the import of Chinese-manufactured clothing. The Chinese Commerce Ministry fired back that the new limit would "seriously damage the confidence of Chinese businesses and people in the international trade environment since China joined WTO."[30]

The ultimate quota is the **embargo**—a complete ban on the import of a product. Since 1960, the United States has maintained an embargo against Cuba in protest of Fidel Castro's dictatorship and policies such as expropriation of property and disregard for human rights. Not only do the sanctions prohibit Cuban exports—cigars and sugar are the island's best-known products—to enter the country, but they also apply to companies that profit from property that Cuba's communist government expropriated from Americans following the Cuban revolution. However, many leading U.S. executives oppose the embargo. They know that they are losing the opportunity to develop the Cuban market while foreign rivals establish production and marketing facilities there. Several years ago, the discovery of mad cow disease and the potential for contaminated beef resulted in a number of embargoes. Japan, which was the world's largest purchaser of American beef, shut its doors after the first case of mad cow disease was discovered in the United States. However, the Japanese beef industry later confirmed cases of mad cow disease in its own herds.[31]

Other trade barriers include **subsidies.** Airbus, the European aircraft consortium, often comes under attack from U.S. trade officials because it is so heavily subsidized by the European Union. The Europeans, on the other hand, argue that Boeing and Lockheed Martin benefit from research done by NASA, the Pentagon, and other U.S. agencies.[32] Some nations also limit foreign ownership in the business sectors. And still another way to block international trade is to create so many regulatory barriers that it is almost impossible to reach target markets. China presents a maze of regulations controlling trade. However, one barrier that was recently lifted was the requirement that a foreign firm enter into a joint venture with a Chinese firm. But most experienced businesspeople agree that it is still easier to navigate all the regulations with a Chinese partner than to try to go it alone.[33]

Foreign trade can also be regulated by exchange control through a central bank or government agency. **Exchange control** means that firms that gain foreign exchange by exporting must sell foreign currencies to the central bank or other foreign agency, and importers must buy foreign currencies from the same organization. The exchange control authority can then allocate, expand, or restrict foreign exchange according to existing national policy.

DUMPING

The practice of selling a product in a foreign market at a price lower than it commands in the producer's domestic market is called **dumping.** Critics of free trade often argue that foreign governments give substantial support to their own exporting companies. Government support may permit these firms to extend their export markets by offering lower prices abroad. In retaliation for this kind of interference with free trade, the United States adds import tariffs to products that foreign firms dump on U.S. markets to bring their prices in line with those of domestically produced products. However, businesses often complain that charges of dumping must undergo a lengthy investigative and bureaucratic procedure before the government assesses import duties. U.S. firms that claim dumping threatens to hurt their business can file a complaint with the U.S. International Trade Commission (ITC), which—on average—rejects about half the claims it receives.

In a move against the dumping of cheap leather shoes into the European market by Chinese and Vietnamese manufacturers, the EU applied import duties starting at 4 percent and increasing to 19.4 percent on the Chinese shoes and 16.8 percent on the Vietnamese shoes. According to EU officials, more than 1.2 billion pairs of Chinese shoes had been sold at cheap prices in Europe the previous year. The duties would last for six months while the EU investigated the dumping allegations but could continue for as long as five years.[34]

 assessment check

1. What are the three criteria that determine a nation's prospects as a host for international business expansion?
2. What is an FCN treaty?
3. What are the two major categories of trade barriers?

MULTINATIONAL ECONOMIC INTEGRATION

A noticeable trend toward multinational economic integration has developed over the six decades since the end of World War II. Multinational economic integration can be set up in several ways. The simplest approach is to establish a **free-trade area** in which participating nations agree to the free trade of goods among themselves, abolishing tariffs and trade restrictions. A **customs union** establishes a free-trade area plus a uniform tariff for trade with nonmember nations. A **common market** extends a customs union by seeking to reconcile all government regulations affecting trade. Despite the many factors in its favor, not everyone is enthusiastic about free trade, particularly Americans who hear news reports of U.S. jobs being outsourced to lower-wage nations such as China, India, and Bulgaria—and worry that their jobs may be affected. So it is important to consider both sides of the issue. Although productivity and innovation are said to grow more quickly with free trade, American workers face pay-cut demands and potential job loss as more companies move their operations overseas. But many firms view the change as a collaboration, and a way to offer superior service. Consider U.S.-based firm Penske Truck Leasing and its outsourcing partner, India-based Genpact. When Penske buys a new truck for lease, Genpact can obtain state titles, registrations, and permits electronically. When the truck is returned to Penske, Genpact receives the driver's log, taxes, fuel, and toll documents. Genpact forwards all the electronic information to its own remote office in Mexico, where workers enter the data into Penske's computer system. Penske claims that its new system solves problems more quickly and efficiently.[35]

3 Outline the basic functions of GATT, WTO, NAFTA, FTAA, CAFTA-DR, and the European Union.

GATT AND THE WORLD TRADE ORGANIZATION

The **General Agreement on Tariffs and Trade (GATT),** a trade accord that has sponsored several rounds of major tariff negotiations, substantially reducing worldwide tariff levels, has existed for six decades. In 1994, a seven-year series of GATT conferences, called the Uruguay Round, culminated in one of the biggest victories for free trade in decades.

The Uruguay Round reduced average tariffs by one-third, or more than $700 billion. Among its major victories were the following:

General Agreement on Tariffs and Trade (GATT) International trade accord that has helped reduce world tariffs.

- reduced farm subsidies, which opened vast new markets for U.S. exports

- increased protection for patents, copyrights, and trademarks

- included services under international trading rules, creating opportunities for U.S. financial, legal, and accounting firms

- phased out import quotas on textiles and clothing from developing nations, a move that cost textile workers thousands of jobs when their employers moved many of these domestic jobs to lower-wage countries, but benefited U.S. retailers and consumers

World Trade Organization (WTO) Organization that replaces GATT, overseeing GATT agreements, making binding decisions in mediating disputes, and reducing trade barriers.

A key outcome of the GATT talks was establishment of the **World Trade Organization (WTO),** a 149-member organization that succeeds GATT. The WTO oversees GATT agreements, mediates disputes, and continues the effort to reduce trade barriers throughout the world. Unlike GATT, WTO decisions are binding. Countries that seek to become members of the WTO must participate in rigorous rounds of negotiations. China, the world's largest nation, is one of the newest members of the WTO, and its entrance into the organization has not been without disagreements. As a market, China holds enormous potential for exporters, but the nation's government has traditionally made it very difficult for foreign firms to operate there. But as China relaxed some of its trade barriers, it was admitted to the WTO.

To date, the WTO has made slow progress toward its major policy initiatives—liberalizing world financial services, telecommunications, and maritime markets. Trade officials have not agreed on the direction for the WTO. Its activities have focused more on complaint resolution than on removing global trade barriers. The United States has been the most active plaintiff in WTO dispute courts. Big differences between developed and developing areas create a major roadblock to WTO progress. These conflicts became apparent at the first WTO meeting in Singapore in the late 1990s. Asian nations want trade barriers lifted on their manufactured goods, but they also want to protect their own telecommunications companies. In addition, they oppose monitoring of corruption and local labor practices by outsiders. The United States wants free trade for telecommunications, more controls on corruption, and establishment of international labor standards. Europe wants standard rules on foreign investments and removal of profit repatriation restrictions but is not as concerned with worker rights. Currently, six major players in the WTO—the EU, the United States, Japan, Australia, Brazil, and India—are trying to negotiate more liberalized farm trade and the opening of markets for industrial products, but no major agreement has been reached.[36]

THE NAFTA ACCORD

North American Free Trade Agreement (NAFTA) Accord removing trade barriers between Canada, Mexico, and the United States.

More than a decade after the passage of the **North American Free Trade Agreement (NAFTA),** an agreement between the United States, Canada, and Mexico that removes trade restrictions among the three nations over a period, negotiations among the nations continue. The three nations insist that they will not create a trade bloc similar to the European Union—that is, they will not focus on political integration but instead on economic cooperation.[37] NAFTA is particularly important to U.S. marketers because Canada and Mexico are this country's largest trading partners. Proponents of NAFTA claim that the treaty has been good for the American economy, citing an increase in U.S.

industrial production and productivity, among other benefits. Critics charge that U.S. and Canadian workers have lost jobs to cheap Mexican labor. However, NAFTA supporters point out that the availability of cheap labor has allowed the prices of some goods to drop, leaving Americans with more money to spend and stimulating the economy. Every day, NAFTA countries conduct nearly $2.2 billion in trade with each other, with a GDP growth of 49 percent for Canada, 48 percent for the United States, and 40 percent for Mexico since the passage of the agreement.[38]

THE FREE TRADE AREA OF THE AMERICAS AND CAFTA-DR

NAFTA was the first step toward creating a **Free Trade Area of the Americas (FTAA),** stretching the length of the entire Western Hemisphere, from Alaska's Bering Strait to Cape Horn at South America's southern tip, encompassing 34 countries, a population of 800 million, and a combined gross domestic product of more than $11 trillion. The FTAA would be the largest free-trade zone on earth, including the European Union, and would offer low or nonexistent tariffs, streamlined customs, and no quotas, subsidies, or other barriers to trade. In addition to the United States, Canada, and Mexico, countries expected to be members of the proposed FTAA include Argentina, Brazil, Chile, Colombia, Ecuador, Guatemala, Jamaica, Peru, Trinidad and Tobago, Uruguay, and Venezuela. The United States is a staunch supporter of the FTAA, which still has many hurdles to overcome as countries wrangle for conditions that are most favorable to them.[39]

As FTAA negotiations continue, the United States has entered into an agreement with the Dominican Republic and Central American nations known as the **Central American Free Trade Agreement-DR (CAFTA-DR).** Some of its provisions took effect immediately, while others will be phased in over the next two decades. Supporters of the agreement say it will help American workers, farmers, and small businesses thrive and grow; critics worry that more American agricultural and manufacturing jobs will be lost. However, both sides agree that CAFTA's economic impact is likely to be relatively small compared with that of NAFTA.[40]

THE EUROPEAN UNION

The best-known example of a multinational economic community is the European Union (EU). As Figure 7.2 shows, 25 countries make up the EU: Finland, Sweden, Denmark, the United Kingdom, Ireland, the Netherlands, Belgium, Germany, Luxembourg, France, Austria, Italy, Greece, Spain, Portugal, Hungary, Poland, the Czech Republic, the Slovak Republic, Slovenia, Estonia, Latvia, Lithuania, Malta, and Cyprus. Four countries—Turkey, Bulgaria, Romania, and Croatia—have applicant status.[41] With a total population of approximately 500 million people, the EU forms a huge common market.

The goal of the EU, whose council is based in Belgium, is eventually to remove all barriers to free trade among its members, making it as simple and painless to ship products between England and Spain as it is between New Jersey and Pennsylvania. Also involved is the standardization of currencies and regulations that businesses must meet. Instead of having to comply with multiple currencies and laws, companies will be able to streamline their efforts. In addition to simplifying transactions among members, the EU seeks to strengthen its position in the world as a political and economic power.[42]

European Union (EU)
Customs union that is moving in the direction of an economic union by adopting a common currency, removing trade restrictions, and permitting free flow of goods and workers throughout the member nations.

figure 7.2

The 25 Members of the European Union

In some ways, the EU is making definite progress toward its economic goals. It is drafting standardized eco-labels to certify that products are manufactured according to certain environmental standards, as well as creating guidelines governing marketers' uses of customer information. Marketers can also protect some trademarks throughout the entire EU with a single application and registration process through the Community Trademark (CTM), which simplifies doing business and eliminates having to register with each member country. Yet marketers still face challenges when selling their products in the EU. Customs taxes differ, and no uniform postal system exists. Using one toll-free phone number for several countries will not work, either, because each country has its own telephone system for codes and numbers.

Mexico has successfully negotiated a trade agreement with the EU that makes it easier for European companies to set up their operations in Mexico, which benefits EU companies by giving them the same privileges enjoyed by the United States and Canada and brings new investors to Mexico.

✓ assessment check

1. What is the World Trade Organization (WTO)?
2. What countries are parties to the NAFTA accord?
3. What is the goal of the European Union (EU)?

GOING GLOBAL

Globalization affects almost every industry and every individual throughout the world, at least in some way. Traditional marketers who decide to take their firms global may do so because they already have strong domestic market shares or their target market is too saturated to offer any substantial growth. Sometimes, by evaluating key indicators of the marketing environment, marketers can move toward globalization at an optimal time. The German footwear firm Adidas made a big jump into the global market after its successful ad campaign that ran under the slogan, "Impossible Is Nothing." Adidas announced it would purchase its rival Reebok in an effort to obtain the number one spot in the world from giant competitor Nike. Using the benefits of the European Union while also making a play for the Asian market, Adidas marketers believe they have a good chance at winning the global game. Making deals with athletes such as British soccer legend David Beckham and Chinese-born basketball star Yao Ming, as well as licensing agreements for major U.S. athletic leagues, has helped Adidas strengthen its brand in major markets around the world. Recently, the firm scored one of its biggest goals yet: sponsorship of the Beijing Summer Olympics. Adidas plans to have 2,400 retail outlets open in China by the time the Olympics start.[43]

Most large firms—and many smaller businesses—already participate in global commerce, and virtually every domestic marketer, large or small, recognizes the need to investigate whether to market its products overseas. It is not an easy step to take, requiring careful evaluation and preparation of a strategy. Common reasons that marketers cite for going global include globalization of customers, new customers in emerging markets, globalization of competitors, reduced trade barriers, advances in technology, and enhanced customer responsiveness.

© RABIH MOGHRABI/AFP/GETTY IMAGES

Dubai-based Emirates is one of the fastest-growing airlines in the world.

FIRST STEPS IN DECIDING TO MARKET GLOBALLY

Successful global marketing starts at the top. Without the enthusiasm and support of senior managers, export efforts are likely to fail. But before a firm even begins to formulate a strategy, marketers must ask themselves:

- Will our product sell well in the new target culture?

- Is our target market familiar yet with our product, or our name?

- Do we feel comfortable doing business in this particular country and culture? Will it be a good fit?

- How well developed is the infrastructure? Can we deliver our product successfully to the marketplace?[44]

Once these questions are answered, a firm can take the following steps:

1. *Prepare an international business plan.* The plan should include an evaluation of the firm's needs and goals.

2. *Conduct research into foreign markets.* The U.S. Department of Commerce is an excellent source for this.

3. *Evaluate distribution possibilities.* Should this be a joint venture with a local firm?

4. *Evaluate methods for financing the expansion.*

5. *Learn all the rules and regulations for bringing the product to market in the new country.*[45]

STRATEGIES FOR ENTERING FOREIGN MARKETS

4 Identify the alternative strategies for entering foreign markets.

Once marketers have completed their research, they may choose from three basic strategies for entering foreign markets: importing and exporting; contractual agreements such as franchising, licensing, and subcontracting; and international direct investment. As Figure 7.3 shows, the level of risk and the firm's degree of control over international marketing increase with greater involvement. Firms often use more than one of these entry strategies.

A firm that brings in goods produced abroad to sell domestically or to be used as components in its products is an importer. In making import decisions, the marketer must assess local demand for the product, taking into consideration factors such as the following:

- ability of the supplier to maintain agreed-to quality levels

- flexibility in filling orders that might vary considerably from one order to the next

- response time in filling orders

- total costs—including import fees, packaging, and transportation—in comparison with costs of domestic suppliers

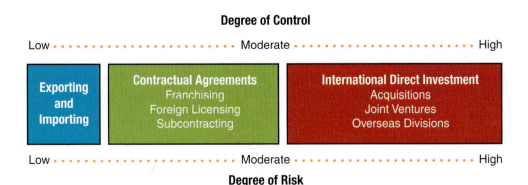

figure 7.3

Levels of Involvement in Global Marketing

Exporting, another basic form of global marketing, involves a continuous effort in marketing a firm's merchandise to customers in other countries. Many firms export their products as the first step in reaching foreign markets. Furniture manufacturer IKEA has built an entire exporting strategy around what it does best: making modular furniture. Because IKEA's furniture is lightweight and comes in components—customer assembly required—the firm can ship its goods almost anywhere in the world at a low cost, unlike manufacturers of traditional furniture.[46]

First-time exporters can reach foreign customers through one or more of three alternatives: export-trading companies, export-management companies, or offset agreements. An export-trading company (ETC) buys products from domestic producers and resells them abroad. While manufacturers lose control over marketing and distribution to the ETC, it helps them export through a relatively simple and inexpensive channel, in the process providing feedback about the overseas market potential of their products.

The second option, an export-management company (EMC), provides the first-time exporter with expertise in locating foreign buyers, handling necessary paperwork, and ensuring that its goods meet local labeling and testing laws. However, the manufacturer retains more control over the export process when it deals with an EMC than if it were to sell the goods outright to an export-trading company. Smaller firms can get assistance with administrative needs such as financing and preparation of proposals and contracts from large EMC contractors.

The final option, entering a foreign market under an offset agreement, teams a small firm with a major international company. The smaller firm essentially serves as a subcontractor on a large foreign project. This entry strategy provides new exporters with international experience, supported by the assistance of the primary contractor in such areas as international transaction documentation and financing.

franchise Contractual arrangement in which a wholesaler or retailer agrees to meet the operating requirements of a manufacturer or other franchiser.

foreign licensing Agreement that grants foreign marketers the right to distribute a firm's merchandise or to use its trademark, patent, or process in a specified geographic area.

Louisville, Kentucky–based Papa John's Pizza has more than 2,000 franchises throughout the United States. But the company is also expanding globally—with approximately 400 foreign franchises.

CONTRACTUAL AGREEMENTS

As a firm gains sophistication in global marketing, it may enter contractual agreements that provide several flexible alternatives to exporting. Both large and small firms can benefit from these methods. Franchising and foreign licensing, for example, are good ways to take services abroad. Subcontracting agreements may involve either production facilities or services.

Franchising

A **franchise** is a contractual arrangement in which a wholesaler or retailer (the franchisee) agrees to meet the operating requirements of a manufacturer or other franchiser. The franchisee receives the right to sell the products and use the franchiser's name as well as a variety of marketing, management, and other services. Fast-food companies such as McDonald's have been active franchisers around the world.

One advantage of franchising is risk reduction by offering a proven concept. Standardized operations typically reduce costs, increase operating efficiencies, and provide greater international recognizability. However, the success of an international franchise depends on its willingness to balance standard practices with local customer preferences. McDonald's, Pizza Hut, and Domino's are all expanding into India with special menus that feature lamb, chicken, and vegetarian items, in deference to Hindu and Muslim customers who do not eat beef and pork.

Foreign Licensing

A second method of going global through the use of contractual agreements is **foreign licensing.** Such an agreement grants foreign marketers the right to distribute a firm's merchandise or to use its trademark, patent, or process in a specified geographic area. These arrangements usually set certain time limits, after which agreements are revised or renewed.

Licensing offers several advantages over exporting, including access to local partners' marketing information and distribution channels and protection from various legal barriers. Because licensing does not require capital outlays, many firms, both small and large, regard it as an attractive entry strategy. Like franchising, licensing allows a firm to quickly enter a foreign market with a known product. The arrangement also may provide entry into a market that government restrictions close to imports or international direct investment. The World Poker Tour has grown tremendously, partly due to foreign licensing agreements. Following the model of golf's PGA Tour, founder of the poker tournament TV show Steve Lipscomb created a way for individual poker enthusiasts to sign up and play in tournaments around the world. By licensing the show in different countries such as France and Italy, Lipscomb maintains a company standard that can be translated—literally—to different markets. The televised tournaments on the World Poker Tour have become extremely popular, having already awarded players around the globe a total of $100 million in prize money.[47]

Subcontracting

A third strategy for going global through contractual agreements is **subcontracting,** in which the production of goods or services is assigned to local companies. Using local subcontractors can prevent mistakes involving local culture and regulations. Manufacturers might subcontract with a local company to produce their goods or use a foreign distributor to handle their products abroad or provide customer service. Manufacturing within the country can provide protection from import duties and may be a lower-cost alternative that makes it possible for the product to compete with local offerings. European aircraft manufacturer Airbus is negotiating with the Chinese government to build an assembly plant in China, which is rapidly becoming a substantial market for Airbus.[48]

INTERNATIONAL DIRECT INVESTMENT

Another strategy for entering global markets is international direct investment in foreign firms, production, and marketing facilities. Because the United States is the world's largest economy, its foreign direct investment inflows and outflows—the total of American firm investments abroad and foreign firm investments in the United States—are one-third greater than Germany's and twice as much as Japan's, its two largest competitors. U.S. direct investment abroad is now more than $2.2 trillion, with its greatest presence in Canada, the United Kingdom, and the Netherlands. On the other hand, foreign direct investment in the United States is led by the United Kingdom, Japan, the Netherlands, and Germany.[49]

Although high levels of involvement and high risk potential are characteristics of investments in foreign countries, firms choosing this method often have a competitive advantage. Direct investment can take several forms. A company can acquire an existing firm in a country where it wants to do business, or it can set up an independent division outside its own borders with responsibility for production and marketing in a country or geographic region. Chinese firms have been seeking to purchase U.S. businesses, mostly in industries involving natural resources

DAVID G. MCINTYRE/BLACK STAR/STOCKPHOTO

Chinese computer manufacturer Lenovo Group recently purchased IBM's personal-computer division. Shown here are former IBM employees touring Lenovo's innovation center in Beijing.

such as oil, natural gas, metals, and coal. However, they have been making inroads in consumer products and technology companies as well. For instance, the Lenovo Group, China's largest computer manufacturer, purchased the personal-computer division of IBM.[50]

Companies may also engage in international marketing by forming joint ventures, in which they share the risks, costs, and management of the foreign operation with one or more partners. These partnerships join the investing companies with nationals of the host countries. While some companies choose to open their own facilities overseas, others share with their partners. Because India does not yet allow foreign direct investment, Starbucks decided to form several joint ventures with local firms to enter the market there. Starbucks will have its own store but will be working with an Indian real estate company as well as at least one retailer in the venture.[51]

Although joint ventures offer many advantages, foreign investors have encountered problems in several areas throughout the world, especially in developing economies. Lower trade barriers, new technologies, lower transport costs, and vastly improved access to information mean that many more partnerships will be involved in international trade.

✓ assessment check

1. What are the three basic strategies for entering foreign markets?
2. What is a franchise?
3. What is international direct investment?

FROM MULTINATIONAL CORPORATION TO GLOBAL MARKETER

A **multinational corporation** is a firm with significant operations and marketing activities outside its home country. Examples of multinationals include General Electric, Siemens, and Mitsubishi in heavy electrical equipment, and Timex, Seiko, and Citizen in watches. Since they first became a force in international business in the 1960s, multinationals have evolved in some important ways. First, these companies are no longer exclusively U.S. based. Today, it is as likely for a multinational to be based in Japan, Germany, or Great Britain as in the United States. Second, multinationals no longer think of their foreign operations as mere outsourcing appendages that carry out the design, production, and engineering ideas conceived at home. Instead, they encourage constant exchanges of ideas, capital, and technologies among all the multinational operations.

Multinationals often employ huge foreign workforces relative to their American staffs. More than half of all Ford and IBM personnel are located outside the United States. These workforces are no longer seen merely as sources of cheap labor. On the contrary, many multinationals center technically complex activities in locations throughout the world. Texas Instruments does much of its research, development, design, and manufacturing in East Asia. In fact, it is increasingly common for U.S. multinationals to bring product innovations from their foreign facilities back to the States.

Multinationals have become global corporations that reflect the interdependence of world economies, the growth of international competition, and the globalization of world markets. However, many people worry that this globalization means that U.S. dominance in many markets will decline and disappear. Sixty percent of households in Hong Kong get their television services through ultrahigh-speed broadband connections that turn their TVs into computers, something that is catching on very slowly in the United Sates. European and Asian consumers now use smart cards with embedded memory chips instead of traditional credit cards or cash for retail purchases. And many American travelers discover that their cell phone service works much better when they are overseas. With this in mind, when Internet service provider EarthLink went looking for a partner to launch a cell phone service in the United States, the firm didn't tap Verizon or any other large U.S. firm. Instead, EarthLink went to South Korea, because that country is way ahead of the United States in development of the technology. "They're doing things we haven't even contemplated in the United States," explains EarthLink's founder, Sky Dayton.[52]

Briefly Speaking

"Learn Chinese. There's going to be a lot of action in China."

—Lakshmi Narayanan
CEO, Cognizant Technologies

✓ assessment check

1. What is a multinational corporation?
2. What are two ways in which multinationals have changed since the 1960s?

DEVELOPING AN INTERNATIONAL MARKETING STRATEGY

5 Differentiate between a global marketing strategy and a multidomestic marketing strategy.

In developing a marketing mix, international marketers may choose between two alternative approaches: a global marketing strategy or a multidomestic marketing strategy. A **global marketing strategy** defines a standard marketing mix and implements it with minimal modifications in all foreign markets. This approach brings the advantage of economies of scale to production and marketing activities. Procter & Gamble (P&G) marketers follow a global marketing strategy for Pringles potato chips, its leading export brand. P&G sells one product with a consistent formulation in every country. P&G meets 80 percent of worldwide demand with only six flavors of Pringles and one package design. This standardized approach saves money because it allows large-scale production runs and reinforces the brand's image.

A global marketing perspective can effectively market some goods and services to segments in many nations that share cultures and languages. This approach works especially well for products with strong, universal appeal such as McDonald's, luxury items such as Rolex watches, and high-tech brands such as Microsoft. Global advertising outlets, such as international editions of popular consumer and business magazines and international transmissions of TV channels such as CNN, MTV, and the CNBC financial network, help marketers deliver a single message to millions of global viewers. International satellite television channels such as StarTV reach 260 million Asian viewers through a host of sports, news, movie, music, and entertainment channels programmed in eight languages.

A global marketing strategy can also be highly effective for luxury products that target upscale consumers everywhere. Marketers of diamonds and luxury watches, for instance, typically use advertising with little or no copy—just a picture of a beautiful diamond or watch with the name discreetly displayed on the page.

But a global strategy doesn't always work. After a quick spike in sales of its computers in China, Dell saw just as rapid a decline. The firm discovered that competitors such as Hewlett-Packard and the Chinese firm Lenovo were more successful at selling their computers through retail stores. Dell's well-known practice of building computers to order and shipping them directly to consumers was not succeeding in China. So the firm had to re-evaluate its marketing strategy there to include a retail presence.[53]

A major benefit of a global marketing strategy is its low cost to implement. Most firms, however, find it necessary to practice market segmentation outside their home markets and tailor their marketing mixes to fit the unique needs of customers in specific countries. This **multidomestic marketing strategy** assumes that differences between market characteristics and competitive situations in certain nations require firms to customize their marketing decisions to effectively reach individual marketplaces. Many marketing experts believe that most products demand multidomestic marketing strategies to give them realistic global marketing appeal. Cultural, geographic, language, and other differences simply make it difficult to send the same message to many countries. Specific situations may allow marketers to standardize some parts of the marketing process but customize others.

✓ *assessment check*

1. What is the difference between a global marketing strategy and a multidomestic marketing strategy?

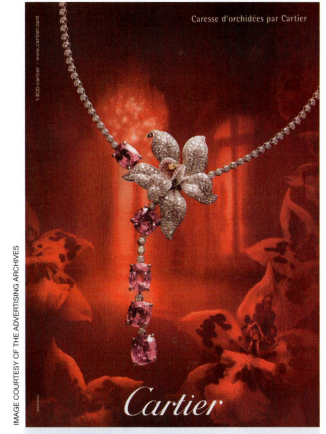

Caresse d'orchidées par Cartier

Cartier

IMAGE COURTESY OF THE ADVERTISING ARCHIVES

A global marketing strategy is effective for luxury name-brand items.

6 Describe the alternative marketing mix strategies used in global marketing.

INTERNATIONAL PRODUCT AND PROMOTIONAL STRATEGIES

Global marketers can choose from among five strategies for selecting the most appropriate product and promotion strategy for a specific foreign market: straight extension, promotion adaptation, product adaptation, dual adaptation, and product invention. As Figure 7.4 indicates, the strategies center on whether to extend a domestic product and promotional strategy into international markets or adapt one or both to meet the target market's unique requirements.

A firm may follow a one-product, one-message straight extension strategy as part of a global marketing strategy. This strategy permits economies of scale in production and marketing. Also, successful implementation creates universal recognition of a product for consumers from country to country. After pursuing a strategy of adapting its dolls to reflect the looks and styles of 40 different nationalities, marketers for Mattel Toys discovered that children around the world just wanted regular Barbies. "Blond Barbies sell just as well in Asia as in the United States," the marketing research told them. So Mattel went back to its one-product, one-message strategy. Its subsequent introduction of Rapunzel Barbie, complete with ankle-length blond locks, to 59 countries was the firm's biggest product launch ever.[54]

Other strategies call for product adaptation, promotion adaptation, or both. In Latin America, Nike relies on local soccer stars instead of Michael Jordan to promote its products. David Beckham represents Pepsi in his home country of England. Some marketing research has revealed that consumers around the world are becoming less enamored of major American brands, so marketers are taking this into consideration when creating global messages.[55]

Finally, a firm may select product invention to take advantage of unique foreign market opportunities. To match user needs in developing nations, an appliance manufacturer might introduce a hand-powered washing machine even though such products became obsolete in industrialized countries years ago. Although Chapter 12 discusses the idea of branding in greater detail, it is important to note here the importance of a company's recognizable name, image, product, or even slogan around the world.

INTERNATIONAL DISTRIBUTION STRATEGY

Distribution is a vital aspect of overseas marketing. Marketers must set up proper channels and anticipate extensive physical distribution problems. Foreign markets may offer poor transportation systems and warehousing facilities—or none at all. Global marketers must adapt promptly and efficiently to these situations to profit from overseas sales.

A distribution decision involves two steps. First, the firm must decide on a method of entering the foreign market. Second, it must determine how to distribute the product within the foreign market through that entry channel. The next auto imports are likely to come from Chinese manufacturer Geely (pronounced *Jeely*). The firm decided to unveil its initial models at the North American Auto Show in Detroit, where dealers and car buffs could catch the first glimpse of the Free Cruiser and Beauty Leopard. Some dealers took the cars seriously—and asked for more information about importing and selling them. "What you're seeing is the first stage," predicts Mike Hanley, a global director for Ernst & Young. "Everybody recognizes that Chinese cars will end up in North America. It's a matter of time."[56]

figure 7.4

Alternative International Product and Promotional Strategies

		Product Strategy		
		Same Product	**Product Adaptation**	**New Product**
Promotion Strategy	**Same Promotion**	**Straight Extension** Wrigley's gum Coca-Cola Eastman Kodak cameras and film	**Product Adaptation** Campbell's soup Exxon gasoline	**Product Invention** Nonelectric sewing machines Manually operated washing machines
	Different Promotion	**Promotion Adaptation** Bicycles/motorcycles Outboard motors	**Dual Adaptation** Coffee Some clothing	

PRICING STRATEGY

Pricing can critically affect the success of an overall marketing strategy for foreign markets. Considerable competitive, economic, political, and legal constraints often limit pricing decisions. Global marketers can succeed if they thoroughly understand these requirements.

Companies must adapt their pricing strategies to local markets and change them when conditions change. In India, Unilever's partner Hindustan Lever offers "penny packets" of shampoo to lower-income consumers, who typically cannot afford to buy an entire bottle of shampoo. Although local firms follow the same practice, Hindustan Lever wants to develop loyalty among these consumers so that if they move up the income scale, they will be more apt to by the firm's higher-priced products as well.[57]

An important development in pricing strategy for international marketing has been the emergence of commodity marketing organizations that seek to control prices through collective action. The Organization of the Petroleum Exporting Countries (OPEC) is a good example of this kind of collective export organization. Pricing agreements such as fair trade pricing in the coffee industry, described in the "Solving an Ethical Controversy" feature, have drawn criticism from those who believe that the agreements do not benefit everyone.

COUNTERTRADE

In a growing number of nations, the only way a marketer can gain access to foreign markets is through **countertrade**—a form of exporting in which a firm barters products rather than selling them for cash. Less developed nations sometimes impose countertrade requirements when they lack sufficient foreign currency to attain goods and services they want or need from exporting countries. These nations allow sellers to exchange their products only for domestic products as a way to control their balance-of-trade problems.

countertrade Form of exporting whereby goods and services are bartered rather than sold for cash.

Countertrade became popular two decades ago, when companies wanted to conduct business in eastern European countries and the former Soviet Union. Those governments did not allow exchanges of hard currency, so this form of barter facilitated trade. PepsiCo made one of the largest countertrades ever when it exchanged $3 billion worth of Pepsi-Cola for Russian Stolichnaya vodka, a cargo ship, and tankers from the former Soviet Union.

Barter activity continues to thrive around the globe. Malaysia and Indonesia are bartering palm oil in exchange for eighteen Russian jet fighters. Libya is bartering fuel to Zimbabwe in exchange for beef, coffee, and tea. China has set up the Yangpu Oil Barter Exchange, the world's first such barter exchange for oil and gas.[58]

 assessment check

1. What are the five strategies for selecting the most appropriate product and promotion strategy for a specific foreign market?
2. What is countertrade?

THE UNITED STATES AS A TARGET FOR INTERNATIONAL MARKETERS

 7 Explain the attractiveness of the United States as a target market for foreign marketers.

Foreign marketers regard America as an inviting target. It offers a large population of nearly 300 million people. In addition, U.S. consumers have a high levels of discretionary income, with a per-capita income estimated at more than $24,000 and a median family income of almost $54,000.[59] Risks to foreign marketers are also low due to the United States' political stability, generally favorable attitude toward foreign investment, and growing economy.

South Korean consumer electronics giant LG Electronics counts the United States as its second most profitable market; Asia ranks first. A few years ago, the company established a North American headquarters, and it expects sales there to top $10 billion annually. The firm plans to grow its U.S. cell phone market share to 20 percent from 18 percent. In comparison, it controls about 9 percent of the worldwide cell phone market. And LG has entered the U.S. portable media player market to compete against Apple's iPod.[60]

Solving an Ethical Controversy

Fair-Trade Pricing for Coffee Growers: Is it Fair to Everyone?

If you think your morning cup of coffee is liquid gold, you're right: coffee is the world's second most valuable traded commodity after oil. But until recently, the farmers who grow the coffee—largely in developing nations such as Mexico, Nicaragua, Guatemala, Colombia, Peru, Ethiopia, and Indonesia—saw very little profits. In fact, they spent generations in poverty because of the low prices commanded by their crops. Now the practice of fair trade—paying farmers better prices regardless of world market prices—is taking hold in companies ranging from Equal Exchange, one of the original fair trade firms, to Starbucks. It is also taking hold in the minds of consumers. No one doubts the benefits to the farmers, who now have a better standard of living with more money to invest in their farms, schools, and healthcare. But some question whether consumers should bear the burden of artificially higher prices.

Is fair-trade pricing for coffee growers also fair to consumers?

PRO

1. Most consumers are happy to pay a higher price for fair-trade goods because it appeals to their sense of social responsibility. "The whole concept of fair trade goes to the heart of American values and the sense of right and wrong. Nobody wants to buy something that was made by exploiting someone else," says Ben Cohen of Ben & Jerry's ice cream, which uses fair-trade coffee products in its ice cream. Cohen's firm actually absorbs the full cost of the switch to fair trade.

2. Fair-trade coffee products are usually of superior quality because farmers have the cash to invest in their farms. So the higher price reflects value. Consumers become connoisseurs of coffee from these regions. "They don't just want French roast," explains Paul Rice, head of the nonprofit organiza-

tion that certifies fair trade. They want Guatemalan Antiguan, and they know where Antigua is."

CON

1. Prices should reflect true fluctuations in world markets, as in the case of oil. Consumers should not be forced to pay artificially increased prices.

2. Consumers are unlikely to pay more if they don't have to, and they may shift to less expensive brands that are available. "I think [fair trade] will be a minor part of consumer spending," predicts Bill Conerly of the National Center for Policy Analysis. "Most consumers are looking for good value. Americans are not willing to pay extra to help American workers. I think it's unlikely they're going to pay extra to help foreign workers."

Summary

In a free-market economy such as in the United States, marketers can usually choose what price to charge for products, and consumers can decide whether they want to pay that price. The concept of fair trade reflects the desire of consumers to purchase high-quality goods and services that are produced by workers who are earning a fair wage or profit. "There's a growing demand by consumers and a growing need by the [coffee] industry for a fair trade model that will take care of these works," says Paul Rice. But if fair-trade prices rise too high, the average consumer may switch to a less expensive brand of morning coffee.

Sources: "Fair Trade Coffee," Global Exchange, **http://www.globalexchange.org**, accessed March 24, 2006; Margot Roosevelt, "The Coffee Clash," *Time*, **http://www.time.com**, accessed March 24, 2006; Jeffrey MacDonald, "How to Brew Justice," *Time Inside Business*, January 2006, pp. A16–A18; Joyce King, "Java Becomes Star in War on Unfair Trade," *USA Today*, October 21, 2005, **http://www.usatoday.com**; Terence Chea, "Coffee Ice Cream Brings Fair Trade Label into Frozen Foods," *San Francisco Chronicle*, April 19, 2005, **http://www.sfgate.com**.

Among the best-known industries in which foreign manufacturers have established U.S. production facilities is automobiles. Most of the world's leading auto companies have built assembly facilities in the United States: Honda, Hyundai, and Mercedes-Benz in Alabama; BMW in South Carolina; Toyota in Kentucky; Nissan and Honda in Tennessee, Mississippi, and Ohio. Recently, South Korean manufacturer Kia announced plans to build its first U.S. plant in Georgia, while Toyota says it will be building Camrys at a Subaru plant in Indiana.[61]

As we discussed earlier, foreign investment continues to grow in the United States. Foreign multinationals will probably continue to invest in U.S. assets as they seek to produce goods locally and control distribution channels. Major U.S. companies owned by foreign firms include Random House and Arista Records, owned by Bertelsmann AG (Germany); Pillsbury, owned by Grand Metropolitan (UK), and Ralph Lauren, owned by L'Oréal (France).[62]

 assessment check

1. What characteristics of the United States make it an inviting target for foreign marketers?
2. Why would U.S. automobile manufacturing be a target for foreign companies?

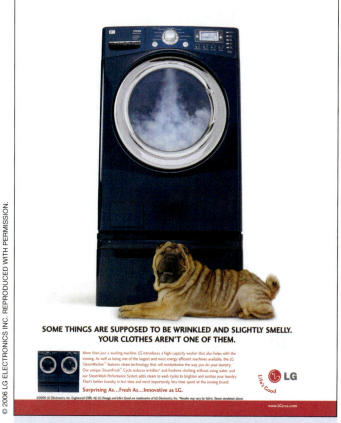

SOME THINGS ARE SUPPOSED TO BE WRINKLED AND SLIGHTLY SMELLY. YOUR CLOTHES AREN'T ONE OF THEM.

Korean consumer electronics marketer LG Electronics targets U.S. consumers.

Strategic Implications of Marketing in the 21st Century

The first decade of the new century has marked a new era of truly global marketing, in which the world's marketplaces are accessible to nearly every firm. Marketers in both small, localized firms and giant businesses need to reevaluate the strengths and weaknesses of their current marketing practices and realign their plans to meet the new demands of this era.

Marketers are the pioneers in bringing new technologies to developing nations. Their successes and failures will determine the direction global marketing will take and the speed with which it will be embraced. Actions of international marketers will influence every component of the marketing environment: competitive, economic, social-cultural, political-legal, and technological.

The greatest competitive advantages will belong to marketers who capitalize on the similarities of their target markets and adapt to the differences. In some instances, the actions of marketers today help determine the rules and regulations of tomorrow.

Marketers need flexible and broad views of an increasingly complex customer. Goods and services will likely become more customized as they are introduced in foreign markets—yet some recognizable brands, such as Mattel's Barbie dolls, seem to remain universally popular just as they are. New and better products in developing markets will create and maintain relationships for the future.

REVIEW OF CHAPTER OBJECTIVES

1   Describe the importance of global marketing from the perspectives of the individual firm and the nation.

Global marketing expands a company's market, allows firms to grow, and makes them less dependent on their own country's economy for success. For the nation, global trade provides a source of needed raw materials and other products not available domestically in sufficient amounts, opens up new markets to serve with domestic output, and converts countries and their citizens into partners in the search for high-quality products at the lowest possible prices. Companies find that global marketing and international trade can help them meet customer demand, reduce certain costs, provide information on markets around the world, and increase employment.

2   Identify the major components of the environment for global marketing.

The major components of the international environment are economic, social-cultural, technological, political-legal, and competitive. A country's infrastructure also plays an important role in determining how effective marketers will be in manufacturing, promoting, and distributing their goods and services.

3   Outline the basic functions of GATT, WTO, NAFTA, FTAA, CAFTA-DR, and the European Union.

The General Agreement on Tariffs and Trade is an accord that has substantially reduced tariffs. The World Trade Organization oversees GATT agreements, mediates disputes, and tries to reduce trade barriers throughout the world. The North American Free Trade Agreement removes trade restrictions among Canada, Mexico, and the United States. The proposed Free Trade Area of the Americas seeks to create a free-trade area covering the entire Western Hemisphere. As another step in that direction, the United States has made an agreement with the Dominican Republic and Central American nations known as the Central American Free Trade Agreement-DR (CAFTA-DR). The European Union is a customs union whose goal is to remove all barriers to free trade among its members.

4   Identify the alternative strategies for entering foreign markets.

Several strategies are available to marketers, including exporting, importing, franchising, foreign licensing, subcontracting, and direct investment. This progression moves from the least to the most involvement by a firm.

5   Differentiate between a global marketing strategy and a multidomestic marketing strategy.

A global marketing strategy defines a standard marketing mix and implements it with minimal modifications in all foreign markets. A multidomestic marketing strategy requires firms to customize their marketing decisions to reach individual marketplaces.

6   Describe the alternative marketing mix strategies used in global marketing.

Product and promotional strategies include the following: straight extension, promotion adaptation, product adaptation, dual adaptation, and product invention. Marketers may also choose among distribution, pricing, and countertrade strategies.

7   Explain the attractiveness of the United States as a target market for foreign marketers.

The United States has a large population, high levels of discretionary income, political stability, a favorable attitude toward foreign investment, and a steadily growing economy.

assessment check **answers**

1.1 Define *importing* and *exporting*.

Importing involves purchasing foreign goods and services. Exporting refers to marketing domestically produced goods and services abroad.

1.2 What is the largest category of exports from the United States?

The largest category of exports from the United States is services.

1.3 What must global marketers be able to do effectively to reach foreign markets?

Global marketers must be able to adapt their goods and services to local preferences.

2.1 What are the three criteria that determine a nation's prospects as a host for international business expansion?

A nation's size, per-capita income, and stage of economic development determine its prospects as a host for international business expansion.

2.2 What is an FCN treaty?

FCN stands for friendship, commerce, and navigation. These treaties set terms for various aspects of commercial relations with other countries.

2.3 What are the two major categories of trade barriers?

The two categories of trade barrier are tariffs and nontariffs.

3.1 What is the World Trade Organization?

The World Trade Organization (WTO) oversees GATT agreements and mediates disputes. It also continues efforts to reduce trade barriers around the world.

3.2 What countries are parties to the NAFTA accord?

The United States, Canada, and Mexico are parties to NAFTA.

3.3 What is the goal of the European Union (EU)?

The European Union seeks to remove all barriers to free trade among its members and strengthen its position in the world as an economic and political power.

4.1 What are the three basic strategies for entering foreign markets?

The three basic strategies are importing and exporting, contractual agreements, and international direct investment.

4.2 What is a franchise?

A franchise is a contractual agreement in which a wholesaler or retailer (the franchisee) agrees to meet the operating requirements of a manufacturer or other franchiser.

4.3 What is international direct investment?

International direct investment is direct investment in foreign firms, production, and marketing facilities.

5.1 What is a multinational corporation?

A multinational corporation is a firm with significant operations and marketing activities outside the home country.

assessment check **answers**

5.2 What are two ways in which multinationals have changed since the 1960s?

Two ways these firms have changed are that they are no longer exclusively U.S. based, and they no longer think of their foreign operations as mere outsourcing appendages.

5.3 What is the difference between a global marketing strategy and a multidomestic marketing strategy?

A global marketing strategy defines a marketing mix and implements it with minimal modifications in all foreign markets. A multidomestic marketing strategy requires that firms customize their marketing decisions to reach individual marketplaces.

6.1 What are the five strategies for selecting the most appropriate product and promotion strategy for a specific foreign market?

The five strategies are the following: straight extension, promotion adaptation, product adaptation, dual adaptation, and product invention.

6.2 What is countertrade?

Countertrade is a form of exporting in which a firm barters products rather then selling them for cash.

7.1 What characteristics of the United States make it an inviting target for foreign marketers?

The characteristics making the United States an attractive target for foreign marketers are a large population to sell products to and high levels of discretionary income that make purchases possible. In addition, it has low risks to foreign marketers due to a stable political environment, favorable attitude toward foreign investment, and a growing economy.

7.2 Why would U.S. automobile manufacturing be a target for foreign companies?

Because the United States has a large population and high income levels, foreign car manufacturers would find the country an attractive and lucrative market. The size and weight of cars make them bulky to transport long distances, so firms might find local manufacturing a profitable alternative to exporting.

MARKETING TERMS YOU NEED TO KNOW

exporting 212
importing 212
exchange rate 218
tariff 221
import quota 222

General Agreement on Tariffs and Trade
    (GATT) 224
World Trade Organization (WTO) 224
North American Free Trade Agreement
    (NAFTA) 224

European Union (EU) 225
franchise 228
foreign licensing 228
countertrade 233

OTHER IMPORTANT MARKETING TERMS

related party trade 213
infrastructure 217
political risk assessment (PRA) 220
friendship, commerce, and navigation (FCN)
    treaties 220
ISO (International Organization for
    Standardization) certification 220
revenue tariff 222

protective tariff 222
embargo 222
subsidy 223
exchange control 223
dumping 223
free-trade area 223
customs union 223
common market 223

Free Trade Area of the Americas (FTAA) 225
Central American Free Trade Agreement-DR
    (CAFTA-DR) 225
subcontracting 229
multinational corporation 230
global marketing strategy 231
multidomestic marketing strategy 231

ASSURANCE OF LEARNING REVIEW

1. What are the benefits to firms that decide to engage in global marketing?
2. Why is a nation's infrastructure an important factor for global marketers to consider?
3. What are the two different classifications of tariff? What is each designed to do?
4. How does an import quota restrict trade?
5. What are two major victories achieved by the Uruguay Round of GATT conferences?
6. Why has the progress of the WTO been slow?
7. What are the three alternatives for first-time exporters to reach foreign customers?
8. Define and describe the different types of contractual agreements that provide flexible alternatives to exporting.
9. In what conditions is a global marketing strategy generally most successful?
10. What type of nation benefits most from countertrade? Why?

PROJECTS AND TEAMWORK EXERCISES

1. Imagine that you and a classmate are marketers for one of the following companies: Apple Computer, Burger King, General Mills, or Mattel Toys. Choose one of the following markets into which your company could expand: Mexico, India, or China. Research the country's infrastructure, social-cultural environment, technological environment, and any possible trade barriers your firm might encounter. Then present your findings to the class, with a conclusion on whether you think the expansion would be beneficial.

2. Assume that you work for Domino's Pizza, which already has 3,000 outlets in more than 46 countries. With a classmate, identify a country that Domino's has not yet reached and write a brief plan for entering that country's market. Then create a print ad for that market (you can write the ad copy in English). It may be helpful to visit Domino's Web site for some ideas.

3. London is hosting the 2012 Summer Olympics. By yourself or with a classmate, identify a company that might benefit from promoting its goods or services at the London Olympics. In a presentation, describe which strategy you would use: straight extension, product or promotion adaptation, dual adaptation, or product invention. Consider the fact that England is a member of the European Union.

4. Suppose you work for a firm that is getting ready to introduce an MP3 player to the Chinese marketplace. With a classmate, decide which strategies your firm could use most effectively for entering this market. Present your ideas either in writing or to the class.

5. With a classmate, research the Chinese auto manufacturer Geely to find out more about the cars it plans to launch in the United States. Then create an ad for the firm, targeting U.S. consumers.

CRITICAL-THINKING EXERCISES

1. Few elements in the global marketing environment are more difficult to overcome than the unexpected, such as natural disasters or outbreaks of disease such as the avian flu. Travel may be curtailed or halted by law, by a breakdown in infrastructure, or simply by fear on the part of consumers. Suppose you work for a firm that has resorts on several continents. As a marketer, what kinds of contingency plans might you recommend for your firm in the event of an unexpected disaster?

2. Zippo lighters have been around for decades. But as the number of smokers in the United States continues to decline, Zippo has spent the last half century scouting the world for new markets. Today, Zippo is a status symbol among Chinese consumers, who prefer U.S. products. To reduce the sale of made-in-China knockoffs, Zippo's ads show Chinese consumers how to identify a real Zippo. In addition, Zippo has worked with U.S. government officials to find a safe way to package its lighters for air travel.[63] Both of these examples demonstrate a firm adapting to requirements of a new marketplace. Do you think a global marketing strategy or a multidomestic strategy would work best if Zippo decided to enter other markets? Explain the reasons for your choice.

3. Do you agree with the goals and ideas of the proposed FTAA? Why or why not?

4. Do you agree with countertrade as a legitimate form of conducting business? Why or why not? Describe a countertrade agreement that Microsoft might make in another country.

5. Foreign investment continues to grow in the United States. Do you think this is a positive trend for U.S. businesses and consumers? Why or why not?

ETHICS EXERCISE

Cheap—and illegal—copies of pirated popular movies, video games, and music are often available for sale in Asia within days of their worldwide release. The entertainment industry has so far had little success in stopping the flow of these copies into consumers' hands. Do you think multinational economic communities should be more effective at combating piracy? Why or why not? What actions could they take?

INTERNET EXERCISES

1. **The European Union.** To answer the following questions, you'll need to visit the EU Web site (http://europa.eu.int). A Google or Yahoo! news search may also be required.
   a. What are the purposes of the EU and the benefits for EU members? From the perspective of a U.S. marketer, what are some of the challenges and opportunities presented by the EU?
   b. Which countries have adopted the euro? Which countries have not adopted the euro? What are the advantages and disadvantages of a single European currency?
   c. Review several recent trade disputes involving the EU. What products and countries are involved? What are the primary issues? How can trade disputes complicate the marketing of U.S. products in Europe?
2. **International promotional strategies.** Visit the Web sites of two U.S. companies that do extensive business in international markets (examples include McDonald's, Ford, Boeing, Coca-Cola, and Procter & Gamble). Also, visit the Web sites of two non-U.S. companies that have extensive U.S. operations and sales (examples include Toyota, Unilever, Nestlé, and Philips). Review the material on the Web sites and perform the following exercises.
   a. Note two or three differences in promotional strategies you found between the companies' products sold in the United States and those sold in other countries.
   b. Note two or three similarities among promotional strategies used by companies in different countries.
   c. Based on your findings, did you find any differences between the U.S. and non-U.S. companies?

Note: Internet Web addresses change frequently. If you don't find the exact site listed, you may need to access the organization's home page and search from there or use a search engine such as Google.

 CASE 7.1   Hyundai Gets a Second Chance

Second chances are rare in marketing. Once consumers decide a product's quality is substandard, the brand—if not the entire company—is probably doomed. When South Korean automaker Hyundai rolled its first model—the Excel—onto U.S. roads in 1986, consumers were lured by Excel's low price tag. Being able to drive away from the dealership for less than $5,000 seemed like a good deal. But soon Hyundai owners discovered they were getting what they'd paid for. Excels began to reveal quality-control problems, requiring frequent repairs or part replacements. It wasn't long before the name Hyundai became synonymous with poor quality, and the target of jokes by late-night TV hosts. In an industry that has been dominated by American, Japanese, and German auto giants, how could a family-owned South Korean start-up with a bad reputation return to the ring after being knocked out so soundly?

Upon his father's retirement, Chung Mong Koo took over Hyundai as its chairman. He spent several years studying Toyota's success with its philosophy of *kaizen,* or continuous improvement. Then he established a zero-defect policy for all of Hyundai's factories. And he hammered the message home to every single Hyundai executive, manager, and worker. He visited the factories and inspected the cars himself. Finally, he unleashed the new Hyundais to the world marketplace, with a ten-year warranty. Consumers who were experiencing sticker shock at some of the new models from other manufacturers, and who liked the security of the new warranty, gave the Sonata a try. They found that the car performed exactly as advertised. Industry watchdogs such as *Consumer Reports* and J. D. Power and Associates took a grudging second look. And they liked what they saw. In less than six years, Hyundai rose to second place in J. D. Power and Associates' survey of initial car quality, tied with Honda behind Toyota. *Consumer Reports* named the Sonata as the most reliable car in the United States.

Hyundai has raised the bar even higher. The latest Sonata has six air bags—most other manufacturers offer only four as a standard feature—a six-speaker CD and MP3 player, and an advanced antilock braking system—all for a price tag of less than $20,000. Competitors not only are paying attention, they are worried. "Hyundai has quality and prices that have caught customers' attention, not to mention ours," admitted Toyota vice chairman Fujio Cho. Yukitoshi Funo, chairman of Toyota Motor Sales USA, agrees with his colleague. "We're worried about them," he says. In fact, Hyundai has become the fastest-growing major automaker in the world, spending $1.6 billion a year on research and development of new products. "I have an unlimited account," says Lee Hyun Soon, a senior executive in R&D. The firm has also spent billions on new manufacturing facilities around the world, in countries such as the United States and China—both huge markets for trucks and cars. Under the watchful eye of Chung Mong Koo, Hyundai is making the most of its second chance. "We can't allow any defects to damage our cars," he insists. It is a simple marketing philosophy that resonates around the world.

Questions for Critical Thinking

1. How does a focus on quality convey a universal message to all of Hyundai's potential customers?
2. Do you think that Hyundai's pricing strategy will be effective in all markets? Why or why not?
3. What steps might Toyota and Honda have to take to compete effectively with Hyundai?

Sources: Kim Tae-jin, "Alabama Plant Is a Hyundai Success Story," *International Herald Tribune*, February 27, 2006, **http://www.iht.com**; "Toyota Sees Hyundai as Threat in America," MSNBC, January 10, 2006, **http://www.msnbc.msn.com**; Cheryl Jensen, "2006 Hyundai Sonata: Filling the Camry's Rearview Mirror," *New York Times*, November 6, 2005, **http://www.nytimes.com**; "Hyundai to Set Up $1.3 Billion China Venture," Livedoor, June 22. 2005, **http://www.livedoorinc.com**; Michael Schuman, "Hyundai Revs Up," *Time Asia*, April 25, 2005, **http://www.time.com**.

VIDEO CASE 7.2   Lonely Planet Brings You the World

The written video case on Lonely Planet appears on page VC-9. The recently filmed Lonely Planet video is designed to expand and highlight the concepts in this chapter and the concepts and questions covered in the written video case.

Talking about Marketing Careers with. . .

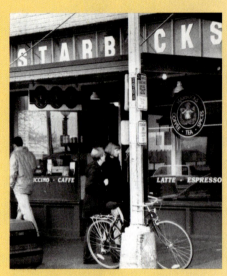

ANNE SAUNDERS
SENIOR VICE PRESIDENT, GLOBAL BRAND
STRATEGY & COMMUNICATIONS
STARBUCKS COFFEE COMPANY

Millions of people around the world just can't start their day off right without a steaming cup of Starbucks coffee. Whether they opt for the full Starbucks experience at a retail store, grind and brew their own cups at home, or serve themselves at a hotel breakfast buffet or their college's foodservice, consumers can satisfy their craving for rich, flavorful coffees or other beverages nearly anytime they choose. And that's the way Starbucks planned it. It has outlets in all 50 U.S. states and the District of Columbia and operates in 37 countries worldwide. The firm has more than 12,000 locations globally to serve customers—from Australia to Japan to Chile and on through the United Arab Emirates, to name just a few.

The company's attention to quality in its roasting and blending process is legendary. So no matter where you prefer to relax with your latte or espresso, you'll find the same premium drink you have come to expect from Starbucks. The firm is even working with other business partners to bring its products to new communities and venues, such as vending machines. Anne Saunders, senior vice president of Global Brand Strategy & Communications, took some time recently to discuss her firm's expansion plans and her own marketing career with us.

Q: Anne, most students would jump at the chance to be part of such a respected company as Starbucks. How did your education and career stepping stones prepare you for your current position with the company?
A: Prior to joining Starbucks, I was the chief executive officer and president of E-Society, a business-to-business e-commerce company. I also spent nine years at AT&T in a variety of positions, including corporate officer. I joined AT&T via its acquisition of McCaw Communications where I led the marketing function.

My undergraduate work was at Northwestern University, where I majored in economics, and I later earned a master's degree in management from Fordham University.

I consider myself a management generalist, with a strong interest in marketing and branding activities. In terms of "stepping stones," I advise people to develop their strength as leaders and to get experience in the basics of management—planning, setting direction, and delivering measurable results. While functional experience is extremely helpful, in a fast-growing company like Starbucks, we find that attributes like the ability to deal with ambiguity and to create a productive work environment are the most valuable leadership skills.

Q: What is involved in managing global brand strategy day to day? Do you have a team helping you with major activities? If so, would you describe their roles briefly?
A: Starbucks's brand has been developed through a unique approach. Rather than relying on traditional advertising, we have essentially considered our stores as our billboards and also leveraged public relations activities to build connections with the communities we serve.

Our brand strategy team includes our Creative department, Communications (which works as much with our partners [employees] and other stakeholders as it does with the media), and other teams who work in concert with our Marketing department. Each function is led by a vice president, who helps to set the vision and strategy for the team and ensures a cohesive approach between departments.

Q: Coffee is enjoyed in many societies around the world. But does Starbucks need to tailor its selection of beverages or other products for different countries? Can you give us an example?
A: We pride ourselves on delivering a consistent experience throughout our entire organization. If you order a nonfat latte in Sheboygan, Wisconsin, it should taste the same as the one that you ordered last week in London. But we definitely adjust our food and beverage offerings to local tastes. For instance, one of our most popular Frappuccino blended beverages in our Asia market has cubes of coffee jelly in it. Our Strawberries & Cream Frappuccino blended beverage was developed in our United Kingdom market and was later released in North America.

Q: Starbucks opened its first coffeehouse in Japan a decade ago. What drives the company in its global expansion? What are its goals in reaching more people?
A: Starbucks has always been a growth company, and we see enormous untapped potential both in North America and certainly around the world. There are more than 12,000 Starbucks stores as of this writing, and we believe that we will ultimately have at least 40,000 locations worldwide, with at least half of those outside the United States. And beyond our

store projections, we want to be available everywhere that our customers want to experience Starbucks—in foodservice locations, at home, and more.

Q: There is often a lot of skepticism in the world about the motivations and actions of large companies. In many instances, companies that market or communicate their corporate social responsibility activities risk being accused of "greenwashing." How does Starbucks approach this subject?

A: Effectively communicating a company's social responsibility efforts can be one of the greatest challenges in marketing. At Starbucks, we try to "bake in" corporate social responsibility messaging throughout all of our internal and external communications. We also do our best to ensure that those messages are clearly linked to our overall commitment to be a positive member of the communities we serve—and to the coffee farmers who supply our beans. Perhaps our most crucial tool is our annual corporate social responsibility report. By providing audited, verifiable updates on the key issues that Starbucks and our stakeholders value, we demonstrate our commitment to economic transparency and to upholding our own guiding principles.

Q: How do you get the message out about Starbucks in countries outside the U.S.? What sort of promotions do you plan? Do local partners provide assistance with your marketing? And do you need to adjust the messages or means of communication from country to country or region to region?

A: As in North America, we do very little traditional advertising in our international markets. We use local public relations agencies and leverage our teams in Europe, the Middle East and Africa, the Asia-Pacific region, and Latin America to create locally relevant promotions. We also have a number of business partners who use their experience to find just the right mix of local taste with Starbucks brand.

Q: We've seen Starbucks coffee in many places other than retail coffeehouses these days. What type of business relationships have you developed with other companies? How do you select a partner who would be a good fit? Is anything new on the horizon?

A: Over the years, Starbucks has formed a number of very successful strategic partnerships. By teaming with Pepsi, for instance, we were able to offer bottled Frappuccino® in the grocery aisle and to create Starbucks DoubleShot®. We have a variety of business relationships, from joint ventures to partnerships to licensing, which allow us to both expand the reach of the *Starbucks Experience* and ensure that our brand is communicated consistently. When we explore potential partnerships, we use our Mission Statement and Guiding Principles as the benchmark. It's important that our organizations have similar values and approaches to business in general. Then we match up our capabilities to see whether there is a complementary fit that benefits us both.

Q: What would you advise students to help them get a solid start in a marketing career? Do internships or other experiences play a role?

A: Internships, job shadowing, and other types of exploratory experiences are a great way to get started in any profession. I definitely recommend that students start actively working in the field during their school years. There are usually many short-term opportunities on campus or with nonprofit organizations. There is nothing like getting that experience in the basics—writing press releases, managing events, contributing content to newsletters or websites—to get a jump start on your career. I also encourage students to keep moving and trying new roles either within a large, growing organization such as Starbucks or by exploring various types of companies and organizations. Getting a wide range of experiences and "sampling" provides a strong base from which to go in any direction your career may take.

Spreading Laughs in Unexpected Places

The first audience exposed to The Compass Players (precursor to The Second City) didn't know that they were about to see a revolutionary mix of sketch and improvisational comedy. The Compass Players began the Second City legacy of groundbreaking comedy in a small tavern in 1959. Their first audience had, in fact, not paid a dime for the entertainment they stumbled on. They found a comedy show based on contemporary headlines, rooted in cutting-edge humor, and spawned from improvisation. Soon after, Second City was formed, opening in a converted Chinese laundry. Word of the fearless cast of actors spread across the Midwest. While The Second City developed its technique, it defined a role for itself in the market. It has entertained a continuously growing body of consumers and has identified a market for custom work in the world of business, which is, ironically, a world that is frequently lampooned on their stages.

The Second City was created by artists—young, hip, intelligent actors, who educated themselves on politics, cultural sentiment, and social hierarchy. It was the early 1960s, and as America was entering a decade of cultural change, The Second City developed a voice that challenged the core values of the day. It attracted a body of consumers who were interested in the comedic take on controversial issues such as civil rights, Vietnam, and the Cold War. Bernie Sahlins, Second City's principal founder, said that SC's comedy spoke to this changing cultural climate. Within eight months of opening, Second City had grabbed national attention. Its product, its comedy, began to take shape as a creative innovation worthy of more expansive entrepreneurial ventures.

In the entertainment industry, two features define the consumer perception of The Second City. It's the launchpad for globally recognized comedic talent, and the live theatre venue dedicated to satire and improvisation. As Second city has developed a variety of related business ventures, it has aimed to, in the words of VP Kelly Leonard, "stay true to their core." Its continued focus on the SC style of comedy has distinguished it from competitors. Consumers interested in live comedic theater have very few alternatives if they also seek satire and improvisation. The Second City legacy is, similarly, exclusive to its business. As tourists come to Chicago looking for a night of entertainment, The Second City is a recognizable brand that has stuck to its roots throughout five decades of expansion.

Capitalizing on Second City's reputation is its communications division. As the modern businessperson faces a workplace in which communication is critical, The Second City has found a key place as teacher, creator, and entertainer.

Tom Yorton, president of Second City Communications, comes from an extensive corporate background. His experience in numerous industries, including high-tech, Internet, retail, automotive, airlines, fitness, restaurants, lodging, financial services, and healthcare, have helped make him accessible to businesses seeking SC's expertise. Second City Communications performs the most sophisticated business-to-business marketing employed by the organization. Yorton's small team of professionals collaborates with a variety of businesses, including Pepsi and Motorola, designing hilarious and subject-specific performances for their corporate events.

Enriching the buyer–seller relationship with corporate clients is fundamental to the success of SC Communications. While Second City's theatrical casts have always been well versed on topical issues, the SC Communications team must understand the challenges of its client. Throughout the buying process, SC Communications educates itself on its client. It often relays potential script ideas to the clients and gains feedback from the corporate heads of these businesses. Yorton reports that through quality interactions with companies, SC Communications has let its marketing work for itself.

SC Communications has become the fastest-growing division of the company and established a reputation that leads businesses to seek out SC Communication. Keith Kramer, president of Chicago Faucets, recently hired SC Communications to help in a presentation for a global conglomerate acquiring his company. He is quoted as saying, "I could either inflict death by PowerPoint, or bring in Second City. I chose Second City." Second City's B2B marketing uses the language of business and the efficiency of comedy to show its relevance in today's corporate world.

After all, in high-pressured business, in which thinking quickly on your feet, trusting your instincts, and taking big risks is paramount, it makes for good business to train with the masters of improvisation. SC Communications provides numerous training options to executives looking for techniques in active listening, presentation skills, teamwork, customer service, and creativity. The Second City Web site hosts a number of "case studies" that detail how it has designed training events based on the specific needs of the client. SC Communications is making impressive strides in video technology to address public relations and training methods for large companies with thousands of employees across the country. The corporate market has come to know Second City and is delighted by its sense of humor and impressed by its sense of business.

The Second City is adept at understanding its consumer base—perhaps because approval of its product has been as clear as the sound of laughter. By commenting on modern culture for nearly 50 years, the Second City has become a social influence all its own. Its recognizable characteristics have enabled its jump into the corporate world. No matter what project the varied teams at The Second City are focusing on, its signatures skills of improvisation make any material suitable for the stage.

Questions

1. Describe who you might think the average audience member at a Second City show might be.
2. What is the consumer perception of Second City?
3. Why do you think that Second City Communications is helpful to businesses?
4. What are some of the techniques that Second City uses to help business people in their work?

PART 3
Target Market Selection

CHEVROLET UNLEASHES THE NEW CORVETTE

New with 4-wheel disc brakes
'65 CORVETTE

'73 CORVETTE
We gave it radials, a quieter ride, guard beams and a nose job.

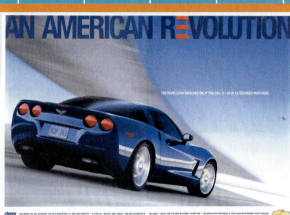
AN AMERICAN REVOLUTION

CHAPTER 8

Abacus: Getting to Know You

Suppose you worked for the outdoor apparel maker Patagonia, and you wanted to promote the company's first line of surf gear with a beautiful—and expensive—40-page mailing. Would you send it to your entire customer mailing list, including thousands of hikers, backpackers, joggers, birders, and other outdoor enthusiasts who do not surf? Not if you knew Abacus.

Abacus is a database marketing company that tracks shoppers' buying habits. The firm collects information from almost 2,000 retailers, including Patagonia and companies such as Restoration Hardware and Sharper Image, that anonymously contribute data to Abacus's database on about 90 million shoppers. Because the input is anonymous, Abacus can pool the information into a shared ("cooperative") base and

provide reports to its clients without compromising anyone's marketing strategies or other proprietary information. Only those who contribute to the pool can request reports from the database.

Abacus CEO Brian Raney says, "We believe past purchases are the best determination of what you'll buy in the future," but the company doesn't limit its client reports to projections of buying behavior. In addition to information about past purchases of everything from appliances to trivets, the data include details about household income, education, and age and gender of household members including children. Abacus even supplements its data with outside information such as post office records so that it can keep up with households that change address. Why does it care about such

moves? A change of address is a flag that tells Abacus you might soon be in the market for certain items, such as rugs or housewares.

Based partly on Abacus's success—the company is worth more than $111 million—the Direct Marketing Association is predicting catalog sales to rise 6 percent, even though the number of catalog shoppers has grown little. "Abacus's focus is on getting every last penny from people who already shop via catalogs," instead of trying to wring catalog sales from Internet or store shoppers, according to one industry observer.

Abacus achieves its results by cross-referencing data about shoppers so that it can locate, say, single males whose recent purchases included short boards or wet suits from any sporting goods retailer. Those young

Marketing Research and Sales Forecasting

Chapter Objectives

1 Describe the development of the marketing research function and its major activities.

2 Explain the steps in the marketing research process.

3 Distinguish between primary and secondary data and identify the sources of each type.

4 Explain the different sampling techniques used by marketing researchers.

5 Identify the methods by which marketing researchers collect primary data.

6 Explain the challenges of conducting marketing research in global markets.

7 Outline the most important uses of computer technology in marketing research.

8 Identify the major types of forecasting methods.

---

men received Patagonia's surf catalog. Abacus can also tell Vermont Country Stores which of the gardeners in its database are over age 50 and might be interested in a cast-iron apple peeler.

Consumers have objected to cross-referencing of purchasing behavior data in the past and succeeded in blocking plans by DoubleClick, the online ad company, to do the same thing. Abacus, which is owned by Hellman & Friedman, the same company that now owns DoubleClick, does more than just sift data for marketing appeals, however. It helps its clients prune their mailing lists and develop strategies to reactivate old customers and retain current ones. In fact, its clients are so happy with the more complete picture of their customers they can get from Abacus that Patagonia's direct-mail director says, "We wouldn't be in business without Abacus."[1]

evolution *of a* brand

Abacus is a successful database marketing company that focuses on direct marketers. For instance, the company helps catalog retailers target customers who would most likely be interested to receive mailings. With printing and postage costs continually rising, direct marketers need to be able to identify potential customers accurately and time their mailings for maximum responses.

- In 1990, Abacus introduced the first cooperative database for catalog marketers. Clients shared data to create a database of their best customers and from the pooled information could generate prospect lists. How could such lists aid direct marketers? How could they assist consumers? What are the drawbacks of this information sharing?

- With all of the different methods available today for customers to purchase products, do you think that catalog retailers—and marketing research firms such as Abacus—will continue to grow and be profitable? Make a list of the challenges and advantages. How can Abacus continue to remain viable in this changing industry? Now research the current status of Abacus to see how accurately you predicted the brand's future.

Chapter Overview

Collecting and managing information about what customers need and want is a challenging task for any marketer. **Marketing research** is the process of collecting and using information for marketing decision making. Data comes from a variety of sources. Some results come from well-planned studies designed to elicit specific information. Other valuable information comes from sales force reports, accounting records, and published reports. Still other data emerges from controlled experiments and computer simulations. Thanks to new database technologies, some data that companies collect is compiled for them by companies like Abacus. Marketing research, by presenting pertinent information in a useful format, aids decision makers in analyzing data and in suggesting possible actions.

This chapter discusses the marketing research function. Marketers use research to understand their customers, target customer segments, and develop long-term customer relationships—all keys to profitability. Information collected through marketing research underlies much of the material on market segmentation discussed in the following chapter. Clearly, the marketing research function is the primary source of the information needed to make effective marketing decisions. The use of technology to mine data and gather business and competitive intelligence is also discussed, as is technology's vast impact on marketing research decision making and planning. This chapter also explains how marketing research techniques are used to make accurate sales forecasts, a critical component of marketing planning.

marketing research Process of collecting and using information for marketing decision making.

Briefly Speaking

"If we knew what it was we were doing, it would not be called research, would it?"

—Albert Einstein
(1879–1955)
Nobel Prize–winning physicist

THE MARKETING RESEARCH FUNCTION

Before looking at how marketing research is conducted, we must first examine its historical development, the people and organizations it involves, and the activities it entails. Because an underlying purpose of research is to find out more about consumers, research is clearly central to effective customer satisfaction and customer relationship programs. Media technologies such as the Internet and virtual reality are opening up new channels through which researchers can tap into consumer information.

1 Describe the development of the marketing research function and its major activities.

DEVELOPMENT OF THE MARKETING RESEARCH FUNCTION

More than 125 years have passed since advertising pioneer N. W. Ayer conducted the first organized marketing research project in 1879. A second important milestone in the development of marketing research occurred 32 years later, when Charles C. Parlin organized the nation's first commercial research department at Curtis Publishing, publisher of *The Saturday Evening Post*.

Parlin got his start as a marketing researcher by counting soup cans in Philadelphia's garbage. Here is what happened. Parlin, an ad salesman, was trying to persuade the Campbell Soup Company to advertise in *The Saturday Evening Post*. Campbell Soup resisted, believing that the *Post* reached primarily working-class readers, who they thought preferred to make their own soup. Campbell Soup marketers were targeting higher-income people who could afford to pay for the convenience of soup in a can. To prove Campbell wrong, Parlin began counting soup cans in the garbage collected from different neighborhoods. His research revealed that working-class families bought more canned soup than wealthy households, who had servants to cook for them. Campbell Soup soon became a regular *Saturday Evening Post* client. It is interesting to note that garbage remains a good source of information for marketing researchers even today. Prior to the current cutbacks in food service, some airlines studied the leftovers from onboard meals to determine what to serve passengers.

Most early research gathered little more than written testimonials from purchasers of firms' products. Research methods became more sophisticated during the 1930s as the development of statistical techniques led to refinements in sampling procedures and greater accuracy in research findings.

In recent years, advances in computer technology have significantly changed the complexion of marketing research. Besides accelerating the pace and broadening the base of data collection, computers have aided marketers in making informed decisions about problems and opportunities. Simulations, for example, allow marketers to evaluate alternatives by posing "what-if" questions. Marketing researchers at many consumer goods firms simulate product introductions through computer programs to determine whether to risk real-world product launches or even to subject products to test marketing.

From the Collections of The Henry Ford Museum, copy and reuse restrictions apply.

From the Collections of The Henry Ford (G3807)

This testimonial letter from a satisfied "customer"—allegedly written by Clyde Barrow of the infamous Bonnie and Clyde gang of the 1930s—was received by Henry Ford before the two gangsters were shot by law enforcement officers on May 23, 1934.

WHO CONDUCTS MARKETING RESEARCH?

The size and organizational form of the marketing research function are usually tied to the structure of the company. Some firms organize research units to support different product lines, brands, or geographic areas. Others organize their research functions according to the types of research they need to perform, such as sales analysis, new-product development, advertising evaluation, or sales forecasting.

Many firms outsource their research needs and depend on independent marketing research firms. These independent organizations might specialize in handling just part of a larger study, such as conducting consumer interviews. Firms can also contract out entire research studies.

Marketers usually decide whether to conduct a study internally or through an outside organization based on cost. Another major consideration is the reliability and accuracy of the information collected by an outside organization. Because collecting marketing data is what these outside organizations do full time, the information they gather is often more thorough and accurate than that collected by less experienced in-house staff. Often an outside marketing research firm can provide technical assistance and expertise not available within the company's marketing department. Interaction with outside suppliers also helps ensure that a researcher does not conduct a study only to validate a favorite viewpoint or preferred option.

Marketing research companies range in size from sole proprietorships to national and international firms such as ACNielsen, Information Resources, and Arbitron. They can be classified as syndicated services, full-service suppliers, or limited-service suppliers depending on the types of services they offer to clients. Some full-service organizations are also willing to take on limited-service activities.

Briefly
Speaking

"You can give people responsibility and authority, but without information they are helpless. Knowledge is the ultimate power tool."

—Bill Gates (b. 1955)
Chairman and chief software architect, Microsoft

Syndicated Services

An organization that regularly provides a standardized set of data to all customers is called a **syndicated service.** Mediamark Research, for example, operates a syndicated product research service based on personal interviews with adults regarding their exposure to advertising media. Clients include advertisers, advertising agencies, magazines, newspapers, broadcasters, and cable TV networks.

Another syndicated service provider is J. D. Power and Associates, a global marketing information firm headquartered in California that specializes in surveying customer satisfaction, product quality, and buyer behavior. Among its customers are companies in the telecommunications, travel and hotel, marine, utilities, healthcare, building, consumer electronics, automotive, and financial services industries.[2]

Full-Service Research Suppliers

An organization that contracts with clients to conduct complete marketing research projects is called a **full-service research supplier.** Brain Group, a Mexican marketing research firm, provides quantitative and qualitative research and various field studies, including face-to-face and telephone interviews, online interviews, multinational studies, B2B interviews, and even "mystery shopper" research to collect information about retail outlets. The company also studies public opinion and buyer behavior and evaluates Web pages and work environments. Its editing department reviews questionnaires before they are used, under strict supervision, by Brain Group's staff in interviews, focus groups, and other types of observation techniques including video.[3] A full-service supplier becomes the client's marketing research arm, performing all of the steps in the marketing research process (discussed later in this chapter).

COURTESY OF BRAIN GROUP

Brain Group is a full-service marketing research company specializing in the markets of Mexico and Latin America.

Limited-Service Research Suppliers

A marketing research firm that specializes in a limited number of activities, such as conducting field interviews or performing data processing, is called a **limited-service research supplier.** Working almost exclusively for major movie studios, Nielsen National Research Group specializes in testing promotional materials for and marketing of motion pictures.[4] The firm also prepares studies to help clients develop advertising strategies and to track awareness and interest. Syndicated services can also be considered a type of limited-service research supplier.

CUSTOMER SATISFACTION MEASUREMENT PROGRAMS

In their marketing research, firms often focus on tracking the satisfaction levels of current customers. Austin, Texas–based Bazaarvoice charges a monthly fee to clients and does everything from designing and managing a firm's customer feedback area on its Web site to moderating online discussion groups and analyzing comments.[5] Some marketers have also gained valuable insights by tracking the dissatisfaction that led customers to abandon certain products for those of competitors. Some customer defections are only partial; customers may remain somewhat satisfied with a business but not completely satisfied. Such attitudes could lead them to take their business elsewhere. Studying the underlying causes of customer defections, even partial defections, can be useful for identifying problem areas that need attention. Market Research Insight conducts research and analysis to help companies and political campaigns develop marketing strategies.[6]

Some organizations conduct their own measurement programs through online polls and surveys. The U.S. Environmental Protection Agency (EPA), for instance, posted a short customer satisfaction questionnaire on its Web site to collect user feedback on how easy or difficult it is to navigate around the site and find desired information.[7]

THE MARKETING RESEARCH PROCESS

2 Explain the steps in the marketing research process.

As discussed earlier, business executives rely on marketing research to provide the information they need to make effective decisions regarding their firm's current and future activities. The chances of making good decisions improve when the right information is provided at the right time during decision making. To achieve this goal, marketing researchers often follow the six-step process shown in Figure 8.1. In the initial stages, researchers define the problem, conduct exploratory research, and formulate a hypothesis to be tested. Next, they create a design for the research study and collect needed data. Finally, researchers interpret and present the research information. The following sections take a closer look at each step of the marketing research process.

DEFINE THE PROBLEM

A popular anecdote advises that well-defined problems are half solved. A well-defined problem permits the researcher to focus on securing the exact information needed for the solution. Clearly defining the question, that research needs to answer increases the speed and accuracy of the research process.

Researchers must carefully avoid confusing symptoms of a problem with the problem itself. A symptom merely alerts marketers that a problem exists. For example, suppose that a maker of frozen pizzas sees its market share drop from 8 to 5 percent in six months. The loss of market share is a symptom of a problem the company must solve. To define the problem, the firm must look for the underlying causes of its market share loss.

A logical starting point in identifying the problem might be to evaluate the firm's target market and marketing mix elements. Suppose, for example, a firm has recently changed its promotional strategies. Research might then seek to answer the question "What must we do to improve the effectiveness of our marketing mix?" The firm's marketers might also look at possible environmental changes. Perhaps a new competitor entered the firm's market. Decision makers will need information to help answer the question, "What must we do to distinguish our company from the new competitor?"

When Subway wanted to determine whether it should enter the breakfast market, where giants such as McDonald's and Burger King already compete successfully, it chose the area around Buffalo, New York, to test the idea with a specially prepared menu of breakfast sandwiches and other products such as hash browns, two different kinds of stuffed French toast, and cinnamon rolls. The chain's 83 stores in the area were set to open at 7 A.M. to offer the items. "This is something we always wanted to do in this market," said the company's regional director of operations. "We will be watching to see what items sell and which are perceived as being customer-friendly." The chain currently offers six breakfast sandwiches.[8]

figure 8.1

The Marketing Research Process

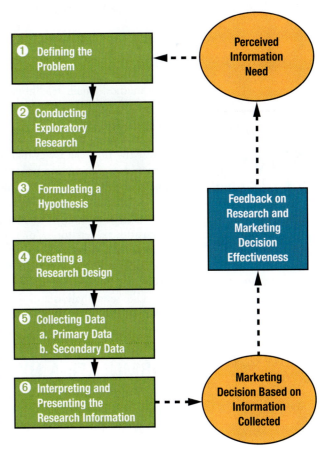

CONDUCT EXPLORATORY RESEARCH

Once a firm has defined the question it wants to answer, researchers can begin exploratory research. **Exploratory research** seeks to discover the cause of a specific problem by discussing the problem with informed sources both within and outside the firm and by examining data from other information sources. Marketers at Romano's Macaroni Grill (part of Dallas-based Brinker International), for example, might talk with their customers, suppliers, and retailers. Executives at Brinker might also ask for input from the sales force or look for overall market clues.

In addition to talking with employees, exploratory research can include evaluation of company records, such as sales and profit analyses, and available competitive data. Marketing researchers often refer to internal data collection as situation analysis. The term *informal investigation* is often used for exploratory interviews with informed people outside the researchers' firms.

Using Internal Data

Marketers can find valuable data in their firm's own internal records. Pulte Homes has been so successful building residential communities in the Chicago area that it has begun buying land for new developments at a record pace. The company, which hopes to expand nationwide, is paying as much attention to marketing research as it is to construction details. Internal research from consumer surveys and demographic data is helping it learn how to build homes for every major demographic group around the country by figuring out what customers want. "There's not an attractive part of the market that Pulte isn't hitting," says one real estate executive. In an industry dominated by small firms, Pulte is building 100 homes a day in 28 states and holds a seven-year supply of housing tracts.[9]

Other typical sources of internal data are sales records, financial statements, and marketing cost analyses. Marketers analyze sales performance records to gain an overall view of company efficiency and to find clues to potential problems. Easily prepared from company invoices or a computer database system, this **sales analysis** can provide important details to management. The study typically compares actual and expected sales based on a detailed sales forecast by territory, product, customer, and salesperson. Once the sales quota—the level of expected sales to which actual results are compared—has been established, it is a simple process to compare actual results with expected performance. Mikuni Coca-Cola Bottling Company, a Coca-Cola bottler in Japan, relies on data about unit sales, sellouts, and mechanical failures to monitor and supply its vending machines. Salespeople gather the information with handheld terminals when they visit each vending location.[10]

Other possible breakdowns for sales analysis separate transactions by customer type, product, sales method (mail, telephone, or personal contact), type of order (cash or credit), and order size. Sales analysis is one of the least expensive and most important sources of marketing information available to a firm.

Accounting data, as summarized in the firm's financial statements, can be another good tool for identifying financial issues that influence marketing. Using ratio analysis, researchers can compare performance in current and previous years against industry benchmarks. These exercises may hint at possible problems, but only more detailed analysis would reveal specific causes of indicated variations.

A third source of internal information is *marketing cost analysis*—evaluation of expenses for tasks such as selling, warehousing, advertising, and delivery to determine the profitability of particular customers, territories, or product lines. Firms often examine the allocation of costs to products, customers, and territories. Marketing decision makers then evaluate the profitability of particular customers and territories on the basis of the sales produced and the costs incurred in generating those sales. Sometimes internal data can produce remarkably detailed customer profiles.

Like sales analysis and financial research, marketing cost analysis is most useful when it provides information linked to other forms of marketing research. A later section of this chapter will address how computer technologies can accomplish these linkages and move information among a firm's units.

FORMULATE A HYPOTHESIS

After defining the problem and conducting an exploratory investigation, the marketer needs to formulate a **hypothesis**—a tentative explanation for some specific event. A hypothesis is a statement about the relationship among variables that carries clear implications for testing this relationship. It sets the stage for more in-depth research by further clarifying what researchers need to test. For example, Olive Garden restaurants might want to see whether good customer service is related to its increased sales, so its marketers would conduct a survey of customers to test this hypothesis.

Not all studies test specific hypotheses. However, a carefully designed study can benefit from the rigor introduced by developing a hypothesis before beginning data collection and analysis.

CREATE A RESEARCH DESIGN

To test hypotheses and find solutions to marketing problems, a marketer creates a **research design,** a master plan or model for conducting marketing research. In planning a research project, marketers must be sure that the study will measure what they intend to measure. A second important research design consideration is the selection of respondents. Marketing researchers use sampling techniques (discussed later in the chapter) to determine which consumers to include in their studies.

Cadbury Schweppes, the candy and gum manufacturer, trains "sensory panelists" for several months to test gum by, for instance, chewing at a steady rate for set periods of time, usually three minutes. After each chewing session, the testers clear their palates with salted crackers and water and then use computers to record their feedback about flavor and texture.[11]

COLLECT DATA

Marketing researchers gather two kinds of data: secondary data and primary data. **Secondary data** is information from previously published or compiled sources. Census data is an example. **Primary data** refers to information collected for the first time specifically for a marketing research study. An example of primary data is statistics collected from a survey that asks current customers about their preferences for product improvements. Global research firm Synovate collects primary data in the Americas, Asia, Europe, and the Middle East for its clients. The company operates in over 50 different countries and reports it has "5,000 curious employees, over 600 qualitative research specialists, and 2,500 research professionals."

Secondary data offers two important advantages: (1) it is almost always less expensive to gather than primary data, and (2) researchers usually spend less time to locate and use secondary data. A research study that requires primary data may take three to four months to complete, while a researcher can often gather secondary data in a matter of days.

Secondary data does have limitations that primary data does not. First, published information can quickly become obsolete. A marketer analyzing the population of various areas may discover that even the most recent census figures are already out of date because of rapid growth and changing demographics. Second, published data collected for an unrelated purpose may not be completely relevant to the marketer's specific needs. For example, census data do not reveal the brand preferences of consumers.

Although research to gather primary data can cost more and take longer, the results can provide richer, more detailed information than secondary data offers. The choice between secondary and primary data is tied to cost, applicability, and effectiveness. Many marketing research projects combine secondary and primary data to fully answer marketing questions. This chapter examines specific methods for collecting both secondary and primary data in later sections.

3 Distinguish between primary and secondary data and identify the sources of each type.

secondary data Previously published information.

primary data Information collected specifically for the investigation at hand.

COURTESY OF SYNOVATE

Synovate uses many methods to collect primary data around the world—personal interviews, surveys of customer feedback, focus groups, direct observation, media research, and field studies.

INTERPRET AND PRESENT RESEARCH INFORMATION

The final step in the marketing research process is to interpret the findings and present them to decision makers in a format that allows managers to make effective judgments. Possible differences in interpretations of research results may occur between marketing researchers and their audiences due to differing backgrounds, levels of knowledge, and experience. Both oral and written reports should be presented in a manner designed to minimize such misinterpretations.

Marketing researchers and research users must cooperate at every stage in the research process. Too many studies go unused because management fears that the results are of little use, once they hear lengthy discussions of research limitations or unfamiliar terminology. Marketing researchers must remember to direct their reports toward management and not to other researchers. They should spell out their conclusions in clear and concise terms that can be put into action. Reports should confine technical details of the research methods to an appendix, if they are included at all.

By presenting research results to all key executives at a single sitting, researchers can ensure that everyone will understand the findings. Decision makers can then quickly reach consensus on what the results mean and what actions need to be taken.

assessment check

1. What are the six steps in the marketing research process?
2. What is the goal of exploratory research?

MARKETING RESEARCH METHODS

Clearly, data collection is an integral part of the marketing research process. One of the most time-consuming parts of collecting data is determining what method the marketer should use to obtain the data. This section discusses the most commonly used methods by which marketing researchers find both secondary and primary data.

SECONDARY DATA COLLECTION

Secondary data comes from many sources. The overwhelming quantity of secondary data available at little or no cost challenges researchers to select only data that is relevant to the problem or issue being studied.

Secondary data consists of two types: internal and external data. Internal data, as discussed earlier, includes sales records, product performance reviews, sales force activity reports, and marketing cost reports. External data comes from a variety of sources, including government records, syndicated research services, and industry publications. Computerized databases provide access to vast amounts of data from both inside and outside an organization. The following sections on government data, private data, and online sources focus on databases and other external data sources available to marketing researchers.

Government Data

The federal government is the nation's most important source of marketing data. Census data provides the most frequently used government statistics. A census of population is conducted every ten years and is made available at no charge in local libraries, on computer disks, and via the Internet. The U.S. Census Bureau also conducts a periodic census of housing, population, business, manufacturers, agriculture, minerals, and governments.

The U.S. Census of Population contains a wealth of valuable information for marketers. It breaks down the population by very small geographic areas, making it possible to determine population traits by city block or census tract in large cities. It divides the populations of nonmetropolitan areas into census tracts. Census tracts are important for marketing analysis because they highlight populations of about 1,500 to 8,000 people with similar traits. This data helps marketers such as local retailers and shopping center developers gather vital information about customers in an immediate neighborhood without spending time or money to conduct comprehensive surveys. The Census Bureau uses a variety of statistical techniques to group households into homogeneous clusters of people who have similar lifestyles and spending habits and who listen to similar kinds of broadcast media.[12]

Marketing researchers find even more valuable resources in the government's computerized mapping database called the TIGER system, for Topographically Integrated Geographic Encoding and Referencing system. This system overlays topographic features such as railroads, highways, and rivers with census data such as household income figures. TIGER data is available on DVD, making the Census Bureau one of the first federal agencies to use this technology to publish huge amounts of digital data. The DVDs contain both database management software and mapping software, making TIGER data highly accessible to marketers.[13]

Marketers often get other information from the federal government, such as the following:

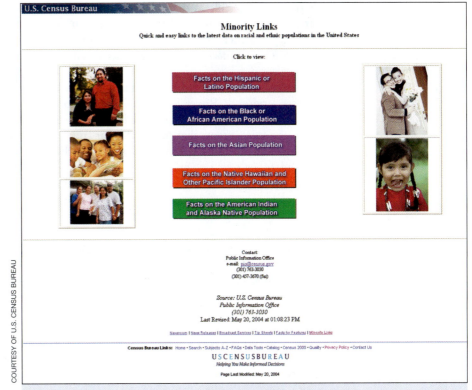

The U.S. Census Bureau collects a wealth of data that can be used for marketing research. For instance, it collects information on ethnic and racial minority populations in many categories—population, geographical distribution, social characteristics, and employment and income levels, to name just a few.

- *Monthly Catalog of United States Government Publications* and *Statistical Abstract of the United States*, published annually and available online as the *Catalog of U.S. Government Publications (CGP)*

- *Survey of Current Business*, updated monthly by the Bureau of Economic Analysis

- *County and City Data Book*, typically published every three years and also available on CD-ROM, providing data on each county and city of more than 25,000 residents

State and city governments serve as additional important sources of information on employment, production, and sales activities. In addition, university bureaus of business and economic research frequently collect and disseminate valuable information.

Private Data

Many private organizations provide information for marketing decision makers. A trade association may be an excellent source of data on activities in a particular industry. Thomson Gale's *Encyclopedia of Associations*, available in many libraries, can help marketers track down trade associations that may have pertinent data. Also, the advertising industry continuously collects data on audiences reached by various media.

Business and trade magazines also publish a wide range of valuable data. Ulrich's *Guide to International Periodicals*, another common library reference, can point researchers in the direction of trade publications that conduct and publish industry-specific research. General business magazines can also be good sources. *Sales & Marketing Management*, for instance, publishes an annual *Survey of Media Markets* that combines statistics for population, effective buying income (EBI), and retail sales into buying power indexes that indicate each geographic market's ability to buy.

Data security is always an issue in marketing research firms. The "Marketing Success" feature explores how one database firm dealt with a security breach.

Because few libraries carry specialized trade journals, the best way to gather data from them is either directly from the publishers or through online periodical databases such as ProQuest Direct's

ABI/Inform, available at many libraries. Increasingly, trade publications maintain Web home pages that allow archival searches. Larger libraries can often provide directories and other publications that can help researchers find secondary data. For instance, Guideline's *FindEx: The Directory of Market Research Reports, Studies, and Surveys* lists a tremendous variety of completed research studies that are available for purchase.

Several national firms offer information to businesses by subscription. RoperASW is a global database service; its Roper Reports Worldwide provides continuing data on consumer attitudes, life stages, lifestyle, and buying behavior for more than 30 developed and developing countries.

Electronic systems that scan UPC bar codes speed purchase transactions, and they also provide data used for inventory control, ordering, and delivery. Scanning technology is widely used by grocers and other retailers, and marketing research companies such as ACNielsen and Information Resources store this data in commercially available databases. These scanner-based information services track consumer purchases of a wide variety of UPC-coded products. Retailers can use this information to target customers with the right merchandise at the right time.

Newer techniques that rely on radio-frequency identification (RFID) technology are in growing use. Wal-Mart has run successful tests showing that RFID reduced out-of-stocks and cut down dramatically on manual orders and excess inventory.[14] Use of RFID to track individuals' purchase and use of products is, however, controversial because of privacy concerns. Currently, the technology is used for aggregate data.

ACNielsen SalesNet uses the Internet to deliver scanner data quickly to clients. Data is processed as soon as it is received from supermarkets and is then forwarded to marketing researchers so they can perform more in-depth analysis. At the same time, Nielsen representatives summarize the data in both graphic and spreadsheet form and post it on the Internet for immediate access by clients.

Online Sources of Secondary Data

The tools of cyberspace sometimes simplify the hunt for secondary data. Hundreds of databases and other sources of information are available online. A well-designed, Internet-based marketing research project can cost less yet yield faster results than offline research.

The Internet has spurred the growth of research aggregators—companies that acquire, catalog, reformat, segment, and then resell premium research reports that have already been published. Aggregators put valuable data within reach of marketers who lack the time or the budget to commission custom research. Because Web technology makes their databases easy to search, aggregators such as Datamonitor and eMarketer can compile detailed, specialized reports quickly and cost-effectively.[15]

Internet search tools such as Google and Yahoo! can find specific sites that are rich with information. Discussion groups may also provide information and insights that can help answer some marketing questions. Additionally, a post to a chat room or newsgroup may draw a response that

 marketing success   Acxion Strengthens Safeguards on Customer Data

Background. Acxiom Corp.—based in Little Rock and Conway, Arkansas—processes billions of records each month to help its clients manage information, maintain data quality, and build the best possible customer relationships. Among its clients are nearly all of the fifteen biggest credit card companies and the top six retail banks, as well as seven of the top ten auto manufacturers.

The Challenge. Like all customer information databases, Acxiom faces the constant possibility that unauthorized users will gain access to its stored data. As the company's chief privacy officer testified before Congress, "The

bad guys are smart and getting more organized. They will make use of all of the skills available to them to try to find ways to obtain the information they need to commit fraud." Then 1 billion records were stolen from the company by an employee at a company that had a business relationship with Acxiom. The thief used decryption software to find passwords that allowed him to access areas of the database to which he had no authorization.

The Strategy. Investigators from the FBI and the U.S. Secret Service on a separate case uncovered the theft and retrieved the stolen data, preventing it from being used in any identify thefts or credit card frauds.

uncovers previously unknown sources of secondary data. Umbria is a market research firm in Boulder, Colorado, whose software is designed to use keywords to scour blogs for useful consumer information on the Internet. "The blogosphere is overflowing with brutally honest opinion," says Umbria's CEO Howard Kaushansky. "Our goal is to track those opinions down."[16]

Researchers must, however, carefully evaluate the validity of information they find on the Internet. People without in-depth knowledge of the subject matter may post information in a newsgroup. Similarly, Web pages might contain information that has been gathered using questionable research methods. The phrase *caveat emptor* ("let the buyer beware") should guide evaluation of secondary data on the Internet.

SAMPLING TECHNIQUES

Before undertaking a study to gather primary data, researchers must first identify which participants to include in the study. **Sampling** is the process of selecting survey respondents or research participants. It is one of the most important aspects of research design because if a study fails to involve consumers who accurately reflect the target market, the research is likely to yield misleading conclusions. Studies of working women, for example, can be vulnerable to error when samples are small, because in recent years the career options available for women have expanded, making generalized conclusions harder to develop.[17]

The total group of people that the researcher wants to study is called the **population** or **universe.** For a political campaign study, the population would be all eligible voters. For research about a new lipstick line, it might be all women in a certain age bracket. The sample is a representative group chosen from this population. Researchers rarely gather information from a study's total population, resulting in a census. Unless the total population is small, the costs of a census are simply too high. Sometimes limitations can reduce the size of the sample. For instance, although public health agencies are charged with collecting health data about people with disabilities, questions often arise about how well those with hearing, speaking, or cognitive difficulty can actively participate in telephone surveys, a common tool of such research.[18]

Samples can be classified as either probability samples or nonprobability samples. A **probability sample** is one that gives every member of the population a chance of being selected. Types of probability samples include simple random samples, stratified samples, and cluster samples.

In a **simple random sample,** every member of the relevant universe has an equal opportunity of selection. The draft lottery of the Vietnam era is an example. The days of the year were drawn and set into an array. The placement of a person's birthday in this list determined his likelihood of being called for service. In a **stratified sample,** randomly selected subsamples of different groups are represented in the total sample. Stratified samples provide efficient, representative groups that are relatively homogeneous for a certain characteristic for such studies as opinion polls, in which groups of individuals share various divergent viewpoints. In a **cluster sample,** researchers select a sample of

4 Explain the different sampling techniques used by marketing researchers.

sampling Process of selecting survey respondents or research participants.

probability sample Sample that gives every member of the population a chance of being selected.

subgroups (or clusters) from which they draw respondents. Each cluster reflects the diversity of the whole population being sampled. This cost-efficient type of probability sample is widely used when the entire population cannot be listed or enumerated.

nonprobability sample
Sample that involves personal judgment somewhere in the selection process.

In contrast, a **nonprobability sample** relies on personal judgment somewhere in the selection process. In other words, researchers decide which particular groups to study. Types of nonprobability samples are convenience samples and quota samples. A **convenience sample** is a nonprobability sample selected from among readily available respondents; this sample is often called an *accidental sample* because those included just happen to be in the place where the study is being conducted. Mall intercept surveys and TV call-in opinion polls are good examples. Marketing researchers sometimes use convenience samples in exploratory research but not in definitive studies. A **quota sample** is a nonprobability sample that is divided to maintain the proportion of certain characteristics among different segments or groups as is seen in the population as a whole. In other words, each field worker is assigned a quota that specifies the number and characteristics of the people to contact. It differs from a stratified sample, in which researchers select subsamples by some random process; in a quota sample, they handpick participants.

✔ *assessment check*

1. What is sampling?
2. Explain the different types of probability samples.
3. Identify the types of nonprobability samples.

5 Identify the methods by which marketing researchers collect primary data.

PRIMARY RESEARCH METHODS

Marketers use a variety of methods for conducting primary research, as Figure 8.2 shows. The principal methods for collecting primary data are observation, surveys, and controlled experiments. The choice among these methods depends on the issues under study and the decisions that marketers need to make. In some cases, researchers may decide to combine techniques during the research process.

Observation Method

In observational studies, researchers view the overt actions of subjects being studied. Marketers trying to understand how consumers behave in certain situations find observation to be a useful technique. Observation tactics may be as simple as counting the number of cars passing by a potential site for a fast-food restaurant or checking the license plates at a shopping center near a state line to determine where shoppers live.

Technological advances provide increasingly sophisticated ways for observing consumer behavior. The television industry relies on data from people meters, which are electronic remote-control devices that record the TV viewing habits of individual household members to measure the popularity of TV shows. Traditional people meters require each viewer to press a button each time he or she turns on the TV, changes channels, or leaves the room.

Marketers have long worried that some viewers do not bother to push people meter buttons at appropriate times, skewing research findings. In response, Arbitron recently tested a portable people meter (PPM) that participants keep with them at all times. Throughout the day, the PPM picks up and stores codes embedded in radio and broadcast, cable, and satellite TV programming as well as Internet content and cinema advertising. At night, the participant puts the PPM into a docking station, from

figure 8.2

Types of Primary Research

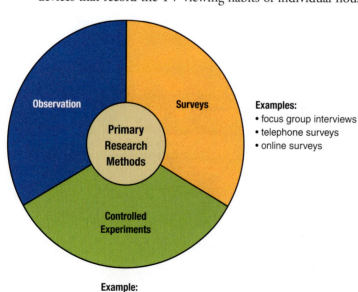

Examples:
- traffic counts
- Nielsen television ratings
- taping shopping habits

Examples:
- focus group interviews
- telephone surveys
- online surveys

Example:
- test market

which the data is uploaded to Arbitron. The PPM even has a built-in motion detector to ensure that it is not abandoned midtest. Wendy's International recently selected the Arbitron meter to collect data about radio listening patterns in order to get better value for its radio advertising dollars.[19]

Acknowledging the growing prevalence of TiVo and other digital video recording (DVR) technologies in households, Nielsen Media Research, in partnership with DVR market leader TiVo, has begun distributing its well-known television ratings in three versions: live, live plus 24 hours (to count viewers who play back shows within a day of recording them), and live plus seven days (to count those who play back shows within a week). The technology allows broadcasters to track viewing habits in the 7 percent of TV households that now use digital video recording to tailor their viewing. Marketers may soon be able to make media decisions knowing how many people are "timeshifting" shows—and the accompanying advertising—to watch them after the broadcast date.[20]

Videotaping consumers in action is also gaining acceptance as a research technique. Cookware manufacturers may videotape consumers cooking in their own kitchens to evaluate how they use their pots and pans. A toothbrush manufacturer asked marketing research firm E-Lab to videotape consumers brushing their teeth and using mouthwash in its quest to develop products that would leave behind the sensation of cleanliness and freshness.

In an effort to understand what makes younger consumers tick, a trend-forecasting firm called Teenage Research Unlimited (TRU) has auditioned and hired a panel of more than 300 "diverse, trend-setting, savvy teens" for its Trendwatch Panel. The teens participate in focus group discussions and respond to research queries on the company's online bulletin board.[21]

Interpretative Research

Another type of primary research is **interpretative research,** a method in which a researcher observes a customer or group of customers in their natural setting and interprets their behavior based on an understanding of the social and cultural characteristics of that setting. We discuss interpretative research in more detail later.

SURVEY METHOD

Observation alone cannot supply all of the desired information. Researchers must ask questions to get information on attitudes, motives, and opinions. It is also difficult to get exact demographic information—such as income levels—from observation. To discover this information, researchers can use either interviews or questionnaires. Philadelphia-based Dorland Healthcare Information provides market research for the healthcare and managed-care market and relies heavily on mail, phone, and fax surveys as well as interviews with knowledgeable sources.[22]

Telephone Interviews

Telephone interviews are a quick and inexpensive method for obtaining a small quantity of relatively impersonal information. Simple, clearly worded questions are easy for interviewers to pose over the phone and are effective at drawing appropriate responses. Telephone surveys have relatively high response rates, especially with repeated calls; calling a number once yields a response rate of 50 to 60 percent, but calling the same number five times raises the response rate to 85 percent. To maximize responses and save costs, some researchers use computerized dialing and digitally synthesized voices that interview respondents.

However, phone surveys have several drawbacks. Most important, many people refuse to take part in them. Their reasons include lack of time, the nuisance factor, negative associations of phone surveys with telemarketing, and poorly designed surveys or questions that are difficult to understand.[23] The National Do Not Call Registry, which regulates telemarketing, excludes calls made for research purposes.[24]

Many respondents are hesitant to give personal characteristics about themselves over the telephone. Also, results may be biased by the omission of typical households in which adults are off working during the day. Other households, particularly market segments such as single women and physicians, are likely to have unlisted numbers. While computerized random dialing can give access to unlisted numbers, it is restricted in several states.

interpretative research
Observational research method developed by social anthropologists in which customers are observed in their natural setting and their behavior is interpreted based on an understanding of social and cultural characteristics; also known as *ethnography*, or "going native."

Briefly
Speaking

"The more the data banks record about each one of us, the less we exist."

—Marshall McLuhan (1911–1980)
Canadian communications theorist

Etiquette Tips for Marketing Professionals

How to Conduct Phone Surveys

Telephone surveys are a common method of conducting marketing research because they're simple to develop and easy to do. But that doesn't mean they don't require preparation to make the process efficient for you and for participants. Respect their time and input with a few courteous tips.

1. Develop and test your research questions ahead of time. They should be brief, clear, and easy to tabulate. Time your questionnaire before you begin.
2. Prepare your opener by knowing how you'll introduce yourself and your purpose, but if you can, avoid writing or memorizing a script. Try for a natural, conversational greeting and introduction.
3. Explain the purpose of your survey and say how much time it will take. Be brief, upbeat, and polite, and make it clear that you aren't selling anything.
4. If the respondent is reluctant, try gentle persuasion, but say thank you and hang up if the resistance is firm.
5. Ask the respondent to verify his or her name and any other contact information you're collecting.
6. Read each question carefully and in its entirety and record the answer. Listen carefully, stay on topic, and avoid introducing comments that could influence the respondent's answers.
7. Thank the respondent for participating.
8. Organize and evaluate your results.

Sources: "Conducting Your Phone Survey," SurveyGold, **http://surveygold. com**, accessed March 22, 2006; "How to Conduct a Telephone Survey," eHow, **http://www.ehow.com**, accessed March 22, 2006; "How to Write a Survey or Questionnaire," eHow, **http://www.ehow.com**, accessed March 22, 2006; "Is Cold Calling Painful for You?" Unlock the Game, **http://www.unlockthegame.com**, accessed March 22, 2006.

The popularity of Caller ID systems to screen unwanted calls is another obstacle for telephone researchers. State laws on Caller ID vary. Some require vendors to offer a blocking service to callers who wish to evade the system. Marketers face other problems in obtaining responses from a representative sample of respondents using phone surveys: consumer perception of intrusion into their privacy and the number of consumers in the national Do Not Call Registry. The "Etiquette Tips for Marketing Professionals" feature lists some helpful tips on conducting phone surveys.

Other obstacles restrict the usefulness of telephone surveys abroad. In areas where telephone ownership is rare, survey results will be highly biased. Telephone interviewing is also difficult in countries that lack directories or charge landline telephone customers on a per-minute basis, or where call volumes congest limited phone line capacity.

Personal Interviews

The best means for obtaining detailed information about consumers is usually the personal interview, because the interviewer can establish rapport with respondents and explain confusing or vague questions. In addition to contacting respondents at their homes or workplaces, marketing research firms can conduct interviews in rented space in shopping centers, where they gain wide access to potential buyers of the merchandise they are studying. These locations sometimes feature private interviewing space, videotape equipment, and food preparation facilities for taste tests. As mentioned earlier, interviews conducted in shopping centers are typically called **mall intercepts.** Downtown retail districts and airports provide other valuable locations for marketing researchers.

focus group Simultaneous personal interview of a small group of individuals, which relies on group discussion about a certain topic.

Focus Groups

Marketers also gather research information through the popular technique of focus group interviews. A **focus group** brings together eight to twelve individuals in one location to discuss a subject of interest.

Unlike other interview techniques that elicit information through a question-and-answer format, focus groups usually encourage a general discussion of a predetermined topic. Focus groups can provide quick and relatively inexpensive insight into consumer attitudes and motivations.

In a focus group, the leader, or moderator, typically begins by explaining the purpose of the meeting and suggesting an opening topic. The moderator's main purpose, however, is to stimulate interaction among group members to encourage their discussion of numerous points. The moderator may occasionally interject questions as catalysts to direct the group's discussion. The moderator's job is difficult, requiring preparation and group facilitation skills.

Focus group sessions often last one or two hours. Researchers usually record the discussion on tape,

COURTESY OF IRWIN

Marketing research firm Irwin specializes in personal interviews of consumers, especially focus groups.

and observers frequently watch through a one-way mirror. Some research firms also allow clients to view focus groups in action through videoconferencing systems.

Focus groups are a particularly valuable tool for exploratory research, developing new-product ideas, and preliminary testing of alternative marketing strategies. They can also aid in the development of well-structured questionnaires for larger scale research.

Focus groups do have drawbacks. John B. Osborne, CEO of ad agency BBDO, explains what many think is one of the biggest problems in focus groups—that people are just not honest in front of others. "There's peer pressure in focus groups that gets in the way of finding the truth about real behavior and intentions," he says. Yahoo's chief marketing officer also voices dissatisfaction with focus groups and prefers "immersion groups" in which the company's product developers meet to talk informally with a handful of users and without professional moderators.[25]

Researchers are finding ways to re-create the focus group environment over the Internet. With experienced moderators who have the technical skills to function fluently online, it is possible to gain valuable qualitative information at a fraction of the cost of running a traditional focus group session.

ACNielsen reports that online focus groups can be both cost and time efficient, with immediate results in the form of chat transcripts. The convenience of online conversations tends to improve attendance as well, particularly among those who are otherwise difficult to include such as professionals and people who travel frequently, and the problem of peer pressure is virtually eliminated. Some drawbacks include the lack of access to body language and nonverbal cues, the difficulty of testing any products in which taste or smell is relevant, and the potential for samples to be nonrepresentative because they are limited to those who have Internet access and a certain comfort level with technology.[26]

Mail Surveys

Although personal interviews can provide very detailed information, cost considerations usually prevent an organization from using personal interviews in a large-scale study. A mail survey can be a cost-effective alternative. Mail surveys can provide anonymity that may encourage respondents to give candid answers. They can also help marketers track consumer attitudes through ongoing research and sometimes provide demographic data that may be helpful in market segmentation.

Mail questionnaires do, however, have several limitations. First, response rates are typically much lower than for personal interviews. Second, because researchers must wait for respondents to complete and return questionnaires, mail surveys usually take a considerably longer time to conduct. A third limitation is that questionnaires cannot answer unanticipated questions that occur to respondents as they complete the forms. In addition, complex questions may not be suitable for a mail questionnaire. Finally, unless they gather additional information from nonrespondents through other means, researchers must worry about possible bias in the results stemming from differences between respondents and nonrespondents.

Researchers try to minimize these limitations by carefully developing and pretesting questionnaires. Researchers can boost response rates by keeping questionnaires short and by offering incentives—typically, discount coupons or a dollar bill.

Fax Surveys

The low response rates and long follow-up times associated with mail surveys have spurred interest in the alternative of faxing survey documents. In some cases, faxes may supplement mail surveys; in others, they may be the primary method for contacting respondents. Because millions of households do not have fax machines, securing a representative sample of respondents is a difficult undertaking in fax surveys of final consumers. As a result, most of these surveys focus on business-related research studies.

The federal junk fax law prohibits the sending by fax of "any material advertising the commercial availability or quality of any property, goods, or services which is transmitted to any person without that person's prior express invitation or permission, in writing or otherwise." The first page of any fax solicitation must now include information for the recipient about how to "opt out" of similar messages in the future.[27]

SurveySpot maintains proprietary online panels in many countries around the world and specializes in providing diverse and reliable samples for its clients.

Online Surveys and Other Internet-Based Methods

The growing population of Internet users has spurred researchers to conduct online surveys. Using the Web, they are able to speed the survey process, increase sample sizes, ignore geographic boundaries, and dramatically reduce costs. While a standard research project can take up to eight weeks to complete, a thorough online project may take two weeks or less. Less intrusive than telephone surveys, online research allows participants to respond at their leisure. The novelty and ease of answering online may even encourage higher response rates. Intelliseek, an online marketing research firm, found that among 660 consumers who consistently avoid ads on TV and the Internet, most were actually more likely to participate in online product discussions at product review sites or in blogs and to post comments on Web sites more often.[28] Survey Sampling International manages online survey panels in more than 30 countries around the world, including 3.8 million households.

Businesses are increasingly including questionnaires on their Web pages to solicit information about consumer demographics, attitudes, and comments and suggestions for improving goods and services or improving marketing messages. Marketers are also experimenting with electronic bulletin boards as an information-gathering device. On a password-protected Web site, moderators pose questions to selected respondents—usually just 15 to 25—over a predetermined period of time. Respondents have a chance to try out new products and are able to submit feedback at their leisure. Online polling is also increasingly popular. KGO-TV in San Francisco uses online polls to produce unique news stories. "Online polling allows us to poll our market more frequently than we ever could if we were doing traditional telephone surveys," says the station's news director. KGO-TV has a pool of about 5,000 people recruited on air and online whom it rotates through various polls. The station finds that many people are glad to be included in the polls and that the online method avoids the problem that telephone surveys often face: their samples are skewed toward the elderly simply because they are the only ones home.[29]

The growth of the Internet is creating a need for new research techniques to measure and capture information about Web site visitors. At present, no industrywide standards define techniques for measuring Web use. Some sites ask users to register before accessing the pages; others merely keep track of the number of "hits" or number of times a visitor accesses a page. Marketers have tried to place a value on a site's "stickiness" (longer-lasting site visits) as a means of measuring effectiveness. Others use "cookies," which, as Chapter 4 explained, are electronic identifiers deposited on viewers' computers, to track click-through behavior—the paths users take as they move through the site. However, because some consumers change their Internet service providers frequently, and special software is available to detect and remove them, cookies have lost some of their effectiveness.

Intelliseek helps marketers track blog topics with a combination of text analysis technology and human insight. Polaroid recently used its services to discover that blogging photographers talk about archiving problems and photo longevity, bumping the topic to a priority product development issue for the camera company.[30]

Some software can monitor the overall content that a person is viewing and display banner advertisements likely to be of interest. For example, a search using the keyword "car" might call up a banner ad for General Motors or Ford. CMG Information Services offers a service called Engage.Knowledge, which collects profiles of Web users from numerous sites and organizes the data into 800 categories, including sports and hobbies. Researchers can use this information to develop marketing strategies. In addition, the popularity of video games has led to the emergence of a new advertising platform, "advergames." Sony Pictures' Web site for the horror film *The Cave* featured a complex advergame with an attention-grabbing storyline, and Unilever promoted its Axe line of men's products with an online dating game called *Mojo Master*. Said Unilever's Axe development manager, "As long as they perceive value in the [game] experience, they don't mind that they're being marketed to."[31]

Experimental Method

The third—and least-used—method for collecting primary data is the **controlled experiment.** A marketing research experiment is a scientific investigation in which a researcher controls or manipulates a test group (or groups) and compares the results with those of a control group that did not receive the experimental controls or manipulations.

The most common use of this method by marketers is **test marketing,** or introducing a new product in a specific area and then observing its degree of success. Up to this point, a product development team may have gathered feedback from focus groups. Other information may have come from shoppers' evaluations of competing products. Test marketing is the first stage at which the product performs in a real-life environment.

Carla Graham enjoyed the experience of pilot-testing an Internet-enabled kitchen in her Boston home. The collaborative project paired IBM, Whirlpool, and other marketers in setting up such prototypes as a cook range with both hot and cold modes, a refrigerator with a mobile Web tablet that could send shopping orders directly from the kitchen to Peapod, the grocery delivery service, and an under-cabinet entertainment center with a flip-down screen that held a VCR, DVD player, television, radio, and Internet access. Graham could interact with all the appliances via cell phone. Said Whirlpool's director for corporate innovation and technology of the findings, "These guys behaved different while using these products. They ate more home-cooked meals."[32]

Some firms omit test marketing and move directly from product development to full-scale production. These companies cite three problems with test marketing:

1. Test marketing is expensive. A firm can spend more than $1 million depending on the size of the test market city and the cost of buying media to advertise the product.

2. Competitors quickly learn about the new product. By studying the test market, competitors can develop alternative strategies.

3. Some products are not well suited to test marketing. Few firms test market long-lived, durable goods such as cars because of the major financial investments required for their development, the need to establish networks of dealers to distribute the products, and requirements for parts and servicing.

Companies that decide to skip the test-marketing process can choose several other options. A firm may simulate a test-marketing campaign through computer-modeling software. By plugging in data on similar products, it can develop a sales projection for a new product. Another firm may offer an item in just one region of the United States or in another country, adjusting promotions and advertising based on local results before going to other geographic regions. Another option may be to limit a product's introduction to only one retail chain to carefully control and evaluate promotions and results.

  assessment check

1. Distinguish between primary and secondary data.
2. What are the major methods of collecting secondary data?
3. What are the major methods of collecting primary data?

6 Explain the challenges of conducting marketing research in global markets.

CONDUCTING INTERNATIONAL MARKETING RESEARCH

As corporations expand globally, they need to gather correspondingly more knowledge about consumers in other countries. Although marketing researchers follow the same basic steps for international studies as for domestic ones, they often face some very different challenges.

U.S. organizations can tap many secondary resources as they research global markets. One major information source is the U.S. government, particularly the Department of Commerce. The Department of Commerce regularly publishes two useful reports, *Export America* magazine (monthly) and *Overseas Business Reports* (annual), that discuss marketing activities in more than 100 countries. The Department of State offers commercial guides to almost every country in the world, compiled by the local embassies. Other government sources include state trade offices and small-business development centers.

When conducting international research, companies must be prepared to deal with both language issues—communicating their message in the most effective way—and cultural issues, or capturing local citizens' interests while avoiding missteps that could unintentionally offend them. Companies also need to take a good look at a country's business environment, including political and economic conditions, trade regulations affecting research studies and data collection, and the potential for short- and long-term growth. Many marketers recommend tapping local researchers to investigate foreign markets.

Businesses may need to adjust their data collection methods for primary research in other countries because some methods do not easily transfer across national frontiers. Face-to-face interviewing, for instance, remains the most common method for conducting primary research outside the United States.

While mail surveys are a common data collection method in developed countries, they are useless in many other nations because of low literacy rates, unreliable mail service, and a lack of address lists. Telephone interviews may also not be suitable in other countries, especially those where many people do not have phones. Focus groups can be difficult to arrange because of cultural and social factors. In Latin American countries, for example, highly educated consumers make up a sought-after and opinionated minority, but they have little time to devote to lengthy focus group discussions. Middle- to lower-income Latin Americans may not be accustomed to articulating their opinions about products and grow reticent in the presence of others, whereas in some countries where violence and kidnapping are common, affluent consumers are reluctant to attend any meetings with strangers. To help with such difficulties, a growing number of international research firms offer experience in conducting global studies.

 assessment check

1. What are some U.S. organizations that can serve as sources of international secondary marketing data?
2. What is the most common method of primary data collection outside the United States?

INTERPRETATIVE RESEARCH

We mentioned earlier that interpretative research is a method that observes a customer or group of customers in their natural settings and then interprets their behavior based on an understanding of social and cultural characteristics of that setting. Interpretative research has attracted considerable interest in recent years. Developed by social anthropologists as a method for explaining behavior that operates below the level of conscious thought, interpretative research can provide insights into consumer behavior and the ways in which consumers interact with brands. The researcher first spends an extensive amount of time studying the culture, and for that reason, the studies are often called *ethnographic* studies. The word *ethnographic* means that a researcher takes a cultural perspective of the population being studied. For that reason, interpretative research is often used to interpret consumer behavior within a foreign culture, where language, ideals, values, and expectations are all subject to different cultural influences. But ethnographic research is also used domestically by looking at the consumer behavior of different groups of people.

Interpretative research focuses on understanding the meaning of a product or the consumption experience in a consumer's life. Its methods capture consumers interacting with products in their environment—in other words, capturing what they actually do, not what they say they do. Typically, subjects are filmed in specific situations, such as socializing with friends in a bar for research into beverage consumption, or for extended periods of time for paid participants. Paid participants may be followed by a videographer who records their day-to-day movements and interactions, or they may film themselves. Kimberly-Clark has been conducting research for several years by paying consumers to wear mini video cameras attached to visors and linked to a sound recorder. The Consumer Vision System, as it's called, records consumer behavior while participants are shopping or doing chores.[33]

Cost is an issue in interpretative research. This type of study takes time and money—a typical ethnographic project can cost about $1,250 to $1,750 per subject, so for instance to study ten people's cooking habits would cost about $15,000.[34] Because of its expense, interpretative research is used only when a company needs detailed information about how consumers use its products.

 ✓ *assessment check*

1. How is interpretative research typically conducted?

2. When should ethnographic research be employed?

COMPUTER TECHNOLOGY IN MARKETING RESEARCH

 7 Outline the most important uses of computer technology in marketing research.

In a world of rapid change, the ability to quickly gather and analyze business intelligence can create a substantial strategic advantage. As noted earlier, computer databases provide a wealth of data for marketing research, whether they are maintained outside the company or designed specifically to gather important facts about its customers. Chapter 10 explores how companies are leveraging internal databases and customer relationship management technology as a means of developing long-term relationships with customers. This section addresses important uses of computer technology related to marketing research: marketing information systems (MISs), marketing decision support systems (MDSSs), data mining, business intelligence, and competitive intelligence.

MARKETING INFORMATION SYSTEMS (MISs)

In the past, many marketing managers complained that their information problems resulted from too much rather than too little information. Reams of data were difficult to use and not always relevant. At times, information was almost impossible to find. Modern technological advances have made constraints like these obsolete.

A **marketing information system (MIS)** is a planned, computer-based system designed to provide decision makers with a continuous flow of information relevant to their areas of responsibility. A component of the organization's overall management information system, a marketing information system deals specifically with marketing data and issues.

A well-constructed MIS serves as a company's nerve center, continually monitoring the market environment—both inside and outside the organization—and providing instantaneous information. Marketers can store data for later use, classify and analyze that data, and retrieve it easily when needed.

MARKETING DECISION SUPPORT SYSTEMS (MDSSs)

marketing decision support system (MDSS)
Marketing information system component that links a decision maker with relevant databases and analysis tools.

A **marketing decision support system (MDSS)** consists of software that helps users quickly obtain and apply information in a way that supports marketing decisions. Taking MIS one step further, it allows managers to explore and connect such varying information as the state of the market, consumer behavior, sales forecasts, competitors' actions, and environmental changes. MDSSs consist of four main characteristics: they are interactive, investigative, flexible, and accessible. An MDSS can create simulations or models to illustrate the likely results of changes in marketing strategies or market conditions.

While an MIS provides raw data, an MDSS develops this data into information useful for decision making. For example, an MIS might provide a list of product sales from the previous day. A manager could use an MDSS to transform this raw data into graphs illustrating sales trends or reports estimating the impact of specific decisions, such as raising prices or expanding into new regions.

DATA MINING

Data mining is the process of searching through computerized data files to detect patterns. It focuses on identifying relationships that are not obvious to marketers—in a sense, answering questions that marketing researchers may not even have thought to ask. The data is stored in a huge database called a *data warehouse*. Software for the marketing decision support system is often associated with the data warehouse and is used to mine data. Once marketers identify patterns and connections, they use this intelligence to check the effectiveness of different strategy options.

Data mining is an efficient way to sort through huge amounts of data and to make sense of that data. It helps marketers create customer profiles, pinpoint reasons for customer loyalty or the lack thereof, analyze potential returns on changes in pricing or promotion, and forecast sales. Data mining offers considerable advantages in retailing, the hotel industry, banking, utilities, and many other areas and holds the promise of providing answers to many specific strategic questions.

Data-mining software also helps Eastman Kodak check out its competitors' patent filings, lets Mayo Clinic researchers plumb doctors' notes for evidence about whether treatments were effective, and flags insider trading or possible terrorist groups for government agencies. Cleveland, Ohio–based NACCO Industries uses data mining to scan warranty claims for common problems in its cargo-vehicle division that get fast attention from the quality improvement team.[35]

BUSINESS INTELLIGENCE

Business intelligence is the process of gathering information and analyzing it to improve business strategy, tactics, and daily operations. Using advanced software tools, marketers gather information from both within and outside the organization. Business intelligence can thus tell the firm how its own sales operation is doing or what its top competitors are up to.

The key is not only gathering the information but also getting it into a form that employees can make sense of and use for decision making and strategizing. Software can help users collect, aggregate, and create reports with outside information available on the Web from such databases as, say, Dun & Bradstreet. Hewlett-Packard used a business intelligence application from SmartOrg to identify market opportunities for its image display technology. "You have all these great plans and you can only do a couple," said an HP executive. "You need something that is fast and quick to sort through the potentials." Thanks to its ability to sort through data and answer questions, business intelligence software is expected to grow at about twice the rate of the rest of the business software industry.[36]

COMPETITIVE INTELLIGENCE

Competitive intelligence is a form of business intelligence that focuses on finding information about competitors using published sources, interviews, observations by salespeople and suppliers in the industry, government agencies, public filings such as patent applications, and other secondary sources including the Internet. Its aim is to uncover the specific advantages a competitor has, such as new-product launches, new features in existing goods or services, or new marketing or promotional strategies. Even a competitor's advertising can provide clues. Marketers use competitive intelligence to make better decisions that strengthen their own competitive strategy in turn.

 assessment check

1. Distinguish between an MIS and an MDSS.
2. What is data mining?
3. Describe the process of collecting business and competitive intelligence.

SALES FORECASTING

8 Identify the major types of forecasting methods.

A basic building block of any marketing plan is a **sales forecast,** an estimate of a firm's revenue for a specified future period. Sales forecasts play major roles in new-product decisions, production scheduling, financial planning, inventory planning and procurement, distribution, and human resources planning. An inaccurate forecast may lead to incorrect decisions in each of these areas. The accompanying "Solving an Ethical Controversy" feature discusses the possible misuse of sales forecasts.

sales forecast Estimate of a firm's revenue for a specified future period.

Marketing research techniques are used to deliver effective sales forecasts. A sales forecast is also an important tool for marketing control because it sets standards against which to measure actual performance. Without such standards, no comparisons can be made.

Planners rely on short-run, intermediate, and long-run sales forecasts. A short-run forecast usually covers a period of up to one year, an intermediate forecast covers one to five years, and a long-run forecast extends beyond five years. Although sales forecasters use an array of techniques to predict the future—ranging from computer simulations to studying trends identified by futurists—their methods fall into two broad categories: qualitative and quantitative forecasting.

Qualitative forecasting techniques rely on subjective data that reports opinions rather than exact historical data. **Quantitative forecasting** methods, by contrast, use statistical computations such as trend extensions based on past data, computer simulations, and econometric models. As Table 8.1 shows, each method has benefits and limitations. Consequently, most organizations use a combination of both techniques.

table 8.1   Benefits and Limitations of Various Forecasting Techniques

TECHNIQUES	BENEFITS	LIMITATIONS
Qualitative Methods		
Jury of executive opinion	Opinions come from executives in many different departments; quick; inexpensive	Managers may lack background knowledge and experience to make meaningful predictions
Delphi technique	Group of experts can accurately predict long-term events such as technological breakthroughs	Time consuming; expensive
Sales force composite	Salespeople have expert customer, product, and competitor knowledge; quick; inexpensive	Inaccurate forecasts may result from low estimates of salespeople concerned about their influence on quotas
Survey of buyer intentions	Useful in predicting short-term and intermediate sales for firms that serve selected customers	Intentions to buy may not result in actual purchases; time consuming; expensive
Quantitative Methods		
Market test	Provides realistic information on actual purchases rather than on intent to buy	Alerts competition to new-product plans; time consuming; expensive
Trend analysis	Quick; inexpensive; effective with stable customer demand and environment	Assumes the future will continue the past; ignores environmental changes
Exponential smoothing	Same benefits as trend analysis, but emphasizes more recent data	Same limitations as trend analysis, but not as severe due to emphasis on recent data

Solving an Ethical Controversy

Did Microsoft Control the Supply of Xbox 360s or Just Forecast Too Low?

Although it was launched with great fanfare, Microsoft's Xbox 360 was so hard to find during its first five weeks on the market that only 600,000 units were sold in that time, about half the number of the first Xbox a few years before. Microsoft expected to meet its six-month sales target of about 5 million units anyway, and it added production capacity at a third Xbox factory. But some critics of its strategy say that the launch was flawed by the shortage and that Microsoft worsened the problem not just by underproducing but also by diverting units to Europe and Japan, where they didn't sell. Shortages of new products are commonplace in the electronics business, but are they deliberate?

Do companies artificially whip up consumer demand for new products by deliberately reducing sales forecasts and then withholding supply?

PRO

1. Product shortages can help a new product succeed by generating "buzz" and mystique that makes it even more desirable.
2. Companies use high initial price to generate profits for new products. They then lower prices when supply is plentiful later.

CON

1. Companies do not want to alienate customers by deliberately limiting supplies. It merely annoys consumers to hear the marketing pitch for a product they know they won't be able to find.
2. Global product rollouts can be difficult to control. When a company launches a new product worldwide over a short time span, temporary shortages are bound to occur.

Summary

Microsoft claimed that as production ramped up for its unprecedented worldwide release of the Xbox 360, the shortages that did occur were unfortunate but temporary and that simultaneous release of new products would become the standard in the industry. Some analysts thought the strategy was too ambitious and the shortages a disaster, while others thought that although consumers might have hated it, the Xbox shortage was a brilliant idea and that the real disaster would have been having too many units in stock.

Sources: Nicholas Varchaver, "Xbox vs. PlayStation: Playing Hard to Get," *Fortune*, February 6, 2006, p. 26; Tim Harford, "Xbox Economics," *Slate*, December 21, 2005, **http://www.slate.com**; Nick Wingfield and Robert A. Guth, "Shortages of Hot Gifts: A Christmas Ritual," *Deseret Morning News*, December 11, 2005, **http://deseretnews.com**; Todd Bishop, "Questions Surround Xbox 360 Shortage," *Seattle Post-Intelligencer*, November 18, 2005, **http://seattlepi.nwsource.com**.

Briefly *Speaking*

"It's tough to make predictions, especially about the future."

—Yogi Berra (b. 1925)
American baseball player, coach, and manager

QUALITATIVE FORECASTING TECHNIQUES

Planners apply qualitative forecasting methods when they want judgmental or subjective indicators. Qualitative forecasting techniques include the jury of executive opinion, Delphi technique, sales force composite, and survey of buyer intentions.

Jury of Executive Opinion

The technique called the **jury of executive opinion** combines and averages the outlooks of top executives from such areas as marketing, finance, production, and purchasing. Top managers bring the following capabilities to the process: experience and knowledge about situations that influence sales, open-minded attitudes toward the future, and awareness of the bases for their judgments. This quick and inexpensive method generates good forecasts for sales and new-product development. It works best for short-run forecasting.

Delphi Technique

Like the jury of executive opinion, the **Delphi technique** solicits opinions from several people, but it also gathers input from experts outside the firm, such as academic researchers, rather than relying completely on company executives. It is most appropriately used to predict long-run issues, such as technological breakthroughs, that could affect future sales and the market potential for new products.

The Delphi technique works as follows: A firm selects a panel of experts and sends each a questionnaire relating to a future event. After combining and averaging the answers, the firm develops another questionnaire based on these results and sends it back to the same people. The process continues until it identifies a consensus. Although firms have successfully used Delphi to predict future technological breakthroughs, the method is both expensive and time consuming.

Sales Force Composite

The **sales force composite** technique develops forecasts based on the belief that organization members closest to the marketplace—those with specialized product, customer, and competitive knowledge—offer the best insights concerning short-term future sales. It typically works from the bottom up. Management consolidates salespeople's estimates first at the district level, then at the regional level, and finally nationwide to obtain an aggregate forecast of sales that reflects all three levels.

The sales force composite approach has some weaknesses, however. Because salespeople recognize the role of their sales forecasts in determining sales quotas for their territories, they are likely to make conservative estimates. Moreover, their narrow perspectives from within their limited geographic territories may prevent them from considering the impact on sales of trends developing in other territories, forthcoming technological innovations, or the major changes in marketing strategies. Consequently, the sales force composite gives the best forecasts in combination with other techniques.

Survey of Buyer Intentions

A **survey of buyer intentions** gathers input through mail-in questionnaires, online feedback, telephone polls, and personal interviews to determine the purchasing intentions of a representative group of present and potential customers. This method suits firms that serve limited numbers of customers but often proves impractical for those with millions of customers. Also, buyer surveys gather useful information only when customers willingly reveal their buying intentions. Moreover, customer intentions do not necessarily translate into actual purchases. These surveys may help a firm predict short-run or intermediate sales, but they employ time-consuming and expensive methods.

QUANTITATIVE FORECASTING TECHNIQUES

Quantitative techniques attempt to eliminate the subjectiveness of the qualitative methods. They include such methods as market tests, trend analysis, and exponential smoothing.

Test Markets

One quantitative technique, the test market, frequently helps planners assess consumer responses to new-product offerings. The procedure typically begins by establishing one or more test markets to

COURTESY OF C&R RESEARCH

Need A Superhero For Your Qualitative Mission?

Let one of our InVision moderators lead the way!

C&R Research
500 N. Michigan Ave.
Chicago, IL 60611
800.621.5022
www.crresearch.com

inVision
Insights you can use.

C&R Research conducts both qualitative and quantitive studies. The company's qualitative division, InVision, uses experienced moderators to conduct in-depth research about such customer segments as kids' or baby boomers' preferences.

gauge consumer responses to a new product under actual marketplace conditions. Market tests also permit experimenters to evaluate the effects of different prices, alternative promotional strategies, and other marketing mix variations by comparing results among different test markets.

The primary advantage of test markets is the realism they provide for the marketer. On the other hand, these expensive and time-consuming experiments may also communicate marketing plans to competitors before a firm introduces a product to the total market.

Trend Analysis

Trend analysis develops forecasts for future sales by analyzing the historical relationship between sales and time. It implicitly assumes that the collective causes of past sales will continue to exert similar influences in the future. When historical data is available, planners can quickly and inexpensively complete trend analysis. Software programs can calculate the average annual increment of change for the available sales data. This average increment of change is then projected into the future to come up with the sales forecast. So if the sales of a firm have been growing $15.3 million on average per year, this amount of sales could be added to last year's sales total to arrive at next year's forecast.

Of course, trend analysis cannot be used if historical data is not available, as in new-product forecasting. Also, trend analysis makes the dangerous assumption that future events will continue in the same manner as the past. Any variations in the determinants of future sales will cause deviations from the forecast. In other words, this method gives reliable forecasts during periods of steady growth and stable demand. If conditions change, predictions based on trend analysis may become worthless. For this reason, forecasters have applied more sophisticated techniques and complex, new forecasting models to anticipate the effects of various possible changes in the future.

Exponential Smoothing

A more sophisticated method of trend analysis, the **exponential smoothing** technique, weighs each year's sales data, giving greater weight to results from the most recent years. Otherwise, the statistical approach used in trend analysis is applied here. For example, last year's sales might receive a 1.5 weight, while sales data from two years ago could get a 1.4 weighting. Exponential smoothing is considered the most commonly used quantitative forecasting technique.

 assessment check

1. Describe the jury of executive opinion.
2. What is the Delphi technique?
3. How does the exponential smoothing technique forecast sales?

Strategic Implications of Marketing in the 21st Century

Marketing research can help an organization develop effective marketing strategies. Approximately 75 percent of new products eventually fail to attract enough buyers to remain viable. Why? A major reason is the seller's failure to understand market needs.

Consider, for example, the hundreds of dot-com companies that went under. A characteristic shared by all of those failing businesses is that virtually none of them was founded on sound marketing research. Very few used marketing research techniques to evaluate product potential, and even fewer studied consumer responses after the ventures were initiated. While research might not have prevented every dot-com meltdown, it may have helped a few of those businesses survive the waning economy in which they were launched.

Marketing research ideally matches new products to potential customers. Marketers also conduct research to analyze sales of their own and competitors' products, to gauge the performance of existing products, to guide the development of promotional campaigns and product enhancements, and to develop and refine products. All of these activities enable marketers to fine-tune their marketing strategies and reach customers more effectively and efficiently.

Marketing researchers have at their disposal a broad range of techniques with which to collect both quantitative and qualitative data on customers, their lifestyles, behaviors, attitudes, and perceptions. Vast amounts of data can be rapidly collected, accessed, interpreted, and applied to improve all aspects of business operations. Because of customer relationship management technology, that information is no longer generalized to profile groups of customers—it can be analyzed to help marketers understand every customer.

REVIEW OF CHAPTER OBJECTIVES

1 Describe the development of the marketing research function and its major activities.

Marketing research, or the collection and use of information in marketing decision making, reached a milestone when Charles C. Parlin, an ad salesman, counted empty soup cans in Philadelphia's trash in an effort to persuade the Campbell Soup Company to advertise in *The Saturday Evening Post*. Today, the most common marketing research activities are (1) determining market potential, market share, and market characteristics and (2) conducting sales analyses and competitive product studies. Most large consumer goods companies now have internal marketing research departments. However, outside suppliers still remain vital to the research function. Some perform the complete research task, while others specialize in a limited area or provide specific data services.

2 Explain the steps in the marketing research process.

The marketing research process can be divided into six specific steps: (1) defining the problem, (2) conducting exploratory research, (3) formulating hypotheses, (4) creating a research design, (5) collecting data, and (6) interpreting and presenting the research information. A clearly defined problem focuses on the researcher's search for relevant decision-oriented information. Exploratory research refers to information gained outside the firm. Hypotheses, tentative explanations of specific events, allow researchers to set out specific research designs—that is, the series of decisions that, taken together, comprise master plans or models for conducting the investigations. The data collection phase of the marketing research process can involve either or both primary (original) and secondary (previously published) data. After the data is collected, researchers must interpret and present it in a way that will be meaningful to management.

3 Distinguish between primary and secondary data and identify the sources of each type.

Primary data can be collected by the firm's own researchers or by independent marketing research companies. Three principal methods of primary data collection are observation, survey, and experiment. Secondary data can be classified as either internal or external. Sources of internal data include sales records, product evaluation, sales force reports, and records of marketing costs. Sources of external data include the government and private sources, such as business magazines. Both external and internal data can also be obtained from computer databases.

4 Explain the different sampling techniques used by marketing researchers.

Samples can be categorized as either probability samples or nonprobability samples. A probability sample is one in which every member of the population has a known chance of being selected. Probability samples include simple random samples, in which every item in the relevant universe has an equal opportunity to be selected; stratified samples, which are constructed such that randomly selected subsamples of different groups are represented in the total sample; and cluster samples, in which geographic areas are selected from which respondents are drawn. A nonprobability sample is arbitrary and does not allow application of standard statistical tests. Nonprobability sampling techniques include convenience samples, in which readily available respondents are picked, and quota samples, which are divided so that different segments or groups are represented in the total sample.

5   Identify the methods by which marketing researchers collect primary data.

Observation data is gathered by observing consumers via devices such as people meters or videotape. Survey data can be collected through telephone interviews, mail or fax surveys, personal interviews, focus groups, or a variety of online methods. Telephone interviews provide more than half of all primary marketing research data. They give the researcher a fast and inexpensive way to get small amounts of information but generally not detailed or personal information. Personal interviews are costly but allow researchers to get detailed information from respondents. Mail surveys are a means of conducting national studies at a reasonable cost; their main disadvantage is potentially inadequate response rates. Focus groups elicit detailed, qualitative information that provides insight not only into behavior but also into consumer attitudes and perceptions. Online surveys can yield fast responses but face obstacles such as the adequacy of the probability sample. The experimental method creates verifiable statistical data through the use of test and control groups to reveal actual benefits from perceived benefits.

6   Explain the challenges of conducting marketing research in global markets.

Many resources are available to help U.S. organizations research global markets. Government resources include the Department of Commerce, state trade offices, small-business development centers, and foreign embassies. Private companies, such as marketing research firms and companies that distribute research from other sources, are another resource. Electronic networks offer online international trade forums, in which marketers can establish global contacts.

7   Outline the most important uses of computer technology in marketing research.

Important uses of computer technology in marketing research include (1) a marketing information system (MIS)—a planned, computer-based system designed to provide managers with a continuous flow of information relevant to their specific decision-making needs and areas of responsibility; (2) a marketing decision support system (MDSS)—a marketing information system component that links a decision maker with relevant databases and analysis tools; (3) data mining—the process of searching through consumer information files or data warehouses to detect patterns that guide marketing decision making; (4) business intelligence—the process of gathering information and analyzing it to improve business strategy, tactics, and daily operations; and (5) competitive intelligence—the form of business intelligence that focuses on finding information about competitors using published sources, interviews, observations by salespeople and suppliers in the industry, government agencies, public filings such as patent applications, and other secondary methods including the Internet.

8   Identify the major types of forecasting methods.

There are two categories of forecasting methods. Qualitative methods are more subjective because they are based on opinions rather than exact historical data. They include the jury of executive opinion, the Delphi technique, the sales force composite, and the survey of buyer intentions. Quantitative methods include more factual and numerical measures such as test markets, trend analysis, and exponential smoothing.

✓ *assessment check* **answers**

1.1   Identify the different classifications of marketing research suppliers and explain how they differ from one another.
Marketing research suppliers can be classified as syndicated services, which regularly send standardized data sets to all customers; full-service suppliers, which contract to conduct complete marketing research projects; or limited-service suppliers, which specialize in selected activities.

1.2   What research methods can be used to measure customer satisfaction?
Some companies look at feedback from existing customers, for instance, hiring marketing research firms to collect and analyze customer feedback at their Web sites. Other firms collect feedback about customer defections—why a customer no longer uses a product. Other organizations conduct research through online polls and surveys.

assessment check **answers**

2.1   What are the six steps in the marketing research process?

The marketing research process can be divided into six specific steps: (1) defining the problem, (2) conducting exploratory research, (3) formulating hypotheses, (4) creating a research design, (5) collecting data, and (6) interpreting and presenting the research information.

2.2   What is the goal of exploratory research?

Exploratory research seeks to discover the cause of a specific problem by discussing the problem with informed sources within and outside the firm and examining data from other information sources.

3.1   Distinguish between primary and secondary data.

Primary data is original; secondary data has been previously published.

3.2   What are the major methods of collecting secondary data?

Sources of internal data include sales records, product evaluation, sales force reports, and records of marketing costs.

3.3   What are the major methods of collecting primary data?

Three principal methods of primary data collection are observation, survey, and experiment.

4.1   What is sampling?

Sampling is the process of selecting representative survey respondents or research participants from the total universe of possible participants.

4.2   Explain the different types of probability samples.

Types of probability samples include simple random samples, stratified samples, and cluster samples.

4.3   Identify the types of nonprobability samples.

Nonprobability samples are convenience samples and quota samples.

5.1   How is interpretative research typically conducted?

Interpretative research observes a customer or group of customers in their natural setting and interprets their behavior based on social and cultural characteristics of that setting.

5.2   When should ethnographic research be employed?

Ethnographic research is used domestically to look at the consumer behavior of different groups of people.

6.1   What are some U.S. organizations that can serve as sources of international secondary marketing data?

The Departments of Commerce and State offer reports and guides to many countries. Other sources include state trade offices, small-business development centers, and U.S. embassies in various nations.

6.2   What is the most common method of primary data collection outside the United States?

Face-to-face interviewing remains the most common method for conducting primary research outside the United States.

7.1   Distinguish between an MIS and an MDSS.

A marketing information system (MIS) is a planned, computer-based system designed to provide managers with a continuous flow of information relevant to their specific decision-making needs and areas of responsibility. A marketing decision support system (MDSS) is a marketing information system component that links a decision maker with relevant databases and analysis tools to help ask "what-if" questions.

7.2   What is data mining?

Data mining is the process of searching through huge consumer information files or data warehouses to detect patterns that can help marketers ask the right questions and guide marketing decision making.

7.3   Describe the process of collecting business and competitive intelligence.

Business intelligence is the process of gathering information and analyzing it to improve business strategy, tactics, and daily operations. Competitive intelligence focuses on finding information about competitors using published sources, interviews, observations by salespeople and suppliers in the industry, government agencies, public filings such as patent applications, and other secondary methods including the Internet.

assessment check **answers**

8.1 Describe the jury of executive opinion.

The jury of executive opinion combines and averages the outlooks of top executives from areas such as marketing, finance, production, and purchasing.

8.2 What is the Delphi technique?

The Delphi technique solicits opinions from several people but also includes input from experts outside the firm such as academic researchers.

8.3 How does the exponential smoothing technique forecast sales?

Exponential smoothing weighs each year's sales data, giving greater weight to results from the most recent years.

MARKETING TERMS YOU NEED TO KNOW

marketing research 248

exploratory research 252

secondary data 253

primary data 253

sampling 257

probability sample 257

nonprobability sample 258

interpretative research 259

focus group 260

marketing decision support system
  (MDSS) 266

sales forecast 267

OTHER IMPORTANT MARKETING TERMS

syndicated service 250

full-service research supplier 250

limited-service research supplier 250

sales analysis 252

hypothesis 252

research design 253

population (universe) 257

simple random sample 257

stratified sample 257

cluster sample 257

convenience sample 258

quota sample 258

mall intercept 260

controlled experiment 263

test marketing 263

marketing information system (MIS) 265

data mining 266

qualitative forecasting 267

quantitative forecasting 267

jury of executive opinion 268

Delphi technique 269

sales force composite 269

survey of buyer intentions 269

trend analysis 270

exponential smoothing 270

ASSURANCE OF LEARNING REVIEW

1. Outline the development and current status of the marketing research function.

2. What are the differences between full-service and limited-service research suppliers?

3. List and explain the steps in the marketing research process. Trace a hypothetical study through the stages in this process.

4. Distinguish between primary and secondary data. When should researchers collect each type of data?

5. What is sampling? Explain the differences between probability and nonprobability samples and identify the various types of each.

6. Distinguish among surveys, experiments, and observational methods of primary data collection. Cite examples of each method.

7. Define and give an example of each of the methods of gathering survey data. Under what circumstances should researchers choose a specific approach?

8. Describe the experimental method of collecting primary data and indicate when researchers should use it.

9. Describe business intelligence.

10. Contrast qualitative and quantitative sales forecasting methods.

PROJECTS AND TEAMWORK EXERCISES

1. ACNielsen offers data collected by optical scanners from the United Kingdom, France, Germany, Belgium, the Netherlands, Austria, Italy, and Finland. This scanner data tracks sales of UPC-coded products in those nations. In small teams, imagine that you are Nielsen clients in the United States. One team might be a retail chain, another an Internet company, and still another a toy manufacturer. Discuss the types of marketing questions this data might help you answer. Share your list with other teams.

2. Set up two class teams to debate the use of the Internet to research new domestic markets. What other research options are available?

3. Today, one in three new homes sold in America is likely to be a manufactured home. New manufactured homes are built using higher-quality materials than those of the past. As a result, the market for manufactured homes has grown to include more affluent buyers. Alabama-based Southern Energy Homes tries to appeal to upscale buyers by custom-building its homes according to customer specifications. What type of data and information should Southern Energy gather through its ongoing marketing intelligence to predict demand for its products? Would primary or secondary methods work best? Name some specific secondary sources of data that Southern Energy might study to find useful business intelligence.

4. Discuss some of the challenges Pizza Hut might face in conducting marketing research in potential new international markets. What types of research would you recommend the company use in choosing new countries for expansion?

5. Which sales forecasting technique(s) are most appropriate for each of the following products? Prepare your arguments in pairs or teams:
   a. Post Shredded Wheat breakfast cereal
   b. Coach handbags
   c. Kinko's copy shops
   d. *Time* magazine

6. Assume you are responsible for launching a new family of skin-care products for teens, with separate product lines for males and females. You would like to collect primary data from a sampling of each market before you prepare your marketing campaign. Let one team make the case for using a focus group and another team devise a plan supporting the use of an online chat room. Present the class with the benefits of each method and the ways in which each team plans to overcome its method's possible shortcomings. Now take this project one step further by having a classroom discussion on whether a decision support system could enhance the data collected from each method. How could an MDSS make the data more useful?

7. Interpretative research offers marketing researchers many possibilities, including the opportunity to improve product features such as packaging for food or over-the-counter medication that is difficult for seniors or the disabled to open. List some other ways in which you think this observation method can help make existing product offerings more appealing or more useful to specific kinds of users. What kind of products would you choose, and how would you test them?

8. Use the Internet to research the details of the National Do Not Call Registry and prepare a report outlining what it does and does not allow marketers to do. Research the effects of the registry to date. Do you think the public understands the purpose of the registry? Why or why not, and if not, what do you think marketers can do to clarify it?

9. McDonald's conducts extensive marketing research for all its new products, including new menu items for its overseas stores. Because of cultural and other differences and preferences, the company cannot always extrapolate its results from one country to another. For instance, Croque McDo fried ham-and-cheese sandwiches are unlikely to be as popular in the United States as they are in France, which invented the *croque monsieur* sandwich on which the McDonald's product is based. Can you think of any other kinds of firms that share this limitation on global applications of their research? In contrast, what sorts of questions *could* multinational firms answer on a global basis? Why?

10. Outdoor advertising, including billboards, ads on bus shelters, and shopping mall displays, accounts for only a tiny portion of the $110 billion spent on advertising in a typical year in the United States. ACNielsen is giving global positioning devices to 700 Chicagoans so it can track how many times they pass by specially coded billboards in the city. List some other ways you can think of to research the effectiveness of outdoor advertising and cite the pros and cons of each.

CRITICAL-THINKING EXERCISES

1. Some companies are broadening their markets by updating classic products to appeal to younger people's tastes and preferences. For example, Wrigley's has introduced two new Juicy Fruit flavors that it hopes will duplicate the success of Altoids and Mountain Dew in becoming revitalized and popular brands. What primary and secondary market information would you want to have if you were planning to reinvigorate an established brand in each of the following categories? Where and how would you obtain the information?
   a. household cleaner
   b. moist packaged cat food
   c. spray starch
   d. electrical appliances

2. Marketers sometimes collect primary information by using so-called *mystery shoppers* who visit stores anonymously (as if they were customers) and note such critical factors as store appearance and ambiance, items in stock, and quality of service including waiting time and courtesy of employees. (The CEO of Staples has gone on mystery shopper trips and sometimes asked his mother to make similar trips.) Prepare a list of data that you would want to obtain from a mystery shopper surveying a chain of gas stations in your area. Devise a format for gathering the information that combines your need to compile the data electronically and the researcher's need to remain undetected while visiting the stores.

3. Select a sales forecasting method (or combination of methods) for each of the following information needs and explain your pick(s).

   a. prediction of next year's sales based on last year's figures
   b. prediction of next year's sales based on weighted data from the last five years
   c. expected sales categorized by district and by region
   d. estimated product usage for the next year by typical consumers
   e. probable consumer response to a new product

4. The Internet provides ready access to secondary market information but is also a portal to an almost limitless store of primary information via message boards, chat rooms, e-mail questionnaires, newsgroups, and Web site registration forms. What are some specific drawbacks of each of these methods for obtaining primary information from customers?

ETHICS EXERCISE

Consumer groups sometimes object to marketers' methods of collecting primary data from customers. They object to such means as product registration forms; certain types of games, contests, or product offers; and "cookies" and demographic questionnaires on company Web sites. Marketers believe that such tools offer them an easy way to collect market data. Most strictly control the use of such data and never link identifying information with consumers' financial or demographic profiles. However, the possibility of abuse or error always exists.

Research the code of ethics of the American Marketing Association (AMA). Note especially the guidelines for use of the Internet in marketing research.

1. Check the Web sites of a few large consumer products companies. How effectively do you think these sites are at informing visitors about the use of "cookies" on the sites? Do you think marketers could or should improve their protection of visitors' privacy? If so, how?

2. Do you think the AMA's code of ethics would be violated if marketers compiled a mailing list from information provided on warranty and product registration cards and then used the list to send customers new-product information? Why or why not? Does your opinion change if the company also sends list members special discount offers and private sale notices?

INTERNET EXERCISES

1. **Marketing research tools.** Chapter 8 describes tools used by marketing researchers to collect and analyze data. The following exercises are designed to help you learn more about several of these marketing research tools.

   a. Focus groups: Visit http://www.managementhelp.org/evaluatn/focusgrp.htm, which describes how a focus group should be conducted. Read through the guidelines and prepare a summary you can use during a class discussion of the topic.

   b. Marketing research on the Web: As noted in the chapter, many organizations find it efficient and effective to use the Web when conducting marketing research. Go to http://www.decisionanalyst.com/online.asp and list the advantages of Web-based marketing research.

   c. Statistical tools: SAS and SPSS have products that are widely used by marketing professionals. Both, for instance, offer data-mining packages. Visit either the SAS (http://www.sas.com) or the SPSS (http://www.spss.com) Web site and learn more about the data mining packages, including actual customer experiences. What other products do SAS or SPSS offer to assist marketing researchers?

2. **Online data sources.** An enormous amount of statistical data is online, and much of it can be obtained for free. To give you an idea of the scope of data available online, go to the main Web page for the *Statistical Abstract of the United States* (http://www.census.gov/statab/www/). Click on the most recent year and answer the following questions.

   a. Under the population section, what are the ten largest metropolitan areas in the United States? What are the five fastest-growing metropolitan areas in the United States?

   b. Under the population section, which metropolitan areas have the highest number of Hispanics? Of African Americans? Of Asian–Pacific Islanders?

   c. Under the income section, what is the median income of American households? Which state has the highest median income? What is the relationship between the household median income and the age of the so-called householder (head of household)?

Note: Internet Web addresses change frequently. If you don't find the exact site listed, you may need to access the organization's home page and search from there or use a search engine such as Google.

CASE 8.1 Forecasting Pitfalls for SUV Makers

Consumers' thirst for big fuel-guzzling SUVs seemed unquenchable. Then, after holding steady for years, sales of large SUVs suddenly dropped nearly 20 percent recently. One factor behind the slump was soaring gas prices. Uncertainty about how high fuel prices would stay—and for how long—led some car buyers to switch from SUVs to more fuel-efficient family-sized cars and minivans. Some buyers looked for smaller cars, and still others turned to hybrids, creating long waiting lists at hybrid dealers' showrooms. That shift in buying habits hurt General Motors, which is well known for its SUVs and pickup trucks. "Obviously, if we have a serious supply constraint in motor fuels that will hurt vehicles with higher fuel consumption," said GM's vice chairman Bob Lutz. "But we can't predict that."

Perhaps they couldn't. SUV makers had committed to their current level of production two years before the rise in fuel prices, when the price of filling the tank was much less of an issue for consumers. New models of the Chevrolet Tahoe, the Chevrolet Suburban, the GMC Yukon, the Ford Expedition, and the Cadillac Escalade were already rolling out. Chrysler released its big new Aspen, with three rows of seats.

Auto industry executives remained upbeat about SUVs, agreeing with GM's Lutz that "people still love these things." Ford CEO Jim Padilla said, "Big SUVs are alive and well." But the National Automobile Dealers Association's chief economist admitted that "every time gas prices go up another 20 cents, you know you see some people making a [buying] decision based on that."

Dealers fell back on incentives to boost sales, offering cash back, lower prices, and new technology that cuts eight cylinders back to four at certain speeds to save fuel. Even Nissan, which avoids discounts, was willing to deal in order to keep its big Armada SUV moving off the lot. "I don't know if we can launch the Aspen without incentives, just because it's the nature of the market in that segment," said Chrysler's vice president of global sales and marketing.

Perhaps Detroit has learned something about the difficulties of forecasting sales in a particularly uncertain world of rising fuel costs. GM, which is increasing production of its most profitable SUVs, has plans for a hybrid Tahoe. But where will the price of gas be when it rolls off the assembly line?

Questions for Critical Thinking

1. Should the auto industry base its sales forecasts more heavily on qualitative or quantitative techniques? Why?

2. What forecasting techniques would help auto industry executives more accurately forecast movements in the price of oil? How should they factor these forecasts into their sales projections?

Sources: Michael Ellis, "Fulfilling Demand: GM to Boost Output of Its Large SUVs," *Detroit Free Press*, March 22, 2006, **http://www.freep.com**; Josee Valcourt, "SUVs Roll Out, Despite Gas Woes," *Detroit News*, January 10, 2006, **http://www.detnews.com**; "High Gas Prices Changing Auto Market," Fox News, September 26, 2005, **http://www.foxnews.com**.

VIDEO CASE 8.2 Nielsen Media Research Plays the Rating Game

The written video case on Nielsen Media Research appears on page VC-10. The recently filmed Nielsen Media Research video is designed to expand and highlight the concepts in this chapter and the concepts and questions covered in the written video case.

American Idol Is a Hit with Teens

Some adults admit to watching Fox network's *American Idol*. Others don't. But teens and preteens are wild about the reality talent show, and they aren't hiding their obsession. Ask a teen, and you'll get a complete rundown of all the winners and runners-up. After several seasons on the air, the show remains a ratings hit for Fox. One season premiere brought the highest entertainment ratings in Fox's history, with an astounding 35.5 million viewers. Viewership didn't fall off after that either. The audience remained steady at about 34 million on Tuesdays and 31 million on Wednesdays. When slotted head-to-head against another musical event—the Grammy Awards show—*Idol* won hands down by more than 10 million viewers. This may seem an ironic twist of fate, because the contestants on *American Idol* hope to take home their own Grammy someday.

Idol is the biggest hit with teen girls, despite the producers' decision to raise the age limit of contestants to 28. Of the 166 network programs currently aired, *Idol* attracts 134 percent more teen girls than any other show. "To me, the best part of the show is all the singers," explains one teen. "I like to watch them as they try out and see if I can pick the one that's going to make it all the way." Executive producer Ken Warwick points out the social aspect of the show for teens at school. "When they go to school the next day, it's become *the* show to watch, and if they haven't seen it, they've got a problem," he observes. Parents note that there aren't many shows targeted for their teens and preteens—many shows are pitched to younger kids, while shows for adults contain too much sex and violence.

Teens aren't just watching the show on television. They visit the show's Web site in huge numbers, even between seasons. The site averages 3 million visitors each season, a statistic that includes adults as well as children. Fox executives now view the site as a year-round business unit, not just a support structure for the show while it is airing.

Although teens are perhaps the most passionate *Idol* fans, they aren't the only ones. Marketing research reveals that adults who watch reality-talent television have certain characteristics. They tend to be active in sports such as jogging, swimming, and golf. They gravi-

Market Segmentation, Targeting, and Positioning

Chapter Objectives

1 Identify the essential components of a market.

2 Outline the role of market segmentation in developing a marketing strategy.

3 Describe the criteria necessary for effective segmentation.

4 Explain the geographic, demographic, and psychographic approaches to segmenting consumer markets.

5 Describe product-related segmentation.

6 Identify the steps in the market segmentation process.

7 Discuss four basic strategies for reaching target markets.

8 Summarize the types of positioning strategies, and explain the reasons for positioning and repositioning products.

tate toward new cars and cell phone services. And they eat at fast-food restaurants ten or more times a month. These findings help Fox and its advertisers create commercials and other marketing messages that target the right audience.

But *Idol* doesn't exclude its younger viewers from marketing efforts. Parents who are searching for the latest birthday party theme can let their kids host their very own *American Idol* party. Through retailer Birthday Express, parents can order an entire *Idol* birthday party package—complete with invitations, party favors, decorations, contestant numbers, and a piñata in the shape of a microphone. The kit includes party tips and a list of supplies, such as a CD player and karaoke machine.

The success of *American Idol* through several seasons illustrates how vital it is for marketers to identify and target a market with their messages. If they hit just the right note, their messages may reach the stars.[1]

evolution *of a* brand

American Idol is more than a television show—it's a cultural phenomenon. From its very first season, the show has tapped into teens' desire for stardom and fame. And its first winner, Kelly Clarkson, received two Grammys, which only boosted the show's profile in the music industry. Tried-and-true stars Stevie Wonder, Kenny Rogers, and Barry Manilow saw their CD sales jump after appearing on the show, bringing their music to a new generation. The brand is a true success story and aims to remain on top.[2]

- Ratings for *American Idol* continue to climb. DVDs of the show have ranked number one on their release. The *American Idol* Web site also draws steady traffic. Why do you think *American Idol* is so popular? Make a list of the different media outlets for the show and explain how they reach and fill a need in their target market—teens.

- *Idol* judges Randy Jackson, Paula Abdul, and Simon Cowell are now household names. *Idol* winners such as Kelly Clarkson—and even some losers, such as Clay Aiken—have become stars with a loyal following. People get involved in the drama of the performances and the judges' reactions and root for their favorites. Research how the show's producers maintain the audience's interest level. How long do you think they can keep the show on the air? Give your reasons.

Chapter Overview

Each of us is unique. We come from different backgrounds, live in different households, and have different interests and goals. You and your best friend may shop at different stores, listen to different music, play different sports, and take different courses in college. Suppose you like country music, but your best friend prefers oldies hits. Marketers for all kinds of music-related products, ranging from CDs to live concerts, want to capture your interest as well as that of your friends. Do you play an instrument or sing, or are you a fan who goes to clubs and downloads music? Marketers look at customers and potential customers to figure out what their characteristics are, whether they can identify certain subgroups, and how they can best offer products to meet their needs. Your interests and needs, your lifestyle and income, the town where you live, and your age all contribute to the likelihood that you will listen to and buy certain types of music. All of these factors make up a market. A **market** is composed of people with sufficient purchasing power, authority, and willingness to buy. And marketers must use their expertise to understand the market for a good or service, whether it's a download by the latest *American Idol* winner, a new radio station, or a twelve-string guitar.

Many markets include consumers with different lifestyles, backgrounds, and income levels. Nearly everyone buys toothpaste, but that does not mean every consumer has the same lifestyle, background, or income. So it is unusual for a single marketing mix strategy to attract all sectors of a market. By identifying, evaluating, and selecting a target market to pursue, such as consumers who prefer toothpaste made with all-natural ingredients or those who want an extra-whitening formula, marketers are able to develop more efficient and effective marketing strategies. On the other hand, some products—such as luxury sports cars and fly-fishing supplies—are intended for a more specific market. In either case, the **target market** for a product is the specific segment of consumers most likely to purchase a particular product.

Marketing now takes place on a global basis more than ever, incorporating many target markets. To identify those markets, marketers must determine useful ways for segmenting different populations and communicating with them successfully. This chapter discusses useful ways to accomplish this objective, explaining the steps of the market segmentation process and surveying strategies for reaching target markets. Finally, it looks at the role of positioning in developing a marketing strategy.

market Group of people with sufficient purchasing power, authority, and willingness to buy.

target market Group of people to whom a firm decides to direct its marketing efforts and ultimately its goods and services.

 1 Identify the essential components of a market.

consumer products Products bought by ultimate consumers for personal use.

business products Goods and services purchased for use either directly or indirectly in the production of other goods and services for resale.

TYPES OF MARKETS

Products are usually classified as either consumer products or business products. **Consumer products** are bought by ultimate consumers for personal use, such as cell phones, sports tickets, or fashion magazines. **Business products** are goods and services purchased for use either directly or indirectly in the production of other goods and services for resale. Most goods and services purchased by individual consumers, such as DVDs and restaurant meals, are considered consumer products. Rubber and raw cotton are examples of items generally purchased by manufacturers and are, therefore, classified as business products. Goodyear buys rubber to manufacture tires; textile manufacturers such as Burlington Industries convert raw cotton into cloth.

However, in many cases, a single product can serve different uses. Tires purchased for the family car constitute consumer products. But tires purchased by General Motors to be mounted on its Chevy Tahoe are business products because they become part of another product destined for resale. Or a product that was once a business product might be modified for consumer use, and vice versa. A line of professional cookware sold to restaurants—a business product—could be adapted by its manufacturer to become a line of cookware for home use—a consumer product. If you want to determine the classification of an item, just think about who is going to buy the product, who will use it, and how or why the product will be used. The bottle of mouthwash you buy at the supermarket is a consumer product, but if a large hotel chain purchases large quantities of the same mouthwash from a wholesaler, it becomes a business product.

THE ROLE OF MARKET SEGMENTATION

There are 6.5 billion people in the world today, 300 million of whom live in the United States.[3] In today's business world, there are too many variables in consumer needs, preferences, and purchasing power to attract all consumers with a single marketing mix. That's not to say that firms must actually change products to meet the needs of different market segments—although they often do—but they must attempt to identify the factors that affect purchase decisions and then group consumers according to the presence or absence of these factors. Finally, they adjust marketing strategies to meet the needs of each group.

Consider motor vehicles. Unlike a century ago, when Henry Ford pronounced that customers could order any color of car they liked—as long as it was black—today there is a make, model, and color for every taste and budget. But auto manufacturers need to adjust their messages for different markets. And savvy marketers are looking toward markets that show growth, such as the U.S. Hispanic population, which is now the largest ethnic group in the country, and aging baby boomers, whose needs for goods and services are changing.

The division of the total market into smaller, relatively homogeneous groups is called **market segmentation.** Both profit-oriented and not-for-profit organizations practice market segmentation.

CRITERIA FOR EFFECTIVE SEGMENTATION

Segmentation doesn't automatically guarantee success in the marketing arena; instead, it is a tool for marketers to

assessment check

1. Define *target market*.
2. Distinguish between a consumer product and a business product.

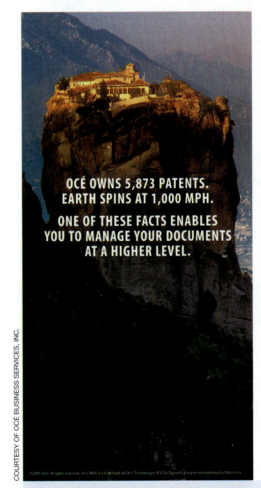

OCÉ OWNS 5,873 PATENTS.
EARTH SPINS AT 1,000 MPH.

ONE OF THESE FACTS ENABLES YOU TO MANAGE YOUR DOCUMENTS AT A HIGHER LEVEL.

For over a century, Océ has led a quiet revolution that advanced the level of achievement in printing technology by orders of magnitude. Twenty-five years ago, Océ Business Services determined to set a new standard in outsourced document process management. Our specialists have successfully introduced a variety of enterprise cultures to considerable savings, higher efficiency and best practices in print, copy, mail, imaging and records management throughout the document lifecycle. Now we can proudly announce another innovation: Océ MAX™. It is a unique Six Sigma® based business performance management application that will advance document process management to the next level. We intend to make it one of many. Keep an eye on Océ. For a free white paper on document process management, visit www.oceusa.com/obs or call 1-888-390-1513.

Océ Business Services
ADVANCING
DOCUMENT PROCESS MANAGEMENT
TO A HIGHER LEVEL

Business products help other firms create and market their goods and services. Océ Business Services offers outsourcing of printing, copying, mailing, imaging, and records management for other companies' documents.

market segmentation Division of the total market into smaller, relatively homogeneous groups.

 Outline the role of market segmentation in developing a marketing strategy.

assessment check

1. Define *market segmentation*.
2. Describe the role of market segmentation.

3 Describe the criteria necessary for effective segmentation.

The personal-care market is segmented into products tailored to the needs of different users. Johnson Products' Ultra Sheen produces conditioners blended specifically for the African American market.

figure 9.1

The Purchasing Power of Women

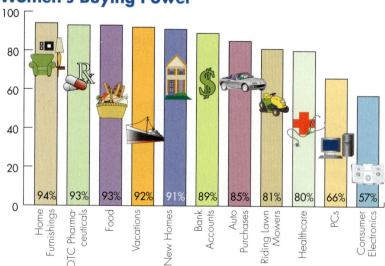

Source: Data from The Business and Professional Women's Foundation, TrendSight, and Business Women's Network, cited in "Women's Buying Power," About.com, **http://womensissues.about.com**, accessed April 10, 2006.

use. Its effectiveness depends on the following four basic requirements.

First, the market segment must present measurable purchasing power and size. With jobs, incomes, and decision-making power, female consumers represent a hefty amount of purchasing power. In fact, they account for 85 percent of all consumer purchases, and carry 76 million credit cards—8 million more than men.[4] In a recent year, women spent more than men—$55 billion of the $96 billion—on electronics gear. Women also represent more than half of Internet use.[5] Figure 9.1 illustrates the percentage of consumer purchases made by women in the United States.

The Lowe's home improvement chain recognizes the role of women in its success. Armed with research showing that women initiate more than 80 percent of home improvement projects—especially large ones such as remodeling a kitchen or adding a bathroom—the chain refocused its marketing efforts to target women. Lowe's has made its stores more comfortable for browsing, with wide aisles, clear signs to direct shoppers, and call buttons that customers can use to summon a salesperson. The company also stocks more appliances and home décor items—including birdfeeders, Pergo laminate floors, and Jacuzzi tubs. The firm also promotes home improvement products as Mother's Day gifts, such as outdoor furniture and gardening items. Such efforts have built the company's excellent reputation, and its competitiveness, in the home improvement retail market.[6]

Second, marketers must find a way to promote effectively to and to serve the market segment. Because women now wield such purchasing power in the technology market, marketers need to find different ways to appeal to them. Some companies have taken this advice to heart. T-Mobile and BlackBerry have created ads featuring working moms.

Third, marketers must then identify segments that are sufficiently large to give them good profit potential. The $55 billion of electronics purchases by women represents plenty of profit potential by that industry. Radio Shack reports that women now constitute 40 percent of its customer base—up from 20 percent seven years ago. Like Lowe's, Radio Shack also promotes Mother's Day gifts, with ads featuring brightly colored iPod covers, trendy laptop bags, and sleek phones and cameras.[7]

Fourth, the firm must aim for segments that match its marketing capabilities. Targeting a large number of small markets can be an expensive, complex, and inefficient strategy, so smaller firms may decide to stick with a particular niche, or target market. To compete for women's business, an electronics retailer could install a supervised play area for children while their mothers shop. It could create showrooms made to look like real living rooms and family rooms with the latest entertainment equipment installed, so women could see how the products would look in their own homes.

✓ *assessment check*

1. Identify the four criteria for effective segmentation.

SEGMENTING CONSUMER MARKETS

Market segmentation attempts to isolate the traits that distinguish a certain group of consumers from the overall market. An understanding of the group's characteristics—such as age, gender, geographic location, income, and buying patterns—plays a vital role in developing a successful marketing strategy. In most cases, marketers seek to pinpoint a number of factors affecting buying behavior in the target segment. Marketers in the travel industry consider employment trends, changes in income levels and buying patterns, age, lifestyle, and other factors when promoting their goods and services. To boost flagging attendance at its theme parks, Disney World has been advertising to adults who are "empty nesters" and groups of friends instead of focusing entirely on families with young children. Marketers rarely identify totally homogeneous segments, in which all potential customers are alike; they almost always encounter some differences among members of a target group. But they must be careful to ensure that their segments accurately reflect consumers.

In the next sections, we discuss the four common bases for segmenting consumer markets: geographic segmentation, demographic segmentation, psychographic segmentation, and product-related segmentation. These segmentation approaches can give important guidance for marketing strategies, provided they identify significant differences in buying behavior.

4 Explain the geographic, demographic, and psychographic approaches to segmenting consumer markets.

GEOGRAPHIC SEGMENTATION

Marketers have long practiced **geographic segmentation**—dividing an overall market into homogeneous groups based on their locations. Geographic location does not ensure that all consumers in a location will make the same buying decisions, but this segmentation approach does help identify some general patterns. Campbell Soup uses this approach for some of its products, as described in the "Marketing Success" feature.

The 300 million people who live in the United States are not scattered evenly across the country. For instance, many are concentrated in major metropolitan areas. New York is the largest U.S. city, with more than 8.1 million citizens. But the metropolitan area surrounding it includes 18.7 million people. Los Angeles is second, with 3.8 million, and a surrounding area of 12.9 million.[8] Figure 9.2 shows populations of the ten largest cities in the United States and the ten states with the largest populations. California tops the list at 36 million residents. Wyoming is the least-populated state, with 509,000. In addition to total population, marketers need to look at the *fastest-growing* states in order to plan their strategies for the future. The five states with the fastest-growing populations are Nevada, Arizona, Florida, Texas, and Georgia.[9]

A look at the worldwide population distribution illustrates why so many firms are pursuing customers around the globe. China has the most citizens, with 1.3 billion people, and India is second with 1.1 billion. The United States is third with about 300 million, and Indonesia is fourth with 248 million. Japan is a distant tenth with 127 million.[10] As in the United States, much of the world's population lives in urban environments. The two largest cities in the world are Shanghai, China, with 14.6 million and Bombay, India, with 12.6 million. The two largest metropolitan areas are Tokyo, Japan, with almost 37 million and New York, with nearly 19 million.[11]

Population size alone, however, may not be reason enough for a business to expand into a specific country. Businesses also need to look at a wide variety of economic variables. Some businesses may decide to combine their marketing efforts for countries that share similar population and product-use patterns instead of treating each country as an independent segment. This grouping is taking place with greater frequency throughout the European Union as the currency and trade laws of the member nations are becoming more unified.

geographic segmentation Division of an overall market into homogeneous groups based on their locations.

Briefly *Speaking*

"Consumers are statistics. Customers are people."

—Stanley Marcus (1905–2002) American merchant

figure 9.2

The Ten Largest Cities and Ten Most Populous States in the United States

Source: "Annual Estimates of the Population for Incorporated Places over 100,000," U.S. Census Bureau, **http://www.census.gov**, accessed May 11, 2006; and data on state populations from the U.S. Census Bureau, cited in Stephen Ohlemacher, "South, West Gaining Population," *Morning News*, December 22, 2005, p. 2B.

10. San Jose; .9 million
2. Los Angeles; 3.8 million
6. Phoenix; 1.4 million
7. San Diego; 1.3 million
3. Chicago; 2.9 million
9. Dallas; 1.2 million
4. Houston; 2.0 million
8. San Antonio; 1.2+ million
1. New York; 8.1 million
5. Philadelphia; 1.5 million

Ranking State Populations
1. California 36.1 mil.
2. Texas 22.9 mil.
3. New York 19.3 mil.
4. Florida 17.8 mil.
5. Illinois 12.8 mil.
6. Penn. 12.4 mil.
7. Ohio 11.5 mil.
8. Michigan 10.1 mil.
9. Georgia 9.1 mil.
10. New Jersey 8.7 mil.

While population numbers indicate the overall size of a market, other geographic indicators such as job growth can also give useful guidance to marketers depending on the type of products they sell. Automobile manufacturers might segment geographic regions by household income because it is an important factor in the purchase of a new car.

Geographic areas also vary in population migration patterns. Recent census data indicates that 40 million Americans live in a different home from the one they lived in a year ago. They might make this move for a number of reasons—job transfer, a change in job status such as a promotion or loss of a job, proximity to extended family, retirement, and the like. U.S. census data also indicate two major population shifts: migration toward the Sun Belt states of the Southeast and Southwest and toward the West. In recent years, the West has experienced the fastest population growth at nearly 20 percent, with the South just behind at 17 percent. As mentioned earlier, Nevada is the fastest-growing individual state. Researchers expect these trends to continue, despite the fact that the highest-paying jobs continue to lie in the East.[12] However, it is important to note another trend: people who leave the East Coast aren't necessarily jumping to the West, and vice versa. New Yorkers tend to gravitate to the South or even to Connecticut or New Jersey. Californians tend to move to other western states instead of coming east.

The move from urban to suburban areas after World War II created a need to redefine the urban marketplace. This trend radically changed cities' traditional patterns of retailing and led to decline in many downtown shopping areas—although recent trends have been toward the revitaliza-

 marketing success Campbell's Segments Its Soups

Background. Your supermarket no doubt has at least one shelf filled with Campbell's Soups. Whether you want classic chicken noodle or something trendier, you have plenty of recipes from which to choose. But if you visit a supermarket in a different part of the country, you might see different selections. That's because Campbell's has figured out how to target the populations of diverse markets.

The Challenge. Not everyone in the United States wants tomato or chicken and rice soup for lunch. Some prefer New England clam chowder, while others crave Tuscan-style meatball or chicken cheese enchilada style.

Still others are watching carbs or calories and want their soup to be low in either or both. And some consumers follow a low-salt diet, so they want their tomato or chicken soup to be a low-sodium concoction. Campbell's has figured out not only who wants what but also what their ethnic background is and where they live.

The Strategy. Campbell's has identified a range of market segments, including ethnic and regional components. In addition to serving these markets in the United States, Campbell's has operations overseas in countries such as Mexico, France, and Ireland, where it offers products created specifi-

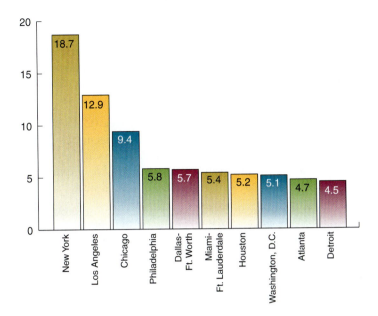

figure 9.3

The Ten Largest Metropolitan Areas in the United States

Source: Data from U.S. Census Bureau, *Statistical Abstract of the United States: 2006*, **http://www.census.gov**.

tion of downtown areas. Subsequently, traditional city boundaries became almost meaningless for marketing purposes.

In an effort to respond to these changes, the government now classifies urban data using the following categories:

- The category of **core based statistical area (CBSA)** became effective in 2000 and refers collectively to metropolitan and micropolitan statistical areas. Each CBSA must contain at least one urban area with a population of 10,000 or more. Each metropolitan statistical area must have at least one urbanized area of 50,000 or more inhabitants. Each micropolitan statistical area must have at least one urban cluster with a population of at least 10,000 but less than 50,000. There are 361 metropolitan and 575 micropolitan statistical areas in the United States. Of the 361 metropolitan statistical areas, 170 of them are classified as being large, meaning that they contain more than 250,000 people.[13]

- A **metropolitan statistical area (MSA)** is a freestanding urban area with a population in the urban center of at least 50,000 and a total metropolitan statistical area population of 100,000 or more. Buyers in metropolitan statistical areas exhibit social and economic homogeneity. They usually border on nonurbanized counties. Examples include Rochester, New York; Albuquerque, New Mexico; and Kalamazoo–Battle Creek, Michigan. Figure 9.3 identifies the ten largest metropolitan areas in the United States.

---

cally for the tastes of those consumers. People who want Mexican flavors can enjoy tortilla soup; French consumers prefer *Liebig*, which is soup packaged in cartons. For consumers who are health conscious, Campbell's has created its Carb Request line of soups, including a roasted chicken, penne, and garden vegetable recipe.

The Outcome. By segmenting consumers, Campbell's has been able to serve up exactly what each segment wants in its soup bowls. The firm continues to create new recipes, and it recently won the Spirit of Innovation Award for its foodservice line, which includes its V8 soups, entrees, and chilis.

Sources: Cambell's Web site, **http://www.campbellsoupcompany.com**, accessed April 11, 2006; "Mining for Drivers of Consumer Behavior," Manifold Data Mining, April 11, 2006, **http://www.manifolddatamining.com**; Tom Zind, "Stirring up the Pot," *Prepared Foods*, May 2005, **http://www.findarticles.com**; William A. Roberts, "Soup's On; Sides, Too," *Prepared Foods*, May 2005, **http://www.findarticles.com**.

- A **micropolitan statistical area** is an area that has at least one town of 10,000 to 49,999 people—it can have several such towns—and proportionally few of its residents commuting outside the area. Recently, the government counted 575 such areas in the continental United States. Examples of micropolitan statistical areas include Granbury, Texas; Marion, Ohio; Alamogordo, New Mexico; and Yazoo City, Mississippi.

- The category of **consolidated metropolitan statistical area (CMSA)** includes the country's 25 or so urban giants such as Detroit–Ann Arbor–Flint, Michigan; Los Angeles–Riverside–Orange County, California; and Philadelphia–Wilmington–Atlantic City. (Note that in the third example, three states are involved—Pennsylvania, Delaware, and New Jersey.) A CMSA must include two or more primary metropolitan statistical areas, discussed next.

- A **primary metropolitan statistical area (PMSA)** is an urbanized county or set of counties with social and economic ties to nearby areas. PMSAs are identified within areas of 1-million-plus populations. Olympia, Washington, is part of the Seattle–Tacoma–Bremerton PMSA. Bridgeport, Connecticut, is part of the New York–Northern New Jersey–Long Island PMSA, and Riverside–San Bernardino, California, is a PMSA within the Los Angeles–Riverside–Orange County PMSA.[14]

USING GEOGRAPHIC SEGMENTATION

Demand for some categories of goods and services can vary according to geographic region, and marketers need to be aware of how these regions differ. Marketers of major brands are particularly interested in defining their **core regions,** the locations where they get 40 to 80 percent of their sales.

Residence location *within* a geographic area is an important segmentation variable. City dwellers often rely on public transportation and may get along fine without automobiles, whereas those who live in the suburbs or rural areas depend on their own cars and trucks. Also, those who live in the suburbs spend more on lawn and garden care products than do people in the city. Climate is another important segmentation factor. Consumers in chilly northern states eat more soup than people who live in warmer southern markets. But here's a surprise—they also eat the most ice cream!

Geographic segmentation provides useful distinctions when regional preferences or needs exist. A consumer may not want to invest in a snowblower or flood insurance, but may *have* to because of the location of his or her home. But it's important for marketers not to stop at geographic location as a segmentation method, because distinctions among consumers also exist within a geographic location. Consider those who relocate from one region to another for work or family reasons. They may bring with them their preferences from other parts of the country. Using multiple segmentation variables is probably a much better strategy for targeting a specific market.

GEOGRAPHIC INFORMATION SYSTEMS (GISs)

Super Bowl Sunday is more than a sporting event—it is also the single biggest sales day of the year for a pizza company such as Domino's. On that day alone, Domino's delivers 1.5 million pizzas around the nation, a 36 percent increase over a normal Sunday. The firm built its reputation as the number one pizza delivery company in the world, which means that its delivery system must be as streamlined and efficient as possible. "Our teams around the country are poised and ready to deliver," says a Domino's spokesperson.[15] To achieve its objectives, Domino's invested in a geographic information system. Once used mainly by the military, **geographic information systems (GISs)** are computer systems that assemble, store, manipulate, and display data by their location. GISs simplify the job of analyzing marketing information by relating data to their locations. The result is a geographic map overlaid with digital data about consumers in a particular area. A growing number of companies benefit from using a GIS to locate new outlets, assign sales territories, plan distribution centers—and map out the most efficient delivery routes. Although the earliest geographic information systems were prohibitively expensive for all but the largest companies, recent technological advances have made GIS software available at a much lower cost, increasing usage among smaller firms. Google Earth is a recent application of GIS technology that allows computer users to view different parts of the country up close. Users simply type in an address and zoom into it, whether it's a house, a theme park, a school, or a store.[16] Marketers will be able to make many uses of this application, starting with deliveries.

Etiquette Tips for Marketing Professionals

How to Say (and Do) the Right Thing

Throughout your career, you'll work with people of all shapes and sizes. You'll probably serve a great variety of customers as well. Recently, some customers have complained that they have received poor service from retailers and other businesspeople because of their weight. Researchers have conducted studies, sending shoppers out to investigate, and learned that the complaints are generally valid. Overweight shoppers were ignored or treated rudely, and they often left the store without purchasing anything.

Discrimination of any kind is unethical, and to overlook or mistreat a customer based on appearance, including obesity, is a poor marketing practice. Every customer deserves to be treated with dignity. But a good marketer can turn the situation into a win-win for both parties simply by approaching each customer with respect and friendliness. The customer will feel better, is more likely to make a purchase, and may even return. Here are a few ways you can monitor your own behavior toward others so that you say (and do) the right thing:

1. Don't stare. Instead, make eye contact with the person with whom you are dealing. Focus on the issue at hand. Maybe you are making a sales call for your firm. Or perhaps a customer has asked for your help in finding an item your store sells. Concentrate on ways to serve your customer.

2. Be aware of your tone of voice. Regardless of a person's appearance, do not be condescending or impatient. You never know; he or she may be about to make a major purchase from you.

3. Don't assume anything. If an overweight shopper visits the department store where you work, don't automatically direct her to the plus sizes—she might be in the store to purchase a baby gift for her grandchild. Instead, ask, "How may I help you today?"

4. Remember that beauty is in the eye of the beholder. Your ideas about attractiveness with regard to weight may be vastly different from someone else's. In fact, these ideals vary from culture to culture. Some countries view slenderness as a sign of poverty, while others view it as an attribute of the upper class.

Sources: "Obese Shoppers Are Discriminated in Stores: Study," Fashion Monitor, **http://toronto.fashion-monitor.com**, accessed April 11, 2006; Anne Harding, "Most Obese People Don't See Themselves That Way," Medicine Online Inc., April 4, 2006, **http://www.medicineonline.com**, "Surprise! Pretty People Earn More," CNN Money.com, April 11, 2005, **http://money.cnn.com**; ABC News, March 8, 2005, **www.abcnews.go.com**.

DEMOGRAPHIC SEGMENTATION

The most common method of market segmentation—**demographic segmentation**—defines consumer groups according to demographic variables such as gender, age, income, occupation, education, sexual orientation, household size, and stage in the family life cycle. This approach is also called *socioeconomic segmentation*. Marketers review vast quantities of available data to complete a plan for demographic segmentation. One of the primary sources for demographic data in the United States is the Census Bureau. Marketers can obtain many of the Census Bureau's statistics online at **http://www.census.gov**.

The following discussion considers the most commonly used demographic variables. Keep in mind, however, that while demographic segmentation is helpful, it can also lead to stereotyping—a preconception about a group of people—which can alienate a potential market or cause marketers to miss a potential market altogether, as discussed in "Etiquette Tips for Marketing Professionals" feature. The idea is to use segmentation as a starting point, not as an end point.

demographic segmentation Division of an overall market into homogeneous groups based on variables such as gender, age, income, occupation, education, sexual orientation, household size, and stage in the family life cycle; also called *socioeconomic segmentation*.

SEGMENTING BY GENDER

Gender is an obvious variable that helps define the markets for certain products. But segmenting by gender can be tricky. In some cases, the segmenting is obvious—lipstick for women, facial shaving products for men. But in recent years, the lines have increasingly blurred. Men sometimes wear earrings and use skin-care products, once both the province of women. Women purchase power tools and pickup trucks, once considered traditionally male purchases. So marketers of cars and trucks, power tools, jewelry, and skin-care products have had to change the way they segment their markets. Dell recently increased its advertising in women's magazines such as *O at Home* and *Ladies' Home Journal. O at Home* and *Real Simple* featured Dell's laser printer, plasma TV, and notebook computer in their "must-have" gift sections.[17] Nivea, well-known for its skin-care products for women and babies, created an entire line of men's skin-care products called Nivea for Men.

Some companies successfully market the same—or similar—products to both men and women. Sony developed a campaign for its flat screen TV aimed at both genders. Calling its brand "The World's First Television for Men and Women," Sony created ads with the tagline, "Coveted by Men, Admired by Women."[18]

As the balance of purchasing power in many families has shifted toward women, marketers have learned that working women who regularly use the Internet make most of the decisions about retail items (such as clothing), healthcare goods and services, and fitness products. Decisions about vacations, financial investments, and home improvement products are often shared equally. In the category of consumer electronics, women edge ahead of men by about 10 percent.[19] Marketers who understand these trends can develop more effective strategies and messages for consumers.

SEGMENTING BY AGE

Age is another variable that marketers use to segment their markets. As with gender, age seems to be an easy distinction to make—baby food for babies, retirement communities for seniors. But also like gender, the distinctions become blurred as consumers' roles and needs change and as age distribution shifts and projected changes in each group take place. St. Joseph's baby aspirin is no longer marketed just to parents for their infants; now it is also marketed to adults to help prevent heart disease.

The Cohort Effect

Marketers can learn from a sociological concept called the **cohort effect,** the tendency of members of a generation to be influenced and bound together by significant events occurring during their key formative years, roughly age 17 to 22. These events help define the core values of the age group that eventually shape consumer preferences and behavior. For seniors, who are discussed later in this section, the events would be the Great Depression and World War II because many were in this age bracket at that time. For older baby boomers, it would be the Vietnam War and the civil rights movement. Marketers have already labeled people who were in the 17-to-22 age bracket at the time of the September 11, 2001, terrorist attacks the **9/11 Generation.** Clearly, this group's previous priorities and values changed, and those changes will become more evident as time passes.

The significance of the cohort effect for marketers lies in understanding the general characteristics of each group as it responds to its defining life events. The social and economic influences that each group experiences help form their long-term beliefs and goals in life—and can have a lasting effect on their buying habits and the product choices they make. For marketers to be effective in reaching their targeted age segments, they need to understand some basic characteristics of each age group. We highlight a few of the distinguishing characteristics next and briefly discuss how some marketers are providing products to meet each age segment's wants and needs.

School-Age Children

School-age children—and those who are even younger—exert considerable influence over family purchases, as marketers are keenly aware, particularly in the area of food. Children as young as 2 can begin to make choices about what they want to eat, play with, and wear. Breakfast cereals, snack foods, and beverages of all kinds are designed to attract the attention of children—who in turn try to persuade their families to purchase them. With childhood obesity on the rise, some nutritionists were concerned about the types of beverages available to children in school vending machines. So beverage marketers Cadbury Schweppes, The Coca-Cola Company, and PepsiCo voluntarily agreed to remove high-calorie soft drinks from schools, substituting lower-calorie choices in smaller serving sizes.[20] Also, some firms, such as Kraft Foods and General Mills, are making efforts to market more healthful alternatives for foods children traditionally like.

Tweens and Teens

Tweens—also called *preteens*—and teens are a rapidly growing market. As a group, tweens and teens spend $159 billion annually on everything from snacks to clothing to electronics.[21] But they also influence billions of dollars' worth of purchases made by their families. According to the Roper Youth Report, one in four tweens and teens advise their parents on purchases of products such as cell phones, Internet service, and the family car.[22] Marketers are noting one important way of reaching this age group: three-quarters of U.S. teens between age 15 and 17 have cell phones.[23] Researchers have also found that members of this group, often referred to as *Generation Y,* don't fall into a single category—although the most popular consumer items they purchase across the board are candy, soft drinks, clothing, CDs, and video games.[24]

Retailers such as Hot Topic, American Eagle Outfitters, and Aeropostale—all of which market directly to teens—have had success where classics such as The Gap and department stores like Sears have lost some ground. That may be because of their image in advertisements and store décor rather than the clothes themselves. Restaurant chain Wendy's International has begun to focus on teens as well, offering breakfast foods, new salads and deli sandwiches, and a 99-cent chicken sandwich.[25] Entrepreneur Addie Swartz recognized a gap in entertainment for preteen girls and developed a series of books called *Beacon Street Girls* that feature strong, realistic characters who face challenges. Swartz's company also offers accessories—mini-backpacks and duffels, with clothing and tech items on the drawing board—to go with the books. The series has been successful because Swartz identified a market and developed products attractive to that market.[26]

© TERRI MILLER/E-VISUAL COMMUNICATIONS, INC.

Children influence many family purchases, such as their favorite foods. Kraft's Supermac and Cheese is fortified with whole grains, calcium, and vitamins.

Generation X

The group born between 1966 and 1981—who are now between ages 25 and 40—are often referred to as *Generation X.* This group of about 44 million faced some economic and career challenges as they began their adult lives and started families: housing costs were high and debt associated with college loans and credit cards was soaring. But their financial squeeze should ease as they enter their prime earning years. This group is very family oriented—not defining themselves by their careers as much as previous generations—well educated, and optimistic. Because they grew up with television, this generation of consumers is far more technologically savvy than their elders.[27] Marketers who understand these traits can appeal to this group of consumers, particularly if they ask Gen Xers directly what they want or need, especially in new technology products.

Baby Boomers

Baby boomers—people born between 1946 and 1965—are a popular segment to target because of their numbers and income levels. Approximately 77 million people were born during this period.[28] The values of this age group were influenced both by the Vietnam War era and the career-driven era that followed. They also came of age with early television, with TV commercials

Want younger looking skin in 14 days?

NEW Breakthrough
Patented Formula

Susan Sarandon is wearing Age Defying Light Makeup in Medium.
revlon.com

AGE DEFYING
light makeup now with BOTAFIRM™

Reduces lines nearly 50% in 2 weeks*

Featuring an exclusive formula with Botafirm, a patented blend of hexapeptide and botanicals, for younger looking skin. SPF 30. Lightweight coverage and feel that keeps up with your active lifestyle.

REVLON®

*Diminished appearance in clinical tests.

Marketers are increasingly targeting baby boomers in advertisements and promotions because of their high level of disposable income and their desire to look and feel healthy and vibrant.

serving as a backdrop to most of their lives. They tried new breakfast cereals, ate TV dinners, and recall when cigarettes were advertised on television.

Not surprisingly, baby boomers are a lucrative segment for many marketers. Baby boomers over age 50 will have a total disposable income of $1 trillion within the next few years, which is why businesses are trying to woo this group. Different subgroups within this generation complicate segmentation and targeting strategies. Some boomers put off having children until their 40s, while others their age have already become grandparents. Boomers tend to value health and quality of life—a fact not lost on marketers for products such as organic foods, financial investments, travel, and fitness. Bally Total Fitness launched its "Build Your Own Membership" campaign, aimed at baby boomers who want to get fit with water aerobics, walking, and other exercises that spare the joints. "We're moving away from that ad that only shows young, beautiful people with a Greek-god physique," explains Jim McDonald, Bally's chief marketing officer.[29]

Vespa Motor Scooters is another firm that has boomers clearly in its sight. When the firm rolled its scooters back onto U.S. streets after a fifteen-year absence, marketers discovered that consumers age 50 and older were snapping them up. It seemed that these consumers were nostalgic for the old candy-colored bikes of their childhood, and the new scooters made them feel good. Baby boomers also have money to spend on leisure products. "The boomers are particularly attractive because . . . they're less likely to be raising young children, and their careers are established and stable," explains Paolo Timoni, CEO of Vespa's parent company Piaggio USA.[30]

Seniors

As Americans continue to live longer, the median age of the U.S. population has dramatically increased. More than 36 million people are now over age 65.[31] In the United States, heads of households of age 55-plus control about three-quarters of the country's total financial assets. Their discretionary incomes and rates of home ownership are higher than those of any other age group. They account for about 40 percent of new-car sales and most of the travel dollars spent. These numbers show why many marketers should target this group. Some refer to these prosperous consumers as WOOFs—Well-Off Older Folks. Although many seniors live on modest, fixed incomes, those who are well off financially have both time and money to spend on leisure activities and luxury items. Knowing this, some unethical marketers try to take advantage of seniors, as discussed in the "Solving an Ethical Controversy" feature.

Because they are healthier, are living longer, and have money to spend, seniors want marketers to know that they are more active. Grand Circle Travel understands this desire and caters most of its upscale trips to adventurous seniors. On one trip, travelers may cruise along the Yangtze River on a small ship, where they can take tai chi classes on deck. On a trip to Egypt, travelers can opt to ride camels.[32]

SEGMENTING BY ETHNIC GROUP

According to the Census Bureau, America's racial and ethnic makeup is constantly changing. The three largest and fastest-growing racial/ethnic groups are Hispanics, African Americans, and Asian

Solving an Ethical Controversy

Scams and Seniors

While most marketers who target senior citizens do so for legitimate and ethical purposes, consumer groups are increasingly concerned that seniors may also become targets for unethical schemes. Investment or insurance scams, particularly combined with telemarketing, are just two areas that have industry watchers and other experts worried. "The impending retirement of the baby boomers will mean that very soon, the vast majority of our nation's net worth will be in the hands of the newly retired," says Christopher Cox, chairman of the Securities and Exchange Commission (SEC). "Scam artists will swarm like locusts over this increasingly vulnerable group."

Should marketers help prevent consumer fraud against seniors?

PRO

1. Although people age 60 and older make up 15 percent of the U.S. population, they account for 30 percent of fraud victims, which means they are particularly vulnerable to unethical behavior by marketers.
2. Marketers who behave ethically and support efforts by consumer advocates and regulators will not only establish better relationships with their customers—seniors—but will also build a positive image for their firms and industries as a whole.

CON

1. It is the responsibility of the SEC, the Food & Drug Administration (FDA), consumer groups, and other agencies—not marketers—to protect seniors from unethical behavior by companies.

2. Seniors are free to make choices in the marketplace, just as other consumers are, which means that sometimes they make mistakes. The free enterprise system provides a variety of selections of goods and services, and it is the responsibility of consumers to decide which ones they want to purchase.

Summary

Older Americans are more likely than any other age group to have accumulated savings, which makes them vulnerable to unethical marketing tactics that are designed to encourage them to spend that money. Some firms now offer education programs to help seniors make informed choices. Linda Sherry, director of National Priorities for Consumer Action, encourages seniors to protect themselves by becoming educated and aware of scams. "Seniors should really be on the lookout for Medicare drug plan schemes, home equity schemes, travel schemes, investment schemes, [and] confidence games where somebody's trying to convince them of something that isn't in their best interest," she advises. Both regulators and consumer advocates agree that, as the population continues to age, the problem is likely to grow. "This is an area that will remain one of the hottest topics for the next several decades," predicts Patricia Struck, head of the North American Securities Administrators Association.

Sources: "Seniors as Predominant Telemarketing Fraud Victims," **http://www.crimes-of-persuasion.com**, accessed April 11, 2006; "Fraud Target: Senior Citizens," Federal Bureau of Investigation, **http://www.fbi.gov**, accessed April 11, 2006; Greg Farrell, "SEC Targets Investment Scams Aimed at Seniors," *USA Today*, March 26, 2006, **http://www.usatoday.com**; Kathy Chu, "Financial Scams Expected to Boom as Boomers Age," *USA Today*, February 6, 2006, **http://www.usatoday.com**; "30 Percent of Seniors Fall Victim to Financial Fraud Scams," PR Newswire, October 31, 2005, **http://www.prnewswire.com**.

Americans. From a marketer's perspective, it is important to note that spending by these groups is rising at a faster pace than for U.S. households in general.

Hispanics and African Americans

Hispanics and African Americans are currently the largest racial/ethnic minority groups in the U.S., with Hispanics edging out African Americans at more than 41 million, according to the most recent census data.[33] The Hispanic population is growing much faster than the African American population and will account for 46 percent of all population growth in the United States over the next 20 years.[34] Just as

¿Has comido proteína hoy?™

Cuando tú anotas tu familia gana. Prueba las chicken wings de Tyson® y pon arriba el marcador. Son alitas de pollo ricas y fáciles de preparar, y son una fuente de proteína y energía para que todos se sientan como campeones.

Tyson appeals to the Hispanic American market by asking, "*Has comido proteína hoy*"—"Have you had your protein today?"

COURTESY OF TYSON FOODS, INC.

important for marketers, U.S. Hispanics' disposable income has increased by nearly one-third over a two-year period, double the rate of the rest of the population—although it is still significantly less than that of non-Hispanic whites.[35]

Many marketers have focused their efforts on the Hispanic population in the United States. Procter & Gamble, General Motors, The Coca-Cola Company, and Wal-Mart are among the largest advertisers to this group of consumers.[36] Major League Baseball (MLB) has made a major effort to attract Hispanic Americans to its ballparks. The Florida Marlins, Los Angeles Dodgers, and Arizona Diamondbacks regularly broadcast their games in Spanish. The Diamondbacks designate five nights a week as Hispanic nights, with special T-shirts and other promotions. Still, one survey shows that Hispanics cite football as their favorite sport.

As is the case with Hispanics—whose origins may be from a variety of distinct countries—African Americans do not represent a single category. Smart marketers know that to capture their share of the $1 trillion in purchases made by African Americans each year, they must be able to reach different segments within the African American population. TV One serves nearly 30 million African American households with lifestyle and entertainment programs, movies, fashion, and music designed to "inform and inspire a diverse audience of adult African American viewers," says the company, which has teamed up with Time Warner and Comcast to distribute its programming.[37] Recently, pharmaceutical giant Pfizer joined with Radio One, the NAACP, the National Black Nurses Association, and other organizations to launch a campaign to encourage health education and awareness among African Americans, offering clinics and other resources to this population.[38] And research shows that more and more African Americans are gaining access to the Internet, where marketers can reach them.

Asian Americans

Although Asian Americans represent a smaller segment than either the African American or Hispanic populations, they are the second-fastest-growing segment of the U.S. population. The Census Bureau, which includes Pacific Islanders in its Asian segment, estimates that this group will grow to 23 million by 2020. Asian Americans are an attractive target for marketers because they also have the fastest-growing income.[39]

The Asian American population is concentrated in fewer geographic areas than are other ethnic markets. Half of Asians live in the West, and 95 percent live in metropolitan areas. However, they are very diverse, representing more than fifteen different cultures and speaking languages that include Cantonese, Hawaiian, Hindi, Japanese, Korean, Mandarin, Tagalog, Urdu, and Vietnamese.[40] Companies can target Asian American consumers by advertising in appropriate local markets rather than on a national scale. Honda's first Asian American advertising campaign, called "Calligraphy," was launched in Los Angeles. The top four advertisers to Asian Americans are AT&T, Verizon, Ford, and General Motors.[41]

Native Americans

Another important minority group is Native Americans, whose current population numbers about 2.8 million. Add to that number the 4 million people who claim Native American heritage and another 7 million who claim "some" Native American ancestry.[42]

In addition to the Great Plains, South, and Southwest tribes, such as the Cherokee, Choctaw, and Navajo, the Census Bureau also includes Alaska native tribes, such as the Inuit and Tlingit, in this population segment. The Native American population is growing at double the rate of the U.S. population in general. Four of ten Native Americans live in the West, and three in ten live in the South.

In addition to population growth, Native American businesses are growing. There are roughly 200,000 Native American businesses in the United States, with $34 billion in revenues. Native American businesses are increasing in the service, construction, and retail areas in particular. Reservation-based casinos and related gaming activities make up a $5 billion industry, but plenty of other businesses exist as well.[43] *Rez Biz,* a new magazine published by the Navajo Nation, aims to encourage entrepreneurial ventures and economic development on reservations and locations where Native Americans are concentrated. "A magazine like this, it's going to spread like wildfire," predicts Frank Dayish Jr., vice president of the Navajo Nation.[44]

PEOPLE OF MIXED RACE

U.S. residents completing census forms now have the option of identifying themselves as belonging to more than one racial category. Marketers need to be aware of this change. In some ways, it benefits marketers by making racial statistics more accurate. On the other hand, marketers may find it difficult to compare the new statistics with data from earlier censuses.

SEGMENTING BY FAMILY LIFE CYCLE STAGES

Still another form of demographic segmentation employs the stages of the **family life cycle**—the process of family formation and dissolution. The underlying theme of this segmentation approach is that life stage, not age per se, is the primary determinant of many consumer purchases. As people move from one life stage to another, they become potential consumers for different types of goods and services.

An unmarried person setting up an apartment for the first time is likely to be a good prospect for inexpensive furniture and small home appliances. This consumer probably must budget carefully, ruling out expenditures on luxury items. On the other hand, a young single person who is still living at home will probably have more money to spend on products such as a car, entertainment, and clothing. As couples marry, their consumer profiles change. Couples without children are frequent buyers of personalized gifts, power tools, furniture, and homes. Eating out and travel may also be part of their lifestyles.

The birth or adoption of a first child changes any consumer's profile considerably; parents must buy cribs, changing tables, baby clothes, baby food, car seats, and similar products. Parents usually spend less on the children who follow because they have already bought many essential items for the first child. Today, the average woman gives birth to fewer children than she did a century ago and usually waits until she is older to have them. Although the average age for American women to have their first child is 25, many women wait much longer, often into their 30s and even 40s.[45] This means that if they work outside the home, older women are likely to be more established financially with more money to spend. However, if a woman chooses to stay home after the birth of a child, income can drop dramatically.

Families typically spend the most during the years their children are growing—on everything including

COURTESY OF WILSON-ART FLOORING

On the days YOU'LL ACTUALLY SEE IT, *it's beautiful.*

Wilsonart® Flooring
1-800-710-8846
wilsonartflooring.com

The birth or adoption of a child brings with it a need for all kinds of products.

housing, food, clothing, braces, and college. Thus, they often look to obtain value wherever they can. Marketers can create satisfied and loyal customers among this group by giving them the best value possible.

Once the children are grown and on their own—or at least off to college—married couples enter the "empty nest" stage. Empty nesters may have the disposable incomes necessary to purchase premium products once college tuitions and mortgages are paid off. They may travel more, eat out more often, redecorate the house, or go back to school themselves. They may treat themselves to a new and more luxurious car or buy a vacation home. In later years, empty nesters may decide to sell their homes and become customers for retirement or assisted-living communities. They may require home-care services or more healthcare products as well. However, one in twelve older adults report that their incomes in retirement do not meet their needs for housing, healthcare, food, and clothing, meaning that they do not have money to spend on luxuries—and are more likely to be looking for lower-priced goods and services.[46]

One trend noted by researchers in the past decade is an increase in the number of grown children who have returned home to live with their parents. Called "boomerangs," some of these grown children bring along families of their own. Another trend is the growing number of grandparents who care for grandchildren on a regular basis—making them customers all over again for baby and child products such as toys, food, and safety devices.

SEGMENTING BY HOUSEHOLD TYPE

The first U.S. census in 1790 found an average household size of 5.8 people. Today, that number is below 3. The U.S. Department of Commerce cites several reasons for the trend toward smaller households: lower fertility rates (including the decision to have fewer children or no children at all), young people's tendency to postpone marriage, the frequency of divorce, and the ability and desire of many people to live alone.

Today's U.S. households represent a wide range of diversity. They include households with a married couple and their children; households that are blended through divorce or loss of a spouse and remarriage; those headed by a single parent, same-sex parents, or grandparents; couples without children; groups of friends; and single-person households.

Couples without children may be young or old. If they are seniors, their children may have already grown and be living on their own. Some older couples choose to live together without marriage because they prefer to keep their finances separate and because they could lose valuable health or pension benefits if they married. Couples who are younger and do not have children are considered attractive to marketers because they often have high levels of income to spend. These couples typically eat out often, take expensive vacations, and buy luxury cars.

Same-sex couples who share households—with or without children—are on the rise. According to the Urban Institute, 22 percent of gay couples and 34 percent of lesbian couples are now raising children.[47] While the social debate over same-sex marriage and civil unions continues, marketers recognize these households as important customers. Wal-Mart has introduced a line of wedding cards and commitment rings designed for same-sex couples.[48]

People live alone for a variety of reasons—sometimes by choice and sometimes by necessity such as divorce or widowhood. In response, marketers have modified their messages and their products to meet the needs of single-person households. Food industry manufacturers are downsizing products, offering more single-serve foods including from soup and macaroni and cheese.

SEGMENTING BY INCOME AND EXPENDITURE PATTERNS

Part of the earlier definition of *market* described people with purchasing power. Not surprisingly, then, a common basis for segmenting the consumer market is income. Marketers often target geographic areas known for the high incomes of their residents. Or they might consider age or household type when determining potential buying power.

Engel's Laws

How do expenditure patterns vary with income? Over a century ago, Ernst Engel, a German statistician, published what became known as **Engel's laws**—three general statements based on his studies

of the impact of household income changes on consumer spending behavior. According to Engel, as household income increases, the following will take place:

1. A smaller percentage of expenditures goes for food.

2. The percentage spent on housing, household operations, and clothing remains constant.

3. The percentage spent on other items (such as recreation and education) increases.

Are Engel's laws still valid? Recent studies say yes, with a few exceptions. Researchers note a steady decline in the percentage of total income spent on food, beverages, and tobacco as income increases. Although high-income families spend greater absolute amounts on food items, their purchases represent declining percentages of their total expenditures compared with low-income families. The second law remains partly accurate. However, the percentage of fixed expenditures for housing and household operations has increased over the past 30 years. And the percentage spent on clothing rises with increased income because of choice. Also, expenditures may vary from region to region. In general, residents of the Northeast and West spend more on housing than people who live in the South.[49] The third law remains true, with the exception of medical and personal-care costs, which appear to decline as a percentage of increased income.

Engel's laws can help marketers target markets at all income levels. Regardless of the economic environment, consumers still buy luxury goods and services. One reason is that some companies now offer their luxury products at different price levels. Mercedes-Benz has its lower-priced C-class models, while Tiffany sells a $100 sterling silver heart pendant with chain. Both of these firms continue to offer their higher-priced items as well but have chosen to broaden their market by serving other consumers.

DEMOGRAPHIC SEGMENTATION ABROAD

Marketers often face a difficult task in obtaining the data necessary for demographic segmentation abroad. Many countries do not have scheduled census programs. Germany skipped counting from 1970 to 1987, and France conducts a census about every seven years. By contrast, Japan and Canada conduct censuses every five years; however, the mid-decade assessments are not as complete as the end-of-decade counts.

Also, some foreign data include demographic divisions not found in the U.S. census. Canada collects information on religious affiliation, for instance. On the other hand, some of the standard segmentation data for U.S. markets are not available abroad. Many nations do not collect income data. Great Britain, Japan, Spain, France, and Italy are examples. Similarly, family life cycle data are difficult to apply in global demographic segmentation efforts. Ireland acknowledges only three marital statuses—single, married, and widowed—while Latin-American nations and Sweden count their unmarried cohabitants.

One source of global demographic information is the International Programs Center (IPC) at the U.S. Census Bureau. The IPC provides a searchable online database of population statistics for many countries on the Census Bureau's Web page. Another source is the United Nations, which sponsors national statistical offices that collect demographic data on a variety of countries. In addition, private marketing research firms can supplement government data.

PSYCHOGRAPHIC SEGMENTATION

Marketers have traditionally referred to geographic and demographic characteristics as the primary bases for dividing consumers into homogeneous market segments. Still, they have long recognized the need for fuller, more lifelike portraits of consumers in developing their marketing programs. As a result, psychographic segmentation can be a useful tool for gaining sharper insight into consumer purchasing behavior.

WHAT IS PSYCHOGRAPHIC SEGMENTATION?

Psychographic segmentation divides a population into groups that have similar psychological characteristics, values, and lifestyles. Lifestyle refers to a person's mode of living; it describes how an individual

psychographic segmentation Division of a population into groups that have similar psychological characteristics, values, and lifestyles.

operates on a daily basis. Consumers' lifestyles are composites of their individual psychological profiles, including their needs, motives, perceptions, and attitudes. A lifestyle also bears the mark of many other influences, such as family, job, social activities, and culture.

The most common method for developing psychographic profiles of a population is to conduct a large-scale survey that asks consumers to agree or disagree with a collection of several hundred AIO statements. These **AIO statements** describe various activities, interests, and opinions. The resulting data allow researchers to develop lifestyle profiles. Marketers can then develop a separate marketing strategy that closely fits the psychographic makeup for each lifestyle segment.

Marketing researchers have conducted psychographic studies on hundreds of goods and services, such as beer and air travel. Hospitals and other healthcare providers use such studies to assess consumer behavior and attitudes toward health care in general, to learn the needs of consumers in particular marketplaces, and to determine how consumers perceive individual institutions. Many businesses turn to psychographic research in an effort to learn what consumers in various demographic and geographic segments want and need.

VALS™

A quarter century ago, the research and consulting firm SRI International developed a psychographic segmentation system called VALS. Today VALS is owned and managed by SRI Consulting Business Intelligence (SRIC-BI), an SRI spin-off. VALS originally stood for "values and lifestyles" because it categorized consumers by their social values—how they felt about issues such as legalization of marijuana or abortion rights. A decade later, SRIC-BI revised the system to link it more closely with consumer buying behavior. The revised VALS system categorizes consumers by psychological characteristics that correlate with purchase behavior. It is based on two key concepts: resources and self-motivation. **VALS** divides consumers into eight psychographic categories: Actualizers, Thinkers, Achievers, Experiencers, Believers, Strivers, Makers, and Survivors. Figure 9.4 details the profiles for these categories and their relationships.

The VALS framework in the figure displays differences in resources as vertical distances, and primary motivation is represented horizontally. The resource dimension measures income, education, self-confidence, health, eagerness to buy, and energy level. Primary motivations divide consumers into three groups: principle-motivated consumers who have a set of ideas and morals—principles—that they live by; achievement-motivated consumers who are influenced by symbols of success; and action-motivated consumers who seek physical activity, variety, and adventure.

SRIC-BI has created several specialized segmentation systems based on this approach. GeoVALS™, for instance, estimates the percentage of each VALS type in each U.S. residential zip code. Marketers can identify zip codes with the highest concentrations of the segment they want to reach; they can use the information to choose locations for retail outlets; and they can tailor marketing messages for a local audience.[50] JapanVALS™ was developed to help companies understand Japanese consumers, and U.K.VALS™ segments consumers in the United Kingdom. SRIC-BI used the VALS segmentation information in conjunction with marketers in consulting projects and on a subscriber basis. Product, service, and media data are available by VALS types from companies' databases.

Other tools available include LifeMatrix, developed by RoperASW and Mediamark Research. LifeMatrix crunches the numbers on hundreds of personal variables that include political views, religious affiliations, and social attitudes and comes up with ten psychographic categories that reflect today's lifestyles. Depending on your own variables, you might be a "priority parent" or "tribe wired." LifeMatrix subdivides the categories even further, making conclusions about personality traits such as "caring" or "altruistic."[51]

figure 9.4

The VALS Network

Source: SRI Consulting Business Intelligence (SRIC-BI); www.sric-bi.com/VALS

PSYCHOGRAPHIC SEGMENTATION OF GLOBAL MARKETS

As JapanVALS suggests, psychographic profiles can cross national boundaries. RoperASW, a marketing research firm that is now part of Germany-based GfK Group, has surveyed 7,000 people in 35 countries.[52] From the resulting data, Roper identified six psychographic consumer segments that exist in all 35 nations, although to varying degrees:

- *Strivers,* the largest segment, value professional and material goals more than the other groups. One-third of the Asian population and one-fourth of Russians are strivers. They are slightly more likely to be men than women.

- *Devouts* value duty and tradition. While this segment comprises 22 percent of all adults, they are most common in Africa, the Middle East, and developing Asia. They are least common in western Europe and developed Asian countries. Worldwide, they are more likely to be female.

- *Altruists* emphasize social issues and societal well-being. Comprising 18 percent of all adults, this group shows a median age of 44 and a slightly higher percentage of women. Altruists are most common in Latin America and Russia, with a significant number of young Chinese adults.[53]

- *Intimates* value family and personal relationships. They are divided almost equally between males and females. One American or European in four would be categorized as intimates, but only 7 percent of consumers in developing Asia fall into this category.

- *Fun seekers,* as you might guess from their name, focus on personal enjoyment and pleasurable experiences. They comprise 12 percent of the world's population, with a male–female ratio of 54 to 46. Many live in developed Asia.

- *Creatives,* the smallest segment, account for just 10 percent of the global population. This group seeks education, technology, and knowledge, and their male–female ratio is roughly equal. Many creatives live in western Europe and Latin America, although 17 percent of China's young adult market can be identified as such.[54]

Roper researchers note that some principles and core beliefs—such as protecting the family—apply to more than one psychographic segment.

USING PSYCHOGRAPHIC SEGMENTATION

No one suggests that psychographic segmentation is an exact science, but it does help marketers quantify aspects of consumers' personalities and lifestyles to create goods and services for a target market. Psychographic profile systems such as those of Roper and SRIC-BI can paint useful pictures of the overall psychological motivations of consumers. These profiles produce much richer descriptions of potential target markets than other techniques can achieve. The enhanced detail aids in matching a company's image and product offerings with the types of consumers who use its products.

Identifying which psychographic segments are most prevalent in certain markets helps marketers plan and promote more effectively. Often segments overlap. Consumers who are most likely to be the first to buy new tech products could live in Virginia or Colorado, they could just as easily be status oriented as action oriented, and they might be creatives or fun seekers. What they do have in common is the tendency to be the first on their block to purchase the latest tech devices.[55]

Psychographic segmentation is a good supplement to segmentation by demographic or geographic variables. For example, marketers may have access to each consumer type's media preferences in network television, cable television, radio format, magazines, and newspapers. Psychographic studies may then refine the picture of segment

✓ *assessment check*

1. Under what circumstances are marketers most likely to use geographic segmentation?

2. What is demographic segmentation?

3. What are the major categories of demographic segmentation?

4. What is psychographic segmentation?

5. Name the eight psychographic categories of the U.S.VALS.

5 Describe product-related segmentation.

characteristics to give a more elaborate lifestyle profile of the consumers in the firm's target market. A psychographic study could help marketers of goods and services in Chicago, New Orleans, or Las Vegas predict what kinds of products consumers in those cities would be drawn to and eliminate those that are not attractive.

product-related segmentation Division of a population into homogeneous groups based on their relationships to the product.

PRODUCT-RELATED SEGMENTATION

Product-related segmentation involves dividing a consumer population into homogeneous groups based on their relationships to the product. This segmentation approach can take several forms:

1. segmenting based on the benefits that people seek when they buy a product
2. segmenting based on usage rates for a product
3. segmenting according to consumers' brand loyalty toward a product

SEGMENTING BY BENEFITS SOUGHT

This approach focuses on the attributes that people seek and the benefits they expect to receive from a good or service. It groups consumers into segments based on what they want a product to do for them.

Consumers who quaff Starbucks premium coffees are not just looking for a dose of caffeine. They are willing to pay extra to savor a pleasant experience, one that makes them feel pampered and appreciated. Women who work out at Curves want to look their best and feel healthy. Pet owners who feed their cats and dogs Science Diet believe that they are giving their animals a great-tasting, healthful pet food.

Even if a business offers only one product line, however, marketers must remember to consider product benefits. Two people may buy the same product for very different reasons. A box of Arm & Hammer baking soda could end up serving as a refrigerator freshener, a toothpaste substitute, an antacid, or a deodorizer for a cat's litter box.

GO AHEAD
SMILE
OUT LOUD

with the
#1 Whitening System
Recommended
by Cosmetic Dentists
Worldwide.

Created by **DR. IRWIN SMIGEL,** President of The American Society for Dental Aesthetics and the world-renowned father of aesthetic dentistry.

Available at: Barneys, Nordstrom, Bath & Body Works, C.O. Bigelow, Clyde Clennels, Victoria's Secret.com, Supersmile.com

Supersmile is pleased to support **AUTISM SPEAKS.** A percentage of all retail sales of the Supersmile Whitening System has been earmarked for donation.

supersmile.
JUST BRUSH AND WHITEN

COURTESY OF SUPERSMILE

Marketers such as Supersmile segment products based on the benefits consumers seek—in this case, bright teeth.

SEGMENTING BY USAGE RATES

Marketers may also segment a total market by grouping people according to the amounts of a product that they buy and use. Markets can be divided into heavy-user, moderate-user, and light-user segments. The **80/20 principle** holds that a big percentage of a product's revenues—maybe 80 percent—comes from a relatively small, loyal percentage of total customers, perhaps 20 percent. The 80/20 principle is sometimes referred to as *Praedo's law*. Although the percentages need not exactly equal these figures, the general principle holds true: Relatively few heavy users of a product can account for much of its consumption.

Depending on their goals, marketers may target heavy, moderate, or light users as well as nonusers. A company may attempt to lure heavy users of another product away from their regular brands to try a new brand. Nonusers and light users may be attractive prospects because other companies are ignoring them. Usage rates can also be linked to other segmentation methods such as demographic and psychographic segmentation.

SEGMENTING BY BRAND LOYALTY

A third product-related segmentation method groups consumers according to the strength of the brand loyalty they feel toward a product. A classic example of brand loyalty segmentation is the frequent-purchase program—it might be frequent flyer, frequent stay, or frequent purchase of shoes or gasoline. Other companies attempt to segment their market by developing brand loyalty over a period of time, through consumers' stages of life. Children whose parents dress them in Lands' End Kids clothes may grow up to wear Lands' End adult clothing—and purchase home furnishings and luggage from the company as well.

Consumers may develop loyalty to seemingly similar brands but for different reasons. One study showed that retailers Wal-Mart and Target have loyal customers whose definition of value is different. Wal-Mart shoppers prefer to do all of their household shopping at one store—which also happens to offer low prices. Target shoppers, who desire low prices as well, are more focused on the store's stylish clothing offerings from well-known designers. "Convenience and price are important to the Wal-Mart-exclusive shopper, whereas style and selection appear to hold more weight with the Target-exclusive shopper," explains Alisa Joseph of Scarborough Research.[56]

Target shoppers want style and selection.

USING MULTIPLE SEGMENTATION BASES

Segmentation is a tool that can help marketers increase their accuracy in reaching the right markets. Like other marketing tools, segmentation is probably best used in a flexible manner—for instance, combining geographic and demographic segmentation techniques or dovetailing product-related segmentation with segmentation by income and expenditure patterns. The important point to keep in mind is that segmentation is a tool to help marketers get to know their potential customers better and ultimately satisfy their needs with the appropriate goods and services.

✓ *assessment check*

1. List the three approaches to product–related segmentation.
2. What is the 80/20 principle?

THE MARKET SEGMENTATION PROCESS

To this point, the chapter has discussed various bases on which companies segment markets. But how do marketers decide which segmentation base—or bases—to use? Firms may use a management-driven method, in which segments are predefined by managers based on their observation of the behavioral and demographic characteristics of likely users. Or they may use a market-driven method, in which segments are defined by asking customers which attributes are important. Then marketers follow a four-stage process.

6 Identify the steps in the market segmentation process.

DEVELOP A RELEVANT PROFILE FOR EACH SEGMENT

After identifying promising segments, marketers should understand the customers in each one. This in-depth analysis of customers helps managers accurately match buyers' needs with the firm's marketing offers. The process must identify characteristics that both explain the similarities among customers within each segment and account for differences among segments.

The task at this stage is to develop a profile of the typical customer in each segment. Such a profile might include information about lifestyle patterns, attitudes toward product attributes and brands, product-use habits, geographic locations, and demographic characteristics.

FORECAST MARKET POTENTIAL

In the second stage, market segmentation and market opportunity analysis combine to produce a forecast of market potential within each segment. Market potential sets the upper limit on the demand that competing firms can expect from a segment. Multiplying by market share determines a single firm's maximum sales potential. This step should define a preliminary go or no-go decision from management because the total sales potential in each segment must justify resources devoted to further analysis. For example, if electronics firms are trying to determine whether to market a new product to teens, they need to determine what the demand for it would be and the disposable income of that group.

FORECAST PROBABLE MARKET SHARE

Once market potential has been estimated, a firm must forecast its probable market share. Competitors' positions in targeted segments must be analyzed, and a specific marketing strategy must be designed to reach these segments. These two activities may be performed simultaneously. Moreover, by settling on a marketing strategy and tactics, a firm determines the expected level of resources it must commit—that is, the costs it will incur to tap the potential demand in each segment.

Apple's iPod took the marketplace by storm, and some believe the iPod is poised to increase Apple's market share of desktop computer sales as loyal iPod users drop their PCs in favor of Mac computers. Researchers predict that as consumers abandon obsolete PCs, instead of upgrading to a new PC, they will switch to a Mac. Because the iPod is already well established, instead of causing a brief downturn in PC sales, a long-term shift toward Apple's Macs and related products might occur.[57]

SELECT SPECIFIC MARKET SEGMENTS

The information, analysis, and forecasts accumulated throughout the entire market segmentation decision process allow management to assess the potential for achieving company goals and to justify committing resources in developing one or more segments. Demand forecasts, together with cost projections, determine the profits and the return on investment (ROI) that the company can expect from each segment. Marketing strategy and tactics must be designed to reinforce the firm's image, yet keep within its unique organizational capabilities.

At this point in the analysis, marketers weigh more than monetary costs and benefits; they also consider many difficult-to-measure but critical organizational and environmental factors. The firm may lack experienced personnel to launch a successful attack on an attractive market segment. Similarly, a firm with 60 percent of the market faces possible legal problems with the Federal Trade Commission if it increases its market concentration. This assessment of both financial and nonfinancial factors is a difficult but vital step in the decision process.

 assessment check

1. Identify the four stages of market segmentation.
2. Why is forecasting important to market segmentation?

STRATEGIES FOR REACHING TARGET MARKETS

Marketers spend a lot of time and effort developing strategies that will best match their firm's product offerings to the needs of particular target markets. An appropriate match is vital to the firm's marketing success. Marketers have identified four basic strategies for achieving consumer satisfaction: undifferentiated marketing, differentiated marketing, concentrated marketing, and micromarketing.

7 Discuss four basic strategies for reaching target markets.

UNDIFFERENTIATED MARKETING

A firm may produce only one product or product line and promote it to all customers with a single marketing mix; such a firm is said to practice **undifferentiated marketing,** sometimes called *mass marketing*. Undifferentiated marketing was much more common in the past than it is today.

While undifferentiated marketing is efficient from a production viewpoint, the strategy also brings inherent dangers. In the past, consumers often preferred to identify themselves with a mass-marketed brand because of a higher perceived quality and a sense of status associated with the brand. But this is no longer the case.[58] A firm that attempts to satisfy everyone in the market with one standard product may suffer if competitors offer specialized alternatives to smaller segments of the total market and better satisfy individual segments. In fact, firms that implement strategies of differentiated marketing, concentrated marketing, or micromarketing may capture enough small segments of the market to defeat another competitor's strategy of undifferentiated marketing.

undifferentiated marketing Strategy that focuses on producing a single product and marketing it to all customers; also called *mass marketing*.

DIFFERENTIATED MARKETING

Firms that promote numerous products with differing marketing mixes designed to satisfy smaller segments are said to practice **differentiated marketing.** By providing increased satisfaction for each of many target markets, a company can produce more sales by following a differentiated marketing strategy than undifferentiated marketing would generate. Oscar Mayer, a marketer of a variety of meat products, practices differentiated marketing. It increased its sales by introducing Lunchables, aimed at children. The original Lunchables were so successful that Oscar Mayer introduced more choices in the line—including snack versions. In general, however, differentiated marketing also

differentiated marketing Strategy that focuses on producing several products and pricing, promoting, and distributing them with different marketing mixes designed to satisfy smaller segments.

raises costs. Production costs usually rise because additional products and variations require shorter production runs and increased setup times. Inventory costs rise because more products require added storage space and increased efforts for record keeping. Promotional costs also rise because each segment demands a unique promotional mix.

Despite higher marketing costs, however, an organization may be forced to practice differentiated marketing to remain competitive. The travel industry now recognizes the need to target smaller groups of travelers with specialized interests. Elderhostel, for instance, targets seniors with specialized trips that may focus on history, hiking, golf, cooking, or other special interests. Old Sturbridge Village in Massachusetts targets people who are interested in American history.

© JOE RAEDLE/GETTY IMAGES

Oscar Mayer developed more versions of its popular Lunchables for different markets.

CONCENTRATED MARKETING

concentrated marketing Focusing marketing efforts on satisfying a single market segment; also called *niche marketing*.

Rather than trying to market its products separately to several segments, a firm may opt for a concentrated marketing strategy. With **concentrated marketing** (also known as **niche marketing**), a firm focuses its efforts on profitably satisfying a single market segment. This approach can appeal to a small firm that lacks the financial resources of its competitors and to a company that offers highly specialized goods and services. American Express, a large firm with many financial products, recently introduced two new credit cards designed for very specific markets: The Knot, for engaged couples, and The Nest, for newlyweds.[59]

Peanut Butter & Co. appeals to the peanut butter lovers of the world with its proprietary brand of gourmet peanut butter flavors including Smooth Operator, Dark Chocolate Dreams, and Cinnamon Raisin Swirl, blended specifically for breakfast. Fans can visit the flagship store in New York City, where they can sample such favorite recipes as "ants on a log" or grilled peanut butter, banana, honey, and bacon sandwiches, or they can shop for their favorite blends online.[60] But along with its benefits, concentrated marketing has its dangers. Because the strategy ties a firm's growth to a specific segment, sales can suffer if new competitors appeal successfully to the same target. If another firm targets peanut butter lovers in the same manner, Peanut Butter & Co. may face a struggle. In addition, errors in forecasting market potential or customer buying habits can lead to severe problems, particularly if the firm has spent substantially on product development and promotion. If more people—children in particular—continue to develop peanut allergies, sales of Peanut Butter & Co.'s products may begin to decline.

Briefly
Speaking

"Put all your eggs in one basket, and watch the basket."

—Mark Twain (1835–1910)
American author

MICROMARKETING

micromarketing Targeting potential customers at very narrow, basic levels, such as by zip code, specific occupation, or lifestyle—possibly even individuals themselves.

The fourth targeting strategy, still more narrowly focused than concentrated marketing, is **micromarketing,** which involves targeting potential customers at a very basic level, such as by zip code, specific occupation, or lifestyle. Ultimately, micromarketing can target even individuals themselves. The salesperson at your favorite clothing boutique may contact you when certain merchandise that she thinks you might like arrives at the store. The Internet allows marketers to make micromarketing even more effective. By tracking specific demographic and personal information, marketers can send e-mail directly to individual consumers who are most likely to buy their products. Consumers who purchase an iPod may receive e-mails about new accessories and other Apple equipment. If you purchase a book via Amazon.com, the company offers to send you e-mail notices about other books that may be of interest.

But micromarketing, like niche marketing, can become too much of a good thing if companies spend too much time, effort, and marketing dollars to unearth a market that is too small and specialized to be profitable. In addition, micromarketing may cause a company to lose sight of other larger markets.

✓ assessment check

1. Explain the difference between undifferentiated and differentiated marketing strategies.
2. What are the benefits of concentrated marketing?

SELECTING AND EXECUTING A STRATEGY

Although most organizations adopt some form of differentiated marketing, no single best choice suits all firms. Any of the alternatives may prove most effective in a particular situation. The basic determinants of a market-specific strategy are (1) company resources, (2) product homogeneity, (3) stage in the product life cycle, and (4) competitors' strategies.

A firm with limited resources may have to choose a concentrated marketing strategy. Small firms may be forced to select small target markets because of limitations in their sales force and advertising budgets. On the other hand, an undifferentiated marketing strategy suits a firm selling items perceived by consumers as relatively homogeneous. Marketers of grain, for example, sell standardized grades of generic products rather than individual brand names. Some petroleum companies implement undifferentiated marketing to distribute their gasoline to the mass market.

The firm's strategy may also change as its product progresses through the stages of the life cycle. During the early stages, undifferentiated marketing might effectively support the firm's effort to build initial demand for the item. In the later stages, however, competitive pressures may force modifications in products and in the development of marketing strategies aimed at segments of the total market.

The strategies of competitors also affect the choice of a segmentation approach. A firm may encounter obstacles to undifferentiated marketing if its competitors actively cultivate smaller segments. In such instances, competition usually forces each firm to adopt a differentiated marketing strategy.

Having chosen a strategy for reaching their firm's target market, marketers must then decide how best to position the product. The concept of positioning seeks to put a product in a certain position, or place, in the minds of prospective buyers. Marketers use a positioning strategy to distinguish their firm's offerings from those of competitors and to create promotions that communicate the desired position. Anheuser-Busch introduced its lower-calorie Budweiser Select, positioning it as a more upscale version of its original Budweiser. The company launched the new beer with special events across the country, along with television commercials featuring well-dressed partygoers.[61]

To achieve the goal of positioning, marketers follow a number of positioning strategies. Possible approaches include positioning a product according to the following categories:

1. *Attributes*—Kraft Foods, "Good food in every bite."

2. *Price/quality*—Omega watches, "We measure the 100th of a second that separates winning from taking part."

3. *Competitors*—Nantucket Nectars, "Real is better."

4. *Application*—Merry Maids, "Relax, it's done."

5. *Product user*—Crane's stationery "for the writer somewhere in each of us."

6. *Product class*—BMW, the "ultimate driving machine."

Whatever strategy they choose, marketers want to emphasize a product's unique advantages and to differentiate it from competitors' options. A **positioning map** provides a valuable tool in helping managers position products by graphically illustrating consumers' perceptions of competing products within an industry. Marketers can create a competitive positioning map from information solicited from consumers or from their accumulated knowledge about a market. A positioning map might present two different characteristics—price and perceived quality—and show how consumers view a product and its major competitors based on these traits. The hypothetical positioning map in Figure 9.5 compares selected retailers based on possible perceptions of the prices and quality of their offerings.

Sometimes changes in the competitive environment force marketers to **reposition** a product—changing the position it holds in the minds of prospective buyers relative to the positions of competing products. Repositioning may even be necessary for already successful products or firms in order to gain greater market share. Fast-food restaurants such as McDonald's

positioning Placing a product at a certain point or location within a market in the minds of prospective buyers.

Versace positions its fashion lines at the top of the market by promoting their style and exclusivity.

IMAGE COURTESY OF THE ADVERTISING ARCHIVES

8   Summarize the types of positioning strategies, and explain the reasons for positioning and repositioning products.

figure 9.5

Hypothetical Positioning Map for Selected Retailers

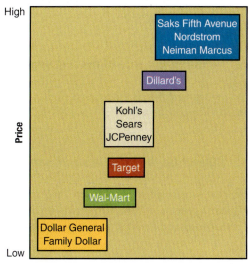

✓ *assessment check*

1. What are the four determinants of a market-specific strategy?

2. What is the role of positioning in a marketing strategy?

and Burger King have repositioned themselves several times over the years in response to shifts in consumer preferences. They have changed ingredients and menu items, and created new marketing campaigns to appeal to different segments of the population. McDonald's current campaign carries the tagline "I'm lovin' it" in an appeal to young urban consumers.

Strategic Implications of Marketing in the 21st Century

To remain competitive, today's marketers must accurately identify potential customers. They can use a variety of methods to accomplish this, including segmenting markets by gender and segmenting by geographic location. The trick is to figure out the best combination of methods for segmentation to identify the most lucrative, long-lasting potential markets. Marketers must also remain flexible, responding to markets as they change—for instance, following a generation as it ages or reaching out to new generations by revamping or repositioning products.

The greatest competitive advantage will belong to firms that can pinpoint and serve markets without segmenting them to the point at which they are too small or specialized to garner profits. Marketers who can reach and communicate with the right customers have a greater chance of attracting and keeping those customers than marketers who are searching for the wrong buyers in the wrong place.

REVIEW OF CHAPTER OBJECTIVES

1   Identify the essential components of a market.

A market consists of people and organizations with the necessary purchasing power, willingness, and authority to buy. Consumer products are purchased by the ultimate consumer for personal use.

Business products are purchased for use directly or indirectly in the production of other goods and services. Certain products may fall into both categories.

2   Outline the role of market segmentation in developing a marketing strategy.

Market segmentation is the process of dividing a total market into several homogeneous groups. It is used in identifying a target market for a good or service. Segmentation is the key to deciding a marketing strategy.

3   Describe the criteria necessary for effective segmentation.

Effective segmentation depends on these four basic requirements: (1) the segment must have measurable purchasing power and size, (2) marketers can find a way to promote to and serve the market, (3) marketers must identify segments large enough for profit potential, and (4) the firm can target a number of segments that match its marketing capabilities.

4   Explain the geographic, demographic, and psychographic approaches to segmenting consumer markets.

Geographic segmentation divides the overall market into homogeneous groups according to population locations. Demographic segmentation classifies the market into groups based on characteristics such as age, gender, and income level. Psychographic segmentation uses behavioral profiles developed from analyses of consumers' activities, opinions, interests, and lifestyles to identify market segments.

5   Describe product-related segmentation.

Product-related segmentation can take three basic forms: segmenting based on the benefits that people seek when they buy a product; segmenting based on usage rates for a product; and segmenting according to consumers' brand loyalty toward a product.

6   Identify the steps in the market segmentation process.

Market segmentation is the division of markets into relatively homogeneous groups. Segmentation follows a four-step sequence: (1) developing user profiles, (2) forecasting the overall market potential, (3) estimating market share, and (4) selecting specific market segments.

7   Discuss four basic strategies for reaching target markets.

Four strategies are (1) undifferentiated marketing, which uses a single marketing mix; (2) differentiated marketing, which produces numerous products, each with its own mix; (3) concentrated marketing, which directs all the firm's marketing resources toward a small segment; and (4) micromarketing, which targets potential customers at basic levels, such as zip code or occupation.

8   Summarize the types of positioning strategies, and explain the reasons for positioning and repositioning products.

Positioning strategies include positioning a good or service according to attributes, price/quality, competitors, application, product user, and product class.

 assessment check **answers**

1.1   Define *target market.*
A target market is the specific segment of consumers most likely to purchase a particular product.

1.2   Distinguish between a consumer product and a business product.
A consumer product is purchased by the ultimate buyer for personal use. A business product is purchased for use directly or indirectly in the production of other goods and services.

2.1   Define *market segmentation.*
Market segmentation is the process of dividing a total market into several homogeneous groups.

2.2   Describe the role of market segmentation.
The role of market segmentation is to identify the factors that affect purchase decisions and then group consumers according to the presence or absence of these factors.

3.1   Identify the four criteria for effective segmentation.
The four criteria for effective segmentation are as follows: (1) the market segment must present measurable purchasing power and size, (2) marketers must find a way to promote effectively and to serve the market segment, (3) marketers must identify segments that are sufficiently large to give them good profit potential, and (4) the firm must aim for segments that match its marketing capabilities.

assessment check **answers**

4.1   Under what circumstances are marketers most likely to use geographic segmentation?

Marketers usually use geographic segmentation when regional preferences exist and when demand for categories of goods and services varies according to geographic region.

4.2   What is demographic segmentation?

Demographic segmentation defines consumer groups according to demographic variables such as gender, age, income, occupation, household, and family life cycle.

4.3   What are the major categories of demographic segmentation?

The major categories of demographic segmentation are gender, age, ethnic group, family life cycle, household type, income, and expenditure patterns.

4.4   What is psychographic segmentation?

Psychographic segmentation divides a population into groups that have similar psychological characteristics, values, and lifestyles.

4.5   Name the eight psychographic categories of U.S. VALS.

The eight categories are the following: actualizers, thinkers, achievers, experiencers, believers, strivers, makers, and survivors.

5.1   List the three approaches to product-related segmentation.

The three approaches are segmenting by benefits sought, segmenting by usage rates, and segmenting by brand loyalty.

5.2   What is the 80/20 principle?

The 80/20 principle states that a big percentage (80 percent) of a product's revenues comes from a relatively small number (20 percent) of loyal customers.

6.1   Identify the four stages of market segmentation.

The four stages are developing user profiles, forecasting the overall market potential, estimating market share, and selecting specific market segments.

6.2   Why is forecasting important to market segmentation?

Forecasting is important because it can define a preliminary go or no-go decision based on sales potential. It can help a firm avoid a disastrous move or point out opportunities.

7.1   Explain the difference between undifferentiated and differentiated marketing strategies.

Undifferentiated marketing promotes a single product line to all customers with a single marketing mix. Differentiated marketing promotes numerous products with different marketing mixes designed to satisfy smaller segments.

7.2   What are the benefits of concentrated marketing?

Concentrated marketing can allow a firm to focus on a single market segment, which is especially appealing to smaller firms and those that offer highly specialized goods and services.

8.1   What are the four determinants of a market-specific strategy?

The four determinants are company resources, product homogeneity, stage in the product life cycle, and competitors' strategies.

8.2   What is the role of positioning in a marketing strategy?

Positioning places a product in a certain position in the minds of prospective buyers so that marketers can create messages that distinguish their offerings from those of competitors.

MARKETING TERMS YOU NEED TO KNOW

market 280
target market 280
consumer products 280
business products 280
market segmentation 281

geographic segmentation 283
demographic segmentation 287
psychographic segmentation 295
product-related segmentation 298
undifferentiated marketing 301

differentiated marketing 301
concentrated marketing 302
micromarketing 302
positioning 303

OTHER IMPORTANT MARKETING TERMS

core based statistical area (CBSA) 285
metropolitan statistical area (MSA) 285
micropolitan statistical area 286
consolidated metropolitan statistical area
    (CMSA) 286
primary metropolitan statistical area
    (PMSA) 286

core region 286
geographic information system (GIS) 286
cohort effect 288
9/11 Generation 288
baby boomers 289
family life cycle 293
Engel's laws 294

AIO statements 296
VALS 296
80/20 principle 298
niche marketing 302
positioning map 303
repositioning 303

ASSURANCE OF LEARNING REVIEW

1. What is the difference between a market and a target market?
2. What are core regions? Why do marketers try to identify these regions?
3. What is the cohort effect? What event—or events—do you consider significant enough to have influenced and bound together your generation?
4. What are the two largest racial/ethnic minority groups in the United States? Why is it important for marketers to understand these and other ethnic/racial groups?
5. Describe the three changes that will take place as a household income increases, according to Engel. Do Engel's laws still hold true?

6. Identify and describe the six psychographic segments that exist in all 35 nations studied by JapanVALS researchers.
7. Identify a branded product to which you are loyal, and explain why you are loyal to the product. What factors might cause your loyalty to change?
8. Choose another branded product. Create a relevant profile for the marketing segment that product serves.
9. Describe a situation in which you think micromarketing would be especially successful.
10. Under what circumstances might marketers decide to reposition a product?

PROJECTS AND TEAMWORK EXERCISES

1. On your own or with a partner, choose a consumer product that you think could serve a business market. Create an advertisement that shows how the product can serve businesses.
2. Choose your favorite activity—it may be a sport, an artistic pursuit, a volunteer opportunity, or something similar. Then identify the best basis for segmenting the market for this activity. Next, identify your target market. Finally, write a brief plan outlining your strategy for reaching your target market.
3. Find an advertisement that uses product-related segmentation as part of its strategy for reaching consumers. Present the ad to the class, identifying specific aspects of the ad, such as segmenting by benefits sought, segmenting by usage rates, or segmenting by brand loyalty.
4. With a partner, identify a product that you are familiar with that is either niche marketed or micromarketed. How might

the firm's marketers widen the audience for the product? Present your ideas and discuss them in class.
5. On your own or with a classmate, select one of the following products. Visit the firm's Web site to see how the product is positioned. Present your findings to the class, detailing how—and why—the product is positioned the way it is.
   a. Slim-Fast bars and shakes
   b. Tyson chicken nuggets
   c. Kleenex
   d. Starwood Hotels
   e. Roots clothing
   f. Porsche automobiles
6. Now discuss how you might reposition your product—and why. Create an ad illustrating your product's new positioning strategy.

CRITICAL-THINKING EXERCISES

1. Create a profile of yourself as part of a market segment. Include such factors as where you live, your age and gender, and psychographic characteristics.
2. Select one of the following products and explain how you would use segmentation by income and expenditure patterns to determine your targeted market.
   a. Busch Gardens theme parks
   b. Sony Cyber-shot camera
   c. Stouffer's Lean Cuisine
   d. Porsche Boxster

3. How do you think the Internet has affected differentiated marketing techniques?
4. Think of a product that reminds you of your childhood—a particular candy, a toy or game, a television show or movie, or a brand of clothing. Describe how you would reposition that product for today's marketplace. Would you try to appeal to children or a different market segment?

ETHICS EXERCISE

Marketers are making a new pitch to men—at the risk of political incorrectness. Marketers for firms such as Unilever and Wendy's have been frustrated at not being able to reach young male consumers with their messages. After searching for clues about what this crowd likes, these firms have created marketing campaigns designed to grab their attention—perhaps at the expense of other consumers. A spokesperson at ad agency J. Walter Thompson says that means advertising built on "bad boy" attitudes, lowbrow humor, and sex.[62]

1. What are some of the pitfalls of this kind of segmentation?
2. Do you think these ads will be successful in the long run? Why or why not?
3. Should marketers be concerned about offending one market segment when trying to reach another? Why or why not?

INTERNET EXERCISES

1. **How companies segment their markets.** Visit the following companies' Web sites. How does each company segment its markets (such as geographic, product-related, demographic, or brand loyalty)? Does the company use more than one method of product segmentation? Why or why not?
   a. John Deere (http://www.deere.com)
   b. ConAgra Foods (http://www.conagrafoods.com)
   c. Harley-Davidson (http://www.harley-davidson.com)
2. **Demographic and geographic segmentation.** As discussed in the chapter, the U.S. Census Bureau is an important source of data used by marketers when making demographic and geographic segmentation decisions. Visit the Census Bureau's Web site (http://www.census.gov) and click on *People & Households* and then *Estimates*. Use the data to answer the following questions.

   a. Which age groups are expected to grow the fastest (slowest) over the next few years? Which states are expected to grow the fastest (slowest) over the next few years?
   b. Which minority groups are expected to grow the fastest over the next few years? Where is most of this growth expected to be concentrated?
   c. What is the current distribution of the U.S. population by age and sex? How is this distribution expected to change over the next decade?

Note: Internet Web addresses change frequently. If you don't find the exact site listed, you may need to access the organization's home page and search from there or use a search engine such as Google.

CASE 9.1   Golden Boy Enterprises Aims for the Hispanic Market

Oscar De La Hoya isn't Rocky. But his story is true. Now in his mid-thirties, the 1992 Olympic gold medal winner in the welterweight class of boxing is hanging up his gloves and putting on a business suit. His loyal fans say he looks terrific in either outfit, and they are willing to support him in every endeavor.

De La Hoya is as much an entrepreneur as he is a fighter. He intends to make the most of his Hispanic background and culture as a businessman. De La Hoya and his group of investors have plans for restaurants, health clubs, and real estate bearing De La Hoya's name, and they are targeting the rapidly growing Hispanic market. "I understand the Hispanic market," says De La Hoya. "I have lived it." De La Hoya even intends to open a bank with his name tied to it. "There are Asian banks, [and] Cuban banks, [but] no banks for Mexican Americans," he explains.

In its largest project to date, De La Hoya's business firm—called Golden Boy Enterprises, after the nickname given to the boxer when he won his gold medal—recently entered a joint venture with another firm in which the two will invest $100 million over three years in real estate developments in Hispanic areas of southern California. According to the U.S. Census Bureau, Hispanics now comprise one-third of California's total population, and they are expected to become the largest population segment by 2030. The Golden Boy Partners venture intends to refurbish and rebuild old, urban areas to make them safe and family friendly, with all the services available to residents of the suburbs, as well as jobs for local workers. "Golden Boy Partners is not just about real estate development," says De La Hoya. "It is about building communities and changing lives."

Although some marketers compare De La Hoya's business ventures to those of basketball legend Earvin "Magic" Johnson, others contend that De La Hoya has positioned himself differently. Johnson "crossed over to a much wider audience than just African Americans," notes David Carter, a sports marketing consultant. "You see him pushing T.G.I. Friday's, not soul food." De La Hoya, on the other hand, tends to remain focused on the Hispanic audience. Skeptics point out that while the Hispanic market is growing tremendously—its per-capita income is expected to increase more than 8 percent annually over the next few years—Hispanic consumers don't spend as much as other groups. But De La Hoya and his backers don't see this as an obstacle. They believe that if Hispanic consumers have the opportunity to purchase goods and services that are tailored to their preferences, they will do so. "Fighting is what I do," says De La Hoya, whether it's in the boxing ring or in the business arena. And he usually wins.

Questions for Critical Thinking

1. Golden Boy Enterprises segments by geographic region and ethnic group. Can you think of other ways in which De La Hoya's firm might segment its market?
2. What type of strategy would likely be best for reaching De La Hoya's target market? Why?
3. Create a slogan for Golden Boy Enterprises that you think reflects the right positioning for its goods and services.

Sources: Golden Boy Partners Web site, **http://goldenboypartners.com,** accessed April 11, 2006; Michael Mullen, "Oscar De La Hoya Interview," February 4, 2006, **http://videogames.aol.com;** "Team De La Hoya Hispanic Business," Ahorre.com, August 9, 2005, **http://www.ahorre.com;** "Online Extra: De La Hoya, Battling Businessman," *BusinessWeek,* August 8, 2005, **http://www.businessweek.com;** Ronald Grover, "The Selling of the Golden Boy," *BusinessWeek,* August 8, 2005, pp. 66–67.

VIDEO CASE 9.2   Harley-Davidson Rules the Road by Understanding Its Customers

The written case on Harley-Davidson appears on page VC-11. The recently filmed Harley-Davidson video is designed to expand and highlight the concepts in this chapter and the concepts and questions covered in the written video.

CHAPTER 10

TOP PHOTO: IMAGE COURTESY OF THE ADVERTISING ARCHIVES
BOTTOM PHOTO: CHARLIE ARCHAMBAULT FOR U.S. NEWS AND WORLD REPORT

Best Buy Bets on Customers

Personal computing technology is becoming more and more sophisticated. Most consumers need more and more assistance to make their way through the retail maze. They must decide not only what to buy but how to install and network the equipment. And then there's maintenance and service. With all of these complications, where can customers turn for help?

Best Buy has an answer. The $30 billion consumer electronics retailer has carefully studied its customers, their needs and habits, its own sales figures, census data, and the layout and appearance of its 900-plus stores, and it has formulated an innovative strategy for retaining its nearly 20 percent share of the U.S. and Canadian markets. In the past, says Brad Anderson,

Best Buy's CEO, "We were treating every customer as though they were the same." But its research showed that the company was earning nearly half its sales from 10 percent of its customers. So Best Buy set out to court these big spenders with a new "centricity" approach that customizes the layouts of its stores and the services they offer for five separate categories of customers, which bear people's names.

"Barry" stores cater to the young-professional tech enthusiast with upscale TVs and home theater systems. "Buzz" stores appeal to young gadget lovers and boast game consoles and a big selection of DVDs and CDs set amid inviting-looking black leather chairs. "Jill" stores try to soften the warehouse style of Best Buy's stores

because research showed that female shoppers strongly disliked it. Personal shopping assistants at "Jill" stores are available to walk female customers through the purchase decision. "Ray" stores are pitched at the budget-conscious family man and emphasize flexible financing options, while "Mr. Storefront" locations are specialized for the small-business owner.

The centricity concept, backed by extensive sales and demographic research to identify the best personality for each individual store location, has been overwhelmingly successful. So Best Buy has accelerated its transformation to bring more of its stores into the centricity model sooner. "Barry" stores predominate, but some stores target more than one of the five profiles,

Relationship Marketing and Customer Relationship Management (CRM)

Chapter Objectives

1   Contrast transaction-based marketing with relationship marketing.

2   Identify and explain the four basic elements of relationship marketing, as well as the importance of internal marketing.

3   Identify the three levels of the relationship marketing continuum.

4   Explain how firms can enhance customer satisfaction and how they build buyer–seller relationships.

5   Explain customer relationship management (CRM) and the role of technology in building customer relationships.

6   Describe the buyer–seller relationship in business-to-business marketing and identify the four types of business partnerships.

7   Describe how business-to-business marketing incorporates national account selling, electronic data interchange and Web services, vendor-managed inventories (VMI), CPFaR, managing the supply chain, and creating alliances.

8   Identify and evaluate the most common measurement and evaluation techniques within a relationship marketing program.

such as "Jill and Barry" stores, and a few are designed to appeal to all five at once. Best Buy is even exploring three additional profiles—"Carrie," the young single woman, and "Helen and Charlie," the empty nesters.

The company typically spends hundreds of thousands of dollars per store to redo lighting and fixtures in its physical centricity transformation. But its biggest per-store investments are on training employees in specialized selling and customer relationship techniques and in financial measures that help them gauge for themselves the effectiveness of in-store marketing strategies.

And the customer-centric focus doesn't stop at the stores. The company's inventory and supply system is being revamped to add flexibility that allows stores to stock different goods for their own local markets. The service arm of Best Buy has also been beefed up with the purchase and expansion of the Geek Squad, a 24-hour computer service and sup-

port team. The Geek Squad boasts nearly 10,000 members, who staff Best Buy's in-store service counters and make emergency house calls for fees that range up to about $300 for troubleshooting and repair.

evolution *of a* brand

Opened in 1966 as the Sound of Music, Best Buy adopted its current name in 1983. The Richfield, Minnesota–based chain operated with its warehouse format for many years. But recently the competition in the consumer electronics market has been heating up, especially from the likes of discounter Wal-Mart and direct marketer Dell. So Best Buy's management team decided to focus on something the discount and direct-to-consumer models didn't offer—personalized customer service.

- At the time of writing, Best Buy had converted roughly one-fourth of its stores over to its new

Best Buy's competition is paying attention. Costco has formed a partnership with a company that installs flat-screen TVs and surround-sound systems, Circuit City is testing a variation on Best Buy's "centricity" concept

customer-centric format. Sales at those stores were nearly double that of the other stores in the chain. Do research about Best Buy's conversion to the new models. How many stores are operating as customer-centric stores and how are they doing? What is the company's overall position in its industry now? Was the change in format a good decision in your opinion? Provide your reasons.

- If possible, visit a Best Buy store near you to identify which of the models it uses—Jill, Buzz, Ray, Barry, or Mr. Storefront. While you are there, explore the Geek Squad customer services

in its stores, and Dell is offering higher levels of customer service than ever—for a fee.

But Best Buy has done its homework, and its customers are pleased. Said one visitor to a Minnesota store, "They have the help when you need the help. Over the last few years, it's become the place to go."[1]

Chapter Overview

As Best Buy's success demonstrates, marketing revolves around relationships with customers and with all the business processes involved in identifying and satisfying them. The shift from **transaction-based marketing,** which focuses on short-term, onetime exchanges, to customer-focused relationship marketing is one of the most important trends in marketing today. Companies know that they cannot prosper simply by identifying and attracting new customers; to succeed, they must build loyal, mutually beneficial relationships with both new and existing customers, suppliers, distributors, and employees. This strategy benefits the bottom line because retaining customers costs much less than acquiring new ones. Building and managing long-term relationships between buyers and sellers are the hallmarks of relationship marketing. **Relationship marketing** is the development, growth, and maintenance of cost-effective, high-value relationships with individual customers, suppliers, distributors, retailers, and other partners for mutual benefit over time.

Relationship marketing is based on promises: the promise of low prices, the promise of high quality, the promise of prompt delivery, the promise of superior service. A network of promises—within the organization, between the organization and its supply chain, and between buyer and seller—determines whether a relationship will grow. A firm is responsible for ensuring that it keeps or exceeds the agreements it makes, with the ultimate goal of achieving customer satisfaction.

This chapter examines the reasons organizations are moving toward relationship marketing and customer relationship management, explores the impact this move has on producers of goods and services and their customers, and looks at ways to evaluate customer relationship programs.

transaction-based marketing Buyer and seller exchanges characterized by limited communications and little or no ongoing relationship between the parties.

relationship marketing Development, growth, and maintenance of long-term, cost-effective relationships with individual customers, suppliers, employees, and other partners for mutual benefit.

---

1 Contrast transaction-based marketing with relationship marketing.

THE SHIFT FROM TRANSACTION–BASED MARKETING TO RELATIONSHIP MARKETING

Since the Industrial Revolution, most manufacturers have run production-oriented operations. They have focused on making products and then promoting them to customers in the hope of selling enough to cover costs and earn profits. The emphasis has been on individual sales or transactions. In transaction-based marketing, buyer and seller exchanges are characterized by limited communications and little or no ongoing relationships. The primary goal is to entice a buyer to make a purchase through such inducements as low price, convenience, or packaging. The goal is simple and short term: Sell something—now.

Some marketing exchanges remain largely transaction based. In residential real estate sales, for example, the primary goal of the agent is to make a sale and collect a commission. While the agent may seek to maintain the appearance of an ongoing buyer–seller relationship, in most cases, the possibility of future transactions is fairly limited. The best an agent can hope for is to represent the seller again in a subsequent real-estate deal that may be several years down the line or, more likely, to gain positive referrals to other buyers and sellers.

Today, many organizations have embraced an alternative approach. Relationship marketing views customers as equal partners in buyer–seller transactions. By motivating customers to enter a long-term relationship in which they repeat purchases or buy multiple brands from the firm, mar-

keters obtain a clearer understanding of customer needs over time. This process leads to improved goods or customer service, which pays off through increased sales and lower marketing costs. In addition, marketers have discovered that it is less expensive to retain satisfied customers than it is to attract new ones or to repair damaged relationships.

The move from transactions to relationships is reflected in the changing nature of the interactions between customers and sellers. In transaction-based marketing, exchanges with customers are generally sporadic and in some instances disrupted by conflict. As interactions become relationship oriented, however, conflict changes to cooperation, and infrequent contacts between buyers and sellers become ongoing exchanges.

As Figure 10.1 illustrates, relationship marketing emphasizes cooperation rather than conflict between

© SCOTT OLSON/GETTY IMAGES

The Coca-Cola Company emphasizes the importance of close relationships with its customers, who are increasingly concerned about childhood obesity. The company offers low-calorie drinks, juices, sports drinks, and waters in its product lineup and has modified its promotional activities in response to customer feedback.

all of the parties involved. This ongoing collaborative exchange creates value for both parties and builds customer loyalty. Customer relationship management goes a step further and integrates the customer's needs into all aspects of the firm's operations and its relationships with suppliers, distributors, and strategic partners. It combines people, processes, and technology with the long-term goal of maximizing customer value through mutually satisfying interactions and transactions.

Twenty-first-century marketers now understand that they must do more than simply create products and then sell them. With so many goods and services to choose from, customers look for added value from their marketing relationships. Owners of GM cars enrolled in the OnStar program, for instance, now get not only the vehicle with their purchase but also the benefits of OnStar's free Vehicle Diagnostics feature, now standard on all GM vehicles. Vehicle Diagnostics operates through OnStar's cellular-based system to perform checkups remotely and let customers know the status of their engine and transmission, air bags, and antilock brakes, as well as when to come in for an oil change or a recall. Says GM North America's vice president of vehicle sales, service, and marketing, "OnStar is not a program, it's a philosophy."[2] Not to be left out,

figure 10.1

Forms of Buyer–Seller Interactions from Conflict to Integration

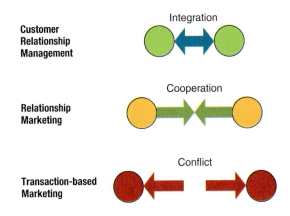

Customer Relationship Management — Integration

Relationship Marketing — Cooperation

Transaction-based Marketing — Conflict

Volvo offers an extensive Aftersales program aimed at increasing parts and service business at Volvo retailers. The Volvo Aftersales Challenge offers awards and incentives to increase dealer participation in this relationship marketing program.[3]

In general, the differences between the narrow focus of transaction marketing and the much broader view of relationship marketing can be summarized as follows:

Relationship marketing:

- focuses on the long term rather than the short term

- emphasizes retaining customers over making a sale

- ranks customer service as a high priority

- encourages frequent customer contact

- fosters customer commitment with the firm

- bases customer interactions on cooperation and trust

- commits all employees to provide high-quality products

As a result, the buyer–seller bonds developed in a relationship marketing partnership last longer and cover a much wider scope than those developed in transaction marketing.

 assessment check

1. **What are the major differences between transaction-based marketing and relationship marketing?**

ELEMENTS OF RELATIONSHIP MARKETING

2 Identify and explain the four basic elements of relationship marketing, as well as the importance of internal marketing.

To build long-term customer relationships, marketers need to place customers at the center of their efforts. When a company integrates customer service and quality with marketing, the result is a relationship marketing orientation.

But how do firms achieve these long-term relationships? They build them with four basic elements.

1. They gather information about their customers. Database technology, discussed later in this chapter, helps a company identify current and potential customers with selected demographic, purchase, and lifestyle characteristics.

2. They analyze the data they have collected and use it to modify their marketing mix to deliver differentiated messages and customized marketing programs to individual consumers.

3. Through relationship marketing, they monitor their interactions with customers. They can then assess the customer's level of satisfaction or dissatisfaction with their service. Marketers can also calculate the cost of attracting one new customer and figure out how much profit that customer will generate during the relationship. Information is fed back, and they are then able to seek ways to add value to the buyer–seller transaction so that the relationship will continue.

4. With customer relationship management (CRM) software, they use intimate knowledge of customers and customer preferences to orient every part of the organization, including both its internal and external partners, toward building a unique company differentiation that is based on strong, unbreakable bonds with customers. Sophisticated technology and the Internet help make that happen.

INTERNAL MARKETING

The concepts of customer satisfaction and relationship marketing are usually discussed in terms of **external customers**—people or organizations that buy or use a firm's goods or services. But marketing in organizations concerned with customer satisfaction and long-term relationships must also address **internal customers**—employees or departments within the organization whose success depends on the work of other employees or departments. A person processing an order for a new piece of equipment is the internal customer of the salesperson who completed the sale, just as the person who bought the product is the salesperson's external customer. Although the order processor might never directly encounter an external customer, his or her performance can have a direct impact on the overall value the firm is able to deliver.

Internal marketing involves managerial actions that enable all members of an organization to understand, accept, and fulfill their respective roles in implementing a marketing strategy. Good internal customer satisfaction helps organizations attract, select, and retain outstanding employees who appreciate and value their role in the delivery of superior service to external customers. With time to market growing ever shorter, Procter & Gamble, for instance, has to make sure that collaboration and the sharing of information among its more than 100,000 employees—and between them and suppliers, distributors, and retailers—is as quick and easy as possible. The company recently adopted a five-product package of Microsoft software that includes instant messaging, a document-sharing program, and a conference service in order to maximize these internal communications.[4]

Sharing information between more than 100,000 employees internationally can be a daunting task in internal marketing. Procter & Gamble is known worldwide for making internal marketing a priority of each aspect of their business.

Employee knowledge and involvement are important goals of internal marketing. Companies that excel at satisfying customers typically place a priority on keeping employees informed about corporate goals, strategies, and customer needs. Employees must also have the necessary tools to address customer requests and problems in a timely manner. Companywide computer networks aid the flow of communications between departments and functions. Several companies—such as Procter & Gamble—also include key suppliers on their networks to speed and ease communication of all aspects of business from product design to inventory control.

Employee satisfaction is another critical objective of internal marketing. Employees can seldom, if ever, satisfy customers when they themselves are unhappy. Dissatisfied employees are likely to spread negative word-of-mouth messages to relatives, friends, and acquaintances, and these reports can affect purchasing behavior. Satisfied employees buy their employer's products, tell friends and families how good the customer service is, and ultimately send a powerful message to customers. One recommended strategy for offering consistently good service is to attract good employees, hire good employees, and retain good employees.[5] Nordstrom, renowned for its world-class customer service, relies on empowering its salespeople with the freedom to make decisions and the management support to back them up. Putting yourself "in the shoes of the customer" is not a strategy for Nordstrom; it's a way of life. Says Robert Spector, who coauthored a best-selling book about Nordstrom's customer service, "At Nordstrom, . . . they're not in the apparel business, shoe business, or cosmetic business, they're in the customer business."[6]

Briefly
Speaking

"The team that trusts—their leader and each other—is more likely to be successful."

—Mike Krzyzewski (b. 1947)
Basketball coach, Duke University

 assessment check

1. **What are the four basic elements of relationship marketing?**
2. **Why is internal marketing important to a firm?**

THE RELATIONSHIP MARKETING CONTINUUM

3 Identify the three levels of the relationship marketing continuum.

Like all other interpersonal relationships, buyer–seller relationships function at a variety of levels. As an individual or firm progresses from the lowest level to the highest level on the continuum of relationship marketing, as shown in Table 10.1, the strength of commitment between the parties grows. The likelihood of a continuing, long-term relationship grows as well. Whenever possible, marketers

table 10.1 Three Levels of Relationship Marketing

CHARACTERISTIC	LEVEL 1	LEVEL 2	LEVEL 3
Primary bond	Financial	Social	Structural
Degree of customization	Low	Medium	Medium to high
Potential for sustained competitive advantage	Low	Moderate	High
Examples	DaimlerChrysler's 5-year no-interest financing plan	MySpace.com's site design	Barnes & Noble's member program of discounts and special offers online and in stores

Source: Adapted from information in Leonard L. Berry, "Relationship Marketing of Services—Growing Internet, Emerging Perspectives," *Journal of the Academy of Marketing Science,* Fall 1995, p. 240.

want to move their customers along this continuum, converting them from Level 1 purchasers, who focus mainly on price, to Level 3 customers, who receive specialized services and value-added benefits that may not be available from another firm.

FIRST LEVEL: FOCUS ON PRICE

Interactions at the first level of relationship marketing are the most superficial and the least likely to lead to a long-term relationship. In the most prevalent examples of this first level, relationship marketing efforts rely on pricing and other financial incentives to motivate customers to enter into buying relationships with a seller. U.S. automakers have used extensive discounts and sales incentives to attract customers, for instance. In one recent month the industry—led by GM, Ford, and Chrysler—spent nearly $3 billion on incentives. DaimlerChrysler offered five-year no-interest financing on select vehicles, and Chrysler also offered cash back and reduced interest rates, or a bonus on leased cars. Ford matched customers' down payments.[7] Sometimes the price savings appears in the form of service, such as Internet phone provider Vonage's program that provides unlimited long-distance calling or Time Warner's plan that includes free Caller ID. As one industry analyst says, "If someone calls up their phone company and asks for a lower price, the company is now more likely to give them what they want. . . . They would rather keep that customer, even if they're getting a little less money from him."[8]

Although these programs can be attractive to users, they may not create long-term buyer relationships. Because the programs are not customized to the needs of individual buyers, they are easily duplicated by competitors. The lesson is that it takes more than a low price or other financial incentives to create a long-term relationship between buyer and seller.

SECOND LEVEL: SOCIAL INTERACTIONS

As buyers and sellers reach the second level of relationship marketing, their interactions develop on a social level—one that features deeper and less superficial links than the financially motivated first level. Sellers have begun to learn that social relationships with buyers can be very effective marketing tools. Customer service and communication are key factors at this stage.

Social interaction can take many forms. The owner of a local shoe store or dry cleaner might chat with customers about local events. A local wine shop may host a wine-tasting reception. The service department of an auto dealership might call a customer after a repair to see whether the customer is satisfied or has any questions. An investment firm might send holiday cards to all its customers. MySpace.com, the hugely popular social networking site, is all about social interaction. "The secret to our success is our one-to-one relationship with our users," says Chris DeWolfe, co-founder of the service and its CEO. "All the site's features have stemmed from users' requests." Despite the recent acquisition of MySpace by News Corp., DeWolfe says, "We don't plan to change that at all."[9]

THIRD LEVEL: INTERDEPENDENT PARTNERSHIP

At the third level of relationship marketing, relationships are transformed into structural changes that ensure that buyer and seller are true business partners. As buyer and seller work more closely together, they develop a dependence on one another that continues to grow over time. Barnes & Noble maintains a "member program" that rewards members with a 10 percent discount on nearly every item in the store and online, plus member-only special offers and discounts, for a membership fee of $25 a year. Both the store and the customer benefit from the program—the store develops a loyal customer who makes repeat purchases, and the customer gets discounts and other offers that offset the membership fee.[10]

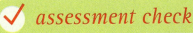
assessment check

1. Identify the three levels of the marketing relationship.
2. Which level is the most complicated? Why?

ENHANCING CUSTOMER SATISFACTION

4 Explain how firms can enhance customer satisfaction and how they build buyer–seller relationships.

Marketers monitor customer satisfaction through various methods of marketing research. As part of an ongoing relationship with customers, marketers must continually measure and improve how well they meet customer needs. As Figure 10.2 shows, three major steps are involved in this process: understanding customer needs, obtaining customer feedback, and instituting an ongoing program to ensure customer satisfaction.

UNDERSTANDING CUSTOMER NEEDS

Knowledge of what customers need, want, and expect is a central concern of companies focused on building long-term relationships. This information is also a vital first step in setting up a system to measure **customer satisfaction.** Marketers must carefully monitor the characteristics of their product that really matter to customers. They also must remain constantly alert to new elements that might affect satisfaction.

Satisfaction can be measured in terms of the gaps between what customers expect and what they perceive they have received. Such gaps can produce favorable or unfavorable impressions. Goods or services may be better or worse than expected. If they are better, marketers can use the opportunity to create loyal customers.

If goods or services are worse than expected, a company may start to lose customers. A survey by the University of Michigan found that Dell's customer satisfaction rating fell more than 6 percent, a big drop for the company that used to head the list of top performers on customer service. The Better Business Bureau logged 23 percent more complaints about Dell in a recent year, and another 5 percent the following year. In the past, dependable customer support has allowed Dell to grow its market share to just below one-third of the U.S. consumer market, helped by low prices and a convenient direct-to-customer sales model. But some observers predict that unhappy customers will spread the word. In the meantime, Dell is improving its service by shortening

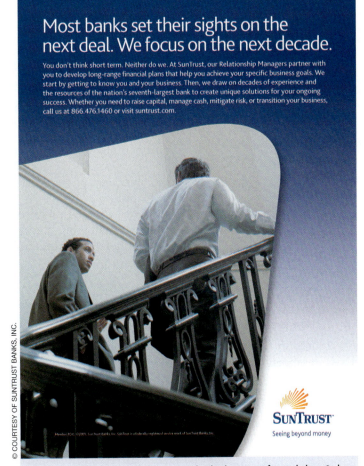

© COURTESY OF SUNTRUST BANKS, INC.

Most banks set their sights on the next deal. We focus on the next decade.

You don't think short term. Neither do we. At SunTrust, our Relationship Managers partner with you to develop long-range financial plans that help you achieve your specific business goals. We start by getting to know you and your business. Then, we draw on decades of experience and the resources of the nation's seventh-largest bank to create unique solutions for your ongoing success. Whether you need to raise capital, manage cash, mitigate risk, or transition your business, call us at 866.476.1460 or visit suntrust.com.

SUNTRUST
Seeing beyond money

SunTrust Banks helps its corporate customers develop long-range financial plans. Such a focus demonstrates a Level 3 marketing relationship—one based on true partnership principles.

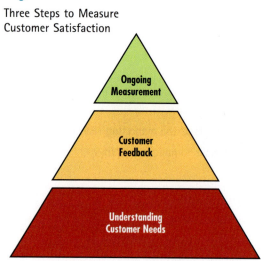

figure 10.2

Three Steps to Measure Customer Satisfaction

Ongoing Measurement

Customer Feedback

Understanding Customer Needs

wait times to speak with a technician, offering remote assistance that lets its technicians access the customer's PC software and fix it, and providing one-year service-desk memberships through which Dell users can customize the level of support they want. However, all these options come with a fee or only with the purchase of a higher-end computer. Even "free shipping" now means shipping to the nearest post office for pickup by the customer.[11]

To avoid unfavorable service gaps, marketers need to keep in touch with the needs of current and potential customers. They must look beyond traditional performance measures and explore the factors that determine purchasing behavior to formulate customer-based missions, goals, and performance standards.

OBTAINING CUSTOMER FEEDBACK AND ENSURING CUSTOMER SATISFACTION

The second step in measuring customer satisfaction is to compile feedback from customers regarding present performance. Increasingly, marketers try to improve customers' access to their companies by including toll-free 800 numbers or Web site addresses in their advertising. Most firms rely on reactive methods of collecting feedback. Rather than solicit complaints, they might, for example, monitor Usenet, other online discussion groups, and popular blogs to track customer comments and attitudes about the value received. Some companies hire mystery shoppers who visit or call businesses posing as customers to evaluate the service they receive. Their unbiased appraisals are usually conducted semiannually or quarterly to monitor employees, diagnose problem areas in customer service, and measure the impact of employee training.

At Oracle's recent Open World conference, CEO Larry Ellison spoke for only fifteen minutes before opening the floor to questions from the customers who attended his keynote address. Applause greeted his promise to look into one client's complaint about a long delay for a call back from customer service. Many were impressed at how well the company had improved its customer relations and image in recent years.[12]

Any method that makes it easier for customers to complain actually benefits a firm. Customer complaints offer firms the opportunity to overcome problems and prove their commitment to service. People often have greater loyalty to a company after a conflict has been resolved than if they had never complained at all.

Many organizations also use proactive methods to assess customer satisfaction, including visiting, calling, or mailing out surveys to clients to find out their level of satisfaction. Companies are also paying more and more attention to the estimated 12 million bloggers on the Internet. U.S. Cellular benefited from the blog watching conducted by its ad agency WPP Group, which helped inspire a new promotion aimed at teenagers. WPP used special technology to identify the demographics of online groups by comparing their speech patterns and discussion topics. The agency found that teen cell phone users resented the fact that incoming calls were charged to their allowable minutes, leading U.S. Cellular to offer unlimited "call me" minutes in its next promotion.[13]

✔ *assessment check*

1. How is customer satisfaction measured?

2. Identify two ways that marketers may obtain customer feedback.

BUILDING BUYER–SELLER RELATIONSHIPS

Marketers of consumer goods and services have discovered that they must do more than simply create products and then sell them. With a dizzying array of products to choose from, many customers are seeking ways to simplify both their business and personal lives, and relationships provide a way to do this.

One reason consumers form continuing relationships is their desire to reduce choices. Through relationships, they can simplify information gathering and the entire buying process as well as decrease the risk of dissatisfaction. They find comfort in brands that have become familiar through their ongoing relationships with companies. Such relationships may lead to more efficient decision making by customers and higher levels of customer satisfaction.

A key benefit to consumers in long-term buyer–seller relationships is the perceived positive value they receive. Relationships add value because of increased opportunities for frequent customers to save money through discounts, rebates, and similar offers; via special recognition from the relationship programs; and through convenience in shopping.

Marketers should also understand why consumers end relationships. Computerized technologies and the Internet have made consumers better informed than ever before by giving them unprecedented abilities to compare prices, merchandise, and customer service. If they perceive that a competitor's product or customer service is better, customers may switch loyalties. Many consumers dislike feeling that they are locked into a relationship with one company, and that is reason enough for them to try a competing item next time they buy. Some customers simply become bored with their current providers and decide to sample the competition.

frequency marketing
Frequent-buyer or user marketing programs that reward customers with cash, rebates, merchandise, or other premiums.

HOW MARKETERS KEEP CUSTOMERS

One of the major forces driving the push from transaction-based marketing to relationship marketing is the realization that retaining customers is far more profitable than losing them. A recent study by research firm Marketing Metrics found that marketers, on average,

- have a 60 to 70 percent chance of selling again to the same customer

- have a 20 to 40 percent chance of winning back an ex-customer

- have only a 5 to 20 percent chance of converting a prospect into a customer[14]

Also, customers usually enable a firm to generate more profits with each additional year of the relationship. A good example of this is the Marriott Rewards program, which now boasts more than 17 million members. Members spend an average of 2.5 times as much at Marriott hotels as nonmembers and account for 40 percent of Marriott's total sales. Members have more than 250 reward options, earning airline miles or points toward hotel stays and merchandise. They can receive 33 percent savings through Marriott Rewards Pointsavers, and during certain time periods they may earn double Marriott rewards or double upgrade points with Hertz.[15]

Programs like Marriott's are an example of **frequency marketing.** These programs reward top customers with cash, rebates, merchandise, or other premiums. Buyers who purchase an item more often earn higher rewards. Frequency marketing focuses on a company's best customers with the goal of increasing their motivation to buy even more of the same or other products from the seller.

rewards that make you feel like a kid in a candy store: priceless

COURTESY OF MASTERCARD INTL.; BLAISE HAYWARD/PHOTOGRAPHER

MasterCard practices frequency marketing by offering a rewards program for use of its card.

affinity marketing Marketing effort sponsored by an organization that solicits responses from individuals who share common interests and activities.

Many different types of companies use frequency programs: fast-food restaurants, retail stores, telecommunications companies, and travel firms. Popular programs include airline frequent-flyer programs, such as Northwest Airlines' WorldPerks, and retail programs, such as Hallmark's Gold Crown Card.

The Internet is proving a fertile medium for frequency marketing initiatives. Borrowing from the airlines' frequent-flyer model, Harrah's Casino has created a Web-based program to reward its frequent customers. About 80 percent of the customers who visit Harrah's properties each day are members of the Total Rewards program. Loyalty cards are swiped on the casino floor to monitor time spent at slot machines or card tables and to total up the sums gambled. A Web site allows members to view their points and learn how to earn more benefits as they gamble their way up to platinum or diamond status. The program also identifies which so-called high rollers yield the highest profits.[16]

In addition to frequency programs, companies use **affinity marketing** to retain customers. Each of us holds certain things dear. Some may feel strongly about Eastern Michigan University, while others admire the Dallas Cowboys or the Chicago White Sox. These examples, along with an almost unending variety of others, are subjects of affinity programs. An affinity program is a marketing effort sponsored by an organization that solicits involvement by individuals who share common interests and activities. With affinity programs, organizations create extra value for members and encourage stronger relationships.

American Express offers an affinity card for golfers and fans of Tiger Woods.

ASSOCIATED PRESS, AP

Affinity credit cards are a popular form of this marketing technique. The sponsor's name appears prominently in promotional materials, on the card itself, and on monthly statements. Bank of America now offers online sign-up for more than 200 affinity credit cards aligned with sports teams, charities, and universities around the country.[17] Starbucks' affinity card offers $10 off the first use in the store and Starbucks credits equal to 1 percent of the cardholder's Visa purchases. With the first Visa purchase, Starbucks makes a $5 donation to the Starbucks Foundation, which benefits a preschool mentoring organization called Jumpstart, among other charities.[18]

Not all affinity programs involve credit cards. WNET, the New York public television station, thanks members who contribute more than $40 a year with a card that entitles them to discounts at participating restaurants, museums, theaters, hotels, and car rental companies.[19]

DATABASE MARKETING

database marketing Use of software to analyze marketing information, identifying and targeting messages toward specific groups of potential customers.

The use of information technology to analyze data about customers and their transactions is referred to as **database marketing.** The results form the basis of new advertising or promotions targeted to carefully identified groups of customers. Database marketing is a particularly effective tool for building relationships because it allows sellers to sort through huge quantities of data from multiple sources on the buying habits or preferences of thousands or even millions of customers. Companies can then track buying patterns, develop customer relationship profiles, customize their offerings and sales promotions, and even personalize customer service to suit the needs of targeted groups of customers. Properly used, databases can help companies in several ways, including these:

- identifying their most profitable customers
- calculating the lifetime value of each customer's business

- creating a meaningful dialogue that builds relationships and encourages genuine brand loyalty

- improving customer retention and referral rates

- reducing marketing and promotion costs

- boosting sales volume per customer or targeted customer group

Where do organizations find all the data that fill these vast marketing databases? Everywhere! Credit card applications, software registration, and product warranties all provide vital statistics of individual customers. Point-of-sale register scanners, customer opinion surveys, and sweepstakes entry forms may offer not just details of name and address but information about preferred brands and shopping habits. Web sites offer free access in return for personal data, allowing companies to amass increasingly rich marketing information.

AOL has built a large marketing database that allows it to e-mail its members with newsletters, real-time messages about member service events, cross-selling and pop-up advertising, and other targeted communications to increase customer retention.[20] Microsoft has a database of information about PCs that are enrolled in its Windows OneCare service, a group of antivirus, firewall, tune-up, and data backup programs available to Windows users. The data includes the frequency with which the user backs up data, changes made to the firewall, and the general "health" of the system, including viruses it encounters. To monitor machines this carefully, OneCare also must identify each individual PC with a specific identifier.[21]

New technologies such as radio frequency identification (RFID) allow retailers to identify shipping pallets and cargo containers, but most observers anticipate that in the near future RFID will be cost effective enough to permit tagging of individual store items, allowing retailers to gather information about the purchaser as well as managing inventory and deterring theft, but raising privacy concerns.[22]

Interactive television promises to deliver even more valuable data—information on real consumer behavior and attitudes toward brands. Linked to digital television, sophisticated set-top boxes such as TiVo and Replay TV already collect vast amounts of data on television viewer behavior, organized in incredible detail. As the technology makes its way into more homes, marketers receive firsthand knowledge of the kind of programming and products their targeted customers want. In addition, rather than using television to advertise to the masses, they can talk directly to the viewers most interested in their products. At a click of a button, viewers can skip ads, but they also can click to a full-length infomercial on any brand that captures their interest. About 75 million U.S. households subscribe to pay television, and about half of them also subscribe to interactive services ranging from home shopping to games.[23]

As database marketing has become more complex, a variety of software tools and services enable marketers to target consumers more and more narrowly while enriching their communications to selected groups. After all, a huge repository of data is not valuable unless it can be turned into information that is useful to a firm's marketers. **Application service providers (ASPs)** assist marketers by providing software when it is needed to capture, manipulate, and analyze masses of consumer data. One type of software collects data on product specifications and details, which marketers can use to isolate products that best meet a customer's needs. This feature would be particularly important in selling business products that are expensive and require high involvement in making a purchase decision. Convio provides such database services to nonprofit organizations that are trying to cultivate a wider base of members and supporters. Convio supplies software and online services designed to help groups such as Easter Seals, the American Diabetes Association, Mothers Against Drunk Driving, the Avon Foundation, museums, and other organizations identify and communicate with contributors. HCI Direct, a large direct marketing company selling hosiery products in the United States, the United Kingdom, and Canada, has about 2 million active customers worldwide. It works with Donnelley Marketing and Yesmail to build a database that allows HCI to conduct offline and one-to-one communication with current and prospective customers.[24]

Firms can also use database marketing to rebuild customer relationships that may have lapsed. NCO Telecommunications Services provides voice, e-mail, and chat capabilities for its corporate clients to help them customize sales and marketing programs to gain new customers and win lost customers back.[25]

Solving an Ethical Controversy

Too Much Data, Not Enough Protection?

Datran Media, a leading e-mail marketer, was accused of making unauthorized use of personal data it "mined" from other unsuspecting firms, including 6 million e-mail addresses of consumers across the country who were then sent unwanted electronic advertising messages. The case, called the largest deliberate breach of Internet privacy so far discovered, was settled with a $1.1 million fine and an agreement that Datran would change its practices.

In another case, the theft of data from Polo Ralph Lauren forced banks and credit card companies to inform about 180,000 MasterCard holders that their credit card information might have been exposed to criminals and to admit that other cards might be at risk. Other companies that have disclosed the theft of customer data include ChoicePoint, DSW Shoe Warehouse, and LexisNexis.

Are marketers doing enough to protect the information they collect about customers?

PRO

1. Marketers are doing the best they can. There is no uniform federal privacy law to guide companies about how to protect data.
2. Companies realize the importance of their databases, but there is little a company can do against a determined thief.

CON

1. Companies are collecting more data than they have the resources to protect. They need to take a hard look at what data they actually need and develop policies to limit data collection.
2. Organizations need to spend more resources to secure valuable customer data. If they can't, the government should regulate how much data can be gathered and the uses companies can make of it.

Summary

The U.S. House Energy and Commerce Committee has unanimously passed legislation that forces data brokers to at least notify the public of security breaches that pose a "reasonable risk" of identify theft and to put effective security in place to prevent unauthorized access to data. Said the committee chair, "Nobody needs to be left in the dark when their data has been compromised by a crook."

Sources: Christopher Wolf, "Dazed and Confused: Data Law Disarray," *BusinessWeek*, April 3, 2006, **http://www.businessweek.com**; Roy Mark, "Data-Breach Disclosure Bill Passes House Panel," Internetnews.com, March 30, 2006, **http://www.internetnews.com**; Michael Gormley, "Firm to Pay $1.1M to Settle E-Mail Case," Associated Press, March 12, 2006, **http://news.yahoo.com**; "Polo Ralph Lauren Customers' Data Stolen," Associated Press, April 14, 2005, **http://story.news.yahoo.com**.

With the ability to gather almost unlimited amounts of customer information comes the responsibility for safeguarding it and protecting customers from unauthorized use. The "Solving an Ethical Controversy" feature provides some insight into the debate over how much protection is enough.

CUSTOMERS AS ADVOCATES

Recent relationship marketing efforts are focusing on turning customers from passive partners into active proponents of a product. **Grassroots marketing** involves connecting directly with existing and potential customers through nonmainstream channels. The grassroots approach relies on marketing strategies that are unconventional, nontraditional, not by the book, and extremely flexible. Grassroots marketing is sometimes characterized by a relatively small budget and lots of legwork, but its hallmark is the ability to develop long-lasting, individual relationships with loyal customers.

With **viral marketing,** firms let satisfied customers get the word about products out to other consumers—like a spreading virus. In the mid-1990s, Hotmail's founders added a simple line of text at the end of every e-mail sent, offering recipients their own free Hotmail accounts. The result brought 8.7 million users in eighteen months, and online viral marketing was born. Video clips are a popular tactic for viral marketing efforts on the Internet, according to a recent survey, and the most popular means of encouraging recipients to spread the news are encouraging them to forward an e-mail and including an easy way to refer others to a Web site, such as a "tell a friend" box to click.[26] Burger King has found viral marketing especially useful in reversing sales declines because it is an effective way to reach the food chain's core target market, young men.[27]

Buzz marketing gathers volunteers to try products and then relies on them to talk about their experiences with their friends and colleagues. "Influencers," or early adopters of products, are ideal carriers of buzz marketing messages because their credibility makes their choices valuable among their peers. They are often recruited online through chat rooms, blogs, and instant messaging. Word-of-mouth, the idea behind buzz marketing, isn't new, but technology has made many more applications possible. Vespa used buzz marketing to introduce its scooters to people who talked about their "cool factor," and Ford lent its Focus cars to drivers for six months, hoping they would make personal recommendations to others.[28] Techniques in this area are still evolving, and the Word of Mouth Marketing Association is developing rules and standards for transparency in buzz marketing efforts that it hopes will prevent fraud and preserve the value of buzz marketing.[29]

CUSTOMER RELATIONSHIP MANAGEMENT

5 Explain customer relationship management (CRM) and the role of technology in building customer relationships.

Emerging from—and closely linked to—relationship marketing, **customer relationship management (CRM)** is the combination of strategies and technologies that empowers relationship programs, reorienting the entire organization to a concentrated focus on satisfying customers. Made possible by technological advances, it leverages technology as a means to manage customer relationships and to integrate all stakeholders into a company's product design and development, manufacturing, marketing, sales, and customer service processes.

CRM represents a shift in thinking for everyone involved with a firm—from the CEO down and encompassing all other key stakeholders, including suppliers, dealers, and other partners. All recognize that solid customer relations are fostered by similarly strong relationships with other major stakeholders. Because CRM goes well beyond traditional sales, marketing, or customer service functions, it requires a top-down commitment and must permeate every aspect of a firm's business. Technology makes that possible by allowing firms—regardless of size and no matter how far-flung their operations—to manage activities across functions, from location to location, and among their internal and external partners.

customer relationship management (CRM) Combination of strategies and tools that drives relationship programs, reorienting the entire organization to a concentrated focus on satisfying customers.

BENEFITS OF CRM

CRM software systems are capable of making sense of the vast amounts of customer data that technology allows firms to collect. Illinois-based Molex makes electrical connectors and was looking for a way to track pending sales to forecast revenue more accurately. With CRM software from the German firm SAP, the company has been able to improve its forecasts dramatically and also set up more efficient workflows, such as identifying sales prospects with preset criteria and routing them to the appropriate area for follow-up.[30]

Another key benefit of customer relationship management systems is that they simplify complex business processes while keeping the best interests of customers at heart. SAP service-industry software also helped Palo Alto, California–based Varian Medical Systems track customer feedback about its medical devices. Thanks to improved technology, both companies seamlessly integrated SAP's software into their existing systems.[31]

DHL EXPRESS, INC., (USA)

1-800-CALL DHL   www.dhl.com

WE EAT, DRINK AND SLEEP YOUR BUSINESS.
THEN WE COME BACK FOR SECONDS.

Customer service is back in shipping.

DHL

With its advertising theme, "Customer Service is back in shipping," package delivery service DHL emphasizes its commitment to forging solid customer relationships.

Selecting the right CRM software system can be critical to the success of a firm's entire CRM program. CRM can be used at three different levels—individual, server-based, and Internet-based— or combine them. Most business applications are server-based (designed for several people to use) or Internet-based (with almost unlimited flexibility and value but some loss of privacy).[32] A firm may choose to buy a system from a company such as SAP or Oracle or rent hosted CRM applications through Web sites such as Salesforce.com or Salesnet. Purchasing a customized system can cost a firm millions of dollars and take months to implement, while hosted solutions—rented through a Web site—are cheaper and quicker to get up and running. But purchasing a system allows a firm to expand and customize, whereas hosted systems are more limited. Experienced marketers also warn that it is easy to get mired in a system that is complicated for staff to use.

Software solutions are just one component of a successful CRM initiative. The most effective companies approach customer relationship management as a complete business strategy, in which people, processes, and technology are all organized around delivering superior value to customers. Successful CRM systems share the following qualities:

- They are results driven. The firm must decide on specific goals and benefits before attempting to implement a CRM strategy.

- They communicate effectively across functions. Effective customer relationship management depends on cross-disciplinary teams, such as sales and customer service, that work together to solve customer problems.

- They are streamlined. A concentrated focus on customers allows firms to weed out wasteful business practices.

- They provide a complete and up-to-date picture of the customer that is easily shared within the company.

- They help identify new markets and sales opportunities.

- They reduce response time and increase customer retention.

- They constantly seek improvement. By tracking and measuring results, firms can continuously improve relationships with customers.[33]

Once the groundwork has been laid, technology solutions drive firms toward a clearer understanding of each customer and his or her needs.

figure 10.3

Annual Customer
Defection Rates

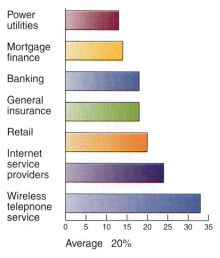

Power utilities

Mortgage finance

Banking

General insurance

Retail

Internet service providers

Wireless telephone service

0   5   10   15   20   25   30   35

Average 20%

Source: Data from Andrew Greenyer, "The Danger of Defection," *CRM Today*, February 17, 2006, http://www.crmtoday.com.

PROBLEMS WITH CRM

CRM is not a magic wand. The strategy needs to be thought out in advance, everyone in the firm must be committed to it, and everyone must understand how to use it. If no one can put the system to work, it is an expensive mistake.

Experts explain that failures with CRM often result from failure to organize—or reorganize—the company's people and business processes to take advantage of the benefits the CRM system can offer. Such planning failures can be prevented by mapping out the organization's existing structure and ensuring that CRM's information flows will be directed to the right employees, who will be trained to use them.[34] Other problems arise when data is not input to the CRM program accurately and on a regular basis. A number of human workflow processes need to be made automatic in order for a CRM system to yield the information it was designed to produce.[35] As one CRM specialist says, "Just reorganizing a company around a new customer focus doesn't mean that a company is doing CRM. Even applying new technologies to enable that customer focus isn't necessarily CRM. CRM is not only changing that focus but changing the business processes around that focus to support a new customer focus, and it's applying technologies to automate those new business processes."[36]

RETRIEVING LOST CUSTOMERS

Customers defect from an organization's goods and services for a variety of reasons. They might be bored, they might move away from the region, they might not need

Etiquette Tips for Marketing Professionals

How to Deal with Rude People

Nearly 70 percent of respondents to a recent poll said that rudeness is on the rise in the United States, spurred by gadgets such as PDAs and cell phones that encourage users to focus on themselves rather than on the people around them. Other factors blamed are the demand for instant gratification, the hurried pace of modern life, and a general decline of formality and rules for behavior. How can you best deal with others who are rude? Here are some tips.

In the office:

- Set the example by always exhibiting thoughtful behavior.

- If someone is rude, control your first reaction, which might be anger or annoyance, and look for some good in the individual, or in the skills or abilities he or she brings to the workplace.

- Remember that everyone has a bad day once in awhile.

- Let the person know, politely and quietly, that rudeness in your firm is counterproductive.

- Ask specific questions about the person's behavior to try to find out the reason for it. It might be a situation you can deal with or change.

In the retail environment:

- Ask polite questions to understand what will best satisfy the customer.

- Immediately and calmly take whatever steps you are authorized to in order to correct the situation that prompted the customer complaint. Refer the problem to a manager if you must.

- After ensuring that you've done everything you can, thank the customer for bringing the situation to your attention.

On the road:

- On your way to the office or a meeting, avoid rush-hour traffic, where aggressive or reckless driving most often occurs.

- Allow plenty of time to get to your destination so you won't be tempted to invite rude behavior with your own anxiety.

Finally:

- Remember that other people's rudeness is not your fault. Don't let their behavior influence yours.

Sources: Peter Murphy, "How to Quickly and Easily Deal with Rude People," Ezine Articles, **http://ezinearticles.com**, accessed April 4, 2006; Loretta Chao, "As Workloads Increase, So Does Office Rudeness," *Wall Street Journal*, January 23, 2006, accessed at **http://www.collegejournal.com**; Donna Cassata, "Poll Shows Rudeness Growing within U.S.," *Morning News*, October 15, 2005, p. 1B.

the product anymore, or they might have tried—and preferred—competing products. Figure 10.3 illustrates the yearly defection rates for some industries. An increasingly important part of an effective CRM strategy is **customer winback,** the process of rejuvenating lost relationships with customers.

In many cases, a relationship gone sour can be sweetened again with the right approach. After the poor customer service ratings mentioned earlier in the chapter, Dell announced plans to open two large new customer service centers to help speed response time and improve the quality of help provided. Survey respondents had indicated that their problems were not with Dell's computers, but with the company's service time and service quality.[37] A good rule for service providers is to anticipate where problems will arise and figure out in advance how to prevent them in the first place. The second part of this strategy is to accept that mistakes will occur in even the best system and to have a high-quality recovery effort in place that employees are empowered to enact.[38]

Sometimes firms may need to change some of their strategies to win back customers or make them more profitable to a seller. To attract baby boom women to its new antiaging cosmetics line, Cover Girl is reintroducing modeling superstar Christie Brinkley, now in her early 50s, who promoted the Cover Girl line for nearly 20 years until 1996. "The Advanced Radiance line is about advanced makeup that delivers beautiful radiance," said the vice president for global cosmetics at Procter & Gamble, which makes Cover Girl products.[39]

One of the easiest ways to lose a customer, or to damage any business relationship, is rudeness. But good manners are a two-way street. The "Etiquette Tips for Marketing Professionals" feature (on page 325) gives some suggestions for salvaging relationships when other people are rude to you.

 assessment check

1. Define *customer relationship management.*
2. What are the two major types of CRM systems?
3. Describe two steps a firm can take to rejuvenate a lost relationship.

6 Describe the buyer–seller relationship in business-to-business marketing and identify the four types of business partnerships.

BUYER–SELLER RELATIONSHIPS IN BUSINESS-TO-BUSINESS MARKETS

Customer relationship management and relationship marketing are not limited to consumer goods and services. Building strong buyer–seller relationships is a critical component of business-to-business marketing as well.

Business-to-business marketing involves an organization's purchase of goods and services to support company operations or the production of other products. Buyer–seller relationships between companies involve working together to provide advantages that benefit both parties. These advantages might include lower prices for supplies, quicker delivery of inventory, improved quality and reliability, customized product features, and more favorable financing terms.

A **partnership** is an affiliation of two or more companies that help each other achieve common goals. Partnerships cover a wide spectrum of relationships from informal cooperative purchasing arrangements to formal production and marketing agreements. In business-to-business markets, partnerships form the basis of relationship marketing.

A variety of common goals motivate firms to form partnerships. Companies may want to protect or improve their positions in existing markets, gain access to new domestic or international markets, or quickly enter new markets. Expansion of a product line—to fill in gaps, broaden the product line, or differentiate the product—is another key reason for joining forces. Other motives include sharing resources, reducing costs, warding off threats of future competition, raising or creating barriers to entry, and learning new skills.

partnership Affiliation of two or more companies that help each other achieve common goals.

 marketing failure   The Perils of Big Partners

Background. LookSmart is an online media company that offers consumers, advertisers, and publishers the ability to find, save, and share articles. Based in San Francisco, the company was happy to count Microsoft among its early customers, in a relationship that accounted for a whopping 70 percent of LookSmart's revenue. Buoyed by the profitable partnership, the company had been growing rapidly and holding its own against rivals Google and Yahoo!. Revenue increased 50 percent a year, and LookSmart's share price tripled in twelve months.

The Marketing Problem. LookSmart's dependence on Microsoft proved to be a mistake. When the software giant suddenly decided not to renew its license for the Web directory that LookSmart markets, the company's stock fell 52 percent in one day.

The Outcome. Revenues are down by more than half, and the company is still struggling to recoup from the loss of its giant customer. LookSmart has not had a profitable quarter since losing Microsoft's business. A new CEO was brought in. He promptly fired the company's senior managers and has been looking for ways to diversify the business and create long-term growth.

CHOOSING BUSINESS PARTNERS

How does an organization decide which companies to select as partners? The first priority is to locate firms that can add value to the relationship—whether through financial resources, contacts, extra manufacturing capacity, technical know-how, or distribution capabilities. The greater the value added, the greater the desirability of the partnership. In many cases, the attributes of each partner complement those of the other; each firm brings something to the relationship that the other party needs but cannot provide on its own. Other partnerships join firms with similar skills and resources to reduce costs.

Organizations must share similar values and goals for a partnership to succeed in the long run. McDonald's formed a congenial partnership with Wild Planet, for instance, and gave away Spy Gear and Mighty Kids Happy Meals during a short promotion based on the Wild Planet toy lines. "We chose McDonald's specifically because they share our audience and offer unparalleled exposure to opportunities," said Wild Planet's Spy Gear brand manager.[40]

TYPES OF PARTNERSHIPS

Companies form four key types of partnerships in business-to-business markets: buyer, seller, internal, and lateral partnerships. This section briefly examines each category.

In a **buyer partnership,** a firm purchases goods and services from one or more providers. Jet-Blue Airways purchased spa products from Bliss, the international spa and beauty product firm, to give away on its redeye flights between the West and East Coast. The kits contain eye masks, ear plugs, moisturizer, lip balm, and a Bliss promotional offer. JetBlue recently ranked first in airline quality in a national survey. "They've always moved in a different direction," said an aviation industry watcher. "That's why they've stayed alive. This is another out-of-the-box marketing play. It cost them almost nothing, and it gets people to think JetBlue."[41]

When a company assumes the buyer position in a relationship, it has a unique set of needs and requirements that vendors must meet to make the relationship successful. Although buyers want sellers to provide fair prices, quick delivery, and high quality levels, a lasting relationship often requires more effort. To induce a buyer to form a long-term partnership, a supplier must also be responsive to the purchaser's unique needs. Buyer relationships can be particularly risky when the seller is small and the buyer is very large, as LookSmart found in its partnership with Microsoft (see the "Marketing Failure" feature).

Seller partnerships set up long-term exchanges of goods and services in return for cash or other consideration. Sellers, too, have specific needs as partners in ongoing relationships. Most prefer to develop long-term relationships with their partners. Sellers also want prompt payment.

The importance of **internal partnerships** is widely recognized in business today. The classic definition of the word *customer* as the buyer of a good or service is now more carefully defined in

"One of our ironclad rules is 'Never do business with anybody you don't like.' If you don't like somebody, there's a reason. Chances are it's because you don't trust him and you're probably right. I don't care who he is or what guarantees you get— cash in advance or whatever. If you do business with somebody you don't like, sooner or later you'll get screwed."

–Harry V. Quadracci
(1936–2002)
American entrepreneur and founder of Quad/Graphics

Briefly
Speaking

Lessons Learned. The new CEO has promised never again to rely on one customer for such a large portion of the company's business. "It is critical that we are organized in a way that lets us move quickly and have leaders who can set a tone of performance, speed and urgency," he said. "I believe we have accomplished this and we will be in better shape to realize the company's goals."

Sources: LookSmart Web site, **http://www.looksmart.com**, accessed April 27, 2006; "Interchange Corporation Chooses LookSmart's Furl to Power Local.com's Page Saving and Archiving System," Business Wire, accessed at **http://www.findarticles.com**, December 13, 2005; Kurt Badenhausen, "Your Big Best Friend—or Not," *Forbes*, October 31, 2005, pp. 182–184; Matt Hicks, "LookSmart Hits More Financial Snags," *eWeek*, accessed at **http://www.findarticles.com**, January 2005.

© BARRY SWEET/BLOOMBERG NEWS/LANDOV

A prime example of a comarketing relationship is the Starbucks coffee bars that are located in Barnes & Noble bookstores.

terms of external customers. However, customers within an organization also have their own needs. Internal partnerships are the foundation of an organization and its ability to meet its commitments to external entities. If the purchasing department selects a parts vendor that fails to ship on the dates required by manufacturing, production will halt, and products will not be delivered to customers as promised. As a result, external customers will likely seek other more reliable suppliers. Without building and maintaining internal partnerships, an organization will have difficulty meeting the needs of its external partnerships.

Lateral partnerships include strategic alliances with other companies or with not-for-profit organizations and research alliances between for-profit firms and colleges and universities. The relationship focuses on external entities—such as customers of the partner firm—and involves no direct buyer–seller interactions. Strategic alliances are discussed in a later section of this chapter.

COBRANDING AND COMARKETING

Two other types of business marketing relationships include cobranding and comarketing. **Cobranding** joins two strong brand names, perhaps owned by two different companies, to sell a product. The automotive world is packed with cobranded vehicles. A car buyer can pick up the Columbia Edition of the Jeep Liberty and wear home a new Columbia ski jacket in the bargain. Subaru and L. L. Bean have a multiyear agreement in which Subaru becomes the official car of the outdoor retail giant, featured at L. L. Bean stores and in its catalogs. Eddie Bauer markets a special edition of the Ford Expedition. Stella McCartney by Adidas is the newest cobranded sportswear collection, using style and practicality to achieve marketing success neither brand might have done so well or so quickly on its own.[42]

In a **comarketing** effort, two organizations join to sell their products in an allied marketing campaign. Wal-Mart Stores is transferring its online DVD rental business to market leader Netflix, offering its customers the chance to continue their Wal-Mart subscriptions with Netflix at their current price. In return, Netflix will remind subscribers to its own service that they can purchase DVDs from Wal-Mart's online store, Walmart.com.[43]

cobranding Cooperative arrangement in which two or more businesses team up to closely link their names on a single product.

comarketing Cooperative arrangement in which two businesses jointly market each other's products.

IMPROVING BUYER–SELLER RELATIONSHIPS IN BUSINESS-TO-BUSINESS MARKETS

Organizations that know how to find and nurture partner relationships, whether through informal deals or contracted partnerships, can enhance revenues and increase profits. Partnering often leads to lower prices, better products, and improved distribution, resulting in higher levels of customer satisfaction. Partners who know each other's needs and expectations are more likely to satisfy them and forge stronger long-term bonds. Often partnerships can be cemented through personal relationships, no matter where firms are located.

In the past, business relationships were conducted primarily in person, over the phone, or by mail. Today, businesses are using the latest electronic, computer, and communications technology to link up. E-mail, the Internet, and other telecommunications services allow businesses to communicate anytime and anyplace. Chapter 4 discussed the business role of the Internet in detail. The following sections explore other ways that buyers and sellers cooperate in business-to-business markets.

NATIONAL ACCOUNT SELLING

Some relationships are more important than others due to the large investments at stake. Large manufacturers such as Procter & Gamble and Clorox pay special attention to the needs of major retailers such as Wal-Mart and Target. Manufacturers use a technique called **national account selling** to serve their largest, most profitable customers. The large collection of supplier offices in northwestern Arkansas—near Wal-Mart's home office—suggests how national account selling might be implemented. These offices are usually called *teams* or *support teams.*

The advantages of national account selling are many. By assembling a team of individuals to serve just one account, the seller demonstrates the depth of its commitment to the customer. The buyer–seller relationship is strengthened as both collaborate to find solutions that are mutually beneficial. Finally, cooperative buyer–seller efforts can bring about dramatic improvements in both efficiency and effectiveness for both partners. These improvements find their way to the bottom line in the form of decreased costs and increased profits.

BUSINESS-TO-BUSINESS DATABASES

As noted earlier, databases are indispensable tools in relationship marketing. They are also essential in building business-to-business relationships. Using information generated from sales reports, scanners, and many other sources, sellers can create databases that help guide their own efforts and those of buyers who resell products to final users.

ELECTRONIC DATA INTERCHANGE AND WEB SERVICES

Technology has transformed the ways in which companies control their inventories and replenish stock. Gone are the days when a retailer would notice stocks were running low, call the vendor, check prices, and reorder. Today's **electronic data interchanges (EDIs)** automate the entire process. EDI involves computer-to-computer exchanges of invoices, orders, and other business documents. It allows firms to reduce costs and improve efficiency and competitiveness. Retailers such as Wal-Mart, Dillard's, and Lowe's all require vendors to use EDI as a core **quick-response merchandising** tool. Quick-response merchandising is a just-in-time strategy that reduces the time merchandise is held in inventory, resulting in substantial cost savings. RFID Expediter uses electronic data interchange to send required shipping documents to the Department of Defense's (DoD) electronic network. The program allows DoD suppliers to fully meet government requirements for custom-coded cases and pallets shipped to DoD depots without having to invest in RFID technology themselves.[44] An added advantage of EDI is that it opens new channels for gathering marketing information that is helpful in developing long-term business-to-business relationships.

Web services provide a way for companies to communicate even if they are not running the same or compatible software, hardware, databases, or network platforms. Companies in a customer–supplier relationship, or a partnership such as airlines and car rental firms, may have difficulty getting their computer systems to work together or exchange data easily. Web services are platform-independent information exchange systems that use the Internet to allow interaction between the firms. They are usually simple, self-contained applications that can handle functions from the simple to the complex.[45]

VENDOR-MANAGED INVENTORY

The proliferation of electronic communication technologies and the constant pressure on suppliers to improve response time have led to another way for buyers and sellers to do business. **Vendor-managed inventory (VMI)** has replaced buyer-managed inventory in many instances. It is an inventory management system in which the seller—based on an existing agreement with the buyer—

---

7 Describe how business-to-business marketing incorporates national account selling, electronic data interchange and Web services, vendor-managed inventories (VMI), CPFaR, managing the supply chain, and creating alliances.

electronic data interchange (EDI) Computer-to-computer exchanges of invoices, orders, and other business documents.

vendor-managed inventory (VMI) Inventory management system in which the seller—based on an existing agreement with a buyer—determines how much of a product is needed.

determines how much of a product a buyer needs and automatically ships new supplies to that buyer. The entertainment division of Mosaic, a sales and marketing company, provides vendor-managed inventory services to its motion picture studio clients, handling in-store merchandising and restocking of DVDs in outlets such as Target, Wal-Mart, and Best Buy.[46]

Some firms have modified VMI to an approach called **collaborative planning, forecasting, and replenishment (CPFaR).** This approach is a planning and forecasting technique involving collaborative efforts by both purchasers and vendors. TruServ, the wholesale hardware cooperative owned by 6,200 independent True Value retailers, relies on its 50 trading partners to use computer-assisted ordering. At the company's twelve distribution centers, inventory has been reduced from $600 to $250 million, while service levels have climbed above 97 percent. Shorter lead times, more accurate forecasting, and faster reactions to marketplace trends are other benefits TruServ has realized from its CPFaR program.[47]

MANAGING THE SUPPLY CHAIN

supply chain Sequence of suppliers that contribute to the creation and delivery of a good or service.

Good relationships between businesses require careful management of the **supply chain,** sometimes called the *value chain*, which is the entire sequence of suppliers that contribute to the creation and delivery of a product. This process affects both upstream relationships between the company and its suppliers and downstream relationships with the product's end users. The supply chain is discussed in greater detail in Chapter 13.

Effective supply chain management can provide an important competitive advantage for a business marketer that results in the following:

- increased innovation

- decreased costs

- improved conflict resolution within the chain

- improved communication and involvement among members of the chain

By coordinating operations with the other companies in the chain, boosting quality, and improving its operating systems, a firm can improve speed and efficiency. Because companies spend considerable resources on goods and services from outside suppliers, cooperative relationships can pay off in many ways.

BUSINESS-TO-BUSINESS ALLIANCES

Strategic alliances are the ultimate expression of relationship marketing. A **strategic alliance** is a partnership formed to create a competitive advantage. These more formal long-term partnership arrangements improve each partner's supply chain relationships and enhance flexibility in operating in today's complex and rapidly changing marketplace. The size and location of strategic partners are not important. Strategic alliances include businesses of all sizes, of all kinds, and in many locations; it is what each partner can offer the other that is important.

Companies can structure strategic alliances in two ways. Alliance partners can establish a new business unit in which each takes an ownership position. In such a joint venture, one partner might own 40 percent, while the other owns 60 percent. Alternatively, the partners may decide to form a cooperative relationship that is less formal and does not involve ownership—for example, a joint new-product design team. The cooperative alliance can operate more flexibly and can change more easily as market forces or other conditions dictate. In either arrangement, the partners agree in advance on the skills and resources that each will bring into the alliance to achieve their mutual objectives and gain a competitive advantage. Resources typically include patents, product lines, brand equity, product and market knowledge, company and brand image, and reputation for product quality, innovation, or customer service. Relationships with customers and suppliers are also desirable resources, as are a convenient manufacturing facility, economies of scale and scope, information technology, and a large sales force. Skills that alliance partners can contribute include marketing skills such as innovation and product development, manufacturing skills including low-cost or flexible manufacturing, and planning and research and development expertise.

Companies form many types of strategic alliances. Some create horizontal alliances between firms at the same level in the supply chain; others define vertical links between firms at adjacent stages. The firms may serve the same or different industries. Alliances can involve cooperation among rivals who are market leaders or between a market leader and a follower. IBM helped the All England Lawn Tennis and Croquet Club improve the way the press and photographers sent copy and photographs from the Wimbledon matches to their editors' sports desks, using onsite workstations equipped to allow instant transfers of words and pictures from courtside. To design and implement the wireless networking facilities it needed, IBM formed a strategic alliance with Cisco Systems.[48]

 assessment check

1. Name four technologies businesses can use to improve buyer–seller relationships in B2B markets.

2. What are the benefits of effective supply chain management?

EVALUATING CUSTOMER RELATIONSHIP PROGRAMS

8 Identify and evaluate the most common measurement and evaluation techniques within a relationship marketing program.

One of the most important measures of relationship marketing programs, whether in consumer or business-to-business markets, is the **lifetime value of a customer.** This concept can be defined as the revenues and intangible benefits such as referrals and customer feedback that a customer brings to the seller over an average lifetime, less the amount the company must spend to acquire, market to, and serve the customer. Long-term customers are usually more valuable assets than new ones because they buy more, cost less to serve, refer other customers, and provide valuable feedback. The "average lifetime" of a customer relationship depends on industry and product characteristics. Customer lifetime for a consumer product such as microwave pizza may be very short, while that for an automobile or computer will last longer.

For a simple example of a lifetime value calculation, assume that a Chinese takeout restaurant determines that its average customer buys dinner twice a month at an average cost of $25 per order over a lifetime of five years. That business translates this calculation to revenues of $600 per year and $3,000 for five years. The restaurant can calculate and subtract its average costs for food, labor, and overhead to arrive at the per-customer profit. This figure serves as a baseline against which to measure strategies to increase the restaurant's sales volume, customer retention, or customer referral rate.

Another approach is to calculate the payback from a customer relationship, or the length of time it takes to break even on customer acquisition costs. Assume that an Internet service provider spends $75 per new customer on direct mail and enrollment incentives. Based on average revenues per subscriber, the company takes about three months to recover that $75. If an average customer stays with the service 32 months and generates $800 in revenues, the rate of return is nearly eleven times the original investment. Once the customer stays past the payback period, the provider should make a profit on that business.

In addition to lifetime value analysis and payback, companies use many other techniques to evaluate relationship programs, including the following:

- tracking rebate requests, coupon redemption, credit card purchases, and product registrations

- monitoring complaints and returned merchandise and analyzing why customers leave

- reviewing reply cards, comment forms, and surveys

- monitoring "click-through" behavior on Web sites to identify why customers stay and why they leave

These tools give the organization information about customer priorities so that managers can make changes to their systems, if necessary, and set appropriate, measurable goals for relationship programs.

One writer suggests that in developing the kind of loyalty that makes lifetime customers valuable, attracting the right buyers is just as important as treating them well. Lexus, for example, targets

lifetime value of a customer Revenues and intangible benefits such as referrals and customer feedback that a customer brings to the seller over an average lifetime, less the amount the company must spend to acquire, market to, and service the customer.

former owners of Mercedes and Cadillac cars, while Infiniti, with its focus on fashion and high performance, looks for younger drivers of sporty BMWs and Jaguars. Because these drivers are less loyal to car companies in general, the Infiniti repurchase rate is about 42 percent compared with 63 percent for the Lexus. Lexus is marketed to older drivers more attracted to long-term values such as service and reliability in the first place.[49]

A hotel chain may set a goal of improving the rate of repeat visits from 44 to 52 percent. A mail-order company may want to reduce time from 48 to 24 hours to process and mail orders. If a customer survey reveals late flight arrivals as the number one complaint of an airline's passengers, the airline might set an objective of increasing the number of on-time arrivals from 87 to 93 percent.

Companies large and small can implement technology to help measure the value of customers and the return on investment from expenditures developing customer relationships. They can choose from among a growing number of software products, many of which are tailored to specific industries or flexible enough to suit companies of varying sizes.

✓ *assessment check*

1. Define *lifetime value of a customer.*

2. Why are customer complaints valuable to evaluating customer relationship programs?

Strategic Implications of Marketing in the 21st Century

A focus on relationship marketing helps companies create better ways to communicate with customers and develop long-term relationships. This focus challenges managers to develop strategies that closely integrate customer service, quality, and marketing functions. By leveraging technology—both through database marketing and through customer relationship management applications—companies can compare the costs of acquiring and maintaining customer relationships with the profits received from these customers. This information allows managers to evaluate the potential returns from investing in relationship marketing programs.

Relationships include doing business with consumers as well as partners, such as vendors, suppliers, and other companies. Partners can structure relationships in many different ways to improve performance, and these choices vary for consumer and business markets. In all marketing relationships, it is important to build shared trust. For long-term customer satisfaction and success, marketers must make—and keep—their promises.

REVIEW OF CHAPTER OBJECTIVES

1 **Contrast transaction-based marketing with relationship marketing.**

Transaction-based marketing refers to buyer–seller exchanges characterized by limited communications and little or no ongoing relationships between the parties. Relationship marketing is the development and maintenance of long-term, cost-effective relationships with individual customers, suppliers, employees, and other partners for mutual benefit.

2 Identify and explain the four basic elements of relationship marketing, as well as the importance of internal marketing.

The four basic elements are database technology, database marketing, monitoring relationships, and customer relationship management (CRM). Database technology helps identify current and potential customers. Database marketing analyzes the information provided by the database. Through relationship marketing, a firm monitors each relationship. With CRM, the firm orients every part of the organization toward building a unique company with an unbreakable bond with customers. Internal marketing involves activities within the company designed to help all employees understand, accept, and fulfill their roles in the marketing strategy.

3 Identify the three levels of the relationship marketing continuum.

The three levels of the relationship marketing continuum are (1) focus on price, (2) social interaction, and (3) interdependent partnership. At the first level, marketers use financial incentives to attract customers. At the second level, marketers engage in social interaction with buyers. At the third level, buyers and sellers become true business partners.

4 Explain how firms can enhance customer satisfaction and how they build buyer–seller relationships.

Marketers monitor customer satisfaction through various methods of marketing research. They look to understand what customers want—including what they expect—from goods or services. They also obtain customer feedback through means such as toll-free numbers and Web sites. Then they use this information to improve. Firms build buyer–seller relationships through frequency marketing programs, affinity marketing, database marketing, and one-to-one marketing.

5 Explain customer relationship management (CRM) and the role of technology in building customer relationships.

Customer relationship management is the combination of strategies and technologies that empowers relationship programs, reorienting the entire organization to a concentrated focus on satisfying customers. Made possible by technological advances, it leverages technology as a means to manage customer relationships and to integrate all stakeholders into a company's product design and development, manufacturing, marketing, sales, and customer service processes. CRM allows firms to manage vast amounts of data from multiple sources to improve overall customer satisfaction. The most effective companies approach CRM as a complete business strategy in which people, processes, and technology are all organized around delivering superior value to customers. A recent outgrowth of CRM is virtual relationships, in which buyers and sellers rarely, if ever, meet face-to-face.

6 Describe the buyer–seller relationship in business-to-business marketing and identify the four types of business partnerships.

By developing buyer–seller relationships, companies work together for their mutual benefit. Advantages may include lower prices for supplies, faster delivery of inventory, improved quality or reliability, customized product features, or more favorable financing terms. The four types of business partnerships are buyer, seller, internal, and lateral. Regardless of the type of partnership, partners usually share similar values and goals that help the alliance endure over time. Two other types of business marketing relationships are cobranding and comarketing.

7 Describe how business-to-business marketing incorporates national account selling, electronic data interchange and Web services, vendor-managed inventories (VMI), CPFaR, managing the supply chain, and creating alliances.

National account selling helps firms form a strong commitment with key buyers, resulting in improvements in efficiency and effectiveness for both parties. The use of electronic data interchanges allows firms to reduce costs and improve efficiency and competitiveness. Web services are software applications that allow firms with different technology platforms to communicate and exchange information over the Internet. Vendor-managed inventory (VMI) is a system in which sellers can automatically restock to previously requested levels. The collaborative planning, forecasting, and replenishment (CPFaR) approach bases plans and forecasts on collaborative seller–vendor efforts. Managing the supply chain provides increased innovation, decreased costs, conflict resolution, and improved communications. Strategic alliances can help both partners gain a competitive advantage in the marketplace.

8 Identify and evaluate the most common measurement and evaluation techniques within a relationship marketing program.

The effectiveness of relationship marketing programs can be measured using several methods. In the lifetime value of a customer, the revenues and intangible benefits that a customer brings to the seller over an average lifetime, less the amount the company must spend to acquire, market to, and service the customer, are calculated. With this method, a company may determine its costs to serve each customer and develop ways to increase profitability.

The payback method calculates how long it takes to break even on customer acquisition costs. Other measurements include tracking rebates, coupons, and credit card purchases; monitoring complaints and returns; and reviewing reply cards, comment forms, and surveys. These tools give the organization information about customer priorities so managers can make changes to their systems and set measurable goals.

 assessment check **answers**

1.1 What are the major differences between transaction-based marketing and relationship marketing?

Transaction-based marketing refers to buyer–seller exchanges involving limited communications and little or no ongoing relationships between the parties. Relationship marketing is the development and maintenance of long-term, cost-effective relationships with individual customers, suppliers, employees, and other partners for mutual benefit.

2.1 What are the four basic elements of relationship marketing?

The four basic elements are database technology, database marketing, monitoring relationships, and customer relationship management (CRM).

2.2 Why is internal marketing important to a firm?

Internal marketing enables all members of the organization to understand, accept, and fulfill their respective roles in implementing a marketing strategy.

3.1 Identify the three levels of the marketing relationship.

The three levels of the relationship marketing continuum are (1) focus on price, (2) social interaction, and (3) interdependent partnership.

3.2 Which level is the most complicated? Why?

The third level is most complex because the strength of commitment between the parties grows.

4.1 How is customer satisfaction measured?

Marketers monitor customer satisfaction through various methods of marketing research.

4.2 Identify two ways that marketers may obtain customer feedback.

Marketers can include a toll-free phone number or Web site address in their advertising; monitor Usenet, other online discussion groups, and blogs; and hire mystery shoppers to personally check on products.

5.1 Define *customer relationship management*.

Customer relationship management is the combination of strategies and technologies that empowers relationship programs, reorienting the entire organization to a concentrated focus on satisfying customers.

✓ *assessment check* **answers**

5.2 What are the two major types of CRM systems?

The two major types of CRM systems are purchased and customized.

5.3 Describe two steps a firm can take to rejuvenate a lost relationship.

Marketers can rejuvenate a lost relationship by changing the product mix if necessary or changing some of their processes.

6.1 What are the four key types of business marketing partnerships?

The four key types of business partnerships are buyer, seller, internal, and lateral.

6.2 Distinguish cobranding and comarketing.

Cobranding joins two strong brand names, perhaps owned by two different companies, to sell a product. In a comarketing effort, two organizations join to sell their products in an allied marketing campaign.

7.1 Name four technologies businesses can use to improve buyer–seller relationships in B2B markets.

The use of electronic data interchanges allows firms to reduce costs and improve efficiency and competitiveness. Web services provide a way for companies to communicate even if they are not running the same or compatible software, hardware, databases, or network platforms. Vendor-managed inventory (VMI) is a system in which sellers can automatically restock to previously requested levels. The collaborative planning, forecasting, and replenishment (CPFaR) approach bases plans and forecasts on collaborative seller–vendor efforts.

7.2 What are the benefits of effective supply chain management?

Managing the supply chain provides increased innovation, decreased costs, conflict resolution, and improved communications.

8.1 Define the term *lifetime value of a customer*.

In the lifetime value of a customer, the revenues and intangible benefits that a customer brings to the seller over an average lifetime, less the amount the company must spend to acquire, market to, and service the customer, are calculated.

8.2 Why are customer complaints valuable to evaluating customer relationship programs?

Customer complaints give the organization information about customer priorities so that managers can make changes to their systems if necessary and set appropriate, measurable goals for relationship programs.

MARKETING TERMS YOU NEED TO KNOW

transaction-based marketing 312
relationship marketing 312
frequency marketing 319
affinity marketing 320
database marketing 320

customer relationship management (CRM) 323
partnership 326
cobranding 328
comarketing 328

electronic data interchange (EDI) 329
vendor-managed inventory (VMI) 329
supply chain 330
lifetime value of a customer 331

OTHER IMPORTANT MARKETING TERMS

external customer 314
internal customer 314
internal marketing 315
employee satisfaction 315
customer satisfaction 317
interactive television 321
application service providers (ASPs) 321
grassroots marketing 322

viral marketing 322
buzz marketing 323
customer winback 325
business-to-business marketing 326
buyer partnership 327
seller partnership 327
internal partnership 327
lateral partnership 328

national account selling 329
quick-response merchandising 329
Web services 329
collaborative planning, forecasting, and
    replenishment (CPFaR) 330
strategic alliance 330

ASSURANCE OF LEARNING REVIEW

1. Describe the benefits of relationship marketing. How does database technology help firms build relationships with customers?
2. What types of factors might the firm monitor in its relationships?
3. What is an affinity marketing program?
4. What is an application service provider (ASP)? How does it work?
5. Distinguish among grassroots marketing, viral marketing, and buzz marketing.
6. Describe at least four qualities of a successful CRM system.
7. Explain how marketers can turn customers into advocates.
8. Describe each of the four types of business partnerships.
9. Give an example of cobranding and comarketing.
10. Why is it important for a firm to manage the relationships along its supply chain?
11. What is the most important factor in a strategic alliance?
12. Explain how a firm goes about evaluating the lifetime value of a customer.

PROJECTS AND TEAMWORK EXERCISES

1. With a teammate, choose one of the following companies. Create a plan to attract customers at the first level of the relationship marketing continuum—price—and move them to the next level with social interactions. Present your plan to the class.
   a. amusement or theme park
   b. health spa
   c. manufacturer of surfboards or snowmobiles
   d. manufacturer of cell phones
2. With a teammate, select a business with which you are familiar and design a frequency marketing program for the firm. Now design a grassroots, viral marketing, or buzz marketing campaign for the company you selected. Present your campaign to the class.
3. A hotel chain's database has information on guests that includes demographics, number of visits, and room preferences. Describe how the chain can use this information to develop several relationship marketing programs. How can it use a more general database to identify potential customers and to personalize its communications with them?
4. Select a local business enterprise. Find out as much as you can about its customer base, marketing strategies, and internal functions. Consider whether a customer relationship management focus would help the enterprise's competitive position. Argue your position in class.
5. Suppose you and a classmate were hired by a local independent bookstore to help its owner win back customers lost to a large chain. Design a plan to win back the store's lost customers and rebuild those relationships. Present your plan in class.
6. Choose a company that makes great stuff—something you really like, whether it is designer handbags, electronics, the tastiest ice cream flavors, or the best jeans. Now come up with a partner for your firm that you think would make a terrific strategic alliance. Write a plan for your alliance, explaining why you made the choice, what you want the two firms to accomplish, and why you think the alliance will be successful.
7. With a teammate, interview a local business owner to find out what methods he or she uses to evaluate customer relationships. You might discover that the businessperson uses very systematic techniques or perhaps just talks to customers. Either way, you will learn something valuable. Discuss your findings in class.

CRITICAL-THINKING EXERCISES

1. Suppose you were asked to be a marketing consultant for a restaurant that specializes in a regional cuisine, such as Tex-Mex, Cuban specialties, or New England clambake. The owner is concerned about employee satisfaction. When you visit the restaurant, what clues would you look for to determine employee satisfaction? What questions might you ask employees?

2. What types of social interaction might be appropriate—and effective—for a local bank to engage in with its customers?

3. What steps might a clothing store take to win back its lost customers?

4. Explain why a large firm such as General Mills might use national account selling to strengthen its relationship with a chain of supermarkets in the Midwest.

5. Why is it important for a company to calculate the lifetime value of a customer?

ETHICS EXERCISE

Suppose you work for a firm that sells home appliances such as refrigerators, microwaves, and washers and dryers. Your company has been slowly losing customers, but no one seems to know why. Employee morale is sliding as well. You believe that the company is run by honest, dedicated owners who want to please their customers. One day, you overhear an employee quietly advising a potential customer to shop at another store. You realize that your firm's biggest problem may be lack of employee satisfaction—which is leading to external customer loss.

1. Would you approach the employee to discuss the problem?

2. Would you ask the employee why he or she is turning customers away?

3. What steps do you think your employer could take to turn the situation around?

INTERNET EXERCISES

1. **Loyalty marketing programs.** Airlines, hotel chains, and rental car companies were among the first to introduce loyalty marketing programs designed to reward frequent customers. Customer loyalty programs have since expanded to a wide variety of other organizations. Visit the following Web sites and review their customer loyalty programs. In what ways do these companies attempt to reward frequent customers?

   a. Barnes & Noble (http://www.bn.com)
   b. L. L. Bean (http://www.llbean.com)
   c. Amazon.com (http://www.amazon.com)

2. **Relationship marketing.** Review the material on relationship marketing in the chapter and then visit the three Web sites that follow. Identify five ways in which the brand's marketers have applied the principles of relationship marketing.

   a. Swiffer (http://www.swiffer.com)
   b. Snapple (http://www.snapple.com)
   c. Armor All (http://www.armorall.com)

Note: Internet Web addresses change frequently. If you don't find the exact site listed, you may need to access the organization's home page and search from there or use a search engine such as Google.

CASE 10.1   The True Cost of Customer Service

Few people believe that airline travel will ever return to the "good old days" when amenities were free and plentiful. Blankets, pillows, meals, and timely arrival with your baggage and a smile seem to have been left permanently on the tarmac. Or have they?

Some analysts believe that the threat of bankruptcy, among other factors, is inducing airlines to improve customer service, often in simple ways that won't hurt the bottom line. "A bankrupt airline is anxious not to lose customers, especially business travelers," said one expert, "and may be wary of cutting service below competitors' levels for fear of confirming passenger suspicions that the company is not long for this world." United Airlines, for instance, scored 64 of a possible 100 in a University of Michigan study of customer satisfaction the year before it filed for bankruptcy protection. One recent passenger, who had abandoned the airline for past rudeness of its employees, said that a cheap fare persuaded her to try again. "It was like flying on a different airline," she said. "The flight attendants were friendly and the service was efficient."

Contrary to what you might think, customer satisfaction may actually improve just before a bankruptcy filing. Companies suffering during hard times often try harder to increase business, including better service or offering deep discounts or other promotions. Some evidence of this extra effort is United's on-time arrival guarantee and promise of 500 free award miles if it doesn't come through. Another troubled airline, Delta, began a service recovery program called First Point of Contact that "focuses on empowering our front-line customer service employees to resolve customer concerns at the first point of contact," according to the company's executive vice president and chief of customer service. The program retrained everyone from phone agents to flight attendants. And Northwest Airlines has broadened stand-by opportunities for customers, added more Spanish-language content to its Web site, and hired more bilingual reservations agents.

Some skeptics, however, point to other recent surveys that give the airline industry failing grades for customer service, with a surge in customer complaints and record-high lost-baggage claims. One industry watcher says that dramatic industry layoffs, combined with a return to pre-9/11 levels of air travel, have created the situation. Employees, he claims, are frustrated by reduced pay and benefits and by having to pick up the slack created by 200,000 fewer workers. And the extras that some airlines are bringing back come with a twist—a fee, ranging from $4 for a snack on American Airlines to $75 for exit-row seats on Virgin Atlantic. Some airlines charge $5 to $30 for curbside baggage checking, for not booking your flight online, or for requesting anything other than a computer-generated ticket. "I always thought when you paid for your ticket, handling your luggage, your beverage and all the other service was included in the price of the ticket," said one passenger. "Now they are telling me everything is extra. I'm disappointed."

Some airlines are defending the new fees by claiming that customers have made it clear they value low-price tickets above all else. The fees are structured so that the additional services or conveniences are paid for only by those who want them. Other carriers claim that customer service was always a priority whether bankruptcy loomed or not. As long as airlines continue to compete on price and try to balance low-cost operations with bankruptcy threats, however, it looks like good customer service remains in the eye of the beholder.

Questions for Critical Thinking

1. Do you think airlines have improved customer service efforts? Why or why not?
2. What advantage do good customer relationships have for airlines on the brink of bankruptcy? Are they worth the cost and effort?
3. Do you think passengers will consider amenities that they pay for to fall under the category of "customer service"? Why or why not? How might their perception affect the airlines' customer service efforts and track record?

Sources: Dawn Gilbertson, "Airline Report Shows Low Marks in Service," *Arizona Republic*, April 4, 2006, **http://www.azcentral.com**; Leslie Miller, "Service on Airlines Gets a Little More Expensive," *CRM Buyer*, April 4, 2006, **http://www.crmbuyer.com**; " 'Service' in the Skies," *USA Today*, March 24, 2006, **http://www.usatoday.com**; Joel J. Smith, "Airline: $15 for Legroom," *Detroit News*, March 14, 2006, **http://www.detnews.com**; Christopher Elliott, "When Fliers Benefit from Airline Bankruptcy," *New York Times*, January 17, 2006, **http://www.nytimes.com**.

VIDEO CASE 10.2   The Little Guys Home Electronics:
Big on Customer Relationships

The written video case on The Little Guys appears on page VC-12. The recently filmed The Little Guys video is designed to expand and highlight the concepts in this chapter and the concepts and questions covered in the written video case.

Talking about Marketing Careers with. . .

LIBBEY PAUL
SENIOR VICE-PRESIDENT, MARKETING
ACNIELSEN HOMESCAN & SPECTRA

Getting into the heads of today's consumers—to understand their needs and offer them products when and where it best serves them—is no easy feat. But marketing research firm ACNielsen attempts to understand the behavior of consumer goods' purchasers so that its clients can meet and exceed customer expectations. ACNielsen works with some big names in consumer goods, such as Wal-Mart and Kraft Foods. With literally millions of dollars at stake, those retailers and manufacturers need to target the right consumers at the right times with the right products to ensure success.

A lot of research and effort goes into what appears to be a simple product sitting on the shelf where you're shopping. We were fortunate to be able to speak with Libbey Paul, Senior Vice-President of Marketing at ACNielsen Homescan & Spectra, a global business unit of ACNielsen, to discuss her career activities and milestones and the processes involved in marketing research, market segmentation, and targeting.

Q: Tell us a bit about your background and the beginnings of your marketing career. How has your career developed through the years?

A: I have an undergraduate degree in business (with an art minor) and an MBA. Some of my most important business training, however, came with my first career stop in Brand Management at Procter & Gamble. P&G has a great reputation for training, and it's well deserved. Two of the lasting lessons I learned there were crisp communication skills, both written and oral, and how to create consumer-centered product concepts and marketing programs. I opted for a more entrepreneurial environment when I left P&G and joined a small, niche micromarketing firm called Spectra, where I started in a consulting and service role with direct client contact. In that role, I put my P&G training to good use and had the opportunity to support and learn from over 15 different consumer packaged goods manufacturers, ranging from Miller Brewing Company to General Mills to Kraft to Con Agra. Six years ago, I moved back into a marketing leadership role at Spectra, helping to create new information and consulting services for this same client base. In the past year, Spectra merged with ACNielsen Homescan to form a consumer insights, segmentation, and targeting business unit.

Q: You head up the product management effort at ACNielsen Homescan & Spectra. What does your position involve? What other team members assist you and what are their roles? How does your job contribute to ACNielsen's overall goals?

A: Like any company, new products are the lifeblood of our company. My department creates the new solutions and software that our service team takes to our clients. Like most marketing departments, we interface with many other groups—clients, client service, research, software development, database management, legal, and finance—to create profitable, client-centered services.

Let me give you an example. Our clients came to us with a challenge: *Give us more precise consumer insights. Tell us how to grow sales in existing stores with this consumer insight. We know historical sales, but where could we sell more by better meeting*

local consumer needs? We had several assets to apply to the problem—Consumer Trade Areas tell us which consumers shop across different stores, and a demand forecasting model tells us how to project volume using consumer attributes. Marketing created business requirements with a clear statement of client needs and the kinds of reporting we'd want to provide to clients to help them solve the problem. We worked with research staff, who created and validated a new algorithm, the Navigator Model, which "consumerizes" store movement data by comparing sales rates to the people shopping in each store. The model output was then used to forecast which stores could be selling more products based on the kinds of shoppers they serve. Research and marketing worked with our development group to build the model into end-user software, with a suite of reporting options. At the same time, marketing worked with legal and finance to develop contracts and a fee structure that created a profitable service model for Spectra. Finally, marketing worked with client service to create sales materials and a sales plan/forecast for this new service offering we called "Opportunity Finder."

Q: What types of problems do your clients typically need to solve, and how does ACNielsen help them? For instance, are they interested in setting strategic marketing plans, developing new products, or devising new advertising campaigns? Where are your clients located—in the U.S. or around the globe?

A: Our manufacturer and retail clients are all trying to drive efficient revenue growth in a flat to declining consumer packaged goods industry. Since many of our clients are global in reach, we are expanding our Spectra solutions beyond North America, though my focus is on the U.S. market. Across all markets, our mission is to help clients realize growth by focusing first on the needs of the consumer. We gather together many consumer insights, create a segmentation construct, called BehaviorScape, to connect those insights to each other and to our

PHOTO: COURTESY OF ACNIELSEN HOMESCAN & SPECTRA

clients' marketing and trade plans, and then measure how our clients moved the needle and impacted their business.

What does this mean in plain English? We start with understanding how people buy products. Consider this example: Who buys Newman's Own Organic snack products? The consumers tend to be in the most affluent neighborhoods that we call Cosmopolitan Centers (upscale cities) and Affluent Suburban Spreads (upscale communities surrounding cities). In fact, people in Cosmopolitan Centers buy at a 70% higher rate than the average U.S. household. This makes sense, as these are the most educated, health-oriented consumers. They're more likely to be effectively managing their weight, physically active, and consuming organic products generally. Armed with this information, we can then tell our clients how to more effectively reach these households. We know where these consumers are more likely to shop overall and, by store, where our clients should place advertising—TV, magazines, Internet. We also know what incentives these consumers respond to, what promotions they'll be interested in seeing. This information helps clients direct spending more intelligently, eliminating waste.

Q: How does ACNielsen Homescan & Spectra get the information it needs to help its clients? Do you observe shopper behavior, conduct focus groups, use telephone or fax questionnaires, collect data electronically, convene consumer panels, do mall intercept surveys—something else? Do you tap other secondary data sources such as U.S. Census Bureau data?

A: We get our information from many sources. With the exception of U.S. Census data and store databases, most sources are consumer panels or large-scale phone, mail, and/or Internet-based surveys.

- U.S. Census provides in-depth demographic and expenditure information down to low-level geographies.
- Trade Dimensions store database covers 350,000+ store outlets across 19 classes of trade, ranging from more conventional channels such as Grocery, Convenience, and Mass Merchandisers to emerging channels such as Pet Superstores.
- ACNielsen Homescan consumer panel data tells us which consumers buy what

products where (how often, how much, and under what conditions), what their attitudes are, what their Internet habits are.

- Nielsen Media Research tells us what television shows people are watching.
- Mediamark Research Inc. (MRI) tells us what magazines people are reading, as well as other lifestyle and media information.
- Scarborough Research does extensive market-level surveys about local media, shopping, and lifestyle activities.
- Additionally, we integrate many client-custom data sources, from attitude and usage surveys to new product testing results. Also, we integrate store movement data either from ACNielsen or directly from retailers.

Q: You must amass a huge amount of data in your research. Does your business unit collect all of that information, or do you partner with other marketing research firms? How do clients use this data and in what form?

A: As indicated, Spectra collects very little information directly. We create store trading areas (called Consumer Trade Areas) and then integrate and apply information to drive greater utility for our clients. As such, partnerships are essential to our business. We have many relationships both with our integration with Homescan and with other ACNielsen businesses that directly gather the information, as well as third-party data sources. To help our clients make sense of all this information, we provide user-friendly software applications, as well as client service consultants, many of whom are on site at client offices.

Q: Do you provide information on specific market segments—based on age, gender, ethnicity, geographic location, or income levels—to your clients? Are they interested in certain target markets? Do your research methods vary from segment to segment?

A: We do many forms of segmentation for our clients, depending on their business needs. A key segmentation framework we have is called BehaviorScape. This segmentation was created by using millions of purchase transaction records from Homescan panel data to understand what household characteristics are associated with purchase behavior changes. From this analysis, we came up with two components for Behav-

iorScape, crossing BehaviorStages (which are created based on age of head of household, age/presence of children, and size of household) by LifeStyle (characterized by a neighborhood's affluence and urbanization). Take my household as an example. I live in a Cosmopolitan Center neighborhood and am in an Older Bustling Family BehaviorStage. Compare that with my best friend who lives in San Francisco—she's an Independent Single who lives in a Struggling Urban Core neighborhood. I guarantee that our refrigerators look totally different!

We have many other types of segmentation depending on the issues that a client is facing—Boomer, Hispanic, Gender, Child/Teen. We believe it is essential to be able to customize our segmentations based on client needs and the rapidly evolving consumer landscape. For example, a key component for Hispanic segmentation is level of acculturation. So we created a model to classify households (and geographies) based on acculturation level.

Q: What words of wisdom can you pass along to students who are preparing for their marketing careers? What work experiences or internships should they seek out to advance?

A: You learn by doing! Seek out classes or educational programs with the case study format; get work experience through internships. Read widely and form an opinion about what you see. *Advertising Age* and *The Wall Street Journal* are two sources, and I'm sure there are many other excellent options. Thoughtfully watch TV—what ads are working, which are not and why? What new products seem like a good idea, which are a bust? Most importantly, though, seek to make a difference in every endeavor you undertake. When talking with prospective employers, use the STAR method to describe your examples:

- **S**ituation: Provide an overview of the situation and any relevant background information. Be specific and succinct.
- **T**ask: Describe the tasks involved in that situation. What goal were you working toward?
- **A**ction: Describe the action you took. How did you make a difference?
- **R**esults: Explain the result of your actions.

A Legacy of Laughter Opens Doors to the Future

The Second City

When the hit show *Whose Line Is It Anyway?* spun prime-time television on its head with completely improvised material, viewers wondered where its talented cast of actors had come from. Two of its cast members, Ryan Stiles and Colin Mochrie, began their careers at The Second City. A similar curiosity surrounds such stars as Mike Myers, who traveled through live comedy venues at a young age before being cast by *Saturday Night Live (SNL)*. Myers has called The Second City his "college," as he began with the troupe after his senior year of high school. SC alumni are behind a long list of entertainment success stories, including *The Simpsons, The Daily Show,* and The Blues Brothers. Many prolific careers began at The Second City, including such stars as Saturday Night Live's former head writer Tina Fey and the iconic Bill Murray. The Second City continues to use its legacy of great talent to capture the hearts of its target market. All of SC's business ventures, big and small, are related to the captivating underlying character of The Second City.

As tourists walk into The Second City, a long list of alumni, including every actor who played in a new revue, occupies a few giant placards at the theater's entrance. Inside, giant photos of the actors in full character adorn the walls. Whether the consumer grew up in the 1960s, while Mike Nichols and Elaine May became a famous comic duo, or more recently when *SNL's* Amy Poehler became a sensation, there are clearly a number of famous faces for anyone to recognize.

Second City's Communication Division has made strategic casting decisions to fit its target market of successful businesspeople. Fred Willard of *Best in Show* and *Everybody Loves Raymond,* a successful SC alum, appears prominently in SC's online and print brochures, His career may be most recognizable to the 50- and 60-year-olds leading some of America's most powerful businesses today, but he's also a cult favorite of young businesspeople making their way up the corporate ladder. Colin Mochrie of *Whose Line Is It Anyway?* and Fred Willard are just two SC actors who have reached great heights in the entertainment industry and continue to directly provide marketing and creative input for their comedic home. SC Communications knows the importance of bringing talented personality right to the customer's door.

Second City theaters market to two important market segments with different approaches. For the tourist market they establish a presence in hotels with marketing materials and concierge contacts. For local residents they stay visible with entertainment listings and public-relations efforts providing reminders that SC still offers fresh, affordable comedy with a local flavor. The Second City Touring Company markets to a larger geographical area and uses several market strategies to reach its market segments, which are primarily college venues and performing arts center venues. For the college market, the marketing approach stresses the show's cutting-edge social commentary. For the performing arts center venues, it stresses the troupe's consistent and successful track record.

Developing a cohesive entertainment business means marketing to, and producing for, a variety of voices and demographics. The Second City has developed an Outreach and Diversity division that has gained an exciting amount of interest from a number of minority communities. By producing such ensembles as Stir-Friday Night, BrownCo, and GayCo, and by offering apprenticeships for participating high school students, The Second City has fostered mutually rewarding bonds with various communities. Archived footage of a diverse range of famous Second City alumni plays a key role in some of the training and workshop programs offered by The Second City Training Center.

SC uses a differentiated marketing strategy, designed to attract various market segments. Throughout its continued expansion, the main focus has always remained its comedy. Since its origin, Second City has been positioned, by virtue of its talent, at the top of the comedy theater market. Second City has continued to take advantage of its status by investing in the newest entertainment medium: the Internet.

The benefits of technology, including self-broadcasting Web sites such as YouTube.com, have opened up the entertainment market to anyone capable of speaking into a microphone or turning on a computer. Second City is prepared to work within the technology/entertainment boom. Kelly Leonard, SC's vice president, recently reported on alliances being formed with media content distribution agencies. "We have realized for some time that this is a major area for The Second City, as we have a tremendous inventory of short form content and the set process for creating a steady stream of this content. These new media forms will serve two or three purposes: exposing us to a youth market, becoming a marketing tool, and eventually a source of income for us." The Second City has begun to use its Web site to market to this youth market segment by producing podcasts and posting interviews and video clips. SC expects to continue to target the plugged-in youth market, which presents significant growth opportunities.

Customer relationship management is an intrinsic part of The Second City, which was created to challenge, surprise, and delight the audience. These original goals of Second City comedy remain integrated throughout all of its business ventures. SC doesn't have to use software systems to tally customer feedback. Laughter can be just as accurate a barometer of customer satisfaction. Second City simply listen to its audience, its corporate partner, its community, and its stars. Speaking on behalf of the stage that launched their careers, Second City's talented alumni make the strongest marketing call. Having alumni such as Hollywood actor Alan Arkin being quoted, saying "The Second City saved my life, quite literally," means that The Second City is as much a marketing success for its actors as it is for its audience.

Questions

1. Where and when did you first hear of The Second City? What first impression did this create?
2. How does the Second City approach its market segmentations?
3. What market segment do you think The Second City has neglected to target?
4. How is The Second City vulnerable in using its celebrity alumni as a major marketing tool?

PART 4

Product Decisions

CHEVROLET UNLEASHES THE NEW CORVETTE

New with 4-wheel disc brakes
'65 CORVETTE

'73 CORVETTE
We gave it radials, a quieter ride, guard beams and a nose job.

AN AMERICAN REVOLUTION

CHAPTER 11

Satellite: The New Sound of Radio

Just when it seemed the life of broadcast radio was dwindling—local stations gobbled up by programming giants and music buffs tuning into iPods instead of their favorite stations—a new sound hit the air waves. Satellite radio is bringing listeners back, and here's why: The signal is strong and clear, and you won't lose it when you're driving in your car. You have your choice of talk, sports, entertainment, and music programs. You get to hear controversial celebrities such as Howard Stern, who isn't on FM anymore. And you won't be bothered by irritating commercials. The catch is that you have to pay for all of these benefits. You buy a satellite radio for between $30 and $300, then you subscribe to one of the two providers currently available: Sirius or XM. Monthly and yearly rates for

the providers are identical: $12.95 per month and $142.45 per year. But if you're a radio buff, the cost is likely to be well worth it. And if you're not, satellite might turn you into one.

It's easy to think of Sirius Satellite Radio and XM Satellite Radio Holdings as the Coke and Pepsi of radio. The technologies are identical and the philosophies are similar, so competition between the two providers is head-to-head and intense. Gaining an advantage at this stage is vital, because satellite radio has moved past the introductory stage in its life cycle and is now beginning to grow. Whoever wins the most fans now could win the long-term game. So, curious consumers might be asking, How do they compare?

In both cases, you need a receiver to get a satellite signal. Before even making this purchase, however, you'll have to decide which provider you want to subscribe to. To operate, a Sirius radio must have a Sirius subscription, and an XM radio requires an XM subscription. Once subscribed, you can purchase anything ranging from a simple car radio to a tabletop radio for your home or office. To find out more about the offerings from a firm, you can visit its Web site, which gives you information about everything from subscription rates to what's on tonight. If you're a football fan, Sirius carries home and away NFL games all season. But if you're a baseball fan, you're better off with XM, which carries home and away MLB games from every team, all season—including spring training. Sirius carries 68 music

Product and Service Strategies

channels, while XM has 67. Sirius has Jimmy Buffett's Margaritaville, while XM has Frank Sinatra's American standards. If you want news and talk, both stations have a variety of world, national, and local news, as well as political commentators. And Sirius has Howard Stern.

Sirius is banking on Stern, the former "shock jock" of FM radio. In his move to Sirius, Stern commanded $500 million in cash and stock over a five-year period, but the firm believes that the cost will be well worth it in new subscribers, advertising revenues, and publicity. Still, Mike Goodman of technology consulting firm The Yankee Group is skeptical of the gamble. "If every single one of Howard Stern's listeners came over, that's more than 10 million subscribers. If that's the only growth for Sirius, that's not a success. It's not Howard Stern radio, it's Sirius radio." But industry experts believe that this type of original content, provided by Stern and others such as Ellen Degeneres, sets satellite radio apart from broadcast radio. "It's this unique programming that

sets them apart," says Goodman. "It is the nonmusic programming, associated or built around celebrity DJs that the other guy doesn't have."

Satellite radio still faces some major challenges, such as persuading radio listeners to pay for the service

and competing against providers of on-demand and iTunes content. Sirius has already entered into an agreement with Sprint to provide some of its streaming programming directly to Sprint customers' cell phones. And as more competitors enter the arena, Sirius and XM

evolution *of a* brand

Sirius and XM are already locked in direct competition for satellite radio listeners. The choices each makes about programming, format, subscription rates, and the radios themselves may determine who comes out ahead as satellite radio expands in the marketplace.

- Strategic partnerships, such as the one between Sirius and Sprint, will likely be vital to each firm's growth. Describe an alliance with another company that the satellite providers might make, in order to provide some type of expanded service. On the other side of the globe, WorldSpace, a satellite radio operator in India, is trying to model itself after Sirius and XM. The firm has two satellites that can broadcast to Asia, western Europe, and Africa, potentially reaching 75 percent of the world's population. But most people in those areas have less money to spend than U.S. consumers do, and they speak many different languages.[1] Should WorldSpace consider linking itself with Sirius or XM to create a stronger brand for both? What would be the advantages for each firm?

- Sirius is relying heavily on one celebrity—Howard Stern—for a certain amount of its

will have to find ways to distinguish themselves from the others. But right now they have a chance to make the most of this new medium—and they are going to do everything they can to get you to tune in.[2]

evolution *of a* **brand**

success. Is this the best way to gain a competitive advantage? List the benefits and limitations of this marketing strategy. Does Sirius run the risk of being known as "Howard Stern Radio"? How might Sirius's place in the market change in five or ten years? What can the firm do to remain viable?

Chapter Overview

We've discussed how marketers conduct research to determine unfilled needs in their markets, how customers behave during the purchasing process, and how firms expand their horizons overseas. Now our attention shifts to a company's **marketing mix,** the blend of four elements of a marketing strategy—product, distribution, promotion, and price—to satisfy the target market. This chapter focuses on how firms select and develop the goods and services they offer, starting with planning which products to offer. The other variables of the marketing mix—distribution channels, promotional plans, and pricing decisions—must accommodate the product strategy selected.

Marketers develop strategies to promote both tangible goods and intangible services. Any such strategy begins with investigation, analysis, and selection of a particular target market, and it continues with the creation of a marketing mix designed to satisfy that segment. Tangible goods and intangible services both intend to satisfy consumer wants and needs, but the marketing efforts supporting them may be vastly different. Sirius and XM sell both types of products—they offer subscriptions to radio service, and they sell the radios that subscribers need to hear the service. This is the case with many companies, as you'll see in this chapter.

This chapter examines both the similarities and the differences in marketing goods and services. It then presents basic concepts—product classifications, development of product lines, and the product life cycle—that marketers apply in developing successful products. Finally, the chapter discusses product deletion and product mix decisions.

marketing mix Blending of the four strategy elements—product, distribution, promotion, and price—to fit the needs and preferences of a specific target market.

Briefly
Speaking

"It has always been my private conviction that any man who pits his intelligence against a fish and loses has it coming."

—John Steinbeck
(1902–1968)
American novelist

---

1 Define *product* and distinguish between goods and services and how they relate to the goods–services continuum.

WHAT IS A PRODUCT?

At first, you might think of a product as an object you hold in your hand, such as a baseball or a toothbrush. You might also think of the car you drive as a product. But this doesn't take into account the idea of a service as a product. Nor does it consider the idea of what the product is used for. So a television is more than a box with a screen and a remote control. It's really a means of providing entertainment—your favorite movies, news programs, or reality shows. Marketers acknowledge this broader conception of product; they realize that people buy *want satisfaction* rather than objects. Want satisfaction can apply to the purchase of products or even the giving of gifts, as described in the "Etiquette Tips for Marketing Professionals" feature.

Etiquette Tips for Marketing Professionals

Giving the Right Gift

When holidays and other special occasions roll around, you want to do the right thing for your co-workers, your boss, and your staff (if you are a manager). While it may have seemed easy to choose gifts for your parents, siblings, and friends when you were growing up, giving gifts at work is a completely different matter. To whom should you give a gift? How much should you spend? What should you give? When and where do you present it to the person? Here are a few suggestions for giving the right gift—to the right person:

1. *Check your firm's gift-giving rules.* Many companies have their own rules or guidelines about gift giving, which will answer many of your questions. Ask someone in the human resources department.
2. *Ask a co-worker who has been at the firm longer than you have.* Someone who has worked there longer and been through a few holiday seasons can give you good pointers.
3. *If you are still uncertain about whether to give and to whom, ask your boss.* Then follow his or her guidelines.
4. *If there is a dollar limit, follow it.* Don't think you have to spend more on your boss just to impress him or her. If you want to spend more for a co-worker who is a close friend, arrange to exchange gifts outside the office. If the limit is too high for you, ask a few co-workers if they want to chip in for group gifts.

5. *Give something consumable.* Gifts of food—homemade cookies or chocolates from the specialty shop around the corner—are appreciated by everyone, and they don't collect dust on someone's shelf. Gift cards to Starbucks, iTunes, Amazon.com, or other stores are welcome, too. However, avoid gifts of alcohol.
6. *Give something appropriate to your industry or useful on the job.* A dish or basket to collect paper clips on a desk, a good pen, a cell phone case, a travel mug or water bottle—something as simple as these items can make a person's job easier.
7. *Be equitable.* If everyone in the office is exchanging gifts, try to do cookies or gift cards for everyone (unless someone has an allergy or other condition that requires a different gift).
8. *Remember, it really is the thought that counts.* Office gifts are a way to say "thank you" to co-workers for their support, to a boss who has given you an opportunity, and to support staff who went the extra mile to meet that project deadline.

Sources: Donna L. Mataldo, "Gift-Giving Guidelines for the Office," About.com, **http://couponing.about.com**, accessed May 1, 2006; Amy Keyishan, "Office Gift-Giving Etiquette," *Ladies' Home Journal*, **http://www.lhj.com**, accessed May 1, 2006; Marshall Loeb, "Office Gift-Giving Etiquette: Santa's Rules Change at Work," *Career Journal.com*, December 8, 2005, **http://www.careerjournal.com**.

You might feel a need for a television to satisfy a want for entertainment. You might not know a lot about how the device itself works, but you understand the results. If you are entertained by watching TV, then your wants are satisfied. If, however, the television is working just fine but you don't like the programming offered, you may need to satisfy your desire for entertainment by changing your cable service or purchasing satellite service. Each of those services is a product.

Marketers think in terms of a product as a compilation of package design and labeling, brand name, price, availability, warranty, reputation, image, and customer-service activities that add value for the customer. Consequently, a **product** is a bundle of physical, service, and symbolic attributes designed to satisfy a customer's wants and needs.

product Bundle of physical, service, and symbolic attributes designed to satisfy a customer's wants and needs.

 assessment check

1. Define *product*.
2. Why is the understanding of want satisfaction so important to marketers?

WHAT ARE GOODS AND SERVICES?

services Intangible tasks that satisfy the needs of consumer and business users.

goods Tangible products that customers can see, hear, smell, taste, or touch.

Services are intangible products. A general definition identifies **services** as intangible tasks that satisfy the needs of consumer and business users. But you can't hold a service in your hand the way you can **goods,** which are tangible products that customers can see, hear, smell, taste, or touch such as the television just described. Most service providers cannot transport or store their products; customers simultaneously buy and consume these products, such as haircuts, car repairs, and visits to the dentist. One way to distinguish services from goods is the **goods–services continuum,** as shown in Figure 11.1.

This spectrum helps marketers visualize the differences and similarities between goods and services. A car is a pure good, but the dealer may also offer repair and maintenance services, or include the services in the price of a lease. The car falls at the pure good extreme of the continuum because the repair or maintenance services are an adjunct to the purchase. A dinner at an exclusive restaurant is a mix of goods and services. It combines the physical goods of gourmet food with the intangible services of an attentive wait staff, elegant surroundings, and perhaps a visit to your table by the chef or restaurant owner to make sure that your meal is perfect. At the other extreme, a dentist provides pure service—cleaning teeth, filling cavities, taking X-rays. The dentist's office may also sell items such as electric toothbrushes or night guards, but it's the service that is primary in patients' minds.

You can begin to see the diversity of services. Services can be distinguished from goods in several ways:

1. *Services are intangible.* Services do not have physical features that buyers can see, hear, smell, taste, or touch prior to purchase. Service firms essentially ask their customers to buy a promise—that the haircut will be stylish, that the insurance will cover injuries, that the lawn will be mowed.

2. *Services are inseparable from the service providers.* Consumer perceptions of a service provider become their perceptions of the service itself. The name of a doctor, lawyer, or hair stylist is synonymous with the service they provide. A bad haircut can deter customers, while a good one will attract more to the salon. A house-cleaning service such as Merry Maids depends on its workers to leave each house spotless, because its reputation is built on this service.

3. *Services are perishable.* Providers cannot maintain inventories of their services. A day spa can't stockpile facials or pedicures. A travel agent can't keep quantities of vacations on a shelf. For this reason, some service providers, such as airlines and hotels, may raise their prices during times of peak demand—such as during spring break from school—and reduce them when demand declines.

4. *Companies cannot easily standardize services.* However, many firms are trying to change this. Most fast-food chains promise that you'll get your meal within a certain number of minutes and that it will taste the way you expect it to. A hotel chain may have the same amenities at each location—a pool, fitness room, free breakfast, or HBO movies.

5. *Buyers often play important roles in the creation and distribution of services.* Service transactions frequently require interaction between buyer and seller at the production and distribution stages. MasterCard introduced MasterCard Card Customization Services, a program that allows card issuers to offer consumers and small businesses the capability to create their own, customized credit, debit, or prepaid cards. In a survey, 70 percent of consumers and 85 percent of small business owners expressed strong interest in the card.[3]

6. *Service standards show wide variations.* New York City's posh Le Cirque and your local Pizza Hut

figure 11.1

The Goods–Services Continuum

Pure Good — Car

Pure Service — Dentist

Dinner in an Exclusive Restaurant

are both restaurants. Depending on your expectations, both can be considered good restaurants. But the service standards at each vary greatly. At LeCirque, you'll experience finely prepared cuisine served by a highly trained wait staff. At Pizza Hut, you may serve yourself fresh pizza from the buffet.

Keep in mind that a product often blurs the distinction between services and goods. Avis is a service that provides rental cars, which are goods. LensCrafters provides eye examinations—services from optometrists—while also selling eyeglasses and contact lenses (goods).

IMPORTANCE OF THE SERVICE SECTOR

2 Explain the importance of the service sector in today's marketplace.

You would live a very different life without service firms to fill many needs. You could not place a phone call, log on to the Internet, flip a switch for electricity, or even take a college course if organizations did not provide such services. During an average day, you probably use many services without much thought, but these products play an integral role in your life.

The service sector makes a crucial contribution to the U.S. economy in terms of both products and jobs. Two of *Fortune*'s top ten most admired U.S. companies are pure service firms—Federal Express and Southwest Airlines. But the other eight firms, all listed in Figure 11.2, provide highly regarded services in conjunction with the goods they sell.[4]

The U.S. service sector now makes up more than two-thirds of the economy, as the shift from a goods-producing economy to a service-producing economy continues. According to the U.S. Department of Labor, service industries are expected to account for 18.7 million of the 18.9 million new jobs that are expected to be generated over the next decade.[5]

Services also play a crucial role in the international competitiveness of U.S. firms. While the U.S. runs a continuing trade deficit in goods, it has maintained a trade surplus in services for every year since 1970.[6] However, although some economists think that more precise measurements of service exports would reveal an even larger surplus, others worry about the effect of offshoring service jobs such as customer-service call centers to nations such as India. While some firms have found success with offshoring their call centers, others such as 1-800-FLOWERS.com have decided against it. After a pilot program using call representatives from India, the flower vendor chose to bring its calls home because of differences in cultural understanding between customers and the representatives. But when he realized that these same representatives wrote eloquent prose, executive Lou Orsi opted to offshore the e-mail portion of customer services.[7]

In another emerging trend, firms are beginning to engage in **homeshoring,** which essentially entails hiring contract workers to do jobs from their homes. Not only do firms save on office space, furnishings, and supplies, most also save on healthcare and other benefits. Jet-Blue is one well-known firm practicing homeshoring—all of its 1,400 reservation agents

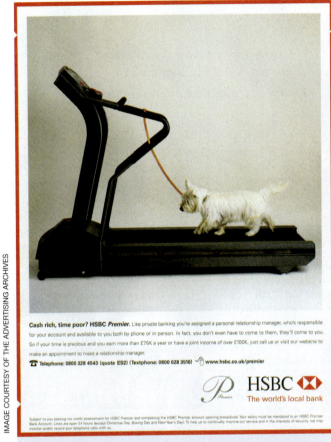

Cash rich, time poor? HSBC Premier. Like private banking you're assigned a personal relationship manager, who's responsible for your account and available to you both by phone or in person. In fact, you don't even have to come to them, they'll come to you. So if your time is precious and you earn more than £75K a year or have a joint income of over £100K, just call us or visit our website to make an appointment to meet a relationship manager.

☎ Telephone: 0800 328 4543 (quote ES2) | (Textphone: 0800 028 3516) | www.hsbc.co.uk/premier

P Premier   **HSBC** ◆◇
The world's local bank

IMAGE COURTESY OF THE ADVERTISING ARCHIVES

HSBC, a global financial services provider, helps customers handle their banking and investment needs.

✓ **assessment check**

1. Describe the goods–services continuum.

2. List the six characteristics that distinguish services from goods.

figure 11.2

America's Most Admired Companies

Source: "America's Most Admired Companies 2006," *Fortune*, accessed April 24, 2006, **http://money.cnn.com**.

homeshoring Hiring workers to do jobs from their homes.

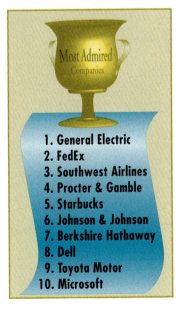

Most Admired Companies

1. General Electric
2. FedEx
3. Southwest Airlines
4. Procter & Gamble
5. Starbucks
6. Johnson & Johnson
7. Berkshire Hathaway
8. Dell
9. Toyota Motor
10. Microsoft

consumer (B2C) product Product destined for use by ultimate consumers.

business-to-business (B2B) product Product that contributes directly or indirectly to the output of other products for resale; also called industrial or organizational product.

3 List the classifications of consumer goods and services and briefly describe each category.

work from home. But JetBlue treats them as office employees with benefits, while most other homeshore workers are independent contractors. Office Depot and J. Crew both use homeshore workers. "Offshoring's under-estimated sibling, homeshoring, is about to hit a growth spurt," predicts one industry watcher.[8]

Observers cite several reasons for the growing importance of services, including consumer desire for speed and convenience and technological advances that allow firms to fulfill this demand. Services that involve wireless communications, data backup and storage, and even meal preparation for busy families are on the rise. Grocery chain Trader Joe's is benefitting from this need for quick meals by offering partially cooked, fully cooked, and flash-frozen entrées that can be picked up and prepared in less time than meals from scratch. Consumers are also looking to advisors to help plan for a financially secure future and insurance to protect their homes and families.

Most service firms emphasize marketing as a significant activity for two reasons. First, the growth potential of service transactions represents a vast marketing opportunity. Second, the environment for services is changing. For instance, increased competition is forcing traditional service industries to differentiate themselves from their competitors. Providing superior service is one way to develop long-term customer relationships and compete more effectively. As we discussed earlier, relationship marketing is just one of the ways service firms can develop and solidify their customer relationships.

CLASSIFYING GOODS AND SERVICES FOR CONSUMER AND BUSINESS MARKETS

A firm's choices for marketing a good or service depend largely on the offering itself and on the nature of the target market. Product strategies differ for consumer and business markets. **Consumer products** (sometimes called **B2C products**) are those destined for use by ultimate consumers, while **business products,** or **B2B products** (also called *industrial* or *organizational products*), contribute directly or indirectly to the output of other products for resale. Marketers further subdivide these two major categories into more specific categories, as discussed in this section.

Some products fall into both categories. A case in point is prescription drugs. Traditionally, pharmaceuticals companies marketed prescription drugs to doctors, who then made the purchase decision for their patients by writing the prescription. Thus, the medications could be classified as a business product. However, many drug companies now advertise their products in consumer-oriented media, including magazines and television. A recent report revealed that of the $19.1 billion spent promoting drugs in one year, $2.7 billion was spent on advertising aimed at consumers, with the rest aimed at doctors.[9]

TYPES OF CONSUMER PRODUCTS

The most widely used product classification system focuses on the buyer's perception of a need for the product and his or her buying behavior.

figure 11.3

Classification of Consumer Products

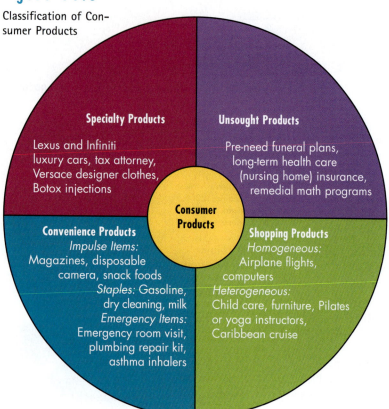

However, **unsought products** are marketed to consumers who may not yet recognize any need for them. Examples of unsought products are long-term-care insurance and funeral services.

However, relatively few products fall into the unsought category. Most consumers recognize their own needs for various types of consumer purchases and actively seek them, so the customer buying-behavior variations are the key to distinguishing the various categories. The most common classification scheme for sought products divides consumer goods and services into three groups based on customers' buying behavior: convenience, shopping, and specialty. Figure 11.3 illustrates samples of these three categories, together with the unsought classification.

Convenience Products

Convenience products refer to goods and services that consumers want to purchase frequently, immediately, and with minimal effort. Milk, bread, and toothpaste are convenience products. Convenience services include 24-hour quick-stop stores, walk-in hair or nail salons, copy shops, and dry cleaners.

Marketers further subdivide the convenience category into impulse items, staples, or emergency items. **Impulse goods and services** are purchased on the spur of the moment, such as a visit to a car wash or a pack of gum tossed in at the register. Some marketers have even come up with ways to make impulse shopping on the Internet attractive. Last-minute shoppers can use GiftBaskets.com's Gift Basket Emergency Service to choose and ship gifts quickly. They can select such items as Little Angel (for a new baby) or Chocolate Lover's Dream (for a birthday or anniversary) by 1 p.m. Monday through Friday and be assured their gift will be delivered the same day. Emergency gifts don't come cheap—they range in price from about $40 to $125—but they fulfill an immediate need for goods and services. Shoppers can also sign up for the firm's reminder service, which sends them e-mail reminders of loved ones' birthdays, anniversaries, and any other occasion that might require a gift.[10]

Staples are convenience goods and services that consumers constantly replenish to maintain a ready inventory; gasoline, shampoo, and dry cleaning are good examples. Marketers spend many hours and dollars creating messages for consumers about these products, partly because there are so many competitors.

Emergency goods and services are bought in response to unexpected and urgent needs. A snow blower purchased during a snowstorm and a visit to a hospital emergency room to treat a broken ankle are examples. Depending on your viewpoint, the products offered by GiftBaskets' emergency service could also fall into this category.

convenience products
Goods and services that consumers want to purchase frequently, immediately, and with minimal effort.

© PR NEWS FOTO/WM. WRIGLEY JR. COMPANY

Wrigley's Thin Ice Strips could be considered a convenience product.

Because consumers devote little effort to convenience product purchase decisions, marketers must strive to make these exchanges as simple as possible. Store location can boost a convenience product's visibility. Marketers compete vigorously for prime locations, which can make all the difference between a consumer choosing one gas station, vending machine, or dry cleaner over another.

In addition, location *within* a store can make the difference between success and failure of a product, which is why manufacturers fight so hard for the right spot on supermarket shelves. Typically, the larger and more powerful grocery manufacturers such as Sara Lee, Kellogg, and General Mills get the most visible spots. Kraft Foods has eight or ten special displays in many supermarkets. Brands such as Miracle Whip, Ritz crackers, Philadelphia cream cheese, Kool-Aid, and Oreo cookies all belong to Kraft—and enjoy prime shelf space. But visibility to consumers sometimes comes at a price, often through a practice called **slotting allowances,** or slotting fees—money paid by producers to retailers to guarantee display of their merchandise. According to retailers, the purpose of slotting allowances is to cover their losses if products don't sell. But the Federal Trade Commission (FTC) has investigated the practice of slotting allowances and found that these fees are far from uniform; they vary greatly across product categories, in both whether fees are charged and, if they are, how large the fees will be.[11] In addition, a new trend regarding slotting allowances is emerging: growth in the private-label goods category has been so great over the last few years that retailers are willing to forfeit the allowances they might receive so that they can get into the manufacturing end themselves. This is particularly true of private-label organic and ethnic foods.[12]

Shopping Products

shopping products
Products that consumers purchase after comparing competing offerings.

In contrast to the purchase of convenience items, consumers buy **shopping products** only after comparing competing offerings on such characteristics as price, quality, style, and color. Shopping products typically cost more than convenience purchases. This category includes tangible items such as clothing, furniture, electronics, and appliances, as well as services such as child care, auto repairs, insurance, and hotel stays. The purchaser of a shopping product lacks complete information prior to the buying trip and gathers information during the buying process.

Several important features distinguish shopping products: physical attributes, service attributes such as warranties and after-sale service terms, prices, styling, and places of purchase. A store's name and reputation have considerable influence on people's buying behavior. The personal selling efforts of salespeople also provide important promotional support.

Buyers and marketers treat some shopping products, such as refrigerators and washing machines, as relatively homogeneous products. To the consumer, one brand seems largely the same as another. Marketers may try to differentiate homogeneous products from competing products in several ways. They may emphasize price and value, or they may attempt to educate buyers about less obvious features that contribute to a product's quality, appeal, and uniqueness.

Other shopping products seem heterogeneous because of basic differences among them. Examples include furniture, physical-fitness training, vacations, and clothing. Differences in features often separate competing heterogeneous shopping products in the minds of consumers. Perceptions of style, color, and fit can all affect consumer choices.

©2004 Dooney & Bourke

PR NEWS WIRE DOONEY & BOURKE

A Dooney & Bourke bag falls into the category of shopping products because consumers would spend time to compare features and quality before making a final selection.

Specialty Products

specialty products Products that offer unique characteristics that cause buyers to prize those particular brands.

Specialty products offer unique characteristics that cause buyers to prize those particular brands. They typically carry high prices, and many represent well-known brands. Examples of specialty goods include Hermès scarves, Kate Spade handbags, Ritz-Carlton resorts, Tiffany jewelry, and Hummer automobiles. Specialty services include professional services such as financial advice, legal counsel, and cosmetic surgery.

Purchasers of specialty goods and services know exactly what they want—and they are willing to pay accordingly. These buyers begin shopping with complete information, and they refuse to accept substitutes. Because consumers are willing to exert considerable effort to obtain specialty products, producers can promote them through relatively few retail locations. In fact, some firms intentionally limit the range of retailers that carry their products to add to their cachet. Both highly personalized service by sales associates and image advertising help marketers promote specialty items. Because these products are available in so few retail outlets, advertisements frequently list their locations or give toll-free telephone numbers that provide customers with this information.

In recent years some makers of specialty products, such as Coach handbags and Donna Karan clothing, have broadened their market by selling some of their goods through company-owned discount outlets. The stores attract consumers who want to own specialty items but who cannot or do not wish to pay their regular prices. The goods offered, however, are usually last season's styles. Tiffany has taken a different approach—broadening its base within its own store. Shoppers who visit the store on Fifth Avenue in New York City can take the elevator to the second floor, where they may purchase a variety of items in sterling silver at prices significantly lower than those for gold and gemstone jewelry. A number of these items are also available in Tiffany's mail-order catalog.

CLASSIFYING CONSUMER SERVICES

Like tangible goods, services are also classified based on the convenience, shopping, and specialty products categories. But added insights can be gained by examining several factors that are unique to classifying services. Service firms may serve consumer markets, business markets, or both. A firm offering architectural services may design either residential or commercial buildings or both. A cleaning service may clean houses, offices, or both. In addition, services can be classified as equipment based or people based. A car wash is an equipment-based service, whereas a law office is people based. Marketers may ask themselves any of these five questions to help classify certain services:

1. What is the nature of the service?

2. What type of relationship does the service organization have with its customers?

3. How much flexibility is there for customization and judgment on the part of the service provider?

4. Do demand and supply for the service fluctuate?

5. How is the service delivered?[13]

A person attempting to classify the activities of a boarding kennel would answer these questions in one way; a person evaluating a lawn care service would come up with different answers. For example, customers would bring their pets to the kennel to receive service, while the lawn care staff would travel to customers' homes to provide service. Workers at the kennel are likely to have closer interpersonal relationships with pet owners—and their pets—than lawn care workers, who might not meet their customers at all. Someone assessing demand for the services of a ski resort or a food concession at the beach is likely to find fluctuations by season. And a dentist has flexibility in making decisions about a patient's care, whereas a delivery service must arrive with a package at the correct destination, on time.

APPLYING THE CONSUMER PRODUCTS CLASSIFICATION SYSTEM

The three-way classification system of convenience, shopping, and specialty goods and services helps guide marketers in developing a successful marketing strategy. Buyer behavior patterns differ for the three types of purchases. For example, classifying a new food item as a convenience product leads to insights about marketing needs in branding, promotion, pricing, and distribution decisions. Table 11.1 summarizes the impact of this classification system on the development of an effective marketing mix.

The classification system, however, also poses a few problems. The major obstacle to implementing this system results from the suggestion that all goods and services must fit within one of the three categories. Some fit neatly into one category, but others share characteristics of more than one category. How would you classify the purchase of a new automobile? Before classifying the expensive good, which is handled by a few exclusive dealers in the area, as a specialty product, consider other characteristics. New-car buyers often shop extensively among competing models and dealers before deciding on the best deal. And there is a wide range of models, features, and prices to consider. At

table 11.1 Marketing Impact of the Consumer Products Classification System

	CONVENIENCE PRODUCTS	SHOPPING PRODUCTS	SPECIALTY PRODUCTS
Consumer Factors			
Planning time involved in purchase	Very little	Considerable	Extensive
Purchase frequency	Frequent	Less frequent	Infrequent
Importance of convenient location	Critical	Important	Unimportant
Comparison of price and quality	Very little	Considerable	Very little
Marketing Mix Factors			
Price	Low	Relatively high	High
Importance of seller's image	Unimportant	Very important	Important
Distribution channel length	Long	Relatively short	Very short
Number of sales outlets	Many	Few	Very few; often one per market area
Promotion	Advertising and promotion by producer	Personal selling and advertising by both producer and retailer	Personal selling and advertising by both producer and retailer

one end of the spectrum is a basic Kia or Ford that could be purchased for less than $20,000. At the other end is what people are calling European supercars such as the Porsche Carrera GT or the Mercedes-Benz SLR McLaren, both costing $500,000 or more. These cars are fast, powerful, and hard to find—which boosts their value.[14]

So it's a good idea to think of the categorization process in terms of a continuum representing degrees of effort expended by consumers. At one end of the continuum, they casually pick up convenience items; at the other end, they search extensively for specialty products. Shopping products fall between these extremes. In addition, car dealers may offer services, both during and after the sale, that play a big role in the purchase decision. On this continuum, the new car purchase might appear between the categories of shopping and specialty products but closer to specialty products.

A second problem with the classification system emerges because consumers differ in their buying patterns. One person may walk into a hair salon and request a haircut without an appointment, while another may check references and compare prices before selecting a stylist. But the first consumer's impulse purchase of a haircut does not make hair styling services a convenience item. Marketers classify goods and services by considering the purchase patterns of the majority of buyers.

 assessment check

1. What are the three major classifications of consumer products?
2. Identify five factors marketers should consider in classifying consumer services.

4   Describe each of the types of business goods and services.

TYPES OF BUSINESS PRODUCTS

Business buyers are professional customers. Their job duties require rational, cost-effective purchase decisions. For instance, General Mills applies much of the same purchase decision process to buying flour that Pillsbury does.

The classification system for business products emphasizes product uses rather than customer buying behavior. B2B products generally fall into one of six categories for product uses: installations, accessory equipment, component parts and materials, raw materials, supplies, and business services.[15] Figure 11.4 illustrates the six types of business products.

Installations

The specialty products of the business market are called **installations.** This classification includes major capital investments for new factories and heavy machinery and for telecommunications systems. Purchases of new Boeing 787 Dreamliner airplanes by Qantas and Kenya Airways are considered installations for those airlines.

Because installations last for long periods of time and their purchases involve large sums of money, they represent major decisions for organizations. Negotiations often extend over several months and involve numerous decision makers. Vendors often provide technical expertise along with tangible goods. Representatives who sell custom-made equipment work closely with buying firms' engineers and production personnel to design the most satisfactory products possible.

Price typically does not dominate purchase decisions for installations, although a single order of 115 new Dreamliners by Qantas will net Boeing $14.4 billion.[16] A purchasing firm buys such a product for its efficiency and performance over its useful life. The firm also wants to minimize breakdowns. Downtime is expensive because the firm must pay employees while they wait for repairs on the machine. Installations are major investments often designed specifically for the purchasers.

Training of the buyer's workforce to operate the equipment correctly, along with significant after-sale service, is usually also involved. As a result, marketers of these systems typically focus their promotional efforts on employing highly trained sales representatives, often with technical backgrounds. Advertising, if the firm uses it at all, emphasizes company reputation and directs potential buyers to contact local sales representatives.

Most installations are marketed directly from manufacturers to users. Even a onetime sale may require continuing contacts for regular product servicing. Some manufacturers prefer to lease extremely expensive installations to customers rather than sell the items outright, and they assign personnel directly to the lessees' sites to operate or maintain the equipment.

Accessory Equipment

Only a few decision makers may participate in a purchase of **accessory equipment**—capital items that typically cost less and last for shorter periods than installations. Although quality and service exert important influences on purchases of accessory equipment, price may significantly affect these decisions. Accessory equipment includes products such as power tools, computers, smart phones, and cell phones. Although these products are considered capital investments and buyers depreciate their costs over several years, their useful lives generally are much shorter than those of installations.

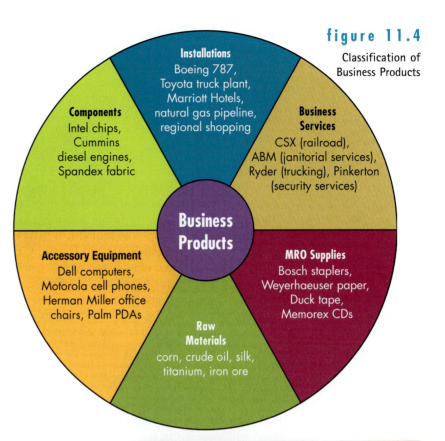

figure 11.4

Classification of Business Products

Business Products

Installations
Boeing 787, Toyota truck plant, Marriott Hotels, natural gas pipeline, regional shopping

Components
Intel chips, Cummins diesel engines, Spandex fabric

Business Services
CSX (railroad), ABM (janitorial services), Ryder (trucking), Pinkerton (security services)

Accessory Equipment
Dell computers, Motorola cell phones, Herman Miller office chairs, Palm PDAs

MRO Supplies
Bosch staplers, Weyerhaeuser paper, Duck tape, Memorex CDs

Raw Materials
corn, crude oil, silk, titanium, iron ore

Space Garden by Diarmuid Gavin

Canon
Imaging across networks

IMAGE COURTESY OF THE ADVERTISING ARCHIVES

A Canon printer is part of a business's accessory equipment because the purchaser would compare prices of competing products, as well as features. Advertising plays a strong role in the marketing of accessory equipment.

Marketing these products requires continuous representation and dealing with the widespread geographic dispersion of purchasers. To cope with these market characteristics, a wholesaler—often called an *industrial distributor*—might be used to contact potential customers in its own geographic area. Customers usually do not require technical assistance, and a manufacturer of accessory equipment often can distribute its products effectively through wholesalers. Advertising is an important component in the marketing mix for accessory equipment.

Component Parts and Materials

Whereas business buyers use installations and accessory equipment in the process of producing their own final products, **component parts and materials** represent finished business products of one producer that become part of the final products of another producer. Some materials, such as flour, undergo further processing before becoming part of finished products. Textiles, paper pulp, and chemicals are also examples of component parts and materials. Bose supplies its luxury sound systems to auto manufacturers such as Audi, Infiniti, Cadillac, and Ferrari. Marketers for the auto manufacturers believe that Bose systems are a good match between premium sound and their luxury vehicles, comparing the high performance of the Bose sound systems to the high performance of their cars.[17]

Purchasers of component parts and materials need regular, continuous supplies of uniform-quality products. They generally contract to purchase these items for set periods of time. Marketers commonly emphasize direct sales, and satisfied customers often become regular buyers. Wholesalers sometimes supply fill-in purchases and handle sales to smaller purchasers.

Raw Materials

Farm products, such as beef, cotton, eggs, milk, poultry, and soybeans, and natural resources, such as coal, copper, iron ore, and lumber, constitute **raw materials.** These products resemble component parts and materials in that they become part of the buyers' final products. Cargill supplies many of the raw materials for finished food products—dry corn ingredients, flour, food starch, oils and shortenings, soy protein and sweeteners, and beef and pork. Food manufacturers then take and turn these materials into finished products including cake and barbecued ribs.[18]

Most raw materials carry grades determined according to set criteria, assuring purchasers of the receipt of standardized products of uniform quality. As with component parts and materials, vendors commonly market raw materials directly to buying organizations, typically according to contractual terms. Wholesalers are increasingly involved in purchasing raw materials from foreign suppliers.

Price is seldom a deciding factor in a raw materials purchase since the costs are often set at central markets, determining virtually identical transactions among competing sellers. Purchasers buy raw materials from the firms they consider best able to deliver the required quantities and qualities.

WE KNEW WE HAD TO HAVE THE CHOPS TO HANG WITH THIS CROWD.

Cargill markets raw materials, such as pork, to other businesses.

REPRINTED WITH PERMISSION OF CARGILL, INCORPORATED

Supplies

If installations represent the specialty products of the business market, operating supplies are its convenience products. **Supplies** constitute the regular expenses that a firm incurs in its daily operations. These expenses do not become part of the buyer's final products.

Supplies are also called **MRO items** because they fall into three categories: (1) maintenance items, such as brooms, filters, and lightbulbs; (2) repair items, such as nuts and bolts used in repairing equipment; and (3) operating supplies, such as fax paper, Post-it notes, and pencils. Office Max sells all kinds of supplies to small, medium, and large businesses. Companies can purchase everything from paper and labels to filing cabinets, lighting, computers, and copiers. The firm also offers print services, downloadable forms, and the production of custom artwork.[19]

A purchasing manager regularly buys operating supplies as a routine job duty. Wholesalers often facilitate sales of supplies because of the low unit prices, the small order size, and the large number of potential buyers. Because supplies are relatively standardized, heavy price competition frequently keeps costs under control. However, a business buyer spends little time making decisions about these products. Exchanges of products frequently demand simple telephone, Web, or EDI orders or regular purchases from a sales representative of a local wholesaler.

Business Services

The **business services** category includes the intangible products that firms buy to facilitate their production and operating processes. Examples of business services are financial services, leasing and rental services that supply equipment and vehicles, insurance, security, legal advice, and consulting. As mentioned earlier, many service providers sell the same services to both consumers and organizational buyers—telephone, gas, and electricity, for example—although service firms may maintain separate marketing groups for the two customer segments.

Organizations also purchase many adjunct services that assist their operations but are not essentially a part of the final product. WebEx offers businesses services that include Web conferencing, videoconferencing, audioconferencing, and Webcasts. Marketers for the firm point out that WebEx's services can help a company demonstrate goods and services any time, anywhere; deliver live, interactive training; and manage geographically scattered teams.[20]

Price may strongly influence purchase decisions for business services. The buying firm must decide whether to purchase a service or provide that service internally. This decision may depend on how frequently the firm needs the service and the specialized knowledge required to provide it.

Purchase decision processes vary considerably for different types of business services. A firm may purchase window-cleaning services through a routine and straightforward process similar to that for buying operating supplies. By contrast, a purchase decision for highly specialized environmental engineering advice requires complex analysis and perhaps lengthy negotiations similar to those for purchases of installations. This variability of the marketing mix for business services and other business products is outlined in Table 11.2.

business services Intangible products that firms buy to facilitate their production and operating processes.

table 11.2 Marketing Impact of the Business Products Classification System

FACTOR	INSTALLATIONS	ACCESSORY EQUIPMENT	COMPONENT PARTS AND MATERIALS	RAW MATERIALS	SUPPLIES	BUSINESS SERVICES
Organizational Factors						
Planning time	Extensive	Less extensive	Less extensive	Varies	Very little	Varies
Purchase frequency	Infrequent	More frequent	Frequent	Infrequent	Frequent	Varies
Comparison of price and quality	Quality very important	Quality and price important	Quality important	Quality important	Price important	Varies
Marketing Mix Factors						
Price	High	Relatively high	Low to high	Low to high	Low	Varies
Distribution channel length	Very short	Relatively short	Short	Short	Long	Varies
Promotion method	Personal selling by producer	Advertising	Personal selling	Personal selling	Advertising by producer	Varies

The purchase of the right business services can make a difference in a firm's competitiveness. The Regus Group provides businesses with facilities for meetings and conferences in 350 cities across 60 countries. Not only are these facilities staffed by experts available for assistance, but they are also equipped with every electronic medium and amenity a business could possibly need. Regus offers expertise as well as lower prices than hotels, where many firms routinely conduct conferences and other meetings.[21]

✔ assessment check

1. What are the six main classifications of business products?
2. What are the three categories of supplies?

---

5 Explain how quality is used by marketers as a product strategy.

QUALITY AS A PRODUCT STRATEGY

No matter how a product is classified, nothing is more frustrating to a customer than having a new item break after just a few uses or having it not live up to expectations. The cell phone that hisses static at you unless you stand still or the seam that rips out of your new jacket aren't life-altering experiences, but they do leave an impression of poor quality that likely will lead you to make different purchases in the future. Then there's the issue of service quality—the department store that seems to have no salespeople or the computer help line that leaves you on hold for 20 minutes.

total quality management (TQM) Continuous effort to improve products and work processes with the goal of achieving customer satisfaction and world-class performance.

Quality is a key component to a firm's success in a competitive marketplace. The efforts to create and market high-quality goods and services have been referred to as **total quality management (TQM).** TQM expects all of a firm's employees to continually improve products and work processes with the goal of achieving customer satisfaction and world-class performance. This means that engineers design products that work, marketers develop products that people want, and salespeople deliver on their promises. Managers are responsible for communicating the goals of total quality management to all staff members and for encouraging workers to improve themselves and take pride in their work. Of course, achieving maximum quality is easier said than done, and the process is never complete.

WORLDWIDE QUALITY PROGRAMS

Although the movement began in the United States in the 1920s as an attempt to improve product quality by improving the manufacturing process, it was during the 1980s that the quality revolution picked up speed in U.S. corporations. The campaign to improve quality found leadership in large manufacturing firms such as Ford, Xerox, and Motorola that had lost market share to Japanese competitors. Smaller companies that supplied parts to large firms then began to recognize quality as a requirement for success. Today, commitment to quality has spread to service industries, not-for-profit organizations, government agencies, and educational institutions.

Congress established the Malcolm Baldrige National Quality Award to recognize excellence in quality management. Named after the late secretary of commerce Malcolm Baldrige, the award is the highest national recognition for quality that a U.S. company can receive. The award works toward promoting quality awareness, recognizing quality achievements of U.S. companies, and publicizing successful quality strategies.

The quality movement is also strong in European countries. The European Union's **ISO 9002** standards define international criteria for quality management and quality assurance. These standards were originally developed by the International Organization for Standardization in Switzerland to ensure consistent quality among products manufactured and sold throughout the nations of the European Union (EU). The standards now include criteria for systems of management as well. Many European companies require suppliers to complete ISO certification, which is a rigorous fourteen-month process, as a condition of doing business with them. The U.S. member body of ISO is the National Institute of Standards and Technology (NIST).[22]

BENCHMARKING

Firms often rely on an important tool called **benchmarking** to set performance standards. The purpose of benchmarking is to achieve superior performance that results in a competitive advantage in the marketplace. A typical benchmarking process involves three main activities: identifying manufacturing or business processes that need improvement, comparing internal processes to those of industry leaders, and implementing changes for quality improvement. The practice of benchmarking has been around for a long time. Henry Ford is known to have developed his own version of the assembly line by observing Armour Meat Packing and also adapting some of Sears, Roebuck's scheduling procedures.[23]

Benchmarking requires two types of analyses: internal and external. Before a company can compare itself with another, it must first analyze its own activities to determine strengths and weaknesses. This assessment establishes a baseline for comparison. External analysis involves gathering information about the benchmark partner to find out why the partner is perceived as the industry's best. A comparison of the results of the analysis provides an objective basis for making improvements. Large firms that have engaged in benchmarking include 3M, Bank of America, DuPont, General Mills, Kraft Foods, and Sun Microsystems. These firms conduct formal, complex programs, but smaller firms may decide to use benchmarking as well.[24]

QUALITY OF SERVICES

Everyone has a story about bad and good service—the waiter who forgot a dinner order, a car mechanic who offered a ride to and from the repair shop. As a consumer, your perception of the quality of the service you have purchased is usually determined during the **service encounter**—the point at which the customer and service provider interact. Employees such as bank tellers, cashiers, and customer service representatives have a powerful impact on their customers' decision to return or not. You might pass the word to your friends about the friendly staff at your local breakfast eatery, the slow cashiers at a local supermarket, or the huge scoops of ice cream you got at the nearby ice cream stand. Those words form powerful marketing messages about the services you received.

Service quality refers to the expected and perceived quality of a service offering, and it has a huge effect on the competitiveness of a company. Toyota is so committed to service that it recently opened a National Customer Center at its manufacturing facility in Indiana. Aimed primarily at the dealers who sell its trucks, the center is designed to provide guests with information, support, and motivation. "Our customers drive our business," says Shankar Basu, president and CEO of Toyota Material Handling, USA.[25] In an entirely different industry, winter resorts have discovered that ski lessons tailored to individual needs and interests—particularly those of beginners—are helping their business grow. "A private instructor is a coach, companion, guide, and concierge, and our instructors understand that they fulfill all of these roles instead of teaching a straightforward lesson," explains Dee Byrne, ski school director at Vail Mountain in Colorado.[26] Unfortunately, poor service can cut into a firm's competitiveness, as Comcast found when dealing with frustrated customers who had been put on hold, disconnected, transferred to the wrong department—and sent the wrong bill.[27] When customers receive this level of service, they often switch to a competitor.

Service quality is determined by five variables:

1. *Tangibles,* or physical evidence. A tidy office and clean uniforms are examples.

Singapore Airlines is well known for its service quality. The company continually invests in training its staff to be top performers, and it solicits feedback from its customers to find ways to improve.

2. *Reliability,* or consistency of performance and dependability. "The right technology. Right away," asserts software solutions provider CDW.

3. *Responsiveness,* or the willingness and readiness of employees to provide service. "What's your request?" is the tag line for Wyndham Hotels & Resorts advertisements.

4. *Assurances,* or the confidence communicated by the service provider. "Relax, it's FedEx," say ads for the delivery firm.

5. *Empathy,* or the service provider's efforts to understand the customer's needs and then individualize the service. "Managing the economy that means most: yours," says American Express to reassure its customers.

If a gap exists between the level of service that customers expect and the level they think they have received, it can be favorable or unfavorable. If you get a larger steak than you expected or your plane arrives ahead of schedule, the gap is favorable, and you are likely to try that service again. But if your steak is tiny, overcooked, and cold or your plane is two hours late, the gap is unfavorable, and you will probably seek out another restaurant or decide to drive the next time. Some wine store owners have found a way to capitalize on the dissatisfaction that many consumers feel with the service they have received when shopping for wine. Instead of conveying a snobbish attitude that intimidates customers—and often turns them away from the store—some shop owners are going out of their way to make customers feel comfortable and welcome. They create handwritten signs, offer a basket of bargain wines, and arrange the store to facilitate browsing and shopping. They also train their staff to smile and offer friendly assistance. "Wine shopping should be fun," explain two food writers. "If it looks like it's a chore to work or shop there, you may want to steer clear."[28]

Briefly
Speaking

"If you can't smile, don't open a store."

—Chinese proverb

assessment check

1. What is TQM?
2. What are the five variables of service quality?

6 Explain why firms develop lines of related products.

product line Series of related products offered by one company.

DEVELOPMENT OF PRODUCT LINES

Few firms today market only one product. A typical firm offers its customers a **product line**—that is, a series of related products. Designer Ralph Lauren has a range of product lines, beginning with men's and women's clothing (Polo), moving on to home furnishings (Ralph Lauren Home), and adding its new Rugby brand. Each line encompasses a variety of products. For example, Polo offers clothing such as polo shirts and slacks; accessories such as sunglasses; and fragrances such as Polo Black for men. Ralph Lauren Home offers sheets and pillowcases, comforters and blankets, and towels.[29]

The motivations for marketing complete product lines rather than concentrating on a single product include the desire to grow, enhancing the company's position in the market, optimal use of company resources, and exploiting the product life cycle. The following subsections examine each of the first three reasons. The final reason, exploiting the stages of the product life cycle, is discussed in the main section that focuses on strategic implications of the product life cycle concept.

© MICHAEL NEWMAN/PHOTO EDIT

Ralph Lauren has created a number of product lines. One is the Polo Ralph Lauren clothing and fragrance line.

DESIRE TO GROW

A company limits its growth potential when it concentrates on a single product, even though the company may have started that way, as retailer L. L. Bean did with its single style of boots called Maine Hunting Shoes. Now the company sells boots for men, women, and children, along with apparel, outdoor and travel gear, home furnishings, and even products for pets. The company, which has grown into a large mail-order and online retailer with a flagship store in Freeport, Maine, is nearly a century old. It is unlikely that the company would have grown to its current size if the successors of Leon Leonwood Bean had stuck to manufacturing and selling a single style of his original Maine Hunting Shoes.[30]

ENHANCING THE COMPANY'S POSITION IN THE MARKET

A company with a line of products often makes itself more important to both consumers and marketing intermediaries than a firm with only one product. A shopper who purchases a tent often buys related camping items. For instance, L. L. Bean now offers a wide range of products so that consumers can completely outfit themselves for outdoor activities or travel. They can purchase hiking boots, sleeping bags and tents, fishing gear, duffel bags, kayaks and canoes, snowshoes and skis, as well as clothing for their adventures. In addition, the firm offers its Outdoor Discovery Schools programs, which teach customers the basics of kayaking, fly fishing, and other sports directly related to the products they purchase from the retailer. Few would know about L. L. Bean if the company only sold its original boots. Business buyers often expect a firm that manufactures a particular product to offer related items as well.[31]

Servicing the variety of products that a company sells can also enhance its position in the market. Bean's Outdoor Discovery Schools programs are a form of service, as are its policy to accept returns no matter what. Schoolchildren who purchase the firm's book backpacks can return them anytime for a new one—even if the child has simply outgrown the pack. Policies like this make consumers feel comfortable about purchasing many different products from L. L. Bean.

OPTIMAL USE OF COMPANY RESOURCES

By spreading the costs of its operations over a series of products, a firm may reduce the average production and marketing costs of each product. Hospitals have taken advantage of idle facilities by adding a variety of outreach services. Many now operate health and fitness centers that, besides generating profits themselves, also feed customers into other hospital services. For example, a blood pressure check at the fitness center might result in a referral to a staff physician.

✓ *assessment check*

1. List the four reasons for developing a product line.

THE PRODUCT MIX

A company's **product mix** is the assortment of product lines and individual product offerings that the company sells. The right blend of product lines and individual products allows a firm to maximize sales opportunities within the limitations of its resources. Marketers typically measure product mixes according to width, length, and depth.

7 Describe the way marketers typically measure product mixes and make product mix decisions.

PRODUCT MIX WIDTH

The *width* of a product mix refers to the number of product lines the firm offers. As Table 11.3 shows, Johnson & Johnson offers a broad line of retail consumer products in the U.S. market, as well as business-to-business products to the medical community. Consumers can purchase over-the-counter medications, nutritional products, dental care products, and first-aid products, among others. Healthcare professionals can obtain prescription drugs, medical and diagnostic devices, and wound treatments. LifeScan, one of Johnson & Johnson's subsidiaries, offers the OneTouch Ultra 2

Blood Glucose Monitoring System, which is designed to simplify blood-sugar testing for people with diabetes. In conjunction with the testing system, LifeScan provides Simple Start educational materials, which teach patients how to use the device and also offer tips on managing diabetes that include understanding portion control and monitoring carbohydrate intake.[32]

PRODUCT MIX LENGTH

The *length* of a product mix refers to the number of different products a firm sells. Table 11.3 identifies some of the hundreds of healthcare products offered by Johnson & Johnson. Some of J&J's most recognizable brands are Band-Aid, Motrin, Tylenol, and Neutrogena.

PRODUCT MIX DEPTH

Depth refers to variations in each product that the firm markets in its mix. Johnson & Johnson's Band-Aid brand bandages come in a variety of shapes and sizes, including Finger-Care Tough Strips, Comfort-Flex and Activ-Flex for elbows and knees, and Advance Healing Blister bandages.

PRODUCT MIX DECISIONS

Establishing and managing the product mix have become increasingly important marketing tasks. Adding depth, length, and width to the product mix requires careful thinking and planning; otherwise, a firm can end up with too many products, including some that don't sell well. To evaluate a firm's product mix, marketers look at the effectiveness of its depth, length, and width. Has the firm ignored a viable consumer segment? It may improve performance by increasing product line depth to offer a product variation that will attract the new segment. Can the firm achieve economies in its sales and distribution efforts by adding complementary product lines to the mix? If so, a wider product mix may seem appropriate. Does the firm gain equal contributions from all products in its portfolio? If not, it may decide to lengthen or shorten the product mix to increase revenues. Schick recently added a battery-powered, four-blade model to its product line, called the Quattro Power Razor. The kit, which includes the razor, one cartridge, a stand, and a battery, sells for $10.99. Rival Gillette—now part of Procter & Gamble—tried to block the sale of the new Schick product, claiming that its patent on three-bladed razors included four-bladed razors as well, but the claim was struck down in court.[33]

Another way to add to the mix is to purchase product lines from other companies. Or a firm can acquire entire companies through mergers or acquisitions. Boeing acquired aerospace parts supplier Aviall, which allowed Boeing to expand its operations as it received more orders for new planes.[34]

table 11.3   Johnson & Johnson's Mix of Healthcare Products

ALLERGY, COLDS, FLU	NUTRITIONALS	SKIN AND HAIR CARE	DENTAL CARE	MEDICAL DEVICES AND DIAGNOSTICS
Motrin pain reliever	Lactaid digestive aid	Aveeno lotions	ACT fluoride rinse	VITROS chemistry immunodiagnostics
Tylenol pain reliever	Splenda artificial sweetener	Clean & Clear facial cleansers and toners	REACH dental floss	Diabetes management products
Simply cough cough syrup	Viactiv calcium supplement	Johnson's Baby Shampoo	ARESTIN antibiotic treatment	Orthopedic joint replacement products
		Neutrogena soaps and shampoos	REACH toothbrushes	MAMMOTOME Breast Biopsy System

Source: Information from Johnson & Johnson Web site, **http://www.jnj.com**, accessed May 1, 2006.

A firm should assess its current product mix for another important reason: to determine the feasibility of a line extension. A **line extension** adds individual offerings that appeal to different market segments while remaining closely related to the existing product line. Recognizing that winter sports enthusiasts want to enjoy their favorite tunes while on the slopes, Burton Snowboards and Motorola developed Burton Audex Snowboard Jackets, which use Motorola's Bluetooth technology to give wireless connectivity to wearers for their cell phones and iPods—without having to pull the devices out of their pockets. The Audex has a microphone embedded in the collar, a mini caller ID sewn into the sleeve, and a control pane that lets users receive or make phone calls and manage music on their iPods.[35]

The marketing environment also plays a role in a marketer's evaluation of a firm's product mix. In the case of Burton and Motorola, the social-cultural environment had shifted so that consumers were looking for more ways to use their communications and music devices.

Careful evaluation of a firm's current product mix can also help marketers make decisions about brand management and new-product introductions. Chapter 12 examines the importance of branding, brand management, and the development and introduction of new products.

✓ *assessment check*

1. Define *product mix.*
2. How do marketers typically measure product mixes?

THE PRODUCT LIFE CYCLE

Products, like people, pass through stages as they age. Successful products progress through four basic stages: introduction, growth, maturity, and decline. This progression, known as the **product life cycle,** is shown in Figure 11.5.

The product life cycle concept applies to products or product categories within an industry, not to individual brands. For instance, camera cell phones are currently in the introductory stage but rapidly moving to the growth stage. Digital cameras are now in the growth stage, while traditional film cameras in the United States are in decline. There is no set schedule or time frame for a particular stage of the life cycle. Some products pass through certain stages rapidly, while others move more slowly. DVD players have shot through the introductory stage, while the Segway human transporter seems to be stuck in the introductory stage.

INTRODUCTORY STAGE

During the **introductory stage** of the product life cycle, a firm works to stimulate demand for the new market entry. Products in this stage might bring new technology to a product category. Because the product is unknown to the public, promotional campaigns stress information about its features. Additional promotions try to induce distribution channel members to carry the product. In this phase, the public becomes acquainted with the item's merits and begins to accept it. Entrepreneurs such as Roger Shiffman thrive on the introductory stage of their products' life cycles, as described in the "Marketing Success" feature.

A recent product whose introductory stage has been successful is the CD burner, which plays and creates a

> **Briefly**
> *Speaking*
>
> "Competition brings out the best in products and the worst in people."
>
> —David Sarnoff
> (1891–1971)
> Founder and president, RCA

8 Explain the concept of the product life cycle and identify the different stages.

product life cycle Progression of a product through introduction, growth, maturity, and decline stages.

figure 11.5

Stages in the Product Life Cycle

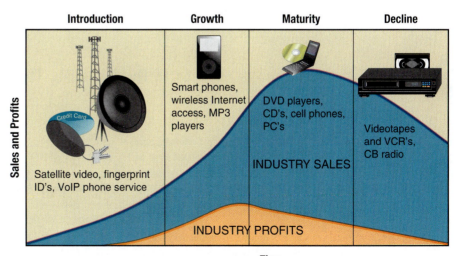

new CD—although it won't burn over an existing CD.[36] Other successful new products include Spa Cuisine frozen meals from Nestlé, which are frozen dinners made with whole grains, and Freschetta Brick Oven frozen pizzas.[37] Both of these food products are designed for busy consumers.

Technical problems and financial losses are common during the introductory stage as companies fine-tune product design and spend money on advertising. Many users remember early problems with the Internet—jammed portals, order fulfilling glitches, dot-coms that went bust. But DVD players and camera phones have experienced few of these setbacks. Although the photos taken by camera phones lack the clarity of full-featured cameras, new models will eventually catch up. And consumers don't seem to mind this, perhaps because they are still enjoying taking pictures with their phones. But another problem has cropped up—the issue of privacy. Camera phones are already so widespread that they have been banned from fitness centers, schools, and similar venues because officials fear that someone might post photos from the locker room or other private areas on the Internet.

GROWTH STAGE

Sales volume rises rapidly during the **growth stage** as new customers make initial purchases and early buyers repurchase the product, such as DVD players and camera phones. The growth stage usually begins when a firm starts to realize substantial profits from its investment. Word-of-mouth reports, mass advertising, and lowered prices all encourage hesitant buyers to make trial purchases of new products. In the case of big-screen TVs, both the plasma and LCD versions, low prices have not been a factor—many cost several thousand dollars. Big-screen simply means anything larger than 40 inches—which, by today's standards, may seem small. As sales volume rises, competitors enter the marketplace, creating new challenges for marketers. As companies with competing technologies vie for dominance, the TVs themselves get bigger and bigger. Recently, L. G. Philips LCD

© 2006 HEWLETT PACKARD DEVELOPMENT COMPANY

Digital photo printers for the home are in their growth stage. HP promotes its Photosmart color printers, which can print either 4" × 6" or 5" × 7" photos, or both, and can store 1,000 images.

marketing success   Is iZ the Next Big Thing?

Background. Maybe you remember Furby, the endearing electronic furball that chatted with you like a friend. Its inventor, Roger Shiffman, left Hasbro—in fact, left toys altogether—several years ago to pursue a relaxing retirement. But he's back with a new company and a new gadget. The company is called Zizzle and the gadget is call iZ.

The Challenge. For several years after Shiffman's successful launch of Furby, the toy industry in general was flagging. And Shiffman didn't quite

settle into retirement. Instead, he formed a new company. "We need a shake-up in toys," observes Avi Arad, CEO of Marvel Studios.

The Strategy. As Shiffman grew restless in retirement, he decided the marketplace needed a new toy. Instead of relying on focus groups, surveys, and other marketing research, he followed his instinct for good toys. He hired Jeff Breslow, president of design firm Big Monster Toys, to develop the new toy. "I want another Furby," he told Breslow.

announced its new 100-inch LCD, to compete against Samsung's 102-inch plasma, which was upstaged by Panasonic's 103-inch plasma. Consumers who want something for less than $2,000 will have to settle for V-Inc's 42-inch plasma.[38]

MATURITY STAGE

Sales of a product category continue to grow during the early part of the **maturity stage,** but eventually, they reach a plateau as the backlog of potential customers dwindles. By this time, many competitors have entered the market, and the firm's profits begin to decline as competition intensifies.

At this stage in the product life cycle, differences between competing products diminish as competitors discover the product and promotional characteristics most desired by customers. Available supplies exceed industry demand for the first time. Companies can increase their sales and market shares only at the expense of competitors, so the competitive environment becomes increasingly important. Cell phones are now in the maturity stage—and they are so commonplace that their use in public is considered disruptive by some, as described in the "Solving an Ethical Controversy" feature.

In the maturity stage, heavy promotional outlays emphasize any differences that still separate competing products, and brand competition intensifies. Some firms try to differentiate their products by focusing on attributes such as quality, reliability, and service. Others focus on redesign or other ways of extending the product life cycle. Remember the soft drink Tab? When it was introduced in 1963, it was the first low-calorie cola. With its slogan, "just one calorie," Tab revolutionized the soft-drink industry. Now in its maturity, Tab is new again—its parent, Coca-Cola, has introduced Tab Energy, formulated specifically for women. Tab Energy is pink and contains only 5 calories per can. Recognizing that women are major consumers of energy drinks, the firm hopes to use this opportunity to extend the life

© TERRI MILLER/E-VISUAL COMMUNICATIONS, INC.

Ritz crackers are a longtime favorite, so the product is at its maturity stage. Kraft offers serving suggestions at its Nabisco site to give consumers new ideas for the product's use.

The Outcome. The result of this assignment was iZ—a posable, animatronic creature that plays catchy beats when you poke its belly. It emits musical leads and rhythms when its ears are twisted, and its antennae produce all kinds of sound effects, including giggles and burps. iZ will also receive and play music from just about any source, including CD players and iPods. Kids like iZ because it allows them to create new sounds and songs every time they play with it. So do adults. "It's certainly unique," reports John Sullivan, senior vice president at Toys "R" Us. "We have yet to carry something that appeals to so broad a range of people."

Sources: Zizzle Web site, **http://www.zizzle.com**, accessed May 1, 2006; Wendy Cole, "Toyland's Savior?" *Time Inside Business*, September 2005, p. A19; "A Happy Tune for Zizzle's iZ?" *BusinessWeek*, August 23, 2005, **http://www.businessweek.com**.

Solving an Ethical Controversy

Silencing Cell Phones in Movie Theaters

When you go to a movie theater, you're there to watch the movie. Presumably, so are the other moviegoers sitting around you. But what about the one person whose cell phone trills just as the main character zeroes in on the key to the mystery? Movie theater owners are keenly aware of this problem and have tried all kinds of ways to encourage moviegoers to turn off their cell phones—or at least to refrain from engaging in audible conversations—during movies. They've had ushers sweep the aisles looking for offenders. They've shown advertisements on the big screen asking viewers to shut off their phones. But now they are considering an approach that, while effective, has some consumer and civil rights groups concerned. Theater owners have petitioned the Federal Communications Commission (FCC) to remove the ban on cell phone jammers so that they can legally block cell phone signals.

Should movie theater owners be allowed to use technologies that block unwanted cell phone signals during movie screenings?

PRO

1. Customers who have paid to see a movie should be allowed to do so without the interruption of those who have chosen not to abide by the theater's rules or requests.
2. If customers are notified of the theater's practice, and if all signals are blocked in a theater, then all customers are treated equally. If they prefer, consumers may choose to go to another theater that does not use this technology.

CON

1. There's no need to block cell phone signals—offending patrons can be asked to leave the building.
2. People should have the ability to be reached in emergencies; if signals are blocked, they might miss a vital call.

Summary

Currently, companies are developing new technologies to address this problem. One product is a high-tech paint manufactured by Natural Nano that actually blocks out unwanted signals on demand. The paint uses nanotechnology to blend particles of copper into paint that will deflect radio signals. "You could use this in a concert hall [or movie theater], to allow cell phones to work before the concert and during breaks, but shutting them down during the performance," explains Michael Riedlinger, president of Natural Nano. This product could represent a compromise that representatives of both sides of the argument could accept.

Sources: Gloria Goodale, "Theaters in a Cellphone Jam," *Christian Science Monitor*, March 24, 2006, **http://www.csmonitor.com**; "Movie Theaters May Ask to Jam Cell Phones," Reuters, March 15, 2006, **http://news.yahoo.com**; Jon Van, "Slapping on a Coat of Silence," *Chicago Tribune*, March 1, 2006, sec. 1, pp. 1, 8.

Briefly
Speaking

"In business, you get what you want by giving other people what they want."

—Alice Foote MacDougall
(1867–1945)

Pioneering U.S. businesswoman

of Tab. "The energy drink category is growing, but a lot of brands are ignoring the fact that 40 percent of the consumption comes from women," explains Mary Merrill of Coca-Cola North America. "We are the first brand to go out there and directly target those women."[39]

DECLINE STAGE

In the **decline stage** of a product's life, innovations or shifts in consumer preferences bring about an absolute decline in industry sales. Dial telephones became touch-tone phones, which evolved to portable phones, which are now being replaced by conventional cell phones, which in turn are being replaced by camera phones. Thirty-five-millimeter home-movie film was replaced by videotape, which is now being replaced by DVD technology.

Some manufacturers refuse to give up in the decline stage. Zippo lighters have been around for more than 70 years; the company reports that it has made more than 350 million lighters to date. While the firm dominates the market for refillable lighters, the market itself has been on the decline.

But in recent years, collectors have started to rejuvenate the market—as tobacco collectibles become hotter in the market, Zippo lighters have increased again in popularity. Vintage Zippos are particularly sought after.[40] Although this secondary market doesn't bring revenue directly to Zippo, it does shine a new light on the old firm. Meanwhile, Zippo itself has launched new products, including its Zippo Multi-Purpose Lighter made to do nonsmoking chores like lighting candles, fireplaces, grills, and camping lanterns. The firm has hosted concerts aimed at aging baby boomers who recall holding their Zippos aloft to encourage rock groups to play encores. And Zippo is licensing products that focus on its brand image as the flame that never goes out—such as tiki torches and patio heaters.[41] The next section of this chapter discusses more specific strategies for extending the life cycle of a product.

It is important to remember that the traditional product life cycle differs from fad cycles. Fashions and fads profoundly influence marketing strategies. Fashions are currently popular products that tend to follow recurring life cycles. For example, bell-bottom pants that were popular in the 1960s and 1970s have returned as flares or boot-cut pants. In contrast, fads are products with abbreviated life cycles. Most fads experience short-lived popularity and then quickly fade, although some maintain residual markets among certain segments. Beanie Babies and power beads are examples of fads.

> ✓ *assessment check*
>
> 1. Identify the four stages of the product life cycle.
> 2. During which stage or stages are products likely to attract the most new customers?

EXTENDING THE PRODUCT LIFE CYCLE

9 Describe how a firm can extend a product's life cycle, and explain why certain products may be deleted.

Marketers usually try to extend each stage of the life cycles for their products as long as possible. Product life cycles can stretch indefinitely as a result of decisions designed to increase the frequency of use by current customers, increase the number of users for the product, find new uses, or change package sizes, labels, or product quality.

INCREASING FREQUENCY OF USE

During the maturity stage, the sales curve for a product category reaches a maximum point if the competitors exhaust the supply of potential customers who previously had not made purchases. However, if current customers buy more frequently than they formerly did, total sales will rise even though no new buyers enter the market.

For instance, consumers buy some products during certain seasons of the year. Marketers can boost purchase frequency by persuading these people to try the product year round. For decades, most people used sunscreen only during warm and sunny seasons of the year. With greater warnings about the risks of sun damage and skin cancer, however, companies now advertise the benefits of using sunscreen year round. In another change, Mars Inc. now releases special-edition M&Ms for different holidays, including Halloween and Easter. The firm also recently introduced Custom Printed M&Ms, which allow consumers to order their own initials or sayings printed on a box of M&Ms.

ASSOCIATED PRESS, AP

Mars extends the life cycle of M&Ms by increasing their use. The company offers a selection of seventeen colors and personalized messages for special occasions.

INCREASING THE NUMBER OF USERS

A second strategy for extending the product life cycle seeks to increase the overall market size by attracting new customers who previously have not used the product. Marketers may find their products in different stages of the life cycle in different countries. This difference can help firms extend product growth. Items that have reached the maturity stage in the United States may still be in the introductory stage somewhere else.

In recent years, the Walt Disney Company has spent time and money on advertising its theme parks to attract adults in addition to young families. Television commercials portray empty nesters taking off to Disney World for a second honeymoon once their children are grown. Dance studios are reaching out to all kinds of people who just want to stay in shape—not just aspiring ballerinas or competitive ballroom dancers. The American Council on Exercise reports that dancing for exercise is a growing trend in many regions of the United States. "People are looking for a more engaging alternative to their traditional workout," says Dr. Cedric Bryant, vice president of the organization. Dance studios are responding by offering beginner and novice classes to customers who want to get fit, lose weight, and learn a few moves.[42]

FINDING NEW USES

Finding new uses for a product is an excellent strategy for extending a product's life cycle. New applications for mature products include oatmeal as a cholesterol reducer, antacids as a calcium supplement, and aspirin for promoting heart health.

Marketers sometimes conduct contests or surveys to identify new uses for their products—often, consumers are the ones who have come up with the new ideas. The WD-40 company conducted one such survey to find the top 2,000 uses for its oil, which had always been used for cleaning metal parts and lubricating squeaky door hinges. The firm discovered that the State of New York was using it to protect the Statue of Liberty from weather, while Philadelphia was rubbing it into the Liberty Bell to keep it from squeaking.[43] Duct tape is another product with many uses—its maker, 3M, even includes a Duct Tape Workshop on its Web site, where consumers can learn how to make such items as a Duct Tape wallet.[44]

CHANGING PACKAGE SIZES, LABELS, OR PRODUCT QUALITY

Many firms try to extend their product life cycles by introducing physical changes in their offerings. Alternatively, new labels or changes in product size can lengthen a product's life cycle. Food marketers have brought out small packages designed to appeal to one-person households and extra-large containers for customers who want to buy in bulk. Other firms offer their products in convenient packages for use away from home or for use at the office. Kraft recently introduced its 100-calorie Snack Packs, which contain just the right portion of Oreos, Chips Ahoy cookies, and Nabisco crackers. After selling more than $100 million of these snack packs in the first year, the firm added more choices, including 100-calorie Snack Packs of Ritz Chips and Wheat Thins Multigrain Chips.[45]

Nabisco cookies and crackers come in convenient 100-calorie packs for consumers who like to snack without completely blowing their diets.

© ASSOCIATED PRESS, AP

PRODUCT DELETION DECISIONS

To avoid wasting resources promoting unpromising products, marketers must sometimes prune product lines and eliminate marginal products. Marketers typically face this decision during the late maturity and early decline stages of the product life cycle. Periodic reviews of weak products should justify either eliminating or retaining them.

A firm may continue to carry an unprofitable item to provide a complete line for its customers. For example, while most grocery stores lose money on bulky, low-unit-value items such as salt, they continue to carry these items to meet shopper demand.

Shortages of raw materials sometimes prompt companies to discontinue production and marketing of previously profitable items. A firm may even drop a profitable item that fails to fit into its existing product line, or fails to fit the direction in which the firm wants to grow. Some of these products return to the market carrying the names of other firms that purchase these "orphan brands" from the original manufacturers.

 assessment check

1. Describe the four strategies for extending a product's life cycle.
2. Under what circumstances do firms decide to delete a product from their line?

Strategic Implications of Marketing in the 21st Century

Marketers who want their businesses to succeed continue to develop new goods and services to attract and satisfy customers. They engage in continuous improvement activities, focusing on quality and customer service. And they continually evaluate their company's mix of products.

Marketers everywhere are constantly developing new and better products that fit their firm's overall strategy. Technological innovations are one area in which new products quickly replace old ones. Marketers are sometimes faced with the dilemma of lagging sales for formerly popular products. They must come up with ways to extend the lives of certain products to extend their firms' profitability and sometimes must recognize and delete those that no longer meet expectations.

REVIEW OF CHAPTER OBJECTIVES

1   Define *product* and distinguish between goods and services and how they relate to the goods–services continuum.

Marketers define a product as the bundle of physical, service, and symbolic attributes designed to satisfy customers' wants and needs. Goods are tangible products that customers can see, hear, smell, taste, or touch. Services are intangible tasks that satisfy the needs of customers. Goods represent one end of a continuum, and services represent the other.

2   Explain the importance of the service sector in today's marketplace.

The service sector makes a crucial contribution to the U.S. economy in terms of products and jobs. The U.S. service sector now makes up more than two-thirds of the economy. Services have grown because of consumers' desire for speed, convenience, and technological advances.

3   List the classifications of consumer goods and services and briefly describe each category.

Consumer products—both goods and services—are classified as convenience products (frequently purchased items), shopping products (products purchased after comparison), and specialty products (those that offer unique characteristics that consumers prize).

4   Describe each of the types of business goods and services.

Business products are classified as installations (major capital investments), accessory equipment (capital items that cost less and last for shorter periods than installations), component parts and materials (finished business products of one producer that become part of the final products of another producer), raw materials (natural resources such as lumber, beef, or cotton), supplies (the regular expenses that a firm incurs in daily operations), and business services (the intangible products that firms buy to facilitate their production and operating processes).

5   Explain how quality is used by marketers as a product strategy.

Many companies use total quality management (TQM) in an effort to encourage all employees to participate in producing the best goods and services possible. Companies may also participate in ISO 9002 certification or benchmarking to evaluate and improve quality. Consumers often evaluate service quality on the basis of tangibles, reliability, responsiveness, assurance, and empathy, so marketers of service firms strive to excel in all of these areas.

6   Explain why firms develop lines of related products.

Companies usually produce several related products rather than individual ones to achieve the objectives of growth, optimal use of company resources, and increased company importance in the market, and to make optimal use of the product life cycle.

7   Describe the way marketers typically measure product mixes and make product mix decisions.

Marketers must decide the right width, length, and depth of product lines. Width is the number of product lines. Length is the number of products a company sells. Depth refers to the number of variations of a product available in a product line. Marketers evaluate the effectiveness of all three elements of the product mix. They may purchase product lines from other companies or extend the product line, if necessary. Firms may also acquire entire companies and their product lines through mergers and acquisitions.

8   Explain the concept of the product life cycle and identify the different stages.

The product life cycle outlines the stages that a product goes through during its "life," including introduction, growth, maturity, and decline.

9   Describe how a firm can extend a product's life cycle, and explain why certain products may be deleted.

Marketers can extend the product life cycle by increasing frequency of use or number of users; finding new uses for the product; or changing package size, label, or quality. If none of these is successful, or if the product no longer fits a firm's line, the firm may decide to delete it from its line.

✓ *assessment check* **answers**

1.1 Define the term *product*.

A product is a bundle of physical, service, and symbolic attributes designed to satisfy a customer's wants and needs.

1.2 Why is the understanding of want satisfaction so important to marketers?

The understanding of want satisfaction is important to marketers because it helps them understand why people purchase certain goods and services.

1.3 Describe the goods–services continuum.

The goods–services continuum is a spectrum that helps marketers visualize the differences and similarities between goods and services.

1.4 List the six characteristics that distinguish services from goods.

The six characteristics distinguishing services from goods are the following: (1) services are intangible; (2) services are inseparable from the service providers; (3) services are perishable; (4) companies cannot easily standardize services; (5) buyers often play important roles in the creations and distribution of services; (6) service standards show wide variations.

2.1 Identify two reasons why services are important to the U.S. economy and business environment.

The service sector makes an important contribution to the economy in terms of products and jobs. Services also play a vital role in the international competitiveness of U.S. firms.

2.2 Why do service firms emphasize marketing?

The growth of potential service transactions represents a vast marketing opportunity, and the environment for services is changing—so marketers need to find new ways to reach customers.

3.1 What are the three major classifications of consumer products?

The three major classifications are convenience products, shopping products, and specialty products.

3.2 Identify five factors marketers should consider in classifying consumer services.

Five factors are the following: (1) the nature of the service, (2) the relationship between the service organization and its customers, (3) flexibility for customization, (4) fluctuation of supply and demand, and (5) the way the service is delivered.

4.1 What are the six main classifications of business products?

The six main classifications of business products are the following: (1) installations, (2) accessory equipment, (3) component parts and materials, (4) raw materials, (5) supplies, and (6) business services.

4.2 What are the three categories of supplies?

The three categories of supplies are maintenance items, repair items, and operating supplies.

5.1 What is TQM?

TQM stands for total quality management, a process that expects all of a firm's employees to continually improve its products and work processes.

5.2 What are the five variables of service quality?

The five variables of service quality are tangibles, reliability, responsiveness, assurances, and empathy.

✓ *assessment check* **answers**

6.1 List the four reasons for developing a product line.

The four reasons why firms want to develop product lines are the following: (1) a desire to grow, (2) enhancing the company's position in the market, (3) optimal use of company resources, and (4) exploiting the stages of the product life cycle.

7.1 Define *product mix.*

The product mix is a company's assortment of product lines and individual product offerings.

7.2 How do marketers typically measure product mixes?

The product mix is measured by width, length, and depth.

8.1 Identify the four stages of the product life cycle.

The four stages are introduction, growth, maturity, and decline.

8.2 During which stage or stages are products likely to attract the most new customers?

Products usually attract the most new customers during the introductory and growth stages.

9.1 Describe the four strategies for extending a product's life cycle.

The four strategies are increasing frequency of use, increasing the number of users, finding new users, and changing packaging or quality.

9.2 Under what circumstances do firms decide to delete a product from their line?

Firms may decide to delete a product if none of the strategies work, if raw materials become unavailable, or if the product no longer fits the existing or future product line.

MARKETING TERMS YOU NEED TO KNOW

marketing mix 346	consumer (B2C) product 350	business services 357
product 347	business-to-business (B2B) product 350	total quality management (TQM) 358
services 348	convenience products 351	product line 360
goods 348	shopping products 352	product life cycle 363
homeshoring 349	specialty products 352	

OTHER IMPORTANT MARKETING TERMS

goods–services continuum 348	component parts and materials 356	product mix 361
unsought products 351	raw materials 356	line extension 363
impulse goods and services 351	supplies 356	introductory stage 363
staples 351	MRO items 356	growth stage 364
emergency goods and services 351	ISO 9002 358	maturity stage 365
slotting allowances 351	benchmarking 358	decline stage 366
installations 355	service encounter 359	
accessory equipment 355	service quality 359	

ASSURANCE OF LEARNING REVIEW

1. Give an example of a product that blurs the distinction between goods and services, and explain why it does.
2. What are the differences between consumer products and B2B products?
3. What are unsought products? Give an example of an unsought product, and explain how it might be marketed.
4. What important features distinguish shopping products from one another?
5. How does marketing for installations and accessory equipment differ?
6. How do firms use benchmarking?
7. Describe briefly how L. L. Bean has achieved each of the objectives for developing a product line.
8. What is a line extension? Describe how *one* of the following might create a line extension:
   a. Kleenex tissues
   b. Kraft Ritz crackers
   c. Renuzit air fresheners
   d. Twinings tea
9. What types of challenges do marketers face with products that are in the introductory stage? What steps can they take to overcome these hurdles?
10. Provide an example of a product whose life cycle was extended by increasing its frequency of use, finding new users, finding new uses, or changing the packaging. Your product may have undergone a combination of these.

PROJECTS AND TEAMWORK EXERCISES

1. On your own or with a classmate, choose one of the following goods. Then create a marketing strategy for developing services to support your good.
   a. Purina cat or dog food
   b. Skechers shoes
   c. Lean Cuisine frozen meals
   d. Odwalla juices
   e. Ikea furniture
2. The next time you go grocery shopping—by yourself or with your roommate—keep a list of all the convenience products you buy. When you get home, make a table showing which of these products are impulse, staple, and emergency goods.
3. Consider a customer service experience you have had in the last month or so. Was it positive or negative? Describe your experience to the class and then discuss how the firm might improve the quality of its customer service—even if it is already positive.
4. With a classmate, choose a firm that interests you. Visit the firm's Web site and measure its product mix. Then create a chart like the one for Johnson & Johnson in Table 11.3, identifying the company's major product lines, along with a few specific examples.
5. With the same classmate, create a plan for further extending one of the firm's product lines. Describe the strategy you would recommend for extending the line as well as new products that might be included.

CRITICAL-THINKING EXERCISES

1. Draw a line representing the goods–services continuum. Then place each of the following along the continuum. Briefly explain your decision.
   a. Google
   b. Amazon.com
   c. Starbucks coffee
   d. Godiva chocolate
   e. Curves for Women
2. Think of a shopping product you purchased in the past year. Describe your decision process, including which attributes you used in comparing competitors. Have you been satisfied with your purchase? Why or why not? Would you make the purchase again, or go to a competitor?
3. Why is the service encounter so important to a firm's relationships with its customers? When is a service gap favorable? When is it unfavorable?
4. Why is it important for even a small firm to develop a line of products?
5. Choose one of the following products, and describe your strategy for taking it to the next stage in its product life cycle. For products in the maturity or decline stage, describe a strategy for extending their life cycle.
   a. Camera phone (growth)
   b. SUV (maturity)
   c. Day spa (growth)
   d. Answering machine (maturity)
   e. VCR (decline)
6. Describe a fad that has come and gone during your lifetime, such as Beanie Babies. Did you take part in the fad? Why or why not? How long did it last? Why do you think it faded?

ETHICS EXERCISE

Suppose you work for a firm that is planning to delete a certain item or service from its product line. Yet the firm is still selling the product, despite the fact that within months there will be no replacement parts or customer service in place to handle any problems that consumers might have with it. Would you continue to market the product without telling customers about its upcoming deletion, or would you inform them and suggest an alternative? Explain your decision.

INTERNET EXERCISES

1. **Product classification.** Visit the Web sites of each of the following companies. Review their product offerings and classify each as being a convenience, shopping, or specialty product.
   a. Colgate: http://www.colgate.com
   b. Tiffany: http://www.tiffany.com
   c. Philips: http://www.usa.philips.com
2. **Managing the product life cycle.** Dozens of products have been around for many, many years. The firms behind these products seem adept at managing and extending the product life cycle. Visit each of the Web sites listed. Prepare a report on how the companies behind each of these products has managed the product life cycle.
   a. Arm and Hammer: http://www.armandhammer.com
   b. Band Aid: http://www.bandaid.com
   c. Clorox: http://www.clorox.com

Note: Internet Web addresses change frequently. If you don't find the exact site listed, you may need to access the organization's home page and search from there or use a search engine such as Google.

CASE 11.1   Pampering Pets: Lavishing Our Friends with Love

Sometimes an industry can sprout an entirely new arm— or leg or tail. That's the case with the pet-care industry, which until recently consisted of the basics: food, collars, leashes, litter, and a few toys. Today, pet owners have a choice of goods and services that rival those of humans.

At Best Friends Pet Care, pampered pooches may receive fitness sessions, play time, ice cream breaks, story time, and, of course, walks. Depending on the services selected, owners may pay $135 a day, per dog, if their pets stay overnight as well. The array of services and the price resemble nothing else so much as a spa—and that's the general idea of the kennel's owners. Best Friends operates 42 locations across the country, and its marketers say that demand has driven the firm's growth. In other words, pet owners want luxury for their animal companions, and they are willing to pay for it.

PetSmart, one of the leading pet supply firms, reports that services have become a significant part of its business. During a recent quarter, the firm scooped up nearly $72 million from its services alone. Several years ago, the retail chain opened 35 PetsHotels across the nation. One popular—if unusual—service at the hotels is that traveling owners can phone their dogs. Other boarding facilities offer birthday parties and spa treatments, all at a premium. "It's the art of the upsell," explains Charlotte Reed, vice president of the National Association of Pet Sitters.

It's not just hotels for pets that are catering to animals; human hotels are getting into the act, as well. For years, certain hotels and inns have allowed pets to stay with their owners. But some have added layers of luxury. New York–based Loews Hotels offers a package called "The Hound of Music." For $1,600, doggy customers get to ride in a limousine to a recording studio where a coach helps them record their first CD. They can bark, howl, yip, or whine their way through a song accompanied by a guitarist, harmonica player, or karaoke machine. Then they go back to the hotel, where lodging is provided.

In addition to services, today's Fido or FiFi can have all the gimmicks, gadgets, and gewgaws he or she wants. You'd expect a firm like PetSmart to offer a variety of pet items, but how about Target, Macy's, T. J. Maxx, and Old Navy? Target has a whole new line of designer pet products—a signature dog collar by Isaac Mizrahi ($13), a black-and-white polka dot food bowl by the same designer ($10), and a doghouse by British architect Michael Graves ($100). Target also offers an array of trench coats, booties, and even a pink faux crocodile carrier for little pooches to ride in. Those who want to walk or run with their companions—without a leash—can purchase an SUV pet stroller for $299 from Kittywalk.com, or a $200 pet jogger from Petgearinc.com.

Not surprisingly, pet food has come a long way from the original cans of mystery meat. Gourmet foods from a wide range of makers have already hit the shelves. Food giant Nestlé Purina recently launched Beneful Prepared Meals, a line of 18 entrées in such lip-smacking flavors as roasted chicken with pasta, carrots, and spinach; and turkey medley with corn, wild rice, peas, and barley. Merrick Pet Care, a small business based in Texas, has offered a gourmet line for several years. One popular dinner product is a pot pie made with chicken, snow peas, and apples. "We use ingredients you would find in a fine restaurant—very appealing ingredients," says Ken Wilks, vice president of sales. Other firms make and sell a wide range of cookies and other baked treats for pets, shipping them locally or nationwide.

What's behind the demand for all these new pet products? Bob Vetere, president of the American Pet Products Manufacturers Association, attributes it to empty nesters, people whose children are grown and gone. "The house is suddenly quiet and because the pet is replacing the children, you tend to humanize them a little bit," he explains. Michael San Filippo of the American Veterinary Medical Association (AVMA) says, "There's probably guilt there. You might be away on business or vacation and you might be overcompensating with some pampering." Bonnie Beaver, also of the AVMA, points out, "The products are designed to the con-

sumers buying them, not necessarily the consumers using them." Whether it's guilt, a bit of loneliness, or just the desire to have the latest thing on the market, consumers are snapping up these new goods and services. Pets may not know the difference between a can of Alpo and gourmet turkey medley, but their owners do.

Questions for Critical Thinking

1. How does PetSmart benefit by offering goods *and* services to pet owners? Describe how the firm might offer both in the same location. Visit PetSmart's Web site at http://www.petsmart.com and create a chart illustrating the mix of some of the firm's pet-care products.

2. Suppose you were a marketer for a firm like Merrick Pet Care. Describe how you would market the firm's gourmet pet dinners to extend their product life cycle. (Be sure to use what you know about why consumers buy these products.)

Sources: Jim Salter, "Gourmet Offerings Cater to Pampered Pooch," Associated Press, April 26, 2006, **http://news.yahoo.com**; Kim Campbell Thornton, "New Products for Pampered Pets," MSNBC, March 29, 2006, **http://www.msnbc.msn.com**; Deborah Yao, "Pet Boarding Industry Finds Pampering Pays," Associated Press, February 27, 2006, **http://news.yahoo.com**; Christopher Elliott, "Diamonds in the Ruff," *U.S. News & World Report*, March 28, 2005, pp. 68, 70.

VIDEO CASE 11.2   Wild Oats Natural Marketplace:
Offering Products at their Peak

The written case on Wild Oats appears on page VC-13. The recently filmed Wild Oats video is designed to expand and highlight the concepts in this chapter and the concepts and questions covered in the written video case.

CHAPTER 12

Conquering Floors with P&G's Swiffer

Who wants to spend time thinking about cleaning? Consumer goods giant Procter & Gamble does—so that you don't have to. The firm markets branded products in nearly 50 categories, including Tide laundry detergent, Pampers diapers, and Crest toothpaste. Its recent push to create a new cleaning tool that would be unique in its product category resulted in a triumph of design. The Swiffer is a simple electrostatic sweeper for hardwood floors with a rectangular head and a long swiveling pole for hard-to-reach nooks and crannies. Although the Swiffer is not a glamorous product, it has proven wildly successful among consumers. Its name has even entered the lexicon of pop culture, as users talk about how they "Swiffer" their floors.

And, in what is probably a first for a household cleaning product, the Swiffer appeared on the cover of *Rolling Stone*. Says the vice president for research and development at P&G's home-care division. "If you would have bet me that one of P&G's brands would have been on the cover of *Rolling Stone* with Jessica Simpson, I would have lost that bet." Already one of the company's most profitable items, the Swiffer is now also the centerpiece of a whole new brand.

The Swiffer relies on a phenomenon called *entrainment*, which means that instead of simply pushing dirt around the floor as many conventional cleaning devices do, its disposable wet or dry cloths immediately capture it. Add to this obvious competitive advantage P&G's decision to package the product partially disassembled

so that its box could be sold on a supermarket shelf in the well-traveled cleaning products aisle, and a spectacularly successful product was born.

The Swiffer now has a 75 percent share of the market for quick household cleaning tools and earns about $750 million a year for P&G. Following up on the Swiffer's success, P&G's design teams tackled other household cleaning problems and soon came up with the Swiffer Max Cleaning System, the Swiffer WetJet Power Mop, The Swiffer Duster, the Swiffer Sweep-Vac, and the newest entry, the Swiffer CarpetFlick.

P&G didn't relish getting into the vacuum cleaner business, but with three-fourths of the country's floors covered with carpet, the company eventually asked the question whether it was possible to "Swiffer" a rug. A

Developing and Managing Brand and Product Categories

Chapter Objectives

1 Explain the benefits of category and brand management.

2 Identify the different types of brands.

3 Explain the strategic value of brand equity.

4 Discuss how companies develop strong identities for their products and brands.

5 Identify and briefly describe each of the new-product development strategies.

6 Describe the consumer adoption process.

7 List the stages in the new-product development process.

8 Explain the relationship between product safety and product liability.

"lightweight sweeper for quick carpet cleanups between vacuuming," the CarpetFlick is the result of an extensive research process that began with P&G teams interviewing consumers in their homes, taking pictures and asking them about their household cleaning problems and preferences. Months later, the team returned with prototypes to demonstrate to the same consumers, and the trials were so successful that no one wanted to give the prototypes back.

But more long months of design tinkering followed, while the team looked for the best way to make the basic carpet product into something "Swifferesque." They experimented with sticky paper to trap dirt, a hinged lid for removing captured dirt from the head, and even sandpaper and steel wool pads to boost its power to trap fuzz and hair. After several iterations and tests, the design team arrived at a model that worked, and all that remained was to choose the color. To let consumers know that the CarpetFlick was for a task different from the familiar blue-green Swiffer for hardwood floors, P&G decided to make it a bright orange.

Follow-up tests with consumers proved the new product a hit, and the CarpetFlick was launched. With people continually looking for ways to simplify household chores, P&G is cleaning up with its innovative products.[1]

evolution *of a* brand

Procter & Gamble released the Swiffer Sweeper for hardwood floors in 1999. The brand quickly became a success, eventually capturing three-fourths of the quick home-cleaning tools market. But because most homes have carpeting, the company decided to develop a product for cleanups between regular vacuuming.

- In addition to the Swiffer Sweeper, the company's designers have come up with an entire family of related products—the Sweep-Vac, Dusters, Max, and WetJet. Research these products. How well do they fit with the concept of the original Swiffer Sweeper? Can you think of any additional products that P&G might want to develop in the line? Make a list of suggestions. Have there been any improvements in the original products?

- The Swiffer CarpetFlick at first seemed to be a line that stretched P&G's product mix. The company was reluctant to enter a market segment that encompassed traditional vacuum cleaners. But to capitalize on the success of the original Sweeper, P&G's research team decided to accelerate its development, compressing the time from concept to launch to a quick eighteen months. What benefits and drawbacks would this present to the firm's researchers? How has the CarpetFlick done in the marketplace? Do you think it will continue to be successful? How important are new products to a firm such as P&G?

Chapter Overview

Brands play a huge role in our lives. We try certain brands for all kinds of reasons: on recommendations from friends, because we want to associate ourselves with the images certain brands possess, or because we remember colorful advertisements. We develop loyalty to certain brands and product lines for varying reasons as well—quality of a product, price, and habit are a few examples. This chapter examines the way companies make decisions about developing and managing the products and product lines that they hope will become consumer necessities. Developing and marketing a product and product line and building a desired brand image are costly propositions. To protect its investment and maximize the return on it, a specialized marketer called a *category manager,* who is responsible for an entire product line, must carefully nurture both existing and new products.

This chapter focuses on two critical elements of product planning and strategy. First, it looks at how firms build and maintain identity and competitive advantage for their products through branding. Second, it focuses on the new-product planning and development process. Effective new-product planning and meeting the profit responsibility that a category manager has for a product line require careful preparation. The needs and desires of consumers change constantly, and successful marketers manage to keep up with—or stay just ahead of—those changes.

1 Explain the benefits of category and brand management.

MANAGING BRANDS FOR COMPETITIVE ADVANTAGE

Think of the last time you went shopping for groceries. As you moved through the store, chances are your recognition of various brand names influenced many of your purchasing decisions. Perhaps you chose Colgate toothpaste over competitive offerings or loaded Heinz ketchup into your cart instead of the store brand. Walking through the snack food aisle, you might have reached for Orville Redenbacher popcorn or Lay's potato chips without much thought.

Marketers recognize the powerful influence that products and product lines have on customer behavior, and they work to create strong identities for their products and protect them. Branding is the process of creating that identity. A **brand** is a name, term, sign, symbol, design, or some combination that identifies the products of one firm while differentiating these products from competitors' offerings. The tradition of excellence created by the Gucci Group is carried through in all the brands in its lineup—Gucci, Yves Saint Laurent, Boucheron, Stella McCartney, and Balenciaga, to name a few.

As you read this chapter, consider how many brands you are aware of—both those you are loyal to and those you have never tried or have tried and abandoned. Table 12.1 shows some selected brands, brand names, and brand marks. Satisfied buyers respond to branding by making repeat purchases of the same product because they identify the item with the name of its producer. One buyer might derive satisfaction from an ice cream bar with the brand name Dove; another might derive the same satisfaction from one with the name Ben & Jerry's.

brand Name, term, sign, symbol, design, or some combination that identifies the products of one firm while differentiating them from the competition's.

BRAND LOYALTY

Brands achieve widely varying consumer familiarity and acceptance. A snowboarder might insist on a Burton snowboard, but the same consumer might show little loyalty to particular brands in another product category such as bath soap. Marketers measure brand loyalty in three stages: brand recognition, brand preference, and brand insistence.

Brand recognition is a company's first objective for newly introduced products. Marketers begin the promotion of new items by trying to make them familiar to the public. Advertising offers one effective way for increasing consumer awareness of a brand. Glad is a familiar brand in U.S. kitchens, and it drew on customers' recognition of its popular sandwich bags and plastic wraps when it introduced a new plastic food wrap that seals around items with just the press of a finger.

Other tactics for creating brand recognition include offering free samples or discount coupons for purchases. Once consumers have used a product, seen it advertised, or noticed it in stores, it moves from the unknown to the known category, which increases the probability that some of those consumers will purchase it.

At the second level of brand loyalty, **brand preference,** buyers rely on previous experiences with the product when choosing it, if available, over competitors' products. You may prefer Steve Madden shoes or Juicy Couture clothes to other brands and buy their new lines as soon as they are offered. If so, those products have established brand preference.

Brand insistence, the ultimate stage in brand loyalty, leads consumers to refuse alternatives and to search extensively for the desired merchandise. A product at this stage has achieved a monopoly position with its consumers. Although many firms try to establish brand insistence with all consumers, few achieve this ambitious goal. Companies that offer specialty or luxury goods and services, such as Tiffany diamonds or Lexus automobiles, are more likely to achieve this status than those that offer mass-marketed goods and services.

IMAGE COURTESY OF THE ADVERTISING ARCHIVES

The Gucci brand is instantly recognizable on this high-quality handbag, with its interlocking Gs.

✓ *assessment check*

1. What is a brand?
2. Differentiate between brand recognition, brand preference, and brand insistence.

table 12.1   Selected Brands, Brand Names, and Brand Marks

Brand type	Dr. Pepper or A&W root beer
Private brand	Metro7 clothing (Wal-Mart) or ACE brand tools
Family brand	RAID insect sprays or Progresso soups
Individual brand	Purex or Clorox
Brand name	Kleenex and Cheetos
Brand mark	Colonel Sanders for KFC or the Gecko for Geico insurance

brand recognition Consumer awareness and identification of a brand.

brand preference Consumer reliance on previous experiences with a product to choose that product again.

brand insistence Consumer refusal of alternatives and extensive search for desired merchandise.

TYPES OF BRANDS

Companies that practice branding classify brands in many ways: private, manufacturer's or national, family, and individual brands. In making branding decisions, firms weigh the benefits and disadvantages of each type of brand.

My Moment. My Dove.™

New DOVE® Cookies.

The only cookie baked with luscious DOVE® Chocolate chunks and coated with a layer of silky smooth DOVE® Chocolate. New DOVE® Cookies create a moment like no other.

Look for DOVE® Beyond Chocolate Chunk, Chocolate Walnut Oasis and Chocolate Walnut Rendezvous in the cookie aisle.

Dove
Beyond Chocolate Chunk

New!

Mars hopes that customer familiarity with its Dove chocolates will carry over to its Dove Cookies and generate brand preference.

Some firms, however, sell their goods without any efforts at branding. These items are called **generic products.** They are characterized by plain labels, little or no advertising, and no brand names. Common categories of generic products include food and household staples. These no-name products were first sold in Europe at prices as much as 30 percent below those of branded products. This product strategy was introduced in the U.S. three decades ago. The market shares for generic products increase during economic downturns but subside when the economy improves. However, many consumers request generic substitutions for certain brand-name prescriptions at the pharmacy whenever they are available.

Manufacturers' Brands versus Private Brands

Manufacturers' brands, also called *national brands,* define the image that most people form when they think of a brand. A **manufacturer's brand** refers to a brand name owned by a manufacturer or other producer. Well-known manufacturers' brands include Hewlett-Packard, Sony, Pepsi Cola, Dell, and French's. In contrast, many large wholesalers and retailers place their own brands on the merchandise they market. The brands offered by wholesalers and retailers are usually called **private brands** (or private labels). Although some manufacturers refuse to produce private-label goods, most regard such production as a way to reach additional market segments. Target offers many private-label products at its stores, including its Squeaky Clean kitchen products and Restore & Recycle home improvement items such as shelving and do-it-yourself products.[2]

The growth of private brands has paralleled that of chain stores in the United States. Manufacturers not only sell their well-known brands to stores but also put the store's own label on similar products. Such leading manufacturers as Westinghouse, Armstrong Rubber, and Heinz generate ever-increasing percentages of their total incomes by producing goods for sale under retailers' private labels. Private brands now account for one of every five items sold in the United States, bringing in more than $50 billion in retail sales. They also make up about 16 percent of all global retail sales and are especially popular in western European countries such as Germany and the United Kingdom.[3]

Staples, the office supply retailer, sells more than 1,000 products under its own brand name. But the firm also invests heavily in product design, development, and packaging, as a product manufacturer would. And it filed for more than 25 patents in a recent year.[4]

Captive Brands

The nation's major discounters—such as Wal-Mart, Target, and Kmart—have come up with a spin-off of the private label idea. So-called **captive brands** are national brands that are sold exclusively by a retail chain. Captive brands typically provide better profit margins than private labels. Target's captive brands include housewares and apparel by Michael Graves and Mossimo Giannulli, bedding by Cyn-

generic products Products characterized by plain labels, no advertising, and the absence of brand names.

manufacturer's brand Brand name owned by a manufacturer or other producer.

thia Rowley, furniture by Thomasville and Shabby Chic, and moderate-priced clothing by Isaac Mizrahi.[5] Similarly, Wal-Mart sells General Electric brand small appliances, even though these items are actually made by other manufacturers.

Family and Individual Brands

A **family brand** is a single brand name that identifies several related products. For example, KitchenAid markets a complete line of appliances under the KitchenAid name, and Johnson & Johnson offers a line of baby powder, lotions, plastic pants, and baby shampoo under its name. All Pepperidge Farm products, including bread, rolls, and cookies, carry the Pepperidge Farm brand. Frito-Lay markets both chips and salsa under its Tostitos family brand.

Alternatively, a manufacturer may choose to market a product as an **individual brand,** which uniquely identifies the item itself, rather than promoting it under the name of the company or under an umbrella name covering similar items. Unilever, for example, markets Knorr, Bertolli, Lipton, and Slim-Fast food products; Pond's and Sunsilk beauty products; and Lifebuoy, Lux, and Dove soaps. PepsiCo's Quaker Oats unit markets Aunt Jemima breakfast products, Life and Cap'n Crunch Cereals, and Rice-a-Roni side dishes along with Quaker oatmeal. Its Frito-Lay division makes Lays, Ruffles, and Doritos chips and Smartfood popcorn, while the Pepsi-Cola brands include Mountain Dew, Sierra Mist, Sobe juices and teas, and Aquafina water. Individual brands cost more than family brands to market because the firm must develop a new promotional campaign to introduce each new product to its target market. Distinctive brands are extremely effective aids in implementing market segmentation strategies, however.

On the other hand, a promotional outlay for a family brand can benefit all items in the line. Family brands also help marketers introduce new products to both customers and retailers. Because supermarkets stock thousands of items, they hesitate to add new products unless they are confident they will be in demand.

Family brands should identify products of similar quality, or the firm risks harming its overall product image. If Rolls-Royce marketers were to place the Rolls name on a low-end car or a line of discounted clothing, they would severely tarnish the image of the luxury car line. Conversely, Lexus, Infiniti, and Porsche put their names on luxury sport-utility vehicles to capitalize on their reputations and to enhance the acceptance of the new models in a competitive market.

Individual brand names should, however, distinguish dissimilar products. Kimberly-Clark markets two different types of diapers under its Huggies and Pull-Ups names. Procter & Gamble offers shaving products under its Gillette name; laundry detergent under Cheer, Tide, and other brands; and dishwasher detergent under Cascade.

100% All Natural

COURTESY OF FRITO-LAY, INC.

Great-tasting TOSTITOS® Salsa is made with 100% all-natural ingredients like tomatoes, peppers and onions, and it contains no additives or preservatives. It's the perfect companion to TOSTITOS® Tortilla Chips.

MEET YOU AT THE TOSTITOS®

TOSTITOS, TOSTITOS Logo and MEET YOU AT THE TOSTITOS are trademarks used by Frito-Lay. ©2006 Frito-Lay North America, Inc.

The Tostitos name and logo are found not just on chips but also on the salsa that goes with them. Tostitos is the family brand name for both products.

family brand Single brand name that identifies several related products.

✓ *assessment check*

1. Identify the different types of brands.
2. How are generic products different from branded products?

BRAND EQUITY

As individuals, we often like to say that our strongest asset is our reputation. The same is true of organizations. A brand can go a long way toward making or breaking a company's reputation. A strong brand identity backed by superior quality offers important strategic advantages for a firm.

3 Explain the strategic value of brand equity.

First, it increases the likelihood that consumers will recognize the firm's product or product line when they make purchase decisions. Second, a strong brand identity can contribute to buyers' perceptions of product quality. Branding can also reinforce customer loyalty and repeat purchases. A consumer who tries a brand and likes it will probably look for that brand on future store visits. All of these benefits contribute to a valuable form of competitive advantage called *brand equity*.

Brand equity refers to the added value that a certain brand name gives to a product in the marketplace. Brands with high equity confer financial advantages on a firm because they often command comparatively large market shares and consumers may pay little attention to differences in prices. Studies have also linked brand equity to high profits and stock returns. Service companies are also aware of the value of brand equity. SBC Communications had not owned long-distance carrier AT&T for very long before it dropped the SBC brand and renamed itself after the newest but most venerable of its acquisitions, with a brand name that had long stood for quality and dependability, as the "Marketing Success" feature discusses.

In global operations, high brand equity often facilitates expansion into new markets. Currently, Coca-Cola is the most valuable—and most recognized—brand in the world.[6] Similarly, Disney's brand equity allows it to market its goods and services in Europe and Japan—and now China. What makes a global brand powerful? According to Interbrand, which measures brand equity in dollar values, a strong brand has the power to increase a company's sales and earnings. A global brand is generally defined as one that sells at least 20 percent outside its home country, as Coca-Cola does. Interbrand's top ten global brands include Microsoft, IBM, GE, McDonald's, and Nokia.[7]

Global advertising agency Young & Rubicam (Y&R) developed another brand equity system called the Brand Asset Valuator. Y&R interviewed more than 9,000 consumers and collected information on 2,500 U.S. brands to help create this measurement system. According to Y&R, a firm builds brand equity sequentially on four dimensions of brand personality. These four dimensions are differentiation, relevance, esteem, and knowledge:

- *Differentiation* refers to a brand's ability to stand apart from competitors. Brands such as Porsche and Victoria's Secret stand out in consumers' minds as symbols of unique product characteristics.

- *Relevance* refers to the real and perceived appropriateness of the brand to a big consumer segment. A large number of consumers must feel a need for the benefits offered by the brand. Brands with high relevance include Microsoft and Hallmark.

- *Esteem* is a combination of perceived quality and consumer perceptions about the growing or declining popularity of a brand. A rise in perceived quality or in public opinion about a brand enhances a brand's esteem. But negative impressions reduce esteem. Brands with high esteem include Starbucks and Honda.

brand equity Added value that a respected, well-known brand name gives to a product in the marketplace.

marketing success   AT&T's Brand Is Back

Background. In 1984, before wireless computing, cell phones, and the Internet, the federal government broke up AT&T, affectionately known as Ma Bell. At the time, AT&T was virtually the sole provider of local and long-distance phone services, and the government wanted to introduce competition in the phone market. With the breakup, AT&T became only a long-distance provider. Southwestern Bell was one of the local-service telephone companies spun off from the company. Later renamed SBC Communications, that firm has been gradually buying back various components of the original company.

The Challenge. After adding wireless, cable, and Internet operations in the late 1990s, AT&T spun off or sold everything but the long-distance company. Then, with its purchase by Cingular Wireless, it looked as though the AT&T brand name would finally disappear. But SBC was one of Cingular's parent companies, and after the merger, it decided to resurrect the nationally known AT&T brand.

The Strategy. To reinvent the AT&T name, the company is spending $1 billion on the biggest advertising campaign in its history. A dozen TV spots, more than 30 print ads, a billboard in Times Square, and sponsorship of the

- *Knowledge* refers to the extent of customers' awareness of the brand and understanding of what a good or service stands for. Knowledge implies that customers feel an intimate relationship with a brand. Examples include Jell-O and Band-Aid.[8]

Sometimes a brand requires a makeover. After running into customer complaints about shoddy design in its lower-priced C-class SUVs, Mercedes dropped to fourteenth place in the J. D. Power quality survey. The low finish spurred the company to start a broad quality-improvement effort, streamlining its manufacturing processes, buying better component parts, and simplifying overcomplicated passenger comfort features, including eliminating 600 electronic functions that weren't being used. Although Mercedes has since climbed back to fifth in the quality survey, the company plans to do more to regain its reputation for durability and dependability.[9]

THE ROLE OF CATEGORY AND BRAND MANAGEMENT

Because of the tangible and intangible value associated with strong brand equity, marketing organizations invest considerable resources and effort in developing and maintaining these dimensions of brand personality. Traditionally, companies assigned the task of managing a brand's marketing strategies to a **brand manager.** Today, because they sell about 80 percent of their products to national retail chains, major consumer goods companies have adopted a strategy called **category management.** In this strategy a manufacturer's *category manager* maximizes sales for the retailer by overseeing an entire product line, often tracking sales history with data from the retail checkout point and aggregating it with sales data for the entire category (obtained from third-party vendors) and qualitative data such as customer surveys.[10]

Unlike traditional product managers, category managers have profit responsibility for their product group and also help the retailer's category buyer maximize sales for the whole category, not just the particular manufacturer's product. These managers are assisted by associates usually called *analysts.* Part of the shift to category management was initiated by large retailers, which realized they could benefit from the marketing muscle of large grocery and household goods producers such as Kraft and Procter & Gamble. As a result, producers began to focus their attention on in-store merchandising instead of mass-market advertising. Some manufacturers that are too small to dedicate a category manager to each retail chain assign a category manager to each major channel, such as grocery, convenience, drugstore, and so on.[11]

Some of the steps companies follow in the category management process include defining the category based on the target market's needs, identifying the role of the retailer in that category (such as a preferred provider or a convenience provider), finding opportunities for growth, setting performance targets and establishing a means to measure progress (such as a category scorecard), and creating a marketing strategy (such as building traffic, enhancing image, or defending turf). An

category management
Product management system in which a category manager—with profit and loss responsibility—oversees a product line.

Masters golf tournament are just the beginning. A new campaign slogan, "Your world. Delivered," will be adapted for Internet advertising, and the campaign even has a theme song—the 1990s pop hit, "All Around the World." As the company also completes its purchase of BellSouth, the advertising budget is reaching $2 billion.

The Outcome. The new AT&T is currently the largest telecommunications company in the world, with $120 billion in sales, and the long journey to return its brand name to prominence is complete. "It is one of the classic American brands," said one industry observer. "Particularly for older Americans, the Ma Bell name stands for quality and reliability." The company is betting that "AT&T" means enough to make it worth jettisoning the brand names SBC, Bell South, and Cingular, which together cost $10.5 billion to promote.

Sources: Tim Doyle, "A Battered Brand, Reborn," *Forbes,* April 24, 2006, pp. 58–60; Yuki Noguchi, "Revival of the Fittest," *Washington Post,* March 7, 2006, http://www.washingtonpost.com; Harry R. Weber, "AT&T Bids for Bell South, Job Cuts Feared," Associated Press, March 6, 2006, http://news.yahoo.com.

assessment check

1. What is brand equity?
2. What are the four dimensions of brand personality?
3. How does category management help retailers?

important next step is choosing the marketing mix by selecting the category product assortment and choosing price, promotion, and supply chain strategies. Finally, the category manager is ready to roll out the plan and review performance on a regular basis.[12]

Hershey's vending division offers category management services to its institutional customers, providing reduced inventory costs, improved warehouse efficiency, and increased sales.[13] Manufacturers of frozen breakfast items have improved sales for Kellogg and General Mills with category management strategies.[14]

 4 Discuss how companies develop strong identities for their products and brands.

PRODUCT IDENTIFICATION

Organizations identify their products in the marketplace with brand names, symbols, and distinctive packaging. Almost every product that is distinguishable from another gives buyers some means of identifying it. Sunkist Growers, for instance, stamps its oranges with the name Sunkist. Iams stamps a paw print on all of its pet food packages. For nearly 100 years, Prudential Insurance has used the Rock of Gibraltar as its symbol. Fellowes shredders demonstrate their power by featuring a bulldog.

Choosing how to identify a firm's output represents a major strategic decision for marketers. Produce growers will soon have another option to choose from, other than paper stickers. A new technology employs laser tattoos to mark fruits and vegetables with their names, identification numbers, and country of origin. The tattoos are visible and edible, good news for consumers who are tired of peeling tiny stickers from their apples and tomatoes. The numbers on the produce stickers provide valuable information in the form of price look-up (PLUS) codes, which operate similarly to traditional bar codes by identifying the product to the retailer's computer system and then retrieving the price for grocery checkout. But the stickers have their drawbacks. "If they are sticky enough to stay on the fruit through the whole distribution and sales network," said the general manager of one Georgia onion grower, "they are so sticky that the customer can't get them off." The laser tattoos will include the four- or five-digit PLUS number and avoid the sticky labels.[15]

THE WORLD'S TOUGHEST SHREDDERS® **Fellowes**

© COURTESY OF FELLOWES, INC.

The CD-eating dog illustrates Fellowes's brand of powerful paper shredders.

BRAND NAMES AND BRAND MARKS

A name plays a central role in establishing brand and product identity. The American Marketing Association defines a **brand name** as the part of the brand consisting of words or letters that form a name that identifies and distinguishes the firm's offerings from those of its competitors. The

brand name Part of a brand consisting of words or letters that form a name that identifies and distinguishes a firm's offerings from those of its competitors.

brand name is, therefore, the part of the brand that people can vocalize. Firms can also identify their brands by brand marks. A **brand mark** is a symbol or pictorial design that distinguishes a product, such as Mr. Peanut for Planters nuts.

Effective brand names are easy to pronounce, recognize, and remember. Short names, such as Nike, Ford, and Bounty, meet these requirements. Marketers try to overcome problems with easily mispronounced brand names by teaching consumers the correct pronunciations. For example, early

Etiquette Tips for Marketing Professionals

Avoiding Technical Jargon

If you're like most people, you become annoyed with technical jargon when you aren't sure what it means. Worse yet, jargon can have negative effects on a business conversation if it clouds the meaning of a message. On the other hand, jargon serves as useful shorthand in a conversation between two people who clearly understand what is being said. In general, it's best to use common sense—and err on the side of clarity. Here are a few tips on when—and when *not*—to use technical jargon.

When to use technical jargon:

1. Use an abbreviation without explanation if you are certain everyone with whom you are communicating knows it. Use a term like *CAD*, for instance, which stands for computer-aided design, only if you are communicating with people who work in that field and already know what computer-aided design is.
2. Use a technical term such as *category management*, if necessary, but surround it with conventional terms that reflect its meaning, to help listeners unfamiliar with it.

3. Keep technical terms to a minimum so that the necessary ones have impact.

When *not* to use technical jargon:

1. Avoid technical jargon when you are communicating with an audience outside your industry, including customers. Instead of referring to an *output device* on a computer, simply say *printer*.
2. Eliminate jargon when speaking or writing to someone from another country or someone whose first language is not English.
3. Stay away from acronyms specific to your organization when you're communicating with someone outside it. Exceptions can be made for terms such as IBM and GE because they are so well known.

Sources: Nancy Halligan, "Technical Writing," **http://www.technical-writing-course.com**, accessed April 19, 2006; Michael Bernhardt, "Seven Sins to Avoid with Your Next Public Speaking Engagement," **http://www.refresher.com/!sevensins.html**, accessed April 19, 2006; Joe Fleischer, "You Don't Need a Hero," *Call Center Magazine*, October 1, 2005, **http://www.callcentermagazine.com**.

advertisements for the Korean carmaker Hyundai explained that the name rhymes with *Sunday*. Sensitivity to clear communication doesn't end with the choice of brand name; marketers should also be aware of how well they get their point across in interpersonal communications. The "Etiquette Tips for Marketing Professionals" feature provides some tips for avoiding technical jargon in business.

A brand name should also give buyers the correct connotation of the product's image. Nissan's X-Terra connotes youth and extreme sports to promote the off-road SUV, while Kodak's EasyShare tells consumers how simple printing digital pictures can be. Con Agra's Healthy Choice food line presents an alternative to fast foods that may be high in sodium or fat, and the iPod Nano uses a name that aptly suggests its tiny size.

© TERRI MILLER/E-VISUAL COMMUNICATIONS, INC.

The dapper Mr. Peanut is the brand mark for Planters nuts.

A brand name must also qualify for legal protection. The Lanham Act of 1946 states that registered trademarks must not contain words or phrases in general use, such as *automobile* or *suntan lotion*. These generic words actually describe particular types of products, and no company can claim exclusive rights to them.

Marketers feel increasingly hard-pressed to coin effective brand names, as multitudes of competitors rush to stake out brand names for their own products. Some companies register names before they have products to fit the names to prevent competitors from using them. Few, however, have found as memorable a name for their product as Louisiana pharmacist George Boudreaux, whose highly successful diaper rash cream is called Boudreaux's Butt Paste. "If I had called it George's Diaper Rash Ointment," Boudreaux asked a reporter, "would we be talking now?" The product has spun off remedies for heat rash, acne, bed sores, chicken pox, shingles, razor burn, poison ivy, and even simple chapped lips, but the Butt Paste name is still the most talked-about sponsor at NASCAR races.[16]

When a class of products becomes generally known by the original brand name of a specific offering, the brand name may become a descriptive generic name. If this occurs, the original owner loses exclusive claim to the brand name. The generic names nylon, aspirin, escalator, kerosene, and zipper started as brand names. Other generic names that were once brand names include cola, yo-yo, linoleum, and shredded wheat.

Marketers must distinguish between brand names that have become legally generic terms and those that seem generic only in many consumers' eyes. Consumers often adopt legal brand names as descriptive names. Jell-O, for instance, is a brand name owned exclusively by Kraft Foods, but many consumers casually apply it as a descriptive name for gelatin desserts. Similarly, many people use the term Kleenex to refer to facial tissues. English and Australian consumers use the brand name Hoover as a verb for vacuuming. One popular way to look something up on the Internet is now to "Google it." Xerox is such a well-known brand name that people frequently—though incorrectly—use it as a verb to mean photocopying. To protect its valuable trademark, Xerox Corporation has created advertisements explaining that Xerox is a brand name and registered trademark and should not be used as a verb.

TRADEMARKS

Businesses invest considerable resources in developing and promoting brands and brand identities. The high value of brand equity encourages firms to take steps in protecting the expenditures they invest in their brands.

trademark Brand for which the owner claims exclusive legal protection.

A **trademark** is a brand for which the owner claims exclusive legal protection. A trademark should not be confused with a trade name, which identifies a company. The Coca-Cola Company is a trade name, but Coke is a trademark of the company's product. Some trade names duplicate companies' brand names. For example, Stride Rite is the children's shoe brand name of Stride Rite Corporation.

Protecting Trademarks

Trademark protection confers the exclusive legal right to use a brand name, brand mark, and any slogan or product name abbreviation. It designates the origin or source of a good or service.

Frequently, trademark protection is applied to words or phrases, such as *Bud* for Budweiser or *the Met* for the New York Metropolitan Opera. Or it can even protect a piece of fruit. Paul McCartney and Ringo Starr, with the widow of John Lennon and the estate of George Harrison, sued Apple Computer for alleged violation of a 1991 agreement that the Beatles say prohibited the maker of the iPod from entering the music business. The Beatles' own record label, Apple Corps, has operated in the industry since 1968, and they claimed that Apple's iTunes music-downloading service violated their agreement. But London's High Court ruled that Apple Computer was not in the business of creating music, just selling it through its online store. The Apple Corps label says it will appeal the decision.[17]

Firms can also receive trademark protection for packaging elements and product features such as shape, design, and typeface. U.S. law has fortified trademark protection in recent years. The Federal Trademark Dilution Act of 1995 gives a trademark holder the right to sue for trademark infringement even if other products using its brand are not particularly similar or easily confused in the minds of consumers. The infringing company does not even have to know that it is diluting another's trademark. The act also gives a trademark holder the right to sue if another party imitates its trademark.

The Internet may be the next battlefield for trademark infringement cases. Some companies are attempting to protect their trademarks by filing infringement cases against companies using similar Internet addresses.

Trade Dress

Visual cues used in branding create an overall look sometimes referred to as **trade dress.** These visual components may be related to color selections, sizes, package and label shapes, and similar factors. For example, the McDonald's "golden arches," Merrill Lynch's bull, and the yellow of Shell's seashell are all part of these products' trade dress. Owens Corning has registered the color pink to distinguish its insulation from the competition. A combination of visual cues may also constitute trade dress. Consider a Mexican food product that uses the colors of the Mexican flag: green, white, and red.

Trade dress disputes have led to numerous courtroom battles but no apparent consensus from the Supreme Court. "The essential question is whether you can use trademark law to protect the design of a product," says one law professor. "And the messy answer is: Well, it depends." Unilever has filed suit against Albert Heijn, part of the giant European supermarket company Ahold, alleging trademark and trade dress infringement in its margarine brands, Lipton iced tea, and Bertolli olive oil.[18]

DEVELOPING GLOBAL BRAND NAMES AND TRADEMARKS

Cultural and language variations make brand-name selection a difficult undertaking for international marketers; an excellent brand name or symbol in one country may prove disastrous in another. An advertising campaign for E-Z washing machines failed in the UK because the British pronounce *z* as "zed." A firm marketing a product in multiple countries must also decide whether to use a single brand name for universal promotions or tailor names to individual countries. Most languages contain *o* and *k* sounds, so *okay* has become an international word. Most languages also have a short *a,* so Coca-Cola, Kodak, and Texaco work as effective brands abroad.

General Motors recently reached a settlement with Chinese automaker Chery Automobile, which GM had accused not only of pirating a minicar design but also of adopting a name that sounds too much like its own brand, Chevy. Chery agreed not to sell its forthcoming products, including five new cars headed for the American market, under the Chery name in the United States.[19]

SIENTE CÓMO LIMPIA.

MIRA CÓMO BLANQUEA.

IMAGE COURTESY OF THE ADVERTISING ARCHIVES

GlaxoSmithKline markets Aquafresh toothpaste as a single brand throughout the world.

PACKAGING

A firm's product strategy must also address questions about packaging. Like its brand name, a product's package can powerfully influence buyers' purchase decisions.

Marketers are applying increasingly scientific methods to their packaging decisions. Rather than experimenting with physical models or drawings, more and more package designers work on special computer graphics that create three-dimensional images of packages in thousands of colors, shapes, and typefaces. Another software program helps marketers design effective packaging by simulating the displays shoppers see when they walk down supermarket aisles.

Companies conduct marketing research to evaluate current packages and to test alternative package designs. For instance, André Lurton, a Bordeaux wine producer, is enthusiastic about its innovative screwcap tops, especially for white wine, because screw caps prevent "cork taint" and oxidation. But the company is sensitive to consumers' perceptions of screw caps. In fact, marketing research by SOFRES, a French marketing survey firm, showed that nearly 4 of 5 regular wine drinkers prefer corks. So, Lurton's red Bordeaux wines remain corked, for now.[20]

A package serves three major objectives: (1) protection against damage, spoilage, and pilferage; (2) assistance in marketing the product; and (3) cost effectiveness. Let's briefly consider each of these objectives.

Protection against Damage, Spoilage, and Pilferage

The original objective of packaging was to offer physical protection for the merchandise. Products typically pass through several stages of handling between manufacturing and customer purchases, and a package must protect its contents from damage. Furthermore, packages of perishable products must protect the contents against spoilage in transit and in storage until purchased by the consumer. The American Plastics Council developed an advertising campaign to promote the benefits of using plastics in food packaging, asserting that plastic bottles, wraps, and containers reduce the chance of food contamination and that tamper-resistant plastic seals provide product safety assurance.[21]

Fears of product tampering have forced many firms to improve package designs. Over-the-counter medicines are sold in tamper-resistant packages covered with warnings informing consumers not to purchase merchandise without protective seals intact. Many grocery items and light-sensitive products are packaged in tamper-resistant containers as well. Products in glass jars, such as spaghetti sauce and jams, often come with vacuum-depressed buttons in the lids that pop up the first time the lids are opened.

Even prescription medicine packaging can be revolutionized for the consumer's benefit, as Target recently found. It accepted a proposal from a visual arts graduate student who came up with a way to improve traditional pill bottles. Target bought Deborah Adler's design and began marketing flattened pill bottles with easy-to-read labels and color-coded plastic rings to identify each person's own prescriptions. The bottles also rest on their caps, so the label that wraps around the top can be seen from above. "We've all been concerned about font size and readability," said a pharmacy safety consultant about the new design. "I think this improves that dramatically."[22]

Many packages offer important safeguards for retailers against pilferage. Shoplifting and employee theft cost retailers several billion dollars each year. To limit this activity, many packages feature oversized cardboard backings too large to fit into a shoplifter's pocket or purse. Efficient packaging that protects against damage, spoilage, and theft is especially important for international marketers, who must contend with varying climatic conditions and the added time and stress involved in overseas shipping.

The prescription bottle proves that even simple packaging can be improved. These bottles got a makeover from Target, with a little help from a design student who wanted to avoid confusing her medication with her grandmother's.

© MONIKA GRAFF/UPI/LANDOV

Assistance in Marketing the Product

The proliferation of new products, changes in consumer lifestyles and buying habits, and marketers' emphasis on targeting smaller market segments have increased the importance of packaging as a promotional tool. Many firms are addressing consumer concerns about protecting the environment by designing packages made of biodegradable and recyclable materials. To demonstrate serious concern regarding environmental protection, Procter & Gamble, Coors, McDonald's, BP Chemical, and other firms have created ads that describe their efforts in developing environmentally sound packaging.

In a grocery store where thousands of different items compete for notice, a product must capture the shopper's attention. Marketers combine colors, sizes, shapes, graphics, and typefaces to establish distinctive trade dress that sets their products apart from the products of competitors. Packaging can help establish a common identity for a group of items sold under the same brand name. Like the brand name, a package should evoke the product's image and communicate its value.

Packages can also enhance convenience for buyers. Pump dispensers, for example, facilitate the use of products ranging from mustard to insect repellent. Squeezable bottles of honey and ketchup make the products easier to use and store. Packaging provides key benefits for convenience foods such as meals and snacks packaged in microwavable containers, juice drinks in aseptic packages, and frozen entrees and vegetables packaged in single-serving portions.

Pfizer Inc. found that a change in product packaging actually induced a change in user behavior. Sales of its Listerine mouthwash grew by more than 10 percent when the company introduced a built-in hand grip and larger cap for the club-store-sized bottle of its popular product. It seems that the grip makes lifting the big bottle easier, and the wider mouth encourages users to swish more of the product around in their mouths, finishing the bottles quicker than before and sending them back to the store for more.[23]

Some firms increase consumer utility with packages designed for reuse. Empty peanut butter jars and jelly jars have long doubled as drinking glasses. Parents can buy bubble bath in animal-shaped plastic bottles suitable for bathtub play. Packaging is a major component in Avon's overall marketing strategy. The firm's decorative, reusable bottles have even become collectibles.

Cost-Effective Packaging

Although packaging must perform a number of functions for the producer, marketers, and consumers, it must do so at a reasonable cost. Sometimes changes in the packaging can make packages both cheaper and better for the environment. Compact disc manufacturers, for instance, once packaged music CDs in two containers, a disc-sized plastic box inside a long, cardboard box that fit into the record bins in stores. Consumers protested against the waste of the long boxes, and the recording industry finally agreed to eliminate the cardboard outer packaging altogether. Now CDs come in just the plastic cases, with plastic shrink-wrapping.

Labeling

Labels were once a separate element that was applied to a package; today, they are an integral part of a typical package. Labels perform both promotional and informational functions. A **label** carries an item's brand name or symbol, the name and address of the manufacturer or distributor, information about the product's composition and size, and recommended uses. The right label can play an important role in attracting consumer attention and encouraging purchases.

Consumer confusion and dissatisfaction over such descriptions as giant economy size, king size, and family size led to the passage of the Fair Packaging and Labeling Act in 1966. The act requires that a label offer adequate information concerning the package contents and that a package design facilitate value comparisons among competing products.

The Nutrition Labeling and Education Act of 1990 imposes a uniform format in which food manufacturers must disclose nutritional information about their products. In addition, the Food and Drug Administration (FDA) has mandated design standards for nutritional labels that provide clear guidelines to consumers about food products. The FDA has also tightened definitions for loosely used terms such as *light, fat free, lean,* and *extra lean,* and it mandates that labels list the amounts of fat, sodium, dietary fiber, calcium, vitamins, and other components in typical servings. The latest ruling requires food manufacturers to include on nutritional labels the total amount of trans fats—hydrogenated oils that improve texture and freshness but contribute to high levels of cholesterol—in each product.

Solving an Ethical Controversy

Is Seafood Labeling Protecting Consumers?

Recent investigations suggest that although the FDA has told consumers that light tuna is safe to eat, it may contain dangerously high levels of mercury. The reason is that yellowfin tuna, a large fish that is known to contain higher than acceptable levels of the poisonous metal—especially for pregnant women and children—is often packaged and labeled as "light tuna," which is supposed to be from the smaller skipjack tuna. Consumer groups and members of Congress have asked the FDA to conduct more frequent and consistent testing for mercury levels in canned tuna, instead of the sporadic testing it has done in the past. They have also asked tuna producers to respond to concerns about mercury levels and about the accuracy of labeling of their products.

Should tuna producers be required to add mercury warnings to their product labels?

PRO

1. Because of the danger of mercury to developing fetuses and growing children, mercury levels should be included on every can sold to inform consumers of the content.

2. Instead of allowing the tuna industry to decide, the FDA should mandate labeling changes. Assuring safety is of greatest importance.

CON

1. No government study has ever found evidence of mercury contamination in anyone who consumed canned tuna, even at above-normal rates. The industry should be allowed to continue as it is.

2. The studies showing light tuna to be high in mercury have been misinterpreted and not consistent, and no one is at risk.

Summary

The debate over the labeling of tuna continues. The tuna industry says tuna is safe and that fish is an important part of a healthy diet. A recent lawsuit brought by the California State Attorney General to require the top three tuna brands to carry mercury warnings was denied by the judge. But *Consumer Reports* analyzed FDA data and came to a different conclusion. The organization found that most cans labeled as light tuna contained one-third the mercury on average of those labeled as white tuna. Still, with some of the light tuna cans containing at least as much mercury as albacore tuna and with no certainty about the safety of even brief exposure of unborn fetuses' and children's developing nervous systems to mercury, the organization advised pregnant women to avoid canned tuna altogether and young children up to 45 pounds to consume no more than four to five ounces of canned light tuna per week.

Sources: "Mercury in Tuna: New Safety Concerns," *Consumer Reports,* July 2006, **http://www.consumerreports.org**; Frank Green, "Tuna Mercury Warnings Unnecessary, Judge Rules," *San Diego Union-Tribune,* May 13, 2006, **http://www.signonsandiego.com**; "Durbin Calls on Tuna Industry to Address Mercury Levels," U.S. Senate, February 2, 2006, **http://www.senate.gov**; "Tuna Industry Confirms FDA Findings on Safety of Canned Tuna," PRNewswire, January 27, 2006, **http://www.prnewswire.com**; Sam Roe and Michael Hawthorne, "How Safe Is Tuna?" *Chicago Tribune,* December 13, 2005, **http://www.chicagotribune.com**.

The new Food Allergen Labeling and Consumer Protection Act took effect at the beginning of 2006 and requires that food labeling disclose all major food allergens in terms that the average consumer can understand. According to the Food and Drug Administration, eight allergens account for 90 percent of documented allergic reactions to food, and all must be identified. They are milk, eggs, peanuts, tree nuts (almonds, cashews, walnuts), fish (such as bass, cod, and flounder), shellfish (crab, lobster, shrimp), soy, and wheat.[24]

Other labeling issues and standards can be quite controversial, particularly if compliance is voluntary. See the "Solving an Ethical Controversy" feature for the debate over the labeling of canned tuna.

Labeling requirements differ elsewhere in the world. In Canada, for example, labels must provide information in both English and French. The type and amount of information required on labels also vary among nations. International marketers must carefully design labels to conform to the regulations of each country in which they market their merchandise.

The **Universal Product Code (UPC)** designation is another important aspect of a label or package. Introduced in 1974 as a method for cutting expenses in the supermarket industry, UPCs are numerical bar codes printed on packages. Optical scanner systems read these codes, and computer systems recognize items and print their prices on cash register receipts. Although UPC scanners are costly, they permit both considerable labor savings over manual pricing and improved inventory control. The Universal Product Code is also a major asset for marketing research. However, many consumers feel frustrated when only a UPC is placed on a package without an additional price tag, because they do not always know how much an item costs if the price labels are missing from the shelf.

brand extension Strategy of attaching a popular brand name to a new product in an unrelated product category.

Radio-frequency identification (RFID) tags—electronic chips that carry encoded product identification—may replace some of the functions of UPC codes, such as price identification and inventory tracking. But consumer privacy concerns about the amount of information RFID tracking can accumulate may limit their use to aggregate packaging such as pallets, rather than units sized for individual sale. When the FDA decided to require drug makers and marketers to place a scannable code on all drugs sold to U.S. hospitals at the level of patient unit doses, it chose UPC codes.[25]

BRAND EXTENSIONS

Some brands become so popular that marketers may decide to use them on unrelated products in pursuit of instant recognition for the new offerings. The strategy of attaching a popular brand name to a new product in an unrelated product category is known as **brand extension.** This practice should not be confused with **line extensions,** which refers to new sizes, styles, or related products. A brand extension, in contrast, carries over from one product nothing but the brand name. In establishing brand extensions, marketers hope to gain access to new customers and markets by building on the equity already established in their existing brands. This is the strategy behind Nautica's brand extension from fashion to furniture and bedding.

Working with a handful of trendy designers, Mattel has extended its Barbie fashion doll brand into a line of high-end designer clothing and accessories for women from their teens through their 30s. "It's not Mattel's usual target audience," admits the company's senior vice president of global consumer marketing and entertainment. "Our target market is the fashionista." Barbie-themed jeans, shirts, handbags, and jewelry under the label Barbie Luxe are being designed by the likes of Anna Sui, Anya Hindmarch, Judith Lieber, Nickel, Not Rational, and Paper Denim & Cloth. The company hopes to revise the Barbie brand by tapping into the doll's grown-up fans.[26]

© TERRI MILLER/E-VISUAL COMMUNICATIONS, INC.

Fashion marketer Nautica's brand extension includes furniture, bedding and towels, and tableware.

BRAND LICENSING

A growing number of firms have authorized other companies to use their brand names. Even colleges have licensed their logos and trademarks. This practice, known as **brand licensing,** expands a firm's exposure in the marketplace, much as a brand extension does. The brand name's owner also receives an extra source of income in the form of royalties from licensees, typically 4 to 8 percent of wholesale revenues.

United Media Licensing handles licensing of such famous popular culture icons as the Peanuts characters, Dilbert, and Precious Moments figures. It licenses Snoopy to appear in MetLife Insurance Company promotions.

Brand experts note several potential problems with licensing, however. Brand names do not transfer well to all products. Harley-Davidson, for instance, didn't do well with its cake-decorating kits.[27] But Virgin's heroic failures in PCs, vodka, clothing, and cosmetics have made the brand stronger, in part because CEO Richard Branson (whose highly publicized round-the-world ballooning efforts have also all ended in failure) has quickly acknowledged and resolved the slip-ups.[28] On the other hand, if a licensee produces a poor-quality product or an item ethically incompatible with the original brand, the arrangement could damage the reputation of the brand.

Overextension is another problem. Pierre Cardin was a high-end couture brand that extended into cologne, wine, and bicycles. "It just got nuts," says the chief marketing officer of apparel maker Haggar. "Their logo was on everything—at every sort of price point and at every channel distribution. You could buy it at the drugstore, or you could buy it at Bloomingdale's. Short term, somebody may have made an awful lot of money through the licensing. But long term, they also messed up the brand."[29]

NEW-PRODUCT PLANNING

As its offerings enter the maturity and decline stages of the product life cycle, a firm must add new items to continue to prosper. Regular additions of new products to the firm's line help protect it from product obsolescence.

New products are the lifeblood of any business, and survival depends on a steady flow of new entries. Some new products may implement major technological breakthroughs. Other new products simply extend existing product lines. In other words, a new product is one that either the company or the customer has not handled before. Only about 10 percent of new-product introductions bring truly new capabilities to consumers.

PRODUCT DEVELOPMENT STRATEGIES

A firm's strategy for new-product development varies according to its existing product mix and the match between current offerings and the firm's overall marketing objectives. The current market positions of products also affect product development strategy. Figure 12.1 identifies four alternative development strategies as market penetration, market development, product development, and product diversification.

A **market penetration strategy** seeks to increase sales of existing products in existing markets. Firms can attempt to extend their penetration of markets in several ways. They may modify products, improve product quality, or promote new and different ways to use products. Packaged-goods marketers often pursue this strategy to boost market share for mature products in mature markets. Product positioning often plays a major role in such a strategy.

Product positioning refers to consumers' perceptions of a product's attributes, uses, quality, and advantages and disadvantages relative to competing brands. Marketers often conduct marketing research studies to analyze

assessment check

1. Distinguish between a brand name and a trademark.
2. What are the three purposes of packaging?
3. Describe brand extension and brand licensing.

5 Identify and briefly describe each of the new-product development strategies.

figure 12.1

Alternative Product Development Strategies

	Old Product	New Product
Old Market	Market Penetration	Product Development
New Market	Market Development	Product Diversification

consumer preferences and to construct product positioning maps that plot their products' positions in relation to those of competitors' offerings.

Method is an upstart marketer of brightly colored household cleaning products in innovative packages. Based in San Francisco, the company has positioned itself as a purveyor of environmentally friendly products, such as a patented nonaerosol air freshener in six scents, sold in bottles that resemble vases, sculptures, bowling pins, and figure eights. To further clinch its position, Method, which has 45 employees compared with Procter & Gamble's 140,000, uses recyclable packaging materials and keeps its products biodegradable by avoiding bleach and chlorine. "When you run through the legs of Goliath," says company co-founder Eric Ryan, "you need to spend a lot of time thinking about how to act so you don't put yourself in a place you can be stepped on."[30]

A **market development strategy** concentrates on finding new markets for existing products. Market segmentation, discussed in Chapter 9, provides useful support for such an effort. Bank of America has succeeded in developing a new market by targeting Asian residents in San Francisco with special television commercials aimed at Chinese, Korean, and Vietnamese consumers. Starbucks' market development strategy is based on opening as many stores as possible, even though they are sometimes very close.[31]

The strategy of **product development** refers to the introduction of new products into identifiable or established markets. LucasFilm, George Lucas's entertainment firm, entered the video game market. Its LucasArts division collaborated with the company's biggest unit, Industrial Light & Magic, the special-effects shop. The goal, inspired by rapidly improving technology, is to combine the fast-paced culture of the game division with ILM's state-of-the-art animation and special-effects tools to create new and better products in both divisions, which are now housed in the same San Francisco location.[32]

IMAGE COURTESY OF THE ADVERTISING ARCHIVES

in the eye
of the storm
i am
still
jennifer lopez

www.jenniferlopez.com/fragrances

a new fragrance premiere by jennifer lopez

ROBINSONS-MAY   HECHT'S   FILENE'S   FOLEY'S

Still is a flanker brand to Jennifer Lopez's popular Glow fragrance line.

Firms may also choose to introduce new products into markets in which they have already established positions to try to increase overall market share. These new offerings are called *flanker brands*. The fragrance industry uses this strategy extensively when it develops scents that are related to their most popular products. The flanker scents are related in both their smell and their names. Jennifer Lopez, whose Glow family of scents—Glow, Miami Glow, Still, and Live—has been a hit for Coty, envisioned her next fragrance as "the dark side of Glow . . . a black-tie, nighttime version of Glow, for an older demographic."[33]

Finally, a **product diversification strategy** focuses on developing entirely new products for new markets. Some firms look for new target markets that complement their existing markets; others look in completely new directions. Cisco Systems, the networking company, is entering the consumer electronics market with radios, telephones, and home theater equipment that will all tap into its expertise in developing computer routers and mine its relationship with portals such as Yahoo! and Google. Cisco's purchase of the big set-top box maker Scientific-Atlanta will give it another advantage in the consumer electronics market.[34] Oakley is marketing the world's first digital audio eyewear, a music system built into an optical frame and powered by a 75 MHz digital signal processor.

 assessment check

1. Distinguish between market penetration and market development strategies.

2. What is product development?

3. What is product diversification?

In selecting a new-product strategy, marketers should keep in mind an additional potential problem: **cannibalization.** Any firm wants to avoid investing resources in a new-product introduction that will adversely affect sales of existing products. A product that takes sales from another offering in the same product line is said to cannibalize that line. A company can accept some loss of sales from existing products if the new offering will generate sufficient additional sales to warrant its investment in its development and market introduction.

6 Describe the consumer adoption process.

THE CONSUMER ADOPTION PROCESS

In the **adoption process,** consumers go through a series of stages from first learning about the new product to trying it and deciding whether to purchase it regularly or to reject it. These stages in the consumer adoption process can be classified as follows:

adoption process Stages that consumers go through in learning about a new product, trying it, and deciding whether to purchase it again.

1. *Awareness.* Individuals first learn of the new product, but they lack full information about it.

2. *Interest.* Potential buyers begin to seek information about it.

3. *Evaluation.* They consider the likely benefits of the product.

4. *Trial.* They make trial purchases to determine its usefulness.

5. *Adoption/Rejection.* If the trial purchase produces satisfactory results, they decide to use the product regularly.

Marketers must understand the adoption process to move potential consumers to the adoption stage. Once marketers recognize a large number of consumers at the interest stage, they can take steps to stimulate sales by moving these buyers through the evaluation and trial stages. Schick, for example, gave away 200,000 new Quattro for Women razors in major cities such as New York, Chicago, Philadelphia, and San Francisco. The razors were packed in kits with calendar/planners and sampled outside high-traffic office buildings as part of a six-month campaign in ten markets. Other samples were handed out at spas, gyms, stadiums, and concert halls. Customers could also request a sample at a special Web site that racked up 4 million hits and ended up exhausting its supply within a month. "Short of sampling at home in the shower, we look to find unconventional ways to reach high-performance women," said the company's senior brand manager. "We're not just sampling the product, we're delivering the brand message."[35]

consumer innovator People who purchase new products almost as soon as the products reach the market.

ADOPTER CATEGORIES

First buyers of new products, the so-called **consumer innovators,** are people who purchase new products almost as soon as these products reach the market. Later adopters wait for additional information and rely on the experiences of initial buyers before making trial purchases. Consumer innovators welcome innovations in each product area. Some computer users, for instance, rush to install new software immediately after each update becomes available. Some physicians pioneer the uses of new pharmaceutical products for AIDS patients.

A number of studies about the adoption of new products have identified five categories of purchasers based on relative times of adoption. These categories, shown in Figure 12.2, are consumer innovators, early adopters, early majority, late majority, and laggards.

While the adoption process focuses on individuals and the steps they go through in making the ultimate decision of whether to become repeat purchasers of the new product or reject it as a failure to satisfy their needs, the

figure 12.2

Categories of Adopters Based on Relative Times of Adoption

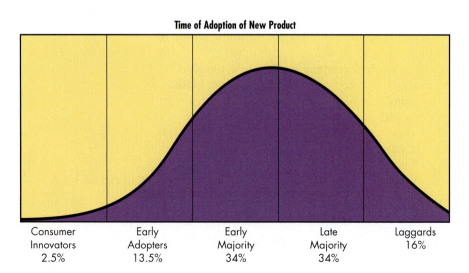

Time of Adoption of New Product

| Consumer Innovators 2.5% | Early Adopters 13.5% | Early Majority 34% | Late Majority 34% | Laggards 16% |

diffusion process focuses on all members of a community or social system. The focus here is on the speed at which an innovative product is accepted or rejected by all members of the community.

Figure 12.2 shows the diffusion process as following a normal distribution from a small group of early purchasers (called *innovators*) to the final group of consumers (called *laggards*) to make trial purchases of the new product. A few people adopt at first and then the number of adopters increases rapidly as the value of the product becomes apparent. The adoption rate finally diminishes as the number of potential consumers who have not adopted, or purchased, the product diminishes. Typically, innovators make up the first 2.5 percent of buyers who adopt the new product; laggards are the last 16 percent to do so. Figure 12.2 excludes those who never adopt the product.

diffusion process Process by which new goods or services are accepted in the marketplace.

IDENTIFYING EARLY ADOPTERS

It's no surprise that identifying consumers or organizations that are most likely to try a new product can be vital to a product's success. By reaching these buyers early in the product's development or introduction, marketers can treat these adopters as a test market, evaluating the product and discovering suggestions for modifications. Because early purchasers often act as opinion leaders from whom others seek advice, their attitudes toward new products quickly spread to others. Acceptance or rejection of the innovation by these purchasers can help forecast its expected success. New-car models are multiplying, for instance, and many are sporting a dizzying variety of options such as ports to accommodate—and integrate—the driver's iPod, wireless phone, and laptop. Improved stability controls, collision warnings, and "smart engines" that save fuel are also available. Toyota Motor's president says the auto is "going through a technological revolution that is the most profound in the last 100 years," and one marketing researcher says of the new models hitting showrooms, "the all-purpose family car is a dying breed." Advances in design, manufacturing, and materials are bringing customization to the driving experience, and automakers will be anxiously watching early adopters to gauge the rest of the market.[36]

A large number of studies have established the general characteristics of first adopters. These pioneers tend to be younger, have higher social status, are better educated, and enjoy higher incomes than other consumers. They are more mobile than later adopters and change both their jobs and addresses more often. They also rely more heavily than later adopters on impersonal information sources; more hesitant buyers depend primarily on company-generated promotional information and word-of-mouth communications.

Rate of Adoption Determinants

Frisbees progressed from the product introduction stage to the market maturity stage in a period of six months. By contrast, the U.S. Department of Agriculture tried for thirteen years to persuade corn farmers to use hybrid seed corn, an innovation capable of doubling crop yields. Five characteristics of a product innovation influence its adoption rate:

1. *Relative advantage.* An innovation that appears far superior to previous ideas offers a greater relative advantage—reflected in terms of lower price, physical improvements, or ease of use—and increases the product's adoption rate.

2. *Compatibility.* An innovation consistent with the values and experiences of potential adopters attracts new buyers at a relatively rapid rate. Consumers already comfortable with the miniaturization of communications technology are likely to be attracted to camera phones, for instance, and the video iPod with its 2½-inch screen.

3. *Complexity.* The relative difficulty of understanding the innovation influences the speed of acceptance. In most cases, consumers move slowly in adopting new products that they find difficult to understand or use. Farmers' cautious acceptance of hybrid seed corn illustrates how long an adoption can take.

4. *Possibility of trial use.* An initial free or discounted trial of a good or service means that adopters can reduce their risk of financial or social loss when they try the product. A coupon for a free item or a free night's stay at a hotel can accelerate the rate of adoption.

5. *Observability.* If potential buyers can observe an innovation's superiority in a tangible form, the

adoption rate increases. In-store demonstrations or even advertisements that focus on the superiority of a product can encourage buyers to adopt a product.

Marketers who want to accelerate the rate of adoption can manipulate these five characteristics at least to some extent. An informative promotional message about a new allergy drug could help consumers overcome their hesitation in adopting this complex product. Effective product design can emphasize an item's advantages over the competition. Everyone likes to receive something for free, so giving away small samples of a new product lets consumers try it at little or no risk. In-home demonstrations or trial home placements of items such as furniture or carpeting can achieve similar results. Marketers must also make positive attempts to ensure the innovation's compatibility with adopters' value systems.

ORGANIZING FOR NEW-PRODUCT DEVELOPMENT

A firm needs to be organized in such a way that its personnel can stimulate and coordinate new-product development. Some companies contract with independent design firms to develop new products. Many assign product-innovation functions to one or more of the following entities: new-product committees, new-product departments, product managers, and venture teams.

New-Product Committees

The most common organizational arrangement for activities in developing a new product is to center these functions in a new-product committee. This group typically brings together experts in such areas as marketing, finance, manufacturing, engineering, research, and accounting. Committee members spend less time conceiving and developing their own new-product ideas than reviewing and approving new-product plans that arise elsewhere in the organization. The committee might review ideas from the engineering and design staff or perhaps from marketers and salespeople who are in constant contact with customers.

Because members of a new-product committee hold important jobs in the firm's functional areas, their support for any new-product plan likely foreshadows approval for further development. However, new-product committees in large companies tend to reach decisions slowly and maintain conservative views. Sometimes members compromise so they can return to their regular responsibilities.

New-Product Departments

Many companies establish separate, formally organized departments to generate and refine new-product ideas. The departmental structure overcomes the limitations of the new-product committee system and encourages innovation as a permanent full-time activity. The new-product department is responsible for all phases of a development project within the firm, including screening decisions, developing product specifications, and coordinating product testing. The head of the department wields substantial authority and typically reports to the chief executive officer, chief operating officer, or a top marketing executive.

Product Managers

A **product manager** is another term for a brand manager, a function mentioned earlier in the chapter. This marketer supports the marketing strategies of an individual product or product line. Procter & Gamble, for instance, assigned its first product manager in 1927, when it made one person responsible for Camay soap.

Product managers set prices, develop advertising and sales promotion programs, and work with sales representatives in the field. In a company that markets multiple products, product managers fulfill key functions in the marketing department. They provide individual attention for each product and support and coordinate efforts of the firm's sales force, marketing research department, and advertising department. Product managers often lead new-product development programs, including creation of new-product ideas and recommendations for improving existing products.

However, as mentioned earlier in the chapter, most consumer-goods companies such as Procter & Gamble and General Mills have either modified the product manager structure or done away with it altogether in favor of a category management structure. Category managers have profit and loss responsibility, which is not characteristic of the product management system. This change has largely come about because of customer preference, but it can also benefit a manufacturer by avoiding duplication of some jobs and competition among the company's own brands and its managers.

Venture Teams

A **venture team** gathers a group of specialists from different areas of an organization to work together in developing new products. The venture team must meet criteria for return on investment, uniqueness of product, serving a well-defined need, compatibility of the product with existing technology, and strength of patent protection. Although the organization sets up the venture team as a temporary entity, its flexible life span may extend over a number of years. When purchases confirm the commercial potential of a new product, an existing division may take responsibility for that product, or it may serve as the nucleus of a new business unit or of an entirely new company.

Some marketing organizations differentiate between venture teams and task forces. A new-product task force assembles an interdisciplinary group working on temporary assignment through their functional departments. Its basic activities center on coordinating and integrating the work of the firm's functional departments on a specific project.

Unlike a new-product committee, a venture team does not disband after every meeting. Team members accept project assignments as major responsibilities, and the team exercises the authority it needs to both plan and implement a course of action. To stimulate product innovation, the venture team typically communicates directly with top management, but it functions as an entity separate from the basic organization.

 assessment check

1. Who are consumer innovators?
2. What characteristics of a product innovation can influence its adoption rate?
3. What is the role of a venture team in new-product development?

THE NEW-PRODUCT DEVELOPMENT PROCESS

Once a firm is organized for new-product development, it can establish procedures for moving new-product ideas to the marketplace. Developing a new product is often time-consuming, risky, and expensive. Usually, firms must generate dozens of new-product ideas to produce even one successful product. In fact, the failure rate of new products averages 80 percent. Products fail for a number of reasons, including inadequate market assessments, lack of market orientation, poor screening and project evaluation, product defects, and inadequate launch efforts. And these blunders cost a bundle: Firms invest nearly half of the total resources devoted to product innovation on products that become commercial failures.

A new product is more likely to become successful if the firm follows the six-step development process shown in Figure 12.3: (1) idea generation, (2) screening, (3) business analysis, (4) development, (5) test marketing, and (6) commercialization. Of course, each step requires decisions about whether to proceed further or abandon the project. And each step involves a greater financial investment.

Traditionally, most companies have developed new products through phased development, which follows the six steps in an orderly sequence. Responsibility for each phase passes first from product planners to designers and engineers, to manufacturers, and finally to marketers. The phased development method can work well for firms that dominate mature markets and can develop variations on existing products. But with rapid changes in technology and markets, many companies feel pressured to speed up the development process.

 List the stages in the new-product development process.

figure 12.3

Steps in the New-Product Development Process

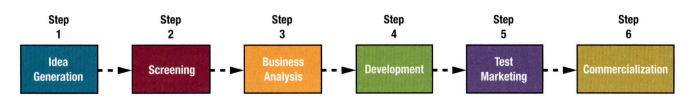

Step 1	Step 2	Step 3	Step 4	Step 5	Step 6
Idea Generation	Screening	Business Analysis	Development	Test Marketing	Commercialization

This time pressure has encouraged many firms to implement accelerated product development programs. These programs generally consist of teams with design, manufacturing, marketing, and sales personnel who carry out development projects from idea generation to commercialization. This method can reduce the time needed to develop products because team members work on the six steps concurrently rather than in sequence.

Whether a firm pursues phased development or parallel product development, all phases can benefit from planning tools and scheduling methods such as the program evaluation and review technique (PERT) and the critical path method (CPM). These techniques, originally developed by the U.S. Navy in connection with construction of the Polaris missile and submarine, map out the sequence of each step in a process and show the time allotments for each activity. Detailed PERT and CPM flow charts help marketers coordinate all activities in the development and introduction of new products.

Method, discussed earlier as an example of positioning, kept its time-to-market cycle to months instead of years by using one name for all its products and outsourcing its manufacturing. The tiny organization is based on innovating, and innovating fast.[37]

IDEA GENERATION

New-product development begins with ideas from many sources: suggestions from customers, the sales force, research-and-development specialists, competing products, suppliers, retailers, and independent inventors. Marissa Mayer is Google's Director of Consumer Web Products, but her function is to champion innovation, encouraging the company's intensely creative employees to produce a constant flow of new ideas.[38] Ray Ozzie, the creator of Lotus Notes, has been hired by Microsoft to integrate its entire product line to tap into the power of the Internet. "Ray really starts with the customer," says one Microsoft executive. "He looks at things 'outside in,' as he says, not technology-out."[39] Similarly, Target's new prescription drug packaging, mentioned earlier in the chapter, was suggested by a customer.[40]

SCREENING

Screening separates ideas with commercial potential from those that cannot meet company objectives. Some organizations maintain checklists of development standards in determining whether a project should be abandoned or considered further. These checklists typically include factors such as product uniqueness, availability of raw materials, and the proposed product's compatibility with current product offerings, existing facilities, and present capabilities. The screening stage may also allow for open discussions of new-product ideas among different parts of the organization.

BUSINESS ANALYSIS

A product idea that survives the initial screening must then pass a thorough business analysis. This stage consists of assessing the new product's potential market, growth rate, and likely competitive strengths. Marketers must evaluate the compatibility of the proposed product with organizational resources.

Concept testing subjects the product idea to additional study prior to its actual development. This important aspect of a new product's business analysis represents a marketing research project that attempts to measure consumer attitudes and perceptions about the new-product idea. Focus groups and in-store polling can contribute effectively to concept testing. The Wrigley Science Institute is a multimillion-dollar effort by Wrigley, makers of chewing gum, to test "emerging research" that suggests that chewing gum might actually be good for you. The institute consists of an international advisory panel of independent scientists and researchers who will look at the potential benefits of gum for stress management, weight management, and alertness and concentration. The company's senior director of corporate relations explained, "We're doing this to learn more about our business and the products that we sell, as well as a brand-new science. But clearly, at the end of the day it has to deliver value. If you can get people to think about chewing gum in a new way, it's good for the category. And we're the category leader."[41]

Briefly
Speaking

"Product testing should not be the basis for introducing a new product because 90 percent of the failures have had successful product test results."

—Richard H. Buskirk
(1927–1994)
American marketing educator

The screening and business analysis stages generate extremely important information for new-product development because they (1) define the proposed product's target market and customers' needs and wants and (2) determine the product's financial and technical requirements. Firms that are willing to invest money and time during these stages tend to be more successful at generating viable ideas and creating successful products.

DEVELOPMENT

Financial outlays increase substantially as a firm converts an idea into a visible product. The conversion process is the joint responsibility of the firm's development engineers, who turn the original concept into a product, and of its marketers, who provide feedback on consumer reactions to the product design, package, color, and other physical features. Many firms implement computer-aided design systems to streamline the development stage, and prototypes may go through numerous changes before the original mock-up becomes a final product. Oakley (see photo) uses a design approach called *sculptural physics,* which they deem as the discipline of wrapping science with art. Their ideas are born using CAD/CAM engineering and are given form as three-dimensional prototypes. New products are evaluated and field-tested by the world's top athletes. Once finalized, they are released to the general public.

TEST MARKETING

As discussed in Chapter 8, many firms test-market their new-product offerings to gauge consumer reaction. After a company has developed a prototype, it may decide to test-market it to measure consumer reactions under normal competitive conditions. Test marketing's purpose is to verify that the product will perform well in a real-life environment. If the product does well, the company can proceed to commercialization. If it flops, the company can fine-tune certain features and reintroduce it or pull the plug on the project altogether. Industries that rely heavily on test marketing are snack foods, automobiles, and movies. Of course, even if a product tests well and reaches the commercialization stage, it may still take a while to catch on with the general public.

MUSIC PLAYERS AND MOBILE PHONES NOW HAVE SOMETHING IN COMMON. THE BEST OPTICS ON EARTH.

O ROKR uses Motorola technology featuring Bluetooth® wireless connectivity to let you enjoy music without tangling in cords. All you need is a compatible Bluetooth enabled mobile phone or Bluetooth Stereo Adapter for your iPod®. You can also use O ROKR to answer calls because it works like a Bluetooth wireless headset, only better. Because all this comes with the unbeatable clarity of Oakley High Definition Optics™ lenses. So the technologies you need are built into what you're wearing. And you're wearing the best optics on earth.

MOTOROLA   OAKLEY

WORKS WITH YOUR iPod.

Oakley's O ROKR, co-developed with Motorola, integrates Bluetooth technology into a sunglass chassis creating a hands-free link to a user's mobile phone or wireless digital music device.

COMMERCIALIZATION

When a new-product idea reaches the commercialization stage, it is ready for full-scale marketing. Commercialization of a major new product can expose the firm to substantial expenses. It must establish marketing strategies, fund outlays for production facilities, and acquaint the sales force, marketing intermediaries, and potential customers with the new product. The marketing team at Method, for instance, brainstormed to determine which competitive advantages

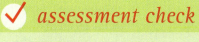

✓ *assessment check*

1. Where do ideas for new products come from?

2. What is concept testing?

3. What happens in the commercialization stage?

of its new air-freshener line to promote, considering environmentally friendly, long-lasting, nonstaining, effective, safe, economical and nonaerosol before settling on "nonaerosol," "concentrated," and "effective."[42]

8   Explain the relationship between product safety and product liability.

PRODUCT SAFETY AND LIABILITY

A product can fulfill its mission of satisfying consumer needs only if it ensures safe operation. Manufacturers must design their products to protect users from harm. Products that lead to injuries, either directly or indirectly, can have disastrous consequences for their makers. **Product liability** refers to the responsibility of manufacturers and marketers for injuries and damages caused by their products. Chapter 3 discussed some of the major consumer protection laws that affect product safety. These laws include the Flammable Fabrics Act of 1953, the Fair Packaging and Labeling Act of 1966, the Poison Prevention Packaging Act of 1970, and the Consumer Product Safety Act of 1972.

Federal and state legislation play a major role in regulating product safety. The Poison Prevention Packaging Act requires drug manufacturers to place their products in packaging that is child resistant yet accessible to all adults, even ones who have trouble opening containers. The Consumer Product Safety Act created a powerful regulatory agency—the Consumer Product Safety Commission (CPSC). This agency has assumed jurisdiction over every consumer product category except food, automobiles, and a few other products already regulated by other agencies. The CPSC has the authority to ban products without court hearings, order recalls or redesigns of products, and inspect production facilities. It can charge managers of negligent companies with criminal offenses. The CPSC is especially watchful of products aimed at babies and young children.

The federal Food and Drug Administration (FDA) must approve food, medications, and health-related devices such as wheelchairs. The new Food Allergen Labeling and Consumer Protection Act mentioned earlier increased the requirements for food labeling. The FDA can also take products off the market if concerns arise about the safety of these products.

The number of product liability lawsuits filed against manufacturers has skyrocketed in recent years. Marketers' exposure to potential liability and litigation is also on the rise in many overseas markets.[43] Although many of these claims reach settlements out of court, such as a recent case in which 340 consumers sued Matrixx Initiatives, alleging loss of their sense of smell following use of Zicam Cold Remedy Nasal Gel, juries have decided on many others, sometimes awarding multimillion-dollar settlements.[44] This threat has led most companies to step up efforts to ensure product safety. Safety warnings appear prominently on the labels of such potentially hazardous products as cleaning fluids and drain cleaners to inform users of the dangers of these products, particularly to children. Changes in product design have reduced the hazards posed by such products as lawn mowers, hedge trimmers, and toys. Product liability insurance has become an essential element for any new or existing product strategy. Premiums for this insurance have risen alarmingly, however, and insurers have almost entirely abandoned some kinds of coverage.

Regulatory activities and the increased number of liability claims have prompted companies to sponsor voluntary improvements in safety standards. Wal-Mart has worked with the Consumer Product Safety Commission to create an innovative Retailer Reporting Model, for instance. Wal-Mart provides CPSC with detailed weekly reports about customer product safety complaints and concerns. CPSC says of the new model, "This type of information will help us keep more consumers safe in the future."[45] Safety planning is now a vital element of product strategy, and many companies now publicize the safety planning and testing that go into the development of their products. Volvo, for example, is well known for the safety features it designs into its automobiles, and consumers recognize that fact when they decide to purchase a Volvo.

 assessment check

1. What is the role of the Consumer Product Safety Commission (CPSC)?

2. What safety issues come under the jurisdiction of the Food and Drug Administration (FDA)?

Strategic Implications of Marketing in the 21st Century

Marketers who want to see their products reach the marketplace successfully have a number of options for developing them, branding them, and developing a strong brand identity among consumers and business customers. The key is to integrate all of the options so that they are compatible with a firm's overall business and marketing strategy and ultimately the firm's mission. As marketers consider ideas for new products, they need to be careful not to send their companies in so many different directions as to dilute the identities of their brands, making it nearly impossible to keep track of what their companies do well. Category management can help companies develop a consistent product mix with strong branding, while at the same time meeting the needs of customers. Looking for ways to extend a brand without diluting it or compromising brand equity is also an important marketing strategy. Finally, marketers must continue to work to produce high-quality products that are also safe for all users.

REVIEW OF CHAPTER OBJECTIVES

1 Explain the benefits of category and brand management.

Category management is beneficial to a business because it gives direct responsibility for creating profitable product lines to category managers and their product group. Consumers respond to branding by making repeat purchases of favored goods and services. Therefore, managing brands and categories of brands or product lines well can result in a direct response from consumers, increasing profits and revenues for companies and creating consumer satisfaction. Brand and category managers can also enhance relationships with business customers such as retailers.

2 Identify the different types of brands.

A generic product is an item characterized by a plain label, no advertising, and no brand name. A manufacturer's brand is a brand name owned by a manufacturer or other producer. Private brands are brand names placed on products marketed by a wholesaler or retailer. A family brand is a brand name that identifies several related products. An individual brand is a unique brand name that identifies a specific offering within a firm's product line to avoid grouping it under a family brand.

3 Explain the strategic value of brand equity.

Brand equity provides a competitive advantage for a firm because consumers are more likely to buy a product that carries a respected, well-known brand name. Brand equity also smooths the path for global expansion

4 Discuss how companies develop strong identities for their products and brands.

Effective brands communicate to a buyer an idea of the product's image. Trademarks, brand names, slogans, and brand icons create an association that satisfies the customer's expectation of the benefits that using or having the product will yield.

5 **Identify and briefly describe each of the new-product development strategies.**

The success of a new product can result from four product development strategies: (1) market penetration, in which a company seeks to increase sales of an existing product in an existing market; (2) market development, which concentrates on finding new markets for existing products; (3) product development, which is the introduction of new products into identifiable or established markets; and (4) product diversification, which focuses on developing entirely new products for new markets.

6 **Describe the consumer adoption process.**

In the adoption process, consumers go through a series of stages from learning about the new product to trying it and deciding whether to purchase it again. The stages are called awareness, interest, evaluation, trial, and adoption/rejection.

7 **List the stages in the new-product development process.**

The stages in the six-step process are: (1) idea generation, (2) screening, (3) business analysis, (4) development, (5) test marketing, and (6) commercialization. These steps may be performed sequentially or, in some cases, concurrently.

8 **Explain the relationship between product safety and product liability.**

Product safety refers to the goal of manufacturers to create products that can be operated safely and will protect consumers from harm. Product liability is the responsibility of marketers and manufacturers for injuries and damages caused by their products. Major consumer protection laws are in place to protect consumers from faulty products.

✓ *assessment check* answers

1.1 What is a brand?
A brand is a name, term, sign, symbol, design, or some combination that identifies the products of one firm while differentiating these products from competitors' offerings.

1.2 Differentiate between brand recognition, brand preference, and brand insistence.
Brand recognition is a company's first objective for newly introduced products and aims to make these items familiar to the public. Brand preference means buyers rely on previous experiences with the product when choosing it over competitors' products. Brand insistence leads consumers to refuse alternatives and to search extensively for the desired merchandise.

2.1 Identify the different types of brands.
The different types of brands are manufacturer's (or national) brands, private brands, captive brands, family brands, and individual brands.

2.2 How are generic products different from branded products?
Generic products are characterized by plain labels, little or no advertising, and no brand names.

3.1 What is brand equity?
Brand equity refers to the added value that a certain brand name gives to a products in the marketplace.

assessment check **answers**

3.2 What are the four dimensions of brand personality?

The four dimensions of brand personality are differentiation, relevance, esteem, and knowledge.

3.3 How does category management help retailers?

Category management helps retailers by providing a person—a category manager—to oversee an entire product line and maximize sales for that retailer. It teams the consumer-goods producer's marketing expertise with the retailer's in-store merchandising efforts to track and identify new opportunities for growth.

4.1 Distinguish between a brand name and a trademark.

A brand name is the part of the brand consisting of words or letters that forms a name distinguishing a firm's offerings from competitors. A trademark is a brand for which the owner claims exclusive legal protection.

4.2 What are the three purposes of packaging?

A package serves three major objectives: (1) protection against damage, spoilage, and pilferage; (2) assistance in marketing the product; and (3) cost effectiveness.

4.3 Describe brand extension and brand licensing.

Brand extension is the strategy of attaching a popular brand name to a new product in an unrelated product category. Brand licensing is the strategy of authorizing other companies to use a brand name.

5.1 Distinguish between market penetration and market development strategies.

In a market penetration strategy, a company seeks to increase sales of an existing product in an existing market. In a market development strategy, the company concentrates on finding new markets for existing products.

5.2 What is product development?

Product development refers to the introduction of new products into identifiable or established markets.

5.3 What is product diversification?

A product diversification strategy focuses on developing entirely new products for new markets.

6.1 Who are consumer innovators?

Consumer innovators are the first buyers of new products—people who purchase new products almost as soon as these products reach the market.

6.2 What characteristics of a product innovation can influence its adoption rate?

Five characteristics of a product innovation influence its adoption rate: relative advantage, compatibility, complexity, possibility of trial use, and observability.

6.3 What is the role of a venture team in new-product development?

A venture team gathers a group of specialists from different areas of an organization to work together in developing new products.

7.1 Where do ideas for new products come from?

New-product development begins with ideas from many sources: suggestions from customers, the sales force, research-and-development specialists, assessments of competing products, suppliers, retailers, and independent inventors.

assessment check answers

7.2　What is concept testing?

Concept testing subjects the product idea to additional study prior to its actual development.

7.3　What happens in the commercialization stage?

When a new-product idea reaches the commercialization stage, it is ready for full-scale marketing.

8.1　What is the role of the Consumer Product Safety Commission (CPSC)?

The Consumer Product Safety Commission is a powerful regulatory agency with jurisdiction over every consumer product category except food, automobiles, and a few other products already regulated by other agencies.

8.2　What safety issues come under the jurisdiction of the Food and Drug Administration (FDA)?

The Food and Drug Administration must approve food, medications, and health-related devices such as wheelchairs.

MARKETING TERMS YOU NEED TO KNOW

brand 378

brand recognition 379

brand preference 379

brand insistence 379

generic products 380

manufacturer's brand 380

family brand 381

brand equity 382

category management 383

brand name 384

trademark 386

brand extension 391

adoption process 394

consumer innovator 394

diffusion process 395

OTHER IMPORTANT MARKETING TERMS

private brand 380

captive brand 380

individual brand 381

brand manager 383

brand mark 384

trade dress 387

label 389

Universal Product Code (UPC) 391

line extension 391

brand licensing 391

market penetration strategy 392

product positioning 392

market development strategy 393

product development 393

product diversification strategy 393

cannibalization 394

product manager 396

venture team 397

concept testing 398

product liability 400

ASSURANCE OF LEARNING REVIEW

1. What are the three stages marketers use to measure brand loyalty?
2. Identify and briefly describe the different types of brands.
3. Why is brand equity so important to companies?
4. What are the characteristics of an effective brand name?
5. What role does packaging play in helping create brand loyalty and brand equity?
6. What is category management and what role does it play in the success of a product line?
7. Describe the different product development strategies.
8. What are the five stages of the consumer adoption process?
9. Describe the different ways companies can organize to develop new products.
10. List the six steps in the new-product development process.

PROJECTS AND TEAMWORK EXERCISES

1. Locate an advertisement for a product that illustrates an especially effective brand name, brand mark, packaging, and overall trade dress. Explain to the class why you think this product has a strong brand identity.

2. With a classmate, go shopping in the grocery store for a product that you think could benefit from updated or new package design. Then sketch out a new package design for the product, identifying and explaining your changes as well as your reasons for the changes. Bring the old package and your new package design to class to share with your classmates.

3. What category of consumer adopter best describes you? Do you follow the same adoption pattern for all products, or are you an early adopter for some and a laggard for others? Create a graph or chart showing your own consumer adoption patterns for different products.

4. With a classmate, choose a firm that interests you and together generate some ideas for new products that might be appropriate for the company. Test your ideas out on each other and then on your classmates. Which ideas make it past this review? Which don't? Why?

5. Consider the steps in the new-product development process. Do you think this process accounts for products that come into being by chance or accident? Why or why not? Defend your answer.

6. With a classmate, visit a couple of supermarkets and look for generic products. How many did you find and in what product categories? Are there any products you think could be successfully marketed as generics that are not now? Why do you think they would be successful?

7. Which product labels do you read? Over the next several days, keep a brief record of the labels you check while shopping. Do you read nutritional information when buying food products? Do you check care labels on clothes before you buy them? Do you read the directions or warnings on a product you haven't used before? Make notes about what influenced your decision to read or not read the product labels. Did you feel they provided enough information, too little, or too much?

8. Some brands achieve customer loyalty by retaining an air of exclusivity and privilege, even though that often comes with high price tags. Louis Vuitton, the maker of luxury leather goods, is one such firm. "You buy into the dream of Louis Vuitton," says one loyal customer. "We're part of a sect, and the more they put their prices up, the more we come back. They pull the wool over our eyes, but we love it." What kind of brand loyalty is this, and how does Vuitton achieve it?

9. Visit a grocery store, look at print ads, or view television advertising to develop a list of all the different brands of bottled water. How do the producers of bottled water turn this commodity item into a branded product? How does each differentiate its brand from all the others?

10. After its ReNu MoistureLoc contact lens solution was linked with cases of severe fungal eye infections, Bausch & Lomb pulled the product from shelves throughout the world.[46] With a partner, research the steps the company went through to investigate the problem. Why was the product discontinued? What was the FDA's involvement in the case? How did the company handle the recall and how did it make the public aware of the problem?

CRITICAL-THINKING EXERCISES

1. With smoking bans in effect in many places, Zippo Manufacturing, maker of the well-known lighters, is looking for ways to license its brand name to makers of products such as grills, torches, space heaters, and fireplaces. Do you think this is a good strategy for Zippo? Why or why not? Identify another well-known product that you think would profit from a licensing strategy. What kind of companies would make good licensing partners for this firm? Do you think the strategy would be successful? Why or why not?

2. General Mills and several other major food makers have begun producing organic foods. But they have deliberately kept their brand names off the packaging of these new products, thinking that the kind of customer who goes out of his or her way to buy organic products is unlikely to trust multinational brands. Other companies, however, such as Heinz, PepsiCo, and Tyson Foods, are betting that their brand names will prove to be persuasive in the $11 billion organic foods market. Which strategy do you think is more likely to be successful? Why?

3. After the terrorist attacks of 9/11, an ad hoc task force of DDB Worldwide advertising professionals in seventeen countries set out to discover what people abroad thought of the United States. In the course of their research, they developed the concept of "America as a Brand," urged U.S. corporations with overseas operations to help "restore" positive impressions of Brand America around the world, and urged the United States to launch Al Hurra as an alternative to the popular Al Jazeera network. Do you think foreigners' perception of a country and its culture can be viewed in marketing terms? Why or why not?

4. Brand names contribute enormously to consumers' perception of a brand. One writer has argued that alphanumeric brand names, such as the Toyota RAV4, Jaguar's X-Type sedan, the Xbox game console, and the GTI from Volkswagen, can translate more easily overseas than "real" names like Golf, Jetta, Escalade, and Eclipse. What other advantages and disadvantages can you think of for each type of brand name? Do you think one type is preferable to the other? Why?

ETHICS EXERCISE

As mentioned in the chapter, some analysts predict that bar codes may soon be replaced by a wireless technology called *radio-frequency identification (RFID)*. RFID is a system of installing tags containing tiny computer chips on, say, supermarket items. These chips automatically radio the location of the item to a computer network where inventory data are stored, letting store managers know not only where the item is at all times but also when and where it was made and its color and size. Proponents of the idea believe RFID will cut costs and simplify inventory tracking and reordering. It may also allow marketers to respond quickly to shifts in demand, avoid under- and overstocking, and reduce spoilage by automatically removing outdated perishables from the shelves.

Privacy advocates, however, think the chips provide too much product-preference information that might be identified with individual consumers. In the meantime, Wal-Mart is asking its top suppliers to begin using the new technology on products stocked by the giant retailer.

1. Do you think RFID poses a threat to consumer privacy? Why or why not?
2. Do you think the technology's possible benefits to marketers outweigh the potential privacy concerns? Are there also potential benefits to consumers, and if so, what are they?
3. How can marketers reassure consumers about privacy concerns if RFID comes into widespread use?

INTERNET EXERCISES

1. **Patents and trademarks.** In the United States the Patent and Trademark Office is responsible for the registration of patents and trademarks. Visit the USPTO Web site (http://www.uspto.gov) and answer the following questions.
   a. What are the types of patents?
   b. How long does the patent review process take?
   c. What is the so-called Madrid Protocol concerning the international registration of marks?
2. **Packaging.** Companies use packaging to help market their products. Visit each of the following Web sites and prepare a brief report on how each company has used packaging as part of its brand management strategy.
   a. H. J. Heinz: http://www.heinz.com
   b. Campbell Soup: http://www.campbellsoup.com
   c. General Mills (Yoplait Yogurt): http://www.yoplait.com

Note: Internet Web addresses change frequently. If you don't find the exact site listed, you may need to access the organization's home page and search from there or use a search engine such as Google.

CASE 12.1   JCPenney Recaptures Its Cool

What's the first place you think of when you're ready to shop for trendy clothes or accessories? It might not be JCPenney, but if the 103-year-old retailer has its way, that could change. Under the leadership first of Allen Questrom, who retired in 2004, and now of Mike Ullman, the new CEO, JCPenney is working hard to transform its venerable name into a fashion destination rather than a place to shop for sales. Questrom's strategy, which Ullman has continued and refined, is all about brands.

JCPenney already has 35 house brands, which account for 40 percent of its sales—that's more than any other U.S. department store. Among the store's most successful brands are Arizona, Worthington, and St. John's Bay, each of which is a billion-dollar business. But JCPenney believes that these valuable brands can do even more for the bottom line at its 1,000 stores. "We looked at them more as labels," Ullman says. The challenge was to give the brands the same kind of emotional appeal that consumers develop for national brands such as Nike. JCPenney is meeting that challenge with a three-part strategy.

First, the company has identified four separate fashion groups to which it wants to appeal—conservative, traditional, modern, and trendy. It plans to tailor its brands for each of those targets. Second, JCPenney has hired dedicated design teams—and sometimes individual designers such as Nicole Miller—to study the target customer's needs and wants for each of the store's fashion brands. Miller, for instance, recently launched a highly successful new fashion line for

JCPenney called Nicole. Finally, JCPenney has added a new marketing position—brand managers will oversee the top brands and be responsible for ensuring consistency between the brand's image, its clothing designs, and its marketing strategies.

JCPenney is well aware that timing is critical. To make sure it stays ahead of the curve, the company has speeded up the introduction of new styles, successfully launching a.n.a., its most ambitious new brand ever. The a.n.a. brand went through an expedited development process that brought fashions from conceptualization to store racks in only four months, compared with the old norm of at least a year. The next step for a.n.a. is a move into accessories. "We want to outfit [the customer] from head to toe so she has the entire look and it is very easy for her," says a.n.a.'s head designer. "It completes the full brand image."

Early results suggest that JCPenney drive to make customers think, "This is my store, they get me," and shed its image as "your mother's store," is already working. Revenues are up, sales of a.n.a.-branded merchandise are running ahead of estimates, and the chain—which plans to add about 200 new stores—is gaining popularity among women shoppers faster than its rival, Kohl's.

Questions for Critical Thinking

1. What aspects of successful brands is JCPenney counting on in its new growth strategy? Why?
2. Are there other branding strategies the company could use to revive its image? What are they? Why do you think they could be important to the firm?

Sources: "Fashion Retailer JCPenney Introduces a n a Women's Apparel Brand," Fibre2fashion, February 15, 2006, **http://www.fibre2fashion.com**; Robert Berner, "Penney: Back in Fashion," *BusinessWeek*, January 9, 2006, pp. 82–84; Janet Guyon, "Penney's Thoughts," *Fortune*, October 31, 2005, p. 161.

VIDEO CASE 12.2 Rebranding at JPMorgan Chase

The written video case on JPMorgan Chase appears on page VC-15. The recently filmed JPMorgan Chase video is designed to expand and highlight the concepts in this chapter and the concepts and questions covered in the written video case.

Talking about Marketing Careers with. . .

MARK A. MERCURIO
ASSISTANT BRAND MANAGER, MR. CLEAN
MARKETING
PROCTER & GAMBLE

Innovation and growth are two key words that best express Procter & Gamble's approach to the consumer goods market. The company is a global powerhouse, with nearly 98,000 employees working in 80 countries and product lines that include 22 billion-dollar brands. P&G focuses its product development and marketing efforts in four major segments: beauty, family health, household care, and its newest shaving products division, Gillette. If you walk down a supermarket or drugstore aisle, you'll see dozens of P&G brands—such as Cover Girl, Ivory, Pampers, ThermaCare, Tide, Folgers, and Dawn, to name just a few—all created to help simplify your daily life.

One of the tried-and-true brands in P&G's family is Mr. Clean. With a history stretching back nearly 50 years, consumers have come to depend on Mr. Clean products to help maintain their homes and autos. The feeling is mutual—the company relies on and values the trust that consumers place in the brand and want to build on that relationship. To do so, P&G has a dedicated marketing team to oversee its Mr. Clean product line. We were fortunate to be able to have a one-on-one exchange with one of those team members: Mark Mercurio, Assistant Brand Manager for Mr. Clean Marketing. He was kind enough to spend some time to help us understand what is involved in the day-to-day activities in brand management.

Q: Heading up the marketing team for such a recognized brand as Mr. Clean is a great career opportunity. Tell us a little about yourself—what academic and work experiences led you to your current position at Mr. Clean Marketing?

A: I took a roundabout track into brand management. I studied civil engineering at the University of Cincinnati for my undergraduate degree. I realized early in my school years that I didn't want to be an engineer but completed the degree and searched for a job in business. I found my engineering degree really helped with the quantitative nature of my future jobs. After UC, I took a job with Accenture—then Andersen Consulting—doing IT management consulting. I really enjoyed the project management nature of that job, and it gave me a chance to experience a number of different industries. After three years, I decided to go back to school to study marketing, as I wanted to get out of the back-office work of IT and more in the front end of the business, driving business strategies and planning. So I went to the Darden Graduate School of Business at the University of Virginia to get my MBA. Between my first and second years of MBA school, I took an internship in marketing research at P&G. I really loved the aspect of using research techniques to determine the best course for the business—it was a great mix of qualitative and quantitative work. After a couple years, though, I moved into marketing at P&G because it had more strategy setting and overall profit-and-loss business responsibility. And that's where I am today. Definitely the long road there, but I am absolutely certain this is the place for me.

Q: Students will be curious about what is involved in marketing consumer products such as those under the Mr. Clean family brand. How many people are on the Mr. Clean team? Would you outline the different functions of the members and their roles in marketing the brand? What is your role in the overall effort of bringing Mr. Clean products to consumers?

A: Brand management is all about leveraging your team's strengths to get the most out of your team. Within marketing, there are five of us—four assistant brand managers and the brand manager. Marketing's role is to set the strategy for the brand—both in how we communicate and in what we communicate to consumers. We oversee marketing planning and work with our agencies to develop world-class marketing. We also typically lead the new product initiatives for the brand—keeping the team on track, navigating the project through management reviews, etc. Marketing interacts with quite a few functions, including R&D, sales, product supply, marketing research, finance, and increasingly directly with sales teams to coordinate more closely with our retailers.

Q: We often talk about product lines in marketing. Procter & Gamble is a giant in its industry, offering several product lines for consumers. How does Mr. Clean fit into the mix of lines that P&G offers? How does it support the company's overall strategy?

A: Generally, different brands play different roles in the company. Mr. Clean's role in the overall company strategy is to drive discontinuous growth. With innovations like Magic Eraser, AutoDry, and Mr. Clean Magic Reach, we have been successful in that role.

Q: Mr. Clean as a brand name and brand mark has been around nearly 50 years now. How do you and your team keep the brand fresh and relevant in such a competitive marketplace as consumer household goods? How do you decide when and how to add a new product to the line? Do consumers have any input in the process? Can you give us an example?

A: Consumers are at the forefront of our decisions on what to bring to market and how. In fact, we have a mantra at P&G—Consumer is Boss—representing that exact thought. Awhile back, P&G brought in business in new markets by first discovering a new technology and then figuring out how to make it work for consumers. Now, we're much better at letting the consumer drive the innovation. Our product researchers, marketing researchers, marketers, and agencies are constantly engaging in conversations with consumers through our research to understand what they need to make their lives easier. A perfect example of this is our Multi-Surface spray. We observed consumers cleaning their homes and found they have a different cleaner for every surface in their house. So we developed a spray that was suitable for every hard surface—it cleans glass, cuts grease, and kills germs all in one. Once we determine a direction for a new product, we involve the consumers in every aspect of bringing it to market, including how we name it, what benefit we talk about with consumers, what the packaging looks like, how to price it, etc.

Q: In textbooks and in the daily news, we hear about the importance of ensuring the quality of a product. That must be critical to consumer goods such as those you market. What goes into the formulation, testing, and production of a new product?

A: R&D staff have consumers with them the entire way as they formulate the product. Typically, they will have an "expert panel" of consumers who try iteration after iteration of formula design to help us optimize the formula. We also typically do one or two very large quantitative research tests to make sure the product meets all of our standards before releasing it to market.

Q: Mr. Clean is a true celebrity in the marketing world. Nearly everyone would instantly recognize his smiling face and bulging muscles. Could you talk a little about his value to Procter & Gamble? How do you protect his image and name?

A: I don't think I could put a value on Mr. Clean, the icon. In these days of fragmented marketing media, consumers are being drowned with messages—it's hard to stand out and be remembered. But with Mr. Clean, consumers are so accustomed to hearing about new ways to clean your home from Mr. Clean that our commercials are instantly recognized and easily remembered. It is a great asset we leverage in all of our marketing. At the same time, we do have distinct rules on how to use and not use the icon so that we can maintain the integrity of that asset. We have design and advertising development managers who help keep us marketing folks in line with how we want to leverage the icon, and they are constantly reviewing our work to make sure it fits with our objectives. We also track our brand's equity consistently to look for movement in how consumers view our brand.

Q: Many marketers get their start in the industry through work experience and internships. Did that help you on your career path? What advice can you give to students who are interested in getting started in a marketing career?

A: There are a number of ways to get into marketing—some more traditional than others. I took a pretty typical route—through an MBA program after having a few years' work experience. My advice would be to think about the kind of marketing you would like to do and focus on that industry. Then build a network. Try joining the marketing club at school or working on research projects with a professor—anything to help you understand the industry better and increase your chances of meeting a hiring manager. And when you get a chance to interview for a job, make sure you prepare yourself and be confident.

Comedy's the Name of the Game in This Mix

The Second City

On a Friday night at The Second City, the audience line stretches past the box office, down the spiral staircase, and even out onto the streets of Chicago, Detroit, or Toronto. Patrons are shown a seat by the host and generally order a round of drinks for their party. The stage lights come up, and over a backdrop of rock music the cast of The Second City bursts onto the stage. Tonight, the first scene of the show is filled with a lightning-paced musical montage. Comedic bits and melodic vignettes preview the characters about to entertain the night's audience. After the scripted show, the crowd is treated to Second City's signature art form—improvisation. These unscripted scenes are based on single word suggestions from the audience and result in quick and hilarious character dialogues. Whether on the Mainstage in Chicago or starting up a new show in Denver, improvisers at The Second City excel in off-the-cuff comedy. It's easy for a customer to forget that the "product" of The Second City is an artistic creation formed as part of a business model.

The Second City has made significant product decisions to build its brand into an attractive mix of related services. Positioning these services in the market has kept SC competitive in the theatre and entertainment industries. To maintain brand equity throughout expansion, SC has stayed true to its roots. Company co-founder Bernie Sahlins relates Second City's success to its dedication to the stage: "I think that's why SC has survived, because it comes from the theatre. . . . As long as it holds on to that, it's going to do well." With multiple stages, national touring companies, a booming corporate comedy division, and a growing Training Center, the SC product is offered to a number of audiences. Rooted in stage comedy, the Second City brand remains recognizable. Whether in the theater, the classroom, or the corporate staff room, Second City must continue producing an impressive cast of performers.

CEO Andrew Alexander has produced more than 200 Second City revues since joining the company in 1974. He has played a strong role in SC's care and growth, which has included finding, cultivating, and producing great talent. He says that SC "looks for individuals that are intelligent, have a point of view, and the potential to become a good actor . . . and a comedic sensibility doesn't hurt." This general welcoming of talent has brought hundreds of performers of all ages to Second City's door. Because The Second City offers an intangible service to its consumers, standardizing the product throughout the organization is a challenge. To meet this challenge and widen its product line, second City has created an instructional division with Training Centers in six cities.

Since opening its first Training Center in 1985, The Second City has attracted a wide range of aspiring actors, comedy enthusiasts, and casual hobbyists. Vice President Kelly Leonard notes that the reputation of the Second City brand has attracted most of the Training Center's student body. It also markets toward the less theatrically inclined, those who wish to "take a different direction in their life—branch out, get better at communicating." Aptly, Second City offers a versatile program. The Training Center has classes on the techniques of acting, writing, music, directing, and, of course, improvisation. Classes are often taught by the same performers who create shows for the Second City stage. This fosters a recognizable community for Second City participants, wherein famous alumni and acclaimed productions are benchmarked for study or revue. The life cycle of the Second City performer in training can start in kindergarten and con-

tinue on with SC's extensive list of offerings. With around 2,000 students enrolled at any given time, the top management at SC must create a cohesive curriculum rooted in the fundamentals of the brand.

For Kelly Leonard, "Second City's culture is built upon improvisation. We ëyes, and' to ideas. We are always creating." The Second City mantra of "yes, and" is a technique in accepting and building off ideas presented in scenes. The creative power of "yes, and" is strung throughout all aspects of The Second City. The New Product Development Process for the Second City has especially benefited from this radical approach to generating ideas. The Second City Theatricals Division headed by Leonard, produces plays and sketch comedy for performing arts centers and private events. Mr. Leonard saw a unique opportunity to extend the product onto Norwegian Cruise Lines, exclusively producing shows for the exotic traveling company. The operation has become a lucrative new product line for Second City.

Today, a number of Second City ensembles perform on ships and stages around the world. The process of hiring and cultivating performers is paramount to producing quality talent. As television and the Internet create competitive alternatives for consumers, The Second City must position its brand as a reliable source of stage comedy. "I think that as the entertainment universe becomes more loud or more crowded, we will strengthen our position through simple quality. More, decidedly, does not mean better. We have to be rock solid and stay true to the brand," says Kelly Leonard. With SC producer Beth Kligerman and a number of other creative personnel, Leonard oversees the selection process for talent at The Second City. Selecting the best graduates of the Training Center and occasionally a talented walk-in, SC consistently makes quality a fundamental product strategy.

Across the nation, prominent marquees display The Second City's stacked logo above the entrance of each theater. SC adopted this "splotched" style logo during its 25th anniversary year. This "graffiti on the wall" look for the logo signifies its subversive style. Hints to that character are found not only on Second City marquees, but in the nature of its service as well. "In The Second City, culture, authority, and the norm are to be disturbed—creativity and originality are to be celebrated," says Kelly Leonard.

The Second City manages its brand in the same way its performers hit the stage: with a dedication to the core product and an eager sense to accept and build on ideas. This commitment has allowed The Second City to develop an impressive product mix.

Questions

1. Given Second City's welcoming of new ideas, what sort of new product planning do you think the Second City could do? How would you relate it to Second City's focus on the theatre?

2. How does Second City's Training Center function as a separate product line for the business? How does it benefit the company in multiple ways?

3. How would you define the Second City product (specialty, unsought, convenient, or shopping)? Why? How is this reflected in its brand?

4. What advantages might the Second City product have to the traditional life cycles of a product? What disadvantages?

410

PART 5

Distribution Decisions

CHEVROLET UNLEASHES THE NEW CORVETTE

CORVETTE by Chevrolet

New with 4-wheel disc brakes
'65 CORVETTE

CHEVROLET

'73 CORVETTE
We gave it radials, a quieter ride, guard beams and a nose job.

Building a better way to see the U.S.A.

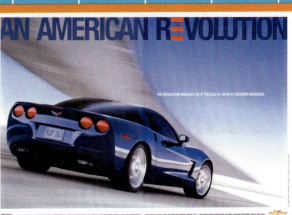

AN AMERICAN REVOLUTION

chevy

Zappos.com Zips Shoes to Your Door

Wandering through a maze of shoes at the mall, searching for the perfect pair, can be frustrating. One store carries your size, but the styles are frumpy. Another has better styles but the wrong colors. A third store has brands you've never heard of and don't want to try. The last shop had the shoes you're looking for—but they sold the last pair yesterday. The people who work at Zappos.com know all about this experience—they've had it themselves. In fact, founder Nick Swinmurn got the inspiration for his firm while on an unsuccessful quest for shoes. The Internet was a still a fairly new way to sell consumer goods in 1999, but he thought he could make it work.

Shoes are a $40 billion market in the United States. In 1999 when Zappos was founded, $2 billion of those sales came from mail order. Brick-and-mortar retailers estimated that they were losing about one of every three sales because they didn't have the right size or color in stock. Swinmurn realized the huge opportunity that lay in front of him. If he could offer one of the largest selections of shoes available and deliver them to consumers' homes as quickly as possible, his firm could fill consumers' needs for shoes in a way no other company had yet been able to.

From the beginning, service and selection have been Zappos.com's mantra. The call center is open round the clock and is staffed by about 200 workers who take and fulfill orders. "We believe that the most important key to our success will be our service-oriented culture, and we spend a lot of time and effort working on ways to constantly improve our culture," says the company's Web site. Every new employee undergoes four weeks of customer service training before starting a job. Because the warehouse is open 24/7, a customer who orders shoes as late as 11 p.m. can still get next-day delivery. Regular shipping and return shipping are free to newcomers, and regular customers quickly get upgraded to overnight or second-day delivery. This strategy has helped the firm grow as it has added new products such as handbags to its lineup. "If customers know that they're going to get the best service from Zappos and they're going to get it overnight, then anytime we're going to add a product category, our customers will be loyal to us," says CEO Tony Hsieh.

Marketing Channels and Supply Chain Management

Service and selection are the perfect fit at Zappos. The firm now carries more than 500 name brands, in 90,000 styles, with about 2 million pairs in stock at the warehouse in Shepherdsville, Kentucky, ready for shipment. Unlike other online retailers, Zappos doesn't accept back orders if shoes are out of stock. Instead, the firm offers an alternative so that customers are never kept waiting for a pair of shoes. The warehouse location is strategic—it's right near the UPS air hub at the Louisville International Airport. "We can get shoes to [customers in] California faster than you could from California," quips Craig Adkins, director of warehouse operations. "We have a very good relationship with UPS. They leave their trailers here, and we fill them up."

To succeed over the long run, Zappos must build and maintain strong relationships with its vendors—the manufacturers and wholesalers that supply the shoes and handbags. Open and frequent communication is the basis of these relationships. Zappos set up an extranet with its vendors so that they can see which brands and models of shoes are selling and how profitable they are. Zappos also hosts a vendor appreciation party to kick off the big shoe trade show each year. "I can see my business from their point of view," explains Tom Austin, manager of the California and Nevada territories for Clarks shoes. "[Zappos] just says, 'I don't want to run out of shoes, you take care of us.' You can't believe how pleasant [Zappos] is to work with."[1]

evolution of a brand

Zappos has rapidly become the leading online retailer of shoes. "The [footwear] industry was in shock when they found out the numbers Zappos is doing and how popular they are," notes an independent sales representative for Simple Shoes and UGG Australia, two popular brands. How did Zappos manage to scoop the competition?[2]

- *Good relations with customers and employees.* "The original concept was to have a great selection and the rest will follow," explains CEO Tony Hsieh. "We found over time that anytime we focused on delivering a great online shopping experience, it generated a lot of repeat customers and a lot of word-of-mouth advertising." Consider the difficulties of developing good relationships with customers when the main point of contact is a Web site. What are the challenges and benefits of delivering products through the Internet? Zappos workers are specifically trained in customer service, no matter what jobs they will undertake when their training is complete. They also receive health and vacation benefits as soon as they are hired. "I would have just never imagined that warehouse workers would get those benefits," says one warehouse employee.

Chapter Overview

Distribution—moving goods and services from producers to customers—is the second marketing mix variable and an important marketing concern. Although a sleek design and stylish photo might motivate consumers to purchase a pair of high-end shoes from Zappos, these strategies are useless if customers don't receive those shoes when they want them—and Zappos knows this. A distribution strategy has two critical components: (1) marketing channels and (2) logistics and supply-chain management.

A **marketing channel**—also called a **distribution channel**—is an organized system of marketing institutions and their interrelationships that enhances the physical flow and ownership of goods and services from producer to consumer or business user. The choice of marketing channels should support the firm's overall marketing strategy. By contrast, **logistics** refers to the process of coordinating the flow of information, goods, and services among members of the marketing channel. **Supply-chain management** is the control of activities of purchasing, processing, and delivery through which raw materials are transformed into products and made available to final consumers. Efficient logistical systems support customer service, enhancing customer relationships—an important goal of any marketing strategy.

A key aspect of logistics is physical distribution, which covers a broad range of activities aimed at efficient movement of finished goods from the end of the production line to the consumer. Although some marketers use the terms *transportation* and *physical distribution* interchangeably, these terms do not carry the same meaning. **Physical distribution** extends beyond transportation to include such important decision areas as customer service, inventory control, materials handling, protective packaging, order processing, transportation, warehouse site selection, and warehousing.

distribution Movement of goods and services from producers to customers.

marketing (distribution) channel System of marketing institutions that enhances the physical flow of goods and services, along with ownership title, from producer to consumer or business user.

logistics Process of coordinating the flow of information, goods, and services among members of the distribution channel.

supply-chain management Control of the activities of purchasing, processing, and delivery through which raw materials are transformed into products and made available to final consumers.

physical distribution Broad range of activities aimed at efficient movement of finished goods from the end of the production line to the consumer.

Briefly
Speaking

"There is no finish line."

—Nike Corporation motto

Well-planned marketing channels and effective logistics and supply-chain management provide ultimate users with convenient ways for obtaining the goods and services they desire. This chapter discusses the activities, decisions, and marketing intermediaries involved in managing marketing channels and logistics. Chapter 14 looks at other players in the marketing channel: retailers, direct marketers, and wholesalers.

THE ROLE OF MARKETING CHANNELS IN MARKETING STRATEGY

1 Describe the types of marketing channels and the roles they play in marketing strategy.

A firm's distribution channels play a key role in its overall marketing strategy because these channels provide the means by which the firm makes the goods and services available to ultimate users. Channels perform four important functions. First, they facilitate the exchange process by reducing the number of marketplace contacts necessary to make a sale. Suppose you want to buy a digital camera. You've had an Olympus camera in the past and been satisfied with it, so when you see an ad for the Stylus 600 you are interested. You visit the Olympus Web site, where you find out that the camera has such features as Bright Capture Technology and an all-weather LCD screen. Then you discover that Olympus also has a digital photo printer, making it convenient to print out individual pictures at home. The site locates a nearby dealer for you, where you can go to see the actual camera and printer. The dealer forms part of the channel that brings you, a potential buyer, and Olympus, the seller, together to complete the exchange process. It's important to keep in mind that all channel members benefit when they work together; when they begin to disagree or—worse yet—compete directly with each other, everyone loses.

Distributors adjust for discrepancies in the market's assortment of goods and services via a process known as *sorting*, the second channel function. A single producer tends to maximize the quantity it makes of a limited line of goods, while a single buyer needs a limited quantity of a wide selection of merchandise. Sorting alleviates such discrepancies by channeling products to suit both the buyer's and the producer's needs.

The third function of marketing channels involves standardizing exchange transactions by setting expectations for products, and it involves the transfer process itself. Channel members tend to standardize payment terms, delivery schedules, prices, and purchase lots, among other conditions. Standardization helps make transactions efficient and fair. However, sometimes standardization causes unforeseen problems. Traditionally, regulations in the state of Washington required beer and wine distributors to sell their products to every retailer at the same price, without offering any volume discounts to retailers such as Costco. Costco sued the state in U.S. district court and won a ruling that the state's system violated several existing laws regarding competition.[3]

© ASSOCIATED PRESS, AP

In a twist on its usual marketing strategy, Dell has opened two stores in busy malls in Texas (shown) and New York so that customers can see and test products in person. But after making their selections, consumers still need to make their purchases online and have them delivered directly to their homes.

The final marketing channel function is to facilitate searches by both buyers and sellers. Buyers search for specific goods and services to fill their needs, while sellers attempt to learn what buyers want. Channels bring buyers and sellers together to complete the exchange process.

Hundreds of distribution channels exist today, and no single channel best serves the needs of every company. Instead of searching for the best channel for all products, a marketing manager must analyze alternative channels in light of consumer needs to determine the most appropriate channel or channels for the firm's goods and services.

Marketers must remain flexible because channels may change over time. Today's ideal channel may prove inappropriate in a few years. Or the way a company uses that channel may have to change. Two decades ago, Michael Dell came up with a revolutionary way to sell computers—by the telephone, directly to consumers. Later, Dell added Internet sales to its operations. Although Dell is still one of the world's largest PC manufacturers, its sales via phone and the Internet have begun to slide as more consumers seem to prefer to visit retail stores to try out new gadgets and features. The shift has caused Dell to re-examine the way it sells computers.[4]

The following sections examine the diverse types of channels available to marketers. They look at the decisions marketers must make to develop an effective distribution strategy that supports their firm's marketing objectives.

TYPES OF MARKETING CHANNELS

The first step in selecting a marketing channel is determining which type of channel will best meet both the seller's objectives and the distribution needs of customers. Figure 13.1 depicts the major channels available to marketers of consumer and business goods and services.

Most channel options involve at least one **marketing intermediary.** A marketing intermediary (or **middleman**) is an organization that operates between producers and consumers or business users. Retailers and wholesalers are both marketing intermediaries. A retail store owned and operated by someone other than the manufacturer of the products it sells is one type of marketing intermediary. A **wholesaler** is an intermediary that takes title to the goods it handles and then distributes these goods to retailers, other distributors, or sometimes end consumers. Although some analysts believed that the Internet would ultimately render many intermediaries obsolete, that hasn't happened. In an unusual partnership, NetBank has joined with UPS to serve its customers. NetBank is a bank that operates only online. Although it is based in Atlanta—as is UPS—it doesn't have branches or ATMs. The Internet may be convenient for many transactions, but how does the average customer deposit a paper check? By stopping in at the nearest UPS store. With 3,800 retail stores nationwide, UPS acts as a convenient branch for NetBank customers.[5]

A short marketing channel involves few intermediaries. By contrast, a long marketing channel involves many intermediaries working in succession to move goods from producers to consumers. Business products usually move through short channels due to geographic concentrations and comparatively fewer business purchasers. Service firms market primarily through short channels because they sell intangible products and need to maintain personal relationships within their channels. Haircuts, manicures, and dental cleanings all operate through short channels. Not-for-profit organizations also tend to work with short, simple, and direct channels. Any marketing intermediaries in such channels usually act as agents, such as independent ticket agencies or fund-raising specialists.

DIRECT SELLING

The simplest and shortest marketing channel is a direct channel. A **direct channel** carries goods directly from a producer to the business purchaser or ultimate user. This channel forms part of **direct selling,** a marketing strategy in which a producer establishes direct sales contact with its product's final users. Direct selling is an important option for goods that require extensive demonstrations in persuading customers to buy.

Direct selling plays a significant role in business-to-business marketing. Most major installations, accessory equipment, and even component parts and raw materials are sold through direct contacts between producing firms and final buyers. Pharmaceutical giants such as Merck, Pfizer, and

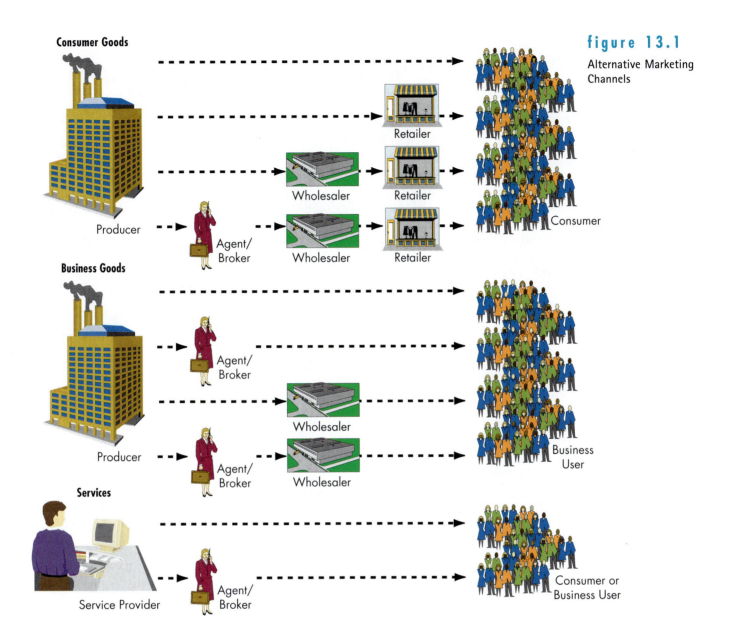

figure 13.1

Alternative Marketing Channels

Upjohn market their prescription medications to physicians and pharmacies with large, well-trained sales forces. Some estimates put the number of such reps at 100,000 nationwide.[6]

Direct selling is also important in consumer-goods markets. Direct sellers such as Avon, Pampered Chef, and Tastefully Simple sidestep competition in store aisles by developing networks of independent representatives who sell their products directly to consumers. Many of these companies practice a direct selling strategy called the *party plan,* originally popularized by Tupperware. A seller attends a gathering at a host customer's home to demonstrate products and take orders. Beijo Bags is one such business. Launched several years ago by entrepreneur Susan Handley, the bags are sold at home-based parties by independent sales reps who are mostly stay-at-home moms—and customers themselves. In just three years, Beijo Bags hit $10 million in sales.[7]

The Internet provides another direct selling channel for both B2B and B2C purchases. Consumers who want to sport designer handbags—but don't want to pay full price for them—can rent them from Bagborrowsteal.com. For those who like to change bags often but can't or won't pay the hundreds or thousands of dollars for Pucci's or Dolce & Gabana's latest, the site may be a real bargain.[8]

Direct mail can be an important part of direct selling—or it can encourage a potential customer to contact an intermediary such as a retailer. Either way, it is a vital communication piece for many marketers, as described in the "Etiquette Tips for Marketing Professionals" feature.

Etiquette Tips for Marketing Professionals

Preparing an Effective Direct-Mail Piece

As a marketer, communicating with your customers—or potential customers—is probably your most important responsibility. Preparing a direct-mail piece can be a particular challenge because it must catch a consumer's eye, keep his or her interest, create a desire for a product, and call for action (such as a phone call or visit to a store). And with consumers' time always a concern, direct marketers need to target the most likely prospects and avoid wasting others' time. Here are a few tips for creating an effective marketing message through direct mail—one that can truly serve customers' needs:

1. Know what your objectives are and communicate them clearly to avoid wasting prospective customers' time and your money. Do you want the consumer to make an immediate purchase or call your organization for more information?
2. Know your target audience and their needs. Sending mail to people who do not buy your type of product only creates an annoyance—junk mail.
3. Write a clear headline directed to your target

audience. Your offer should be featured prominently in the headline or near the beginning of the piece so consumers can quickly determine the intent of your mailing. Be sure the offer is easy to read and understand.
4. In a few sentences—or with a brief list—describe how consumers will benefit from the offer.
5. Provide all the necessary contact information—fax number, e-mail address, Web site address, phone number, mailing address for customer convenience. Potential customers should have a variety of ways to reach you or your company so that they can choose which method best suits them.
6. Create a clean, clear, eye-catching design for your piece. Make sure all illustrations support the text. Clutter only works against you by confusing potential customers.

Sources: "Direct Mail Buyer's Guide," BuyerZone.com, **http://www.buyerzone.com**, accessed May 19, 2006; "Preparing an Effective Direct Mail Piece," BlueGrass, **http://www.bgmailing.com**, accessed May 19, 2006; Joanna L. Krotz, "Sending the Right Message: How to Match a Direct Mailer to Your Marketing," Microsoft, **http://www.microsoft.com/smallbusiness**, accessed May 19, 2006.

CHANNELS USING MARKETING INTERMEDIARIES

Although direct channels allow simple and straightforward marketing, they are not practical in every case. Some products serve markets in different areas of the country or world or have large numbers of potential end users. Other categories of goods rely heavily on repeat purchases. The producers of these goods may find more efficient, less expensive, and less time-consuming alternatives to direct channels by using marketing intermediaries. This section considers five channels that involve marketing intermediaries.

Producer to Wholesaler to Retailer to Consumer

The traditional channel for consumer goods proceeds from producer to wholesaler to retailer to user. This method carries goods between thousands of small producers with limited lines and local retailers. A firm with limited financial resources will rely on the services of a wholesaler that serves as an immediate source of funds and then markets to hundreds of retailers. On the other hand, a small retailer can draw on a wholesaler's specialized distribution skills. In addition, many manufacturers hire their own field representatives to service retail accounts with marketing information. Wholesalers may then handle the actual sales transactions.

Producer to Wholesaler to Business User

Similar characteristics in the organizational market often attract marketing intermediaries to operate between producers and business purchasers. The term *industrial distributor* commonly refers to intermediaries in the business market that take title to the goods.

Producer to Agent to Wholesaler to Retailer to Consumer

In markets served by many small companies, a unique intermediary—the agent—performs the basic function of bringing buyer and seller together. An agent may or may not take possession of the goods but never takes title. The agent merely represents a producer by seeking a market for its products or a wholesaler (which does take title to the goods) by locating a supply source.

Producer to Agent to Wholesaler to Business User

Like agents, brokers are independent intermediaries who may or may not take possession of goods but never take title to these goods. Agents and brokers also serve the business market when small producers attempt to market their offerings through large wholesalers. Such an intermediary, often called a **manufacturers' representative,** provides an independent sales force to contact wholesale buyers. A kitchen equipment manufacturer may have its own manufacturer's representatives to market its goods, for example.

Producer to Agent to Business User

For products sold in small units, only merchant wholesalers can economically cover the markets. A merchant wholesaler is an independently owned wholesaler that takes title to the goods. By maintaining regional inventories, this wholesaler achieves transportation economies, stockpiling goods and making small shipments over short distances. For a product with large unit sales, however, and for which transportation accounts for a small percentage of the total cost, the producer-agent-business user channel is usually employed. The agent in effect becomes the producer's sales force, but bulk shipments of the product reduce the intermediary's inventory management function.

A WASHING MACHINE THAT'S EASIER TO UNLOAD?
(IT'S NOT MAGIC, IT'S WHIRLPOOL)

WE ASKED 40,000 PEOPLE WHAT THEY WANTED FROM A WASHING MACHINE THE RESULT IS A BRAND-NEW MODEL WITH EVERYTHING YOU COULD ASK FOR BUILT INTO IT.

THE BIGGEST DOOR OPENING IN THE MARKET, SO IT'S EASIER TO UNLOAD.

A LARGE WASH DRUM FOR A MORE EFFICIENT WASH

NEW SPECIAL PROGRAMME EXCLUSIVELY FOR SILK

NEW EASY ACCESS WASH FILTER

NEW INTEGRATED HANDLE WITH CHILD-LOCK.

Whirlpool

BRINGS QUALITY TO LIFE

IMAGE COURTESY OF THE ADVERTISING ARCHIVES

Home appliance manufacturer Whirlpool relies on intermediaries to get its products to consumers.

DUAL DISTRIBUTION

Dual distribution refers to movement of products through more than one channel to reach the firm's target market. Nordstrom, for instance, has a three-pronged distribution system, selling through stores, catalogs, and the Internet. Marketers usually adopt a dual distribution strategy either to maximize their firm's coverage in the marketplace or to increase the cost-effectiveness of the firm's marketing effort. TiVo recently made a deal with online video service Brightcove Networks in which TiVo customers will be able to record TV shows and receive Internet-based videos from Brightcove. The alliance works for both firms. TiVo is able to offer more products to its customers, and Brightcove has the opportunity to deliver its videos directly to viewers' TV sets.[9]

REVERSE CHANNELS

While the traditional concept of marketing channels involves the movement of goods and services from producer to consumer or business user, marketers should not ignore **reverse channels**—channels designed to return goods to their producers. Reverse channels have gained increased importance with rising prices for raw materials, increasing availability of recycling facilities, and passage of additional antipollution and conservation laws. Purchase a new set of tires, and you'll find a recycling charge for disposing of the old tires. The intent is to halt the growing litter problem of illegal tire dumps. Automotive batteries contain potentially toxic materials, including 21 pounds of lead and a gallon of sulfuric acid. Despite this, every element in a spent battery can be reclaimed, recycled, and reused in new batteries. Thirty-six states have now passed laws requiring consumers to turn in their old batteries at the time they purchase new ones. To help in this effort, the American Automobile Association (AAA) holds an annual AAA Great Battery Roundup in the United States and Canada, during which consumers can drop off their dead batteries.[10]

Some reverse channels move through the facilities of traditional marketing intermediaries. In states that require bottle deposits, retailers and local bottlers perform these functions in the soft-drink industry. For other products, manufacturers establish redemption centers, develop systems for rechanneling products for recycling, and create specialized organizations to handle disposal and recycling. Staples collects empty printer cartridges at its stores, and some Nike retail outlets collect worn-out sneakers for recycling. Other reverse channel participants include community groups that organize cleanup days and develop recycling and waste disposal systems. Timberland actually gives its employees paid time off to participate in programs that involve cleaning up parks, schools, and other public places.

Reverse channels also handle product recalls and repairs. An appliance manufacturer might send recall notices to the buyers of a washing machine. An auto manufacturer might send notices to car owners advising them of a potential problem and offering to repair it at no cost through local dealerships.

 assessment check

1. Distinguish between a marketing channel and logistics.
2. What are the different types of marketing channels?
3. What four functions do marketing channels perform?

2 Outline the major channel strategy decisions.

CHANNEL STRATEGY DECISIONS

Marketers face several strategic decisions in choosing channels and marketing intermediaries for their products. Selecting a specific channel is the most basic of these decisions. Marketers must also resolve questions about the level of distribution intensity, assess the desirability of vertical marketing systems, and evaluate the performance of current intermediaries.

SELECTION OF A MARKETING CHANNEL

Consider the following questions: What characteristics of a franchised dealer network make it the best channel option for a company? Why do operating supplies often go through both agents and merchant wholesalers before reaching their actual users? Why would a firm market a single product through multiple channels? Marketers must answer many such questions in choosing marketing channels.

A variety of factors affect the selection of a marketing channel. Some channel decisions are dictated by the marketplace in which the company operates. In other cases, the product itself may be a key variable in picking a marketing channel. Finally, the marketing organization may base its selection of channels on its size and competitive factors. Individual firms in a single industry may choose different channels as part of their overall strategy to gain a competitive edge. Book publishers, for instance, may sell through bookstores, directly to consumers on their own Web sites, or through nontraditional outlets including specialty retailers such as craft stores or home improvement stores.[11]

Market Factors

Channel structure reflects a product's intended markets, for either consumers or business users. Business purchasers usually prefer to deal directly with manufacturers (except for routine supplies or small accessory items), but most consumers make their purchases from retailers. Marketers often sell products that serve both business users and consumers through more than one channel.

Other market factors also affect channel choice, including the market's needs, its geographic location, and its average order size. To serve a concentrated market with a small number of buyers, a direct channel offers a feasible alternative. But in serving a geographically dispersed potential trade area in which customers purchase small amounts in individual transactions—the conditions that characterize the consumer-goods market—distribution through marketing intermediaries makes sense.

Product Factors

Product characteristics also guide the choice of an optimal marketing channel strategy. Perishable goods, such as fresh fruit and vegetables, milk, and fruit juice, move through short channels. Trendy or seasonal fashions, such as swimsuits and ski wear, are also examples.

Vending machines represent another short channel. Typically, you can buy a bag of M&Ms, Lay's potato chips, or a Coke from a vending machine. But how about boxers or a beer? If you're a guest at Tokyo's Shibuya Excel Hotel, you can do just that. In addition, you can get a serving of dried squid or a package of batteries. The vending machine, manufactured by Sanyo Electric, is so large that it is really an automated convenience store. "This is four vending machines in one,"

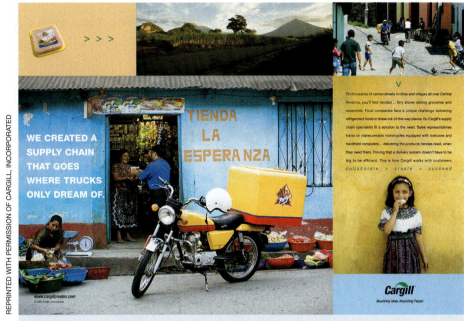

boasts Misao Awane of Sanyo. "It holds 200 different products, at three different temperatures."[12]

Complex products such as custom-made installations and computer equipment are often sold directly to ultimate buyers. In general, relatively standardized items that are also nonperishable pass through comparatively long channels. Products with low unit costs, such as cans of dog food, bars of soap, and packages of gum, typically travel through long channels. Perishable items such as fresh flowers, meat, and produce require much shorter channels.

Organizational and Competitive Factors

Companies with strong financial, management, and marketing resources feel less need for help from intermediaries. A large, financially strong manufacturer can hire its own sales force, warehouse its own goods, and extend credit to retailers or consumers. But a small firm with fewer resources may do better with the aid of intermediaries. Entrepreneur Cheryl Tallman knew she had a unique product—a kit for freezing fresh baby food—but her talent lay in selling, not manufacturing and distribution. So she created partnerships with a manufacturer and a distributor while she concentrated on marketing her Fresh Baby kits to baby boutiques and other retailers. "If we'd tried to develop competencies in all this other stuff, we'd be distracting our attention from what we're really good at," explains Tallman.[13]

A firm with a broad product line can usually market its products directly to retailers or business users because its own sales force can offer a variety of products. High sales volume spreads selling costs over a large number of items, generating adequate returns from direct sales. Single-product firms often view direct selling as unaffordable.

The manufacturer's desire for control over marketing its products also influences channel selection. Some manufacturers sell their products only at their own stores. Manufacturers of specialty or luxury goods such as scarves from Hermès and watches from Rolex limit the number of retailers that can carry their products.

Businesses that explore new marketing channels must be careful to avoid upsetting their channel intermediaries. In the past decade, conflicts frequently arose as companies began to establish an Internet presence in addition to traditional outlets. Today, firms look for new ways to handle both without damaging relationships. Still, some firms feel compelled to develop new marketing channels to remedy inadequate promotion of their products by independent marketing intermediaries. In recent years, insurance giant Allstate has been moving away from its reliance on proprietary agents to sell its products and toward direct retail channels such as the Internet. Allstate has made this move in

table 13.1   Factors Influencing Marketing Channel Strategies

	CHARACTERISTICS OF SHORT CHANNELS	CHARACTERISTICS OF LONG CHANNELS
Market factors	Business users	Consumers
	Geographically concentrated	Geographically dispersed
	Extensive technical knowledge and regular servicing required	Little technical knowledge and regular servicing not required
	Large orders	Small orders
Product factors	Perishable	Durable
	Complex	Standardized
	Expensive	Inexpensive
Organizational factors	Manufacturer has adequate resources to perform channel functions	Manufacturer lacks adequate resources to perform channel functions
	Broad product line	Limited product line
	Channel control important	Channel control not important
Competitive factors	Manufacturer feels satisfied with marketing intermediaries' performance in promoting products	Manufacturer feels dissatisfied with marketing intermediaries' performance in promoting products

order to compete more effectively with lower-cost providers such as Geico.[14] Movie studios have begun to release films to DVD or to on-demand TV service either more quickly or simultaneously with their movie releases, as described in the "Marketing Success" feature.

Table 13.1 summarizes the factors that affect the selection of a marketing channel. The table also examines the effect of each factor on the channel's overall length.

DETERMINING DISTRIBUTION INTENSITY

Another key channel strategy decision is the intensity of distribution. *Distribution intensity* refers to the number of intermediaries through which a manufacturer distributes its goods in a particular market. Optimal distribution intensity should ensure adequate market coverage for a product. Adequate market coverage varies depending on the goals of the individual firm, the type of product, and the consumer segments in its target market. In general, however, distribution intensity varies along a continuum with three general categories: intensive distribution, selective distribution, and exclusive distribution.

 marketing success   Skipping the Box Office Rush

Background. Movie buffs used to have to wait many months after seeing their favorite film on the big screen before being able to view it at home. But in recent years, movie marketers have recognized that the lag time between a theater release and a release of DVD or on-demand service may represent a lost opportunity.

The Challenge. With the popularity of home theaters, on-demand service, and constant entertainment innovations, the movie industry has struggled to find ways to keep its audience interested—at a profit. If studios

released movies simultaneously to theaters and DVD or on-demand channels, would they lose money?

The Strategy. Studios have already begun to shrink the time between a theater debut and the DVD release. Now some companies are pushing the strategy further. "So much great film has fallen by the wayside," explains Jonathan Sehring, president of IFC Entertainment, which has a film production and distribution unit. "The studios are collapsing the window between the theatrical release and the DVD. We're taking that one step further." IFC

Intensive Distribution

An **intensive distribution** strategy seeks to distribute a product through all available channels in a trade area. Because Campbell Soup practices intensive distribution for many of its products, you can pick up a can from its microwavable line just about anywhere—the supermarket, the drugstore, and even Staples. Usually, an intensive distribution strategy suits items with wide appeal across broad groups of consumers.

Selective Distribution

In another market coverage strategy, **selective distribution,** a firm chooses only a limited number of retailers in a market area to handle its line. Italian design firm Versace sells its merchandise only through a limited number of select boutiques worldwide. By limiting the number of retailers, marketers can reduce total marketing costs while establishing strong working relationships within the channel. Moreover, selected retailers often agree to comply with the company's strict rules for advertising, pricing, and displaying its products. *Cooperative advertising,* in which the manufacturer pays a percentage of the retailer's advertising expenditures and the retailer prominently displays the firm's products, can be used for mutual benefit, and marginal retailers can be avoided. Where service is important, the manufacturer usually provides training and assistance to the dealers it chooses.

Exclusive Distribution

When a producer grants exclusive rights to a wholesaler or retailer to sell its products in a specific geographic region, it practices **exclusive distribution.** The automobile industry provides a good example of exclusive distribution. A city with a population of 40,000 may have a single Ford dealer. Exclusive distribution agreements also govern marketing for some major appliance and apparel brands.

Marketers may sacrifice some market coverage by implementing a policy of exclusive distribution. However,

COURTESY OF GEORG JENSEN

Danish luxury jewelry design firm Georg Jensen uses selective distribution for its high-end jewelry pieces.

intensive distribution Distribution of a product through all available channels.

selective distribution Distribution of a product through a limited number of channels.

exclusive distribution Distribution of a product through a single wholesaler or retailer in a specific geographic region.

announced plans to launch six films intended for simultaneous release to independent theaters and on-demand service provided by cable companies.

The Outcome. Committed to this modified way of distributing new movies, IFC has said that it would make more and more movies available this way, including some films from other distributors. Some industry experts are skeptical that the big studios may be slower to react. But producer Steve Tisch disagrees. "I think the industry will resist and resist some more, and then slowly embrace it."

Sources: Jennifer Whitehead, "Winterbottom Film to Get Simultaneous Cinema, DVD, and Online Release," *Digital Bulletin,* February 13, 2006, **http://www.brandrepublic.com**; Sharon Waxman, "Missed It in the Theater Today? See It on DVD Tonight," *New York Times,* January 23, 2006, **http://www.nytimes.com**; Xeni Jardin, "Thinking outside the Box Office," *Wired,* December 2005, **http://www.wired.com**.

Solving an Ethical Controversy

The Funeral Business: Who Should Control the Sale of Caskets?

Death, like taxes or a change in the weather, is inevitable. Death also supports the funeral business, an industry that itself will never die. Like most industries, the funeral business has faced controversy at one time or another, but unlike other industries, consumers have no desire to purchase its goods or services. "We have a product no one wants to buy," says Kenneth Camp, chief executive of Batesville Casket Company.

The most current debate surrounds how much control a company such as Batesville should have over the channels through which it sells its products. Batesville collects about $650 million a year in sales of its caskets through about 16,000 funeral homes across the United States, clearly dominating the market in which its nearest competitor posts only about one-third the amount of its sales.

Does one firm have too much control over the channels for burial caskets?

PRO

1. A consumer group recently filed an antitrust suit against Batesville in California, alleging that the firm artificially inflated casket prices, resulting in overcharges of "hundreds of millions, if not billions, for caskets." Other lawsuits with similar charges are also pending. Batesville denies the allegations.
2. Batesville maintains an extraordinarily close relationship with its customers—funeral homes. The firm hosts executive retreats and provides free casket showroom renovations to some of its best customers. Many funeral directors use Batesville as their exclusive supplier, and in nearly all cases, it is their top seller.

CON

1. Batesville does a superior job of serving its customers—funeral homes—which is why it is the top provider of caskets in the nation. "We try to pamper them, take care of their needs," says CEO Kenneth Camp. Ultimately, the funeral homes themselves decide which caskets to offer consumers.
2. More than 20 years ago, the U.S. government deregulated the casket industry in order to stimulate competition. Consumers no longer have to purchase caskets through funeral homes; they can opt for direct sellers, whose prices are often lower. As a result, consumers do have choices.

Summary

Consumers don't like to think about shopping for caskets, which is why most still purchase these products through a funeral home. They may be in an emotional crisis and not want to dwell on the purchase. This makes consumers somewhat vulnerable to the business practices of firms in the funeral industry. Many of these practices are now being examined by government officials, as well as the industry itself. "The more I looked into it, the more I uncovered the less tasteful aspects of the funeral industry," says Philip Wartel, former owner of a casket store in Massachusetts. After filing a suit against Batesville and a large chain of funeral homes called Service Corp. International, Wartel shut down his shop.

Sources: Batesville Web site, **http://www.batesville.com,** accessed May 19, 2006; Seth Lubove, "Six Feet Under," *Forbes,* October 31, 2005, pp. 136–138; "Batesville Casket Enhances Service through Efficiency," IBM Case Study, June 9, 2005, **http://www-306.ibm.com.**

they often develop and maintain an image of quality and prestige for the product. If it's harder to find a Free People silk dress, the item seems more valuable. In addition, exclusive distribution limits marketing costs because the firm deals with a smaller number of accounts. In exclusive distribution, producers and retailers cooperate closely in decisions concerning advertising and promotion, inventory carried by the retailers, and prices.

Legal Problems of Exclusive Distribution

Exclusive distribution presents potential legal problems in three main areas: exclusive dealing agreements, closed sales territories, and tying agreements. Although none of these practices is illegal per se, all may break the law if they reduce competition or tend to create monopolies, as described in the "Solving an Ethical Controversy" feature.

As part of an exclusive distribution strategy, marketers may try to enforce an **exclusive dealing agreement,** which prohibits a marketing intermediary (a wholesaler or, more typically, a retailer) from handling competing products. Producers of high-priced shopping goods, specialty goods, and accessory equipment often require such agreements to ensure total concentration on their own product lines. Such contracts violate the Clayton Act only if the producer's or dealer's sales volumes represent a substantial percentage of total sales in the market area. While exclusive distribution is legal for companies first entering a market, such agreements violate the Clayton Act if used by firms with a sizable market share seeking to bar competitors from the market. In New York, a court fined two major retailers, Lenox and Waterford Wedgwood, roughly $3 million for an exclusive dealing agreement the firms had made with each other.[15]

Producers may also try to set up **closed sales territories** to restrict their distributors to certain geographic regions, reasoning that the distributors gain protection from rival dealers in their exclusive territories. St. Louis–based ProSource Wholesale Floorcoverings recently announced plans to expand its business through a limited number of closed franchise territories. ProSource, which sells only to professionals in the industry—not directly to consumers—is one of the largest such firms in the nation. "We are the trade professional's showroom serving a unique and growing niche, which makes our concept in extremely high demand," explains David Kraeling, president of the company.[16] But the downside of this practice is that the distributors sacrifice any opportunities in opening new facilities or marketing the manufacturers' products outside their assigned territories. The legality of a system of closed sales territories depends on whether the restriction decreases competition. If so, it violates the Federal Trade Commission Act and provisions of the Sherman and Clayton Acts.

The legality of closed sales territories also depends on whether the system imposes horizontal or vertical restrictions. Horizontal territorial restrictions result from agreements between retailers or wholesalers to avoid competition among sellers of products from the same producer. Such agreements consistently have been declared illegal. However, the U.S. Supreme Court has ruled that vertical territorial restrictions—those between producers and wholesalers or retailers—may meet legal criteria. The ruling gives no clear-cut answer, but such agreements likely satisfy the law in cases in which manufacturers occupy relatively small parts of their markets. In such instances, the restrictions may actually increase competition among competing brands; the wholesaler or retailer faces no competition from other dealers carrying the manufacturer's brand, so it can concentrate on effectively competing with other brands.

The third legal question of exclusive distribution involves **tying agreements,** which allow channel members to become exclusive dealers only if they also carry products other than those that they want to sell. In the apparel industry, for example, an agreement might require a dealer to carry a comparatively unpopular line of clothing to get desirable, fast-moving items. Tying agreements violate the Sherman Act and the Clayton Act when they reduce competition or create monopolies that keep competitors out of major markets. Recently The Coca-Cola Company entered into an agreement with the European Union—which is governed by the European Commission—to refrain from making tying agreements between its most popular brands—such as Coke, Diet Coke, and Sprite—and its lesser-known products.[17]

WHO SHOULD PERFORM CHANNEL FUNCTIONS?

A fundamental marketing principle governs channel decisions. A member of the channel must perform certain central marketing functions. Responsibilities of the different members may vary, however. Although independent wholesalers perform many functions for manufacturers, retailers, and other wholesaler clients, other channel members could fulfill these roles instead. A manufacturer might bypass its wholesalers by establishing regional warehouses, maintaining field sales forces, serving as sources of information for retail customers, or arranging details of financing. For years, auto manufacturers have operated credit units that offer new-car financing; some have even established their own banks.

An independent intermediary earns a profit in exchange for providing services to manufacturers and retailers. This profit margin is low, however, ranging from 1 percent for food wholesalers to 5

Briefly
Speaking

"You can do away with middlemen, but you can't do away with the functions they perform."

—American business saying

percent for durable-goods wholesalers. Manufacturers and retailers could retain these costs, or they could market directly and reduce retail prices—but only if they could perform the channel functions, and match the efficiency of the independent intermediaries.

To grow profitably in a competitive environment, an intermediary must provide better service at lower costs than manufacturers or retailers can provide for themselves. In this case, consolidation of channel functions can represent a strategic opportunity for a company.

3 Describe the concepts of channel management, conflict, and cooperation.

CHANNEL MANAGEMENT AND LEADERSHIP

Distribution strategy does not end with the choice of a channel. Manufacturers must also focus on channel management by developing and maintaining relationships with the intermediaries in their marketing channels. Positive channel relationships encourage channel members to remember their partners' goods and market them. Manufacturers also must carefully manage the incentives offered to induce channel members to promote their products. This effort includes weighing decisions about pricing, promotion, and other support efforts that the manufacturer performs.

Increasingly, marketers are managing channels in partnership with other channel members. Effective cooperation allows all channel members to achieve goals that they could not achieve on their own. Keys to successful management of channel relationships include the development of high levels of coordination, commitment, and trust between channel members.

channel captain Dominant and controlling member of a marketing channel.

Not all channel members wield equal power in the distribution chain, however. The dominant member of a marketing channel is called the **channel captain.** This firm's power to control a channel may result from its control over some type of reward or punishment to other channel members, such as granting an exclusive sales territory or taking away a dealership. Power might also result from contractual arrangements, specialized expert knowledge, or agreement among channel members about their mutual best interests.

In the grocery industry, food producers once were considered channel captains. Today, however, the power has shifted to the retail giants. Kroger, Supervalu, and Safeway operate 6,500 supermarkets nationwide. These three chains also own smaller stores, food warehouse stores, department stores, and even jewelry stores. Manufacturers who want to get their products on the shelves and properly marketed have to pay slotting fees, described in Chapter 11, to do so. Partnering among retailers—including grocery chains—is a growing trend, as firms are recognizing that they can compete more effectively as channel captains if they join forces. Several grocery retailers might form a so-called *value network* to achieve dominance.[18]

Another strategy is the building of supercenters like Wal-Mart's. With the opening of its supercenters, Wal-Mart's grocery sales have reached about $80 billion, making it the largest seller of supermarket goods in the United States.[19]

Cincinnati-based Kroger is one of the largest retail food companies in the United States, so it can be considered a channel captain in the grocery industry.

© ASSOCIATED PRESS, AP

CHANNEL CONFLICT

Marketing channels work smoothly only when members cooperate in well-organized efforts to achieve maximum operating efficiencies. Yet channel members often perform as separate, independent, and even competing forces. Two types of conflict—horizontal and vertical—may hinder the normal functioning of a marketing channel.

Horizontal Conflict

Horizontal conflict sometimes results from disagreements among channel members at the same level, such as two or more wholesalers or two or more retailers, or among marketing intermediaries of the same type, such as two competing discount stores or several retail florists. More often, horizontal conflict causes problems between different types of marketing intermediaries that handle similar products. Google and CBS have announced a partnership in which they will offer current hit TV programs online—the first such agreement between a major broadcast network and an Internet service provider. This agreement further blurs the line between the television set and the computer, a trend that most experts believe will continue. It means that marketers for both types of media—along with advertisers—will have to shift the way they think about delivering entertainment to audiences.[20]

Vertical Conflict

Vertical relationships may result in frequent and severe conflict. Channel members at different levels find many reasons for disputes, as when retailers develop private brands to compete with producers' brands or when producers establish their own retail stores or create mail-order operations that compete with retailers. Producers may annoy wholesalers and retailers when they attempt to bypass these intermediaries and sell directly to consumers. A few years ago, Tupperware—traditionally sold only by independent consultants at in-home parties—tried selling its products through Target stores. The move led to a precipitous drop in party bookings and sales. Tupperware suspended its deal with Target, but by then three-quarters of the sales force had dropped out. Tupperware has since created new incentive programs to try to recruit new and former consultants.[21]

Recently, the European Union imposed a tax of nearly 45 percent on imports of Chinese-made color televisions in an effort to stop Chinese manufacturers from "dumping" thousands of televisions on the market at below-market prices. The practice caused conflict between European retailers, who could sell many of the televisions, and manufacturers, whose prices could not compete. The EU has also investigated Chinese and Vietnamese dumping of leather shoes.[22]

The Gray Market

Another type of channel conflict results from activities in the so-called *gray market*. As U.S. manufacturers license their technology and brands abroad, they sometimes find themselves in competition in the U.S. market against versions of their own brands produced by overseas affiliates. These **gray goods,** goods produced for overseas markets often at reduced prices, enter U.S. channels through the actions of unauthorized foreign distributors. While licensing agreements usually prohibit foreign licensees from selling in the United States, no such rules inhibit their distributors.

When farm equipment manufacturer John Deere discovered that some U.S. importers and exporters were attempting to market its European-made harvesters in the United States, the firm tried to stop the group from doing so, arguing that the harvesters were gray-market goods. After one ruling in Deere's favor, a second ruling directed the U.S. International Trade Commission to re-examine whether the harvesters were actually manufactured differently, and whether this affected sales.[23]

ACHIEVING CHANNEL COOPERATION

The basic antidote to channel conflict is effective cooperation among channel members. Cooperation is best achieved when all channel members regard themselves as equal components of the same organization. The channel captain is primarily responsible for providing the leadership necessary to achieve this kind of cooperation.

Samsung Electronics is committed to achieving channel cooperation to have its products reach as many homes and offices worldwide as possible. The firm believes that one way to achieve this

Briefly
Speaking

"All things being equal, people will do business with a friend. All things being unequal, people will still do business with a friend."

—Mark McCormack
(1930–2003)
American sports agent and founder, IMG Sports Management

coordination is to train its partners thoroughly in marketing its products. One training session focused on the launch of health-conscious air-conditioning products and gathered together partners from the United Arab Emirates, Qatar, Bahrain, Oman, Yemen, and Kuwait. "Samsung always believed in providing world-class training to its partner community, as they are the key interface between the company and its customers, and play a vital role in helping customers make the right decisions," said S. Y. Kim, general manager of the home appliances division at Samsung.[24]

✓ assessment check

1. What is a channel captain? What is its role in channel cooperation?

2. Identify and describe the three types of channel conflict.

 4 Identify and describe the different vertical marketing systems.

vertical marketing system (VMS) Planned channel system designed to improve distribution efficiency and cost-effectiveness by integrating various functions throughout the distribution chain.

VERTICAL MARKETING SYSTEMS

Efforts to reduce channel conflict and improve the effectiveness of distribution have led to the development of vertical marketing systems. A **vertical marketing system (VMS)** is a planned channel system designed to improve distribution efficiency and cost-effectiveness by integrating various functions throughout the distribution chain.

A vertical marketing system can achieve this goal through either forward or backward integration. In **forward integration,** a firm attempts to control downstream distribution. For example, a manufacturer might set up a retail chain to sell its products. **Backward integration** occurs when a manufacturer attempts to gain greater control over inputs in its production process. A manufacturer might acquire the supplier of a raw material the manufacturer uses in the production of its products. Backward integration can also extend the control of retailers and wholesalers over producers that supply them.

A VMS offers several benefits. First, it improves chances for controlling and coordinating the steps in the distribution or production process. It may lead to the development of economies of scale that ultimately saves money. A VMS may also let a manufacturer expand into profitable new businesses. However, a VMS also involves some costs. A manufacturer assumes increased risk when it takes control of an entire distribution chain. Manufacturers may also discover that they lose some flexibility in responding to market changes.

Marketers have developed three categories of VMSs: corporate systems, administered systems, and contractual systems. These categories are outlined in the sections that follow.

CORPORATE AND ADMINISTERED SYSTEMS

When a single owner runs organizations at each stage of the marketing channel, it operates a **corporate marketing system.** Phillips auctioneers runs a corporate marketing system. An **administered marketing system** achieves channel coordination when a dominant channel member exercises its power. Even though Goodyear sells its tires through independently owned and operated dealerships, it controls the stock that these dealerships carry. Other examples of channel captains leading administered channels include McKesson and Costco.

CONTRACTUAL SYSTEMS

Instead of common ownership of intermediaries within a corporate VMS or the exercising of power within an administered system, a **contractual marketing system** coordinates distribution through formal agreements among channel members. In practice, three types of agreements set up these systems: wholesaler-sponsored voluntary chains, retail cooperatives, and franchises.

Wholesaler-Sponsored Voluntary Chain

Sometimes an independent wholesaler tries to preserve a market by strengthening its retail customers through a wholesaler-sponsored voluntary chain. The wholesaler adopts a formal agreement with its retailers to use a common name and standardized facilities and to purchase the wholesaler's goods. The wholesaler may even develop a line of private brands to be stocked by the retailers. This practice often helps smaller retailers compete with rival chains—and strengthens the wholesaler's position as well.

IGA (Independent Grocers Alliance) Food Stores is a good example of a voluntary chain. Other wholesaler-sponsored chains include Associated Druggists, Sentry Hardware, and Western Auto. Because a single advertisement promotes all the retailers in the trading area, a common store name and similar inventories allow the retailers to save on advertising costs.

Retail Cooperative

In a second type of contractual VMS, a group of retailers establishes a shared wholesaling operation to help them compete with chains. This is known as **retail cooperative.** The retailers purchase ownership shares in the wholesaling operation and agree to buy a minimum percentage of their inventories from this operation. The members typically adopt a common store name and develop common private brands. Ace Hardware is an example of a retail cooperative.

Franchise

A third type of contractual vertical marketing system is the **franchise,** in which a wholesaler or dealer (the franchisee) agrees to meet the operating requirements of a manufacturer or other franchiser. Franchising is a huge and growing industry. More than 4,500 U.S. companies distribute goods and services through systems of franchised dealers, and numerous firms also offer franchises in international markets. Nationwide, about 600,000 retail outlets represent franchises.[25] Table 13.2 shows the 20 fastest-growing franchises in the United States, with Subway, Pizza Hut, and Quiznos Subs topping the list.

table 13.2   The Top 20 Fastest-Growing Franchises

RANK	COMPANY AND PRODUCT
1	Subway: sandwiches and salads
2	Pizza Hut: pizza
3	Quiznos Sub: sandwiches and salads
4	Jan-Pro Franchising International: commercial cleaning
5	Curves: women's fitness centers
6	Jani-King: commercial cleaning
7	Jackson Hewitt Tax Service: tax preparation service
8	The UPS Store: postal, business, and communication services
9	Coverall Cleaning Concepts: commercial cleaning
10	CleanNet USA: commercial office cleaning
11	Cold Stone Creamery: ice cream, frozen yogurt
12	RE/MAX International: real estate agents
13	Liberty Tax Service: income tax preparation
14	Bonus Building Care: commercial cleaning
15	Century 21 Real Estate: real estate agents
16	Dunkin' Donuts: donuts and coffee
17	Anago Franchising: commercial cleaning
18	Sylvan Learning Centers: tutoring services
19	Coldwell Banker Real Estate: real estate agents
20	Great Clips: family hair salons

Source: "Fastest-Growing Franchises 2006 Rankings," *Entrepreneur,* http://www.entrepreneur.com, accessed February 24, 2006.

Quiznos is one of the fastest growing franchises in the United States.

© ASSOCIATED PRESS, AP

Franchise owners pay anywhere from several thousand to more than a million dollars to purchase and set up a franchise. Typically, they also pay a royalty on sales to the franchising company. In exchange for these initial and ongoing fees, the franchise owner receives the right to use the company's brand name, as well as services such as training, marketing, advertising, and volume discounts. Major franchise chains justify the steep price of entry because it allows new businesses to sell winning brands. But if the brand enters a slump or the corporation behind the franchise makes poor strategic decisions, franchisees are often hurt.

LOGISTICS AND SUPPLY CHAIN MANAGEMENT

Pier 1 imports its eclectic mix of items from 600 vendors in 55 countries, and more than 80 percent come from small companies. If high-demand items or seasonal products are late into its warehouses or are shipped in insufficient quantities, the company may miss opportunities to deliver popular shopping choices to its 1,200 retail stores and could lose ground to competitors such as Pottery Barn and Crate & Barrel. The situation facing Pier 1 Imports illustrates the importance of logistics. Careful coordination of Pier 1's supplier network, shipping processes, and inventory control is the key to its continuing success. In addition, the store's buyers develop relationships with suppliers in all 55 countries, including Mexico and China.[26]

> ### ✓ assessment check
>
> 1. What are vertical marketing systems (VMSs)? Identify the major types.
> 2. Identify the three types of contractual marketing systems.

Effective logistics requires proper supply-chain management, the control of activities of purchasing, processing, and delivery through which raw materials are transformed into products and made available to final consumers. The **supply chain,** also known as the *value chain,* is the complete sequence of suppliers and activities that contribute to the creation and delivery of goods and services. The supply chain begins with the raw-material inputs for the manufacturing process of a product and then proceeds to the actual production activities. The final link in the supply chain is the movement of finished products through the marketing channel to customers. Each link of the chain benefits the consumers as raw materials move through manufacturing to distribution. The chain encompasses all activities that enhance the value of the finished goods, including design, quality manufacturing, customer service, and delivery. Customer satisfaction results directly from the perceived value of a purchase to its buyer.

5 Explain the roles of logistics and supply-chain management in an overall distribution strategy.

To manage the supply chain, businesses must look for ways to maximize customer value in each activity they perform. Supply-chain management takes place in two directions: upstream and downstream, as illustrated in Figure 13.2. **Upstream management** involves managing raw materials, inbound logistics, and warehouse and storage facilities. **Downstream management** involves managing finished product storage, outbound logistics, marketing and sales, and customer service.

supply chain Complete sequence of suppliers and activities that contribute to the creation and delivery of merchandise.

Companies choose a variety of methods for managing the supply chain. They can include high-tech systems such as radio frequency identification, discussed in the next section, and regular person-to-person meetings. Tyson Foods maintains a close relationship with Fastenal and other suppliers with both of these methods. Tyson also evaluates how quickly suppliers deliver their goods and how long those goods last in relation to their price—in other words, how much the goods cost Tyson.[27]

Logistics plays a major role in giving customers what they need when they need it and thus is central in the supply chain. Another important component of this chain, *value-added service,* adds some improved or supplemental service that customers do not normally receive or expect. The following sections examine methods for streamlining and managing logistics and the supply chain as part of an overall distribution strategy.

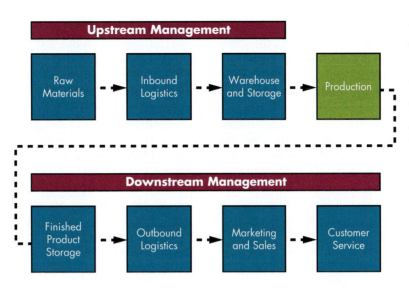

figure 13.2

The Supply Chain of a Manufacturing Company

Source: Adapted from Figure 2.2, Ralph M. Stair and George W. Reynolds, *Principles of Information Systems,* 7th edition. Boston: Course Technology, © 2006.

RADIO FREQUENCY IDENTIFICATION (RFID)

One tool that marketers are using to help manage logistics is **radio frequency identification (RFID)** technology. With RFID, a tiny chip with identification information that can be read by a radio frequency scanner from a distance is placed on an item. These chips are already widely used in tollway pass transmitters, allowing drivers to zip through toll booths without stopping or rolling down their windows to toss change into baskets. They are also embedded in employee ID cards that workers use to open office doors without keys. But businesses such as retail giant Wal-Mart, manufacturer Procter & Gamble, credit card firms MasterCard and American Express, and German retailer Metro AG are eagerly putting the technology to wider use; they say it will speed deliveries, make consumer bar codes obsolete, and provide marketers with valuable information about consumer preferences. Wal-Mart is pushing its biggest suppliers to attach RFID tags to pallets and cases of products such as Coca-Cola and Dove soap, saying that the technology will vastly improve its ability to track inventory and keep the right amount of products in stock.

As mentioned previously, Tyson Foods relies on RFID as well. The firm ships about 500 million cases of food products to retailers each year, so finding the quickest, most accurate method of tracking those products—and the supplies that go into their manufacture—is vital to Tyson's business. Knowing where a case of Tyson chicken tenders is—in the warehouse, on the truck, or in the store—makes a difference, as does knowing when a supermarket is out of stock of those tenders. "RFID is more than a technology," explains Paul Lothian, Tyson's director of information systems

radio frequency identification (RFID) Technology that uses a tiny chip with identification information that can be read by a scanner using radio waves from a distance.

RFID technology helps firms manage logistics.

and manufacturing integration. "It's a tool." Lothian emphasizes the importance of the whole company—and if possible, the whole supply chain—being on board with RFID.[28]

Kimberly-Clark, maker of such household staples as Kleenex and Huggies, is another large firm that has embraced RFID technology for supply-chain management, tagging more than 144 of the products in its current line. In addition, the company has built a 5,000-square-foot warehouse for the purpose of experimenting with and testing uses for RFID. "RFID should give us visibility into our whole supply chain," muses CEO Terry Assink. "From our supplier's supplier all the way to the shelf—not the pantry, mind you, but the store shelf. Think about that."[29]

Some privacy groups have expressed concern about the data obtained from RFID tags, but one survey revealed that 58 percent of respondents would not mind the technology if they were assured that it would be disabled before they left the store with a purchased product. That's not much different from a clerk mechanically removing the big plastic tag from an item of clothing. But analysts encourage businesses to adopt specific codes of conduct surrounding the use of RFID technology—for their own good as well as for the protection of consumers. "Without clarification about how RFID works," warns Forrester Research staffer Christine Overby, "consumers will base their opinion on the Big Brother stories currently making the headlines."[30]

ENTERPRISE RESOURCE PLANNING

Software is an important aspect of logistics management and the supply chain. An **enterprise resource planning (ERP) system** is an integrated software system that consolidates data from among the firm's units. Roughly two-thirds of ERP system users are manufacturers concerned with production issues such as sequencing and scheduling. Dow Corning is one such firm. The company adopted several programs from German software giant SAP AG to help it streamline processes and reduce costs globally. In addition, Dow uses SAP's software in its human resources department—also on a global basis.[31]

As valuable as it is, ERP and its related software aren't always perfect. For example, ERP failures were blamed for Hershey's inability to fulfill all of its candy orders during one Halloween period, when a fall-off in sales was blamed on a combination of shipping delays, inability to fill orders, and partial shipments while candy stockpiled in warehouses. The nation's major retailers were forced to shift their purchases to other candy vendors.

LOGISTICAL COST CONTROL

In addition to enhancing their products by providing value-added services to customers, many firms are focusing on logistics for another important reason: to cut costs. Distribution functions currently represent almost half of a typical firm's total marketing costs. To reduce logistical costs, businesses are re-examining each link of their supply chains to identify activities that do not add value for customers. By eliminating, reducing, or redesigning these activities, they can often cut costs and boost efficiency. As just described, new technologies such as RFID can save businesses millions—or even billions—of dollars.

Because of increased security requirements in recent years, businesses involved in importing and exporting have faced a major rise in logistical costs. Despite heated debates in the U.S. Congress over how much cargo should be inspected, and at what cost, everyone agrees on the need for enhanced security. The most recent bill to be approved by Congress involves screening 98 percent of all cargo for radiological materials at seaports.[32]

Third-Party Logistics

Some companies try to cut costs and offer value-added services by outsourcing some or all of their logistics functions to specialist firms. **Third-party (contract) logistics firms** (3PL firms) specialize in handling logistical activities for their clients. Third-party logistics is a huge industry, estimated at $333 billion worldwide, $115 billion of which takes place in North America alone. Penske Logistics, UPS, and European-based Schenker are three of the largest 3PL firms worldwide, with major operations in China and Russia. Such companies are also gaining strong footholds in other Asian countries, India, Europe, and Latin America.[33]

Through such outsourcing alliances, producers and logistical service suppliers cooperate in developing innovative, customized systems that speed goods through carefully constructed manufacturing and distribution pipelines. Although many companies have long outsourced transportation and warehousing functions, today's alliance partners use similar methods to combine their operations.

 assessment check

1. What is upstream management? What is downstream management?

2. Identify three methods for managing logistics.

PHYSICAL DISTRIBUTION

6 Identify the major components of a physical distribution system.

A firm's physical distribution system is an organized group of components linked according to a plan for achieving specific distribution objectives. It contains the following elements:

1. *Customer service.* What level of customer service the distribution activities should support.

2. *Transportation.* How the firm should ship its products.

3. *Inventory control.* How much inventory the firm should maintain at each location.

4. *Protective packaging and materials handling.* How the firm can package and efficiently handle goods in the factory, warehouse, and transport terminals.

5. *Order processing.* How the firm should handle orders.

6. *Warehousing.* Where the distribution system will locate stocks of goods and the number of warehouses the firm should maintain.

All of these components function in interrelated ways. Decisions made in one area affect efficiency in others. The physical distribution manager must balance each component so that the system avoids stressing any single aspect to the detriment of overall functioning. A firm might decide to reduce transportation costs by shipping its products by less costly—but slow—water transportation. But slow deliveries would likely force the firm to maintain higher inventory levels, raising those costs. This mismatch between system elements often leads to increased production costs. So balancing the components is crucial.

The general shift from a manufacturing economy to a service economy in the United States has affected physical distribution in two key ways. First, customers require more flexible—yet reliable—transportation service. Second, the number of smaller shipments is growing much faster than the number of large shipments. Although traditional, high-volume shipments will continue to grow, they will represent a lower percentage of the transportation industry's revenues and volume.[34]

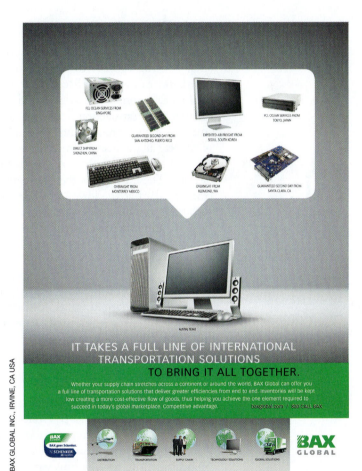

© BAX GLOBAL INC., IRVINE, CA USA

BAX Global offers a full range of services designed to help businesses manage distribution.

THE PROBLEM OF SUBOPTIMIZATION

Logistics managers seek to establish a specified level of customer service while minimizing the costs of physically moving and storing goods. Marketers must first decide on their priorities for customer service and then figure out how to fulfill those goals by moving goods at the least cost. Meshing together all the physical distribution elements is a huge challenge that firms don't always meet.

Suboptimization results when the managers of individual physical distribution functions attempt to minimize costs, but the impact of one task on the others leads to less than optimal results. Imagine a hockey team composed of record-holding players. Unfortunately, despite the individual talents of the players, the team fails to win a game. This is an example of suboptimization. The same thing can happen at a company when each logistics activity is judged by its own accomplishments instead of the way it contributes to the overall goals of the firm. Suboptimization often happens when a firm introduces a new product that may not fit easily into its current physical distribution system.

Effective management of the physical distribution function requires some cost trade-offs. By accepting relatively high costs in some functional areas to cut costs in others, managers can minimize their firm's total physical distribution costs. Of course, any reduction in logistical costs should support progress toward the goal of maintaining customer-service standards.

 assessment check

1. What are the six major elements of physical distribution?
2. What is suboptimization?

CUSTOMER-SERVICE STANDARDS

Customer-service standards state the goals and define acceptable performance for the quality of service that a firm expects to deliver to its customers. Internet retailers such as Zappos.com and Giftbaskets.com thrive because of their ability to ship within hours of receiving an order. 1-800-FLOWERS.com offers same-day delivery, every day of the week, nationwide, with a 100 percent guarantee of satisfaction.[35] A pizza parlor might set a standard to deliver customers' pizzas hot and fresh to their homes within 30 minutes of their order. An auto repair shop might set a standard to complete all oil changes in a half hour.

Designers of a physical distribution system begin by establishing acceptable levels of customer service. These designers then assemble physical distribution components in a way that will achieve this standard at the lowest possible total cost. This overall cost breaks down into five components: (1) transportation, (2) warehousing, (3) inventory control, (4) customer service/order processing, and (5) administrative costs.

TRANSPORTATION

The transportation industry was largely deregulated a number of years ago. Deregulation has been particularly important for motor carriers, railroads, and air carriers. Today, an estimated 2.6 million tractor-trailers transport goods nationwide; about 82 percent of U.S. communities rely entirely on trucking for the delivery of goods.[36] Railroads are enjoying a new boom—once hauling mostly commodities like corn and grain, they now transport cross-country the huge loads of goods that come into California ports from Asia.[37]

Typically adding about 10 percent to the cost of a product, transportation and delivery expenses represent the largest category of logistics-related costs for most firms. Also, for many items—particularly perishable ones such as fresh fish or produce—transportation makes a central contribution to satisfactory customer service.

Many logistics managers have found that the key to controlling their shipping costs is careful management of relationships with shipping firms. Freight carriers use two basic rates: class and commodity rates. A class rate is a standard rate for a specific commodity moving between any pair of destinations. A carrier may charge a lower commodity rate, sometimes called a *special rate,* to a favored shipper as a reward for either regular business or a large-quantity shipment. Railroads and inland water carriers frequently reward customers in this way.

In addition, the railroad and motor carrier industries sometimes supplement this rate structure with negotiated, or contract, rates. In other words, the two parties finalize terms of rates, services, and other variables in a contract.

Classes of Carriers

Freight carriers are classified as common, contract, and private carriers. **Common carriers,** often considered the backbone of the transportation industry, provide transportation services as for-hire carriers to the general public. The government still regulates their rates and services, and they cannot conduct their operations without permission from the appropriate regulatory authority. Common carriers move freight via all modes of transport. FedEx is a major common carrier serving businesses and consumers. One way the firm remains competitive is by developing new methods for enhancing customer service. Recently, FedEx introduced a service called Insight, which essentially reverses the package-tracking process—instead of following a package from shipment to delivery, customers can go online to find out what is going to be delivered to them that day. One FedEx customer that has benefited greatly from this new service is a firm that conducts bone-marrow-sample testing. Time is essential for the delivery of these samples. Now the firm can find out exactly how many completed test kits will be arriving in the lab each day.[38]

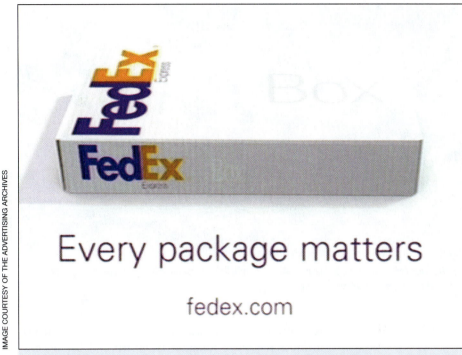

IMAGE COURTESY OF THE ADVERTISING ARCHIVES

Tennessee-based FedEx is a major common carrier serving businesses and consumers worldwide.

Contract carriers are for-hire transporters that do not offer their services to the general public. Instead, they establish contracts with individual customers and operate exclusively for particular industries, such as the motor freight industry. These carriers operate under much looser regulations than do common carriers.

Private carriers do not offer services for hire. These carriers provide transportation services solely for internally generated freight. As a result, they observe no rate or service regulations. The Interstate Commerce Commission (ICC), a federal regulatory agency, permits private carriers to operate as common or contract carriers as well. Many private carriers have taken advantage of this rule by operating their trucks fully loaded at all times.

Major Transportation Modes

Logistics managers choose among five major transportation alternatives: railroads, motor carriers, water carriers, pipelines, and air freight. Each mode has its own unique characteristics. Logistics managers select the best options for their situations by matching the situation features to their specific transportation needs.

7 Compare the major modes of transportation.

Railroads

Railroads continue to control the largest share of the freight business as measured by ton-miles. The term *ton-mile* indicates shipping activity required to move one ton of freight one mile. Rail shipments quickly rack up ton-miles because this mode provides the most efficient way for moving bulky commodities over long distances. Rail carriers generally transport huge quantities of coal, chemicals, grain, nonmetallic minerals, lumber and wood products, and automobiles. The railroads have improved their service standards through a number of innovative concepts, such as unit trains, run-through trains, **intermodal operations,** and double-stack container trains. Unit trains carry much of the coal, grain, and other high-volume commodities shipped, running back and forth between single loading points (such as a mine) and single destinations (such as a power plant) to deliver a single commodity. Run-through trains bypass intermediate terminals to speed up schedules. They work similarly to unit trains, but a run-through train may carry a variety of commodities.

intermodal operations Combination of transport modes such as rail and highway carriers (piggyback), air and highway carriers (birdyback), and water and air carriers (fishyback) to improve customer service and achieve cost advantages.

© ASSOCIATED PRESS, AP

Business has been booming for Burlington Northern Santa Fe Railway. The company experienced back-to-back years of record-breaking volume shipments.

In piggyback operations, one of the intermodal operations, highway trailers and containers ride on railroad flatcars, thus combining the long-haul capacity of the train with the door-to-door flexibility of the truck. A double-stack container train pulls special rail cars equipped with bathtub-shaped wells so they can carry two containers stacked on top of one another. By nearly doubling train capacity and slashing costs, this system offers enormous advantages to rail customers.

As mentioned earlier, the railroad industry is enjoying a resurgence—which also means that it must build a better infrastructure to handle the increase in demand. Cities such as Chicago are making large investments in track and switching improvements, while firms such as BNSF Railway (which includes the old Burlington Northern and Santa Fe lines) are sinking cash into new storage and intermodal facilities. The Association of American Railroads predicts that in one year, the major rail freight carriers will invest $8.2 billion in new track, equipment, and infrastructure. Manufacturers and retailers are jumping on the rails by building warehouses and distribution centers near the new railroad hubs. Wal-Mart recently opened a 3.4 million-square-foot distribution center right next to the BNSF facility in Illinois.[39]

Motor Carriers

The trucking industry is alive and well. About 500,000 trucking companies are operating in the United States, employing more than 9 million people. Many of these companies are small businesses, operating fleets of 20 trucks or fewer. The American Trucking Association estimates that the trucking industry hauls about 64 percent of the total freight tonnage transported in the United States.[40]

Osceola Mills, Pennsylvania–based T. L. Bainey is one of those small trucking firms. His fleet is made up of eight company trucks and four owner-operators. Mostly, his firm hauls freight from distribution centers to retailers. Bainey believes that the reason for his firm's success is the relationships he maintains with his drivers. He gives them full responsibility to do their jobs right and makes sure that his equipment is high quality and well maintained. Bainey is philosophical about shifts in demand. "Sometimes we have more trucks than we have work, but that's how the trucking industry goes, you have to be flexible and adaptable."[41]

Trucking offers some important advantages over the other transportation modes, including relatively fast shipments and consistent service for both large and small shipments. Motor carriers concentrate on shipping manufactured products, while railroads typically haul bulk shipments of raw materials. Motor carriers, therefore, receive greater revenue per ton shipped, because the cost for shipping raw materials is higher than for shipping manufactured products.

Technology has also improved the efficiency of trucking. Many trucking firms now track their fleets via satellite communications systems, and in-truck computer systems allow drivers and dispatchers to make last-minute changes in scheduling and delivery. The Internet is also adding new features to motor carrier services.

Water Carriers

Two basic types of transport methods move products over water: inland or barge lines and oceangoing, deepwater ships. Barge lines efficiently transport bulky, low-unit-value commodities such as grain, gravel, lumber, sand, and steel. A typical lower Mississippi River barge line may stretch more than a quarter mile across. Large ships also operate on the Great Lakes, transporting materials such as iron ore from Minnesota and harvested grain for market. These lake carrier ships range in size from roughly 400 feet to more than 1,000 feet in length.

Oceangoing ships carry about $522 billion of containerized freight between the United States and foreign ports each year.[42] New supertankers from global companies such as Maersk Line are the size of three football fields, almost doubling the capacity of other vessels. At full capacity, the ships can cut the cost of shipping a container across the Pacific by a fifth. Shippers that transport goods via water carriers incur very low costs compared with the rates for other transportation modes. Standardized modular shipping containers maximize savings by limiting loading, unloading, and other handling.

Ships often carry large refrigerated containers called "reefers" for transporting everything from fresh produce to medical supplies. These containers, along with their nonrefrigerated counterparts, improve shipping efficiency because they can easily be removed from a ship and attached to trucks or trains. Although shipping by water has traditionally been less expensive than other modes of transportation, as explained earlier, costs for this mode have increased dramatically because of tightened security measures.

Pipelines

Although the pipeline industry ranks third after railroads and motor carriers in ton-miles transported, many people scarcely recognize its existence. More than 140,000 miles of pipelines crisscross the United States in an extremely efficient network for transporting natural gas and oil products.[43] Oil pipelines carry two types of commodities: crude (unprocessed) oil and refined products, such as gasoline, jet fuel, and kerosene. In addition, one so-called *slurry pipeline* carries coal in suspension after it has been ground up into a powder and mixed with water. The Black Mesa Pipeline, owned by Union Pacific, moves the coal mined by Peabody Coal from northern Arizona 290 miles south into southern Nevada.

Although pipelines offer low maintenance and dependable methods of transportation, a number of characteristics limit their applications. They have fewer locations than water carriers, and they can accommodate shipments of only a small number of products. Finally, pipelines represent a relatively slow method of transportation; liquids travel through this method at an average speed of only three to four miles per hour.

Air Freight

Although the air freight industry grew steadily for many years, recently that growth has leveled off—at least in certain market sectors, such as overnight delivery service. Although U.S. domestic air shipments in one recent year totaled nearly $2.5 billion and generated revenue of roughly $32 billion, this actually represented a decline in the number of shipments. The reason is simple: cost-conscious businesses are thinking twice about paying a premium for overnight delivery, and are instead relying on less-expensive, guaranteed ground deliveries. FedEx recently announced that it expected to carry more domestic ground shipments than air shipments in one year—for the first time in the company's history. "If our projections are accurate, this trend will persist for years to come with surface transport representing an ever-larger share of FedEx's U.S. shipping mix," says one industry watcher. "This reflects the growing role of ground transportation in the national economy." The U.S. Postal Service is still the largest domestic air shipper, followed by FedEx Express, UPS Air, and DHL.[44]

© CLEVE BRYANT/PHOTOEDIT

The U.S. Postal Service is the largest domestic air carrier.

Comparing the Five Modes of Transport

Table 13.3 compares the five transportation modes on several operating characteristics. Although all shippers judge reliability, speed, and cost in choosing the most appropriate transportation methods, they assign varying importance to specific criteria when shipping different goods. For example, while motor carriers rank highest in availability in different locations, shippers of petroleum products frequently choose the lowest-ranked alternative, pipelines, for their low cost.

Examples of types of goods most often handled by the different transports include the following:

- *Railroads.* Lumber, iron, steel, coal, automobiles, grain, chemicals

- *Motor carriers.* Clothing, furniture, fixtures, lumber, plastic, food, leather, machinery

- *Water carriers.* Fuel, oil, coal, chemicals, minerals, and petroleum products; automobiles and electronics from foreign manufacturers; low-value products from foreign manufacturers

- *Pipelines.* Oil, diesel fuel, jet fuel, kerosene, natural gas

- *Air freight.* Flowers, medical testing kits, gourmet food products sent directly to consumers

 assessment check

1. Identify the five major modes of transport.
2. Which mode of transport is currently being replaced by ground delivery, and why?

8 Discuss the role of transportation intermediaries, combined transportation modes, and warehousing in improving physical distribution.

Freight Forwarders and Supplemental Carriers

Freight forwarders act as transportation intermediaries, consolidating shipments to gain lower rates for their customers. The transport rates on less-than-truckload (LTL) and less-than-carload (LCL) shipments often double the per-unit rates on truckload (TL) and carload (CL) shipments. Freight forwarders charge less than the highest rates but more than the lowest rates. They profit by consolidating shipments from multiple customers until they can ship at TL and CL rates. The customers gain two advantages from these services: lower costs on small shipments and faster delivery service than they could achieve with their own LTL and LCL shipments.

In addition to the transportation options reviewed so far, a logistics manager can ship products via a number of auxiliary, or supplemental, carriers that specialize in small shipments. These carriers include UPS, FedEx, DHL Express, and the U.S. Postal Service.

Intermodal Coordination

Transportation companies emphasize specific modes and serve certain kinds of customers, but they sometimes combine their services to give shippers the service and cost advantages of each. *Piggyback* service, mentioned in the section on rail transport, is the most widely used form of intermodal coordination. *Birdyback* service, another form of intermodal coordination, sends motor carriers to pick up a shipment locally and deliver that shipment to local destinations; an air carrier takes it between

MODE	SPEED	DEPENDABILITY IN MEETING SCHEDULES	FREQUENCY OF SHIPMENTS	AVAILABILITY IN DIFFERENT LOCATIONS	FLEXIBILITY IN HANDLING	COST
Rail	Average	Average	Low	Low	High	Average
Water	Very slow	Average	Very low	Limited	Very high	Very low
Truck	Fast	High	High	Very extensive	Average	High
Pipeline	Slow	High	High	Very limited	Very low	Low
Air	Very fast	High	Average	Average	Low	Very high

table 13.3 Comparison of Transport Modes

airports near those locations. *Fishyback* service sets up a similar intermodal coordination system between motor carriers and water carriers.

Intermodal transportation generally gives shippers faster service and lower rates than either mode could match individually because each method carries freight in its most efficient way. However, intermodal arrangements require close coordination between all transportation providers.

Recognizing this need, multimodal transportation companies have formed to offer combined activities within single operations. Piggyback service generally joins two separate companies—a railroad and a trucking company. A multimodal firm provides intermodal service through its own internal transportation resources. Shippers benefit because the single service assumes responsibility from origin to destination. This unification prevents disputes over which carrier delayed or damaged a shipment.

WAREHOUSING

Products flow through two types of warehouses: storage and distribution warehouses. A storage warehouse holds goods for moderate to long periods in an attempt to balance supply and demand for producers and purchasers. For example, controlled-atmosphere—also called *cold storage*—warehouses in Yakima and Wenatchee, Washington, serve nearby apple orchards. By contrast, a distribution warehouse assembles and redistributes goods, keeping them moving as much as possible. Many distribution warehouses or centers physically store goods for less than 24 hours before shipping them to customers.

Logistics managers have attempted to save on transportation costs by developing central distribution centers. A manufacturer might send a single, large, consolidated shipment to a break-bulk center—a central distribution center that breaks down large shipments into several smaller ones and delivers them to individual customers in the area. Many Internet retailers use break-bulk distribution centers.

Wal-Mart operates an enormous distribution network that includes more than 100 centers in the United States and nearly 60 overseas. The retail giant continues to build more distribution centers in prime U.S. locations—such as the one near the railroad hub in Chicago. The firm recently opened its largest facility in Houston—two 2-million-square-foot bulk storage and distribution warehouse structures.[45] By increasing the number of centers in strategic U.S. locations, Wal-Mart can reduce its transportation distances and costs significantly. In addition, Wal-Mart is rapidly building distribution centers in most of the countries where it operates stores. Each center represents a full supply-chain system that includes all logistics—a large center may have as many as a hundred docking centers. China, which already has 56 Wal-Mart stores, has several distribution centers—with more to come. These centers, as well as the stores, employ tens of thousands of local workers.[46]

Automated Warehouse Technology

Logistics managers can cut distribution costs and improve customer service dramatically by automating their warehouse systems. Although automation technology represents an expensive investment, it can provide major labor savings for high-volume distributors such as grocery chains. A computerized system might store orders, choose the correct number of cases, and move those cases in the desired sequence to loading docks. This kind of warehouse system reduces labor costs, worker injuries, pilferage, fires, and breakage.

Warehouse Locations

Every company must make a major logistics decision when it determines the number and locations of its storage facilities. Two categories of costs influence this choice: (1) warehousing and materials handling costs and (2) delivery costs from warehouses to customers. Large facilities offer economies of scale in facilities and materials handling systems; per-unit costs for these systems decrease as volume increases. Delivery costs, on the other hand, rise as the distance from warehouse to customer increases. As mentioned earlier, Wal-Mart continues to work to increase the number of warehouse locations to reduce distance and cost.

Warehouse location also affects customer service. Businesses must place their storage and distribution facilities in locations from which they can meet customer demands for product availability and delivery times. They must also consider population and employment trends. For example, the rapid growth of metropolitan areas in the southern and western United States has caused some firms to open more distribution centers in these areas.

INVENTORY CONTROL SYSTEMS

Inventory control captures a large share of a logistics manager's attention because companies need to maintain enough inventory to meet customer demand without incurring unneeded costs for carrying excess inventory. Some firms attempt to keep inventory levels under control by implementing just-in-time (JIT) production. Others are beginning to use RFID technology, discussed earlier in this chapter.

Companies such as Costco have shifted responsibility—and costs—for inventory control from retailers back to individual manufacturers. Costco gives Kimberly-Clark access to individual store sales data. Kimberly-Clark uses the information to track inventory levels of its diapers and other products and replenishes stocks as needed.[47] **Vendor-managed inventory (VMI)** systems like this are based on the assumption that suppliers are in the best position to spot understocks or surpluses, cutting costs along the supply chain that can be translated into lower prices at the checkout.

ORDER PROCESSING

Like inventory control, order processing directly affects the firm's ability to meet its customer service standards. A company may have to compensate for inefficiencies in its order-processing system by shipping products via costly transportation modes or by maintaining large inventories at many expensive field warehouses.

Order processing typically consists of four major activities: (1) conducting a credit check; (2) keeping a record of the sale, which involves tasks such as crediting a sales representative's commission account; (3) making appropriate accounting entries; and (4) locating orders, shipping them, and adjusting inventory records. A stockout occurs when an order for an item is not available for shipment. A firm's order-processing system must advise affected customers of a stockout and offer a choice of alternative actions.

As in other areas of physical distribution, technological innovations improve efficiency in order-processing. Many firms are streamlining their order-processing procedures by using e-mail and the Internet. Outdoor-gear retailer REI, for example, pushes customers toward Web ordering, its least costly fulfillment channel, in its catalogs, store receipts, signs, mailers, and membership letters.

PROTECTIVE PACKAGING AND MATERIALS HANDLING

Logistics managers arrange and control activities for moving products within plants, warehouses, and transportation terminals, which together compose the **materials handling system.** Two important concepts influence many materials handling choices: unitizing and containerization.

Unitizing combines as many packages as possible into each load that moves within or outside a facility. Logistics managers prefer to handle materials on pallets (platforms, generally made of wood, on which goods are transported). Unitizing systems often lash materials in place with steel bands or shrink packaging. A shrink package surrounds a batch of materials with a sheet of plastic that shrinks after heating, securely holding individual pieces together. Unitizing promotes efficient materials handling because each package requires minimal labor to move. Securing the materials together also minimizes damage and pilferage. PaR Systems designs, builds, and integrates robotic systems that stack bags onto pallets. For instance, the system can take 96-pound bags of animal feed, convey them onto a pallet, stack them, wrap the entire pallet, and generate the appropriate documentation.[48]

Logistics managers extend the same concept through **containerization**—combining several unitized loads. A container of oil rig parts, for example, can be loaded in Tulsa and trucked to Kansas City, where rail facilities place the shipment on a high-speed run-through train to New York City. There, the parts are loaded on a ship headed to Saudi Arabia.

 assessment check

1. What are the benefits of intermodal transportation?
2. Identify the two types of warehouses and explain their function.

In addition to the benefits outlined for unitizing, containerization also markedly reduces the time required to load and unload ships. Containers limit in-transit damage to freight because individual packages pass through few handling systems en route to purchasers.

Strategic Implications of Marketing in the 21st Century

Several factors, including the burgeoning e-commerce environment, are driving changes in channel development, logistics, and supply-chain management. As the Internet continues to revolutionize the ways manufacturers deliver goods to ultimate consumers, marketers must find ways to promote cooperation between existing dealer, retailer, and distributor networks while harnessing the power of the Web as an alternative channel. This system demands not only delivery of goods and services faster and more efficiently than ever before but also superior service to Web-based customers.

In addition, increased product proliferation—grocery stores typically stock almost 50,000 different items—demands logistics systems that can manage multiple brands delivered through multiple channels worldwide. Those channels must be finely tuned to identify and rapidly rectify problems such as retail shortfalls or costly overstocks. The trend toward leaner retailing, in which the burden of merchandise tracking and inventory control is switching from retailers to manufacturers, means that to be effective, logistics and supply-chain systems must result in cost savings.

REVIEW OF CHAPTER OBJECTIVES

1 Describe the types of marketing channels and the roles they play in marketing strategy.

Marketing (distribution) channels are the systems of marketing institutions that enhance the physical flow of goods and services, along with ownership title, from producer to consumer or business user. In other words, they help bridge the gap between producer or manufacturer and business customer or consumer. Types of channels include direct selling, selling through intermediaries, dual distribution, and reverse channels. Channels perform four functions: facilitating the exchange process, sorting, standardizing exchange processes, and facilitating searches by buyers and sellers.

2 Outline the major channel strategy decisions.

Decisions include selecting a marketing channel and determining distribution intensity. Selection of a marketing channel may be based on market factors, product factors, organizational factors, or competitive factors. Distribution may be intensive, selective, or exclusive.

3 Describe the concepts of channel management, conflict, and cooperation.

Manufacturers must practice channel management by developing and maintaining relationships with the intermediaries in their marketing channels. The channel captain is the dominant member of the channel. Horizontal and vertical conflict can arise when there is disagreement among channel members. Cooperation is best achieved when all channel members regard themselves as equal components of the same organization.

4 Identify and describe the different vertical marketing systems.

A vertical marketing system (VMS) is a planned channel system designed to improve distribution efficiency and cost-effectiveness by integrating various functions throughout the distribution chain. This coordination may be achieved by forward integration or backward integration. Options include a corporate marketing system, operated by a single owner; an administered marketing system, run by a dominant channel member; and contractual marketing systems, based on formal agreements among channel members.

5 Explain the roles of logistics and supply-chain management in an overall distribution strategy.

Effective logistics requires proper supply-chain management. The supply chain begins with raw materials, proceeds through actual production, and then continues with the movement of finished products through the marketing channel to customers. Supply-chain management takes place in two directions: upstream and downstream. Tools that marketers use to streamline and manage logistics include radio-frequency identification (RFID), enterprise resource planning (ERP), and logistical cost control.

6 Identify the major components of a physical distribution system.

Physical distribution involves a broad range of activities concerned with efficient movement of finished goods from the end of the production line to the consumer. As a system, physical distribution consists of six elements: (1) customer service, (2) transportation, (3) inventory control, (4) materials handling and protective packaging, (5) order processing, and (6) warehousing. These elements are interrelated and must be balanced to create a smoothly functioning distribution system and to avoid suboptimization.

7 Compare the major modes of transportation.

The five major modes of transport are railroads, motor carriers, water freight, pipelines, and air freight. Railroads rank high on flexibility in handling products; average on speed, dependability in meeting schedules, and cost; and low on frequency of shipments. Motor carriers are relatively high in cost but rank high on speed, dependability, shipment frequency, and availability in different locations. Water carriers balance their slow speed, low shipment frequency, and limited availability with lower costs. The special nature of pipelines makes them rank relatively low on availability, flexibility, and speed, but they are also low in cost. Air transportation is high in cost but offers very fast and dependable delivery schedules.

8 Discuss the role of transportation intermediaries, combined transportation modes, and warehousing in improving physical distribution.

Transportation intermediaries facilitate movement of goods in a variety of ways, including piggyback, birdyback, and fishyback services—all forms of intermodal coordination. Methods such as unitization and containerization facilitate intermodal transfers.

✓ *assessment check* answers

1.1 Distinguish between a marketing channel and logistics.

A marketing channel is an organized system of marketing institutions and their interrelationships designed to enhance the flow and ownership of goods and services from producer to user. Logistics is the actual process of coordinating the flow of information, goods, and services among members of the marketing channel.

1.2 What are the different types of marketing channels?

The different types of marketing channels are direct selling, selling through intermediaries, dual distribution, and reverse channels.

assessment check **answers**

1.3   What four functions do marketing channels perform?

The four functions of marketing channels are (1) facilitating the exchange process by reducing the number of marketplace contacts necessary for a sale; (2) sorting; (3) standardizing exchange transactions; and (4) facilitating searches by buyers and sellers.

2.1   Identify four major factors in selecting a marketing channel.

The four major factors in selecting a marketing channel are market, product, organizational, and competitive.

2.2   Describe the three general categories of distribution intensity.

Intensive distribution seeks to distribute a product through all available channels in a trade area. Selective distribution chooses a limited number of retailers in a market area. Exclusive distribution grants exclusive rights to a wholesaler or retailer to sell a manufacturer's products.

3.1   What is a channel captain? What is its role in channel cooperation?

A channel captain is the dominant member of the marketing channel. Its role in channel cooperation is to provide the necessary leadership.

3.2   Identify and describe the three types of channel conflict.

Horizontal conflict results from disagreements among channel members at the same level. Vertical conflict occurs when channel members at different levels disagree. The gray market causes conflict because it involves competition in the U.S. market of brands produced by overseas affiliates, which are often lower priced than the same U.S. manufactured goods.

4.1   What are vertical marketing systems (VMSs)? Identify the major types.

Vertical marketing systems are planned channel systems designed to improve the effectiveness of distribution, including efficiency and cost. The three major types are corporate, administered, and contractual.

4.2   Identify the three types of contractual marketing systems.

The three types of contractual systems are wholesale-sponsored voluntary chains, retail cooperatives, and franchises.

5.1   What is upstream management? What is downstream management?

Upstream management involves managing raw materials, inbound logistics, and warehouse and storage facilities. Downstream management involves managing finished product storage, outbound logistics, marketing and sales, and customer service.

5.2   Identify three methods for managing logistics.

Methods for managing logistics include RFID technology, enterprise resource planning (ERP) systems, and logistical cost control.

6.1   What are the six major elements of physical distribution?

The major elements of physical distribution are customer service, transportation, inventory control, materials handling and protective packaging, order processing, and warehousing.

6.2   What is suboptimization?

Suboptimization occurs when managers of individual functions try to reduce costs but create less than optimal results.

7.1   Identify the five major modes of transport.

The five major modes of transport are railroads, motor carriers, water carriers, pipelines, and air freight.

7.2   Which mode of transport is currently being replaced by ground delivery, and why?

Air transport is in many cases being replaced by ground delivery because of cost.

assessment check **answers**

8.1   What are the benefits of intermodal transportation?

Intermodal transportation usually provides shippers faster service and lower rates than a single mode could offer.

8.2   Identify the two types of warehouses and explain their function.

The two types of warehouses are storage and distribution. Storage warehouses hold goods for moderate to long periods of time in order to balance supply and demand. Distribution warehouses assemble and redistribute goods as quickly as possible.

MARKETING TERMS YOU NEED TO KNOW

distribution 414

marketing (distribution) channel 414

logistics 414

supply-chain management 414

physical distribution 414

intensive distribution 423

selective distribution 423

exclusive distribution 423

channel captain 426

vertical marketing system (VMS) 428

supply chain 430

radio frequency identification (RFID) 431

intermodal operations 435

OTHER IMPORTANT MARKETING TERMS

marketing intermediary (middleman) 416

wholesaler 416

direct channel 416

direct selling 416

manufacturers' representative 419

dual distribution 419

reverse channel 419

exclusive dealing agreement 425

closed sales territory 425

tying agreement 425

gray goods 427

forward integration 428

backward integration 428

corporate marketing system 428

administered marketing system 428

contractual marketing system 428

retail cooperative 429

franchise 429

upstream management 430

downstream management 430

enterprise resource planning (ERP)
   system 432

third-party (contract) logistics firm 432

suboptimization 434

common carriers 434

contract carriers 435

private carriers 435

vendor-managed inventory (VMI) 440

materials handling system 440

containerization 440

ASSURANCE OF LEARNING REVIEW

1. What is a marketing intermediary? What is the intermediary's role?
2. Why would marketers use a dual distribution strategy?
3. Describe the three levels of distribution intensity. Give an example of a product in each level.
4. Compare and contrast the two types of channel conflict.
5. What are the benefits of owning a franchise? What are the drawbacks?
6. List some ways companies are streamlining their supply chains.
7. What is suboptimization? How can effective management of the physical distribution function avoid or overcome this problem?

8. Which mode of transport would probably be selected for the following goods?
   a. natural gas
   b. lumber
   c. fresh flowers
   d. oil
   e. clothing made in the United States
   f. a diamond ring
   g. grain
9. Which two categories of costs influence the choice of how many storage facilities a firm might have and where they are located?
10. Describe the two concepts that influence materials handling choices.

PROJECTS AND TEAMWORK EXERCISES

1. Imagine a vending machine that would charge more for soft drinks during hot weather. The Coca-Cola Company has tested such a device. What is your opinion of a temperature-sensitive vending machine? Would your opinion change if there were no nearby alternatives—say, a convenience store or another vending machine? How do you think consumers would react? With a partner, poll your classmates or your dorm or eating facility to find out.

2. The traditional channel for consumer goods runs from producer to wholesaler to retailer to user. With a classmate, select a product from the following list (or choose one of your own) and create a chart that traces its distribution system. You may go online to the firm's Web site for additional information.
   a. a kayak from the L. L. Bean Web site or catalog
   b. a meal at Olive Garden
   c. a CD or DVD from Best Buy

3. On your own or with a classmate, identify, draw, and explain a reverse channel with which you are personally familiar. What purpose does this reverse channel serve to businesses? To the community? To consumers?

4. On your own or with a classmate, choose one of the franchises listed in Table 13.2 and visit the Web site of that company. Based on what you can learn about its contractual marketing system as well as other information about its products, logistics, supply-chain management, and physical distribution system, would you be interested in purchasing a franchise from this company? Why or why not? Present your findings in class.

5. For the franchise you selected, create a chart outlining the physical distribution objectives.

CRITICAL-THINKING EXERCISES

1. Movielink is a joint venture of five Hollywood studios that offers movies over the Internet. Recently, the company signed a deal with Twentieth Century Fox, which means that all the major studios are now offering consumers the option to download certain films—ones to which the studios have Internet distribution rights.[49] How do you think this new arrangement will affect the way movies are distributed to the public in the future?

2. Auto dealerships often have exclusive distribution rights in their local markets. How might this affect the purchase choices consumers make? What problems might a dealership encounter with this type of distribution?

3. The new Airbus 380, the largest passenger jet in existence, has the capacity to carry 550 travelers. It also contains 32,000 major parts. The cockpit is built in France, the front and aft fuselages in Germany, the engines in the United Kingdom and the United States, and the tailcone in Spain. New factories were built to handle the scale and complex-

ity of the Airbus. Some of the parts are so large that there aren't aircraft big enough to transport them. These are just a few of the challenges faced by Airbus.[50] Describe steps that Airbus can take to achieve and maintain channel cooperation during the first years of this venture.

4. In their most basic form, RFID tags track the progress of products from warehouse to retail shelf to checkout counter. But they have great potential to provide marketers with more information about consumers' purchase patterns. In what ways might RFID technology be used to serve customers better? What problems might arise?

5. After a trip to Mexico, where you were inspired by the craftsmanship of a number of artisans you met there, you've decided to establish an import business for home furnishings, accessories, and some toys. What type (or types) of transportation would you use to get the goods to the United States, and why?

ETHICS EXERCISE

McDonald's has been the focus of criticism for many years—from nutrition experts, consumer health groups, and the like. Critics point to the high fat and calorie content of McDonald's burgers, fries, and shakes, claiming that they contribute to obesity and other health problems. McDonald's has responded in a number of ways—by adding salads to its menu, including fruit and other more healthful choices in children's meals, and offering lower-fat, lower-calorie sandwich items. Still, the critics won't go away. "Because we are the biggest and the best, some people like to take shots at us," says J.C. Gonzalez-Mendez, head of McDonald's U.S. supply chain.

So McDonald's is trying a new tactic: opening up the supply chain to the media's view. The company invited Reuters reporters to tour one meat-processing plant to see exactly how its burgers are made. Reporters learned that each box of burger patties has a tracking number that can be traced back to the meatpacker that supplied the beef. In the future, McDonald's plans to add a feature to its Web site that allows consumers to track the source of each ingredient in popular food items such as the Egg McMuffin. By providing this information, McDonald's marketers hope that consumers will focus on the quality of the food they are purchasing.[51]

1. Do you think that opening up the supply chain is an ethical strategy by McDonald's? Why or why not?
2. Do you think the strategy will work, or do you think it might backfire? Explain your answer.

INTERNET EXERCISES

1. **Patents and trademarks.** In the U.S., the Patent and Trademark Office is responsible for the registration of patents and trademarks. Visit the USPTO Web site (http://www.uspto.gov) and answer the following questions.
   a. What are the types of patents?
   b. How long does the patent review process take?
   c. What is the so-called Madrid Protocol concerning the international registration of marks?
2. **Packaging.** Companies use packaging to assist in the marketing of their products. Visit each of the following Web sites and prepare a brief report on how each company has used packaging as part of its brand management strategy.
   a. H.J. Heinz: http://www.heinz.com
   b. Campbell Soup: http://www.campbellsoup.com
   c. Yoplait yogurt: http://www.yoplait.com

Note: Internet Web addresses change frequently. If you don't find the exact site listed, you may need to access the organization's home page and search from there or use a search engine such as Google.

CASE 13.1   Heavy Metal at Hyundai

Shipping is a major mode of transportation in the physical distribution of many products, including oil, cars, electronics, and bathroom tiles. Shipping is a complex industry with few players willing to take on the risks associated with building expensive new ships, handling potential environmental disasters, and negotiating through a complicated array of international regulations. Despite these risks, shipbuilding itself is enjoying a recent boom. The upturn is due to the phaseout of single-hull ships (replaced by new, double-hull vessels), the upswing of China's economy that fuels more trade between Asia and the United States, and the increasing demand for oil from developing countries.

The largest player in the global shipbuilding industry is Korea's Hyundai Heavy Industries, followed by Daewoo and Samsung. Not surprisingly, the world's largest shipyard also belongs to Hyundai. Built more than three decades ago, the yard now runs so efficiently that it can turn out a new $80 million vessel every four days of operation. Despite the firm's current prowess, Hyundai engineers continue to develop plans for even larger, more complex ships. On the drawing board is a supervessel that could carry as many as 10,000 steel containers—or 30 million pairs of sneakers.

Why doesn't the firm feel comfortable with its first-place position? China has been outspoken about its intent to become the leading shipbuilder in the world by 2015. China already puts pressure on leaders in other industries, including U.S. manufacturers of numerous products. With its large workforce and lower wages, China is poised to take on just about any industry it wants. So Hyundai executives continually develop new strategies for improving or enhancing their products as they develop new ones. As the old ore carriers and oil tankers are phased out of the shipping market in general, Hyundai looks for ways to build the enormous container ships. But—just like an auto manufacturer—marketers also seek ways to "load" them with expensive features. "We obviously want the more value-added-type vessel—[liquid natural gas] carriers, more complicated container vessels, ice-glass carriers," explains Han Dae Yoon, chief marketing officer of Hyundai's shipbuilding division. "Shipbuilders have to be selective." By focusing on the higher end of the market—letting Chinese shipbuilders take contracts for simple tankers and bulk carriers—Hyundai keeps itself out front. "Now the South Koreans are moving more toward the Lexus end in order to have an edge over the Chinese," notes Peter E. Bartholomew of Industrial Research and Consulting.

China's exploding economy has also created another potential challenge for Hyundai—a shortage of some building materials such as steel, which can make up 20 percent of the material on one ship. This shortage caused the price of steel plate to jump 70 percent in one year, contributing to a $30 million loss by the firm in one quarter. But Hyundai is still ahead of its competition, perhaps because its leaders take nothing for granted. Even with Hyundai's nine dry docks booked until 2009, with contracts for 102 ships worth a total of more than $8 billion, no one at Hyundai rests. "When you are being chased, you have to do something that the chaser cannot do," says Han Dae Yoon. That means building bigger, better ships—faster.

Questions for Critical Thinking

1. With what types of intermediaries do you think Hyundai must maintain relationships?
2. Describe ways in which Hyundai can manage its supply chain effectively.
3. What role does Hyundai play in the global marketplace?

Sources: James Brooke, "Korean Shipbuilders See China's Shadow," *Seoul Times*, May 20, 2006, **http://theseoultimes.com**; Moon Ihlwan, "Korea's Shipbuilding Industry Sails Ahead," *BusinessWeek*, May 12, 2006, **http://www.businessweek.com**; Hyundai Heavy Industries Web site, **http://english.hhi.co.kr**, accessed May 8, 2006.

VIDEO CASE 13.2   American Apparel: Supply Fits the Demand

The written video case on American Apparel appears on page VC-16. The recently filmed American Apparel video is designed to expand and highlight the concepts in this chapter and the concepts and questions covered in the written video case.

CHAPTER 14

Federated Owns the World of Retail

Every year millions of people around the country watch Macy's Thanksgiving Day parade on television, but Macy's department stores have never advertised during the broadcast. The reason? Until recently, Macy's remained a relatively local brand. But that has changed. Federated Department Stores, the owner of Macy's, is well on its way to making Macy's a national retail brand by transforming dozens of hometown retailers around the country into Macy's stores.

Following a $17 billion merger with May Department Stores, Federated took over such local department stores as Kaufman's in Pittsburgh, Filene's, Strawbridge's of Philadelphia, Robinsons-May in Southern California, and Foley's in Houston, all of which have become Macy's. Even the well-known Marshall Field's of Chicago

has changed its name. "It's now got the potential to be a Godzilla," said one fashion retail consultant about the new Macy's, which numbers more than 900 stores. And according to the CEO of Liz Claiborne, a clothing line carried by Macy's stores, the new Macy's "represents the best chance to stop the decline of the department-store channel."

Department store chains have been losing ground to other stores for years. "Department stores have lost sight of their customer. It's that simple," said a retail strategist. Indeed, in the last 30 years the number of viable department store chains dropped from 35 to only 13, as many were forced to shut their doors despite trying cuts in prices, service, and inventory. With cheaper alternatives such as Wal-

Mart, trendy stores such as Target, and more service-oriented stores such as Nordstrom, not to mention catalog companies and the Internet, department stores couldn't keep up. Customers found their selections boring and their lack of service frustrating, and store chains Gimbels, Wanamakers, and Montgomery Ward closed or were sold. The most successful of the survivors specialize in high-end merchandise or stellar customer service.

But Macy's is working hard for a turnaround. The challenges it faces are many. As a national brand, the store has huge buying power, but it must still recognize regional differences in consumer tastes. "What fashion means in Miami is quite different from Atlanta," acknowledges Terry Lundgren, Federated's CEO. To

TOP PHOTO: IMAGE COURTESY OF THE ADVERTISING ARCHIVES
BOTTOM PHOTO: © TIM BOYLE/GETTY IMAGES

Retailers, Wholesalers, and Direct Marketers

Chapter Objectives

1 Explain the wheel of retailing.

2 Discuss how retailers select target markets.

3 Show how the elements of the marketing mix apply to retailing strategy.

4 Explain the concepts of retail convergence and scrambled merchandising.

5 Identify the functions performed by wholesaling intermediaries.

6 Outline the major types of independent wholesaling intermediaries and the appropriate situations for using each.

7 Compare the basic types of direct marketing and nonstore retailing.

8 Describe how much the Internet has altered the wholesaling, retailing, and direct marketing environments.

solve that problem, the company is setting up seven local buying offices around the country, as well as a centralized national database to let its buyers move merchandise more efficiently. It's focusing on the lifestyle characteristics of four types of core customers—from traditional "Katherine," the code name of the female version of this customer, to the neotraditional "Julie," to the contemporary "Erin," and finally high-fashion customer "Alex." Macy's also has to leverage its private labels, such as Charter Club and INC, as well as national brands such as Tommy Hilfiger and Ralph Lauren to offer an array of choices that consumers won't find elsewhere. Finally, the chain is trying to use that exclusivity to convince shoppers used to endless sales and promotions that its merchandise is worth paying full price for, at least some of the time.

Among Macy's suppliers who hope to benefit from its rise to national prominence are cosmetics companies such as L'Oréal and Estée Lauder, which can now develop national campaigns instead of hav-

ing to create separate promotions for each market. "The branding of Macy's can only help us," says the president of L'Oréal-USA's luxury-products division. "Now that department stores have a clear strategy, they'll be able to bring magic back into their stores."

With wider aisles, a bigger assortment of "affordable luxuries" in more price ranges, more frequent deliveries of new merchandise, and revamped fitting rooms, Macy's stores all over the country are ready for the magic to start.[1]

evolution *of a* brand

After a string of retail failures, Rowland Hussey Macy opened a drygoods store called R. H. Macy & Co. at the corner of New York's Fourteenth Street and Sixth Avenue in 1858. Because he'd been a sailor, Macy chose a red star to symbolize his new store, which took in $11 on its first day. Within 20 years Macy's had expanded to occupy the ground floors of several buildings adjoining its original location, and it was soon calling itself the world's largest store. The first retailer to introduce the tea bag and colored bath towels, Macy's also promoted the first female executive in the retail industry. The store moved to its famous Herald Square location in 1902 and within a generation had grown to occupy 1 million square feet of space. The famous Thanksgiving Day parade began as a Christmas parade organized by employees in 1924, with band, floats, and zoo animals. Federated Department Stores acquired Macy's in 1994.

Says Federated's CEO Terry Lundgren, "The idea behind Macy's is that it can market on a national basis but can respond regionally to consumer fashion, choices, and taste. That's a new model for growth." With that philosophy, Macy's is on the verge of becoming a major national—perhaps even international—brand.

evolution *of a* brand

- Federated Department Stores is putting its resources into Macy's and selling its other department store chain, the upscale Lord & Taylor group. "Lord & Taylor does not fit our strategic focus for building the Macy's national brands," says CEO Lundgren. Research the two department store chains and develop a profile for each. Do you agree that Lord & Taylor is, as one consultant said, "a left shoe on the right foot"?

- Lundgren says the Chinese have expressed interest in having a Macy's store in Beijing because the Macy's brand is better known there than Japanese or European store brands. What would Macy's need to find out about the Chinese market to succeed there? Which of its strengths could it exploit if it expanded to Asia? What challenges would it face?

Chapter Overview

In exploring how today's retailing sector operates, this chapter introduces many examples that explain the combination of activities involved in selling goods to ultimate consumers, as Macy's does in its efforts to attract people who are interested in all sorts of fashions, housewares, and gifts. Then the chapter discusses the role of wholesalers and other intermediaries who deliver goods from the manufacturers into the hands of retailers or other intermediaries. Finally, the chapter looks at nonstore retailing. Direct marketing, a channel consisting of direct communication to consumers or business users, is a major form of nonstore retailing. It includes not just direct mail and telemarketing but also direct-response advertising, infomercials, and Internet marketing. The chapter concludes by looking at a less pervasive but growing aspect of nonstore retailing, automatic merchandising.

RETAILING

retailing Activities involved in selling merchandise to ultimate consumers.

Retailers are the marketing intermediaries who are in direct contact with ultimate consumers. **Retailing** describes the activities involved in selling merchandise to these consumers. Retail outlets serve as contact points between channel members and ultimate consumers. In a very real sense, retailers represent the distribution channel to most consumers because a typical shopper has little contact with manufacturers and virtually no contact with wholesaling intermediaries. Retailers determine locations, store hours, number of sales personnel, store layouts, merchandise selections, and return policies—factors that often influence the consumers' images of the offerings more strongly than consumers' images of the products themselves. Both large and small retailers perform the major channel activities: creating time, place, and ownership utilities.

Retailers act as both customers and marketers in their channels. They sell products to ultimate consumers, and at the same time, they buy from wholesalers and manufacturers. Because of their critical location in the marketing channel, retailers often perform a vital feedback role. They obtain information from customers and transmit that information to manufacturers and other channel members.

EVOLUTION OF RETAILING

The development of retailing illustrates the marketing concept in operation. Early retailing in North America can be traced to the establishment of trading posts, such as the Hudson Bay Company, and to pack peddlers who carried their wares to outlying settlements. The first type of

© SPENCER PLATT/GETTY IMAGES

Barney's New York buys men's suits from manufacturers such as Lanvin to sell to its ultimate consumers—business professionals.

retail institution, the general store, stocked a wide range of merchandise that met the needs of an isolated community or rural area. Supermarkets appeared in the early 1930s in response to consumers' desire for lower prices. In the 1950s, discount stores delivered lower prices in exchange for reduced services. The emergence of convenience-food stores in the 1960s satisfied consumer demand for fast service, convenient locations, and expanded hours of operation. The development of off-price retailers in the 1980s and 1990s reflected consumer demand for brand-name merchandise at prices considerably lower than those of traditional retailers. In recent years, Internet-enabled retailing has increased in influence and importance.

A key concept, known as the **wheel of retailing,** attempts to explain the patterns of change in retailing. According to the wheel of retailing, a new type of retailer gains a competitive foothold by offering customers lower prices than current outlets charge and maintains profits by reducing or eliminating services. Once established, however, the innovator begins to add more services, and its prices gradually rise. It then becomes vulnerable to new low-price retailers that enter with minimum services—and so the wheel turns. The retail graveyard is littered with former giants such as Montgomery Ward, Ames Department Stores, and Weibolts Department Stores.

Many major developments in the history of retailing appear to fit the wheel's pattern. Early department stores, chain stores, supermarkets, discount stores, hypermarkets, and catalog retailers all emphasized limited service and low prices. Most of these retailers gradually increased prices as they added services.

Some exceptions disrupt this pattern, however. Suburban shopping centers, convenience food stores, and vending machines never built their appeals around low prices. Still, the wheel pattern has been a good indicator enough times in the past to make it an accurate indicator of future retailing developments.

1 Explain the wheel of retailing.

wheel of retailing
Hypothesis that each new type of retailer gains a competitive foothold by offering lower prices than current suppliers charge; the result of reducing or eliminating services.

✓ assessment check

1. What is retailing?
2. Explain the wheel-of-retailing concept.

figure 14.1
Components of Retail Strategy

RETAILING STRATEGY

Like manufacturers and wholesalers, a retailer develops a marketing strategy based on the firm's goals and strategic plans. The organization monitors environmental influences and assesses its own strengths and weaknesses in identifying marketing opportunities and constraints. A retailer bases its key decisions on two fundamental steps in the marketing strategy process: (1) selecting a target market and (2) developing a retailing mix to satisfy the chosen market. The retailing mix specifies merchandise strategy, customer-service standards, pricing guidelines, target market analysis, promotion goals, location/distribution decisions, and store atmosphere choices. The combination of these elements projects a desired retail image. Retail image communicates the store's identity to consumers. Kohl's, for instance, counts on its trendy, contemporary image to attract consumers. As Figure 14.1 points out, components of retailing strategy must work together to create a consistent image that appeals to the store's target market.

One retailer that has emphasized a retail image consistent with its simple but flavorful products is Chipotle Grill. Says CEO and founder Steve Ells, "The atmosphere says something about the brand beyond just decoration. . . . In our case, it uses very simple materials like plywood, concrete, and steel. Through architecture and good design, you elevate these materials to something extraordinary. It's the same for the food at Chipotle. We use basic building blocks, such as rice, beans, and meat, but it's the use of great cooking techniques and fresh herbs and citrus that elevates those ingredients to something extraordinary."[2]

SELECTING A TARGET MARKET

2 Discuss how retailers select target markets.

A retailer starts to define its strategy by selecting a target market. Factors that influence the retailer's selection are the size and profit potential of the market and the level of competition for its business. Retailers pore over demographic, geographic, and psychographic profiles to segment markets. In the end, most retailers identify their target markets in terms of certain demographics.

The importance of identifying and targeting the right market is dramatically illustrated by the erosion of department store retailing. While mall anchor stores fight to hold on to customers, stand-alone store Target, known for its chic but cheap casual clothes, has solidified its niche. The store attracts style-conscious consumers with fashionable lines under its own designer labels, such as cosmetics from Kashuk and sleek kitchenware from Michael Graves. The trendy but affordable lines draw shoppers with conservative tastes away from traditional department stores.[3]

Deep-discount chains such as Family Dollar Stores and Dollar General, with their less glamorous locations and low-price merchandise crammed into narrow aisles, target lower-income bargain hunters. Attracted by cents-off basics such as shampoo, cereal, and laundry detergent, customers typically pick up higher-margin goods—toys or chocolates—on their way to the checkout.[4]

Target attracts style-conscious customers who like a large assortment of goods at reasonable prices.

© ASSOCIATED PRES, AP

By broadening its product lines and adding services that appeal to women as well as men, hardware chain Lowe's competes with archrival Home Depot. Wide aisles, clean presentation, friendly service, and a broad selection of high-end merchandise, such as Laura Ashley paints, have boosted the store's popularity with female shoppers, who now account for half of all home improvement store customers.[5]

After identifying a target market, a retailer must then develop marketing strategies to attract these chosen customers to its stores or Web site. The following sections discuss tactics for implementing different strategies.

assessment check

1. How does a retailer develop a marketing strategy?
2. How do retailers select target markets?

MERCHANDISING STRATEGY

A retailer's merchandising strategy guides decisions regarding the items it will offer. A retailer must decide on general merchandise categories, product lines, specific items within lines, and the depth and width of its assortments. At Claire's Stores, a chain of accessories stores catering to teen girls, CEOs and sisters Marla and Bonnie Schaefer introduced a higher-margin product mix after inheriting the business from their father. Focusing more on jewelry, they have introduced a new line of pieces selected by Mariah Carey as well as a Mary-Kate and Ashley brand of cosmetics.[6]

To develop a successful merchandise mix, a retailer must weigh several priorities. First, it must consider the preferences and needs of its previously defined target market, keeping in mind that the competitive environment influences these choices. The retailer must also consider the overall profitability of each product line and product category.

3 Show how the elements of the marketing mix apply to retailing strategy.

Category Management

As mentioned in Chapter 12, a popular merchandising strategy is *category management,* in which a category manager oversees an entire product line for both vendors and retailers and is responsible for the profitability of the product group. Category management seeks to improve the retailer's product category performance through more coordinated buying, merchandising, and pricing. Rather than focusing on the performance of individual brands, such as Flex shampoo or Kleenex tissue, category management evaluates performance according to each product category. Laundry detergent, skin-care products, and paper goods, for example, are each viewed as individual profit centers, and different category managers supervise each group. Those that underperform are at risk of being dropped from inventory, regardless of the strength of individual brands. To improve their profitability, for example, some department stores have narrowed their traditionally broad product categories to eliminate high-overhead, low-profit lines such as toys, appliances, and furniture.

The Battle for Shelf Space

As discussed in Chapter 13, large-scale retailers are increasingly taking on the role of channel captain within many distribution networks. Some have assumed traditional wholesaling functions, while others dictate product design and specifications to manufacturers. The result is a shift in power from the manufacturers of top-selling brands to the retailer who makes them available to customers.

Adding to the pressure is the increase in the number of new products and variations on existing products. To identify the varying items within a product line, retailers refer to a specific product offering as a **stock-keeping unit (SKU).** Within the skin-care category, for example, each facial cream, body moisturizer, and sunscreen in each of a variety of sizes and formulations is a separate SKU. The proliferation of new SKUs has resulted in a fierce battle for space on store shelves.

Increasingly, major retailers such as JCPenney make demands in return for providing shelf space. They may, for example, seek pricing and promotional concessions from manufacturers as conditions for selling their products. Retailers—such as Wal-Mart—also routinely require that manufacturers participate in their electronic data interchange (EDI) and quick-response systems. Manufacturers unable to comply may find themselves unable to penetrate the marketplace.

Slotting allowances, described in Chapter 11, are just one of the range of nonrefundable fees grocery retailers receive from manufacturers to secure shelf space for new products. A manufacturer can

stock-keeping unit (SKU) Offering within a product line such as a specific size of liquid detergent.

pay a national retailer as much as $40,000 per item just to get its new products displayed on store shelves.[7] Other fees include failure fees, which are imposed if a new product does not meet sales projections; annual renewal fees, a "pay to stay" inducement for retailers to continue carrying brands; trade allowances; discounts on high-volume purchases; survey fees for research done by the retailers; and even fees to allow salespeople to present new items.

It's not just a yard.

It's a playground for children of all ages.

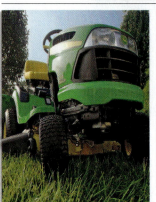

For over 60 years, Lowe's has understood your home is your dream. That's why only Lowe's offers you these three brands; John Deere, Troy-Bilt and Husqvarna, and the most complete after sales service, including 24 hour phone assistance. If you find the same item at a lower price elsewhere, we'll meet it and beat it by 10%.* That's our promise. For the store nearest you call 1-800-44-LOWES.

Lowe's offers a full array of quality, healthy live plants all backed with a 1-year plant guarantee.

LOWE'S
Improving Home Improvement®

CELEBRATING 60 YEARS

*See store for details. Visit Lowes.com. © 2006 by Lowe's. All rights reserved. Lowe's and the gable design are registered trademarks of LF, LLC.

Lowe's home improvement stores follow a customer service strategy, promising customers it will beat competitors' prices by 10 percent and offering 24-hour telephone assistance to do-it-yourselfers.

CUSTOMER-SERVICE STRATEGY

Some stores build their retailing strategy around heightened customer services for shoppers. Gift wrapping, alterations, return privileges, bridal registries, consultants, interior design services, delivery and installation, and perhaps even electronic shopping via store Web sites are all examples of services that add value to the shopping experience. A retailer's customer-service strategy must specify which services the firm will offer and whether it will charge customers for these services. Those decisions depend on several conditions: store size, type, and location; merchandise assortment; services offered by competitors; customer expectations; and financial resources. Now consumers can also get "virtual assistance" from companies such as Virtuosity and CallWave, which manage phone calls by allowing users to switch between voice mail, e-mail, and real-time cell and landline calls using voice commands. CallWave also offers call screening and the ability to receive voice-mail messages as e-mail to be retrieved later or saved.[8]

The basic objective of all customer services focuses on attracting and retaining target customers, thus increasing sales and profits. Some services—such as convenient restrooms, lounges, and complimentary coffee—enhance shoppers' comfort. Other services are intended to attract customers by making shopping easier and faster than it would be without the services. Some retailers, for example, offer child-care services for customers. Others, such as Jewel supermarkets, offer the opportunity to pay for purchases using your fingerprint in place of a check or credit card, with a technology marketed by Pay by Touch, a San Francisco biometrics company.[9]

A customer service strategy can also support efforts in building demand for a line of merchandise. Despite the trend toward renovation, redecorating, and do-it-yourself home projects, Home Depot was experiencing slowing sales until its recent decision to revamp its stores, improve customer service, offer a decorating service, and upgrade its marketing efforts. Home Depot is now seeing its best growth in years, assuring its customers with its familiar slogan, "You can do it; we can help."

PRICING STRATEGY

Prices reflect a retailer's marketing objectives and policies. They also play a major role in consumer perceptions of a retailer. Consumers realize, for example, that when they enter a Gucci boutique in Milan, New York, or Tokyo, they will find such expensive products as $275 snakeskin belts and $990 handbags. Customers of the retail chain Dollar Discount Store expect a totally different type of merchandise; true to the name, every product in the store bears the same low price.

Sometimes a pricing strategy can be controversial. The "Solving an Ethical Controversy" feature discusses the hidden fees and charges that can reduce the value of a gift card below its retail price.

Solving an Ethical Controversy

Are Gift Cards Truly a Gift?

More than half of all holiday shoppers bought gift cards in a recent year, totaling about $62 billion in sales. Most retail cards, which make up more than 80 percent of that dollar volume, can be redeemed only at the issuing store, and many charge an "inactivity" fee on unused balances after six months to a year. Some have expiration dates. Bank-issued cards, which can be used almost anywhere, are subject to additional fees that issuers such as Visa, MasterCard, and American Express say they need to keep the cards profitable.

Should gift card issuers be allowed to reduce the value of their cards with handling fees, dormancy fees, and other charges?

PRO

1. The cards provide value and convenience that buyers should be willing to pay for, so the fees cover those costs.
2. The fees are minimal in comparison to the face value on most cards, so they are acceptable.

CON

1. Gift cards are already limited in that they can't be redeemed for cash or replaced if lost or stolen, so reducing their value places further restrictions on their use.
2. The user should get the full face value that the gift giver intended for the card. It's unfair to assess a fee that wouldn't ordinarily be charged with a direct purchase.

Summary

Several states, including Connecticut, Hawaii, New Hampshire, Rhode Island, and Vermont, have passed laws temporarily restricting the use of fees on gift cards. In response, American Express has stopped issuing its gift cards in those states. A similar law is pending in Massachusetts, and New Jersey has temporarily forbidden dormancy fees. Sales of gift cards are expected to continue rising because they're convenient, perfect for those who love to shop, and more personal than a cash gift.

Sources: Bruce Mohl, "Bill Could Run Bank Gift Cards out of Mass.," *Boston Globe*, April 9, 2006, **http://www.boston.com**; Anne D'Innocenzio, "Gift Cards Spurring Sales," *The Morning News*, January 11, 2006, p. 1D; Marianne Lavelle, "The Year of the Gift Card," *U.S. News & World Report*, January 9, 2006, p. 53.

Markups and Markdowns

The amount that a retailer adds to a product's cost to set the final selling price is the **markup.** The amount of the markup typically results from two marketing decisions:

1. *The services performed by the retailer.* Other things being equal, stores that offer more services charge larger markups to cover their costs.

2. *The inventory turnover rate.* Other things being equal, stores with a higher turnover rate can cover their costs and earn a profit while charging a smaller markup.

A retailer's markup exerts an important influence on its image among present and potential customers. In addition, the markup affects the retailer's ability to attract shoppers. An excessive markup may drive away customers; an inadequate markup may not generate sufficient revenue to cover costs and return a profit. Retailers typically state markups as percentages of either the selling prices or the costs of the products.

Marketers determine markups based partly on their judgments of the amounts that consumers will pay for a given product. When buyers refuse to pay a product's stated price, however, or when improvements in other items or fashion changes reduce the appeal of current merchandise, a retailer must take a **markdown.** The amount by which a retailer reduces the original selling price—

markup Amount that a retailer adds to the cost of a product to determine its selling price.

markdown Amount by which a retailer reduces the original selling price of a product.

Chicos distributes its stylish apparel through its own stores, through its catalogs, and on the Web. Tag Heuer specialty watches are available only at selected retail locations.

the discount typically advertised for a sale item—is the markdown. Markdowns are sometimes used to evaluate merchandisers. For example, a department store might base its evaluations of buyers partly on the average markdown percentages for the product lines for which they are responsible.

The formulas for calculating markups and markdowns are provided in the "Financial Analysis in Marketing" appendix at the end of the text.

LOCATION/DISTRIBUTION STRATEGY

Retail experts often cite location as a potential determining factor in the success or failure of a retail business. A retailer may locate at an isolated site, in a central business district, or in a planned shopping center. The location decision depends on many factors, including the type of merchandise, the retailer's financial resources, characteristics of the target market, and site availability.

In recent years, many localities have become saturated with stores. As a result, some retailers have re-evaluated their location strategies. A chain may close individual stores that do not meet sales and profit goals. Other retailers have experimented with nontraditional location strategies. Starbucks cafés are now found in grocery stores, Barnes & Noble, Target, and seemingly on every other street corner.

planned shopping center
Group of retail stores planned, coordinated, and marketed as a unit.

Locations in Planned Shopping Centers

Over the past several decades, retail trade has shifted away from traditional downtown retailing districts and toward suburban shopping centers. A **planned shopping center** is a group of retail stores designed, coordinated, and marketed to shoppers in a geographic trade area. Together, the stores provide a single convenient location for shoppers as well as free parking. They facilitate shopping by maintaining uniform hours of operation, including evening and weekend hours.

There are five main types of planned shopping centers. The smallest, the *neighborhood shopping center,* is likely to consist of a group of smaller stores, such as a drugstore, a dry cleaner, a card and gift shop, and perhaps a hair-styling salon. This kind of center provides convenient shopping for 5,000 to 50,000 shoppers who live within a few minutes' commute. It contains five to fifteen stores, and the product mix is usually confined to convenience items and some limited shopping goods.

A *community shopping center* serves 20,000 to 100,000 people in a trade area extending a few miles from its location. It contains anywhere from 10 to 30 retail stores, with a branch of a local department store or some other large store as the primary tenant. In addition to the stores found in a neighborhood center, a community center probably encompasses more stores featuring shopping goods, some professional offices, a branch bank, and perhaps a movie theater or supermarket. Community shopping centers typically offer ample parking, and tenants often share some promotion costs. With the advent of stand-alone big-box retailers, some community shopping centers have declined in popularity. Some department stores are also moving away from the strategy of locating in shopping centers and opting for freestanding stores, such as the new Bloomingdale's that opened in New York's trendy SoHo neighborhood.[10] Sears began relocating outside malls a few years ago in former Kmart stores. Its newest strategy is to rename these stores Sears Grand, adding CDs, DVDs, milk and convenience foods, and books and magazines to the traditional Sears product mix of DieHard batteries, Kenmore appliances, and Lands' End apparel.[11]

A *regional shopping center* is a large facility with at least 300,000 square feet of shopping space. Its marketing appeal usually emphasizes major department stores with the power to draw customers, supplemented by as many as 200 smaller stores. A successful regional center needs a location within 30 minutes' driving time of at least 250,000 people. A regional center—or a superregional center such as Minnesota's Mall of America—provides a wide assortment of convenience, shopping, and specialty goods, plus many professional and personal service facilities.

A *power center,* usually located near a regional or superregional mall, brings together several huge specialty stores, such as Toys "R" Us, Home Depot, and Bed Bath & Beyond, as stand-alone stores in a single trading area. Rising in popularity during the 1990s, power centers offered value because they were able to underprice department stores while providing a huge selection of specialty merchandise. Heated competition from cost-cutter Wal-Mart and inroads from more upscale discounters such as Target and Kohl's are currently hurting the drawing power of these centers.

Recently, a fifth type of planned center has emerged, known as a *lifestyle center.* This retailing format seeks to offer a combination of shopping, movie theaters, stages for concerts and live entertainment, decorative fountains and park benches in greenways, and restaurants and bistros in an attractive outdoor environment. At around 300,000 to 1 million square feet, the centers are large, but they seek to offer the intimacy and easy access of neighborhood village retailing with a fashionable cachet. Convenience, safety, and pleasant ambiance are also part of the appeal. Here, there are usually no big anchor stores but rather a mix of just the right upscale tenants—Williams-Sonoma, Eddie Bauer, Banana Republic, Ann Taylor, Pottery Barn, and Restoration Hardware, for instance. About 130 lifestyle centers are currently operating or opening in suburbs around the nation as well as in cities such as Tacoma and New York, and some include office parks, townhouses, and condominiums. Well-heeled customers are currently flocking to them.[12]

Retail analysts say the decline of shopping malls and the rising market for luxury goods is fueling the rapid growth of lifestyle centers. "Developers want to take shopping centers closer and closer to where the affluent, professional people live," says one retail expert. "Lifestyle centers are a means to that end." Another explains the lifestyle center's appeal by saying, "This format creates a sort of shopping/leisure destination that's an extension of [a consumer's] personal lifestyle."[13]

Others, however, see the entertainment aspects of these malls as the biggest drawing card. At the Wynn Esplanade in Las Vegas, for example, a two-mile strip of stores is interrupted by a canal with singing gondoliers and a Moroccan-style bazaar with an artificial thunderstorm every half hour.[14]

PROMOTIONAL STRATEGY

To establish store images that entice more shoppers, retailers use a variety of promotional techniques. Through its promotional strategy, a retailer seeks to communicate to consumers information about

JCPenney is using innovative promotions such as its recent "pop-up store" to create a retail turnaround featuring the chain's many brands, including fashion designer Nicole Miller's exclusive offerings.

its stores—locations, merchandise selections, hours of operation, and prices. If merchandise selection changes frequently to follow fashion trends, advertising is typically used to promote current styles effectively. In addition, promotions help retailers attract shoppers and build customer loyalty.

Innovative promotions can pay off, as retailer JCPenney can testify. In addition to sponsorship of the Academy Awards show and a twelve-page magazine spread, a temporary promotional store called a "pop-up" in New York's Times Square helped the chain ring in a marketing turnaround. The three-story "pop-up" store was created in ten days and filled with boutiques and kiosks to showcase JCPenney's new and revitalized brands, as well as plasma video screens showing JCPenney's new ad campaign. "We want to showcase that something has changed at JCPenney," says the company's vice president of marketing. The pop-up store was open to the public for just 24 days, but sales and profits are coming back up after a long decline. [15]

National retail chains often purchase advertising space in newspapers, on radio, and on television. Other retailers are experimenting with promoting over the Internet or using Bluetooth's wireless technology to send marketing messages to customers' cell phones. One research firm estimates that about 140 million U.S. cell phones will soon be Bluetooth-enabled. [16] Sometimes a well-chosen store location aids promotion; the high-end leather-goods retailer Coach has flagship stores in such tony areas as Beverly Hills' Rodeo Drive and New York's Madison Avenue, though most of its 200 stores are in less expensive locations. Most important, its 85 factory outlets are always at least 60 miles from any of its other retail locations, which never offer markdowns or discounts. [17]

Retailers also try to combine advertising with in-store merchandising techniques that influence buyer behavior at the point of purchase. At H&M's trendy clothing stores, for instance, chic new fashions arrive almost daily, and because nothing is overstocked, styles sell out before they need to be marked down. This "fast fashion" strategy encourages customers to stop in more often, sometimes weekly or even every day to browse the new arrivals. [18]

A friendly, well-trained, and knowledgeable salesperson plays a vital role in conveying the store's image to consumers and in persuading shoppers to buy. To serve as a source of information, a salesperson must possess extensive knowledge regarding credit policies, discounts, special sales, delivery terms, layaways, and returns. To increase store sales, the salesperson must persuade customers that the store sells what those customers need. To this end, salespeople should receive training in selling up and suggestion selling.

Good customer service begins the minute a prospective customer walks in the door. The "Etiquette Tips for Marketing Professionals" feature lists some suggestions about how to treat your own customers.

By *selling up,* salespeople try to persuade customers to buy higher-priced items than originally intended. For example, an automobile salesperson might persuade a customer to buy a more expensive model than the car that the buyer had initially considered. Of course, the practice of selling up must always respect the constraints of a customer's real needs. If a salesperson sells customers something that they really do not need, the potential for repeat sales dramatically diminishes.

Another technique, *suggestion selling,* seeks to broaden a customer's original purchase by adding related items, special promotional products, or holiday or seasonal merchandise. Here, too, the sales-

Etiquette Tips for Marketing Professionals

Providing the Personal Touch to Retail Transactions

The retail business is all about the customer, and that means treating people well from the minute they enter your store. What's the best way to greet them? "May I help you?" often invites a "No, just looking" response, and that may waste your best chance to develop a customer relationship.

Here are some tips for greeting shoppers and treating them well.

1. Let customers know right away that they're welcome to the store, and make them feel relaxed and comfortable.
2. Remember that ignoring customers isn't just bad service, it's rude.
3. Try starting with, "Hi! How are you today?" or "Good to see you! What's new?"
4. Follow with some reference to the merchandise the customer is looking at or moving toward, or mention an item you're promoting just now. "Have you seen these yet? They just arrived," is a good follow-up to your initial greeting.
5. Be enthusiastic but not insincere, and pleasant rather than forceful.

6. Make sure you have enough employees on hand to greet everyone who enters the store, and train your staff to do it promptly and well.
7. Once you strike up a conversation, listen to the customer carefully and let him or her express needs and concerns.
8. Ensure that you and your staff know the merchandise thoroughly so you can answer questions and offer suggestions.
9. Avoid hovering or crowding the customer just for the sake of making a sale to someone who then might not feel comfortable enough to return another day.
10. Thank your customers when they leave, and always invite them back.

Sources: "Retail Customer Service Tips," American Marketing Association, **http://www.marketingpower.com**, accessed May 5, 2006; Anne M. Obarski, "Strive for a Positive 5," Retail Industry, **http://retailindustry. about.com**, accessed May 5, 2006; "Greeting the Customer," *Retail Smarts*, **http://www.retailsmarts.servenet.com**, February 10, 2006.

---

person tries to help a customer recognize true needs rather than unwanted merchandise. Beauty advisors in upscale department stores are masters of suggestion selling.

Just as knowledgeable and helpful sales personnel can both boost sales and set retailers apart from competitors, poor service influences customers' attitudes toward a retailer. Increasing customer complaints about unfriendly, inattentive, and uninformed salespeople have prompted many retailers to intensify their attention to training and motivating salespeople. Older training methods are giving way to online learning in many firms. Nike, for instance, logged a 2 percent increase in sales after training 10,000 sales associates worldwide, using an online learning system.[19]

STORE ATMOSPHERICS

While store location, merchandise selection, customer service, pricing, and promotional activities all contribute to a store's consumer awareness, stores also project their personalities through **atmospherics**—physical characteristics and amenities that attract customers and satisfy their shopping needs. Atmospherics include both a store's exterior and interior décor.

A store's exterior appearance, including architectural design, window displays, signs, and entryways, helps identify the retailer and attract its target market shoppers. The Saks Fifth Avenue script logo on a storefront and McDonald's "golden arches" are exterior elements that readily identify these retailers. Other retailers design eye-catching exterior elements aimed at getting customers' attention. Colorfully lifelike recreations of jungle animals flank the theatrically lit entrances of the popular Rainforest Cafés, and the tropical motif carries over to the interiors, decorated with wall-sized aquariums.

atmospherics Combination of physical characteristics and amenities that contribute to a store's image.

COURTESY OF INTERNATIONAL CONCEPT MANAGEMENT

The unique interior and exterior designs of Rainforest Café restaurants provide a dramatic backdrop to the dining experience of its customers.

The interior décor of a store should also complement the retailer's image, respond to customers' interests, and most important, induce shoppers to buy. Interior atmospheric elements include store layout, merchandise presentation, lighting, color, sounds, scents, and cleanliness. One by one, TGI Friday's 531 U.S. restaurants are getting a facelift, updating their jauntily cluttered décor to include pop culture "junk" from the 1960s through the 1990s, including skateboards and surfboards, road signs, *Star Wars* memorabilia, album covers, and other treasures salvaged from garage sales and flea markets. "We've tested a lot of focus groups and they're reacted very well," said the company's decorator of the new theme. The old items on the restaurants' walls "were always designed to be conversation pieces, but people couldn't recognize them anymore."[20]

The New York–based travel-goods boutique Flight 001 was designed to evoke an airplane interior, with its white curving walls and storage bays. The counter resembles an airline ticket counter, and new luggage lines are displayed in the "baggage claim" area. "Their use of design to court the consumer, their attention to detail and environmental design, was novel," says one design consultant. Its integration of a story-telling interior with a trendy mix of travel-related products has helped Flight 001 expand to Los Angeles, San Francisco, Chicago, and Dubai. "We feel like we're creating the market as we speak," says co-founder John Sencion.[21]

When designing the interior and exterior of a store, marketers must remember that many people shop for reasons other than just purchasing needed products. Other common reasons for shopping include escaping the routine of daily life, avoiding weather extremes, fulfilling fantasies, and socializing with family and friends. Retailers expand beyond interior design to create welcoming and entertaining environments that draw shoppers. Forth & Towne, the Gap's newest retail chain, targets women over 35 with a pitch to get out of the house and socialize. "Why would you go out to a store vs. shopping online?" asks the store's architect. "What's going to draw you out? A lot of it is social interaction. . . . Forth & Towne is really about making a commitment to going out in the public realm." To create that interaction, the center of each store boasts a set of carefully designed fitting rooms that all open onto an elegant and comfortable central space. With fresh flowers and water bottles at hand, it is meant to be the real heart of the store.[22]

 assessment check

1. What is an SKU?
2. What are the two components of a markup?
3. What are store atmospherics?

TYPES OF RETAILERS

Because new types of retailers continue to evolve in response to changes in consumer demand, a universal classification system for retailers has yet to be devised. Certain differences do, however, define several categories of retailers: (1) forms of ownership, (2) shopping effort expended by customers, (3) services provided to customers, (4) product lines, and (5) location of retail transactions.

As Figure 14.2 points out, most retailing operations fit in different categories. A 7-Eleven outlet may be classified as a convenience store (category 2) with self-service (category 3) and a relatively broad product line (category 4). It is both a store-type retailer (category 5) and a member of a chain (category 1).

CLASSIFICATION OF RETAILERS BY FORM OF OWNERSHIP

Perhaps the easiest method for categorizing retailers is by ownership structure, distinguishing between chain stores and independent retailers. In addition, independent retailers may join wholesaler-sponsored voluntary chains, band together to form retail cooperatives, or enter into franchise agreements with manufacturers, wholesalers, or service-provider organizations. Each type of ownership has its own unique advantages and strategies.

figure 14.2

Bases for Categorizing Retailers

Chain Stores

Chain stores are groups of retail outlets that operate under central ownership and management and handle the same product lines. Chains have an advantage over independent retailers in economies of scale. Volume purchases allow chains to pay lower prices than their independent rivals must pay. Because a chain may have hundreds of retail stores, it can afford extensive advertising, sales training, and computerized systems for merchandise ordering, inventory management, forecasting, and accounting. Also, the large sales volume and wide geographic reach of a chain may enable it to advertise in a variety of media.

Independent Retailers

The second-largest industry in the United States by number of establishments as well as number of employees, the retailing structure supports a large number of small stores, many medium-size stores, and a small number of large stores. It generates about $3.8 trillion in retail sales every year and accounts for about 12 percent of all business establishments in the United States.[23]

Independent retailers compete with chains in a number of ways. The traditional advantage of independent stores is friendly, personalized service. Cooperatives offer another strategy for independents. For instance, cooperatives such as Ace Hardware and Valu-Rite Pharmacies help independents compete with chains by providing volume buying power as well as advertising and marketing programs.

Coldwater Creek is a highly successful independent retailer that is growing its catalog business, its online business, and its brick-and-mortar business. The "Marketing Success" feature discusses the store's rise.

CLASSIFICATION BY SHOPPING EFFORT

Another classification system is based on the reasons consumers shop at particular retail outlets. This approach categorizes stores as convenience, shopping, or specialty retailers.

Convenience retailers focus their marketing appeals on accessible locations, long store hours, rapid checkout service, and adequate parking facilities. Local food stores, gasoline stations, and dry cleaners fit this category. GreenStop, Canada's new chain of alternative-fuel stations, features convenience stores that sell solar-roasted coffee and organic veggie wraps instead of candy and cigarettes.[24]

Shopping stores typically include furniture stores, appliance retailers, clothing outlets, and sporting-goods stores. Consumers usually compare prices, assortments, and quality levels at competing outlets before making purchase decisions. Consequently, managers of shopping stores attempt to differentiate their outlets through advertising, in-store displays, well-trained and knowledgeable salespeople, and appropriate merchandise assortments.

Specialty retailers combine carefully defined product lines, services, and reputations in attempts to persuade consumers to expend considerable effort to shop at their stores. Examples include Neiman Marcus, Macy's, and Nordstrom.

Nordstrom is one of the most successful specialty retailers.

© TIM BOYLE/GETTY IMAGES

CLASSIFICATION BY SERVICES PROVIDED

Another category differentiates retailers by the services they provide to customers. This classification system consists of three retail types: self-service, self-selection, or full-service retailers.

White Hen Pantry illustrates a self-service store, while Safeway grocery stores and A&P Future Stores are examples of self-selection stores. Both categories sell convenience products that people can purchase frequently with little assistance. In the clothing industry, catalog retailer Lands' End is a self-selection store. Full-service retailers such as Neiman Marcus focus on fashion-oriented merchandise, backed by a complete array of customer services.

CLASSIFICATION BY PRODUCT LINES

Product lines also define a set of retail categories and the marketing strategies appropriate for firms within those categories. Grouping retailers by product lines produces three major categories: specialty stores, limited-line retailers, and general-merchandise retailers.

Specialty Stores

A *specialty store* typically handles only part of a single product line. However, it stocks this portion in considerable depth or variety. Specialty stores include a wide range of retail outlets: Examples include fish markets, grocery stores, men's and women's shoe stores, and bakeries. Although some specialty stores are chain outlets, most are independent small-scale operations. They represent perhaps the greatest concentration of independent retailers who develop expertise in one product area and provide narrow lines of products for their local markets.

 marketing success   Coldwater Creek Finds a Hot Spot in Retail

Background. "We really didn't know what we were doing," says Dennis Pence. "But we had great confidence in ourselves." In 1984, Pence and his wife, Ann, left good marketing jobs in New York for Idaho and a tiny catalog business they ran from their apartment, selling women's accessories and gifts with a Native American flair. Profits were so slim in the early days of Coldwater Creek that Pence rode his bike two miles to drop customer orders off at UPS, saving the package pickup fee.

The Challenge. With the store's survival assured by the mid-1990s, growth became the company's goal. The challenge was to expand without

losing focus on providing both quality fashions and strong customer service to Coldwater Creek's target market, female baby boomers with average incomes of $70,000 a year and a taste for classic styles and unique accessories.

The Strategy. Pence (the couple divorced in 2003) pursued a three-part strategy—strengthening the catalog's appeal by splitting it into several specialty catalogs with a combined audience of 15 million names, opening an online Coldwater Creek store and an aggressive effort to e-mail customers on a regular basis, and moving into the brick-and-mortar retail business, with

Specialty stores should not be confused with specialty products. Specialty stores typically carry convenience and shopping goods. The label *specialty* reflects the practice of handling a specific, narrow line of merchandise. For example, Lady Foot Locker is a specialty store that offers a wide selection of name-brand athletic footwear, apparel, and accessories made specifically for women. Gloria Jean's Coffees sells whole-bean coffees, beverages, and gift baskets.[25]

Limited-Line Retailers

Customers find a large assortment of products within one product line or a few related lines in a **limited-line store.** This type of retail operation typically develops in areas with a large enough population to sufficiently support it. Examples of limited-line stores are IKEA (home furnishings and housewares) and Rubenstein's of New Orleans (clothing). These retailers cater to the needs of people who want to select from complete lines in purchasing particular products.

A unique type of limited-line retailer is known as a **category killer.** These stores offer huge selections and low prices in single product lines. Stores within this category—such as Best Buy, Borders Books, Bed Bath & Beyond, and Home Depot—are among the most successful retailers in the nation. Category killers at first took business away from general-merchandise discounters, which were not able to compete in selection or price. Recently, however, expanded merchandise and aggressive cost cutting by warehouse clubs and Wal-Mart have turned the tables. Competition from Internet companies that can offer unlimited selection and speedy delivery has also taken customers away. While they still remain a powerful force in retailing, especially for local businesses, category killers are not invulnerable.[26]

General-Merchandise Retailers

General-merchandise retailers, which carry a wide variety of product lines that are all stocked in some depth, distinguish themselves from limited-line and specialty retailers by the large number of product lines they carry. The general store described earlier in this chapter was a primitive form of a general-merchandise retailer. This category includes variety stores, department stores, and mass merchandisers such as discount houses, off-price retailers, and hypermarkets.

Variety Stores

A retail outlet that offers an extensive range and assortment of low-price merchandise is called a *variety store.* Less popular today than they once were, many of these stores have evolved into or given way to other types of retailers such as discount stores or hybrid combinations of drugstores and variety stores, such as Walgreen's, with nearly 5,000 stores nationwide and a 14 percent share of the prescription drug market.[27] The nation's variety stores now account for less than 1 percent of all retail sales. However, variety stores remain popular in other parts of the world. Many retail outlets in Spain and Mexico are family-owned variety stores.

nearly 200 stores open in upper-middle-class neighborhoods and plans for 500 more over the next few years.

The Outcome. Coldwater Creek is one of the fastest-growing retailers in the United States, with annual sales of nearly $700 million and profits expected to increase by more than 50 percent. The Web site accounts for one-fourth of the company's revenues, and the retail stores for more than half. Best of all, a National Retail Federation poll named the company number one in customer service among specialty retailers.

Sources: "Coldwater Creek Boosts Sales Margins by Focusing on Email Deliverability," Return Path, **http://www.returnpath.biz**, accessed May 5, 2006; Stanley Holmes, "Coldwater Creek's Hot Run," *BusinessWeek*, December 12, 2005, pp. 68–71; Duff McDonald, "Using One Retail Channel to Fund Another," *CIO Insight*, October 15, 2005, **http://www.cioinsight.com**.

Department Stores

In essence, a **department store** is a series of limited-line and specialty stores under one roof. By definition, this large retailer handles a variety of merchandise, including men's, women's, and children's clothing and accessories; household linens and dry goods; home furnishings; and furniture. It serves as a one-stop shopping destination for almost all personal and household products. Chicago's Macy's (formerly Marshall Field's) is a classic example.

Department stores such as Macy's, profiled in the chapter opening vignette, built their reputations by offering wide varieties of services, such as charge accounts, delivery, gift wrapping, and liberal return privileges. As a result, they incur relatively high operating costs, averaging about 45 to 60 percent of sales.

Department stores have faced intense competition over the past several years. Relatively high operating costs have left them vulnerable to retailing innovations such as discount stores, Internet retailers, and hypermarkets. In addition, department stores' traditional locations in downtown business districts have suffered from problems associated with limited parking, traffic congestion, and population migration to the suburbs.

Department stores have fought back in a variety of ways. Many have closed certain sections, such as electronics, in which high costs kept them from competing with discount houses and category killers. They have added bargain outlets, expanded parking facilities, and opened major branches in regional shopping centers. Marketers have attempted to revitalize downtown retailing in many cities by modernizing their stores, expanding store hours, making special efforts to attract the tourist and convention trade, and serving the needs of urban residents.

In addition to moving beyond the traditional mall locations, Sears is attempting a turnaround under new CEO Aylwin Lewis that focuses on changing the corporate culture. Work flows are being reengineered to get employees back on the selling floor with the customers, and all the chain's nearly 4,000 employees must spend a day working in a store. "Make no mistake," Lewis tells the managers attending a day-long course he runs on Sears's new culture, "we have to change."[28]

Mass Merchandisers

Mass merchandising has made major inroads into department store sales by emphasizing lower prices for well-known brand-name products, high product turnover, and limited services. A **mass merchandiser** often stocks a wider line of items than a department store but usually without the same depth of assortment within each line. Discount houses, off-price retailers, hypermarkets, and catalog retailers are all examples of mass merchandisers.

Discount Houses   A **discount house** charges low prices and offers fewer services. Early discount stores sold mostly appliances. Today, they offer soft goods, drugs, food, gasoline, and furniture.

By eliminating many of the "free" services provided by traditional retailers, these operations can keep their markups 10 to 25 percent below those of their competitors. Some of the early discounters have since added services, stocked well-known name brands, and boosted their prices. In fact, many now resemble department stores.

A discount format that is gaining strength is the *warehouse club*. Costco, BJ's, and Wal-Mart's Sam's Club are the largest warehouse clubs in the United States. These no-frills, cash-and-carry outlets offer consumers access to name-brand products at deeply discounted prices. Selection at warehouse clubs includes gourmet popcorn, fax machines, peanut butter, luggage, and sunglasses sold in vast warehouselike settings. Attracting business away from almost every retailing segment, warehouse clubs now even offer fresh food and gasoline. Customers must be members to shop at warehouse clubs.

Off-Price Retailers   Another version of a discount house is an *off-price retailer*. This kind of store stocks only designer labels or well-known brand-name clothing at prices equal to or below regular wholesale prices and then passes the cost savings along to buyers. While many off-price retailers are located in outlets in downtown areas or in freestanding buildings, a growing number are concentrating in *outlet malls*—shopping centers that house only off-price retailers.

Inventory at off-price stores changes frequently as buyers take advantage of special price offers from manufacturers selling excess merchandise. Off-price retailers such as Loehmann's, Marshall's,

Stein Mart, and T.J. Maxx also keep their prices below those of traditional retailers by offering fewer services. Off-price retailing has been well received by today's shoppers.

Hypermarkets and Supercenters
Another innovation in discount retailing is the creation of **hypermarkets**—giant one-stop shopping facilities that offer wide selections of grocery and general merchandise products at discount prices. Store size determines the major difference between hypermarkets and supercenters. Hypermarkets typically fill up 200,000 or more square feet of selling space, about a third larger than most **supercenters.** Ohio-based Bigg's Hypermarket Shoppes offer a vast array of items in dozens of departments including housewares, groceries, apparel, drugs, hardware, electronics, and photo finishing in stores that average 220,000 square feet. Customer ser-

T. J. Maxx is a popular off-price retailer that gives consumers up to 60 percent discounts off prices found in department stores and specialty retailers. Each store carries a slightly different selection of merchandise.

vice is enhanced by wireless phones carried by 40 key employees at each store.[29] The newest type of hypermarket, now being tested in New Mexico, is AutoCart, a 24-hour drive-through superstore of about 130,000 square feet that can serve up to 12,000 cars a day. Although critics say it will lack the entertainment value of a store like Wal-Mart, AutoCart allows shoppers to phone in their orders ahead of time and will eventually offer dry-cleaning services in addition to groceries, office supplies, prescription drugs, and DVD rentals.[30]

Showroom and Warehouse Retailers These retailers send direct mail to their customers and sell the advertised goods from showrooms that display samples. Back-room warehouses fill orders for the displayed products. Low prices are important to catalog store customers. To keep prices low, these retailers offer few services, store most inventory in inexpensive warehouse space, limit shoplifting losses, and handle long-lived products such as luggage, small appliances, gift items, sporting equipment, toys, and jewelry.

CLASSIFICATION OF RETAIL TRANSACTIONS BY LOCATION

Although most retail transactions occur in stores, nonstore retailing serves as an important marketing channel for many products. In addition, both consumer and business-to-business marketers rely on nonstore retailing to generate orders or requests for more information that may result in future orders.

Direct marketing is a broad concept that includes direct mail, direct selling, direct-response retailing, telemarketing, Internet retailing, and automatic merchandising. The last sections of this chapter will consider each type of nonstore retailing.

RETAIL CONVERGENCE AND SCRAMBLED MERCHANDISING

Many traditional differences no longer distinguish familiar types of retailers, rendering any set of classifications less useful. **Retail convergence,** whereby similar merchandise is available from multiple retail outlets distinguished by price more than any other factor, is blurring distinctions between types of retailers and the merchandise mix they offer. A few years ago, a customer looking for a

4 Explain the concepts of retail convergence and scrambled merchandising.

retail convergence Situation in which similar merchandise is available from multiple retail outlets, resulting in the blurring of distinctions between type of retailer and merchandise offered.

BUBBLE BATH
GRAHAM CRACKERS
5 CT DIAMOND NECKLACE

REGULAR RETAIL $813,000
SAM'S CLUB PRICE $560,000

LUXURY GOODS AT SAM'S CLUB®
WHO KNEW?

COURTESY OF SAM'S CLUB. CHRIS TRAYER—PHOTOGRAPHER. PREMIER GEM CORPORATIONS—NECKLACE

Sam's Club, the membership warehouse division of Wal-Mart, is going upscale in some areas, offering luxury items such as this diamond pendant, which normally sells for $813,000 but is priced at $560,000 at Sam's Club. The ad promotes "Bubble Bath, Graham Crackers, 5 Carat Diamond Necklace."

 assessment check

1. How do we classify retailers by form of ownership?
2. Categorize retailers by shopping effort and by services provided.
3. List several ways to classify retailers by product line.

scrambled merchandising Retailing practice of combining dissimilar product lines to boost sales volume.

wholesaler Channel intermediary that takes title to goods it handles and then distributes these goods to retailers, other distributors, or B2B customers.

wholesaling intermediary Comprehensive term that describes wholesalers as well as agents and brokers.

 5 Identify the functions performed by wholesaling intermediaries.

fashionable coffeepot might have headed straight for Williams-Sonoma or Starbucks. Today, she's just as likely to pick one up at Target or her neighborhood Sam's Club, where she can check out new spring fashions and stock up on paper goods. The Gap is no longer pitted only against Eddie Bauer or American Eagle Outfitters but against designer-label brands at department stores and Kohl's, too. Grocery stores compete with Super Wal-Mart, Sam's Club, and Costco. In turn, Wal-Mart and Sam's Club are changing their product mix to compete with electronics retailer Best Buy, "green" grocer Whole Foods, and fine wine and jewelry stores for the loyalty of affluent customers.[31]

Scrambled merchandising—in which a retailer combines dissimilar product lines in an attempt to boost sales volume—has also muddied the waters. Drugstores not only fill prescriptions but offer cameras, cards, housewares, magazines, and even small appliances. Convenience retailer 7-Eleven recently began offering such services as bill payment, payroll check cashing, money wiring, and ticket purchasing through in-store terminals linked to the Web. Goods ordered through the system are delivered to the store for later pickup.[32]

WHOLESALING INTERMEDIARIES

Recall from Chapter 13 that several distribution channels involve marketing intermediaries called **wholesalers.** These firms take title to the goods they handle and sell those products primarily to retailers or to other wholesalers or business users. They sell to ultimate consumers only in insignificant quantities, if at all. **Wholesaling intermediaries,** a broader category, include not only wholesalers but also agents and brokers, who perform important wholesaling activities without taking title to the goods.

FUNCTIONS OF WHOLESALING INTERMEDIARIES

As specialists in certain marketing functions, as opposed to production or manufacturing functions, wholesaling intermediaries can perform these functions more efficiently than producers or consumers. The importance of these activities results from the utility they create, the services they provide, and the cost reductions they allow.

Creating Utility

Wholesaling intermediaries create three types of utility for consumers. They enhance time utility by making products available for sale when consumers want to purchase them. They create place utility by helping deliver goods and services for purchase at convenient locations. They create ownership (or possession) utility when a smooth exchange of title to the products from producers or intermediaries to final purchasers is complete. Possession utility can also result from transactions in which actual title does not pass to purchasers, as in rental-car services.

Providing Services

Table 14.1 lists a number of services provided by wholesaling intermediaries. The list clearly indicates the marketing utilities—time, place, and possession utility—that wholesaling intermediaries create or enhance. These services also reflect the basic marketing functions of buying, selling, storing, transporting, providing market information, financing, and risk taking.

Of course, many types of wholesaling intermediaries provide varying services, and not all of them perform every service listed in the table. Producer-suppliers rely on wholesaling intermediaries for distribution and selection of firms that offer the desired combinations of services. In general, however, the critical marketing functions listed in the table form the basis for any evaluation of a marketing intermediary's efficiency. The risk-taking function affects each service of the intermediary.

Ingram Micro is a leading technology distributor with business clients in 100 countries and vendors all over the world. Twelfth among the *Fortune* 500, it offers a wide range of information

table 14.1 Wholesaling Services for Customers and Producer-Suppliers

SERVICE	BENEFICIARIES OF SERVICE	
	Customers	Producer-Suppliers
Buying Anticipates customer demands and applies knowledge of alternative sources of supply; acts as purchasing agent for customers.	Yes	No
Selling Provides a sales force to call on customers, creating a low-cost method for servicing smaller retailers and business users.	No	Yes
Storing Maintains warehouse facilities at lower costs than most individual producers or retailers could achieve. Reduces risk and cost of maintaining inventory for producers.	Yes	Yes
Transporting Customers receive prompt delivery in response to their demands, reducing their inventory investments. Wholesalers also break bulk by purchasing in economical carload or truckload lots, then reselling in smaller quantities, thereby reducing overall transportation costs.	Yes	Yes
Providing Marketing Information Offers important marketing research input for producers through regular contacts with retail and business buyers. Provides customers with information about new products, technical information about product lines, reports on competitors' activities and industry trends, and advisory information concerning pricing changes, legal changes, and so forth.	Yes	Yes
Financing Grants credit that might be unavailable for purchases directly from manufacturers. Provides financing assistance to producers by purchasing products in advance of sale and by promptly paying bills.	Yes	Yes
Risk Taking Evaluates credit risks of numerous, distant retail customers and small-business users. Extends credit to customers that qualify. By transporting and stocking products in inventory, the wholesaler assumes risk of spoilage, theft, or obsolescence.	Yes	Yes

figure 14.3

Transaction Economies through Wholesaling Intermediaries

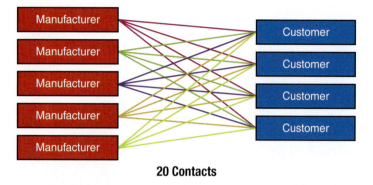

20 Contacts

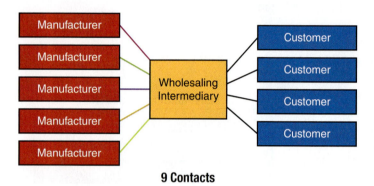

9 Contacts

✔ *assessment check*

1. What is a wholesaler? How does it differ from a wholesaling intermediary?

2. How do wholesaling intermediaries help sellers lower costs?

6   Outline the major types of independent wholesaling intermediaries and the appropriate situations for using each.

technology services for order management and fulfillment, contract manufacturing and warehousing, transportation management, and credit and collection management, as well as distributing and marketing information technology products to businesses worldwide.[33]

Lowering Costs by Limiting Contacts

When an intermediary represents numerous producers, it often cuts the costs of buying and selling. The transaction economies are illustrated in Figure 14.3, which shows five manufacturers marketing their outputs to four different retail outlets. Without an intermediary, these exchanges create a total of 20 transactions. Adding a wholesaling intermediary reduces the number of transactions to 9.

United Stationers is a wholesaler of everything including paper clips and fax machines to discount chains, independent stores, and Internet resellers. While big-box retailers buy in bulk directly from manufacturers, they can order low-volume specialty goods faster and more efficiently from United Stationers. Through Web-enabled orders, mom-and-pop stores have access to more than 35,000 items, delivered either to the store or directly to customers overnight. Positioning itself as a one-stop warehousing, logistics, and distribution network, the company recently expanded beyond its office products roots by establishing a new janitorial supply unit.[34]

TYPES OF WHOLESALING INTERMEDIARIES

Various types of wholesaling intermediaries operate in different distribution channels. Some provide wide ranges of services or handle broad lines of goods, while others specialize in individual services, goods, or industries. Figure 14.4 classifies wholesaling intermediaries by two characteristics: ownership and title flows (whether title passes from manufacturer to wholesaling intermediary). The three basic ownership structures are as follows: (1) manufacturer-owned facilities, (2) independent wholesaling intermediaries, and (3) retailer-owned cooperatives and buying offices. The two types of independent wholesaling intermediaries are merchant wholesalers, which take title of the goods, and agents and brokers, which do not.

Manufacturer-Owned Facilities

Several reasons lead manufacturers to distribute their goods directly through company-owned facilities. Some perishable goods need rigid control of distribution to avoid spoilage; other goods require complex installation or servicing. Some goods need aggressive promotion. Goods with high unit values allow profitable sales by manufacturers directly to ultimate purchasers. Manufacturer-owned facilities include sales branches, sales offices, trade fairs, and merchandise marts.

A *sales branch* carries inventory and processes orders for customers from available stock. Branches provide a storage function like independent wholesalers and serve as offices for sales representatives in their territories. They are prevalent in marketing channels for chemicals, commercial machinery and equipment, and petroleum products.

A *sales office*, in contrast, does not carry inventory, but it does serve as a regional office for a manufacturer's sales personnel. Locations close to the firm's customers help limit selling costs and support active customer service. For example, numerous sales offices in the Detroit suburbs serve the area's automobile industry.

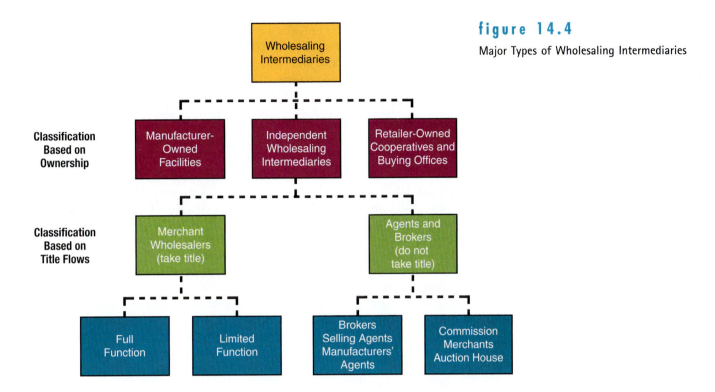

figure 14.4

Major Types of Wholesaling Intermediaries

A *trade fair* (or trade exhibition) is a periodic show at which manufacturers in a particular industry display their wares for visiting retail and wholesale buyers. For example, Interop, held annually for more than 20 years, is the biggest information technology trade show in North America, with about 18,000 attendees visiting the booths of about 375 exhibitors.[35]

A *merchandise mart* provides space for permanent showrooms and exhibits, which manufacturers rent to market their goods. One of the world's largest merchandise marts is Chicago's Merchandise Mart Center, a 7-million-square-foot complex with its own zip code that hosts more than 30 seasonal buying markets each year.[36]

© ASSOCIATED PRESS, AP

Chicago's Merchandise Mart was once open only to professionals in the design trade. But now it offers everyday customers access to unique home decor items through its Design Center.

Independent Wholesaling Intermediaries

Many wholesaling intermediaries are independently owned. These firms fall into two major categories: merchant wholesalers and agents and brokers.

Merchant Wholesalers

A **merchant wholesaler** takes title to the goods it handles. Merchant wholesalers account for roughly 60 percent of all sales at the wholesale level. Further classifications divide these wholesalers into full-function or limited-function wholesalers, as indicated in Figure 14.4.

A full-function merchant wholesaler provides a complete assortment of services for retailers and business purchasers. Such a wholesaler stores merchandise in a convenient location, allowing customers to make purchases on short notice and minimizing inventory requirements. The firm typically maintains a sales force that calls on retailers, makes deliveries, and extends credit to qualified buyers. Full-function wholesalers are common in the drug, grocery, and hardware industries. In the business-goods market, full-function merchant wholesalers (often called *industrial distributors*) sell machinery, inexpensive accessory equipment, and supplies.

A **rack jobber** is a full-function merchant wholesaler that markets specialized lines of merchandise to retailers. A rack jobber supplies the racks, stocks the merchandise, prices the goods, and makes regular visits to refill shelves. Unitime Imports, based in Spokane, Washington, imports, distributes, and guarantees goods such as pens, knives, novelty key rings, batteries, flashlights, sunglasses, film, and other inexpensive "impulse" and seasonal items. CEO Doug Huffman hopes to expand the company's ability to brand its products. He already puts the company's trademark logo on some imported items and says, "We're not interested in bringing in something cheap. We stand behind it, and if I put my name on it, it's going to be something good."[37]

Limited-function merchant wholesalers fit into four categories: cash-and-carry wholesalers, truck wholesalers, drop shippers, and mail-order wholesalers. Limited-function wholesalers serve the food, coal, lumber, cosmetics, jewelry, sporting goods, and general-merchandise industries.

A *cash-and-carry wholesaler* performs most wholesaling functions except for financing and delivery. Although feasible for small stores, this kind of wholesaling generally is unworkable for large-scale grocery stores. Today, cash-and-carry operations typically function as departments within regular full-service wholesale operations. Cash-and-carry wholesalers are commonplace outside the United States, such as in the United Kingdom.

A **truck wholesaler,** or **truck jobber,** markets perishable food items such as bread, tobacco, potato chips, candy, and dairy products. Truck wholesalers make regular deliveries to retailers, perform sales and collection functions, and promote product lines. S. Abraham & Sons is a regional wholesale distributor that delivers brand-name groceries and health and beauty aids to small grocery and convenience stores in the Midwest.[38]

A **drop shipper** such as ONE, Inc., of Tampa, Florida, accepts orders from customers and forwards these orders to producers, which then ship the desired products directly to customers. Although drop shippers take title to goods, they never physically handle or even see the merchandise. These intermediaries often operate in industries selling bulky goods that customers buy in large lots. Coal and lumber would be examples.

A **mail-order wholesaler** is a limited-function merchant wholesaler that distributes physical or online catalogs as opposed to sending sales representatives to contact retail, business, and institutional customers. Customers then make purchases by mail, by phone, or online. Such a wholesaler often serves relatively small customers in outlying areas. Mail-order operations mainly exist in the hardware, cosmetics, jewelry, sporting goods, and specialty food lines as well as in general merchandise. Some popular mail-order products are pharmaceuticals, roasted bean coffee, Christmas trees and wreaths, and popcorn.

Table 14.2 compares the various types of merchant wholesalers and the services they provide. Full-function merchant wholesalers and truck wholesalers rank as relatively high-cost intermediaries because of the number of services they perform, while cash-and-carry wholesalers, drop shippers, and mail-order wholesalers provide fewer services and set lower prices because they incur lower operating costs.

Agents and Brokers

A second group of independent wholesaling intermediaries, agents and brokers, may or may not take possession of the goods they handle, but they never take title. They normally perform fewer services than merchant wholesalers, working mainly to bring together buyers and sellers. Agents and brokers fall into five categories: commission merchants, auction houses, brokers, selling agents, and manufacturers' representatives (reps).

Commission merchants, which predominate in the markets for agricultural products, take possession when producers ship goods such as grain, produce, and livestock to central markets for sale. Commission merchants act as producers' agents and receive agreed-upon fees when they make sales. Because customers inspect the products and prices fluctuate, commission merchants receive

table 14.2 Comparison of the Types of Merchant Wholesalers and Their Services

| SERVICE | Full-Function | LIMITED-FUNCTION WHOLESALER | | | |
		Cash-and-Carry	Truck	Drop Shipper	Mail-Order
Anticipates customer needs	Yes	Yes	Yes	No	Yes
Carries inventory	Yes	Yes	Yes	No	Yes
Delivers	Yes	No	Yes	No	No
Provides market information	Yes	Rarely	Yes	Yes	No
Provides credit	Yes	No	No	Yes	Sometimes
Assumes ownership risk by taking title	Yes	Yes	Yes	Yes	Yes

considerable latitude in marketing decisions. The owners of the goods may specify minimum prices, but the commission merchants sell these goods at the best possible prices. The commission merchants then deduct their fees from the sales proceeds.

An *auction house* gathers buyers and sellers in one location and allows potential buyers to inspect merchandise before submitting competing purchase offers. Auction house commissions typically reflect specified percentages of the sales prices of the auctioned items. Auctions are common in the distribution of tobacco, used cars, artworks, livestock, furs, and fruit. The Internet has led to a new type of auction house that connects customers and sellers in the online world. A well-known example is eBay, which auctions a wide variety of products in all price ranges.

Brokers work mainly to bring together buyers and sellers. A broker represents either the buyer or the seller, but not both, in a given transaction, and the broker receives a fee from the client when the transaction is completed. Intermediaries that specialize in arranging buying and selling transactions between domestic producers and foreign buyers are called *export brokers*. Brokers operate in industries characterized by large numbers of small suppliers and purchasers, such as real estate, frozen foods, and used machinery. Because they provide onetime services for sellers or buyers, they cannot serve as effective channels for manufacturers seeking regular, continuing service. A firm that seeks to develop a more permanent channel might choose instead to use a selling agent or manufacturer's agent.

A **selling agent** typically exerts full authority over pricing decisions and promotional outlays, and it often provides financial assistance for the manufacturer. Selling agents act as independent marketing departments because they can assume responsibility for the total marketing programs of client firms' product lines. Selling agents mainly operate in the coal, lumber, and textiles industries. For a small, poorly financed, production-oriented firm, such an intermediary might prove the ideal marketing channel.

While a manufacturer may deal with only one selling agent, a firm that hires **manufacturers' representatives** often delegates marketing tasks to many of these agents. Such an independent salesperson may work for a number of firms that produce related, noncompeting products. Manufacturers' reps are paid on a commission basis, such as 6 percent of sales. Unlike selling agents, who may contract for exclusive rights to market a product, manufacturers' agents operate in specific territories. They may develop new sales territories or represent relatively small firms and those firms with unrelated lines.

Castle Supply of Pinellas Park, Florida, is a manufacturer's representative serving the plumbing industry, with $15 million worth of inventory from leading manufacturers such as Kohler, Briggs, Moen, and Delta. The firm was recently named Wholesaler of the Year by *Supply House Times* for its commitment to its plumbing contractor customers. CEO Joe White, whose parents founded the company, says, "As time went on, it just became part of our culture to empower all of our people to satisfy the customer. We tell them, 'Act now, ask questions later.'"[39]

broker Agent wholesaling intermediary that does not take title to or possession of goods in the course of its primary function, which is to bring together buyers and sellers.

manufacturers' representative Agent wholesaling intermediary that represents manufacturers of related but noncompeting products and receives a commission on each sale.

table 14.3   Services Provided by Agents and Brokers

SERVICE	Commission Merchant	Auction House	Broker	Manufacturers' Agent	Selling Agent
Anticipates customer needs	Yes	Sometimes	Sometimes	Yes	Yes
Carries inventory	Yes	Yes	No	No	No
Delivers	Yes	No	No	Sometimes	No
Provides market information	Yes	Yes	Yes	Yes	Yes
Provides credit	Sometimes	No	No	No	Sometimes
Assumes ownership risk by taking title	No	No	No	No	No

The importance of selling agents in many markets has declined because manufacturers want better control of their marketing programs than these intermediaries allow. In contrast, the volume of sales by manufacturers' agents has more than doubled and now accounts for 37 percent of all sales by agents and brokers. Table 14.3 compares the major types of agents and brokers on the basis of the services they perform.

 assessment check

1. **What is the difference between a merchant wholesaler and a rack jobber?**

2. **Differentiate between agents and brokers.**

RETAILER-OWNED COOPERATIVES AND BUYING OFFICES

Retailers may assume numerous wholesaling functions in an attempt to reduce costs or provide special services. Independent retailers sometimes band together to form buying groups that can achieve cost savings through quantity purchases. Other groups of retailers establish retailer-owned wholesale facilities by forming cooperative chains. Large chain retailers often establish centralized buying offices to negotiate large-scale purchases directly with manufacturers.

 7 Compare the basic types of direct marketing and nonstore retailing.

direct marketing Direct communications, other than personal sales contacts, between buyer and seller, designed to generate sales, information requests, or store or Web site visits.

DIRECT MARKETING AND OTHER NONSTORE RETAILING

Although most retail transactions occur in stores, nonstore retailing is an important marketing channel for many products. Both consumer and business-to-business marketers rely on nonstore retailing to generate leads or requests for more information that may result in future orders.

Direct marketing is a broad concept that includes direct mail, direct selling, direct-response retailing, telemarketing, Internet retailing, and automatic merchandising. Direct and interactive marketing expenditures amount to hundreds of billions of dollars in yearly purchases. The last sections of this chapter consider each type of nonstore retailing.

DIRECT MAIL

Direct mail is a major component of direct marketing. It comes in many forms: sales letters, postcards, brochures, booklets, catalogs, house organs (periodicals published by organizations to cover internal issues), and video- and audiocassettes. Both not-for-profit and profit-seeking organizations make extensive use of this distribution channel.

Direct mail offers several advantages such as the ability to select a narrow target market, achieve intensive coverage, send messages quickly, choose from various formats, provide complete information, and personalize each mailing piece. Response rates are measurable and higher than other types of advertising. In addition, direct mailings stand alone and do not compete for attention with magazine articles and television programs. On the other hand, the per-reader cost of direct mail is high, effectiveness depends on the quality of the mailing list, and some consumers object strongly to direct mail, considering it "junk mail."

Direct-mail marketing relies heavily on database technology in managing lists of names and in segmenting these lists according to the objectives of the campaign. Recipients get targeted materials, often personalized with their names within the ad's content.

Catalogs are a popular form of direct mail, with more than 10,000 different consumer specialty mail-order catalogs—and thousands more for business-to-business sales—finding their way to almost every mailbox in the United States.

Lands' End made its claim to fame as a catalog retailer of high-quality goods with no-hassle guarantees. Today, shoppers still rely on the service and quality they receive from its catalog division.

In a typical year, mail-order catalogs generate almost $128 billion in sales, of which nearly $50 billion is business-to-business sales. Both consumer and B2B catalog sales are expected to grow by at least 25 percent.[40] Catalogs can be a company's only or primary sales method. Spiegel, L. L. Bean, and Coldwater Creek are well-known examples, along with Herrington, Charles Keath, and Boston Proper. Brick-and-mortar retailers such as Bloomingdale's and Macy's also distribute catalogs.

New technologies are changing catalog marketing. Today's catalogs can be updated quickly, providing consumers with the latest information and prices. Online catalogs allow marketers to display products in three-dimensional views and can include video sequences of product demonstrations. For instance, Nordstrom's online shoe store catalog allows browsers to zoom in and out and view a shoe from different angles and in different colors.

DIRECT SELLING

Through direct selling, manufacturers completely bypass retailers and wholesalers. Instead, they set up their own channels to sell their products directly to consumers. Avon, Pampered Chef, Dell, and party-plan marketers such as Tupperware are all direct sellers. This channel was discussed in detail in Chapter 13.

DIRECT-RESPONSE RETAILING

Customers of a direct-response retailer can order merchandise by mail or telephone, by visiting a mail-order desk in a retail store, or by computer or fax machine. The retailer then ships the merchandise to the customer's home or to a local retail store for pickup.

Many direct-response retailers rely on direct mail, such as catalogs, to create telephone and mail-order sales and to promote in-store purchases of products featured in the catalogs. Some firms, such as Lillian Vernon, make almost all their sales through catalog orders. Mail-order sales have grown at about twice the rate of retail store sales in recent years.

Direct-response retailers are increasingly reaching buyers through the Internet and through unique catalogs. Although catalogs may run into the thousands, with some industry experts estimating that there are 10,000 at any given time, some of which are niche catalogs selling specialty products such as art supplies or boating products, about 500 are from well-established marketers.[41]

assessment check

1. What is direct marketing?
2. What is direct mail?

8 Describe how much the Internet has altered the wholesaling, retailing, and direct marketing environments.

Direct-response retailing also includes home shopping, which runs promotions on cable television networks to sell merchandise through telephone orders. One form of home shopping has existed for years—*infomercials* that run for at least 30 minutes. Such products as Flavor Wave Oven and Turbo Cooker have been featured on these commercials. More recently, TV networks such as Home Shopping Network and QVC have successfully focused exclusively on providing shopping opportunities. Programming ranges from extended commercials to call-in shows to game show formats. Shoppers call a toll-free number to buy featured products, and the retailer ships orders directly to their homes.

TELEMARKETING

Telemarketing refers to direct marketing conducted entirely by telephone. It is the most frequently used form of direct marketing. It provides marketers with a high return on their expenditures, an immediate response, and the opportunity for personalized two-way conversations. Telemarketing is discussed in further detail in Chapter 17.

INTERNET RETAILING

Internet-based retailers sell directly to customers via virtual storefronts on the Web. They usually maintain little or no inventory, ordering directly from vendors to fill customer orders received via their Web sites. In recent years, conventional retailers have anxiously watched the rise—and then the demise—of many poorly planned, financed, and marketed Internet-based retailers. During the dot-com bust, 130 e-tailers failed. Even early successes such as Ezshop, an online home furnishings retailer, eventually ran aground. Traditional retailers, using the Web to support brick-and-mortar stores—the so-called *brick-and-click retailers*—have had much better staying power. The Gap, Best Buy, and Lands' End, for example, succeeded in extending their expertise to the Web. Office Max offers thousands of office supply products on its Web site, which also offers e-mail alerts, favorite-item lists, and a customer loyalty program.[42] Chapter 4 discussed Internet retailing and other forms of e-commerce in more detail.

Although consumers worldwide often use vending machines for fast-food service, U.S. chains and customers have been reluctant to adopt kiosks for their quick meals.

© ASSOCIATED PRESS, AP

AUTOMATIC MERCHANDISING

The world's first vending machines dispensed holy water for five-drachma coins in Egyptian temples around 215 B.C. This retailing method has grown rapidly ever since; today, nearly 6,000 vending machine operators sell more than $7 billion in convenience goods annually to Americans.[43]

Although U.S. vending machines have traditionally been limited to snacks, soft drinks, and lottery tickets, Japanese consumers use automatic merchandising for everything including fresh sushi and new underwear. Recently, U.S. marketers have begun to realize the potential of this under-used marketing tool. Organic yogurt and smoothie marketer Stonyfield

Farms is helping schools install "Healthy Vending Machines" as alternatives for kids.[44] The three major soft-drink companies recently agreed to remove sweetened drinks such as soda and iced tea from vending machines in elementary and high schools nationwide. The calorie-laden drinks will be replaced by bottled water, low-fat milk, and 100 percent fruit juice or sports drinks.[45] As technological advances and credit card payments make it easier to sell high-cost items, even iPods are being sold from vending machines, in airports in Atlanta, San Francisco, and other cities.[46]

 assessment check

1. Describe Internet–based retailers.
2. Explain how the Internet has enhanced retailers' functions.

Strategic Implications of Marketing in the 21st Century

As the Internet revolution steadily becomes a way of life—both for consumers and for the businesses marketing goods and services to them—technology will continue to transform the ways in which retailers, wholesalers, and direct marketers connect with customers.

In the retail sector, the unstoppable march toward lower prices has forced retailers from Neiman Marcus to dollar stores to re-evaluate everything including their logistics and supply networks and their profit margins. Many have used the power of the Internet to strengthen such factors as store image, the merchandising mix, customer service, and the development of long-term relationships with customers.

Although manufacturers first anticipated that Internet technology would enable them to bypass such intermediaries as wholesalers and agents, bringing them closer to the customer, the reality is quite different. Successful wholesalers have established themselves as essential links in the supply, distribution, and customer service network. By leveraging technology, they have carved out new roles, providing such expert services as warehousing and fulfillment to multiple retail clients.

The Internet has empowered direct marketers by facilitating ever more sophisticated database segmentation. Traditional catalog and direct-mail marketers have integrated Internet sites, Web advertising, and e-mailing programs into a cohesive targeting, distribution, and repeat-buying strategy.

REVIEW OF CHAPTER OBJECTIVES

1 Explain the wheel of retailing.

The wheel of retailing is the hypothesis that each new type of retailer gains a competitive foothold by offering lower prices than current suppliers and maintains profits by reducing or eliminating services. Once established, the innovator begins to add more services, and its prices gradually rise, making it vulnerable to new low-price retailers. This turns the wheel again.

2 Discuss how retailers select target markets.

A retailer starts to define its strategy by selecting a target market. The target market dictates, among other things, the product mix, pricing strategy, and location strategy. Retailers deal with consumer behavior at the most complicated level, and a clear understanding of the target market is critical. Strategies for selecting target markets include merchandising, customer services, pricing, location/distribution, and promotional strategies.

3   Show how the elements of the marketing mix apply to retailing strategy.

A retailer must first identify a target market and then develop a product strategy. Next, it must establish a customer-service strategy. Retail pricing strategy involves decisions on markups and markdowns. Location is often the determining factor in a retailer's success or failure. A retailer's promotional strategy and store atmosphere play important roles in establishing a store's image.

4   Explain the concepts of retail convergence and scrambled merchandising.

Retail convergence is the coming together of shoppers, goods, and prices, resulting in the blurring of distinctions between types of retailers and the merchandise mix they offer. Similar selections are available from multiple sources and are differentiated mainly by price. Scrambled merchandising refers to retailers' practice of carrying dissimilar product lines in an attempt to generate additional sales volume. Retail convergence and scrambled merchandising have made it increasingly difficult to classify retailers.

5   Identify the functions performed by wholesaling intermediaries.

The functions of wholesaling intermediaries include creating utility, providing services, and lowering costs by limiting contacts.

6   Outline the major types of independent wholesaling intermediaries and the appropriate situations for using each.

Independent wholesaling intermediaries can be divided into two categories: merchant wholesalers and agents and brokers. The two major types of merchant wholesalers are full-function merchant wholesalers, such as rack jobbers, and limited-function merchant wholesalers, including cash-and-carry wholesalers, truck wholesalers, drop shippers, and mail-order wholesalers. Full-function wholesalers are common in the drug, grocery, and hardware industries.

Limited-function wholesalers are sometimes used in the food, coal, lumber, cosmetics, jewelry, sporting goods, and general-merchandise industries. Agents and brokers do not take title to the products they sell; this category includes commission merchants, auction houses, brokers, selling agents, and manufacturers' reps. Companies seeking to develop new sales territories, firms with unrelated lines, and smaller firms use manufacturers' reps. Commission merchants are common in the marketing of agricultural products. Auction houses are used to sell tobacco, used cars, livestock, furs, and fruit. Brokers are prevalent in the real estate, frozen foods, and used-machinery industries.

7   Compare the basic types of direct marketing and nonstore retailing.

Direct marketing is a distribution channel consisting of direct communication to a consumer or business recipient. It generates orders and sales leads that may result in future orders. Because direct marketing responds to fragmented media markets and audiences, growth of customized products, and shrinking network broadcast audiences, marketers consider it an important part of their planning efforts. While most U.S. retail sales take place in stores, such nonstore retailing activities as direct mail, direct selling, direct-response retailing, telemarketing, Internet retailing, and automatic merchandising are important in marketing many types of goods and services.

8   Describe how much the Internet has altered the wholesaling, retailing, and direct marketing environments.

The Internet has affected everything including how supply networks operate and how relationships are formed with customers. Successful wholesalers have carved out a niche as a source of expertise offering faster, more efficient, Web-enabled distribution and fulfillment. The Internet has allowed retailers to enhance their merchandising mix and their customer service by, among other things, giving them access to much broader selections of goods. Direct marketers have merged their traditional catalog or direct-mail programs with an Internet interface that allows for faster, more efficient, and more frequent contact with customers and prospects.

assessment check **answers**

1.1   What is retailing?

Retailing describes the activities involved in selling merchandise to ultimate consumers.

1.2   Explain the wheel-of-retailing concept.

The wheel of retailing is the hypothesis that each new type of retailer gains a competitive foothold by offering lower prices than current suppliers and maintains profits by reducing or eliminating services.

2.1   How does a retailer develop a marketing strategy?

A retailer develops a marketing strategy based on its goals and strategic plans.

2.2   How do retailers select target markets?

Strategies for selecting target markets include merchandising, customer services, pricing, location/distribution, and promotional strategies.

3.1   What is an SKU?

An SKU or stock-keeping unit is a specific product offering within a product line.

3.2   What are the two components of a markup?

A markup consists of the product's cost and an amount added by the retailer to determine its selling price.

3.3   What are store atmospherics?

Store atmospherics are physical characteristics and amenities that attract customers and satisfy their shopping needs.

4.1   How do we classify retailers by form of ownership?

There are two types of retailers by form of ownership: chain stores and independent retailers.

4.2   Categorize retailers by shopping effort and by services provided.

Convenience retailers and specialty retailers are classified by shopping effort; self-service, self-selection, and full-service describe retailers in terms of services provided.

4.3   List several ways to classify retailers by product line.

Retailers classified by product line include specialty stores, limited-line retailers, and general-merchandise retailers. General-merchandise retailers include variety stores, department stores, and mass merchandisers.

5.1   What is a wholesaler? How does it differ from a wholesaling intermediary?

A wholesaler is a channel intermediary that takes title to goods it handles and then distributes these goods to retailers, other distributors, or B2B customers. A wholesaling intermediary can be a wholesaler, an agent, or a broker and perform wholesaling activities without taking title to the goods.

5.2   How do wholesaling intermediaries help sellers lower costs?

Wholesaling intermediaries lower the number of transactions between manufacturers and retail outlets, thus lowering distribution costs.

6.1   What is the difference between a merchant wholesaler and a rack jobber?

A merchant wholesaler takes title to the goods it handles. A rack jobber is a full-function merchant wholesaler that markets specialized lines of merchandise to retailers.

assessment check **answers**

6.2   Differentiate between agents and brokers.

Agents and brokers may or may not take possession of the goods they handle but they never take title. Brokers work mainly to bring together buyers and sellers. A selling agent typically exerts full authority over pricing decisions and promotional outlays and often provides financial assistance for the manufacturer.

7.1   What is direct marketing?

Direct marketing is a distribution channel consisting of direct communication to a consumer or business recipient. It generates orders and sales leads that may result in future orders.

7.2   What is direct mail?

Direct mail is a form of direct marketing that includes sales letters, postcards, brochures, booklets, catalogs, house organs, and video- and audiocassettes.

8.1   Describe Internet-based retailers.

Internet-based retailers sell directly to customers via virtual storefronts on the Web. They usually maintain little or no inventory, ordering directly from vendors to fill customers' orders.

8.2   Explain how the Internet has enhanced retailers' functions.

The Internet has allowed retailers to enhance their merchandising mix and their customer service by, among other things, giving them access to much broader selections of goods. Direct marketers have merged their traditional catalog or direct-mail programs with an Internet interface that allows for faster, more efficient, and more frequent contact with customers and prospects.

MARKETING TERMS YOU NEED TO KNOW

retailing 450

wheel of retailing 451

stock-keeping unit (SKU) 453

markup 455

markdown 455

planned shopping center 456

atmospherics 459

retail convergence 465

scrambled merchandising 466

wholesaler 466

wholesaling intermediary 466

broker 471

manufacturers' representative 471

direct marketing 472

OTHER IMPORTANT MARKETING TERMS

convenience retailer 461

specialty retailer 461

limited-line store 463

category killer 463

general-merchandise retailer 463

department store 464

mass merchandiser 464

discount house 464

hypermarket 465

supercenter 465

merchant wholesaler 469

rack jobber 470

truck wholesaler (truck jobber) 470

drop shipper 470

mail-order wholesaler 470

commission merchant 470

selling agent 471

ASSURANCE OF LEARNING REVIEW

1. Find some examples of retailers that demonstrate the concept of the wheel of retailing. Explain the stages they went through and are in currently.
2. How do retailers identify target markets? Explain the major strategies by which retailers reach their target markets.
3. Explain the importance of a retailer's location to its strategy.
4. What is retail convergence?
5. Define *scrambled merchandising*. Why has this practice become so common in retailing?
6. What is a wholesaling intermediary? Describe the activities it performs.
7. Distinguish among the different types of manufacturer-owned wholesaling intermediaries. What conditions might suit each one?
8. Differentiate between direct selling and direct-response retailing. Cite examples of both.
9. In what ways has the Internet changed direct-response retailing?
10. Define *automatic merchandising* and explain its role in U.S. retailing today and in the future.

PROJECTS AND TEAMWORK EXERCISES

1. Research and then classify each of the following retailers:
   a. Circuit City
   b. Petite Sophisticate
   c. Limited
   d. Ethan Allen Galleries
   e. Dillard's
2. Visit a local Wal-Mart store and observe such aspects as product placement, shelf placement, inventory levels on shelves, traffic patterns, customer service, and checkout efficiency. Discuss what makes Wal-Mart the world's most successful retailer.
3. Target has become known for trendy clothes and stylish housewares, all readily available in spacious stores at reasonable prices. Visit a local Target store or the company's Web site and compare its product selection to that of your local hardware store and/or a department store. Make a list of each store's advantages and disadvantages, including convenience, location, selection, service, and general prices. Do any of their product lines overlap? How are they different from each other?
4. Match each industry with the most appropriate type of wholesaling intermediary.

_____ hardware	a. drop shipper
_____ perishable foods	b. truck wholesaler
_____ lumber	c. auction house
_____ wheat	d. full-function merchant wholesaler
_____ used cars	e. commission merchant

5. In teams, develop a retailing strategy for an Internet retailer. Identify a target market and then suggest a mix of merchandise, promotion, service, and pricing strategies that would help a retailer reach that market via the Internet. What issues must Internet retailers address that do not affect traditional store retailers?
6. With a classmate, visit two or three retail stores that compete with one another in your area and compare their customer service strategies. (You might wish to visit each store more than once to avoid making a snap judgment.) Select at least five criteria and use them to assess each store. How do you think each store sees its customer service strategy as fitting into its overall retailing strategy? Present your findings in detail to the class.
7. Visit a department store and compare at least two departments' pricing strategies based on the number of markdowns you find and the size of the discount. What, if anything, can you conclude about the success of each department's retailing strategy?
8. Think of a large purchase you make on a nonroutine basis, such as a new winter coat or expensive clothing for a special occasion. Where will you shop for such items? Will you travel out of your way? Will you go to the nearest shopping center? Will you look on the Internet? Once you have made your decision, describe any strategies used by the retailer that led you to this decision. What might make you change your mind about where to shop for this item?
9. Outlet malls are a growing segment of the retail market. Visit a local outlet mall or research one on the Internet. What types of stores are located there? How do the product selection and price compare with typical stores?
10. Torrid is a national chain of about 50 stores that feature clothing for plus-size women. Recommend an appropriate retailing strategy for this type of retailer.

CRITICAL-THINKING EXERCISES

1. Talbots made its name as a retailer of classic sportswear for women, but it has recently expanded its target market to include men and children. Men, however, typically don't enjoy shopping for clothes, and children shop with their parents. Visit http://www.talbots.com and assess how well Talbots is reaching men through its Web site. Do you think Talbots' target market is still women who shop for the men in their lives? Why or why not? How can Talbots widen its appeal on the Internet?

2. Several major retailers have begun to test the extreme markdown strategy that lies behind popular "dollar" stores such as Dollar General and Family Dollar Stores. Kroger, A&P, and Wal-Mart are all opening sections in selected stores that feature items from snacks to beauty supplies priced at $1. Is this experiment simply a test of pricing strategy? What else might motivate these retailers to offer such deep discounts?

3. When Tower Records filed for bankruptcy, it was only one symptom of the general decline of the retail music store. Industry watchers blame everything including music downloading programs and changes in consumers' tastes. Most, however, feel that music stores will somehow remain viable. What are some changes that these retailers could make in their merchandising, customer service, pricing, location, and other strategies to try to reinvent their business?

4. McDonald's has traditionally relied on a cookie-cutter approach to its restaurant design. One store looked essentially like every other—until recently. The chain has decided to loosen its corporate design mandate to fit within special markets and to update its image with customers. Research McDonald's makeover efforts. What types of changes has the company made and where? How have changes in atmospherics helped the chain with customers? Have the changes you researched modified your perception of McDonald's at all? If so, how?

ETHICS EXERCISE

As the largest company in the world, with more than a million employees worldwide and nearly $320 billion in sales in a recent year, Wal-Mart has become big and powerful enough to influence the U.S. economy. It is responsible for 10 percent of total U.S. imports from China and for about 12 percent of U.S. productivity gains since the late 1990s. Some observers believe Wal-Mart is also responsible for the low U.S. inflation rates of recent years. However, its unbeatable buying power and efficiency have forced many local stores to close when Wal-Mart opens a new store in their area.

1. Some economists fear what might happen to the U.S. economy if Wal-Mart has a bad year (so far it has had more than four decades of nonstop growth). Should retailers have that much influence on the economy? Why or why not?

2. Wal-Mart is selective about what it sells—refusing, for instance, to carry music or computer games with mature ratings, magazines with content that it considers too adult, or a popular morning-after pill. Because of its sheer size, these decisions can become influential in the culture. Do you think this is a positive or negative effect of the growth of this retailer? Why?

INTERNET EXERCISES

1. **Retailing strategy.** Visit the Web site of electronics retailer Best Buy (http://www.bestbuy.com). The Web site is classified as a shopping site, or online store. Review the material in the chapter on retailing strategy and store atmospherics. Answer the following questions.
   a. How does the design and layout of the Best Buy Web store appeal to the company's target market(s)?
   b. How would you describe the atmospherics created by the online store? If you can visit a brick-and-mortar store, compare the store's atmospherics to the Web store.
   c. In what ways does Best Buy use its online store to enhance its brick-and-mortar stores?

2. **Retailing statistics.** The U.S. Census Bureau reports regularly on U.S. retail sales. Visit the Bureau's Web site (http://www.census.gov) do a search for "Retail Sales," and answer the following questions:
   a. What is the current level of retail sales in the United States? By how much have retail sales increased during the past year?
   b. Which categories of retail sales are growing the fastest? Which categories are growing the slowest?
   c. Do you see any evidence of a seasonal pattern in retail sales? In which categories does the seasonal pattern appear strongest? Describe any seasonal patterns you find.

Note: Internet Web addresses change frequently. If you don't find the exact site listed, you may need to access the organization's home page and search from there or use a search engine such as Google.

CASE 14.1 Grocery Chains Shop for the Right Retail Strategy

Now that Wal-Mart has become the largest grocery chain in the United States, with sales of $115 billion in one recent year—roughly double those of Kroger, its nearest competitor—the nation's other grocers are pulling out all the stops to remain competitive with the giant, low-price retailer. Kroger itself, which has more than 2,500 stores under several different names, is relying on customer loyalty programs and a broad product mix. Kroger customers can rack up gift points on a special MasterCard or qualify for a frequent-shopper gasoline discount. In some outlets they can pick up a television or some deck furniture along with milk and eggs, while Kroger's "Marketplace" stores offer office supplies and fine jewelry. Those looking for specialty foods can find them in Kroger's Fresh Fare markets, which are concentrated in California, while low-price shoppers browse its Food4Less stores for no-frills, warehouse-style grocery shopping.

Piggly Wiggly stores are investing in sensors that use fingerprint recognition technology to trigger payments from the customer's bank account or credit card. Bloom supermarkets offer hand-held scanners that customers can use to check out items as they shop, stopping at a checkout station where the total has already been calculated. On the low-tech front, Bloom is also promoting a Recipe of the Week at the front of the store and offering 20-minute parking just outside for those who want to use the supermarket as a convenience store. Managers give out their business cards and respond to e-mail, and employees are instructed to form friendly relationships with the regular shoppers.

And just in case there aren't enough supermarket chains in the picture, Tesco, the grocery powerhouse from Britain and the world's fifth-largest retailer, is spending more than $4.5 million on a chain of minisupermarkets to open on the West Coast. Tesco's midsized food marts will compete against all the established U.S. grocers, as well as Home Depot's new gas station/convenience stores, an expanded U.S. roster of Canada's Circle K stores, and an aggressive upgrading of existing convenience stores run by industry leader 7-Eleven, now owned by a Japanese firm. Observers say Tesco is likely to try to make its name by relying on high-tech conveniences, such as the ability to order groceries via cell phone, which British shoppers already enjoy.

In the meantime, Wal-Mart is challenging Kroger on its own turf by opening Supercenters in Ohio, Kentucky, and Indiana. The retail giant is also moving aggressively into yet another food market—the organic-foods market, in which stores such as Whole Foods Market and Trader Joe's have reigned until now. Whole Foods is expected to reposition itself as a low-cost purveyor of traditionally expensive organic and specialty foods in response to Wal-Mart's entry.

Questions for Critical Thinking

1. One retail expert says that because it's planning to locate where Wal-Mart has a relatively small presence, "Tesco is beating them to the punch" in California. Do you agree? How important is location in retailing, and why?

2. "The Krogers of this world are working very hard to create a reason to shop in the traditional supermarkets," said a food industry consultant. "It's about food. It's about what's for dinner tonight. It's about ease of shopping." Wal-Mart, however, competes on price. What do you think grocery shoppers are really looking for? How can Wal-Mart's competitors provide it?

Sources: Dan Sewell, "Grocery Titans Clash in Ohio," *The Morning News,* June 4, 2006, pp. 1D, 6D; Michael Barbaro, "Whole Foods Talks Dollars and Cents," *New York Times,* May 10, 2006, **http://www.nytimes.com**; Kerry Capell, "Tesco: California Dreaming?" *BusinessWeek,* February 27, 2006, p. 38; Dan Sewell, "Grocers Look beyond Mere Aisles," *The Morning News,* December 2, 2005, p. 4D; Blake Eskin, "LCD in Aisle Three," *U.S. News & World Report,* August 15–22, 2005, pp. 67–68.

VIDEO CASE 14.2 BP Connects with Drivers

The written video case on BP appears on page VC-17. The recently filmed BP video is designed to expand and highlight the concepts in this chapter and the concepts and questions covered in the written video case.

Talking about Marketing Careers with. . .

RICHARD YOO
SENIOR DIRECTOR, GLOBAL MENU
MANAGEMENT
MCDONALD'S CORPORATION

The Golden Arches are one of the most recognized brand marks in the world. McDonald's Corporation holds a unique—and enviable—place in the quick-service food retailing industry. The firm is a global leader, with more than 32,000 local restaurants serving nearly 50 million people daily in 118 countries around the world. But McDonald's built its reputation by serving one customer at a time, and it still focuses on the local aspect of its business through strong relationships with its owner/operators, suppliers, and employees.

Key to the chain's success is its emphasis on adapting to local tastes and customs—to serve the needs of its many markets. Here today to talk with us about McDonald's retail strategy and its global supply chain is Richard Yoo, Senior Director, Global Menu Management.

Q: Richard, McDonald's is a true global corporation with worldwide reach. Working for such a visible firm must be both challenging and satisfying. What milestones in your education and career led

you to your current position with one of the world's top brands?

A: It truly is a privilege to work on a brand that has global reach and touches the hearts, minds, (and appetites!) of so many people everyday. My overall approach to problem solving has been shaped by both my liberal arts training at the University of Michigan (BA in English) and my formal business school training at the University of Notre Dame (MBA). I like to think of my education as a powerful combination of right-brain and left-brain development. From a career perspective, my path has taken a similar path in that I started as a brand management generalist and now specialize in product innovation. My marketing experiences in the toy industry (at LEGO) and in retail food (Kraft Foods, Keebler Company) have built a solid foundation of general management skills and also led to my interest in and passion for new product development/product innovation. From my point of view, the on-the-job influence, a creative approach to problem solving, collaboration with other functional areas, and value-based leadership have been important career drivers for me.

Q: Overseeing global menu choices is a huge undertaking for such a large restaurant chain. What is involved in planning and adapting menus for different countries? What types of team members at the corporate and local level help suggest and select menu choices? How does the process work?

A: The process is a collaborative effort, and generally speaking, our development process consists of three stages: discovery, development, and deployment. During the discovery stage, we develop consumer insights; monitor culinary, technology, and cultural trends; collect competitive intelligence; and brainstorm. These ideas are made more powerful by involving cross-functional teams at our home office and collaborating with our Menu Centers of Excellence and our suppliers. These centers

are THE development hubs in Latin America, Europe, Asia, and North America that do the heavy lifting of taking Menu Strategies and ideas and bringing them to life for consumers. It is at this stage that broader food platforms are made locally relevant by developing and testing products that have components that sing at the country level, and that can be executed well in our restaurants to delight our guests.

Q: Students read in this text about the importance of selecting the right target markets. What proportion of your corporation's sales come from global operations? How does your firm decide which markets to enter? Is it still expanding into new countries?

A: At this time, roughly half of our sales are generated outside the U.S. As you might expect, the decision to enter a market is driven by a number of factors. Since 2003, our focus has shifted from growth via new restaurants to growth by serving more customers in our existing restaurants.

Q: Local partners—people who can help bring a firm's marketing vision to life—are critical to a global business such as yours. Because nearly 85 percent of McDonald's restaurants are locally owned and operated, your firm relies heavily on its owner/operators to "localize" the brand. How do their efforts contribute to the success of the firm? What contribution do employees make?

A: Our franchisees are clearly a key pillar of our business. Their energy and passion are critical to our growth and brand sustainability. We engage them in almost every facet of our business. The local store marketing plans that they create and execute bring the corporate vision to life in their respective communities. Our managers and crew are our brand ambassadors and are the key element in delivering our brand promise of uncompromised QSC and V (quality, service, cleanliness and value) to every customer. QSC and V was the foundational operating philosophy of Ray Kroc and still is today.

Q: Suppliers of food and other restaurant products must be critical to the quality of McDonald's menu items. Are your suppliers local or global—or a mix? What efficiencies can your firm achieve by having global operations?

A: We've developed a coordinated supply chain "engine" that provides the ability to leverage global trade dynamics and drive efficiencies at the local level. From food and paper products to media buys, this engine, complemented by our scale and our commitment to social responsibility, is one of our competitive advantages. Wherever possible, we do purchase locally in the countries where we do business.

Q: In the past few years, McDonald's has shifted its marketing strategy to fit the needs of today's health- and quality-conscious but time-pressed consumer. Can you tell us a little bit about the changes featured in the "i'm lovin' it" campaign and the firm's Plan to Win strategy? How do you get the message out to the public? Does this effort extend to global operations, too?

A: "i'm lovin' it"™ is our brand attitude and spirit. It celebrates real people, real passions, and real stories around the globe. The campaign will shift focus from the "i" (consumer-centric stories) to the "it" (the reasons why consumers love their McDonald's experiences). Our customers have told us what "it" is—it is our food. It is the moments they share at our restaurants and the feelings they get before, during, and after they visit McDonald's. We are putting the "it" in "i'm lovin' it." We are also deepening our relationships by connecting customers with the facts about our brand—our food, our people, and our values.

Our Plan to Win Strategy is all about delivering a delightful experience to our customers by creating strategies for and executing the key pillars of our business: People, Product, Promotion, Place, and Price. Since the Plan to Win was implemented in 2003, our business results have been robust.

Q: Many students today are interested in running their own businesses. One of their career paths might involve running a franchise, such as a McDonald's restaurant. What types of educational experiences, training, or internships might help students get a foothold in your industry or advance their marketing career?

A: I often coach students to seek out their career sweet spot, where passion meets capability, and to not necessarily chase a career for the money, prestige, or perks but because you LOVE the content, the people, and the brand. Everything else has a way of falling into place along the way. I'm also a big fan of broad-based curricula, complemented by specialized "trade content" because a balanced thinker who knows how to connect and collaborate is an effective one.

Laughter Coming Your Way

The Second City uses a variety of marketing channels to distribute its product. Whether at the local theater, on the high seas or for a corporate conference, The Second City provides a direct service to its customer. Strategic distribution is essential for making the SC product conveniently available. By using a variety of channels, The Second City increases its accessibility and its utility as a company. Its distribution aids, fashions, and facilitates its product marketing. A tourist who witnesses Second City's flair for off-the-cuff humor may be inclined to hire its Communications division for a business event. So Second City's distribution and marketing departments function as reciprocally related partners.

The Second City operates five different theaters across North America in Chicago, Toronto, Detroit, Denver, and Las Vegas. These locations were chosen largely because they access SC's largest market, the tourist population. Decorated in photos of famous alumni and Second City memorabilia, they project their legacy as a comedic fixture of the entertainment industry. By distributing Second City's product across the country they allow a greater number of consumers to experience it. But The Second City is a small enough company that distribution across the continent presents managerial challenges. To meet the localized needs of its theaters, SC uses different ownership practices for different locations. SC Detroit, for instance, is marketed vertically as the company's only franchise. The Las Vegas theatre is a partnership designed to attract tourists off the glitzy, yet beaten path. Second City Denver is a community-based endeavor working closely with the Denver Center for the Performing Arts. The first two locations, Chicago and Toronto, are the only Second City theaters fully owned by three shareholders who work closely within theater operations.

Lou Carbone, Second City's chief financial officer, says that SC does not have plans to open another theater in the near future. SC's current focus is on finding more innovative ways to dually distribute its comedy far and wide with multiple product lines and services. Second City Theatricals performs classic and new material for a variety of performing arts centers and private events. It often produces shows for youth or traditional theater going audiences to distribute the brand as a specialized product line. It recently joined forces with the Steppenwolf Theater, in which a SC Theatricals production will be represented by the highly acclaimed Chicago venue. SC Theatricals also spawned SC's partnership with Norwegian Cruise Lines. The Second City is exclusively distributed to its target tourist market with full-time companies performing on four NCL ships.

Since the mid 1990s The Second City has produced shows in such locations as Scotland, Vienna, Saudi Arabia, Tokyo, and Hong Kong. These international endeavors are often contractual marketing agreements with organizations that temporarily house a Second City touring company. In America, Second City's national touring company focuses on the nation's college campuses and performing arts centers. By distributing internationally the Second City acquires unique promotion and global awareness. In the United States, its touring companies attract the textbook-reading, socially conscious college population looking for an entertaining study break.

The Second City similarly distributes its brand to the youth and technically adept market through the Internet. Second City Chicago's musical director, Ruby Streak, hosts a weekly podcast called *We'll Be Right Back. Second City Radio,* which was broadcast from Chicago's WCKG-FM and featured current cast and alumni of The Second City, is also offered on the Second City Web site. Video clips from a variety of former SC productions are showcased next to interviews of famous SC alumni. Secondcity .com also features volumes of Second City Television for purchase. *SCTV* was the company's most acclaimed television distribution venture. Launching a variety of impressive careers and securing the brand name throughout the continent, SCTV distribution continues as a company commodity nearly 20 years after production ended.

For Second City Communications, however, the product is customized and sold directly to the buyer. SC Communications offers services in the form of learning and development, event support, entertainment, or video production. Over the last fifteen years, SC Communications has worked with more than 400 *Fortune* 1000 companies. Whether answering Wal-Mart's call to develop an Emmyesque event celebration, or celebrating a lucrative year for Acura with the help of alumnus Martin Short, SC Communications distributes its product directly by addressing the needs of the client. It links the communicative power of improvisation with the corporate need for agility, teamwork and innovation. Its marketing channel is selected by designing the products (and services) to be competitive in the industry. As a result, SC Communications is routinely sought out by businesses for consultation. "People pay us because we're good," SC Communication's Web site declares. It has marketed its product/service throughout the business channel. It has become Second City's most lucrative division and has blazed a trail in an important new market.

Customers of The Second City may see a show only once in their lifetime. They may routinely check out podcasts on the Web site, see a couple of touring company shows in college, or call on Second City Communications to spice up an otherwise stale sales conference for their company. By selecting a variety of distribution channels, The Second City makes its product available to a broad spectrum of consumers. They have excelled as a convenient, unique service provider in the entertainment industry.

Questions

1. Why might The Second City not look to develop more fixed stages in the near future?
2. What is The Second City's location/distribution strategy? How do atmospherics play a role in the company?
3. Name three marketing channels that The Second City has selected. How and Why does it distribute its product in this way?
4. How has Second City Theatricals developed an innovative approach to distribution and marketing?

PART 6

Promotional Decisions

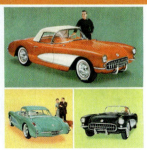

CHEVROLET UNLEASHES THE NEW CORVETTE

CORVETTE by Chevrolet

New with 4-wheel disc brakes
'65 CORVETTE

'73 CORVETTE

We gave it radials, a quieter ride, guard beams and a nose job.

Building a better way to see the U.S.A.

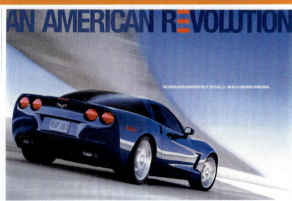

AN AMERICAN REVOLUTION

CHAPTER 15

Gillette Fuses Its Marketing Communications

Razor burn and shaving nicks may soon be history. They will be if Gillette marketers can spread the word to consumers about the firm's new, five-blade Fusion razor. To reach potential customers, Gillette is making sure you'll see the Fusion just about everywhere you go. Naturally, you'll find one if you happen to be in the shaving aisle at the supermarket or drugstore. But you could pick one up in the beer aisle as well—you never know when you might need to shave for an upcoming party. And you might also notice a display in the checkout at a sporting-goods store. If you happened to be in Detroit for a recent Super Bowl, you could have received a free shave before the game. If you weren't there but were glued to the TV for the game, you were exposed to the Fusion commercials dubbed "The Miracle

of Shaving." If you stay up to watch David Letterman—and you're a Ben Roethlisberger fan—you could have watched the late-night talk show host shave the Steelers quarterback's beard on TV. Say you don't watch football but like to head to a NASCAR track; you'll be greeted by Fusion promotions, too. If you are a Hispanic consumer, Gillette has you covered—on the Hispanic networks. All of these strategic placements and information sources are provided in addition to the obvious advertising venues—magazines such as *Sports Illustrated* and *Men's Health*. And if you want to learn more about the Fusion before you shop, you can visit its interactive Web page at Gillettefusion.com.

Gillette, which is owned by Procter & Gamble, is engaged in a well-planned marketing campaign to communicate the message about Fusion through a variety of media and methods, even if the choices seem a little unusual. But the campaign makes sense. "We just want trial," explains Pauline Munroe, marketing director for blades and razors for Gillette. "We're trying to put the product wherever men shop." Gillette marketers believe that if men try the Fusion, which is packed with new shaving technology, they will become loyal users.

The firm wants to develop demand for its new razor in every way possible. In a highly competitive market, this means differentiating the Fusion from competing products such as Schick's Quattro razor. In addition to the five blades—no other razor has that many—Gillette designers placed the blades closer together, which reduces skin irritation. The Fusion

Integrated Marketing Communications

Chapter Objectives

1 Explain how integrated marketing communications relates to the development of an optimal promotional mix.

2 Describe the communication process and how it relates to the AIDA concept.

3 Explain how the promotional mix relates to the objectives of promotion.

4 Identify the different elements of the promotional mix and explain how marketers develop an optimal promotional mix.

5 Describe the role of sponsorships and direct marketing in integrated marketing communications.

6 Discuss the factors that influence the effectiveness of a promotional mix.

7 Contrast pushing and pulling strategies.

8 Explain how marketers budget for and measure the effectiveness of promotion.

9 Discuss the value of marketing communications.

blades have a smoother coating than others, with a strip containing vitamin E and skin-soothing aloe. In addition, the design is high-tech. "The razor does have a futuristic feel and look to it, so we wanted the ads to convey that, too," says Alfred Merrin of the agency that created the Fusion ads.

Although the Fusion may seem to be a luxury grooming purchase—at an initial purchase price of $10 for a kit containing the razor and two replaceable blade cartridges and another $12 for four more replacements—Gillette is emphasizing the value of the purchase over time. For a man who shaves every day, the Fusion should cost only about $50 per year.

Gillette tested the Fusion against its own Mach3 and Schick's Quattro on 9,000 men, and the feedback was positive. "[Participants] preferred Fusion by a 2-to-1 margin over its rivals," claims Peter Hoffman, president of Gillette's blades and razors division. By developing demand for the Fusion, Gillette marketers hope also to increase demand for

its companion products, such as shaving cream and aftershave. In fact, the firm is so confident of Fusion's success that it is launching new related grooming prod-

ucts. "Fusion will get so much attention that it will drive a lot of men to try these grooming products," predicts one consultant.[1]

evolution *of a* brand

Gillette knows how to build and market razors. In many respects, the Fusion follows in the footsteps of its highly successful Gillette predecessor, the Mach3. Launched in 1998, the Mach3 quickly became the leader in men's shavers, despite its higher price tag. The Fusion is poised to make the same move, demonstrating Gillette's expertise in creating a successful brand.

- Consider how the individual pieces of Gillette's marketing plan attempt to achieve dominance in the marketplace. The company is trying to be sure that every male consumer who shaves gets the message about the Fusion. They see it wherever they are likely to buy other products and in entertainment venues that are typically male dominated, such as the Super Bowl and NASCAR events. Where else could the company promote its Fusion? Make a list that you think would be useful to Gillette marketers. Do you think Gillette should get the message to women as well—so they will think of the Fusion line when they purchase shaving and grooming products for husbands, sons, and boyfriends?

- Gillette also introduced a battery-powered Fusion at the same time it debuted its manual model.

Chapter Overview

Two of the four components of the marketing mix—product and distribution strategies—were discussed in previous chapters. The three chapters in Part 6 analyze the third marketing mix variable—promotion. **Promotion** is the function of informing, persuading, and influencing the consumer's purchase decision.

This chapter introduces the concept of integrated marketing communications, briefly describes the elements of a firm's promotional mix—personal and nonpersonal selling—and explains the characteristics that determine the success of the mix. Next, we identify the objectives of promotion and describe the importance of developing promotional budgets and measuring the effectiveness of promotion. Finally, we discuss the importance of the busi-

ness, economic, and social aspects of promotion. Chapter 16 covers advertising, public relations, and other nonpersonal selling elements of the promotional mix, including sponsorships and guerrilla advertising. Chapter 17 completes this part of the book by focusing on personal selling and sales promotion.

Throughout *Contemporary Marketing,* special emphasis has been given to new information that shows how technology is changing the way marketers approach *communication,* the transmission of a message from a sender to a receiver. Consumers receive **marketing communications**—messages that deal with buyer–seller relationships—from a variety of media, including television, radio, magazines, direct mail, the Internet, and cell phones. Marketers can broadcast an ad on the Web to mass markets or design a customized appeal targeted to a small market segment. Each message the customer receives from any source represents the brand, company, or

organization. A company needs to coordinate all these messages for maximum total impact and to reduce the likelihood that the consumer will completely tune them out.

To prevent this loss of attention, marketers are turning to **integrated marketing communications (IMC),** which coordinates all promotional activities—media advertising, direct mail, personal selling, sales promotion, public relations, and sponsorships—to produce a unified, customer-focused promotional message. As you saw in the opening story, Gillette uses IMC to get the message out about its Fusion razor. IMC is a broader concept than marketing communications and promotional strategy. It uses database technology to refine the marketer's understanding of the target audience, segment this audience, and select the best type of media for each segment.

This chapter shows that IMC involves not only the marketer but also all other organizational units that interact with the consumer. Market-

Briefly
Speaking

"When I started college, I think I was good at two things: arguing and asking questions."

—Karen Hughes (b. 1956)
U.S. undersecretary of state for public diplomacy and public affairs

---

promotion Communication link between buyers and sellers; the function of informing, persuading, and influencing a consumer's purchase decision.

marketing communications Messages that deal with buyer–seller relationships.

integrated marketing communications (IMC) Coordination of all promotional activities to produce a unified, customer-focused promotional message.

ing managers set the goals and objectives of the firm's promotional strategy in accordance with overall organizational objectives and marketing goals. Based on these objectives, the various elements of the promotional strategy—personal selling, advertising, sales promotion, direct marketing, publicity, and public relations—are formulated into an integrated communications plan. This plan becomes a central part of the firm's total marketing strategy to reach its selected market segments. The feedback mechanism, including marketing research and field reports, completes the system by identifying any deviations from the plan and suggesting improvements.

INTEGRATED MARKETING COMMUNICATIONS

1 Explain how integrated marketing communications relates to the development of an optimal promotional mix.

Stop and think for a moment about all the marketing messages you receive in a single day. You click on the television for the morning news, and you see plenty of commercials. Listen to the car radio on the way to work or school, and you can sing along with the jingles. You get catalogs, coupons, and flyers in the mail. People even leave promotional flyers under your car's windshield wiper while it sits in the parking lot. When you go online, you're deluged with banner and pop-up ads and even marketing-related e-mail. Marketers know that you are receiving many types of communication. They know they need to compete for your attention. So they look for ways to reach you in a coordinated manner through integrated marketing communications.

Successful marketers use the marketing concept and relationship marketing to develop customer-oriented marketing programs. The customer is at the heart of integrated marketing communications. An IMC strategy begins not with the organization's goods and services but with consumer wants or needs and then works in reverse to the product, brand, or organization. It sends receiver-focused rather than product-focused messages.

Rather than separating the parts of the promotional mix and viewing them as isolated components, IMC looks at these elements from the consumer's viewpoint: as information about the brand, company, or organization. Even though the messages come from different sources—sales presentations, word of mouth, TV, radio, newspapers, billboards, direct mail, coupons, public relations, and online services—consumers may perceive them as "advertising" or a "sales pitch." IMC broadens promotion to include all the ways a customer has contact with an organization, adding to traditional media and direct mail such sources as package design, store displays, sales literature, and online and interactive media. Unless the organization takes an integrated approach to present a unified, consistent message, it may send conflicting information that confuses consumers.

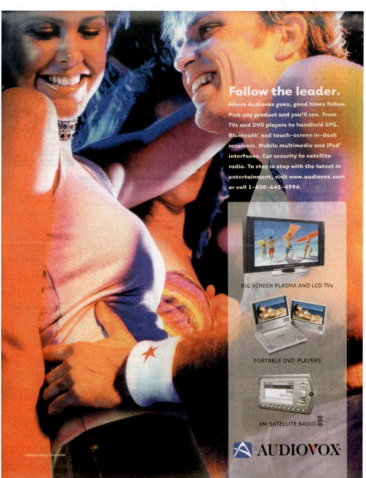

COURTESY OF AUDIOVOX

Marketers use many different methods to attract attention to their products and to provide information. This AudioVox promotion not only shows some of the company's high-tech electronics but also provides a Web site (http://www.audiovox.com) and an 800 number from which interested consumers can obtain more information.

Today's business environment is characterized by many diverse markets and media, creating both opportunities and challenges. The success of any IMC program depends on identifying the members of an audience and understanding what they want. Without accurate, current information about existing and potential customers and their purchase histories, needs, and wants, marketers may send the wrong message. But they cannot succeed simply by improving the quality of the messages or by sending more of them. IMC must not only deliver messages to intended audiences but also gather responses from them. Databases and interactive marketing are important IMC tools that help marketers collect information from customers and then segment markets according to demographics and preferences. Marketers can then design specialized communications programs to meet the needs of each segment.

Young male consumers can be hard to pin down. But marketers for companies including Old Spice, Mountain Dew, and Panasonic have tailored new marketing messages to the lifestyle of this segment. Instead of trying to get these consumers to come to them, marketers are taking their message to young men. In some cases, it means hitting the late-night party circuit—because that's where the guys are. Panasonic now puts its television ads on late-night television, because that's when young men watch TV. Mountain Dew promotes its new energy drink, MDX, with a Web site—BeNocturnal.com—that includes an interactive game about driving around at night. A TV commercial for the drink features owls and bats singing Lionel Richie's song "All Night Long." Old Spice has introduced a line of scents for 18- to 24-year-olds called After Hours, with print ads showing a neon sign that reads, "A good night's sleep just means you had a really boring night."[2]

The increase in media options provides more ways to give consumers product information; however, it can also create information overload. Marketers have to spread available dollars across fragmented media markets and a wider range of promotional activities to achieve their communication goals. Mass media such as TV ads, while still useful, are no longer the mainstays of marketing campaigns. In 1960, a marketer could reach about 90 percent of U.S. consumers by advertising on the three major TV networks—CBS, NBC, and ABC. Today, even though overall TV viewing is at an all-time high, consumers spend less than 20 percent of their viewing hours watching these stations. Basic cable—with channels such as ESPN, CNN, and the Food Network—now accounts for about 45 percent of viewing time, with additional networks such as Fox, the CW, and PBS (public broadcasting) eating up hours as well.[3] So to reach targeted groups of consumers, organizations must turn to niche marketing—advertising in special-interest magazines, purchasing time on cable TV channels, reaching out through telecommunications media such as cell phones and the Internet, and sponsoring events and activities. Without an IMC program, marketers frequently encounter problems within their own organizations because separate departments have authority and responsibility for planning and implementing specific promotional mix elements.

The coordination of an IMC program often produces a competitive advantage based on synergy and interdependence among the various elements of the promotional mix. With an IMC strategy, marketers can create a unified personality for the product or brand by choosing the right elements from the promotional mix to send the message. At the same time, they can develop more narrowly focused plans to reach specific market segments and choose the best form of communication to send a particular message to a specific target audience. IMC provides a more effective way to reach and serve target markets than less coordinated strategies. Establishing an effective IMC program requires teamwork.

IMPORTANCE OF TEAMWORK

IMC requires a big-picture view of promotion planning, a total strategy that includes all marketing activities, not just promotion. Successful implementation of IMC requires that everyone involved in every aspect of promotion—public relations, advertising, personal selling, and sales promotion—function as a team. They must present a consistent, coordinated promotional effort at every point of customer contact with the organization. This way, they save time, money, and effort. They avoid duplication of efforts, increasing marketing effectiveness and reducing costs. Ultimately, it means that the result—the IMC program—is greater than the sum of its parts.

Teamwork involves both in-house resources and outside vendors. It involves marketing personnel; members of the sales force who deal with wholesalers, retailers, and organizational buyers; and customer service representatives. A firm gains nothing from a terrific advertisement featuring a great product, an informational Web site, and a toll-free number if unhelpful salespeople frustrate customers when they answer the phones. The company must train its representatives to send a single positive message to consumers and also to solicit information for the firm's customer database.

IMC also challenges the traditional role of the outside advertising agency. A single agency may no longer fulfill all a client's communications requirements, including traditional advertising and sales promotions, interactive marketing, database development, direct marketing, and public relations. To best serve client needs, an agency must often assemble a team with members from other companies.

ROLE OF DATABASES IN EFFECTIVE IMC PROGRAMS

With the explosive growth of the Internet, marketers have the power to gather more information faster and to organize it more easily than ever before in history. By sharing this detailed knowledge appropriately among all relevant parties, a company can lay the foundation for a successful IMC program.

The move from mass marketing to a customer-specific marketing strategy—a characteristic of online marketing—requires not only a means of identifying and communicating with the firm's target market but also information regarding important characteristics of each prospective customer. As discussed in Chapter 10, organizations can compile different kinds of data into complete databases with customer information, including names and addresses, demographic data, lifestyle considerations, brand preferences, and buying behavior. This information provides critical guidance in designing an effective IMC strategy that achieves organizational goals and finds new opportunities for increased sales and profits. This increased ability to acquire huge amounts of data poses a new challenge: how to sift through it efficiently so that it becomes useful information. Newer technology allows researchers to do exactly that—working with millions of sets of data to make very specific analyses.[4]

Direct sampling is another method frequently used to quickly obtain customer opinions regarding a particular firm's goods and services. If you've ever received a free sample of laundry detergent, air freshener, or even a new magazine in your mailbox, you've been the recipient of direct sampling. In an effort to attract the interest of the 11.5 million women and girls who run, Lady Foot Locker's IMC campaign includes free samples from its own product line and those of partners. Consumers can either sign up for giveaways on a special Web site or attend one of the promotional events sponsored by Asics, Olay, Propel Fitness Water, and Lady Foot Locker.[5]

Today's technology allows marketers to create a customer-specific marketing strategy. Marketing research firms such as Data Recognition Corporation help their clients understand and satisfy their customers' needs.

assessment check

1. Define *promotion*.
2. What is the difference between marketing communications and integrated marketing communications (IMC)?

2
Describe the communication process and how it relates to the AIDA concept.

THE COMMUNICATION PROCESS

When you have a conversation with someone, do you wonder whether the person understood your message? Do you worry that you might not have heard the person correctly? Marketers have the same concerns—when they send a message to an intended audience or market, they want to make sure it gets through clearly and persuasively. That is why the communication process is so important to marketing. The top portion of Table 15.1 shows a general model of the communication process and its application to promotional strategy.

The **sender** acts as the source in the communication system as he or she seeks to convey a **message** (a communication of information, advice, or a request) to a receiver. An effective message accomplishes three tasks:

1. It gains the receiver's attention.

2. It achieves understanding by both receiver and sender.

3. It stimulates the receiver's needs and suggests an appropriate method of satisfying them.

Table 15.1 also provides several examples of promotional messages. Although the types of promotion may vary from a highly personalized sales presentation to such nonpersonal promotions as television advertising and dollar-off coupons, each goes through every stage in the communications process.

AIDA concept Steps through which an individual reaches a purchase decision: attention, interest, desire, and action.

The three tasks just listed are related to the **AIDA concept** (attention interest desire action), the steps consumers take in reaching a purchase decision. First, the promotional message must gain the potential consumer's attention. It then seeks to arouse interest in the good or service. At the next stage, it stimulates desire by convincing the would-be buyer of the product's ability to satisfy his or her needs. Finally, the sales presentation, advertisement, or sales promotion technique attempts to produce action in the form of a purchase or a more favorable attitude that may lead to future purchases.

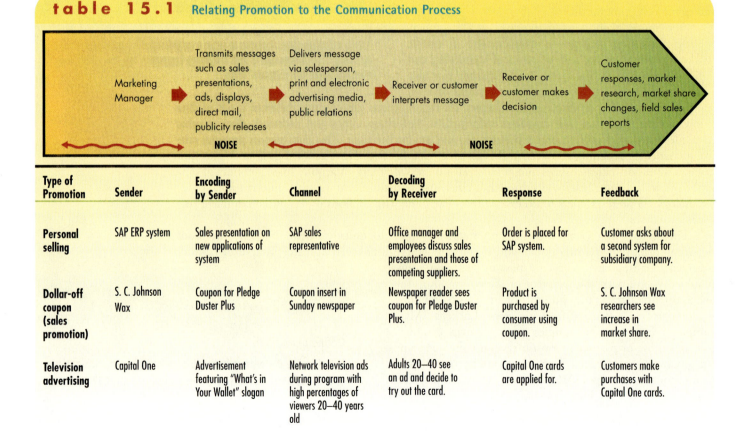

table 15.1 **Relating Promotion to the Communication Process**

Type of Promotion	Sender	Encoding by Sender	Channel	Decoding by Receiver	Response	Feedback
Personal selling	SAP ERP system	Sales presentation on new applications of system	SAP sales representative	Office manager and employees discuss sales presentation and those of competing suppliers.	Order is placed for SAP system.	Customer asks about a second system for subsidiary company.
Dollar-off coupon (sales promotion)	S. C. Johnson Wax	Coupon for Pledge Duster Plus	Coupon insert in Sunday newspaper	Newspaper reader sees coupon for Pledge Duster Plus.	Product is purchased by consumer using coupon.	S. C. Johnson Wax researchers see increase in market share.
Television advertising	Capital One	Advertisement featuring "What's in Your Wallet" slogan	Network television ads during program with high percentages of viewers 20–40 years old	Adults 20–40 see an ad and decide to try out the card.	Capital One cards are applied for.	Customers make purchases with Capital One cards.

The message must be **encoded,** or translated into understandable terms, and transmitted through a communications channel. **Decoding** is the receiver's interpretation of the message. The receiver's response, known as **feedback,** completes the system. Throughout the process, **noise** (in such forms as ineffective promotional appeals, inappropriate advertising media, or poor radio or television reception) can interfere with the transmission of the message and reduce its effectiveness.

The marketer is the message sender in Table 15.1. He or she encodes the message in the form of sales presentations, advertising, displays, or publicity releases. The **channel** for delivering the message may be a salesperson, a public-relations outlet, a Web site, or one of the numerous advertising media. Decoding is often the most troublesome step in marketing communications because consumers do not always interpret promotional messages in the same way that senders do. Because receivers usually decode messages according to their own frames of reference or experiences, a sender must carefully encode a message in a way that matches the frame of reference of the target audience. Consumers today are bombarded daily by hundreds of sales messages through many media channels. This communications traffic can create confusion as noise in the channel increases. Because the typical shopper will choose to process only a few messages, ignored messages waste communications budgets.

The AIDA concept is also vital to online marketers. It is not enough to say a Web site has effective content or high response rates. Marketers must know just how many "eyeballs" are looking at the site, how often they come to view a message, and what they are examining. Most important, they must find out what consumers do besides just look. The bottom line is that if nobody is responding to a Web site, it might as well not exist. Experts advise attracting users' attention by including people in advertisements and other communications in addition to new content and formats. Marketers associated with the FIFA World Cup soccer tournament know that as many as 38 billion viewers watch the tournament during June and July. Yahoo! set up a World Cup Web site, whose traffic was measured by comScore Networks, providing important marketing information to firms involved with the tournament. Europeans visited the site most often, followed by those from the Asia Pacific and Latin America. Africans, Middle Easterners, and North Americans visited the site the least. By using this and other information, marketers can tailor their messages to interested consumers. "Major brands can reach consumers worldwide in a very cost effective manner, as long as they utilize the capabilities of online advertising to adapt their message to the local user," notes Bob Ivins, managing director for comScore in Europe.[6]

Feedback, the receiver's response to the message, provides a way for marketers to evaluate the effectiveness of the message and tailor their responses accordingly. Feedback may take the form of attitude changes, purchases, or nonpurchases. In some instances, organizations use promotion to create favorable attitudes toward their goods or services in the hope of future purchases. Other promotional communications have the objective of directly stimulating consumer purchases. Marketers using infomercials that urge the viewer to call a toll-free number to place orders for music collections, the latest fitness fad, or other products can easily measure their success by counting the number of calls they receive that result in orders.

Even nonpurchases may serve as feedback to the sender. Failure to purchase may result from ineffective communication in which the receivers do not believe the message, don't remember it, or

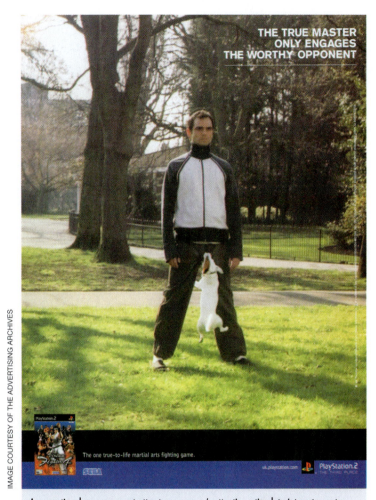

IMAGE COURTESY OF THE ADVERTISING ARCHIVES

THE TRUE MASTER
ONLY ENGAGES
THE WORTHY OPPONENT

The one true-to-life martial arts fighting game.

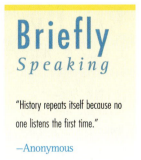

A promotional message must attract a consumer's attention, stimulate interest, create desire for the product, and produce action. Marketers often use humor to gain attention for their products.

¿por qué dejarlo manejar tan pequeño?

Porque con Bounty sí puedes.

Como una esponja de papel.

Usala   Enjuágala   Reúsala   ¡Listo!

Marketers try to avoid noise when communicating in different languages. In its promotion for Bounty paper towels, Procter & Gamble focuses on the universal theme of a child making a mess and provides information on its paper towel's strength and ability to be used and reused.

IMAGE COURTESY OF THE ADVERTISING ARCHIVES

even associate it with another firm's products. Or receivers may remember it correctly, but the message may have failed to persuade them that the firm's products are better than those of the competition. So marketers need to be keenly aware of the reasons that messages fail.

Noise represents interference at some stage in the communication process. It may result from disruptions such as transmissions of competing promotional messages over the same communications channel, misinterpretation of a sales presentation or advertising message, receipt of the promotional message by the wrong person, or random events such as people conversing or leaving the room during a television commercial. Noise can also result from distractions within an advertising message itself. Buzzwords and jargon can create a linguistic jungle for consumers who are just trying to find out more about a product. One investment firm sent a notice to its customers reading, "Please ensure that all registered holders complete and sign the enclosed Form of Renunciation. Due to a temporary issue, we are currently unable to pre-populate all holders' names and addresses." Most recipients probably scratched their heads and asked, "What?" Worse, they may have ignored the message or tossed the letter in the trash.[7]

Noise can be especially problematic in international communications. One problem is that there may be too many competing messages. Italian television channels, for instance, broadcast all advertisements during a single half-hour slot each night. Or technology may be poor, and language translations inaccurate. Nonverbal cues, such as body language and tone of voice, are important parts of the communication process, and cultural differences may lead to noise and misunderstandings. For example, in the United States, the round *O* sign made with the thumb and first finger means "okay." But in Mediterranean countries, the same gesture means "zero" or "the worst." A Tunisian interprets this sign as "I'll kill you," and to a Japanese consumer, it means "money." It's easy to see how misunderstandings could arise from this single gesture.

Perhaps the most misunderstood language for U.S. marketers is English. With 74 English-speaking nations, local terms can confuse anyone trying to communicate globally. The following examples illustrate how easy it can be for marketers to make mistakes in English-language promotional messages:

- *Police:* bobby (Britain), garda (Ireland), Mountie (Canada), police wallah (South Africa)
- *Porch:* stoep (South Africa), gallery (Caribbean)
- *Bar:* pub (Britain), hotel (Australia), boozer (Australia, Britain, New Zealand)
- *Bathroom:* loo (Britain), dunny (Australia)
- *Ghost or monster:* wendigo (Canada), duppy (Caribbean), taniwha (New Zealand)
- *Barbecue:* braai (South Africa), barbie (Australia)
- *Truck:* lorry (Britain and Australia)
- *Festival:* feis (Ireland)

Briefly
Speaking

"England and America are two countries separated by a common language."

—George Bernard Shaw (1856–1950)
Irish playwright

Etiquette Tips for Marketing Professionals

Cultural Considerations in Marketing Messages

Integrated marketing communications requires some skilled decision making—but what about creating an IMC campaign for a diverse audience? Differences in language, social and cultural values, and lifestyle among consumers can create challenges for marketers who want to reach and attract consumers of different backgrounds. Before you become overwhelmed by the possibilities, consider a few questions you might ask to help you learn more about certain groups of consumers in order to serve them and develop a strong relationship:

1. Find out how your group views work—would they accept less pay for a job with less stress? Do they place more emphasis on how much they earn? This may affect the types of goods and services they want or need.
2. What type of relationship does this group generally have toward your category of products— is it something they value or something they can do without? For example, one survey reveals that Hispanic consumers maintain a loyal relationship with certain brands of soft drinks and consumer electronics stores.
3. On what products does this group spend the most money? According to the Department of Commerce, African Americans spend more on books, charitable contributions, education, health care, housing and household furnishings than do Hispanics, who spend the most on consumer electronics, housewares, and sports.
4. How does the group of consumers like to pay for purchases? Asians are more apt to use American Express and Discover cards than other segments, while Anglos are the most frequent users of MasterCard and Visa.

Sources: "Multicultural Snapshot," Allied Media, **http://www.allied-media.com**, accessed June 12, 2006; "Selling Ethnicity Inc.," *Time*, **http://www.time.com**, accessed June 12, 2006; "The Psychology of Consumers," *Consumer Psychologist*, **http://www.consumerpsychologist.com**, accessed June 12, 2006; "How Minorities Are Becoming Markets of Consequence," *Brand Central Station*, January 13, 2006.

- *Sweater:* jumper (England)
- *French fries:* chips (Britain)
- *Soccer:* football (the rest of the world)
- *Soccer field:* pitch (England)

Faulty communications can be especially risky on a global level, where noise can lead to some interesting misinterpretations. Here are three recent international examples:

- *On a sign in a Bucharest hotel lobby:* The lift is being fixed for the next day. During that time, we regret that you will be unbearable.

- *From a Japanese information booklet about using a hotel air conditioner:* Cooles and Heates: If you want just condition of warm in your room, please control yourself.

- *In an Acapulco hotel:* The manager has personally passed all the water served here.

Marketers involved in IMC on an international level—or in the United States, where diverse audiences are involved—can benefit from some of the suggestions offered in the "Etiquette Tips for Marketing Professionals" feature.

 assessment check

1. **What are the three tasks accomplished by an effective message?**
2. **Identify the four steps of the AIDA concept.**
3. **What is noise?**

3 Explain how the promotional mix relates to the objectives of promotion.

OBJECTIVES OF PROMOTION

What specific tasks should promotion accomplish? The answers to this question seem to vary as much as the sources consulted. Generally, however, marketers identify the following objectives of promotion:

1. Provide information to consumers and others.
2. Increase demand.
3. Differentiate a product.
4. Accentuate a product's value.
5. Stabilize sales.

PROVIDE INFORMATION

The traditional function of promotion was to inform the market about the availability of a particular good or service. In fact, marketers still direct much of their current promotional efforts at providing product information to potential customers. An advertisement for a musical performance typically provides information about the performer, time, and place. A commercial for a theme park offers information about rides, location, and admission price. Information can also help differentiate a product from its competitors by focusing on its features or benefits.

In addition to traditional print and broadcast advertising, marketers often distribute a number of high-tech, low-cost tools to give consumers product information. DVDs are currently used for products such as cosmetics, automobiles, and exercise equipment, providing virtual demonstrations of the products. Political candidates even distribute them, packed with scenes from speeches, rallies, and the candidate on the job. Consumers still regard the DVD as a novelty, so they are less likely to consider them junk mail and throw them out. Many companies also send disks containing software that provides information about or sampling of a good or service. Music companies and Internet service providers such as AOL are regular users of this promotional technique.

INCREASE DEMAND

Most promotions pursue the objective of increasing demand for a product. Some promotions are aimed at increasing **primary demand,** the desire for a general product category such as HDTVs or DVD players. Funding for the advertisement of agricultural commodities such as milk and cotton comes from mandatory fees called *checkoffs* charged to farmers on the sale of their products—in order to stimulate primary demand for the entire category of products, not just one brand. The fees, which total $750 million a year, have generated some controversy. Supporters say it's good for everyone in the industry. "I don't care what anybody says, [nearly] a billion dollars' worth of awareness generation makes a difference," says the president of the Mushroom Council. But critics say the program is unfair, pointing out that small farmers are contributing to the advertising budgets of major firms such as Hormel and Smithfield. Still, these funds have generated such memorable slogans as these:

- "Beef. It's what's for dinner."
- "Pork. The other white meat."
- "The incredible edible egg."
- "Cotton. The fabric of our lives."[8]

Primary-demand promotions are also typical for firms holding exclusive patents on significant product improvements and for marketers who decide to expand overseas, creating new markets for their products in other parts of the world. When Procter & Gamble first introduced its Pampers disposable diapers in Hungary, most parents were using overpants with paper inserts to diaper their babies. So early Pampers television ads focused on generating interest in the novel product.

More promotions, however, are aimed at increasing **selective demand,** the desire for a specific brand. Movie studios have been looking for ways to get consumers to watch their films. So they've launched integrated campaigns that include Internet, video podcast, and cell phone marketing efforts. Warner Bros. filmed 27 behind-the-scenes production "diaries" during the filming of *Superman Returns* and posted links to the videos on its Web site, iTunes, and the Superman fan site BlueTights Network. The response was "beyond our wildest expectations," says one marketer. Fans conducted nearly 60 million downloads from the iTunes link alone.[9]

DIFFERENTIATE THE PRODUCT

A frequent objective of the firm's promotional efforts is **product differentiation.**

IMAGE COURTESY OF THE ADVERTISING ARCHIVES

While some advertisements are designed to stimulate primary demand for oranges and their related products in general, this one hopes to stimulate selective demand for Tropicana orange juice.

Homogeneous demand for many products results when consumers regard the firm's output as virtually identical to its competitors' products. In these cases, the individual firm has almost no control over marketing variables such as price. A differentiated demand schedule, in contrast, permits more flexibility in marketing strategy, such as price changes. It may seem difficult to differentiate among the many brands and styles of running shoes, but Reebok is attempting to do just that with its latest campaign. The theme of the campaign is "I am what I am," which is an effort to convey the message that Reebok is inclusive of many types of athletes. Nike's "Just Do It" campaign gives off an aura of exclusivity—only hard-core athletes need apply—while Reebok seeks to celebrate the athlete in everyone. Even so, the firm has gathered a stellar lineup to speak for its products, including NBA players Allen Iverson and Yao Ming and rappers Jay-Z and 50 Cent. "Every other sporting goods commercial is about buying the shoe to become something you're not," says tennis ace Andy Roddick, who is featured in some of the ads. "This is about being yourself."[10]

ACCENTUATE THE PRODUCT'S VALUE

Promotion can explain the greater ownership utility of a product to buyers, thereby accentuating its value and justifying a higher price in the marketplace. This objective benefits both consumer and business products. A firm's promotional messages must build brand image and equity and at the same time deliver a "call to action." Advertising typically offers reasons why a product fits into the consumer's lifestyle. Today, consumers everywhere value their time; the challenge for marketers is to demonstrate how their merchandise will make their lives better.

Marketers must choose their words wisely when creating messages that accentuate their product's value. One expert advises staying away from five words: *quality, value, service, caring,* and *integrity.* These overused words are vague and tend to fall on deaf ears.[11]

STABILIZE SALES

Sales of most goods and services fluctuate throughout the year. These fluctuations may result from cyclical, seasonal, or irregular demand. Ice cream, ski trips, and swimming pools have obvious fluctuations, as do snow shovels and lawn mowers. Sales of bottled water and flashlights might spike just before a storm, while vacation rentals might be canceled in the path of the same oncoming hurricane. Stabilizing these variations is often an objective of promotional strategy. Although it may seem less obvious than ice cream, coffee sales follow a seasonal pattern, rising during colder months and dropping when the weather turns warm. Instead of turning up the temperature on its advertising for hot coffee in the summer, Dunkin' Donuts focuses on its iced coffee drinks. Using its "America Runs on Dunkin'" tagline, Dunkin' Donuts runs ads featuring summer problems like that of bare legs sticking to hot leather car seats—naturally, the antidote is a frosty iced coffee. In another ad, a young woman chugs a Dunkin' Donuts iced latte—and gets so much energy that she does a somersault and climbs a tree to retrieve her 8-year-old child. "We're emotionally connecting with everyday Americans celebrating life," claims vice president of marketing John Gilbert.[12]

✔ *assessment check*

1. What are the objectives of promotion?
2. Why is product differentiation important to marketers?

4 Identify the different elements of the promotional mix and explain how marketers develop an optimal promotional mix.

promotional mix Subset of the marketing mix in which marketers attempt to achieve the optimal blending of the elements of personal and nonpersonal selling to achieve promotional objectives.

ELEMENTS OF THE PROMOTIONAL MIX

Like the marketing mix, the promotional mix requires a carefully designed blend of variables to satisfy the needs of a company's customers and achieve organizational objectives. The **promotional mix** works like a subset of the marketing mix, with its product, distribution, promotion, and pricing elements. With the promotional mix, the marketers attempt to create an optimal blend of various elements to achieve promotional objectives. The components of the promotional mix are personal selling and nonpersonal selling, including advertising, sales promotion, direct marketing, public relations, and guerrilla marketing.

Personal selling, advertising, and sales promotion usually account for the bulk of a firm's promotional expenditures. However, direct marketing, guerrilla marketing, sponsorships, and public relations also contribute to integrated marketing communications. Later sections of this chapter examine the use of guerrilla marketing, sponsorships, and direct marketing, and Chapters 16 and 17 present detailed discussions of the other elements. This section defines the elements and reviews their advantages and disadvantages.

© KAYTE M. DEIOMA/PHOTOEDIT

Many real estate firms offer online home listings and use advertisements such as this one to attract customers. But personal selling through agents is still an important part of most real estate purchases.

PERSONAL SELLING

Personal selling is the oldest form of promotion, dating back as far as the beginning of trading and commerce. Traders vastly expanded both market sizes and product varieties as they led horses and camels along the Silk Road from China to Europe roughly between 300 B.C.E. and A.D. 1600, conducting personal selling at both ends. Personal selling may be defined as a seller's promotional presentation conducted on a person-to-person basis with the buyer. This direct form of promotion may be conducted face-to-face, over the telephone, through videoconferencing, or through interactive computer links between the buyer and seller.

Today, more than 13 million people in the United States have careers in personal sales. They may sell real estate, insurance, and financial investments, or tractors, automobiles, and vacuum cleaners; they may work in retail or wholesaling; they may be regional managers or in the field. In other words, the range of jobs, as well as the products they represent, is huge.[13]

NONPERSONAL SELLING

Nonpersonal selling includes advertising, product placement, sales promotion, direct marketing, public relations, and guerrilla marketing. Advertising and sales promotion are usually regarded as the most important forms of nonpersonal selling. About one-third of marketing dollars spent on nonpersonal selling activities are allocated for media advertising; the other two-thirds fund trade and consumer sales promotions.

Advertising

Advertising is any paid, nonpersonal communication through various media about a business firm, not-for-profit organization, product, or idea by a sponsor identified in a message that is intended to inform, persuade, or remind members of a particular audience. It is a major promotional mix component for thousands of organizations—total ad spending in the United States topped $152 billion during a recent year. Online ad spending reached $15.6 billion.[14] Mass consumption and geographically dispersed markets make advertising particularly appropriate for marketing goods and services aimed at large audiences likely to respond to the same promotional messages. However, the advertisement of some of these products has caused concern, as discussed in the "Solving an Ethical Controversy" feature.

Advertising primarily involves the mass media, such as newspapers, television, radio, magazines, movie screens, and billboards, but it also includes electronic and computerized forms of promotion such as Web commercials, CDs and DVDs, and TV monitors at supermarkets. The rich potential of the Internet as an advertising channel to reach millions of people one at a time has attracted the attention of companies large and small, local and international. As consumers become increasingly savvy—and tune out messages that don't interest them—marketers are finding new ways to grab their attention. Geico has placed ads on 400 turnstiles throughout Chicago's transit system. Home Depot uses the new Parking Stripe ads—vinyl ads installed over parking lot lines. CBS places ads on office water-cooler bottles and laser etches them on eggs in grocery stores for some of its new shows.[15]

Product Placement

Product placement is a form of nonpersonal selling in which the marketer pays a motion picture or television program owner a fee to display his or her product prominently in the film or show. The practice gained attention more than two decades ago in the movie *E.T.: The Extra-Terrestrial* when Elliott, the boy who befriends E.T., lays out a trail of Reese's Pieces for the extraterrestrial to follow, to draw the alien from his hiding place. Product sales for Reese's Pieces candies went through the roof. (Interestingly, this was not the moviemaker's first choice of candy; Mars turned down the opportunity to have its M&Ms appear in the film.) Today, hundreds of products appear in movies and on television shows, and the fees charged for these placements have soared. The opening season of NBC's reality series *Treasure Hunters* featured a host of product placements from companies such as Motorola, Ask.com, Toyota, Genworth Financial, Recreational Equipment, Mountain Hardwear, and Mad River Canoe.

Some firms have moved to the next generation of product placement, seeking new places for their merchandise. One popular venue for product placement is video games. Not only do these placements generate recognition and awareness, but they can also result in an immediate sale. Video game players who are engaged in the online game Everquest II can click an icon for Pizza Hut and have their pizza delivered within 30 minutes. This capability represents a huge opportunity for both game publishers and advertisers. Advertisers reach precisely the market they have targeted, and game publishers stand to gain from placement fees. "Game publishers have to recognize that there are millions, if not billions, of dollars in advertising money coming their way in

Solving an Ethical Controversy

The Marketing of Drugs: Sales or Science?

The pharmaceuticals industry spends somewhere between $3 billion and $4 billion each year advertising its products directly to consumers. In total, the top ten drug companies spend about $80 billion per year in marketing (to doctors and consumers) and administration costs. These same ten firms sink about $42 billion annually into research for new or improved drugs. Critics of the industry point out that some of these firms' biggest sellers don't treat or cure life-threatening diseases; instead, they treat cosmetic or mild conditions. One example is Lamisil, manufactured by Novartis. The drug, which costs $850 for a three-month supply, and on which Novartis spent more than $100 million in advertising, is the firm's fourth best-seller. It treats toenail fungus.

Does the pharmaceutical industry spend too much on marketing, perhaps at the expense of research on lifesaving drugs?

PRO

1. In the last decade, pharmaceutical companies have tripled the number of salespeople who call on doctors, to about 100,000.
2. Television advertising, along with other ads aimed directly at consumers, actually broadens the base of users for particular medicines. "It creates demand where there's not even disease," notes one physician. "I wish they didn't spend all that money on marketing." This happened in the case of Merck's Vioxx, which was intended for a small group of patients whose stomachs couldn't tolerate aspirin. But $550 million in advertising boosted sales to some 20 million people. The firm was later slapped with 10,000 lawsuits seeking billions in alleged damages based

on the argument that Vioxx increased the risk for heart attack.

CON

1. Drug companies argue that their industry is driven by science, not marketing. "We are thought of as monsters, but I don't know of a single case where we have been driven to take risks on a [drug] compound because of a marketing push. I would not let it happen," insists Martin Mackay, chief of research for Pfizer.
2. Firms are still working on lifesaving drugs for targeted groups of people. Genentech developed a drug targeted for only 25 percent of breast cancer patients. Instead of costing the firm, Herceptin is nearing $1 billion in sales. How does Genentech do it? "If you are developing novel drugs, you don't need sales forces of tens of thousands," says CEO Arthur Levinson.

Summary

The debate over pharmaceuticals marketing is an emotional one. "The biggest disconnect for me is between how the industry is portrayed and how people in it actually feel about what they do," says Bristol-Myers Squibb former CEO Peter Dolan. Yet Jurgen Drews, former research chief for Roche, stands firm in his conviction. "The dominance of marketing over research has done real damage to company pipelines," he says. In other words, newly researched drugs are not replacing old ones fast enough—and no amount of marketing can fix that.

Sources: Robert Langreth and Matthew Herper, "Pill Pushers," *Forbes*, May 8, 2006, pp. 94–102; John Curran, "Vioxx Trial Under Way in Merck's Home State," Associated Press, March 6, 2006, **http://news.yahoo.com**; "More States Want Details on Marketing Costs," *AARP Bulletin*, March 2006, pp. 4, 6.

sales promotion Marketing activities other than personal selling, advertising, guerrilla marketing, and public relations that stimulate consumer purchasing and dealer effectiveness.

the next few years," predicts Justin Townsend, CEO of IGA Partners Europe, which places in-game ads for clients.[16]

Sales Promotion

Sales promotion consists of marketing activities other than personal selling, advertising, guerrilla marketing, and public relations that stimulate consumer purchasing and dealer effectiveness. This broad category includes displays, trade shows, coupons, contests, samples, premiums, product demonstrations, and various nonrecurring, irregular selling efforts. Sales promotion provides a short-term incentive, usually in combination with other forms of promotion, to emphasize, assist, supplement, or otherwise support the objectives of the promotional program. Restaurants, including those that serve fast food, often place certain items on the menu at a lower price "for a limited time only." Advertisements may contain coupons for free or discounted items for a specified period of time. Or companies may conduct sweepstakes for prizes such as new cars or vacations, which may even be completely unrelated to the products the companies are selling.

Movie promotional tie-ins are a classic example. Although this is still a popular—and profitable—type of promotion, some companies are discovering they aren't getting the return on their investment that they had hoped for. If the movie flops, it may be bad news for the product as well. So marketers are tweaking the process to get more out of it. Some movie studios are looking to nontraditional partners—firms that haven't been traditionally involved in tie-ins—to create a different image. Disney/Pixar enlisted seventeen promotional partners for its release of *Cars,* most of which produce goods or services that are not necessarily geared for children. Organizations included Hertz, Mack Trucks, NWA World Vacations, and even the U.S. Department of Transportation. In addition, *Cars* producers announced that they were looking for marketing partners willing to deliver messages about childhood obesity.[17]

Sales promotion geared to marketing intermediaries is called **trade promotion.** Companies spend about as much on trade promotion as on advertising and consumer-oriented sales promotion combined. Trade promotion strategies include offering free merchandise, buyback allowances, and merchandise allowances along with sponsorship of sales contests to encourage wholesalers and retailers to sell more of certain items or product lines.

Direct Marketing

Another element in a firm's integrated promotional mix is **direct marketing,** the use of direct communication to a consumer or business recipient designed to generate a response in the form of an order (direct order), a request for further information (lead generation), or a visit to a place of business to purchase specific goods or services (traffic generation). While many people equate direct marketing with direct mail, this promotional category also includes telephone marketing (telemarketing), direct-response advertising and infomercials on television and radio, direct-response print advertising, and electronic media. Direct marketing is such an important element of the promotional mix that it is discussed in depth later in this chapter.

direct marketing Direct communications, other than personal sales contacts, between buyer and seller, designed to generate sales, information requests, or store or Web site visits.

Public Relations and Publicity

Public relations refer to a firm's communications and relationships with its various publics. These publics include customers, suppliers, stockholders, employees, the government, and the general public. Public-relations programs can conduct either formal or informal contacts. The critical point is that every organization, whether or not it has a formally organized program, must be concerned about its public relations.

public relations Firm's communications and relationships with its various publics.

Publicity is the marketing-oriented aspect of public relations. It can be defined as nonpersonal stimulation of demand for a good, service, person, cause, or organization through unpaid placement of significant news about it in a published medium or through a favorable presentation of it on the radio or television. Compared with personal selling, advertising, and even sales promotion, expenditures for public relations are usually low in most firms. Because companies do not pay for publicity, they have less control over the publication by the press or electronic media of good or bad company news. But this often means that consumers find this type of news source more believable than if the information were disseminated directly by the company.

Of course, bad publicity can damage a company's reputation and diminish brand equity. During recent spikes in gasoline prices, oil companies became the target of criticism and charges of price gouging. Federal lawmakers made several attempts to pass legislation about oil companies' pricing practices, publicly lashing out at them for raking in record profits at the expense of consumers.[18]

Every year, the Harris Poll identifies which industries consumers feel serve them best and which are the worst—the publicity can affect each, for better or worse. Supermarkets ranked highest in

Briefly
Speaking

"Propaganda, to be effective, must be believed. To be believed, it must be credible. To be credible, it must be true."

—Hubert Humphrey
(1911–1978)
Former U.S. vice president

service, with tobacco and oil companies hovering at the bottom.[19] Organizations that are enjoying good publicity generally try to make the most of it. Those who have suffered from bad publicity try to turn the situation around. Bill Gates—both admired and criticized, largely because of the power and wealth he has accumulated—announced his retirement from day-to-day operations of Microsoft in order to devote his energy full-time to his charitable organization, the Bill & Melinda Gates Foundation. Many believe that the move will improve his public image. Another businessman, Warren Buffett, announced that he will begin to give away 85 percent of his $40 billion in Berkshire Hathaway stock to five foundations, the largest chunk of which will go to the Bill & Melinda Gates Foundation. That move generated much admiration for Buffett, who could have set up his own foundation to publicize his generosity.[20]

Guerrilla Marketing

Guerrilla marketing uses unconventional, innovative, and low-cost techniques to attract consumers' attention. It is a relatively new approach used by marketers whose firms are underfunded for a full marketing program. Many of these firms can't afford the huge costs involved in the orthodox media of print and broadcasting, so they need to find an innovative, low-cost way to reach their market. But some large companies, such as PepsiCo and Toyota, engage in guerrilla marketing as well.

As mentioned in Chapter 10, *buzz marketing* can be part of guerrilla marketing. This type of marketing works well to reach college students and other young adults. Marketing firms may hire students to mingle among their own classmates and friends, creating buzz about a product. Often called *campus ambassadors,* they may wear logo-bearing T-shirts or caps, leave Post-it notes with marketing messages around campus, and chat about the good or service with friends during class breaks or over meals. JetBlue relies on these buzz marketers to get its message across on campuses. One such student loves his job at MIT—he places flight schedules where classmates can find them, tacks up JetBlue posters, and even secured corporate sponsorship for the school's fall festival. "We're supposed to break the rules a little bit," he says. "Traditional media doesn't work, so you have to go out and be creative."[21]

Viral marketing, also mentioned in Chapter 10, is another form of guerrilla marketing that has rapidly caught on with large and small firms. "People have grown increasingly skeptical of packaged, canned, Madison Avenue–speak," says Russ Klein, chief marketing officer of Burger King. Burger King has used viral marketing to promote its chicken sandwiches and salads online.[22]

The results of guerrilla marketing can be funny and outrageous—even offensive to some people. But they almost always get consumers' attention. Some guerrilla marketers stencil their company and product names anywhere graffiti might appear. Street artists are hired to plaster company and product logos on blank walls or billboards. Neverstop, a marketing firm hired by Starbucks' ad agency, drove a truck to Grand Central Station in New York City and projected a huge image of Starbucks onto the terminal's giant façade. A phone number accompanied the projection, which consumers could dial to hear accompanying tunes.[23]

ADVANTAGES AND DISADVANTAGES OF TYPES OF PROMOTION

As Table 15.2 indicates, each type of promotion has both advantages and shortcomings. Although personal selling entails a relatively high per-contact cost, it involves less wasted effort than do nonpersonal forms of promotion such as advertising. Personal selling often provides more flexible promotion than the other forms because the salesperson can tailor the sales message to meet the unique needs—or objections—of each potential customer.

The major advantages of advertising come from its ability to create instant awareness of a good, service, or idea; build brand equity; and deliver the marketer's message to mass audiences for a relatively low cost per contact. Major disadvantages include the difficulty in measuring advertising effectiveness and high media costs. Sales promotions, by contrast, can be more accurately monitored and measured than advertising, produce immediate consumer responses, and provide short-term sales increases. Direct marketing gives potential customers an action-oriented choice, permits narrow audience segmentation and customization of communications, and produces measurable results. Public-relations efforts such as publicity frequently offer substantially higher credibility than other promotional techniques. Guerrilla marketing efforts can be innovative—and highly effective—at a

table 15.2   Comparison of the Six Promotional Mix Elements

	PERSONAL SELLING	ADVERTISING	SALES PROMOTION	DIRECT MARKETING	PUBLIC RELATIONS	GUERRILLA MARKETING
Advantages	Permits measurement of effectiveness Elicits an immediate response Tailors the message to fit the customer	Reaches a large group of potential consumers for a relatively low price per exposure Allows strict control over the final message Can be adapted to either mass audiences or specific audience segments	Produces an immediate consumer response Attracts attention and creates product awareness Allows easy measurement of results Provides short-term sales increases	Generates an immediate response Covers a wide audience with targeted advertising Allows complete, customized, personal message Produces measurable results	Creates a positive attitude toward a product or company Enhances credibility of a product or company	Is low cost Attracts attention because it is innovative Is less cluttered with competitors trying the same thing
Disadvantages	Relies almost exclusively on the ability of the salesperson Involves high cost per contact	Does not permit totally accurate measurement of results Usually cannot close sales	Is nonpersonal in nature Is difficult to differentiate from competitors' efforts	Suffers from image problem Involves a high cost per reader Depends on quality and accuracy of mailing lists May annoy consumers	May not permit accurate measurement of effect on sales Involves much effort directed toward non-marketing-oriented goals	May not reach as many people If the tactics are too outrageous, they may offend some people

low cost to marketers with limited funds, as long as the tactics are not too outrageous, but it is more difficult to reach people. The marketer must determine the appropriate blend of these promotional mix elements to effectively market the firm's goods and services.

 assessment check

1. **Differentiate between personal and nonpersonal selling.**
2. **What are the six major categories of nonpersonal selling?**

SPONSORSHIPS

One of the most significant trends in promotion offers marketers the ability to integrate several elements of the promotional mix. Commercial sponsorships of an event or activity apply personal selling, advertising, sales promotion, and public relations in achieving specific promotional goals. These sponsorships, which link events with sponsors and with media ranging from TV and radio to print and the Internet, have become a $28 billion business worldwide. Sponsorship spending is growing more rapidly than spending for both advertising and sales promotion.[24]

Sponsorship occurs when an organization provides money or in-kind resources to an event or activity in exchange for a direct association with that event or activity. The sponsor purchases two things: (1) access to the activity's audience and (2) the image associated with the activity. Sponsorships typically involve advertising, direct mail and sales promotion, publicity in the form of media coverage of the event, and personal selling at the event itself. They also involve relationship marketing, bringing

 Describe the role of sponsorships and direct marketing in integrated marketing communications.

sponsorship Relationship in which an organization provides funds or in-kind resources to an event or activity in exchange for a direct association with that event or activity.

© GAVIN LAWRENCE/GETTY IMAGES

Target sponsors a team in the Indy Car Series, Indy Racing League, the centerpiece of which is the ever-popular Indianapolis 500.

together the event, its participants, the sponsoring firms, and their channel members and major customers. Marketers underwrite varying levels of sponsorships depending on the amount their companies wish to spend and the types of events.

Commercial sponsorship is not a new phenomenon. Aristocrats in ancient Rome sponsored gladiator competitions and chariot races featuring teams that were often supported financially by competing businesses. More than 2,000 years ago, wealthy Athenians underwrote drama, musical, and sporting festivals. Craft guilds in 14th-century England sponsored plays (occasionally insisting that the playwrights insert "plugs" for their lines of work in the scripts). In the United States during the 1880s, some local baseball teams were sponsored by streetcar companies.

Today's sponsorships, although they include both commercial and not-for-profit events, are most prevalent in sports—the Olympics, the Super Bowl, the NCAA basketball championships, the Tour de France bicycle race, and thousands of smaller events as well. Local firms may sponsor soccer and baseball teams, while giants such as Anheuser-Busch sponsor the NASCAR racing series.[25] Firms try to associate themselves with sporting events that match the image of their brand. Avon, whose products mostly focus on women, sponsors the annual Avon Walk for Breast Cancer, whose proceeds go to research, treatment, and care.[26] Cadillac sponsors the Super Bowl and the Ryder Cup golf tournament.[27] Rolex sponsors the Rolex Kentucky 3-Day Event (an equestrian event), the Wimbledon tennis tournament, the Rolex Vintage Festival (automobile racing), and the Rolex Regatta in St. Thomas—all highly prestigious sporting events.

Companies may also sponsor concerts or art exhibits, reading and child-care programs, programs that support small businesses and create new jobs, and humanitarian programs such as the Make-a-Wish Foundation and Habitat for Humanity.

HOW SPONSORSHIP DIFFERS FROM ADVERTISING

Even though sponsorship spending and traditional advertising spending represent forms of nonpersonal selling, they are different in a number of ways. These differences include potential cost-effectiveness, the sponsor's degree of control versus that of advertising, the nature of the message, and audience reaction.

Escalating costs of traditional advertising media have made commercial sponsorships a cost-effective alternative. Except for the really large events—which often have multiple sponsors—most are less expensive than an advertising campaign that relies on television, print, and other advertising. In addition, sponsors often gain the benefit of media coverage anyway, as the events they are associated with are covered by the news. And in the case of naming rights of such venues as sports arenas, the name serves as a perpetual advertisement. Examples include the Delta Center in Salt Lake City, the Pepsi Center in Denver, Heinz Field in Pittsburgh, Bank One Ballpark in Phoenix, and Minute Maid Park in Houston.

Marketers have considerable control over the quantity and quality of market coverage when they advertise. But sponsors have little control of sponsored events beyond matching the audiences to profiles of their own target markets. Instead, event organizers control the coverage, which typically focuses on the event—not the sponsor. By contrast, a traditional advertisement allows the marketer to create an individual message containing an introduction, a theme, and a conclusion.

Audiences react differently to sponsorship as a communications medium than to other media. The sponsor's investment provides a recognizable benefit to the sponsored activity that the audience can appreciate. As a result, sponsorship is often viewed more positively than traditional advertising. Some marketers have tried to take advantage of this fact by practicing **ambush marketing,** in which a firm that is not an official sponsor tries to link itself to a major international event, such as the Olympics or a concert tour by a musical group. While it might be tempting to assume that smaller firms with limited marketing budgets would be most likely to engage in ambush marketing, that is not always the case. A recent Lufthansa advertisement featured soccer players, airplanes, and a soccer ball along with the airline's logo. But Emirates—not Lufthansa—was an official airline sponsor of the FIFA World Cup soccer tournament.[28] While creating a vague advertisement is not illegal, some ambush practices clearly are. If a nonsponsor used the Olympic rings in an advertisement, the ad would be an illegal use of a trademark.

To assess the results of sponsorships, marketers use some of the same techniques by which they measure advertising effectiveness. However, the differences between the two promotional alternatives often necessitate some unique research techniques as well. A few corporate sponsors attempt to link expenditures to sales. Other sponsors measure improved brand awareness and image as effectiveness indicators; they conduct traditional surveys before and after the events to secure this information. Still other sponsors measure the impact of their event marketing in public relations terms.

DIRECT MARKETING

Few promotional mix elements are growing as fast as direct marketing. Direct marketing advertising expenditures in the United States topped $161 billion in one recent year. Direct marketing is effective: for every $1 spent, a firm typically receives $11.49 in revenues.[29] Both business-to-consumer and business-to-business marketers rely on this promotional mix element to generate orders or sales leads (requests for more information) that may result in future orders. Direct marketing also helps increase store traffic—visits to the store or office to evaluate and perhaps purchase the advertised goods or services.

Direct marketing opens new international markets of unprecedented size. Electronic marketing channels have become the focus of direct marketers, and Web marketing is international marketing. Even direct mail and telemarketing will grow outside the United States as commerce becomes more global. Consumers in Europe and Japan are proving to be responsive to direct marketing. But most global marketing systems remain undeveloped, and many are almost dormant. The growth of international direct marketing is being spurred by marketing operations born in the United States.

Direct marketing communications pursue goals beyond creating product awareness. Marketers want direct marketing to persuade people to place an order, request more information, visit a store, call a toll-free number, or respond to an e-mail message. In other words, successful direct marketing should prompt consumers to take action. Because direct marketing is interactive, marketers can tailor individual responses to meet consumers' needs. They can also measure the effectiveness of their efforts more easily than with advertising and other forms of promotion. Direct marketing is a very powerful tool that helps organizations win new customers and enhance relationships with existing ones.

The growth of direct marketing parallels the move toward integrated marketing communications in many ways. Both respond to fragmented media markets and audiences, growth in customized products, shrinking network broadcast audiences, and the increasing use of databases to target specific markets. Lifestyles also play a role because today's busy consumers want convenience and shopping options that save them time.

Databases are an important part of direct marketing. Using the latest technology to create sophisticated databases, a company can select a narrow market segment and find good prospects within that segment based on desired characteristics. Marketers can cut costs and improve returns on dollars spent by identifying customers who are most likely to respond to messages and by eliminating others from their lists who are not likely to respond. In fact, mining information about customers is a trend boosted by the growth of e-marketing.

DIRECT MARKETING COMMUNICATIONS CHANNELS

Direct marketing uses many different media forms: direct mailings such as brochures and catalogs; telecommunications initiated by companies or customers; television and radio through special offers, infomercials, or shopping channels; the Internet via e-mail and electronic messaging; print media such as newspapers and magazines; and specialized channels such as electronic kiosks. Each works best for certain purposes, although marketers often combine two or more media in one direct marketing program. As long as it complies with current "do not call" regulations, a company might start with telemarketing to screen potential customers and then follow up by sending more material by direct mail to those who are interested.

DIRECT MAIL

As the amount of information about consumer lifestyles, buying habits, and wants continues to mount, direct mail has become a viable channel for identifying a firm's best prospects. Marketers gather information from internal and external databases, surveys, personalized coupons, and rebates that require responses. **Direct mail** is a critical tool in creating effective direct-marketing campaigns. It comes in many forms, including sales letters, postcards, brochures, booklets, catalogs, *house organs* (periodicals issued by organizations), DVDs, videotapes, and audiocassettes.

Direct mail offers advantages such as the ability to select a narrow target market, achieve intensive coverage, send messages quickly, choose from various formats, provide complete information, and personalize each mailing piece. Response rates are measurable and higher than other types of advertising. In addition, direct mailings stand alone and do not compete for attention with magazine ads and radio and TV commercials. On the other hand, the per-reader cost of direct mail is high, effectiveness depends on the quality of the mailing list, and some consumers object strongly to what they consider "junk mail."

Recently, some firms have been trying a direct-mail tactic that has sparked some debate—sending marketing messages that appear to be from the government, banks, or even a personal friend. One envelope might bear a logo that looks like a government seal; inside is a solicitation for refinancing a loan. Another might have what looks like a handwritten note from a friend—but actually contains an ad for a fitness center. Some envelopes look like bank statements. All are intended to cut through the clutter that appears in consumers' mailboxes. However, "from a consumer perspective, when a mailing misleads consumers as to who sent it and why it was sent, then it could be considered deceptive," warns Patricia Kachura, senior vice president of ethics and consumer affairs for the Direct Marketing Association.[30]

CATALOGS

Catalogs have been a popular form of direct mail in the United States since the late 1800s. During the early 1900s, consumers could even order a house from the famous Sears, Roebuck catalog. More than 10,000 different catalogs fill mailboxes every year. Catalogs fill so many segments that you could probably order just about anything you need for any facet of your life from a catalog. Catalog sales reached more than $160 billion during a recent year, with almost $97 billion attributed to consumers and more than $63 billion attributed to businesses, outpacing the overall growth of retail. "This is consistent with the traditional performance of catalogs and other types of direct marketing, which, because of their efficiency, tend to do well even in times of economic uncertainty," notes H. Robert Wientzen, president and CEO of the Direct Marketing Association.[31]

Pottery Barn, L. L. Bean, and Williams-Sonoma are well known for their catalogs. But these and other retailers have also added online catalogs to their direct marketing lineup. Hammacher Schlemmer, an upscale gift retailer, created an online catalog that replicated each page of its print catalog so that consumers could flip through both and find items on the same "page." Dayna Batemen, director of the firm's Internet marketing, explains the strategy: "What's nice about having a digital approximation of the book itself is that, experientially, it anchors people to a very important part of our story, which is the catalog. There is something very familiar and very reassuring about going to an [online] catalog where you know there's something you wanted on page five and you can flip to that page."[32]

The 21st-century consumer is time-pressed and overloaded with information. To help consumers escape the barrage of mail stuffed into their boxes, the Direct Marketing Association established its Mail Preference Service. This consumer service sends name-removal forms to people who do not wish to receive direct-mail advertising.

TELEMARKETING

Although its use has been limited by a number of "do not call" restrictions enacted by the Federal Trade Commission, telemarketing remains the most frequently used form of direct marketing. It provides marketers with a high return on their expenditures, an immediate response, and the opportunity for personalized two-way conversations. In addition to business-to-consumer direct marketing, business-to-business telemarketing is another form of direct customer contact.

Telemarketing refers to direct marketing conducted entirely by telephone, and it can be classified as either outbound or inbound contacts. Outbound telemarketing involves a sales force that uses only the telephone to contact customers, reducing the cost of making personal visits. The customer initiates inbound telemarketing, typically by dialing a toll-free number that firms provide for customers to use at their convenience to obtain information or make purchases.

New predictive dialer devices improve telemarketing's efficiency and reduce costs by automating the dialing process to skip busy signals and answering machines. When the dialer reaches a human voice, it instantaneously puts the call through to a salesperson. This technology is often combined with a print advertising campaign that features a toll-free number for inbound telemarketing.

© DAVID YOUNG-WOLFF/PHOTOEDIT

Catalogs are a popular and effective method of direct marketing. Pottery Barn is well known for its colorful catalogs of home furnishings.

Because recipients of both consumer and business-to-business telemarketing calls often find them annoying, the Federal Trade Commission passed a *Telemarketing Sales Rule* in 1996. The rule curtailed abusive telemarketing practices by establishing allowed calling hours (between 8 A.M. and 9 P.M.) and regulating call content. Companies must clearly disclose details of any exchange policies, maintain lists of people who do not want to receive calls, and keep records of telemarketing scripts, prize winners, customers, and employees for two years. This regulation was recently strengthened by the passage of amendments, creating the national *Do Not Call Registry.* The new rules prohibit telemarketing calls to anyone who has registered his or her phone number, restrict the number and duration of telemarketing calls generating dead air space with use of automatic dialers, crack down on unauthorized billing, and require telemarketers to transmit their Caller ID information. Violators can be fined as much as $11,000 per occurrence. Exempt from these rules, however, are current customers, charities, opinion pollsters, and political candidates.

DirectTV agreed to pay a $5.34 million settlement for charges made by the FTC that it had violated the new laws. Named in the civil case were DirectTV, the five telemarketing firms it had hired, and the six principals of those firms.[33] Some critics of the new regulations claim that they go too far, while others argue that they don't go far enough. The FTC says it receives about 1,000 to 2,000 complaints of violations every day—yet few fines are actually issued. And under the "current customer" exemption, a business may call someone up to eighteen months after a purchase.[34]

DIRECT MARKETING VIA BROADCAST CHANNELS

Broadcast direct marketing can take three basic forms: brief direct-response ads on television or radio, home shopping channels, and infomercials. Direct-response spots typically run 30, 60, or 90 seconds and include product descriptions and toll-free telephone numbers for ordering. Often shown on cable television and independent stations and tied to special-interest programs, broadcast direct marketing usually encourages viewers to respond immediately by offering them a special price or a gift if they call within a few minutes of an ad's airing. Radio direct-response ads also provide product descriptions and addresses or phone numbers to contact the sellers. However, radio often proves expensive compared with other direct marketing media, and listeners may not pay close enough attention to catch the number or may not be able to write it down because they are driving a car, which accounts for a major portion of radio listening time.

Home shopping channels such as Quality Value Convenience (QVC), Home Shopping Network (HSN), and ShopNBC represent another type of television direct marketing. Broadcasting around the clock, these channels offer consumers a variety of products, including jewelry, clothing, skin-care products, home furnishings, computers, cameras, kitchen appliances, and toys. In essence, home shopping channels function as on-air catalogs. The channels also have Web sites that consumers can browse through to make purchases. In both cases, customers place orders via toll-free telephone numbers and pay for their purchases by credit card.

Infomercials are 30-minute or longer product commercials that resemble regular television programs. Because of their length, infomercials do not get lost as easily as 30-second commercials can, and they permit marketers to present their products in more detail. But they are usually shown at odd hours, and people often watch only portions of them. Think of how many times you have channel-surfed past an infomercial for Bowflex, Proactiv skin care, or Ronco's rotisserie. Infiniti recently launched an innovative program featuring five African American artists—including a dancer, an oil painter, and a music producer—talking about design. For the first 25 minutes, there is no mention of Infiniti. But when the conversation ends, the last 5 minutes of the infomercial focus on images of the various Infiniti models.[35]

Infomercials provide toll-free telephone numbers so that viewers can order products or request more information. Although infomercials incur higher production costs than prime-time 30-second ads on national network TV, they generally air on less expensive cable channels and in late-night time slots on broadcast stations.

ELECTRONIC DIRECT MARKETING CHANNELS

Anyone who has ever visited the Web is abundantly aware of the growing number of commercial advertisements that now clutter their computer screen. Web advertising is a recurring theme throughout this text, corresponding to its importance as a component of the promotional mix. In fact, Chapter 4 explained the vital role e-business now plays in contemporary marketing practices. U.S. spending on online advertising now totals about $16 billion per year, representing more than 5 percent of total advertising spending. Advertising executives now say that more than 18 percent of media budgets are allocated to online advertising.[36] Companies that were once skeptical—or at least slow to adopt—online advertising are now embracing it. General Mills, Kraft Goods, and PepsiCo all say that consumers are spending more time online—and these firms want to be where their customers are.[37]

Web advertising, however, is only one component of electronic direct marketing. E-mail direct marketers have found that traditional practices used in print and broadcast media are easily adapted to electronic messaging. You might receive e-mail notices from retailers from whom you've made past purchases, telling you about special promotions or new products. Antivirus program makers routinely provide new downloads with the latest protection via the Web and notify you by e-mail. Experts agree that the basic rules for online direct marketing mirror those of traditional practices. Any successful offline direct marketing campaign can be applied to e-mail promotions. Electronic media deliver data instantly to direct marketers and help them track customer buying cycles quickly. As a result, they can place customer acquisition programs online for less than the cost of traditional programs.

OTHER DIRECT MARKETING CHANNELS

Print media such as newspapers and magazines do not support direct marketing as effectively as do Web marketing and telemarketing. However, print media and other traditional direct marketing channels are still critical to the success of all electronic media channels. Magazine ads with toll-free telephone numbers enhance inbound telemarketing campaigns. Companies can place ads in magazines or newspapers, include reader-response cards, or place special inserts targeted for certain market segments within the publications. Newspapers are becoming savvy about the Internet, producing online versions of their content—which naturally include online, interactive ads.[38]

Kiosks provide another outlet for electronic sales. Fujifilm has a GetPix Kiosk, which allows consumers to print a single 4-by-6-inch digital photo in eight seconds. Alamo Rent a Car has installed new touch-screen car rental kiosks at airports that reduce check-in time for customers as much as 50 percent. And Sephora stores now have customer loyalty kiosks that provide preferred customers with exclusive information and an all-access pass to a personalized beauty program.[39]

© JOHN FROSCHAUER/BLOOMBERG NEWS/LANDOV

Kiosks are an efficient way of conducting electronic sales. Shown here is the Kodak Picture Maker digital kiosk, which allows customers to print photos from their camera's memory card.

DEVELOPING AN OPTIMAL PROMOTIONAL MIX

By blending advertising, personal selling, sales promotion, and public relations to achieve marketing objectives, marketers create a promotional mix. Because quantitative measures are not available to determine the effectiveness of each mix component in a given market segment, the choice of an effective mix of promotional elements presents one of the marketer's most difficult tasks. Several factors influence the effectiveness of a promotional mix: (1) the nature of the market, (2) the nature of the product, (3) the stage in the product life cycle, (4) the price, and (5) the funds available for promotion.

NATURE OF THE MARKET

The marketer's target audience has a major impact on the choice of a promotion method. When a market includes a limited number of buyers, personal selling may prove a highly effective technique. However, markets characterized by large numbers of potential customers scattered over sizable geographic areas may make the cost of contact by personal salespeople prohibitive. In such instances, extensive use of advertising often makes sense. The type of customer also affects the promotional mix. Personal selling works better in a target market made up of industrial purchasers or retail and wholesale buyers than in a target market consisting of ultimate consumers. Similarly, pharmaceuticals firms use large sales forces to sell prescription drugs directly to physicians and hospitals, but they also advertise to promote over-the-counter and prescription drugs for the consumer market. So the drug firm must switch its promotional strategy from personal selling to consumer advertising based on the market it is targeting.

Subway has begun to use direct marketing—in the form of Jared Fogle, the customer who lost 245 pounds by sticking to a diet of Subway sandwiches. Consumers already know Fogle from Subway's

6 Discuss the factors that influence the effectiveness of a promotional mix.

television advertising campaign; now they can get to know him by phone. Consumers who feel they need a little inspiration to eat more healthful meals and lose weight can sign up online to receive a recorded message from Fogle; they can even specify the time of day they want the call. "It's maybe that mid-afternoon snack attack or maybe you want that call before lunch," explains Tom Seddon, CEO of the Subway Franchisee Advertising Fund Trust. "Getting people to eat better is both good for them and good for us."[40]

NATURE OF THE PRODUCT

A second important factor in determining an effective promotional mix is the product itself. Highly standardized products with minimal servicing requirements usually depend less on personal selling than do custom products with technically complex features or requirements for frequent maintenance. Marketers of consumer products are more likely to rely heavily on advertising than are business products. For example, soft drinks lend themselves more readily to advertising than do large pieces of business machinery.

Promotional mixes vary within each product category. In the B2B market, for example, installations typically rely more heavily on personal selling than does marketing of operating supplies. In contrast, the promotional mix for a convenience product is likely to involve more emphasis on manufacturer advertising and less on personal selling. On the other hand, personal selling plays an important role in the promotion of shopping products, and both personal and nonpersonal selling are important in the promotion of specialty items. A personal-selling emphasis is also likely to prove more effective than other alternatives in promotions for products involving trade-ins.

STAGE IN THE PRODUCT LIFE CYCLE

The promotional mix must also be tailored to the product's stage in the product life cycle. In the introductory stage, both nonpersonal and personal selling are used to acquaint marketing intermediaries and final consumers with the merits of the new product. Heavy emphasis on personal selling helps inform the marketplace of the merits of the new good or service. Salespeople contact marketing intermediaries to secure interest in and commitment to handling the newly introduced item. Trade shows are frequently used to inform and educate prospective dealers and ultimate consumers about its merits over current competitive offerings. Advertising and sales promotion are also used during this stage to create awareness, answer questions, and stimulate initial purchases.

As the product moves into the growth and maturity stages, advertising gains relative importance in persuading consumers to make purchases. Marketers continue to direct personal-selling efforts at marketing intermediaries in an attempt to expand distribution. As more competitors enter the marketplace, advertising begins to stress product differences to persuade consumers to purchase the firm's

 marketing success Beer Grows Up

Background. Beer advertisements used to feature kegs, tailgate parties, even croaking frogs. Beer was considered the lower-end beverage, hardly in the same class with fine wine, gourmet food, or affluent consumers.

The challenge. As the consumer population ages, and as microbreweries develop a loyal following, the larger brewers—such as Anheuser-Busch—are faced with the challenge of coming up with new products and new marketing efforts to attract older, more affluent consumers.

The Strategy. Anheuser-Busch has launched a whole new campaign emphasizing the finer aspects of beer, including the art of brewing and blending flavors, as well as its suitability at more formal gatherings or with upscale foods. Some of the recent ads feature the firm's president, August Busch IV, surrounded by well-dressed friends enjoying an informal gathering— suggesting that this is how the upper class entertains. Robert Lachkey, executive vice president of global industry development for Anheuser-Busch, calls this "romancing the product." The famous brewer of Budweiser has rolled out

brand. In the maturity and early decline stages, firms frequently reduce advertising and sales promotion expenditures as market saturation is reached and newer items with their own competitive strengths begin to enter the market. However, some firms use marketing to breathe new life into mature products, as Anheuser-Busch has done to attract affluent consumers (see the "Marketing Success" feature).

Starbucks, while it is still considered a hot brand, faces many more competitors than it did just a few years ago. So marketers are finding new ways to differentiate Starbucks products from those of competitors. If you think you've seen Ben Affleck and Jennifer Garner toting white coffee cups with the famous green logo, you're right. Despite speculation, Starbucks denies paying the couple for carrying the cups in public. Either way, it gives Starbucks a different kind of exposure.[41]

PRICE

The price of an item is the fourth factor that affects the choice of a promotional mix. Advertising dominates the promotional mixes for low-unit-value products due to the high per-contact costs in personal selling. These costs make the sales call an unprofitable tool in promoting most lower-value goods and services. Advertising, in contrast, permits a low promotional expenditure per sales unit because it reaches mass audiences. For low-value consumer goods, such as chewing gum, soft drinks, and snack foods, advertising is the most feasible means of promotion. Even shopping products can be sold at least partly on the basis of price. On the other hand, consumers of high-priced items such as luxury cars expect lots of well-presented information from qualified salespeople. High-tech direct marketing promotions such as video presentations on a laptop PC or via cell phone, fancy brochures, and personal selling by informed, professional salespeople appeal to these potential customers.

FUNDS AVAILABLE FOR PROMOTION

A real barrier in implementing any promotional strategy is the size of the promotional budget. A single 30-second television commercial during the Super Bowl telecast costs an advertiser $2.5 million. While millions of viewers may see the commercial, making the cost per contact relatively low, such an expenditure exceeds the entire promotional budgets of thousands of firms, a dilemma that at least partially explains how guerrilla marketing got its start. And if a company wants to hire a celebrity to advertise its goods and services, the fee can run into millions of dollars a year. Producers of a recent Super Bowl paid former NFL stars as much as $75,000 to appear at corporate events before the game and to walk onto the field in a tribute during the game's entertainment. Top-dollar players included Super Bowl MVPs Joe Montana, John Elway, and Terry Bradshaw.[42] Table 15.3 summarizes the factors that influence the determination of an appropriate promotional mix.

some new brews for the occasion, including Budweiser Select. In addition, the firm has set up a new Web site in an effort to generate grassroots interest in the new brews and the new outlook for beer.

The Outcome. Some industry watchers worry that Budweiser may lose its base of fans, but others see the effort to change the image of beer as a necessity. "It's a challenge in general to change an image, especially the image of an entire product category," says Patricia Williams, marketing professor at the Wharton School of Business. But Anheuser-Busch isn't waiting around for the fizz in its sales to go flat.

Sources: Clarke Canfield, "Craft Beer Industry Enjoys Resurgence," *Sacramento Bee*, March 27, 2006, **http://www.sacbee.com**; "Tastes Great, Less Filling, and Perfect with Cheese: Beer Tries to Brew Up a New Image," *Knowledge*, January 25, 2006, **http://knowledge.wharton.upenn.edu**; Parija Bhatnagar, "What, No Keg? Beer Gets a Makeover," *CNN Money.com*, January 20, 2006, **http://money.cnn.com**.

table 15.3 Factors Influencing Choice of Promotional Mix

	Emphasis	
	PERSONAL SELLING	**ADVERTISING**
Nature of the market		
Number of buyers	Limited number	Large number
Geographic concentration	Concentrated	Dispersed
Type of customer	Business purchaser	Ultimate consumer
Nature of the product		
Complexity	Custom-made, complex	Standardized
Service requirements	Considerable	Minimal
Type of good or service	Business	Consumer
Use of trade-ins	Trade-ins common	Trade-ins uncommon
Stage in the product life cycle	Often emphasized at every stage; heavy emphasis in the introductory and early growth stages in acquainting marketing intermediaries and potential consumers with the new good or service	Often emphasized at every stage; heavy emphasis in the latter part of the growth stage, as well as the maturity and early decline stages, to persuade consumers to select specific brands
Price	High unit value	Low unit value

 assessment check

1. What are the five factors that affect the choice of a promotional mix?
2. Why is the choice of a mix a difficult task for marketers?

7 Contrast pushing and pulling strategies.

pulling strategy Promotional effort by the seller to stimulate final-user demand, which then exerts pressure on the distribution channel.

pushing strategy Promotional effort by the seller directed to members of the marketing channel rather than final users.

PULLING AND PUSHING PROMOTIONAL STRATEGIES

Marketers may implement essentially two promotional alternatives: a pulling strategy or a pushing strategy. A **pulling strategy** is a promotional effort by the seller to stimulate final-user demand, which then exerts pressure on the distribution channel. When marketing intermediaries stock a large number of competing products and exhibit little interest in any one of them, a firm may have to implement a pulling strategy to motivate them to handle its product. In such instances, this strategy is implemented with the objective of building consumer demand so that consumers will request the product from retail stores. Advertising and sales promotion often contribute to a company's pulling strategy.

In contrast, a **pushing strategy** relies more heavily on personal selling. Here the objective is promoting the product to the members of the marketing channel rather than to final users. To achieve this goal, marketers employ cooperative-advertising allowances to channel members, trade discounts, personal-selling efforts by salespeople, and other dealer supports. Such a strategy is designed to gain marketing success for the firm's merchandise by motivating representatives of wholesalers and/or retailers to spend extra time and effort promoting the products to customers. About half of manufacturers' promotional budgets are allocated for cash incentives used to encourage retailers to stock their products.

Timing also affects the choice of promotional strategies. The relative importance of advertising and selling changes during the various phases of the purchase process. Prior to the actual sale, advertising usually is more important than personal selling. However, one of the primary advantages of a successful advertising program is the support it gives the salesperson who approaches the prospective buyer for the first time. Selling activities are more important than advertising at the time of purchase. Personal selling provides the actual mechanism for closing most sales. In the postpurchase period, advertising regains primacy in the promotional effort. It affirms the customer's decision to buy a particular good or service and—as pointed out in Chapter 5—reminds him or her of the product's favorable qualities by reducing any cognitive dissonance that might occur.

The promotional strategies used by auto marketers illustrate this timing factor. Car, truck, and SUV makers spend heavily on consumer advertising to create awareness before consumers begin the purchase process. At the time of their purchase decisions, however, the personal-selling skills of dealer salespeople provide the most important tools for closing sales. Finally, advertising is used frequently to maintain postpurchase satisfaction by citing awards such as *Motor Trend*'s Car of the Year and results of J. D. Power's customer satisfaction surveys to affirm buyer decisions.

BUDGETING FOR PROMOTIONAL STRATEGY

Promotional budgets may differ not only in amount but also in composition. Business-to-business marketers generally invest larger proportions of their budgets in personal selling than in advertising, while the reverse is usually true of most producers of consumer goods. Cannondale Associates, a leading U.S. sales and marketing consulting firm, conducts an annual survey of trade promotion spending in different industries. Figure 15.1 shows estimated allocations of promotional budgets by consumer packaged-goods manufacturers.

Evidence suggests that sales initially lag behind promotional expenses for structural reasons—funds spent filling up retail shelves, boosting low initial production, and supplying buyer information. This fact produces a threshold effect in which few sales may result from substantial initial investments in promotion. A second phase might produce sales proportionate to promotional expenditures—the most predictable range. Finally, promotion reaches the area of diminishing returns, in which an increase in promotional spending fails to produce a corresponding increase in sales.

For example, an initial expenditure of $40,000 may result in sales of 100,000 units for a consumer-goods manufacturer. An additional $10,000 expenditure during the second phase may generate sales of 30,000 more units, and another $10,000 may produce sales of an additional 35,000 units. The cumulative effect of the expenditures and repeat sales will have generated increasing returns from the promotional outlays. However, as the advertising budget moves from $60,000 to $70,000, the marginal productivity of the additional expenditure may fall to 28,000 units. At some later point, the return may actually become zero or negative as competition intensifies, markets become saturated, and marketers employ less expensive advertising media.

The ideal method of allocating promotional funds would increase the budget until the cost of each additional increment equals the additional

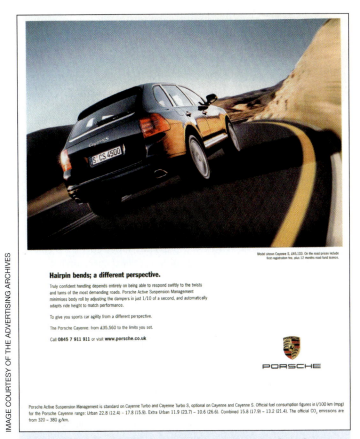

IMAGE COURTESY OF THE ADVERTISING ARCHIVES

Hairpin bends; a different perspective.

Truly confident handling depends entirely on being able to respond swiftly to the twists and turns of the most demanding roads. Porsche Active Suspension Management minimises body roll by adjusting the dampers in just 1/10 of a second, and automatically adapts ride height to match performance.

To give you sports car agility from a different perspective.

The Porsche Cayenne: from £35,560 to the limits you set.

Call 0845 7 911 911 or visit www.porsche.co.uk

PORSCHE

Auto manufacturers rely heavily on advertising to create awareness of—and excitement about—their products. Later, sales associates on dealers' lots close the sale.

✓ *assessment check*

1. What is a pulling strategy?
2. What is a pushing strategy?

8 Explain how marketers budget for and measure the effectiveness of promotion.

figure 15.1

Allocation of Promotional Budgets for Consumer Packaged Goods

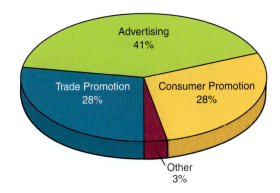

- Advertising 41%
- Consumer Promotion 28%
- Trade Promotion 28%
- Other 3%

Source: Data from Kathleen M. Joyce, "Higher Gear," *Promo,* April 1, 2006, **http://promomagazine.com**.

table 15.4 Promotional Budget Determination

METHOD	DESCRIPTION	EXAMPLE
Percentage-of-sales method	Promotional budget is set as a specified percentage of either past or forecasted sales.	"Last year we spent $10,500 on promotion and had sales of $420,000. Next year we expect sales to grow to $480,000, and we are allocating $12,000 for promotion."
Fixed-sum-per-unit method	Promotional budget is set as a predetermined dollar amount for each unit sold or produced.	"Our forecast calls for sales of 14,000 units, and we allocate promotion at the rate of $65 per unit."
Meeting competition method	Promotional budget is set to match competitor's promotional outlays on either an absolute or relative basis.	"Promotional outlays average 4 percent of sales in our industry."
Task-objective method	Once marketers determine their specific promotional objectives, the amount (and type) of promotional spending needed to achieve them is determined.	"By the end of next year, we want 75 percent of the area high school students to be aware of our new, highly automated fast-food prototype outlet. How many promotional dollars will it take, and how should they be spent?"

incremental revenue received. In other words, the most effective allocation procedure increases promotional expenditures until each dollar of promotional expense is matched by an additional dollar of profit. This procedure—referred to as marginal analysis—maximizes the input's productivity. The difficulty arises in identifying the optimal point, which requires a precise balance between marginal expenses for promotion and the resulting marginal receipts. In addition, as marketing communications become more integrated, it becomes harder to identify exact amounts that companies spend on individual elements of promotion.[43]

Traditional methods used for creating a promotional budget include the percentage-of-sales and fixed-sum-per-unit methods, along with techniques for meeting the competition and achieving task objectives. Each method is briefly examined in Table 15.4.

The **percentage-of-sales method** is perhaps the most common way of establishing promotional budgets. The percentage can be based on sales either from some past period (such as the previous year) or forecasted for a future period (the current year). While this plan is appealingly simple, it does not effectively support the achievement of basic promotional objectives. Arbitrary percentage allocations can't provide needed flexibility. In addition, sales should depend on promotional allocation rather than vice versa.

The **fixed-sum-per-unit method** differs from budgeting based on a percentage of sales in only one respect: It allocates a predetermined amount to each sales or production unit. This amount can also reflect either historical or forecasted figures. Producers of high-value consumer durable goods, such as automobiles, often use this budgeting method.

Another traditional budgeting approach, the **meeting competition method,** simply matches competitors' outlays, either in absolute amounts or relative to the firms' market shares. But this method doesn't help a company gain a competitive edge. A budget that is appropriate for one company may not be appropriate for another.

The **task-objective method** develops a promotional budget based on a sound evaluation of the firm's promotional objectives. The method has two steps:

1. The firm's marketers must define realistic communication goals that they want the promotional mix to achieve. Say that a firm wants to achieve a 25 percent increase in brand awareness. This step quantifies the objectives that promotion should attain. These objectives in turn become integral parts of the promotional plan.

2. Then the company's marketers determine the amount and type of promotional activity required for each objective that they have set. Combined, these units become the firm's promotional budget.

A crucial assumption underlies the task-objective approach: Marketers can measure the productivity of each promotional dollar. That assumption explains why the objectives must be carefully chosen, quantified, and accomplished through promotional efforts. Generally, budgeters should avoid general marketing objectives such as, "We want to achieve a 5 percent increase in sales." A sale is a culmination of the effects of all elements of the marketing mix. A more appropriate promotional objective might be, "We want to achieve an 8 percent response rate from a targeted direct-mail advertisement."

Promotional budgeting always requires difficult decisions. Still, recent research studies and the spread of computer-based models have made it a more manageable problem than it used to be.

MEASURING THE EFFECTIVENESS OF PROMOTION

It is widely recognized that part of a firm's promotional effort is ineffective. John Wanamaker, a leading 19th-century retailer, expressed the problem this way: "Half the money I spend on advertising is wasted; the trouble is, I don't know which half."

Evaluating the effectiveness of a promotion today is a far different exercise in marketing research than it was even a few decades ago. For years, marketers depended on store audits conducted by large organizations such as ACNielsen. Other research groups conducted warehouse withdrawal surveys of shipments to retail customers. These studies were designed to determine whether sales had risen as a direct result of a particular promotional campaign. During the 1980s, the introduction of scanners and automated checkout lanes completely changed marketing research. For the first time, retailers and manufacturers had a tool to obtain sales data quickly and efficiently. The problem was that the collected data was used for little else other than determining how much of which product was bought at what price and at what time.

By the 1990s, marketing research entered another evolutionary period with the advent of the Internet. Now marketing researchers can delve into each customer's purchase behavior, lifestyle, preferences, opinions, and buying habits. All of this information can also be obtained in a matter of seconds. Both Sun Microsystems and IBM now engage in comprehensive evaluations of their trade promotions, using *trade promotion management,* which incorporates a variety of software tools that help manage and analyze promotional spending budgets, in addition to identifying issues that could reduce the effectiveness of trade promotions.[44] The next section explains the impact of electronic technologies on measuring promotional effectiveness. However, marketers today still depend on two basic measurement tools: direct sales results tests and indirect evaluations.

Most marketers would prefer to use a **direct sales results test** to measure the effectiveness of promotion. Such an approach would reveal the specific impact on sales revenues for each dollar of promotional spending. This type of technique has always eluded marketers, however, because of their inability to control other variables operating in the marketplace. A firm may receive $20 million in additional sales orders following a new $1.5 million advertising campaign, but the market success may really have resulted from the products' benefiting from more intensive distribution as more stores decide to carry them or price increases for competing products rather than from the advertising outlays.

Marketers often encounter difficulty isolating the effects of promotion from those of other market elements and outside environmental variables. **Indirect evaluation** helps researchers concentrate on quantifiable indicators of effectiveness, such as recall (how much members of the target market remember about specific products or advertisements) and readership (size and composition of a message's audience). The basic problem with indirect measurement is the difficulty in relating these variables to sales. Will the fact that many people read an ad lead directly to increased sales?

Marketers need to ask the right questions and understand what they are measuring. Promotion to build sales volume produces measurable results in the form of short-term returns, but brand-building programs and efforts to generate or enhance consumers' perceptions of value in a product, brand, or organization cannot be measured over the short term.

MEASURING ONLINE PROMOTIONS

The latest challenge facing marketers is how to measure the effectiveness of electronic media. Early attempts at measuring online promotional effectiveness involved counting hits (user requests for a file) and visits (pages downloaded or read in one session). But as Chapter 4 explained, it takes more than counting "eyeballs" to measure online promotional success. What matters is not how many times a Web site is visited but how many people actually buy something. Traditional numbers that work for other media forms are not necessarily relevant indicators of effectiveness for a Web site. For one thing, the Web combines both advertising and direct marketing. Web pages effectively integrate advertising and other content, such as product information, that may often prove to be the page's main—and most effective—feature. For another consideration, consumers generally choose the advertisements they want to see on the Net, whereas traditional broadcast or print media automatically expose consumers to ads.

One way that marketers measure performance is by incorporating some form of direct response into their promotions. This technique also helps them compare different promotions for effectiveness and rely on facts rather than opinions. Consumers may say they will try a product when responding to a survey question yet not actually buy it. A firm may send out three different direct-mail offers in the same promotion and compare response rates from the groups of recipients receiving each alternative. An offer to send for a sample may generate a 75 percent response rate, coupons might show a 50 percent redemption rate, and rebates might appeal to only 10 percent of the targeted group.

The two major techniques for setting Internet advertising rates are cost per impression and cost per response (click-throughs). **Cost per impression** is a measurement technique that relates the cost of an ad to every thousand people who view it. In other words, anyone who sees the page containing the banner or other form of ad creates one impression. This measure assumes that the site's principal purpose is to display the advertising message. **Cost per response (click-throughs)** is a direct marketing technique that relates the cost of an ad to the number of people who click it. However, not everyone who clicks on an ad makes a purchase. So the **conversion rate** measurement was developed, which is the percentage of Web site visitors who actually make a purchase. All three rating techniques have merit. Site publishers point out that click-through rates are influenced by the creativity of the ad's message. Advertisers, on the other hand, point out that the Web ad has value to those who click it for additional information.

 assessment check

1. What is the most common way of establishing a promotional budget?
2. What is the task-objective budgeting method? Describe its two steps.
3. What is the direct sales results test?
4. What is indirect evaluation?

9　Discuss the value of marketing communications.

THE VALUE OF MARKETING COMMUNICATIONS

The nature of marketing communications is changing as new formats transform the traditional idea of an advertisement or sales promotion. Sales messages are now placed subtly, or not so subtly, in movies and television shows, blurring the lines between promotion and entertainment and changing the traditional definition of advertising. Messages show up at the beach in the form of skywriting, in restrooms, on stadium turnstiles, on buses, and even on police cars.

Despite new tactics by advertisers, promotion has often been the target of criticism. Some people complain that it offers nothing of value to society and simply wastes resources. Others criticize promotion's role in encouraging consumers to buy unnecessary products that they cannot afford. Many ads seem to insult people's intelligence or offend their sensibilities, and they criticize the ethics—or lack thereof—displayed by advertisers and salespeople.

New forms of promotion are considered even more insidious because marketers are designing promotions that bear little resemblance to paid advertisements. Many of these complaints cite issues that constitute real problems. Some salespeople use unethical sales tactics. Some product advertising hides its promotional nature or targets consumer groups that can least afford the advertised goods or services. Many television commercials contribute to the growing problem of cultural pollution. One area that has sparked both criticism and debate is promotion aimed at children.

While promotion can certainly be criticized on many counts, it also plays a crucial role in modern society. This point is best understood by examining the social, business, and economic importance of promotion.

SOCIAL IMPORTANCE

We live in a diverse society characterized by consumer segments with differing needs, wants, and aspirations. What one group finds tasteless may be quite appealing to another. But diversity is one of the benefits of living in our society because it offers us many choices and opportunities. Promotional

Briefly
Speaking

"You can tell the ideals of a nation by its advertising."

—Norman Douglas
(1862–1952)
British author

strategy faces an averaging problem that escapes many of its critics. The one generally accepted standard in a market society is freedom of choice for the consumer. Consumer buying decisions eventually determine acceptable practices in the marketplace, which is why consumers who criticize cigarette ads may also agree that it is acceptable for them to appear.

Promotion has also become an important factor in campaigns aimed at achieving social objectives. Advertising agencies donate their expertise in creating **public service announcements (PSAs)** aimed at promoting such important causes as stopping drug abuse or supporting national parks. The Ad Council recently announced a campaign for the Amber Alert program, which was formed to help recover missing children who are believed to have been abducted. The new campaign includes the opportunity for people to sign up for free wireless Amber Alerts, which are text messages sent to subscribers when a child has been abducted in their geographical area. Included in the messages are vital pieces of information about the child, a potential abductor, or the vehicle in which they may be traveling.[45]

Promotion performs an informative and educational task crucial to the functioning of modern society. As with everything else in life, what is important is how promotion is used rather than whether it is used.

BUSINESS IMPORTANCE

Promotional strategy has become increasingly important to both large and small business enterprises. The well-documented, long-term increase in funds spent on promotion certainly attests to management's faith in the ability of promotional efforts to encourage attitude changes, brand loyalty, and additional sales. It is difficult to conceive of an enterprise that would not attempt to promote its offerings in some manner. Most modern institutions simply cannot survive in the long run without promotion. Business must communicate with its publics.

Nonbusiness enterprises also recognize the importance of promotional efforts. The Government Accountability Office (GAO) reports that seven major federal government departments spend collectively about $648 million per year in advertising.[46]

ECONOMIC IMPORTANCE

Promotion has assumed a degree of economic importance if for no other reason than because it provides employment for millions of people. More important, however, effective promotion has allowed society to derive benefits not otherwise available. For example, the criticism that promotion costs too much isolates an individual expense item and fails to consider its possible beneficial effects on other categories of expenditures.

Promotional strategies increase the number of units sold and permit economies of scale in the production process, thereby lowering the production costs for each unit of output. Lower unit costs allow lower consumer prices, which in turn make products available to more people. Similarly, researchers have found that advertising subsidizes the information content of newspapers and the broadcast media. In short, promotion pays for many of the enjoyable entertainment and educational opportunities in contemporary life as it lowers product costs.

COURTESY OF ACEFITNESS.ORG

Think of her as an exercise machine with hair.

You don't have to join a gym to get a workout. Recent studies show that every hour of moderate physical activity can add two hours to your life. So there's no need to radically alter your exercise habits to improve your health, and live longer! Just enjoy everyday activities like walking the dog. Washing the car. Cutting the grass. Playing golf. Or just taking the stairs instead of the elevator.

Don't sweat it if spinning classes aren't your style. Just get out and do something physical each day. You'll feel better, and live longer. Besides, the stair climber at the gym won't fetch your newspaper.

ACE CERTIFIED
ACE Certified: The Mark of Quality
Look for the ACE symbol of excellence
in fitness training and education.
For more information, visit our website:
www.ACEfitness.org

A Public Service Message brought to you by the American Council on Exercise, a not-for-profit organization committed to the promotion of safe and effective exercise

American Council on Exercise®
4851 PARAMOUNT DRIVE, SAN DIEGO, CA 92123 USA
(800) 825-3636 X653 | WWW.ACEFITNESS.ORG

AMERICA'S AUTHORITY ON FITNESS™

Public service announcements (PSAs) promote important causes such as regular moderate exercise. It may be a surprise for many to learn that the American Council on Exercise recommends regular moderate exercise everyday, rather than major workouts 3 times a week.

✓ *assessment check*

1. **Identify the three areas in which promotion exerts influence.**

Strategic Implications of Marketing in the 21st Century

With the incredible proliferation of promotional messages in the media, today's marketers—who are also consumers themselves—must find new ways to reach customers without overloading them with unnecessary or unwanted communications. Guerrilla marketing has emerged as an effective strategy for large and small companies, but ambush marketing has raised ethical concerns. Product placement has gained in popularity, in movies, television shows, and video games.

In addition, it is difficult to overstate the impact of the Internet on the promotional mix of 21st-century marketers—for small and large companies alike. Even individual entrepreneurs find the Internet to be a lucrative launch pad for their enterprises. But even though cyberspace marketing has been effective in business-to-business transactions and, to a lesser extent, for some types of consumer purchases, a major source of Internet revenues is advertising.

Integrating marketing communications into an overall consumer-focused strategy that meets a company's promotional and business objectives has become more and more critical in the busy global marketplace. Chapter 16 will examine specific ways marketers can use advertising and public relations to convey their messages; then Chapter 17 will discuss personal selling, sales force management, and sales promotion in the same manner.

REVIEW OF CHAPTER OBJECTIVES

1 Explain how integrated marketing communications relates to the development of an optimal promotional mix.

Integrated marketing communications (IMC) refers to the coordination of all promotional activities to produce a unified, customer-focused promotional message. Developing an optimal promotional mix involves selecting the personal and nonpersonal selling strategies that will work best to deliver the overall marketing message as defined by IMC.

2 Describe the communication process and how it relates to the AIDA concept.

In the communication process, a message is encoded and transmitted through a communications channel; then it is decoded, or interpreted by the receiver; finally, the receiver provides feedback, which completes the system. The AIDA concept (attention, interest, desire, action) explains the steps through which a person reaches a purchase decision after being exposed to a promotional message. The marketer sends the promotional message, and the consumer receives and responds to it via the communication process.

3 Explain how the promotional mix relates to the objectives of promotion.

The objectives of promotion are to provide information, stimulate demand, differentiate a product, accentuate the value of a product, and stabilize sales. The promotional mix, which is the blend of numerous variables intended to satisfy the target market, must fulfill the overall objectives of promotion.

4 Identify the different elements of the promotional mix and explain how marketers develop an optimal promotional mix.

The different elements of the promotional mix are personal selling and nonpersonal selling (advertising, product placement, sales promotion, direct marketing, and public relations). Guerrilla marketing is frequently used by marketers with limited funds and firms attempting to attract attention for new-product offerings with innovative promotional approaches. Marketers develop the optimal mix by considering the nature of the market, the nature of the product, the stage in the product life cycle, price, and funds available for promotion.

5 Describe the role of sponsorships and direct marketing in integrated marketing communications.

Sponsorship, which occurs when an organization provides money or in-kind resources to an event or activity in exchange for a direct association with the event or activity, has become a hot trend in promotion. The sponsor purchases access to an activity's audience and the image associated with the activity, both of which contribute to the overall promotional message being delivered by a firm. Direct marketing involves direct communication between a seller and a B2B or final customer. It includes such promotional methods as telemarketing, direct mail, direct-response advertising and infomercials on TV and radio, direct-response print advertising, and electronic media.

6 Discuss the factors that influence the effectiveness of a promotional mix.

Marketers face the challenge of determining the best mix of components for an overall promotional strategy. Several factors influence the effectiveness of the promotional mix: (1) the nature of the market; (2) the nature of the product: (3) the stage in the product life cycle; (4) price; and (5) the funds available for promotion.

7 Contrast pushing and pulling strategies.

In a pulling strategy, marketers attempt to stimulate final-user demand, which then exerts pressure on the distribution channel. In a pushing strategy, marketers attempt to promote the product to channel members rather than final users. To do this, they rely heavily on personal selling.

8 Explain how marketers budget for and measure the effectiveness of promotion.

Marketers may choose among several methods for determining promotional budgets, including percentage-of-sales, fixed-sum-per-unit, meeting competition, or task-objective, which is considered the most flexible and most effective. Today, marketers use either direct sales results tests or indirect evaluation to measure effectiveness. Both methods have their benefits and drawbacks because of the difficulty of controlling variables.

9 Discuss the value of marketing communications.

Despite a number of valid criticisms, marketing communications provide socially important messages, are important to businesses, and contain economic importance. As with every communication in society, it is important to consider how promotion is used rather than whether it is used at all.

 assessment check **answers**

1.1 Define *promotion*.

Promotion is the function of informing, persuading, and influencing the consumer's purchase decision.

1.2 What is the difference between marketing communications and integrated marketing communications (IMC)?

Marketing communications are messages that deal with buyer-seller relationships, from a variety of media. IMC coordinates all promotional activities to produce a unified, customer-focused promotional message.

2.1 What are the three tasks accomplished by an effective message?

An effective message gains the receiver's attention; it achieves understanding by both receiver and sender; and it stimulates the receiver's needs and suggests an appropriate method of satisfying them.

2.2 Identify the four steps of the AIDA concept.

The four steps of the AIDA concept are attention, interest, desire, and action.

2.3 What is noise?

Noise represents interference at some stage in the communication process.

assessment check **answers**

3.1   What are the objectives of promotion?

The objectives of promotion are to provide information to consumers and others, to increase demand, to differentiate a product, to accentuate a product's value, and to stabilize sales.

3.2   Why is product differentiation important to marketers?

Product differentiation, distinguishing a good or service from its competitors, is important to marketers because they need to create a distinct image in consumers' minds. If they can do so, they can then exert more control over variables such as price.

4.1   Differentiate between personal selling and nonpersonal selling.

Personal selling involves a promotional presentation conducted on a person-to-person basis with a buyer. Nonpersonal selling involves communication with a buyer in any way other than on a person-to-person basis.

4.2   What are the six major categories of nonpersonal selling?

The six major categories of nonpersonal selling are advertising, product placement, sales promotion, direct marketing, public relations, and guerrilla marketing.

5.1   Define *sponsorship*.

Sponsorship occurs when an organization pays money or in-kind resources to an event or activity in exchange for a direct association with that event or activity.

5.2   How is sponsorship different from advertising?

Although sponsorship generates brand awareness, the sponsor has little control over the message or even the coverage, unlike advertising.

5.3   Define *direct mail*.

Direct mail is communications in the form of letters, postcards, brochures, and catalogs containing marketing messages and sent directly to a customer or potential customer.

5.4   What are the benefits of electronic direct marketing?

Electronic media deliver data instantly to direct marketers and help them track customer buying cycles quickly.

6.1   What are the five factors that affect the choice of a promotional mix?

The five factors affecting the choice of promotional mix are the nature of the market, the nature of the product, the stage in the product life cycle, price, and the funds available for promotion.

6.2   Why is the choice of a mix a difficult task for marketers?

The choice of a mix is difficult because no quantitative measures are available to determine the effectiveness of each component in a given market segment.

7.1   What is a pulling strategy?

A pulling strategy is a promotional effort by the seller to stimulate final-user demand.

7.2   What is a pushing strategy?

A pushing strategy is an effort to promote a product to the members of the marketing channel.

8.1   What is the most common way of establishing a promotional budget?

The most common method of establishing a promotional budget is the percentage-of-sales method.

8.2   What is the task–objective budgeting method? Describe its two steps.

The task-objective method develops a promotional budget based on an evaluation of the firm's promotional objectives. Its two steps are defining realistic communication goals and determining the amount and type of promotional activity required for each objective set.

assessment check **answers**

8.3   What is the direct sales results test?

The direct sales results test reveals the specific impact on sales revenues for each dollar of promotional spending.

8.4   What is indirect evaluation?

Indirect evaluation helps researchers concentrate on quantifiable indicators of effectiveness.

9.1   Identify the three areas in which promotion exerts influence.

The three areas in which promotion exerts influence are society, business, and the economy.

MARKETING TERMS YOU NEED TO KNOW

promotion 488

marketing communications 488

integrated marketing communications
    (IMC) 488

AIDA concept 492

promotional mix 498

sales promotion 500

direct marketing 501

public relations 501

guerrilla marketing 502

sponsorship 503

pulling strategy 512

pushing strategy 512

OTHER IMPORTANT MARKETING TERMS

sender 492

message 492

encoding 493

decoding 493

feedback 493

noise 493

channel 493

primary demand 496

selective demand 497

product differentiation 497

personal selling 498

nonpersonal selling 500

advertising 500

product placement 500

trade promotion 501

publicity 501

ambush marketing 505

direct mail 506

telemarketing 507

home shopping channel 508

infomercial 508

percentage-of-sales method 514

fixed-sum-per-unit method 514

meeting competition method 514

task-objective method 514

direct sales results test 515

indirect evaluation 515

cost per impression 516

cost per response (click-throughs) 516

conversion rate 516

public service announcements (PSAs) 517

ASSURANCE OF LEARNING REVIEW

1. What is the role of integrated marketing communications (IMC) in a firm's overall marketing strategy? When executed well, what are its benefits?
2. Describe the five stages of communication.
3. What is the difference between primary demand and selective demand?
4. Differentiate between advertising and product placement. Which do you think is more effective, and why?
5. What are the benefits and drawbacks of publicity?
6. Why is sponsorship such an important part of a firm's IMC?
7. For each of the following goods and services, indicate which direct marketing channel or channels you think would be best:

   a.   vacation time share
   b.   denim jacket
   c.   custom-made bracelet
   d.   lawn care service
   e.   magazine subscription

8. How does the nature of the market for a firm's goods or services affect the choice of a promotion method?
9. What is the difference between a pushing strategy and a pulling strategy?
10. What are two major ways of setting Internet advertising rates, and how do they work?

PROJECTS AND TEAMWORK EXERCISES

1. Not-for-profit organizations rely on IMC just as much as for-profit firms do. The Egyptian government, which owns the remains and artifacts of boy pharaoh King Tutankhamun, has sent the King Tut collection on a worldwide tour of selected nations and museums (the exhibit is titled *Tutankhamun and the Golden Age of the Pharaohs*). Many organizers—including *National Geographic* and museums such as the Los Angeles County Museum of Art—have been involved in a multimillion-dollar marketing campaign promoting the exhibit.[47] On your own or with a classmate, conduct online research to learn how museums and other organizers have used IMC to promote this elaborate tour. Present your findings to the class.

2. On your own or with a classmate, select a print advertisement that catches your attention and analyze it according to the AIDA concept (attention, interest, desire, action). Identify features of the ad that catch your attention, pique your interest, make you desire the product, and spur you toward a purchase. Present your findings to the class.

3. Watch a television show and see how many products you can find placed within the show. Present your findings to the class.

4. With a classmate, choose a good or service that you think could benefit from guerrilla marketing. Imagine that you have a limited promotional budget and come up with a plan for a guerrilla approach. Outline several ideas and explain how you plan to carry them out. Present your plan to the class.

5. Evaluate two or three pieces of direct mail that you have received lately. Which items caught your attention and at least made you save the mailing? Which items did you toss in the trash without even opening or considering beyond an initial glance? Why?

CRITICAL-THINKING EXERCISES

1. Choose one of the following products and discuss what you think the objective(s) of promotion should be for the product:
   a. beef
   b. Kraft Macaroni & Cheese
   c. Toyota Prius
   d. T-Mobile cell phone service

2. Identify a corporate sponsorship for a cause or program in your area, or find a local company that sponsors a local charity or other organization. What do you think the sponsor is gaining from its actions? (Be specific.) What does the sponsored organization receive? Do you think this sponsorship is good for your community? Explain.

3. What are some of the advantages and disadvantages of using a celebrity spokesperson to promote a good or service? How might this affect a firm's public-relations efforts?

4. Take a careful look at a direct-mail catalog that you have received recently. Who is the audience for the products? Did the firm target you correctly or not? What is the response the firm is seeking?

5. Describe a public service announcement that you have seen recently. Do you believe that the announcement will help the organization achieve its goals? Why or why not?

ETHICS EXERCISE

Pop-up ads, those unsolicited messages that sometimes pop onto your computer screen and block the site or information you're looking for until you close or respond to them, are inexpensive to produce and cost nearly nothing to send. But they are so annoying to some computer users that dozens of special programs have been written to block them from appearing on the screen during Internet use.

1. Do you think that because they are unsolicited, pop-up ads are also intrusive? Are they an invasion of privacy? Explain your reasoning.

2. Do you consider the use of pop-up ads to be unethical? Why or why not?

INTERNET EXERCISES

1. **Integrated marketing communication.** Promotional mix, guerilla marketing, and sponsorships are all aspects of integrated marketing communication. Review the appropriate chapter material and then complete the following exercises.
   a. Visit two prominent shopping Web sites, including one that has brick-and-mortar stores in addition to its online store. Write a brief report comparing and contrasting the promotional mix used by each retailer.
   b. Guerilla Marketing International (http://www.gmarketing.com/) is an excellent source of information on guerilla marketing. Visit its Web site and research how email can fit into a guerilla marketing campaign. Bring the material to class so you can participate in a group discussion on the subject.
   c. Many companies sponsor a variety of events. Visit Sprint's Web site (http://www.sprint.com/sponsorships) and prepare a report on how Sprint uses sponsorships as part of its integrated marketing communication strategy.

2. **AIDA.** Visit the three Web sites listed below. Write a brief report explaining how the retailers have succeeded in applying the AIDA (attention-interest-desire-action) concept discussed in the chapter.
   a. Blue Nile: http://www.bluenile.com
   b. REI: http://www.rei.com
   c. Tractor Supply: http://www.mytscstore.com/default.asp

Note: Internet Web addresses change frequently. If you don't find the exact sites listed, you may need to access the organization's or company's home page and search from there or use a search engine such as Google.

CASE 15.1 State Slogans and Nicknames: Promoting Where You Live

Quick: Can you reel off your state's nickname? If you're from New Mexico, it's Land of Enchantment. If you were raised in New York, it's the Empire State. If you hail from Hawaii, it's the Aloha State. Arkansas is the Natural State, while Illinois is the Prairie State. It's no surprise that California is the Golden State and New Hampshire is the Granite State. Delaware? Of course, it's the First State. Now dig a little deeper. What's the official slogan of your state? If you're from Kentucky, it's "Unbridled Spirit." If you grew up in Maine, it's "The Way Life Should Be." Louisiana bids you to "Come As You Are. Leave Different." And Wyoming claims to be "Like No Place on Earth."

These nicknames and slogans represent much more than an opportunity to answer trivia questions. Each tries to capture in a few words the essence of the place, the reasons why people should visit, reside, or set up a business there. And each represents a massive marketing effort that includes a variety of communications designed to increase demand—by getting people to visit, move, or open a business. Vacation advertisements point out such features as natural beauty, cultural activities, theme parks, sporting opportunities such as fishing or hiking, and regional cuisine. Marketing messages designed to attract new residents might focus on low housing costs and good schools. Advertising targeted to businesses emphasizes such factors as low taxes and efficient transportation. Generating positive publicity by hosting events and offering special vacation packages can spread the word that a certain state is the place to be. Marketing a state is not unlike marketing other goods and services—the goal is to attract customers who ultimately support the economy.

New Jersey recently launched a campaign to make over its image. Over the years, the Garden State had become better known for dense population, urban decay, chemical plants, pollution, and casinos than it was for its dairy farms, antique homes, and historic sites. But much of New Jersey is rural, with rolling hills, horse farms, small vil-

lages—and gardens. The state also has more than 100 miles of shoreline and wilderness areas such as the Pine Barrens. It is home to Princeton University and the very first U.S. baseball game. So tourism officials decided the time was ripe to generate good publicity about their home state. They began with a contest for a new state slogan, in which residents could phone or e-mail suggestions. "We have the opportunity to craft a new message for our tourist literature to reflect the pride we have in our many parks, open spaces, farmlands, quaint villages, boardwalks, and beaches and our exciting cities," the governor wrote in his message on the state's Web site. Proud citizens responded, submitting more than 6,000 entries—including such gems as "Bada Bing! Choose New Jersey," and "New Jersey: It Always Smells Like This." In the end, the governor chose the winning slogan, which was written by Jeffrey Antman of the NJ Transit department: "New Jersey: Come See for Yourself." The new slogan says it all.

Questions for Critical Thinking

1. Identify the nickname and slogan for your own home state (or one that you like to visit). Suggest your own alternative, and explain why you think it would be effective as a marketing tool.
2. In addition to advertising, select which elements of the promotional mix would best promote your state, and explain why.
3. Describe the social, economic, and business importance of marketing a state.

Sources: "List of U.S. State Slogans," and "List of U.S. State Nicknames," Wikipedia, **http://en.wikipedia.org**, accessed June 30, 2006; Lauren O. Kidd, "New Jersey's New Slogan: 'Come See for Yourself,'" *(Morris County, NJ) Daily Record*, January 13, 2006, **http://www.dailyrecord.com**; John Bacon, "New Jersey: Come See for Yourself," *USA Today*, January 13, 2005, p. 3A; "Bada Bing! NJ Looks for New Slogan," MSNBC, November 14, 2005, **http://www.msnbc.msn.com**, "50 States of Discovery," May 15, 2005, pp. 49–59.

VIDEO CASE 15.2 The Toledo Mud Hens: Family Fun = A Winning Strategy

The written video case on The Toledo Mud Hens appears on page VC-18. The recently filmed Toledo Mud Hens video is designed to expand and highlight the concepts in this chapter and the concepts and questions covered in the written video case.

CHAPTER 16

"Champions get many
a small boy to eat
a good breakfast!"

Betty Crocker

Peyton Manning Wins Big in Endorsements

"Peyton is as important to us as any asset we have."

That's not the coach of the Indianapolis Colts football team talking about his star quarterback Peyton Manning. It's the vice president of team properties at Reebok, one of several consumer-product companies from which Manning earns a combined $10.5 million a year in product endorsements. Despite his team's missing a shot at a recent Super Bowl, Reebok's vice president went on to say of Manning, "It's safe to say he'll be with Reebok as long as he plays football."

Marketers at Gatorade, MasterCard, Direct TV, Microsoft's Xbox division, Sony, Marsh Supermarkets, Kraft, and General Mills—the maker of Wheaties—would probably agree. "He's the nicest guy in the world, and everybody loves him," says the editor of

Sports Business Daily & Journal about Manning. "He will continue to be well fed. And he can always add more if he wins more." In fact, Manning's appeal is so golden that one analyst says, "Peyton is in a league by himself in terms of endorsements. This isn't a guy who got endorsement deals based on his winning the big game. I'm sure he turns down 10 times as many deals as he signs."

Perhaps the most memorable and best loved of Manning's off-the-field performances is his comical commercial for MasterCard, in which he enthusiastically hails ordinary supermarket workers and restaurant waiters and busboys, applauding their efforts ("Great salad bar today!") and begging them for their autographs on a melon or a loaf of bread. The ad turns

upside down the typical scenario of superstars besieged by fans, and one reason it works so well is that Manning is genuine and credible in the role of fan.

Manning's easygoing, folksy persona and lack of bad-boy theatrics on and off the field have helped make him an appealing and credible endorser of everything from Wheaties and milk in the famous "Got Milk?" campaign to banking services, used cars, and computer games.

But it takes more than charm to earn the attention of marketers looking for a powerful spokesperson. When it comes to star quarterbacks, Manning is the real thing. The son and the sibling of two famous NFL quarterbacks—his father Archie Manning played in the NFL for fourteen years, and his brother Eli currently plays

TOP PHOTO: IMAGE COURTESY OF THE ADVERTISING ARCHIVES
BOTTOM PHOTO: © FRANK J. POLICH/UPI/LANDOV

Advertising and Public Relations

Chapter Objectives

1 Identify the three major advertising objectives and the two basic categories of advertising.

2 List the major advertising strategies.

3 Describe the process of creating an advertisement.

4 Identify the major types of advertising appeals and discuss their uses.

5 List and compare the major advertising media.

6 Outline the organization of the advertising function and the role of an advertising agency.

7 Explain the roles of cross-promotion, public relations, publicity, and ethics in an organization's promotional strategy.

8 Explain how marketers assess promotional effectiveness.

for the New York Giants—Manning is nothing if not passionately committed to football. "It's a great feeling to coach a guy like that, who is so driven, who is going to push the offense," says Colts coach Tony Dungy. "He's going to make sure everyone is practicing well. He's going to keep the tempo of practice going. He's going to work hard and never get complacent."

In a professional career scarcely a decade old, Manning has set single-season records for touchdown passes and is already among the game's top quarterbacks for pass completions, passing yards, and touchdowns. Competing quarterbacks view him as a sure bet for the football Hall of Fame, though Manning himself says that figuring out what plays to run and where to set his receivers on the field occupies most of his attention right now. "I always talk about enjoying the journey and not the destination. Right now," he says, "I'm in the middle of it."[1]

evolution *of a* brand

Peyton Manning's appearance on the front of the fabled orange Wheaties box makes him one of a long line of sports heroes to promote the crunchy breakfast cereal. Fabled quarterbacks Brett Favre, Roger Staubach, Steve Young, and Dan Marino are just a few football legends who have served as celebrity spokesmen for Wheaties.

Product endorsement has a long history. But while the link between Wheaties and sports figures has humble beginnings in the 1930s, the evolution of Peyton Manning as the NFL's Most Valuable Player and highest-paid endorsement figure has been carefully planned. Manning works with a professional sports marketing company that also managed the marketing exposure of his famous dad, quarterback Archie Manning. Despite the high demand for his services, Manning burnishes the self-effacing image that makes him

so successful as a marketing spokesperson. Like many successful sports figures, he lends his name and resources to good causes such as the Peyback Foundation to help disadvantaged youth, the Bright Ideas grant program to help teachers meet local educational needs, and special events to benefit at-risk kids, local food pantries, foster-care facilities, and a host of other outreach efforts. Combine that humanitarian profile with his stellar performance as a quarterback, and "Peyton is the gold standard in the NFL," according to the CEO of a national sports marketing firm. "Peyton is a guy you can put your logo on and you know it will be safe in 10 years."

- Not every sports figure has had a successful run as a marketing spokesperson. NBA basketball star Kobe Bryant's standing nose-dived after he was accused of rape. Yet marketing analysts feel sure that not even losing a Super Bowl playoff

evolution *of a* **brand**

game can tarnish Manning's value. What potential missteps must figures such as Manning keep in mind as they pursue their careers on and off the field?

• How important is the match between celebrity endorser and product? What goods or services do you think Peyton Manning might not be able to promote with credibility?

Chapter Overview

From the last chapter, you already know that the nonpersonal elements of promotion include advertising and public relations. Thousands of organizations rely on nonpersonal selling in developing their promotional mixes and integrated marketing communications strategies. Advertising is the most visible form of nonpersonal promotion, and marketers often use it together with sales promotion (discussed in the next chapter) to create effective promotional campaigns. Television is probably the most obvious medium for nonpersonal selling dollars. But recently off-Broadway theatergoers were surprised by a three-minute "play" promoting tourism in London, performed on stage by actors before the curtain rose on the scheduled show. The ad drew mixed reviews from the audience.[2]

More promising, for now, are ads beamed directly to consumers' Bluetooth-enabled cell phones, such as the signals transmitted to waiting passengers in Virgin Atlantic Airways' first-class lounge at London's Heathrow Airport. These messages invited travelers to watch a video ad for the Range Rover Sport SUV on their phone's screen. Similar messages, which use audio and video to leap past the simple text messages many cell phone users already receive, are planned for transmitters at 30 British rail stations, a number of large British shopping malls, and other Heathrow locations. Marketers hope that the popularity of cell phones will help them reach younger consumers, who are spending less time with traditional advertising media such as television, newspapers, and magazines. Though some consumers fear cell phone ads will be intrusive, early results suggest they might be effective with the right audience. EMI Group used 30-second cell phone spots, including music remixed for sound quality and interviews with the musicians, to promote a new album from the band Coldplay, adding new clips at least once a day as the ads were beamed from six London train stations. The album *X&Y* rose to number one in the United Kingdom.[3]

Marketers seeking excitement for new-product launches have recently paid millions for celebrities to promote their products. Catherine Zeta-Jones was recently paid $20 million to promote T-Mobile, while Angelina Jolie earned more than $12 million from the luxury apparel company St. John, and Nicole Kidman's contract with Chanel No. 5 perfume is worth $12 million.[4]

This chapter begins with a discussion of the types of advertising and explains how advertising is used to achieve a firm's objectives. It then considers alternative advertising strategies and the process of creating an advertisement. Next we provide a detailed look at various advertising media channels: television, radio, print advertising, direct mail, and outdoor and interactive media. The chapter then focuses on the importance of public relations, publicity, and cross-promotions. Alternative methods of measuring the effectiveness of both online and offline nonpersonal selling are examined. We conclude the chapter by exploring current ethical issues relating to nonpersonal selling.

ADVERTISING

Twenty-first-century advertising is closely related to integrated marketing communications (IMC) in many respects. While IMC involves a message dealing with buyer–seller relationships, **advertising** consists of paid non-personal communication through various media with the purpose of informing or persuading members of a particular audience. Advertising is used by marketers to reach target markets with messages designed to appeal to business firms, not-for-profit organizations, or ultimate consumers.

America is home to most of the world's leading advertisers. Procter & Gamble, General Motors, Unilever, Ford, and L'Oréal are five of the top advertisers in the world, each spending more than $2 billion annually—an average of almost $6 million a day—on U.S. advertising.[5]

Advertising spending varies among industries as well as companies. The cosmetics industry is widely known for pouring dollars into advertising, as is the auto manufacturing industry. Auto makers and telecommunications companies dominate the top ten megabrands for ad spending, with Verizon, Sprint, and Cingular accounting for nearly $3.2 billion in U.S. advertising spending. Ford, Nissan, Chevrolet, Toyota, and Dodge spend almost $4.3 billion combined. Dell and McDonald's ranked ninth and tenth, respectively, each spending more than $600 million a year.[6]

As previous chapters have discussed, the emergence of the marketing concept, with its emphasis on a company-wide consumer orientation, boosted the importance of integrated marketing communications. This change in turn expanded the role of advertising. Today, a typical consumer is exposed to hundreds of advertising messages each day. Advertising provides an efficient, inexpensive, and fast method of reaching the ever-elusive, increasingly segmented consumer market.

advertising Paid, non-personal communication through various media about a business firm, not-for-profit organization, product, or idea by a sponsor identified in a message that is intended to inform or persuade members of a particular audience.

The cell phone industry relies heavily on advertising to inform consumers of their products' benefits. Here, Verizon promotes its reliability.

TYPES OF ADVERTISING

Advertisements fall into two broad categories: product advertising and institutional advertising. **Product advertising** is nonpersonal selling of a particular good or service. This is the type of advertising the average person usually thinks of when talking about most promotional activities.

Institutional advertising, in contrast, promotes a concept, an idea, a philosophy, or the goodwill of an industry, company, organization, person, geographic location, or government agency. This term has a broader meaning than *corporate advertising,* which is typically limited to nonproduct advertising sponsored by a specific profit-seeking firm. Institutional advertising is often closely related to the public-relations function of an enterprise.

product advertising Nonpersonal selling of a particular good or service.

institutional advertising Promotion of a concept, an idea, a philosophy, or the goodwill of an industry, company, organization, person, geographic location, or government agency.

1 Identify the three major advertising objectives and the two basic categories of advertising.

OBJECTIVES OF ADVERTISING

Marketers use advertising messages to accomplish three primary objectives: to inform, to persuade, and to remind. These objectives may be used individually or, more typically, in conjunction with each

COURTESY OF PEPSI-COLA COMPANY

In a twist on the typical celebrity endorsement, PepsiCo treats its Diet Pepsi as the star in its product promotion.

informative advertising Promotion that seeks to develop initial demand for a good, service, organization, person, place, idea, or cause.

persuasive advertising Promotion that attempts to increase demand for an existing good, service, organization, person, place, idea, or cause.

reminder advertising Advertising that reinforces previous promotional activity by keeping the name of a good, service, organization, person, place, idea, or cause before the public.

other. For example, an ad for a not-for-profit agency may inform the public of the existence of the organization and at the same time persuade the audience to make a donation, join the organization, or attend a function.

Informative advertising seeks to develop initial demand for a good, service, organization, person, place, idea, or cause. The promotion of any new market entry tends to pursue this objective because marketing success at this stage often depends simply on announcing availability. Therefore, informative advertising is common in the introductory stage of the product life cycle, as for hybrid cars such as the Toyota Prius or for camera cell phones.

Persuasive advertising attempts to increase demand for an existing good, service, organization, person, place, idea, or cause. Persuasive advertising is a competitive type of promotion suited to the growth stage and the early part of the maturity stage of the product life cycle. 7Up's recent campaign announces that its original variety is "100% natural," now that an artificial preservative has been removed from the soft drink's formula.[7]

Reminder advertising strives to reinforce previous promotional activity by keeping the name of a good, service, organization, person, place, idea, or cause before the public. It is common in the latter part of the maturity stage and throughout the decline stage of the product life cycle. Procter & Gamble, for instance, seeks to remind consumers, particularly women, about the stain-fighting qualities of its Tide detergent by focusing on the emotional commitment many people have with their clothing.[8]

Figure 16.1 illustrates the relationship between advertising objectives and the stages of the product life cycle. Informative advertising tends to work best during the early stages, while reminder advertising is effective later on. Persuasive advertising, if done well, can be effective through the entire life cycle.

Traditionally, marketers stated their advertising objectives as direct sales goals. A more current and realistic standard, however, views advertising as a way to achieve communications objectives, including informing, persuading, and reminding potential customers of the product. Advertising attempts to condition consumers to adopt favorable viewpoints toward a promotional message. The goal of an ad is to improve the likelihood that a customer will buy a particular good or service. In this sense, advertising illustrates the close relationship between marketing communications and promotional strategy.

To get the best value for a firm's advertising investment, marketers must first determine what that firm's advertising objectives are. Effective advertising can enhance consumer perceptions of quality in a good or service, leading to increased customer loyalty, repeat purchases, and protection against price wars. In addition, perceptions of superiority pay off in the firm's ability to raise prices without losing market share.

Some basic do's and don'ts apply to advertising in general and can help ensure that messages are presented in ways that are effective, not offensive. The "Etiquette Tips for Marketing Professionals" feature outlines a few of these rules.

figure 16.1

Advertising Objectives in Relation to Stage in the Product Life Cycle

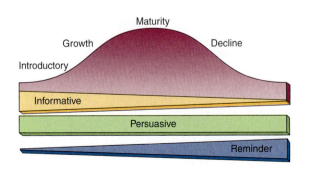

Etiquette Tips for Marketing Professionals

Advertising Do's and Don'ts

As advertising expands its reach to interactive media such as computer games and even cell phones, it will undergo many changes. Some basics, however, never change, including the rules of composing effective advertising messages. Here are a few fundamental do's and don'ts, including some special reminders about advertising in new media.

DO

1. Be clear about whether your objective is to inform, to persuade, or to remind.
2. Keep your message short and simple.
3. Choose visuals and graphics that attract attention in a positive way and that show the product, if illustrated, accurately in all details.
4. Disclose all relevant information about the good or service in the ad.
5. For product placements, make sure the brand is relevant to the context, such as a car added to a video racing game.

DON'T

1. Don't advertise sales or specials unless you've really lowered prices, and don't increase prices just to later be able to afford a "free" giveaway.
2. Don't make claims about the product that you can't substantiate.
3. Don't even think about running tasteless ads. Check a humorous message with a wide variety of readers or viewers before you run with it.
4. Don't waste resources on ads that aren't well targeted.
5. Don't send spam. Ever.

Sources: Farid Aziz, "Online Advertising Mistakes—3 Don'ts for Newbies," *AF Work*, **http://www.allfreelancework.com**, accessed November 6, 2006; "Newspaper Advertising Do's and Don'ts," Workforce Planning for Wisconsin State Government, **http://workforceplanning.wi.gov**, accessed May 31, 2006; "Advertising Do's and Don'ts," Business Infosource, Government of Saskatchewan, **http://www.cbsc.org**, April 1, 2006; Fran Kennish, "In-Game Advertising Dos and Don'ts," iMedia Connection, March 3, 2006, **http://www.imediaconnection.com**; "Super Don'ts," *USA Today*, February 3, 2006, **http://www.usatoday.com**.

ADVERTISING STRATEGIES

If the primary function of marketing is to bring buyers and sellers together, then advertising is the means to an end. Effective advertising strategies accomplish at least one of three tasks: informing, persuading, or reminding consumers. The secret to success in choosing the best strategy is developing a message that best positions a firm's product in the audience's mind. Among the advertising strategies available for use by 21st-century marketers are comparative advertising and celebrity advertising, as well as decisions about global and interactive ads. Channel-oriented decisions such as retail and cooperative advertising can also be devised.

Marketers often combine several of these advertising strategies to ensure that the advertisement accomplishes set objectives. As markets become more segmented, the need for personalized advertising increases. The next sections describe strategies that contemporary marketers may use to reach their target markets.

COMPARATIVE ADVERTISING

Firms whose products are not the leaders in their markets often favor **comparative advertising,** a promotional strategy that emphasizes advertising messages with direct or indirect comparisons to dominant brands in the industry. By contrast, advertising by market leaders seldom acknowledges

 assessment check

1. What are the goals of institutional advertising?
2. At what stage in the product life cycle are informative ads used? Why?
3. What is reminder advertising?

 List the major advertising strategies.

comparative advertising
Advertising strategy that emphasizes messages with direct or indirect promotional comparisons between competing brands.

that competing products even exist, and when they do, they usually do not point out any benefits of the competing brands.

Wireless telecommunications carriers have been battling it out in media advertising, promoting their calling plans and inviting comparison to competitors. Some offer "in" calling, free text messaging, no roaming charges, or extended hours at reduced rates to compete against similar offers from other companies.

A generation ago, comparative advertising was not the norm; in fact, it was frowned on. But the Federal Trade Commission now encourages comparative advertising. Regulators believe such ads keep marketers competitive and consumers better informed about their choices. Generally speaking, when there is competition through advertising, prices tend to go down because people can shop around. This benefit has proved increasingly true for online consumers, who now use shopping bots to help find the best prices on goods and services.

LOOK WHO'S DRINKING BIGELOW GREEN TEA NOW.

"Six years ago, my nutritionist recommended I make it a regular part of my diet, so I did. I've been drinking Bigelow green tea ever since...especially during the game."

Joe Torre
— Joe Torre

BIGELOW

Go to www.gogreentea.com for more information.

COURTESY OF BIGELOW'S GREEN TEA

Joe Torre, Major League Baseball celebrity, endorses the health benefits of Bigelow's Green Tea, saying "My nutritionist recommended I make [green tea] a regular part of my diet. . . . I've been drinking Bigelow green tea ever since . . . especially during the game."

CELEBRITY TESTIMONIALS

A popular technique for increasing advertising readership in a cluttered promotional environment and improving overall effectiveness of a marketing message involves the use of celebrity spokespeople, such as the Colts' quarterback Peyton Manning, discussed in the chapter opener. About one of every five U.S. ads currently includes celebrities. This type of advertising is also popular in foreign countries. In Japan, 80 percent of all ads use celebrities, both local and international stars. U.S. celebrities featured in Japanese ads include actors Harrison Ford for Kirin Beer, Jodie Foster for Keri Cosmetics and Latte Coffee, and Paul Newman for Evance watch stores. Japanese consumers view foreign stars as images more than actual people, which helps marketers sell products. They also associate American stars with quality and idolize, for instance, the Seattle Mariners' right fielder and star hitter Ichiro Suzuki, originally from Kobe, Japan, who currently has more than $10 million in endorsement deals from various U.S. and Japanese firms and has turned down millions more.[9]

Both the number of celebrity ads and the dollars spent on those ads have increased in recent years. Professional athletes such as Ichiro Suzuki are among the highest-paid product endorsers, raking in millions each year. They appear in advertisements for a wide variety of products, many having little or nothing to do with sports. Nike has signed English soccer star Wayne Rooney for more than $9 million, while Suzuki endorses not only sports gear from several Japanese firms but also the services of a brokerage firm, Sato Pharmaceuticals, NTT Communications, and Shin Nippon Oil.[10] But actors, singers, and other media stars top the list of most powerful celebrities in the United States. Those who make the most money and attract the most attention include George Lucas, Steven Spielberg, Madonna, Elton John, and Johnny Depp, along with sports icons Tiger Woods and Shaquille O'Neal. But topping the list is talk show host Oprah Winfrey.[11]

One advantage of associations with big-name personalities is improved product recognition in a promotional environment filled with hundreds of competing 15- and 30-second commercials. Advertisers use the term *clutter* to describe this situation. As e-marketing continues to soar, one inevitable result has been the increase in advertising clutter as companies rush to market their goods and services online. But marketers need to remember that an effective online site must have meaningful content and helpful service.

Another advantage to using celebrities occurs when marketers are trying to reach consumers of another culture. Blockbuster Video and McDonald's have hired Hispanic stars to attract Hispanic consumers to their stores. Actress Daisy Fuentes appeared in ads for McDonald's, while John Leguizamo and Hector Elizondo advertised for Blockbuster.

A celebrity testimonial generally succeeds when the celebrity is a credible source of information for the product being promoted. The most effective ads of this type establish relevant links between the celebrities and the advertised goods or services, such as the models and actresses who endorse Revlon cosmetics. Michelle Wie, already the world's highest-paid female golfer when she was still only 15, has signed deals with Nike and Sony that are reported to be worth about $10 million a year and is represented by the William Morris agency, which has represented far more Hollywood clients than sports figures.[12]

Several studies of consumer responses show that celebrities improve the product's believability, recall of the product, and brand recognition. Celebrity endorsements also create positive attitudes, leading to greater brand equity.

However, a celebrity who endorses too many products may create marketplace confusion. Customers may remember the celebrity but not the product or brand; worse, they might connect the celebrity to a competing brand. Another problem arises if a celebrity is dogged by scandal or legal problems, or if the promotion itself skirts scandal. Sometimes the problem is simply a less than perfect match. Within months of signing an endorsement deal with hair dressing Brylcreem, English soccer star David Beckham shaved his head. Brylcreem declined to renew the contract.[13] And Fidelity, the world's largest mutual fund company, signed former Beatle Paul McCartney as a spokesman in a move that some observers feel is "novel" but that others are skeptical will resonate with the public.[14]

Some advertisers try to avoid problems with celebrity endorsers by using cartoon characters as endorsers. Snoopy, a character in the popular *Peanuts* comic strip and long-running TV animated programs, has appeared in MetLife ads for years. Some advertisers may actually prefer cartoon characters because the characters can never say anything negative about the product, they do exactly what the marketers want them to do, and they cannot get involved in scandals. The only drawback is high licensing fees; popular animated characters often cost more than live celebrities. Companies may create their own cartoon characters or "talking" animals, which eventually become celebrities in their own right as a result of many appearances in advertisements, as is the case with the Keebler elves and the Geico gecko.

In recent years, marketers have begun to consider celebrities as marketing partners rather than pretty or famous faces who can sell goods and services. Tiger Woods has been active in developing Nike's golf gear and apparel. Former supermodel Claudia Schiffer not only agreed to endorse a signature line of Palm Pilots but also helped position the handheld computers in the electronics market by selecting fashionable colors and her own favorite software programs.

RETAIL ADVERTISING

Most consumers are confronted daily with **retail advertising,** which includes all advertising by retail stores that sell goods or services directly to the consuming public. While this activity accounts for a sizable portion of total annual advertising expenditures, retail advertising varies widely in its effectiveness. One study showed that consumers often respond with suspicion to retail price advertisements. Source, message, and shopping experience seem to affect consumer attitudes toward these advertisements.

An advertiser once quipped that the two most powerful words to use in an ad are "New" and "Free"—and these terms are often capitalized on in retail ads. Although "Free" may be featured only in discussions of customer services, the next best term—"Sale"—is often the centerpiece of retail promotions. And "New" typically describes new lines of products being offered. However, many retail stores continue to view advertising as a secondary activity, although that is changing. Local independent retailers rarely use advertising agencies, probably because of the expense involved. Instead, store managers may accept responsibility for advertising in addition to their other duties.

Management can begin to correct this problem by assigning one individual the sole responsibility and authority for developing an effective retail advertising program.

A retailer often shares advertising costs with a manufacturer or wholesaler in a technique called **cooperative advertising.** For example, an apparel marketer may pay a percentage of the cost of a retail store's newspaper advertisement featuring its product lines. Cooperative advertising campaigns originated to take advantage of the media's practice of offering lower rates to local advertisers than to national ones. Later, cooperative advertising became part of programs to improve dealer relations. The retailer likes the chance to secure advertising that it might not be able to afford otherwise. Cooperative advertising can strengthen vertical links in the marketing channel, as when a manufacturer and retailer coordinate their resources. It can also involve firms at the same level of the supply chain. In a horizontal arrangement, a group of retailers—for example, all the Ford dealers in the northeastern United States—might pool their resources.

cooperative advertising
Strategy in which a retailer shares advertising costs with a manufacturer or wholesaler.

IMAGE COURTESY OF THE ADVERTISING ARCHIVES

In this cooperative promotion, Adidas links its well-known sports shoes with up-and-coming fashion designer Stella McCartney. McCartney designs a product line for Adidas.

INTERACTIVE ADVERTISING

Millions of advertising messages float across idle—and active—computer screens in homes and offices around the country every day. Net surfers play games that are embedded with ads from the site sponsors. Companies offer free e-mail service to people willing to receive ads with their personal messages. Video screens on grocery carts display ads for shoppers to see as they wheel down the aisles of grocery stores.

Because marketers realize that two-way communications provide more effective methods for achieving promotional objectives, they are interested in interactive media. **Interactive advertising** involves two-way promotional messages transmitted through communication channels that induce message recipients to participate actively in the promotional effort. Achieving this involvement is the difficult task facing contemporary marketers. Although interactive advertising has become nearly synonymous with e-business and the Web, it also includes other formats such as kiosks in shopping malls and text messages on cell phones. Multimedia technology, the Internet, and commercial online services are changing the nature of advertising from a one-way, passive communication technique to more effective, two-way marketing communications. Interactive advertising creates dialogue between marketers and individual shoppers, providing more materials at the user's request. The advertiser's challenge is to gain and hold consumer interest in an environment where these individuals control what they want to see. "It's not about linear communication," said Robert Greenberg, head of the advertising and communications agency R/GA in New York. "It's about symbols and icons and you click here and you click there, and you control it."[15]

Interactive advertising changes the balance between marketers and consumers. Unlike the traditional role of advertising—providing brief, entertaining, attention-catching messages—interactive media provide information to help consumers throughout the purchase and consumption processes. In a sense, it becomes closer to personal selling as consumers receive immediate responses to questions or requests for more information about goods and services. Interactive advertising provides consumers with more information in less time to help them make necessary comparisons between available products.

Successful interactive advertising adds value by offering the viewer more than just product-related information. An ad on the Web can do more than promote a brand; it can create a company store, provide customer service, and offer additional content. And many marketers at companies both large and small are hoping that such ads will soon be so finely targeted that they can cut through increasing "advertising clutter" and reach only consumers who are ready to hear their messages. The CEO of ClearGauge, an interactive ad agency, hopes that "we can cut the cost of the advertising in half while maintaining customer response." After all, says the chief marketing officer of Claria, a company that offers online tracking services, "If you're starting a high-end pet-food company, you only want to talk to people who have a certain type of pet and are willing to pay a premium to feed it. We can identify those people. Why do you need to reach anyone else?"[16]

Most firms deliver their interactive advertising messages through proprietary online services and through the Web. In fact, online ad spending rose to a new high of $12.5 billion in a recent year and is expected to double that in just the next few years. Search advertising accounts for about 40 percent of total online ad spending, followed by display advertising. Both categories are projected to grow rapidly.[17]

assessment check

1. What is comparative advertising?
2. What makes a successful celebrity testimonial?
3. What is cooperative advertising?

CREATING AN ADVERTISEMENT

3 Describe the process of creating an advertisement.

Marketers spend about $300 billion a year on advertising campaigns in the United States alone.[18] With so much money at stake, they must create effective, memorable ads that increase sales and enhance their organizations' images. They cannot afford to waste resources on mediocre messages that fail to capture consumers' attention, communicate their sales message effectively, or lead to a purchase, donation, or other positive action for the organization.

Research helps marketers create better ads by pinpointing goals that an ad needs to accomplish, such as educating consumers about product features, enhancing brand loyalty, or improving consumer perception of the brand. These objectives should guide the design of the ad. Marketers can also discover what appeals to consumers and can test ads with potential buyers before committing funds for a campaign.

Marketers sometimes face specific challenges as they develop advertising objectives for services. They must find a creative way to fill out the intangible images of most services and successfully convey the benefits that consumers receive. The "You're in Good Hands" message of Allstate Insurance is a classic example of how creative advertising can make the intangible nature of services tangible.

TRANSLATING ADVERTISING OBJECTIVES INTO ADVERTISING PLANS

Once a company defines its objectives for an advertising campaign, it can develop its advertising plan. Marketing research helps managers make strategic decisions that guide choices in technical areas such as budgeting,

IMAGE COURTESY OF THE ADVERTISING ARCHIVES

This promotion from the United Kingdom's Center Parcs is made up of individual photos of guests and nature. Together, the snapshots form a larger image of a tree. Simultaneously featuring fun, nature, and relaxation conveys the heart of a Center Parcs vacation.

figure 16.2

Elements of the Advertising Planning Process

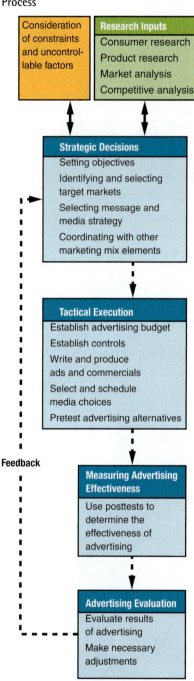

Consideration of constraints and uncontrollable factors

Research Inputs
Consumer research
Product research
Market analysis
Competitive analysis

Strategic Decisions
Setting objectives
Identifying and selecting target markets
Selecting message and media strategy
Coordinating with other marketing mix elements

Tactical Execution
Establish advertising budget
Establish controls
Write and produce ads and commercials
Select and schedule media choices
Pretest advertising alternatives

Feedback

Measuring Advertising Effectiveness
Use posttests to determine the effectiveness of advertising

Advertising Evaluation
Evaluate results of advertising
Make necessary adjustments

4 Identify the major types of advertising appeals and discuss their uses.

advertising campaign
Series of different but related ads that use a single theme and appear in different media within a specified time period.

copywriting, scheduling, and media selection. Posttests, which are discussed in greater detail later in the chapter, measure the effectiveness of advertising and form the basis for feedback concerning possible adjustments. The elements of advertising planning are shown in Figure 16.2. Experienced marketers know the importance of following even the most basic steps in the process, such as market analysis.

As Chapter 9 explained, positioning involves developing a marketing strategy that aims to achieve a desired position in a prospective buyer's mind. Marketers use a positioning strategy that distinguishes their good or service from those of competitors. Effective advertising then communicates the desired position by emphasizing certain product characteristics, such as performance attributes, price/quality, competitors' shortcomings, applications, user needs, and product classes.

ADVERTISING MESSAGES

The strategy for creating a message starts with the benefits a product offers to potential customers and moves to the creative concept phase, in which marketers strive to bring an appropriate message to consumers using both visual and verbal components. Marketers work to create an ad with meaningful, believable, and distinctive appeals—one that stands out from the clutter and is more likely to escape "zapping" by the television remote control.

Usually ads are created not individually but as part of specific campaigns. An **advertising campaign** is a series of different but related ads that use a single theme and appear in different media within a specified time period. General Electric is running an integrated marketing campaign showcasing its "Ecomagination," or dedication to researching clean technologies, reducing greenhouse gases, and improving energy efficiency. Print, TV, and online ads direct visitors from all over the world to a special Web site introducing seventeen environmentally friendly GE products with sound, animation, and pictures.[19]

In developing a creative strategy, advertisers must decide how to communicate their marketing message. They must balance message characteristics, such as the tone of the appeal, the extent of information provided and the conclusion to which it leads the consumer, the side of the story the ad tells, and its emphasis on verbal or visual primary elements.

✓ *assessment check*

1. **What is an advertising campaign?**

2. **What are an advertisement's three main goals?**

ADVERTISING APPEALS

Should the tone of the advertisement focus on a practical appeal such as price or gas mileage, or should it evoke an emotional response by appealing to, say, fear, humor, sex, guilt, or fantasy? This is another critical decision in the creation of memorable ads that possess the strengths needed to accomplish promotional objectives. Recent research suggests that skeptical consumers might actually be more responsive to consumer-product ads that appeal to their emotions than to ads that deliver information. Nonskeptics were found to respond better to informational advertising.[20]

Fear Appeals

In recent years, marketers have relied increasingly on fear appeals. Ads for insurance, autos, healthcare products, and even certain foods imply that incorrect buying decisions could lead to illness, injury, or other bad consequences. Even ads for business services imply that if a company doesn't purchase the advertised services, its competitors will move ahead or valuable information may be lost.

Pharmaceuticals companies spend nearly $4 billion a year on advertising, much of which is directed toward consumer fears—whether fear of hair loss, fear of allergies, or fear of heart attacks and other potentially serious illnesses. These drug advertisements have flourished in both print and broadcast media after the Food and Drug Administration lifted a ban on prescription drug advertising on television. Such ads have become a key component of marketers' pulling channel strategies. Typical ads that the industry categorizes as "disease-state awareness advertising" encourage readers and viewers to ask their doctors whether the medication should be prescribed for their medical needs.[21]

Fear appeals can backfire, however. Viewers are likely to practice selective perception and tune out statements they perceive as too strong or not credible. Some consumer researchers believe that viewer or reader backlash will eventually occur due to the amount of prescription drug advertising based on fear appeals.

Humor in Advertising Messages

A humorous ad, such as CareerBuilder.com's ad campaign that used silly chimps in shirts and ties to poke fun at office workers, seeks to create a positive mood related to a good or service. Humor can improve audience awareness and recall and enhance the consumer's favorable image of the brand. After all, if the ad makes the consumer feel good, then the product may do the same. CareerBuilder's vice president of consumer marketing says that office humor works so well because it's a "common denominator" for the company's target market—young office workers looking for better jobs.[22]

But advertising professionals differ in their opinions of the effectiveness of humorous ads. Some believe that humor distracts attention from brand and product features; consumers remember the humor but not the product. Humorous ads, because they are so memorable, may lose their effectiveness sooner than ads with other kinds of appeals. In addition, humor can be tricky because what one group of consumers finds funny may not be funny at all to another group. Men and women sometimes have a different sense of humor, as do people of different ages. This distinction may become even greater across cultures.

Ads Based on Sex

Ads with sex-based appeals have what is called "stopping power" because they attract the reader's or viewer's attention. Research indicates, however, that sexual content in an ad boosts recall of the ad's content only if the appeal is appropriate to the type of product advertised.[23] A recent risqué TV ad for Carl's Jr. restaurants that featured Paris Hilton and a car drew attention in the media for its eroticism.[24] Some advertisers, including teen clothier Abercrombie & Fitch, which produced a catalog called "XXX Wet, Hot Summer Fun," have begun to tone down their appeals based on sex.[25] The "Solving an Ethical Controversy" feature examines the pros and cons of using sex to sell.

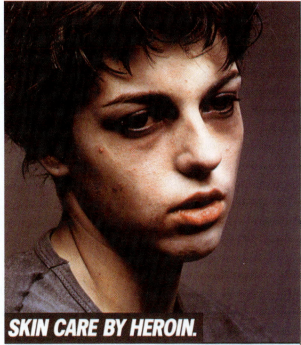

SKIN CARE BY HEROIN.

At first you think you can control heroin.
But before long you'll start looking ill, losing weight and feeling like death.
Then one day you'll wake up knowing that, instead of you controlling heroin, it now controls you.
So, if a friend offers you heroin, you know what to say.

HEROIN SCREWS YOU UP.

This ad uses a frightening visual and an alarming concept—what heroin looks like as it attacks a person's skin—to try to steer people away from using drugs.

Karaoke got you croaky?
Treat your throat

Soothe your dry, scratchy throat with the delicious cooling relief of Halls Fruit Breezers! In no time flat you'll start to feel like yourself again. Now hit that high note—even if it is off key. Use as directed. hallsfruitbreezers.com

HALLS® uses humor to promote its HALLS Fruit Breezers® throat lozenges.

Solving an Ethical Controversy

Using Sex to Sell

Ads that rely on sex appeal are nothing new, nor is the fact that the products advertised, such as toothpaste and vacation packages, sometimes have little connection with the provocative copy and images that promote them. One retail clothing chain, American Apparel, has become widely successful using sexually provocative and even explicit advertising, featuring amateur models who are often company employees. Founder Dov Charney promotes the company's freewheeling atmosphere, publicizing its policy of free massages at work and his own "loving" relationships with employees and colleagues.

While few firms go so far, and the reaction to American Apparel's promotions hasn't all been positive, there's no doubt that sexual appeals for all kinds of products are in wide use and are often effective.

Should marketers use sex to sell products?

PRO

1. There is so much sexuality elsewhere in the culture today that marketers have to keep pushing the barriers just to get noticed.
2. It attracts attention, so it is a legitimate means to sell products. In short, it works.

CON

1. Explicit or provocative ads are demeaning to both men and women and help lower the standards of what is acceptable in our culture.

2. When sex is irrelevant to the good or service, relying on sexual marketing is counterproductive. It can confuse the message.

Summary

Broadcasters must pay large fines for programming deemed "obscene, profane, and indecent." Its effects on the advertising industry remain to be seen. Meanwhile, young teens across the country have begun to protest the marketing of shirts emblazoned with provocative slogans such as "Hottie," "Vixen," and "Maybe You'll Get Lucky." "We use sex to sell everything in this country," says one educator. "Kids must be very perplexed." And employees filed three sexual harassment lawsuits against American Apparel; two have been withdrawn, and one is pending.

Sources: "Bush Signs Broadcast Decency Law," *New York Times,* June 15, 2006, **www.nytimes.com**; Kathleen Wereszynski, "Girl Culture Begets Backlash," Fox News, May 31, 2006, **http://www.foxnews.com**; Beth Potter, "Sex! Now Wanna Buy the Toaster?" *Denver Post,* May 9, 2006, **http://www.denverpost.com**; Dan Glaister, "Nice and Sleazy," *The Guardian,* January 10, 2006, **http://www.guardian.co.uk**; Susan Aschoff, "It's Grrrl Power vs. Abercrombie & Fitch," *St. Petersburg (FL) Times,* November 5, 2005, **http://www.sptimes.com**; Stuart Eskenazi, "Hot Retailer Aims to Recharge Buzz, and Business, on the Ave.," *The Seattle Times,* October 22, 2005, **http://seattletimes.nwsource.com**.

DEVELOPING AND PREPARING ADS

The final step in the advertising process—the development and preparation of an advertisement—should flow logically from the promotional theme selected. This process should create an ad that becomes a complementary part of the marketing mix with a carefully determined role in the total marketing strategy. Preparation of an advertisement should emphasize features such as its creativity, its continuity with past advertisements, and possibly its association with other company products.

What immediate tasks should an advertisement accomplish? Regardless of the chosen target, an advertisement should (1) gain attention and interest, (2) inform and/or persuade, and (3) eventually lead to a purchase or other desired action. It should gain attention in a productive way; that is, it should instill some recall of the good or service. Otherwise, it will not lead to buying action.

Gaining attention and generating interest—cutting through the clutter—can be formidable tasks. "People are tired of commercials that look like commercials," according to the creative director of giant ad agency Saatchi & Saatchi. "People are looking for things that are real," a desire that has led some marketers to create ads that reflect the popularity of reality television, such as a Toyota spot that looks like a home movie or Anheuser-Busch ads meant to look like minidocumentaries about a fictional daredevil.[26] Stimulating buying action is often difficult because an advertisement cannot actually close a sale. Nevertheless, if an ad gains attention and informs or persuades, it probably represents a worthwhile investment of marketing resources. Too many advertisers fail to suggest how audience members can purchase their products if they desire to do so. Creative design should eliminate this shortcoming.

The Ray-Ban ad in Figure 16.3 shows the four major elements of this print advertisement: headline, illustration, body copy, and signature. *Headlines* and *illustrations* (photographs, drawings, or other artwork) should work together to generate interest and attention. *Body copy* informs, persuades, and stimulates buying action. The *signature,* which may include the company name, address, phone number, Web address, slogan, trademark, or simply a product photo, names the sponsoring organization. An ad may also have one or more subheads—headings subordinate to the main headline that either link the main headline to the body copy or subdivide sections of the body copy.

After advertisers conceive an idea for an ad that gains attention, informs and persuades, and stimulates purchases, their next step involves refining the thought sketch into a rough layout. Continued refinements of the rough layout eventually produce the final version of the advertisement design that is ready to be executed, printed, or recorded.

The creation of each advertisement in a campaign requires an evolutionary process that begins with an idea and ultimately results in a finished ad that is ready for distribution through print or electronic media. The idea itself must first be converted into a thought sketch, which is a tangible summary of the intended message.

Advances in technology allow advertisers to create novel, eye-catching advertisements. Innovative computer software packages now allow artists to merge multiple images to create a single image with a natural, seamless appearance. Computer-generated images appeal to younger, computer-literate consumers.

CREATING INTERACTIVE ADS

Web surfers want engaging, lively content that takes advantage of the medium's capabilities and goes beyond what they find elsewhere. The Web's major advantages make it possible for advertisers to provide that, offering speed, information, two-way communications, self-directed entertainment, and personal choice. Web ads are also vibrant in their visual appeal, such as the World Wide Fund for Nature ad that shows a roll of toilet paper unwinding to the floor.[27]

Web ads have grown from information-based home pages to innovative, interactive channels for transmitting messages to cyberaudiences, including banners, pop-ups, keyword ads, advertorials, and interstitials. *Advergames* are either online games created by marketers to promote their products to targeted audiences in an interactive way or ads or product placements inserted into online video games. Automakers are using these product placements to reach younger audiences—those who may not watch their TV commercials as often. Cadillac inserts its cars into a Microsoft Xbox game, and Toyota pays for its Scion to be featured—and "purchased"—in the fictitious world of Whyville.net, an interactive community for 8- to 15-year-old computer users.[28]

Banners, advertisements on a Web page that link to an advertiser's site, are the most common type of advertising on the Web. They can be free of charge or cost thousands of dollars per month depending on the amount of hits the site receives. Online advertisers often describe their Internet ads in terms of "richness," referring to the degree to which new technologies—such as streaming video, 3-D animation, JavaScript, and interactive capabilities—are implemented in the banners.

figure 16.3

Elements of a Typical Ad

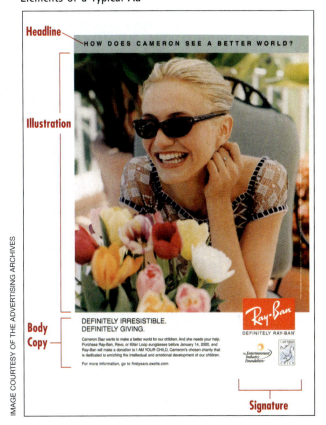

IMAGE COURTESY OF THE ADVERTISING ARCHIVES

Banners have evolved into a more target-specific technique for Internet advertising with the advent of *missiles:* messages that appear on the screen at exactly the right moment. When a customer visits the site of Company A's competitor, a missile can be programmed to appear on the customer's monitor that allows the customer to click a direct link to Company A's site. However, many people feel the use of such missiles is a questionable practice.

The British Broadcasting Company (BBC) is launching a U.S. ad campaign that uses banners to stream relevant BBCNews.com headlines to consumers so that, for example, the headlines for lifestyle stories will appear on entertainment sites while political news will run at national newspaper sites such as **http://www.nytimes.com** and **http://www.washingtonpost.com**.[29]

Keyword ads are an outcropping of banner ads. Used in search engines, keyword ads appear on the results page of a search and are specific to the term being searched. Advertisers pay search engines to target their ads and display the banners only when users search for relevant keywords, allowing marketers to target specific audiences. For example, if a user searched for the term "digital camera," keyword ads might appear for electronic boutiques or camera shops that sell digital cameras and film. Google and Yahoo! have long earned revenue from such ads; Microsoft is ready to join them with its new adCenter, which will be able to accurately target ads to receptive audiences.[30]

Banner designs that have also evolved into larger advertising squares that closely resemble advertisements in the telephone book's Yellow Pages are called *advertorials*. Advertisers quickly expanded on these advertorials with *interstitials*—ads that appear between Web pages of related content. Interstitials appear in a separate browser window while the user waits for a Web page to download.[31]

Then there are pop-ups, which are little advertising windows that appear in front of the top window of a user's computer screen, and "pop-unders," which appear under the top window. Some industry observers believe that pop-ups may be on the decline, partly because several lawsuits have been filed charging deceptive business practices and computer tampering.[32] Indeed, many users complain that interstitials, like pop-ups and missiles, are intrusive and unwanted. Interstitials are more likely to contain large graphics and streaming presentations than banner ads and therefore are more difficult to ignore than typical banner ads. But despite complaints, some studies show that users are more likely to click interstitials than banners.

Perhaps the most intrusive form of online advertising is *adware,* which allows ads to be shown on users' screens through the use of software downloaded to their computers without their consent or through trickery. Such software can be difficult to remove, and some legislators and industry experts believe that reputable marketers should avoid dealing with Internet marketing firms that promote the use of adware.[33]

 assessment check

1. What are some common emotional appeals used in advertising?

2. What are the main types of interactive ads?

 5 List and compare the major advertising media.

MEDIA SELECTION

One of the most important decisions in developing an advertising strategy is the selection of appropriate media to carry a firm's message to its audience. The media selected must be capable of accomplishing the communications objectives of informing, persuading, and reminding potential customers of the good, service, person, or idea being advertised.

Research identifies the ad's target market to determine its size and characteristics. Advertisers then match the target characteristics with the media best able to reach that particular audience. The objective of media selection is to achieve adequate media coverage without advertising beyond the identifiable limits of the potential market. Finally, cost comparisons between alternatives should determine the best possible media purchase.

Table 16.1 compares the major advertising media by noting their shares of overall advertising expenditures. It also compares the advantages and disadvantages of each media alternative. *Broadcast media* include television (network and cable) and radio. Newspapers, magazines, outdoor (out of home) advertising, and direct mail represent the major types of print media. Electronic media include the Internet and kiosks.

table 16.1 Comparison of Advertising Media Alternatives

MEDIA OUTLET	PERCENTAGE OF TOTAL*	ADVANTAGES	DISADVANTAGES
Broadcast			
Broadcast television	17.5	Extensive coverage; repetition; flexibility; prestige	High cost; brief message; limited segmentation
Cable television	8.2	Same strengths as network TV; less market coverage because not every viewer is a cable subscriber	Same disadvantages as network TV, although cable TV ads are targeted to considerably more specific viewer segments
Radio	7.4	Immediacy; low cost; flexibility; segmented audience; mobility	Brief message; highly fragmented audience
Print			
Newspapers	17.7	Tailored to individual communities; ability to refer back to ads	Limited life
Direct mail	19.8	Selectivity; intense coverage; speed; flexibility; opportunity to convey complete information; personalization	High cost; consumer resistance; dependence on effective mailing list
Magazines— Consumer Business	4.6 1.5	Selectivity; quality image reproduction; long life; prestige	Flexibility is limited
Outdoor (out of home)	2.2	Quick, visual communication of simple ideas; link to local goods and services; repetition	Brief exposure; environmental concerns
Electronic			
Internet	2.6	Two-way communications; flexibility; link to self-directed entertainment	Poor image reproduction; limited scheduling options; difficult to measure effectiveness

*An estimated 18.5 percent is spent on a variety of miscellaneous media, including Yellow Pages, business papers, transit displays, point-of-purchase displays, cinema advertising, and regional farm papers.

Source: Data from "U.S. Ad Spending Totals by Media," *FactPack 2006 Edition* (special supplement to *Advertising Age*), February 27, 2006, p. 11.

TELEVISION

Television—network and cable combined—accounts for roughly one of every four advertising dollars spent in the United States. The attractiveness of television advertising is that marketers can reach local and national markets. Whereas most newspaper advertising revenues come from local advertisers, the greatest share of television advertising revenues comes from organizations that advertise nationally. The newest trend in television advertising is virtual ads—banner-type logos and brief messages that are superimposed onto television coverage of sporting events so that they seem to be a part of the arena's signage but cannot be seen by anyone attending the game. Then there are streaming headlines run by some news stations, which are paid for by corporate sponsors whose names and logos appear within the news stream.

Other trends in television advertising are the abbreviated spot—a 15- or 30-second ad that costs less to make and buy and is too quick for most viewers to zap with their remote control—and single-advertiser shows. Chevrolet, for instance, bought all the ad time on an episode of *The Tonight Show* to promote its new HHR vehicle. Sometimes called *ad takeovers,* these single-advertiser spots allow for longer commercials and effectively block competitors from buying time on the same show. Marketers also hope that with takeovers they are "putting so many ads in that you can't possibly TiVo out every last one."[34]

In fact, TiVo is unveiling a new way for advertisers to get their messages across, through small logos called *billboards* that pop up over television commercials as viewers fast-forward through them. These billboards offer contests, giveaways, and links to more ads. If the user selects an ad, TiVo downloads contact information directly to the advertiser, with the viewer's permission. TiVo already gathers collective information about viewers' habits and sells it to networks and marketers. Far from becoming "the weapon of mass destruction of Madison Avenue," as one observer called it, TiVo is now viewed as the "first generation of the TV advertising of the future," according to the vice president of Starcom MediaVest Group, a media-buying company.[35] The "Marketing Success" feature discusses another way television advertisers are trying to "TiVo-proof" their messages.

In the past decade, cable television's share of ad spending and revenues has grown tremendously.[36] Satellite television has contributed to increased cable penetration, which almost three-fourths of all Americans now have installed in their homes. In response to declining ratings and soaring costs, network television companies such as NBC, CBS, ABC, Fox, and the CW (a network formed by the merger of the WB and UPN) are refocusing their advertising strategies with a heavy emphasis on moving onto the Net to capture younger audiences.

As cable audiences grow, programming improves, and ratings rise, advertisers are compelled to earmark more of their advertising budgets for this medium. Cable advertising offers marketers access to more narrowly defined target audiences than other broadcast media can provide—a characteristic referred to as *narrowcasting*. The top five cable network companies, ranked in terms of ad revenues, are ESPN, TNT, MTV, Lifetime, and TBS.[37] The great variety of special-interest channels devoted to subjects such as cooking, golf, history, home and garden, health, fitness, and various shopping channels attract specialized audiences and permit niche marketing.

Television advertising offers the advantages of mass coverage, powerful impact on viewers, repetition of messages, flexibility, and prestige. Its disadvantages include loss of control of the promotional message to the telecaster, which can influence its impact; high costs; and some public distrust. Compared with other media, television can suffer from lack of selectivity because specific TV programs may not reach consumers in a precisely defined target market without a significant degree of wasted coverage. However, the growing specialization of cable TV channels can help resolve the problem.

Finally, some types of products are actually banned from television advertising. Tobacco goods, such as cigarettes, cigars, and smokeless tobacco, fall into this category.

RADIO

Radio advertising has always been a popular media choice for up-to-the-minute newscasts and for targeting advertising messages to local audiences. But in recent years, radio has become one of the fastest-growing media alternatives. As more and more people find they have less and less time, radio

marketing success   HDTV and Super Bowl Advertising

Background. Although technology is creating many new opportunities for advertisers, it also threatens to close some tried-and-true avenues for pushing marketing messages. Television shows can be downloaded from the Internet without their advertising, and digital video recorders and cable video-on-demand allow viewers to skip past commercials even more easily than they did with homemade VHS recordings.

The Challenge. Getting viewers to sit still for advertising is the challenge facing today's top advertisers. With the cost of creating commercials rising

and the sheer number of marketing messages creating a sea of clutter, the stakes are climbing ever higher to beat the ease of zapping past commercials.

The Strategy. High-spending marketers such as FedEx, Bayer, Anheuser-Busch, Visa, MasterCard, and McDonald's are investing millions in two strategies. About 16 million U.S. households have at least one high-definition-capable TV, so marketers are creating high-definition ads. The aim is to ensure viewers a "seamless transition" from ad to programming and to capture attention with the highest-quality images. "When you're watching a

provides immediate information and entertainment at work, at play, and in the car, where, according to a Yankelovich Monitor study, Americans on average spend 2.5 hours each day. In addition, as e-business continues to push the growth in global business, more people are traveling abroad to seek out new markets. For these travelers, radio, because many radio stations are airing over the Internet, is a means of staying in touch with home—wherever that may be. Marketers frequently use radio advertising to reach local audiences. But in recent years, it plays an increasingly important role as a national—and even global—listening favorite. Thousands of online listeners use the Internet to beam in on radio stations from almost every city—tuning in on an easy-listening station in London, a top-40 Hong Kong broadcaster, or a chat show from Toronto. Other listeners equip their vehicles with satellite radio to maintain contact with hometown or destination stations during long trips.

Satellite radio providers offer much higher-quality digital signals than regular radio stations, with many more available channels that are mostly free of Federal Communications Commission oversight and generally commercial free. XM Radio, the first such service to be licensed, began airing commercials on a few of its nearly 200 music, sports, and talk channels. XM and its chief competitor, Sirius Satellite Radio, charge an annual fee; listeners must have a special receiver to decode the signals. By contrast, terrestrial radio stations that combine digital and analog signals to beam multiple types of content called HD radio are both ad and subscription free for the moment.[38]

Advertisers like radio for its ability to reach people while they drive because they are a captive audience. With an increase in commuters, this market is growing. Stations can adapt to local preferences by changing format, such as going from country and western to an all-news or sports station. The variety of stations allows advertisers to easily target audiences and tailor their messages to those listeners. Other benefits include low cost, flexibility, and mobility. Disadvantages include highly segmented audiences (reaching most people in a market may require ads placed on ten or more stations), the temporary nature of messages (unlike print ads, radio and TV ads are instantaneous and must be rebroadcast to reach consumers a second time), and a minimum of research information compared with television.

While most radio listening is often done in cars or with headset-equipped portables, technology has given birth to Net radio. Webcast radio allows customers to widen their listening times and choices through their computers. The potential for selling on this new channel is great. A listener can simply "click here to purchase the song you're hearing." Other goods are easily adapted to click-and-sell possibilities.

NEWSPAPERS

Newspaper advertising continues to dominate local markets, accounting for $47 billion of annual advertising expenditures. In addition to retail advertisements, classified advertising is an important part of newspaper revenues. Although some have predicted the decline of newspaper audiences, if

high-def broadcast, and you see a [standard] commercial come on, it looks like someone put a sheet over your television," says one producer of TV commercials. But high-def ads look great on both kinds of receivers, making them worth the expense for marketers determined to get the word out.

The second strategy is to place ads in programming that goes beyond mere entertainment. Live events such as the Academy Awards, the Olympics, and especially the Super Bowl are the kind of "TiVo-proof" pop-culture moments that still draw huge audiences eager to participate in real time.

The Outcome. Award shows and big sports contests have become a tremendous opportunity for creating memorable advertising that viewers actually want to watch. "The Super Bowl is a huge, rocket shot of creativity,"

says one media buying firm. Some ads created for the Super Bowl broadcast have gone on to have long lives on the Internet, where millions of people play them again and again. What more could an advertiser want?

Sources: Laura Petrecca, "Advertisers Jump on Board Live TV," *USA Today*, January 26, 2006, p. 1B; Paul R. LaMonica, "SB XL Ads: A Druid, Fabio and the King," CNN Money.com, January 22, 2006, **http://money.cnn.com**; Laura Petrecca, "More Super Bowl Marketers Shoot High-Def Ads," *USA Today*, January 13, 2006, p. 1B; Theresa Howard, "Ad Sales Boom for Super Bowl, Olympics," *USA Today*, January 6, 2006, **http://www.usatoday.com**.

online readers are counted in, newspapers are more popular than ever. About 5,000 daily newspapers have Web sites, and research done for the Newspaper Association of America suggests that a record one-third of all Internet users in the United States, or almost 50 million people, visited an online newspaper during one recent month.[39] In fact, online ad revenues have been growing for newspapers—at a rate of nearly 35 percent—compared with sluggish growth in print ads.[40]

Newspapers' primary advantages start with flexibility because advertising can vary from one locality to the next. Newspapers also allow intensive coverage for ads. Readers sometimes keep the advertising message, unlike television or radio advertising messages, and can refer back to newspaper ads.

Newspaper advertising does have some disadvantages: hasty reading (the typical reader spends about 28 minutes reading the newspaper),[41] and relatively poor reproduction quality, although that is changing as technology improves. The high quality of ads in *USA Today* is an example of the recent strides in newspaper ad quality made possible by new technologies.

Newspapers have also begun to struggle to "get through the noise" of other advertisers. To retain big advertisers such as trendy designers and national retailers, some have launched their own annual or semiannual fashion magazines, taking advantage of their finely tuned distribution capabilities.

MAGAZINES

Advertisers divide magazines into two broad categories: consumer magazines and business magazines. These categories are also subdivided into monthly and weekly publications. The top five magazines in terms of circulation are *Parade, Reader's Digest, TV Guide, Better Homes & Gardens,* and *Good Housekeeping.*[42] The primary advantages of magazine advertising include the ability to reach precise target markets, quality reproduction, long life, and the prestige associated with some magazines, such as the *Robb Report.* The primary disadvantage is that magazines lack the flexibility of newspapers, radio, and television.

Media buyers study circulation numbers and demographic information for various publications before choosing optimal placement opportunities and negotiating rates. The same advertising categories have claimed the title for big spenders for several years running. Automotive, retail, and movies and media advertising have held their first, second, and third places, respectively, each year and have continued to show strong growth percentages. Advertisers seeking to promote their products to target markets can reach them by advertising in the appropriate magazines.

DIRECT MAIL

As discussed in Chapter 14, direct-mail advertising includes sales letters, postcards, leaflets, folders, booklets, catalogs, and house organs (periodicals published by organizations to cover internal issues). Its advantages come from direct mail's ability to segment large numbers of prospective customers into narrow market niches, speed, flexibility, detailed information, and personalization. Disadvantages of direct mail include high cost per reader, reliance on the quality of mailing lists, and some consumers' resistance to it.

The advantages of direct mail explain its widespread use. Data are available on previous purchase patterns and preferred payment methods, as well as household characteristics such as number of children or seniors. Direct mail accounts for about 20 percent of U.S. total advertising expenditures, or $52 billion annually, and is the largest single category of ad spending by media.[43]

The downside to direct mail is clutter, otherwise known as *junk mail.* So much advertising material is stuffed into people's mailboxes every day that the task of grabbing consumers' attention and evoking some interest is daunting to direct mail advertisers. Three of every five respondents to a survey about "things most likely to get on consumers' nerves" rated junk mail at the top—above telemarketing, credit card fees, and the fine print on billing statements.

OUTDOOR ADVERTISING

Outdoor advertising, sometimes called *out-of-home advertising,* is perhaps the oldest and simplest media business around. It represents just over 2 percent of total advertising spending. Traditional outdoor advertising takes the form of billboards, painted displays (such as those that appear on the walls of buildings), and electronic displays. Transit advertising includes ads placed both inside and outside buses, subway trains and stations, and commuter trains. Some firms place ads on the roofs of taxicabs, on bus stop shelters and benches, on entertainment and sporting event turnstiles, in public restrooms, and even on parking meters. A section of highway might be cleaned up by a local real estate company or restaurant, with a nearby sign indicating the firm's contribution. All these are forms of outdoor advertising.

Outdoor advertising quickly communicates simple ideas. It also offers repeated exposure to a message, and strong promotion for locally available products. Outdoor advertising is particularly effective along metropolitan streets and in other high-traffic areas.

But outdoor advertising, just like every other type, is subject to clutter. It also suffers from the brevity of exposure to its messages by passing motorists. Driver concerns about rush-hour safety and limited time also combine to limit the length of exposure to outdoor messages. As a result, most of these ads use striking, simple illustrations, short selling points, and humor to attract people interested in products such as beer, vacations, local entertainment, and lodging.

A third problem relates to public concerns over aesthetics. The Highway Beautification Act of 1965, for example, regulates the placement of outdoor advertising near interstate highways. In addition, many cities have local ordinances that set regulations on the size and placement of outdoor advertising messages, and Hawaii prohibits them altogether. Critics have even labeled billboard advertising as "pollution on a stick."

New technologies are helping revive outdoor advertising. Technology livens up the billboards themselves with animation, large sculptures, and laser images. Digital message signboards can display winning lottery num-

PHOTO: DAVE EVERETT, ADSONFEET FOUNDER. AOF STAFF PHOTO BY: DUSTIN CORBETT

Outdoor advertising has gone creative. Boston's AdsOnFeet advertising firm uses chest-mounted flat-screen monitors to advertise everything from job opportunities to upcoming sporting events.

bers or other timely messages such as weather and traffic reports. The best-known digital signboard in the United States is in New York's Times Square. Digital video screens broadcast news, announcements, weather, and advertising in Europe.[44]

INTERACTIVE MEDIA

Interactive media—especially the Internet—are growing up. Keyword ads dominate online advertising, helping online revenues grow for several consecutive years to a new record of more than $12 billion, according to the Interactive Advertising Bureau (IAB). "Interactive advertising continues to experience tremendous growth as marketers experience its overall effectiveness in building brands and delivering online and offline sales," said the chief executive of IAB.[45] Not surprisingly, interactive advertising budgets are being beefed up at a growing number of companies.

Ads are coming to cell phones as well, as video and broadcast capabilities explode. About 90 percent of consumer marketers plan to dive into cell phone advertising, and revenues from such advertising are expected to reach more than $1.3 billion in a few years. To counter consumer resistance, some experts advise offering opt-in features and incentives, such as credits toward the phone bill.[46] Some marketers even envision capitalizing on global positioning systems in some phones to beam ads to users in the vicinity of certain retail stores. By law, however, wireless carriers are not allowed to give out information about a customer's location without permission or to sell phone numbers to telemarketers, making the use of incentives more likely.[47] Virgin Mobile USA already offers SugarMama, the first ad-supported cell phone service in the United States. The program is aimed at teenagers, who can earn up to 75 free minutes a month by watching 30-second commercials on their computers or text messages on their phones—and answering questions about the ads (from Pepsi, Microsoft's Xbox, and Truth, an antismoking campaign) to prove they paid attention.[48]

OTHER ADVERTISING MEDIA

As consumers filter out appeals from traditional as well as Internet ads, marketers need new ways to catch their attention. In addition to the major media, firms use a vast number of other vehicles to communicate their messages. Thousands of U.S. movie theaters accept commercials. The trend began as theater owners realized that a lag of 20 minutes between the time patrons enter the theater until the film actually starts could not be filled with upcoming previews, and they began to fill the time with ads. Theater owners have spent a combined $150 million to install digital projectors just to show these ads.[49] Each year, 1.6 billion tickets are sold, mostly to the teen to 35-year-old category, a prime target for many advertisers.

Ads also appear on T-shirts, inlaid in store flooring, in printed programs of live theater productions, and as previews on movie DVDs. Directory advertising includes the familiar Yellow Pages in telephone books, along with thousands of business directories. Some firms pay to have their advertising messages placed on hot-air balloons, blimps, banners behind airplanes, and scoreboards at sporting events. Johnson & Johnson, Yahoo!, and Dreyer's Ice Cream, among others, pay to have their logos and company messages placed on autos via the company Rush Hour Media, known by their drivers as http://www.autowrapped.com. Rush Hour Media uses regular people to literally drive the advertiser's message home. The drivers are chosen based on their driving habits, routes, occupations, and living and working locations and are paid a monthly fee for the use of the outside of their vehicles as advertising space.

MEDIA SCHEDULING

Once advertisers have selected the media that best match their advertising objectives and promotional budget, attention shifts to **media scheduling**—setting the timing and sequence for a series of advertisements. A variety of factors influence this decision as well. Sales patterns, repurchase cycles, and competitors' activities are the most important variables.

Seasonal sales patterns are common in many industries. An airline might reduce advertising during peak travel periods and boost its media schedule during low travel months. Repurchase cycles may also play a role in media scheduling—products with shorter repurchase cycles will more likely require consistent media schedules throughout the year. Competitors' activities are still other influences on media scheduling. A small firm may avoid advertising during periods of heavy advertising by its rivals.

Advertisers use the concepts of reach, frequency, and gross rating points to measure the effectiveness of media scheduling plans. *Reach* refers to the number of different people or households exposed to an advertisement at least once during a certain time period, typically four weeks. *Frequency* refers to the number of times an individual is exposed to an advertisement during a cer-

COURTESY OF ALABAMA BUREAU OF TOURISM AND TRAVEL; © MARK TUCKER

Seasonal advertisements are timed to attract maximum consumer attention. Ads for family beach vacations on the Gulf Coast appear in spring, when parents are looking ahead to a summer break with the kids.

tain time period. By multiplying reach times frequency, advertisers quantitatively describe the total weight of a media effort, which is called the campaign's *gross rating point (GRP)*.

Recently, marketers have questioned the effectiveness of reach and frequency to measure ad success online. The theory behind frequency is that the average advertising viewer needs a minimum of three exposures to a message to understand it and connect it to a specific brand. For Web surfers, the "wear-out" is much quicker—hence, the greater importance of building customer relationships through advertisements.

A media schedule is typically created in the following way. Say an auto manufacturer wants to advertise a new model designed primarily to appeal to professional consumers in their 30s. The model would be introduced in November with a direct mail piece offering test drives. Outdoor, newspaper, and magazine advertising would support the direct mail campaign but also follow through the winter and into the spring and summer. The newspaper ads might actually be cooperative, for both the manufacturer and local dealers. Early television commercials might air during a holiday television special in mid-December, and then one or more expensively produced, highly creative spots would be first aired during the Super Bowl in late January. Another television commercial—along with new print ads—might be scheduled for fall clearance sales as the manufacturer gets ready to introduce next year's models. This example illustrates how marketers might plan their advertising year for just one product.

> ✓ *assessment check*
>
> 1. What types of products are banned from advertising on television?
>
> 2. What are some advantages radio offers to advertisers? What about newspapers?
>
> 3. Define *media scheduling* and identify the most important factors influencing the scheduling decision.

ORGANIZATION OF THE ADVERTISING FUNCTION

6 Outline the organization of the advertising function and the role of an advertising agency.

Although the ultimate responsibility for advertising decision making often rests with top marketing management, organizational arrangements for the advertising function vary among companies. A producer of a technical industrial product may operate with a one-person department within the company, who works primarily to write copy for submission to trade publications. A consumer-goods company, on the other hand, may staff a large department with advertising specialists.

The advertising function is usually organized as a staff department reporting to the vice president (or director) of marketing. The director of advertising is an executive position with the responsibility for the functional activity of advertising. This position requires not only a skilled and experienced advertiser but also an individual who communicates effectively within the organization. The success of a firm's promotional strategy depends on the advertising director's willingness and ability to communicate both vertically and horizontally. The major tasks typically organized under advertising include advertising research, design, copywriting, media analysis, and in some cases, sales and trade promotion.

ADVERTISING AGENCIES

Most large companies in industries characterized by sizable advertising expenditures hire an independent **advertising agency,** a firm whose marketing specialists help businesses plan and prepare advertisements. Advertising is a huge, global industry. Ranked by worldwide revenue, Japan's Dentsu is the world's largest advertising agency, followed by New York City–based McCann-Erickson Worldwide.[50]

advertising agency Firm whose marketing specialists help advertisers plan and prepare advertisements.

Most large advertisers cite several reasons for relying on agencies for at least some aspects of their advertising. Agencies typically employ highly qualified specialists who provide a degree of creativity and objectivity that is difficult to sustain in a corporate advertising department. Phil Dusenberry, a legendary figure in the world of advertising and longtime chairman of ad agency BBDO in North America before his recent retirement, says, "We live in a world of parity. Most products in the same category are very similar. . . . The only difference is their advertising. So you've got to come up with something that sets your brand apart."[51] Some agencies also manage to reduce the cost of advertising by allowing the advertiser to avoid many of the fixed expenses associated with maintaining an internal advertising department.

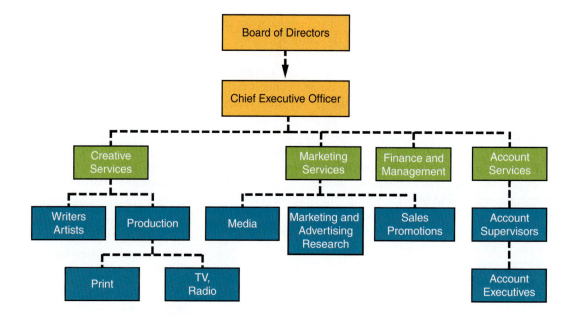

figure 16.4

Advertising Agency Organizational Chart

Figure 16.4 shows a hypothetical organization chart for a large advertising agency. Although job titles may vary among agencies, the major functions may be classified as creative services; account services; marketing services, including media services, marketing research, and sales promotion; and finance and management. Whatever organization structure it selects, an agency often stands or falls on its relationships with its clients. The fast pace and pressure of ad agencies are legendary, but good communication remains paramount to maintaining that relationship. Says Dusenberry, "If you're not on the same page with a client, if you don't have a meeting of the minds, if . . . you don't have a good relationship, then you're skating on thin ice."[52]

 assessment check

1. What is the role of an advertising agency?
2. What are some advantages of using an agency?

 7 Explain the roles of cross promotions, publicity, and ethics in an organization's promotional strategy.

PUBLIC RELATIONS

In Chapter 15, we defined public relations as the firm's communications and relationships with its various publics, including customers, employees, stockholders, suppliers, government agencies, and the society in which it operates. Organizational public relations efforts date back to 1889, when George Westinghouse hired two people to publicize the advantages of alternating-current electricity and to refute arguments originally championed by Thomas Edison for direct-current systems.

Public relations is an efficient, indirect communications channel through which a firm can promote products, although it serves broader objectives than those of other components of promotional strategy. It is concerned with the prestige and image of all parts of the organization. Today, public relations plays a larger role than ever within the promotional mix, and it may emphasize more marketing-oriented information. In addition to its traditional activities, such as surveying public attitudes and creating a good corporate image, PR also supports advertising in promoting the organization's goods and services.

Approximately 188,000 people work in public relations in both the not-for-profit and profit-oriented sectors.[53] Some 1,800 public-relations firms currently operate in the United States. In addition, thousands of one-person operations compete to offer these services.

Public relations is in a period of major growth as a result of increased public pressure on industries regarding corporate ethical conduct and environmental and international issues. International expenditures on public relations are growing more rapidly than those for advertising and sales promotion. Many top executives are becoming more involved in public relations as well. The public expects top managers to take greater responsibility for company actions than they have accepted in the past. Those who refuse are widely criticized and censured.

The PR department is the link between the firm and the media. It provides press releases and holds news conferences to announce new products, the formation of strategic alliances, management changes, financial results, or similar developments. Liz Miller, communications manager for Jan Marini Skin Research, learned the importance of ensuring accuracy in press releases when one item she wrote for the skin-care firm was picked up by a trade publication aimed at dermatologists and spas. The toll-free number Miller gave for readers to call for more information contained a typo and sent respondents to a telephone sex line instead of to Jan Marini. Fortunately, Miller and her employer both survived the mistake.[54] The PR department may also issue its own publications, including newsletters, brochures, and reports.

A PR plan begins much like an advertising plan, with research to define the role and scope of the firm's overall public relations and current challenges. Next come strategic decisions on short-term and long-term goals and markets, analysis of product features, and choices of messages and media channels—or other PR strategies such as speaking engagements or contests—for each market. Plan execution involves developing messages highlighting the benefits that the firm brings to each market. The final step is to measure results.

COURTESY OF ARTISTIC STUDIO BY LORI HELMS AND RHONDA TRENKAMP

In an organized campaign to woo Honda to locate its new assembly plant in Greensburg, Indiana, the townspeople wrote the company letters, put up signs of support, and posed for a photo of themselves in the shape of the Honda logo. The campaign worked—Honda built its plant in Greensburg.

The Internet has actually changed some PR planning, as PR representatives now have more direct access to the public instead of having their messages filtered through journalists and the news media. This direct access gives them greater control over their messages, as Wal-Mart is discovering. Working with its public-relations firm, the world's largest retailer has begun distributing information, news, and topic suggestions to sympathetic bloggers, who spread the word on the Internet. Critics of the company's image-boosting strategy say that some bloggers are misrepresenting the source of the information by posting it word-for-word as their own. Nevertheless, Wal-Mart, which says it discourages its correspondents from cutting and pasting, insists it is simply telling its story. "As more and more Americans go to the Internet to get information from varied, credible, trusted sources, Wal-Mart is committed to participating in that online conversation," says a company spokesperson. The company also continues to rely on more conventional public relations outlets such as full-page newspaper ads to set the record straight about its sometimes criticized employment policies.[55]

MARKETING AND NONMARKETING PUBLIC RELATIONS

Nonmarketing public relations refers to a company's messages about general management issues. When a company makes a decision that affects any of its publics, input from public-relations specialists can help smooth its dealings with those publics. A company that decides to close a plant would need advice on how to deal with the local community. Other examples include a company's attempts to gain favorable public opinion during a long strike or an open letter to Congress published in a newspaper during congressional debates on a bill that would affect a particular industry. Although companies typically organize their public-relations departments separately from their marketing divisions, PR activities invariably affect promotional strategies.

In contrast, **marketing public relations (MPR)** refers to narrowly focused public relations activities that directly support marketing goals. MPR involves an organization's relationships with consumers or other groups about marketing concerns and can be either proactive or reactive.

With proactive MPR, the marketer takes the initiative and seeks out opportunities for promoting the firm's products, often including distribution of press releases and feature articles. For example, companies send press releases about new products to newspapers, television stations, and relevant consumer, business, and trade publications. It is a powerful marketing tool because it adds news coverage that reinforces direct promotion activities.

Reactive MPR responds to an external situation that has potential negative consequences for the organization. When the formula of Bausch & Lomb's ReNu with MoistureLoc contact lens solution was implicated as a possible cause of serious eye infections in more than 100 users in the United States and Asia, the company immediately and voluntarily pulled the product from store shelves, and its CEO appeared on NBC's *Today* show to announce the recall and reassure the public that the company's other eye-care products were safe. The company's quick action undoubtedly contributed to minimizing its losses despite the fact that a complete product recall had to be done.[56]

PUBLICITY

publicity Nonpersonal stimulation of demand for a good, service, place, idea, person, or organization by unpaid placement of significant news regarding the product in a print or broadcast medium.

The aspect of public relations that is most directly related to promoting a firm's products is **publicity:** nonpersonal stimulation of demand for a good, service, place, idea, person, or organization by unpaid placement of significant news regarding the product in a print or broadcast medium. It has been said that if advertising is the hammer, publicity is the nail. It creates credibility for the advertising to follow. Firms generate publicity by creating special events, holding press conferences, and preparing news releases and media kits. Many firms, such as Starbucks and Wal-Mart's Sam's Club, have built their brands with virtually no advertising. After being featured in the *Wall Street Journal* and other publications, GarageTek required no advertising to sell 52 franchises within a year.[57] Pharmaceutical products including Viagra and Prozac became worldwide brands with relatively little advertising, although advertising—including a frequent-user awards program—is now used extensively in competing with a number of newly introduced competitors.

While publicity generates minimal costs compared with other forms of promotion, it does not deliver its message entirely for free. Publicity-related expenses include the costs of employing marketing personnel assigned to create and submit publicity releases, printing and mailing costs, and related expenses.

Firms often pursue publicity to promote their images or viewpoints. Other publicity efforts involve organizational activities such as plant expansions, mergers and acquisitions, management changes, and research breakthroughs. A significant amount of publicity, however, provides information about goods and services, particularly new products.

Because many consumers consider news stories to be more credible than advertisements as sources of information, publicity releases are often sent to media editors for possible inclusion in news stories. The media audiences perceive the news as coming from the communications media, not the sponsors. The information in a publicity release about a new good or service can provide valuable assistance for a television, newspaper, or magazine writer, leading to eventual broadcast or publication. Publicity releases sometimes fill voids in publications, and at other times, they become part of regular features. In either case, they offer firms valuable supplements to paid advertising messages.

CROSS-PROMOTION

cross-promotion Promotional technique in which marketing partners share the cost of a promotional campaign that meets their mutual needs.

In recent years, marketers have begun to combine their promotional efforts for related products using a technique called **cross promotion,** in which marketing partners share the cost of a promotional campaign that meets their mutual needs—an important benefit in an environment of rising media costs. Relationship marketing strategies such as comarketing and cobranding, discussed in Chapter 10, are forms of cross-promotion. Marketers realize that these joint efforts between established brands provide greater benefits in return for both organizations; investments of time and money on such promotions will become increasingly important to many partners' growth prospects.

Cingular Wireless helps promote artists such as Coldplay, Gwen Stefani, and Alicia Keys by featuring their songs as exclusive cell phone ringtones. "When we pick the right artists and package it, we sell more ringtones than we would have otherwise," says Cingular's vice president of consumer data services. "Customers see it as a value-add and the artist sees it as a value-add." All proceeds from the Peter Gabriel song recorded by Alicia Keys were donated to a group providing AIDS medicines to children and families in Africa. Says Cingular, "We think this will expand the appeal of ringtones and help out a great cause."[58]

MEASURING PROMOTIONAL EFFECTIVENESS

Each element of the promotional mix represents a major expenditure for a firm. Although promotional prices vary widely, advertisers typically pay a fee based on cost to deliver the message to viewers, listeners, or readers—the so-called *cost per thousand (CPM)*. Billboards are the cheapest way to spend advertising dollars, with television and some newspapers the most expensive. But while price is an important factor in media selection, it is by no means the only one—or all ads would appear on billboards! Versace's campaign featuring Halle Berry modeling the designer's new collection was promoted on both billboards and magazine covers.[59]

Because promotion represents such a major expenditure for many firms, they need to determine whether their campaigns accomplish appropriate promotional objectives. Companies want their advertising agencies and in-house marketing personnel to demonstrate how promotional programs contribute to increased sales and profits. Marketers are well aware of the number of advertising messages and sales promotions that consumers encounter daily, and they know that these people practice selective perception and simply screen out many messages.

By measuring promotional effectiveness, organizations can evaluate different strategies, prevent mistakes before spending money on specific programs, and improve their promotional programs. As the earlier discussion of promotional planning explained, any evaluation program starts with objectives and goals; otherwise, marketers have no yardstick against which to measure effectiveness. However, determining whether an advertising message has achieved its intended objective is one of the most difficult undertakings in marketing. Sales promotions and direct marketing are somewhat easier to evaluate because they evoke measurable consumer responses. Like advertising, public relations is also difficult to assess on purely objective terms.

COURTESY OF THE PROCTER AND GAMBLE COMPANY

Some Tide detergents incorporate Downy fabric softener, allowing manufacturer Procter & Gamble to cross-promote both brands.

8 Explain how marketers assess promotional effectiveness.

MEASURING ADVERTISING EFFECTIVENESS

Measures to evaluate the effectiveness of advertising, although difficult and costly, are essential parts of any marketing plan. Without an assessment strategy, marketers will not know whether their advertising achieves the objectives of the marketing plan or whether the dollars in the advertising budget are well spent. To answer these questions, marketers can conduct two types of research. **Media research** assesses how well a particular medium delivers the advertiser's message, where and when to place the advertisement, and the size of the audience. Buyers of broadcast time base their purchases on estimated Nielsen rating points, and the networks have to make good if ratings do not reach promised levels. Buyers of print advertising space pay fees based on circulation. Circulation figures are independently certified by specialized research firms.

The other major category, **message research,** tests consumer reactions to an advertisement's creative message. Pretesting and posttesting, the two methods for performing message research, are discussed in the following sections.

Pretesting

To assess an advertisement's likely effectiveness before it actually appears in the chosen medium, marketers often conduct **pretesting.** The obvious advantage of this technique is the opportunity to evaluate ads when they are being developed. Marketers can conduct a number of different pretests, beginning during the concept phase in the campaign's earliest stages, when they have only rough copy of the ad, and continuing until the ad layout and design are almost completed.

Pretesting employs a variety of evaluation methods. For example, focus groups can discuss their reactions to mock-ups of ads using different themes, headlines, or illustrations. CopyTest is an Internet-based advertising pretesting system developed by Decision Analyst that predicts the effectiveness of advertising pieces, including television storyboards, finished television and radio commercials, and magazine, newspaper, and billboard ads.[60]

To screen potential radio and television advertisements, marketers often recruit consumers to sit in a studio and indicate their preferences by pressing two buttons, one for a positive reaction to the commercial and the other for a negative reaction. Sometimes proposed ad copy is printed on a postcard that also offers a free product; the number of cards returned represents an indication of the copy's effectiveness. *Blind product tests* are also frequently used. In these tests, people are asked to select unidentified products on the basis of available advertising copy.

Mechanical devices offer yet another method of assessing how people read advertising copy. One mechanical test uses a hidden camera to photograph eye movements of readers. The results help advertisers determine headline placement and copy length. Another mechanical approach measures the galvanic skin response—changes in the electrical resistance of the skin produced by emotional reactions.

POSTTESTING

Posttesting assesses advertising copy after it has appeared in the appropriate medium. Pretesting generally is a more desirable measurement method than posttesting because it can save the cost of placing ineffective ads. However, posttesting can help in planning future advertisements and in adjusting current advertising programs. For instance, post-test research indicated that Kraft Miracle Whip scored higher in a test of brand selection after both television and print ads appeared supporting the brand. In other posttesting, marketers found that two print exposures benefited Reynolds Crystal Color Plastic Wrap, and two television ads boosted results for Ultra Slim-Fast better than a combination of print and television.[61]

In one of the most popular posttests, the *Starch Readership Report* interviews people who have read selected magazines to determine whether they observed various ads in them. A copy of the magazine is used as an interviewing aid, and each interviewer starts at a different point in the magazine. For larger ads, respondents are also asked about specifics, such as headlines and copy. Figure 16.5 shows a magazine advertisement with its Starch scores. All such *readership tests,* also called recognition tests, assume that future sales are related to advertising readership.

Unaided recall tests are another method of posttesting the effectiveness of advertisements. Respondents do not see copies of the magazine after their initial reading but are asked to recall the ads from memory. In a recent study of cell phone users who responded to a contest at a sponsored event, half reported unaided recall of the event's sponsor. Aided recall reached 62 percent.[62]

Inquiry tests are another popular form of posttest. Advertisements sometimes offer gifts—generally product samples—to people who respond to them. The number of inquiries relative to the advertisement's cost forms a measure of its effectiveness.

Split runs allow advertisers to test two or more ads at the same time. Although advertisers traditionally place different versions in newspapers and magazines, split runs on cable television systems frequently test the effectiveness of TV ads. With this method, advertisers divide the cable TV audience or a publication's subscribers in two; half view advertisement A and the other half view advertisement B. The relative effectiveness of the alternatives is then determined through inquiries or recall and recognition tests.

Regardless of the exact method they choose, marketers must realize that pretesting and posttesting are expensive efforts. As a result, they must plan to use these techniques as effectively as possible.

figure 16.5

Magazine Advertisement with Starch Scores

"Noted %" indicates the percentage of readers interviewed who saw any part of the advertisement. 64% noted this ad.

"Associated %" indicates the percentage of readers interviewed who saw any part of the ad that indicates the brand or advertiser. 62% associated this ad with Chevrolet.

"Read Most %" indicates the percentage of readers interviewed who read more than half of the body copy. 22% read most of this ad.

"Read Some %" indicates the percentage of readers interviewed who read any amount of the body copy. 61% read some of this ad.

GENERAL MOTORS CORP. USED WITH PERMISSION, GM MEDIA ARCHIVES

MEASURING PUBLIC-RELATIONS EFFECTIVENESS

As with other forms of marketing communications, organizations must measure PR results based on their objectives both for the PR program as a whole and for specific activities. In the next step, marketers must decide what they want to measure. This choice includes determining whether the message was heard by the target audience and whether it had the desired influence on public opinion.

The simplest and least costly level of assessment measures outputs of the PR program: whether the target audience received, paid attention to, understood, and retained the messages directed to them. To make this judgment, the staff could count the number of media placements and gauge the extent of media coverage. They could count attendees at any press conference, evaluate the quality of brochures and other materials, and pursue similar activities. Formal techniques include tracking publicity placements, analyzing how favorably their contents portrayed the company, and conducting public-opinion polls.

To analyze PR effectiveness more deeply, a firm could conduct focus groups, interviews with opinion leaders, and more detailed and extensive opinion polls. The highest level of effectiveness measurement looks at outcomes: Did the PR program change people's opinions, attitudes, and behavior? PR professionals measure these outcomes through before-and-after polls (similar to pretesting and posttesting) and more advanced techniques such as psychographic analysis (discussed in Chapter 5).

EVALUATING INTERACTIVE MEDIA

Marketers employ several methods to measure how many users view Web advertisements: *hits* (user requests for a file), *impressions* (the number of times a viewer sees an ad), and *click-throughs* (when the user clicks the ad to get more information). *View-through* rates measure responses over time. However, some of these measures can be misleading. Because each page, graphic, or multimedia file equals one hit, simple interactions can easily inflate the hit count, making it less accurate. To increase effectiveness, advertisers must give viewers who do click through their site something good to see. Successful Web campaigns use demonstrations, promotions, coupons, and interactive features.

Internet marketers price ad banners based on cost per thousand (CPM). Web sites that sell advertising typically

 assessment check

1. What is CPM and how is it measured?
2. Distinguish between media research and message research.
3. Describe several research techniques used in posttesting.

guarantee a certain number of impressions—the number of times an ad banner is downloaded and presumably seen by visitors. Marketers then set a rate based on that guarantee times the CPM rate.

ETHICS IN NONPERSONAL SELLING

Chapter 3 introduced the topic of marketing ethics and noted that promotion is the element in the marketing mix that raises the most ethical questions. People actively debate the question of whether marketing communications contribute to better lives. The final section of this chapter takes a closer look at ethical concerns in advertising and public relations.

ADVERTISING ETHICS

Even though advertising to children and advertising beer are legal, these types of promotions continue to be debated as important ethical issues. One area of controversy is advertising aimed at children. When it comes to influencing parents' purchase decisions, nothing beats influencing kids. By promoting goods and services directly to children, firms can sell not only to them but to the rest of the household, too. But many parents and consumer advocates question the ethics of promoting directly to children. Their argument: at a time when kids need to learn how to consume thoughtfully, they are being inundated with promotional messages teaching the opposite. To woo younger consumers, especially teens and those in their 20s, advertisers attempt to make these messages appear as different from advertisements as possible; they design ads that seem more like entertainment.

Alcoholic beverage advertising on television is another controversial area. Beer marketers advertise heavily on television and spend far more on advertising in print and outdoor media than do marketers of hard-liquor brands. Some members of Congress want much stricter regulation of all forms of such advertising on television and other media. This change would restrict ads in magazines with a 15 percent or more youth readership to black-and-white text only. Critics decry advertisements with messages implying that drinking the right beer will improve a person's personal life. Many state and local authorities are considering more restrictive proposals on both alcohol and tobacco advertising. A new study of several thousand U.S. young people age 15 to 26, randomly chosen in 24 media markets over several years, suggests that young people who watch more alcohol ads do tend to drink more.[63]

In cyberspace ads, it is often difficult to separate advertising from editorial content because many sites resemble magazine and newspaper ads or television infomercials. Another ethical issue surrounding advertising online is the use of **cookies,** small text files that are automatically downloaded to a user's computer whenever a site is visited. Each time the user returns to that site, the site's server accesses the cookie and gathers information: What site was visited last? How long did the user stay? What was the next site visited? Marketers claim that this device helps them determine consumer preferences and argue that cookies are stored in the user's PC, not the company's Web site. The problem is that cookies can and do collect personal information without the user's knowledge.

Puffery and Deception

Puffery refers to exaggerated claims of a product's superiority or the use of subjective or vague statements that may not be literally true. A company might advertise the "most advanced system" or claim that its product is "most effective" in accomplishing its purpose.

Exaggeration in ads is not new. Consumers seem to accept advertisers' tendencies to stretch the truth in their efforts to distinguish their products and get consumers to buy. This inclination may provide one reason that advertising does not encourage purchase behavior as successfully as sales promotions do. A tendency toward puffery does raise some ethical questions, though: Where is the line between claims that attract attention and those that provide implied guarantees? To what degree do advertisers deliberately make misleading statements?

The *Uniform Commercial Code* standardizes sales and business practices throughout the United States. It makes a distinction between puffery and any specific or quantifiable statement about product quality or performance that constitutes an "express warranty," which obligates the company to stand behind its claim. General boasts of product superiority and vague claims are puffery, not warranties. They are considered so self-praising or exaggerated that the average consumer would not rely on them to make a buying decision.

A quantifiable statement, on the other hand, implies a certain level of performance. For example, tests can establish the validity of a claim that a brand of long-life lightbulbs outlasts three regular lightbulbs.

ETHICS IN PUBLIC RELATIONS

Several public-relations issues open organizations to criticism. Various PR firms perform services for the tobacco industry; publicity campaigns defend unsafe products. Also, marketers must weigh ethics before they respond to negative publicity. For example, do firms admit to problems or product deficiencies, or do they try to cover them up? It should be noted that PR practitioners violate the Public Relations Society of America's Code of Professional Standards if they promote products or causes widely known to be harmful to others.

Strategic Implications of Marketing in the 21st Century

Greater portions of corporate ad budgets will migrate to the Web in the near future. This trend means that marketers must be increasingly aware of the benefits and pitfalls of Internet advertising. But they should not forget the benefits of other types of advertising as well.

Promotion industry experts agree that e-business broadens marketers' job tasks, though many promotional objectives still remain the same. Today, advertisers need 75 different ways to market their products in 75 countries in the world and innumerable market segments. In years to come, advertisers also agree that channels will become more homogeneous while markets become more fragmented.

REVIEW OF CHAPTER OBJECTIVES

1 Identify the three major advertising objectives and the two basic categories of advertising.

The three major objectives of advertising are to inform, to persuade, and to remind. The two major categories of advertising are product advertising and institutional advertising. Product advertising involves the nonpersonal selling of a good or service. Institutional advertising is the nonpersonal promotion of a concept, idea, or philosophy of a company or organization.

2 List the major advertising strategies.

The major strategies are comparative advertising, which makes extensive use of messages with direct comparisons between competing brands; celebrity, which uses famous spokespeople to boost an advertising message; retail, which includes all advertising by retail stores selling products directly to consumers; and interactive, which encourages two-way communication either via the Internet or kiosks.

3 Describe the process of creating an advertisement.

An advertisement evolves from pinpointing goals, such as educating consumers, enhancing brand loyalty, or improving a product's image. From those goals, marketers move to the next stages: creating a plan, developing a message, developing and preparing the ad, and selecting the appropriate medium (or media). Advertisements often appeal to consumers' emotions with messages focusing on fear, humor, or sex.

4 Identify the major types of advertising appeals and discuss their uses.

Advertisers often focus on making emotional appeals to fear, humor, sex, guilt, or fantasy. While these can be effective, marketers need to recognize that fear appeals can backfire; people's sense of humor can differ according to sex, age, and other factors; and use of sexual imagery must not overstep the bounds of taste.

5 List and compare the major advertising media.

The major media include broadcast (television and radio), newspapers and magazines, direct mail, outdoor, and interactive. Each medium has benefits and drawbacks. Newspapers are flexible and dominate local markets. Magazines can target niche markets. Interactive media encourage two-way communication. Outdoor advertising in a high-traffic location reaches many people every day; television and radio reach even more. Direct mail allows effective segmentation.

6 Outline the organization of the advertising function and the role of an advertising agency.

Within a firm, the advertising department is usually a group that reports to a marketing executive. Advertising departments generally include research, art and design, copywriting, and media analysis. Outside advertising agencies assist and support the advertising efforts of firms. These specialists are usually organized by creative services, account services, marketing services, and finance.

7 Explain the roles of cross-promotion, public relations, publicity, and ethics in an organization's promotional strategy.

Cross-promotion, illustrated by tie-ins between popular movies and fast-food restaurants, permits the marketing partners to share the cost of a promotional campaign that meets their mutual needs. Public relations consists of the firm's communications and relationships with its various publics, including customers, employees, stockholders, suppliers, government, and the society in which it operates. Publicity is the dissemination of newsworthy information about a product or organization. This information activity is frequently used in new-product introductions. Although publicity is welcomed by firms, negative publicity is easily created when a company enters a gray ethical area with the use of its promotional efforts. Therefore, marketers should be careful to construct ethically sound promotional campaigns, avoiding such practices as puffery and deceit.

8 Explain how marketers assess promotional effectiveness.

The effectiveness of advertising can be measured by both pretesting and posttesting. Pretesting is the assessment of an ad's effectiveness before it is actually used. It includes such methods as sales conviction tests and blind product tests. Posttesting is the assessment of the ad's effectiveness after it has been used. Commonly used posttests include readership tests, unaided recall tests, inquiry tests, and split runs.

✓ *assessment check* **answers**

1.1 What are the goals of institutional advertising?

Institutional advertising promotes a concept, an idea, a philosophy, or the goodwill of an industry, company, organization, person, geographic location, or government agency.

1.2 At what stage in the product life cycle are informative ads used? Why?

Informative ads are common in the introductory stage of the product life cycle.

1.3 What is reminder advertising?

Reminder advertising strives to reinforce previous promotional activity by keeping the name of a good, service, organization, person, place, idea, or cause before the public.

assessment check **answers**

2.1   What is comparative advertising?

Comparative advertising makes extensive use of messages with direct comparisons between competing brands.

2.2   What makes a successful celebrity testimonial?

Successful celebrity ads feature figures who are credible sources of information for the product being promoted.

2.3   What is cooperative advertising?

In cooperative advertising a manufacturer or wholesaler shares advertising costs with a retailer.

3.1   What is an advertising campaign?

An advertising campaign is a series of different but related ads that use a single theme and appear in different media within a specified time period.

3.2   What are an advertisement's three main goals?

Advertising's three main goals are to educate consumers about product features, enhance brand loyalty, and improve consumer perception of the brand.

4.1   What are some common emotional appeals used in advertising?

Advertisers often focus on making emotional appeals to fear, humor, sex, guilt, or fantasy.

4.2   What are the main types of interactive ads?

Interactive ads include Internet banners, pop-ups, keyword ads, advertorials, advergames, and interstitials.

5.1   What types of products are banned from advertising on television?

Tobacco goods such as cigarettes, cigars, and smokeless tobacco are banned from television advertising.

5.2   What are some advantages radio offers to advertisers? What about newspapers?

Radio ads allow marketers to target a captive audience and also offer low cost, flexibility, and mobility. Newspaper ads are flexible and provide intensive coverage of the market. Readers can also refer back to newspaper ads.

5.3   Define *media scheduling* **and identify the most important factors influencing the scheduling decision.**

Media scheduling sets the timing and sequence for a series of advertisements. Sales patterns, repurchase cycles, and competitors' activities are the most important variables in the scheduling decision.

6.1   What is the role of an advertising agency?

An advertising agency's role is to help businesses plan and prepare advertisements.

6.2   What are some advantages of using an agency?

Advantages of using an ad agency are the availability of highly qualified specialists who provide creativity and objectivity, and sometimes cost savings.

7.1   Distinguish between marketing public relations and nonmarketing public relations.

Marketing public relations refers to narrowly focused public-relations activities that directly support marketing goals. Nonmarketing public relations refers to a company's messages about general issues.

7.2   What is publicity?

Publicity is nonpersonal stimulation of demand for a good, service, place, idea, person, or organization by unpaid placement of significant news regarding the product in a print or broadcast medium.

assessment check **answers**

7.3   What are the advantages of cross-promotion?

Cross-promotion divides the cost of a promotional campaign that meets the mutual needs of marketing partners and provides greater benefits for both in return.

8.1   What is CPM and how is it measured?

CPM is cost per thousand, a fee based on cost to deliver the advertisers' message to viewers, listeners, or readers.

8.2   Distinguish between media research and message research.

Media research assesses how well a particular medium delivers the advertiser's message, where and when to place the ad, and the size of the audience. Message research tests consumer reactions to an advertisement's creative message.

8.3   Describe several research techniques used in posttesting.

Commonly used posttests include readership tests, unaided recall tests, inquiry tests, and split runs.

MARKETING TERMS YOU NEED TO KNOW

advertising 527	persuasive advertising 528	advertising campaign 534
product advertising 527	reminder advertising 528	advertising agency 545
institutional advertising 527	comparative advertising 529	publicity 548
informative advertising 528	cooperative advertising 532	cross-promotion 548

OTHER IMPORTANT MARKETING TERMS

retail advertising 531	marketing public relations (MPR) 548	split runs 551
interactive advertising 532	media research 550	cookies 552
banners 537	message research 550	puffery 552
media scheduling 544	pretesting 550	
nonmarketing public relations 547	posttesting 550	

ASSURANCE OF LEARNING REVIEW

1. Identify and define the two broad categories of advertising. Give an example of each.
2. Describe each of the four major advertising strategies.
3. What variables might marketers consider in creating an advertising message for a firm that offers financial services, including retirement accounts, credit cards, and other investments?
4. What are the advantages and disadvantages of the types of emotional appeals in advertising?
5. Identify and describe the different advertising media. Give an example of one type of product that could best be advertised in each.

6. How is advertising through interactive media different from advertising in traditional media? Describe how you think a chain of golf resorts could use interactive advertising effectively.
7. What is the role of an advertising agency?
8. How can firms use marketing public relations (MPR) to their advantage?
9. Describe the ways in which marketers assess promotional effectiveness.
10. Identify the major ethical issues affecting advertising, sales promotion, and public relations.

PROJECTS AND TEAMWORK EXERCISES

1. With a classmate, review a number of advertising messages across several media and identify two effective messages and two you think are ineffective. Describe why you think each is effective or ineffective. Bring at least two of the ads to class to discuss with classmates.

2. Choose a magazine that interests you and analyze the advertisements in one issue. Describe who you think the magazine's readers are by reviewing the ads.

3. With a classmate, find an example of cross-promotion. If possible, bring it to class to discuss its effectiveness. Then create your own plan for cross-promoting two products that you think would be good candidates for cross-promotion.

4. Access the Internet and surf around to some sites that interest you. How many banner ads or pop-ups do you see? Do you like to view these ads, or do you find them intrusive? Which are most appealing? Which are least?

5. Select two different advertisers' television or print ads for the same product category (cars or soft drinks, for instance) and decide what emotion each appeals to. Which ad is more effective and why?

6. Which kind of appeal do you think would be most effective in advertising each of the following? Why?
   a. whitening toothpaste
   b. wireless Internet access
   c. diamond jewelry
   d. antilitter campaign
   e. anticavity toothpaste
   f. discount shoe store

7. Do outdoor ads and pop-up ads have any characteristics in common? What are they?

8. Research suggests that advertising appeals based on sex are successful only when they are appropriate to the type of product being advertised. With a classmate, discuss whether each of you agrees or disagrees with this observation. Prepare to present your reasoning to the class.

9. List as many advertisements as you can that you remember seeing, reading, or hearing in the last week. Narrow your list down to five or six ads you can recall with some detail and accuracy. What was memorable about each of these ads?

10. Think back to any good or bad publicity you have heard about a company or its products recently. If it was good publicity, how was it generated and what media were used? If it was bad publicity, where did you find out about it and how did the firm try to control or eliminate the situation?

CRITICAL-THINKING EXERCISES

1. Design a print ad, with rough-draft copy and an image (or a description of an image), for an electronics store you visit frequently. Be sure to include the elements of a typical ad and identify the appeal you chose.

2. One writer says that children exposed to puffery in ads grow into teens who are healthily skeptical of advertising claims. Find several print ads aimed at children, and identify what you think might be puffery in these ads. Select one ad that you think children would be influenced by, and rewrite the ad without the puffery.

3. Comparative advertising, in which marketers directly compare the advertised product with a competitor's, is controversial. The advertising industry is self-regulating on this issue, and disputes between companies regarding incorrect or misleading comparative ads are likely to result in lawsuits. Consequently, because the law provides few specific guidelines, advertisers who use comparative ads are responsible for monitoring the honesty and fairness of their messages. What do you think advertisers' criteria for fairness should be? Locate two or three comparative ads and compare the advertisers' criteria to your own. Which set of guidelines is stricter, yours or the advertisers'? Use the ads to illustrate a presentation to your class.

4. Some marketers believe that marketing in schools—through advertisements on book covers, product placement in lesson plans, and ads in educational videos and other programs—is acceptable only if the ads are designed to help schools financially by giving them supplies they cannot afford or helping them get money to buy these items. Others feel advertising has no place in schools at all. But most expect it to increase in the future. Find out about advertiser participation in the schools in your area. Do you agree that it has a benefit? Why or why not? Interview a few high school students you know and find out what they think. Prepare a brief report about your findings.

ETHICS EXERCISE

Major League Baseball recently canceled plans to plant a temporary Spider-Man logo on first, second, and third base to promote the film *Spider-Man 2* after sports fans voiced strong objections. Shocked by this sacrilege and convinced that, once advertising moved from signage to the field of play, the uniforms of players, coaches, and umpires would be covered with more brand images than a NASCAR race car, tradition-oriented fans cried foul. They wrote letters; they called sports talk radio programs. Their vocal media complaints proved successful, and baseball commissioner Bud Selig announced that the *Spider-Man* logo "proposal" had been rejected. But one sports marketing executive predicted that "marketers will always push the envelope, and I think somebody will try something like this again." New York Yankee pitching great Whitey Ford said of the proposed ads, "With the salaries they're paying now, they have to make money. . . . Today, television calls the shots."

1. Do you think marketing at sporting events and stadiums will become more aggressive if salaries for top players continue to climb? If the alternative is to charge higher ticket prices, which is preferable in the short term? In the long term? Why?

2. Some fans and sportswriters were outraged at the proposal to market a movie by using the bases, even though the plan was quickly canceled. Do you think advertisers should "test the waters" first for certain types of ads? Why or why not? If yes, what sort of feedback mechanism would you suggest marketers use?

INTERNET EXERCISES

1. **Public relations.** Complete the following exercises to learn more about public relations and apply what you learned in the chapter.

   a. Visit http://aboutpublicrelations.net/toolkit.htm. Prepare a brief report on how to use photos and graphics for public relations.

   b. Read the summary in the *Occupational Outlook Handbook* (http://www.bls.gov/oco/ocos086.htm) for public-relations specialists. What is the nature of the work? Who employs public-relations specialists? How much do they earn? What is the job outlook for public-relations specialists?

   c. A couple of years ago, many retailers came under criticism for selling clothing produced in factories where workers were poorly paid, often abused, and subjected to hazardous working conditions. In response, retailers instituted new standards for vendors. Some retailers went even further. Visit the Web site of The Gap Stores (http://www.gap.com). Click on About Gap Inc. and then *Social Responsibility*. Read about the company's annual social audit and its other efforts to protect garment workers. Explain how these efforts are examples of the effective use of public relations and publicity as described in the chapter.

2. **Advertising.** Visit the *Advertising Age* Web site to access information on advertising during the 20th century (http://www.adage.com/century). Answer the following questions:

   a. Who were the top ten advertisers?

   b. What were the top five advertising campaigns? What were the top three advertising jingles? What were the top two advertising slogans? Who were the top ten ad icons?

   c. Are any of the top campaigns, slogans, jingles, or icons still in use today? What significant changes have occurred since the beginning of the 21st century?

Note: Internet Web addresses change frequently. If you don't find the exact site listed, you may need to access the organization's home page and search from there or use a search engine such as Google.

CASE 16.1   Wacky Advertising

Elise Harp of Georgia recently earned $8,800 promoting an online casino. Her story isn't unusual, only the ad: a temporary tattoo Harp wore on her belly while pregnant. Do we have your attention?

"The more media messages we get, the fewer we listen to," says one writer. With consumers awash in messages, advertisers are looking hard for attention-getting tactics. People routinely sell ad space on their bodies via eBay, and Lease Your Body.com has 2,500 members who agree that body advertising is the wave of the future. Maybe it is—Toyota and Dunkin' Donuts have already given it a try.

Sony paid artists in several big cities to paint fake graffiti of kids and its PSP game player. The ads appeared on rented private property, and some gamers and bloggers thought them "cheeky" and "creative." Others likened the graffiti to vandalism, and some thought it was a smear campaign by a Sony competitor.

New York City pedestrians are bumping into models wearing flat-screen TVs that show videos promoting everything from job openings at Verizon to pay-per-view sports events from HBO. Created by a college student who dropped out after getting a D for the idea, AdsOnFeet charges $2,500 a day to carry messages to trade shows, sports events, and train stations.

Subway cars in Washington, D.C., are wrapped with ads and carry TV screens showing commercials. The transit system may sell naming rights to its stations.

Ads appear on school buses from Massachusetts to Arizona. Fire trucks in Phoenix advertise the logo of a local hospital. Ad space on the bottom of the city's public swimming pools is available.

CBS advertises on overhead video screens installed in 1,300 supermarkets across the country. Other firms broadcast ten-second commercials from tiny monitors attached to the grocery shelves.

A Brooklyn baseball team, a local mall, Entenmann's Bakery, and 1-800-FLOWERS picked up $75,000 of expenses in sponsoring the Long Island wedding of Dave Kerpen and Caroline Fisher, who tied the knot before 500 guests and 7,500 ticket holders in KeySpan Park.

Snapple bought all the ad time on WFNX (Boston) for a 40-day period in the summer. Instead of traditional commercials, Snapple offered an array of promotions and giveaways, a special Web site, music and ringtones for downloading, and text messaging to tout its teas, juices, and other drinks. Snapple's marketing vice president summed up the new rules. "If you want to break through, you have to connect in a way that fits with [people's] lifestyles, in a way they can't tune you out."

Questions for Critical Thinking

1. Advertising messages follow consumers as they work, shop, commute, vacation, recuperate, and even visit public restrooms. Marketers are enthusiastic about innovative advertising, but does it work? Do you think wildly unusual advertising is effective? Why or why not?

2. What else can marketers do to break through advertising clutter? Are they merely creating even more clutter by advertising on everything including police cars, sports team uniforms, and park benches?

Sources: Heather Fletcher, "This Wedding Is Brought to You by . . . ," *New York Times*, June 11, 2006, **http://www.nytimes.com**; Stuart Elliott, "A Station with a One-of-a-Kind Campaign: All Snapple, All the Time," *New York Times*, May 25, 2006, **http://www.nytimes.com**; "Advertising Gets Fruity," Seedlings, March 23, 2006, **http://seedlings.wordpress.com**; "Executive Decisions: Craving AV," eMediaLive, May 31, 2006, **http://www.emedialive.com**; Raina Kumra, "Hijacking the Urban Screen: Trends in Outdoor Advertising and Predictions for the Use of Video Art and Urban Screens," *First Monday*, February 2006, **http://www.firstmonday.org**; Emily Bazar, "Advertisers Catch the School Bus," *USA Today*, December 27, 2005, **http://www.usatoday.com**; James Brightman, "Sony's Urban PSP Campaign Irritates Residents," *GameDaily*, December 5, 2005, **http://biz.gamedaily.com**; Linda Stern, "Hands Off My Knobs!" *Newsweek*, November 28, 2005, p. E2; "Ad Blockers in Public Spaces," *Christian Science Monitor*, May 17, 2005, **http://www.csmonitor.com**; Christopher Simmons, "Body Advertising: Pittsburgh Waitress Paid to Wear Lease Your Body Tattoo," Send2Press, August 19, 2005, **http://www.send2press.com**; Maria Puente, "Rent This Space: Bodies Double as Billboards," *USA Today*, March 2, 2005, **http://www.usatoday.com**.

VIDEO CASE 16.2   BP: Beyond Petroleum

The written video case on BP appears on page VC-19. The recently filmed BP video is designed to expand and highlight the concepts in this chapter and the concepts and questions covered in the written video case.

Another "unexpected" **GT** from Mustang...new

Top Execs: The Ultimate Sales Force

In today's tough, competitive environment, organizations must operate efficiently and effectively. For some, that means rethinking their tried-and-true processes to accomplish goals with fewer staff. Others that are tops in their industries may stay there by acquiring competitors or innovators to keep their edge. Still others refocus their efforts to take advantage of new opportunities in their markets. Three top executives have faced these challenges recently and met them head on. Once the plans were laid for change, they tackled the job of selling the new ideas and directions to their employees, investors, and customers. Their success in connecting with the various stakeholders, understanding their needs, and persuading them to a course of action are at the heart of effective personal selling. And their

companies' survival and dominance depend on how well they can sell their ideas.

When Bill Ford was named CEO of his family's firm, critics immediately pointed to his inexperience. They called him naïve, too young for the job—he was in his early forties—not qualified to steer the giant Ford Motor Company. He had to sell himself to the media and to customers. To do that, he had to figure out how to turn around a company that seemed to be sputtering against Japanese competitors such as Toyota and Honda. He had to create a plan to build better cars. And he had to sell them—to skeptical dealers and consumers. Ford has traditionally made most of its profits on pickup trucks and SUVs. But with the soaring price of gasoline and pressure to produce vehicles with

better gas mileage—including hybrids—Bill Ford had to come up with an alternative. So he began a company overhaul called "Way Forward" that included the redesign of processes as well as vehicles—and unpopular layoffs of tens of thousands of workers. "We recognize we've been too dependent upon a very few vehicles," he explained, "and that we couldn't count on hitting home runs in the future, even though we'd love to do it. Therefore, our business structure had to be such that all of our vehicles had profit potential and that we were going to try and hit a lot of singles and doubles." Ford convinced his audience that it would be better to build and sell a number of different vehicles—including those that compete directly with Toyota and Honda—than to rely solely on a few models. His

Personal Selling and Sales Promotion

1 Describe the role of today's salesperson.

2 Describe the four sales channels.

3 Describe the major trends in personal selling.

4 Identify and briefly describe the three basic sales tasks.

5 Outline the seven steps in the sales process.

6 Identify the seven basic functions of a sales manager.

7 Explain the role of ethical behavior in personal selling.

8 Describe the role of sales promotion in the promotional mix, and identify the different types of sales promotions.

---

plans also included finding his own replacement—a new CEO to head up the turnaround. Ford tapped former Boeing executive vice president Alan Mulally, who had revamped Boeing's commercial airplane division and brought it back to the top of its industry. Bill Ford retained his position as executive chairman to continue helping with strategy.

Larry Ellison and Steve Ballmer are both giants in the computer world. Ellison is the founder and CEO of Oracle; Ballmer is CEO of Microsoft. Both compete in an industry that initiates and responds to rapid change. Like Bill Ford, they must be able to sell their vision of their companies—and their products—to investors, critics, consumers, and business customers. Ellison is a tenacious, flamboyant competitor, in and out of the business world. Personally worth an estimated $18.4 billion, he has funded several America's Cup racing teams. At Oracle, he gobbles up smaller companies such as Siebel Systems and PeopleSoft. Under Ellison, Oracle has historically pitched its own technology to business customers instead of asking them what they

wanted in software and then building it for them. Ellison believes that his engineers and designers know best how to deliver what customers need—and many believe in the power of the growing Oracle empire.

If Ellison is flashy, Steve Ballmer is the opposite. He's a technician who knows exactly what his company's products can do. He talks with passion about Microsoft software and the ways it can help people.

evolution *of a* brand

All three executives described represent firms that have very strong brands. Bill Ford took the wheel of the firm that literally brought automobiles to consumers a century ago. Larry Ellison founded a firm whose name—Oracle—has proved to be prophetic. Steve Ballmer now heads what may be the most powerful software company in the world. Each of these brands has already had a significant impact on its own industry and on the marketplace. Yet each must be guided carefully to meet the competitive challenges of the 21st century.

- Ford Motor Company is responsible for producing such well-loved models as the Explorer and the Mustang. Now it is focusing on producing models such as the Fusion, which has already received praise for its sleek styling and agile handling. Its goal is to meet and beat the competition with a new CEO who has a strong background in engineering, manufacturing, and product development.

- Oracle has achieved much of its prominence by acquiring smaller firms such as PeopleSoft and Siebel Systems. CEO Larry Ellison believes that only the strongest in the industry will survive.

Chapter Overview

Bill Ford, Larry Ellison, and Steve Ballmer illustrate how important it is for top executives to become the ultimate salespeople for their firms. In exploring personal selling strategies, this chapter gives special attention to the relationship-building opportunities that the selling situation presents.

Personal selling is the process of a seller's person-to-person promotional presentation to a buyer. The sales process is essentially interpersonal, and it is basic to any enterprise. Accounting, engineering, human resources management, production, and other organizational activities produce no benefits unless a seller matches the needs of a client or customer. The 16

million people employed in sales occupations in the United States testify to the importance of selling.[2] Personal selling is much more costly and time-consuming than other types of promotion because of its direct contact with customers. This makes personal selling the single largest marketing expense in many firms.

Personal selling is a primary component of a firm's promotional mix when one or more of several well-defined factors are present: (1) customers are geographically concentrated; (2) individual orders account for large amounts of revenue; (3) the firm markets goods and services that are expensive, are technically complex, or require special handling; (4) trade-ins are involved; (5) products move through short channels; or (6) the firm markets to relatively few potential customers. For example, personal

selling is an important component of the promotional mix for a car dealer, although both dealers and manufacturers also rely heavily on advertising. Because cars and trucks are expensive, customers usually like to go to a dealership to compare models, discuss a purchase, or obtain service, and trade-ins are often involved. So a dealer's salespeople provide valuable assistance to the customer. Table 17.1 summarizes the factors that influence the importance of personal selling in the overall promotional mix based on four variables: consumer, product, price, and marketing channels. This chapter also explores *sales promotion,* which includes all marketing activities other than personal selling, advertising, and publicity that enhance consumer purchasing and dealer effectiveness.

personal selling Interpersonal influence process involving a seller's promotional presentation conducted on a person-to-person basis with the buyer.

table 17.1 Factors Affecting the Importance of Personal Selling in the Promotional Mix

VARIABLE	CONDITIONS THAT FAVOR PERSONAL SELLING	CONDITIONS THAT FAVOR ADVERTISING
Consumer	Geographically concentrated	Geographically dispersed
	Relatively low numbers	Relatively high numbers
Product	Expensive	Inexpensive
	Technically complex	Simple to understand
	Custom made	Standardized
	Special handling requirements	No special handling requirements
	Transactions frequently involve trade-ins	Transactions seldom involve trade-ins
Price	Relatively high	Relatively low
Channels	Relatively short	Relatively long

THE EVOLUTION OF PERSONAL SELLING

1 Describe the role of today's salesperson.

Selling has been a standard business activity for thousands of years. As long ago as 2000 B.C., the Code of Hammurabi protected the rights of the Babylonian salesman, who was referred to as a *peddler*. Throughout U.S. history, selling has been a major factor in economic growth. Even during the 1700s, Yankee peddlers pulled their carts full of goods from village to village and farm to farm, helping expand trade among the colonies. Today, professional salespeople are problem solvers who focus on satisfying the needs of customers before, during, and after sales are made. Armed with knowledge about their firm's goods or services, those of competitors, and their customers' business needs, salespeople pursue a common goal of creating mutually beneficial long-term relationships with customers.

Personal selling is a vital, vibrant, dynamic process. As domestic and foreign competition increases the emphasis on productivity, personal selling is taking on a more prominent role in the marketing mix. Salespeople must communicate the advantages of their firms' goods and services over those of competitors. They must be able to do the following:

- Focus on customers' needs and problems, and offer solutions.

- Follow through with phone calls and other communications.

- Develop knowledge about the industry in general as well as their own firms' goods and services and those of the competition, including any technical expertise required.

- Go the extra mile. This means making an extra effort to fulfill customers' needs—beyond their expectations.[3]

Relationship marketing affects all aspects of an organization's marketing function, including personal selling. This means that marketers in both internal and external relationships must develop different sales skills. Instead of working alone, many salespeople now unite their efforts in sales teams. The customer-focused firm wants its salespeople to form long-lasting relationships with buyers by providing high levels of customer service rather than going for quick sales. Even the way salespeople perform their jobs is constantly changing. Growing numbers of companies have integrated communications and computer technologies into the sales routine. These trends are covered in more detail later in the chapter.

✓ *assessment check*

1. **What is personal selling?**
2. **What is the main focus of today's salespeople?**

Personal selling is an attractive career choice for today's college students. According to the Bureau of Labor Statistics, jobs in sales and related fields are expected to grow by about 10 percent over the next decade.[4] Company executives usually recognize a good salesperson as a hard worker who can solve problems, communicate clearly, and be consistent. In fact, many corporations are headed by executives who began their careers in sales.

2 Describe the four sales channels.

THE FOUR SALES CHANNELS

Personal selling occurs through several types of communication channels: over-the-counter selling (including online selling), field selling, telemarketing, and inside selling. Each of these channels includes both business-to-business and direct-to-customer selling. Although telemarketing and online selling are lower-cost alternatives, their lack of personal interaction with existing or prospective customers often makes them less effective than personalized, one-to-one field selling and over-the-counter channels. In fact, many organizations use a number of different channels. Dreyfus uses advertising, a toll-free number, and a Web site address to encourage prospective customers to talk with its professional advisors about investment opportunities.

OVER-THE-COUNTER SELLING

The most frequently used sales channel, **over-the-counter selling,** typically describes selling in retail and some wholesale locations. Most over-the-counter sales are direct-to-customer, although business customers are frequently served by wholesalers with over-the-counter sales reps. Customers typically visit the seller's location on their own initiative to purchase desired items. Some visit their favorite stores because they enjoy shopping. Others respond to many kinds of appeals including direct mail, personal letters of invitation from store personnel, and advertisements for sales, special events, and new-product introductions.

Marketers are getting increasingly creative in their approach to over-the-counter selling. Borsheim's jewelry store in Omaha offers an annual free pizza and beer night to attract male shoppers to the store. The evening has been so successful over the past five years that the store now hosts a ladies' night (with free wine and Perrier, along with pastries) during which women can fill out wish lists to give to their husbands before they shop.[5]

Electronics giant Best Buy continues to outsell its competitors; with 700 stores, the firm's sales hover around $34 billion. Perhaps Best Buy's success is because of the training its salespeople receive. The training focuses on the firm's mantra: CARE Plus. *C* stands for contact with the customer. *A* means asking questions to learn what the customer needs.

Is it time?

You've worked hard and saved right. Retirement's right around the corner, and you might be more prepared than you think. Talk to your advisor or visit Dreyfus.com to learn how our wide range of investments can help make your transition to retirement easier.

What's Your Story? Enter Our Contest at Dreyfus.com
We're looking for an inspirational story from a current retiree about how careful planning allowed you to retire from your career and re-invent yourself by pursuing a hobby, a dream or a passion. The winner will be featured in a Dreyfus ad in an upcoming issue of FORTUNE® magazine. The winning entry will be selected on a subjective basis by Dreyfus and only the winner will be contacted. Your privacy rights will be respected. More complete guidelines appear on Dreyfus.com.

Dreyfus.com | 1-800-896-2647

Investors should consider the investment objectives, risks, charges and expenses of the fund carefully before investing. Ask your advisor for a prospectus that contains this and other information about the fund and read it carefully before investing.

DREYFUS PRESENTS
NEW BEGINNINGS
A PRACTICAL LOOK AT RETIREMENT

YOU, YOUR ADVISOR AND
Dreyfus
A MELLON FINANCIAL COMPANY

Dreyfus uses several channels—including sales promotion in the form of a contest—to promote its services.

over-the-counter selling
Personal selling conducted in retail and some wholesale locations in which customers come to the seller's place of business.

R represents making recommendations to the customer. *E* stands for encouragement, praising the customer for a wise purchase.

Local retailers often know their customers by name. They also know their customers' likes and dislikes. The owner of a bookstore in your hometown might call you when a new book by your favorite author arrives. Taking a page from this type of selling, Amazon.com creates personalized messages for its customers as well—even though its salespeople have never met their customers in person. Amazon's software can send you reminders for gift purchases, recommend related purchases or even stop you from making the same purchase twice. The site also welcomes you by name when you log on.[6]

Regardless of a retailer's innovation, a few things remain the same in over-the-counter selling. One survey reveals the things that customers *don't* want to hear salespeople say:

- "That's not my department."

- "If it's not on the rack [or shelf], we don't have it."

- "That's the policy."

- "I'm new here."

- "I'm closing," or "I'm on a break."

- "The computer is down."[7]

While these quotes may seem humorous, they also ring true—you've probably heard them yourself. Each conveys the message that the salesperson is not willing or able to serve the customer—exactly the opposite of what every retailer wants to convey.

FIELD SELLING

Field selling involves making sales calls on prospective and existing customers at their businesses or homes. Some situations involve considerable creative effort, such as the sale of major computer installations. Often the salesperson must convince customers first that they need the good or service and then that they need the particular brand the salesperson is selling. Field sales of large industrial installations such as Boeing's 787 Dreamliner also often require considerable technical expertise.

Largely because it involves travel, field selling is considerably more expensive than other selling options. During the last 25 years, the cost of a single sales call has increased from $126 to $379.[8] This means that firms need to find ways to trim costs while increasing productivity. Some have replaced certain travel with conference calls, while others require salespeople to stay in less expensive hotels and spend less on meals. Some firms have simply shortened the time allowed for trips.

In fairly routine field selling situations, such as calling on established customers in industries such as food, textiles, or wholesaling, the salesperson basically acts as an order taker who processes regular customers' orders. But more complex situations may involve weeks of preparation, formal presentations, and many hours of postsales call work. Field selling is a lifestyle that many people enjoy; they also cite some of the negatives, such as travel delays, impact on family life, high costs of fuel, and understanding cultural differences.[9]

Some firms view field selling as a market in itself—and have developed goods and services designed to help salespeople do their jobs. Ford and Microsoft have partnered to produce the Stargate Mobile—a tablet computer loaded with Microsoft Office software, a wireless broadband card from Sprint, and a connection to Slingbox, which uses the Internet to access live television programming. In short, the two firms have created a mobile office. The computer is wrapped in a rubber case and mounted on a swiveling floor mount—but can be unlocked and carried like a laptop.[10]

Taking their cue from the successes of businesses such as Avon, Mary Kay Cosmetics, and Tupperware, thousands of smaller businesses now rely on field selling in customers' homes. Often called **network marketing,** this type of personal selling relies on lists of family members and friends of the salesperson or "party host," who organizes a gathering of potential customers for an in-home demonstration of products. Rags Land sells children's clothing this way, while Silpada sells jewelry. Tastefully Simple also operates this way, offering packaged mixes for gourmet appetizers, breads, and desserts. The firm has used this method of selling to grow from $100,000 in sales to $119 million in sales in just one decade. The costs of this type of field selling are minimal compared with those of traditional firms. "From a purely business standpoint, it's a very appealing way to do business because there is robust cash flow and low overhead," explains Amy Robinson, spokesperson for the Direct Selling Association. These selling parties generate a total of about $6.3 billion in sales each year.

Briefly
Speaking

"Sometimes the better part of innovation is responsiveness, listening to your customers."

—Steve Ballmer (b. 1956)
CEO, Microsoft

field selling Sales presentations made at prospective customers' locations on a face-to-face basis.

© DAVID COATES/THE DETROIT NEWS

Tastefully Simple senior sales consultant Jennifer Raybaud uses network marketing to sell the firm's gourmet appetizers, soups, breads, and desserts. Raybaud organizes parties at which customers can sample many of the company's products.

TELEMARKETING

Telemarketing, a channel in which the selling process is conducted by phone, serves two general purposes (sales and service) and two general markets (business-to-business and direct-to-customer). Both inbound and outbound telemarketing are forms of direct marketing.

Outbound telemarketing involves a sales force that relies on the telephone to contact customers, reducing the substantial costs of personal visits to customers' homes or businesses. Technologies such as predictive dialers, autodialing, and random-digit dialing increase chances that telemarketers will reach customers at home. *Predictive dialers* weed out busy signals and answering machines, nearly doubling the number of calls made per hour. *Autodialing* allows telemarketers to dial numbers continually; when a customer

telemarketing Promotional presentation involving the use of the telephone on an outbound basis by salespeople or on an inbound basis by customers who initiate calls to obtain information and place orders.

answers the phone, the call is automatically routed to a sales representative. However, the Telephone Consumer Protection Act of 1991 prohibits the use of autodialers to contact (or leave messages) on telephone devices such as answering machines.[11] *Random-digit dialing* allows telemarketers to reach unlisted numbers and block Caller ID.

A major drawback of telemarketing is that most consumers dislike the practice, and 100 million have signed up for the national Do Not Call Registry.[12] If an unauthorized telemarketer does call any of these numbers, the marketer is subject to an $11,000 fine. Organizations that are exempt from the fine include not-for-profits, political candidates, companies that have obtained the customer's permission, and firms that have an existing business relationship with the customer.

Why do some firms still use telemarketing? The average call still costs only about $3, and companies still point to a significant rate of success. According to the Direct Marketing Association, about 6 million people are employed in telemarketing jobs.[13]

Inbound telemarketing typically involves a toll-free number that customers can call to obtain information, make reservations, and purchase goods and services. When a customer calls a toll-free number, the caller can be identified and routed to the representatives with whom he or she has done business before, creating a human touch not possible before. This form of selling provides maximum convenience for customers who initiate the sales process. Many large catalog merchants, such as Pottery Barn, L. L. Bean, Lands' End, and Performance Bike, keep their inbound telemarketing lines open 24 hours a day, 7 days a week.

Some firms are taking dramatic steps to incorporate inbound telemarketing into their overall marketing strategy. Retailer Office Depot closed ten of its twelve U.S. call centers and replaced them with home-based telemarketers—workers who handle the calls from their own homes. JetBlue Airways is well known for the fact that all of its 1,400 reservation agents take their calls at home. Other firms continue to run call centers in the United States and overseas, including India, Hungary, Jamaica, and China. "Today in China you're able to attract some of the best people [in telemarketing]," says S. Gopalakrishnan, COO of Infosys.[14]

INSIDE SELLING

inside selling Selling by phone, mail, and electronic commerce.

The role of many of today's telemarketers is a combination of field selling techniques applied through inbound and outbound telemarketing channels with a strong customer orientation, called **inside selling.** Inside sales reps perform two primary jobs: They turn opportunities into actual sales, and they support technicians and purchasers with current solutions. Inside sales reps do far more than read a canned script to unwilling prospects. Their role goes beyond taking orders to solving problems, providing customer service, and selling. A successful inside sales force relies on close working relationships with field representatives to solidify customer relationships.

The NBA's Detroit Pistons has more than a dozen inside sales representatives who support the team's various marketing efforts such as special events for season ticket holders, including backstage tours, scavenger hunts, and privileges such as getting into games 30 minutes early.[15]

INTEGRATING THE VARIOUS SELLING CHANNELS

Figure 17.1 illustrates how firms are likely to blend alternative sales channels—from over-the-counter selling and field selling to telemarketing and inside selling—to create a successful cost-effective sales organization. Existing customers whose business problems require complex solutions are likely to be best served by the traditional field sales force. Other current customers who need answers but not the same attention as the first group can be served by inside sales reps who contact them as needed. Over-the-counter sales reps serve existing customers by supplying information and advice and completing sales transactions. Telemarketers may be used to strengthen communication with customers or to reestablish relationships with customers that may have lapsed over a few months.

figure 17.1

Alternative Sales Channels for Serving Customers

 assessment check

1. **What is over-the-counter selling?**
2. **What is field selling?**
3. **Distinguish between outbound and inbound telemarketing.**

TRENDS IN PERSONAL SELLING

In today's complex marketing environment, effective personal selling requires different strategies from those used by salespeople in the past. As pointed out in the discussion of *buying centers* in Chapter 6, rather than selling one-on-one, in B2B settings it is now customary to sell to teams of corporate representatives who participate in the client firm's decision-making process. In business-to-business sales situations involving technical products, customers expect salespeople to answer technical questions—or bring along someone who can. They also want representatives who understand technical jargon and can communicate using sophisticated technological tools. Patience is also a requirement because the B2B sales cycle, from initial contact to closing, may take months or even years. To address all of these concerns, companies rely on three major personal selling approaches: relationship selling, consultative selling, and team selling. Regardless of the approach, however, experts agree on a few basic guidelines for conducting successful personal selling.

 Describe the major trends in personal selling.

RELATIONSHIP SELLING

Most firms now emphasize **relationship selling,** a technique for building a mutually beneficial partnership with a customer through regular contacts over an extended period. Such buyer–seller bonds

relationship selling
Regular contacts between sales representatives and customers over an extended period to establish a sustained buyer–seller relationship.

table 17.2   What Buyers Expect from Salespeople

Buyers prefer to do business with salespeople who:

- Orchestrate events and bring to bear whatever resources are necessary to satisfy the customer
- Provide counseling to the customer based on in-depth knowledge of the product, the market, and the customer's needs
- Solve problems proficiently to ensure satisfactory customer service over extended time periods
- Demonstrate high ethical standards and communicate honestly at all times
- Willingly advocate the customer's cause within the selling organization
- Create imaginative arrangements to meet buyers' needs
- Arrive well prepared for sales calls

Briefly Speaking

"There are no problems we cannot solve together, and very few we can solve by ourselves."

—Lyndon B. Johnson (1908–1973)

36th president of the United States

become increasingly important as companies cut back on the number of suppliers and look for companies that provide high levels of customer service and satisfaction. Salespeople must also find ways to distinguish themselves and their products from competitors. To create strong, long-lasting relationships with customers, salespeople must meet buyers' expectations. Table 17.2 summarizes the results of several surveys that indicate what buyers expect of professional salespeople.

The success of tomorrow's marketers depends on the relationships they build today in both the business-to-consumer and business-to-business markets. Merrill Lynch recently refocused its 10,000-plus U.S. brokers on a relationship selling approach. The company redirected its brokers to concentrate on wealthy clients with $1 million or more to invest. Investors with more modest assets are now handled by call centers. The change not only has cut costs but positions Merrill Lynch for faster growth, because brokers are able to offer more sophisticated advice to fewer but more profitable clients.[16]

Relationship selling is equally important in business-to-business sales, if not more so. Firms may invest millions of dollars in goods and services from a single firm, so creating relationships is vital. The Dubai-based Emirates airline now gives building specifications to Boeing and Airbus, not the other way around. But Emirates rewards these firms by ordering more new planes than any other carrier.[17] Boeing's most successful salesperson, Larry Dickenson, is profiled in the "Marketing Success" feature.

 ## marketing success   Star Salesman Lifts Boeing's Profits

Background. A jet is an expensive and complex purchase for an airline. So manufacturers such as Boeing must do everything they can to make the purchase process as smooth and attractive as possible. One sale can mean billions of dollars, and it can all rest on the shoulders of a salesperson such as Boeing's Larry Dickenson.

The Challenge. Asia and the Pacific region are the world's fastest-growing markets for aircraft. Airlines based there are also the largest buyers of the new, longer-range widebody jets. Boeing wanted to grab the biggest portion of the market, which also meant dealing with foreign government officials, regulations, and agencies. So the firm turned to Larry Dickenson, who already had 20 years of experience in commercial jet sales in Asia.

The Strategy. "I'm just a jet salesman. We have good products, and we try to demonstrate [their] value," says Dickenson. But selling jets is a lot more complicated than that. Dickenson plans each sales call right down to the last detail, including the wording of press releases. He devises creative solutions for pricing, financing, leasing, training, and service. He also hosts events designed to bring people together in a relaxed setting where they can talk—such as golf tournaments. Golf is popular among Asian businesspeople, so every November Dickenson hosts a lavish tournament in Hawaii for about

CONSULTATIVE SELLING

Field representatives and inside sales reps require sales methods that satisfy today's cost-conscious, knowledgeable buyers. One such method, **consultative selling,** involves meeting customer needs by listening to customers, understanding—and caring about—their problems, paying attention to details, and following through after the sale. It works hand in hand with relationship selling in building customer loyalty. Xerox has turned itself around by employing consultative selling. "About five years ago we really started shifting to the consultative selling model," recalls Keith Stock, vice president of education and learning for North America. "We've become very focused on the customer and helping them solve their business problems, rather than just placing another piece of equipment. We identify opportunities at the customer site and turn that into sales for Xerox."[18]

As rapid technological changes drive business at an unprecedented pace, selling has become more complex, often changing the role of salespeople. At West Chester, Pennsylvania–based ZEKS Compressed Air Solutions, for instance, every sales representative has a background in engineering. With the job title Application Engineer, they bring technical proficiency to the sales situation. The change in title has helped the company overcome resistance to sales calls, because the expertise offered brings extra value to the buyer–seller relationship.

Online companies have instituted consultative selling models to create long-term customers. Particularly for complicated, high-priced products that require installation or specialized service, Web sellers must be able to quickly communicate the benefits and features of their products. They accomplish this through consultative selling.

Sometimes consultative selling takes place outside the workplace—in restaurants or on golf courses, as described in the "Etiquette Tips for Marketing Professionals" feature. Regardless of the venue, however, it is important for salespeople to maintain a professional attitude and demeanor.

Similar to consultative selling, **cross-selling**—offering multiple goods or services to the same customer—is another technique that capitalizes on a firm's strengths. It costs a bank five times as much to acquire a new customer as to cross-sell to an existing one. Moreover, research shows that the more a customer buys from an institution, the less likely that person is to leave. So a customer who opens a checking account at a local bank may follow with a safe-deposit box, retirement savings account, and a mortgage loan. Starwood Hotels & Resorts practices cross-selling not only among its various hotel brands such as Westin and Sheraton but also under partnerships with firms such as Time Warner. Time Warner places specific magazines and books in guest rooms of Sheraton and Westin hotels and provides content from its cartoon network to Starwood's "Westin Kids Club." Starwood is exploring a partnership with Sprint Nextel that would provide hotel guests with free ten-minute calling cards at check-in, with the opportunity to purchase more minutes during their stay.[19]

consultative selling
Meeting customer needs by listening to them, understanding their problems, paying attention to details, and following through after the sale.

---

100 invited guests. "When you play four hours of golf a day, you get to know your team," he explains.

The Outcome. In a recent year, Dickenson landed $26 billion in Asian sales for Boeing. He orchestrated the sale of 115 Boeing 787 Dreamliners to Quantas, totaling about $10 billion. And he sold an order for sixteen 777 widebody jetliners to Cathay Pacific Airways. Experts estimate that Boeing now controls about 60 percent of the Asian market for widebody jets. But Dickenson won't rest on his laurels. He is always watching his competition, particularly John Leahy of Airbus. "I'm always nervous when John is in Asia," he says. Boeing predicts that China alone will need about 2,600 new aircraft over the next 20 years—and Larry Dickenson plans to be the person to sell them.

Sources: James Wallace, "Aerospace Notebook: Boeing Doubles up on Retreats," *Seattle Post-Intelligencer*, June 7, 2006, **http://seattlepi.nwsource.com**; Brad Wong, "Boeing: Need for Planes Keeps Growing," *Seattle Post-Intelligencer*, April 15, 2006, **http://seattlepi.nwsource.com**; Stanley Holmes, "Boeing's Jet Propellant," *BusinessWeek*, December 26, 2005, p. 40.

Etiquette Tips for Marketing Professionals

Good Golfing Manners

If horse racing is the sport of kings, golf is the sport of businesspeople. Many business and marketing discussions take place on the golf course and in the clubhouse. That's why so many managers with their eyes on the prize—whether it's an important deal or a top company position—take golf lessons. In addition to improving their swing and their knowledge of the rules, golfers must learn a fairly strict code of etiquette that not only affects the game but may also determine the business outcome of a golf outing. Here are a few tips:

1. Arrive well before your tee time in order to greet others, get ready, and warm up.
2. Check your scorecard for any local course rules. Be sure to abide by all the rules—there is no referee to check up on you.
3. Do not swing your golf club until you know that other players are standing at a safe distance. Also make sure you stand at a safe distance from other players who are getting ready to swing.
4. Maintain a reasonable pace when you are playing. Be prepared to take your shot when it is your turn. Always leave the green when your group has finished putting.
5. Take care of the course. Replace any divots and ball marks you create. Obey cart rules. Rake sand traps after hitting.
6. Be quiet while on the course. Never talk during someone else's swing. Do not yell after a shot—whether it's good or bad.
7. In general, be courteous to everyone you encounter—in your group, on the course, and in the clubhouse. Not only is this good sportsmanship, it is also an indicator of your temperament; and it may influence a business decision later.

Sources: Brent Kelley, "Golf Etiquette Is about More Than Just Manners," Your Guide to Golf, **http://golf.about.com**, accessed June 26, 2006; "Guidelines from the Rules of Golf," USGA, Bill Purdin, "The 10 Commandments of Golf Etiquette," *Legendinc*, **http://www.legendinc.com**, accessed June 26, 2006.

TEAM SELLING

team selling Selling situation in which several sales associates or other members of the organization are recruited to help the lead sales representative reach all those who influence the purchase decision.

One of the latest developments in the evolution of personal selling is **team selling**, in which the salesperson joins with specialists from other functional areas of the firm to complete the selling process. Teams can be formal and ongoing or created for a specific short-term selling situation. Although some salespeople have hesitated to embrace the idea of team selling, preferring to work alone, a growing number believe that team selling brings better results. Customers often prefer the team approach, which makes them feel well served. Consider a restaurant meal. If the host, servers, wine steward, chef, kitchen crew, and dishwashers are all working well together as a team, your experience at the restaurant is likely to be positive. But if the service stops and starts, your order is recorded wrong, the food is cold, the silverware is dirty, and the staff seems grouchy, you probably won't eat at that restaurant again. In fact, you may not even finish the meal.

Another advantage of team selling is the formation of relationships between companies rather than between individuals. In sales situations that call for detailed knowledge of new, complex, and ever-changing technologies, team selling offers a distinct competitive edge in meeting customers' needs. In most computer software B2B departments, a third of the sales force is made up of technically trained, nonmarketing experts such as engineers or programmers. A salesperson continues to play the lead role in most sales situations, but technical experts bring added value to the sales process. Some companies establish permanent sales-and-tech teams that conduct all sales presentations together; others have a pool of engineers or other professionals who are on call for different client visits.

Some resourceful entrepreneurs have begun building a **virtual sales team**—a network of strategic partners, suppliers, and others who are qualified and willing to recommend a firm's goods or services. Merrimack, New Hampshire–based McMahon Worldwide is a small but powerful sales and management company founded a decade ago by Tim McMahon. The firm's clients include Canon USA, IBM, and The Guardian Insurance. McMahon Worldwide offers its customers strategies and software for creating their own virtual sales forces—products such as SalesConference.Net, a fully collaborative training and consulting program. MacMahon and his partner Jonathan Narducci practice their own advice by conducting many virtual sessions with clients.[20]

SALES TASKS

Today's salesperson is more concerned with establishing long-term buyer–seller relationships and helping customers select the correct products for meeting their needs than with simply selling whatever is available. Where repeat purchases are common, the salesperson must be certain that the buyer's purchases are in his or her best interest; otherwise, no future relationship will be possible. The seller's interests are tied to the buyer's in a mutually beneficial relationship.

While all sales activities help the customer in some manner, they are not all alike. Three basic sales tasks can be identified: (1) order processing, (2) creative selling, and (3) missionary sales. Most of today's salespeople are not limited to performing tasks in a single category. Instead, they often perform all three tasks to some extent. A sales engineer for a computer firm may be doing 50 percent missionary sales, 45 percent creative selling, and 5 percent order processing. Most sales positions are classified on the basis of the primary selling task performed.

Then there's the philosophy that *everyone* in the organization, regardless of what his or her job description is, should be engaged in selling. Chandler, Arizona–based Microchip Technology achieved this—and retrieved itself from a downward slide—by eliminating sales commissions. Seen as a radical move by other firms (and their sales forces), the change actually brought all sales workers at Microchip together. Instead of sales commissions, employees now receive company stock based on Microchip's overall performance—so they have a stake in how well they sell.[21]

ORDER PROCESSING

Order processing, which can involve both field selling and telemarketing, is most often typified by selling at the wholesale and retail levels. For instance, a Pepsi-Cola route salesperson who performs this task must take the following steps:

1. *Identify customer needs.* The route salesperson determines that a store has only 7 cases left in stock when it normally carries an inventory of 40 cases.

2. *Point out the need to the customer.* The route salesperson informs the store manager of the inventory situation.

"WILL WE BE ABLE TO AFFORD COLLEGE AND TAKE TRIPS LIKE THIS? WHAT IF THERE'S LAW SCHOOL? OR MED SCHOOL? WOULD THOSE BE CONSIDERED ROCKS OR BOULDERS?"

For 150 years, people have been coming to Northwestern Mutual to put their minds at ease.

 Northwestern Mutual®
the quiet company®

northwesternmutual.com   insurance / investments / ideas™

Financial services firms such as Northwestern Mutual offer many different products to clients, such as insurance, retirement planning, education funding, and estate planning. So the firm can gain by cross-selling those services to meet clients' needs.

✓ assessment check

1. **Identify the three major personal selling approaches.**
2. **Distinguish between relationship selling and consultative selling.**

4 Identify and briefly describe the three basic sales tasks.

order processing Selling, mostly at the wholesale and retail levels, that involves identifying customer needs, pointing them out to customers, and completing orders.

3. *Complete (write up) the order.* The store manager acknowledges the need for more of the product. The driver unloads 33 cases, and the manager signs the delivery slip.

My work says I'm the graphic designer to watch.

Unfortunately, my Web site traffic says I'm the one you can't find.

We can help customers find your Web site with better search engine results, online directory listings and online banner ads. Call or visit us to learn more, and to find out all the ways we can help take your business farther.

Easy Build-It-Myself Web Site™
Do-It-For-Me Web Site Design™
Real-Person Customer Service™
Personalized E-mail
Online Sales & Marketing Tools

from $24.95 mo
for online marketing services

Network**Solutions**.
Go Farther ➢

Call or click: 1.866.455.2005 | www.networksolutions.com

Order processing can be facilitated by technology. Network Solutions creates e-commerce websites that allow customers to sell their products online, as well as provide effective online sales and marketing tools.

Order processing is part of most selling positions. It becomes the primary task in situations in which needs can be readily identified and are acknowledged by the customer. Even in such instances, however, salespeople whose primary responsibility involves order processing will devote some time persuading their wholesale or retail customers to carry more complete inventories of their firms' merchandise or to handle additional product lines. They also are likely to try to motivate purchasers to feature some of their firms' products, increase the amount of shelf space devoted to these items, and improve product location in the stores.

Technology now streamlines order-processing tasks. In the past, salespeople wrote up an order on the customer's premises but spent much time later, after the sales visit, completing the order and transmitting it to headquarters. Today, many companies have automated order processing. With portable computers and state-of-the-art software, the salesperson can place an order on the spot, directly to headquarters, and thus free up valuable time and energy. Computers have even eliminated the need for some of the traditional face-to-face contacts for routine reorders. JCPenney has placed kiosks in its stores that allow salespeople to select, create, and transmit accurate orders in 30 minutes or less. The kiosks are particularly useful for such transactions as orders for custom blinds. The complete order is automatically transmitted electronically to a manufacturer, and a confirmation receipt is returned immediately to the salesperson. Three weeks after the kiosks' installation, JCPenney's percentage of accurate orders had increased significantly, and the lead time required by manufacturers to fulfill custom orders dropped by one week.[22]

CREATIVE SELLING

creative selling Personal selling that involves situations in which a considerable degree of analytical decision making on the buyer's part results in the need for skillful proposals of solutions for the customer's needs.

When a considerable amount of decision making is involved in purchasing a good or service, an effective salesperson uses **creative selling** techniques to solicit an order. In contrast to the order-processing task, which deals mainly with maintaining existing business, creative selling generally is used to develop new business either by adding new customers or by introducing new goods and services. New products or upgrades to more expensive items often require creative selling. The salesperson must first identify the customer's problems and needs and then propose a solution in the form of the item being offered. Creative selling techniques are used in over-the-counter selling, field selling, inside selling, and telemarketing (when attempting to expand an existing business relationship).

Sometimes creative selling can rejuvenate an old product. Newell Rubbermaid's Phoenix program is designed to train young, entry-level salespeople to do whatever it takes to sell Rubbermaid products. They may be found stocking shelves, demonstrating new products, or organizing in-store scavenger hunts. Phoenix program trainees are energetic and enthusiastic—and they have helped turn the company around. As employees progress in their careers, they take part in additional training seminars that teach advanced selling skills, product and channel marketing, negotiating skills, and leadership skills.[23]

MISSIONARY SELLING

Missionary selling is an indirect approach to sales. Salespeople sell the firm's goodwill and provide their customers with information and technical or operational assistance. A cosmetics company salesperson may call on retailers to check on special promotions and overall product movement, even though a wholesaler takes orders and delivers merchandise. Large pharmaceuticals companies are the most aggressive of missionary sales operations. Through free samples, educational seminars, and incentives, teams of sales reps typically court doctors (the indirect customer) in the hope of persuading them to prescribe a particular brand to patients. They also provide physicians with glossy product literature. Here, the doctor is clearly the decision maker, even though the transaction is not complete until the patient hands the prescription over to a pharmacist.

Pharmaceutical firms are not the only ones who offer **sales incentives,** however. Three Florida homebuilders—Cambridge Homes, Mercedes Homes, and Holiday Builders—have been offering customer incentives. Cambridge Homes recently offered a $20,000 Mini Cooper, $20,000 in upgrades, or a lower interest rate to customers who sign on. Mercedes Homes is offering $15,000 in upgrades and will pay closing costs. Holiday Builders tosses in a $2,000 gas card after closing. All three firms have reported an increase in sales—although only one customer took the Mini Cooper deal, because state law required a tax paid on delivery.[24]

Missionary sales may involve both field selling and telemarketing. Many aspects of team selling can also be seen as missionary sales, as when technical support salespeople help design, install, and maintain equipment; when they train customers' employees; and when they provide information or operational assistance.

> **missionary selling** Indirect type of selling in which specialized salespeople promote the firm's goodwill among indirect customers, often by helping customers use products.

THE SALES PROCESS

✓ *assessment check*

1. **What are the three major tasks performed by salespeople?**
2. **What are the three steps of order processing?**

If you have worked in a retail store, or if you've sold magazine subscriptions or candy to raise money for your school or sports team, you will recognize many of the activities involved in the following list of steps in the sales process. Personal selling encompasses the following sequence of activities: (1) prospecting and qualifying, (2) approach, (3) presentation, (4) demonstration, (5) handling objections, (6) closing, and (7) follow-up.

As Figure 17.2 indicates, these steps follow the AIDA concept (attention, interest, desire, action). Once a sales prospect has been qualified, an attempt is made to secure his or her attention. The presentation and demonstration steps are designed to generate interest and desire. Successful handling of buyer objections should arouse further desire. Action occurs at the close of the sale.

Salespeople modify the steps in this process to match their customers' buying processes. A neighbor who eagerly looks forward to the Girl Scout cookie sale each year needs no presentation—except for details about new types of cookie offerings. But the same neighbor would expect a demonstration from an auto dealer when looking for a new car or might appreciate a presentation of dinner specials by the server prior to ordering a meal at a restaurant.

5 Outline the seven steps in the sales process.

figure 17.2

The AIDA Concept and the Personal Selling Process

PROSPECTING AND QUALIFYING

Prospecting, the process of identifying potential customers, may involve hours, days, or weeks of effort, but it is a necessary step. Leads about prospects come from many sources: the Internet, computerized databases, trade show exhibits, previous customers, friends and neighbors, other vendors, nonsales employees in the firm, suppliers, and social and professional contacts. Although a firm may emphasize personal selling

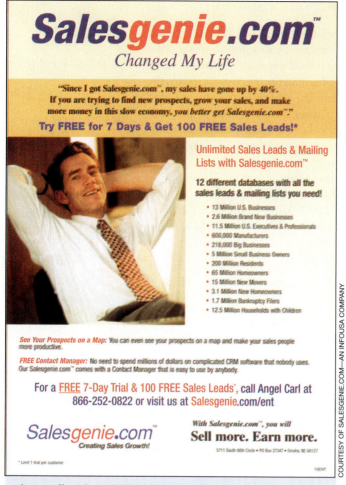

Salesgenie offers salespeople help in leads and mailing lists to generate new customers.

as the primary component of its overall promotional strategy, direct mail and advertising campaigns are also effective in identifying prospective customers.

As a salesperson, before you begin your prospecting effort, you must be clear about what your firm is selling. But don't limit your thoughts to a narrow definition of the product offerings. Customers are generally looking for solutions to problems, or ways to make their lives better or businesses more successful. In addition, you need to be well informed about the goods and services of the industry in general. Find out how other goods are marketed and packaged. Try out a service yourself. Understand how the industry operates so you will understand what your prospective customers need and want—and how you can serve them.[25]

Qualifying—determining that the prospect really is a potential customer—is another important sales task. Not all prospects are qualified to make purchase decisions. Even though an employee in a firm might like your products, he or she might not be authorized to make the purchase. A consumer who test-drives a Porsche might fall in love with it—but not be able to afford the purchase price. Qualifying can be a two-way street. As a sales representative, you might determine that a certain prospect is qualified to make a purchase. But the prospect must agree in order for the process to go forward. If either you or the prospect determine at the outset that there's no chance for a purchase, then it's best to move on.

APPROACH

Once you have identified a qualified prospect, you need to collect all available, relevant information and plan an **approach**—your initial contact with the prospective customer. If your firm already has a relationship with the customer or has permission to contact the person, you may use telemarketing. But before you do so, gather as much information as you can.

Information gathering makes **precall planning** possible. As mentioned earlier, educate yourself about the industry in general, as well as goods and services offered by competitors. Read any marketing research that is available. Go to trade shows—you can learn a lot about many companies and their products at one location, usually in one day. Also learn as much as you can about the firm you are planning to approach—browse the company's Web site, find online news articles and press releases about the company, talk with other people in the industry. Know its product offerings well. If possible, buy at least one of the firm's products and use it yourself. Identify ways you can help the firm do whatever it does better. Without invading an individual customer's privacy, see if there is anything you have in common—perhaps you grew up in the same state, or you both like to play golf.[26] All of this planning will help you make an effective approach.

As you plan your approach, try to answer the following questions:

• Whom am I approaching and what are their jobs within the company?

• What is their level of knowledge? Are they already informed about the idea I am going to present?

• What do they want or need? Should I speak in technical terms or provide general information?

• What do they need to hear? Do they need to know more about specific products or how those products can serve them? Do they need to know how the product works? Do they need to know about cost and availability?

If you are a retail salesperson, you can ask a shopper questions to learn more about his or her needs and preferences. Say you work at a large sporting-goods store. You might ask a young male shopper whether he works out at home, what equipment he already has, what his fitness goals are. The answers to these questions should lead you in the direction of a sale.

PRESENTATION

In your **presentation,** you convey your marketing message to the potential customer. You will describe the product's major features, point out its strengths, and cite other customers' successes with the product. One popular form of presentation is a "features-benefits" framework wherein you talk about the good or service in terms that are meaningful to the buyer. If you work for a car dealership, you might point out safety features such as side airbags and built-in car seats to a young couple. You probably wouldn't provide them with engine specifications.

Your presentation should be well organized, clear, and concise. If appropriate, you might use visual sales support materials such as a chart, a brochure, a CD, or even streaming video from your laptop. If this is your first presentation to a potential customer, it will likely be more detailed than a routine call to give an existing customer some updates. Regardless of the situation, though, be attuned to your audience's response so you can modify your presentation—even on the spur of the moment—to meet their needs.

© ASSOCIATED PRESS, AP

A runway fashion show is a form of sales presentation by a designer such as Ralph Lauren.

Many presentations now use computer-based multimedia, which can offer everything from interactivity to current pricing information. CNN Headline News salespeople previously used ordinary PowerPoint presentations to sell ads to cable operators. But when the Atlanta-based company decided to change the look and feel of its 24-hour cable news network, the sales presentation material changed as well to include audio, video, and high-tech graphics.

However, technology must be used efficiently to be effective. For example, a company's Web site can be an excellent selling tool if it is easy for salespeople to present and buyers to use. Experts recommend that a site offer obvious links to products directly from the home page. A salesperson can actually use the site during a presentation by showing a potential customer how to use it to learn about and purchase products.[27]

In a **cold calling** situation, the approach and presentation often take place at the same time. Cold calling means phoning or visiting the customer without a prior appointment—and making a sales pitch on the spot. Cold calling requires nerve, skill, and creativity—but salespeople who are successful at it still point to the importance of preparation. "Before I pick up the phone, I read up on the company—its current strategies, key products, revenues, growth," says Scott Vincent Borba, CEO and founder of Beverly Hills–based Borba, a firm that makes vitamin-infused beauty products. "The worst thing you can do is pitch a top executive and know nothing about his business."[28]

DEMONSTRATION

One of the most important advantages of personal selling is the opportunity to demonstrate a product. During a **demonstration,** the buyer gets a chance to try the product or at least see how it works. A demonstration might involve a test-drive of the latest hybrid car or an in-store cooking class using pots and pans that are for sale.

Many firms use new technologies to make their demonstrations more outstanding than those of their competitors. Multimedia interactive demonstrations are now common. Visitors to the Black & Decker Web site can click on video demonstrations of such products as the Alligator Lopper (an electric branch clipper) and the Grass Hog String Trimmer and Edger.[29]

The key to an outstanding demonstration—one that gains the customer's attention, keeps his or her interest, is convincing, and stays in the customer's memory—is planning. But planning should also include time and space for improvisation. During your demonstration, you should be prepared to stop and answer questions, redemonstrate a certain feature, or even let the customer try the product firsthand.

HANDLING OBJECTIONS

Potential customers often have legitimate questions and concerns about a good or service they are considering. **Objections** are expressions of resistance by the prospect, and it is reasonable to expect them. Objections might appear in the form of stalling or indecisiveness. "Let me call you back," your prospect might say, or "I just don't know about this." Or your buyer might focus on something negative such as high price.

You can answer objections without being aggressive or rude. Use an objection as an opportunity to reassure your buyer about price, features, durability, availability, and the like. If the objection involves price, you might be able to suggest a less-expensive model or a payment plan. If the objection involves a comparison to competitive products, point out the obvious—and not so obvious—benefits of your own. If the objection involves a question about availability, a few clicks on your laptop should be able to show how many items are in stock and when they can be shipped.

CLOSING

The moment of truth in selling is the **closing**—the point at which the salesperson asks the prospect for an order. If your presentation has been effective and you have handled all objections, a closing would be the natural conclusion to the meeting. But you may still find it difficult to close the sale. Closing does not have to be thought of in terms of a "hard sell." Instead, you can ask your customer, "Would you like to give this a try?" or, "Do I have your approval to proceed?"

Other methods of closing include the following:

1. Addressing the prospect's major concern about a purchase and then offering a convincing argument. ("If I can show you how the new heating system will reduce your energy costs by 25 percent, would you be willing to let us install it?")

2. Posing choices for the prospect in which either alternative represents a sale. ("Would you prefer the pink sweater or the green one?")

3. Advising the buyer that a product is about to be discontinued or will go up in price soon. (But be completely honest about this—you don't want a customer to learn later that this was not true.)

4. Remaining silent so the buyer can make a decision on his or her own.

5. Offering an extra inducement designed to motivate a favorable buyer response, such as a quantity discount, an extended service contract, or a low-interest payment plan.

Even if the meeting or phone call ends without a sale, the effort is not over. "Never, ever forget the power of a simple, handwritten thank-you note. It's become a lost art in our fast-moving, high-tech society," says one sales expert.[30] You can use a written note or an e-mail to keep communication open, letting the buyer know that you are ready and waiting to be of service.

FOLLOW-UP

The word *close* can be misleading because the point at which the prospect accepts the seller's offer is where much of the real work of selling begins. In today's competitive environment, the most successful salespeople make sure that today's customers will also be tomorrow's.

It is not enough to close the sale and move on. Relationship selling involves reinforcing the purchase decision and making sure the company delivers the highest-quality merchandise. As a salesperson, you must also ensure that customer service needs are met and that satisfaction results from all of a customer's dealings with your company. Otherwise, some other company may get the next order.

These postsale activities, which often determine whether a person will become a repeat customer, constitute the sales **follow-up.** Some sales experts believe in a wide array of follow-up techniques, ranging from expensive information folders to holiday cards to online greetings. Others recommend phone calls at regular intervals. Some prefer automatic e-mail reminders when it is time to renew or reorder.[31] At the very least, however, you should try to contact customers to find out whether they are satisfied with their purchases. This step allows you to psychologically reinforce the customer's original decision to buy. It also gives you an opportunity to correct any problems and ensure the next sale. Follow-up helps strengthen the bond you are trying to build with customers in relationship selling. You have probably experienced follow-up as a customer—if your auto dealership called to see if you were satisfied with recent service, or if your doctor phoned to find out if you were feeling better.

 assessment check

1. Identify the seven steps of the sales process.
2. Why is follow-up important to the sales effort?

MANAGING THE SALES EFFORT

The overall direction and control of the personal selling effort are in the hands of a firm's sales managers. In a typical geographic sales structure, a district or divisional sales manager might report to a regional or zone manager. This manager in turn reports to a national sales manager or vice president of sales.

Currently, there are about 337,000 sales managers in the United States.[32] The sales manager's job requires a unique blend of administrative and sales skills, depending on the specific level in the sales hierarchy. Sales skills are particularly important for first-level sales managers because they are involved daily in the continuing process of training and directly leading the sales force. But as people rise in the sales management hierarchy, they require more managerial skills and fewer sales skills to perform well. Ann Livermore, executive vice president of Hewlett-Packard, is passionate about her job. While her company has traditionally maintained an engineering focus, she has recently steered it toward a sales focus by hiring upper-level managers and executives with sales backgrounds. "There's a new energy about closing deals—about hating to lose," she says. "It's easier for an engineer to analytically describe why you lost a deal. But sales managers are much more emotional about it. There's a different hunger. With a truly great sales executive, you can almost see the blood on their teeth."[33]

Sales force management links individual salespeople to general management. The sales manager performs seven basic managerial functions: (1) recruitment and selection, (2) training, (3) organization, (4) supervision, (5) motivation, (6) compensation, and (7) evaluation and control. Sales managers perform these tasks in a demanding and complex environment. They must manage an increasingly diverse sales force that includes more women and minorities. Women account for almost half of U.S. professional salespeople, and their numbers are growing at a faster rate than that for men. As the workforce composition continues to change, an even more diverse blend of people will be needed to fill a growing number of sales positions. In fact, employment opportunities for sales and related fields are expected to increase faster than the average for all occupations through the next decade.[34]

6 Identify the seven basic functions of a sales manager.

RECRUITMENT AND SELECTION

Recruiting and selecting successful salespeople are among the sales manager's greatest challenges. After all, these workers will collectively determine just how successful the sales manager is. New salespeople—like you—might come from colleges and universities, trade and business schools, other companies, and even the firm's current nonsales staff. A successful sales career offers satisfaction in all of the following five areas that a person generally considers when deciding on a profession:

1. *Opportunity for advancement.* Studies have shown that successful sales representatives advance rapidly in most companies.

2. *Potential for high earnings.* Salespeople have the opportunity to earn a very comfortable living.

3. *Personal satisfaction.* A salesperson derives satisfaction from achieving success in a competitive environment and from helping customers satisfy their wants and needs.

4. *Job security.* Selling provides a high degree of job security because there is always a need for good salespeople.

5. *Independence and variety.* Salespeople often work independently, calling on customers in their territory. They have the freedom to make important decisions about meeting their customers' needs and frequently report that no two workdays are the same.

Careful selection of salespeople is important for two reasons. First, a company invests a substantial amount of time and money in the selection process. Second, hiring mistakes can damage relationships with customers and overall performance, and are also costly to correct.

Most large firms use a specific seven-step process in selecting sales personnel: application screening, initial interview, in-depth interview, testing, reference checks, physical examination, and hiring decision. An application screening is typically followed by an initial interview. If the applicant looks promising, an in-depth interview takes place. During the interview, a sales manager looks for the person's enthusiasm, organizational skills, ambition, persuasiveness, ability to follow instructions, and sociability.

Next, the company may administer aptitude, interest, and knowledge tests. One testing approach gaining in popularity is the assessment center. This technique, which uses situational exercises, group discussions, and various job simulations, allows the sales manager to measure a candidate's skills, knowledge, and ability. Assessment centers enable managers to see what potential salespeople can do rather than what they say they can do. Before hiring a candidate, the firm checks references, reviews company policies, and may request a physical examination.

TRAINING

To shape new sales recruits into an efficient sales organization, managers must conduct an effective training program. The principal methods used in sales training are on-the-job training, individual instruction, in-house classes, and external seminars.

Popular training techniques include instructional videos or DVDs, lectures, role-playing exercises, and interactive computer programs. Simulations can help salespeople improve their selling techniques. Many firms supplement their training by enrolling salespeople in executive development programs at local colleges and by hiring specialists to teach customized training programs. In other instances, sales reps attend courses and workshops developed by outside companies.

Best Buy is committed to training. Several years ago, its sales managers realized that customers were leaving their stores without buying anything because salespeople didn't know how to explain the electronics they were supposed to sell. If a customer asked which speakers worked well with which plasma screen, the sales staff couldn't always reply. So every new salesperson now receives four hours of classroom training the first day on the job, supplemented by twelve hours of Web-based training. Then the new hire shadows an experienced salesperson on the job until a supervisor says he or she is ready to navigate alone. Salespeople continue to receive product training so that they become adept at selling. Overall, the training focuses on everything from product features to customer interaction.[35]

Candy Bouquet offers training to new sales consultants.

Still, ongoing sales training is also important for veteran salespeople. Sales managers often conduct this type of training informally, traveling with field reps and then offering constructive criticism or suggestions. Sales meetings, classes, and workshops are other ways to reinforce training. Mentoring is also a key tool in training salespeople. Best Buy's shadowing technique is a form of mentoring.

ORGANIZATION

Sales managers are responsible for the organization of the field sales force. General organizational alignments, which are usually made by top marketing management, may be based on geography, products, types of customers, or some combination of these factors. Figure 17.3 presents a streamlined organizational chart illustrating each of these alignments.

A product sales organization is likely to have a specialized sales force for each major category of the firm's products. This approach is common among industrial business companies that market large numbers of highly technical, complex products that are sold through different marketing channels.

Firms that market similar products throughout large territories often use geographic specialization. Multinational corporations may have different sales divisions on different continents and in different countries. A geographic organization may also be combined with one of the other organizational methods.

However, many companies are moving away from using territorial sales reps as they adopt customer-focused sales forces. For example, a single territory that contains two major customers might be redefined so the same sales rep covers both customers. Customer-oriented organizations use different sales force strategies for each major type of customer served. Some firms assign separate sales forces for their consumer and organizational customers. Others have sales forces for specific industries, such as financial services, educational, and automotive. Sales forces can also be organized by customer size, with a separate sales force assigned to large, medium, and small accounts.

A growing trend among firms using a customer-oriented organizational structure is the **national accounts organization.** This structure strengthens a firm's relationship with its largest customers by assigning senior sales personnel or sales teams to major accounts in each market. Organizing by national accounts helps sales representatives develop cooperation among departments to meet special needs of the firm's most important customers. An example of national account selling is the relationship between Wal-Mart and its major vendors. S. C. Johnson, Unilever, H. J. Heinz, Johnson & Johnson, Kimberly-Clark, Kraft, Nestlé, Hormel, and Colgate Palmolive are just some of the companies that have sales offices near Wal-Mart's headquarters in Bentonville, Arkansas.

As companies expand their market coverage across national borders, they may use a variant of national account sales teams. These global account teams may be staffed by local sales representatives in the countries in which a company is operating. In other instances, the firm selects highly trained sales executives from its domestic operations. In either case, specialized training is critical to the success of a company's global sales force.

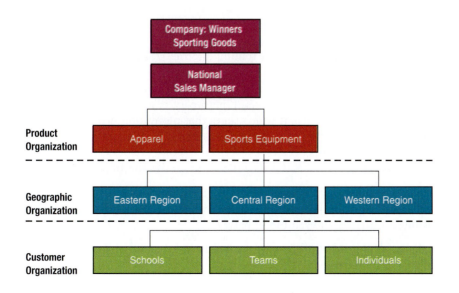

figure 17.3

Basic Approaches to Organizing the Sales Force

The individual sales manager also must organize the sales territories within his or her area of responsibility. Factors such as sales potential, strengths and weaknesses of available personnel, and workloads are considered in territory allocation decisions.

SUPERVISION

Sales managers have differing opinions about the supervision of a sales force. Individuals and situations vary, so it is impossible to write a recipe for the exact amount of supervision needed in all cases. However, a concept known as **span of control** helps provide some general guidelines. Span of control refers to the number of sales representatives who report to first-level sales managers. The optimal span of control is affected by such factors as complexity of work activities, ability of the individual sales manager, degree of interdependence among individual salespeople, and the extent of training each salesperson receives. A 6-to-1 ratio has been suggested as the optimal span of control for first-level sales managers supervising technical or industrial salespeople. In contrast, a 10-to-1 ratio is recommended if sales representatives are calling on wholesale and retail accounts.

MOTIVATION

What motivates salespeople to perform their best? The sales manager is responsible for finding the answer to this question. The sales process involves problem solving, which sometimes includes frustration—particularly when a sale is delayed or falls through. Information sharing, recognition, bonuses, incentives, and benefits can all be used to help defray frustration and motivate a sales staff. Developing an enthusiastic sales staff who are happy at their jobs is the goal of the sales manager. Motivation is an important part of a company's success; according to research by the Forum Corporation, firms that score high on "motivational climate" surveys also score high on sales performance.[36]

Creating a positive, motivating environment doesn't necessarily mean instituting complex or expensive incentive programs. Monetary reward—cash—is often considered king. But sometimes simple recognition—a thank-you, a dinner, a year-end award—can go a long way. It is important for the sales manager to figure out what types of incentives will be most effective with his or her particular group of employees. Some firms go all out, dangling luxury items such as computers, digital cameras, or trips in front of the sales force as rewards. A Caribbean cruise, a trip to Disney World, or a weekend at a luxury spa could be the carrot that works, particularly if family members are included. Some firms purchase gift cards from retailers such as L. L. Bean or Lowe's to distribute to sales staff who perform well. "Some people are motivated by winning—not only cash," observes Dan Moynihan of Upper Saddle River, New Jersey–based Compensation Resources. "There is more interest in noncash prizes, such as trips and TVs, because they hold a certain value and can be flaunted."[37]

But not all incentive programs are effective at motivating employees. A program with targets that are set too high, that isn't publicized, or that allows only certain sales personnel to participate can actually backfire. So it is important for sales management to plan carefully for an incentive program to succeed.

Sales managers can improve sales force productivity by understanding what motivates individual salespeople. They shouldn't overlook the importance of their own influence on their employees. "Lots of research says a person's immediate boss is key in retention," observes Ron Koprowski, head of Boston-based Forum Corporation's sales training practice. "Sales managers represent the company, so the day-to-day climate is essential."[38]

Sales managers can also gain insight into the subject of motivation by studying the various theories of motivation developed over the years. One theory that has been applied effectively to sales force motivation is **expectancy theory,** which states that motivation depends on the expectations an individual has of his or her ability to perform the job and on how performance relates to attaining rewards that the individual values.

Sales managers can apply the expectancy theory of motivation by following a five-step process:

1. Let each salesperson know in detail what is expected in terms of selling goals, service standards, and other areas of performance. Rather than setting goals just once a year, many firms do so on a semiannual, quarterly, or even monthly basis.

2. Make the work valuable by assessing the needs, values, and abilities of each salesperson and then assigning appropriate tasks.

3. Make the work achievable. As leaders, sales managers must inspire self-confidence in their sales-people and offer training and coaching to reassure them.

4. Provide immediate and specific feedback, guiding those who need improvement and giving positive feedback to those who do well.

5. Offer rewards that each salesperson values, whether it is an incentive as described previously, opportunity for advancement, or a bonus.

COMPENSATION

Money is an important part of any person's job, and the salesperson is no exception. So deciding how best to compensate the sales force can be a critical factor in motivation. Sales compensation can be based on a commission, a straight salary, or a combination of both. Bonuses based on end-of-year results are another popular form of compensation. The increasing popularity of team selling has also forced companies to set up reward programs to recognize performance of business units and teams. Today, about 25 percent of firms rewards business-unit performance.

A **commission** is a payment tied directly to the sales or profits that a salesperson achieves. A salesperson might receive a 5 percent commission on all sales up to a specified quota, and a 7 per-cent commission on sales beyond that point. This approach to sales compensation is increasingly popular. But while commissions reinforce selling incentives, they may cause some sales force members to overlook nonselling activities, such as completing sales reports, delivering promotion materi-als, and servicing existing accounts. In addition, salespeople who operate entirely on commission may become too aggressive in their approach to potential customers, which could backfire.

A **salary** is a fixed payment made periodically to an employee. A firm that bases compensation on salaries rather than commissions might pay a salesperson a set amount every week, twice a month, or once a month. A company must balance benefits and disadvantages in paying predeter-mined salaries to compensate managers and sales personnel. A straight salary plan gives management more control over how sales personnel allocate their efforts, but it may reduce the incentive to find new markets and land new accounts.

Many firms have found that it's best to develop compensation programs that combine features of both salary and commission plans. A new salesperson often receives a base salary while in training, even if he or she moves to full commission later on. If the salesperson does a lot of driving as part of the job, he or she may receive a vehicle. If the person works from home, there might be an allowance toward setting up an office there.

Total compensation packages vary according to industry, with the finance, insurance, and real estate industries coming out on top, followed closely by general services. They also vary according to years of experience in sales. Figure 17.4 shows the average annual pay for sales representatives during a recent year.

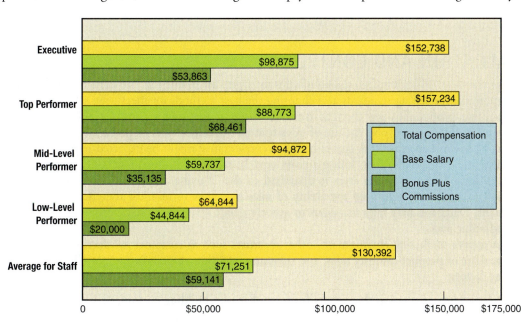

figure 17.4

Average Annual Pay for Sales Representatives

Source: Data from Christine Galea, "The 2005 Compensa-tion Survey," *Sales & Marketing Management*, May 2006, p. 31.

Solving an Ethical Controversy

Sales Quotas—Are They Fair?

Most firms that rely on personal selling set quotas for their salespeople to meet during a certain period of time. A sales quota is a target level of sales that the salesperson is expected to achieve. While managers often argue that quotas are the best way to set goals and measure performance, critics point out that they may not always be fair to the salesperson or even the firm's customers.

Are sales quotas good for salespeople, customers, and the firms they are designed to promote?

PRO

1. Realistic quotas act as goals for salespeople and can be positive motivators.
2. Sales quotas that are tied to compensation plans attract and retain the most qualified sales staff, and they provide focus on the firm's overall marketing strategy and performance.

CON

1. Sales quotas can cause salespeople to focus on new accounts at the expense of servicing existing accounts—with the result that existing customers may grow frustrated and choose a competitor instead.

2. When a salesperson meets or exceeds a quota one year, the quota is often increased by managers the following year. This practice only creates frustration among salespeople—not productivity.

Summary

Sales quotas—especially those that are developed or applied unfairly—can reduce morale, motivation, and productivity in a sales force. Quotas that are set too high may cause reps to give up. Quotas that are set too low may leave opportunities untapped. Either way, customers aren't served, sales staff are unhappy, and the firm loses ground. But some experts argue that realistic sales goals—if they are developed with a knowledge of the market, an analysis of sales territories, and industry standards—can create energy and enthusiasm throughout a sales force.

Sources: "Dictionary of Marketing Terms," American Marketing Association, **http://www.marketingpower.com**, accessed June 26, 2006; Donna Siegel, "Setting Sales Quotas for Your Sales Team," Sales MBA, **http://www.salesmba.com**, accessed June 26, 2006; Paul Dorf, "Sales Compensation: One Size Does Not Fit All," *Marketing Times*, Spring 2006, **http://www.emcmarketing.com**; Jeffrey Moses, "Setting Sales Quotas without Sacrificing Customer Service," National Federation of Independent Business, March 30, 2006, **http://www.nfib.com**.

EVALUATION AND CONTROL

Perhaps the most difficult tasks required of sales managers are evaluation and control. Sales managers are responsible for setting standards and choosing the best methods for measuring sales performance. Sales volume, profitability, and changes in market share are the usual means of evaluating sales effectiveness. They typically involve the use of **sales quotas**—specified sales or profit targets that the firm expects salespeople to achieve. A particular sales representative might be expected to generate sales of $720,000 in his or her territory during a given year. In many cases, the quota is tied to the compensation system. The sales quota issue is described in the "Solving an Ethical Controversy" feature. Technology has greatly improved the ability of sales managers to monitor the effectiveness of their sales staffs. Databases help sales managers to quickly divide revenues by salesperson, by account, and by geographic area.

In today's marketing environment, other measures such as customer satisfaction, profit contribution, share of product-category sales, and customer retention also come into play. This is the result of three factors:

1. A long-term orientation that results from emphasis on building customer relationships.

2. The fact that evaluations based on sales volume alone may lead to overselling and inventory problems that may damage customer relationships.

3. The need to encourage sales representatives to develop new accounts, provide customer service, and emphasize new products. Sales quotas tend to put focus on short-term selling goals rather than long-term relationships.

The sales manager must follow a formal system that includes a consistent series of decisions. This way, the manager can make fair and accurate evaluations. The system helps the sales manager answer three general questions:

1. *Where does each salesperson's performance rank relative to predetermined standards?* This comparison takes into consideration any uncontrollable variables on sales performance, such as a natural disaster or unforeseen change in the industry. Each adjusted rank is stated as a percentage of the standard.

2. *What are the salesperson's strong points?* The manager might list areas of the salesperson's performance in which he or she has performed above the standard. Or strong points could be placed in such categories as technical ability, processes, and end results.

3. *What are the salesperson's weak points?* No one likes to hear criticism, but when it is offered constructively, it can be motivation to improve performance. The manager and employee should establish specific objectives for improvement and set a timetable for judging the employee's improvement.

In completing the evaluation summary, the sales manager follows a set procedure so that all employees are treated equally:

- Each aspect of sales performance for which a standard exists should be measured separately. This helps prevent the so-called *halo effect*, in which the rating given on one factor influences those on other performance variables.

- Each salesperson should be judged on the basis of actual sales performance rather than potential ability. This is why rankings are important in the evaluation.

- Sales managers must judge each salesperson on the basis of sales performance for the entire period under consideration, rather than for a few particular incidents.

- The evaluation should be reviewed by a third party— such as the manager's boss or a human resources manager—for completeness and objectivity.

Once the evaluation is complete, both manager and salesperson should focus on positive action—whether it is a drive toward new goals or correcting a negative situation. An evaluation should be motivation for improved performance.

 assessment check

1. **What are the seven basic functions performed by a sales manager?**

2. **Define** *span of control.*

3. **What are the three main questions a sales manager must address as part of a salesperson's evaluation?**

ETHICAL ISSUES IN SALES

7 Explain the role of ethical behavior in personal selling.

Promotional activities can raise ethical questions, and personal selling is no exception. A difficult economy or highly competitive environment may tempt some salespeople—particularly those new to the business—to behave in ways that they might later regret. They might use the company car for a family trip or pad an expense report. They might give personal or expensive gifts to customers. They might try to sell a product that they know is not right for a particular customer's needs. But today's experienced, highly professional salespeople know that long-term success requires a strong code of ethics. They also know that a single breach of ethics could have a devastating effect on their careers.

Some people believe that ethical problems are inevitable because of the very nature of the sales function. And in the wake of corporate scandals in which top executives have benefited at the expense of customers, employees, and shareholders, ethical managers are working harder than ever to dispel the notion that many salespeople cannot be trusted.

Sales managers and top executives can do a lot to foster a corporate culture that encourages honesty and ethical behavior. Here are some characteristics of such a culture:

- *Employees understand what is expected of them.* A written code of ethics—which should be reviewed by all employees—in addition to ethics training helps educate employees in how to conduct ethical business.

- *Open communication.* Employees who feel comfortable talking with their supervisors are more apt to ask questions if they are uncertain about situations or decisions and to report any violations they come across.

- *Managers lead by example.* Workers naturally emulate the ethical behavior of managers. A sales manager who is honest with customers, doesn't accept inappropriate gifts, and leaves the company car at home during vacation is likely to be imitated by his or her sales staff.

Regardless of corporate culture, every salesperson is responsible for his or her own behavior and relationship with customers. If, as a new salesperson, you find yourself uncertain about a decision, ask yourself these questions. The answers should help you make the ethical choice.

 assessment check

1. Why is it important for salespeople to maintain ethical behavior?

2. What are the characteristics of companies that foster corporate cultures that encourage ethical behavior?

1. Does my decision affect anyone other than myself and the bottom line?

2. Is my success based on making the sale or creating a loyal customer?

3. Is my service of a customer based on ethical behavior?

4. What price will I pay for this decision?[39]

---

8 Describe the role of sales promotion in the promotional mix, and identify the different types of sales promotions.

sales promotion Marketing activities other than personal selling, advertising, and publicity that enhance consumer purchasing and dealer effectiveness.

SALES PROMOTION

Sales promotion includes marketing activities other than personal selling, advertising, and publicity designed to enhance consumer purchasing and dealer effectiveness. Sales promotion can be traced back as far as the ruins of Pompeii and Ephesus. In the United States, companies have been giving away trinkets and premiums for more than 100 years.

Sales promotion techniques were originally intended as short-term incentives aimed at producing an immediate response—a purchase. Today, however, marketers recognize sales promotion as an integral part of the overall marketing plan, and the focus has shifted from short-term goals to long-term objectives of building brand equity and maintaining continuing purchases. A frequent-flyer program enables a new airline to build a base of loyal customers. A frequent-stay program allows a hotel chain to attract regular guests.

Both retailers and manufacturers use sales promotions to offer consumers extra incentives to buy. These promotions are likely to stress price advantages, giveaways, or special offerings. The general objectives of sales promotion are to speed up the sales process and increase sales volume. Promotions can also help build loyalty. Through a consumer promotion, a marketer encourages consumers to try the product, use more of it, and buy it again. The firm also hopes to foster sales of related items and increase impulse purchases. Skype, a Web telephone company, announced that its U.S. customers and Canada could make free calls to conventional landline and mobile phones for a limited period of time. The promotion was designed to attract more users and put pressure on competitor Vonage.[40]

Experts warn that creating a loyalty program is more important to companies than ever before because consumers have so many more choices among products than in the past. According to one study, the number of shoppers who identified themselves as "longtime loyal customers" dropped from 84 percent to 77 percent in one year.[41] This means that marketers must find ways to build loyalty among customers.

Because sales promotion is so important to a marketing effort, an entire promotion industry exists to offer expert assistance in its use and to design unique promotions, just as the entire advertising industry offers similar services for advertisers. These companies, like advertising agencies, provide other firms with assistance in promoting their goods and services. Figure 17.5 shows current spending by companies for different types of sales promotions, many of which are conducted by these firms.

Sales promotions often produce their best results when combined with other marketing activities. Ads create awareness, while sales promotions lead to trial or purchase. After a presentation, a salesperson may offer a potential customer a discount coupon for the good or service. Promotions encourage immediate action because they impose limited time frames. Discount coupons and rebates usually have expiration dates. In addition, sales promotions produce measurable results, making it relatively easy for marketers to evaluate their effectiveness. If more people buy shoes during a buy-one-get-one-free promotion at a shoe store, its owners know the promotion was successful.

It is important to understand what sales promotions can and cannot do. They can encourage interest in both new and mature products, help introduce new products, encourage trial and repeat purchases, increase usage rates, neutralize competition, and reinforce advertising and personal selling

© SUSAN VAN ETTEN/PHOTOEDIT

Sales promotions such as instant coupon machines, special offers, and additional product information can help create and serve loyal customers.

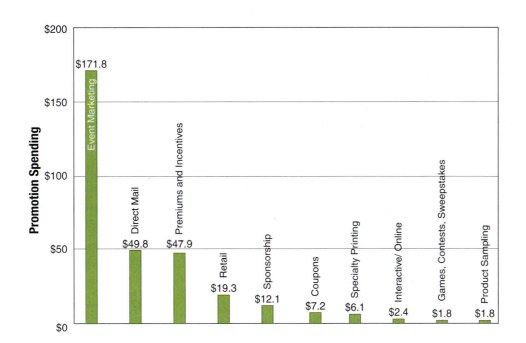

figure 17.5

Current Spending by Companies for Different Sales Promotions (in billions)

Source: Data from Kathleen M. Joyce, "Higher Gear," *Promo*, April 1, 2006, **http://promomagazine.com**.

efforts. On the other hand, sales promotions cannot overcome poor brand images, product deficiencies, or poor training for salespeople. While sales promotions increase volume in the short term, they may not lead to sales and profit growth in the long run.

Sales promotion techniques may serve all members of a marketing channel. In addition, manufacturers may use trade promotion methods to promote their products to resellers. Promotions generally are employed selectively. Sales promotion techniques include the following consumer-oriented promotions: coupons, refunds, samples, bonus packs, premiums, contests, sweepstakes, and specialty advertising. Trade-oriented promotions include trade allowances, point-of-purchase advertising, trade shows, dealer incentives, contests, and training programs.

CONSUMER-ORIENTED SALES PROMOTIONS

In the promotion industry, marketers use all types of sales promotions, including games, contests, sweepstakes, and coupons to persuade new and existing customers to try their products. Consumer-oriented sales promotions encourage repurchases by rewarding current users, boosting sales of complementary products, and increasing impulse purchases. These promotions also attract consumer attention in the midst of advertising clutter.

It's important for marketers to use sales promotions selectively because if they are overused, consumers begin to expect price discounts at all times, which ultimately diminishes brand equity. The following sections describe the various forms of consumer-oriented sales promotions.

Coupons and Refunds

Coupons, the most widely used form of sales promotion, offer discounts on the purchase price of goods and services. Consumers can redeem the coupons at retail outlets, which receive the face value of the coupon plus a handling fee from the manufacturer. The $5 billion coupon industry has been somewhat clipped in recent years due to more complex accounting rules that make couponing less attractive to some marketers, as well as the growing clout of retailers. In addition, consumers receive so many coupons that they can't possibly redeem them all. One estimate says that although 342 billion coupons are offered in the United States each year, only about 3.2 billion are redeemed.[42]

Mail, magazines, newspapers, package inserts, and, increasingly, the Internet are the standard methods of distributing coupons. A new channel for distributing coupons has emerged: cell phones. California-based Moonstorm has been testing its cell phone–based coupon technology with selected customers and believes it will be a success. Users can download free software from Moonstorm's Web site to their phones and receive targeted offers from such firms as Hollywood Video, Finish Line, Supercuts, Boston Market, and Sharper Image.[43]

Refunds, or rebates, offer cash back to consumers who send in proof of purchasing one or more products. Refunds help packaged-goods companies increase purchase rates, promote multiple purchases, and reward product users. Although many consumers find the refund forms too bothersome to complete, plenty still do so.

Coupons and rebates are a popular form of sales promotion.

© PATTI MCCONVILLE/THE IMAGE BANK/GETTY IMAGES

Samples, Bonus Packs, and Premiums

Marketers are increasingly adopting the "try it, you'll like it" approach as an effective means of getting consumers to try and then purchase their goods and services. **Sampling** refers to the free distribution of a product in an attempt to obtain future sales. Samples may be distributed door-to-door, by mail, online, via demonstrations in stores or at events, or by including them in packages with other products.

Sampling produces a higher response rate than most other promotions. About three-quarters of the consumers who receive samples try them, particularly if they have requested the samples, and total annual spending on this sales promotion technique has topped $1 billion. A recent survey showed that 92 percent of consumers preferred receiving free samples rather than coupons. With sampling, marketers can target potential customers and be certain that the product reaches them. Sampling provides an especially useful way to promote new or unusual products because it gives the consumer a direct product experience. It also has a "Wow!" factor. During one week in December, 1 million customers who ordered pizzas delivered from Domino's received a free 20-ounce bottle of Coca-Cola Zero and a coupon toward future purchases of both Coke Zero and pizza. Coca-Cola marketers believe it was an excellent way to build awareness of the new Coke Zero; consumers got something for free, and followed up with more purchases from the coupons.[44]

A major disadvantage of sampling is the high cost involved. Firms spent about $1.8 billion on sampling in one recent year.[45] Not only must the marketer give away small quantities of a product that might otherwise have generated revenues through regular sales, but the market is also in effect closed for the time it takes consumers to use up the samples. In addition, the marketer may encounter problems in distributing the samples. Hellman's marketers once annoyed consumers instead of pleasing them when the firm distributed sample packets of Italian and French salad dressing in home-delivered copies of the *New York Times*. Many of the packets burst when the papers hit the driveways.

A **bonus pack** is a specially packaged item that gives the purchaser a larger quantity at the regular price. For instance, Camay soap recently offered three bars for the price of two, and Salon Selectives is known to increase the size of its shampoos and conditioners for the same price as regular sizes.

Premiums are items given free or at reduced cost with purchases of other products. For example, Pantene frequently attaches a purse-size bottle of hairspray to the sides of its other hair-care products. Premiums have proven effective in motivating consumers to try new products or different brands. A premium should have some relationship with the product or brand it accompanies, though. For example, a home improvement center might offer free measuring tapes to its customers.

Contests and Sweepstakes

Firms often sponsor contests and sweepstakes to introduce new goods and services and to attract additional customers. **Contests** require entrants to complete a task such as solving a puzzle or answering questions in a trivia quiz, and they may also require proofs of purchase. **Sweepstakes,** on the other hand, choose winners by chance, so no product purchase is necessary. They are more popular with consumers than contests because they do not take as much effort for consumers to enter. Marketers like them, too, because they are inexpensive to run and the number of winners is predetermined. With some contests, the sponsors cannot predict the number of people who will correctly complete the puzzles or gather the right number of symbols from scratch-off cards.

Marketers are increasingly turning to the Internet for contests and sweepstakes, because of its relatively low cost and its ability to provide data immediately. Interactivity is also a key part of the online experience—as consumers become more engaged in the contest or sweepstakes event, they also build a relationship with the firm's products. Best Buy blends both online and offline sweepstakes to promote its back-to-school sales. Its Tech 101 sweepstakes awarded MP3 players, dorm refrigerators, and notebooks to winners. Best Buy reported that its Web site received more than 1 million hits during the promotion, and 300,000 consumers signed up for company e-mails.[46] With the recent rash of court rulings and legal restrictions, the use of contests requires careful administration. A firm contemplating this promotional technique might consider the services of online promotion specialists such as WebStakes or NetStakes.

Specialty Advertising

The origin of specialty advertising has been traced to the Middle Ages, when artisans gave wooden pegs bearing their names to prospects, who drove them into the walls at home to serve as convenient hangers for armor. Corporations began putting their names on a variety of products in the late 1800s, as newspapers and print shops explored new methods to earn additional revenues from their expensive printing presses. Today, just about everyone owns a cap or T-shirt with the name or logo of a company, organization, or product displayed on it.

Specialty advertising is a sales promotion technique that places the advertiser's name, address, and advertising message on useful articles that are then distributed to target consumers. Marketers spend more than $17.8 billion on specialty advertising items each year.[47] Wearable products are the most popular, accounting for nearly a third of specialty advertising sales. Pens, mugs, glassware, and calendars are other popular forms.

Advertising specialties help reinforce previous or future advertising and sales messages. Consumers like these giveaways, which generate stronger responses to direct mail, resulting in three times the dollar volume of sales compared with direct mail alone. Companies use this form of promotion to highlight store openings and new products, motivate salespeople, increase visits to trade show booths, and remind customers about their products.

TRADE-ORIENTED PROMOTIONS

Sales promotion techniques can also contribute effectively to campaigns aimed at retailers and wholesalers. **Trade promotion** is sales promotion that appeals to marketing intermediaries rather than to final consumers. Marketers use trade promotions in push strategies by encouraging resellers to stock new products, continue to carry existing ones, and promote both effectively to consumers. The typical firm actually spends half of its promotional budget on trade promotion—as much money as it spends on advertising and consumer-oriented sales promotions combined. Successful trade promotions offer financial incentives. They require careful timing and attention to costs and are easy to implement by retailers. These promotions should bring quick results and improve retail sales.

Trade Allowances

Among the most common trade promotion methods are **trade allowances**—special financial incentives offered to wholesalers and retailers that purchase or promote specific products. These offers take various forms. A buying allowance gives retailers a discount on goods. They include off-invoice allowances through which retailers deduct specified amounts from their invoices or receive free goods, such as one free case for every ten ordered. When a manufacturer offers a promotional allowance, it agrees to pay the reseller a certain amount to cover the costs of special promotional displays or extensive advertising that features the manufacturer's product. The goal is to increase sales to consumers by encouraging resellers to promote their products effectively.

As mentioned in previous chapters, some retailers require vendors to pay a special slotting allowance before they agree to take on new products. These fees guarantee slots, or shelf space, for newly introduced items in the stores. This practice is common in large supermarket chains. Retailers defend these fees as essential to cover the added costs of carrying the products, such as redesigning display space and shelves, setting up and administering control systems, managing inventory, and taking the risks inherent in stocking new products. The fees can be sizable, from several hundred dollars per store to many thousands of dollars for a retail chain and millions of dollars for nationally distributed products.

Point-of-Purchase Advertising

A display or other promotion located near the site of the actual buying decision is known as **point-of-purchase (POP) advertising.** This method of sales promotion capitalizes on the fact that buyers make many purchase decisions within the store, so it encourages retailers to improve on-site merchandising. Product suppliers assist the retailer by creating special displays designed to stimulate sales of the item being promoted. Although it is difficult to obtain concrete measures of spending on POP advertising, one estimate suggests that it gathers about $17 billion a year in spending.[48]

Freestanding POP promotions often appear at the ends of shopping aisles. On a typical trip to the supermarket, you might see a POP display for Disney videos, Coppertone sunscreen, or Pepsi's new reduced-calorie drink. Warehouse-style retailers such as Home Depot and Sam's Club, along with Staples and Kmart, all use POP advertising displays frequently. Electronic kiosks, which allow consumers to place orders for items not available in the store, have begun to transform the POP display industry, as creators of these displays look for ways to involve consumers more actively as well as entertain them.

Trade Shows

To influence resellers and other members of the distribution channel, many marketers participate in **trade shows**. These shows are often organized by industry trade associations; frequently, they are part of these associations' annual meetings or conventions. Vendors who serve the industries display and demon-

© HARUYOSHI YAMAGUCHI/BLOOMBERG NEWS/LANDOV

Trade shows attract marketers and customers.

strate their products for members. Every year, more than 4,300 different shows in the United States and Canada draw more than 1.3 million exhibitors and 85 million attendees. Industries that hold trade shows include manufacturers of sporting goods, medical equipment, electronics, automobiles, clothing, and home furnishings. Service industries include hair styling, health care, travel, and restaurant franchises. Los Angeles, one of the major trade show locations in the United States, reports continued growth in the number and size of trade shows each year.[49]

Because of the expense involved in trade shows, a company must assess the value of these shows on several criteria, such as direct sales, any increase in product awareness, image building, and any contribution to the firm's marketing communications efforts. Trade shows give especially effective opportunities to introduce new products and to generate sales leads. Some types of shows reach ultimate consumers as well as channel members. Home, recreation, and automobile shows, for instance, allow businesses to display and demonstrate home improvement, recreation, and other consumer products to entire communities.

Dealer Incentives, Contests, and Training Programs

Manufacturers run dealer incentive programs and contests to reward retailers and their salespeople who increase sales and, more generally, to promote specific products. These channel members receive incentives for performing promotion-related tasks and can win contests by reaching sales goals. Manufacturers may offer major prizes to resellers such as trips to exotic places. **Push money** (which retailers commonly refer to as *spiffs*) is another incentive that gives retail salespeople cash rewards for every unit of a product they sell. This benefit increases the likelihood that the salesperson will try to persuade a customer to buy the product rather than a competing brand.

For more expensive and highly complex products, manufacturers often provide specialized training for retail salespeople. This background helps sales personnel explain features, competitive advantages, and other information to consumers. Training can be provided in several ways: a manufacturer's sales representative can conduct training sessions during regular sales calls, or the firm can distribute sales literature and DVDs.

✓ *assessment check*

1. Define *sales promotion.*

2. Identify at least four types of consumer-oriented sales promotions.

3. Identify at least three types of trade-oriented sales promotions.

Strategic Implications of Marketing in the 21st Century

Today's salespeople are a new breed. Richly nourished in a tradition of sales, their roles are strengthened even further through technology. However, as many companies are discovering, nothing can replace the power of personal selling in generating sales and in building strong, loyal customer relationships.

Salespeople today are a critical link in developing relationships between the customer and the company. They communicate customer needs and wants to co-workers in various units within an organization, enabling a cooperative, company-wide effort in improving product offerings and in better satisfying individuals within the target market. For salespeople, the greatest benefit of electronic technologies is the ability to share knowledge when it is needed with those who need to know, including customers, suppliers, and employees.

Because buyers are now more sophisticated, demanding more rapid and lower-cost transactions, salespeople must be quick and creative as they find solutions to their customers' problems. Product life cycles are accelerating, and customers who demand more are likely to switch from one product to another. Recognizing the long-term impact of keeping satisfied buyers—those who make repeat and cross-purchases and provide referrals—versus dissatisfied buyers, organizations are increasingly training their sales forces to provide superior customer service and rewarding them for increasing satisfaction levels.

The traditional skills of a salesperson included persuasion, selling ability, and product knowledge. But today's sales professional is more likely to possess communication skills, problem-solving skills, and knowledge of products, customers, industries, and applications. Earlier generations of sales personnel tended to be self-driven; today's sales professional is more likely to be a team player as well as a customer advocate who serves his or her buyers by solving problems.

The modern professional salesperson is greatly assisted by the judicious use of both consumer- and trade-oriented sales promotions. Sales promotion is often overlooked in discussions of high-profile advertising; the typical firm allocates more promotional dollars for sales promotion than for advertising. The proven effectiveness of sales promotion makes it a widely used promotional mix component for most B2C and B2B marketers.

REVIEW OF CHAPTER OBJECTIVES

1 Describe the role of today's salesperson.

Today's salesperson seeks to form long-lasting relationships with customers by providing high levels of customer service rather than going for the quick sale. Firms have begun to integrate their computer and communications technologies into the sales function, so people involved in personal selling have an expanded role.

2 Describe the four sales channels.

Over-the-counter (retail) selling takes place in a retail location, and usually involves providing product information and completing a sale. Field selling involves making personal sales calls to customers. Under certain circumstances, telemarketing is used to provide product information and answer questions from customers who call. Inside selling relies on phone, mail, and e-commerce to provide sales and product services for customers on a continuing basis.

3 Describe the major trends in personal selling.

Companies are turning to relationship selling, consultative selling, and team selling. Relationship selling occurs when a salesperson builds a mutually beneficial relationship with a customer on a regular basis over an extended period. Consultative selling involves meeting customer needs by listening to customers, understanding and caring about their problems, paying attention to the details, and following through after the sale. Team selling occurs when the salesperson joins with specialists from other functional areas of the firm to complete the selling process.

4 Identify and briefly describe the three basic sales tasks.

Order processing is the routine handling of an order. It characterizes a sales setting in which the need is made known to and is acknowledged by the customer. Creative selling is persuasion aimed at making the prospect see the value of the good or service being presented. Missionary selling is indirect selling, such as making goodwill calls and providing technical or operational assistance.

5 Outline the seven steps in the sales process.

The basic steps in the sales process are prospecting and qualifying, approach, presentation, demonstration, handling objections, closing, and follow-up.

6 Identify the seven basic functions of a sales manager.

A sales manager links the sales force to other aspects of the internal and external environments. The manager's functions are recruitment and selection, training, organization, supervision, motivation, compensation, and evaluation and control.

7 Explain the role of ethical behavior in personal selling.

Ethical behavior is vital to building positive, long-term relationships with customers. Although some people believe that ethical problems are inevitable, employers can do much to foster a corporate culture that encourages honesty and ethical behavior. In addition, each salesperson is responsible for his or her own behavior and relationship with customers.

8 Describe the role of sales promotion in the promotional mix, and identify the different types of sales promotions.

Sales promotion includes activities other than personal selling, advertising, and publicity designed to enhance consumer purchasing and dealer effectiveness. Sales promotion is an integral part of the overall marketing plan, intended to increase sales and build brand equity. Promotions often produce their best results when combined with other marketing activities.

Consumer-oriented sales promotions include coupons, refunds, samples, bonus packs, premiums, contests and sweepstakes, and specialty advertising. Trade-oriented promotions include trade allowances, point-of-purchase (POP) advertising, trade shows, dealer incentives, contests, and training programs.

✓ *assessment check* **answers**

1.1 What is personal selling?
Personal selling is the process of a seller's person-to-person promotional presentation to a buyer.

1.2 What is the main focus of today's salespeople?
The main focus of today's salespeople is to build long-lasting relationships with customers.

2.1 What is over-the-counter selling?
Over-the-counter selling describes selling in retail and some wholesale locations. Most of these transactions take place directly with customers.

assessment check **answers**

2.2   What is field selling?

Field selling involves making sales calls on prospective and existing customers at their businesses or homes.

2.3   Distinguish between outbound and inbound telemarketing.

Outbound telemarketing takes place when a salesperson phones customers; inbound telemarketing takes place when customers call the firm.

3.1   Identify the three major personal selling approaches.

The three major personal selling approaches are relationship selling, consultative selling, and team selling.

3.2   Distinguish between relationship selling and consultative selling.

Relationship selling is a technique for building a mutually beneficial partnership with a customer. Consultative selling involves meeting customer needs by listening to, understanding, and paying attention to their problems, then following up after a sale.

4.1   What are the three major tasks performed by salespeople?

The three major tasks are order processing, creative selling, and team selling.

4.2   What are the three steps of order processing?

The three steps of order processing are identifying customer needs, pointing out the need to the customer, and completing the order.

5.1   Identify the seven steps of the sales process.

The seven steps of the sales process are prospecting and qualifying, approach, presentation, demonstration, handling objections, closing, and follow-up.

5.2   Why is follow-up important to the sales effort?

Follow-up allows the salesperson to reinforce the customer's purchase decision, strengthen the bond, and correct any problems.

6.1   What are the seven basic functions performed by a sales manager?

The seven basic functions of a sales manager are recruitment and selection, training, organization, supervision, motivation, compensation, and evaluation and control.

6.2   Define *span of control*.

Span of control refers to the number of sales representatives who report to first-level sales managers.

6.3   What are the three main questions a sales manager must address as part of a salesperson's evaluation?

The three main questions a sales manager must address are: Where does each salesperson's performance rank relative to predetermined standards? What are the salesperson's strong points? What are the salesperson's weak points?

7.1   Why is it important for salespeople to maintain ethical behavior?

Salespeople need to maintain ethical behavior because it is vital to their firm's relationships with customers and because they are representing their company. A breach of ethics could also be detrimental to an individual's career.

7.2   What are the characteristics of companies that foster corporate cultures that encourage ethical behavior?

Characteristics of corporations fostering ethical behavior include the following: employees who understand what is expected of them, open communication, and managers who lead by example.

8.1   Define *sales promotion*.

Sales promotion includes marketing activities other than personal selling, advertising, and publicity designed to enhance consumer purchasing and dealer effectiveness.

8.2   Identify at least four types of consumer-oriented sales promotions.

Consumer-oriented sales promotions include coupons, refunds, samples, bonus packs, premiums, contests, sweepstakes, and specialty advertising.

8.3   Identify at least three types of trade-oriented sales promotions.

Trade-oriented sales promotions include trade allowances, POP advertising, trade shows, dealer incentives, contests, and training programs.

MARKETING TERMS YOU NEED TO KNOW

personal selling 562
over-the-counter selling 564
field selling 565
telemarketing 566

inside selling 566
relationship selling 567
consultative selling 569
team selling 570

order processing 571
creative selling 572
missionary selling 573
sales promotion 584

OTHER IMPORTANT MARKETING TERMS

network marketing 565
outbound telemarketing 566
inbound telemarketing 566
cross-selling 569
virtual sales team 570
sales incentives 573
prospecting 573
qualifying 574
approach 574
precall planning 574
presentation 575
cold calling 575

demonstration 575
objection 576
closing 576
follow-up 577
national accounts organization 579
span of control 580
expectancy theory 580
commission 581
salary 581
sales quota 582
coupon 586
refund 586

sampling 587
bonus pack 587
premium 587
contest 587
sweepstakes 587
specialty advertising 588
trade promotion 588
trade allowance 588
point-of-purchase (POP) advertising 588
trade show 589
push money 589

ASSURANCE OF LEARNING REVIEW

1. How does each of the following factors affect the decision to emphasize personal selling or nonpersonal advertising and/or sales promotion?
   a. geographic market concentration
   b. length of marketing channels
   c. degree of product technical complexity
2. Which of the four sales channels is each of the following salespeople most likely to use?
   a. salesperson in a Blockbuster Video store
   b. Coldwell Banker real estate sales agent
   c. route driver for Keebler snack foods (sells and delivers to local food retailers)
   d. technical support for Dell
3. What is team selling? Describe a situation in which you think

it would be effective.
4. Why is it important for a salesperson to understand order processing regardless of the type of selling he or she is engaged in?
5. What is the role of a sales incentive?
6. Suppose you are hired as a salesperson for a firm that offers prep courses for standardized tests. What would be your first step in the sales process? Where might you find some leads?
7. What is expectancy theory? How do sales managers use it?
8. What is the role of sales promotion in the marketing effort?
9. What are the benefits of sampling? What are the drawbacks?
10. What is trade promotion? What are its objectives?

PROJECTS AND TEAMWORK EXERCISES

1. Cross-selling can be an effective way for a firm to expand. On your own or with a classmate, locate an advertisement for a firm that you believe could benefit from cross-selling. List ways it could offer multiple goods or services to the same customer. Then create a new ad illustrating the multiple offerings.
2. With a partner, choose one of the following sales situations. Then take turns coming up with creative ways to close the deal—one of you plays the customer and the other plays the salesperson. Present your closing scenarios to the class.
   a. You are a new sales associate at a car dealership, and a potential customer has just test-driven one of your

newest models. You have handled all the customer's objections and settled on a price. You don't want the customer to leave without agreeing to purchase the car.
   b. You operate a lawn-care business and have visited several homeowners in a new development. Three of them have already agreed to give your service a try. You are meeting with the fourth and want to close that sale, too.
3. As sales representatives for a cooperative of organic farmers, you and a classmate are invited to make a sales presentation to a national supermarket chain. List the most important messages you wish to relate and then role-play the sales presentation.

4. On your own or with a classmate, go online and research a firm such as Kraft, General Mills, Ford, or Burger King to find out what kinds of consumer-oriented promotions the company is conducting for its various brands or individual products. Which promotions seem the most appealing to you as a consumer? Why? Present your findings to the class.

5. With a classmate, design a specialty advertising item for one of the following companies or its products, or choose one of your own. Present your design sketches to the class.

    a. Sea World or Busch Gardens
    b. Dunkin' Donuts
    c. Porsche
    d. Verizon Wireless
    e. Equal Exchange coffee
    f. Apple iPod

CRITICAL-THINKING EXERCISES

1. Since the implementation of the national Do Not Call Registry, Americans have noticed an increase in door-to-door selling as well as e-mails containing sales messages. As a marketer, do you think this type of selling is effective? Why or why not?

2. Green Mountain Coffee Roasters is well known for its specialty coffees, which are available in many retail outlets such as supermarkets and convenience stores. But visit a medical office or a car dealership, and you might find it there as well—in one-cup dispensers, ready for individuals to brew while waiting for service from the doctor or the car dealer.[50] This requires personal selling to office managers, doctors, and the like. What role does relationship selling play in this situation? What kind of training might Green Mountain sales reps receive?

3. Imagine that you want to sell your parents on the idea of your taking a trip, buying a car, attending graduate school—something that is important to you. Outline your approach and presentation as a salesperson would.

4. Why is the recruitment and selection stage of the hiring process one of a sales manager's greatest challenges?

5. InterContinental Hotels Group began offering its Priority Club members free nights at "any hotel, anywhere"—including those of competitors—as part of a sales promotion.[51] Do you think this would be a successful promotion? Why or why not?

ETHICS EXERCISE

You have been hired by a discount sporting-goods retailer in an over-the-counter sales position. You have completed a training course that includes learning about the products, assisting customers, and cross-selling. You have made several good friends in the training course and sometimes get together after work to go running, play golf, or have dinner. You've noticed that one of your friends has really taken the training course to heart, and has adopted a very aggressive attitude toward customers in the store, pushing them to buy just about anything, whether they need it or not. Your friend even boasted about selling a boogie board to the father of a boy who didn't know how to swim.

1. Do you agree with your friend's actions? Why or why not?

2. Should you discuss the situation with your friend? Should you discuss it with your supervisor? Explain your response.

INTERNET EXERCISES

1. **Sales careers.** The College Board's Web site contains helpful information about many careers. Visit the Web site (http://www.collegeboard.com/csearch/majors_careers/profiles/careers/104714.html) and answer the following questions.

    a. What types of skills are important for salespeople?
    b. What is the job outlook for sales professionals?
    c. Approximately how much do sales professionals earn?

2. **Using the Internet.** The chapter discussed how many marketers are using the Internet to support personal selling and enhance sales promotion activities. Review the chapter material and then complete the following exercises.

    a. Many companies now use the Internet to demonstrate their products. Visit http://www.blackberry.com/products/handhelds/demos/index.shtml and view the product presentations. Make a list of your observations and bring your list to class to participate in a class discussion on the subject.

    b. ValPak.com is a major source of online coupons. Visit the ValPak.com Web site (http://www.valpak.com). Write a brief report summarizing what you learned and your impressions of online coupons.

    c. Sweepstakes Online is a Web site that lists and provides links to dozens of online sweepstakes and contests. Visit the firm's Web site (http://www.sweepstakesonline.com). How many online sweepstakes and contests are currently available? What kinds of products or prizes are available? What is your overall assessment of online sweepstakes and contests?

Note: Internet Web addresses change frequently. If you don't find the exact site listed, you may need to access the organization's home page and search from there or use a search engine such as Google.

CASE 17.1   Sears Ties Up with Ty Pennington

He's tall and skinny, with hair that sticks straight up on its own. His raspy voice sounds like sandpaper—especially when bellowing through a bullhorn. He never sits still. In fact, he never *stands* still. But audiences—particularly women—love him. That's what Sears is banking on, having signed TV host and designer Ty Pennington for a new line of bedding, bath, and tabletop products to be sold online and in its stores.

Ty sells. The former carpenter and host of *Trading Spaces* is now a superstar of home design and furnishings as the host of ABC's "Extreme Makeover: Home Edition," which is sponsored by Sears. The weekly show features a total makeover—often including complete demolition—of one deserving family's home, with soup-to-nuts design, craftsmanship, furnishing, and decorating. Ty leads the team through the project while the family has been whisked off to vacation somewhere glamorous and far away. Sears supplies almost all of the appliances, fixtures, furniture, bedding, and accessories for each project, and the company has received hundreds of e-mails from viewers complimenting the firm on its goodwill. But Ty is the face of the show, and the new face of Sears. Marketing experts applaud the relationship as a good fit.

Pennington's popularity—along with the popularity of other home-improvement show hosts, including Martha Stewart—has most likely contributed to an 18 percent increase in such projects throughout the United States during the last five years. This trend gives Sears a double boost—consumers watch the TV show that features its products, then shop at Sears for everything from tools to appliances to Pennington's own line. Ty Pennington Style actually features seven different lines, with varying designs and color palettes. But each line includes bedding, rugs, pillows, bath towels and shower cur-tains, lamps, dishware, and flatware, along with accessories such as candleholders and placemats. All are priced affordably compared with higher-end department stores; accessories start at $6, while entire bedding sets can be purchased for $120 to $200. And all bear Ty's name.

While experts agree that a celebrity name alone doesn't sell a product—it has to be what the customer wants—someone as popular as Pennington can attract customers to the store. Consumers are influenced by a celebrity's credibility and integrity—Pennington's association with "Extreme Makeover: Home Edition" reinforces those qualities in consumers' minds. They believe he knows how to do these projects himself, and they trust his sense of design. They also appreciate his—and Sears's—contributions to the community. Pennington is just as complimentary of his relationship of Sears. "Designing for Sears is very cool," he says, "because they understand today's families have to create modern, casual living spaces." Sears has confidence that whatever Pennington sells, their customers will buy.

Questions for Critical Thinking

1. How might Sears use its relationship with Ty Pennington as a motivator for its retail sales force?
2. Describe a sales promotion that Sears might create for Ty Pennington Style.

Sources: "Ty Pennington Style," Sears, **www.sears.com**, accessed June 26, 2006; "Retailing Today," International Council of Shopping Centers, **http://www.icsc.org**, accessed June 26, 2006; Holly M. Sanders, "Tiger Woods You Believe, But Trust Trump? Uh-Uh," *New York Post*, April 25, 2006, **http://www.nypost.com**; Susan Chandler, "Is Sears Trading Faces?" *Chicago Tribune*, March 2, 2006, sec. 3, pp. 1, 4.

VIDEO CASE 17.2   Harley-Davidson: Selling the Thrill

The written video case on Harley-Davidson appears on page VC-20. The recently filmed Harley-Davidson video is designed to expand and highlight the concepts in this chapter and the concepts and questions covered in the written video case.

Talking about Marketing Careers with. . .

ANDREW SWINAND
PRESIDENT, CHIEF CLIENT OFFICER
STARCOM WORLDWIDE

Starcom Worldwide is a major player in the media marketing communications industry; in fact, it is one of the largest full-service media divisions in the world. As part of the Starcom MediaVest Group, which has global operations in 89 markets worldwide and nearly 3,500 employees, the Chicago division specializes in media selection and buying to help leading companies position and build their brands.

Starcom's media experts develop integrated marketing communications programs, providing marketing research and promotional services for their clients. Staying on top of the fragmented media market can be challenging these days because of the spread of digital and online communications. We were able to take a few minutes to discuss the changes in the advertising and media industry with Andrew Swinand of Starcom Worldwide, and he explained his role in helping clients take advantage of those new developments.

Q: Having a career in a creative field such as media communications is a job many marketing students dream of having one day. How did your educational experience prepare you to work in this field? What jobs have you held along the way, and how did they help you reach your current position?

A: Prior to working at Starcom, I was in the U.S. Army, worked in account management at BBDO Worldwide [advertising agency], and was in brand management at Procter & Gamble. I also majored in economics and marketing in school. All contributed to my knowledge and success. That said, I believe the two most important qualities for success in any marketing job are curiosity and discipline. You must have a curious mind to succeed. A mind that causes you to constantly ask why—Why do consumers prefer this versus that? Why is this important to them? etc. Second, you must have the discipline to follow through on those questions with rigor. Marketing is becoming more analytical, and clients are demanding a greater degree of accountability. Successful marketers must be able to both conceptualize the ideas, and actualize the results.

Q: What are your duties and responsibilities as President and Chief Client Officer at Starcom? What strengths and skills do you draw on in your daily work? How are your work teams organized—are they specialized into different functions or units, based on the client or industry, or some other criteria?

A: Our agency is split into two job functions. One group works directly with the clients to manage their media strategy, media planning, consumer understanding, and accountability. The second group works directly with media vendors to activate these plans through strategic media investment by stewarding the media buys, negotiating rates, and negotiating added value such as accountability programs. My job is to ensure our client teams are delivering the best ideas, strategy, and service to our clients.

The one thing I can say about my job is that no two days are ever alike. As Chief Client Officer, I work with teams that support clients in marketing everything from technology and databases to selling cereal or dog food. Every client has different marketing challenges and a different relationship with consumers. Part of our challenge is to be flexible enough to adjust our approach to each situation yet still have enough discipline and uniformity to our process to ensure a successful result.

Q: We know that Starcom works with some very prominent clients, such as Disney, Kellogg's, Oracle, and Procter & Gamble. How do you help your clients create a cohesive marketing message? What types of promotions do you arrange—sponsorships, event marketing, direct marketing messages?

A: I think the key to any effective strategy is to start with solid consumer understanding. Many people think the goal of integrated communications is to do a little of everything and ensure it looks similar. We are finding that as consumers become more and more bombarded with messages, understanding their relationship with both the brand and the media is critically important. In what context are they watching TV, searching for information on the Internet, or seeking streaming content? Then, how do we strategically place the right content into that environment to ensure consumers are captivated by our clients' messaging? The goal is not breadth of exposure but depth of experience resulting in engagement.

Q: Today's media outlets are so numerous—network and cable TV, traditional and subscriber radio, print and online newspapers, magazines and e-zines, new interactive media, to name just a few—that companies have many different avenues through which to reach their target audiences. How do you create a strategy for your clients? What relationship does your team have with the various media outlets to be able to offer expertise on media selections?

A: It has been said that more has changed in media in the last 36 months than the previous 36 years. I believe this to be true and find it one of the most exciting parts of the job. I think a big change is that it is not long enough for us to do research on how consumers feel about brands. We now must constantly research how consumers are interacting with media to understand both the context of the interaction and the value they are looking to get out of the experience. At Starcom, we have created a new role called Consumer Context Planning that is dedicated to researching and discovering the links between consumers' experiences with brands, media, and advertising.

Q: What objectives do your clients have in their media campaigns? Can you give us an example? How do you gauge the effectiveness of an individual media buy—or its part in a larger campaign?

A: Accountability in advertising has become increasingly important. Clients now expect agencies to be able to provide proof of performance for the dollars they are given. In the past, agencies provided this proof in the form of *input*-based accountabilities (i.e., a certain reach and fre-

quency, or TRPs [television rating points]). Today, clients want *output*-based accountability in addition. They want to know if the ads achieved the desired goals of increasing awareness, driving purchase intent, capturing consumer information, or directly driving sales. To support this need, Starcom has invested in tools that allow us to better track and report what actions consumers have taken after viewing our clients' advertising. I do not believe Starcom, or the industry, has completely solved the accountability puzzle yet, and I feel that this is an exciting area of focus for the industry.

Q: Being so involved with media communications, you must have some great advice for students on developing contacts and relationships to get started in their marketing careers. What can students do now to get a good start? What types of skills would you look for in a student interested in your field?

A: I think there are three things that everyone starting a career in marketing should do:

1. Define your brand: I always tell people if you can't market yourself, you probably won't be able to successfully

sell soap. I would encourage students to define what is their unique selling proposition and what makes them different from or better than the competition. If candidates can effectively articulate this, it goes a long way.

2. Recognize that you are a consumer: Marketers spend millions of dollars each year to talk to consumers. When you go on an interview, go with an opinion on the products the company sells or advertises. One, they will be interested in your feedback. Two, it demonstrates that you are engaged in their business (see my comments about "curiosity" at the beginning of the interview).

3. Do your homework: It is always amazing to me how many people come into an interview unprepared. If you want to be successful in the communications industry, you must be a great communicator. Great communications come from preparation (see #1 and #2 here).

Promoting Awareness through Humor

The Second City

With its eyes and ears on the nation's front page, The Second City has hilariously relayed political tensions, economic fluctuations, and cultural trends back to its audience, its consumers. The nature of The Second City product has set the stage for its broad mix of promotional activities. Across its many business ventures a mix of personal and non-personal selling distributes its product. The value of the Second City is promoted with the support of its strong topical, entertaining, and consumer-oriented brand.

Each of Second City's Theaters frequently updates its shows to respond to current events. When new revues are being produced, their titles function as brief, humorous advertisements. Gripping titles like *Piñata Full of Bees* and *Holy War, Batman* appeal to tourists and locals alike looking for entertainment with an edge. Captivating pictures of the cast are placed with hotel concierges, convention bureaus, and other visitors and tourist-related publications. The Second City has experimented with radio and TV spots, but had little success. Its theaters perpetuate word-of-mouth promotion by maintaining creative relevance as satirists. As with its improvisational technique used on stages, promotional decisions are sometimes made best as quick reactions to a given situation. When the local market began taking Second City's presence for granted, its noticed a difference in sales. SC responded by promoting a differentiated product of more eclectic off-night revues to attract the local crowd. As an innovative entertainment company, its promotional opportunities are nearly limitless. It has, however, avoided sponsorship, which allows it free rein to satirize anyone and everyone. "Second City does not presently allow for corporate sponsorship, for fear that we, as satirists, would put ourselves in a potentially vulnerable position," explains vice president Kelly Leonard. Alternatively, The Second City has been able to play with some guerilla marketing, such as chalk-writing announcements of new shows on the sidewalks of Chicago.

For Second City's Touring Companies, promotional decisions target the college and performing arts center markets. East Coast Entertainment, a talent-booking agency focusing on the college market, sells on Second City's behalf at conferences and through continued networking. Predominantly, Second City uses phone sales to book shows around the nation. Over the summer, when the college market is less active, SC touring companies promote themselves locally to stabilize sales. They provide regional showcases and develop new material with a variety of unique performances.

For the Second City Training Center, promotional efforts are based on relationship selling. Celebrity testimonials throughout SC's evolution have garnered consistent interest from the ever-growing market of aspiring actors. This consumer base seeks out The Second City for services and training. The Training Center focuses promotional efforts on regular consumers looking to broaden their creative horizons. It offers a wide range of classes for all age levels and interests. It uses an informative group e-mail list that unifies its student body and fosters a mutually beneficial relationship. It offers discounted shows to students, welcomes student feedback, and posts job openings.

Second City's Web site embodies its total advertising campaign. Each division of the company is represented by its own electronic promotion. Each theater has interactive advertisements that lead consumers to newspaper reviews and cast biographies. The Web site is entirely inclusive. A customer who visits to purchase tickets will also notice the myriad of classes offered by the theater. Second City has also integrated its marketing with each city in which it operates. A customer who is in town can peruse SC's Web site for information on local restaurants, hotels, museums, and music venues. Most of SC's retail advertising is offered through the Web site. Bernie Sahlins, co-founder of the company, published *Days and Nights at the Second City*, which details his experience with the influential theater company. Books like his, and a number of others on the art and history of improvisation, promote the brand to those already invested in or curious about the company. Other merchandise, such as apparel, is attractive to tourists. A company advertisement then returns home with the consumer wearing a Second City T-shirt or baseball cap.

The Second City Communications Division has been creating virtual comedy shorts to promote the theater and its services through the Internet. One such video introduces the "Yes, and" principle by presenting a mock business meeting. When communication between employees has broken down, the practice of accepting each other's ideas and building on them enables the group to function as a team. Teamwork is a guiding practice for the Second City. Its focus on collaboration has given each division the autonomy to communicate its own promotional messages while still remaining a part of the team of Second City product offerings.

Second City Communications promotes its services through personal selling. It conducts business by creatively approaching the specific, complex problems of the client. Case studies on SC's Web site describe how it has succeeded in addressing consumer needs. As a consultant, SC must listen to its customers and build customer loyalty. Success from the Communications division has eliminated the first few steps of a traditional sales process. Clients come to SC's door without much prospecting or approach. SC Communications specializes in presenting and demonstrating its product throughout the production process by fashioning the product to meet customer expectations. Tom Yorton, president of Second City Communications, and his team routinely communicate with clients before and after the sales process. They also partner with an outside publicist to design high-quality print and media promotional materials.

SC Theatricals' exclusive deal with Norwegian Cruise Lines has its cast presenting a series of comedic revues at sea. It also offers customized corporate workshops that capitalize on SC's expertise in the business market and promote the brand to a captive target audience.

The promotional mix supporting The Second City brand simultaneously grows the divisions of the company. By integrating its marketing communications, the Second City promotes their product from a variety of positions . . . and spreads laughter in their wake.

Questions

1. How does the nature of Second City's product function as a promotional tool for the company?
2. Do you think Second City allocates a relatively large amount of funds for promotion? Why or not why? How does this relate to Second City's stage in the product life cycle?
3. Which advertising strategy do you think is most advantageous to The Second City? Does it change for different divisions?
4. What challenges does the Second City find when attempting a sponsorship arrangement? What can you determine from this about the nature of The Second City's promotional strategy?

PART 7
Pricing Decisions

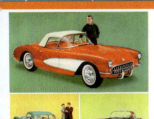

CHAPTER 18

Discount Stores Lures Shoppers with Cheap Gas

Filling the gas tank has become a painful prospect for many drivers as oil prices continue to climb. But it's easier than ever before to offset that bite by combining trips—for example, getting your weekly grocery shopping done at the place you fill up. Costco, Sam's Clubs, Giant Eagle, Kroger, Wal-Mart, and Meijer are some of the biggest food retailers in the United States, and they're also becoming a major force at the pump. All sell gasoline outside at some of their stores, and according to one industry watcher, "It must be pretty attractive. Giant Eagle is adding stations. Kroger is adding stations. Safeway is adding stations."

Some stores, such as Big Three in Ohio, tie their gasoline sales to customer loyalty programs. Others, such as Giant Eagle, offer gasoline discounts to grocery shoppers. Said one Ohio shopper, "I save [the discounts] up until they accumulate. My personal best is $1.40 off per gallon of gas. I was ecstatic." A Meijer spokesperson explained retailers' motivation for the jump in the number of food stores—more than five times the number a few years ago—that sell gas across the country: "Clearly we do it for our customers," she said. "It's more of our one-stop-shopping concept."

Still, most food retailers adding pumps also report an uptick in sales of food and other items within the store. "If you've already got them in the parking lot, chances are they'll run in to grab a rotisserie chicken for dinner," admits one Costco executive. But dinner or not, everyone is looking for cheap gas. "If there's a lot of fuel competition [nearby] or it's a low-traffic location, you could get into a price war," says one industry observer. Local and independent service stations and convenience stores are fighting back by offering their own discounts, but at Costco, for instance, the goal for its 227 U.S. stores selling gas is to beat the prices offered at the five nearest gas stations.

Selling gas is not without risk. In entering the fuel business, giant food retailers have had to take on the expense of buying or leasing land for gas stations and the costs associated with operating them. As a result, most of them do little more than break even on their gasoline sales. And when the price of gas climbs too steeply, it reduces their profits from gas sales, which account for about one-third of the revenue of many

Pricing Concepts

Chapter Objectives

1 Outline the legal constraints on pricing.

2 Identify the major categories of pricing objectives.

3 Explain price elasticity and its determinants.

4 List the practical problems involved in applying price theory concepts to actual pricing decisions.

5 Explain the major cost-plus approaches to price setting.

6 List the chief advantages and shortcomings of using breakeven analysis in pricing decisions.

7 Explain the use of yield management in pricing decisions.

8 Identify the major pricing challenges facing online and international marketers.

retail stores, not to mention the hit to overall profits, too.

But at least one expert believes that the combination of price-driven gasoline sales and customer loyalty programs is such a successful marketing tool that consumers can expect to see it expand into other types of retail businesses. "The price of fuel isn't going down that much," he said, "so they're using it as a marketing tool. Imagine a restaurant, say an Olive Garden, where you could spend $100 and get a $5 Shell gas coupon."[1]

evolution *of a* brand

Issaquah, Washington–based Costco is just one of the discount wholesale chains to provide gas pumps at its store locations. Competition in the discount retail market is fierce, with each chain fighting to attract and retain customers. Historically, Costco has fared better than most discount chains in this tough environment.

- Consider Costco's motives for placing gas pumps at its stores. What do you think might be the reasons executives made this move? Do you think this is a good strategy for Costco? Do some research into the company's current financial

condition and write a paragraph on whether selling gas was a wise decision for the chain.

- The cost of gasoline has reached all-time highs nationwide recently. How might chains such as Costco affect the overall price of gas at the pump? Explain how this added competition could affect consumers, the major oil producers, and other gas retailers. Back up your explanations with research to support your points.

Chapter Overview

One of the first questions shoppers ask is, "How much does it cost?" Marketers understand the critical role that price plays in the consumer's decision-making process. For products as varied as lipstick and perfume, automobiles and gasoline, and doughnuts and coffee, marketers must develop strategies that price products to achieve their firms' objectives.

As a starting point for examining pricing strategies, consider the meaning of the term *price*. A **price** is the exchange value of a good or service—in other words, it represents whatever that product can be exchanged for in

price Exchange value of a good or service.

the marketplace. Price does not necessarily denote money. In earlier times, the price of an acre of land might have been 20 bushels of wheat, three head of cattle, or one boat. Even though the barter process continues to be used in some transactions, in the 21st century, price typically refers to the amount of funds required to purchase a product.

Prices are both difficult to set and dynamic; they shift in response to a number of variables. A higher-than-average price can convey an image of prestige, while a lower-than-average price may connote good value. In other instances, though, a price that is much lower than average may be interpreted as an indicator of inferior

quality, and a higher price, like the increasing price of gasoline, may reflect both high demand and scarce supply. And price certainly affects a company's overall profitability and market share, as discount food chains that sell cheap gas are discovering.

This chapter discusses the process of determining a profitable but justifiable (fair) price. The focus is on management of the pricing function, including pricing strategies, price–quality relationships, and pricing in various sectors of the economy. The chapter also looks at the effects of environmental conditions on price determination, including legal constraints, competitive pressures, and changes in global and online markets.

---

1 Outline the legal constraints on pricing.

PRICING AND THE LAW

Pricing decisions are influenced by a variety of legal constraints imposed by federal, state, and local governments. Included in the price of products are not only the cost of the raw materials, processing and packaging, and profit for the business but also the various taxes that governments require providers to charge. For instance, excise taxes are levied on a variety of products—including real estate transfers, alcoholic beverages, and motor fuels. Sales taxes are charged on food, clothing, furniture, and many other purchases.

In the global marketplace, prices are directly affected by special types of taxes called *tariffs*. These taxes—levied on the sale of imported goods and services—often make it possible for firms to protect their local markets while still setting prices on domestically produced goods well above world market levels. The average tariff on fruits and vegetables around the world is more than 50 percent, although it varies considerably from country to country. The United States levies tariffs of less than 5 percent on more than half its fruit and vegetable imports, and in transactions with its largest trading partners in the produce market, Mexico and Canada, tariffs for both imports and exports are minimal or zero.[2] In other instances, tariffs are levied to prevent foreign producers from engaging in a practice described in Chapter 7: *dumping* foreign-produced products in international markets at prices lower than those set in their domestic market.

The United States is not the only country to use tariffs to protect domestic suppliers. Canada and the European Union recently levied a 15 percent penalty tariff on imports of a wide range of consumer products such as clothing, paper products, cigarettes, sweet corn, and oysters from the United States in retaliation for American government subsidies to domestic producers that the World Trade Organization ruled illegal.[3] These tariffs will raise the prices overseas consumers must pay to purchase U.S. goods.

Not every "regulatory" price increase is a tax, however. Rate increases to cover costly government regulations imposed on the telecommunications industry have been appearing on Internet and cell phone bills as "regulatory cost recovery fees"

© ASSOCIATED PRESS, AP

The U.S. levies minimal tariffs on fruits and vegetables from other countries.

or similarly named costs. But these charges are not taxes, because the companies keep all the income from the fees and apply only some of it to complying with the regulations. In essence, such "recovery fees" are a source of additional revenues in an industry so price-sensitive that any announced price increase is likely to send some customers fleeing to competitors.[4]

Almost every person looking for a ticket to a high-demand sporting or concert event has encountered an expensive—and often illegal—form of pricing called *ticket scalping*. Scalpers camp out in ticket lines (or hire someone else to stand in line) to purchase tickets they expect to resell at a higher price. Although some cities have enacted laws prohibiting the practice, it continues to occur in many locations.

But the ticket reselling market is both highly fragmented and susceptible to fraud and distorted pricing. In response, buyers and sellers are finding that the Internet is helping create a market in which both buyers and sellers can compare prices and seat locations. Web firms such as StubHub.com and TicketsNow.com act as ticket clearinghouses for this secondary market and have signed deals with several professional sports teams that allow season ticket holders to sell unwanted tickets and for buyers to purchase them with a guarantee. Its partnership with StubHub has been a success for the University of Southern California, among others.[5]

Pricing is also regulated by the general constraints of U.S. antitrust legislation, as outlined in Chapter 3. The following sections review some of the most important pricing laws for contemporary marketers.

ROBINSON–PATMAN ACT

The **Robinson-Patman Act** (1936) typifies Depression-era legislation. Known as the Anti-A&P Act, it was inspired by price competition triggered by the rise of grocery store chains—in fact, the original draft was prepared by the U.S. Wholesale Grocers Association. Enacted in the midst of the Great Depression, when legislators viewed chain stores as a threat to employment in the traditional retail sector, the act was intended primarily to save jobs.

The Robinson-Patman Act was technically an amendment to the Clayton Act, enacted 22 years earlier, which had applied only to price discrimination between geographic areas, which injured local sellers. Broader in scope, Robinson-Patman prohibits price discrimination in sales to wholesalers, retailers, and other producers. It rules that differences in price must reflect cost differentials and prohibits selling at unreasonably low prices to drive competitors out of business. Supporters justified the amendment by arguing that the rapidly expanding chain stores of that era might be able to attract substantial discounts from suppliers anxious to secure their business, while small, independent stores would continue to pay regular prices.

Robinson-Patman Act
Federal legislation prohibiting price discrimination that is not based on a cost differential; also prohibits selling at an unreasonably low price to eliminate competition.

Price discrimination, in which some customers pay more than others for the same product, dates back to the very beginnings of trade and commerce. Today, however, technology has added to the frequency and complexity of price discrimination, as well as the strategies marketers adopt to get around it. For example, marketers may encourage repeat business by inviting purchasers to become "preferred customers," entitling them to average discounts of 10 percent. As long as companies can demonstrate that their price discounts and promotional allowances do not restrict competition, they avoid penalties under the Robinson-Patman Act. Direct-mail marketers frequently send out catalogs of identical goods but with differing prices for different catalogs. Zip-code areas that traditionally consist of high spenders get the higher-price catalogs, while price-sensitive zip-code customers receive a low-price catalog with lower prices. Victoria's Secret, Staples, and Simon & Schuster are among the hundreds of companies that employ legal price discrimination strategies.

Firms accused of price discrimination often argue that they set price differentials to meet competitors' prices and that cost differences justify variations in prices. When a firm asserts that it maintains price differentials as good-faith methods of competing with rivals, a logical question arises: What constitutes good-faith pricing behavior? The answer depends on the particular situation.

A defense based on cost differentials works only if the price differences do not exceed the cost differences resulting from selling to various classes of buyers. Marketers must then be prepared to justify the cost differences. Many authorities consider this provision one of the most confusing areas in the Robinson-Patman Act. Courts handle most charges brought under the act as individual cases. Therefore, domestic marketers must continually evaluate their pricing actions to avoid potential Robinson-Patman violations.

unfair-trade laws State laws requiring sellers to maintain minimum prices for comparable merchandise.

fair-trade laws Statutes enacted in most states that once permitted manufacturers to stipulate a minimum retail price for their product.

Luxury products, such as Prada clothing and accessories, are offered in limited outlets to protect their image of exclusivity.

IMAGE COURTESY OF THE ADVERTISING ARCHIVES

UNFAIR-TRADE LAWS

Most states supplement federal legislation with their own **unfair-trade laws,** which require sellers to maintain minimum prices for comparable merchandise. Enacted in the 1930s, these laws were intended to protect small specialty shops, such as dairy stores, from so-called *loss-leader* pricing tactics, in which chain stores might sell certain products below cost to attract customers. Typical state laws set retail price floors at cost plus some modest markup.

Although most unfair-trade laws have remained on the books for the past 70 years, marketers had all but forgotten them until recently when several lawsuits were brought against different warehouse clubs over their practice of loss-leader gasoline pricing. Most were found to violate no laws.

FAIR-TRADE LAWS

The concept of fair trade has affected pricing decisions for decades. **Fair-trade laws** allow manufacturers to stipulate minimum retail prices for their products and to require dealers to sign contracts agreeing to abide by these prices.

Fair-trade laws assert that a product's image, determined in part by its price, is a property right of the manufacturer. Therefore, the manufacturer should have the authority to protect its asset by requiring retailers to maintain a minimum price. Exclusivity is one method manufacturers use to achieve this. By severely restricting the number of retail outlets that carry their upscale clothing and accessories, designers can exert more control over their prices and avoid discounting, which might adversely affect their image.

Like the Robinson-Patman Act, fair-trade legislation has its roots in the Depression era. In 1931, California became the first state to enact fair-trade legislation. Most other states soon followed; only Missouri, the District of Columbia, Vermont, and Texas failed to adopt such laws.

A U.S. Supreme Court decision invalidated fair-trade contracts in interstate commerce, and Congress responded by passing the Miller-Tydings Resale Price Maintenance Act (1937). This law exempted interstate fair-trade contracts from compliance with antitrust requirements, thus freeing states to keep these laws on their books if they so desired.

Over the years, fair-trade laws declined in importance as discounters emerged and price competition gained strength as a marketing strategy component. These laws became invalid with the passage of the Consumer Goods Pricing Act (1975), which halted all interstate enforcement of resale price maintenance provisions, an objective long sought by consumer groups.

In a new use of the term *fair trade*, some retailers are charging higher-than-market prices for commodities such as coffee, bananas, and chocolate as part of an international campaign to help farmers earn a living wage in poor countries where such products are grown. Although thousands of farmers have already benefited from the funds, which pay for education, healthcare, and training projects, it remains to be seen whether experience with the practice in U.S. stores will be similar to that in Europe, where some retailers have simply used higher markups so that they can benefit as well. It's often difficult for consumers to know how much of the added price is going to help those in need. But as one official of the London-based Fairtrade Foundation says, "We're helping to create an atmosphere in which many people can play their part in many different ways. What we want to create is a situation where it is no longer acceptable to do nothing, where every company, and every individual, has to do something to make the world fairer."[6]

assessment check

1. What was the purpose of the Robinson–Patman Act?

2. What laws require sellers to maintain minimum prices for comparable merchandise?

3. What laws allow manufacturers to set minimum retail prices for their products?

PRICING OBJECTIVES AND THE MARKETING MIX

2 Identify the major categories of pricing objectives.

The extent to which any or all of the factors of production—natural resources, capital, human resources, and entrepreneurship—are employed depends on the prices those factors command. A firm's prices and the resulting purchases by its customers determine the company's revenue, influencing the profits it earns. Overall organizational objectives and more specific marketing objectives guide the development of pricing objectives, which in turn lead to the development and implementation of more specific pricing policies and procedures.

A firm might, for instance, set a major overall goal of becoming the dominant producer in its domestic market. It might then develop a marketing objective of achieving maximum sales penetration in each region, followed by a related pricing objective of setting prices at levels that maximize sales. These objectives might lead to the adoption of a low-price policy implemented by offering substantial price discounts to channel members.

Price affects and is affected by the other elements of the marketing mix. Product decisions, promotional plans, and distribution choices all impact the price of a good or service. For example, products distributed through complex channels involving several intermediaries must be priced high enough to cover the markups needed to compensate wholesalers and retailers for services they provide. Basic so-called *fighting brands* are intended to capture market share from higher-priced, options-laden competitors by offering relatively low prices. Those cheaper products are intended to entice customers to give up some options in return for a cost savings.

Pricing objectives vary from firm to firm, and they can be classified into four major groups: (1) profitability objectives, (2) volume objectives, (3) meeting competition objectives, and (4) prestige objectives. Not-for-profit organizations as well as for-profit companies must consider objectives of one kind or another when developing pricing strategies. Table 18.1 outlines the pricing objectives marketers rely on to meet their overall goals.

table 18.1 Pricing Objectives

OBJECTIVE	PURPOSE	EXAMPLE
Profitability objectives	Profit maximization Target return	Microsoft's initially high price for the Xbox 360
Volume objectives	Sales maximization Market share	Southwest Airlines' low fares in new markets
Meeting competition objectives	Value pricing	Wal-Mart's lower prices on private house brands
Prestige objectives	Lifestyle Image	High-priced luxury autos such as Lexus and stereo equipment by Bose
Not-for-profit objectives	Profit maximization Cost recovery Market incentives Market suppression	Reduced or zero tolls for high-occupancy vehicles to encourage carpooling

PROFITABILITY OBJECTIVES

Marketers at for-profit firms must set prices with profits in mind. Even not-for-profit organizations realize the importance of setting prices high enough to cover expenses and provide a financial cushion to cover unforeseen needs and expenses. As the Russian proverb says, "There are two fools in every market: One asks too little, one asks too much." For consumers to pay prices that are either above or below what they consider the going rate, they must be convinced that they are receiving fair value for their money.

Economic theory is based on two major assumptions. It assumes, first, that firms will behave rationally and, second, that this rational behavior will result in an effort to maximize gains and minimize losses. Some marketers estimate profits by looking at historical sales data; others use elaborate calculations based on predicted future sales. It has been said that setting prices is an art, not a science. The talent lies in a marketer's ability to strike a balance between desired profits and the customer's perception of a product's value.

Marketers should evaluate and adjust prices continually to accommodate changes in the environment. The technological environment, for example, forces Internet marketers to respond quickly to competitors' pricing strategies. New search capabilities performed by shopping bots (described in Chapter 4) allow customers to compare prices locally, nationally, and globally in a matter of seconds.

Intense price competition—sometimes conducted even when it means forgoing profits altogether or reducing services—often results when rivals battle for leadership positions. Passenger airlines have been cutting costs for years in order to compete on pricing. Computer technology has allowed them to automate many services and put passengers in charge of others, such as making reservations online and checking in at electronic kiosks. Some amenities, such as in-flight meals, have almost disappeared. A drive for efficiency and reduced fuel consumption helps American Airlines, and United is saving an hour or more on long-distance flights to Asia by routing planes across the North Pole, relying on improved relationships with China, which grants United permission to cross its air space.[7]

Profits are a function of revenue and expenses:

$$\text{Profits} = \text{Revenue} - \text{Expenses}$$

Revenue is determined by the product's selling price and number of units sold:

$$\text{Total Revenue} = \text{Price} \times \text{Quantity Sold}$$

Therefore, a profit-maximizing price rises to the point at which further increases will cause disproportionate decreases in the number of units sold. A 10 percent price increase that results in only an

8 percent cut in volume will add to the firm's revenue. However, a 10 percent price hike that results in an 11 percent sales decline will reduce revenue.

Economists refer to this approach as **marginal analysis.** They identify profit maximization as the point at which the addition to total revenue is just balanced by the increase in total cost. Marketers must resolve a basic problem of how to achieve this delicate balance when they set prices. Relatively few firms actually hit this elusive target. A significantly larger number prefer to direct their effort toward more realistic goals.

Consequently, marketers commonly set target-return objectives—short-run or long-run goals usually stated as percentages of sales or investment. The practice has become particularly popular among large firms in which other pressures interfere with profit-maximization objectives. Target-return objectives offer several benefits for marketers in addition to resolving pricing questions. For example, these objectives serve as tools for evaluating performance. They also satisfy desires to generate "fair" profits as judged by management, stockholders, and the public.

profit maximization Point at which the additional revenue gained by increasing the price of a product equals the increase in total costs.

target-return objective Short-run or long-run pricing objectives of achieving a specified return on either sales or investment.

VOLUME OBJECTIVES

Some economists and business executives argue that pricing behavior actually seeks to maximize sales within a given profit constraint. In other words, they set a minimum acceptable profit level and then seek to maximize sales (subject to this profit constraint) in the belief that the increased sales are more important in the long-run competitive picture than immediate high profits. As a result, companies should continue to expand sales as long as their total profits do not drop below the minimum return acceptable to management.

Sales maximization can also result from nonprice factors such as service and quality. Marketers succeeded in increasing sales for Dr. Scholl's new shoe insert, Dynastep, by advertising heavily in magazines. The ads explained how the Dynastep insert would help relieve leg and back pain. Priced around $14 for two inserts—twice as much as comparable offerings—Dynastep ran over its competitors to become number one in its category.

Another volume-related pricing objective is the **market-share objective**—the goal of controlling a specified minimum share of the market for a firm's good or service. Apple is using this strategy to retain its dominant 83 percent share of the market for digital music downloads, the key to which is the iPod player. Apple recently cut the price of the basic iPod Shuffle model to $69 from $99 and introduced a 1 GB Nano at $149, or 25 percent cheaper than the next-higher-capacity model. These moves "make it really hard for others to compete," says one industry watcher.[8]

The PIMS Studies

Market-share objectives may prove critical to the achievement of other organizational objectives. High sales, for example, often mean more profits. The Profit Impact of Market Strategies (PIMS) project, an extensive study conducted by the Marketing Science Institute, analyzed more than 2,000 firms and revealed that two of the most important factors influencing profitability were product quality and market share. Companies such as outdoor gear maker REI and Best Buy, the electronics giant, are introducing loyalty programs as a means of retaining customers and protecting their market share. Retail clothier Banana Republic offers its Luxe program for customers who spend at least $800 a year at its stores. Luxe members receive free clothing alterations and basic shipping at no charge.[9]

Profit Impact of Market Strategies (PIMS) project Research that discovered a strong positive relationship between a firm's market share and product quality and its return on investment.

The relationship between market share and profitability is evident in PIMS data that reveal an average 32 percent return on investment (ROI) for firms with market shares above 40 percent. In contrast, average ROI decreases to 24 percent for firms whose market shares are between 20 and 40 percent. Firms with a minor market share (less than 10 percent) generate average pretax investment returns of approximately 13 percent.[10]

The relationship also applies to a firm's individual brands. PIMS researchers compared the top four brands in each market segment they studied. Their data revealed that the leading brand typically generates after-tax ROI of 18 percent, considerably higher than the second-ranked brand. Weaker brands, on average, fail to earn adequate returns.

Marketers have developed an underlying explanation of the positive relationship between profitability and market share. Firms with large shares accumulate greater operating experience and lower

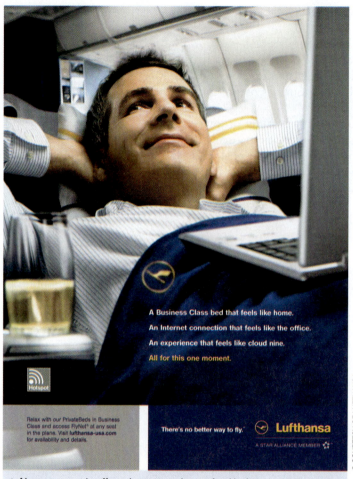

Lufthansa competes by offering business travelers comfortable sleeping accommodations and Internet connections rather than trumpeting the lowest fares.

overall costs relative to competitors with smaller market shares. Accordingly, effective segmentation strategies might focus on obtaining larger shares of smaller markets and on avoiding smaller shares of larger ones. A firm might achieve higher financial returns by becoming a major competitor in several smaller market segments than by remaining a relatively minor player in a larger market.

Meeting Competition Objectives

A third set of pricing objectives seeks simply to meet competitors' prices. In many lines of business, firms set their own prices to match those of established industry price leaders.

Price is a pivotal factor in the ongoing competition between long-distance telephone services and wireless carriers. Some cell phone companies are reviving prepaid calling plans to compete with reduced-rate and unlimited calling plans. These plans allow customers to pay up front for their minutes at lower costs than before, avoid overage fees, and eliminate long-term contracts. [11]

Pricing objectives tied directly to meeting prices charged by major competitors deemphasize the price element of the marketing mix and focus more strongly on nonprice variables. Pricing is a highly visible component of a firm's marketing mix and an easy and effective tool for obtaining a differential advantage over competitors. It is, however, a tool that other firms can easily duplicate through price reductions of their own. Airline price competition in recent years exemplifies the actions and reactions of competitors in this marketplace. Rather than emphasizing the lowest fares of any carrier, most airlines choose to compete by offering convenient arrival and departure times, enhanced passenger comfort with more room between each row, an attractive frequent-flyer program, and customer-focused alliances with automobile rental, lodging, and other partners. Southwest Airlines countered free-flight vouchers offered by a rival airline with a six-week free-drink offer. [12] Some airlines even returned to providing passenger meals on long flights, a practice that had been discontinued in a cost-cutting effort. Even when price increases are needed to remain profitable, an announced price hike by one airline will be implemented only if its major competitors match the new price. Because price changes directly affect overall profitability in an industry, many firms attempt to promote stable prices by meeting competitors' prices and competing for market share by focusing on product strategies, promotional decisions, and distribution—the nonprice elements of the marketing mix.

Value Pricing

When discounts become normal elements of a competitive marketplace, other marketing mix elements gain importance in purchase decisions. In such instances, overall product value, not just price, determines product choice. In recent years, a new strategy—**value pricing**—has emerged that emphasizes the benefits a product provides in comparison to the price and quality levels of competing offerings. This strategy typically works best for relatively low-priced goods and services, although Fred Franzia of Bronco Wine, a California winery ranked fourth largest in the U.S., believes value pricing is the way to protect the American wine industry from high-priced imports. "We've stupidly foreclosed major market share to ourselves," he says. "There's not a bottle of wine made worth more than $5. Ten dollars would be a stretch. Everyone's too greedy. We should be trying to make wine accessible to the average person, to give them something they can drink every day." He sells his

Briefly
Speaking

"Price is what you pay. Value is what you get."

—Warren Buffett (b. 1930)
American investor

value pricing Pricing strategy emphasizing benefits derived from a product in comparison to the price and quality levels of competing offerings.

NapaCreek wines at $3.99 to provide consumers with good quality at reasonable prices.[13]

Value-priced products generally cost less than premium brands, but marketers point out that value does not necessarily mean *inexpensive*. The challenge for those who compete on value is to convince customers that low-priced brands offer quality comparable to that of a higher-priced product. An increasing number of alternative products and private-label brands has resulted in a more competitive marketplace in recent years. Trader Joe's, a rapidly growing grocery chain that began in the Los Angeles area and has since expanded throughout the West, Midwest, and mid-Atlantic states, stands out from other specialty food stores with its cedar plank walls, nautical décor, and a captain (the store manager), first mate (the assistant manager), and the other employees (known as crew members) all attired in colorful Hawaiian shirts. The chain uses value pricing for the more than 2,000 upscale food products it develops or imports and generates annual sales of more than $2 billion by selling wines, cheeses, meats, fish, and other unique gourmet items at closeout prices, mostly under its own brand names. If the high quality doesn't persuade customers at its 210 stores to buy, they can also take comfort from the fact that Trader Joe's tuna are caught without environmentally dangerous nets, its dried apricots contain no sulfur preservatives, and its peanut butter is organic.[14]

Value pricing is perhaps best seen in the personal computer industry. In the past few years, PC prices have collapsed, reducing the effectiveness of traditional pricing strategies intended to meet competition. In fact, despite rising costs for several standard PC components such as memory chips and LCD screens, PCs priced at less than $600 are now the fastest-growing segment of the market. This category now accounts for almost 20 percent of PCs sold in stores. Industry leaders such as Dell, Hewlett-Packard, and Gateway cannot continue to cut prices, so they are adding features such as increased memory and 3-D graphics accelerator cards that increase speed. Dell has even launched a home installation plan to offset tumbling prices in the PC market, and Apple has introduced the Mac Mini for $499.[15]

IMAGE COURTESY OF THE ADVERTISING ARCHIVES

Top 5.99 H&M www.hm.com

Retailer H&M offers value-priced clothing to draw customers to stores frequently. Selections change often so that customers can see something new on each visit.

PRESTIGE OBJECTIVES

The final category of pricing objectives, unrelated to either profitability or sales volume, is prestige objectives. Prestige pricing establishes a relatively high price to develop and maintain an image of quality and exclusiveness that appeals to status-conscious consumers. Such objectives reflect marketers' recognition of the role of price in creating an overall image of the firm and its product offerings.

Prestige objectives affect the price tags of such products as Waterford crystal, Alfa Romeo sports cars, Omega watches, and Tiffany jewelry. When a perfume marketer sets a price of $400 or more per ounce, this choice reflects an emphasis on image far more than the cost of ingredients. Analyses have shown that ingredients account for less than 5 percent of a perfume's cost. Thus, advertisements for Joy that promote the fragrance as the "costliest perfume in the world" use price to promote product prestige. Diamond jewelry also uses prestige pricing to convey an image of quality and timelessness.

In the business world, private jet ownership imparts an image of prestige, power, and high price tags—too high for most business travelers to consider. Recognizing that cost is the primary factor that makes jet ownership prohibitive, companies such as Flight Options and NetJets have

IMAGE COURTESY OF THE ADVERTISING ARCHIVES

One of the hallmarks of prestige pricing as a marketing strategy is to omit any mention of price from product advertising. This ad for men's clothing from Valentino creates an image of luxury.

 assessment check

1. What are target–return objectives?
2. What is value pricing?
3. How do prestige objectives affect a seller's pricing strategy?

created an alternative—fractional ownership. In San Francisco, Torbin Fuller adapted their business model to create Club Sportiva, a classic-car club that boasts a fleet including a Rolls Royce Corniche II, a 1989 Ferrari 348 GTB, and a 1977 Aston Martin V8. With 200 club members paying up to $8,500 a year to drive the cars for a few days at a time, Fuller plans a nationwide rollout—and has attracted several competitors, too.[16]

PRICING OBJECTIVES OF NOT-FOR-PROFIT ORGANIZATIONS

Pricing is also a key element of the marketing mix for not-for-profit organizations. Pricing strategy can help these groups achieve a variety of organizational goals:

1. *Profit maximization.* While not-for-profit organizations by definition do not cite profitability as a primary goal, there are numerous instances in which they do try to maximize their returns on single events or a series of events. A $1,000-a-plate political fund-raiser is a classic example.

2. *Cost recovery.* Some not-for-profit organizations attempt to recover only the actual cost of operating the unit. Mass transit, toll roads and bridges, and most private colleges and universities are common examples. The amount of recovered costs is often dictated by tradition, competition, or public opinion. A more unusual case is Indiana's decision to lease its 157-mile toll road to a team of Australian and Spanish companies for the next 75 years, creating a source of almost $4 billion in revenue to fund needed transportation projects in the state.[17]

3. *Market incentives.* Other not-for-profit groups follow a lower-than-average pricing policy or offer a free service to encourage increased usage of the good or service. Seattle's bus system offers free service in the

 marketing success   Variable Pricing to Ease Your Commute

Background. California governor Arnold Schwarzenegger spoke for many of the nation's frustrated truckers and commuters when he said, "Californians can't get from place to place on little fairy wings. We are a car-centered state. We need roads." The country has outgrown its massive interstate highway system, and clogged lanes and congestion now cost the average commuter 46 hours a year of sitting idle in a car. Miles driven have increased more than 80 percent in a generation. The number of new highway lanes has gone up just 4 percent in the same period.

The Challenge. To alleviate congestion, save fuel, reduce pollution, increase safety, and cut driving time, states need to repair and upgrade the existing highway systems and in some cases create new ones to serve growing communities. But federal money for public highway projects is often hard to come by.

The Strategy. A number of ideas are being tested around the country, but one of the most promising is variable pricing to replace standard pay-as-you-

downtown area in an attempt to reduce traffic congestion, encourage retail sales, and minimize the effort required to access downtown public services.[18]

4. *Market suppression.* Price can also discourage consumption. High prices help accomplish social objectives independent of the costs of providing goods or services. Illustrations include tobacco and alcohol taxes (the so-called sin taxes), parking fines, tolls, and gasoline excise taxes. California voters recently considered a 300 percent hike in cigarette taxes to help cover the healthcare costs associated with smoking—and to encourage smokers to quit.[19]

The "Marketing Success" feature discusses some ingenious pricing techniques that state governments are trying out as they attempt to cover budget shortfalls with increased revenue from highway tolls.

METHODS FOR DETERMINING PRICES

Marketers determine prices in two basic ways—by applying the theoretical concepts of supply and demand and by completing cost-oriented analyses. During the first part of the 20th century, most discussions of price determination emphasized the classical concepts of supply and demand. During the last half of the century, however, the emphasis began to shift to a cost-oriented approach. Hindsight reveals certain flaws in both concepts.

Treatments of this subject often overlook another concept of price determination—one based on the impact of custom and tradition. **Customary prices** are retail prices that consumers expect as a result of tradition and social habit. Candy makers have attempted to maintain traditional price levels by greatly reducing overall product size. Similar practices have prevailed in the marketing of soft drinks as bottlers attempt to balance consumer expectations of customary prices with the realities of rising costs.

Wrigley, manufacturer of chewing gum favorites Juicy Fruit, Doublemint, and Big Red, took advantage of the weakness in the industry's customary pricing strategy by introducing a smaller-quantity pack at a lower price. While competitors continued to offer only seven-piece packs for 35 cents, Wrigley priced its five-piece packs at 25 cents. To spur impulse buying, the company prominently displayed the price on the package. The strategy was so successful that within two years of its inception, Wrigley discontinued selling seven-stick gum packs.

The soaring price of U.S. gasoline presents another example of supply and demand. As average prices for a gallon of gas rose above the $3-a-gallon mark and crude oil soared to more than $70 a barrel, frustrated drivers began demanding to know who, if anyone, was cashing in on the price spike. Even though the United States is the world's largest refiner of gasoline, strong demand has led to an increase in oil imports.

Although profits at U.S. refineries have reached record levels, they continue to struggle to produce enough gasoline to meet demand. Recent Gulf Coast hurricanes only multiplied the problems,

customary prices Traditional prices that customers expect to pay for certain goods and services.

---

go tolls. Some proposals would levy higher-than-normal tolls during peak travel times and offer reduced tolls and discounts during off-peak hours, particularly in the middle of the night. Others provide special commuter lanes guaranteed to move at the maximum speed limit, for a hefty fee.

The Outcome. It remains to be seen how effectively variable pricing can spread road use more effectively over any given 24-hour period. A proposal to offer an optional permanent fast lane for an extra fee in Wisconsin could painlessly generate millions in revenue to support highway rebuilding projects. But one observer says a potential flaw in a steep discount to encourage truckers to drive at night is that they may face closed yards and warehouses when they arrive.

Sources: "Study Calls for Variable-Priced Lanes to Be Part of Freeway Plans," Reason Foundation news release, February 28, 2006, http://www.reason.org; "States Introduce Discounted Off-Hour Tolls to Relieve Congestion," National Governors Association, October 20, 2005, http://www.nga.org; Larry Copeland, "Off-Hour Tools Aimed at 'Chokepoint,'" *USA Today*, October 11, 2005, p. 1A; Timothy Egan, "Paying on the Highway to Get Out of First Gear," *New York Times*, April 28, 2005, http://www.nytimes.com.

Etiquette Tips for Marketing Professionals

Tipping Do's and Don'ts

Tips are part of the price of dining out or using the services of door attendants, taxi drivers, bellhops, porters, valets, maitre d's, and others with whom businesspeople come in contact. Tipping is meant to thank anyone who performs a special service for you or who makes your travel more convenient or your meal more enjoyable. Many service workers depend on tips to make ends meet.

But many people are confused by tipping. Who gets a tip and who doesn't? How much is appropriate? What if the service offered isn't deserving of a tip? Here are a few guidelines to remember about tipping in the United States.

1. If the service is poor, give your server the benefit of the doubt and leave the standard 15 percent tip. But talk to the manager about improving service.
2. Don't make up for high prices by cutting back on the tip. If adding the tip makes the service a stretch for your budget, patronize the service less often or find a cheaper one.
3. Tip hairdressers and manicurists 10 to 20 percent of the total; skycaps and bellhops or door attendants receive $1 per bag (more if the bags are heavy).
4. Tip your taxi, limo, or van driver 15 percent of the total fare, but never less than $1. Add more for help with your bags. Tip a valet or parking attendant $2 to $5 for returning your car, but not for parking it.

5. Tip the hotel maid daily; different maids take care of your room each day. Leave $1 to $3 on your pillow each time, including the day you check out.
6. Tip the hotel concierge $5 to $10 at the end of your stay if he or she has been helpful with dinner or theater reservations.
7. Tip for room service as you would for service in a restaurant—15 to 20 percent of the total charge.
8. No tip is required if the maitre d' merely seats you in a restaurant. If he or she gets you a special table or a table without a reservation during a busy hour, tip $5 to $10 or more, depending on the average price of a meal.
9. Tip jars at coffee shops, cafeterias, and concessions stands can usually be safely ignored because no extraordinary or personal service is offered.
10. For holiday gifts to those you see regularly, such as doormen, hairdressers, manicurists, and personal trainers, give within your means, or ask the shop owner or manager or your colleagues about what is appropriate. Skip the homemade goodies; cash and gift certificates are still the most widely appreciated gifts.

Sources: James G. Lewis, "Tipping Etiquette," Findalink, **http://www. findalink.net**, accessed June 16, 2006; "Proper Tipping Etiquette," Essortment, **http://msms.essortment.com**, accessed June 16, 2006; "Tipping Etiquette," About.com, **http://hotels.about.com**, accessed June 16, 2006; Eileen Alt Powell, "Tipping Shouldn't Break Bank," *The Morning News*, December 11, 2005, p. 11D.

when refineries were temporarily knocked out of service. Adding to the supply problem is the fact that no new refineries have been built in three decades, and oil companies are reluctant to build more out of concerns for returns on their investment.[20]

Higher gas prices have effects on other consumer costs as well. With prices at record highs, hybrid cars are in greater demand than ever before, and some dealers have months-long waiting lists even at premium prices. Retail businesses that use trucks and cars to deliver their products—such as pizza restaurants and florists—feel the pinch at the pump. Although riding a bike might be a good alternative for some, bicycle shops are paying more for deliveries, too. Leigh Sorrells, owner of a Connecticut bike shop, is cutting back on freebies such as accessories to avoid raising prices. "It's all going to come around," he says, "and that's the downside. Whether it's food, my stuff, this stuff, that stuff—everything is going to get more expensive."[21]

Rising energy costs affect the costs of running a Laundromat, patrolling the streets in a police cruiser, painting a house with oil-based paint, bringing produce to supermarkets, and even driving to the store to buy it. The alternative-rock band Kill Hannah saw profits from its recent tour get eaten away by the rising cost of hauling its 5,000-pound equipment trailer around the Midwest. "You can't raise ticket prices," says the band's bass guitarist, Greg Corner, "but we're spending as much money in gas as a band that's selling out a 3,000-seat arena. This tour is really a learning experience."[22]

One price that's often difficult for businesspeople to set is the size of a tip. The "Etiquette Tips for Marketing Professionals" feature offers guidelines for acknowledging the services of waiters, bellhops, taxi drivers, personal trainers and hairdressers, and others.

 assessment check

1. What goals does pricing strategy help a not-for-profit organization achieve?

2. What are the two basic ways in which marketers determine prices?

PRICE DETERMINATION IN ECONOMIC THEORY

Microeconomics suggests a way of determining prices that assumes a profit-maximization objective. This technique attempts to derive correct equilibrium prices in the marketplace by comparing supply and demand. It also requires more complete analysis than actual business firms typically conduct.

Demand refers to a schedule of the amounts of a firm's product that consumers will purchase at different prices during a specified time period. **Supply** refers to a schedule of the amounts of a good or service that will be offered for sale at different prices during a specified period. These schedules may vary for different types of market structures. Businesses operate and set prices in four types of market structures: pure competition, monopolistic competition, oligopoly, and monopoly.

Pure competition is a market structure with so many buyers and sellers that no single participant can significantly influence price. Pure competition presupposes other market conditions as well: homogeneous products and ease of entry for sellers due to low start-up costs. The agricultural sector exhibits many characteristics of a purely competitive market, making it the closest actual example. But more than 1,000 U.S. ranchers have switched their beef herds to an all-grass diet in an attempt to differentiate their product from those raised in feedlots.[23]

Monopolistic competition typifies most retailing and features large numbers of buyers and sellers. These diverse parties exchange heterogeneous, relatively well-differentiated products, giving marketers some control over prices.

Relatively few sellers compete in an **oligopoly.** Pricing decisions by each seller are likely to affect the market, but no single seller controls it. High start-up costs form significant barriers to entry for new competitors. Each firm's demand curve in an oligopolistic market displays a unique kink at the current market price. Because of the impact of a single competitor on total industry sales, competitors usually quickly match any attempt by one firm to generate additional sales by reducing prices. Price cutting in such industry structures is likely to reduce total industry revenues. Oligopolies operate in the petroleum refining, automobile, tobacco, and airline industries.

With demand for air travel surging at the same time that many airlines are

© ASSOCIATED PRESS, AP

Farmers such as these in Kansas are typical sellers in purely competitive markets.

table 18.2 Distinguishing Features of the Four Market Structures

	TYPE OF MARKET STRUCTURE			
CHARACTERISTICS	PURE COMPETITION	MONOPOLISTIC COMPETITION	OLIGOPOLY	MONOPOLY
Number of competitors	Many	Few to many	Few	No direct competitors
Ease of entry into industry by new firms	Easy	Somewhat difficult	Difficult	Regulated by government
Similarity of goods or services offered by competing firms	Similar	Different	Can be either similar or different	No directly competing goods or services
Control over prices by individual firms	None	Some	Some	Considerable
Demand curves facing individual firms	Totally elastic	Can be either elastic or inelastic	Kinked; inelastic below kink; more elastic above	Can be either elastic or inelastic
Examples	Illinois soybean farm	Best Buy stores	Verizon Wireless	Waste Management

retiring older, larger planes, fewer seats are available on domestic flights than ever before. Prices are skyrocketing with almost no impact on demand—proof, according to industry analysts, that U.S. consumers are willing to pay to fly.[24]

A **monopoly** is a market structure in which only one seller of a product exists and for which there are no close substitutes. Antitrust legislation has nearly eliminated all but temporary monopolies, such as those created through patent protection. Regulated industries constitute another form of monopoly. The government allows regulated monopolies in markets in which competition would lead to an uneconomical duplication of services. In return for such a license, government reserves the right to regulate the monopoly's rate of return.

The four types of market structures are compared in Table 18.2 on the following bases: number of competitors, ease of entry into the industry by new firms, similarity of competing products, degree of control over price by individual firms, and the elasticity or inelasticity of the demand curve facing the individual firm. Elasticity—the degree of consumer responsiveness to changes in price—is discussed in more detail in a later section.

figure 18.1

Determining Price by Relating Marginal Revenue to Marginal Cost

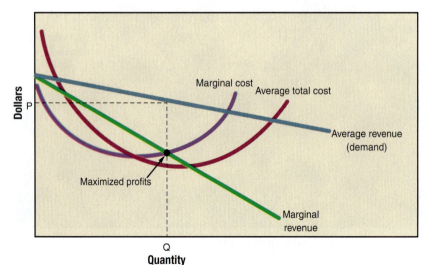

COST AND REVENUE CURVES

Marketers must set a price for a product that generates sufficient revenue to cover the costs of producing and marketing it. A product's total cost is composed of total variable costs and total fixed costs. **Variable costs** (such as raw materials and labor costs) change with the level of production, and **fixed costs** (such as lease payments or insurance costs) remain stable at any production level within a certain range. **Average total costs** are calculated by dividing the sum of the variable and fixed costs by the number of units produced. Finally, **marginal cost** is the change in total cost that results from producing an additional unit of output.

table 18.3 Price Determination Using Marginal Analysis

PRICE	NUMBER SOLD	TOTAL REVENUE	MARGINAL REVENUE	TOTAL COSTS	MARGINAL COSTS	PROFITS (TOTAL REVENUE MINUS TOTAL COSTS)
–	–	–	–	–	–	($50)
$34	1	$34	$34	57	$7	(23)
32	2	64	30	62	5	2
30	3	90	26	66	4	24
28	4	112	22	69	3	43
26	5	130	18	73	4	57
24	6	144	14	78	5	66
22	7	154	10	84	6	70
20	8	160	6	91	7	69
18	9	162	2	100	9	62
16	10	160	(2)	110	11	50

The demand side of the pricing equation focuses on revenue curves. Average revenue is calculated by dividing total revenue by the quantity associated with these revenues. Average revenue is actually the demand curve facing the firm. Marginal revenue is the change in total revenue that results from selling an additional unit of output. Figure 18.1 shows the relationships of various cost and revenue measures; the firm maximizes its profits when marginal costs equal marginal revenues.

Table 18.3 illustrates why the intersection of the marginal cost and marginal revenue curves is the logical point at which to maximize revenue for the organization. Although the firm can earn a profit at several different prices, the price at which it earns maximum profits is $22. At a price of $24, $66 in profits is earned—$4 less than the $70 profit at the $22 price. If a price of $20 is set to attract additional sales, the marginal costs of the extra sales ($7) are greater than the marginal revenues received ($6), and total profits decline.

THE CONCEPT OF ELASTICITY IN PRICING STRATEGY

Although the intersection of the marginal cost and marginal revenue curves determines the level of output, the impact of changes in price on sales varies greatly. To understand why it fluctuates, one must understand the concept of elasticity.

Elasticity is the measure of the responsiveness of purchasers and suppliers to price changes. The price elasticity of demand (or elasticity of demand) is the percentage change in the quantity of a good or service demanded divided by the percentage change in its price. A 10 percent increase in the price of eggs that results in a 5 percent decrease in the quantity of eggs demanded yields a price elasticity of demand for eggs of 0.5. The price elasticity of supply of a product is the percentage change in the quantity of a good or service supplied divided by the percentage change in its price. A 10 percent increase in the price of shampoo that results in a 25 percent increase in the quantity supplied yields a price elasticity of supply for shampoo of 2.5.

Consider a case in which a 1 percent change in price causes more than a 1 percent change in the quantity supplied or demanded. Numerically, that means an elasticity measurement greater than 1.0. When the elasticity of demand or supply is greater than 1.0, that demand or supply is said to be elastic. If a 1 percent change in price results in less than a 1 percent change in quantity, a product's elasticity of demand or supply will be less than 1.0. In that case, the demand or supply is called

3 Explain price elasticity and its determinants.

elasticity Measure of responsiveness of purchasers and suppliers to a change in price.

Solving an Ethical Controversy

Energy from Ethanol: Hope or Hype?

Gasoline and petroleum-based products drive the U.S. economy. Demand for the fuel remains strong despite all-time highs in the price of a gallon of oil. But with supplies tight and worldwide demand for oil increasing, consumers are taking a harder look at corn-based ethanol to help ease the energy crunch. Yet it is not clear how much ethanol can reduce U.S. dependence on foreign oil imports. That's not stopping some marketers, who point to a future of renewable energy resources and cleaner air. If Brazil can use its sugar cane to become energy independent, they argue, why can't the United States use its abundant corn crop to wean itself from oil, which often comes from unstable—and sometimes hostile—parts of the world? Consumers are left to try to sort fact from fiction.

Is ethanol a viable replacement for petroleum in the market, or are producers overpromising its benefits?

PRO

1. Ethanol is produced from a renewable resource: corn. Existing cars can run on a 10 percent ethanol mixture without any modifications. With minor engine modifications—some experts say about $100 of tinkering—cars could run on 85 percent ethanol power. And corn is domestically produced, creating a reliable supply.
2. Ethanol burns clean, reducing pollution. Federal government mandates to increase the amount of biofuels mixed into gasoline until the year 2012 encourage research and development in efficient ethanol production. So producers already have a set minimum demand for their product. If gas prices continue to rise or the supply is in doubt, then demand for ethanol will continue to surge beyond those minimums.

CON

1. Ethanol production uses considerable amounts of energy. Experts estimate that ethanol produces about 20 to 40 percent more energy than it uses. But transporting the fuel to markets outside its Midwest production area consumes even more energy, making the fuel very costly in other areas of the United States.
2. Ethanol dissolves in water, and current transportation and storage methods are not completely watertight. So new distribution systems would need to be built to handle ethanol. Also, corn is used in many food products and is exported to other countries, so increasing corn-based ethanol could drive up the price of food products and reduce revenue from exports.

Summary

Major companies and individuals—agricultural giant Archer Daniels Midland, British entrepreneur Richard Branson, and Bill Gates and Paul Allen of Microsoft fame, among others—are investing in ethanol research and development. So supply of the renewable fuel is set to increase. In addition, because corn is not the most efficient source of ethanol (high-sugar crops such as sugarcane are cheaper sources), researchers are looking into other alternatives. So-called *cellulosic ethanol*—ethanol produced from waste products such as wood chips, straw, corn husks, and a perennial grass—could be viable alternatives to corn. But the enzymes needed to make this type of production cost-effective are not widely available at present. So, for the time being, the dream of an economy running on ethanol remains a mix of hope and hype.

Sources: Mark Clayton, "Ethanol's Rise Prompts Worries of a Corn Crunch," *Christian Science Monitor*, July 26, 2006, **http://www.csmonitor.com**; Amanda Paulson, "Where Corn Is King, a New Fuel Is Prince," *Christian Science Monitor*, July 19, 2006, **http://www.csmonitor.com**; Steve Hargreaves, "Super Ethanol Is on the Way," CNN Money, June 29, 2006, **http://money.cnn.com**; Chris Taylor, "Ethanol War Brewing," *Business 2.0*, June 27, 2006, **http://money.cnn.com**; Rob Kelley, "Ethanol Fueling Growth for ADM," CNN Money, June 16, 2006, **http://money.cnn.com**; Libby Quaid, "Ethanol Dazzles Wall Street, White House," Associated Press, June 3, 2006, **http://news.yahoo.com**.

inelastic. For example, the demand for cigarettes is relatively inelastic; research studies have shown that a 10 percent increase in cigarette prices results in only a 4 percent sales decline.

Prices in Zimbabwe are rising at unheard-of rates, the result of hyperinflation that threatens to surpass 1,000 percent a year. Toilet paper recently climbed to $417 for a single two-ply sheet, or almost $150,000 a roll—contrast that with a price of about 69 cents in the United States. Although under ordinary inflation, people will continue to buy necessities with relatively inelastic demand such as food, under hyperinflation such as Zimbabwe's, even staples such as bread, margarine, meat, and tea become unattainable luxuries for the country's 13 million people, many of whom face food shortages and more than 70 percent of whom are unemployed.[25]

Determinants of Elasticity

Why is the elasticity of supply or demand high for some products and low for others? What determines demand elasticity? One major factor influencing the elasticity of demand is the availability of substitutes or complements. If consumers can easily find close substitutes for a good or service, the product's demand tends to be elastic. A product's role as a complement to the use of another product also affects its degree of price elasticity. For example, the relatively inelastic demand for motor oil reflects its role as a complement to a more important product, gasoline. With record high prices of gasoline recently, interest in and demand for energy alternatives has reached a fever pitch, as the "Solving an Ethical Controversy" feature describes.

As increasing numbers of buyers and sellers complete their business transactions online, the elasticity of a product's demand is drastically affected. Take major discounters and other price-competitive stores, for example. Small businesses and individual do-it-yourselfers shop Home Depot for tools, such as wheelbarrows; parents look for birthday gifts at Wal-Mart; and homeowners go to Circuit City for new refrigerators or stoves. Today, however, the Internet lets consumers contact many more providers directly, often giving them better selections and prices for their efforts with service sites such as Shopzilla.com for consumer goods and electronics, Net-a-Porter.com for high fashion clothing, *Kayak.com* for travel bargains, and Shoebuy.com for shoes from dozens of different manufacturers.[26] The increased options available to shoppers combine to create a market characterized by demand elasticity.

Elasticity of demand also depends on whether a product is perceived as a necessity or a luxury. The Four Seasons chain of luxury hotels and resorts enjoys such a strong reputation for service, comfort, and exclusiveness that it has become a favorite among affluent individual travelers and business professionals. In other contexts, specialty shops such as Starbucks are considered necessities by some consumers today.

Most people regard high-fashion clothes, such as a $2,500 Escada embroidered silk suit at Neiman Marcus, as luxuries. If prices for designer outfits increase dramatically, people can respond by purchasing lower-priced substitutes instead. In contrast, medical and dental care are considered necessities, so price changes have little effect on the frequency of visits to the doctor or dentist.

However, under the continuing influence of higher prices, some products once regarded as necessities may be dismissed as luxuries, leading to decreasing demand. Formerly booming personal computer sales have shown little or no growth in recent years.

Elasticity also depends on the portion of a person's budget that he or she spends on a good or service. People no longer really need matches. They can easily find good substitutes. Nonetheless, the demand for matches remains very inelastic because people spend so little on them that they hardly notice a price change. In contrast, the demand for housing or transportation is not totally inelastic, even though they are necessities, because both consume large parts of a consumer's budget.

Elasticity of demand also responds to consumers' time perspectives. Demand often shows less elasticity in the short run than in the long run. Consider the demand for home air conditioning. In the short run, people pay rising energy prices because they find it difficult to cut back on the quantities they use. Accustomed to living with specific temperature settings and dressing in certain ways, they prefer to pay more during a few months of the year than to explore other possibilities. Over time, though, with global warming becoming a real and present danger, they may find ways to economize. They can better insulate their homes, experiment with alternative cooling systems, or plant shade trees.

Sometimes the usual patterns do not hold true, though. Alcohol and tobacco, which are not necessities but do occupy large shares of some personal budgets, are also subject to inelastic demand.

Elasticity and Revenue

The elasticity of demand exerts an important influence on variations in total revenue as a result of changes in the price of a good or service. Assume, for example, that San Francisco's Bay Area Rapid

Transit (BART) officials are considering alternative methods of raising more money for their budget. One possible method for increasing revenues would be to change rail pass fares for commuters. But should BART raise or lower the price of a pass? The correct answer depends on the elasticity of demand for subway rides. A 10 percent decrease in fares should attract more riders, but unless it stimulates more than a 10 percent increase in riders, total revenue will fall. A 10 percent increase in fares will bring in more money per rider, but if more than 10 percent of the riders stop using the subway, total revenue will fall. A price cut will increase revenue only for a product with elastic demand, and a price increase will raise revenue only for a product with inelastic demand. BART officials seem to believe that the demand for rapid rail transit is inelastic; they raise fares when they need more money.

assessment check

1. What are the determinants of elasticity?
2. What is the usual relationship between elasticity and revenue?

PRACTICAL PROBLEMS OF PRICE THEORY

4 List the practical problems involved in applying price theory concepts to actual pricing decisions.

Marketers may thoroughly understand price theory concepts but still encounter difficulty applying them in practice. What practical limitations interfere with setting prices?

First, many firms do not attempt to maximize profits. Economic analysis is subject to the same limitations as the assumptions on which it is based—for example, the proposition that all firms attempt to maximize profits. Second, it is difficult to estimate demand curves. Modern accounting procedures provide managers with a clear understanding of cost structures, so managers can readily comprehend the supply side of the pricing equation. But they find it difficult to estimate demand at various price levels. Demand curves must be based on marketing research estimates that may be less exact than cost figures. Although the demand element can be identified, it is often difficult to measure in real-world settings.

assessment check

1. List the three reasons why it is difficult to put price theory into practice.

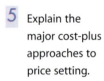

PRICE DETERMINATION IN PRACTICE

5 Explain the major cost-plus approaches to price setting.

The practical limitations inherent in price theory have forced practitioners to turn to other techniques. **Cost-plus pricing,** the most popular method, uses a base-cost figure per unit and adds a markup to cover unassigned costs and to provide a profit. The only real difference among the multitude of cost-plus techniques is the relative sophistication of the costing procedures employed. For example, a local apparel shop may set prices by adding a 45 percent markup to the invoice price charged by the supplier. The markup is expected to cover all other expenses and permit the owner to earn a reasonable return on the sale of clothes.

In contrast to this rather simple pricing mechanism, a large manufacturer may employ a complex pricing formula requiring computer calculations. However, this method merely adds a more complicated procedure to the simpler, traditional method for calculating costs. In the end, someone still must make a decision about the markup. The apparel shop and the large manufacturer may figure costs differently, but they are remarkably similar in completing the markup side of the equation.

Cost-plus pricing often works well for a business that keeps its costs low, allowing it to set its prices lower than those of competitors and still make a profit. Wal-Mart keeps costs low by buying most of its inventory directly from manufacturers, using a supply chain that slashes inventory costs by quickly replenishing inventory as items are sold, and relying on wholesalers and other intermediaries only in special instances such as localized items. This strategy has played a major role in the discounter's becoming the world's largest retailer.

ALTERNATIVE PRICING PROCEDURES

The two most common cost-oriented pricing procedures are the full-cost method and the incremental-cost method. **Full-cost pricing** uses all relevant variable costs in setting a product's price. In addition, it allocates fixed costs that cannot be directly attributed to the production of the specific item being priced. Under the full-cost method, if job order 515 in a printing plant amounts to 0.000127 percent of the plant's total output, then 0.000127 percent of the firm's overhead expenses are charged to that job. This approach allows the marketer to recover all costs plus the amount added as a profit margin.

The full-cost approach has two basic deficiencies. First, there is no consideration of competition or demand for the item. Perhaps no one wants to pay the price the firm has calculated. Second, any method for allocating overhead (fixed expenses) is arbitrary and may be unrealistic. In manufacturing, overhead allocations often are tied to direct labor hours. In retailing, the square footage of each profit center is sometimes the factor used in computations. Regardless of the technique employed, it is difficult to show a cause–effect relationship between the allocated cost and most products.

One way to overcome the arbitrary allocation of fixed expenses is with **incremental-cost pricing,** which attempts to use only costs directly attributable to a specific output in setting prices. Consider a very small-scale manufacturer with the following income statement:

Sales (10,000 units at $10)		$100,000
Expenses:		
Variable	$50,000	
Fixed	40,000	90,000
Net Profit		$ 10,000

Suppose the firm is offered a contract for an additional 5,000 units. Because the peak season is over, these items can be produced at the same average variable cost. Assume that the labor force would otherwise be working on maintenance projects. How low should the firm price its product to get the contract?

Under the full-cost approach, the lowest price would be $9 per unit. This figure is obtained by dividing the $90,000 in expenses by an output of 10,000 units. The incremental approach, on the other hand, could permit any price above $5, which would significantly increase the possibility of securing the additional contract. This price would be composed of the $5 variable cost associated with each unit of production plus a $0.10-per-unit contribution to fixed expenses and overhead. With a $5.10 proposed price, the income statement now looks like this:

Sales (10,000 at $10; 5,000 at $5.10)		$125,500
Expenses:		
Variable	$75,000	
Fixed	40,000	115,000
Net Profit		$ 10,500

Profits thus increase under the incremental approach.

Admittedly, the illustration is based on two assumptions: (1) the ability to isolate markets such that selling at the lower price will not affect the price received in other markets and (2) the absence of legal restrictions on the firm. The example, however, does illustrate that profits can sometimes be enhanced by using the incremental approach.

✓ assessment check

1. What is full-cost pricing?
2. What is incremental-cost pricing?

BREAKEVEN ANALYSIS

Breakeven analysis is a means of determining the number of goods or services that must be sold at a given price to generate sufficient revenue to cover total costs. Figure 18.2 graphically depicts this process. The total cost curve includes both fixed and variable segments, and total fixed cost is represented by a horizontal line. Average variable cost is assumed to be constant per unit as it was in the example for incremental pricing.

breakeven analysis Pricing technique used to determine the number of products that must be sold at a specified price to generate enough revenue to cover total cost.

The breakeven point is the point at which total revenue equals total cost. In the example in Figure 18.2, a selling price of $10 and an average variable cost of $5 result in a per-unit contribution to fixed cost of $5. The breakeven point in terms of units is found by using the following formula, in which the per-unit contribution equals the product's price less the variable cost per unit:

$$\text{Breakeven Point (in units)} = \frac{\text{Total Fixed Cost}}{\text{Per-Unit Contribution to Fixed Cost}}$$

$$\text{Breakeven Point (in units)} = \frac{\$40,000}{\$5} = 8,000 \text{ units}$$

The breakeven point in dollars is found with the following formula:

$$\text{Breakeven Point (in dollars)} = \frac{\text{Total Fixed Cost}}{1 - \text{Variable Cost per Unit Price}}$$

$$\text{Breakeven Point (in dollars)} = \frac{\$40,000}{1 - (\$5/\$10)} = \frac{\$40,000}{0.5} = \$80,000$$

figure 18.2

Breakeven Chart

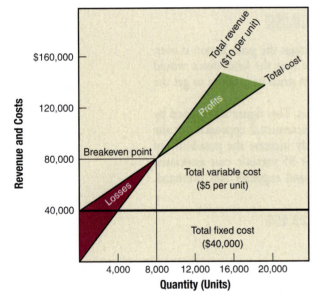

Sometimes breakeven is reached by reducing costs. Ford Motor Company aims to bring its North American operations back to profitability by slashing costs. Soaring gas prices have reduced the popularity of gas-guzzling SUVs, which were a former bright spot in Ford's lineup. So Bill Ford, Jr., announced a 15 percent cutback in production, closing fourteen plants and laying off up to 30,000 factory jobs in North America. The goal is profitability by 2008.[27]

Once the breakeven point has been reached, sufficient revenues will have been obtained from sales to cover all fixed costs. Any additional sales will generate per-unit profits equal to the difference between the product's selling price and the variable cost of each unit. As Figure 18.2 reveals, sales of 8,001 units (1 unit above the breakeven point) will produce net profits of $5 ($10 sales price less per-unit variable cost of $5). Once all fixed costs have been covered, the per-unit contribution will become the per-unit profit.

Target Returns

Although breakeven analysis indicates the sales level at which the firm will incur neither profits nor losses, most firms' managers include a targeted profit in their analyses. In some instances, management sets a desired dollar return when considering a proposed new product or other marketing strategy. A retailer may set a desired profit of $250,000 in considering whether to expand to a second location. In other instances, the target return may be expressed in percentages, such as a 15 percent return on sales. These target returns can be calculated as follows:

$$\text{Breakeven Point (including specific dollar target return)} = \frac{\text{Total Fixed Cost} + \text{Profit Objective}}{\text{Per-Unit Contribution}}$$

$$\text{Breakeven Point (in units)} = \frac{\$40,000 + \$15,000}{\$5} = 11,000 \text{ units}$$

If the target return is expressed as a percentage of sales, it can be included in the breakeven formula as a variable cost. Suppose the marketer in the preceding example seeks a 10 percent return on sales. The desired return is $1 for each product sold (the $10 per-unit selling price multiplied by the 10 percent return on sales). In this case, the basic breakeven formula will remain unchanged, although the variable cost per unit will be increased to reflect the target return, and the per-unit contribution to fixed cost will be reduced to $4. As a result, the breakeven point will increase from 8,000 to 10,000 units:

$$\text{Breakeven Point} = \frac{\$40,000}{\$4} = 10,000 \text{ units}$$

✓ assessment check

1. Give the formula for finding the breakeven point, in units and in dollars.

2. What adjustments to the basic breakeven calculation must be made to include target returns?

Evaluation of Breakeven Analysis

Breakeven analysis is an effective tool for marketers in assessing the sales required for covering costs and achieving specified profit levels. It is easily understood by both marketing and nonmarketing executives and may help them decide whether required sales levels for a certain price are realistic goals. However, it has its shortcomings.

First, the model assumes that costs can be divided into fixed and variable categories. Some costs, such as salaries and advertising outlays, may be either fixed or variable depending on the particular situation. In addition, the model assumes that per-unit variable costs do not change at different levels of operation. However, these may vary because of quantity discounts, more efficient use of the workforce, or other economies resulting from increased levels of production and sales. Finally, the basic breakeven model does not consider demand. It is a cost-based model and does not directly address the crucial question of whether consumers will purchase the product at the specified price and in the quantities required for breaking even or generating profits. The marketer's challenge is to modify the breakeven analysis and the other cost-oriented pricing approaches to incorporate demand analysis. Pricing must be examined from the buyer's perspective. Such decisions cannot be made by considering only cost factors.

 6 List the chief advantages and shortcomings of using breakeven analysis in pricing decisions.

✓ assessment check

1. What are the advantages of breakeven analysis?

2. What are the disadvantages of breakeven analysis?

THE MODIFIED BREAKEVEN CONCEPT

Traditional economic theory considers both costs and demand in determining an equilibrium price. The dual elements of supply and demand are balanced at the point of equilibrium. In actual practice, however, most pricing approaches are largely cost oriented. Because purely cost-oriented approaches to pricing violate the marketing concept, modifications that add demand analysis to the pricing decision are required.

Consumer research on such issues as degree of price elasticity, consumer price expectations, existence and size of specific market segments, and buyer perceptions of strengths and weaknesses of substitute products is necessary for developing sales estimates at different prices. Because much of the resulting data involves perceptions, attitudes, and future expectations of present and potential customers, such estimates are likely to be less precise than cost estimates.

The breakeven analysis method illustrated in Figure 18.2 assumes a constant $10 retail price regardless of quantity. But what happens at different retail prices? As Figure 18.3 shows, a more sophisticated approach called **modified breakeven analysis** combines the traditional breakeven analysis model with an evaluation of consumer demand.

Table 18.4 summarizes both the cost and revenue aspects of a number of alternative retail prices. The $5 per-unit variable cost and the $40,000 total fixed cost are based on the costs used in the basic breakeven model. The expected unit sales for each specified retail price are obtained from marketing research. The table contains the information necessary for calculating the breakeven point for each of the five retail price alternatives. These points are shown in Figure 18.3(a).

modified breakeven analysis Pricing technique used to evaluate consumer demand by comparing the number of products that must be sold at a variety of prices to cover total cost with estimates of expected sales at the various prices.

figure 18.3

Modified Breakeven Chart: Parts A and B

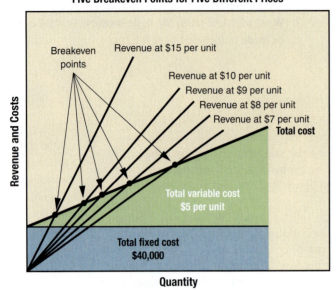

(a)
Five Breakeven Points for Five Different Prices

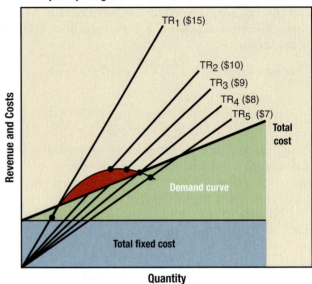

(b)
Superimposing a Demand Curve on the Breakeven Chart

The data shown in the first two columns of Table 18.4 represent a demand schedule that indicates the number of units consumers are expected to purchase at each of a series of retail prices. As Figure 18.3(b) shows, these data can be superimposed onto a breakeven chart to identify the range of feasible prices for the marketer to charge.

Figure 18.3 reveals that the range of profitable prices exists from a low of approximately $8 ($TR_4$) to a high of $10 ($TR_2$), with a price of $9 ($TR_3$) generating the greatest projected profits. Changing the retail price produces a new breakeven point. At a relatively high $15 ($TR_1$) retail price, the breakeven point is 4,000 units; at a $10 retail price, it is 8,000 units; and at the lowest price considered, $7 ($TR_5$), it is 20,000 units.

The contribution of modified breakeven analysis is that it forces the marketer to consider whether the consumer is likely to purchase the number of units required for achieving breakeven at a given price. It demonstrates that a large number of units sold does not necessarily produce added profits, because—other things equal—lower prices are necessary for stimulating additional sales. Consequently, it is important to consider both costs and consumer demand in determining the most appropriate price.

table 18.4 Revenue and Cost Data for Modified Breakeven Analysis

		Revenues		Costs			
PRICE	QUANTITY DEMANDED	TOTAL REVENUE	TOTAL FIXED COST	TOTAL VARIABLE COST	TOTAL COST	BREAKEVEN POINT (NUMBER OF SALES REQUIRED TO BREAK EVEN)	TOTAL PROFIT (OR LOSS)
$15	2,500	$37,500	$40,000	$12,500	$52,500	4,000	$(15,000)
10	10,000	100,000	40,000	50,000	90,000	8,000	10,000
9	13,000	117,000	40,000	65,000	105,000	10,000	12,000
8	14,000	112,000	40,000	70,000	110,000	13,334	2,000
7	15,000	105,000	40,000	75,000	115,000	20,000	(10,000)

YIELD MANAGEMENT

7 Explain the use of yield management in pricing decisions.

When most of a firm's costs are fixed over a wide range of outputs, the primary determinant of profitability will be the amount of revenue generated by sales. **Yield management** strategies allow marketers to vary prices based on such factors as demand, even though the cost of providing those goods or services remains the same. For example, ticket prices for Broadway hit *The Color Purple*, based on Alice Walker's Pulitzer Prize–winning novel, range from $66 to well over $100 for most performances. Wednesday matinees, which are usually less convenient for theatergoers, carry lower prices—$51 to $101—which are designed to fill the theater. With a production cost of more than $12 million and operating costs of about $500,000 a week, the show's producers estimated that it would take one year to recoup the show's investment if every performance had 75 percent attendance at full price.[28]

yield management Pricing strategy that allows marketers to vary prices based on such factors as demand, even though the cost of providing those goods or services remains the same.

Similar yield management strategies typify the marketing of such goods and services as the following:

- *Sports teams*—the San Francisco Giants charge more for weekend games, and the Colorado Rockies raise ticket prices based on the crowd-pleasing power of visiting teams

- *Lodging*—lower prices in the off-season and higher prices during peak-season periods; low-priced weekend rates (except in locations such as Las Vegas, New Orleans, and Charleston, South Carolina, with high weekend tourist visits)

- *Auto rental*—lower prices on weekends when business demand is low and higher prices during the week when business demand is higher

- *Airfares*—lower prices on nonrefundable tickets with travel restrictions such as advance-purchase and Saturday-night stay requirements and penalties for flight changes and higher prices on refundable tickets that can be changed without penalty

The following example from the airline industry demonstrates how yield management maximizes revenues in situations in which costs are fixed.[29]

Airlines constantly monitor reservations on every flight. Beginning approximately 330 days before the flight, space is allocated between full-fare, discount-fare, and free tickets for frequent flyers who qualify for complimentary tickets. This allocation is monitored and adjusted at regular intervals until the flight departs.

Assume, for example, that Northwest Airlines has scheduled a 180-seat plane as Flight 1480 with an 8 a.m. departure from Memphis to Minneapolis on October 23. When Flight 1480 leaves its gate, all costs associated with the flight (fuel, crew, and other operating expenses) are fixed. The pricing that maximizes revenues on this flight will also maximize profits. An examination of past sales indicates that Northwest could sell 40 to 60 round-trip, full-fare tickets at $600 per passenger and 100 to 150 round-trip restricted-fare tickets at $200 per passenger. Demand for frequent-flyer space should be at least 10 seats.

If Northwest reserves 60 seats for full-fare passengers and accepts reservations for 110 restricted-fare tickets but sells only 40 full-fare tickets (leaving 20 vacant seats), total revenues will be as follows:

$$\text{Revenues} = (40 \times \$600) + (110 \times \$200) = \$46,000$$

On the other hand, if Northwest's pricing decision makers want to reduce vacancies, they might decide to reduce the number of full-fare tickets to 20 and increase the restricted-fare tickets to 150. If the plane leaves the gate at full capacity, the flight will generate the following total revenues:

$$\text{Revenues} = (20 \times \$600) + (150 \times \$200) = \$42,000$$

Instead of rigidly maintaining the allocations established nearly a year before the flight, Northwest will use yield management to maximize the revenue per flight. In this example, the airline initially holds 60 full-fare seats and accepts reservations for up to 110 restricted-fare seats. Thirty days before the October 23 departure, updated computer projections indicate that 40 full-fare seats are likely to be sold. The allocation is now revised to 40 full-fare and 130 restricted-fare tickets. A full flight leaves the gate and revenues are as follows:

$$\text{Revenues} = (40 \times \$600) + (130 \times \$200) = \$50,000$$

assessment check

1. What is modified breakeven analysis?
2. Explain the goal of yield management.

Applying yield management for the Memphis–Minneapolis flight increases revenues by at least $4,000 over the inflexible approach of making advance allocations and failing to adjust them based on passenger reservations and other data.

8   Identify the major pricing challenges facing online and international marketers.

GLOBAL ISSUES IN PRICE DETERMINATION

It is equally important for a firm engaging in global marketing to use a pricing strategy that reflects its overall marketing strategy. Prices must support the company's broader goals, including product development, advertising and sales, customer support, competitive plans, and financial objectives.

In general, firms can use five pricing objectives to set prices in global marketing. Four of them are the same pricing objectives that we discussed earlier in the chapter: profitability, volume, meeting competition, and prestige. In addition, international marketers work to achieve a fifth objective: price stability.

In the global arena, marketers may choose profitability objectives if their company is a price leader that tends to establish international prices. Profitability objectives also make sense if a firm is a low-cost supplier that can make a good profit on sales.

Volume objectives become especially important when nations lower their trade barriers to expose domestic markets to foreign competition. As the European Union lowered economic barriers between countries, for instance, competition for customers soared. A recent trend has been mergers of European firms to form larger companies that can achieve volume objectives. Luxembourg steel company Arcelor bought big stakes in two Costa Rican firms and one Turkish firm and made a hostile takeover bid for Dofasco, Canada's biggest steel producer. German drug company Merck initiated a hostile bid for rival Schering.[30]

Increased competition in Europe has also spurred firms to work toward the third pricing objective of meeting competitors' prices. The widespread adoption of the euro, the currency of the European Union, has become a driving force in price convergence. "In 2002, the span of prices from the cheapest to the most expensive country was 71 percent," according to the CEO of the marketing research firm ACNielsen Europe. "Today, for identical international brand products, we see that gap reduced to 50 percent. Among Europe's larger markets, stagnating growth and flat consumer demand combined with an increasing competitive retailing industry, are forcing prices down." The company's Euro Price Barometer surveyed the cost of 160 products sold at more than 25,000 grocery stores, supermarkets, and hypermarkets in fifteen European countries to find that the introduction of the euro had increased price competition.[31]

Prestige is a valid pricing objective in international marketing when products are associated with intangible benefits, such as high quality, exclusiveness, or attractive design. The greater a product's perceived benefits, the higher its price can be. Marketers must be aware, however, that cultural perceptions of quality can differ from one country to the next. Sometimes items that command prestige prices in the United States are considered run-of-the-mill in other nations; sometimes products that are anything but prestigious in America seem exotic to overseas consumers. American patrons, for instance, view McDonald's restaurants as affordable fast-food eateries, but in China, they are seen as fashionable and relatively expensive.

© ASSOCIATED PRESS, AP

Wal-Mart not only gets many of its products from China but has entered the competitive Chinese market.

The fifth pricing objective, price stability, is desirable in international markets, although it is difficult to achieve. Wars, terrorism, economic downturns, changing governments and political parties, and shifting trade policies can alter prices. A challenge for Wal-Mart in the years ahead will be making substantial inroads in China, where it plans to grow and where local retailers control about 90 percent of the market through price dominance. Wal-Mart will also have to surpass the freshness and quality of the food products offered by the country's many street vendors, who sell everything from live chickens to reptiles with no overhead at prices that are hard to beat. Further hampering Wal-Mart's ability to compete on price may be the expected high costs of training local workers and managers who are not very loyal and dealing with costly problems of piracy and corruption.[32]

Price stability can be especially important for producers of commodities—goods and services that have easily accessible substitutes that other nations can supply quickly. Countries that export international commodities, such as wood, chemicals, and agricultural crops, suffer economically when their prices fluctuate. A nation such as Nicaragua, which exports sugarcane, can find that its balance of payments changes drastically when the international price for sugar shifts. This makes it vulnerable to stiff price competition from other sugarcane producers.

In contrast, countries that export value-oriented products, rather than commodities, tend to enjoy more stable prices. Prices of electronic equipment and automobiles tend to fluctuate far less than prices of crops such as sugarcane and bananas.

 assessment check

1. What are five pricing objectives in global and online marketing?

2. Why is price stability difficult to achieve in online and global marketing?

Strategic Implications of Marketing in the 21st Century

This chapter has focused on traditional pricing concepts and methods—principles that are critical to all marketing strategies, especially in e-business. Consumers can now compare prices quickly, heightening the already intense competitive pricing environment. The Web allows for prices to be negotiated on the spot, and anything can be auctioned. For products as varied as airline tickets and automobiles, the Web allows consumers to name their price.

While Internet shopping has not resulted in massive price cutting, it has increased the options available for consumers. Online price comparison engines, known as *shopping bots,* promise to help consumers find the lowest price for any good or service. Reverse auctions offered by sites such as Priceline.com, which allow customers to submit the highest price they are willing to pay for airline tickets, could conceivably be extended to other types of goods and are already gaining in popularity in business-to-business purchasing.

Electronic delivery of music, books, and other goods and services will only lead to further price reductions. E-business has smoothed out the friction of time, which kept pricing relatively static. The current obsession with time and the ability to measure it will change the perceptions and pricing of tangible goods. A growing number of products are not made until they are ordered, and increasingly, their prices are no longer fixed; instead, prices can shift up and down in response to changing market conditions.

REVIEW OF CHAPTER OBJECTIVES

1   Outline the legal constraints on pricing.

A variety of laws affect pricing decisions. Antitrust legislation provides a general set of constraints. The Robinson-Patman Act amended the Clayton Act to prohibit price discrimination in sales to other producers, wholesalers, or retailers that are not based on a cost differential. This law does not cover export markets or sales to the ultimate consumer. At the state level, unfair-trade laws require sellers to maintain minimum prices for comparable merchandise. These laws have become less frequently enforced in recent years. Fair-trade laws represented one legal barrier to competition that was removed in the face of growing price competition. These laws permitted manufacturers to set minimum retail prices for products and to require their dealers to sign contracts agreeing to abide by such prices. The Consumer Goods Pricing Act banned interstate use of fair-trade laws.

2   Identify the major categories of pricing objectives.

Pricing objectives should be the natural consequence of overall organizational goals and more specific marketing goals. They can be classified into four major groups: (1) profitability objectives, including profit maximization and target returns; (2) volume objectives, including sales maximization and market share; (3) meeting competition objectives; and (4) prestige objectives.

3   Explain price elasticity and its determinants.

Elasticity is an important element in price determination. The degree of consumer responsiveness to price changes is affected by such factors as (1) availability of substitute or complementary goods, (2) the classification of a good or service as a luxury or a necessity, (3) the portion of a person's budget spent on an item, and (4) the time perspective.

4   List the practical problems involved in applying price theory concepts to actual pricing decisions.

Three problems are present in using price theory in actual practice. First, many firms do not attempt to maximize profits, a basic assumption of price theory. Second, it is difficult to accurately estimate demand curves. Finally, inadequate training of managers and poor communication between economists and managers make it difficult to apply price theory in the real world.

5   Explain the major cost-plus approaches to price setting.

Cost-plus pricing uses a base-cost figure per unit and adds a markup to cover unassigned costs and to provide a profit. It is the most commonly used method of setting prices today. There are two primary cost-oriented pricing procedures. Full-cost pricing uses all relevant variable costs in setting a product's price and allocates those fixed costs that cannot be directly attributed to the production of the specific item being priced. Incremental-cost pricing attempts to use only those costs directly attributable to a specific output in setting prices to overcome the arbitrary allocation of fixed expenses. The basic limitation of cost-oriented pricing is that it does not adequately account for product demand.

6   List the chief advantages and shortcomings of using breakeven analysis in pricing decisions.

Breakeven analysis is a means of determining the number of goods or services that must be sold at a given price to generate revenue sufficient for covering total costs. It is easily understood by managers and may help them decide whether required sales levels for a certain price are realistic goals. Its shortcomings are as follows. First, the model assumes that cost can be divided into fixed and variable categories and ignores the problems of arbitrarily making some allocations. Second, it assumes that per-unit variable costs do not change at different levels of operation, ignoring the possibility of quantity discounts, more efficient use of the workforce, and other possible economies. Third, the basic breakeven model does not consider demand. It is a cost-based model and fails to directly address the crucial question of whether consumers will actually purchase the product at the specified price and in the quantities required for breaking even or generating profits.

7 Explain the use of yield management in pricing decisions.

Breakeven analysis is a means of determining the number of products that must be sold at a given price to generate sufficient revenue to cover total costs. The modified breakeven concept combines traditional breakeven analysis with an evaluation of consumer demand. It directly addresses the key question of whether consumers will actually purchase the product at different prices and in what quantities. Yield management pricing strategies are designed to maximize revenues in situations in which costs are fixed, such as airfares, auto rentals, and theater tickets.

8 Identify the major pricing challenges facing online and international marketers.

In general, firms can choose from among five pricing objectives to set prices in global marketing. Four of these objectives are the same pricing objectives discussed earlier: profitability, volume, meeting competition, and prestige. The fifth objective is price stability, which is difficult to achieve because wars, border conflicts, terrorism, economic trends, changing governments and political parties, and shifting trade policies can alter prices. The same types of changes can alter pricing in online marketing.

✓ *assessment check* **answers**

1.1 What was the purpose of the Robinson–Patman Act?

The Robinson-Patman Act amended the Clayton Act to prohibit price discrimination in sales to other producers, wholesalers, or retailers that are not based on a cost differential.

1.2 What laws require sellers to maintain minimum prices for comparable merchandise?

At the state level, unfair-trade laws require sellers to maintain minimum prices for comparable merchandise.

1.3 What laws allow manufacturers to set minimum retail prices for their products?

Fair-trade laws permitted manufacturers to set minimum retail prices for products and to require their dealers to sign contracts agreeing to abide by such prices.

2.1 What are target-return objectives?

Target-return objectives are short-run or long-run goals that are usually stated as percentages of sales or investment.

2.2 What is value pricing?

Value pricing emphasizes the benefits a product provides in comparison to the price and quality levels of competing offerings.

2.3 How do prestige objectives affect a seller's pricing strategy?

Prestige pricing establishes a relatively high price to develop and maintain an image of quality that appeals to status-conscious customers. The seller uses price to create an overall image of the firm.

2.4 What goals does pricing strategy help a not-for-profit organization achieve?

Pricing strategy helps not-for-profit organizations achieve a variety of goals: profit maximization, cost recovery, market incentives, and market suppression.

2.5 What are the two basic ways in which marketers determine prices?

Marketers determine prices by applying the theoretical concepts of supply and demand and by completing cost-oriented analysis.

assessment check **answers**

3.1   What are the determinants of elasticity?

The degree of consumer responsiveness to price changes—elasticity—is affected by such factors as (1) availability of substitute or complementary goods, (2) the classification of a good or service as a luxury or a necessity, (3) the portion of a person's budget spent on an item, and (4) the time perspective.

3.2   What is the usual relationship between elasticity and revenue?

A price cut increases revenue only for a product with elastic demand, and a price increase raises revenue only for a product with inelastic demand.

4.1   List the three reasons why it is difficult to put price theory into practice.

A basic assumption of price theory is that all firms attempt to maximize profits. This does not always happen in practice. A second reason is that demand curves can be extremely difficult to estimate. Finally, managers can be inadequately trained, causing poor communication between economists and managers, which makes it difficult to apply price theory in the real world.

5.1   What is full-cost pricing?

Full-cost pricing uses all relevant variable costs in setting a product's price.

5.2   What is incremental-cost pricing?

Incremental-cost pricing attempts to use only costs directly attributable to a specific output in setting prices to overcome the arbitrary allocation of fixed expenses.

5.3   Give the formula for finding the breakeven point, in units and in dollars.

Breakeven point (in units) = Total fixed cost/Per-unit contribution to fixed cost. Breakeven point (in dollars) = Total fixed cost/ (1 − Variable cost per unit price).

5.4   What adjustments to the basic breakeven calculation must be made to include target returns?

Breakeven point (including specific dollar target return) = (Total fixed cost + Profit objective)/Per-unit contribution.

6.1   What are the advantages of breakeven analysis?

Breakeven analysis is easily understood by managers and may help them decide whether required sales levels for a certain price are realistic goals.

6.2   What are the disadvantages of breakeven analysis?

First, the model assumes that cost can be divided into fixed and variable categories and ignores the problems of arbitrarily making some allocations. Second, it assumes that per-unit variable costs do not change at different levels of operation, ignoring the possibility of quantity discounts, more efficient use of the workforce, and other possible economies. Third, the basic breakeven model does not consider demand.

7.1   What is modified breakeven analysis?

The modified breakeven concept combines traditional breakeven analysis with an evaluation of consumer demand. It directly addresses the key question of whether consumers will actually purchase the product at different prices and in what quantities.

7.2   Explain the goal of yield management.

Yield management pricing strategies are designed to maximize revenues in situations in which costs are fixed, such as airfares, auto rentals, and theater tickets.

assessment check **answers**

8.1   What are five pricing objectives in global and online marketing?

Five pricing objectives in global and online marketing are profitability, volume, meeting competition, prestige, and price stability.

8.2   Why is price stability difficult to achieve in online and global marketing?

Price stability is difficult to achieve because wars, border conflicts, terrorism, economic trends, changing governments and political parties, and shifting trade policies can alter prices.

MARKETING TERMS YOU NEED TO KNOW

price 602
Robinson-Patman Act 603
unfair-trade laws 604
fair-trade laws 604
profit maximization 607

target-return objective 607
Profit Impact of Market Strategies (PIMS) project 607
value pricing 608
customary prices 611

elasticity 615
breakeven analysis 619
modified breakeven analysis 621
yield management 623

OTHER IMPORTANT MARKETING TERMS

marginal analysis 607
market-share objective 607
demand 613
supply 613
pure competition 613

monopolistic competition 613
oligopoly 613
monopoly 614
variable costs 614
fixed costs 614

average total costs 614
marginal cost 614
cost-plus pricing 618
full-cost pricing 618
incremental-cost pricing 619

ASSURANCE OF LEARNING REVIEW

1. Distinguish between fair-trade and unfair-trade laws. As a consumer, would you support either fair-trade or unfair-trade laws? Would your answer change if you were the owner of a small store?
2. Give an example of each of the major categories of pricing objectives.
3. What are the major price implications of the PIMS studies? Suggest possible explanations for the relationships the PIMS studies reveal.
4. Identify each factor influencing elasticity and give a specific example of how it affects the degree of elasticity in a good or service.

5. What are the practical problems in applying price theory concepts to actual pricing decisions?
6. Explain the advantages and drawbacks of using incremental-cost pricing rather than full-cost pricing.
7. How can locating the breakeven point assist in price determination?
8. Explain the advantage of modified breakeven analysis over the basic breakeven formula.
9. Explain how the use of yield management can result in greater revenue than other pricing strategies.

PROJECTS AND TEAMWORK EXERCISES

1. In small teams, categorize each of the following as a specific type of pricing objective. Suggest a company or product likely to use each pricing objective. Compare your findings.
   a. 5 percent increase in profits over the previous year
   b. prices no more than 6 percent higher than prices quoted by independent dealers
   c. 5 percent increase in market share
   d. 25 percent return on investment (before taxes)
   e. setting the highest prices in the product category to maintain favorable brand image

2. In pairs, discuss the market situations that exist for the following products. Defend your answers and present them to the class.
   a. DVD players
   b. golf clubs
   c. soybeans
   d. remote control car alarms
   e. razors

3. How are the following prices determined and what do they have in common?
   a. ticket to a local museum
   b. your college tuition
   c. local sales tax rate
   d. printing of business cards
   e. lawn mowers

4. WebTech Development of Nashville, Tennessee, is considering the possible introduction of a new product proposed by its research and development staff. The firm's marketing director estimates that the product can be marketed at a price of $70. Total fixed cost is $278,000, and average variable cost is calculated at $48.
   a. What is the breakeven point in units for the proposed product?
   b. The firm's CEO has suggested a target profit return of $214,000 for the proposed product. How many units must be sold to both break even and achieve this target return?

5. The marketing research staff at Cleveland-based Cyber Novelties has developed the following sales estimates for a proposed new item the firm plans to market through direct mail sales:

PROPOSED SELLING PRICE	SALES ESTIMATE (UNITS)
$8	55,000
10	22,000
15	14,000
20	5,000
24	2,800

The new product has a total fixed cost of $60,000 and a $7 variable cost per unit.
   a. Which of the proposed selling prices would generate a profit for Cyber Novelties?
   b. Cyber Novelties' director of marketing also estimates that an additional $0.50 per-unit allocation for extra promotion will produce the following sales increases: 60,000 units at an $8 unit selling price, 28,000 units at $10, 17,000 units at $15, 6,000 units at $20, and 3,500 units at $24. Indicate the feasible range of prices if this proposal is implemented and results in the predicted sales increases.
   c. Indicate the feasible price or prices if the $0.50 per-unit additional promotion proposal is not implemented but management insists on a $25,000 target return.

6. Research the price schedule at your local movie theater multiplex. What pricing strategy accounts for any price differentials you discover? Why don't matinee prices constitute price discrimination against those who don't qualify for the discounts?

7. Why is it more expensive to buy beer and a hot dog at a Major League Baseball game than it is to buy them at local retail stores?

8. Public funding of national parks has been declining for many years. What would you expect to happen to entry and use fees in this case? Research fees at parks in your state or region to verify your answer and report to the class.

9. How do cell phone companies make money by charging a flat rate per month for a set number of minutes, such as $35 for 300 minutes? Can you think of another plan that would be more profitable? Would it appeal to consumers?

10. Some airline industry executives believe that lower, simpler fares for the major carriers will earn goodwill from customers and send a clear marketing message that they are ready to compete with low-cost rivals. But few big airlines are embracing a new pricing system, frequently opting to launch new no-frills discount airlines to compete with AirTran, JetBlue, Southwest, and the other low-cost carriers. Why do you think they are hesitating?

CRITICAL-THINKING EXERCISES

1. Prices at amusement parks are expected to rise because operators such as Disney and Universal Studios are adding new rides and coping with the rising cost of fuel; they are also copying each other's prices. List as many things as you can think of that parks like these offer patrons in return for their money. Which of these do you think are directly reflected in the price of admission?

2. Musical artists earn only about 9 percent in royalties per CD, using a royalty base of retail price less 25 percent for packaging costs. The rest goes to the producer and to cover recording costs, promotion, copies given away to radio stations and reviewers, and other costs such as videos. What do you think happens to the artist's royalties when a CD is marked down to sell faster? Consider two cases: (1) the marked-down CD sells more copies, and (2) it sells the same number of copies as before.

3. One writer advises consumers not to worry about rising gasoline prices, the cost of which can easily be covered by forgoing one takeout meal a month, but to worry about how high energy prices will affect the rest of the economy. For example, each dollar-a-barrel price increase is equivalent to a $20 million-a-day "tax" on the economy. Explain what this means.

4. Ajax Motor Company recently announced that it will rely less on high-volume strategies such as discounts and rebates to improve its profitability. Another strategy it will employ is to sell fewer cars to rental fleets, which eventually return the cars to Ajax for sale at low auction prices. How do these types of sales affect Ajax's profitability?

ETHICS EXERCISES

You work for a major bank in your town. The bank has decided it needs new sources of revenue to cover costs for its free checking account customers. As a result, management implements an automatic courtesy-overdraft fee for people who overdraw their free checking accounts with a debit card or ATM withdrawal. Under this service, the bank will automatically cover the overdraft and charge the customer a $30 fee—but it won't notify the customer ahead of time. The bank does not plan to advertise this fee to account holders. Managers at the bank maintain that this fee will save customers the embarrassment of having their purchases denied and any returned check fees from merchants.[33]

1. You know that the bank advertises its free checking account service widely in the local media. But the new fees are not advertised, and it bothers you. What course of action would you take?

2. The bank also has a program in which customers can sign up to cover bounced checks through an automatic savings account transfer. That service is less costly to the account holder, but it doesn't generate as much revenue. A customer has just come to you to open a free checking account. Do you explain the two options in detail to the customer, or because the courtesy overdraft is a routine feature of free checking, do you sign the customer up for the "free" account?

INTERNET EXERCISES

1. **Legal and ethical issues in pricing.** As noted in the chapter, numerous legal and ethical issues result from pricing. Review each of the following and prepare summaries you can bring to class to participate in a discussion on pricing.
   a. *Dumping.* Many trade disputes involve a practice called dumping. Visit http://www.wto.org/english/tratop_e/adp_e/adp_e.htm to learn more about dumping including several recent dumping cases.
   b. *Price fixing.* In most communities, all real estate agents charge sellers a 6 percent commission. Critics contend that this amounts to price fixing. Using a search engine such as Google, find several recent articles on real estate commissions and price fixing. Where do the National Association of Realtors (http://www.realtor.org) and the Federal Trade Commission (http://www.ftc.gov) stand on the issue of fixed real estate commissions?
   c. *Price discrimination.* In the United States, hospitals and physicians often charge different patients different amounts depending on their insurance coverage. Using Google or another search engine, find two or three recent articles on the topic of the pricing of health care services. Why are these practices not violations of the Robinson-Patman Act?

2. **Yield management.** Airlines, hotels, and rental car companies all practice yield management. Complete the following exercises. Relate your experience to the discussion of yield management found in the chapter.

   a. Assume you wish to fly round trip between the New York City area and Southern California. You are flexible in terms of day of travel, time of travel, and departure and arrival airports. Visit at least two airline Web sites along with a travel site such as Expedia (http://www.expedia.com) or Orbitz (http://www.orbitz.com). Record and summarize the different fares you find. Why are some fares higher than others?
   b. Now, assume you want to stay in a hotel in a popular vacation area, such as Maui, Las Vegas, or Orlando. Visiting at least two hotel chains and travel Web sites, research hotel rates for varying lengths of stay, during different times of the year. Summarize your findings. How much variation did you find in rates for the same hotel?
   c. You would like to rent a car in each of the following cities: Seattle; Charleston, South Carolina; and Cleveland. Visiting at least two car rental and travel Web sites, research car rental rates during different times of year, on different days of the week, and for different lengths of time. Record your findings and note any patterns you see.

Note: Internet Web addresses change frequently. If you don't find the exact site listed, you may need to access the organization's home page and search from there or use a search engine such as Google.

CASE 18.1   Value Menus Fill Customer Cravings

Value menus, one of the fast-food industry's most successful pricing strategies, started by accident. Back in 1988, Taco Bell managers were trying to figure out how to increase sales of their new steak and chicken fajitas, which were high-priced by fast-food standards. One day they heard about a Las Vegas franchise that was successfully competing against its local McDonald's by reducing prices, driving up sales volume. Taco Bell jumped at the opportunity, tested the concept, and quickly introduced value menus in all its stores. Sales rebounded by more than 20 percent, and the fast-food landscape was reshaped.

Value menu strategies remained popular with many fast-food chains for years, despite the reduced profitability they brought. Higher volume—especially among young consumers age 18 to 24—and long hours of operation, sometimes around the clock, helped compensate for the crippling price wars between McDonald's, Burger King, Wendy's, KFC, and many others. Then more competition appeared in the form of quick-serve chains such as Baja Fresh and Panera Bread Company, whose popularity grew by serving alternatives to burgers. Finally, however, fast-food outlets began to suffer from widespread criticism of their high-calorie meals and from the sameness of their menu offerings. Consumers began to worry about weight gain, diabetes, and high-fat, high-sodium food served in giant portions. Some chains began to decline. McDonald's reported its first quarterly loss as sales dropped and its stock price fell. Some stores did away with their value menus to prop up their profits.

Healthier offerings soon cropped up on fast-food menus, including fresh fruits, salads, and reduced-fat, reduced-calorie offerings. Some were more successful than others, and after a trial period, some fast-food outlets reverted to their old standbys. Wendy's took out its salad bars, and McDonald's dropped the McLean burger. "What Americans say they want and what they actually do are two different things," says one marketing research executive about the public's experiment with healthier fast food. But both chains, in time, offered packaged salads in their menus for those concerned about calories.

And later, value menus also returned. Wendy's offers a 99-cent value menu, KFC has a 99-cent chicken sandwich, and Burger King's extensive value menu features a $1 Whopper Junior. McDonald's, which has improved both its appearance and its service and made a dramatic profit turnaround, offers a Dollar Menu of popular food items. McDonald's promotes its dollar menu with hip and stylish advertising.

The next phase in fast-food pricing might be tiered pricing, with some value-menu items priced at $1.29. The innovator? It's Taco Bell again.

Questions for Critical Thinking

1. Do you think value pricing and dollar pricing are effective strategies for increasing market share in the fast-food market even if they reduce the profit stores can earn on each meal? Why or why not?

2. Fast-food chains may face renewed challenges to their menu offerings as health concerns about obesity and other ills increase, and as alternatives such as Panera Bread and Baja Fresh continue to grow. Do you think pricing strategies can continue to protect the fast-food giants against these threats? Why or why not?

Sources: Melanie Warner, "Salads or No, Cheap Burgers Revive McDonald's," *New York Times*, April 19, 2006, **http://www.nytimes.com**; Stuart Morris, "Redefining the Value Menu Will Reinvigorate Sales, Profits for Quick-Service Operations," *Nation's Restaurant News*, February 6, 2006, **http://www.findarticles.com**; Jyoti Thottam, "Fast-Food Face-Off," *Time*, July 2005, **http://www.time.com**.

VIDEO CASE 18.2   Washburn Guitars: How Much Is the Maya Worth?

The written video case on Washburn Guitars appears on page VC-21. The recently filmed Washburn Guitars video is designed to expand and highlight the concepts in this chapter and the concepts and questions covered in the written video case.

CHAPTER 19

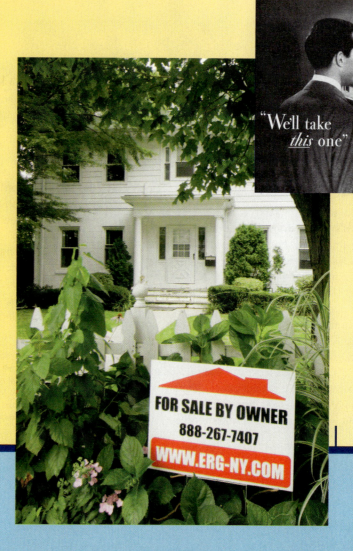

"We'll take *this* one"

How Much Does It Cost to Sell Your Home?

Buying a home is one of the biggest purchases you make during your lifetime. So when you think about its price, you usually think about how much it costs to buy it. But in the real estate market, the seller often pays a hefty sum—about 6 percent of the purchase price—to a real estate agent as a commission for selling the property. This fee and the exclusivity that surrounds the listing of homes have sparked debate among buyers, sellers, and the National Association of Realtors. It has even prompted a lawsuit against the association by the Justice Department, which claims that the association's rules for listings create an unfair disadvantage against online brokers and owners who prefer to sell on their own.

Enter entrepreneurs such as Mary Clare Murphy, Christie Miller, and Colby Sambrotto. Murphy and Miller, who live in Madison, Wisconsin, decided together that houses in their area could be sold more reasonably. So they started a Web site called FsboMadison.com, where homeowners could list their houses for sale and buyers could view them. They charge only $150 to list a home at the site and include a signature teal-blue yard sign. When a seller is experiencing financial hardship, Murphy and Miller waive the $150 fee. They do not accept referral fees from real estate agents, attorneys, or other professionals associated with the home-selling business. And they don't accept credit cards. Instead, they insist on payment by personal check because, they claim, it reduces impulse decisions. Murphy and Miller collect much less in fees than they would if they sold the same number of houses—about 1,440 in one

year—as real estate agents. But they still make a comfortable living. "I don't think we've done anything unusual," says Murphy. "We are not out to take over the market, to eliminate the real estate world. We're just here to offer this service."

Colby Sambrotto also runs an Internet site for home sales, called ForSalebyOwner.com. Unlike most traditional real estate agents, Sambrotto looks forward to slowdowns in the real estate market. That's because during a slowdown, both buyers and sellers are looking to cut costs. If a seller can cut the cost of a real estate agent's commission, he or she can reduce the sale price of the home to make it more attractive to buyers and still make a profit. It costs sellers only $250 to list their homes for six months, including a yard sign and a slide

TOP PHOTO: IMAGE COURTESY OF THE ADVERTISING ARCHIVES
BOTTOM PHOTO: © ASSOCIATED PRESS

Pricing Strategies

1 Compare the alternative pricing strategies and explain when each strategy is most appropriate.

2 Describe how prices are quoted.

3 Identify the various pricing policy decisions that marketers must make.

4 Relate price to consumer perceptions of quality.

5 Contrast competitive bidding and negotiated prices.

6 Explain the importance of transfer pricing.

7 Compare the three alternative global pricing strategies.

8 Relate the concepts of cannibalization, bundle pricing, and bots to online pricing strategies.

---

presentation at the ForSalebyOwner.com site. Sambrotto has expanded his business from the East Coast across the country, but not without resistance from real-estate organizations. ForSalebyOwner.com has had as many as 50,000 listings in a year, and it is targeted to grow to 200,000 annually, which is small in comparison with the Multiple Listing Service (MLS) that licensed Realtors put together.

But Sambrotto recently made a deal with The Home Depot, which will carry ForSalebyOwner.com's CD-ROM tutorial package on selling a home in its stores. He notes that Internet home sales continue to rise, even as the real estate market in general has cooled. "The residential real estate market has changed more in the past five years than it did in the previous 90 years combined," he observes. "Most of that is due to the Internet. It's a great tool for buying and selling a home." In fact, nearly 80 percent of buyers in one survey said they used the Internet to look for a new home, compared with 2 percent a decade ago.

Most homeowners still hire professional real estate agents, who can market properties and help smooth the path toward a good price. "[Consumers] understand that to market [a home] themselves is a 24/7 job," says Thomas M. Stevens, president of the National Association of Realtors. "They have to be available for people to view their home all the time." Still, those extra dollars can add substantially to a profit—and sometimes make a difference in what a seller can purchase the next time around.[1]

evolution *of a* brand

The real estate market is constantly evolving and—like most other industries—has been affected tremendously by the Internet. Traditionally, real-estate agents charged the seller a percentage of the purchase price as a commission, but that practice is changing as Internet services help buyers and sellers connect directly, without the assistance of a broker. ForSalebyOwner.com and FsboMadison.com have already begun to establish a presence in the real estate market. Sellers who list homes with these two online services help develop the brands simply by placing signs in their yards. Word of mouth, especially for successful transactions, also enhances the brand. And as more and more buyers and sellers turn to the Internet in general to look for or list houses, each of these firms will find ways to distinguish themselves from others.

- Describe two or three ways that online listing services such as ForSalebyOwner.com and FsboMadison.com could attract new buyers and sellers.

- The National Association of Realtors emphasizes that its members create value for buyers and sellers by marketing homes in creative ways, reducing stress, and avoiding legal snags—thus earning their commission. But online listing services are gaining ground because of price. How might Realtors combat this competition?

Chapter Overview

Setting prices is neither a one-time decision nor a standard routine. As you learned in the story on real estate sales, sometimes pricing creates debate, and sometimes it is the catalyst for change. Pricing is a dynamic function of the marketing mix. While about half of all companies change prices once a year or less frequently, one in ten does so every month. Online companies, which face enormous price pressures, may adjust prices more often depending on what they are selling. Some firms negotiate prices on the spot, as in the case of a car dealership or an antique shop.

Companies translate pricing objectives into pricing decisions in two major steps. First, someone takes responsibility for making pricing decisions and administering the resulting pricing structure. Second, someone sets the overall pricing structure—that is, basic prices and appropriate discounts for channel members, quantity purchases, and geographic and promotional considerations.

The decision to make price adjustments is directly related to demand. Most businesses slowly change the amounts they charge cus-tomers, even when they clearly recognize strong demand. Instead of raising prices, they may scale down customer service or add fees to cover rising costs. They may also wait to raise prices until they see what their competitors will do.

Significant price changes in the retail gasoline and airline industries occur in the form of a **step out**, in which one firm raises prices and then waits to see if others follow suit. If competitors fail to respond by increasing their prices, the company making the step out usually reduces prices to the original level. In an eighteen-month period, U.S. airlines succeeded in raising and maintaining higher fares in the industry 21 times, but they failed to do so 17 times. United, American, and Delta Airlines recently attempted a $10 hike in round-trip business fares, but they soon reversed course because others did not follow suit. "We rescinded because we did not see other airlines match the increase," said a United spokesperson.[2]

Few businesses want the distinction of being the first to charge higher prices. Because many firms base their prices on manufacturing costs rather than consumer demand, they may wait for increases in their own costs before responding with price changes. These increases generally emerge more slowly than changes in consumer demand. Finally, because many business executives believe that steady prices help preserve long-term relationships with customers, they are reluctant to raise prices even when strong demand probably justifies the change.

Chapter 18 introduced the concept of price and its role in the economic system and marketing strategy. This chapter examines various pricing strategies and price structures, such as reductions from list prices, and geographic considerations. It then looks at the primary pricing policies, including psychological pricing, price flexibility, product-line pricing, and promotional pricing, as well as price–quality relationships. Competitive and negotiated prices are discussed, and one section focuses entirely on transfer pricing. Finally, the chapter concludes by describing important factors in pricing goods and services for online and global markets.

PRICING STRATEGIES

The specific strategies that firms use to price goods and services grow out of the marketing strategies they formulate to accomplish overall organizational objectives. One firm's marketers may price their products to attract customers across a wide range; another group of marketers may set prices to appeal to a small segment of a larger market; still another group may simply try to match competitors' price tags. In general, firms can choose from three pricing strategies: skimming, penetration, and competitive pricing. The following sections look at these choices in more detail.

SKIMMING PRICING STRATEGY

Derived from the expression "skimming the cream," **skimming pricing strategies** are also known as **market-plus pricing.** They involve intentionally setting a relatively high price compared with the prices of competing products. Although some firms continue to use a skimming strategy throughout most stages of the product life cycle, it is more commonly used as a market entry price for distinctive goods or services with little or no initial competition. When the supply begins to exceed demand, or when competition catches up, the initial high price is dropped.

Such was the case with high-definition televisions (HDTVs), whose average price was $19,000, including installation, when they were first introduced. The resulting sticker shock kept them out of the range of most household budgets. But nearly a decade later, price cuts have brought both LCD and plasma models into the reach of mainstream consumers. One of Sharp's most popular LCD models sells for $1,700. But competition among the high-end firms is not the sole reason for these price drops. Budget brands such as Syntax and Westinghouse are pressuring the market. Syntax offers an LCD that competes with Sharp's for around $1,100.[3]

A company may practice a skimming strategy in setting a market-entry price when it introduces a distinctive good or service with little or no competition. Or it may use this strategy to market higher-end goods such as HDTVs. British vacuum cleaner manufacturer Dyson has used this practice. Offering entirely new design and engineering, Dyson sells its vacuum cleaners for between $420 and $620, far more than the average vacuum, which goes for around $100. Even iRobot's automated Roomba retails for about $200—and that machine, claims the company, does all the work for you. In fact, the

1   Compare the alternative pricing strategies and explain when each strategy is most appropriate.

Pricing in the real estate market depends on a variety of factors, such as whether a seller chooses to use a real estate agent. Coldwell Banker, one of the largest U.S. real-estate firms, uses different divisions such as Previews International to market homes in various price ranges.

skimming pricing strategy Pricing strategy involving the use of a high price relative to competitive offerings.

Dyson emphasizes the unique engineering and design of its vacuums. The firm uses a skimming pricing strategy.

Roomba followed quickly on the heels of the first robotic vacuum for consumers, the Electrolux Trilobite, which sold for $2,000. At first, vacuum manufacturers believed they had a premium product with the robotic vacuum. But their hopes were dashed when a robotics company decided they could make one and sell it much more cheaply.[4]

In some cases, a firm may maintain a skimming strategy throughout most stages of a product's life cycle. The jewelry category is a good example. Although discounters such as Costco, HSN, and QVC offer heavier gold pieces for a few hundred dollars, firms such as Tiffany and Cartier command prices ten times that amount just for the brand name. Exclusivity justifies the pricing—and the price, once set, rarely falls.

Sometimes maintaining a high price through the product's life cycle works, but sometimes it does not. High prices can drive away otherwise loyal customers. Baseball fans may shift from attending major league games to minor league games because of ticket, parking, and food prices. Amusement park visitors may shy away from high admission prices and head to the beach instead. If an industry or firm has been known to cut prices at certain points in the past, consumers—and retailers—will expect it. If the price cut doesn't come, consumers must decide whether to pay the higher tab. This has been the case with Sony's PlayStation 3 and Microsoft's Xbox 360. Both firms have traditionally cut prices during the fall, but they did not do so during one recent season. As word leaked during the summer that there would be no price drop, consumers scrambled to make their purchases early.[5]

Despite the risk of backlash, a skimming strategy does offer benefits. It allows a manufacturer to quickly recover its research and development (R&D) costs. Pharmaceuticals companies, which fiercely protect their patents on new drugs, justify high prices because of astronomical R&D costs—an average of 16 cents of every sales dollar, compared with 8 cents for computer makers and 4 cents in the aerospace industry. To protect their brand names from competition from lower-cost generics, drug makers frequently make small changes to their products—such as combining the original product with a complementary prescription drug that treats different aspects of the ailment.

A skimming strategy also permits marketers to control demand in the introductory stages of a product's life cycle and then adjust productive capacity to match changing demand. A low initial price for a new product could lead to fulfillment problems and loss of shopper goodwill if demand outstrips the firm's production capacity. The result is likely to be consumer and retailer complaints and possibly permanent damage to the product's image. Excess demand occasionally leads to quality issues, as the firm strives to satisfy consumer desires for the product with inadequate production facilities.

During the late growth and early maturity stages of its life cycle, a product's price typically falls for two reasons: (1) the pressure of competition and (2) the desire to expand its market. Figure 19.1 shows that 10 percent of the market may buy Product X at $10.00, and another 20 percent could be added to its customer base at a price of $8.75. Successive price declines may expand the firm's market size and meet challenges posed by new competitors.

A skimming strategy has one inherent chief disadvantage: It attracts competition. Potential competitors see innovative firms reaping large financial returns and decide to enter the market. This new supply may force the price of the original product even lower than its eventual level under a sequential skimming procedure. However, if patent protection or some other unique proprietary ability allows a firm to exclude competitors from its market, it may extend a skimming strategy.

PENETRATION PRICING STRATEGY

A **penetration pricing strategy** sets a low price as a major marketing weapon. Marketers often price products noticeably lower than competing offerings when they enter new industries characterized by dozens of competing brands. Once the product achieves

penetration pricing strategy Pricing strategy involving the use of a relatively low entry price compared with competitive offerings, based on the theory that this initial low price will help secure market acceptance.

figure 19.1

Price Reductions to Increase Market Share

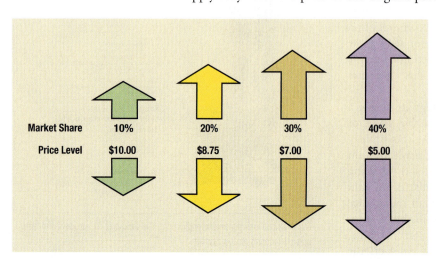

| Market Share | 10% | 20% | 30% | 40% |
| Price Level | $10.00 | $8.75 | $7.00 | $5.00 |

some market recognition through consumer trial purchases stimulated by its low price, marketers may increase the price to the level of competing products. Marketers of consumer products such as detergents often use this strategy. A penetration pricing strategy may also extend over several stages of the product life cycle as the firm seeks to maintain a reputation as a low-price competitor.

A penetration pricing strategy is sometimes called *market-minus pricing* when it implements the premise that a lower-than-market price will attract buyers and move a brand from an unknown newcomer to at least the brand-recognition stage or even to the brand-preference stage. Because many firms begin penetration pricing with the intention of increasing prices in the future, success depends on generating many trial purchases. Penetration pricing is common among credit card firms, which typically offer low or zero interest rates for a specified introductory period, then raise the rates.

If competitors view the new product as a threat, marketers attempting to use a penetration strategy often discover that rivals will simply match their prices. Crocs—those soft, rubbery clogs that come in bright colors—may be a fad, but their makers did everything they could to cash in while the weather was hot and the shoes are cool. Crocs got their name because they can wade through water and are tough enough for the garden or the boat. They slip on and off with ease, and fans claim they are the most comfortable shoes they've ever worn. Food service employees, factory workers, and hair stylists love Crocs because they cushion their feet. Some believers have eight or nine pairs and have no intention of stopping there. Crocs, which come in about 20 colors, sell for $30 to $60—a bargain compared with a pair of brand-name running shoes or Birkenstocks, either of which can top $100. But Crocs' competitors are never far behind. Similar shoes have appeared on the shelves of Skechers, Wal-Mart, and Target stores. Crocs' maker is fighting back with new styles— flip-flops, slides, hiking shoes, even a calf-high boot and Mary Jane shoes.[6]

Retailers may use penetration pricing to lure shoppers to new stores. Strategies might take such forms as zero interest charges for credit purchases at a new furniture store, two-for-one offers for dinner at a new restaurant, or an extremely low price on a single product purchase for first-time customers to get them to come in and shop.

Penetration pricing works best for goods or services characterized by highly elastic demand. Large numbers of highly price-sensitive consumers pay close attention to this type of appeal. The strategy also suits situations in which large-scale operations and long production runs result in low production and marketing costs. Finally, penetration pricing may be appropriate in market situations in which introduction of a new product will likely attract strong competitors. Such a strategy may allow a new product to reach the mass market quickly and capture a large share prior to entry by competitors. Research shows that about 25 percent of companies use penetration pricing strategies on a regular basis.

Some auto manufacturers have been using penetration pricing for some new models to attract customers who might not otherwise consider purchasing a vehicle during a given year or who might be looking at a more expensive competitor. DaimlerChrysler plans to launch the next generation of its two-seat Smart car in the United States soon, after its success in Europe. The car gets an average of 40 miles per gallon in combined city and highway driving and will be priced at less than $15,000. Although skeptics warn that the car is just too small for the American market, chairman Dieter Zetsche notes that the price of gas is driving the U.S. introduction. "We may never see cheap gas again," he predicts. He believes that the car is perfect for congested urban areas and that the low sticker price will be attractive to consumers.[7]

Everyday Low Pricing

Closely related to penetration pricing is **everyday low pricing (EDLP),** a strategy devoted to continuous low prices as opposed to relying on short-term, price-cutting tactics such as cents-off coupons, rebates, and special sales. EDLP can take two forms. In the first, retailers such as Wal-Mart and Lowe's compete by consistently offering consumers low prices on a broad range of items. Through its EDLP policy, Lowe's offers not only to match any price the consumer sees elsewhere but also to take off an additional 10 percent. Wal-Mart states that it achieves EDLP by negotiating better prices from suppliers and by cutting its own costs. Its executives fly coach and empty their own wastebaskets. "Every penny we save is a penny in our customers' pockets," claims the company Web site.[8]

The second form of the EDLP pricing strategy involves its use by the manufacturer in dealing with channel members. Manufacturers may seek to set stable wholesale prices that undercut offers that competitors make to retailers, offers that typically rise and fall with the latest trade promotion deals. Many marketers reduce list prices on a number of products while simultaneously reducing promotion allowances to retailers. While reductions in allowances mean that retailers may not fund such in-store promotions as shelf merchandising and end-aisle displays, the manufacturers hope that stable low prices will stimulate sales instead.

Some retailers oppose EDLP strategies. Many grocery stores, for instance, operate on "high–low" strategies that set profitable regular prices to offset losses of frequent specials and promotions. Other retailers believe that EDLP will ultimately benefit both sellers and buyers. Supporters of EDLP in the grocery industry point out that it already succeeds at two of the biggest competitors—Wal-Mart and warehouse clubs such as Costco.

One popular pricing myth is that a low price is a sure sell. Low prices are an easy means of distinguishing the offerings of one marketer from other sellers, but such moves are easy to counter by competitors. Unless overall demand is price elastic, overall price cuts will mean less revenue for all firms in the industry. In addition, low prices may generate an image of questionable quality.

COMPETITIVE PRICING STRATEGY

competitive pricing strategy Pricing strategy designed to deemphasize price as a competitive variable by pricing a good or service at the general level of comparable offerings.

Although many organizations rely heavily on price as a competitive weapon, even more implement **competitive pricing strategies.** These organizations try to reduce the emphasis on price competition by matching other firms' prices and concentrating their own marketing efforts on the product, distribution, and promotion elements of the marketing mix. As pointed out earlier, while price offers a dramatic means of achieving competitive advantage, it is also the easiest marketing variable for competitors to match. In fact, in industries with relatively homogeneous products, competitors must match each other's price reductions to maintain market share and remain competitive.

Retailers such as The Home Depot and Lowe's both use price-matching strategies, assuring consumers that they will meet—and beat—competitors' prices. Grocery chains such as Kroger's and Stop & Shop may compete with seasonal items: soft drinks and hot dogs in the summer, hot chocolate and turkeys in the winter. As soon as one store lowers the price of an item, the rest follow suit.

Another form of competitive pricing is setting an **opening price point** within a category. Retailers often achieve this by pricing a quality private-label product below the competition. Wal-Mart recently advertised its private-label DVD player at less than $40 and a 23-inch LCD TV at $898—both lower than competing brand-name products and attractive to consumers.[9]

When companies continually match each other's prices, prices can really drop, as has been evident periodically in the airline and computer industries. But competitive pricing can be tricky; a price reduction affects not only the first company but also the entire industry as other firms match the reduction. Unless the lower prices can attract new customers and expand the overall market enough to offset the loss of per-unit revenue, the price cut will leave all competitors with less revenue. Research shows that nearly two-thirds of all firms set prices using competitive pricing as their primary pricing strategy. Some firms that are forced to the edge by competitive pricing strategies eventually decide to declare Chapter 11 bankruptcy to become more competitive in their markets.

What happens when one discounter undercuts another? Although many retailers fear competition from Wal-Mart, one type of store seems well positioned against the powerful chain: the so-called dollar stores. Dollar General and Family Dollar are posting better-

My job is saving you money.

I love my job.

Get a FREE rate quote today.   1-800-947-AUTO

COURTESY OF GEICO

In certain industries, such as insurance, competitive pricing strategies are typical. Here GEICO offers to provide a free car insurance quotation to consumers.

than-expected profits because they cater to middle- and lower-income shoppers who are struggling with rising energy costs—both at the gas pump and for home heating.[10] Today's equivalent of the five-and-dime variety stores of the 20th century, dollar stores sell inexpensive items such as cleaning supplies, paper plates, toothpaste, greeting cards, and other household products—and compete on price and convenience, especially parking and easy access to the goods. Although these stores have yet to threaten Wal-Mart's position—their combined annual sales total just over $20 billion while Wal-Mart total sales are nearly $320 billion annually—the retail giant is paying attention. As these dollar store chains expand, adding more brand-name products and attracting more price-conscious customers, Wal-Mart is likely to take some competitive action.

Once competitors are routinely matching each other on price, marketers must turn away from price as a marketing strategy, emphasizing other variables to develop areas of distinctive competence and to attract customers. Airlines, which are famous for competition based on price, must constantly look for other ways to get people to fly with them.

✓ assessment check

1. **What are the three major pricing strategies?**

2. **What is EDLP?**

PRICE QUOTATIONS

2 Describe how prices are quoted.

The choice of the best method for quoting prices depends on many industry conditions, including competitive trends, cost structures, and traditional practices, along with the policies of individual firms. This section examines the reasoning and methodology behind price quotation practices.

Most price structures are built around **list prices**—the rates normally quoted to potential buyers. Marketers usually determine list prices by one or a combination of the methods discussed in Chapter 18. The sticker price on a new automobile is a good example: It shows the list price for the basic model and then adds the prices of options. The sticker price on a new Ford Fusion lists the car at $20,625. But when options such as a power moonroof, antilock brakes, and a sport package are added, the price can increase to $23,000 or more. This doesn't include any taxes, dealer prep charges, or other costs that will be added to the price at the time of purchase.[11]

list price Established price normally quoted to potential buyers.

The price of oil is equally important to consumers—particularly those who drive cars—because it directly affects the list price of gasoline. Factors such as hurricanes and wars affect the price of oil, and ultimately the price that drivers pay at the pump. Prices may also fluctuate seasonally, as demand for gasoline rises and falls. U.S. demand for gasoline in the summer reaches more than 9 million barrels per day.[12] Figure 19.2 illustrates where the money from a gallon of gas goes on its journey from the oil field to your gas tank.

REDUCTIONS FROM LIST PRICE

The amount that a consumer pays for a product—its **market price**—may or may not equal the list price. Discounts and allowances sometimes reduce list prices. A list price often defines a starting point from which discounts set a lower market price. Marketers offer discounts in several classifications: cash, trade, and quantity discounts.

market price Price that a consumer or marketing intermediary actually pays for a product after subtracting any discounts, allowances, or rebates from the list price.

figure 19.2

Components of Retail Gasoline Prices

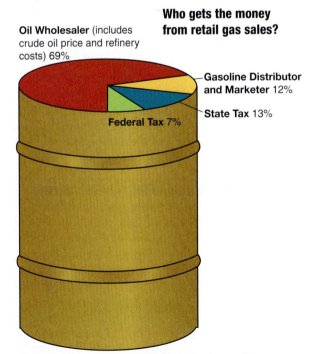

Who gets the money from retail gas sales?

Oil Wholesaler (includes crude oil price and refinery costs) 69%

Gasoline Distributor and Marketer 12%

State Tax 13%

Federal Tax 7%

Note: Percentages do not total 100% due to rounding.

Source: Data from Energy Information Administration, "Components of Retail Gasoline Prices," *Annual Energy Outlook 2006,* **http://www.eia.doc.gov,** accessed July 17, 2006.

Cash Discounts

Consumers, industrial purchasers, or channel members sometimes receive reductions in price in exchange for prompt payment of bills; these price cuts are known as **cash discounts.** Discount terms usually specify exact time periods, such as 2/10, net 30. This notation means that the customer must pay within 30 days, but payment within 10 days entitles the customer to subtract 2 percent from the amount due. Consumers may receive a cash discount for immediate payment—say, paying with cash instead of a credit card at the gas pump or paying the full cash amount up front for elective healthcare services such as braces for teeth. Cash discounts represent a traditional pricing practice in many industries. They fulfill legal requirements provided that all customers can take the same reductions on the same terms.

In recent years, sellers have increasingly attempted to improve their own liquidity positions, reduce their bad-debt losses, and cut collection expenses by moving to a form of *negative cash discount.* Confronted with purchasers who may defer paying their bills as long as possible, a new notice has begun to appear on customer statements:

> **Due on Receipt.** A FINANCE CHARGE of 1.5% per month (18% A.P.R.) is computed on and added to the unpaid balance as of the statement date.

Past-due accounts may be turned over to collection agencies.

Trade Discounts

Payments to channel members for performing marketing functions are known as **trade discounts,** or functional discounts. Services performed by various channel members and the related costs were discussed in Chapters 13 and 14. A manufacturer's list price must incorporate the costs incurred by channel members in performing required marketing functions and expected profit margins for each member.

Trade discounts initially reflected the operating expenses of each category, but they have become more or less customary practices in some industries. The Robinson-Patman Act allows trade discounts as long as all buyers in the same category, such as all wholesalers or all retailers, receive the same discount privileges.

Figure 19.3 shows how a chain of trade discounts works. In the first instance, the trade discount is "40 percent, 10 percent off list price" for wholesalers. In other words, the 40 percent discount on the $40 product is the trade discount the retailer receives to cover operating expenses and earn a profit. The wholesaler receives 10 percent of the $24 price to retailers to cover expenses and earn a profit. The manufacturer receives $21.60 from the wholesaler for each order.

In the second example, the manufacturer and retailer decide to bypass the wholesaler. The producer offers a trade discount of 45 percent to the retailer. In this instance, the retailer receives $18 for each product sold at its list price, and the manufacturer receives the remaining $22. Either the retailer or the manufacturer must assume responsibility for the services previously performed by the wholesaler, or they can share these duties between them.

figure 19.3

Chain of Trade Discounts

"40 PERCENT, 10 PERCENT OFF" TRADE DISCOUNT

List Price	–	Retail Trade Discount	–	Wholesale Trade Discount	=	Manufacturer Proceeds
$40	–	$16 ($40 × 40%)	–	$2.40 ($24 × 10%)	=	$21.60 ($40 – $16 – $2.40)

"45 PERCENT" TRADE DISCOUNT

List Price	–	Retail Trade Discount	=	Manufacturer Proceeds
$40	–	$18 ($40 × 45%)	=	$22 ($40 – $18)

Quantity Discounts

Price reductions granted for large-volume purchases are known as **quantity discounts.** Sellers justify these discounts on the grounds that large orders reduce selling expenses and may shift some costs for storage, transportation, and financing to buyers. The law allows quantity discounts provided they are applied on the same basis to all customers.

Quantity discounts may specify either cumulative or noncumulative terms. **Cumulative quantity discounts** reduce prices in amounts determined by purchases over stated time periods. Annual purchases of at least $25,000 might entitle a buyer to a 3 percent rebate, and purchases exceeding $50,000 would increase the refund to 5 percent. These reductions are really patronage discounts because they tend to bind customers to a single supply source.

Noncumulative quantity discounts provide onetime reductions in the list price. For example, a firm might offer the following discount schedule for a product priced at $1,000 per unit:

1 unit	List: $1,000
2–5 units	List less 10 percent
6–10 units	List less 20 percent
Moe than 10 units	List less 25 percent

Many businesses have come to expect quantity discounts from suppliers. Online discount office supplier Rapid Supplies offers quantity discounts on all 35,000 of its products, including business cards, computers, and office furniture.[13] Sony ImageStation offers quantity discounts on photo gifts ordered online. Customers who order 25 or more photo mugs pay a quantity discount price of $9.74 instead of the everyday low price of $12.99. The price of a leather photo book drops from $34.99 to $26.99.[14]

Marketers typically favor combinations of cash, trade, and quantity discounts. See's Candies offers a quantity discount for a minimum purchase of 50 pounds of candy ($492.50), upon which customers also receive free delivery and continued savings throughout the year.[15]

Allowances

Allowances resemble discounts by specifying deductions from list price. The major categories of allowances are trade-ins and promotional allowances. **Trade-ins** are often used in sales of durable goods such as automobiles. The new product's basic list price remains unchanged, but the seller accepts less money from the customer along with a used product—usually the same kind of product as the buyer purchases.

allowance Specified deduction from list price, including a trade-in or promotional allowance.

Promotional allowances reduce prices as part of attempts to integrate promotional strategies within distribution channels. Manufacturers often return part of the prices that buyers pay in the form of advertising and sales-support allowances for channel members. Automobile manufacturers frequently offer allowances to retail dealers to induce them to lower prices and stimulate sales. In an effort to alert consumers to the difference between a car's sticker price and the price the dealer actually pays to the manufacturer, *Consumer Reports* recently began selling car and truck buyers a breakdown on dealers' wholesale costs. The information reveals undisclosed dealer profits such as manufacturers' "holdbacks"—amounts as high as 3 percent of the full sticker price—that are refunded to dealers after sales are completed. The breakdown also reveals allowances for the dealers' advertising and other promotional costs. Once they are aware of the dealer's actual cost, car buyers are better able to negotiate a fair purchase price.[16] Dealers dislike the move to reveal their markups, arguing that no other retail sector is forced to give consumers details of their promotional allowances.

Minimum advertised pricing (MAP) occurs when a manufacturer pays a retailer not to advertise a product below a certain price. The music industry came under scrutiny for this policy, which in effect raised prices per CD by $1 to $2 across the board, eliminating most price competition. Under pressure from the Federal Trade Commission, major companies such as Bertelsmann, Sony, and EMI agreed to discontinue MAP allowances.[17]

Rebates

In still another way to reduce the price paid by customers, marketers may offer a **rebate**—a refund of a portion of the

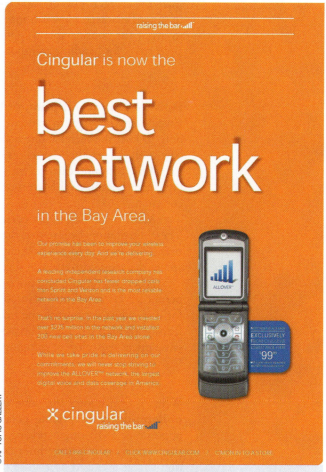

Cingular offers a $50 mail-in rebate on a Motorola RAZR with a two-year service agreement.

purchase price. Rebates appear everywhere—on appliances, electronics, and auto promotions—by manufacturers eager to get consumers to try their products or to move products during periods of slow sales. Mattress manufacturer Sealy has successfully used rebates to move consumers up to more expensive models in its product line, offering the biggest rebates for its top-priced mattresses.

Rebates can have their problems. Many consumers complain of the amount of paperwork they have to fill out to get a rebate, particularly on larger items such as computers and kitchen appliances. Others report never receiving the rebate at all. In response to this, Dell has announced that it will phase out rebates and other sales promotions but reduce its regular prices over time. "Customers don't like rebates," explains Ro Parra, senior vice president for Dell's Home and Small Business Group. "They want immediate savings at the time of purchase."[18] OfficeMax has made a similar announcement, citing the same reasons—that customers want savings at the cash register, not later on.[19] However, Staples is continuing with its Easy Rebate program—a promotion that allows consumers to submit their rebates online and track them.[20]

GEOGRAPHIC CONSIDERATIONS

In industries dominated by catalog and online marketers, geographic considerations weigh heavily on the firm's ability to deliver orders in a cost-effective manner at the right time and place. In other instances, geographic factors affect the marketer's ability to receive additional inventory quickly in response to demand fluctuations. And although geographic considerations strongly influence prices when costs include shipping heavy, bulky, low-unit-value products, they can also affect lightweight, lower-cost products.

Buyers and sellers can handle transportation expenses in several ways: (1) The buyer pays all transportation charges, (2) the seller pays all transportation charges, or (3) the buyer and the seller share the charges. This decision has major effects on a firm's efforts to expand its geographic coverage to distant markets. How can marketers compete with local suppliers in distant markets who are able to avoid the considerable shipping costs that their firms must pay? Sellers can implement several alternatives for handling transportation costs in their pricing policies.

FOB Pricing

FOB (free on board) plant, or **FOB origin,** prices include no shipping charges. The buyer must pay all freight charges to transport the product from the manufacturer's loading dock. The seller pays only to load the merchandise aboard the carrier selected by the buyer. Legal title and responsibility pass to the buyer after the seller's employees load the purchase and get a receipt from the representative of the common carrier. Firms such as Wal-Mart often handle freight charges over the entire supply chain. Because Wal-Mart sources so many products from China, "FOB China" is now becoming common.

Many marketing intermediaries sell only on FOB plant terms to downstream channel members. These distributors believe that their customers have more clout than they do in negotiating with carriers. They prefer to assign transportation costs to the channel members in the best positions to secure the most cost-effective shipping terms.

Sellers may also quote prices as **FOB origin-freight allowed,** or **freight absorbed.** These terms permit buyers to subtract transportation expenses from their bills. The amount such a seller receives for its product varies with the freight charged against the invoice. This alternative is popular among firms with high fixed costs because it helps them expand their markets considerably by quoting the same prices regardless of shipping expenses.

Uniform-Delivered Pricing

When a firm quotes the same price, including transportation expenses, to all buyers, it adopts a **uniform-delivered pricing** policy. This method of handling transportation expenses is the exact opposite of FOB origin pricing. The uniform-delivered system resembles the pricing structure for mail service, so it is sometimes called **postage-stamp pricing.** The price quote includes a transportation charge averaged over all of the firm's customers, meaning that distant customers actually pay a smaller share of shipping costs while nearby customers pay what is known as *phantom freight* (the amount by which the average transportation charge exceeds the actual cost of shipping).

Zone Pricing

Zone pricing modifies a uniform-delivered pricing system by dividing the overall market into different zones and establishing a single price within each zone. This pricing structure incorporates average transportation costs for shipments within each zone as part of the delivered price of goods sold there; by narrowing distances, it greatly reduces but does not completely eliminate phantom freight. The primary advantage of zone pricing comes from its simplified administration that helps a seller compete in distant markets. The U.S. Postal Service's parcel rates depend on zone pricing.

Zone pricing helps explain why gasoline can cost more in one suburb than it costs in a neighborhood just two or three miles down the road. One way in which gasoline marketers boost profits is by mapping out areas based on formulas that factor in location, affluence, or simply what the local market will bear. Dealers are then charged different wholesale prices, which are reflected in the prices paid at the pump by customers. Some dealers argue that zone pricing should be prohibited. When drivers shop around for cheaper gas in other zones, stations in high-price zones are unable to compete. Ironically, many consumers suspect the local dealer, not just the major oil company, of price gouging.

Basing-Point Pricing

In **basing-point pricing,** the price of a product includes the list price at the factory plus freight charges from the basing-point city nearest the buyer. The basing point specifies a location from which freight charges are calculated—not necessarily the point from which the goods are actually shipped. In either case, the actual shipping point does not affect the price quotation. Such a system seeks to equalize competition between distant marketers because all competitors quote identical transportation rates. Few buyers would accept a basing-point system today, however.

For many years, the best-known basing-point system was the Pittsburgh-plus pricing structure common in the steel industry. Steel buyers paid freight charges from Pittsburgh regardless of where the steel was produced. As the industry matured, manufacturing centers emerged in Chicago; Gary, Indiana; Cleveland; and Birmingham. Still, Pittsburgh remained the basing point for steel pricing, forcing a buyer in Atlanta who purchased steel from a Birmingham mill to pay phantom freight from Pittsburgh.

 assessment check

1. What are the three major types of discounts?
2. Identify the four alternatives for handling transportation costs in pricing policies.

PRICING POLICIES

 Identify the various pricing policy decisions that marketers must make.

Pricing policies contribute important information to buyers as they assess the firm's total image. A coherent policy provides an overall framework and consistency that guide day-to-day pricing decisions. Formally, a **pricing policy** is a general guideline that reflects marketing objectives and influences specific pricing decisions.

Decisions concerning price structure generally tend to focus on technical, detailed questions, but decisions concerning pricing policies cover broader issues. Price-structure decisions take the firm's pricing policy as a given, from which they specify applicable discounts. Pricing policies have important strategic effects, particularly in guiding competitive efforts. They form the basis for more practical price-structure decisions.

Firms implement variations of four basic types of pricing policies: psychological pricing, price flexibility, product-line pricing, and promotional pricing. Specific policies deal effectively with various competitive situations; the final choice depends on the environment within which marketers must make their pricing decisions.

PSYCHOLOGICAL PRICING

Psychological pricing applies the belief that certain prices or price ranges make products more appealing than others to buyers. No research offers a consistent foundation for such thinking, how-

psychological pricing
Pricing policy based on the belief that certain prices or price ranges make a good or service more appealing than others to buyers.

HomeGoods practices odd pricing in its home decorating products by using prices ending in 9.

© TERRI MILLER/E-VISUAL COMMUNICATIONS INC.

ever, and studies often report mixed findings. Nevertheless, marketers practice several forms of psychological pricing. Prestige pricing, discussed in Chapter 18, sets a relatively high price to convey an image of quality and exclusiveness. Two more psychological pricing techniques are odd pricing and unit pricing.

In **odd pricing,** marketers set prices at odd numbers just under round numbers. Many people assume that a price of $4.95 appeals more strongly to consumers than $5.00, supposedly because buyers interpret it as $4.00 plus change. Odd pricing originated as a way to force clerks to make change, thus serving as a cash-control device, and it remains a common feature of contemporary price quotations. One recent survey revealed that consumers believe that a price of $19.95 instead of $20 means that a retailer has worked hard to plan its prices and save the customer every penny possible.[21]

Some producers and retailers practice odd pricing but avoid prices ending in 5, 9, or 0. These marketers believe that customers view price tags of $5.95, $5.99, or $6.00 as regular retail prices, but they think of an amount such as $5.97 as a discount price. Others, such as Wal-Mart, avoid using 9s as ending prices for their items.

Unit pricing states prices in terms of some recognized unit of measurement (such as grams and liters) or a standard numerical count. Unit pricing began to be widely used during the late 1960s to make price comparisons more convenient following complaints by consumer advocates about the difficulty of comparing the true prices of products packaged in different sizes. These advocates thought that posting prices in terms of standard units would help shoppers make better informed purchases. However, unit pricing has not improved consumers' shopping habits as much as supporters originally envisioned. Instead, research shows that standard price quotes most often affect purchases only by relatively well-educated consumers with high earnings.

PRICE FLEXIBILITY

Marketing executives must also set company policies that determine whether their firm will permit **price flexibility**—that is, the decision of whether to set one price that applies to every buyer or to permit variable prices for different customers. Generally, one-price policies suit mass-selling marketing programs, whereas variable pricing is more likely to be applied in marketing programs based on individual bargaining. In a large department store, customers do not expect to haggle over prices with retail salespeople. Instead, they expect to pay the amounts shown on the price tags. Generally, customers pay less only when the retailer replaces regular prices with sale prices or offers discounts on damaged merchandise. Variable pricing usually applies to larger purchases such as automobiles, real estate, and hotel room rates. While variable pricing adds some flexibility to selling situations, it may conflict with provisions of the Robinson-Patman Act. It may also lead to retaliatory pricing by competitors, and it may stir complaints among customers who find that they paid higher prices than necessary. Although all Netflix subscribers pay the same price, some complain that they are receiving less service than others, as described in the "Solving an Ethical Controversy" feature.

One service that is taking off is fractional jet ownership. Fractional jet ownership works something like a time-share—customers buy an ownership stake that includes a certain number of flying

Solving an Ethical Controversy

Netflix Throttles Its Best Customers

If you paid the same rate to the same company as your classmate for a service, wouldn't you expect to get the identical service? That's the question that some of Netflix's best customers—and critics—are asking. Recently, Netflix has been criticized for "throttling" the customers who rent the most movies in a short period of time. What that means is that Netflix subscribers who are tagged as heavy renters by the firm's automated system often experience delays in receiving the movies they request, or they receive their second and third choices instead. The top-choice movies get funneled to new customers or those who rent less frequently. Still, all customers who sign up for the same plan pay the same monthly fee.

Should customers who pay a firm the same rate for a service receive the same service?

PRO

1. All customers should be treated fairly. Firms should not differentiate among customers who are paying the same fee for a service. Some customers are more profitable than others, but firms should set prices that accommodate those fluctuations.
2. A firm that makes this kind of differentiation most likely will suffer from bad publicity and lose customers over the long run. It is much better to treat consumers fairly and develop positive relationships.

CON

1. Netflix cannot afford to send out more than a certain number of movies to each customer per month. The firm's most loyal customers have been renting as many as two dozen DVDs every month, causing a drain on Netflix's profits.
2. Netflix's user agreement explicitly states that heavy renters will be more likely to experience shipping delays and less likely to receive their top choices on the first try. So consumers are informed about the firm's practices when they subscribe.

Summary

A class-action suit was filed against Netflix by an unhappy customer—a heavy renter—charging that the firm had failed to keep its promise of one-day delivery. Perhaps the best course of action for Netflix would be to set a limit on the number of movies customers may receive for their monthly fee. If they want to see more, they can pay more. Or they can wait until the following month.

Sources: Jeff Zabin, "The Netflix Paradox: Are Loyal Customers Sinking Your Stock?" *Chief Marketer*, February 20, 2006, **http://chiefmarketer.com**; Michael Liedtke, "Netflix's Throttling Tactics Anger Some," *USA Today*, February 13, 2006, p. 13B; Dan Bell, "Netflix Algorithm Penalizes Heavy Renters with Fewer Movies," *CD Freaks*, February 11, 2006, **http://www.cdfreaks.com**; Mike Elgan, "How to Hack Netflix," *Information Week*, January 30, 2006, **http://www.informationweek.com**.

hours per year on a private jet. For example, the company Fraction Air charges a onetime fee of $225,000 for each one-sixteenth stake in an eight-person Beechjet. The share, plus monthly management and maintenance fees, buys the customer 60 hours of flying time. Other firms offer similar programs—MarquisJet sells 25 hours of flying time for $115,000, which does not include an ownership stake in the plane or involve monthly fees. Although fractional jet ownership isn't cheap, it is a bargain for business travelers and others who want the service of a private jet, but do not want to pay $5 million to own one outright.[22]

PRODUCT-LINE PRICING

Because most firms market multiple product lines, an effective pricing strategy must consider the relationships among all of these items instead of viewing each in isolation. **Product-line pricing** is the practice of setting a limited number of prices for a selection of merchandise. For example, one well-known clothier might offer three lines of men's suits—one priced at $450, a second at $695, and the most expensive at $1,295. These price points help the retailer define important product characteristics that differentiate the three product lines and help the customer decide on whether to trade up or trade down.

product-line pricing
Practice of setting a limited number of prices for a selection of merchandise and marketing different product lines at each of these price levels.

FOR SCHOOL. FOR HOME. FOR $99.*
HP ALL-IN-ONE PRINTERS.

School is competitive. Give your kids an edge with an HP All-in-One printer. They print, copy and scan. And with HP Vivera Inks, you can also create lab-quality photos for as little as 24¢ a page with some printers. All from HP. PC Magazine's Readers' Choice for Service and Reliability for 14 straight years. Brilliantly Simple.

BEGINNER
HP Photosmart C3180.
Print, copy and scan up to 20 color pages a minute using this compact photo All-in-One.**
$99.99*

INTERMEDIATE
HP Photosmart C4180.
Does everything the C3180 does, plus prints up to 24 color pages a minute while viewing and editing on a 2.4-inch display.**
$149.99*

ADVANCED
HP Photosmart 3210.
From photos to homework. Print, copy and scan. It's the world's fastest All-in-One.**
$299.99*

Visit hp.com/go/hpallinone. Call 1-800-HP-PHOTO. Visit Best Buy,® Circuit City, CompUSA, Office Depot or Staples.

*Estimated retail price. Prices may vary. ¹Based on estimated retail price of HP 95 series 200-sheet 4x6 Photo Value Pack, three-ink printing. Actual cost may vary based on printer used, images printed and other factors. **Speed comparisons in default and fastest modes, when printing from a computer, based upon HP internal testing of comparable consumer photo printing products available as of April 2005. ©2006 Hewlett-Packard Development Company, L.P. Simulated images.

COURTESY OF HEWLETT PACKARD

HP offers three different models—and prices—in its product line of all-in-one printers made for consumers.

Retailers practice extensive product-line pricing. In earlier days, five-and-dime variety stores exemplified this technique. It remains popular, however, because it offers advantages to both retailers and customers. Shoppers can choose desired price ranges and then concentrate on other product variables such as colors, styles, and materials. Retailers can purchase and offer specific lines in limited price categories instead of more general assortments with dozens of different prices. Steve & Barry's University Sportswear offers its entire line of casual clothes—T-shirts, jeans, jackets, and the like—for $10 or less per item, and it has become a strong contender in the marketplace, as described in the "Marketing Success" feature.

Old Navy, also known for is moderate-priced casual clothing that can outfit an entire family, has recently introduced its most expensive line ever—ruffled leather jackets for $129, silk tops for $29.50, and sweater coats for $34.50. In addition, it is adding special touches to its basics—shell buttons on long-sleeved Henley shirts, and a metallic stamp in place of the old sewn-in label. The firm says it is increasing quality as well as price in order to compete with more popular clothing firms such as Abercrombie & Fitch.[23]

A potential problem with product-line pricing is that once marketers decide on a limited number of prices to use as their price lines, they may have difficulty making price changes on individual items. Rising costs, therefore, force sellers to either change the entire price-line structure, which results in confusion, or cut costs through production adjustments. The second option opens the firm to customer complaints that its merchandise is not what it used to be.

PROMOTIONAL PRICING

In **promotional pricing,** a lower-than-normal price is used as a temporary ingredient in a firm's marketing strategy. Some promotional pricing arrangements form part of recurrent marketing initiatives, such as a shoe store's annual "buy one pair, get the second pair for one cent" sale. Another

marketing success   Steve & Barry's Cashes In with Customers

Background. Steve Shore and Barry Prevor began their business by selling T-shirts at the Roosevelt Raceway flea market in Long Island, New York. But they had a dream. They wanted to compete with the big guys such as Wal-Mart and Target. They wanted to sell as much casual clothing to consumers as they could, at a great price.

The Challenge. Steve and Barry didn't have the resources that the big chains have. They had to figure out how to give consumers what they wanted, at the most competitive prices. Here's how they did it.

The Strategy. First, they founded Steve & Barry's University Sportswear. The two partners knew how to obtain mid-quality apparel products at low cost from various suppliers overseas. They also knew their customers—consumers who were less concerned about straight stitches and high-end fabric than about price, such as college students. They began to offer T-shirts, jeans, jackets, hats, and other goods for the whole family at $10 or less per item. Consumers snatched up the clothes, and the two men opened store after store—in shopping malls, old supermarkets, wherever they could get cheap space. They added specialty items such as $6 T-shirts with sayings such as

example would be "7 CDs for 1 cent." This artificially low price attracts customers who must then agree to purchase a set number of CDs at regular prices within a specified time limit. Another firm may introduce a promotional model or brand with a special price to begin competing in a new market.

Managing promotional pricing efforts requires marketing skill. Customers may get hooked on sales and other promotional pricing events. If they know their favorite department store has a one-day sale every month, they are likely to wait to make their purchases on that day. Car shoppers have been offered so many price incentives that it is becoming harder and harder for manufacturers and dealers to take them away. Employee-discount programs have complicated this situation, as auto manufacturers have begun to offer employee discounts to consumers. Called the Employee Pricing Plus program, Chrysler's discount plan essentially offers the same price to consumers as it does to Chrysler employees, during the summer months. Ford and General Motors offer similar plans in an effort to lure consumers their way.[24]

© TERRI MILLER/E-VISUAL COMMUNICATIONS INC.

McDonald's runs many promotional pricing programs, including its Dollar Menu, which rotates some items on and off the list for specified periods of time.

Loss Leaders and Leader Pricing

Retailers rely most heavily on promotional pricing. In one type of technique, stores offer **loss leaders**—goods priced below cost to attract customers who, the retailer hopes, will also buy other, regularly priced merchandise. Loss leaders can form part of an effective marketing program, but states with unfair-trade laws limit the practice. Your Thanksgiving turkey is probably a loss leader. The grocery store might pay 70 cents a pound for holiday turkey and then charge consumers as little as 39 cents a pound. A chain that sells millions of pounds of turkey for the Thanksgiving holiday thus takes a significant loss on this one product. "Historically, what we've

loss leader Product offered to consumers at less than cost to attract them to stores in the hope that they will buy other merchandise at regular prices.

leader pricing Variant of loss-leader pricing in which marketers offer prices slightly above cost to avoid violating minimum-markup regulations and earn a minimal return on promotional sales.

seen across the country is grocers use turkeys as a loss leader," confirms Sherrie Rosenblatt, spokesperson for the National Turkey Federation, whose members sell 98 percent of all turkeys in the United States.[25] But while they are picking up their turkeys, consumers are also shopping for cranberries, rolls, stuffing, apple cider, potatoes, desserts, wine, and other products—all of which are profitable for grocers.

Retailers frequently use a variant of loss-leader pricing called **leader pricing.** To avoid violating minimum-markup regulations and to earn some return on promotional sales, they offer so-called *leader merchandise* at prices slightly above cost. Among the most frequent practitioners of this combination pricing/promotion strategy are supermarkets and mass merchandisers such as Wal-Mart, Target, and Kmart. Retailers sometimes treat private-label products (such as Sam's Choice colas at Wal-Mart stores) as leader merchandise because prices of the store brands average 5 to 60 percent less than those of comparable national brands. While store brand items generate lower per-unit revenues than national brands would produce, higher sales volume will probably offset some of the difference, as will related sales of high-margin products such as toiletries and cosmetics.

The personal computer industry provides an excellent example of this trend in pricing. Little more than a decade ago, PCs cost up to $5,000. Today, you can get a good-quality notebook computer from makers such as Acer and Dell and for around $500. Granted, these machines handle the basics—e-mail, Web surfing, word processing, and a few other chores. Some experts predict that these prices could drop even lower. As long as these machines deliver reliable computing, they should continue to sell well. Marketers assert that these computers provide consumers with more choices. "Now consumers can buy the computer they want, not just the desktop they can afford," says one industry observer.[26]

But marketers should anticipate two potential pitfalls when making a promotional pricing decision:

1. Some buyers are not attracted by promotional pricing.
2. By maintaining an artificially low price for a period of time, marketers may lead customers to expect it as a customary feature of the product. That is the situation currently faced by U.S. car manufacturers; sales of their models lag when they do not offer price incentives.

PRICE–QUALITY RELATIONSHIPS

One of the most thoroughly researched aspects of pricing is its relationship to consumer perceptions of product quality. In the absence of other cues, price serves as an important indicator of a product's quality to prospective purchasers. Many buyers interpret high prices as signals of high-quality products. Prestige is also often associated with high prices. In an unusual pairing, designer firm Dolce & Gabbana teamed up with Motorola to offer a high-style design for Motorola's popular Razr cell phone. The gold Razr V31 model comes with special backgrounds, screensavers, MP3 ring tones, animations, and a gold D&G pendant. The two firms are also offering a line of D&G phone accessories, including a gold leather phone case and gold-wired headphones with a gold volume control. Those who want the prestige of owning the new phone will pay between $424.99 and $479.88 for the privilege, depending on the retailer.[27]

assessment check

1. Define *pricing policy*.
2. Describe the two types of psychological pricing other than prestige pricing.
3. What is promotional pricing?

4 Relate price to consumer perceptions of quality.

JET SET.

HINCKLEY NEWPORT, RI

1-866-HINCKLEY
www.thehinckleycompany.com/T29C
PORTSMOUTH, RI | SOUTHWEST HARBOR, ME
ANNAPOLIS, MD | WEST PALM BEACH, FL | HARBOR SPRINGS, MI

COURTESY OF HINCKLEY YACHTS

Hinckley yachts can cost several million dollars each, and they are perceived by boating enthusiasts to be among the best in the world.

Etiquette Tips for Marketing Professionals

Making Your Complaint—Effectively

We've all been disappointed with a product at some point—either merchandise we bought or a service we tried. Maybe the coffeemaker fizzled out after one pot, or the new clothes iron just didn't get hot enough. Perhaps the hotel lost a reservation or a special restaurant dinner arrived cold. When this happens, we need to make a complaint so that the company knows about the problem and has a chance to correct it.

If you find yourself in this situation, how you handle it can make a difference in how it is resolved. Remember that the mission of a firm is to attract and keep your business—and its employees will likely do their best to help you, especially if you are polite, patient, and persistent. Here are a few tips for expressing your discontent effectively:

1. *Act immediately.* If a product breaks or arrives defective, make the call or visit the store right away. If you wait, you may exceed the return period or warranty. If your restaurant dinner isn't what you expected, speak quietly to the waiter or owner. You could have a new dinner in a matter of minutes.

2. *Focus on the problem, not the person in front of you or on the phone.* Explain the situation as clearly as possible so that the person can take the right corrective steps.

3. *State how you would like the problem to be solved.* Ask for a replacement, a refund, or a rain check. If the seller cannot fulfill your request, listen to the options before making a decision about what to accept. Sometimes it's good to know what your consumer rights are regarding expiration dates, return policies, and so forth in your state.

4. *Be assertive, but polite.* If an employee is unable to help you, ask to speak to a supervisor or someone else who has the authority to make a decision.

5. *Think before you speak.* No matter how frustrated you may become, don't resort to insults or anger. Never raise your voice or lose your cool—if you do, your cause may be lost.

6. *Have a positive attitude.* Generally, people respond better to this than to a sour outlook. If a person has really made an effort to help you, thank him or her. Let the company know an employee has done a good job.

Sources: Mary Mitchell, "Business Etiquette: Avoid These Mistakes," Live and Learn, **http://www.uliveandlearn.com**, accessed July 21, 2006; "Assertive Communication," University Counseling Service, University of Iowa, **http://www.uiowa.edu**, accessed July 21, 2006; Denise Anne Taylor, "Business Etiquette," About.com, March 17, 2006, **http://www.about.com**.

Despite the appeal of prestige, nearly every consumer loves a good deal. Marketers work hard to convince consumers that they are offering high-quality products at the lowest possible price. Shopping networks HSN and QVC have struggled for many years to convince consumers that their low prices do not reflect the quality of their goods. Target's advertisements promote an image of "cheap chic," or affordable style. "Target means style at accessible pricing," explains Robert Passikoff, president of Brand Keys.[28]

Probably the best statement of the price-quality connection is the idea of price limits. Consumers define certain limits within which their product-quality perceptions vary directly with price. A potential buyer regards a price below the lower limit as too cheap, and a price above the higher limit seems too expensive. This perception holds true for both national brands and private-label products. Regardless of the price you've paid for a good or service, however, you want it to deliver what you expect. If it does not, you may need to seek a price adjustment or refund, as described in the "Etiquette Tips for Marketing Professionals" feature.

 assessment check

1. **Describe the price–quality connection.**

2. **What are price limits?**

Briefly
Speaking

"I have discovered in 20 years of moving around a ballpark that the knowledge of the game is usually in inverse proportion to the price of the seats."

—Bill Veeck (1914–1986)
American baseball team owner

COMPETITIVE BIDDING AND NEGOTIATED PRICES

5 Contrast competitive bidding and negotiated prices.

Many government and organizational procurement departments do not pay set prices for their purchases, particularly for large purchases. Instead, they determine the lowest prices available for items that meet specifications through **competitive bidding.** This process consists of inviting potential suppliers to quote prices on proposed purchases or contracts. Detailed specifications describe the good or service that the government agency or business organization wishes to acquire. One of the most important procurement tasks is to develop accurate descriptions of products that the organization seeks to buy. This process generally requires the assistance of the firm's technical personnel, such as engineers, designers, and chemists.

A select group of state troopers test potential police cars every year to determine which will be the best model—and what price—for their organization. While Ford's Crown Victoria Police Interceptor has come out on top for many years, recently Chrysler's Dodge Charger and Magnum have gained ground, taking orders for 3,000 vehicles. Still, the Crown Victoria reigns, with orders for 47,000 cars in a recent year.[29]

In some cases, business and government purchasers negotiate contracts with favored suppliers instead of inviting competitive bids from all interested parties. The terms of such a contract emerge through offers and counteroffers between the buyer and the seller. When only one supplier offers a desired product or when projects require extensive research and development, buyers and sellers often set purchase terms through negotiated contracts. In addition, some state and local governments permit their agencies to skip the formal bid process and negotiate purchases under certain dollar limits— say $500 or $1,000. This policy seeks to eliminate economic waste that would result from obtaining and processing bids for relatively minor purchases. For example, Texas state law requires cities and counties to request competitive, sealed bids for contracts of more than $25,000. Texas cities and towns often lay out stricter laws.[30]

NEGOTIATING PRICES ONLINE

Many people see the Internet as one big auction site. Whether it's toys, furniture, or automobiles, there seems to be an online auction site to serve every person's needs— buyer and seller alike. Auctions are the purest form of negotiated pricing.

Ticket sales are an online auction favorite. Whether it is a Broadway show, a baseball playoff game, or Ozzy Osbourne's Ozzfest concert, you can bid for tickets online. Tickets.com catalogs the dates, times, and locations of events including concerts and museum exhibits. It recently partnered with the Advantix ticketing system to open a sales site for sports venues. In addition, Tickets.com also functions as a reseller through its own online auctions.

Online auctions also take place at sites such as eBay and uBid.com, where consumers can snap up items as varied as Italian gold cufflinks and a home in upstate New York. But recently, eBay reported that 40 percent of its transactions now take place at fixed prices through the "Buy It Now" option, signaling that perhaps consumers prefer to secure an item by paying a set price for it, or that they do not want to wait up to a week for an auction to close.[31]

going, going, gone-on-line.

Buy
Sell

PDA's
MP3 Players
DVD's
In-Car Entertainment
Gaming Consoles
Widescreen TV's
Mobile Internet
Mini Discs
Digital Cameras
Home Cinema
HiFi's
Arcade Machines

You can buy and sell anything on eBay. eBay.co.uk

IMAGE COURTESY OF THE ADVERTISING ARCHIVES

EBay provides online auction and sales opportunities for businesses and consumers.

✓ **assessment check**

1. What is competitive bidding?
2. Describe the benefits of an auction—to the buyer and to the seller.

THE TRANSFER PRICING DILEMMA

6 Explain the importance of transfer pricing.

A pricing problem peculiar to large-scale enterprises is the determination of an internal **transfer price**—the price for moving goods between **profit centers,** which are any part of the organization to which revenue and controllable costs can be assigned, such as a department. As companies expand, they tend to decentralize management and set up profit centers as a control device in the newly decentralized operation.

In a large company, profit centers might secure many needed resources from sellers within their own organization. The pricing problem thus poses several questions: What rate should profit center A (maintenance department) charge profit center B (production department) for the cleaning compound used on B's floors? Should the price be the same as it would be if A did the work for an outside party? Should B receive a discount? The answers to these questions depend on the philosophy of the firm involved.

Transfer pricing can be complicated, especially for multinational organizations. The government closely monitors transfer pricing practices because these exchanges offer easy ways for companies to avoid paying taxes on profits. Recent congressional investigations of the trend for U.S. firms to incorporate in Bermuda have focused on U.S. tax savings made possible by transfer pricing rates used between the firm's production location (U.S.) and its home country (Bermuda), even though no production takes place in Bermuda.

Figure 19.4 shows how this type of pricing manipulation might work. Suppose a South Korean manufacturer of DVD players sells its machines to its U.S. subsidiary for distribution to dealers. Although each unit costs $25 to build, the manufacturer charges the distributor $75. In turn, the distributor sells the DVD players to retailers for $125 each. This arrangement gives the South Korean manufacturer a $50 profit on each machine, on which it pays taxes only in South Korea. Meanwhile, the American distributor writes off $50 for advertising and shipping costs, leaving it with no profits—and no tax liability.

 assessment check

1. Define *transfer price.*
2. What is a profit center?

GLOBAL CONSIDERATIONS AND ONLINE PRICING

Throughout this course, we have seen the impact of the Internet on every component of the marketing mix. This chapter has touched on the outer edges of the Internet's influence on pricing practices. Remember that every online marketer is inherently a global marketer that must understand the wide variety of internal and external conditions that affect global pricing strategies. Internal influences include the firm's goals and marketing strategies; the costs of developing, producing, and marketing its output; the nature of the products; and the firm's competitive strengths. External influences

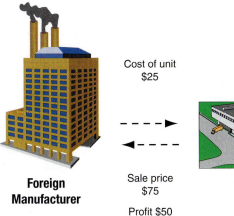

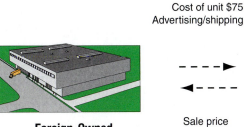

figure 19.4

Transfer Pricing to Escape Taxation

Cost of unit $25

Cost of unit $75
Advertising/shipping $50

Foreign Manufacturer

Sale price $75

Profit $50

Foreign-Owned Distributor

Sale price $125

Profit $0

Retailer

include general conditions in international markets, especially those in the firm's target markets; regulatory limitations; trade restrictions; competitors' actions; economic events; and the global status of the industry.

TRADITIONAL GLOBAL PRICING STRATEGIES

7 Compare the three alternative global pricing strategies.

In general, a company can implement one of three export pricing strategies: a standard worldwide price, dual pricing, or market-differentiated pricing. Exporters often set standard worldwide prices, regardless of their target markets. This strategy can succeed if foreign marketing costs remain low enough that they do not affect overall costs or if their prices reflect average unit costs. A company that implements a standard pricing program must monitor the international marketplace carefully, however, to make sure that domestic competitors do not undercut its prices.

The dual pricing strategy distinguishes prices for domestic and export sales. Some exporters practice cost-plus pricing to establish dual prices that fully allocate their true domestic and foreign costs to product sales in those markets. These prices ensure that an exporter makes a profit on any product it sells, but final prices may exceed those of competitors. Other companies opt for flexible cost-plus pricing schemes that allow marketers to grant discounts or change prices according to shifts in the competitive environment or fluctuations in the international exchange rate.

The third strategy, market-differentiated pricing, makes even more flexible arrangements to set prices according to local marketplace conditions. The dynamic global marketplace often requires frequent price changes by exporters who choose this approach. Effective market-differentiated pricing depends on access to quick, accurate market information.

 assessment check

1. What are the three traditional global pricing strategies?
2. Which is the most flexible global pricing strategy?

CHARACTERISTICS OF ONLINE PRICING

To deal with the influences of the Internet on pricing policies and practices, marketers are applying old strategies in new ways and companies are updating operations to compete with electronic technologies. Some firms offer online specials that do not appear in their stores or mail-order catalogs. These may take such forms as limited-time discounts, free shipping offers, or coupons that are good only online.

The Cannibalization Dilemma

8 Relate the concepts of cannibalization, bundle pricing, and bots to online pricing strategies.

cannibalization Loss of sales of an existing product due to competition from a new product in the same line.

By pricing the same products differently online, companies run the risk of **cannibalization.** The new twist to an old tactic is that companies are self-inflicting price cuts by creating competition among their own products. During the first decade of e-business, marketers debated whether it was worth taking the risk of alienating customers and channel members by offering lower prices for their products online—which then was an unproven retail outlet. But today, marketers are becoming more savvy about integrating marketing channels, including online sites and affiliated stores—different stores owned by the same company.[32] Books-A-Million is the nation's third-largest bookstore chain. Customers who visit its stores may purchase its top 20 bestsellers at 40 percent below list price. But those who order online can pick up the same books at a discount of 46 percent or more. This practice actually gives BAM a chance to compete against Amazon.com, reaching a wider range of customers.

Use of Shopbots

A second characteristic of online pricing is the use of search programs called **bots** or **shopbots**—derived from the word *robots*—that act as comparison shopping agents. Bots search the Web for a specific product and print a list of sites that offer the best prices. In online selling, bots force marketers to keep prices low. However, marketing researchers report that almost four of every five online shoppers check out several sites before buying, and price is not the only variable they consider when making a purchase decision. Service quality and support information are powerful motivators in the decision process. Also, while price is an important factor with products such as books and DVDs, it is not as important with complex or highly differentiated products, such as real estate or investment banking. Brand image and customer service may outweigh price in these purchase decisions.

BUNDLE PRICING

As marketers have watched e-business weaken their control over prices, they have modified their use of the price variable in the marketing mix. Whenever possible, they have moved to an approach called **bundle pricing,** in which customers acquire a host of goods and services in addition to the tangible products they purchase.

> **bundle pricing** Offering two or more complementary products and selling them for a single price.

Nowhere is bundle pricing more prevalent than in the telecommunications industry. Consumers are bombarded daily by advertisements for all kinds of Internet, cell phone, and cable TV packages. AT&T recently offered two packages to new subscribers who were still considering switching from dial-up to broadband service. The packages included ten e-mail accounts with 2 gigabytes of storage, along with rebates on an AT&T wireless gateway or modem. A one-year contract was required, and prices reverted from the special rate of $12.99 and $17.99 to $29.99 and $34.99 at the end of that period. Many marketers believe that bundling for telecom and cable providers is a necessity for retaining customers.[33]

But sometimes consumers resist the practice of bundling, claiming that they are being forced to pay for services they don't want in order to receive the ones they do. This is particularly the case with cable television. Cable firms explain that they have spent billions of dollars to expand their networks and technology and would be left with unused capacity if they sold only a few channels at a time. But Charles F. Dolan, chairman of Cablevision Systems Corporation, disagrees, saying that he supports *à la carte* pricing, or giving consumers the option to choose and pay for only the channels they want. This practice, he argues, "will result in a more affordable service for all with more programming options. Consumers should not be obliged directly or indirectly to buy services they do not want."[34]

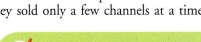

✓ assessment check

1. What is cannibalization?
2. What is bundle pricing?

Strategic Implications of Marketing in the 21st Century

Price has historically been the marketing variable least likely to be used as a source of competitive advantage. However, using price as part of a marketing program designed to meet a firm's overall organizational objectives can be a powerful strategy.

Technology has forever changed the marketplace, which affects the pricing function. Traditional geographic boundaries that allowed some businesses to operate have been broken by the Internet as well as mass merchandisers who offer a larger selection and lower prices. A customer in Wyoming might want to purchase an individually carved and painted walking cane from Kenya or an ornamental fan from Kyoto. Not a problem—the Web connects buyers and sellers around the globe. Similarly, the cost of shipping an overnight FedEx package from New York to California is no more than shipping it to a nearby city.

Not only is it possible to escape the boundaries of time and space on the Internet, but price is no longer a constant in the marketing process.

With the increasing number of auction sites and search technologies such as bots, customers now have more power to control the prices of goods and services. Consumers can find the lowest prices on the market, and they can also negotiate prices for many of the products they buy. To succeed, marketers will continue to offer value—fair prices for quality goods and services—and superior customer service. Those traditions will always be in style.

REVIEW OF CHAPTER OBJECTIVES

1   Compare the alternative pricing strategies and explain when each strategy is most appropriate.

The alternative pricing strategies are skimming pricing strategy, penetration pricing strategy, and competitive pricing strategy. Skimming pricing is commonly used as a market-entry price for distinctive products with little or no initial competition. Penetration pricing is used when there is a wide array of competing brands. Everyday low pricing (EDLP), a variant of penetration pricing, is used by discounters that attempt to hold the line on prices without having to rely heavily on short-term coupons, rebates, and other price concessions. Competitive pricing is employed when marketers wish to concentrate their competitive efforts on marketing variables other than price.

2   Describe how prices are quoted.

Methods for quoting prices depend on such factors as cost structures, traditional practices in the particular industry, and policies of individual firms. Price quotes can involve list prices, market prices, cash discounts, trade discounts, quantity discounts, and allowances such as trade-ins, promotional allowances, and rebates. Shipping costs often figure heavily into the pricing of goods. A number of alternatives for dealing with these costs exist: FOB plant pricing, in which the price includes no shipping charges; FOB origin-freight allowed, or freight absorbed, which allows the buyer to deduct transportation expenses from the bill; uniform-delivered price, in which the same price, including shipping expenses, is charged to all buyers; and zone pricing, in which a set price exists within each region.

3   Identify the various pricing policy decisions that marketers must make.

A pricing policy is a general guideline based on pricing objectives and is intended for use in specific pricing decisions. Pricing policies include psychological pricing, unit pricing, price flexibility, product-line pricing, and promotional pricing.

4   Relate price to consumer perceptions of quality.

The relationship between price and consumer perceptions of quality has been the subject of considerable research. In the absence of other cues, price is an important influence on how the consumer perceives the product's quality. A well-known and accepted concept is that of price limits—limits within which the perception of product quality varies directly with price. The concept of price limits suggests that extremely low prices may be considered too cheap, thus indicating inferior quality.

5   Contrast competitive bidding and negotiated prices.

Competitive bidding and negotiated prices are pricing techniques used primarily in the B2B sector and in government and organizational markets. Sometimes prices are negotiated through competitive bidding, in which several buyers quote prices on the same service or good. Buyer specifications describe the item that the government or B2B firm wishes to acquire. Negotiated contracts are another possibility in many procurement situations. The terms of the contract are set through negotiations between buyer and seller.

6   Explain the importance of transfer pricing.

A phenomenon in large corporations is transfer pricing, in which a company sets prices for transferring goods or services from one company profit center to another. The term *profit center* refers to any part of the organization to which revenue and controllable costs can be assigned. In large companies whose profit centers acquire resources from other parts of the firm, the prices charged by one profit center to another will directly affect both the cost and profitability of the output of both profit centers.

7   Compare the three alternative global pricing strategies.

Companies can choose from three export pricing strategies: a standard worldwide price, dual pricing, or market-differentiated pricing. A standard worldwide price may be possible if foreign marketing costs are so low that they do not affect overall costs or if the price is based on an average unit cost. The dual pricing approach establishes separate domestic and export price strategies. Some exporters use cost-plus pricing methods to establish

dual prices that fully allocate their true domestic and foreign costs to their product; others choose flexible cost-plus pricing. Market-differentiated pricing is the most flexible export pricing strategy, because it allows firms to price their products according to marketplace conditions. It requires easy access to quick, accurate market information.

8   Relate the concepts of cannibalization, bundle pricing, and bots to online pricing strategies.

To deal with the influences of the Internet on pricing policies and practices, marketers are applying old strategies in new ways, and companies are updating operations to compete with electronic technologies. Cannibalization secures additional sales through

lower prices that take sales away from the marketer's other products. Bots, also known as shopbots, act as comparison-shopping agents. Bundle pricing is offering two or more complementary products and selling them for a single price.

 ✓ *assessment check* **answers**

1.1 What are the three major pricing strategies?

The three major pricing strategies are skimming, penetration, and competitive.

1.2 What is EDLP?

EDLP stands for everyday low pricing. It is a variation of penetration pricing often used by discounters.

2.1 What are the three major types of discounts?

The three major types of discounts are cash discounts, trade discounts, and quantity discounts.

2.2 Identify the four alternatives for handling transportation costs in pricing policies.

The four alternatives for handling transportation costs are FOB pricing, uniform-delivered pricing, zone pricing, and basing-point pricing.

3.1 Define *pricing policy*.

A pricing policy is a general guideline that reflects marketing objectives and influences specific pricing decisions.

3.2 Describe the two types of psychological pricing other than prestige pricing.

The two additional types of psychological pricing are odd pricing, in which marketers set prices at odd numbers just under round numbers, and unit pricing, which states prices in terms of a recognized unit of measurement.

3.3 What is promotional pricing?

Promotional pricing is a lower-than-normal price for a set period of time.

4.1 Describe the price–quality connection.

Price serves as an important indicator of a product's quality. However, many marketers now work hard to convince consumers that they are offering high-quality products at the lowest possible price.

4.2 What are price limits?

Price limits indicate certain boundaries within which consumers' product-quality perceptions vary directly with price. A price set lower than expected seems too cheap, and one set above the expected limit is seen as too expensive.

assessment check **answers**

5.1 What is competitive bidding?

Competitive bidding consists of inviting potential suppliers to quote prices on proposed purchases or contracts.

5.2 Describe the benefits of an auction—to the buyer and to the seller.

An auction can provide buyers with opportunities to buy goods and services at very low prices. It can also offer the seller an opportunity to sell to a wider audience (online) perhaps at a higher price than otherwise would be possible, if the item is particularly popular.

6.1 Define *transfer price*.

A transfer price is the price for moving goods between profit centers.

6.2 What is a profit center?

A profit center is any part of the organization to which revenue and controllable costs can be assigned.

7.1 What are the three traditional global pricing strategies?

The three global pricing strategies are standard worldwide pricing, dual pricing, and market-differentiated pricing.

7.2 Which is the most flexible global pricing strategy?

The most flexible global pricing strategy is market-differentiated pricing, which allows firms to set prices according to actual conditions.

8.1 What is cannibalization?

Cannibalization involves cutting prices in one selling channel, which creates direct competition with a firm's own products.

8.2 What is bundle pricing?

Bundle pricing involves combining a number of goods or services together and offering them at a set price.

MARKETING TERMS YOU NEED TO KNOW

OTHER IMPORTANT MARKETING TERMS

ASSURANCE OF LEARNING REVIEW

1. Under what circumstances is a skimming pricing strategy most likely to be used? What are its benefits? Drawbacks?
2. Why is competitive pricing risky for marketers?
3. What is the difference between a list price and a market price?
4. What are the benefits and drawbacks to rebates—for both buyers and sellers?
5. How is product-line pricing helpful to both retailers and their customers?
6. What is leader pricing? Why do retailers use it?
7. What is the difference between a competitive bid and a negotiated price?
8. In what ways is transfer pricing somewhat complicated?
9. Describe briefly the three traditional global pricing strategies. Give an example of a firm or product that would be likely to adopt one of the three approaches, and explain why.
10. Although cannibalization generally forces price cuts, in what ways can it actually benefit a firm?

PROJECTS AND TEAMWORK EXERCISES

1. Skimming pricing, penetration pricing, and competitive pricing are three alternative pricing strategies. Divide your class into three teams. Then assign each team one of the three strategies and ask them to prepare a brief argument discussing the merits of their assigned pricing strategy for the following five products. Ask them to share their findings with the rest of the class. Once all three presentations have been completed, ask the class to vote on the most appropriate strategy for each product.
   a. video game
   b. cell phone with camera feature
   c. monitored burglar, smoke, and fire alarm
   d. special section of the supermarket that stocks only locally grown produce
   e. new brand of skin- and hair-care products
2. On your own or with a classmate, figure out how much it will cost to buy and own one of the following cars (or select another model), new, from a dealership. What is the list price? What price do you plan to negotiate?
   a. Toyota Prius
   b. Saturn Vue
   c. Ford Mustang
   d. Volkswagen Beetle
3. Assume that a product sells for $100 per ton and that Pittsburgh is the basing-point city for calculating transportation charges. Shipping from Pittsburgh to a potential customer in Cincinnati costs $10 per ton. The actual shipping costs of suppliers in three other cities are $8 per ton for Supplier A, $11 per ton for Supplier B, and $10 per ton for Supplier C. Using this information, answer the following questions:

   a. What delivered price would a salesperson for Supplier A quote to the Cincinnati customer?
   b. What delivered price would a salesperson for Supplier B quote to the Cincinnati customer?
   c. What delivered price would a salesperson for Supplier C quote to the Cincinnati customer?
   d. How much would each supplier net (after subtracting actual shipping costs) per ton on the sale?
4. On your own or with a classmate, browse through a local newspaper to find examples of promotional pricing. Tear out a few ads and evaluate them for their effectiveness. Does the promotional pricing make you want to purchase the products being advertised? Why or why not? Present your opinions to the class.
5. Target is a retailer that goes to great lengths to offer consumers the highest-quality goods at the lowest possible prices. To do this, Target makes alliances with popular top designers who agree to create special product lines for the store. One such talent is Luella Bartley, a British designer whose high-end goods are coveted worldwide—her popular Giselle tote bag retails for about $800. Bartley has recently signed an agreement with Target for a new Luella Target product line of clothing and accessories that will be priced from $9.99 to $149.99. Other designers are considering similar agreements with Target.[35] On your own or with a classmate, describe your plan for marketing the Luella Target product line in such a way that uses the price-quality connection to the best advantage.

CRITICAL-THINKING EXERCISES

1. As a consumer, would you rather shop at a store that features a sale once a month or a store that practices everyday low pricing (EDLP)? Why?

2. Go online and search for some items that offer rebates. What types of products did you find? Do you think rebates are an effective enticement to purchase? Why or why not?

3. Visit your supermarket or flip through your local newspaper and note the prices for different types of products. Which firms seem to use psychological pricing? Do competing firms seem to use the same pricing policies?

4. Are you a bargain hunter, or do you routinely pay full price when you shop? Make a list of the items for which price is a major consideration in your purchase decision. Then make a second list of the products for which price is either secondary or hardly a consideration at all. As a class, discuss your lists.

5. Frequent-purchase programs are discount offers designed by retailers and service providers to build loyalty among customers. Do these programs always work? What potential drawbacks might they contain?

ETHICS EXERCISE

Cell phone companies are well known for charging penalty fees to subscribers who want to terminate their service contracts early—a practice that has customers and consumer advocate groups grumbling. But in a break with the industry, Verizon Wireless has announced that it will now prorate its termination fee so that customers will only pay an amount that is proportionate to the time left in their contracts. Prior to this plan, Verizon Wireless subscribers would have to pay $175 to cancel their contracts. "The number of complaints on this issue is the single largest that our customers have," notes CEO Denny Strigl. "It's a legitimate complaint: if they leave in one month or month 23, they pay the same charge."[36]

1. The high termination fee effectively keeps wireless consumers tied to their plans and unable to respond to offers by other firms. Do you think Verizon Wireless is making a good move from a pricing standpoint? From an ethical standpoint? Why or why not?

2. Do you think that other firms will follow Verizon Wireless's lead?

INTERNET EXERCISES

1. **Pricing strategies.** Shopzilla.com (http://www.shopzilla.com) is a so-called shopping bot. Enter a product and Shopzilla.com searches through online retailers and identifies those that sell that particular product along with the price. Visit Shopzilla.com and go shopping for the following products (specify a model). Do the prices of these products vary from online retailer to online retailer? Do some products cost the same regardless of where they are purchased? Prepare a brief report on your findings and what they tell you about the pricing strategies used by various companies.
   a. A Nikon digital camera.
   b. A Bose home theater system.
   c. An HP notebook computer.

2. **Price markups.** Pick three makes and models of new vehicles. Choose different manufacturers and different body styles. Visit Edmunds.com (http://www.edmunds.com). Enter each vehicle you selected and answer the following questions:

   a. What is the difference between the invoice price and suggested retail price for each vehicle? Does each vehicle have the same markup?

   b. Does some optional equipment have higher markups than other equipment? Does the markup on optional equipment vary from manufacturer to manufacturer?

   c. Edmunds.com also reports something it calls the TVM® price—the price the consumer should expect to pay for the vehicle. For each vehicle is the TVM price closer to the invoice price of the retail price? Does the relationship between the TVM price, invoice, price, and retail price vary from vehicle to vehicle?

Note: Internet Web addresses change frequently. If you don't find the exact site listed, you may need to access the organization's home page and search from there or use a search engine such as Google.

CASE 19.1 Shopping Networks Price Everything to Sell

If you can't sleep one night, you might click the TV remote through a few channels and land on one of the shopping networks. They can be mesmerizing in the wee hours of the morning. Devotees of this type of shopping will tell you that these networks have the best bargains anywhere—24 hours a day, 7 days a week. That's because they never sell merchandise at the retail price; everything is automatically discounted, the minute it hits the air. The goods for sale include fine and costume jewelry, cosmetics, clothing, food, dolls, tools, small appliances, big-screen TVs, furniture, bedding—you name it. Consumers can snap up brand-name items made by manufacturers such as Dooney & Bourke, Sony, and KitchenAid, or they can select goods from the networks' own private-label lineup. Entrepreneurs clamor to get their products on the air—doing so can mean big bucks for small businesses, even if the prices are low, because the networks sell such a huge volume of goods.

The two largest networks—Home Shopping Network (HSN) and QVC (which stands for Quality, Value, Convenience) have been competing head to head for two decades now, with no signs of letting up. HSN has been in business for 29 years, while QVC has racked up 20. HSN claims to reach 89 million households in the United States, while QVC claims 87 million. Each has a 24-hour television channel and a Web site offering items and online promotions not available on TV. Despite its emphasis on TV as *the* way to shop—combining the convenience of mail order with the immediacy of live demonstrations of products by hosts and vendors—QVC also has a full-line store at the Mall of America in Minnesota, plus six outlet stores. HSN teams up with other mail-order firms such as Territory Ahead, Ballard Designs, and TravelSmith, offering shows devoted to products from these firms—at a lower price than is found in the catalogs. Both networks feature celebrities who either represent their own product lines or endorse those of others, including chef Wolfgang Puck, singer Patti Labelle, and NASCAR driver Jeff Gordon.

Prices at both networks follow a kind of reverse order of sale—they start at a discounted amount, then increase after a certain amount of time. But there are also special event prices—say, during an entire 24 hours devoted to fashion or jewelry. In some cases, a special price might be good for a day—or an hour. In addition, each network periodically offers payment plans spread over several months. For instance, HSN might offer its Flex-Pay over three months on a pair of earrings priced at $199.95. QVC might offer Easy Pay over two months on a bird bath that costs $87.84. Sometimes shipping & handling (S&H) is offered free, but in general, both networks attach an S&H charge to each item, rather than an entire order, as is the case with other mail-order or online firms.

HSN and QVC each has its loyal fans, much like those who follow certain television shows. Unlike taped shows, the themed broadcasts by the shopping networks are interactive—viewers are encouraged to call in and give testimonials about goods or services. But there are also those who are merely surfing through channels in the middle of the night, happen to land at a demonstration of cookware or jewelry, and stay there. If they watch long enough, they may buy something.

Questions for Critical Thinking

1. Describe the pricing strategy or strategies used by HSN and QVC.
2. Both networks use promotional pricing. What are the benefits and potential drawbacks of this approach?
3. Because both networks are well-known for low prices, how might this affect consumer perceptions of quality? What can the two firms do to combat any misperceptions?

Sources: HSN and QVC Web sites, **http://www.hsn.com** and **http://www.qvc.com**, accessed July 21, 2006; "QVC, Inc.," *Hoover's*, **http://www.hoovers.com**, accessed July 21, 2006; "Customer Success: Home Shopping Network," Business Objects, **http://www.firstlogic.com**, accessed July 21, 2006.

VIDEO CASE 19.2 Whirlpool: Innovation for Every Price Point

The written video case on Whirlpool appears on page VC-22. The recently filmed Whirlpool video is designed to expand and highlight the concepts in this chapter and the concepts and questions covered in the written video case.

Talking about Marketing Careers with. . .

PAUL WILLIAMS
FOUNDER
IDEA SANDBOX

Inspiration is found in some unexpected places—a garage where entrepreneurs tinker with new technology that revolutionizes business, an accidental meeting of the best and brightest minds that sparks an idea. But do we need a garage or face-to-face meetings? Finding creative solutions to marketing problems is the essence of a Web site called the Idea Sandbox. The site combines the free flow of ideas of a brainstorming session with the ease of communicating in the virtual world. It also offers resources—lists of other Web sites, publications, and a blog—to which marketers can turn for inspiration and creative problem solving. The purpose, as the site says, is to help businesses create *wicked good ideas,* which are "innovative, support [a company's] key strategy, and are truly remarkable."

Idea Sandbox is the brainchild of Paul Williams, a marketing professional who has brought a fresh perspective and new strategies to such giants as Disney and Starbucks. He is here to give us some background on his activities.

Q: You've worked for some pretty high- profile companies in your career. How did your education and professional experiences lead you to form Idea Sandbox? Did you always want to be an entrepreneur?

A: I've always considered myself in business for myself. Even when I was working at corporations, in the back of my mind I was working for myself—just at that company. Yes, I was totally loyal, but it allowed me to manage my *own* brand. Having this mindset allowed me to manage my career growth. I've always paid attention to my professional growth. If I hadn't grown in responsibility, maturity, or skills, I would work with my boss to put a plan together. If my growth was stagnant, I would first try to fix it within the company. If that wouldn't work, it indicated that I needed to find a challenge elsewhere.

I graduated in '91 with a bachelor of science degree with a double major in public relations (speech communication program) and business marketing/management. I also had a minor in art with emphasis in commercial and graphic design. Like many students, I didn't really know what I wanted to do when I graduated, so I built my program around subjects that I had enthusiasm for and saw a practical potential for. Public relations helped me be a better problem solver. Business courses helped me think more strategically. Art course work allowed me to communicate with creative people and understand visual composition.

One of my most valuable experiences was doing an internship my final year in college. I worked in the PR department of a medical center, which gave me real experience that could be reflected in my résumé. I recommend that you do as much work related to your potential field as possible. It doesn't matter if it's volunteer or unpaid—you'll get paid with experience.

Q: Students read about different pricing strategies for companies—reaching or maintaining profitability, meeting the competition, and establishing prestige for a product. How did you set a strategy for your company?

A: At Idea Sandbox, I use two different pricing strategies. Occasionally, when working with a smaller client, I may charge a per-day fee or perhaps a flat fee based on how many days' work a project will take. But the key pricing strategy I use is called value-based fees. Hourly rates and even day rates force your work based on the cost of time and materials. Value-based fees are based on the value of the outcome to the client, not the cost of your tasks.

Q: Who are Idea Sandbox clients? What range of services do they obtain? How are your fees set?

A: Idea Sandbox specializes in innovative/creative problem solving for medium to large English-speaking companies in the U.S. and Europe that lack internal expertise or resources or want an external perspective for innovative ideas essential to business success.

We offer problem solving/strategy sessions—a forum where you bring the challenge—and after sessions ranging from several hours to several weeks, we emerge with an effective and meaningful strategy. I also assist companies in improving their innovation process. Finally, other services range from creativity and innovation courses to designing space conducive for brainstorming.

My fees are primarily based on the anticipated value of implementing the programs or ideas I'm assisting to build—value-based fees. While I use key tools and pull from a proven process, every client situation is different. So, each proposal is unique.

Q: In this text students have seen examples of companies that are shifting their strategies to better serve customers and remain competitive. How common is it for companies to switch marketing strategies?

A: The best-run companies have created a mission statement that guides their choices. I'm not talking about some words on paper or posted in the company lunchroom, rather a living mission that everyone in the company believes—its reason for being. When a company faces change, its staff may alter their short-term plans to better meet customer needs, to keep up with technology, to outdo their competitor, etc. But they should stay true to their reason for being. The mission statement serves as a compass to keep the company on the right path.

Q: Today's marketers are using some innovative methods to reach their customers—enlisting consumers in buzz marketing campaigns to serve as brand champions, sending text messages to cell phones—and get the word out cost-effectively. What is the most creative idea you've seen companies use in a marketing campaign?

A: The most creative ideas brands execute are ideas that entertain, make a point, are memorable, are genuine, and connect with me as a customer. It is extremely difficult to do all these things and easy to take a short-cut and go for the quick blast of attention. But ultimately the brand will suffer. Truly understanding your customers and communicating through an appropriate channel is a lot of work—but extremely rewarding both financially and for the brand's reputation. A company that does a great job of this is Apple Computer. Everything they do from the design of the computer to the design of their shipping boxes and shopping bags clearly says "Apple" and "think different."

You may be tempted to do a media stunt to gain attention. But think about the brand of the company as if it were a person with a reputation to uphold. Is the tactic you are considering going to help or hurt that reputation? There are a million cheap and easy ideas out there, but they're just that—cheap and easy.

Q: Because you help marketers generate creative ideas, you must have some unique insight to pass along. What can students do to gain skills and make themselves stand out from the crowd?

A: **Gain Experience!** On your first marketing job interview, they're going to ask you if you have ever managed a budget, created a marketing plan, led an event, led people, managed multiple priorities, taken care of details, increased sales, increased attendance (the same stuff written into an entry-level job description). Now you won't be surprised, and you have plenty of time between now and graduation to work on these skills. Be the treasurer for an organization, write the plan to help the volunteer group gain awareness, be in charge of student elections, raise your hand and be team captain, learn to prioritize and effectively juggle tasks, pay attention to the details, come up with ways to drive sales, get more student participation in an event than in the past. Finally, keep notes of all these activities. It doesn't matter where or for what cause you did these things. It matters that you can say, "Yes, I have," during your first interview.

Read. I know, you're probably sick of reading. I was by the time I finished school. But the more you read, the faster you can read and the more you can process. You may not have to read something because it's on a syllabus but rather because your boss says you could use more organization skills or should be better at managing projects. You'll want to quickly and effectively learn these skills, and reading is your best ally. I recommend reading everything that interests you and is related to your job (or potential job). It's also great to read stuff you would never normally pick up.

Add Value. Your boss asks you to enter some figures in a spreadsheet and you only need to return to her with a completed spreadsheet. But what if you found a way to graph the data so it reads easier than a column of numbers or reformatted the spreadsheet so it fits better in her planner? Or what if you corrected some inconsistencies in the formulas? Bottom line: Always look for a way to add value—to add the brand called YOU to the projects you work on. Leave them better than when you found them.

Arrive with the Solution. One of the first mistakes I made early in my career was alerting my boss to a problem with one of our marketing programs. I thought I was being smart in discovering the issue. What I hadn't done was to think through the steps to fix it. Yes, I raised the issue, but I simply became part of the problem. From that point on, I learned to arrive with the solution to any problem I discovered. If I could, I'd fix the problem and report that. "Hey, the tracking sheets weren't calculating properly, but I reworked the formulas, reran the numbers, and it's all better now." If I couldn't fix it, I'd recommend an approach. It taught me to think through issues and align myself with my boss as a problem solver.

Be Passionate. I've always followed the philosophy, "It's not enough to be good when you dream of being great." Being passionate about what you're doing helps you to get great. Sometimes in your professional career you can skate by—going through the motions gets you where you need to go. But I argue that if you don't have passion for what you are doing, it isn't worth doing. If you aren't challenged, you aren't growing and getting better—you're becoming stagnant. Perhaps it's time to try a new project, take on more work, or find a different role. I know statistics indicate only a small percentage of workers enjoy their jobs. But that's something totally within your control. If you're not passionate about your job, either find a way to make it exciting or do something different. It's up to you.

To Second City, Laughter's Priceless

The Second City

For an entertainment company based on improvised decision-making, Second City's chief financial officer, Lou Carbone, holds a unique responsibility. He operates out of the Chicago office as a strategist, a liaison, a treasurer, and, in his own words, "the father figure who may have to say ëno, you can't play with that toy.'" When Second City Communications negotiates a deal with Microsoft or JPMorgan, it turns to Carbone for analysis and guidance. And when Second City Theatricals sees an exciting opportunity in children's theater, its Lou Carbone measures the financial gain. Lou Carbone and Second City's top management want to make pricing decisions that welcome as many fans as possible. They also want to keep the company adequately funded.

The Second City's ticket prices are set competitively for the live entertainment industry. Intended to attract the general market, tickets are priced at, around, or just below the traditional theater rate. Kelly Leonard, Second City's vice president, explains SC's use of a flexible pricing strategy: "We've been sensitive to not underprice ourselves in the marketplace when demand is highest. Therefore, the weekend tickets are significantly more than the weekday prices." This maneuver capitalizes on tourist activity at each of SC's main city theaters. In Detroit, Toronto, Las Vegas, and Chicago, the ticket prices fluctuate from $12 to $24, depending on the night. For Second City Los Angeles, which opened with a smaller studio theater, ticket prices penetrate the industry at a comparatively lower rate of $15 a seat. Conversely, Second City Denver's partnership with the Denver Center for the Performing Arts has set market-plus prices at $28 for a Friday night show. This introduces an evening at The Second City as a prestigious outing for the new Colorado market. SC theaters offer only general-admission seating, so audiences arrive early to get a good seat. This creates more excitement prior to the show and boosts bar sales.

Pricing strategy takes a more complicated, varied approach for Second City Communications. In such negotiations Lou Carbone brings financial savvy to a company otherwise focused on creating an ideal acting environment. Tom Yorton, president of Second City Communications, collaborates regularly with Carbone. "Thank God for Lou," says Yorton. "The fact is that none of us really have a finance background. He can help educate us to make the place run better. We're an improv theater, so we make it up as we go along. Finance is one area where you really can't make it up as you go along." SC Communications negotiates with its clients on the assumption that the quality of the product relates directly to the price. Because this division is offering *Fortune* 1000 clients a product that responds to their need for presentations at specific events or training, it negotiates at an appropriate price for each project and strives to secure long-term relationships. It also offers discounts to nonprofit and educational organizations,

For the Training Center, pricing is designed to make The Second City accessible to a wide variety of consumers. Focusing on volume, SC Training Center sets their price at a competitive, slightly below-market rate. The Training Center student has a variety of incentives. For instance, the SC Training Center produces shows for students in the writing, acting, and improvisation programs. The students enjoy trying their hand at the exciting art form without having to rent the theater, while Second City acquires a certain percentage of ticket sales. Once a student is involved in the program, ticket prices for Second City's resident shows are discounted. Class prices can be reduced for those involved in internships, and a variety of summer camps and work-

shops are offered to attract students with limited funds.

Second City also sells a variety of products: DVDs, CDs and books, T-shirts and hats, and beverages from the bar served in the theater. Each of these items has a different price and a different pricing strategy.

Over the last two years, Lou Carbone has been meeting one on one with department heads to train them in streamlined financial reporting. This practice has also provided The Second City a more consistent strategy for pricing ventures.

No matter which division of Second City is determining price, assessing the cost of production is fundamental. Many innovative ideas, according to Lou Carbone, are challenged by the practical assessment of production costs, travel expenses, labor fees, and unexpected market fluctuations. Forty to 50 percent of all revenue for the Second City goes toward covering labor costs. It employs approximately 325 people in the United States and 50 in Canada. Though it has a relatively small entertainment company, The Second City operates theaters in two countries as well as a number of touring companies, and offers its product mix of business consultation and training internationally. Its main source of revenue remains, however, its resident stages. Kelly Leonard explains that while this may fluctuate, Second City continues to see its stages as its "financial base." Second City stages are the division of the company most capable of self-sustenance. As new project proposals are generated within the Second City team, its core product of live sketch comedy is often the creative and financial backdrop for the venture. Competitive ticket pricing at the Chicago stages generates consistent sellouts and has given the company a reliable financial resource to nurture each facet of its growing business. SC Toronto, for instance, has been challenged by a struggling economy in that region throughout the last decade. The Second City Chicago has been able to pull from reserves and credit lines to back the operation.

The Second City has evolved from humble financial beginnings to become an iconic fixture of the entertainment industry. It has made pricing decisions that have provided solid returns and have resulted in financial stability. This stability gives Second City the confidence to be innovative and take risks. Exciting project proposals are consistently handed to Lou Carbone and he "has to be the one to pull in the reins." But Carbone says that for a CFO, The Second City is the best place to work. "We're always laughing here," says Carbone, and you can't put a price on that.

Questions

1. Explain The Second City's use of flexible pricing for its resident stages. What are a couple of major factors in determining show ticket prices?

2. Why does Second City Communications use the most negotiating in its pricing?

3. What incentives exist for consumers of SC's Training Center? How do you think these function in SC's long-term relationship with its students?

4. Which division of The Second City's product mix does the company consider its "financial base"? Why? How has its pricing strategy benefited the whole company?

appendix

Financial Analysis in Marketing

A number of basic concepts from accounting and finance offer invaluable tools to marketers. Understanding the contributions made by these concepts can improve the quality of marketing decisions. In addition, marketers often must be able to explain and defend their decisions in financial terms. These accounting and financial tools can be used to supply quantitative data to justify decisions made by marketing managers. In this appendix we describe the major accounting and finance concepts that have marketing implications and explain how they help managers make informed marketing decisions.

FINANCIAL STATEMENTS

All companies prepare a set of financial statements on a regular basis. Two of the most important financial statements are the income statement and balance sheet. The analogy of a motion picture is often used to describe an *income statement,* because it presents a financial record of a company's revenues, expenses, and profits over a period of time, such as a month, quarter, or year. By contrast, the *balance sheet* is a snapshot of what a company owns (called *assets*) and what it owes (called *liabilities*) at a point in time, such as at the end of the month, quarter, or year. The difference between assets and liabilities is referred to as *owner's, partners',* or *shareholders' equity*—the amount of funds the firm's owners have invested in its formation and continued operations. Of the two financial statements, the income statement contains more marketing-related information.

A sample income statement for Composite Technology is shown in Figure 1. Headquartered in a Boston suburb, Composite Technology is a B2B producer and marketer. The firm designs and manufactures a variety of composite components for manufacturers of consumer, industrial, and government products. Total sales revenues for 2007 amounted to $675.0 million. Total expenses, including taxes, for the year were $583.1 million. The year 2007 proved to be profitable for Composite Technology—the firm reported a profit, referred to as net income, of $91.9 million. While total revenue is a fairly straightforward number, several of the expenses shown on the income statement require additional explanation.

For any company that makes its own products (a manufacturer) or simply markets one or more items produced by others (an importer, retailer, or wholesaler), the largest single expense is usually a category called *cost of goods sold.* This reflects the cost, to the firm, of the goods that it markets to its customers. In the case of Composite Technology, the cost of goods sold represents the cost of components and raw materials, as well as the cost of designing and manufacturing the composite panels the firm produces and markets to its business customers.

The income statement illustrates how cost of goods sold is calculated. The calculation begins with the value of the firm's inventory at the beginning of 2007. Inventory is the value of raw materials, partially completed products, and finished products held by the firm at the end of some time period, say the end of the year. The cost of materials Composite Technology purchased during the year and the direct cost of manufacturing the finished products are then added to the beginning inventory figure. The result is cost of goods the firm has available for sale during the year. Once the firm's accountants subtract the value of inventory held by the firm at the end of 2007, they know the cost of goods sold. By simply subtracting cost of goods sold from total sales revenues generated during the year, they determine that Composite achieved gross profits of $270.0 million in 2007.

Operating expenses are another significant cost for most firms. This broad category includes such marketing outlays as sales compensation and expenses, advertising and other promotions, and the expenses

figure 1

Composite Technology 2007 Income Statement

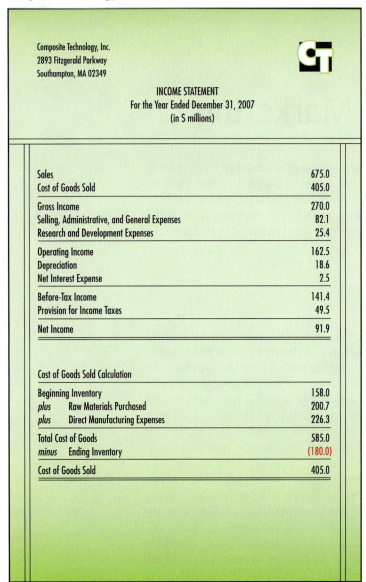

Composite Technology, Inc.
2893 Fitzgerald Parkway
Southampton, MA 02349

INCOME STATEMENT
For the Year Ended December 31, 2007
(in $ millions)

Sales	675.0
Cost of Goods Sold	405.0
Gross Income	270.0
Selling, Administrative, and General Expenses	82.1
Research and Development Expenses	25.4
Operating Income	162.5
Depreciation	18.6
Net Interest Expense	2.5
Before-Tax Income	141.4
Provision for Income Taxes	49.5
Net Income	91.9

Cost of Goods Sold Calculation

Beginning Inventory		158.0
plus	Raw Materials Purchased	200.7
plus	Direct Manufacturing Expenses	226.3
Total Cost of Goods		585.0
minus	Ending Inventory	(180.0)
Cost of Goods Sold		405.0

involved in implementing marketing plans. Accountants typically combine these financial outlays into a single category with the label *Selling, Administrative, and General Expenses.* Other expense items included in the operating expenses section of the income statement are administrative salaries, utilities, and insurance.

Another significant expense for Composite Technology is research and development (R&D). This category includes the cost of developing new products and modifying existing ones. Firms such as pharmaceuticals, biotechnology, and computer companies spend significant amounts of money each year on R&D. Subtracting selling, administrative, and general expenses and R&D expenses from the gross profit equals the firm's operating income. For 2007, Composite had operating income of $162.5 million.

Depreciation represents the systematic reduction over time in the value of certain company assets, such as production machinery, office furniture, or laptops provided for the firm's sales representatives. Depreciation is an unusual expense in that it does not involve an actual cash expense. However, it does reflect the reality that equipment owned by the company is physically wearing out over time from use and/or from technological obsolescence. Also, charging a portion of the total cost of these long-lived items to each of the years in which they are used results in a more accurate determination of the total costs involved in the firm's operation each year.

Net interest expense is the difference between what a firm paid in interest on various loans and what it collected in interest on investments it might have made during the time period involved. Subtracting depreciation and net interest expense from the firm's operating profit reveals the firm's taxable income. Composite had depreciation of $18.6 million and a net interest expense of $2.5 million for the year, so its 2007 taxable income was $141.4 million.

Profit-seeking firms pay taxes calculated as a percentage of their taxable income to the federal government, as well as state income taxes in most states. Composite paid $49.5 million in taxes in 2007. Subtracting taxes from taxable income gives us the firm's *net income,* $91.9 million.

PERFORMANCE RATIOS

Managers often compute a variety of financial ratios to assess the performance of their firm. These ratios are calculated using data found on both the income statement and the balance sheet. Ratios are then compared with industry standards and with data from previous years. Several ratios are of particular interest to marketers.

A number of commonly used financial ratios focus on *profitability measures.* They are used to assess the firm's ability to generate revenues in excess of expenses and earn an adequate rate of return. Profitability measures include gross profit margin, net profit margin, and return on investment (or sales).

Gross Profit Margin

The gross profit margin equals the firm's gross profit divided by its sales revenues. In 2007, Composite had a gross profit margin of

$$\frac{\text{Gross Profit}}{\text{Sales}} = \frac{\$270.0 \text{ million}}{\$675.0 \text{ million}} = 40\%$$

The gross profit margin is the percentage of each sales dollar that can be used to pay other expenses and meet the firm's profit objectives. Ideally, businesses would like to see gross profit margins that are equal to or higher than those of other firms in their industry. A declining gross profit margin may indicate that the firm is under some competitive price pressure.

Net Profit Margin

The net profit margin equals net income divided by sales. For 2007, Composite had a net profit margin of

$$\frac{\text{Net Income}}{\text{Sales}} = \frac{\$91.9 \text{ million}}{\$675.0 \text{ million}} = 13.6\%$$

The net profit margin is the percentage of each sales dollar that the firm earns in profit, or keeps after all expenses have been paid. Companies generally want to see rising, or at least stable, net profit margins.

Return on Assets (ROA)

A third profitability ratio, return on assets, measures the firm's efficiency in generating sales and profits from the total amount invested in the company. For 2007, Composite's ROA is calculated as follows:

$$\frac{\text{Sales}}{\text{Average Assets}} \times \frac{\text{Net Income}}{\text{Sales}} = \frac{\text{Net Income}}{\text{Average Assets}}$$

$$\frac{\$675.0 \text{ million}}{\$595.0 \text{ million}} \times \frac{91.9 \text{ million}}{\$675.0 \text{ million}} = 1.13 \times 13.6\% = 15.4\%$$

The ROA ratio actually consists of two components. The first component, called *asset turnover,* is the amount of sales generated for each dollar invested. The second component is *net profit margin*. Data for total assets are found on the firm's balance sheet.

Assume that Composite began 2007 with $560 million in assets and ended the year with $630 million in assets. Its average assets for the year would be $595 million. As was the case for the other profitability ratios, Composite's ROI should be compared with that of other firms in the industry and with its own previous performance to be meaningful.

Inventory Turnover

Inventory turnover is typically categorized as an activity ratio because it evaluates the effectiveness of the firm's resource use. Specifically, it measures the number of times a firm "turns" its inventory each year. The ratio can help answer the question of whether the firm has the appropriate level of inventory. Inventory turnover equals sales divided by average inventory. From the income statement, we see that Composite Technology began 2007 with $158 million in inventory and also ended the year with $180 million in inventory. Therefore, the firm's average inventory was $169 million. The firm's inventory turnover ratio equals

$$\frac{\text{Sales}}{\text{Average Inventory}} = \frac{\$675.0 \text{ million}}{\$169.0 \text{ million}} = 3.99$$

For 2007, Composite Technology turned its inventory almost four times a year. While a faster inventory turn is usually a sign of greater efficiency, to be really meaningful the inventory turnover ratio must be compared with historical data and appropriate peer firm averages. Different organizations can have very different inventory turnover ratios, depending on the types of products they sell. For instance, a supermarket such as Safeway might turn its inventory every three weeks for an annual rate of roughly 16 times per year. By contrast, a large furniture retailer is likely to average only about 2 turns per year. Again, the determination of a "good" or "inadequate" inventory turnover rate depends on typical rates in the industry and the firm's performance in previous years.

Accounts Receivable Turnover

Another activity ratio that may be of interest to marketers is accounts receivable turnover. This ratio measures the number of times per year a company "turns" its receivables. Dividing accounts receivable turnover into 365 gives us the average age of the company's receivables.

Companies make sales on the basis of either cash or credit. Credit sales allow the buyer to obtain a product now and pay for it at a specified later date. In essence, the seller is providing credit to the buyer. Credit sales are common in B2B transactions. It should be noted that sales to buyers using credit cards such as MasterCard and Visa are counted as cash sales because the issuer of the credit card, rather than the seller, is providing credit to the buyer. Consequently, most B2C sales are counted as cash sales.

Receivables are uncollected credit sales. Measuring accounts receivable turnover and the average age of receivables are important for firms in which credit sales make up a high proportion of total sales. Accounts receivable turnover is defined as follows:

$$\text{Accounts Receivable Turnover} = \frac{\text{Credit Sales}}{\text{Average Accounts Receivable}}$$

Assume that all of Composite Technology's sales are credit sales. Also assume that the firm began 2007 with $50 million in receivables and ended the year with $60 million in receivables (both numbers can be found on the balance sheet). Therefore, it had an average of $55 million in receivables. The firm's receivables turnover and average age equal:

$$\frac{\$675.0 \text{ million}}{\$55.0 \text{ million}} = 12.3 \text{ times}$$

$$\frac{365}{12.3} = 29.7 \text{ days}$$

Composite turned its receivables slightly more than 12 times per year. The average age of its receivables was slightly less than 30 days. Because Composite expects its customers to pay outstanding invoices within 30 days, these numbers appear appropriate. As with other ratios, however, receivables turnover and average age of receivables should also be compared with peer firms and historical data.

MARKUPS AND MARKDOWNS

In earlier chapters, we discussed the importance of pricing decisions for firms. This section expands on our prior discussion by introducing two important pricing concepts: markups and markdowns. They can help establish selling prices and evaluate various pricing strategies, and they are closely tied to a firm's income statement.

Markups

The amount that a marketer adds to a product's cost to set the final selling price is the markup. The amount of the markup typically results from two marketing decisions:

1. The services performed by the marketer. Other things being equal, retailers who offer more services charge larger markups to cover their costs.
2. The inventory turnover rate. Other things being equal, retailers with a higher turnover rate can cover their costs and earn a profit while charging a smaller markup.

A marketer's markup exerts an important influence on its image among present and potential customers. In addition, the markup affects the retailer's ability to attract shoppers. An excessive markup may drive away customers; an inadequate markup may fail to generate sufficient income to cover costs and return a profit.

Markups are typically stated as percentages of either the selling prices or the costs of the products. The formulas for calculating markups are as follows:

$$\text{Markup Percentage on Selling Price} = \frac{\text{Amount Added to Cost (Markup)}}{\text{Selling Price}}$$

$$\text{Markup Percentage on Cost} = \frac{\text{Amount Added to Cost (Markup)}}{\text{Cost}}$$

Consider a product with an invoice of 60 cents and a selling price of $1. The total markup (selling price less cost) is 40 cents. The two markup percentages are calculated as follows:

$$\text{Markup Percentage on Selling Price} = \frac{\$0.40}{\$1.00} = 40\%$$

$$\text{Markup Percentage on Cost} = \frac{\$0.40}{\$0.60} = 66.7\%$$

To determine the selling price knowing only the cost and markup percentage on selling price, a marketer applies the following formula:

$$\text{Price} = \frac{\text{Cost in Dollars}}{(100\% - \text{Markup Percentage on Selling Price})}$$

In the previous example, to determine the correct selling price of $1, the marketer would calculate as follows:

$$\text{Price} = \frac{\$0.60}{(100\% - 40\%)} = \$1.00$$

Similarly, you can convert the markup percentage from a specific item based on the selling price to one based on cost and the reverse using the following formulas:

$$\text{Markup Percentage on Selling Price} = \frac{\text{Markup Percentage on Cost}}{(100\% + \text{Markup Percentage on Cost})}$$

$$\text{Markup Percentage on Cost} = \frac{\text{Markup Percentage on Selling Price}}{(100\% - \text{Markup Percentage on Selling Price})}$$

Again, data from the previous example give the following conversions:

$$\text{Markup Percentage on Selling Price} = \frac{66.7\%}{(100\% + 66.7\%)} = 40\%$$

$$\text{Markup Percentage on Cost} = \frac{40\%}{(100\% - 40\%)} = 66.7\%$$

Marketers determine markups based partly on their judgments of the amounts that consumers will pay for a given product. When buyers refuse to pay a product's stated price, however, or when improvements in other products or fashion changes reduce the appeal of the current merchandise, a producer or retailer must take a markdown.

Markdowns

A markdown is a price reduction a firm makes on an item. Reasons for markdowns include sales promotions featuring price reductions or a decision that the initial price was too high. Unlike markups, markdowns cannot be determined from the income statement because the price reduction takes place before the sale occurs. The markdown percentage equals dollar markdowns divided by sales. For example, a retailer may decide to reduce the price of an item by $10, from $50 to $40, and sells 1,000 units. The markdown percentage equals:

$$\frac{(1,000 \times \$10)}{(1,000 \times \$40)} = \frac{\$10,000}{\$40,000} = 25\%$$

ASSIGNMENTS

1. Assume a product has an invoice price of $45 and a selling price of $60. Calculate the markup both as a percentage on the selling price and the cost.

2. A product has an invoice price of $92.50. The seller wants a markup on the selling price of 25%. Calculate the selling price.

3. Assume a retailer decides to reduce the price of an item by $5, from $15 to $10, and sells 5,000 units. Calculate the markdown percentage.

4. Obtain a recent income statement and balance sheet for a business of your choosing whose stock is publicly traded. (A good source of recent financial statements is the MSN Investor Web site, http://moneycentral.msn.com/investor.) Use the relevant data included on the income statement to calculate each of the following ratios:
   a. gross profit margin
   b. net profit margin
   c. inventory turnover
   d. return on assets
   e. price markup

5. Match the following set of financial ratios to each of the following firms: 3M, Gap, Pfizer, and Wal-Mart.

FINANCIAL RATIO	FIRM A	FIRM B	FIRM C	FIRM D
Net profit margin	28.4%	3.5%	13.9%	6.5%
Return on assets	20.6%	8.6%	14.6%	10.0%
Inventory turnover	2.1	7.6	3.4	4.9

video case contents

PHOTO: © GETTY IMAGES

VIDEO CASE 1.2   Harley–Davidson Keeps Riders Coming Back

Hog Heaven. That's where Harley-Davidson owners say they are during a ride. "Hogs," as Harley-Davidson motorcycles are affectionately known, represent freedom, adventure, and fun to their devoted owners. Riding one, with its distinctive engine roar and signature teardrop gas tank, is considered a unique experience that symbolizes the best of the American dream. Harley-Davidson bikes have proven to be a surprisingly durable pastime, too: once known as a symbol of rebellion, they now represent a fun indulgence to their owners.

Harley-Davidson, based in Milwaukee, has been manufacturing heavyweight motorcycles for more than a century and has watched them earn an enduring place in America's automotive history—as well as its popular culture. Elvis even rode one. Harley-Davidson knows its customers extremely well. Most are male; only about 11 percent are female. Nearly half have already owned a Harley, and just under a third have already owned a competitor's motorcycle. About 28 percent are first-time bike buyers. The largest group of Harley owners, and the company's target market, consists of 40-something males with a median income of more than $80,000, most of whom have owned a Harley before. The company is adept at using this kind of information about its customers to design its products and accessories and market them successfully.

The only major motorcycle manufacturer based in the United States, Harley-Davidson produces 36 different models and 8 different sport motorcycles. In one recent year its manufacturing plants produced a record number of bikes—350,000—helping fuel the company's steadily climbing annual revenues and earnings. Besides managing its production and distribution to be sure the bikes are ready when and where customers want to purchase them, Harley also makes it easier to own them. It offers its own financing and insurance programs for both dealers and customers.

Among the most successful of Harley's marketing efforts has been its ability to develop long-term relationships with its customers. One result? The number of repeat buyers mentioned earlier. The company uses a number of different relationship-building strategies. First, a full one-year membership in the Harley Owners Group (H.O.G.) comes with every purchase of a new, unregistered Harley-Davidson motorcycle. The company offers associate memberships for H.O.G. family members and passengers, and owner memberships are renewable at a discount. You can even become a member for life, and quite a few owners do. Membership earns owners entry into the members-only part of the company's H.O.G. Web site, several issues of its *Enthusiast* magazine each year, a subscription to the special member publication called *Hogtales*, a membership manual, toll-free customer service, and a touring handbook for trip planning. Harley-Davidson also organizes and sponsors special events for members, such as Pin Stops for awarding commemorative pins, Pit Stops for relaxing and socializing with other members at bike races, touring rallies, factory tours and open houses, and parades and charity functions. There are H.O.G. chapters in the United States and 20 other countries, including Australia, Canada, France, Germany, Italy, Japan, the Netherlands, New Zealand, Sweden, South Africa, and the United Kingdom. Links to each chapter on the company's Web site help connect 1 million members around the world.

Full members in the owner's group can take advantage of the company's online travel service to schedule a Fly & Ride vacation to any of 41 different locations in the United States, Canada, Europe, or Australia, picking up a bike from a local Harley-Davidson dealership on arrival to tour in style or simply renting a bike at selected dealerships. Harley-Davidson has also partnered with the Motorcycle Safety Foundation to sponsor a safe-rider skills program for H.O.G. members, which awards a $50 coupon for those who successfully complete the training.

For H.O.G. members wondering what to spend that $50 on, they can buy items including a black leather jacket or T-shirt emblazoned with the company's well-known logo, collectible patches, and customized accessories and gear for their bikes. The company has more than 1,300 dealerships in 60 countries and satellite stores nearly everywhere. "For Harley-Davidson enthusiasts," says one of the company's repair managers, "the actual motorcycle is only part of the ownership experience; customizing the bike can become an obsession. . . . A large part of Harley mania is due to the company's ability to provide quality custom components and accessories." In fact, it's said that you will rarely see two bikes that look alike. Harley-Davidson is using every means to build customer satisfaction and fulfill its owners' dreams.

Questions for Critical Thinking

1. How does Harley-Davidson provide customers with form, time, place, and ownership utility for its motorcycles?
2. In what ways does Harley-Davidson practice relationship marketing? Explain.
3. How does Harley-Davidson use the Internet in its marketing?
4. Would you say that Harley-Davidson adopts a consumer orientation in its marketing efforts? Explain your answer.

Sources: Harley-Davidson Web site, **http://www.harley-davidson.com**, accessed July 6, 2006; Harley Owners Group Web site, **http://www.hog.com**, accessed July 6, 2006; Harley-Davidson Motor Company brochure, **http://www.harley-davidson.com**; "Hog Heaven: Celebrating 100 Years of the Harley Davidson," The Library of Congress, **http://www.loc.gov**, accessed July 6, 2006; "Lista Storage Units Keep Harley-Davidson Running Fast," *MRO Today*, **http://www.mrotoday.com**, accessed July 6, 2006.

VIDEO CASE 2.2   Timbuk2's Success Is in the Bag

Timbuk2 began like many entrepreneurial businesses—it was started by someone whose need wasn't being met by the marketplace. A San Francisco bike messenger designed a rugged and stylish shoulder bag to carry during his workday. It was so popular with friends and acquaintances that he soon quit his job to start making the custom bags. The new company attracted devoted customers among young professionals both male and female—and fellow bike messengers—but within a few years it was nearly bankrupt.

Backed by private investors and a venture capital firm, Mark Dwight bought Timbuk2 a few years ago and swiftly turned the company around. It now produces more than 30 different products, and its San Francisco factory turns out a bag every fifteen minutes. Business has been so good that Timbuk2 recently distributed a total of $1 million in bonuses to its 40 nonmanagement workers to celebrate a banner year with sales of more than $10 million. Production has doubled; more than 1,000 specialty retailers in the outdoor, bicycle, and personal computer markets carry Timbuk2 bags nationwide. The company's e-business arm has tripled in size. Most important, the firm now operates with a positive cash flow and is solidly profitable.

When he bought the ailing firm, Dwight knew he would have to bring in experienced managers and impose a carefully thought-out vision for the future. He put together a team of industry veterans and with their help mapped out a detailed five-year plan that included hiring a financial controller and a product developer. The biggest challenge was to streamline production and revamp the company's existing production methods. Instead of stockpiling inventory, the firm's executives decided that Timbuk2 employees would make every bag to order and keep none in stock. Doing so would reduce the costs associated with warehousing items. In addition, they looked at the product lineup to decide which merchandise customers could order as standard designs and which customers would choose to customize. The changes met with some staff resistance, but Dwight credits those changes with keeping the factory from going out of business. He still reviews key performance measures with the entire operational staff in San Francisco every day. "Timbuk2 has the fun-loving culture of a start-up and the operational discipline of a mature company," he says proudly.

Another change Dwight brought to Timbuk2 was the concept of "stretch goals," which are revenue and target profits exceeding those in the company's budget by an aggressive margin but those that management believes can be reached with minimal added investment. "Our stretch goal is designed to inspire *esprit de corps* and exceptional effort," he says. "Since the incremental revenue is achieved with min-

imal added expense, it turbo-charges our annual profit sharing—and everyone loves that."

Other changes Dwight and his team planned for were significant additions to the product line, which continues to appeal to both men and women. Innovation began with the design and manufacture of a computer bag. Today, one-third of the company's sales come from computer bags, and the Apple Store is its largest single customer.

To keep its costs low, the firm has moved about half its production work to factories in China, but it still employs more than 50 people in sewing jobs in its Mission District location. "Our San Francisco factory is a novelty in the current age of outsourcing and offshoring," says Dwight. "I am committed to keeping [it] open for as long as possible." Although social responsibility is a big part of Timbuk2's overall goals, there's another reason for keeping production close to customers: "Locally produced bags can be customized to customer requests [via Timbuk2's "Build Your Own Bag" Web site] on a very short lead time," Dwight notes. "That quick response is a unique advantage."

Other elements of Timbuk2's marketing mix are as carefully planned as the company's product line and distribution. For instance, Timbuk2 recently hired a Sausalito marketing firm to manage its branding and marketing activities.

The changes the company instituted have been a resounding success. Its revenues grew 158 percent in a two-year period. That doesn't mean every new idea has worked out well. One big mistake—a short-lived deal to distribute bags in CompUSA stores at lower-than-normal markups—cost the company $50,000 before it was over. But Timbuk2's progress has been on a steady upward track ever since.

Dwight isn't stopping, though. His goals for the future include making Timbuk2 a more environmentally safe operation, so the firm is removing all traces of the dioxin-producing polyvinyl chloride plastic from its bags. This alteration also means changing many of the components in its most popular products to other compatible materials. The company is also planning on making a bigger "footprint" in the retail landscape. It has opened its first retail store, and there's talk of producing lines of apparel and footwear. "I want the Timbuk2 swirl to be as recognizable as the Nike swoosh," says Dwight.

Questions for Critical Thinking

1. What were some of the organizational strengths and weaknesses Mark Dwight inherited with the original Timbuk2, and how did they shape his strategic plans for the firm?

2. Describe how Porter's Five Forces model might apply to the situation facing Timbuk2 today. Be as specific as possible.
3. What are the opportunities and threats facing Timbuk2? How well do you think the company is planning to meet these challenges?
4. What do you think is Timbuk2's product strategy? How effective is it? What suggestions would you make to increase its effectiveness?

Sources: Timbuk2 Web site, **http://www.timbuk2.com**, accessed July 26, 2006; Maya Melenchuk, "In the Sack," *San Francisco Bay Guardian*, **http://www.sfbg.com**, accessed July 26, 2006; "In the Bag: 2005 Fast 50 Winner," *Fast Company*, **http://www.fastcompany.com**, accessed July 26, 2006; Julie McFadden, "Timbuk2 Goes PVC-Free," OutdoorNewswire, **http://www.outdoornewswire.com**, July 3, 2006; "Timbuk2 Taps Sausalito Brand Company," *San Francisco Business Times*, February 28, 2006, **http://www.bizjournals.com**; "Timbuk2 Acquired by Private Equity Investors," Business Wire, October 26, 2005, **http://www.findarticles.com**; David Worrell, "Go for the Gold," *Entrepreneur*, July 2005, **http://www.entrepreneur.com**; "Timbuk2: Delivering an Urban Lifestyle," *San Francisco Business Times*, May 4, 2005, **http://www.biztimes.com**; Andrew Tilin, "Bagging the Right Customers," *Business 2.0*, May 1, 2005, **http://money.cnn.com**.

VIDEO CASE 3.2   Organic Valley Farms: Producing Food That's Good for People and the Earth

Organic Valley's roots are deeply embedded in the welfare of its communities and customers. Organic Valley is a North American organic farming cooperative of more than 750 family farms in 22 states. Its Wisconsin founders laid out its guiding principles: "We think it's a simple truth. The earth's most delicious, most healthful foods are made when farmers work *in harmony with nature.*" That's why Organic Valley's production standards surpass those required by the U.S. Department of Agriculture (USDA) for organic foods, which prohibit the use of antibiotics, synthetic hormones, irradiation, sewage sludge, and genetically modified organisms. Humane treatment of animals is another requirement. All Organic Valley livestock have access to the outdoors, rather than being penned in warehouselike facilities. Its cows live five to ten times as long as those in conventional dairies, and they produce only 50 pounds of milk per day rather than the usual 70.

The cooperative's certified organic foods have won awards and attracted customers since its founding in 1988 by seven farmers who wanted to combine the market demand for more healthful food products with their own desire to produce better products at better prices. Organic Valley's current members are all owners in the business, with a voice in its future and a commitment to its environmental stewardship. The group's central mission is to support family farms and help them achieve both economic success and environmental sustainability "into the next generation." One of the benefits that Organic Valley believes it offers customers with its organically produced dairy products, eggs, juice and soybean beverages, meat, and produce is the right to choose high-quality foods produced in healthful, responsible, and humane ways. It also stresses the value of letting consumers know how their food was produced, with what methods and what ingredients.

In fact, Organic Valley sees itself as a partner with its customers, as well as with the member-farmers and employees who play a role in shaping the cooperative's actions. For instance, as farmers continue to join the co-op, at the rate of about 25 to 50 per year, its managers must balance the supply of food it can produce both with consumer demand and with the need to hire people for additional operations. The co-op's governing body is a national board of directors elected every year, which hears members' opinions through regional executive committees to which any member can belong. Marketing is also done centrally by the cooperative's board. In addition to becoming equity owners in a national food brand, co-op members receive support in their production, in planning, in locating feed for their animals (the USDA requires 100 percent organic feed for organic livestock), and in caring for them through veterinary consultations. A quarterly newsletter keeps members informed about the cooperative's plans and reinforces its goals of independence and price stability with a fair return.

Organic Valley is now the largest source of organic milk in the United States, and it is a leader in the $15 billion organic food industry, which is growing more than 20 percent a year. Although organic farms make up only three-tenths of 1 percent of all farms in the United States, Organic Valley sells its products to more than 10,000 stores nationally and is growing faster than the industry as a whole, at a rate of about 25 percent per year. Its sales in a recent year topped $259 million, and it is investing in a new state-of-the-art and environmentally friendly $15 million distribution warehouse in Wisconsin. But George Siemon, its reluctant CEO who is still a farmer at heart and in practice, says, "We wouldn't mind if the growth slowed down. The most important thing to us is to keep our mission. Organic Valley's not looking to conquer the world. We do things our own way, because we care about things other than business success."

The co-op's profit sharing plan pays 45 percent of profits to its farmers, 45 percent to its employees, and 10 percent to the community. This sharing of the organization's success is a key difference between the way the cooperative functions and the way a traditional company distributes its earnings. In the cooperative, everyone is rewarded for success, not just the shareholders. But the cooperative is also eager to share benefits with its local communities—and even with distant ones. Siemon's son spearheaded an impromptu relief effort in the wake of Hurricane Katrina, organizing a group of students and teachers from the Wisconsin high school where he teaches to set up an emergency kitchen using a school bus filled with cooking equipment and co-op support. Other efforts include a national campaign to save family farms by encouraging them to adopt organic methods, an inspirational Web community (at http://www.moomom.com), educational partnerships with organizations that focus on clean water and children's health, and a Web site where visitors can send instant messages to their elected representatives on topics such as animal cloning and genetically engineered food. After all, as Organic Valley says, "in order to make a difference, companies need to think differently."

Questions for Critical Thinking

1. What types of competition does Organic Valley face? Give an example of each type.
2. How does Organic Valley define its members' rights? What consumer rights does it support? Are these two sets of rights compatible? Why or why not?
3. How does Organic Valley puts its ethical standards into action in its product and pricing strategies? Do you think it is doing a good job of this? Why or why not?
4. How do the ethical standards at Organic Valley translate into acts of social responsibility?

Sources: Organic Valley Web site, **http://organicvalley.coop**, accessed July 31, 2006; "Organic Valley: The Truest Meaning of Organic," United Buying Clubs, **http://www.unitedbuyingclubs.com,** accessed July 31, 2006; Gregg Hoffman, "WisBusiness: Cashton Banking on Green Industries," WisBusiness.com, July 26, 2006, **http://www.wisbusiness.com;** Bryan Welch, "Doing Well by Doing Good," *Mother Earth News*, February 2006, **http://www.motherearthnews.com;** "Local Growers Try to Cultivate Interest in Organic Farming," *Orlando Business Journal*, January 27, 2006, **http://orlando.bizjournals.com;** Tom Hundt and Matt Johnson, "Youth Initiative, Organic Valley Help Feed Masses in Hurricane-Torn South," *Vernon County (WI) Broadcaster*, October 5, 2005, **http://www.vernonbroadcaster.com**.

VIDEO CASE 4.2   Pick Your Bananas Online at Peapod

Peapod, the pioneer of online grocery delivery, has grown since its 1989 founding to become the nation's leading Internet grocer. It has delivered more than 8 million orders in eighteen different U.S. markets. Since its purchase by Dutch international food retailer Royal Ahold, the company has formed partnerships with other Ahold companies such as Stop & Shop and Giant Foods and continues to revolutionize the way U.S. consumers buy everything edible, from soup to nuts.

Peapod is unusual not just for creating a new e-business format but also for surviving the dot-com bust that left so many online entrepreneurs in the dust. Industry observers say other online competitors such as Webvan failed not because there was no market for their offerings but because of overexpansion, overly complex Web sites, and other business errors. Still, shoppers have taken some time to adapt to the idea. One reason only about 3 percent of grocery shoppers place online orders is that delivery service is still not available in all areas, but "after the dotcom bubble burst, people who were shopping online continued to do so at remaining sites," says one industry expert. "The re-education that is hap-

pening is not necessarily from the online consumer. It is a resetting of expectations on the business side." Online grocery sales in the United States recently topped $3 billion and are forecast to more than double by 2009.

One reason for Peapod's nearly 20 years of success is its deliberate and careful approach to expansion. Taking advantage of the fact that it doesn't have to pay to maintain dozens of retail stores, the company instead operates sixteen "warerooms," or distribution centers attached to its partners' stores in five states, along with two giant warehouses in Chicago and Washington, D.C. And Peapod epitomizes what another observer calls "the key dimensions that count in food retailing: quality, price, and service."

When it comes to quality, Peapod stocks the freshest local produce, meat, seafood, prepared foods, party trays, and deli items sliced to order, in categories including natural, organic, low-carb, and kosher. It also sells wine and beer and nonperishables such as pet and school supplies. Its warerooms and warehouses are set up to store food in different climate zones for peak freshness. "It is quality assurance that frozen items like ice cream will arrive rock hard but that delicate perishables like produce won't," says founder and president Andrew Parkinson. Peapod's Stay Fresh delivery system allows clerks to fill orders quickly, pack them in crush-proof containers with dry ice and chill packs, and send delivery vans out at two-hour intervals from 8 a.m. until 1 a.m. most days. Guaranteed same-day delivery is available for an extra fee.

As for service, Peapod promises customers its trained "personal shoppers" will select items, particularly perishables such as produce, as if they were choosing them for their own table. Peapod's Web site makes it possible for shoppers to personalize their orders down to the most finicky detail. If you like unripe bananas, you can order them that way, and Peapod will deliver them unripe to your door. Other features of the Web site include the ability to save past shopping lists for convenient reorders and to sort lists by sales item, price, or nutritional criteria. "One of our greatest advantages is the ability for customers to navigate items to see labeling or ingredients," says one of the company's regional senior vice presidents. "They can sort by carb or fat content or search for organic foods." In fact, he says, when it comes to picking and choosing, "we need to show customers that we can do it better than they do it themselves," and the company does that with a 100 percent customer satisfaction guarantee.

Peapod doesn't claim to compete on price, but its delivery fees are low—$6.95 for orders more than $100 and $9.95 for orders less than $100; the minimum order is $50. Although the online service sets its prices independently of its partner Stop & Shop, its drivers will accept coupons (and tips). The average online grocery order is between $130 and $145.

Parkinson believes Peapod has successfully weathered the dot-com bust to achieve a loyal and growing base of about 155,000 customers. Those who use Peapod include two-career couples and other busy professionals who love the speed of online shopping for basics and the convenience of prepared foods, "foodies" looking for the latest specialty and gourmet items, and new mothers for whom delivery of baby items and health and beauty aids is a welcome benefit. He also believes Peapod is well prepared to face the growing ranks of local, national, and even international competitors. Britain's huge food retailer Tesco already operates online "Express" stores in five countries and plans to expand into the United States shortly. "The biggest hurdle was convincing customers they could shop online and still maintain control over the quality of their picks," Parkinson says. "That's been Peapod's cornerstone all along."

Questions for Critical Thinking

1. Peapod's founder and president, Andrew Parkinson, says of online grocery delivery that "the increasing use of high-speed broadband, advances in portable technologies, and the growing numbers of women in the online shopping ranks are mounting forces that will spur the industry to maturity." Do you agree that these are growth factors for Peapod? Why or why not? What others might exist for online grocers? What factors might delay the growth and maturing of the online grocery business?

2. Parkinson says Peapod is "a lifestyle solution for [customers'] busy lives." What solutions or benefits do you think Peapod offers? Could it offer any that it doesn't currently? How difficult would it be for competitors to copy these benefits?

3. Why do you think Peapod has been able to minimize channel conflicts as it expands its operations? Do you think its solution to this problem is a good model for other e-businesses? Why or why not?

4. How well do you think Peapod rates on the B2C benefit of personalization? How does its ability to personalize customer orders compare with that of other online retailers you're familiar with?

Sources: Peapod Web site, **http://www.peapod.com,** accessed August 8, 2006; Denise Purcell, "The Return of the Online Grocer," Specialty Food, **http://www.gourmetfoodmall.com,** accessed August 8, 2006; "Life after Webvan," *Red Herring,* May 1, 2006, **http://www.redherring.com**; Bruce Mohl, "Like Peapod, Roche Bros. Now Aims to Deliver," *Boston Globe,* October 23, 2005, **http://www.boston.com.**

VIDEO CASE 5.2   Nielsen Media Research Watches the TV Watchers

Choosing what to watch on TV was once a simple matter of flipping through a few channels. It's far from simple today. Cable and satellite television have brought us hundreds of channels, often with specialized content and advertising focusing on shopping, sports, music videos, classic movies, cooking, gardening, and many other options. First VCRs and then digital video recording (DVR) technology allowed audiences to "time shift" their viewing, watching shows not when they were broadcast but when viewers wanted or were able to. This freedom came with an added wrinkle—for the first time, consumers could watch commercial broadcasts without commercials, "zapping" through ads to view only the content.

Now podcasts and Webcasts offer portable and customized viewing, and cell phones can receive highly targeted TV programming, such as mini-episodes of popular shows filmed especially for wireless broadcast and never shown on TV at all. It might soon be possible to share your viewing experience in real time, through online communities that your computer will link to automatically when it senses you have tuned in to a specific show.

Viewers are adopting all the media options with enthusiasm, and advertisers want to know exactly what they think. For 70 years they have been paying Nielsen Media Research to find out.

Nielsen provides the only ratings of TV programs' viewership and market share of audience in the United States. These data are the basis for setting television advertising rates, which can exceed $60 billion a year. Advertisers want to spend that money wisely, and they are eager to get a handle on what viewers are watching—why, when, with whom, and how. Nielsen CEO Susan Whiting says of her clients, "Advertisers are asking for more qualitative information. They're asking how engaged the audience is in the programming. They're asking for more frequent measures of the audience and for commercials' ratings."

That's why new consumer behaviors such as time shifting and ad zapping are such a big concern for marketers. Some ads are time sensitive—marketers want them to be seen when the blockbuster film is about to open or when the dealer's lot is full of this year's SUVs. Says one ad buyer, "If you're not watching a show live, you're most likely not watching the commercials or you're watching them too late to matter." But others argue that as many as half of all DVR users do watch commercials and that ads bear fruit even if viewed after the broadcast date by, for instance, reinforcing brand image. Whichever view is correct—and perhaps they both are—consumer behavior is a topic of intense interest to the advertising industry and to Nielsen Media Research.

So how do people watch TV today? Do they watch the shows that others are discussing at work because they want to feel "in the know"? Do they select personalized programming, such as Spanish-language soap operas or European soccer matches? Is TV a family event, with everyone gathered around the set to watch the new fall lineup and a sitcom together after dinner? Or is a parent TiVo-ing a movie broadcast in the family room while the kids download *SpongeBob SquarePants* episodes to their iPods for viewing on the school bus? Whatever the case, viewers are certainly more fragmented, more demanding, and more mobile than ever before.

Nielsen still collects most of its information about local broadcasts with paper-and-pencil surveys given to randomly selected households, who are asked to record their daily viewing habits as truthfully as possible. More accurate and more sophisticated electronic measures are becoming a bigger and bigger part of Nielsen's arsenal, however.

One way Nielsen is coping with changes in both consumer behavior and technology is in its tracking of DVR viewing. Only about 8 percent of U.S. homes have a DVR today, but that number is expected to reach 40 percent by 2011. Nielsen hopes to keep ahead of the wave by publishing tracking reports three times a day instead of once. The first report measures how many people watched a show at its broadcast time; the second incorporates the number who recorded the show and watched it within 24 hours. The third report adds the number who played back the show within seven days of its original air date.

Nielsen is exploring ways to measure Internet viewing behavior as well as viewing choices made on handheld devices such as cell phones and iPods. "The pace of change is incredible," says Whiting. Arbitron, which primarily researches radio audiences, says that fully 15 percent of TV viewing across all age and demographic segments already takes place outside the home.

Questions for Critical Thinking

1. What cultural and social influences do you think are helping change consumer behavior among TV viewers today? Which ones have changed your behavior, and how?

2. Do you think TV viewers go through a formal decision process in selecting programming? Why or why not? Which steps in the process do you think are the most important for marketers to know about? Why?

3. What aspects of consumer behavior can Nielsen Media Research effectively measure? For instance, can the company currently measure attitudes and perceptions? If you answered no, how could the company achieve this goal?

4. Which behavioral influences on viewer behavior—cultural, social, personal—are most relevant to Nielsen Media Research and its advertising industry clients? Are any influences irrelevant?

Sources: Jason Lee Miller, "Google's Next Rival: Nielsen Media Research," WebProNews.com, June 16, 2006, **http://www.webpronews.com**; David Lieberman, "Nielsen Media Has Cool Head at the Top," *USA Today*, March 27, 2006, **http://www.usatoday.com**; Coco Masters, "The Rating Game," *Time Inside Business*, March 2006, p. A18; Brooks Barnes, "New TV Ratings Will Produce Ad-Price Fight," *Wall Street Journal*, December 22, 2005, **http://online.wsj.com**; John Borland, "Nielsen's Mobile-TV Challenge," CNet News, December 12, 2005, **http://news.com.com**; Laura Rich, "She Watches Who's Watching What," *New York Times*, June 18, 2005, **http://www.nytimes.com**.

VIDEO CASE 6.2   High Sierra Sport Company Excels in B2B

You can buy almost anything online today, but you can't buy any of High Sierra Sport Company's dozens of outdoor products at its Web site. In fact, you can't buy a High Sierra duffel bag, sport bag, laptop case, briefcase, luggage set, or backpack in a High Sierra retail store. The 28-year-old Illinois company doesn't sell anything on its Web site or operate a single retail outlet.

You might then be wondering how High Sierra—a privately owned company originally founded as the H. Bernbaum Import & Export Company in 1979—has grown to become the tenth-largest outdoor company in the United States, with a staff of only 40 people and no stores. The answer is that it has developed extraordinary expertise in business-to-business (B2B) sales. It markets its products around the world through more than 1,500 retailers and 2,250 corporate accounts, including the U.S. Olympic Ski and Snowboarding teams, which it also sponsors.

High Sierra's success is due in large part to its carefully designed product assortment and its smart segmentation of the B2B market. Its high-quality, high-fashion bags and luggage are tailored to outdoor enthusiasts, adventure lovers, athletes, travelers, students, and business professionals. The products offer an array of attractive features: padded interiors, multiple compartments, ventilated sections for cooling off your laptop after stowing it away, adjustable and ergonomic padded straps and handles, drawstring and zipper closures, wheels, frames, mesh pockets, corner protectors, water bottle pockets, and on and on.

With dozens of products to choose from, High Sierra's distributors might have trouble selecting what to offer their retail customers. But the company's product lines are organized into clear functional categories, such as wheeled book bags, business travel, day packs, duffels, wheeled duffels, luggage, lumbar packs, urban messenger bags, and sport and technical bags. The company also characterizes its products by activity—for example, running and cycling, school use, skiing and snowboarding, travel, and messenger—and by "collection," which focuses on the style characteristics of its wide selection. Brand names in this category include A.T. Gear Access, A.T. Gear Ballistic, AT3 Sierra-Lite, Cove Island, Cross-Sport, and RSX.

Trendy styling is important, even though High Sierra's customers aren't the ultimate consumers of its bags. And times have changed. Says the company's national sales manager, "People don't frown on you these days if you're dressed corporate casual and you're carrying a backpack. Ten years ago people would have raised an eyebrow at that." One of the company's newer models, the Sonic Pack, is an attaché with a removable holder for a CD player and a headphone port. The company expects it to be a best seller because of its versatility. "I think we're getting a lot more play on this type of bag because it hits such a broad target of people," says the sales manager.

Business bags are also big sellers to distributors of promotional products. High Sierra does a lot of business with financial services companies, for instance, and recently sold 18,000 units to a financial consulting company promoting a new product line. Insurance firms and food companies are also major customers, along with corporate training programs and trade shows. High Sierra recently won a Microsoft Business Solutions Pinnacle Award for excellence in customer service. Although consumers ultimately drive the company's product decisions—and online retailer eBags.com named it "best of the best" for consumer satisfaction—High Sierra is obviously also doing a very good job of keeping its business customers happy, too.

Questions for Critical Thinking

1. How does High Sierra segment its B2B market? Can you think of any other useful segmentation strategy it could use? What is it, and what advantage would it offer the company?

2. What kind of market demand does High Sierra face (derived, volatile, joint, inelastic, inventory)? Give examples to support your answer.

3. What advantages and disadvantages would High Sierra have to consider if it wanted to start selling directly to consumers? Why do you think it doesn't do so?

4. Assume you are a buyer for a company looking for a promotional item to use in rewarding your top salespeople. In which stage(s) of the organizational buying process will High Sierra's wide variety of products be most important to you? Why?

Sources: U.S. Ski Team Web site, **http://www.usskiteam.com,** accessed August 18, 2006; High Sierra Sport Web site, **http://www.highsierrasport .com,** accessed July 6, 2006; "High Sierra Sport Company," Google Finance Company Profile, **http://www.google.com/finance,** accessed July 6, 2006; "About High Sierra," Luggage.com, **http://www.luggage.com,** accessed July 6, 2006; "High Sierra Sport Company," Gear Trends, **http://www.geartrends.com,** accessed July 6, 2006; "High Sierra Sport Company Wins Microsoft Pinnacle Award," Sikich Worldwide press release, April 14, 2006, **http://www.icsadvantage.com.**

VIDEO CASE 7.2   Lonely Planet Brings You the World

Australia-based guidebook publisher Lonely Planet knows all about expanding your horizons around the world—in business as well as in travel. Started in the 1970s by Tony and Maureen Wheeler after the intrepid pair backpacked, penniless, through Asia, the firm has grown enormously. From its first product—a stack of hand-collated sheets about that Asian trip stapled into a yellow cover—Lonely Planet has become the purveyor of 650 different guidebooks in a dozen languages that cover 150 regions and countries, from aboriginal Australia to Zion National Park.

"If people are going somewhere odd," says Tony Wheeler, "the first thing they think of is Lonely Planet." He personally researched the company's new travel guide to East Timor, which has almost no tourist traffic—yet.

Lonely Planet is the world's leading independent publisher of travel guides, with offices in Australia; Oakland, California; and London. It has a staff of approximately 400 and about 150 seasoned authors from more than 20 countries. Its annual gross revenues are about $72 million on sales of more than 6 million books, which are distributed around the world. The company's second title, *Southeast Asia on a Shoestring,* remains one of its most popular, with more than 500,000 copies sold.

Lonely Planet offers curious travelers a wide array of walking, snorkeling, and cycling guides; maps and atlases; phrasebooks, food guides, and calendars; and a series of travel literature titles, all in addition to hundreds of $12.99 paperback guides with maps, highlights of things to see, language guidance, health and emergency information, and trusted recommendations for sightseeing, entertainment, shopping, dining, and, of course, accommodations. Competition in the market for guidebooks has surged over the years, with California-based Moon Travel Guides and English firm Rough Guides in particular grabbing distinct market shares among the daring and the budget-minded. But Lonely Planet has adapted as it has grown, and its original audience of committed—if frugal—backpackers has been successfully expanded to include families, businesspeople, and serious but savvy travelers of all kinds.

"Our Hawaii book used to be written for people who were picking their own guava and sneaking into the resort pool," says one Lonely Planet writer. "We were getting killed by the competition. So we relaunched it for a more typical two-week American mid-market vacation." The publisher of *Frommer's Travel Guides,* another competitor, sees Wheeler's operation as edging into the upscale market Frommer's targets, and indeed the whole Lonely Planet series was revamped with more focus on "highlights" and "itineraries"

and almost none of the original discussions of local history and economics. The once-outspoken guides now take a middle road on questions of local politics as well. For instance, it now publishes a guide to Myanmar (formerly Burma), which has been the object of international sanctions for its repressive government, that tells readers travel itself is a form of communication that can topple barriers.

Yet the guides still don't carry advertising, although the company's Web site does. And the company donates 5 percent of its profits to charity. It has long held to Tony Wheeler's original advice to travelers—"Just go!" But now it's "go" with a difference. For the long term, the company is embracing an "information model" for its guides. "When Tony washed up on the deserted shores of Bali thirty years ago," says the company's digital-product manager, "it was great to 'just go.' If you just went to Bali now, you might not have a place to stay. We're thinking about every phase of the travel cycle—dream, plan, book, go, come back—and trying to fill each one with Lonely Planet content."

In fact, the company has come a long way from its beginnings, when "we had no idea how independent travel would become and what a huge part of the global economy tourism would become," says Wheeler. Lonely Planet now offers newsletters; a branded phone card; a Web site that features English, Italian, Spanish, French, and German versions and logs 3 million hits a day; an active online bulletin board called the Thorn Tree; news commentary; blogs; an online shop; and a professional digital travel-image library with more than 100,000 downloadable high-resolution images. Lonely Planet Television is its new television production arm; its "Six Degrees" travel series now airs in more than 30 countries and is available on DVD.

The Lonely Planet Web site—both English-language and some international versions—offers an array of partnered travel-service offerings including air travel, hotel reservations, travel insurance, rail passes, and expedition bookings. B2B partners include Virgin Atlantic, Eurosport, Sony, Nokia, and AOL. Browsers on the main Web site can see how Lonely Planet solved some of its corporate challenges such as generating brand awareness and building sales online through "Lonely Planet Business Solutions," which also offers corporate gifts and incentive and promotional products. The company has also adopted a new automated publishing system to shorten the production cycle of its core product—books.

Looking ahead, however, Wheeler is mindful of the declining road that print encyclopedias have trod. The travel guide of the future, he believes, is "a mobile phone, my handheld computer, and global positioning system all molded together. You call up Italian restaurants, and find one that looks nice, and then a little arrow points in that direction for 480 meters, and then it phones up for you and books a table." That's quite a distance from a stapled guide to Asia.

Questions for Critical Thinking

1. What elements of the international economic and social-cultural environment can affect Lonely Planet's business, and how?
2. How well do you think Lonely Planet is meeting the technological challenges of the international environment? What do you think it could do that it isn't yet?

3. How could the movement toward economic integration affect Lonely Planet?
4. What kind of international product and promotional strategies does Lonely Planet appear to use?

Sources: Lonely Planet Web site, **http://www.lonelyplanet.com**, accessed August 22, 2006; Lonely Planet Images Web site, **http://www.lonelyplanetimages.com,** accessed August 22, 2006; Lonely Planet B2B Web site, **http://www.lonelyplanet.biz**, accessed August 22, 2006; "Lonely Planet: 'Best of' Eastern Europe," Associated Press, August 21, 2006, **http://news.yahoo.com;** "Lonely Planet Adopts Typefi Publishing System," PR Web, August 4, 2006, **http://www.prweb.com;** Tad Friend, "The Parachute Artist," *The New Yorker,* April 18, 2005, **http://www.newyorker.com**; Chris Brummit, "Lonely Planet Boss Travels the World in Style," *Deseret Morning News,* January 2, 2005, **http://deseretnews.com**.

VIDEO CASE 8.2   Nielsen Media Research Plays the Rating Game

For 70 years Nielsen Media Research has held a monopoly on collecting data about television viewing in the United States. Its eagerly awaited viewership counts and other statistics are the basis for the advertising rates broadcasters charge to marketers placing commercials on local and national stations every week. The research that Nielsen does has a huge impact in the industry; organizations spend about $60 billion a year on television advertising. In those 70 years, Nielsen has seen viewer habits change dramatically as VCRs, DVDs, iPods, digital video recording (DVR), video on demand, and even cell phones have expanded viewing options.

Though the marketing research firm still relies heavily on television meters and handwritten daily viewing diaries filled out by thousands of randomly selected consumers in all 50 states each week, the explosion of media technology has forced the company to find new ways to keep up with rapidly changing viewer behavior. A $2.5 million research effort is under way at Nielsen to find innovative methods to collect data about who watches what, when, and how. And with portable viewing via iPod and cell phone becoming easier all the time, even *where* we watch is a variable Nielsen wants to capture.

In response to criticism that it has undercounted minority viewers in the past—with corresponding effects on television advertisers' marketing decisions—Nielsen is focusing particular attention on African Americans and Hispanic Americans, as well as on viewers under 35 and DVR and video-on-demand users. The company plans to offer its clients data on conventional television viewing and also on less traditional

methods—Internet use, media viewing in airports and other public places, college dorms, and cell phones and iPods.

The ultimate goal for Nielsen and its advertising clients, of course, is not only to know how many people watch, say, *24* via TiVo three days after the broadcast but also to know how many of them—given the option to skip the ads—watched them instead and how deeply they were "engaged" with the marketing messages. In fact, says one media buyer, "The problem with the way Nielsen has approached the problem is that their focus has been completely on the program. We want to know the truth about who's actually watching the ads we're putting out on television."

"Advertisers need even more information on how you're using television differently," agrees Nielsen's CEO, Susan Whiting. These research efforts will be expensive for the firm. "We are managing a business with increased requirements for quality, technology, [and] speed, and at a time when clients also have more pressure on their budgets," says Whiting. "It's a challenge to balance both things."

One innovation Nielsen is experimenting with is the portable people meter (PPM), a small wearable device now in the testing phase that can pick up audio signals from cell phone viewing. "But for iPods," says Whiting, "we can either measure what you download from your PC—and even how often you're using it at your PC—or put it in a little attachment that would go onto the headset. For cell phones, we would probably use a software application. We have them working in our labs now." In fact, says the company's chief technology officer, when it comes to broadcasting media, "We've never met a device we couldn't measure." Nielsen even anticipates someday having the ability to use the PPM to track actual purchases, by having consumers scan the products they buy.

What might be the result of all Nielsen's television research? Whiting says the future of advertising could hold a lot of experimentation and change: If viewing is measured 365 days a year, the need for programming around the traditional "sweeps" weeks will change. Commercials could be as short as five seconds, product placement in programming could continue to grow, and advertisers might return to one of the oldest sponsorship ideas in the business—supporting an entire show without any interruptions for traditional ads.

Another change could well be in store for Nielsen—competition. TiVo can already tell advertisers what customers are watching, and Google is looking into developing interactive wireless applications that will link your computer and your television, allowing the company not only to track what you're watching but also to send you real-time information, chat, and advertising based on your viewing choices.

Questions for Critical Thinking

1. Nielsen has sister companies that track Internet activity around the world, box office receipts, and the retail sales of audio and video entertainment products and books. Who are the likely clients of these companies, and how would they use its research?

2. Could Nielsen's random sampling return unbiased results? Why or why not? Why do you think the company is dedicating two of its many television indexes to the national and local Hispanic audience?

3. Much of Nielsen's research is still reported manually by the subjects of its surveys. Do you think this method provides reliable and unbiased results? Why or why not? Why do you think Nielsen has a policy of prohibiting volunteer participants in its television surveys?

4. What are some advantages and disadvantages of the newer methods of automated data collection that both Nielsen and Google are exploring? Are there any privacy questions at issue in these new methods? How would a marketing research company deal with them?

Sources: Jason Lee Miller, "Google's Next Rival: Nielsen Media Research," WebProNews.com, June 16, 2006, **http://www.webpronews.com;** David Lieberman, "Nielsen Media Has Cool Head at the Top," *USA Today*, March 27, 2006, **http://www.usatoday.com**; Coco Masters, "The Rating Game," *Time Inside Business*, March 2006, p. A18; Brooks Barnes, "New TV Ratings Will Produce Ad-Price Fight," *Wall Street Journal*, December 22, 2005, **http://online.wsj.com**; John Borland, "Nielsen's Mobile-TV Challenge," *CNet News*, December 12, 2005, **http://news.com.com**; Laura Rich, "She Watches Who's Watching What," *New York Times*, June 18, 2005, **http://www.nytimes.com**.

VIDEO CASE 9.2   Harley-Davidson Rules the Road by Understanding Its Customers

Harley-Davidson grew up along with the U.S. automotive industry. Based in Milwaukee, it is the only major U.S. motorcycle manufacturer. More than 100 years old, the company has a venerable history, making products that tap into America's enduring spirit of individualism, adventure, and fun. From its early days, when inventors strapped crude motors onto bicycles, the firm has evolved and now develops different motorcycles for different customers—producing 36 motorcycle models and 8 sport motorcycles.

Along with its products, Harley-Davidson has developed many sophisticated marketing strategies, most prominent of which is its Harley Owners Group (H.O.G.). Any purchaser of a new, unregistered Harley can join. Another marketing effort focuses on helping owners customize their motorcycles. One reason the company knows which marketing strategies to choose is that it has carefully researched and segmented its market so that it knows exactly who its customers are. For instance, the ratio of male to female Harley owners has been holding nearly steady for years at about 9 to 1, with a slight increase in the number of female owners over the last several years, and almost half of all Harley buyers are repeat purchasers. The target market for Harley-Davidson is males with a median age just over 45 and a median annual income around $80,000. Most of these buyers are previous Harley owners, too. And for those who prefer sport motorcycles, the company's Buell Motorcycle line offers a number of choices.

Harley-Davidson promotes—and actively supports—a feeling of "one big happy family" among owners, particularly with its owners' group. But there are many different kinds of "family" members, and the company can pinpoint them accurately. So although its Web site features many pictures of men on their bikes, women are shown, too. And there's a special owners' membership group called Ladies of Harley (LOH) that women can join. Non-Harley owners who are Harley enthusiasts can buy associate memberships in H.O.G., and devotees can even sign on for lifetime memberships. The company offers H.O.G. members so many different membership benefits and activities to participate in all over the country and the world that it ends up offering something for nearly everyone. If you like long-distance solo rides, you can just head out for the open road with nothing more than a map, free from Harley, to guide you on your way. Or if you're the sociable type, you can join in parades, group rides, parties, rallies, charitable events, and other group activities orchestrated by local H.O.G. chapters in every state and in 20 foreign countries. There are nearly 1 million H.O.G. members worldwide, and it's easy for them to contact each other on Harley's members-only Web site (another benefit of membership). If you're not just a social rider but also enjoy volunteering, your local H.O.G. chapter offers plenty of opportunities for leadership and service in your community. As the H.O.G. Web site says, "Whether you want to simply come along for the ride, take it year by year, or devote the rest of your life to becoming the best H.O.G. member you can be, there's a membership to match your passion."

With so many H.O.G. chapters, each sponsored by a local dealership, Harley-Davidson can maintain accurate demographic information about a large proportion of its members, even though not all Harley owners join H.O.G. Many do, and by encouraging members to make full use of all their benefits, including almost unlimited opportunities to get together for social, educational, and fund-raising events and live the Harley lifestyle, the company ensures that owners around the world know that they mean more to the company than just a sale.

For customers who want more than a motorcycle off the dealer's lot, there are many options to customize their bikes. The company's broad line of parts and accessories allows rid-

ers thousands of options for making their motorcycles truly their own, expressing their individuality and increasing their satisfaction in the Harley experience. In fact, because customization is such a big part of Harley-Davidson's brand, the company recently upgraded its customizing manufacturing operations in the Milwaukee headquarters. For consumers who want to have the Harley look themselves, the company also offers a full line of MotorClothes apparel, including the iconic black leather jacket emblazoned with the company's familiar logo and dozens of other pieces of riding gear. However you want to shape your riding experience, Harley-Davidson is there to help.

Questions for Critical Thinking

1. Does Harley-Davidson's target market meet the criteria for effective segmentation? Explain your answer.
2. Which targeting strategies do you think Harley-Davidson is currently using? Which do you think it should be using? Explain.
3. How well do you think Harley-Davidson applies psychographics to its marketing activities? Give examples.
4. Are there any demographic groups that could be Harley-Davidson customers but are not? If so, how can segmentation help the company's marketers reach them?

Sources: Harley-Davidson Web site, **http://www.harley-davidson.com**, accessed July 6, 2006; Harley Owners Group Web site, **http://www.hog.com**, accessed July 6, 2006; Harley-Davidson Motor Company brochure, **http://www.harley-davidson.com**; "Hog Heaven: Celebrating 100 Years of the Harley Davidson," Library of Congress, **http://www.loc.gov**, accessed July 6, 2006; "Lista Storage Units Keep Harley-Davidson Running Fast," *MRO Today*, **http://www.mrotoday.com**, accessed July 6, 2006.

VIDEO CASE 10.2 The Little Guys Home Electronics: Big on Customer Relationships

When it comes to close relationships, most people probably would not think about their local home electronics store. But if you're a customer of The Little Guys, you just might.

The Little Guys, a family-owned home electronics retailer founded in the 1990s in a Chicago suburb, now earns more than $10 million a year from sales of electronics of all kinds, including amplifiers, CD players, DVD players and recorders, iPod accessories, speakers, and especially plasma and flat-screen TVs and entertainment systems. The brands carried range from Apple to Zenith and include innovators such as

Sharp, Sony, Bose, Onkyo, Hitachi, Mitsubishi, and Epson.

But what makes The Little Guys different from its competitors is its deep-seated commitment to customer service. The Little Guys is so eager to make customers feel at home that it even lists the names of its salespeople on the company's Web site, with photos and brief biographies.

They aren't just ordinary salespeople, either. They are enthusiastic experts in home electronics who are continually trained by the manufacturers whose products they sell. As a result, they can help customers assess their needs, select the right product, answer the most basic or the most technical questions about it, and even help install it and show customers how to get the most from their purchases. In fact, The Little Guys will work with customers who are installing home entertainment centers well before they are ready to buy a plasma TV or other components. For custom jobs, they will even work with the customer's architect and contractor to design and plan everything needed to support the entertainment center, from wiring during the construction phase to final installation.

The company is proud of its ability to become a partner in the home electronics purchase and installation process. "We've worked with interior designers, architects, and builders," explains the Little Guys Web site. "We'll meet you at your home or office. If you need custom cabinetry, we work with furniture designers who can create it for you. We can design any audio/video system in any room, including the bathroom." Four full-time installation crews take measurements, connect components, and hook up cable and satellite connections to make sure customers are able to just click the "on" button to begin enjoying their purchase. To keep up to date with technology trends, the company maintains membership in trade associations such as the Custom Electronic Design & Installation Association, Home Theater Specialists of America, and PARA, a nonprofit group that supports personalized, relationship-based shopping coupled with expert technical support.

But what if you're not sure what a home theater would look like in *your* home? The Little Guys can show you. In its "house within a store," a kitchen, bedroom, and bathroom are all on display to show customers how the latest home electronics equipment can function in just about every room of the house. The display even includes a set of fully equipped home theater rooms to provide ideas and give customers the opportunity to see state-of-the-art equipment in action in a realistic setting. Browsing is OK, too—the sales staff do not pressure anyone to buy until they are ready.

And if you can't come to the store but live within 100 miles, you can fax The Little Guys a sketch of your room and your requirements, or you can fill out a quick questionnaire about your project on the firm's Web site. Even if you're not sure how much you want to spend, you'll still get a speedy and informative answer. The Web site also offers a long list of common questions that customers have about what to buy,

how it works, and how to use it, with space to ask a new question of your own.

If even that outlet doesn't give you what you're looking for, you can tune in to The Little Guys' weekly one-hour radio show and phone in to chat with staff members about home theater, high-definition TV, surround sound, whole-house audio, and whatever other product questions you might have.

In a recent consumer behavior survey of 3,000 adults, "helpful and knowledgeable staff" was among the most important factors cited by consumer electronics shoppers, ahead of product availability, financing offers, and rebates. The Little Guys seems to have found an effective way to leverage the power of its own sales staff. Customer relationships are what The Little Guys is all about. "The biggest change in the industry," says co-founder Evie Wexler, "is that five years ago brands drove people to our store. Today, the manufacturers' brands are everywhere, so the brand is now us. It's 'The Little Guys' name that's most important." Maintaining The Little Guys' personal touch has never been a better marketing strategy.

Questions for Critical Thinking

1. How well has The Little Guys achieved each of the four basic elements of long-term customer relationships? Explain your answer.
2. "The single best thing about our store is the people who work here," says The Little Guys Web site. Why can the company make this claim, and how does it reflect the firm's customer relationships?
3. At which level or levels of the relationship marketing continuum shown in Table 10.1 are The Little Guys' customers? Explain your answer.
4. What does The Little Guys do in order to understand customer needs? What more, if anything, do you think it could do?

Sources: The Little Guys Web site, **http://www.thelittleguys.com**, accessed July 27, 2006; Alan Wolf, "Consumers Cutting Back on CE Purchases This Summer," *This Week in Consumer Electronics*, July 17, 2006, **http://www.twice.com**; Lisa Johnston, "Study: Brand-Name Importance Drops for CE Shoppers," *This Week in Consumer Electronics*, July 3, 2006, **http://www.twice.com**; Alan Wolf, "Glikes to HTSA: Stay Ahead of the Curve," *This Week in Consumer Electronics*, April 24, 2006, **http:// www.twice.com**.

VIDEO CASE 11.2 Wild Oats Natural Marketplace: Offering Products at their Peak

Think of your local farmer's market or corner produce stand. It's the place where you pick up fresh corn, sweet strawberries, tart raspberries, and crisp lettuce. If you want to make a peach

pie, you buy your peaches there, knowing they were plucked from the tree yesterday. If you're planning on a rich, homemade spaghetti sauce, you put half a dozen sun-drenched tomatoes from the stand in your paper bag. Now imagine an entire grocery store with foods like this: fresh organic produce, dairy products, juices, meat and poultry—even natural tortilla chips and salsa. Add to the list environmentally friendly household and personal products, and you're beginning to get the full flavor of Wild Oats Natural Marketplace.

Wild Oats began its journey with one store in Boulder, Colorado. Today the company operates more than 110 stores in 40 cities and 24 states and Canada. And all sell natural and organic foods. Wild Oats maintains rigorous criteria for its selection of products, including those under its private label. None of the foods carried by Wild Oats contains hydrogenated oils, artificial colors, flavors, or preservatives. Many are certified organic according to the USDA's National Organic Program, including meat, poultry, seafood, and produce. The seafood is even labeled with its country of origin so that customers know they are purchasing fish from companies that do not engage in controversial seal hunts or related activities. And the eggs are certified to be laid by hens that are humanely treated.

In addition, Wild Oats has a new Choose Local program that showcases products from local growers and producers throughout the country during the summer months. "So many times people don't have a connection to where their food comes from," explains Perry Odak, president and CEO of Wild Oats. "They think milk comes from a grocery store. Through our Local Fest we . . . create a unique, authentic experience for Wild Oats customers—the chance to meet and talk with the people who actually grow and produce the foods we eat."

All of these factors—certified organic foods, environmentally friendly sources, locally grown products—combine to make up the Wild Oats private label. Many supermarket chains have launched their own line of products, reaping the full benefit of offering their own goods, usually at a lower price than national brands, without having to share the profits with outside manufacturers. "Private label can play an important role in merchandising strategy," notes Laura Copeland of Wild Oats. But Wild Oats operates under the strictest standards—every product has to fit certain criteria to bear the Wild Oats label. The firm decided to differentiate its goods based first on quality, then on price.

As part of its strategy, Wild Oats decided to go big. "We started with the large volume [product] categories first," recalls Copeland. "We had a lot to tackle, so we started with the biggest part of the business. The first products we launched were pantry items, the things that people buy on a regular basis." These products included pasta and pasta sauces, and bottled or canned juices. "Over time, we've incorporated more specialty items. And we're always looking for new products, new categories. We now sell more than 1,000 private-label products," continues Copeland.

Wild Oats now offers three of its own product lines: Wild Oats Organic, Wild Oats Natural, and Wild Oats Living. Each product line has distinctive qualities. The Organic line is in accordance with the U.S. National Organic Program. The Natural line features products that are not organic but meet Wild Oats's own standards for foods with no high-fructose syrup, no hydrogenated oils, and no synthetic ingredients. The Wild Oats Living line offers environmentally friendly household products, such as cleaners and paper goods. Wild Oats is intent on competing with the big supermarket chains with as many private-label products as possible. "We want to be able to meet our customers' needs across all categories," says Copeland. But the company has to approach this carefully. "The concern about introducing a private-label selection is that consumers will simply switch from the established brand to the private-label brand, cannibalizing sales of the established brand," Copeland explains.

What's next for Wild Oats? Other retailers want to sell Wild Oats products in their stores and on their Web sites. Wild Oats now offers some of its products through Amazon.com and through online grocer Peapod. "Natural and organic products are available in a limited area of the country," says Copeland. "We're looking to extend our brand beyond our four walls as much as possible."

Questions for Critical Thinking

1. How would you classify most of the consumer goods that are sold by Wild Oats? How does this affect the way they are marketed?

2. What are the benefits to Wild Oats of creating three private-label product lines?

3. Large firms such as Johnson & Johnson and General Mills have product mixes with a huge assortment of product lines and individual offerings. Visit the Wild Oats Web site at http://www.wildoats.com and sketch out the firm's product mix, showing its width, length, and depth. You don't need to list every product, just a few examples that demonstrate each of the three components in the mix.

4. At what stage would you place the organic foods category in the product life cycle? Based on this answer, describe the approach you think Wild Oats should take toward marketing its Wild Oats Organic line.

Sources: Wild Oats Web site, **http://www.wildoats.com**, accessed September 12, 2006; "Wild Oats Urges Customers to 'Choose Local,'" PR Newswire, July 17, 2006, **http://biz.yahoo.com**; "Food Fest at Wild Oats," *Saugus (MA) Advertiser*, July 13, 2006, **http://www.townonline.com**; "Wild Oats to Sell Eggs Certified as Humanely Raised," *New Mexico Business Weekly*, June 14, 2006, **http://www.bizjournals.com**.

VIDEO CASE 12.2   Rebranding at JPMorgan Chase

Some brand names and logos are so familiar that they are part of American culture. When we see the logo, we know which brand it represents. Maybe it's the NBC peacock, the Tommy Bahama palm tree, or one of the most recognizable of all, the McDonald's "golden arches." But what about a bank? Marketers at JPMorgan Chase want to make their logo instantly recognizable, too. In a massive campaign to re-create the bank's brand—after the merger of financial institutions JPMorgan and Chase Manhattan—JPMorgan Chase marketers are hard at work. "We want our logo to be as big as the Nike swoosh," says a spokesperson. "Branding is extremely important; it speaks to our reputation and depth of our products."

While the JPMorgan division encompasses all of the firm's subsidiaries and serves governments, large corporations, and institutional investors, the Chase brand is designated for the U.S. consumer and commercial banking businesses that serve small businesses, individuals, consumer and business credit card customers, commercial real estate transactions, and the like. The firm's octagon logo is attached to both the JPMorgan and Chase brands.

How does a financial institution get its brand to stand out the way a fast-food or clothing brand does? As smaller banks and financial firms are folded into the larger entity, fresh signs and advertisements help create awareness of a new identity. The merger of JPMorgan Chase with Bank One a few years ago was a golden opportunity for marketers to create a new bond with business customers and consumers in such places as Illinois and Texas, where JPMorgan Chase branches replaced those of the former Bank One. Now called Chase Bank, the new bank has engaged in an intensive rebranding effort through various media. Radio and TV spots, print ads, billboards, bus signs, and other outdoor advertising—including a presence at the commuter rail stations in downtown Chicago—blanketed the area when the changeover took place. One television commercial featured the Beatles' 1967 hit tune "Hello Goodbye"—with the message that customers could say good-bye to the old and hello to the new. In addition, Chase Bank conducted a sweepstakes whose prizes included up to 1 million mileage points on United Airlines, which is based in Chicago.

Incorporating the Chase name was a major part of the strategy. "Chase is well known," explains Bill Lozito, president of Strategic Name Development. "It opens the door to breaking the emotional bond that consumers may have with Bank One." Although rebranding is often about change, it also helps if some things stay the same. "The same employees are in [Chase Bank], and the employees seem to be well trained and are buying into the change," says Lozito. If familiar faces are behind the counter and at managers' desks—and seem comfortable with the change—then customers can

feel relaxed about it as well. But to achieve this positive atmosphere, the vision and values of the new company must be communicated effectively to employees, so that they convey a message of confidence to their customers.

One way to reinforce awareness of the JPMorgan Chase logo is to stamp it on credit cards that are used daily by thousands of customers. The new Chase Freedom Visa has a sky-blue background with the company's octagon prominently printed on it. The card offers consumers the following options: earning cash back for their purchases or points toward rewards. Customers can earn 3 percent cash back on purchases at participating grocery stores, gas stations, and quick service restaurants, or 1 percent for every dollar spent elsewhere. If they prefer a rewards system instead, they can earn points toward hotel stays, car rentals, or airline travel. Once they become established customers, they may switch back and forth between the two programs. The idea is to get consumers to associate the Chase octagon with greater purchasing freedom.

JPMorgan Chase also sponsors events as part of its rebranding effort. The firm has sponsored the JPMorgan Chase Corporate Challenge—a road race in Boston—for more than two decades. The popularity of the 3.5-mile race, which attracts about 12,000 runners from 617 Boston-based companies, supports the rebranding of the firm. Money raised by entry fees and donations goes to a specific beneficiary each year, such as the Boston Arts Festival. Like a road race, rebranding is a true challenge for any firm. The marketplace, like the starting line, is jammed with images. But only a few top competitors cross the finish line in the lead.

Questions for Critical Thinking

1. Describe the brand equity that JPMorgan Chase already has.
2. Using the four dimensions of brand personality on the Brand Asset Valuator, describe the JPMorgan Chase brand.
3. Do you think the JPMorgan Chase octagon will become as recognizable as the Nike swoosh or the McDonald's "golden arches"? Do you think the firm's brand name will have equal success? Why or why not?
4. Describe a new product that JPMorgan Chase might choose to introduce as part of its rebranding effort. Why do you think it would succeed?

Sources: Chase Freedom Web site, **http://www.chasefreedomnow.com**, accessed September 19, 2006; JPMorgan Chase Web site, **http://www.jpmorganchase.com**, accessed August 14, 2006; "JPMorgan Chase Corporate Challenge," June 15, 2006, **http://www.jpmorganchasecc.com**; Judy Artunian, "Change of Name Can Come with Risk," *Chicago Tribune*, May 29, 2006, **http://www.chicagotribune.com**; "Chase Says Hello in Illinois," Chase press release, October 20, 2005, **http://investor.shareholder.com/jpmorganchase**.

VIDEO CASE 13.2   American Apparel: Supply Fits the Demand

American Apparel makes hip T-shirts and other clothing for young urban consumers. Based in Los Angeles, the company was founded in 1997 as a wholesale T-shirt manufacturer by offbeat entrepreneur Dov Charney. The company now operates 131 brick-and-mortar retail stores, as well as a Web store, with sales of more than $250 million a year. American Apparel is not just a patriotic name. Its Los Angeles plant is the largest garment factory in the country, and the clothing truly is designed and made in the United States. With so many manufacturers—particularly in the clothing industry—moving their production overseas, how does a relatively small, independent firm such as American Apparel manage to keep its production profitable in the United States and compete against giants such as The Gap?

Founder Dov Charney and vice president of operations Marty Bailey maintain that the answer to this question lies in vertical integration. "Vertical integration means that all elements of production are carried out under one roof. Design, cutting and sewing, even marketing and photography, all takes place in one building," explains Bailey. Essentially, vertical integration reduces production time. Because everything takes place at one plant, no time is lost shipping materials or components from one facility to another. In addition, all the processes are completed by teams, which Bailey instituted when he joined the firm. A sewing team consists of four to twelve workers, depending on how complicated the garment is. By converting to a team organization, the factory tripled its production output—from 30,000 pieces a day to 90,000.

Meeting demand is critical to success in the ever-changing apparel industry. "Being vertically integrated gives us the ability to respond quickly to changing needs," says Bailey. "If we need to produce more pieces of one color or style, we can change production immediately. You can only do that if all your production is together."

This flexibility helps American Apparel manage its supply chain while meeting the demand for certain styles, sizes, and colors. The manufacturing process starts with the yarn itself—American Apparel buys raw yarn and knits it into fabric. Knitting machines at the factory are capable of creating smooth jersey or baby ribbed fabric—whatever the design calls for. "Then the fabric is dyed," says Bailey. "We dye as much as we need in the colors we need. If we change colors, or a color becomes hot, it's easy for us to adjust." If one of the 30 colors available in the unisex T-shirt fades in popularity and another is suddenly a hit, the factory can make fewer of one and more of the other. Or it can quickly add swimsuits, if necessary, or back off on T-shirt dresses. In addition, the factory can modify a style immediately. "We can adjust a pattern this morning and have workers sewing it this afternoon," notes Bailey. "Since our success is based on the design and fit of our garments, this flexibility is important to us."

Just as vital as changes in demand is the flexibility in design to remain ahead of constantly shifting fashion trends. Because both design and production are under one roof, new styles can be created and produced rapidly. "We can develop a product on Monday and have it in stores by Friday," boasts Bailey. This gives American Apparel a competitive edge if a celebrity appears in a certain style one day and consumers are clamoring for it the next. It doesn't take months to design, produce, and ship from a factory overseas. Finally, vertical integration assures quality and the ability to respond to a crisis. "We can see the pieces in real time, as they are produced, instead of waiting for a shipment, examining the quality, and maybe sending it back or waiting for a new shipment," Bailey points out. And if there's a problem with a garment, the factory can usually correct it within hours, instead of weeks.

For the first five years of business, American Apparel sold its garments strictly to wholesalers, who then resold to retailers. In 2002, the company opened its first retail store and now sells directly to consumers through its Web site. Founder Dov Charney likes the advantage the company stores give his firm. "They allow us to reach the customer directly," he notes. "It's more direct contact than through a Web site or a third party. Stores also provide immediate feedback. We can see what products sell and what colors and styles people are interested in. Then we can adjust what we make."

American Apparel's young urban image is reinforced by the fact that everything is made by the factory in L.A. "If you have the right product, the right business model, and the ability to serve your customer well, you can be successful," observes Marty Bailey. "I believe we have all of those things."

Questions for Critical Thinking

1. Which types of marketing channels does American Apparel use? What are the benefits of each to the company?

2. In what ways does American Apparel gain an advantage over its competition by being vertically integrated?

3. Although most of American Apparel's processes take place at one facility, what outside components of the supply chain does the firm still have to manage?

4. Suppose American Apparel decided to move its manufacturing operations to Mexico. How would this move affect its physical distribution system?

Sources: American Apparel Web site, **http://www.americanapparel.net,** accessed September 13, 2006; Jennifer Ordonez, "California Hustlin'," *Newsweek,* June 18, 2006, **http://www.msnbc.msn.com**; Stephen Franklin, "More Pay American's Way," *Chicago Tribune,* May 30, 2006, sec. 3, pp. 1, 3.

VIDEO CASE 14.2   BP Connects with Drivers

You're staring down a long road. You've got miles to travel before you reach your destination, and your fuel gauge says you're running low on gas. It's after dinnertime and getting late. You're hungry and you could use a decent cup of coffee to keep you awake for the trip ahead. Suddenly you see a welcome sign: BP Connect. You slow down and pull in, sliding next to the pump. After you fill the tank, you head inside the warmly lit shop where other customers are chatting with the clerk, choosing sandwiches and fresh pastries, and filling huge mugs with steaming hot coffee. Now you know you're going to survive the drive.

BP is well known worldwide as a source of fuel. But the firm has been opening its BP Connect convenience stores at a rapid pace. BP Connect stores are different from the average convenience store—they are set up for travelers who want to grab a snack for the road or those who want a break from driving. In fact, the Wild Bean Café located inside each BP Connect convenience store offers gourmet coffee, herbal teas, fountain beverages, fresh-baked breads and pastries, hot specialty soups, custom-made sandwiches, and fresh salads.

This retail strategy comes in response to a changing market—and new opportunities. "Twenty years ago, buying snacks at a gas station was unusual," notes BP spokesperson Polly Flinn. "You didn't buy food from the same guy who worked on your car. In the past fifteen years, it's become something to think twice about." BP has done much more than think about it. The firm has developed a strategy to serve consumers who spend more and more time in their cars, who may be on the road during mealtimes, and who want higher-quality food than a bag of chips or a packaged doughnut. "The latest data show more than 60 percent of consumers do not eat breakfast at home any longer," says Flinn. So BP Connect offers an alternative. "Our strategy hinges on the fact that the same kind of people who had to get over buying a Snickers bar at a gas station will now feel comfortable seeing these locations as a place to get a sandwich and a cup of coffee on the go," notes Flinn.

Another important reason for BP's new retailing strategy is the fuel industry itself. Growth in the gasoline industry has been flat or negative for the past few years, while the growth in convenience items—particularly fresh food—has been steady. "The gross margin on food is twice that on convenience [items] and four times what we make on a gallon of gas," Flinn explains. So, as BP invests more in its convenience stores and cafés, these profitable locations begin to offset the ups and downs of the fuel industry. Deciding where to put a BP Connect store is easy—they can fit right in to your local BP gas station. "Our existing BP locations are some of the most convenient corners in the world," Flinn points out. "Right in, right out . . . The challenge is how to take advantage of these convenient corners and adapt them to consumers' ever-changing tastes."

Those tastes now run more toward fresh gourmet food and beverages and to a more welcoming atmosphere, both of which are served by the Wild Bean Café. The café operates like a store within a store. "This helps create the separation between food and fuel in the customer's mind," says Flinn. "It also creates greater credibility for the Wild Bean brand." Upon finding that consumers wanted to customize their snacks and meals—and save time—BP created a unique system that fulfills both needs. "At Connect, we've implemented the New Wild Bean Café Screen that allows customers to create the sandwich they want on a touchscreen, order it, and walk away and shop the rest of the store," explains Flinn. "They are controlling their time, rather than having a cashier control their time while they are standing there waiting."

With all of these innovations, BP Connect stores still stock the basics—candy, gum, mints, bottled water, soda, chips, and the like. Every item is placed carefully according the marketing planogram, a sort of map that illustrates where everything goes. And the stores are kept stocked—Flinn explains that a retailer's nightmare is running out of an item that customers want. But she observes that BP Connect's regular customers tend to make purchases several times a week. "So far, we're pleased with our customer satisfaction and loyalty," says Flinn.

Questions for Critical Thinking

1. Describe the target market for BP Connect and Wild Bean Café stores.
2. How do the elements of the marketing mix apply to BP's retailing strategy (see Figure 14.1)?
3. Using the five different categories discussed in the chapter, how would you classify BP Connect stores as retailers?
4. In what ways does BP Connect represent scrambled merchandising? How does this strategy boost sales?

Sources: BP Web site, **http://www.bp.com**, accessed August 22, 2006; "BP Re-Energizes Its Store Brands," *Convenience Store News,* **http://www.csnews.com**, accessed August 22, 2006, "BP Rebranding in Sunshine State," *CSP Daily News,* May 17, 2006, **http://www.cspnet.com**.

VIDEO CASE 15.2 The Toledo Mud Hens: Family Fun = A Winning Strategy

How does a minor league baseball team set a team attendance record and become the league leader in ticket sales revenue, food and beverage sales, merchandise sales, and corporate sales?

How does a minor league baseball team succeed when the parent major league club controls everything from the ballplayers' compensation to which players stay with the club and for how long? How does the club attract fans when it's difficult to predict or promise which ballplayers the fans will be seeing at the ballpark on a given night?

In the case of the Toledo Mud Hens, the top (Triple-A) minor league affiliate of the Detroit Tigers, they succeed by seeing the club as a marketing, promotion, and sales organization. The Mud Hens marketing team has done a thorough marketing analysis of what draws fans to the ballpark, what interests them, and what keeps them coming back.

The Toledo Mud Hens' Marketing Team's marketing slogans are "Toledo's Family Fun Park" and "The Joy of Mudville." Marketing research reveals that fans come to the ballpark to see baseball, and to see famous or soon-to-be famous baseball players, as well as for the fun, entertainment, and an affordable family outing. They come because they know it will be a special family event, regardless of who is playing, how the team is doing, or what the score that night might be because there is a lot going on at the ballpark in addition to the baseball game.

With a clear receiver-focused marketing campaign target established, the Mud Hens have created their strategy in reverse. What mix of experiences will it take to fulfill the wishes of any fan and any family who attends a game at Fifth Third Field? What will it take to translate that loyalty into advanced or "pre-sale" ticket purchases to make it possible for the Mud Hens to offer more and more value for the family investment?

The Mud Hens sell out 284 corporate suites each year. Group sales to anyone organizing 25 or more people can include a picnic area package. Long concession lines, common at many sporting events, are rare at a Mud Hens game. With the receiver-focused planning aiming at family fan enjoyment at an affordable price, the quality, service, and value of the food service has been a critical ingredient to sales success. Revenue for the food and beverage service equals revenue from ticket sales.

The stadium was also designed with a team store, dubbed The Swamp Shop, to market the large variety of popular Mud Hens merchandise. Here again, long lines, typical at other stadiums, are rare here. Also much more emphasis is placed on a myriad of promotions for the fans and family enjoyment. Birthday parties, Boy Scout Sleepovers, High School Baseball, Baseball Camp, Red Hat Ladies, Senior Days, Youth Baseball and Softball Days, Summer Recreation Days, and Home Run Derbies are major promotions throughout the season. Muddy's Knothole Club, tricycle races, musical chairs, fireworks, and many contests during the games provide a kaleidoscope of fun activities before, during, and after the games.

In order to promote this unique family experience to the fans, the Mud Hens marketing team has created an effective Integrated Marketing Communications strategy. The Mud Hens have created an atmosphere that the players love, which boosts team morale and attracts good players. This has turned a long-struggling team into a team that has won two straight league championships and a club that has supplied more that half of the players on the American League Champion Detroit Tigers.

One third of the tickets sold are season ticket holders, mini plans, and suite sales. Another third of the tickets sold are group sales, and the last third of tickets sold are on an individual sales basis. Two thirds of the tickets are pre-sold from a week to six months before the games. The Mud Hens average 75% of capacity at their ball park throughout the season. 65% of all tickets are pre-sold, which greatly benefits the clubs cash flow and planning.

Since a high percentage of sales are to loyal, repeat customers, direct mail brochures are a major vehicle in the marketing and sales mix. Currently, 40% of the advertising budget is used for direct marketing. 60% of the ad budget mix is for TV, radio, and newspaper advertising to attract individual purchases and keep "top of mind" awareness in the community. Plans are to raise direct marketing gradually to 75% as the loyalty of repeat customers trends upwards.

Thirty-five marketing vehicles are now in place to promote and advertise "The Joy of Mudville" at "Toledo's Family Fun Park." The most powerful marketing vehicle is the "pocket schedule," 300,000 of which are distributed annually via retail stores in the Toledo-area. The stadium's video boards, LED message centers, and electronic signs also play a prominent role in the marketing strategy.

Direct mail and email for target marketing is particularly effective, especially to repeat customers. Direct mail efforts rely on their large database, which is carefully maintained. CRM (Customer Relations Management) software is used to fully develop and efficiently utilize the database for newsletters and direct messages, as well as to accurately track the campaigns.

Their advertising and PR presence in area newspapers, and on TV and radio, is an important part of the mix to attract new interest to discover "The Joy of Mudville," and show how minor league baseball is significantly different from major league baseball. 50-60 games per year are televised in Toledo on the local sports cable station. TV and radio games are also effective marketing tools, generating interest and reminding fans that the team is home, while also generating advertising revenue.

The "Joy of Mudville" at "Toledo's Family Fun Park" message is tightly coordinated through all advertising, PR, and direct sales by the marketing director to promote the large community block party experience that has become a highly important slice of the Toledo quality of family life.

Questions for Critical Thinking

1. In what ways is the Toledo Mud Hens marketing campaign "receiver-focused?"
2. Why does the marketing strategy intend to raise the direct sales mix to 75% of the total?
3. Why is it important to increase the number of pre-sold tickets and how does the marketing strategy address this target?
4. Why is the food and beverage sales program playing a significant role in the success of the marketing and sales strategy?

VIDEO CASE 16.2   BP: Beyond Petroleum

Nearly a decade ago, two of the world's energy giants merged: British Petroleum and Amoco became BP. Consolidating the two organizations—and the two brands—was a massive undertaking. Getting the message out to the public that this was a new company with a new image was part of the marketing objective. With increasing energy prices, public perception of oil companies in general has had its ups and downs, so BP marketers had their work cut out for them. But the merger offered the perfect opportunity to create a fresh image in consumers' minds.

Instead of focusing on selling products, BP marketers went straight to selling a new perception of the company itself by launching an ad campaign called "BP on the Street." "When you undertake an image campaign, it's critical that you know what you want to do," says BP spokesperson Kathy Leech. "We had two tasks. The first was informative. We had to let people know who BP was. The second was positioning. The goal was to lift BP from the negative aura that surrounds energy companies in the mind of the public. We positioned ourselves as a different kind of energy company."

The tag line of the new campaign was catchy: "Beyond Petroleum." But it also conveyed the message that BP is more than a company that sells fossil fuels. BP is interested in doing more than filling consumers' gas tanks. In fact, BP is willing to face head on some of the tough questions concerning the energy industry. "It is the responsibility of an energy company to provide heat, light, and mobility to people. But you have to recognize that there are environmental costs," says Leech. "And you have a responsibility to mitigate those effects as much as possible." BP was the first large energy company to acknowledge the existence of global warming and to take steps to reduce the impact of its operations on the environment. The firm has invested in new sources of energy such as solar and hydrogen, research in climate change, and energy security—and these programs are featured in the advertising campaign, explaining to consumers why these activities are important to everyone.

If one part of the challenge is to make people aware of the new BP brand as well as its name, another part is to get them to relate to the message. So BP marketers created advertisements featuring real people voicing their concerns about energy issues. "The big issue in any sort of advertising is that people are cynical," admits Kathy Leech. "They are especially cynical about oil companies. By using real people [in the ads], speaking in unscripted situations, we hoped to cut through some of that cynicism."

The ads were originally launched in a few selected cities—Chicago; New York; Washington, D.C.; and London. The idea was to test some local markets and observe how viewers responded to the message. Although consumers liked the underlying principle, the ads were not wildly popular. "The first year, the ads came across as too negative," says Kathy Leech. "Consumers don't like negative advertising." So BP marketers went back to the drawing board and fine-tuned the ads. "The ads are now provocative without being negative," Leech continues. "Also, we are seeking a partnership with consumers. Rather than focusing on what BP is doing, we try to focus on what we can do together." BP has refined its ad campaign further, now targeting an audience that it refers to as opinion holders—those who vote, who follow decisions made by Congress, who may even write to their representatives. "You can't reach everyone," Leech explains. "Instead, we target people who are more informed, who other people go to for their information."

As the "BP on the Street" campaign moved from local advertising outlets to national and eventually international media, targeting its audience became even more important because it allowed BP to better monitor its advertising costs. The cost of advertising rises tremendously as media outlets expand. Despite this expansion, however, BP makes local refinements wherever necessary. Leech notes that American consumers are receptive to British accents, but British consumers don't respond well to American speakers in commercials. German consumers don't care for "person on the street" ads, so BP creates an "expert on the street."

Because of the high cost of an advertising campaign, and because conveying the right message is so crucial, BP marketers track the progress of "BP on the Street" carefully. "We do what is called a key learning summary at the end of each period," says Leech. "We've made adjustments based on what we learn. For example, last year we found that we were presenting too many messages. So we scaled back."

Moving beyond petroleum is essential for an energy firm like BP as it competes in the 21st century. As the firm transforms itself to meet new challenges, it also changes the messages it transmits to the public.

Questions for Critical Thinking

1. What are the objectives of the "BP on the Street" advertising campaign? How would you categorize the campaign?
2. Would celebrity advertising be as effective for "BP on the Street" as the use of average citizens? Why or why not? If BP decided to use include a celebrity spokesperson in its campaign, whom would you suggest and why?
3. What kind of appeal do you think would be most effective for the "BP on the Street" advertisements? Why?
4. What role do the "BP on the Street" advertisements play in BP's public relations efforts?

Sources: BP Web site, **http://www.bp.com**, accessed August 29, 2006; "Ogilvy Wins BP CO$_2$ Reduction Drive," *Marketing Week*, August 24, 2006, **http://www.mad.co.uk**; Wendy Melillo and Steve Miller, "Companies Find It's Not Easy Marketing Green," *Brandweek*, July 24, 2006, **http://www.brandweek.com**.

VIDEO CASE 17.2   Harley-Davidson: Selling the Thrill

When the first Harley-Davidson motorbikes rolled onto the street in 1903, people didn't rush to buy them. They were curious but skeptical, despite the fact that a coal-powered, steam engine motorcycle and a gas-powered wooden bike had been introduced in the late 1880s by other inventors. After all, who would put an engine on a perfectly good bicycle? What kind of chaos and harm would result? In fact, founders William Harley, Arthur Davidson, and Walter Davidson understood that their new bike would have to prove itself in another arena before they could market it as a mode of transportation for the public. They had to promote it—get people to notice it and want it—before they could sell it.

The team decided to enter their motorcycle in races, where it would be seen by spectators who might be convinced of its quality and desirability. Over the next few years, the Harley-Davidson motorcycle set record after record for speed and for gas mileage—in 1908, a Harley achieved a whopping 188.234 miles per gallon during

one race. In 1910, the Harley won seven motorcycle races, and in 1916 a Harley-Davidson Sidecar won the first annual race up Pikes Peak in Colorado. People were taking notice. Meanwhile, William Harley and the Davidsons had offered a distributorship to Chicago businessman C. H. Lange. Consumers in Chicago, who already demonstrated a love for motoracing and auto touring, caught on quickly to the new trend, and soon Lange was asking for more motorcycles to sell. In 1906, the firm's manufacturing operations had to move to larger quarters in Milwaukee. By 1912, there were 200 Harley-Davidson distributorships across the nation.

Rev the engines forward to the 1960s, when Harleys won seven consecutive titles at the Daytona 200. In the 1970s, Harleys won the AMA Grand National Championship four times and broke world records for speed. This visibility on the racetrack through the decades has been a distinctive part of Harley-Davidson's promotional strategy. People like to be part of a winning team. Harley riders have always had a personal relationship with their motorcycles. They appreciate the high quality, smooth ride, and power of a Harley. They take good care of their bikes. And they like to associate with other Harley riders.

Harley-Davidson has promoted this relationship right from the beginning, through the Harley Owners Group (H.O.G.) and other outreach efforts. H.O.G. boosts dealers' selling efforts by creating a membership in a club of like-minded consumers. Purchasers of new cycles automatically become members for a year, and their families can join as associates at a discount. In addition, Harley-Davidson sponsors special events for customers, including training programs, rallies, factory tours, and parades. Nearly half of the nation's Harley dealers now send their customers localized e-zines that contain announcements of special events, updates on local rides, news items, tips for maintenance, trip planners, and the like. These e-zines are entirely the creation of dealers—not Harley-Davidson's corporate staff—as an effort to stay in close touch with their customers.

The Harley-Davidson Rider's Edge program goes a step further, attracting spectators or motorcycle enthusiasts and turning them into actual riders. These motorcycle training classes, offered by dealerships around the country, are aimed at teaching new and potential customers the basics of riding and maintaining a motorcycle—how to shift, turn, and brake—as well as the purpose of all the dials and knobs on a Harley. The idea is to boost customers' confidence with hands-on experience before they hit the road.

Dealers also hold open houses during the early fall to showcase the year's new models. Consumers can visit a showroom, meet the dealer personally, enjoy games and events, and even test-drive the Harley they've always dreamed about. "We've been doing a lot of things to increase our outreach," says James Ziemer, Harley-Davidson's president and CEO. That means getting more people out on the open road—on Harleys.

Questions for Critical Thinking

1. Describe the role of a salesperson at a Harley-Davidson dealership.
2. Which personal selling approach do Harley-Davidson dealers use? Give an example of how the approach is used.
3. Why is demonstration an important part of the selling process at Harley-Davidson? How does the firm use this technique to its best advantage?
4. How has Harley-Davidson used promotion techniques in its past? What types of sales promotions might a Harley-Davidson dealer use during an open house to encourage consumers to purchase a motorcycle?

Sources: Traci Purdum, "Harley-Davidson Inc: Global Road Trips, Training Programs Prove Profitable," *Industry Week*, July 20, 2006, **http://www.industryweek.com**; Harley Owners Group Web site, **http://www.hog.com**, accessed July 6, 2006; "Hog Heaven," Library of Congress, **http://www.loc.gov**, accessed July 6, 2006; Ray Schultz, "Harley-Davidson E-Zines Go Their Own Way," *Chief Marketer*, April 12, 2006, **http://chiefmarketer.com**.

 # VIDEO CASE 18.2   Washburn Guitars: How Much Is the Maya Worth?

What is your most prized possession? It might be a bracelet worn by your grandmother. It might be your car. Perhaps it's your collection of vintage baseball cards or your array of current CDs. If you play a musical instrument, maybe you value your violin or keyboard. If you're a guitar player, it could be a Washburn. Now try to put a price on your prize. Perhaps you inherited it, or someone gave it to you. Maybe you bought it or made it yourself. Assigning a price might be difficult, but that's what marketers do every day. If you're considering a high-end electric guitar like the Washburn Maya, you'd have to think in terms of $1,500 or $2,700. The Maya isn't cheap—the average electric guitar goes for about $500 to $600. But people who own it—or any other Washburn guitar—say it's well worth the price.

Washburn has been manufacturing high-quality, high-end guitars in the United States since 1883. Based in Illinois,

the firm's parent company is now U.S. Music Corporation, which includes a number of different brands such as Randall Amplifiers, Vinci Strings and Accessories, SoundTech Professional Audio, and Oscar Schmidt folk instruments. Still, the firm is best known for its Washburn guitars.

Washburn makes a number of different lines and models of guitars. The Maya series is one of its most recent, used and endorsed by Dan Donegan, the lead guitarist for the rock band Disturbed. Although Donegan's personal guitar isn't for sale—it may end up in the Rock and Roll Hall of Fame someday—guitarists can purchase either the Maya Pro for a list price of $2,699 or the Maya Standard, which lists for $1,499. The Pro model has a few additional features, including a mahogany neck and abalone finger dots. Donegan, who helped design the line, says he's pleased with the results. "Washburn really went above and beyond to make sure my guitars are to my exact specification," he says. "I really wanted to create a guitar that is somewhat unique but appeals to artists of all musical genres." Washburn benefits from creating signature lines such as the Maya, which is associated with high-profile performers such as Donegan. "Signature models are used to increase the appeal of products in many fields," explains Kevin Lello, vice president of marketing. "Guitar enthusiasts follow the leading guitarists and sometimes choose the same equipment, like the Maya. This strengthens our relationship with Dan and his millions of fans."

Washburn promises that "each guitar represents the finest quality at the best possible price." To achieve this standard, the highest-quality materials must be used while costs are monitored so that consumers may purchase Washburn's products at a reasonable price. "We track quality and costs for everything in our guitar production process, to maximize quality and minimize price . . . from the man and machine hours to the sandpaper and cleaning supplies," says Gil Vasquez, production manager. Guitar prices vary depending on where they are manufactured. Guitars made in the United States, where Washburn guitars are built, usually command the highest prices because customers believe they are made to the highest standards.

Kevin Lello notes that the Maya series is a "showpiece" for Washburn. The materials used are expensive, as is the handcrafting involved in building the instruments. In addition, the line was designed with the help of Dan Donegan, so the musician receives a royalty on the guitars sold. "We spend a little more in marketing this model as well, with print and

Web campaigns," Lello says. But the Maya is not intended to be a high-volume product. Lello observes that although the list price for the Maya Pro is $2,699, some retailers discount the price a bit in order to sell it more easily.

While the Maya series is at the upper end of the price range, Washburn also manufactures lower-priced guitars. However, Lello admits that the lower-priced models have hurt the firm's image for high quality. So the firm is trying to turn this around. He believes this is possible because consumers are willing to pay for quality. If they want a $99 guitar, they can purchase one elsewhere. "Demand for good guitars is relatively inelastic," Lello says. Those words are pure music to Washburn.

Questions for Critical Thinking

1. What are the pricing objectives for the Maya series of guitars?
2. Why does Kevin Lello say that the demand for good guitars is relatively inelastic?
3. Would cost-plus pricing be appropriate for the Maya series? Why or why not?
4. What challenges might Washburn face as it markets its products overseas?

Sources: Washburn Guitars Web site, **http://www.washburn.com**, accessed August 29, 2006; NexTag Web site, **http://www.nextag.com**, accessed August 29, 2006; Dan Moran, "U.S. Music Corp.'s Washburn Guitars No Strangers to Fame," *Suburban Chicago News*, **http://www .suburbanchicagonews.com**, accessed April 17, 2006; "Washburn Guitars," Answers.com, **http://www.answers.com**, accessed April 17, 2006; "Disturbed Dan Donegan Signature Series Washburn Guitar at Winter NAMM," All About Jazz, March 3, 2006, **http://www.allaboutjazz.com**.

 VIDEO CASE 19.2   Whirlpool: Innovation for Every Price Point

The Whirlpool logo says a lot about the company. It evokes whirling water, constant change, and innovation within a circle that consumers can trust. "Inspired by bold innovations and designs, customers around the globe trust Whirlpool to make their lives easier," says the company Web site. "More than ever before, our brands are connecting with customers in ways that will last a lifetime." These brands include Whirlpool, KitchenAid, Roper, and Consul, along with others that are distributed to more than 170 countries worldwide. The Michigan-based firm has been innovating since 1911, when Louis, Frederick, and Emory Upton created the Upton Machine Company to produce the first electric, motor-driven wringer washers. Today Whirlpool is a global manufacturer of

major home appliances with 68,000 employees and nearly 50 manufacturing and research facilities around the world.

Like many large manufacturers, Whirlpool offers consumers different brands at different prices. By the 1980s, the firm had developed a three-level brand structure in order to give consumers a clear purchasing choice. The KitchenAid brand represents high-end, higher-priced appliances, including its popular stand mixer, coffee mills and grinders, microwave ovens, built-in ovens and cooktops, refrigerators, dishwashers, and washers and dryers. The smaller appliances are sold at retailers known for their cutting-edge design, such as Target, while the larger items—which can run as much as $3,800 for a combination microwave and wall oven from the Architect Series—are carried by specialized high-end appliance and electronics retailers such as Chicago-based Abt Electronics, which sells both the large and small KitchenAid products.

The Whirlpool brand, which represents midlevel pricing, is carried by Best Buy, Lowe's, and Sears—a reflection of Whirlpool's relationship with Sears, Roebuck dating back to 1916, when the retailer reported that it was selling Upton washers faster than the manufacturer could make them. Consumers can choose from washers and dryers, refrigerators, microwaves, ovens, dishwashers, trash compactors, and more. They can furnish entire kitchens and laundry rooms with Whirlpool products at midlevel prices, spending as little as $449 for a dishwasher and as much as $2,799 for a built-in microwave/oven combination. Whirlpool believes in innovation that offers choice—there are 46 refrigerator models with a variety of features, including side-by-side design, top or bottom freezers, ice and water dispensers, and Spill-guard shelves. All are certified with the Energy Star rating.

Whirlpool refers to its Roper brand as the "work-horse"—simple, sturdy, dependable, and affordable. Consumers can take home a washing machine for as little as $249 and a dishwasher from $229 to $379. Refrigerators top out at $999.

Whirlpool can offer such a wide range of products and prices because of its focus on innovation. "Without innovation and differentiation, the fundamental basis for competition was just price," notes president and CEO Jeff Fettig. "But our view was that for us to truly [be able to] execute a differentiated, value-creating strategy, we needed to do something dramatically different. From day one, we took the approach that innovation was not the privilege of a few; it was a right of the masses." This strategy means that whether they are purchasing the most expensive KitchenAid product or the lowest-priced Roper product, consumers get the benefits of innovation in design, construction, and technology.

Innovation is also a factor in appealing to consumers' perception of the price-quality relationship. Consumers who purchase Whirlpool's top-of-the-line KitchenAid appliances believe that they are getting the best products as demonstrated by high-quality design and features. But consumers who purchase Whirlpool's Roper line feel they are getting a good deal because the firm promotes the dependability and durability of these appliances, characteristics that are also

achieved through design. Those who select Whirlpool feel that the brand is designed for them, because the brand's slogan is "Inspired by You." So each group of purchasers perceives that the products they are buying provide value and quality. Across all three brands, price increases as the number and complexity of innovative features increase, which consumers view as acceptable and reasonable. With this strategy, consumers have the opportunity to choose which features are important to them and how much they want to pay for an appliance.

As crucial as they are, consumers aren't Whirlpool's only customers. Because Whirlpool is a manufacturer, the firm must also satisfy the needs of its channel members, including retailers such as Target and Sears. Whirlpool provides different types of price breaks to retailers, including volume rebates and discounts if a retailer sends its own truck to pick up goods at the factory rather than having them delivered. Consumer rebates actually benefit retailers as well, because they give consumers an incentive to purchase Whirlpool products. "We're a high innovation company," remarks Fettig. You could say that Whirlpool has been making a stir in the marketplace for a long time.

Questions for Critical Thinking

1. What types of reductions from list price does Whirlpool use? Is this an effective marketing strategy? Why or why not?

2. Describe how Whirlpool uses the product lines in its three brands to promote a positive relationship between price and quality.

3. Do you think consumers would have different price limits across the three Whirlpool brands? Explain your answer.

4. Whirlpool sells its products in many different countries. Which of the three alternative global pricing strategies presented in the chapter do you think would work best for the company? Why?

Sources: Roper Web site, **http://www.roperappliances.com**, accessed September 27, 2006; Whirlpool Web sites, **http://www.whirlpoolcorp.com** and **http://www.whirlpool.com**, accessed September 12, 2006; KitchenAid Web site, **http://www.kitchenaid.com**, accessed September 12, 2006; "Whirlpool's Future Won't Fade," *BusinessWeek*, May 8, 2006, **http://www.businessweek.com**.

notes

Prologue

1. Grohe America Web site, http://www.groheamerica.com, accessed August 18, 2006; Sarah E. Needleman, "Marketing Exec Juggles a Multitude of Tasks," CareerJournal, July 18, 2006, http://www.careerjournal.com; Allison Deerr, "Hit the Showers!" **Reeves Journal**, November 10, 2005, http://www.reevesjournal.com; "Conversations at ISH Frankfurt," *Supply House Times,* June 30, 2005, http://www.supplyht.com.

2. U.S. Department of Labor, "Advertising, Marketing, Promotions, Public Relations, and Sales Managers," *Occupational Outlook Handbook,* 2006–2007 edition, Bureau of Labor Statistics, http://www.bls.gov, accessed August 4, 2006.

3. Deshundra Jefferson, "Most Lucrative College Degrees," CNN Money.com, February 8, 2006, http://money.cnn.com.

4. Bureau of Labor Statistics, "Employment Projections," July 26, 2006, http://www.bls.gov.

5. William M. Bulkeley, "In-House Bloggers Offer an Insider's View," *Career Journal,* April 4, 2006, www.careerjournal.com; Sarah E. Needleman, "As Blogging Goes Corporate, It Becomes a Full-Time Job," CareerJournal, May 31, 2005, http://www.careerjournal.com.

6. "SalesJobs.com," <I>Forbes<$> Best of the Web, http://www.forbes.com, accessed September 8, 2006; Sarah E. Needleman, "Career Sites for Women: Most Also Welcome Men," *CollegeJournal,* June 28, 2005, http://www.careerjournal.com.

7. Amanda Loudin, "Career Solutions: Playing the Board Game," Inbound Logistics, December 2005, http://www.inboundlogistics.com.

8. Enterprise Rent-A-Car Web site, http://www.erac.com/recruit, accessed August 16, 2006.

9. Stephanie Glaittli, "Internships Increasing in Importance for Landing a Job," *Daily Utah Chronicle,* June 12, 2006, http://www.dailyutahchronicle.com.

10. "Internships," Michigan State University Libraries, May 26, 2006, http://www.lib.msu.edu.

11. "Your Guide to Resume Writing," JobWeb.com, http://www.jobweb.com, accessed August 16, 2006.

12. Kim Isaacs, "Ten Cover Letter Don'ts," Monster.com, December 20, 2005, http://www.monster.com.

13. "How to Apply Online and Get an Employer's Attention," JobWeb.com, http://www.jobweb.com, accessed August 17, 2006.

14. "Interviewing Tips," Sam M. Walton College of Business, http://waltoncollege.uark.edu, accessed August 17, 2006.

15. U.S. Department of Labor, "Advertising, Marketing, Promotions, Public Relations, and Sales Managers," *Occupational Outlook Handbook,* 2006–2007 edition, Bureau of Labor Statistics, http://www.bls.gov, accessed August 4, 2006.

16. Ibid.

17. Ibid.

18. Ibid.

19. "Advertising and Public Relations Services," The 2006–2007 Career Guide to Industries, December 20, 2005, http://www.bls.gov.

20. Ibid

21. Ibid.

22. Ibid.

23. U.S. Department of Labor, "Purchasing Managers, Buyers, and Purchasing Agents," *Occupational Outlook Handbook,* 2006–2007 edition, Bureau of Labor Statistics, http://www.bls.gov, accessed August 4, 2006.

24. Ibid.

25. U.S. Department of Labor, "Market and Survey Researchers," *Occupational Outlook Handbook,* 2006–2007 edition, Bureau of Labor Statistics, http://www.bls.gov, accessed August 4, 2006.

26. U.S. Department of Labor, "Market and Survey Researchers," *Occupational Outlook Handbook,* 2006–2007 Edition, http://www.bls.gov, accessed August 4, 2006.

27. U.S. Department of Labor, "Management, Business, and Financial Occupations," *Occupational Outlook Handbook,* 2006–2007 edition, Bureau of Labor Statistics, http://www.bls.gov, accessed August 4, 2006.

Chapter 1

1. April Y. Pennington, "Primal Need," *Entrepreneur,* February 2006, p. 20; "Starbucks to Promote Movie, Sell DVDs," Reuters, January 12, 2006, http://news.yahoo.com; William Meyers, "Conscience in a Cup of Coffee," *U.S. News & World Report,* October 31, 2005, pp. 48–50; "Starbucks Launches New Ready-to-Drink Coffee Beverage in Japan and Taiwan," Business Wire, September 26, 2005, http://www.businesswire.com; "Starbucks: The Next Generation," *Fortune,* April 4, 2005, p. 30; Peter Kafka, "Bean Counter," *Forbes,* February 28, 2005, pp. 78–80; Jon D. Markman, "Starbucks Genius Blends Community, Caffeine," MSN Money, February 16, 2005, http://moneycentral.msn.com.

2. Brad Stone, "Can Amazon Catch Apple?" *Newsweek,* February 13, 2006, p. 46.

3. Johnnie L. Robertson, "Murdoch's New Groove," *Newsweek,* February 13, 2006, pp. 42–44.

4. Sara Wilson, "Right of Fashion," *Entrepreneur,* February 2006, p. 30.

5. Greg Sandoval, "Podcasting Spurs a Media 'Land Grab,'" Associated Press, July 16, 2005, http://news.yahoo.com.

6. Joseph P. Guiltinian and Gordon W. Paul, *Marketing Management,* 6th ed. (New York: McGraw-Hill), 1996, pp. 3–4.

7. "AMA Adopts New Definition of Marketing," American Marketing Association, http://www.marketingpower.com, accessed January 31, 2006.

8. Ron Scherer, "Oil Prices Climb to Katrina Levels," *Christian Science Monitor,* January 23, 2006, http://www.csmonitor.com.

9. Mike Dolan, "Consumers Not the Root of GDP Shock," Reuters, January 27, 2006, http://news.yahoo.com.

10. "Fuji Photo Film to Slash 5,000 Jobs, Shift Production to China," Agence France Presse, January 31, 2006, http://www.afp.com.

11. Geri Smith, "Online Extra: Can Latin America Challenge India?" *BusinessWeek,* January 27, 2006, http://www.businessweek.com.

12. "Top 20 Innovative Companies in the World," *BusinessWeek,* August 1, 2005, p. 64.

13. Peter Burrows and Ronald Grover, "Steve Jobs's Magic Kingdom," *BusinessWeek,* January 26, 2006, http://www.businessweek.com.

14. Arnie Williams, "PTC Helps Airbus Megajet Take Off," LookSmart, March 2005, http://www.findarticles.com.

15. Steve Rosenbush, "Why WiMax Could Hit the Hotspot," *BusinessWeek,* October 5, 2005, http://www.businessweek.com.

16. Kristin Ohlson, "Burst of Energy," *Entrepreneur,* February 2006, pp. 46–47.

17. Robert Stein, "Williamsburg Living History Gets a Little Livelier," *Newsweek,* February 13, 2006, p. 10.

18. "Target House," http://www.target.com, accessed January 31, 2006.

19. America's Second Harvest, http://www.secondharvest.org, accessed January 31, 2006.

20. Timothy McNulty, "Bono's Red Line Will Fight AIDS," *Pittsburgh Post-Gazette,* January 28, 2006, http://www.post-gazette.com.

21. Sam Farmer, "Roethlisberger Turns Blue Collar into Green," *Los Angeles Times,* January 27, 2006, http://www.latimes.com; Lacey Rose, "The World's Best-Paid Young Celebrities," Forbes.com, January 11, 2006, http://www.forbes.com.

22. Tim Jones, "Sheboygan Wants to Be the Big Cheese in Space," *Chicago Tribune,* January 29, 2006, sec. 1, pp. 1, 12.

23. "West Virginia: Little-Known Ski Town a Hidden Gem," CNN.com, November 23, 2005, http://cnn.worldnews.com.

24. ASPCA Web site, http://www.aspca.org, accessed February 2, 2006.

25. Stuart Elliott, "At $83,333 a Second, Ads Chase Super Bowl Score," *International Herald Tribune,* February 2, 2006, http://www.iht.com.

26. "Adidas Bets on Beijing Olympics," *International Herald Tribune,* January 30, 2006, http://www.iht.com.

27. Keith Spera, "Jazzfest, Shell to Work in Harmony," *(New Orleans, AL) Times-Picayune,* February 1, 2006, http://www.nola.com; Mimi Hall, "Women of the Storm Push for More Katrina Funding," *USA Today,* January 31, 2006, http://www.usatoday.com.

28. *Kiplinger's Personal Finance,* February 2006, p. 86.

29. "U.S. Army Reaches Influencers with Four New Commercials," Leo Burnett, April 18, 2005, http://www.leoburnett.com.

30. Katrina Brooker, "The Pepsi Machine," *Fortune,* February 6, 2006, pp. 68–72.

31. Allison Linn, "Microsoft Plans Launch of Internet Research Lab," TechNewsWorld, January 30, 2006, http://www.technewsworld.com.

32. "E-Tailers Try New Holiday Tricks." *BusinessWeek,* December 12, 2005, http://www.businessweek.com.

33. Rodrique Ngowi, "Cell Phone Use Changes Life in Africa," Yahoo! News, October 16, 2005, http://news.yahoo.com.

34. Pamela Parker, "Kleenex Hopes to Tap Olympic Emotions Online," ClickZ Network, January 25, 2006, http://www.clickz.com.

35. "E-Tailers Try New Holiday Tricks."

36. "Internet Protocol Television," Webopedia, http://www.webopedia.com, accessed February 15, 2006; Brucey Meyerson, "Interactive TV Poised for a Rollout," *USA Today,* February 14, 2005, http://www.usatoday.com.

37. Pamela Parker, "Mobile Video in Real Time," ClickZ Network, January 27, 2006, http://www.clickz.com.

38. Ibid.

39. "Where Is Mobile Marketing Headed?" eMarketer, February 3, 2005, http://www.emarketer.com.

40. Michael Meltzer, "Customer Dialogue Builds Loyalty & Profit," *CRM Today,* http://www.crm2day.com, accessed February 2, 2006.

41. James M. Pethokoukis, "Spreading the Word," *U.S. News & World Report,* December 5, 2005, pp. EE1–EE6.

42. Ibid.

43. May Wong, "Yahoo, TiVo Join to Blend TV, Web Services," Yahoo! News, November 7, 2005, http://news.yahoo.com.

44. Timberland Web site, http://www.timberland.com, accessed March 3, 2006.

45. "Home Room," *O at Home,* Spring 2006, pp. 66–71.

46. "Cisco Systems, Grand Circle, and KaBOOM! Win CECP Awards Honoring Excellence in Corporate Philanthropy," Business Wire, February 27, 2006, http://home.businesswire.com.

Chapter 2

1. Gene Sloan, "Fine Bedding Helps Lull Passengers to Sleep," *USA Today,* February 23, 2006, http://www.usatoday.com; Rosemary Barnes, "In Selling a Hotel, the Bed's the Thing," *San Antonio Express-News,* October 27, 2005, http://www.expressnews.com; Michael Martinez, "Hotel Chains Compete in a Bid to Provide the Comfiest Night's Sleep," *San Jose Mercury News,* June 27, 2005, http://www.mercurynews.com; Kitty Bean Yancey, "Westin's Heavenly Venture," *USA Today,* April 28, 2005, http://www.usatoday.com.

2. Jay Greene, "Three-Part Harmony for Microsoft?" *BusinessWeek,* September 12, 2005, http://www.businessweek.com.

3. Cloud Star Web site, http://www.cloudstar.com, accessed February 7, 2006; Nichole L. Torres, "Cloud Star Corp.," in Amanda Kooser et al., "Beyond Their Years," *Entrepreneur,* November 2003, pp. 74–85.

4. Laurie Sullivan, "Oracle Seals Siebel Deal," *TechWeb,* January 31, 2006, http://www.techweb.com; Sarah Lacey, "Now, Oracle May Finally Rest," *BusinessWeek,* September 13, 2005, http://www.businessweek.com.

5. "What's Kodak's Strategy?" interview with Brad Stone, *Newsweek,* January 16, 2006, p. 46.

6. Guy Trebay, "Influencers Are Forever," *New York Times,* June 26, 2005, http://www.nytimes.com.

7. Margaret Webb Pressler, "Hold the Health, Serve that Burger," *Washington Post,* August 18, 2005, http://www.washingtonpost.com; Miriam Gottfried, "Restaurant Lets You Know What You Eat," *(Tacoma, WA) News Tribune,* March 29, 2005, http://www.thenewstribune.com.

8. Linda Stern, "Finance: Buying a Car? Drive a Bargain," Reuters, February 22, 2006, http://news.yahoo.com.

9. Josh Getlin, "Small Record Stores Rocked by Hard Times," *Chicago Tribune,* January 8, 2006, Sec. 1, p. 11.

10. Justin Ewers, "Maxims in Need of a Makeover," *U.S. News & World Report,* March 27, 2006, pp. EE2-EE6.

11. "iTunes: 1 Billion Served," *Red Herring,* February 23, 2006, http://www.redherring.com; Steve Alexander, "iTunes Trumpets a New Milestone: 1 Billion Downloads Sold," TechNewsWorld, February 23, 2006, http://www.technewsworld.com.

12. Jon Birger, "Second-Mover Advantage," *Fortune,* March 20, 2006, pp. 20–21.

13. "Google, Earthlink Bid to Offer Wireless Access," *Los Angeles Times,* February 23, 2006, http://www.latimes.com; "AT&T Expands Global Network," *America's Network,* February 23, 2006, http://www.americasnetwork.com; "Fortune Names AT&T Best U.S. Telecom Co.," United Press International, February 22, 2006, http://www.upi.com; "AT&T, Yahoo Link Web to Cingular Mobile Phones," Reuters, February 21, 2006, http://news.yahoo.com; Dan Beucke, "The Big Picture," *BusinessWeek,* January 9, 2006, p. 9; "At SBC, It's All about 'Scale and Scope,'" interview with Roger O. Crockett, *BusinessWeek,* November 7, 2005, http://www.businessweek.com.

14. Derek F. Abell, "Strategic Windows," *Journal of Marketing,* vol. 42, mo. 3 (July 1978), pp. 21–26.

15. "Cars in China: Dream Machines," *The Economist,* June 2, 2005, http://www.economist.com.

16. David Kiley, "Toyota Builds a Truck Even Bubba May Love," *BusinessWeek,* February 3, 2006, http://www.businessweek.com.

17. "Hispanic Population in U.S. Soars," CBS News, June 9, 2005, http://www.cbsnews.com.

18. Barbara De Lollis, "More Hotels Try to Offer What Women Want: Security, Luxury," *USA Today,* November 8, 2005, p. 5B.

19. Duncan Martell, "HP Charges into Retail Photo Printing Market," Reuters, February 22, 2006, http://news.yahoo.com.

20. Seth Sutel, "Dow Jones Announces Reorganization," Associated Press, February 22, 2006, http://news.yahoo.com.

21. Jason Roberson, "New Marketing Strategy Planned: Higher Sales, New Vehicles Boost Outlook of Mitsubishi," *Detroit Free Press,* January 10, 2006, http://www.freep.com.

22. Dody Tsiantar, "Competing for Business Class," *Time,* December 2005, p. A24.

23. May Wong, "Lenovo Makes Global Push with Computers," Associated Press, February 23, 2006, http://news.yahoo.com.

24. Ian Austen, "BlackBerry Service to Continue," *New York Times,* March 4, 2006, http://www.nytimes.com; Anne Broache, "BlackBerry Saved," *New York Times,* March 3, 2006, http://www.nytimes.com; Stephanie Stoughton, "End to BlackBerry Patent Feud May Finally Be at Hand," *USA Today,* February 19, 2006, http://www.usa.today.com.

25. Betsy Streisand and Richard J. Newman, "The New Media Elites," *U.S. News & World Report,* November 14, 2005, pp. 54–63.

26. As mentioned in Jagdish Sheth and Rajendra Sisodia, *Surviving and Thriving in Competitive Markets* (New York: Free Press, 2002).

27. "JetBlue's Neeleman Sees Possible Partnerships, Addresses Embraer 190 Glitches," *ATW Daily News,* January 30, 2006, http://www.atwonline.com; Andrew Blum, "JetBlue's Terminal Takes Wing," *BusinessWeek,* July 21, 2005, http://www.businessweek.com; Wendy Zellner, "Is JetBlue's Flight Plan Flawed?" *BusinessWeek,* February 16, 2004, pp. 72–75.

28. Ed Sutherland, "HP to Split Handhelds, Notebooks," Internetnews.com, February 13, 2006, http://www.internetnews.com.

29. Matt Krantz, "Ask Matt: Take a Bite of Apple?" *USA Today,* February 2, 2006, http://www.usatoday.com; Jefferson Graham, "Jobs Has a Knack for Getting His Way," *USA Today,* January 25, 2006, http://www.usatoday.com.

30. Annys Shin, "New CEO's Theme for Six Flags Is Change," *Washington Post,* December 15, 2005. http://www.washingtonpost.com.

Appendix

1. "Corporate Information," Google Web site, http://www.google.com, accessed June 28, 2006.

2. T. Shawn Taylor, "What Works in Bridging the Digital Divide," *Chicago Tribune,* May 16, 2006, sec. 7, p. 3.

3. Starbucks Web site, http://www.starbucks.com, accessed June 28, 2006.

4. Ken Thomas, "Flexible-Fuel Vehicle Production to Rise," Associated Press, June 28, 2006, http://news.yahoo.com.

5. Daren Fonda, "Jim Sinegal, Costco's Discount CEO," *Time,* May 8, 2006, p. 148.

6. Ann Meyer, "Taking on Giants: The Small Shop That Fought Back," *Chicago Tribune,* May 16, 2006, sec. 7, p. 5.

7. Chelsea Emery and Yung Kim, "J. Crew Shares Surge 28 Pct in Market Debut," Reuters, June 28, 2006, http://news.yahoo.com; Anne D'Innocenzio, "J. Crew Prepares to Go Public," Associated Press, June 23, 2006, http://news.yahoo.com; Emily Scardino, "J. Crew Walks Down the Aisle," *DSN Retailing Today,* February 28, 2005, http://www.findarticles.com.

8. Yian Q. Mui, "Retailers Redesign as Boomers Hit 60," *Washington Post,* January 17, 2006, http://www.washingtonpost.com.

9. Brooks Barnes, "Toyota Aims Young, Sponsors Fox Spinoff for Cellphone Screens," *Wall Street Journal,* April 24, 2006, http://online.wsj.com.

10. Clayton Collins, "Pitches to Tweens Target Parents, Too," *Christian Science Monitor,* April 28, 2006, http://www.csmonitor.com.

11. "Nokia Launches New Online Retail Distribution Channel for N-Gage Games," June 6, 2006, "Nokia and Gameloft Announce Expanded Mobile Gaming Collaboration," May 9, 2006, and "Nokia Simplifies Creation of Online Gaming Communities for Java Technology Games," March 20, 2006, Nokia press releases, http://www.n-gage.com; Grant Gross, "Nokia Slashes N-Gage Price," *PC World,* March 15, 2005, http://www.pcworld.com.

12. Wheat Montana Web site, http://www.wheatmontana.com, accessed July 17, 2006; Adelle Waldman, "Turning Wheat into Dough," *Wall Street Journal,* July 27, 2005, http://online.wsj.com.

13. Kyle Peterson, "Cendant Agrees to Sell Travel Unit for $4.3 Bln," Reuters, June 30, 2006, http://news.yahoo.com.

14. Choe Sang-Hun, "Wal-Mart Selling Stores and Leaving South Korea," *New York Times,* May 23, 2006, http://www.nytimes.com.

Chapter 3

1. Lauran Neergaard, "Officials Warn of Scarce Bird Flu Vaccine," Associated Press, June 6, 2006, http://news.yahoo.com; Roche Pharmaceuticals Web site, http://www.rocheusa.com, accessed June 5, 2006; "U.S. Shipping Tamiflu Stockpile to Asia," Associated Press, May 22, 2006, http://news.yahoo.com; David Brown, "Run on Drug for Avian Flu Has Physicians Worried," *Washington Post,* October 22, 2005, http://www.washingtonpost.com.

2. Elizabeth Weise, "Poultry Industry Knows Bird Flu Drill," *USA Today,* April 12. 2006, p. 8D; ABC News, March 13, 2006; "Business Braces for Disaster," *Kiplinger's,* March 2006, pp. 19–20; "More Tamiflu Ordered for Federal Stockpile," Associated Press, March 2, 2006, http://news.yahoo.com; "FDA Initiative Helps Expedite Development of Seasonal and Pandemic Flu Vaccines," U.S. Food and Drug Administration, March 2, 2006, http://www.fda.gov; "Feds Move to Speed Flu Vaccine Development," Associated Press, March 2, 2006, http://news.yahoo.com; "Japanese Researchers Find a New Way to Make Tamiflu," Reuters, March 2, 2006, http://news.yahoo.com; Kristen Scharnberg, "Hawaii on Front Lines for Bird Flu," *Chicago Tribune,* March 1, 2006, sec. 1, pp. 1, 18; Richard Cowan, "Bird Flu Likely in US Flocks Soon: Health Secretary," Reuters, March 1, 2006, http://news.yahoo.com; Joe De Capua, "Bird Flu Affects Trade and Consumption," Voice of America, February 28, 2006, http://www.voanews.com; Lauren Neergaard, "FDA

Clears a Third Flu-Vaccine Supplier," *Washington Post,* August 31, 2005, http://www.washingtonpost.com.

3. Dee-Ann Durbin, "GM to Cut 30,000 Jobs, Close 9 Plants," Associated Press, November 21, 2005, http://news.yahoo.com.

4. Kana Inagaki, "Japan Seeks Assurances for U.S. Beef," Associated Press, February 21, 2006, http://news.yahoo.com; "State Dept: South Korea Agrees to Lift Partially Ban on U.S. Beef Exports," HT Media Ltd., January 13, 2006, http://www.fednews.com.

5. Ryan G. Murphy, "FDA to Revisit Drug Marketing," *Los Angeles Times,* November 2, 2005, http://www.latimes.com; Robert Pear, "Drug Industry Is Said to Work on an Ad Code," *New York Times,* May 17, 2005, http://www.nytimes.com.

6. Kees Cools and Alexander Roos, "After a Pause, the Return of Business Alliances," *Christian Science Monitor,* January 30, 2006, http://www.csmonitor.com.

7. "AT&T," *Hoover's,* http://www.hoovers.com, accessed March 14, 2006; Marguerite Reardon, "Phone Options Expand Despite Telecom Mergers," CNet News.com, March 31, 2006, http://www.com.com.

8. Byron Acohido, "Microsoft Rivals File Antitrust Complaint," *USA Today,* February 22, 2006, http://www.usatoday.com.

9. "Synergy Brands to Sell Designer Brand Luxury Goods to Costco through PHS Group," Sys-Con Media, February 1, 2006, http://www.sys-con.com.

10. Kozo Mizoguchi, "Japanese Make Gasoline from Cattle Dung," Associated Press, March 3, 2006, http://news.yahoo.com; Patrick O'Driscoll, "Utahans Wary of Renewed Interest in Uranium," *USA Today,* January 20, 2006, http://www.usatoday.com; Terence Chea, "California Energy Regulators OK Solar Program," Associated Press, January 12, 2006, http://news.yahoo.com.

11. "Wi-Fi on the Farm," CNN, http://www.cnn.com, accessed October 19, 2005.

12. Kristen Kennedy, "Intel Endorses Wi-MAX with New Line of Chips for Standard," *Computer Reseller News,* http://www.lexis-nexis.com, accessed October 17, 2005.

13. "Wi-Fi on the Farm."

14. John Schmeltzer, "New McDonald's Brew," *Chicago Tribune,* February 28, 2006, http://www.chicagotribune.com; "French Giant Sells Dunkin' Donuts," CBS News, December 12, 2005, http://www.cbsnews.com.

15. Nancy Gohring, "Google News Goes Mobile," *PC World,* March 1, 2006, http://www.pcworld.com; "Apple Unveils iPod Home Stereo, Mini-Computer with Intel Chip," Agence France Presse, March 1, 2006, http://www.afp.com.

16. Byron Acohido and Jon Swartz, "FTC Launches Site to Fight Cybercrime," *USA Today,* January 11, 2006, http://www.usatoday.com.

17. "National Do Not Call Registry," Federal Trade Commission, http://www.ftc.gov, updated September 1, 2005.

18. Andrew Bridges, "FDA Panel Recommends Ban on Some Inhalers," Associated Press, January 24, 2006, http://news.yahoo.com.

19. Paul Adams, "Lights Go Dim for Electricity Deregulation," *Chicago Tribune,* April 2, 2006, sec. 5, p. 3; "Status of Electric Industry Restructuring Activity," Energy Information Administration, http://www.eia.doe.gov, accessed March 1, 2006; "Fact Sheet on Effects of Electric Utility Deregulation," U.S. Nuclear Regulatory Commission, May 2, 2005, http://www.nrc.gov.

20. Renin Paul, "New Standardized Credit Scoring System Launched," *Earth Times,* March 15, 2006, http://www.earthtimes.org.

21. "Fire Service, Health, and Consumer Organizations Ask Tobacco Companies to Produce Only Fire-Safe Cigarettes," PR Newswire, March 16, 2006, http://www.prnewswire.com.

22. Megan McCloskey, "Animal-Rights Groups Target Human Association," *San Jose Mercury News,* March 15, 2006, http://www.mercurynews.com.

23. "The DMA Member Logo," Direct Marketing Association, http://www.the-dma.org, accessed March 3, 2006.

24. Sonia Arrison, "Don't Tax the Internet," TechNewsWorld, March 3, 2006, http://www.technewsworld.com.

25. James Mehrin, "Vital Signs for the Week of February 27," *BusinessWeek,* March 1, 2006, http://www.businessweek.com.

26. Aleksandrs Rozens, "Sector Growth Indicates Robust Economy," Associated Press, March 3, 2006, http://news.yahoo.com.

27. "Economics for Investment," American Express Bank Ltd., December 9, 2005.

28. "U.S. Initial Jobless Claims Rose Last Week to 294,000," Bloomberg.com, March 2, 2006, http://www.bloomberg.com; "Weekly U.S. Jobless Claims Post an Increase," MSNBC, March 2, 2006, http://www.msnbc.com.

29. "Personal Income, Consumer Spending Rose in January," Bureau of Economic Analysis, March 1, 2006, http://www.bea.gov.

30. Madlen Read, "Oil Prices Rise on Supply Fears," Associated Press, March 3, 2006, http://news.yahoo.com; "Gasoline and Diesel Fuel Update," Energy Information Administration, February 27, 2006, http://tonto.eia.doe.gov; "Q&A: Saudi Oil Attack," BBC News, February 24, 2006, http://news.bbc.co.uk.

31. Crystal Kua, "Reverse Vending," *Honolulu StarBulletin,* July 13, 2005, http://starbulletin.com.

32. Frank Hornig and Wieland Wagner, "China, the US and Battle to Lead a Globalized World," *Der Spiegel,* February 3, 2006, http://service.spiegel.de; Pete Engardio, "Substan-

tial Benefits from China Trade?" *BusinessWeek,* February 8, 2006, http://www.businessweek.com.

33. David J. Lynch, "World Economy Grows, Faces Dangerous Balancing Act," *USA Today,* January 12, 2006, http://www.usatoday.com.

34. Douglas Quan and John Welsh, "Technology Tracks Goods, Now People," *(Riverside, CA) Press-Enterprise,* January 20, 2006, http://www.pe.com.

35. "The Emerging Carbohydrate Economy," *Sacramento Bee,* February 26, 2006, http://www.evworld.com.

36. "Research Universities Join Effort to Reduce Costs of Drug Development, Manufacturing," Purdue University, November 3, 2005, http://news.uns.purdue.edu.

37. "Sales of Chinese-Branded Cars Soaring," Comtex News Network, January 12, 2006, http://0-web.lexis-nexis.com.library.uark.edu.

38. L.S. Sya, "Wi-Fi to March Ahead," RedOrbit, February 5, 2006, http://www.redorbit.com.

39. "About Vonage," http://www.vonage.com, accessed January 23, 2006.

40. Bruce Meyerson, "Momentum Grows to Meld Tech Platforms," Associated Press, November 27, 2005, http://news.yahoo.com.

41. Linda Stern, "How to Ride That Aging Baby-Boomer Wave," Reuters, March 4, 2006, http://news.yahoo.com.

42. Wilson Lievan, "Satellite, Cable Companies Target Hispanics," *Wall Street Journal,* March 3, 2006, http://www.hispanicbusiness.com.

43. Alexei Barrionuevo, "Egg Producers Relent on Industry Seal," *New York Times,* October 4, 2005, http://www.nytimes.com.

44. "PepsiCo to Change Tropicana Drinks' Labels," Associated Press, August 11, 2005, http://news.yahoo.com.

45. "Snowboard Bindings Recalled Due to Fall Hazards," U.S. Consumer Product Safety Commission, March 3, 2006, http://www.cpsc.gov.

46. Marilyn Geewax, "Wal-Mart Wants Ethics Chief to Help Improve Its Image," Indystar.com, March 3, 2006, http://www.indystar.com.

47. Carol D. Leonnig, "Tobacco Escapes Huge Penalty," *Washington Post,* June 8, 2005, http://www.washingtonpost.com.

48. Alan Stafford, "Privacy in Peril," *PC World,* November 2005, http://www.pcworld.com.

49. "ChoicePoint Settles Data Security Breach Charges," Federal Trade Commission, January 26, 2006, http://www.ftc.gov.

50. Alan Stafford, "Privacy in Peril."

51. Marilynn Marchione, "A Hard Stance against Soft Drinks," *Fort Worth Star-Telegram,* March 5, 2006, http://www.star-telegram.com.

52. Emily Bazar, "Advertisers Catch the School Bus," *USA Today,* December 27, 2005, http://www.usatoday.com; "Junk Food Infiltrating Schools," CBS News, September 7, 2005, http://www.cbsnews.com.

53. John Schmeltzer and Leon Lazaroff, "Kraft Competitors Face Tough Choice," *Chicago Tribune,* January 13, 2005, sec. 3, pp. 1, 8.

54. Bruce Horovitz, "Alcohol Makers on Tricky Path in Marketing to College Crowd," *USA Today,* November 17, 2005, http://www.usatoday.com; Alan Mozes, "Alcohol Merchandise Encourages Underage Drinking," Yahoo! News, May 17, 2005, http://story.news.yahoo.com.

55. Kevin G. Demarrais, "Sunoco Agrees to Pay $325,000 to Settle Price-Gouging Suit," NorthJersey.com, February 7, 2006, http://www.northjersey.com.

56. Deborah Mendenhall, "Keep Your Credit under Control," *Family Circle,* March 2006, pp. 42–49.

57. Marc Gunther, "Social Investing That Hits Home," *Fortune,* November 14, 2005, p. 228.

58. "When the Bits Bite the Dust," *CIO,* October 1, 2005, http://www.cio.com.

59. Theresa Howard, "Being Eco-Friendly Can Pay Economically," *USA Today,* August 15, 2005, http://www.usatoday.com.

60. Jane Brissett, "Organic Food Sales Grow as Consumers Push for Chemical-Free," *Duluth News Tribune,* January 4, 2006, http://0-web.lexis-nexis.com.library.uark.edu.

61. Brian Grow, "The Great Rebate Runaround," *BusinessWeek,* December 5, 2005, pp. 34–37.

62. "Yucca Mountain Project," Office of Civilian Radioactive Waste Management, http://www.ocrwm.doe.gov, accessed March 6, 2006.

Chapter 4

1. Southwest Airlines Web site, http://www.southwest.com, accessed May 22, 2006; "Southwest Airlines Online Partner Marketing Campaign," Spur Digital, http://www.spurdigital.com, accessed May 22, 2006; "Southwest Airlines Introduces Wireless Check-In," PR Newswire, January 23, 2006, http://www.prnewswire.com; "Now Your Complete Southwest Airlines Vacation Package Is Just One Click Away on Southwest.com," PR Newswire, January 20, 2006, http://www.prnewswire.com.

2. "Quarterly Retail E-Business Sales," U.S. Census Bureau, http://www.census.gov, accessed April 17, 2006.

3. Internet World Statics, http://www.internetworldstats.com, accessed April 24, 2006; Rob McGann, "Web Usage Growth," ClickZ Network, http://www.clickz.com, accessed April 24, 2006.

4. Pew Internet and American Life Project, http://www.pewinternet.org, accessed April 24, 2006.
5. Rob McGann, "Internet Edges Out Family Time More Than TV Time," ClickZ Network, http://www.clickz.com, accessed March 11, 2006; Bobbie Johnson, "Britain Turns Off—and Logs On," *The Guardian*, March 8, 2006, http://www.guardian.co.uk.
6. Scott Miller, "Store Closing to Concentrate on Online Sales," Knight Ridder Tribune Business News, February 22, 2006.
7. Robert Hof, "Don't Cut Back Now," *BusinessWeek*, http://www.businessweek.com, accessed April 24, 2006.
8. Rob McGann, "Web-to-Store Consumers Spend, Shop More at Local Stores," ClickZ Network, http://www.clickz.com, accessed April 11, 2006.
9. U.S. Census Bureau, "E-Stats," http://www.census.gov, accessed April 24, 2006.
10. "Web Integration: Then and Now," *Network World*, http://www.infotrac.com, accessed April 16, 2006.
11. David Hannon, "Exchanges Are Dead, but Collaboration Is Not," *Purchasing*, http://www.purchasing.com, accessed April 9, 2006; Cara Cannella, "Why Online Exchanges Died," *Inc.*, http://www.inc.com, accessed April 9, 2005; Arundhati Parmar, "A Focus on Services Helped Revive B2B E-Exchanges," *Marketing News*, http://www.marketingpower.com, accessed April 26, 2006.
12. "The Role of E-Marketplaces in Relationship-Based Supply Chains: A Survey," *IBM Systems Journal*, http://www.infotrac.com, accessed March 27, 2006.
13. "Ariba at Work: Customer Spotlight," Ariba, http://www.ariba.com, accessed March 30, 2006.
14. "General Information" and "Benefits," State of North Carolina E-Procurement Program, http://www.ncgov.com/eprocurement/asp/section/ep_index.asp, accessed April 26, 2006.
15. "Quarterly Retail E-Business Sales," U.S. Census Bureau, http://www.census.gov, accessed April 28, 2006.
16. Laura Rush, "E-Business Growth Spurred by Maturation," ClickZ Network, http://www.clickz.com, accessed March 8, 2006.
17. Bob Tedeschi, "Where Is Wal-Mart's Fancy Stuff? Try Online," *New York Times*, http://www.nytimes.com, accessed April 28, 2006.
18. Pew Internet and American Life Project.
19. Rob McGann, "Broadband: High Speed, High Spend," ClickZ Network, http://www.clickz.com, accessed April 28, 2006.
20. "Women Out-Shop Men Online for the First Time in '05 Holiday Season, Study Says," *Internet Retailer*, http://www.internetretailer.com, accessed May 1, 2006.
21. Robyn Greenspan, "E-Tailers Will See Green," ClickZ Network, http://www.clickz.com, accessed September 1, 2006.
22. "Trends," Pew Internet and American Life Project, http://www.pewinternet.org, accessed May 6, 2005.
23. "Women Out-Shop Men Online for First Time in '05 Holiday Season, Study Says."
24. Laura Rush, "Women, Comparison Shopping Help Boost Holiday Revenues," ClickZ Network, http://www.clickz.com, accessed March 10, 2005.
25. "Irrelevance through Constant Consumer Analysis," Jupiter Media Metrix, http://www.jmm.com, accessed April 6, 2006.
26. "About VeriSign," http://www.verisign.com, accessed May 12, 2006.
27. "One in Four Consumers Won't Holiday Shop Because of Security Concerns," *Internet Retailer*, http://www.internetretailer.com, accessed May 1, 2006.
28. "Personal Data of 59,000 People Stolen," Associated Press, http://news.yahoo.com, accessed May 1, 2006.
29. "2005 Annual Report," Internet Crime Complaint Center, http://www.ic3.gov, accessed May 3, 2006.
30. "How Not to Get Hooked by a Phishing Scam," *FTC Consumer Alert*, http://www.ftc.gov, accessed May 1, 2006.
31. "Online Merchants Fight Fraud," CBS News, http://www.cbsnews.com, accessed April 20, 2006.
32. "2005 Holiday Web Shopper Report," WebSurveyor, http://www.internetretailer.com, accessed May 3, 2006.
33. "Negative Online Experience Poses Risk to Retailer's Brands, Survey Says," *Internet Retailer*, http://www.internetretailer.com, accessed May 1, 2006.
34. "Online Shoppers Want Satisfaction," *Sales and Marketing Management*, http://www.smm.com, accessed April 17, 2006.
35. "One in Four Consumers Won't Holiday Shop Because of Security Concerns."
36. Kate Zernike, "Tired of TiVo? Beyond Blogs? Podcasts are Here," *New York Times*, http://www.nytimes.com, accessed April 28, 2006.
37. Riva Richmond, "Blogs Keep Internet Customers Coming Back," *Wall Street Journal*, http://www.wsj.com, accessed May 6, 2006.
38. "News Analysis: How Blogs Help Brands Build Trust Online," *Revolution*, http://www.infotrac.com, accessed May 6, 2006.
39. Thomas Mucha, "Why GM's Blog Works," *Business 2.0*, http://money.cnn.com, accessed May 3, 2006.
40. Kevin Dugan, Strategic Public Relations, http://prblog.typepad.com, accessed May 3, 2006.
41. Stuart Elliott, "More Agencies Investing in Marketing with a Click," *New York Times*, http://www.nytimes.com, accessed May 3, 2006.
42. Rob McGann, "Web-to-Store Consumers Spend, Shop More at Local Stores."
43. "Success Stories," Coremetrics, http://www.coremetrics.com, accessed April 22, 2006.

Chapter 5

1. "The Dollars & Sense of Hybrids," *Consumer Reports*, April 2006, http://www.consumerreports.org; Jack Speer, "New Tax Credit Benefits Buyers of Hybrid Cars," *Morning Edition*, National Public Radio, March 10, 2006, http://www.npr.org; Chris Birk, "Drivers Devouring Hybrid $$," *(Scranton, PA) Times-Tribune*, March 10, 2006, http://thetimes-tribune.com; Miguel Llanos, "Consumer Reports Fixes Error on Hybrid Costs," MSNBC, March 9, 2006, http://www.msnbc.msn.com; "Hybrid Car Buyers to Receive Tax Credits," *USA Today*, December 31, 2005, http://www.usatoday.com.
2. "Music City Motorplex Targeting Hispanic Customers," *Nashville Business Journal*, May 6, 2005, http://nashville.bizjournals.com.
3. "Kraft Foods Helps Latina Moms and Families Celebrate Their Heritage," *Hispanic PR Wire*, March 15, 2006, http://hispanicprwire.com.
4. Ann Zimmerman, "Wal-Mart's Hispanic Outreach," *Wall Street Journal*, May 31, 2005, http://www.mindfully.org.
5. Tom Zeller, Jr., "A Generation Serves Notice: It's a Moving Target," *New York Times*, January 22, 2006, http://www.nytimes.com.
6. Randall Frost, "Global Packaging: What's the Difference?" Brand channel.com, January 16, 2006, http://www.brandchannel.com.
7. Mike Bergman, "More Diversity, Slower Growth," U.S. Census Bureau, March 14, 2006, http://www.census.gov.
8. "Hispanics: A People in Motion," *Pew Research Center Report: Trends 2005*, January 20, 2005, http://pewresearch.org.
9. Ibid.
10. Mike Bergman, "More Diversity, Slower Growth."
11. Mike Beirne, "Reports: African American Buying Power Soaring," *Brandweek*, February 23, 2006, http://www.brandweek.com.
12. "Magazine Targeting African Americans Set to Launch," UrbanMecca.com, March 2, 2006, http://www.urbanmecca.com.
13. Mike Bergman, "More Diversity, Slower Growth."
14. Kassidy Emmerson, "Best Clothing Stores for Asian American Women," AsianAmericans.com, February 15, 2006, http://www.asianamericans.com.
15. "The Invisible Market," *Brandweek*, February 1, 2006, http://www.brandweek.com.
16. Michael Fielding, "Luxe Life," *Marketing News*, December 15, 2005, pp. 11–12.
17. Elizabeth, Weise, "Idea of Simple Life Takes Hold," *USA Today*, March 23, 2006, pp. 1D–2D.
18. Michael Fielding, "Luxe Life."
19. Rebecca A. Clay, "Advertising to Children? Is It Ethical?" *Monitor on Psychology*, February 24, 2006, http://www.apa.org.
20. Kristin Arnold, "Exclusive Cards, Exclusive Services," Bankrate.com, March 17, 2006, http://biz.yahoo.com.
21. Trent Edwards, "A Lot Like Lance," *Calgary Herald*, August 11, 2005, http://www.canada.com/calgaryherald.
22. Christopher Farrell and Ann Therese Palmer, "The Overworked, Networked Family," *BusinessWeek*, September 23, 2005, http://www.businessweek.com.
23. Chelsea Emery, "In Terms of Purchasing, It's a Woman's World: Study," Reuters, January 27, 2006, http://news.yahoo.com.
24. Tom Van Riper, "Brand Me," *Forbes*, February 10, 2006, http://www.forbes.com.
25. "Families Drawn Together by Communication Revolution," Pew Research Center, February 21, 2006, http://pewresearch.org.
26. Gary Levin, "Ad Glut Turns Off Viewers," *USA Today*, October 11, 2005, http://www.usatoday.com.
27. Ibid.
28. Jim McKnight, "Marketers Use Word of Mouth to Pop the Top on Retro Beer," *USA Today*, June 12, 2005, http://www.usatoday.com.
29. Wendy Melillo, "What Neuroscience Can Tell Us about Marketing," AdWeek.com, January 16, 2006, http://www.adweek.com.
30. "Consumer Focus: It's All in the Name," *Carpet & Floorcoverings Review*, January 9, 2006, http://0-web.lexis-nexis.com.library.uark.edu.
31. Heather Landy, "Wal-Mart Courts Upscale Shoppers," MiamiHerald.com, March 23, 2006, http://www.miamiherald.com.
32. Theresa Howard, "Citi's Ads Tell Clients of Faster Rewards," *USA Today*, June 13, 2005, http://www.usatoday.com.
33. Allison Enright, "Samples Eliminate Fear Factor," *Marketing News*, October 15, 2005, http://0-web.lexis-nexis.com.library.uark.edu.
34. Michael Liedtke, "Online Shopping Comparison Sites on the Rise," Associated Press, November 18, 2005, http://news.yahoo.com.
35. Joshua Freed, "Big TVs Make Big Splash for Big Game," *USA Today*, January 13, 2006, http://www.usatoday.com.

Chapter 6

1. Jad Mouawed, "Gulf Energy Firms Hurting," *Arizona Republic,* March 6, 2006, www .azcentral.com; "Katrina Liability Limits Sought," CNN Money.com, September 20, 2005, http://money.cnn.com; Jeff D. Ophdyke and Christopher Cooper, "New Orleans Officials Criticize Contracts," *Real Estate Journal,* September 14, 2005, www.realestatejournal .com; Yochi J. Dreazen, "U.S. Names Five Firms to Build Housing," *Real Estate Journal,* September 12, 2005, http://www.realestatejournal.com; Alex Frangos, "Can Rebuilding Create a Better New Orleans?" *Real Estate Journal,* September 6, 2005, http://www.realestatejournal.com.

2. Anne Rochell Konigsmark, "Census Outlines Face of Today's New Orleans," *USA Today,* June 7, 2006, http://www.usatoday.com; Christopher Cooper, "Governor Seeks Oil Revenue for Louisiana," *The Wall Street Journal,* June 5, 2006, http://online.wsj.com; Bret Schulte, "Turf Wars," *U.S. News & World Report,* February 27, 2006, pp. 60–71.

3. U.S. Department of Defense, http://www.dod.gov, accessed March 3, 2006.

4. "E-Stats," U.S. Census Bureau, http://www.census.gov/estats, May 11, 2005, accessed March 24, 2006.

5. Nortel Web site, http://www.nortel.com, accessed May 2, 2006.

6. Allison Enright, "It Takes a Committee to Buy into B-to-B," *Marketing News,* February 15, 2006, pp. 11–13.

7. Jan-Pro Web site, http://www.jan-pro.com, accessed March 8, 2006.

8. Paulette Thomas, "Manufacturing Your Product," *Startup Journal,* May 16, 2005, http://www.startupjournal.com.

9. Gary Stoller, "Sale of Airports' Banned Items Proves Bountiful," *USA Today,* February 7, 2006, http://www.usatoday.com.

10. "E-Stats," U.S. Census Bureau.

11. Thomas J. Baskind, "Eight Key Steps to Building B2B Major Account Client Alliances," National Business Association, http://www.nationalbusiness.org, accessed March 8, 2006.

12. Scott Shepard, "The Seam's Success in Cotton Generates Added Commodity in Trading: Peanuts," *Memphis Business Journal,* August 15, 2005, http://memphis.bizjournals.com.

13. Mark Calvey, "BofA to Enhance Array of Small Business Services," *San Francisco Business Times,* March 3, 2006, http://sanfrancisco.bizjournals.com.

14. Tetra Tech Web site, http://www.tetratech.com, accessed March 8, 2006.

15. "North American Industry Classification System (NAICS)," U.S. Census Bureau, http://www.census.gov, accessed March 16, 2006.

16. Direction Web site, http://www.directron.com, accessed March 8, 2006.

17. "The Manufacturing Core," U.S. Department of State, http://usinfo.state.gov, accessed March 8, 2006.

18. Bob Tita, "Chicago's Ford Plant May Get Boost from Closures," *Crain's ChicagoBusiness,* January 23, 2006, http://chicagobusiness.com.

19. "Success Story—Taxi and Logistics Division at Seoul City Hall," Sun Microsystems, http://www.sun.com, accessed March 10, 2006.

20. "Wal-Mart and CMN," http://www.walmartfoundation.org, accessed March 10, 2006.

21. Elizabeth Esfahani, "Thinking Locally, Succeeding Globally," *Business 2.0,* December 2005, pp. 96–98.

22. Office Depot Web site, http://www.officedepot.com, accessed March 10, 2006.

23. Richard Ripley, "Coldwater Fattens Up Key Margin," *Journal of Business,* May 5, 2005, p. 1.

24. "Unisys Predicts 2006 Outsourcing Trends," Business Wire, December 12, 2005, http://www.businesswire.com.

25. Andrea Tan, "Around Asia's Markets: Optimism Returns for Singapore Chip Firm," *International Herald Tribune,* March 7, 2006, http://www.iht.com.

26. "Procter & Gamble Feature," Wal-Mart Stores, http://www.walmartstores.com, accessed March 10, 2006.

27. Xerox Web site, http://www.xerox.com, accessed March 10, 2006.

28. S. Mitra Kalita, "Hope and Toil at India's Call Centers," *Washington Post,* December 27, 2005, http://www.washingtonpost.com.

29. Richard J. Newman, "Coming and Going," *U.S. News & World Report,* January 23, 2006, pp. 50–52.

30. Ed Frauenheim, "Report: China's Outsourcing Industry Lags India's," CNet News.com, February 3, 2005, http://www.news.com.com; Fareed Sakaria, "Does the Future Belong to China?" MSNBC, May 9, 2005, http://www.msnbc.com.

31. Newman, "Coming and Going."

32. Ibid.

33. John W. Miller, "Eastern Europe Becomes Hub for 'Nearshoring' Call-Center Jobs," *Wall Street Journal, CareerJournal Europe.com,* March 17, 2005, http://www.careerjournaleurope .com.

34. "Signed, Sealed and Procured," CDIT, http://www.cdit.com, accessed March 16, 2006.

35. Fred Tannenbaum, "Fueling Firm's Growth," *Charlotte Business Journal,* March 10, 2006, http://www.bizjournals.com.

36. Keurig Web site, http://www.keurig.com, accessed February 3, 2006; Michelle Leder, "Taking a Niche Player Big-Time," *Inc.,* January 2004, pp. 34, 37.

37. Keurig Web site, http://www.keurig.com.

38. Ibid.

39. Laurie Sullivan, "DHL Taps Several Vendors for RFID Project," *Information Week,* March 8, 2006, http://www.informationweek.com.

40. Ibid.

41. "Flexible Platforms: The Springboard to B2B Success," *Supply Chain Management Review,* http://www.manufacturing.net, accessed March 8, 2006.

42. Office Depot Web site, http://mediarelations.officedepot.com, accessed March 13, 2006; Mike Troy, "Office Depot Shifts Store Expansion to M2 Format," *DSN Retailing Today,* July 24, 2004, accessed at http://www.findarticles.com, March 17, 2006.

43. Sumner Lemon, "Chinese Vendors Face Cultural Challenge," *CIO,* May 25, 2005, http://cio-asia.com.

44. "Supplier Diversity," U.S. Postal Service, http://www.usps.com, accessed March 8, 2006.

45. "Get It Right," U.S. General Services Administration, http://www.gsa.gov, accessed March 13, 2006; David Perera, "Three Tips on How to Get It Right," FCW.com, September 5, 2005, http://www.fcw.com.

46. "GSA Advantage Web site, http://www.gsaadvantage.gov, accessed March 13, 2006.

47. "Interactions with the Pharmaceutical Industry," American College of Physicians, http://ea.acponline.org, accessed March 13, 2006.

48. Greg Burns, "New Doctors Are Allergic to Freebies," *Chicago Tribune,* March 12, 2006, sec. 5, pp. 1, 14.

Chapter 7

1. Nokia Web site, http://www.nokia.com, accessed April 6, 2006; Tom Wright, "Finland Again Ranks First among Global Competitors," *New York Times,* September 29, 2005, http://www.nytimes.com; "Tapping into Good Ideas," *Financial Times,* September 13, 2005, http://www.ft.com; Robert G. Kaiser, "Innovation Gives Finland a Firm Grasp on its Future," *Washington Post,* July 14, 2005, http://www.washingtonpost.com.

2. "A Bright Vision, a Solid Record," *2006 U.S. Trade Policy Agenda: Asset Upload,* Office of the U.S. Trade Representative, http://www.ustr.gov, accessed March 27, 2006.

3. Ibid.

4. "U.S. Goods Trade: Imports & Exports by Related Parties," *U.S. Census Bureau News,* April 12, 2005, http://www.census.gov.

5. "A Bright Vision, a Solid Record."

6. Ibid.

7. Bernard Condon, Michael Freedman, and Naazneen Karmali, "Globetrotter," *Forbes,* April 18, 2005, http://www.forbes.com.

8. "Customer Case Study/Blue Jeans Cable," Paypal Web site, http://www.paypal.com, accessed March 26, 2006.

9. Dexter Roberts and David Rocks, "Let a Thousand Brands Bloom," *BusinessWeek,* October 17, 2005, pp. 58-60.

10. "China to Become World's No. 1 Tourist Destination in 2017: Official," *Xinhua General News Service,* November 4, 2005, http://www.xinhuanet.com/english.

11. Jack Ewing, "Bulgarian Back Lot, Hollywood Dreams," *BusinessWeek,* January 23, 2006, pp. 50–53.

12. Jason Bush, "Shoppers Gone Wild," *BusinessWeek,* February 20, 2006, pp. 46–47.

13. Dexter Roberts and David Rocks, "Let a Thousand Brands Bloom."

14. Sherri Daye Scott, "Like the Big Boys Do It," *QSR Magazine,* September 2005, http://www.qsrmagazine.com.

15. Central Intelligence Agency, *World Factbook,* January 10, 2006, http://www.cia.gov.

16. David Cohen, "The Global Reverb of China and India," *BusinessWeek,* February 9, 2006, http://www.businessweek.com.

17. Ibid.

18. Philip Bowring, "On Trade, the U.S. and China Need to Go Global," *International Herald Tribune,* March 27, 2006, http://www.iht.com.

19. Amelia Gentleman, "The I, Me, My Generation: A Buyers' Market," *International Herald Tribune,* January 26, 2006, http://www.iht.com.

20. "Internet Usage Statistics—The Big Picture," Internet World Stats, http://www. internetworldstats.com, accessed December 5, 2005.

21. "European Court Overrules Popular Ban on Genetically Engineered Crops in 164 Regions," Organic Consumers Association, October 5, 2005, http://www.organic-consumers.org.

22. Jan Silva, "Dock Workers Attack EU Building in France," Associated Press, January 16, 2006, http://news.yahoo.com.

23. "ISO 9000 and ISO 14000—in Brief," International Organization for Standardization, http://www.iso.org, accessed March 27, 2006.

24. "A Closer Look at the Helms-Burton Law," Global Exchange, March 10, 2005, http://www.globalexchange.org.

25. G. Jeffrey MacDonald, "Congress's Dilemma: When Yahoo in China's Not Yahoo," *Christian Science Monitor,* February 14, 2006, http://www.csmonitor.com; G. Jeffrey MacDonald, "Google's Dilemma: Privacy vs. Police," *Christian Science Monitor,* January 26, 2006, http://www.csmonitor.com.

26. Michael Fielding, "CAFTA-DR to Build Options over Time," *Marketing News,* February 1, 2006, pp. 13–14.

27. Bruce Odessey, "Bush Advisers View Sugar Program as Hurting U.S. Consumers," Bureau of International Information Programs, U.S. Department of State, February 13, 2006, http://usinfo.state.gov.

28. Bruce Odessey, "EU Must Cut Farm Tariffs in Trade Talks, United States Insists," Bureau of International Information Programs, U.S. Department of State, December 12, 2005, http://usinfo.state.gov.

29. "WTO Arbitrators Once Again Reject EU's Proposed Banana Import Tariff," *Bridges,* November 2, 2005, http://www.ictsd.org/weekly.

30. Chris Buckley, "China Assails U.S. Textile Quotas," *International Herald Tribune,* May 16, 2005, http://www.iht.com.

31. "Japan Officials Confirm 1st Mad Cow Case," Associated Press, March 17, 2006, http://news.yahoo.com.

32. Sam Cage, "U.S. Asks WTO to Eye New Airbus Subsidies," ABC News, February 2, 2006, http://abcnews.go.com.

33. Jaksa Kivela, "Doing Business in the People's Republic of China," AllBusiness, May 2005, http://www.allbusiness.com.

34. "EU to Act on Asian Shoe Imports," CNN, March 23, 2006, http://www.cnn.com.

35. Pete Engardio, "The Future of Outsourcing," *BusinessWeek,* January 30, 2006, pp. 50–58.

36. "Key WTO Members Fail to Plug Gaps in Talks to Promote Doha Round+," TMCnet, March 11, 2006, http://www.tmcnet.com.

37. Steven Chase, "Partners Hold Watershed NAFTA Talks," *Globe and Mail,* March 25, 2006, http://www.theglobeandmail.com.

38. "NAFTA: A Strong Record of Success," Office of the U.S. Trade Representative, March 2006, http://www.ustr.gov.

39. Carlos To Echeverria P., "What Is FTAA and What Is Its Current Status?" *Fair Economy,* September 16, 2005, http://www.faireconomy.org. 40. Warren Vieth, "Bush Wins Approval of Trade Pact," *Los Angeles Times,* July 28, 2005, http://www.latimes.com.

41. "European Union Member States," European Union Web site, *http://europa.eu.int,* accessed March 27, 2006.

42. "European Union," *World Factbook,* January 10, 2006, http://www.cia.gov.

43. Joellen Perry, "Global Goal," *U.S. News & World Report/Executive Edition,* February 27, 2006, pp. EE2–EE4.

44. "Grow Your Business," *Entrepreneur,* December 5, 2005, http://www.entrepreneur.com.

45. Ibid.

46. Diana Farrell, "Are You Ready to Go Global?" *Working Knowledge,* Harvard Business School, January 31, 2005, http://hbswk.hbs.edu.

47. "WTP Enterprises, Inc. Announces Results for the First Quarter 2005," http://www.shareholder.com/wpt, accessed March 27, 2006.

48. "Chinese Premier Visits Airbus as France Waits for Contracts," *Associated Press,* December 4, 2005, http://0-web.lexis-nexis.com.library.uark.edu.

49. Jennifer L. Koncz and Daniel R. Yorgason, "Direct Investment Positions," *Survey of Current Business,* Bureau of Economic Analysis, July 2005, pp. 40–53.

50. Abe De Ramos, "China's Growing Appetite," *CFO,* November 1, 2005, http://www.cfo.com.

51. Ratna Bhushan, "Starbucks Set to Finalise India JV," *The Times of India,* July 20, 2005, http://0-web.lexis-nexis.com.library.uark.edu.

52. Richard J. Newman, "Can America Keep Up?" *U.S. News & World Report,* March 27, 2006, pp. 48–56.

53. Louise Lee, Peter Burrows, and Bruce Einhorn, "Dell May Have to Reboot in China," *BusinessWeek,* November 7, 2005, p. 46.

54. Gary Cross, "Japan, the U.S. and the Globalization of Children's Consumer Culture," *Journal of Social History,* Summer 2005, http://www.findarticles.com.

55. Pete Gumber, "Branding America," *Time,* February 20, 2005, http://www.time.com.

56. Daren Fonda, "China's Fast-Moving Vehicles," *Time,* January 16, 2006, pp. 60–61.

57. S. Dinakar, "A Penny a Packet," *Forbes,* November 28, 2005, pp. 186, 188.

58. "Barter Happenings around the Globe," *BarterNews,* http://www.barternews.com, accessed March 31, 2006.

59. "United States American Community Survey: Data Profile Highlights," U.S. Census Bureau, http://www.census.gov, accessed May 9, 2006.

60. "LG Electronics Inc. Company Profile," Yahoo! Finance, http://biz.yahoo.com, accessed May 9, 2006; "Expo—LG Electronics to Gain U.S. Cell Phone Share," *The San Diego Union-Tribune,* January 4, 2006, http://www.signonsandiego.com; Martyn Williams, "LG to Enter U.S. Portable Media Device Market," *PC World,* January 4, 2006, http://www.pcworld.com.

61. Yuri Kageyama, "Kia, Toyota Will Build Here, Create 5,500 U.S. Jobs," *USA Today,* March 13, 2006, http://www.usatoday.com.

62. Mark Tatge and Miriam Gottfried, "The British Are Coming!" *Forbes,* February 13, 2006, pp. 51–52.

63. Joe Sharkey, "Change in Rules Ignites Hope for Zippo-Toting Air Travelers," *Ventura County (CA) Star,* August 7, 2005, http://www.venturacountystar.com.

Chapter 8

1. Abacus Web site, www.abacus-us.com, accessed May 16, 2006; Amy Syracuse, "Co-op Databases Offer Savings, Services for Those Willing to Share," *BtoB,* February 13, 2006,

http://www.btobonline.com; Helen Coster, "Consumer Spy," *Forbes,* January 6, 2006, p. 91; Mark Del Franco, "The Latest Matchback Tools," *Catalog Age,* April 1, 2005, http://preview.catalogagemag.com.

2. J. D. Power and Associates Web site, http://www.jdpower.com, accessed March 17, 2006.

3. "Quantitative Research," http://www.brain-research.com, accessed March 17, 2006.

4. "Welcome to a New Way of Looking at Nielsen," http://www.nielsenmedia.com, accessed March 17, 2006.

5. Oliver Ryan, "Putting Your Customers to Work," *Fortune,* March 20, 2006, p. 30.

6. "Who Is MRI?" *The Topline,* http://www.mri-research.com, accessed March 17, 2006.

7. U.S. Environmental Protection Agency, "Customer Satisfaction Questionnaire," http://www.epa.gov, accessed March 17, 2006.

8. James Fink, "Subway Chooses WNY to Sample Breakfast," *Buffalo Business First,* January 27, 2005, http://www.bizjournals.com/buffalo.

9. Thomas Mucha, "The Builder of Boomtown," CNN Money.com, September 1, 2005, http://money.cnn.com.

10. Karen D. Schwartz, "Decisions at the Touch of a Button," Teradata, http://www.teradata.com, accessed March 20, 2006.

11. Deborah Ball, "As Chocolate Sags, Cadbury Gambles on a Piece of Gum," *Wall Street Journal,* January 12, 2006, http://online.wsj.com.

12. "Census Tracts and Block Numbering Areas," U.S. Census Bureau, http://www.census.gov, accessed March 17, 2006.

13. "TIGER® Overview," U.S. Census Bureau, http://www.census.gov, accessed March 17, 2006.

14. Barbara Thau, "Tests Back Wal-Mart's Faith in RFID," *HFN,* November 28, 2005, http://www.hfnmag.com.

15. "Research Distributors," KnowThis.com, http://www.knowthis.com, accessed March 20, 2006.

16. Justin Martin, "Blogging for Dollars," *Fortune,* December 12, 2005, p. S178.

17. Reyhan Harmanci, "Women's Pages: Next Time You Read about 'What Women Want,' Check the Research," *San Francisco Chronicle,* January 4, 2006, http://www.sfgate.com.

18. Susan Kinne, "Inclusion of People with Disabilities in Telephone Health Surveillance Surveys," *American Journal of Public Health,* March 2005, pp. 512ff.

19. "Portable People Meters—A Future-Proof Audience Measurement Solution," Arbitron, http://www.arbitron.com, accessed March 21, 2006; "Wendy's International Selects Arbitron Portable People Meter Radio Ratings Service," Arbitron news release, March 6, 2006.

20. Stuart Elliott, "How to Value Ratings with DVR Delay?" *New York Times,* February 13, 2006, http://www.nytimes.com.

21. TRU Web site, http://www.teenresearch.com, accessed March 21, 2006.

22. Dorland Healthcare Information Web site, http://www.dorlandhealth.com, accessed March 21, 2006.

23. "Surveys and Non Response," SuperSurvey Knowledge Base, http://knowledge-base.supersurvey.com, accessed March 21, 2006.

24. Rob Fargman, "Has the Do Not Call Registry Turned Out to Be a Survey Researcher's Best Friend?" Edison Media Research, http://www.edisonresearch.com, accessed March 28, 2006.

25. David Kiley, "Shoot the Focus Group," *BusinessWeek,* November 14, 2005, p. 120.

26. Sonali Desai, "Conducting Multi-Country Focus Group Discussions on the Net," ACNielsen, http://www.acnielsen.com, accessed March 21, 2006.

27. Chris Kelleher, "The New Junk Fax Law: An Overview," *Entrepreneur,* September 19, 2005, http://www.entrepreneur.com.

28. Alex Mindlin, "The Ad-Averse: Finicky and Opinionated," *New York Times,* October 3, 2005, http://www.nytimes.com.

29. "Online Polling Provides Cost-Effective Local Content," *The Rundown,* August 22, 2005, http://www.tvrundown.com.

30. William M. Bulkeley, "Marketers Scan Blogs for Brand Insights," *Wall Street Journal,* June 23, 2005, http://online.wsj.com.

31. "Ad Watch Year-End Recap—Part Two," GameDaily, January 9, 2006, http://www.gamedaily.com.

32. Kitty Crider, "Wired Kitchens of Tomorrow Ace Real-Families Test," *Chicago Tribune,* August 7, 2005, p. 6.

33. Todd Wasserman, "Kimberly-Clark Tries Seeing Things from Consumer's POV," *Brandweek,* September 5, 2005, http://www.brandweek.com.

34. Lauren Gibbons Paul, "Ethnography: What Does It Cost?" *CMO,* http://www.cmomagazine.com, accessed March 21, 2006.

35. Brian Bergstein, "Companies Using Tech Analysis on Themselves," Associated Press, August 7, 2005, http://news.yahoo.com.

36. Michael Kahn, "Business Intelligence Software Looks to Future," Reuters Limited, January 15, 2006, http://news.yahoo.com.

Chapter 9

1. "American Idol Birthday Party," Amazing Moms.com, http://www.amazingmoms.com, accessed April 12, 2006; "Americanidol.com This Season," March 9, 2006, http://www.americanidol.com; Ann Oldenburg, "Welcome to Idol Nation," *USA Today,* February 13, 2006, http://www.usatoday.com; "American Idol Crushes Grammys in Rat-

ings," MSNBC, February 9, 2006, http://www.msnbc.com; Craig Berman, "American Idol Isn't Kind to Teens," MSNBC, March 30, 3005, http://www.msnbc.com; "Atlanta Ratings Reign for American Idol," Nielsen Media, January 18, 2005, http://www.nielsen-media.com.

2. Ann Oldenburg, "Welcome to Idol Nation," *USA Today,* February 13, 2006, http://www.usatoday.com; "Atlanta Ratings Reign for American Idol," Nielsen Media Research, January 18, 2005, http://www.nielsenmedia.com.

3. U.S. Census Bureau, International Database, http://www.census.gov, accessed May 23, 2006.

4. "Women's Buying Power," About.com, http://womensissues.about.com, accessed April 10, 2006.

5. "Tech Savvy Women Wield Purchasing Power of $55 Billion Annually," PR Newswire, February 14, 2006, http://www.sys-con.com.

6. Lowe's Web site, http://www.lowes.com, accessed May 1, 2006.

7. Radio Shack Web site, http://www.radioshack.com, accessed May 1, 2006.

8. U.S. Census Bureau, http://www.census.gov, accessed March 17, 2006.

9. Ibid.

10. International Data Base, U.S. Census Bureau, http://www.census.gov, accessed April 10, 2006.

11. "World City Populations," http://www.world-gazetteer.com, accessed April 10, 2006.

12. Stephen Ohlemacher, "Highest Wages in East, Lowest in South," Yahoo! News, November 29, 2005, http://news.yahoo.com.

13. U.S. Census Bureau, *Statistical Abstract of the United States: 2006,* http://www.census.gov, accessed March 17, 2006.

14. U.S. Census Bureau, http://www.census.gov, accessed March 17, 2006.

15. "Domino's Pizza Has Its Own Winning Game Plan," PR Newswire, January 31, 2006, http://www.prnewswire.com.

16. "Google Earth—Explore, Search, and Discover," Google Earth Home, http://earth.google.com, accessed March 19, 2006.

17. Pallavi Gogoi, "Meet Jane Geek," *BusinessWeek,* November 23, 2005, http://www.businessweek.com.

18. Michele Gershberg, "Sony Makes Style Pitch to Women for Flat TV," Reuters, September 28, 2005, http://news.yahoo.com.

19. "Household Decision Making Balance of Power," Working Women Online, *Washington Post,* http://www.washingtonpost.com, accessed April 10, 2006.

20. Caroline E. Mayer, "Sugary Drinks to Be Pulled from Schools," *Washington Post,* May 3, 2006, http://www.washingtonpost.com.

21. "Industry Snapshot: Teen Shoppers," *Investor's Business Daily,* January 17, 2006, http://www.investors.com.

22. "Rising Individualism and Growing Wallets among Teens and Tweens," Growth from Knowledge, http://www.gfkamerica.com, accessed March 15, 2006.

23. Alex Williams, "Nag Factor Has Parents of Teens in a Material Spin," *Chicago Tribune,* May 30, 2005, sec. 1, p. 9.

24. "Rising Individualism and Growing Wallets among Teens and Tweens."

25. "Wendy's to Target Younger Generation," Associated Press, February 6, 2006, http://news.yahoo.com.

26. Nadine Heintz, "Case Study: Addie Swartz," *Inc.,* March 2005, pp. 44–45.

27. Melinda Crowley, "Generation X Speaks Out on Civic Engagement and the Decennial Census," U.S. Census Bureau, http://www.census.gov, accessed May 23.2006; Kelly Barry, "Young Earners Face Intense Financial Challenge," *USA Today,* January 24, 2006, http://www.usatoday.com.

28. Anne Thompson, "Baby Boomers Create New Marketing Frontier," MSNBC, March 17, 2005, http://www.msnbc.com.

29. Candice Choi, "Gyms Going after Boomers, and Those Older," Associated Press, October 3, 2005, http://news.yahoo.com.

30. "Love Those Boomers," *BusinessWeek,* October 24, 2005, www.businessweek.com.

31. National Center for Health Statistics, National Vital Statistics Reports, http://www.cdc.gov, accessed March 2006.

32. "Small Ship Travel," Grand Circle Travel catalog, http://www.gct.com, accessed May 4, 2006.

33. U.S. Census Bureau, http://www.census.gov, accessed March 19, 2006.

34. "Inside America's Largest Minority," *Time,* August 22, 2005, p. 56.

35. Ibid.

36. "10 Largest Advertisers to the Hispanic Market," *Marketing News,* July 15, 2005, p. 23.

37. "TV One Adds Nearly Four Million New Subscribers in First Quarter of 2006," *Target Market News,* April 10, 2006, http://www.targetmarketnews.com.

38. Nakia Herring, "Pfizer Health Information Campaign Encourages Blacks to Be Powerful," *Target Market News,* April 10, 2006, http://www.targetmarketnews.com.

39. "Snapshot of the Asian-American Market," *Asian-American Market Profile,* Magazine Publishers of America, http://www.magazine.org/marketprofiles, accessed April 10, 2006.

40. Ibid.

41. "Top Advertisers to Asian Americans," *Asian-American Market Profile,* Magazine Publishers of America, http://www.magazine.org/marketprofiles, accessed April 10, 2006.

42. U.S. Census Bureau, *2006 Statistical Abstract of the United States,* http://www.census.gov; "Targeting Native Americans," AllBusiness, http://www.allbusiness.com, accessed April 10, 2006.

43. "Targeting Native Americans."

44. Susan Montoya Bryan, "Magazine for American Indians Debuts," Yahoo! News, September 30, 2005, http://news.yahoo.com.

45. *National Vital Statistics Reports,* U.S. Census Bureau, December 29, 2005, p. 2.

46. Barbara Butrica, Joshua H. Goldwyn, and Richard W. Johnson, "Understanding Expenditure Patterns in Retirement," Urban Institute, January 18, 2005, http://www.urban.org.

47. Michelle Conlin, "Unmarried America," *BusinessWeek,* accessed March 2006, pp. 106–166.

48. Heather Timmons, "Wal-Mart Unit Hears Gay Wedding Bells," *New York Times,* December 7, 2005, http://www.nytimes.com.

49. "Regional Spending Patterns in the U.S. and Metropolitan Areas in the Midwest," News, Bureau of Labor Statistics, March 9, 2006, http://www.bls.gov.

50. SRI Consulting Web site, http://www.sric-bi.com, accessed April 13, 2006.

51. RoperASW Web site, http://www.roperasw.com/products/lifematrix.html, accessed April 13, 2006.

52. "Sale of NOP World to GfK for 383 Million Pounds," GfK Web site, April 15, 2005, http://www.gfk.com.

53. "A Thousand Chinese Desires Bloom," *BusinessWeek,* August 22, 2005, http://www.businessweek.com.

54. Ibid.

55. Mindy Fetterman and Barbara Hansen, "Techies: They're Everywhere," *USA Today,* October 18, 2005, http://www.usatoday.com.

56. "The One-Stop Wal-Mart Shoppers vs. The Style-Oriented Target Shoppers," Scarborough Research, September 19, 2005, http://www.scarborough.com.

57. Peter Judge, "iPod Tipped to Boost Apple's Desktop Share," ZDNet UK, March 21, 2005, http://news.zdnet.co.uk.

58. Michel Jensen and Roland van Kralingen, "The End of Traditional Mass Brands," Brandchannel.com, http://www.brandchannel.com, accessed April 12, 2006.

59. Steve McKee, "Growing Big by Thinking Narrow," *BusinessWeek,* January 18, 2006, http://www.businessweek.com.

60. "The Sandwich Chronicle," New York First, http://www.newyorkfirst.com, accessed April 14, 2006; "Peanut Butter & Co.," *New York,* http://www.nymetro.com, accessed April 14, 2006; Peanut Butter & Co. Web site, http://www.ilovepeanutbutter.com, accessed January 24, 2006.

61. Melanie Warner and Stuart Elliott, "From Suds to Suave, Beers Aim Upmarket," *Chicago Tribune,* sec. 1, p. 19.

62. Theresa Howard, "Ads Take Bite Out of Political Sensitivity," *USA Today,* May 31, 2006, http://www.usatoday.com.

Chapter 10

1. Matthew Boyle, "Best Buy's Giant Gamble," CNN Money.com, March 29, 2006, http://money.cnn.com; Nisha Ramachandran, "Best Buy Shapes Up the Big Box," *U.S. News & World Report,* October 17, 2005, pp. 39–41; Don Peppers and Martha Rogers, "Best Buy Counts Customers," *CIO,* July 1, 2005, http://www.cio.com; "Best Buy's Customer-Centric Model Pays Off," *Forbes,* June 14, 2005, http://www.forbes.com.

2. Jessica Howell, "OnStar Vehicle Diagnostics," *Road and Travel Magazine,* http://www.roadandtravel.com, accessed April 3, 2006.

3. "Aftersales Challenge Promotion," *Relationship Marketing,* http://www.rmarketing.com, accessed February 8, 2006.

4. John Foley, "Selling Soap, Razors—and Collaboration," *InformationWeek,* November 14, 2005, http://www.informationweek.com.

5. Michelle Nichols, "Great Employees Make a Great Business," *BusinessWeek,* March 31, 2006, http://www.businessweek.com.

6. Colin Beasty, "Required Reading: Nordstrom's Class of Service," Destination CRM.com, May 2, 2005, http://www.crm.com.

7. Jui Chakravorty, "Automakers Extend Deals, Hope Discounts Abate," Reuters, March 3, 2006, http://news.yahoo.com.

8. Sanford Nowlin, "Telecoms Compete for Customers," *San Antonio Express-News,* September 28, 2005, http://www.express-news.com.

9. Carly Mayberry, "MySpace Intent on Staying User-Friendly," Reuters, January 18, 2006, http://news.yahoo.com.

10. "Barnes & Noble Member Program," http://www.barnesandnoble.com, accessed April 3, 2006.

11. Louise Lee, "Hanging Up on Dell?" *BusinessWeek,* September 30, 2005, http://www.businessweek.com.

12. Sarah Lacy, "Oracle: Nice Guys Finish. . . ," *BusinessWeek,* September 23, 2005, http://www.businessweek.com.

13. William M. Bulkeley, "Marketers Scan Blogs for Brand Insights," *Wall Street Journal,* June 25, 2005, http://online.wsj.com.

14. Jill Griffin, "Winning Back 'Lost' Customers," CustomerSat, January 2006, http://www.customersat.com.

15. Mariott Web site, http://marriott.com, accessed April 3, 2006.

16. Thomas Hoffman, "Harrah's Bets on Loyalty Program in Caesars Deal," *Computerworld,* June 27, 2005, http://www.computerworld.com.

17. "Bank of America Begins Sales of Affinity Credit Cards Online," Yahoo! Finance, January 25, 2006, http://biz.yahoo.com.

18. "Starbucks: A New Twist on Affinity Credit Cards," Cause Marketing Forum, http://www.causemarketingforum, accessed April 3, 2006.

19. WNET New York, http://support.thirteen.org, accessed April 12, 2006.

20. "America Online Collaboration with Abacus and DoubleClick Redefines E-Mail Database Marketing," PR Newswire, December 13, 2005, http://www.prnewswire.com.

21. Gregg Keizer, "Microsoft Data Collection Troubles Some Users," *InternetWeek,* January 20, 2006, http://internetweek.cmp.com.

22. Randall Frost, "RFID: Beyond the Barcode," Brandchannel.com, January 2, 2006, http://www.brandchannel.com.

23. Matt Stump, "Interactive TV Unchained," *Multichannel News,* October 31, 2005, http://www.multichannel.com.

24. "Donnelly Marketing and Yesmail Chosen by HCI Direct, Inc. to Build Customer Database," CRM Directory.com, February 23, 2006, http://www.crmdirectory.com.

25. "NCO Telecommunications Services," http://www.ncogroup.com, accessed April 3, 2006.

26. "Special Report: Viral Marketing 2006," *Marketing Sherpa,* March 28, 2006, http://www.marketingsherpa.com.

27. Therese Howard, "'Viral' Advertising Spreads through Marketing Plans," *USA Today,* June 23, 2005, http://www.usatoday.com.

28. "Buzz Marketing," CRM.com, http://searchcrm.techtarget.com, accessed April 3, 2006; "What's the Buzz about Buzz Marketing?" Marketing/Wharton, http://knowledge.wharton.upenn.edu, January 12, 2005.

29. Mike Hofman, "Lies, Damn Lies, and Word of Mouth," *Inc.,* April 2006, pp. 25–27.

30. Todd Spangler, "Late Bloomer," *Baseline,* November 8, 2005, http://www.baselinemag.com.

31. Ibid.

32. Michelle Nichols, "A Primer in CRM," *BusinessWeek,* March 17, 2006, http://www.businessweek.com.

33. "Why Is CRM Important," Oracle/Siebel, http://www.siebel.com, accessed April 3, 2006; "Five Benefits of Integrated CRM," Microsoft Dynamics, http://www.microsoft.com, updated November 18, 2005; Kathleen Cholewka, "CRM: The Failures Are Your Fault," *emanager,* January 2002, pp. 23–24.

34. Michael Meltzer, "Getting Started with CRM," *CRM Today,* http://www.crmtoday.com, accessed April 3, 2006.

35. Rashid Khan, "Stop Blaming CRM for Your Customer Service Failures," ContactCenterWorld.com, September 30, 2005, http://www.centerworld.com.

36. Danielle Dunne, "The CRM Backlash," interview with Jill Dyché, *CIO,* http://www.cio.com, accessed April 3, 2006.

37. "Study: Dell Customer Rating Plunges, Apple Leads Pack," IT World.com, August 16, 2005, http://www.itworld.com.

38. "Keeping Customers Happy Keeps Customers," *CRM Buyer,* April 1, 2006, http://www.crmbuyer.com.

39. "Christie Brinkley Returns as Face of CoverGirl," *Promo,* August 23, 2005, http://promomagazine.com.

40. Tina Benitez, "Wild Planet, McDonald's Team Up," Playthings.com, March 16, 2006, http://www.playthings.com.

41. Adam Goldman, "JetBlue Adds Spa Amenities on Redeyes," Associated Press, April 4, 2006, http://news.yahoo.com.

42. Rob Mitchell, "Is Fashion Design a Team Sport?" Brandchannel.com, May 9, 2005, http://www.brandchannel.com.

43. "Wal-Mart, Netflix Join Forces," CBS News, May 19, 2005, http://www.cbsnews.com.

44. "RFID Leaders Team to Provide Nationwide Compliance Service to DoD Suppliers," Business Wire, February 2, 2006, http://www.businesswire.com.

45. Eric Puller and Hugh Taylor, "SOA for B2B Commerce," JavaWorld, November 28, 2005, http://www.javaworld.com.

46. "Mosaic Leverages GXS Managed Services to Improve Vendor-Managed Inventory Solutions," Business Wire, September 21, 2005, http://www.businesswire.com.

47. "$2 Billion TruServ Reduces Inventory 41% and Improves Service Level to Above 97% with JDA Portfolio," JDA Software Group, http://www.jda.com, accessed April 4, 2006.

48. "The Perfect Doubles Match: Wimbledon Press Scores with Wireless System from IBM and Cisco," IBM Success Stories, http://www.03.ibm.com, accessed April 4, 2006.

49. Arthur Middleton Hughes, "The Loyalty Effect: A New Look at Lifetime Value," DB Marketing, April 4, 2006, http://www.dbmarketing.com.

Chapter 11

1. Peter Svensson, "Satellite Radio for the Rest of the World, If They'll Listen," *USA Today,* October 27, 2005, http://www.usatoday.com.

2. Ryan D'Agostino, "Sound Advice," *Money,* February 2006, pp. 139–142; "Is Howard Worth It?" *BusinessWeek,* January 23, 2006, p. 40; Lay Lyman, "Will Stern Push Satellite Radio to Mainstream?" *eCommerce Times,* January 4, 2006, http://www.ecommercetimes.com; Keith Regan, "Sprint Adding Sirius Satellite Radio to Mobile Service," *eCommerce Times,* June 14, 2005, http://www.ecommercetimes.com.

3. "MasterCard Launches Card Customization Services," Business Wire, November 14, 2005, http://www.businesswire.com.

4. "America's Most Admired Companies 2006," CNN Money.com, http://money.cnn.com, accessed April 24, 2006.

5. "Tomorrow's Jobs," *Occupational Outlook Handbook,* U.S. Department of Labor, Bureau of Labor Statistics, http://www.bls.gov, accessed April 12, 2006.

6. "U.S International Trade in Goods and Services Highlights," U.S. Census Bureau, http://www.census.gov, accessed April 12, 2006.

7. Michelle Conlin, "Call Centers in the Rec Room," *BusinessWeek,* January 23, 2006, http://www.businessweek.com.

8. Ibid.

9. Anita Manning, "Plugged into Prescription Drugs," *USA Today,* February 14, 2005, http://www.usatoday.com.

10. Gift Baskets.com Web site, http://www.giftbaskets.com, accessed May 18, 2006.

11. "FTC Releases Grocery Industry Slotting Allowance Report," http://www.ftc.gov, accessed April 24, 2006.

12. Kathleen Kiley, "Private-Label Brands Enter the High-End Food Market," *KPMG Consumer Markets Insider,* September 16, 2005, http://www.kpmginsider.com.

13. Concept introduced by Christopher H. Lovelock, "Classifying Services to Gain Strategic Marketing Insights," *Journal of Marketing,* Summer 1983, p. 10.

14. Matt Vella, "Europe's Supercars," *BusinessWeek,* April 24, 2006, http://www.businessweek.com.

15. Michael D. Hutt and Thomas W. Speh, *Business Marketing Management,* 8th ed. (Mason, OH: South-Western, 2004).

16. "Qantas Orders 65 New Boeing 787 Aircraft," MSNBC, December 14, 2005, http://www.msnbc.msn.com.

17. Bose Web site, http://www.bose.com, accessed April 28, 2006.

18. Cargill Web site, http://www.cargillfoods.com, accessed April 28, 2006.

19. Office Max Web site, http://www.officemax.com, accessed April 28, 2006.

20. Web Ex Web site, http://www.webex.com, accessed April 28, 2006.

21. Regus Group Web site, http://www.regus.com, accessed April 28, 2006.

22. International Organization for Standardization Web site, http://www.iso.org, accessed April 28, 2006.

23. Rosemary A. Baczewski, "Four Methods for Improving Performance: A Comparison," Healthcare Financial Management Association, July 2005, http://www.findarticles.com.

24. "Improving the Quality Function: Driving Organizational Impact & Efficiency," *Benchmarking Reports,* http://www3.best-in-class.com, accessed May 26, 2006.

25. "Toyota Unveils National Customer Center, New Customer Experience," Thomas.net, August 2, 2005, www.thomas.net.

26. "Beginner Lessons Help Keep Ski Industry Growing," CNN.com, December 20, 2005, http://www.cnn.com.

27. Scott Goldstein, "And the Customer Service Award Does NOT Go to . . ." *Chicago Tribune,* August 17, 2005, sec. 1, pp. 1, 19.

28. Dorothy J. Gaiter and John Brecher, "Attention, Wine Shoppers," *SmartMoney,* February 2006, pp. 110–111.

29. "Ralph Lauren Fragrances," Sephora, http://www.sephora.com, accessed April 2006; Rodney Reid, "The New Look of Polo Ralph Lauren," *Viewpoints,* http://www.hs.ttu.edu/viewpoints, accessed April 12, 2006.

30. L. L. Bean Web site, http://www.llbean.com, accessed May 1, 2006.

31. Ibid.

32. "New Meter Can Help People with Diabetes," Johnson & Johnson, April 26, 2006, http://www.jnj.com.

33. "Schick Introduces Battery-Powered Quattro Razor," Reuters, August 31, 2005, http://news.yahoo.com.

34. "Boeing to Buy Parts Supplier Aviall for $1.7 billion," Reuters, May 1, 2006, http://news.yahoo.com.

35. Bary Alyssa Johnson, "Snowboarders Stay Connected with Wireless Winter Wear," *PC Magazine,* October 28, 2005, http://www.pcmag.com.

36. "Understand CD/DVD Burners," CNet Burner Buying Guide, http://reviews.cnet.com, accessed May 1, 2006.

37. "On the Go: Whether Fresh, Frozen, or Hand-Held, New Prepared Foods Appeal to Busy Consumers," *Stagnito's New Products Magazine,* September 2005, http://www.newproducts.com.

38. "Big-Screen TVs and What to Watch on Them," *PC World,* April 17, 2006, http://www.pcworld.com.

39. Lori Dahm, "When Old Is New Again," *New Products Magazine,* March 2006, http://www.newproductsmagazine.com.

40. Larry Cantwell, "Tobacco Collectibles are Smokin' at H.S.B.," *St. Louis Post-Dispatch,* September 10, 2005, http://www.stltoday.com.

41. Zippo Web site, http://www.zippo.com, accessed May 23, 2006; Ellen Neuborne, "Zippo—Inc.com Case Study," *Inc.,* http://www.pf.inc.com/magazine, accessed February 20, 2006.
42. Daniel Yee, "More People Choosing Dance for Exercise," Associated Press, January 26, 2006, http://news.yahoo.com.
43. WD-40 Web site, http://www.wd40.com, accessed May 23, 2006.
44. 3M Web site, http://www.3m.com, accessed May 23, 2006.
45. Bruce Horovitz, "In the Newest Snack Packs, Less Is More," *USA Today,* April 23, 2006, http://www.usatoday.com.

Chapter 12

1. "Procter & Gamble—Swiffer," Design Continuum, http://www.dcontinuum.com, accessed April 19, 2006; "Swiffer," http://www.pg.com, accessed April 18, 2006; Sarah Lacy, "How P&G Conquered Carpet," *BusinessWeek,* September 23, 2005, http://www.businessweek.com.
2. J. B. Davis, "The Six-Legged Horse Race: Why Store Branding Matters in the Battle between Walgreens and CVS," Brandchannel, http://www.brandchannel.com, accessed April 18, 2006.
3. Laurie Sullivan, "Retailers Ply Their Own Brands," *InformationWeek,* April 18, 2006, http://www.informationweek.com.
4. Ibid.
5. Pallavi Gogoi, "How Target Found Its Grooviness," *BusinessWeek,* October 3, 2005, http://www.businessweek.com.
6. "The 100 Top Brands," *BusinessWeek,* August 1, 2005, p. 90.
7. Ibid.
8. Al Ehrbar, "Breakaway Brands," *Fortune,* October 31, 2005, pp. 153-170; "Young & Rubicam Inc. Launches the Media Edge," Young & Rubicam press release, http://www.youngandrubicam.com/news, accessed May 11, 2006.
9. Alex Taylor III, "Buffing Up a Faded Star," *Fortune,* October 31, 2005, p. 166.
10. "What Is Category Management?" Association for Category Development Professionals, http://www.cpgcatnet.org, accessed February 22, 2006.
11. Ibid.
12. Al Heller, "Consumer-Centric Category Management: A Fresh Spin on Maximizing Performance," *Consumer Insight,* Summer 2005, pp. 6–10.
13. "Category Management," Hershey's Vending Info Center, http://www.hersheys.com, accessed February 22, 2006.
14. "Breakfast of Champions," *Frozen Food Age,* October 2005, http://www.frozenfoodage.com.
15. Elizabeth Levermore, "Light Branding Replaces Labels," *Southland Times* (New Zealand), February 7, 2006, accessed at http://0-web.lexis-nexis.com; Julia Moskin, "Tattooed Fruit Is on Way," *The New York Times,* July 10, 2005, http://www.nytimes.com; Rachel Yang, "Produce Labels: A Sticky Subject," American Chemical Society, July 5, 2005, http://www.chemistry.org.
16. Ron Lemasters, Jr., "Butt Paste Produces Sponsor Dollars, Laughs," NASCAR, April 6, 2005, http://www.nascar.com; "Itch Doctor," *People,* October 20, 2003, p. 130.
17. "Beatles Lose Apple Court Battle," BBC News, May 8, 2006, http://news.bbc.co.uk; "Apple vs. Apple Gets Down to the Core," CBS News, March 28, 2006, http://www.cbsnews.com.
18. Jeff Neff, "Marketers Put Foot Down on Private-Label Issue," *Advertising Age,* April 4, 2005, p. 14; Kevin Rayburn, "Copy Those Festive Umbrellas at Your Peril," *Impact,* Spring 2005, accessed at http://php.louisville.edu.
19. Dee-Ann Durbin, "GM Reaches Settlement with China's Chery," ABC News, November 18, 2005, http://abcnews.go.com.
20. "French Winemakers Mull Screw Cap vs. Cork," Agence France-Presse, March 1, 2006, http://news.yahoo.com.
21. "Plastics: Made Possibly by Chemistry," American Chemistry Council, http://www.americanchemistry.com, accessed February 22, 2006.
22. "New Prescription: Target ClearRx Bottle," *BusinessWeek,* December 19, 2005, p. 91; Joshua Freed, "Target Redesigns the Pill Bottle," *Boston Globe,* April 28, 2005, http://www.boston.com.
23. David Goldenberg, "Fresh Breath, Fresher Packaging," CNN Money.com, December 1, 2005, http://money.cnn.com.
24. "Food Allergies: New Food-Labeling Requirements," Mayo Clinic, http://www.mayoclinic.com, accessed January 20, 2006; "FDA to Require Food Manufacturers to List Food Allergens," U.S. Food and Drug Administration news release, December 20, 2005, http://www.fda.gov.
25. Stacy Lawrence, "Compliance Lagging for FDA's Bar-Code Mandate," *Baseline,* March 29, 2006, http://www.baselinemag.com.
26. Angela Moore, "Mattel Launches Barbie Clothes for Women," Reuters, October 14, 2005, http://news.yahoo.com.
27. Kenneth Hein, "Living with Your 'Ex': A Brand New World," *Brandweek,* December 5, 2005, pp. 4ff.
28. Adam Bass, "The Growth in Corporate Brand Licensing," BrandChannel.com, http://www.brandchannel.com, accessed April 18, 2006.
29. Constantine von Hoffman, "Overextended," *CMO,* February 2005, http://www.cmo-magazine.com.
30. Stephanie Clifford, "Running through the Legs of Goliath," *Inc.,* February 2006, pp. 102–109.
31. Ed Gold, "With Roughly 9,000 Stores, Starbucks Serves It Up by Design," *St. Charles County Business Record,* May 13, 2005, p. 1.
32. "The New Force at LucasFilm," *BusinessWeek,* March 27, 2006, http://www.businessweek.com.
33. Julia Boorstin, "The Scent of Celebrity," CNN Money.com, November 14, 2005, http://money.cnn.com.
34. "Cisco to Pack Retail Shelves," *Red Herring,* January 16, 2006, http://www.redherring.com.
35. Betsy Spethmann, "Schick Revived Quattro with Sampling," *Promo,* December 26, 2005, http://www.promomagazine.com.
36. Lee Walczak and David Welch, "Dream Machines," *BusinessWeek,* January 6, 2006, http://www.businessweek.com.
37. Stephanie Clifford, "Running through the Legs of Goliath."
38. Ben Elgin, "Managing Google's Idea Factory," *BusinessWeek,* September 26, 2005, http://www.businessweek.com.
39. David Kirkpatrick, "Microsoft's New Brain," CNN Money.com, April 18, 2006, http://money.cnn.com.
40. "New Prescription: Target ClearRx Bottle."
41. Dave Carpenter, "Wrigley Looks to Science for Gum Benefits," Associated Press, March 29, 2006, http://news.yahoo.com.
42. Clifford, "Running through the Legs of Goliath."
43. Kenneth Ross, "Product Liability Goes Global," *Risk Management,* February 2006, pp. 10ff.
44. Legal Issues: Agreement Reached in Litigation Regarding Alleged Loss of Smell after Using Cold Remedy," *Obesity, Fitness & Wellness Week,* February 18, 2006, p. 1047.
45. "U.S. CPSC Logs Record Year for Recalls, Civil Penalties, and Reports of Dangerous Products," M2 Presswire, October 28, 2005, http://www.m2.com.
46. Julie Steenhuysen, "Bausch Extends Lens Solution Recall Worldwide," Reuters, May 15, 2006, http://news.yahoo.com.

Chapter 13

1. Zappos Web site, http://www.zappos.com, accessed May 18, 2006; Karla Ward, "High on Heels," Kentucky.com, April 3, 2006, http://www.kentucky.com; Kimberly Weisul, "A Shine on Their Shoes," *BusinessWeek,* December 5, 2005, pp. 84–85; Brian Moore, "Success Fits Shoe Shipper," *(Louisville, KY) Courier-Journal,* February 16, 2005, http://www.courier-journal.com.
2. Kimberly Weisul, "A Shine on Their Shoes"; Brian Moore, "Success Fits Shoe Shipper."
3. Monica Soto Ouchi, "State to Appeal Costco Wine Ruling," *Seattle Times,* May 3, 2006, http://seattletimes.nwsource.com.
4. Louise Lee, "It's Dell vs. the Dell Way," *BusinessWeek,* March 6, 2006, pp. 61–62.
5. UPS Web site, http://www.ups.com, accessed June 16, 2006; Tom Steinert-Threlkeld, "UPS Delivers Real Presence for Virtual Bank," *Baseline,* September 7, 2005, http://www.baselinemag.com.
6. Jim Callandrillo, "Sales Management: Sales Growth, for What?" *Pharmaceutical Executive,* http://www.pharmexec.com, accessed May 10, 2006.
7. Beijo Bags Web site, http://www.beijobags.com, accessed June 16, 2006; Kimberly L. McCall, "Bags to Riches," *Entrepreneur,* May 2005, http://www.entrepreneur.com.
8. "Status Faux," *Indianapolis Star,* January 5, 2006, http://www.indystar.com; Christine Van Dusen, "Many Who Crave Luxury Are Content to Rent," *Atlanta Journal-Constitution,* March 2, 2005, http://www.ajc.com.
9. May Wong, "TiVo Inks Deal to Offer Web-Based Videos," Associated Press, May 10, 2006, http://news.yahoo.com.
10. "Battery Recycling Tips," *Road & Travel Magazine,* http://www.roadandtravel.com, accessed May 10, 2006.
11. Jim Milliott, "Bucking the Odds," *Publishers Weekly,* March 7, 2005, http://www.publishersweekly.com.
12. Ginny Parker, "Vending the Rules," *Time,* May 10, 2006, http://www.time.com.
13. "Key Move: Artful Outsourcing," *Forbes,* March 8, 2006, http://www.forbes.com.
14. Tim Smart, "Allstate Weathers the Storm," *U.S. News & World Report,* January 23, 2006, pp. EE8–EE10.
15. Gordon Schnell, "Exclusive Dealing; Antitrust Law," *National Law Journal,* September 5, 2005, http://www.nlj.com.
16. ProSource Web site, www.pswholesale.com, accessed June 17, 2006; "ProSource Offers Limited Number of Exclusive Franchise Territories," Bizjournals, July 7, 2005, http://http://bizjournals.bison.com.
17. Heba M. Hamouda, "Agreement with Coca-Cola Ends the European Union's Five Year Inquiry into a Potential Abuse of a Dominant Position," Loyola University Chicago School of Law, http://www.luc.edu, accessed May 15, 2006.
18. Allen F. Wysocki, "A Frictionless Marketplace Operating in a World of Extremes," *Choices,* 4th Quarter 2005, pp. 263–291.

19. Wal-Mart Web site, http://www.walmart.com, accessed June 17, 2006; Joseph Agnese, "Supermarkets Face Supersize Rivals," *BusinessWeek,* July 14, 2005, www.businessweek.com.

20. Phil Rosenthal, "Increasingly, the TV Set Is Becoming Optional," *Chicago Tribune,* January 7, 2006, pp. 1, 12.

21. Jennifer Barrett, "Can a '50s Icon Do It Again?" *Newsweek,* March 20, 2006, p. E20.

22. "EU Imposes 44.6pct Anti-Dumping Duty on Imports of China Color TVs," *Forbes,* March 30, 2006, www.forbes.com.

23. Eric Duff, "Ruling Deals Setback for John Deere's Fight against Grey Market Goods," *The Business Review,* April 3, 2006, http://albany.bizjournals.com.

24. Stuart Wilson, "Samsung Chills Out with Home Appliance Partners," ITP Technology, May 9, 2006, www.itp.net.

25. "How to See Beyond the Burgers in Franchising," *The Globe and Mail,* http://www.theglobeandmail.com, accessed May 15, 2006.

26. Pier 1 Imports Web site, http://www.pier1.com, accessed May 15, 2006.

27. Tyson Foods Web site, http://www.tyson.com, accessed June 19, 2006; Shea Van Hoy, "Tyson Stresses Supply Chain," *The Morning News,* November 3, 2005, pp. D1, D2.

28. Shea Van Hoy, "Tyson Stresses Supply Chain."

29. Michael Fitzgerald, "True Believers," *CIO Insight,* December 5, 2005, http://www.cioinsight.com.

30. Mark Long, "RFID Scare Tactics and the Push to Adopt," News Factor Network, January 10, 2006, http://www.newsfactor.com.

31. "MySAP ERP Human Capital Management at Dow Corning," SAP, http://www.sap.com, accessed May 15, 2006.

32. Lara Jakes Jordan, "House Approves Cargo Screening at Ports," Associated Press, May 4, 2006, http://news.yahoo.com.

33. Thomas A. Foster and Richard Armstrong, "Top 25 Third-Party Logistics Providers: Bigger and Broader," Global Logistics and Supply Chain Strategies, May 2005, www.glscs.com.

34. "Freight Transportation in a Changing Business Environment," U.S. Department of Transportation, Federal Highway Administration, January 7, 2005, http://ops.fhwa.dot.gov, accessed June 19, 2006.

35. 1-800-FLOWERS Web site, http://www.1800flowers.com, accessed June 14, 2006.

36. "Industry Overview," IdleAire, http://www.idleaire.com, accessed May 15, 2006.

37. Greg Burns, "Railroads on Track to Revival," *Chicago Tribune,* March 27, 2006, sec. 1, pp. 1, 10.

38. Geoffrey Colvin, "The FedEx Edge," CNN Money.com, March 20, 2006, http://money.cnn.com.

39. Greg Burns, "Railroads on Track to Revival."

40. "Frequently Asked Questions," TWNA, http://www.twna.org, accessed May 15, 2006.

41. T. L. Bainey Web site, http://www.tlbainey.com, accessed June 19, 2006; "Tip of the Iceberg," SelecTrucks, Fall 2005, http://www.selectrucks.com.

42. "Global Container Trade and Industry Information and Statistics," IBM, September 2005, http://www.ibm.com.

43. *Survey of Current Business,* 2006 Edition, U.S. Census Bureau, http://www.census.gov.

44. "UPS in Deal to Carry Mail for U.S. Postal Service," Reuters, June 28, 2006, http://news.yahoo.com; "Expedited Cargo Market Set to Grow; Ground Trumps Air," *Multichannel Merchant,* December 7, 2005, http://www.multichannelmerchant.com; "Logistics Trends: FedEx to Handle More Ground Shipments than Air in '05," *Supply & Demand Chain Executive,* May 23, 2005, http://www.sdcexec.com.

45. "Giant Wal-Mart Distribution Center Has an Equally Large Impact," *Houston Business Journal,* April 28, 2006, http://houston.bizjournals.com.

46. "Wal-Mart Reshapes the Retail World," *Forbes,* January 24, 2006, http://moneycentral.msn.com.

47. Kimberly-Clark Web site, www.kimberly-clark.com, accessed June 20, 2006; "Pampers out, Huggies in at Some Costcos," *Promo,* June 16, 2005, http://promomagazine.com.

48. PaR Systems Web site, http://www.par.com, accessed May 17, 2006.

49. Gary Gentile, "Fox to Offer Movies Online via Movielink," Associated Press, November 21, 2005, http://news.yahoo.com.

50. Aida Edemariam, "Wings of Desire," *The Guardian,* February 23, 2006, http://www.guardian.co.uk.

51. McDonald's Web site, www.mcdonalds.com, accessed June 20, 2006; Nichola Groom, "McDonald's Touts Quality in Ad Campaign," Reuters, October 24, 2005, http://news.yahoo.com.

Chapter 14

1. "Macy's: A History," Federated Department Stores Web site, http://www.fds.com, accessed May 16, 2006; Dody Tsiantar, "Department-Store Superstar," *Time Inside Business,* March 2006, pp. A1–A6; "Here's Mr. Macy," interview, *Fortune,* November 28, 2005, pp. 138–142; Lorrie Grant, "Some Famous Store Names to Disappear," *USA Today,* July 29, 2005, p. 6B.

2. Lea Davis, "The QSR Interview: Steve Ells," *QSR Magazine,* February 2005, http://www.qsrmagazine.com.

3. Target Web site, http://www.target.com, accessed May 12, 2006.

4. Brook Stockberger, "More Bang for the Buck," *Knight Ridder Tribune Business News,* February 13, 2006, p. 1.

5. Lowe's Web site, http://www.lowes.com, accessed May 12, 2006; Kara Rhodes, "See Jane Hammer," *Knight Ridder Tribune Business News,* January 26, 2006, p. 1.

6. Dean Foust, "A Sister Act That's Wowing Them," *BusinessWeek,* March 13, 2006, pp. 84–86.

7. K. Sudhir and Vithala R. Rao, "Are Slotting Allowances Efficiency-Enhancing or Anti-Competitive?" Yale School of Management, http://mba.yale.edu, accessed May 3, 2006.

8. Scott Kirsner, "Virtual Assistance," *Fast Company,* April 2006, p. 34.

9. Alex Halperin, "Biometrics: Payments at Your Fingertips," *BusinessWeek,* March 28, 2006, http://www.businessweek.com.

10. Bloomingdale's Web site, http://www.bloomingdales.com, accessed May 12, 2006.

11. Lorrie Grant, "Sears Shifts Strategy for Off-Mall Stores," *USA Today,* February 24, 2006, http://www.usatoday.com.

12. Debra Hazel, "Wide-Open Spaces," *Chain Store Age,* November 2005, p. 120; Andrew Blum, "The Mall Goes Undercover," *Slate,* April 6, 2005, http://www.slate.com.

13. Parija Bhatnagar, "Not a Mall, It's a Lifestyle Center," CNN Money.com, January 12, 2005, http://money.cnn.com.

14. Sally Horchow, "Las Vegas Meets Shoppertainment," *International Herald Tribune,* January 15, 2006, http://www.iht.com.

15. Mindy Fetterman, "J.C. Penney Sells with an Attitude," *USA Today,* March 3, 2006, pp. 1B, 3B.

16. Jessie Seyfer, "Personal Shopper," *San Jose Mercury News,* December 19, 2005, http://www.mercurynews.com.

17. Diane Brady, "Coach's Split Personality," *BusinessWeek,* November 7, 2005, pp. 60–62.

18. Rana Foroohar, "A New Fashion Frontier," *Newsweek,* March 20, 2006, accessed at MSNBC, http://www.msnbc.msn.com.

19. Claire Schooley, "Retailers Adopt eLearning to Groom Smarter Store Associates," Forrester Research, http://www.forrester.com, accessed May 4, 2006; "Exclusive Interview with Mr. Frank Russell, CEO and President, Geolearning, Inc.," Distance-Educator.com, February 28, 2005, http://www.distance-educator.com.

20. Michael Tunison, "A Side of Décor," *Washington Post,* December 8, 2005, http://www.washingtonpost.com.

21. Tom Vanderbilt, "Flight 001: Ready for Takeoff," *BusinessWeek,* September 30, 2005, http://www.businessweek.com.

22. Andrew Blum, "Forth & Towne: The Store's the Thing," *BusinessWeek,* September 20, 2005, http://www.businessweek.com.

23. "Retail Industry Profile," About.com, http://retailindustry.about.com, accessed May 4, 2006.

24. Georgia Flight, "Whole Fuels," *Business 2.0,* December 2005, p. 78.

25. Gloria Jean's Web site, http://www.gloriajeans.com, accessed May 12, 2006.

26. Nadia Alvarado, "Retail Revolution," American Independent Business Alliance, August 14, 2005, http://www.amiba.net.

27. Matthew Boyle, "Drug Wars," *Fortune,* June 13, 2005, pp. 79–84.

28. Robert Berner, "At Sears, A Great Communicator," *BusinessWeek,* October 31, 2005, pp. 50–52.

29. "Corporate Information," http://www.biggs.com, accessed May 12, 2006; "Bigg's Hypermarket," http://www.spectralink.com, accessed May 4, 2006.

30. Georgia Flight, "A Speedier Superstore," *Business 2.0,* December 2005, p. 38.

31. Melanie Warner, "Wal-Mart Eyes Organic Foods," *New York Times,* May 12, 2006, http://www.nytimes.com; David Keonig, "Wal-Mart Wants to Be Where You Go for $500 Wine," *USA Today,* March 23, 2006, p. 28; Barbara Thau, "Wal-Mart's Upscale Push Hits Electronics," *HFN,* November 7, 2005, http://www.hfnmag.com.

32. "Products & Services," http://www.7-eleven.com, accessed May 12, 2006; "7-Eleven, Inc. Signs Deal with NCR to Expand Financial Services Initiative and 24-Hour Check-Cashing Program," NCR News Release, November 17, 2005, http://www.ncr.com.

33. "About Ingram Micro," http://www.ingrammicro.com, accessed May 4, 2006; "Fortune 500," CNN Money.com, April 17, 2006, http://money.cnn.com.

34. "United Stationers Inc.," Yahoo! Finance Profile, http://finance.yahoo.com, accessed May 4, 2006; Jack Hough, "Office-Supplies Politics," *SmartMoney,* April 10, 2006, http://yahoo.smartmoney.com.

35. Matt Hamblen, "Bigger Interop in Store This Week," *Computerworld,* May 1, 2006, http://www.computerworld.com.

36. "Merchandise Mart," Citysearch, http://chicago.citysearch.com, accessed May 4, 2006.

37. Unitime Imports Web site, http://www.unitimeimports.com, accessed May 5, 2006; Kim Crompton, "Counting on 'Counter Impulse,'" *Journal of Business,* http://www.spokanejournal.com, accessed May 5, 2006.

38. "S. Abraham & Sons, Inc.," Yahoo! Finance Company Profile, http://biz.yahoo.com, accessed May 5, 2006.

39. Jim Olsztynski, "2005 Wholesaler of the Year: Castle Supply," Eclipse, November 30, 2005, http://www.eclipse.intuit.com.

40. "Directory of Mail Order Catalogs, 2006 Edition," National Mail Order Association, http://www.nmoa.org, accessed May 5, 2006; "Directory of Business to Business Cata-

logs, 2006 Edition," *National Mail Order Association,* http://www.nmoa.org accessed May 5, 2006.

41. Karen E. Klein, "Making It with Mail-Order," *BusinessWeek,* January 24, 2006, http://www.businessweek.com.

42. Office Max Web site, http://www.officemax.com, accessed May 5, 2006.

43. "Sales Size of Establishments for the United States—Vending Machine Operators," *Retail Trade—Subject Series,* U.S. Census Bureau Economic Census, http://www.census.gov, accessed May 4, 2006.

44. Vicki Koenig, "Menu for Change: A Year's Progress," Stonyfield Farm, http://www.stonyfield.com, accessed May 5, 2006.

45. Marian Burros and Melanie Warner, "Bottlers Agree to a School Ban on Sweet Drinks," *New York Times,* May 4, 2006, http://www.nytimes.com.

46. Victor Mihailescu, "iPod Vending Stations Are a Great Success," Softpedia, April 10, 2006, http://news.softpedia.com.

Chapter 15

1. Cliff Peale, P&G Angles for Fusion Razor," *The (Cincinnati, OH) Enquirer,* February 8, 2006, http://news.enquirer.com; Jenn Abelson, "For Fusion, Gillette Plans a Super Bowl Blitz," *Boston Globe,* January 27, 2006, http://www.boston.com; Claudia Deutsch, "Can a Razor Ever Have Enough Blades?" *New York Times,* January 27, 2006, http://www.nytimes.com; William C. Symonds, "Gillette's Five-Blade Wonder," *Business-Week,* September 15, 2005, http://www.businessweek.com.

2. Julie Bosman, "If It's after Midnight, Then It's Time to Market to Young Men," *New York Times,* November 28, 2005, http://www.nytimes.com.

3. Ed Papazian, "Ed's Forum: Waiting for TV to Lose Favor Is a Poor Option for Rival Media," *Media Industry Newsletter,* January 30, 2006, vol. 59, no. 5, p. 1.

4. Michael Fielding, "Global Insights," *Marketing News,* May 15, 2006, pp. 41–42.

5. "Girls on the Move Running Club," Lady Foot Locker, http://www.ladyfootlocker.com, accessed June 5, 2006.

6. Fiona Torrance, "comScore: World Cup Web Analysis," iMedia Connection, May 31, 2006, http://www.imediaconnection.com.

7. Paul Majendie, "Fanboys and Overdogs Muscling into English Language," Reuters, October 24, 2005, http://news.yahoo.com.

8. "U.S. Agricultural Campaigns Are at Risk," National Cattlemen's Beef Association, http://www.beefusa.org, accessed June 7, 2006.

9. Laura Petrecca, "Movie Promotions Get Smaller to Reach Bigger Audience," *USA Today,* May 15, 2006, http://www.usatoday.com.

10. Reebok Web site, http://www.reebok.com, accessed June 6, 2006; Michael McCarthy, "New Theme for Reebok," *USA Today,* February 10, 2005, http://www.usatoday.com.

11. Steve McKee, "Five Words to Never Use in an Ad," *BusinessWeek,* June 7, 2006, http://www.businessweek.com.

12. Pallavi Gogol, "Dunkin' Donuts' Cheap Chic," *BusinessWeek,* April 11, 2006, http://www.businessweek.com; "Life Might Take Visa but 'American Runs on Dunkin'," *Adrants,* April 10, 2006, http://www.adrants.com.

13. "Occupational Groups: Sales and Related," *Occupational Outlook Quarterly,* Spring 2006, http://www.bls.gov.

14. Kate Maddox, "Ad Spending to Grow in 2006," *B to B,* February 13, 2006, http://www.mediabusinessonline.com.

15. David S. Joachim, "For CBS's Fall Lineup, Check Inside Your Refrigerator," *New York Times,* July 17, 2006, http://www.nytimes.com; "Catch 'Em Where You Can," *Business-Week,* January 23, 2006, p. 16.

16. Gary Gentile, "Products Placed Liberally in Video Games," Associated Press, May 22, 2005, http://news.yahoo.com.

17. Gail Schiller, "Brave New World for Summer Tie-Ins," Reuters, May 30, 2006, http://news.yahoo.com.

18. "FTC Chief Cool about Price Gouging Law," *USA Today,* May 23, 2006, http://www.usatoday.com.

19. "The Harris Poll," Harris Interactive, April 25, 2006, http://www.harrisinteractive.com.

20. Carol J. Loomis, "Warren Buffett Gives It Away," *Fortune,* July 10, 2006, pp. 57-69.

21. Sarah Schweitzer, "Building a Buzz on Campus," *Boston Globe,* October 24, 2005, http://www.boston.com.

22. Theresa Howard, "Viral Advertising Spreads through Marketing Plans," *USA Today,* June 23, 2005, http://www.usatoday.com.

23. "Guerilla Marketing Sparks Controversy," UPI, December 9, 2005, http://0-web.lexis-nexis.com.library.uark.edu.

24. "Sponsorship," Cascade Bicycle Club, http://www.cascade.org, accessed May 6, 2006.

25. "Dale Jr. to Race Vintage Earnhardt Paint Scheme on Father's Day," Anheuser-Busch, May 31, 2006, http://www.anheuser-busch.com.

26. Avon Foundation, http://www.avonfoundation.org, accessed June 9, 2006.

27. Laura Clark Geist, "Automakers Open Wallets to Event Sponsorship," *Automotive News,* February 13, 2006, http://www.autonews.com.

28. Doreen Carvajal, "Can't Tell the Sponsors without a Scorecard," *International Herald Tribune,* May 31, 2006, http://www.iht.com.

29. "DMA CEO Unveils New Association Brand Identity and Reveals Latest Industry Market Numbers at DMA05," Direct Marketing Association, October 17, 2005, http://www.the-dma.org. accessed June 6, 2006.

30. Caroline E. Mayer, "Marketers Dress Up Pitches to Look Official," *Washington Post,* November 1, 2005, http://www.washingtonpost.com.

31. "Catalog Sales Growth Continues to Outpace Overall Retail Growth," About.com, http://www.about.com, accessed June 9, 2006.

32. Ken Magill, "From Print to Screen: Virtual Catalogs," *Multichannel Merchant,* June 1, 2006, http://www.multichannelmerchant.com.

33. Andrew Bridges, "FTC Tells DirectV to Pay Up," *Chicago Tribune,* December 14, 2005, sec. 1, p. 21.

34. "Telemarketers Settle FTC Charges of Costly 'Free' Samples, Do Not Call Violations, and Worthless Weight-Loss Patches," Federal Trade Commission, January 17, 2006, http://www.ftc.gov; Christopher Conkey, "Do-Not-Call Lists under Fire," *Wall Street Journal,* September 28, 2005, http://online.wsj.com.

35. "Infiniti's 30-Minute Spot: Don't Call it an Infomercial," Adweek.com, January 4, 2006, http://www.adweek.com.

36. "Online Advertising on the Rise," eMarketer, January 24, 2006, http://www.imediaconnection.com.

37. Kevin J. Delaney, "Once-Wary Industry Giants Embrace Internet Advertising," *Wall Street Journal,* April 17, 2006, http://online.wsj.com.

38. Julie Bosman, "Papers' Online Ads Outpace Print," *International Herald Tribune,* June 6, 2006, http://www.iht.com.

39. "Creative Interactive Merchandising," *Creative Online Weekly,* April/May 2006, http://www.creativemag.com.

40. "Getting Help with Your Weight Loss," MediaLink, January 2, 2006, http://biz.yahoo.com; "Subway's Jared to Phone Dieters," CBS News, December 27, 2005, http://www.cbsnews.com.

41. Vivian Manning-Schaffel, "Brands Get Celebrity Exposure," *Brandchannel.com,* February 13, 2006, http://www.brandchannel.com.

42. Mark Hyman, "Super Guests for the Super Bowl," *BusinessWeek,* January 30, 2006, p. 16.

43. Kathleen M. Joyce, "Higher Gear," *Promo,* April 1, 2006, http://promomagazine.com.

44. "Trade Funds Investment," IBM, http://www-1.ibm.com, accessed June 12, 2006; "Trade Promotion Management," Sun Microsystems, December 2005, http://www.sun.com.

45. "Wireless AMBER Alerts," AdCouncil, http://www.adcouncil.org, accessed June 12, 2006.

46. Ira Teinowitz, "GAO Report: White House Spent $1.62 Billion for Advertising," *Advertising Age,* February 13, 2006, http://adage.com.

47. Tara Burghart, "King Tut Returns to Chicago," Associated Press, May 30, 2006, http://news.yahoo.com; Maria Puente, "King Tut Reigns Again," *USA Today,* June 8, 2005, http://www.usatoday.com.

Chapter 16

1. Wheaties Web site, http://www.wheaties.com/ourhistory.asp, accessed June 16, 2006; "Peyton Manning 2005 Biography," http://www.peytonmanning.com, accessed June 16, 2006; Phillip B. Wilson, "Marketers Won't Sack Manning," *Indianapolis Star,* January 28, 2006, http://www.indystar.com; Les Winkeler, "Manning's MasterCard Commercial Takes Me Back," *The Southern Illinoisan,* December 28, 2005, http://www.southernillinoisan.com; Michael Klitzing, "Manning, by the Numbers," *North County (CA) Times,* December 15, 2005, http://www.nctimes.com.

2. Clyde Haberman, "NYC: Broadway, Or Was It Madison Ave.?" *New York Times,* May 26, 2006, http://www.nytimes.com.

3. Aaron O. Patrick, "Commercials by Cellphone," *Wall Street Journal,* August 22, 2005, http://online.wsj.com.

4. "AdWeek Ranks Top Celebrity Advertising Earners," *AdRants,* April 2006, http://www.adrants.com.

5. "Top 25 Global Marketers," *FactPack2006* (special supplement to *Advertising Age*), February 27, 2006, p. 15.

6. "Top 25 U.S. Megabrands," *FactPack2006,* February 28, 2006, p. 9.

7. Theresa Howard, "Food, Beverage Marketers Seek Healthier Images," *USA Today,* April 20, 2006, http://www.usatoday.com.

8. Robert Berner, "Detergent Can Be So Much More," *BusinessWeek,* May 1, 2006, p. 66.

9. Eric Engleman, "Ichiro Inc.: The M's True Impact Player," *Puget Sound Business Journal,* February 28, 2005, http://seattle.bizjournals.com.

10. Barbara Wall, "Celebrity Cachet Has Firms Banking on What's in a Name," *International Herald Tribune,* May 12, 2006, http://www.iht.com; Eric Engleman, "Ichiro Inc."

11. "Oprah Tops Powerful Celebs List," CBS News, June 17, 2005, http://www.cbsnews.com.

12. "Golfer Michelle Wie, 15, Turns Pro," CBS News, October 5, 2005, http://www.cbsnews.com; John Hawkins, "Wie to Turn Professional before 16th Birthday," ESPN, September 12, 2005, http://sports.espn.go.com.

13. Barbara Wall, "Celebrity Cachet Has Firms Banking on What's in a Name."

14. Renee Alexander, "Fidelity and McCartney: Mutually Invested," *Brandchannel.com,* November 14, 2005, http://www.brandchannel.com.

15. Timothy L. O'Brien, "Clearing Out Advertising's Clutter," *International Herald Tribune,* February 12, 2006, http://www.iht.com.

16. David H. Freedman, "The Future of Advertising Is Here," *Inc.,* August 2005, pp. 70–77.

17. Elinor Mills, "How Deep Is the Online-Ad Well?" ZDNet News, May 9, 2006, http://news.zdnet.com.

18. "U.S. Ad Spending Totals by Media," *FactPack2006,* February 27, 2006, p. 10.

19. General Electric Web site, http://www.ge.com, accessed May 30, 2006; Mickey Alam Khan, "GE Glows Green for Ecomagination Campaign," *DM News,* July 15, 2005, http://www.dmnews.com.

20. "Emotional, Not Factual, Ads Win Skeptical Consumers, Study Shows," *Medical News Today,* August 16, 2005, http://www.medicalnewstoday.com.

21. Jim Edwards, "New Pharma Ad Rules Result In . . . More Ads," *Brandweek,* May 8, 2006, http://www.brandweek.com; Rich Thomaselli, "Sleep Drugs Keep DTC Ad Spending up to $4B," *Advertising Age,* November 21, 2005, p. 4.

22. Michael McCarthy, "CareerBuilder Ads Find Humor in the Workplace," *USA Today,* May 15, 2005, http://www.usatoday.com.

23. Terence A. Shimp, *Advertising, Promotion, and Supplemental Aspects of Integrated Marketing Communications,* 6th ed. (Mason, OH: South-Western, 2003), pp. 306–309.

24. David Kiley, "Feedback from Carl's Jr Paris Hilton Ad as Spicey as the Ad," *BusinessWeek,* May 30, 2005, http://www.businessweek.com.

25. Mark Levit, "Sex in Advertising: Does It Sell?" *Ezine,* http://www.ezinearticles.com, accessed May 30, 2006.

26. Suzanne Vranica and Brian Steinberg, "Ads Reach for 'Reality,'" *Wall Street Journal,* December 21, 2005, http://online.wsj.com.

27. Sarah Boxer, "Got Wit? Make It Visual in Ads Online," *New York Times,* October 3, 2005, http://www.nytimes.com.

28. Julie Bosman, "Hey, Kid, You Want to Buy a Toyota Scion?" *New York Times,* June 14, 2006, p. C2; Yuki Noguchi, "Advertisers Push Deeper into Online Games," *Washington Post,* April 27, 2006, http://www.washingtonpost.com.

29. Brian Morrissey, "Advertisers Fight Banner Blindness with News Feeds," *Adweek,* September 20, 2005, http://www.adweek.com.

30. Allison Linn, "Microsoft Plans Launch of Search Ad System," Associated Press, January 13, 2006, http://news.yahoo.com.

31. "Interstitials," *AdLink,* http://www.adlink.com, accessed May 30, 2006.

32. Brad Stone, "The Web: Are We Nearing the End of Pop-Up Ads?" *Newsweek,* April 17, 2006, http://www.msnbc.msn.com.

33. "Who Is Responsible for Adware?" *Wall Street Journal,* April 12, 2006, http://online.wsj.com.

34. Jenn Abelson, "And Now, a Few (More) Words from Our (One) Sponsor," *Boston Globe,* October 24, 2005, http://www.boston.com.

35. Gina Piccalo, "TiVo Will No Longer Skip Past Advertisers," *Los Angeles Times,* November 17, 2005, http://www.latimes.com.

36. "U.S. Ad Spending Totals by Media," *FactPack2006,* February 27, 2006, p. 10.

37. "TV and Cable Network Ad Revenue," *FactPack2006,* February 27, 2006, p. 37.

38. Olga Khariff, "Coming Soon to XM: More Commercials," *BusinessWeek,* April 13, 2006, http://www.businessweek.com; "The Battle for America's Ears Has Begun," About.com, http://stereos.about.com, accessed May 30, 2006.

39. Jennifer Saba, "Dispelling the Myth of Readership Decline," *Editor & Publisher,* http://www.editorandpublisher.com, November 28, 2005; Jason Lee Miller, "Online Newspaper Readership Spikes," *WebProNews,* November 18, 2005, http://www.webpronews.com.

40. Seth Sutel, "Newspapers Seek more Online Viewers, Ads," Associated Press, June 21, 2006, http://biz.yahoo.com.

41. "Consumers, Media & U.S. Newspapers," Readership Institute, Media Management Center at Northwestern University, http://www.readership.org, accessed June 16, 2006.

42. "Top 10 Magazines by Gross Revenue" (also showing paid subscribers), *FactPack2006,* February 27, 2006, p. 35.

43. "U.S. Ad Spending Totals by Media," *FactPack2006,* February 27, 2006, p. 11.

44. Tomas Pukas, "Outdoor Video Screen Business: A Network of Success," Sign Industry.com, May 1, 2006, http://www.signindustry.com.

45. Anick Jesdanun, "Online Ad Revenues Grow for 3rd Yr. in Row," Associated Press, April 20, 2006, http://news.yahoo.com.

46. David Kiley, "Call It a Sell Phone," *BusinessWeek,* April 3, 2006, p. 55.

47. Matt Richtel, "Marketers Interested in Small Screen," *New York Times,* January 16, 2006, http://www.nytimes.com.

48. Matt Richtel, "Earn Cell Minutes By Watching Ads," *New York Times,* May 29, 2006, http://www.nytimes.com.

49. Laura Petrecca and David Lieberman, "Film Fans Can Export More Advertising on Big Screen," *USA Today,* December 6, 2005, http://www.usatoday.com.

50. "World's Top 10 Core Agency Brands," *FactPack2006,* February 27, 2006, p. 41.

51. Curt Schleier, "Striving for the 'Wow' Factor," *Investor's Business Daily,* September 20, 2005, http://www.investors.com.

52. Ibid.

53. U.S. Department of Labor, *Occupational Outlook Handbook,* 2006–2007 edition, Bureau of Labor Statistics, http://www.bls.gov.

54. Lora Kolodny, "The Art of the Press Release," *Inc.,* March 2005, p. 36.

55. Michael Barbaro, "Wal-Mart Enlists Bloggers in P.R. Campaign," *New York Times,* March 7, 2006, http://www.nytimes.com; Chuck Bartels, "Wal-Mart's CEO on Offensive against Critics," *Associated Press,* January 13, 2005, http://story.news.yahoo.com.

56. Bill Berkrot, "CDC Report Supports Bausch & Lomb Recall," Reuters, May 19, 2006, http://news.yahoo.com.

57. Mark Siebert, "Turn Good Publicity into Franchising Success," *Entrepreneur,* January 24, 2005, http://www.entrepreneur.com.

58. Sue Marek, "Ringing in the New Year," *Wireless Week,* January 1, 2006, http://www.wirelessweek.com.

59. "Halle Berry Dazzles in New Versace Ads," Hellomagazine.com, January 25, 2006, http://www.hellomagazine.com.

60. Decision Analyst Web site, http://www.decisionanalyst.com, accessed May 31, 2006.

61. "The Advertising Impact of Magazines in Conjunction with Television," Magazine Publishers of America, http://www.magazine.org, accessed May 31, 2006.

62. Kathy Prentice, "Connect Your Client by Text Message," *Media Life,* April 24, 2006, http://www.medialifemagazine.com.

63. "Alcohol Ads Linked to Teen Drinking," ConsumerAffairs.com, January 2, 2006, http://www.consumeraffairs.com.

Chapter 17

1. Tom Krishner, "Boeing Exec to Take Reins at Ford," Associated Press, September 6, 2006, http://news.yahoo.com. "Lawrence Ellison," *Forbes,* http://www.forbes.com, accessed June 26, 2006; Oracle Web site, http://www.oracle.com, accessed June 26, 2006; Jeffrey McCracken, "Ford's Way Forward Restructuring Plan Faces Setback," *Pittsburgh Post-Gazette,* May 5, 2006, http://www.post-gazette.com; Telios Demos, "The Sleeping Giant Goes on the Offensive," *Fortune,* April 3, 2006, http://money.cnn.com; Daniel Lyons, "Ballmer, Bemused," *Forbes,* March 23, 2006, http://www.forbes.com; "My Goal Is to Fight Toyota," *Time,* January 30, 2006, p. 47; Michael Liedtke, "Ellison, Old Friends in Software Showdown," Associated Press, October 30, 2005, http://news.yahoo.com; "Steve Ballmer Shrugs Off the Critics," *BusinessWeek,* September 26, 2005, http://www.businessweek.com; Jim Kerstetter, "Siebel and Ellison: Software's Odd Couple," CNet News.com, September 13, 2005, http://news.com.com; Sharon Silke Carty, "Bill Ford Carries on Family Name with Grace," *USA Today,* March 4, 2005, http://www.usatoday.com.

2. U.S. Census Bureau, *Statistical Abstract of the United States,* 2006 edition, http://www.census.gov.

3. Barry Farber, "Star Qualities," *Entrepreneur,* May 2006, http://www.entrepreneur.com.

4. Bureau of Labor Statistics, U.S. Department of Labor, "Tomorrow's Jobs," http://www.bls.gov, accessed June 22, 2006.

5. Borsheim's Web site, http://www.borsheims.com, accessed August 10, 2006; Emily Fredrix, "Stores Woo Male Shoppers," *The Morning News,* December 17, 2005, p. 8D.

6. Amazon.com Web site, http://www.amazon.com, accessed August 10, 2006; "Amazon Knows Who You Are," *Wired News,* March 27, 2005, http://www.wired.com.

7. "Annoying Quotes from Sales Clerks Listed," Associated Press, October 25, 2005, http://news.yahoo.com.

8. "How to Convert Prospects to Sales Faster with Pre-Call Planning," *Hoover's,* http://www.hoovers.com, accessed June 22, 2006.

9. Tom Belden, "The Long and Wearying Road," *Sales & Marketing Management,* June 2006, http://www.salesandmarketing.com.

10. Mike Wendland, "Ford Puts Computer in Truck; Delphi Hypes Satellite Radio," *USA Today,* January 12, 2006, http://www.usatoday.com.

11. "Telemarketing and the Telephone Consumer Protection Act," Electronic Privacy Information Center, http://www.epic.org, accessed May 15, 2006.

12. Carolyn Duffy Marsan, "Registry Proves Critics Wrong," *Network World,* October 3, 2005, http://www.networkworld.com.

13. "Telemarketing Industry Stats & Facts," Direct Marketing Association, http://www.the-dma.org, accessed June 2006.

14. Kerry A. Dolan, "Offshoring the Offshorers," *Forbes,* April 17, 2006, pp. 74–76; Michelle Conlin, "Call Centers in the Rec Room," *BusinessWeek,* January 23, 2006, pp. 76–77; Adam Geller, "Homeshoring Means That Call Center Might Be in Someone's Bedroom," *Seattle Post-Intelligencer,* May 9, 2005, http://seattlepi.nwsource.com.

15. Detroit Pistons Web site, http://www.nba.com/pistons, accessed June 23, 2006.

16. Eleanor Laise and William Mauldin, "Hook the Right Broker," Smart Money.com, August 1, 2005, http://www.smartmoney.com.

17. Carol Matlack, "An Airline with a Deafening Roar," *BusinessWeek,* March 27, 2006, p. 46.

18. Chris Taylor, "Changing Gears," *Sales & Marketing Management,* October 2005, http://0-proquest.umi.com.library.uark.edu.

19. Jim Cole, "Marketing Study Touts Cross-Selling over Cold Calling," *American Banker,* February 22, 2006, http://0-proquest.umi.com.library.uark.edu.

20. "MacMahon Worldwide/SalesConference.Net," Groove Networks, http://www.groove.net, accessed June 23, 2006.

21. Marilyn Alva, "Managing for Success," *Investor's Business Daily,* June 9, 2006, http://www.investors.com.
22. "JCPenney Improves Operating Efficiencies," *Investor's Business Daily,* June 20, 2005, http://www.investors.com.
23. Newell Rubbermaid Web site, http://www.newellrubbermaid.com, accessed June 23, 2006.
24. Kurt Schultheis, "Cars, Free Gas among Incentives Thrown at Home Buyers," MSNBC, June 18, 2006, http://msnbc.msn.com.
25. Barry Farber, "Break on Through," *Entrepreneur,* March 2006, http://www.entrepreneur.com.
26. Ibid.; Paul Kaihla, "Firing Up Your Cold Calls," *Business 2.0,* December 2005, pp. 60–65.
27. Kristin Zhivago, "The Tools Your Sellers Need from Your Website," *Revenue Journal,* May 25, 2006, http://www.revenuejournal.com.
28. Scott Vincent Borba, "15 Cold Calls a Day, $5 Million in Sales," Fortune Small Business, June 20, 2006, http://money.cnn.com.
29. Black & Decker Web site, http://www.blackanddecker.com, accessed June 23, 2006.
30. Barry Farber, "Hanging Tough," *Entrepreneur,* April 2006, http://www.entrepreneur.com.
31. Michelle Nichols, "A Hands-On Guide to Staying in Touch," *BusinessWeek,* October 7, 2005, http://www.businessweek.com.
32. U.S. Department of Labor, *Occupational Outlook Handbook,* 2006–2007 edition, Bureau of Labor Statistics, http://www.bls.gov, accessed June 23, 2006.
33. "The Livermore Way at HP," *BusinessWeek,* January 30, 2006, http://www.businessweek.com.
34. *Occupational Outlook Handbook.*
35. Lesley Kump, "Teaching the Teachers," *Forbes,* December 12, 2005.
36. Julia Chang, "Ultimate Motivation Guide: Happy Sales Force, Happy Returns," *Sales & Marketing Management,* March 2006, http://www.salesandmarketing.com.
37. Christine Galea, "The 2005 Compensation Survey," *Sales & Marketing Management,* May 2005, pp. 23–29.
38. Julia Chang, "Ultimate Motivation Guide."
39. Frank Bucaro, "Sales Ethics: Oxymoron or Opportunity?" *Negotiator Magazine,* http://www.negotiatormagazine.com, accessed June 23, 2006.
40. Eric Auchard, "Skype Launches Free Call Promotion in U.S., Canada," Reuters, May 15, 2006, http://news.yahoo.com.
41. Ken Burke, "Get with the Loyalty Program," *Multichannel Merchant,* May 1, 2006, http://multichannelmerchant.com.
42. Jim Wasserman, "Touchtone Discounts Taking Clip at Coupons," *(Fort Wayne, TX) Journal Gazette,* January 1, 2006, http://www.fortwayne.com.
43. Ibid.
44. Andrew Scott, "Try Me!" *Promo,* April 1, 2006, http://promomagazine.com.
45. Ibid.
46. Amy Johannes, "Playing the Game," *Promo,* April 1, 2006, http://promomagazine.com.
47. Joe Mandese, "Promo Products Outpace Ad Spending, Now Greater than Cable, Outdoor, Online Display," MediaPost Publications, April 17, 2006, http://publications.mediapost.com.
48. "P&G, Wal-Mart Bail on In-Store Ad Study," *Media Buyer Planner,* June 13, 2006, http://www.mediabuyerplanner.com.
49. "Growth Spurt Continues into the First Quarter," *Trade Show Week,* http://www.tradeshowweek.com, accessed June 23, 2006.
50. "Green Mountain Coffee Roasters," Corporate Dynamics, http://www.corpdyn.com, accessed March 13, 2006.
51. "InterContinental Hotel's Customer Loyalty Program, Priority Club, Now Provides Free Nights at Competitors' Hotels," Hotel Online, June 18, 2005, http://www.hotel-online.com.

Chapter 18

1. Kathy Showalter, "Grocers See Gold in Gas, Add Discounted Pumps," MSNBC, June 11, 2006, http://www.msnbc.msn.com; "Gas Prices Squeeze Costco Profits," MSNBC, June 1, 2006, http://www.msnbc.msn.com; Tom Molloy, "Gas Customers Rage about Pump Prices," *USA Today,* May 29, 2006, http://www.usatoday.com; Lauren Young, "Why Costco Is All Pumped Up," *BusinessWeek,* September 12, 2005, p. 13.
2. Barry Krissoff and John Wainio, "U.S. Fruit and Vegetable Imports Outpace Exports," *Amber Waves,* U.S. Department of Agriculture's Economic Research Service, June 2005, http://www.ers.usda.gov.
3. "Canada and EU Hit U.S. with Retaliatory Tariffs," *International Herald Tribune,* May 2, 2005, http://www.iht.com.
4. Ben Charny, "Net Telephone Fees Have Users Fuming," CNet News, January 27, 2005, http://news.com.com.
5. Greg Sandoval, "Can the Net Make Ticket Scalping Legit?" CNet News, June 5, 2006, http://news.com.com.
6. "Ethical Eating: How Much Do You Swallow," *Guardian Unlimited,* February 26, 2006, http://observer.guardian.co.uk.
7. Dean Foust, "Making Every Gallon Count," *BusinessWeek,* May 8, 2006, pp. 54–55; Mark Skertic, "United Takes Polar Express on Flights to China, Japan," *Chicago Tribune,* April 4,

2006, p. B1; Roger Yu, "Airline Services Evolves into Do-It-Yourself," *CRM Buyer,* February 26, 2006, http://www.crmbuyer.com.
8. Jefferson Graham, "Apple Rolls Out $69 iPods, New Showtime Downloads," *USA Today,* February 8, 2006, http://www.usatoday.com.
9. Ken Burke, "Get with the Loyalty Program," *Multichannel Merchant,* May 1, 2006, http://multichannelmerchant.com.
10. Robert D. Buzzell and Frederick D. Wiersema, "Successful Share Building Strategies," *Harvard Business Review,* January–February 1981, pp. 135–144.
11. Ben Patterson, "Prepaid Primer: The What, Why, and How of Prepaid Cell Phones," CNet Networks, April 18, 2006, http://reviews.cnet.com.
12. "Southwest Airlines Uses Free Booze to Lure Passengers," *BostonChannel.com,* June 7, 2006, http://www.thebostonchannel.com.
13. "A Rambunctious Little Vintage," *Los Angeles Times,* January 25, 2006, http://www.latimes.com; Justin Ewers, "Bottoms Up for Bargains," *U.S. News & World Report,* December 5, 2005, pp. EE10, EE12.
14. Trader Joe's Web site, http://www.traderjoes.com, accessed January 26, 2006.
15. Dan Nystedt, "Component Costs Rising, but PC Prices Won't," InfoWorld, August 15, 2005, http://www.infoworld.com; Dan Frakes, "The Mac Mini: Comparing Apples and Oranges," *Macworld,* January 18, 2005, http://www.macworld.com.
16. Olga Kharif, "Car Clubs That Share Classy Wheels," *BusinessWeek,* February 21, 2006, http://www.businessweek.com.
17. Amy Goldstein, "Strapped States Try New Route, Lease Toll Roads to Foreign Firms," *Washington Post,* June 14, 2006, http://www.washingtonpost.com.
18. "Travel Options: Ride Free Area," *Metro Online,* http://transit.metrokc.gov, accessed June 15, 2006.
19. Steve Geissinger, "Prop. 86 Foes Trying to Play Terror Card," *Alameda (CA) Times-Star,* August 6, 2006, http://www.insidebayarea.com.
20. "Report: U.S. Trails in Refinery Growth," CNN Money, December 28, 2005, http://money.cnn.com; Susan Jones, "Bill Aims to Encourage New Refinery Building," Cybercast News Service, September 23, 2005, http://www.cnsnews.com.
21. Jim Surh, "Gas Prices May Impact Pizza, Flower Costs," Associated Press, April 28, 2006, http://news.yahoo.com.
22. Susan Chandler, Kevin Pang, and Robin Jenkins, "The Oil Squeeze," *Chicago Tribune,* April 23, 2006, pp. 1, 20.
23. Margot Roosevelt, "The Grass-Fed Revolution," *Time,* June 16, 2006, http://www.time.com.
24. Tara Weingarten, "Travel: A Better Class of Coach," MSNBC, June 19, 2006, http://www.msnbc.com; Don Teague, "What's Behind the Soaring Cost of Air Travel?" MSNBC, April 14, 2006, http://www.msnbc.com.
25. "Zimbabwe's Inflation Steams Ahead," BBC News, June 9, 2006, http://news.bbc.co.uk; Michael Wines, "How Bad Is Inflation in Zimbabwe?" *New York Times,* May 2, 2006, http://www.nytimes.com.
26. Shopzilla Web site, http://www.shopzilla.com, accessed January 5, 2006; Vicky Hallet, "Ringing Up the Best Bargain," *U.S. News & World Report,* December 5, 2005, p. 58; Kim Clark, "Searching for a Fair Fare," *U.S. News & World Report,* December 5, 2005, p. 65.
27. Poornima Gupta, "Ford Posts Unexpected Loss," Reuters, July 20, 2006, http://news.yahoo.com.
28. Susan Berfield, "The Making of *The Color Purple,*" *BusinessWeek,* November 21, 2005, pp. 104–112.
29. James L. McKenney, *Stouffer Yield Management System,* Harvard Business School Case 9-190-193 (Boston: Harvard Business School, 1994); Anirudh Dhebar and Adam Brandenburger, *American Airlines, Inc.: Revenue Management,* Harvard Business School Case 9-190-029 (Boston: Harvard Business School, 1992).
30. "Europe's Merger Wave," *The Economist,* March 14, 2006, http://www.economist.com; Peter Gumbel, "It's High Time for Mixing Brands," *Time,* December 31, 2005, http://www.time.com.
31. "Breaking News: New ACNielsen Survey Points to Price Convergence in Europe Since the Introduction of the Euro," ACNielsen news release, September 2005, http://www.acnielsen.co.uk.
32. Parija Bhatnaqar, "Wal-Mart's Challenge in China," CNN Money, January 12, 2006, http://money.cnn.com.
33. Kathy Chu, "Rising Bank Fees Hit Consumers," *USA Today,* October 5, 2005, http://www.usatoday.com.

Chapter 19

1. Vicki Lee Parker, "More Selling Homes on Their Own," *(Raleigh, NC) News & Observer,* July 2, 2006, http://www.newsobserver.com; Noelle Knox, "It's Always Open House as Real Estate Goes Online," *USA Today,* May 8, 2006, http://www.usatoday.com; Sandra Fleishman, "For Sale by Owner Means Cutting Commission, at What Cost?" *Washington Post,* April 29, 2006, http://www.washingtonpost.com; Glen Justice, "Lobbying to Sell Your House," *New York Times,* January 12, 2006, http://www.nytimes.com; Jeff Bailey, "Owners' Web Gives Realtors Run for Money," *New York Times,* January 3, 2006, http://www.nytimes.com.

2. Robert Manor, "Airlines Play a Match Game," *Chicago Tribune,* August 22, 2006, section 3, pp. 1, 4.

3. Sean Captain, "High Def, Low Cost: HDTV Prices Plunge," *PC World,* January 2006, http://www.pcworld.com.

4. Electrolux Web site, http://www.electroluxusa.com, accessed August 24, 2006; iRobot Web site, http://www.roombavac.com, accessed August 24, 2006; Faye Musselman, "High-End Sales Not Automatic in Robotic Vacs," *Home Furnishing News,* August 29, 2005, http://www.hfnmag.com; Thomas K. Grose, "The Vacuum's Design Moment," *U.S. News & World Report,* May 23, 2005, pp. EE18, EE20.

5. Patrick Klepek, "Microsoft Erases Hopes of Xbox 360 Price Drop," Extreme Tech, June 27, 2006, http://www.extremetech.com.

6. Joanne Viviano, "Crocs Shoes Making Great Strides," Associated Press, June 30, 2006, http://news.yahoo.com.

7. "Daimler to Launch Smart Car in U.S. in 2008," Associated Press, June 29, 2006, http://www.msnbc.com.

8. Wal-Mart Web site, http://www.walmartstores.com, accessed July 14, 2006.

9. "No Insult Pricing and Promotions," AT Kearney, http://www.atkearney.com, accessed July 14, 2006.

10. Emily Kaiser, "Family Dollar Profit Beats Forecasts," Reuters, June 22, 2006, http://news.yahoo.com.

11. "TMV Pricing Report," Edmunds.com, http://www.edmunds.com, accessed July 2006.

12. Alex Halperin, "Prices: How High Can They Go?" *BusinessWeek,* July 10, 2006, http://www.businessweek.com.

13. Rapid Supplies Web site, http://www.rapidsupplies.com, accessed July 17, 2006.

14. Sony ImageStation Web site, http://www.imagestation.com, accessed July 17, 2006.

15. See's Candies Web site, http://qd.sees.com, accessed July 17, 2006.

16. "New & Used Car Price Service," *Consumer Reports,* http://www.consumerreports.org, accessed July 17, 2006.

17. "Probe May Delay Change in Digital-Music Prices," CNet News.com, January 4, 2006, http://news.com.com.

18. Ben Ames, "Dell Will Use Fewer Rebates in PC Pricing," *PC World,* July 14, 2006, http://www.pcworld.com.

19. Erica Ogg, "OfficeMax Bids Farewell to Mail-In Rebates," CNet News.com, June 30, 2006, http://news.com.com.

20. "Welcome to Staples Rebate Center," Staples.com, http://www.stapleseasyrebates.com, accessed July 17, 2006.

21. Joel R. Evans and Barry Berman, "Pricing and Small Retailers: Questions to Consider," About.com, http://retailindustry.about.com, accessed July 17, 2006.

22. Ryan Underwood, "These Time Shares Have Wings—Fractional Jet Ownership Takes Off," Tennessean.com, January 10, 2006, http://www.tennessean.com.

23. Amy Merrick, "Can Silk and Leather Tempt Shoppers Back to Old Navy?" *Wall Street Journal,* June 30, 2006, http://online.wsj.com.

24. Bradford Wernle, "Chrysler Starts Summer Selling Season with Employee-Discount Program," *AutoWeek,* June 23, 2006, http://www.autoweek.com.

25. Doris Hajewski, "Bargains Gobbled as Stores Eat Loss," *Milwaukee Journal Sentinel,* November 18, 2005, http://www.findarticles.com.

26. Tom Spring, "Solid $500 Laptops," *PC World,* October 31, 2005, http://www.pcworld.com.

27. "Motorola Razr V3I Dolce & Gabbana," CNet.com, http://inktomi-cnet.com, accessed August 18, 2006; Candace Lombardi, "A Razr for Designer-Label Lovers," CNet News.com, June 2, 2006, http://news.com.com.

28. Theresa Howard, "Ads Try to Expand Customer Base," *USA Today,* February 19, 2006, http://www.usatoday.com.

29. Joe Guy Coller, "Chasing the Police," *Detroit Free Press,* June 15, 2006, http://www.freep.com; Peter Valdes-Dapena, "Best Cars for Cops," CNN, January 20, 2006, http://www.cnn.com.

30. Carole Keeton Strayhorn, "To Bid, or Not to Bid," Window on State Government, February 2006, http://www.window.state.tx.us.

31. eBay Web site, http://www.ebay.com, accessed July 19, 2006.

32. Jamie Birch, "Channel Integration, Cannibalization, and the Affiliate's Brand," ReveNews, May 25, 2006, http://www.revenews.com.

33. Ed Sutherland, "AT&T Shuffles Broadband Bundle Pricing," Internet News, February 3, 2006, http://www.internetnews.com.

34. Ken Belson, "Chairman of Cable Giant Urges Industry Shift to Flexible Pricing," *New York Times,* December 2, 2005, http://www.nytimes.com.

35. Kristin Larson, "Affordable Chic: Designer Labels, Discount Prices," MSN, http://lifestyle.msn.com, accessed July 14, 2006.

36. Bruce Meyerson, "Verizon Wireless to Ease up on Fees," Associated Press, June 28, 2006, http://news.yahoo.com.

glossary

80/20 principle Generally accepted rule that 80 percent of a product's revenues come from 20 percent of its total customers.

9/11 Generation People in their formative years at the time of the September 11, 2001, terrorist attacks.

A

accessory equipment Capital items such as desktop computers and printers that typically cost less and last for shorter periods than installations.

acculturation Process of learning a new culture foreign to one's own.

administered marketing system VMS that achieves channel coordination when a dominant channel member exercises its power.

adoption process Stages that consumers go through in learning about a new product, trying it, and deciding whether to purchase it again.

advertising Paid, nonpersonal communication through various media about a business firm, not-for-profit organization, product, or idea by a sponsor identified in a message that is intended to inform or persuade members of a particular audience.

advertising agency Firm whose marketing specialists help advertisers plan and prepare advertisements.

advertising campaign Series of different but related ads that use a single theme and appear in different media within a specified time period.

affinity marketing Marketing effort sponsored by an organization that solicits responses from individuals who share common interests and activities.

AIDA concept Steps through which an individual reaches a purchase decision: attention, interest, desire, and action.

AIO statements Items on lifestyle surveys that describe various activities, interests, and opinions of respondents.

allowance Specified deduction from list price, including a trade-in or promotional allowance.

ambush marketing Attempt by a firm that is not an official sponsor of an event or activity to link itself to the event or activity.

antitrust Laws designed to prevent restraints on trade such as business monopolies.

application service providers (ASPs) Outside companies that specialize in providing both the computers and the application support for managing information systems of business clients.

approach Salesperson's initial contact with a prospective customer.

Asch phenomenon Impact of groups and group norms on individual behavior, as described by S. E. Asch. People often conform to majority rule, even when majority rule goes against their beliefs.

atmospherics Combination of physical characteristics and amenities that contribute to a store's image.

attitudes Person's enduring favorable or unfavorable evaluations, emotions, or action tendencies toward some object or idea.

average total costs Costs calculated by dividing the sum of the variable and fixed costs by the number of units produced.

B

baby boomers People born between 1946 and 1965.

backward integration Process through which a manufacturer attempts to gain greater control over inputs in its production process, such as raw materials.

banner ad Strip message placed in high-visibility areas of frequently visited Web sites.

banners Advertisements on a Web page that link to an advertiser's site.

basing-point pricing System used in some industries during the early 20th century in which the buyer paid the factory price plus freight charges from the basing-point city nearest the buyer.

benchmarking Method of measuring quality by comparing performance against industry leaders.

blog Short for *Web log*—an online journal for an individual or organization.

bonus pack Specially packaged item that gives the purchaser a larger quantity at the regular price.

bot Software program that allows online shoppers to compare the price of a particular product offered by several online retailers.

bottom line Business jargon referring to the overall profitability of an organization.

brand equity Added value that a respected, well-known brand name gives to a product in the marketplace.

brand extension Strategy of attaching a popular brand name to a new product in an unrelated product category.

brand insistence Consumer refusal of alternatives and extensive search for desired merchandise.

brand licensing Firm's authorization of other companies to use its brand names.

brand manager Marketer within an organization who is responsible for a single brand.

brand mark Symbol or pictorial design that distinguishes a product.

brand name Part of a brand consisting of words or letters that form a name that identifies and distinguishes a firm's offerings from those of its competitors.

brand preference Consumer reliance on previous experiences with a product to choose that product again.

brand recognition Consumer awareness and identification of a brand.

brand Name, term, sign, symbol, design, or some combination that identifies the products of one firm while differentiating them from the competition's.

breakeven analysis Pricing technique used to determine the number of products that must be sold at a specified price to generate enough revenue to cover total cost.

broadband technology Extremely high-speed, always-on Internet connection.

broker Agent wholesaling intermediary that does not take title to or possession of goods in the course of its primary function, which is to bring together buyers and sellers.

bundle pricing Offering two or more complementary products and selling them for a single price.

business cycle Pattern of stages in the level of economic activity: prosperity, recession, depression, and recovery.

business plan Formal document that outlines a company's objectives, how they will be met, how the business will obtain financing, and how much money the company expects to earn.

business products Goods and services purchased for use either directly or indirectly in the production of other goods and services for resale.

business services Intangible products that firms buy to facilitate their production and operating processes.

business-to-business (B2B) e-marketing Use of the Internet for business transactions between organizations.

business-to-business (B2B) marketing Organizational sales and purchases of goods and services to support production of other products, for daily company operations, or for resale.

business-to-business (B2B) product Product that contributes directly or indirectly to the output of other products for resale; also called industrial or organizational product.

business-to-consumer (B2C) e-marketing Selling directly to consumers over the Internet.

buyer partnership Relationship in which a firm purchases goods or services from one or more providers.

buyer's market Market in which there are more goods and services than people willing to buy them.

buyer Person who has the formal authority to select a supplier and to implement the procedures for securing a good or service.

buying center Participants in an organizational buying action.

buzz marketing Marketing that gathers volunteers to try products and then relies on them to talk about their experiences with their friends and colleagues.

C

cannibalization Loss of sales of an existing product due to competition from a new product in the same line.

captive brand National brands that are sold exclusively by a retail chain.

cash discount Price reduction offered to a consumer, business user, or marketing intermediary in return for prompt payment of a bill.

category advisor (category captain) Trade industry vendor who develops a comprehensive procurement plan for a retail buyer.

category killer Store that offers huge selections and low prices in single product lines.

category management Product management system in which a category manager—with profit and loss responsibility—oversees a product line.

category Key business unit within diversified firms; also called a *strategic business unit (SBU)*.

cause marketing Identification and marketing of a social issue, cause, or idea to selected target markets.

Central American Free Trade Agreement-DR (CAFTA-DR) Trade agreement among the United States, Central American nations, and the Dominican Republic.

channel Medium through which a message is delivered.

channel captain Dominant and controlling member of a marketing channel.

channel conflicts Conflicts between manufacturers, wholesalers, and retailers.

click-through rate Percentage of people presented with a banner ad who click on it.

closed sales territory Exclusive geographic selling region of a distributor.

closing Stage of the personal selling process in which the salesperson asks the customer to make a purchase decision.

cluster sample Probability sample in which researchers select a sample of subgroups (or clusters) from which they draw respondents; each cluster reflects the diversity of the whole population being sampled.

cobranding Cooperative arrangement in which two or more businesses team up to closely link their names on a single product.

cognitive dissonance Imbalance among knowledge, beliefs, and attitudes that occurs after an action or decision, such as a purchase.

cohort effect Tendency of members of a generation to be influenced and bound together by events occurring during their key formative years—roughly age 17 to 22.

cold calling Contacting a prospect without a prior appointment.

collaborative planning, forecasting, and replenishment (CPFaR) Inventory management technique involving collaborative efforts by both purchasers and vendors.

comarketing Cooperative arrangement in which two businesses jointly market each other's products.

commercial market Individuals and firms that acquire products to support, directly or indirectly, production of other goods and services.

commission merchant Agent wholesaling intermediary who takes possession of goods shipped to a central market for sale, acts as the producer's agent, and collects an agreed-upon fee at the time of the sale.

commission Incentive compensation directly related to the sales or profits achieved by a salesperson.

common carriers Businesses that provide transportation services as for-hire carriers to the general public.

common market Extension of a customs union by seeking to reconcile all government regulations affecting trade.

comparative advertising Advertising strategy that emphasizes messages with direct or indirect promotional comparisons between competing brands.

competitive bidding Inviting potential suppliers to quote prices on proposed purchases or contracts.

competitive environment Interactive process that occurs in the marketplace among marketers of directly competitive products, marketers of products that can be substituted for one another, and marketers competing for the consumer's purchasing power.

competitive pricing strategy Pricing strategy designed to deemphasize price as a competitive variable by pricing a good or service at the general level of comparable offerings.

competitive strategy Methods through which a firm deals with its competitive environment.

component parts and materials Finished business products of one producer that become part of the final products of another producer.

concentrated marketing Focusing marketing efforts on satisfying a single market segment; also called *niche marketing*.

concept testing Method for subjecting a product idea to additional study before actual development by involving consumers through focus groups, surveys, in-store polling, and the like.

consolidated metropolitan statistical area (CMSA) Urban area that includes two or more PMSAs.

consultative selling Meeting customer needs by listening to them, understanding their problems, paying attention to details, and following through after the sale.

consumer (B2C) product Product destined for use by ultimate consumers.

consumer behavior Process through which buyers make purchase decisions.

consumer innovator People who purchase new products almost as soon as the products reach the market.

consumer orientation Business philosophy incorporating the marketing concept that emphasizes first determining unmet consumer needs and then designing a system for satisfying them.

consumer products Products bought by ultimate consumers for personal use.

consumer rights List of legitimate consumer expectations suggested by President Kennedy.

consumerism Social force within the environment that aids and protects the consumer by exerting legal, moral, and economic pressures on business and government.

containerization Process of combining several unitized loads into a single, well-protected load for shipment.

contest Sales promotion technique that requires entrants to complete a task such as solving a puzzle or answering questions on a quiz for the chance to win a prize.

contract carriers For-hire transporters that do not offer their services to the general public.

contractual marketing system VMS that coordinates channel activities through formal agreements among participants.

controlled experiment Scientific investigation in which a researcher manipulates a test group (or groups) and compares the results with those of a control group that did not receive the experimental controls or manipulations.

convenience products Goods and services that consumers want to purchase frequently, immediately, and with minimal effort.

convenience retailer Store that appeals to customers on accessible location, long hours, rapid checkout, and adequate parking.

convenience sample Nonprobability sample selected from among readily available respondents.

conversion rate Percentage of visitors to a Web site who make a purchase.

cookies Controversial techniques for collecting information about online Web site visitors in which small text files are automatically downloaded to a user's computer to gather such data as length of visit and the site visited next.

cooperative advertising Strategy in which a retailer shares advertising costs with a manufacturer or wholesaler.

core based statistical area (CBSA) Collective term for metropolitan and micropolitan statistical areas.

core competencies Activities that a company performs well and that customers value and competitors find difficult to duplicate.

core region Region from which most major brands get 40 to 80 percent of their sales.

corporate marketing system VMS in which a single owner operates the entire marketing channel.

corporate Web site Site designed to increase a firm's visibility, promote its offerings, and provide information to interested parties.

cost per impression Measurement technique that relates the cost of an ad to every thousand people who view it.

cost per response (also called *click-throughs*) Direct marketing technique that relates the cost of an ad to the number of people who click it.

cost-plus pricing Practice of adding a percentage of specified dollar amount—or markup—to the base cost of a product to cover unassigned costs and to provide a profit.

countertrade Form of exporting whereby goods and services are bartered rather than sold for cash.

coupon Sales promotion technique that offers a discount on the purchase price of goods or services.

creative selling Personal selling that involves situations in which a considerable degree of analytical decision making on the buyer's part results in the need for skillful proposals of solutions for the customer's needs.

creativity Human activity that produces original ideas or knowledge, frequently by testing combinations of ideas or data to produce unique results.

critical thinking Determining the authenticity, accuracy, and worth of information, knowledge, claims, and arguments.

cross-promotion Promotional technique in which marketing partners share the cost of a promotional campaign that meets their mutual needs.

cross-selling Selling multiple, often unrelated goods and services to the same customer based on knowledge of that customer's needs.

cue Any object in the environment that determines the nature of a consumer's response to a drive.

culture Values, beliefs, preferences, and tastes handed down from one generation to the next.

cumulative quantity discount Price discount determined by amounts of purchases over stated time periods.

customary prices Traditional prices that customers expect to pay for certain goods and services.

customer relationship management (CRM) Combination of strategies and tools that drives relationship programs, reorienting the entire organization to a concentrated focus on satisfying customers.

customer satisfaction Extent to which customers are satisfied with their purchases.

customer winback Process of rejuvenating lost relationships with customers.

customer-based segmentation Dividing a business-to-business market into homogeneous groups based on buyers' product specifications.

customs union Establishment of a free-trade area plus a uniform tariff for trade with nonmember unions.

D

data mining Process of searching through customer databases to detect patterns that guide marketing decision making.

database marketing Use of software to analyze marketing information, identifying and targeting messages toward specific groups of potential customers.

decider Person who chooses a good or service, although another person may have the formal authority to complete the sale.

decline stage Final stage of the product life cycle, in which a decline in total industry sales occurs.

decoding Receiver's interpretation of a message.

Delphi technique Qualitative sales forecasting method that gathers and redistributes several rounds of anonymous forecasts until the participants reach a consensus.

demand Schedule of the amounts of a firm's product that consumers will purchase at different prices during a specified time period.

demarketing Process of reducing consumer demand for a good or service to a level that the firm can supply.

demographic segmentation Division of an overall market into homogeneous groups based on variables such as gender, age, income, occupation, education, sexual orientation, household size, and stage in the family life cycle; also called *socioeconomic segmentation*.

demonstration Stage in the personal selling process in which the customer has the opportunity to try out or otherwise see how a good or service works before purchase.

department store Large store that handles a variety of merchandise, including clothing, household goods, appliances, and furniture.

deregulation movement Opening of markets previously subject to government control.

derived demand Demand for a resource that results from demand for the goods and services that are produced by that resource.

differentiated marketing Strategy that focuses on producing several products and pricing, promoting, and distributing them with different marketing mixes designed to satisfy smaller segments.

diffusion process Process by which new goods or services are accepted in the marketplace.

direct channel Marketing channel that moves goods directly from a producer to the business purchaser or ultimate user.

direct mail Communications in the form of sales letters, postcards, brochures, catalogs, and the like conveying messages directly from the marketer to the customer.

direct marketing Direct communications, other than personal sales contacts, between buyer and seller, designed to generate sales, information requests, or store or Web site visits.

direct sales results test Method for measuring promotional effectiveness based on the specific impact on sales revenues for each dollar of promotional spending.

direct selling Strategy designed to establish direct sales contact between producer and final user.

discount house Store that charges low prices but may not offer services such as credit.

discretionary income Money available to spend after buying necessities such as food, clothing, and housing.

distribution strategy Planning that ensures that consumers find a firm's products in the proper quantities at the right times and places.

distribution Movement of goods and services from producers to customers.

downstream management Controlling part of the supply chain that involves finished product storage, outbound logistics, marketing and sales, and customer service.

drive Any strong stimulus that impels a person to act.

drop shipper Limited-function merchant wholesaler that accepts orders from customers and forwards these orders to producers, which then ship directly to the customers who placed the orders.

dual distribution Network that moves products to a firm's target market through more than one marketing channel.

dumping Controversial practice of selling a product in a foreign market at a price lower than what it receives in the producer's domestic market.

E

e-business Firm that targets customers by collecting and analyzing business information, conducting customer transactions, and maintaining online relationships with customers.

ecology Relationship between organisms and their natural environment.

economic environment Factors that influence consumer buying power and marketing strategies, including stage of the business cycle, inflation and deflation, unemployment, income, and resource availability.

elasticity Measure of responsiveness of purchasers and suppliers to a change in price.

electronic bulletin board Internet forum that allows users to post and read messages on a specific topic.

electronic data interchange (EDI) Computer-to-computer exchanges of invoices, orders, and other business documents.

electronic exchange Online marketplace that caters to a specific industry's needs.

electronic shopping cart File that holds items that the online shopper has chosen to buy.

electronic signatures Electronic identification that allows legal contracts such as home mortgages and insurance policies to be executed online.

electronic storefront Company Web site that sells products to customers.

electronic wallet Computer data file set up by an online shopper at an e-business site's checkout counter that contains credit card information and owner identification.

e-marketing Strategic process of creating, distributing, promoting, and pricing goods and services to a target market over the Internet or through digital tools.

embargo Complete ban on the import of specified products.

emergency goods and services Products bought in response to unexpected and urgent needs.

employee satisfaction Employee's level of satisfaction in his or her company and the extent to which that loyalty or lack of loyalty is communicated to external customers.

encoding Translating a message into understandable terms.

encryption The process of encoding data for security purposes.

end-use application segmentation Segmenting a business-to-business market based on how industrial purchasers will use the product.

Engel's laws Three general statements about the impact of household income on consumer spending behavior: as household income increases, a smaller percentage of expenditures goes for food; the percentage spent on housing, household operations, and clothing remains constant; and the percentage spent on other items (such as recreation and education) increases.

enterprise resource planning (ERP) system Software system that consolidates data from among a firm's various business units.

environmental management Attainment of organizational objectives by predicting and influencing the competitive, political-legal, economic, technological, and social-cultural environments.

environmental scanning Process of collecting information about the external marketing environment to identify and interpret potential trends.

e-procurement Use of the Internet by organizations to solicit bids and purchase goods and services from suppliers.

ethics Moral standards of behavior expected by a society.

European Union (EU) Customs union that is moving in the direction of an economic union by adopting a common currency, removing trade restrictions, and permitting free flow of goods and workers throughout the member nations.

evaluative criteria Features that a consumer considers in choosing among alternatives.

event marketing Marketing of sporting, cultural, and charitable activities to selected target markets.

everyday low pricing (EDLP) Pricing strategy of continuously offering low prices rather than relying on such short-term price cuts as cents-off coupons, rebates, and special sales.

evoked set Number of alternatives that a consumer actually considers in making a purchase decision.

exchange control Method used to regulate the privilege of international trade among importing organizations by controlling access to foreign currencies.

exchange functions Buying and selling functions of marketing.

exchange process Activity in which two or more parties give something of value to each other to satisfy perceived needs.

exchange rate Price of one nation's currency in terms of another country's currency.

exclusive dealing agreement Arrangement between a manufacturer and a marketing intermediary that prohibits the intermediary from handling competing product lines.

exclusive distribution Distribution of a product through a single wholesaler or retailer in a specific geographic region.

expectancy theory Theory stating that motivation depends on an individual's expectations of his or her ability to perform a job and how that performance relates to attaining a desired reward.

exploratory research Process of discussing a marketing problem with informed sources both within and outside the firm and examining information from secondary sources.

exponential smoothing Quantitative forecasting technique that assigns weights to historical sales data, giving the greatest weight to the most recent data.

exporting Marketing domestically produced goods and services in foreign countries.

extended problem solving Situation that involves lengthy external searches and long deliberation; results when brands are difficult to categorize or evaluate.

external customer People or organizations that buy or use a firm's goods or services.

F

facilitating functions Functions that assist the marketer in performing the exchange and physical distribution functions.

fair-trade laws Statutes enacted in most states that once permitted manufacturers to stipulate a minimum retail price for their product.

family brand Single brand name that identifies several related products.

family life cycle Process of family formation and dissolution.

feedback Receiver's response to a message.

field selling Sales presentations made at prospective customers' locations on a face-to-face basis.

firewall Electronic barrier between a company's internal network and the Internet that limits access into and out of the network.

first mover strategy Theory advocating that the company that is first to offer a product in a marketplace will be the long-term market winner.

fixed costs Costs that remain stable at any production level within a certain range (such as lease payments or insurance costs).

fixed-sum-per-unit method Method of promotional budgeting in which a predetermined amount is allocated to each sales or production unit.

FOB (free on board) plant (FOB origin) Price quotation that does not include shipping charges.

FOB origin-freight allowed (freight absorbed) Price quotation system that allows the buyer to deduct shipping expenses from the cost of purchases.

focus group Simultaneous personal interview of a small group of individuals, which relies on group discussion about a certain topic.

follow-up Postsale activities that often determine whether an individual who has made a recent purchase will become a repeat customer.

foreign licensing Agreement that grants foreign marketers the right to distribute a firm's merchandise or to use its trademark, patent, or process in a specified geographic area.

forward integration Process through which a firm attempts to control downstream distribution.

franchise Contractual arrangement in which a wholesaler or retailer agrees to meet the operating requirements of a manufacturer or other franchiser.

Free Trade Area of the Americas (FTAA) Proposed free-trade area stretching the length of the entire Western Hemisphere and designed to extend free trade benefits to additional nations in North, Central, and South America.

free-trade area Region in which participating nations agree to the free trade of goods among themselves, abolishing tariffs and trade restrictions.

frequency marketing Frequent-buyer or user marketing programs that reward customers with cash, rebates, merchandise, or other premiums.

friendship, commerce, and navigation (FCN) treaties International agreements that deal with many aspects of commercial relations among nations.

full-cost pricing Pricing method that uses all relevant variable costs in setting a product's price and also allocates those fixed costs that cannot be directly attributed to the production of the specific item being priced.

full-service research supplier Marketing research organization that offers all aspects of the marketing research process.

 G

gatekeeper Person who controls the information that all buying center members will review.

General Agreement on Tariffs and Trade (GATT) International trade accord that has helped reduce world tariffs.

general-merchandise retailer Store that carries a wide variety of product lines, stocking all of them in some depth.

generic products Products characterized by plain labels, no advertising, and the absence of brand names.

geographic information systems (GISs) Software packages that assemble, store, manipulate, and display data by their location.

geographic segmentation Division of an overall market into homogeneous groups based on their locations.

global marketing strategy Standardized marketing mix with minimal modifications that a firm uses in all of its domestic and foreign markets.

global sourcing Purchasing goods and services from suppliers worldwide.

goods Tangible products that customers can see, hear, smell, taste, or touch.

goods–services continuum Spectrum along which goods and services fall according to their attributes, from pure good to pure service.

grassroots marketing Efforts that connect directly with existing and potential customers through nonmainstream channels.

green marketing Production, promotion, and reclamation of environmentally sensitive products.

grey goods Products manufactured abroad under license from a U.S. firm and then sold in the U.S. market in competition with that firm's own domestic output.

gross domestic product (GDP) Sum of all goods and services produced by a nation in a year.

growth stage Second stage of the product life cycle, which begins when a firm starts to realize substantial profits from its investment in a product.

guerrilla marketing Unconventional, innovative, and low-cost marketing techniques designed to get consumers' attention in unusual ways.

H

high-involvement purchase decision Buying decision that evokes high levels of potential economic or social consequence.

home shopping channel Television direct marketing in which a variety of products are offered and consumers can order them directly by phone or online.

homeshoring Hiring workers to do jobs from their homes.

hypermarket Giant one-stop shopping facility that offers wide selections of grocery items and general merchandise at discount prices, typically filling up 200,000 or more square feet of selling space (about a third larger than most supercenters).

hypothesis Tentative explanation for some specific event.

I

import quotas Trade restrictions that limit the number of units of certain goods that can enter a country for resale.

importing Purchasing foreign goods and services.

impulse goods and services Products purchased on the spur of the moment.

inbound telemarketing Sales method in which prospects call a toll-free number to obtain information, make reservations, and purchase goods and services.

incremental-cost pricing Pricing method that attempts to use only costs directly attributable to a specific output in setting prices.

indirect evaluation Method for measuring promotional effectiveness by concentrating on quantifiable indicators of effectiveness such as recall and readership.

individual brand Single brand that uniquely identifies a product.

inelastic demand Demand that, throughout an industry, will not change significantly due to a price change.

inflation Rising prices caused by some combination of excess consumer demand and increases in the costs of one or more factors of production.

influencer Typically, technical staff such as engineers who affect the buying decision by supplying information to guide evaluation of alternatives or by setting buying specifications.

informative advertising Promotion that seeks to develop initial demand for a good, service, organization, person, place, idea, or cause.

infomercial Paid 30-minute or longer product commercial that resembles a regular television program.

infrastructure A nation's basic system of transportation networks, communications systems, and energy facilities.

inside selling Selling by phone, mail, and electronic commerce.

installations Business products such as factories, assembly lines, and large machinery that are major capital investments.

institutional advertising Promotion of a concept, an idea, a philosophy, or the goodwill of an industry, company, organization, person, geographic location, or government agency.

integrated marketing communications (IMC) Coordination of all promotional activities to produce a unified, customer-focused promotional message.

intensive distribution Distribution of a product through all available channels.

interactive advertising Two-way promotional messages transmitted through communication channels that induce message recipients to participate actively in the promotional effort.

interactive marketing Buyer–seller communications in which the customer controls the amount and type of information received from a marketer through such channels as the Internet and virtual reality kiosks.

interactive television Television service package that includes a return path for viewers to interact with programs or commercials by clicking their remote controls.

intermodal operations Combination of transport modes such as rail and highway carriers (piggyback), air and highway carriers (birdyback), and water and air carriers (fishyback) to improve customer service and achieve cost advantages.

internal customer Employees or departments within an organization that depend on the work of another employee or department to perform tasks.

internal marketing Managerial actions that help all members of the organization understand, accept, and fulfill their respective roles in implementing a marketing strategy.

internal partnership Relationship involving customers within an organization.

Internet Protocol television (IPTV) Technology that allows a two-way broadcast signal to be sent through a telephone or cable network by way of a broadband connection.

interpretative research Observational research method developed by social anthropologists in which customers are observed in their natural setting and their behavior is interpreted based on an understanding of social and cultural characteristics; also known as *ethnography*, or "going native."

introductory stage First stage of the product life cycle, in which a firm works to stimulate sales of a new market entry.

ISO (International Organization for Standardization) certification Internationally recognized standards that ensure that a company's goods, services, and operations meet established quality levels and that its operations minimize harm to the environment.

ISO 9002 International quality standards developed by the International Organization for Standardization in Switzerland to ensure consistent quality among products manufactured and sold throughout the European Union (EU).

J

joint demand Demand for a product that depends on the demand for another product used in combination with it.

jury of executive opinion Qualitative sales forecasting method that assesses the sales expectations of various executives.

just-in-time (JIT)/just-in-time II (JIT II) Inventory practices that seek to boost efficiency by cutting inventories to absolute minimum levels. With JIT II, suppliers' representatives work at the customer's facility.

L

label Branding component that carries an item's brand name or symbol, the name and address of the manufacturer or distributor, information about the product, and recommended uses.

lateral partnerships Strategic relationships that extend to external entities but involve no direct buyer–seller interactions.

leader pricing Variant of loss-leader pricing in which marketers offer prices slightly above cost to avoid violating minimum-markup regulations and earn a minimal return on promotional sales.

learning Knowledge or skill that is acquired as a result of experience, which changes consumer behavior.

lifetime value of a customer Revenues and intangible benefits that a customer brings to an organization over an average lifetime, minus the investment the firm has made to attract and keep the customer.

limited problem solving Situation in which the consumer invests a small amount of time and energy in searching for and evaluating alternatives.

limited-line store Retailer that offers a large assortment within a single product line or within a few related product lines.

limited-service research supplier Marketing research firm that specializes in a limited number of research activities, such as conducting field interviews or performing data processing.

line extension Development of individual offerings that appeal to different market segments while remaining closely related to the existing product line.

list price Established price normally quoted to potential buyers.

logistics Process of coordinating the flow of information, goods, and services among members of the distribution channel.

loss leader Product offered to consumers at less than cost to attract them to stores in the hope that they will buy other merchandise at regular prices.

low-involvement purchase decision Routine purchase that poses little risk to the consumer, either economically or socially.

M

mail-order wholesaler Limited-function merchant wholesaler that distributes catalogs instead of sending sales representatives to contact customers.

mall intercept Interviews conducted inside retail shopping centers.

manufacturer's brand Brand name owned by a manufacturer or other producer.

manufacturers' representative Agent wholesaling intermediary that represents manufacturers of related but noncompeting products and receives a commission on each sale.

marginal analysis Method of analyzing the relationship between costs, sales price, and increased sales volume.

marginal cost Change in total cost that results from producing an additional unit of output.

markdown Amount by which a retailer reduces the original selling price of a product.

market development strategy Strategy that concentrates on finding new markets for existing products.

market penetration strategy Strategy that seeks to increase sales of existing products in existing markets.

market price Price that a consumer or marketing intermediary actually pays for a product after subtracting any discounts, allowances, or rebates from the list price.

market segmentation Division of the total market into smaller, relatively homogeneous groups.

market share/market growth matrix Framework that places SBUs on a chart that plots market share against market growth potential.

market Group of people with sufficient purchasing power, authority, and willingness to buy.

marketing (distribution) channel System of marketing institutions that enhances the physical flow of goods and services, along with ownership title, from producer to consumer or business user.

marketing communications Messages that deal with buyer–seller relationships.

marketing concept Company-wide consumer orientation with the objective of achieving long-run success.

marketing decision support system (MDSS) Marketing information system component that links a decision maker with relevant databases and analysis tools.

marketing ethics Marketers' standards of conduct and moral values.

marketing information system (MIS) Planned, computer-based system designed to provide managers with a continuous flow of information relevant to their specific decisions and areas of responsibility.

marketing intermediary (middleman) Wholesaler or retailer that operates between producers and consumers or business users.

marketing mix Blending of the four strategy elements—product, distribution, promotion, and pricing—to fit the needs and preferences of a specific target market.

marketing myopia Management's failure to recognize the scope of its business.

marketing plan Detailed description of the resources and actions needed to achieve stated marketing objectives.

marketing planning Implementing planning activities devoted to achieving marketing objectives.

marketing public relations (MPR) Narrowly focused public-relations activities that directly support marketing goals.

marketing research Process of collecting and using information for marketing decision making.

marketing strategy Overall, company-wide program for selecting a particular target market and then satisfying consumers in that market through the marketing mix.

marketing Web site Site whose main purpose is to increase purchases by visitors.

marketing Organizational function and a set of processes for creating, communicating, and delivering value to customers and for managing customer relationships in ways that benefit the organization and its stakeholders.

market-plus pricing The intentional setting of a relatively high price compared with the prices of competing products; also known as *skimming pricing*.

market-share objective Volume-related pricing objective in which the goal is to achieve control of a portion of the market for a firm's good or service.

markup Amount that a retailer adds to the cost of a product to determine its selling price.

mass merchandiser Store that stocks a wider line of goods than a department store, usually without the same depth of assortment within each line.

materials handling system Set of activities that move production inputs and other goods within plants, warehouses, and transportation terminals.

maturity stage Third stage of the product life cycle, in which industry sales level out.

media research Advertising research that assesses how well a particular medium delivers an advertiser's message, where and when to place the advertisement, and the size of the audience.

media scheduling Setting the timing and sequence for a series of advertisements.

meeting competition method Method of promotional budgeting that simply matches competitors' outlays.

merchandisers Trade sector buyers who secure needed products at the best possible prices.

merchant wholesaler Independently owned wholesaling intermediary that takes title to the goods that it handles; also known as an industrial distributor in the business-goods market.

message Communication of information, advice, or a request by the sender to the receiver.

message research Advertising research that tests consumer reactions to an advertisement's creative message.

metropolitan statistical area (MSA) Freestanding urban area with a population in the urban center of at least 50,000 and a total MSA population of 100,000 or more.

micromarketing Targeting potential customers at very narrow, basic levels, such as by zip code, specific occupation, or lifestyle—possibly even individuals themselves.

micropolitan statistical area Area that has at least one town of 10,000 to 49,999 people with proportionally few of its residents commuting to outside the area.

minimum advertised pricing (MAP) Fees paid to retailers that agree not to advertise products below set prices.

mission Essential purpose that differentiates one company from others.

missionary selling Indirect type of selling in which specialized salespeople promote the firm's goodwill among indirect customers, often by helping customers use products.

mobile marketing Marketing messages transmitted via wireless technology.

modified breakeven analysis Pricing technique used to evaluate consumer demand by comparing the number of products that must be sold at a variety of prices to cover total cost with estimates of expected sales at the various prices.

modified rebuy Situation in which a purchaser is willing to reevaluate available options for repurchasing a good or service.

monopolistic competition Market structure involving a heterogeneous product and product differentiation among competing suppliers, allowing the marketer some degree of control over prices.

monopoly Market structure in which a single seller dominates trade in a good or service for which buyers can find no close substitutes.

motive Inner state that directs a person toward the goal of satisfying a need.

MRO items Business supplies that include maintenance items, repair items, and operating supplies.

multidomestic marketing strategy Application of market segmentation to foreign markets by tailoring the firm's marketing mix to match specific target markets in each nation.

multinational corporation Firm with significant operations and marketing activities outside its home country.

multiple sourcing Purchasing from several vendors.

N

national account selling Promotional effort in which a dedicated sales team is assigned to a firm's major customers to provide sales and service needs.

national accounts organization Promotional effort in which a dedicated sales team is assigned to a firm's major customers to provide sales and service needs.

nearshoring Moving jobs to vendors in countries close to the business's home country.

need Imbalance between a consumer's actual and desired states.

network marketing Personal selling that relies on lists of family members and friends of the salesperson, who organizes a gathering of potential customers for a demonstration of products.

new-task buying First-time or unique purchase situation that requires considerable effort by decision makers.

niche marketing Marketing strategy that focuses on profitably satisfying a single market segment; also called *concentrated marketing*.

noise Any stimulus that distracts a receiver from receiving a message.

noncumulative quantity discount Price reduction granted on a one-time-only basis.

nonmarketing public relations Organizational messages about general management issues.

nonpersonal selling Promotion that includes advertising, product placement, sales promotion, direct marketing, public relations, and guerilla marketing—all conducted without being face-to-face with the buyer.

nonprobability sample Sample that involves personal judgment somewhere in the selection process.

norms Values, attitudes, and behaviors that a group deems appropriate for its members.

North American Free Trade Agreement (NAFTA) Accord removing trade barriers between Canada, Mexico, and the United States.

North American Industry Classification System (NAICS) Classification used by NAFTA countries to categorize the business marketplace into detailed market segments.

O

objection Expression of sales resistance by the prospect.

objectives Goals that support a firm's overall mission.

odd pricing Pricing policy based on the belief that a price ending with an odd number just under a round number is more appealing—for instance, $9.97 rather than $10.

offshoring Movement of high-wage jobs from one country to lower-cost overseas locations.

oligopoly Market structure in which relatively few sellers compete and where high start-up costs form barriers to keep out new competitors.

opening price point Setting an opening price below that of the competition, usually on a high-quality private-label item.

opinion leaders Trendsetters who purchase new products before others in a group and then influence others in their purchases.

order processing Selling, mostly at the wholesale and retail levels, that involves identifying customer needs, pointing them out to customers, and completing orders.

organization marketing Marketing by mutual-benefit organizations, service organizations, and government organizations intended to influence others to accept their goals, receive their services, or contribute to them in some way.

outbound telemarketing Sales method in which sales representatives place phone calls to prospects and try to conclude the sale over the phone.

outsourcing Using outside vendors to provide goods and services formerly produced in-house.

over-the-counter selling Personal selling conducted in retail and some wholesale locations in which customers come to the seller's place of business.

P

partnership Affiliation of two or more companies that help each other achieve common goals.

penetration pricing strategy Pricing strategy involving the use of a relatively low entry price compared with competitive offerings, based on the theory that this initial low price will help secure market acceptance.

percentage-of-sales method Method of promotional budgeting in which a dollar amount is based on a percentage of past or projected sales.

perception Meaning that a person attributes to incoming stimuli gathered through the five senses.

perceptual screen Mental filter or block through which all inputs must pass to be noticed.

person marketing Marketing efforts designed to cultivate the attention, interest, and preferences of a target market toward a person (perhaps a political candidate or celebrity).

personal selling Interpersonal influence process involving a seller's promotional presentation conducted on a person-to-person basis with the buyer.

persuasive advertising Promotion that attempts to increase demand for an existing good, service, organization, person, place, idea, or cause.

phishing High-tech scam that uses authentic-looking e-mail or pop-up messages to get unsuspecting victims to reveal personal information.

physical distribution Broad range of activities aimed at efficient movement of finished goods from the end of the production line to the consumer.

place marketing Marketing efforts to attract people and organizations to a particular geographic area.

planned obsolescence Intentional design, manufacture, and marketing of products with limited durability.

planned shopping center Group of retail stores planned, coordinated, and marketed as a unit.

planning Process of anticipating future events and conditions and of determining the best way to achieve organizational objectives.

podcast Online audio or video file that can be downloaded to other digital devices.

point-of-purchase (POP) advertising Display or other promotion placed near the site of the actual buying decision.

political risk assessment (PRA) Units within a firm that evaluate the political risks of the marketplaces in which they operate as well as proposed new marketplaces.

political-legal environment Component of the marketing environment consisting of laws and their interpretations that require firms to operate under competitive conditions and to protect consumer rights.

population (universe) Total group that researchers want to study.

pop-up ad Separate window that pops up with an advertising message.

Porter's Five Forces Model developed by strategy expert Michael Porter that identifies five competitive forces that influence planning strategies: the threat of new entrants, the bargaining power of buyers, the bargaining power of suppliers, the threat of substitute products, and rivalry among competitors.

portfolio analysis Evaluation of a company's products and divisions to determine which are strongest and which are weakest.

positioning map Tool that helps marketers place products in a market by graphically illustrating consumers' perceptions of competing products within an industry.

positioning Placing a product at a certain point or location within a market in the minds of prospective buyers.

postage-stamp pricing System for handling transportation costs under which all buyers are quoted the same price, including transportation expenses; also known as *uniform-delivered price.*

posttesting Research that assesses advertising effectiveness after it has appeared in a print or broadcast medium.

precall planning Use of information collected during the prospecting and qualifying stages of the sales process and during previous contacts with the prospect to tailor the approach and presentation to match the customer's needs.

premium Item given free or at reduced cost with purchases of other products.

presentation Personal selling function of describing a product's major features and relating them to a customer's problems or needs.

pretesting Research that evaluates an ad during its development stage.

price flexibility Pricing policy permitting variable prices for goods and services.

price Exchange value of a good or service.

pricing policy General guideline that reflects marketing objectives and influences specific pricing decisions.

pricing strategy Methods of setting profitable and justifiable prices.

primary data Information collected specifically for the investigation at hand.

primary demand Desire for a general product category.

primary metropolitan statistical area (PMSA) Urbanized county or set of counties with social and economic ties to nearby areas.

private brand Brand offered by a wholesaler or retailer.

private carriers Transporters that provide service solely for internally generated freight.

probability sample Sample that gives every member of the population a chance of being selected.

product advertising Nonpersonal selling of a particular good or service.

product development Introduction of new products into identifiable or established markets.

product differentiation Occurs when consumers regard a firm's products as different in some way from those of competitors.

product diversification strategy Developing entirely new products for new markets.

product liability Responsibility of manufacturers and marketers for injuries and damages caused by their products.

product life cycle Progression of a product through introduction, growth, maturity, and decline stages.

product line Series of related products offered by one company.

product manager Marketer within an organization who is responsible for an individual product or product line; also called a brand manager.

product mix Assortment of product lines and individual product offerings that a company sells.

product placement Form of promotion in which a marketer pays a motion picture or television program owner a fee to display a product prominently in the film or show.

product positioning Consumers' perceptions of a product's attributes, uses, quality, and advantages and disadvantages relative to competing brands.

product strategy Decisions about what goods or services a firm will offer its customers; also includes decisions about customer service, packaging, brand names, and the like.

product Bundle of physical, service, and symbolic attributes designed to satisfy a customer's wants and needs.

production orientation Business philosophy stressing efficiency in producing a quality product, with the attitude toward marketing that "a good product will sell itself."

product-line pricing Practice of setting a limited number of prices for a selection of merchandise and marketing different product lines at each of these price levels.

product-related segmentation Division of a population into homogeneous groups based on their relationships to the product.

profit center Any part of an organization to which revenue and controllable costs can be assigned.

Profit Impact of Market Strategies (PIMS) project Research that discovered a strong positive relationship between a firm's market share and product quality and its return on investment.

profit maximization Point at which the additional revenue gained by increasing the price of a product equals the increase in total costs.

promotion Communication link between buyers and sellers; the function of informing, persuading, and influencing a consumer's purchase decision.

promotional allowance Promotional incentive in which the manufacturer agrees to pay the reseller a certain amount to cover the costs of special promotional displays or extensive advertising.

promotional mix Subset of the marketing mix in which marketers attempt to achieve the optimal blending of the elements of personal and nonpersonal selling to achieve promotional objectives.

promotional pricing Pricing policy in which a lower-than-normal price is used as a temporary ingredient in a firm's marketing strategy.

prospecting Personal selling function of identifying potential customers.

protective tariff Taxes designed to raise the retail price of an imported product to match or exceed that of a similar domestic product.

psychographic segmentation Division of a population into groups that have similar psychological characteristics, values, and lifestyles.

psychological pricing Pricing policy based on the belief that certain prices or price ranges make a good or service more appealing than others to buyers.

public relations Firm's communications and relationships with its various publics.

public service announcements (PSAs) Advertisements aimed at achieving socially oriented objectives by focusing on causes and charitable organizations that are included in print and electronic media without charge.

publicity Nonpersonal stimulation of demand for a good, service, place, idea, person, or organization by unpaid placement of significant news regarding the product in a print or broadcast medium.

puffery Exaggerated claims of a product's superiority, or the use of subjective or vague statements that may not be literally true.

pulling strategy Promotional effort by the seller to stimulate final-user demand, which then exerts pressure on the distribution channel.

pure competition Market structure characterized by homogeneous products in which there are so many buyers and sellers that none has a significant influence on price.

push money Financial incentive that gives retail salespeople cash rewards for every unit of a product they sell.

pushing strategy Promotional effort by the seller directed to members of the marketing channel rather than final users.

Q

qualifying Determining that a prospect has the needs, income, and purchase authority necessary for being a potential customer.

qualitative forecasting Use of subjective techniques to forecast sales, such as the jury of executive opinion, Delphi technique, sales force composite, and surveys of buyer intentions.

quantitative forecasting Use of statistical forecasting techniques such as trend analysis and exponential smoothing.

quantity discount Price reduction granted for a large-volume purchase.

quick-response merchandising Just-in-time strategy that reduces the time a retailer must hold merchandise in inventory, resulting in substantial cost savings.

quota sample Nonprobability sample divided to maintain the proportion of certain characteristics among different segments or groups as the population as a whole.

R

rack jobber Full-function merchant wholesaler that markets specialized lines of merchandise to retail stores.

radio frequency identification (RFID) Technology that uses a tiny chip with identification information that can be read by a scanner using radio waves from a distance.

raw materials Natural resources such as farm products, coal, copper, or lumber that become part of a final product.

rebate Refund of a portion of the purchase price, usually granted by the product's manufacturer.

reciprocity Buying from suppliers that are also customers.

reference groups People or institutions whose opinions are valued and to whom a person looks for guidance in his or her own behavior, values, and conduct, such as family, friends, or celebrities.

refund Cash given back to consumers who send in proof of purchasing one or more products.

reinforcement Reduction in drive that results from a proper response.

related party trade Trade by U.S. companies with their subsidiaries overseas as well as trade by U.S. subsidiaries of foreign-owned firms with their parent companies.

relationship marketing Development, growth, and maintenance of long-term, cost-effective relationships with individual customers, suppliers, employees, and other partners for mutual benefit.

relationship selling Regular contacts between sales representatives and customers over an extended period to establish a sustained buyer–seller relationship.

remanufacturing Efforts to restore older products to like-new condition.

reminder advertising Advertising that reinforces previous promotional activity by keeping the name of a good, service, organization, person, place, idea, or cause before the public.

repositioning Changing the position of a product within the minds of prospective buyers relative to the positions of competing products.

research design Master plan for conducting marketing research.

reseller Marketing intermediaries that operate in the trade sector.

response Individual's reaction to a set of cues and drives.

retail advertising Advertising by stores that sell goods or services directly to the consuming public.

retail convergence Situation in which similar merchandise is available from multiple retail outlets, resulting in the blurring of distinctions between type of retailer and merchandise offered.

retail cooperative Group of retailers that establish a shared wholesaling operation to help them compete with chains.

retailing Activities involved in selling merchandise to ultimate consumers.

revenue tariff Taxes designed to raise funds for the importing government.

reverse channel Channel designed to return goods to their producers.

Robinson-Patman Act Federal legislation prohibiting price discrimination that is not based on a cost differential; also prohibits selling at an unreasonably low price to eliminate competition.

roles Behavior that members of a group expect of individuals who hold specific positions within that group.

routinized response behavior Rapid consumer problem solving in which no new information is considered; the consumer has already set evaluative criteria and identified available options.

rule of three Three dominant companies in an industry that will capture 70 to 90 percent of the market.

S

salary Fixed compensation payment made periodically to an employee.

sales analysis In-depth evaluation of a firm's sales.

sales force composite Qualitative sales forecasting method based on the combined sales estimates of the firm's salespeople.

sales forecasting Estimate of a firm's revenue for a specified future period.

sales incentives Programs that reward salespeople for superior performance.

sales orientation Business assumption that consumers will resist purchasing nonessential goods and services, with the attitude toward marketing that only creative advertising and personal selling can overcome consumers' resistance and persuade them to buy.

sales promotion Marketing activities other than personal selling, advertising, and publicity that enhance consumer purchasing and dealer effectiveness.

sales quota Level of expected sales for a territory, product, customer, or salesperson against which actual results are compared.

sampling In marketing research, the process of selecting survey respondents or research participants; in sales promotion, free distribution of a product in an attempt to obtain future sales.

scrambled merchandising Retailing practice of combining dissimilar product lines to boost sales volume.

search marketing Paying search engines, such as Google, a fee to make sure that the company's listing appears toward the top of the search results.

second mover strategy Theory that advocates observing closely the innovations of first movers and then improving on them to gain advantage in the marketplace.

secondary data Previously published information.

Secure Sockets Layer (SSL) Technology that secures a Web site by encrypting information and providing authentication.

selective distribution Distribution of a product through a limited number of channels.

selective demand Desire for a specific brand within a product category.

self-concept Person's multifaceted picture of himself or herself.

seller partnership Relationship involving long-term exchanges of goods or services in return for cash or other valuable consideration.

seller's market Market in which there are more buyers for fewer goods and services.

selling agent Agent wholesaling intermediary responsible for the entire marketing program of a firm's product line.

sender Source of the message communicated to the receiver.

service encounter Point at which the customer and service provider interact.

service quality Expected and perceived quality of a service offering.

services Intangible tasks that satisfy the needs of consumer and business users.

shaping Process of applying a series of rewards and reinforcements to permit more complex behavior to evolve.

shopping products Products that consumers purchase after comparing competing offerings.

simple random sample Basic type of probability sample in which every individual in the relevant universe has an equal opportunity of being selected.

skimming pricing strategy Pricing strategy involving the use of a high price relative to competitive offerings.

slotting allowances Money paid by vendors to retailers to guarantee display of merchandise.

social responsibility Marketing philosophies, policies, procedures, and actions whose primary objective is the enhancement of society.

social-cultural environment Component of the marketing environment consisting of the relationship between the marketer, society, and culture.

sole sourcing Purchasing a firm's entire stock of an item from just one vendor.

spam Popular name for junk e-mail.

span of control The number of representatives who report to first-level sales managers.

specialty advertising Sales promotion technique that places the advertiser's name, address, and advertising message on useful articles that are then distributed to target consumers.

specialty products Products that offer unique characteristics that cause buyers to prize those particular brands.

specialty retailer Store that combines carefully defined product lines, services, and reputation to persuade shoppers to spend considerable shopping effort there.

split runs Methods of testing alternate ads by dividing a cable TV audience or a publication's subscribers in two, using two different ads, and then evaluating the relative effectiveness of each.

sponsorship Relationship in which an organization provides funds or in-kind resources to an event or activity in exchange for a direct association with that event or activity.

spreadsheet analysis Grid that organizes numerical information in a standardized, easily understood format.

staples Convenience goods and services that consumers constantly replenish to maintain a ready inventory.

status Relative position of any individual member in a group.

step out Pricing practice in which one firm raises prices and then waits to see if others follow suit

stock-keeping unit (SKU) Offering within a product line such as a specific size of liquid detergent.

straight rebuy Recurring purchase decision in which a customer repurchases a good or service that has performed satisfactorily in the past.

strategic alliance Partnership in which two or more companies combine resources and capital to create competitive advantages in a new market.

strategic business units (SBUs) Key business units within diversified firms.

strategic planning Process of determining an organization's primary objectives and adopting courses of action that will achieve these objectives.

strategic window Limited periods during which the key requirements of a market and the particular competencies of a firm best fit together.

stratified sample Probability sample constructed to represent randomly selected subsamples of different groups within the total sample; each subgroup is relatively homogeneous for a certain characteristic.

subcontracting Contractual agreements that assign the production of goods or services to local or smaller firms.

subcultures Smaller groups within a society that have their own distinct characteristics and modes of behavior, defined by ethnicity, race, region, age, religion, gender, social class, or profession.

subliminal perception Subconscious receipt of incoming information.

suboptimization Condition that results when individual operations achieve their objectives but interfere with progress toward broader organizational goals.

subsidy Government financial support of a private industry.

supercenter Large store, usually smaller than a hypermarket, that combines groceries with discount store merchandise.

supplies Regular expenses that a firm incurs in its daily operations.

supply chain Complete sequence of suppliers and activities that contribute to the creation and delivery of merchandise.

supply Schedule of the amounts of a good or service that firms will offer for sale at different prices during a specified time period.

supply-chain management Control of the activities of purchasing, processing, and delivery through which raw materials are transformed into products and made available to final consumers.

survey of buyer intentions Qualitative sales forecasting method that samples opinions among groups of present and potential customers concerning their purchase intentions.

sustainable competitive advantage Superior market position that a firm possesses and can maintain for an extended period of time.

sweepstakes Sales promotion technique in which prize winners are selected by chance.

SWOT analysis Analysis that helps planners compare internal organizational strengths and weaknesses with external opportunities and threats.

syndicated service Organization that provides standardized data on a periodic basis to its subscribers.

systems integration Centralization of the procurement function within an internal division or as a service of an external supplier.

T

tactical planning Planning that guides the implementation of activities specified in the strategic plan.

target market Segment to whom a firm decides to direct its marketing efforts and ultimately its goods and services.

target-return objective Short-run or long-run pricing objectives of achieving a specified return on either sales or investment.

tariff Tax levied against imported goods.

task-objective method Development of a promotional budget based on evaluation of the firm's promotional objectives.

team selling Selling situation in which several sales associates or other members of the organization are recruited to help the lead sales representative reach all those who influence the purchase decision.

technological environment Application to marketing of knowledge based on discoveries in science, inventions, and innovations.

technology Business application of knowledge based on scientific discoveries, inventions, and innovations.

telemarketing Promotional presentation involving the use of the telephone on an outbound basis by salespeople or on an inbound basis by customers who initiate calls to obtain information and place orders.

test marketing Marketing research technique that involves introducing a new product in a specific area and then measuring its degree of success.

third-party (contract) logistics firm Company that specializes in handling logistics activities for other firms.

time-based competition Strategy of developing and distributing goods and services more quickly than competitors.

total quality management (TQM) Continuous effort to improve products and work processes with the goal of achieving customer satisfaction and world-class performance.

trade allowance Special financial incentive offered to wholesalers and retailers that purchase or promote specific products.

trade discount Payment to a channel member or buyer for performing marketing functions; also known as a *functional discount.*

trade dress Visual components that contribute to the overall look of a brand.

trade industries Retailers or wholesalers that purchase products for resale to others.

trade promotion Sales promotion that appeals to marketing intermediaries rather than to consumers.

trade show Product exhibition organized by industry trade associations to showcase goods and services.

trade-in Credit allowance given for a used item when a customer purchases a new item.

trademark Brand for which the owner claims exclusive legal protection.

transaction-based marketing Buyer and seller exchanges characterized by limited communications and little or no ongoing relationships between the parties.

transfer price Cost assessed when a product is moved from one profit center in a firm to another.

trend analysis Quantitative sales forecasting method that estimates future sales through statistical analyses of historical sales patterns.

truck wholesaler Limited-function merchant wholesaler that markets perishable food items; also called a *truck jobber.*

tying agreement Arrangement that requires a marketing intermediary to carry items other than those they want to sell.

U

undifferentiated marketing Strategy that focuses on producing a single product and marketing it to all customers; also called *mass marketing.*

unemployment Proportion of people in the economy who are actively seeking work but do not have jobs.

unfair-trade laws State laws requiring sellers to maintain minimum prices for comparable merchandise.

uniform-delivered pricing Pricing system for handling transportation costs under which all buyers are quoted the same price, including transportation expenses. Sometimes known as *postage-stamp pricing.*

unit pricing Pricing policy in which prices are stated in terms of a recognized unit of measurement or a standard numerical count.

Universal Product Code (UPC) Numerical bar code system used to record product and price information.

unsought products Products marketed to consumers who may not yet recognize a need for them.

upstream management Controlling part of the supply chain that involves raw materials, inbound logistics, and warehouse and storage facilities.

user Individual or group that actually uses a business good or service.

utility Want-satisfying power of a good or service.

V

VALS Segmentation system that divides consumers into eight psychographic categories: actualizers, fulfilleds, believers, achievers, strivers, experiencers, makers, and strugglers.

value analysis Systematic study of the components of a purchase to determine the most cost-effective approach.

value pricing Pricing strategy emphasizing benefits derived from a product in comparison to the price and quality levels of competing offerings.

variable costs Costs that change with the level of production (such as labor and raw materials costs).

vendor analysis Assessment of supplier performance in areas such as price, back orders, timely delivery, and attention to special requests.

vendor-managed inventory (VMI) Inventory management system in which the seller—based on an existing agreement with a buyer—determines how much of a product is needed.

venture team Associates from different areas of an organization who work together in developing new products.

vertical marketing system (VMS) Planned channel system designed to improve distribution efficiency and cost-effectiveness by integrating various functions throughout the distribution chain.

viral marketing Efforts that allow satisfied customers to spread the word about products to other consumers.

virtual sales team Network of strategic partners, suppliers, and others who recommend a firm's goods or services.

VoIP Voice over Internet protocol—a phone connection through a personal computer with any type of broadband Internet connection.

W

Web services platform-independent information exchange systems that use the Internet to allow interaction between the firms.

Web-to-store shoppers Consumers who use the Internet as a tool to aid them at brick-and-mortar retailers.

wheel of retailing Hypothesis that each new type of retailer gains a competitive foothold by offering lower prices than current suppliers charge; the result of reducing or eliminating services.

wholesaler Channel intermediary that takes title to goods it handles and then distributes these goods to retailers, other distributors, or B2B customers.

wholesaling intermediary Comprehensive term that describes wholesalers as well as agents and brokers.

wiki Web page that anyone can edit.

wireless technology Technology that allows communications connections without cables or wires.

World Trade Organization (WTO) Organization that replaces GATT, overseeing GATT agreements, making binding decisions in mediating disputes, and reducing trade barriers.

Y

yield management Pricing strategy that allows marketers to vary prices based on such factors as demand, even though the cost of providing those goods or services remains the same.

Z

zone pricing Pricing system for handling transportation costs under which the market is divided into geographic regions and a different price is set in each region.

name and company index

A

Abacus, 246, 247, 248
ABC News, 20
ABC Television Network, 490, 595
Abdul, Paula, 279
Abell, Derek, 46
Abercrombie & Fitch, 11, 648
ABM, 355
Ace Hardware, 429, 461
ACE Tools, 379
Acer Computers, 650
ACNielsen, 134, 249, 256, 261, 515, 624
Acxiom Corp., 256, 257
Adelstein, Jonathan, 109
Adidas, 17, 226, 328, 532
Adler, Deborah, 388
Adobe, 128
Adopt-a-Pet, 16
ADP, 186
AdsOnFeet, 543
Advanced Micro Devices, 209
Advantage Group, 164
Advantix, 652
Aeropostale, 289
Aetna, 158
Affleck, Ben, 511
Ahold, 387
Aiken, Clay, 279
Airbus, 179, 180, 185, 223, 229, 568, 569
AirTran, 162
Al Hurra Television Network, 405
Al Jazeera Television Network, 405
Alamo Rent-a-Car, 509
Albercrombie & Fitch, 535
Albert Heijn, 387
Alcatel, 191
All England Lawn Tennis and Croquet Club, 331
Alley, Kirstie, 15
Allstate Insurance, 215, 421, 533
Almquist, Wendy, 181
Alpo, 375
Amazon.com, 4, 114, 117, 121, 122, 124, 125, 302, 337, 347, 373, 564, 565, 654
Amerada Hess, 99
America Online, 21, 82, 190, 321
America West Airlines, 162, 163
American Airlines, 338, 636
American Apparel, 536
American Association of Retired Persons, 85
American Automobile Association, 420
American Eagle Outfitters, 11, 167, 289
American Express, 13, 17, 139, 155, 158, 164, 190, 208, 215, 302, 360, 431, 495
American Heart Association, 12
American Humane Association, 85
American Kennel Club, 12
American Leather, 127
American Society for the Prevention of Cruelty to Animals, 16
American Trucking Association, 436
America's Second Harvest, 13
Anderson, Brad, 310

Andre Lurton, 388
Anheuser-Busch, 142, 303, 504, 510, 511, 537
Ann Taylor, 457
Anna Sui, 391
Antman, Jeffrey, 523
Anya Hindmarch, 391
A&P Future Store, 462
Apple Computer, 4, 7, 10, 45, 53, 76, 81, 107, 114, 128, 140, 141, 157, 209, 234, 239, 300, 302, 386, 594, 607, 609
Applebee's, 174
Arad, Avi, 364
Arbitron, 249, 258, 259
Ariba, 118
Arista Records, 235
Arizona Diamondbacks, 292
Arm & Hammer, 298, 374
Armor All, 337
Armour Meat Packing, 359
Armstrong, Lance, 155
Armstrong Rubber, 380
Artezen, 114
Asch, S. E., 154
Asics, 491
Ask.com, 132, 500
Assink, Terry, 432
Associated Druggists, 429
Association of American Railways, 436
AT&T, 11, 20, 46, 78, 142, 215, 292, 382, 383, 655
Audi, 356
AutoCart, 465
Aviall, 362
Avis Rental Cars, 349
Avon, 389, 417, 473, 504, 565
Ayer, N. W., 248

B

Bainey, T.L., 436
Baja Fresh, 632
Baldrige, Malcolm, 358
Ballard Designs, 661
Ballmer, Steve, 37, 561, 562
Bally Total Fitness, 290
Banana Republic, 457, 607
Bank of America, 52, 119, 120, 121, 182, 320, 359, 393
Barnes & Noble, 120, 316, 317, 337
Barney's New York, 451
Bartholomew, Peter E., 447
Bartley, Luella, 659
Basu, Shankar, 359
Batemen, Dayna, 506
Batesville Casket Company, 424
Bausch & Lomb, 405
Bay Area Rapid Transit, 617–618
Bayer, 159
Bazaarvoice, 250
BBDO, 261, 545
Bean, Leon Leonwood, 361
Beans Wax Candle Company, 181
Beatles, 386
Beaver, Bonnie, 375
Bechtel National, 176
Beckham, David, 226, 232, 531
Bed, Bath & Beyond, 463
Beijo Bags, 417
Bellagio Hotel, 159

BellSouth, 78
Ben & Jerry's, 233, 378
Berry, Halle, 549
Berkshire Hathaway, 502
Bertelsmann, 643
Bertelsmann AG, 235
Best Buy, 115, 119, 310, 311, 312, 330, 463, 466, 474, 564, 578, 587, 607
Best Friends Pet Care, 374
Better Homes & Gardens, 542
Bezos, Jeff, 50
Big Monster Toys, 364
Big Three, 600
Bigelow's Green Tea, 530
Bigg's Hypermarket Shoppes, 465
BJ's, 464
Black, Clint, 15
Black & Decker, 576
Black Mesa Pipeline, 437
Bliss, 327
Blockbuster Video, 531, 593
Bloom supermarkets, 481
Bloomingdale's, 154, 392, 457
Blue Jeans Cable, 215
Bluetooth, 458
BMW, 191, 235, 303, 332
BN.com, 115
BNSF Railway, 436
Boeing, 47, 92, 179, 180, 181, 185, 191, 207, 214, 223, 240, 355, 362, 561, 565, 568, 569
Bono, 13
Books-A-Million, 654
Borba, 575
Borba, Scott Vincent, 575
Borders Books, 463
Borsheim's Jewelry Store, 564
Bosch, 355
Bose, 356, 660
Boston Consulting Group, 10, 52
Boston Market, 586
Boston Proper, 473
Botox, 350
Boudreaux, George, 386
Bounty, 384
Bowflex, 508
Boyana Film Studios, 216
Bradshaw, Terry, 511
Brain Group, 250
Brand Keys, 651
Branson, Richard, 392
Breslow, Jeff, 364
Brightcove Networks, 419
Brin, Sergey, 18
Brinker International, 252
Brinkley, Christie, 326
Bristol-Myers Squibb, 499
British Airways, 185
British Broadcasting Company, 538
British Petroleum, 213, 389
Bronco Wine, 608
Brooks, Tim, 160
Brown, Michael, 25
Bryant, Cedric, 368
Bryant, Kobe, 525
Buffett, Jimmy, 345
Buffett, Warren, 502
Build-a-Bear Workshop, 22
Bureau of Economic Analysis, 88

Burger King, 43, 174, 175, 239, 251, 304, 323, 502, 594
Burns, Jim, 85
Burton Snowboards, 363
Busch Gardens, 105, 107, 308, 594
Byrne, Dee, 359

C

Cablevision, 93, 655
Cadbury Schweppes, 129, 253, 288
Cadillac, 277, 332, 356, 504
Cairo.com, 18
CallWave, 454
Camay Soap, 587
Cambridge Homes, 573
Camp, Kenneth, 424
Campbell Soup Company, 13, 232, 248, 271, 283, 284, 285, 406, 423
Cannondale Associates, 513
Canon, 5, 571
Capital One, 492
CardSystems, 97
CareerBuilder.com, 535
Carey, Mariah, 453
Carl Jr's., 535
Carli, Elizabeth, 157
Carlson Marketing Group, 181
Carmax.com, 44
Carson, Scott E., 92
Carter, David, 309
Cartier, 638
Castle Supply, 471
Caterpillar, 180, 214
Cathay Pacific Airways, 569
CBS, 14, 81, 426, 490, 500
CDW, 360
Center for Science in the Public Interest, 94
Center Parcs, 533
Centers for Disease Control, 74
Charles Keath, 473
Charles Schwab, 119
Charney, Dov, 536
Chase/Bank One, 120
Chef's Catalog, 126
Chelsea, Chris, 74
Chery Automobile, 387
Chevrolet, 146, 161, 277, 539
Chevron, 177, 213
Chicago White Sox, 320
Chicos, 456
Children's Miracle Network, 187
Chipotle Grill, 452
Chiron, 75
CH2M Hill, 176
Cho, Fujio, 241
ChoicePoint, 97, 124, 322
Chrysler, 277, 316, 649, 652
Cingular, 78, 79, 109, 382, 383, 527, 549
Circle K, 481
Circuit City, 311
Cisco Systems, 24, 331, 393
Citibank, 120, 164
CitiGroup, 97, 214, 215
Citizen, 230
Claire's Stores, 453
Claria, 533
Clarkson, Kelly, 279
ClearGauge, 533

subject index

international index